Essential

WORLD ATLAS

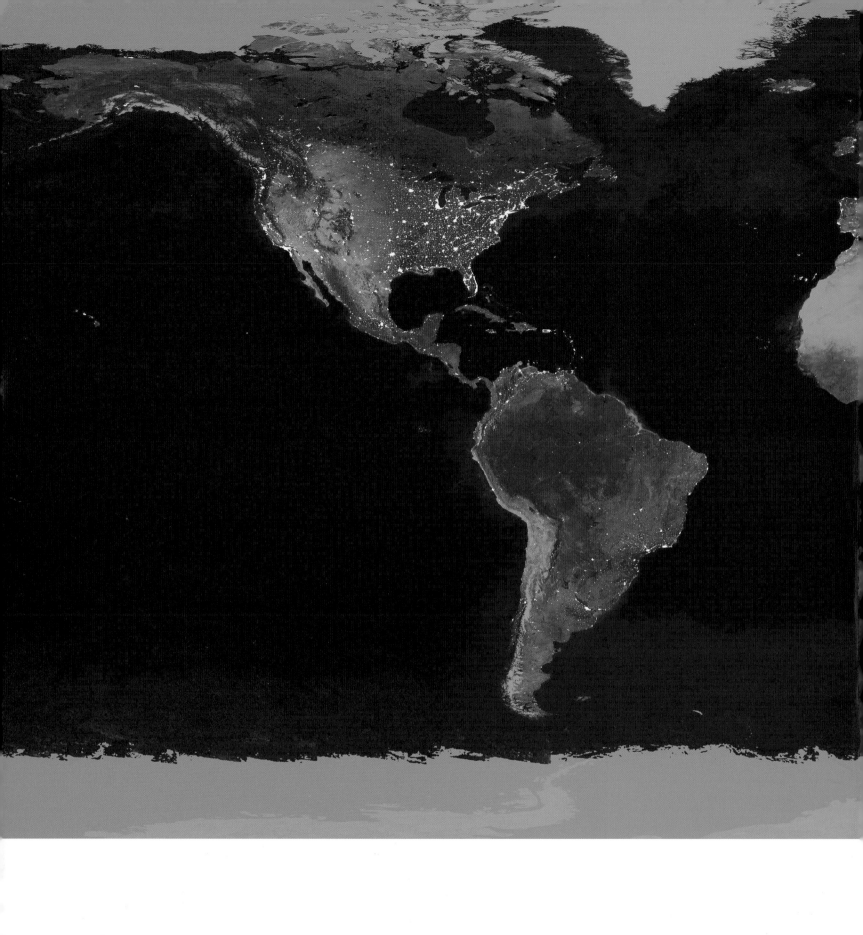

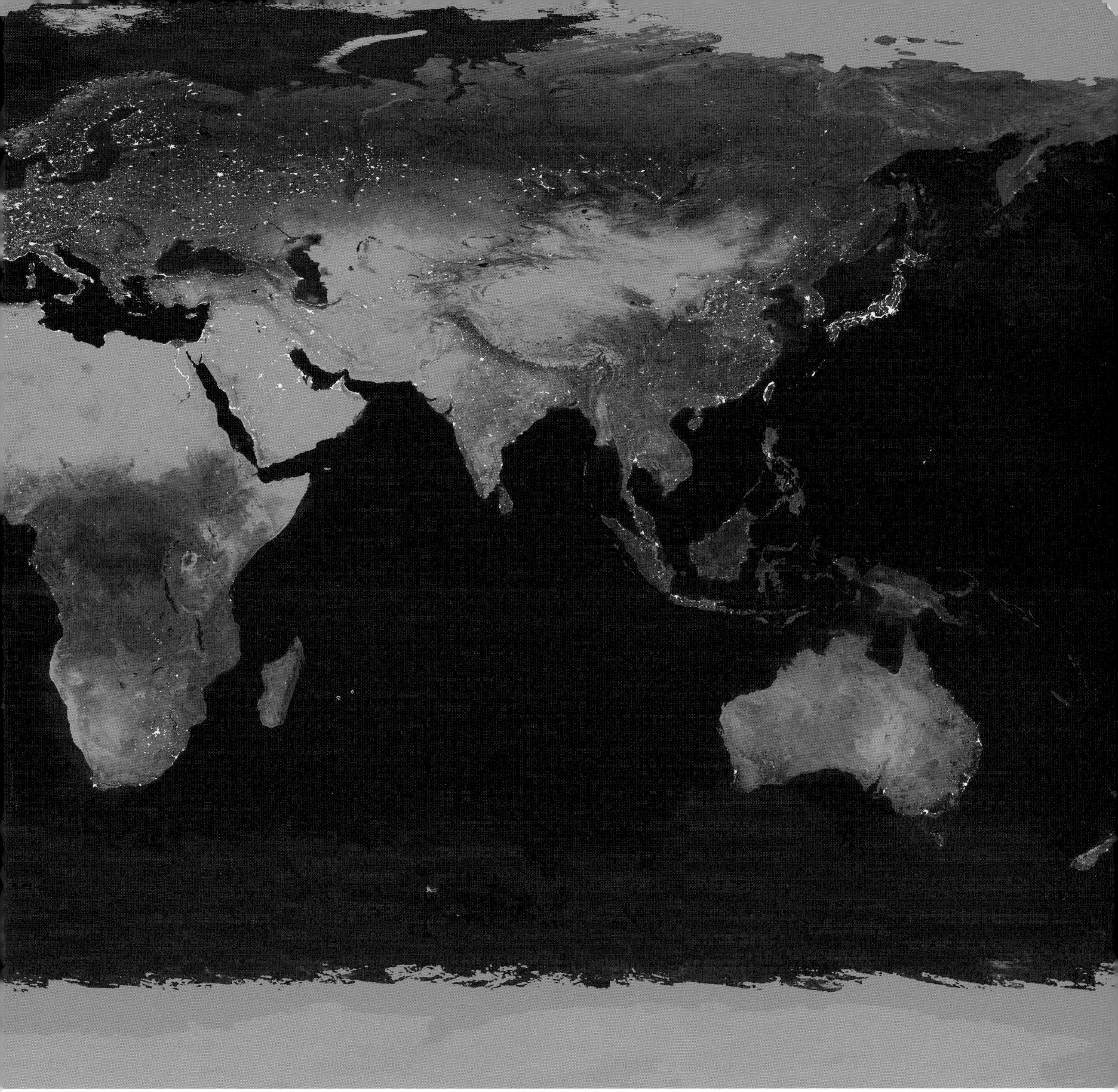

Essential WORLD ATLAS

WELDON OWEN

Published by Weldon Owen Pty Ltd
59–61 Victoria Street
McMahons Point
Sydney, NSW 2060
Australia

Copyright ©2005 Weldon Owen Pty Ltd

ISBN 978-1-921530-41-8

Color reproduction by Colourscan Overseas Co Pte Ltd
Printed in Singapore by Craft Print International Ltd

A WELDON OWEN PRODUCTION

Top: At the southern tip of South America is the mountainous Patagonia region, an area progressively sculpted by glacial action. In this image vegetation appears as red, the glacier white.

Bottom: Surrounded by sand dunes, Lake Disappointment is an ephemeral salt lake in one of the most remote areas of Western Australia.

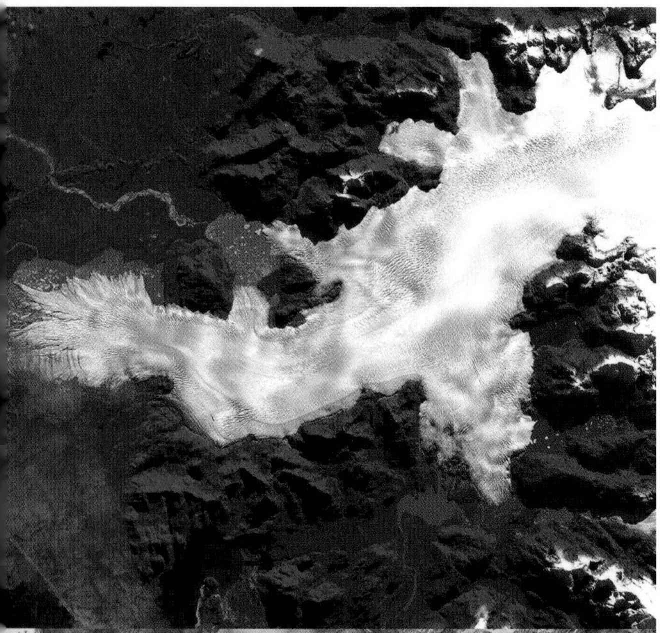

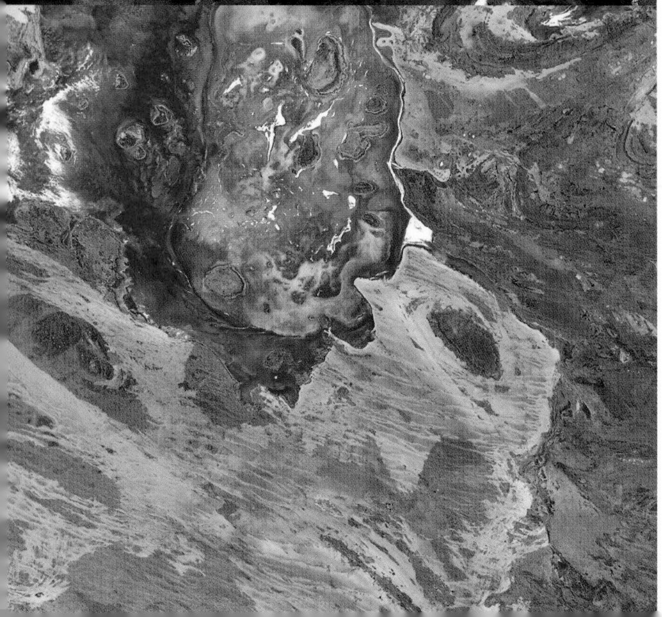

Cartographic Consultants

Dr William Cartwright
Associate Professor in Multimedia Cartography
School of Mathematical and Geospatial Sciences
RMIT University, Melbourne, Australia
Vice-President, International
Cartographic Association

Professor Michael P. Peterson
Department of Geography/Geology
University of Nebraska at Omaha, U.S.A.
Chair, International Cartographic Association
Commission on Maps and the Internet

Regional Mapping Consultants

Imran Ali
Cartographer, Pakistan

M. (John) Balodis
FMSIA Adjunct Professor
Curtin University, Perth, Australia

Professor Jean Carrière
Professeur titulaire
Directeur du Département de géographie
Université du Québec à Montréal, Canada

Dr Prem Chetri
School of Mathematical and Geospatial Sciences
RMIT University, Melbourne, Australia

Professor Benjamin Cohen
Department of Photogrammetry and Cartography
University of Architecture, Civil Engineering and Geodesy,
Sofia, Bulgaria

Igor Drecki
Geographics Unit Manager
School of Geography and Environmental Science
University of Auckland, Auckland, New Zealand

Dr Francisco Escobar
Profesor Titular de Análisis Geográfico Regional
Departamento de Geografía
Universidad de Alcalá de Henares, Spain

Dr David Fairbairn
School of Civil Engineering and Geosciences
University of Newcastle, Newcastle, U.K.

Steve Foldi
Cartographer, Windsor, Australia

Scott Furey
School of Mathematical and Geospatial Sciences
RMIT University, Melbourne, Australia

Professor Dr Georg Gartner
Institut für Kartographie und Geo-Medientechnik
Technische Universitat Wien, Vienna, Austria

Ibrahim Hanna
Hydrogeologist, Syria

Hashim al Hashimi
Geo-Information Analyst
Environmental Research and Wildlife
Development Agency, United Arab Emirates

Dr Stephen Hutchinson
Southampton Oceanography Centre
University of Southampton, Southampton, U.K.

Dr Simon Jones
School of Mathematical and Geospatial Sciences
RMIT University, Melbourne, Australia

Professor Milan Konecny
Department of Geography, Faculty of Science
Masaryk University, Brno, Czech Republic
President, International Cartographic Association

Professor Alexandra Koussoulakou
Department of Cadastre, Photogrammetry
and Cartography
The Aristotle University, Thessaloniki, Greece

Colin Kropman
Geographic Consultant, Sydney, Australia

Hyun Jong (David) Lee
Sung Kyun Kwan University, Seoul, South Korea

Antonio Hernández Navarro
Geodetic Coordinator
National Institute of Statistics,
Geography and Informatics (INEGI)
National Mapping Agency of Mexico,
Aguascaliente, Mexico

Professor Ferjan Ormeling
University of Utrecht, Netherlands
Secretary-General, International
Cartographic Association

Will Pringle
Cartographic Director
Australian Geographic Pty Ltd,
Sydney, Australia

Professor Patrick Quilty
Honorary Research Professor
School of Earth Sciences
University of Tasmania, Hobart, Australia

Cristhiane da Silva Ramos
School of Mathematical and Geospatial Sciences
RMIT University, Melbourne, Australia

Rushan Gul Rozi
School of Mathematical and Geospatial Sciences
RMIT University, Melbourne, Australia

Afshin Alizadeh Shabini
University of Tehran, Tehran, Iran

Hussein Tawansi
Fellow Member, Institute of Quarrying
Sydney, Australia

Professor Dr Theodor Wintges
Munich University of Applied Sciences,
Munich, Germany

Assistant Professor Hiroyuki Yoshida
Faculty of Policy Management
SFC, Keio University, Endo, Japan

Jason Zhang
School of Mathematical and Geospatial Sciences
RMIT University, Melbourne, Australia

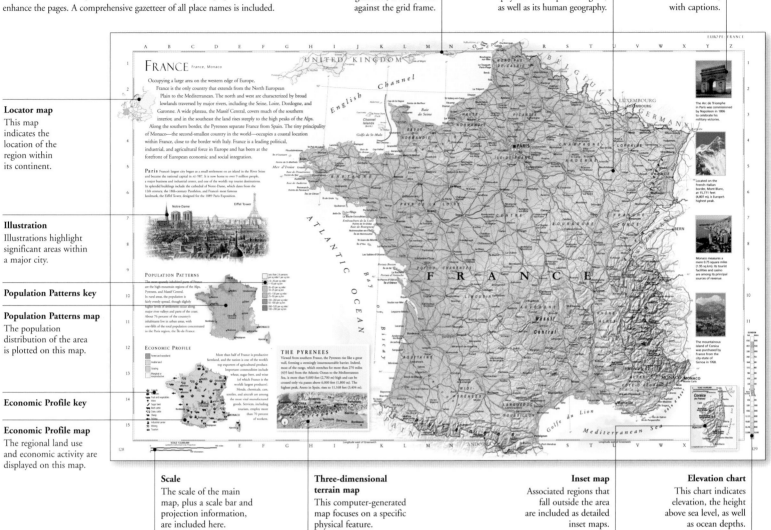

How to Use this Atlas

Essential World Atlas contains two world maps—physical and political—and 67 regional spreads, arranged by continent. Each of these features a detailed regional map, supplemented by smaller maps plotting population patterns and an economic profile of the area. Three-dimensional terrain maps, evocative illustrations and photographs, and an informative text enhance the pages. A comprehensive gazetteer of all place names is included.

Grid reference
The location of each place, as listed in the gazetteer, is referenced against the grid frame.

Regional map
Each regional map includes detailed information on the physical landscape of a region, as well as its human geography.

Photographs
Photographs of natural features and human structures are included, with captions.

Locator map
This map indicates the location of the region within its continent.

Illustration
Illustrations highlight significant areas within a major city.

Population Patterns key

Population Patterns map
The population distribution of the area is plotted on this map.

Economic Profile key

Economic Profile map
The regional land use and economic activity are displayed on this map.

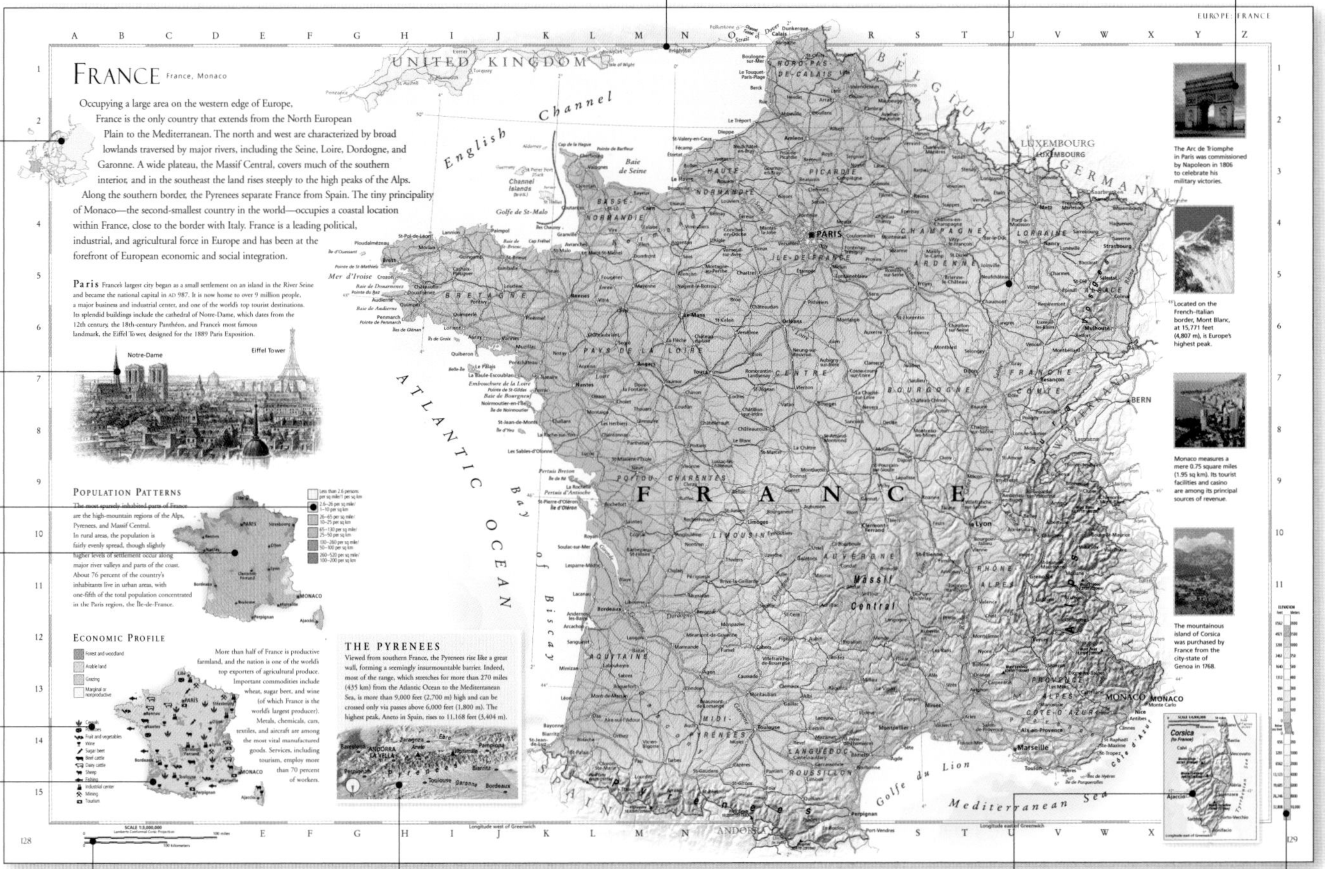

Scale
The scale of the main map, plus a scale bar and projection information, are included here.

Three-dimensional terrain map
This computer-generated map focuses on a specific physical feature.

Inset map
Associated regions that fall outside the area are included as detailed inset maps.

Elevation chart
This chart indicates elevation, the height above sea level, as well as ocean depths.

Key to Maps

PHYSICAL FEATURES

ELEVATION

Feet	Meters
6562	2000
4921	1500
3281	1000
2461	750
1640	500
1312	400
984	300
656	200
328	100
0	0
Below sea level	
0	0
656	200
3281	1000
6562	2000
13,123	4000
19,685	6000
26,246	8000
32,808	10,000

PHYSICAL FEATURES

- □ Ice cap
- □ Ice shelf
- ▲ *Mountain peak/volcano Height, feet (meters)*
- + *Pole*
- △ *Geomagnetic Pole*
- ▲ *Seamount*
- ▼ *Sea trench Depth, feet (meters)*

WATER FEATURES

- *Lake*
- *Salt pan/Dry/Intermittent lake*
- Coastline
- *Major river*
- *Minor river*
- ✖ *River source*
- ▼ *Waterfall*

GRATICULE FEATURE

- 125° Graticule number
- Graticule line
- --- Tropics/polar circle
- Equator

BORDERS

- International border
- Defined maritime boundary
- Equidistant lines
- Disputed border
- •••• Demarcation/line of control/ceasefire line
- State/territory border (Australia, Canada, U.S.A.)
- International Date Line

TRANSPORT

- Major road
- Main road
- Minor road
- Railway

NATIONAL/DEPENDENT TERRITORY CAPITAL CITIES

Over 5 million	■	**LONDON**
1--5 million	●	**OTTAWA**
100,000--1 million	✪	**HELSINKI**
100,000--1 million	✪	**KINGSTON**
0--100,000	✪	**HONIARA**
0--100,000	✪	**BELMOPAN**

STATE/TERRITORY CAPITAL CITIES (Australia, Canada, U.S.A.)

Over 5 million	■	**Toronto**
1--5 million	●	**Sydney**
100,000--1 million	✪	**Québec**
0--100,000	✪	Columbia

OTHER CITIES OR TOWNS

Over 5 million	■	**São Paulo**
1--5 million	●	**Calicut**
100,000--1 million	○	**Luxor**
0--100,000	○	Lillehammer
	□	Research base
		Built-up area

TYPOGRAPHIC KEY

POLITICAL FEATURES

Country	**BELIZE**
Dependent territory with parent state	VIRGIN ISLANDS ***(to U.S.A.)***
Internal administrative region	***UMBRIA***
State/Territory (Australia, Canada, U.S.A.)	**VICTORIA**

PHYSICAL FEATURES

Mountain range	***Allegheny Mountains***
Mountain peak	***Mt Davis***
Geographic feature	***Nullarbor Plain***
Peninsula	***Cape York Peninsula***
Headland/point/cape	*Cabo de São Vincent*
Island group	***Solomon Islands***
Island	***New Caledonia***
Pole	***North Pole***

WATER FEATURES

Ocean	*PACIFIC OCEAN*
Sea	*Irish Sea*
Bay/gulf	*Gulf of Mexico*
Channel/strait	*Bass Strait*
Undersea ridge	***Carlsberg Ridge***
Seamount/Sea trench	***Golden Dragon Seamount***
Lake/Salt pan/Dry/Intermittent lake	*Lake Titicaca*
Major river	*Nile*
Minor river	*Salween*
River source	***Source of the Amazon***
Waterfall	***Angel Falls***

GRATICULE FEATURES

Tropics/polar circle/equator	Tropic of Capricorn
Date line	International Date Line

CONTENTS

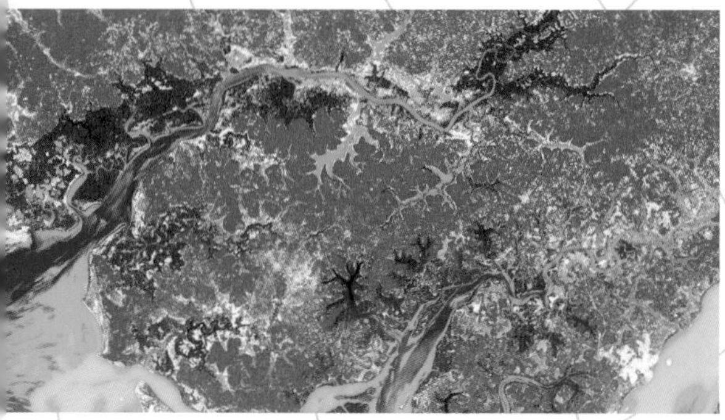
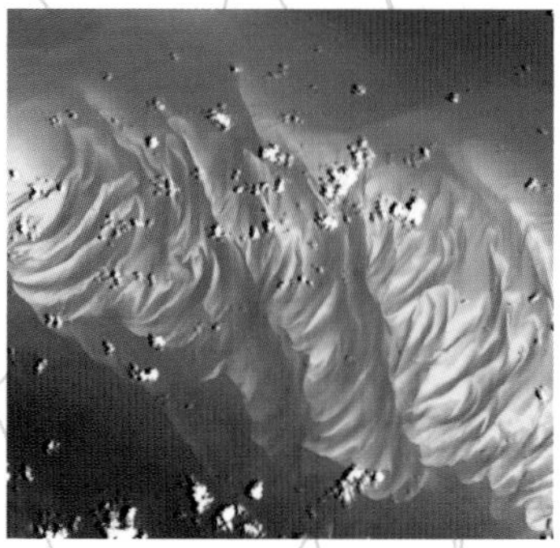
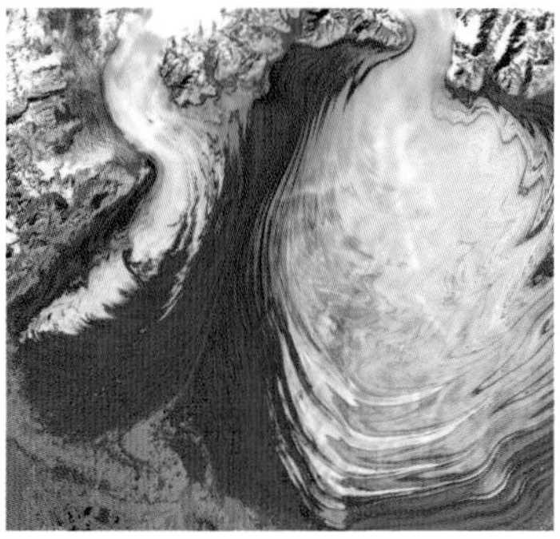
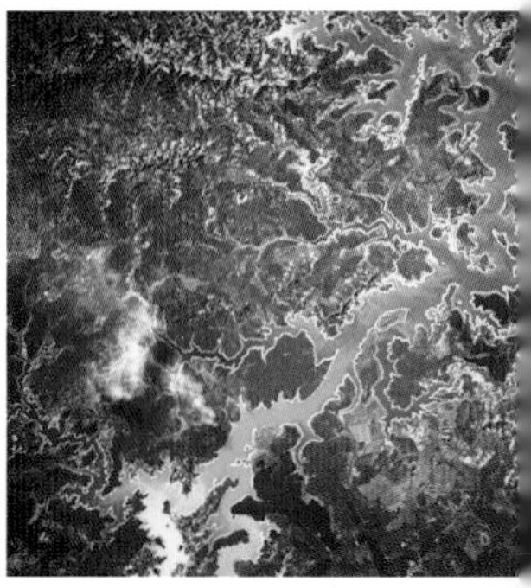

THE WORLD

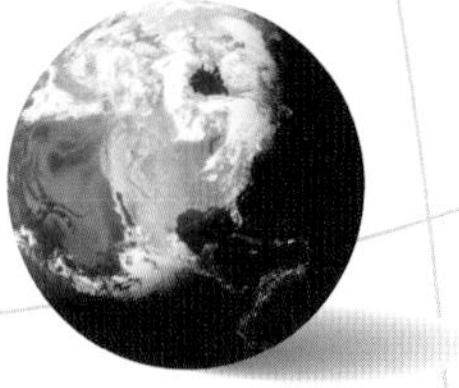

NORTH AMERICA

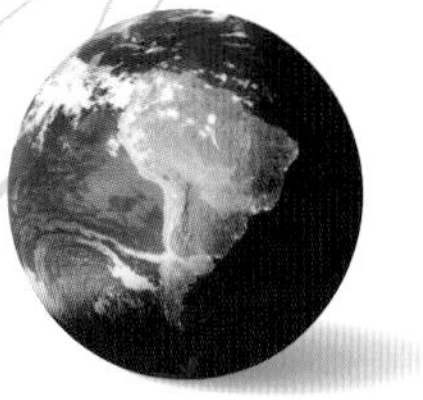

SOUTH AMERICA

EUROPE

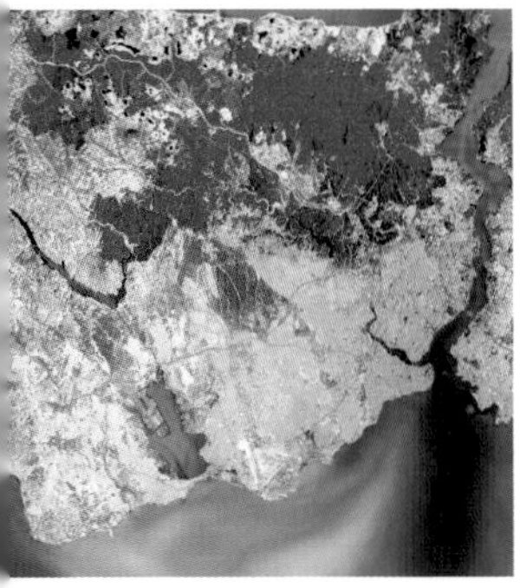

ASIA

AFRICA

OCEANIA

THE POLES

THE PHYSICAL WORLD

Oceans and seas dominate the globe, covering 70.8 percent of its surface. The land between these large bodies of water is traditionally divided into seven major landmasses or continents: Europe, Asia, North America, South America, Africa, Australia, and Antarctica. Europe and Asia form a single landmass, known as Eurasia, but are conventionally identified as separate continents because of their distinct peoples and histories. Though technically a continent in itself, Australia is usually considered part of the large region of Oceania, which includes the other islands of the southwestern Pacific Ocean.

NORTHERN HEMISPHERE

The Northern Hemisphere encompasses more than two-thirds of Earth's land, including all of Europe and North America, and most of Asia and Africa. Its areas of open ocean are further reduced by the presence of a permanent ice cap that surrounds the North Pole, covering most of the Arctic Ocean.

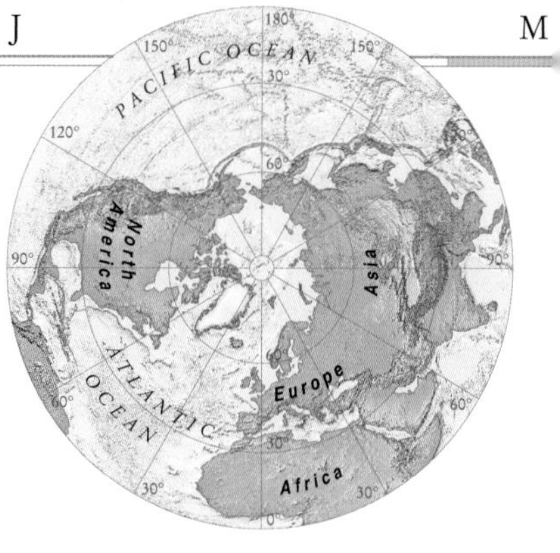

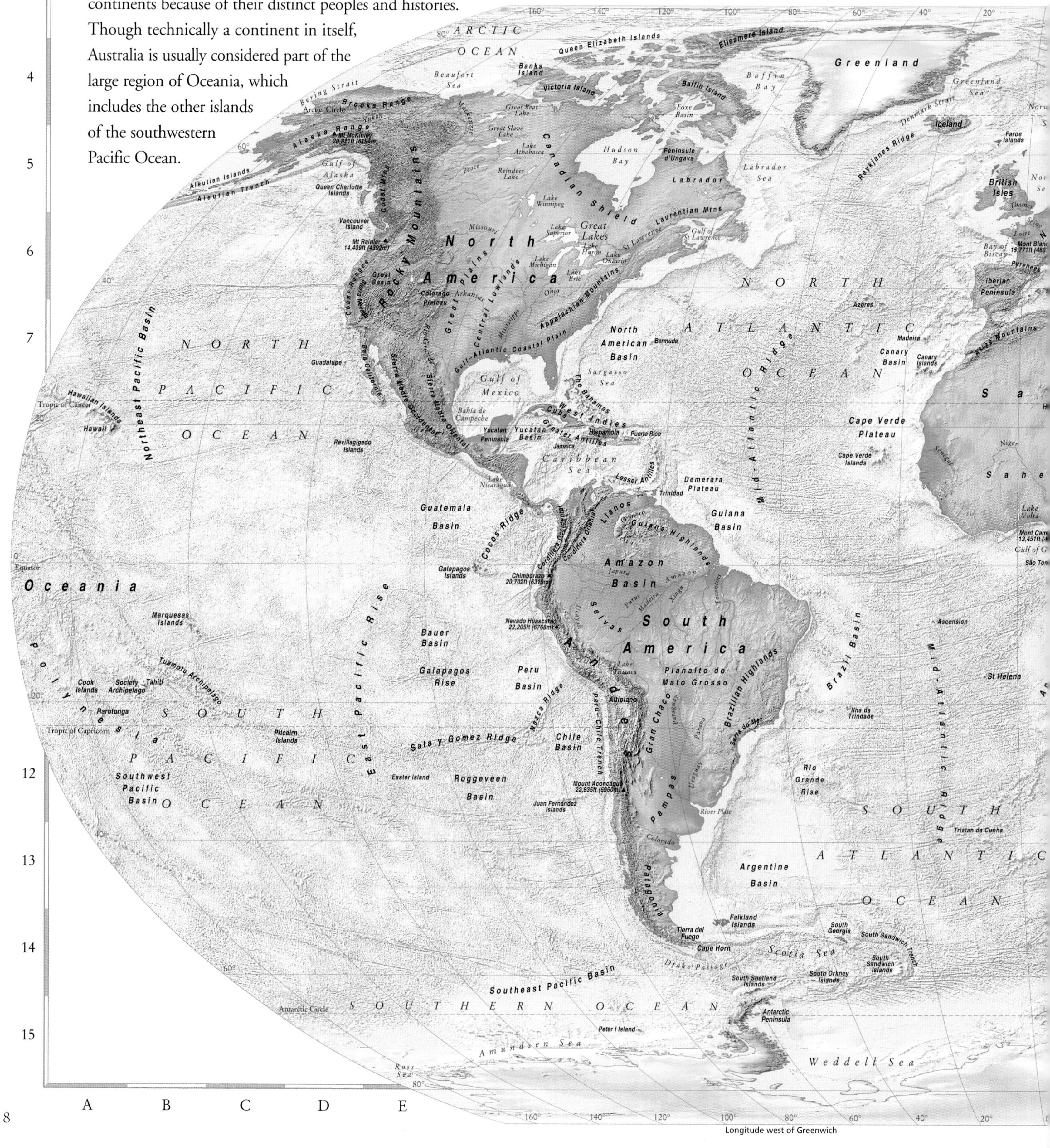

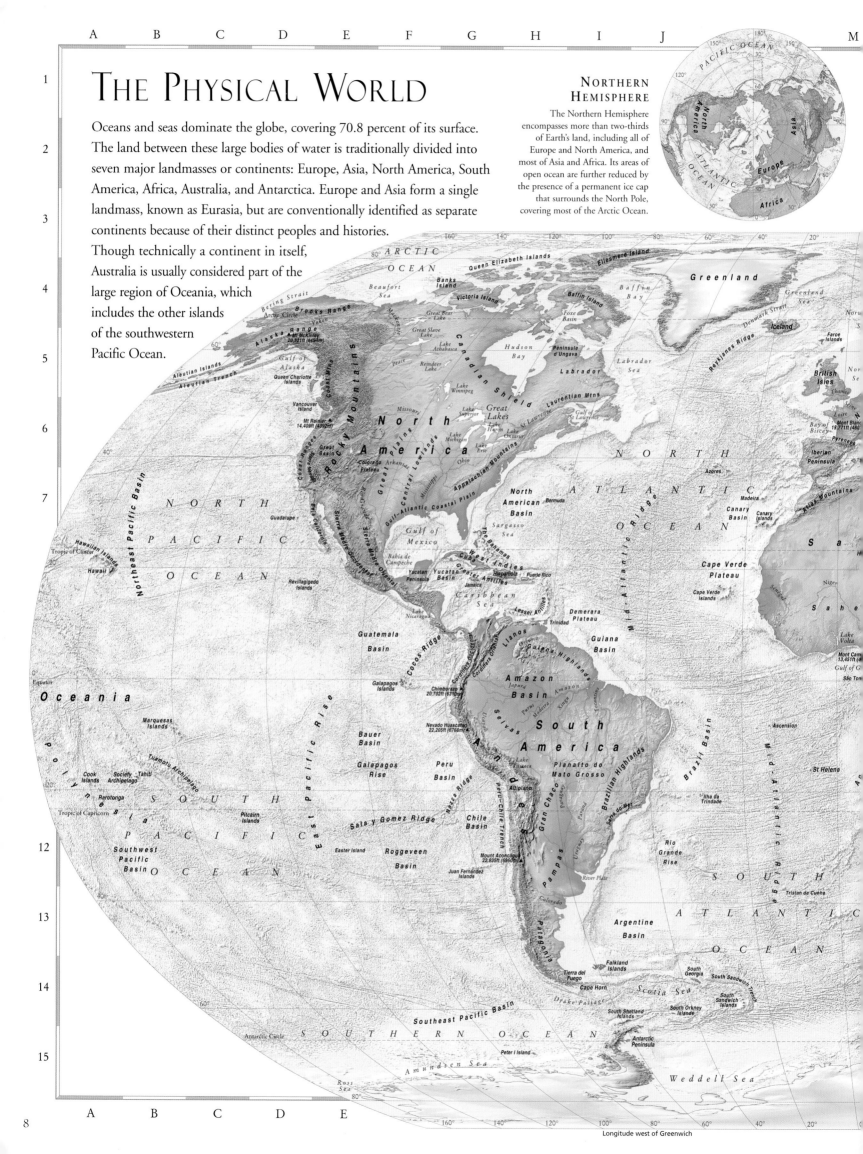

N Q R S T U V W X Y Z

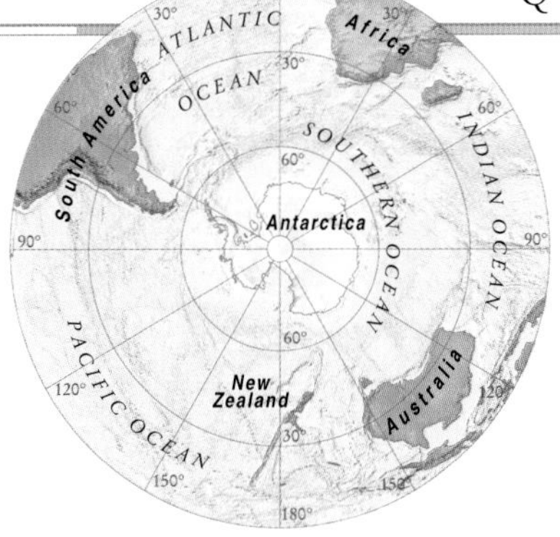

Southern Hemisphere

Although the South Pole is surrounded by the continent of Antarctica, the Southern Hemisphere has a much higher proportion of sea than the Northern Hemisphere. Vast expanses of the Indian, Pacific, Atlantic, and Southern oceans separate South America, southern Africa, Australia, and Antarctica.

Water Resources

Most of Earth's water is contained in its oceans and seas, and is therefore salt water. Of the small proportion that is fresh water, almost four-fifths is locked up in ice caps and glaciers, and another fifth lies below the ground. Just one percent of all the water on Earth is readily accessible surface fresh water. More than half of this is in lakes, one percent is in rivers, and the rest is in the soil and air.

THE DISTRIBUTION OF WATER ON EARTH

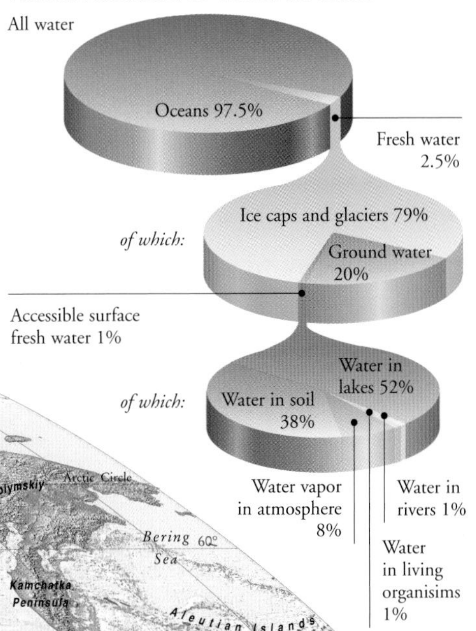

1 2 3 4 5 6 7 12

V W

SCALE 1:70,329,670
Robinson Projection
0 2000 miles
0 2000 kilometers

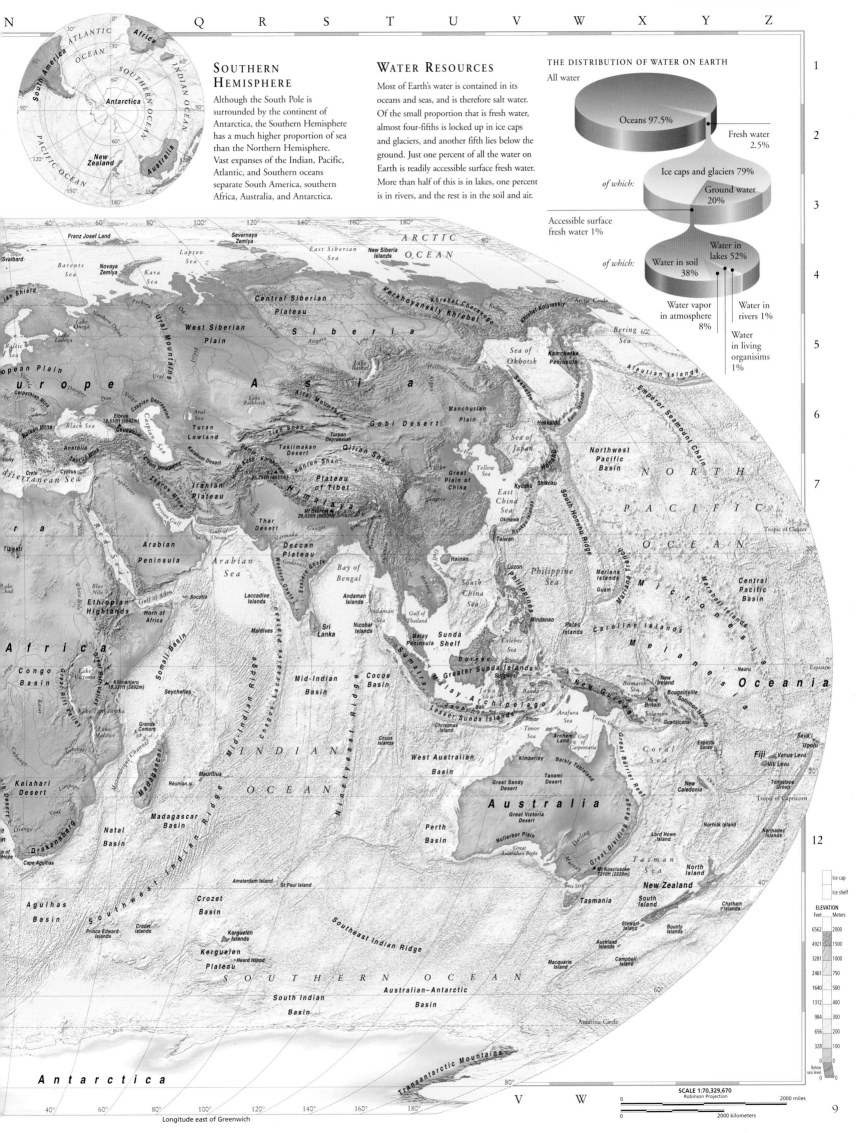

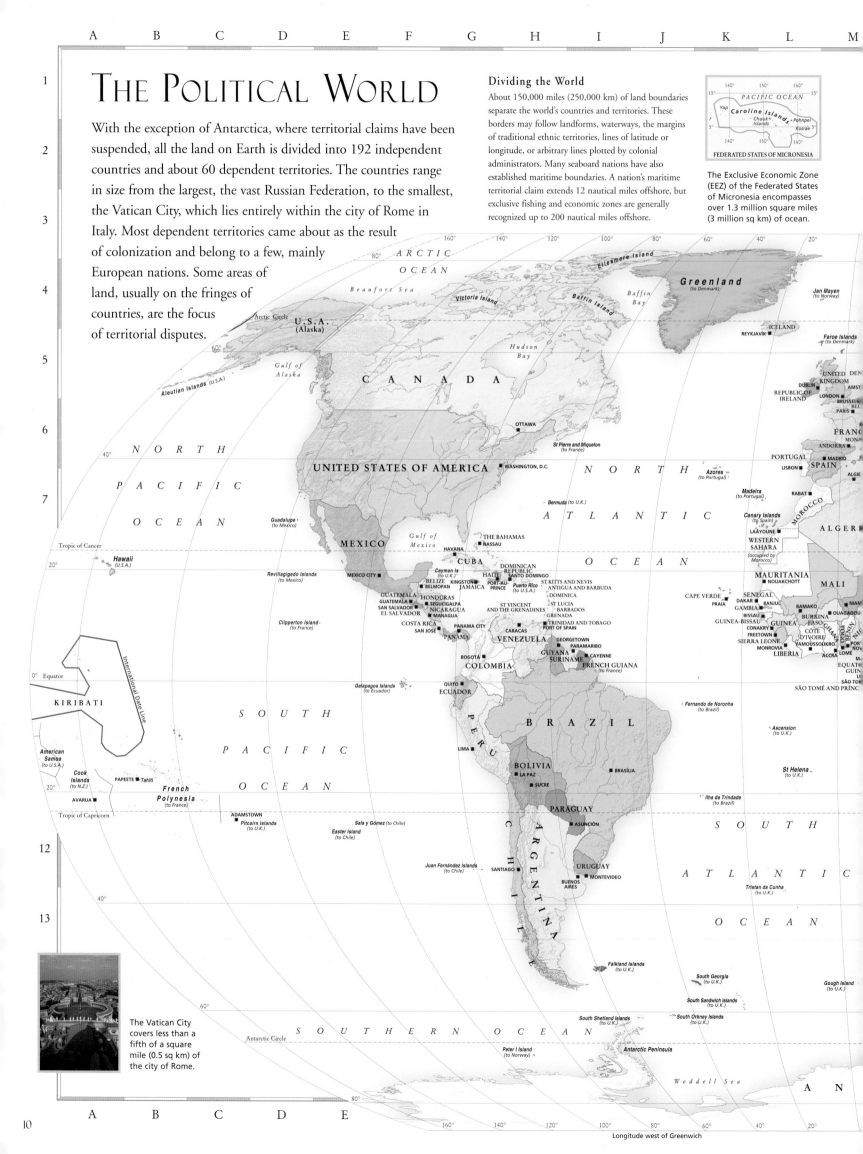

The Political World

With the exception of Antarctica, where territorial claims have been suspended, all the land on Earth is divided into 192 independent countries and about 60 dependent territories. The countries range in size from the largest, the vast Russian Federation, to the smallest, the Vatican City, which lies entirely within the city of Rome in Italy. Most dependent territories came about as the result of colonization and belong to a few, mainly European nations. Some areas of land, usually on the fringes of countries, are the focus of territorial disputes.

Dividing the World

About 150,000 miles (250,000 km) of land boundaries separate the world's countries and territories. These borders may follow landforms, waterways, the margins of traditional ethnic territories, lines of latitude or longitude, or arbitrary lines plotted by colonial administrators. Many seaboard nations have also established maritime boundaries. A nation's maritime territorial claim extends 12 nautical miles offshore, but exclusive fishing and economic zones are generally recognized up to 200 nautical miles offshore.

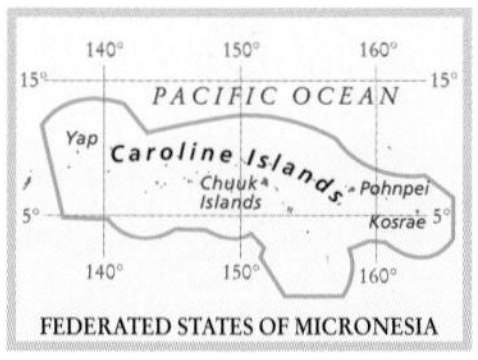

The Exclusive Economic Zone (EEZ) of the Federated States of Micronesia encompasses over 1.3 million square miles (3 million sq km) of ocean.

The Vatican City covers less than a fifth of a square mile (0.5 sq km) of the city of Rome.

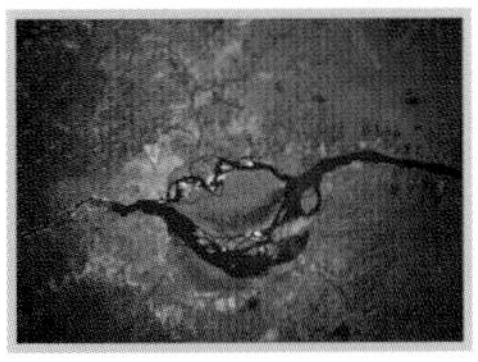

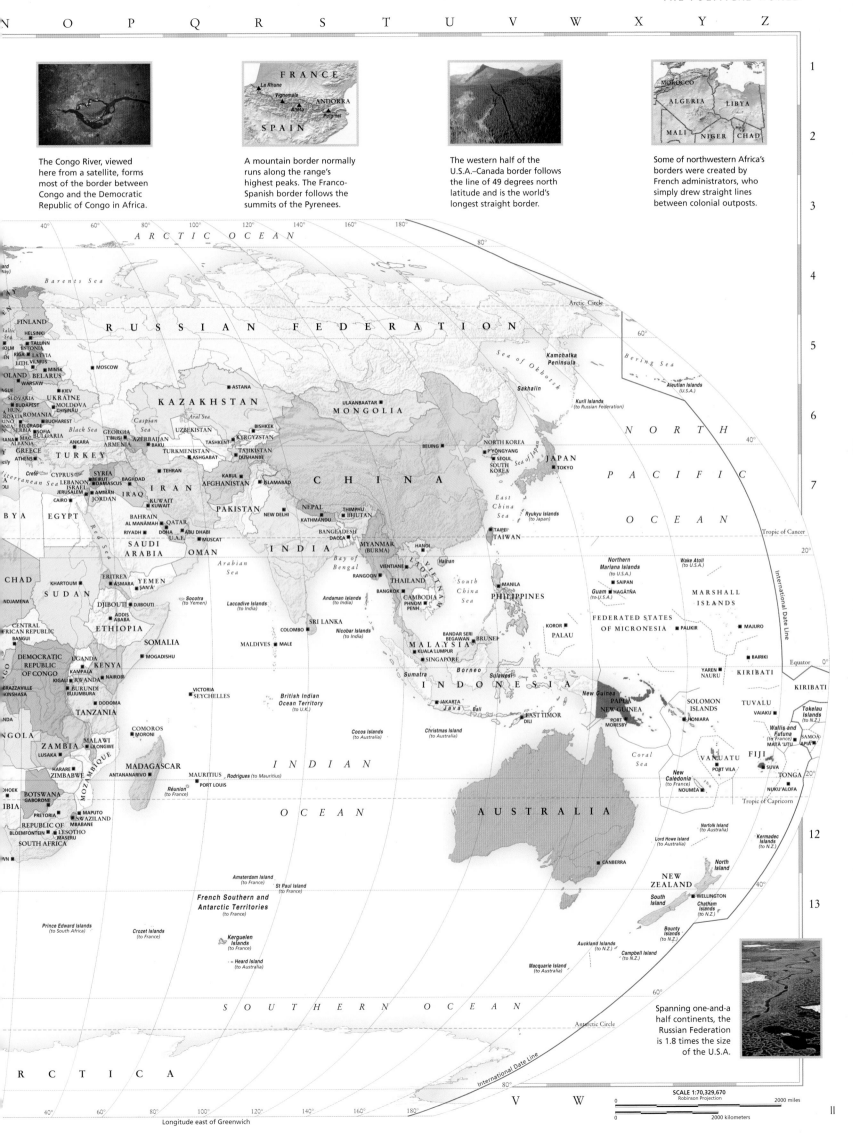

The Congo River, viewed here from a satellite, forms most of the border between Congo and the Democratic Republic of Congo in Africa.

A mountain border normally runs along the range's highest peaks. The Franco-Spanish border follows the summits of the Pyrenees.

The western half of the U.S.A.–Canada border follows the line of 49 degrees north latitude and is the world's longest straight border.

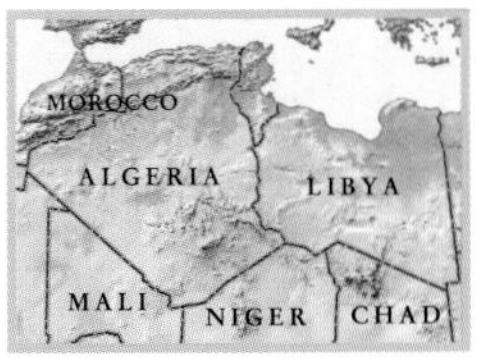

Some of northwestern Africa's borders were created by French administrators, who simply drew straight lines between colonial outposts.

Spanning one-and-a half continents, the Russian Federation is 1.8 times the size of the U.S.A.

United States of America

A federal republic made up of 50 states, the United States of America (U.S.A.) is the world's third-largest country by size and population. Its contiguous 48 states span the center of North America, from the Pacific Ocean to the Atlantic shoreline. The other two states are Alaska, in the far northwest of the continent, and the island state of Hawaii, in the central Pacific Ocean. On the western side of the lower 48, coastal ranges and the central Rocky Mountains enclose a series of high, arid plateaus and peaks. Plains predominate in the center and east, the much-eroded Appalachian Mountains dividing the vast Mississippi River Basin from the Atlantic Coastal Plain. The U.S.A. declared independence from British rule in 1776 and, with help from France, defeated Britain in the Revolutionary War. It has since flourished to become the world's leading economic and political power.

The Rockies attain their highest elevations in Colorado, which has 53 peaks above 14,000 feet (4,270 m).

The Mississippi River nears the end of its 2,339-mile (3,765-km) journey at New Orleans in Louisiana.

Population Patterns

The U.S.A. has a large population, but it is distributed over a wide area. Density is higher in the eastern half of the country, especially on the northeastern seaboard, but California is the most populous state. Although the western interior is the least densely inhabited area, it has the fastest-growing state populations. The majority of Americans, 69.1 percent, are non-Hispanic whites; Hispanics make up 12.5 percent of the population, blacks 12.3 percent, Asians 3.6 percent, and Native Americans 0.9 percent.

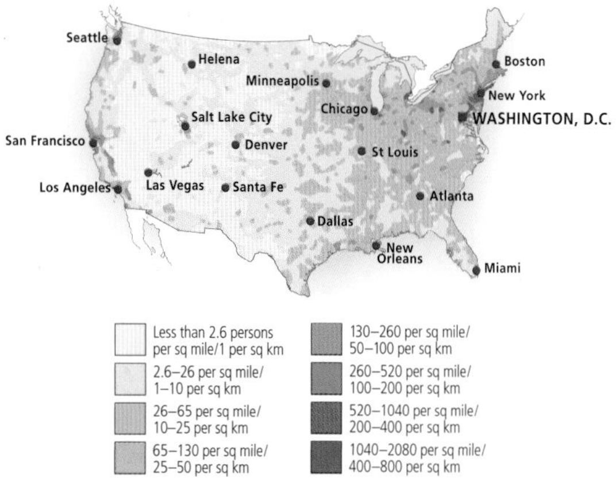

Economic Profile

The U.S.A. is the most productive nation on Earth. It has the world's largest coal reserves and generates 40 percent of its oil. Intensive farming of rich agricultural lands yields half of the world's corn, one-fifth of its meat, and one-tenth of its wheat. The U.S.A. is also the top producer of soybeans and the biggest source of timber. Forestry, mining, and agriculture are far surpassed, however, in terms of contribution to GDP, by manufacturing—led by transport equipment, industrial machinery, electronic components, and computers—and services, which employ 73.5 percent of workers, primarily in the financial and health sectors.

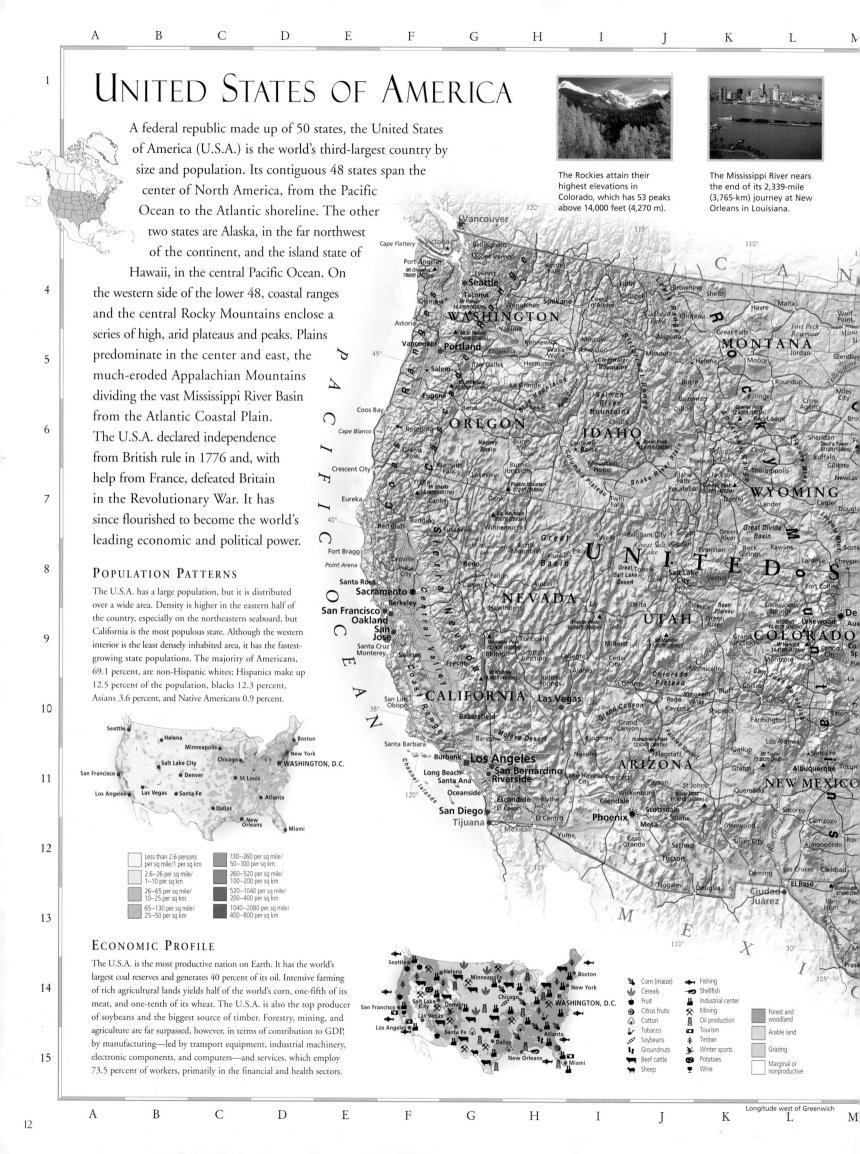

Divided between the U.S.A. and Canada, Lake Superior is 383 miles (616 km) wide and fed by about 200 rivers.

Washington, D.C. In 1790, 10 square miles (26 sq km) on the Potomac River were selected by Congress as the site of a new national capital and named the District of Columbia after Christopher Columbus. George Washington commissioned French engineer Pierre-Charles L'Enfant to plan a city, subsequently named after the president. Although L'Enfant was later dismissed, his plan for a rectangular grid and avenues radiating out from grand government buildings was broadly followed. The Capitol Building, home of the House of Representatives and the Senate, was commenced in 1793 and first hosted Congress in 1800.

SCALE 1:13,186,813
Lamberts Conformal Conic Projection
0 400 miles
0 400 kilometers

The world's tallest trees, redwoods grow on California's rainy north coast.

NORTHEASTERN U.S.A.

Connecticut, Maine, Massachusetts, New Hampshire, New Jersey, New York, Pennsylvania, Rhode Island, Vermont

The site of some of the continent's earliest European settlements and subsequently the entry point to North America for millions of immigrants, the northeastern seaboard is the most densely populated part of the U.S.A. On the southern half of the coastal plain lies a string of cities that have merged to form one massive, almost continuous urban area. Running from Boston south to Washington, D.C., it is sometimes referred to as the megalopolis or BosWash corridor.

In the north, the shoreline is less developed and more rugged, deep bays and promontories lining southern Maine. To the west, the coastal plain is hemmed in by the ancient, forested peaks of the Appalachian Mountains. Studded with lakes and breached by rivers, including the Hudson, Delaware, and Connecticut, the Appalachians reach west to the shores of the Great Lakes, to the Adirondack Mountains, and north into Canada.

Measuring 3,500 miles (5,630 km) in length, the heavily indented Maine coast is fringed by rocky inlets and 1,200 islands.

The strongest winds ever measured were recorded on top of Mount Washington in New Hampshire's White Mountains.

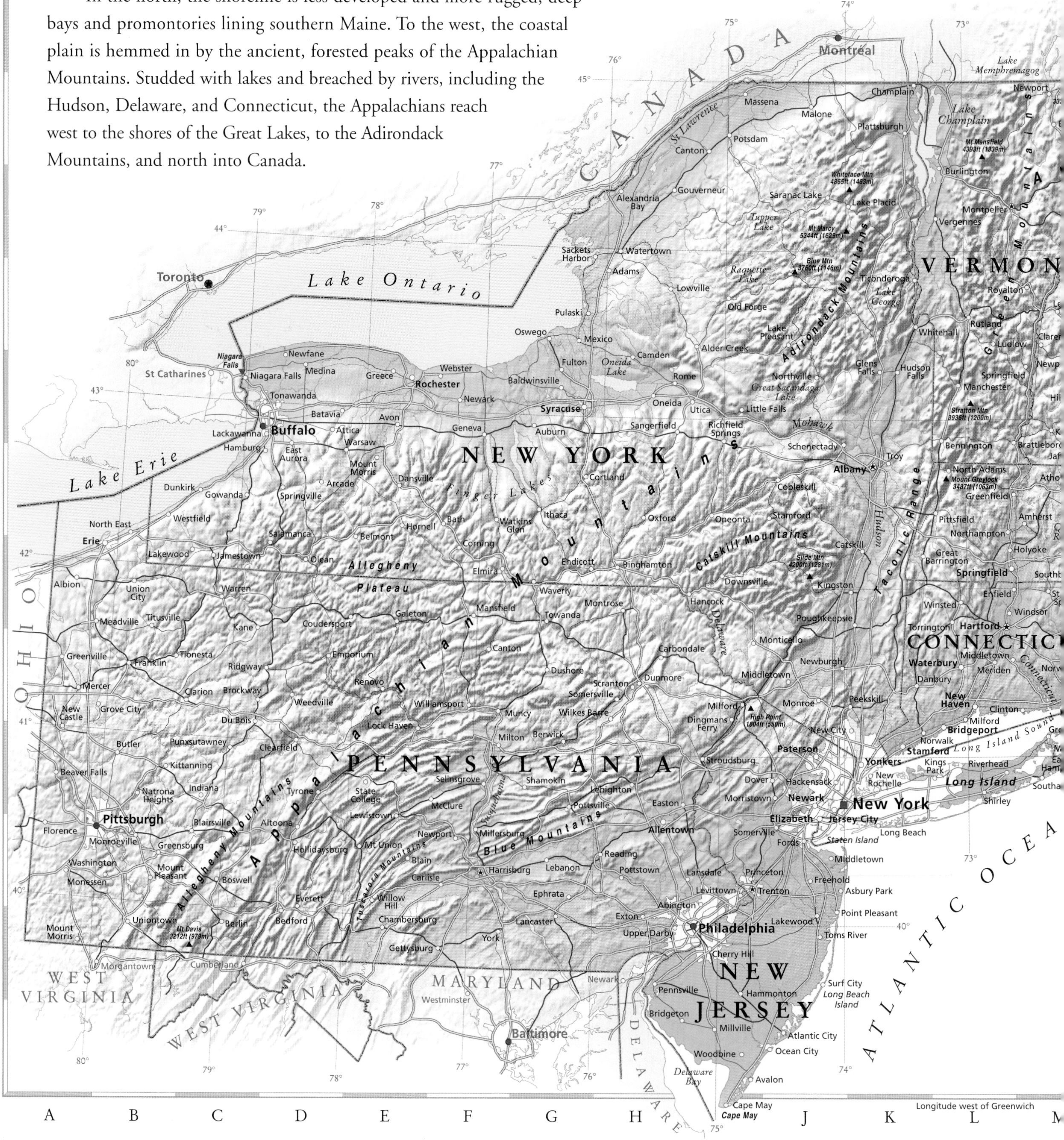

A B C D E F G H I J K L M
1 4 5 6 7 8 9 10 11 12 13 14 15
CANADA
Montreal
Lake Memphremagog
Lake Champlain
Lake Ontario
Lake Erie
Toronto
St Catharines
NEW YORK
PENNSYLVANIA
NEW JERSEY
VERMONT
CONNECTICUT
MARYLAND
WEST VIRGINIA
OHIO
DELAWARE
ATLANTIC OCEAN
Adirondack Mountains
Green Mountains
Catskill Mountains
Taconic Range
Allegheny Plateau
Allegheny Mountains
Appalachian Mountains
Blue Mountains
Tuscarora Mountains
Finger Lakes
Mohawk
Hudson
Delaware
Susquehanna
St Lawrence
Long Island
Long Island Sound
Whiteface Mtn 4865ft (1483m)
Mt Marcy 5344ft (1629m)
Blue Mtn 3760ft (1146m)
Mt Mansfield 4393ft (1339m)
Stratton Mtn 3936ft (1200m)
Mount Greylock 3487ft (1063m)
Slide Mtn 4200ft (1281m)
High Point 1804ft (550m)
Mt Davis 3212ft (979m)
Buffalo
Rochester
Syracuse
Albany
Erie
Pittsburgh
Harrisburg
Philadelphia
Trenton
New York
Newark
Jersey City
Hartford
Baltimore
Cape May
Longitude west of Greenwich

N O P Q R S T U V W X Y Z
1 2 3 4 5 6 7 8 9 10 11
CANADA
MAINE
NEW HAMPSHIRE
MASSACHUSETTS
RHODE ISLAND
Gulf of Maine
Appalachian Mountains
New England
White Mountains
Madawaska
Van Buren
Eagle Lake
Limestone
Caribou
Presque Isle
Ashland
Eagle Lake
Chamberlain Lake
Houlton
Chesuncook Lake
Patten
Mt Katahdin 5269ft (1606m)
Sherman Mills
Moosehead Lake
Chiputneticook Lakes
Danforth
Millinocket
Vanceboro
Jackman
White Cap Mountain 3645ft (1111m)
Greenville
Mattawamkeag
Lincoln
Bingham
Milo
Woodland
Calais
Flagstaff Lake
West Grand Lake
Guilford
Stratton
Wesley
Old Town
Rangeley
Solon
Bangor
Brewer
Lubec
Grand Manan Channel
Colebrook
Skowhegan
Pittsfield
Machias
Errol
Farmington
Ellsworth
Cross Island
Grand Manan Island
Groveton
Wilton
Winslow
Searsport
Belfast
Blue Hill
Milbridge
Great Wass Island
Lancaster
Bethel
Bar Harbor
Mt Washington 6293ft (1918m)
Augusta
Camden
Mount Desert Island
South Paris
Rockland
Deer Isle
Swans Island
Lewiston
Isle au Haut
Bridgton
Vinalhaven Island
Conway
Lisbon Falls
Wiscasset
Bath
Brunswick
Sebago Lake
Portland
Small Point
Casco Bay
Cape Elizabeth
Lake Winnipesaukee
Laconia
Biddeford
Sanford
Kennebunkport
Rochester
Concord
Dover
York Harbor
Newmarket
Portsmouth
Manchester
Hampton
Derry
Newburyport
Lawrence
Cape Ann
Lowell
Gloucester
Salem
Cambridge
Massachusetts Bay
Boston
Newton
Weymouth
Provincetown
Brockton
Cape Cod
Plymouth
Cape Cod Bay
Taunton
Orleans
Providence
Fall River
Barnstable
Monomoy Island
New Bedford
Nantucket Sound
Buzzards Bay
Newport
Oak Bluffs
Rhode Island Sound
Martha's Vineyard
Nantucket
Nantucket Island
Block Island
47°
46°
45°
44°
43°
42°
71°
70°
69°
68°
67°

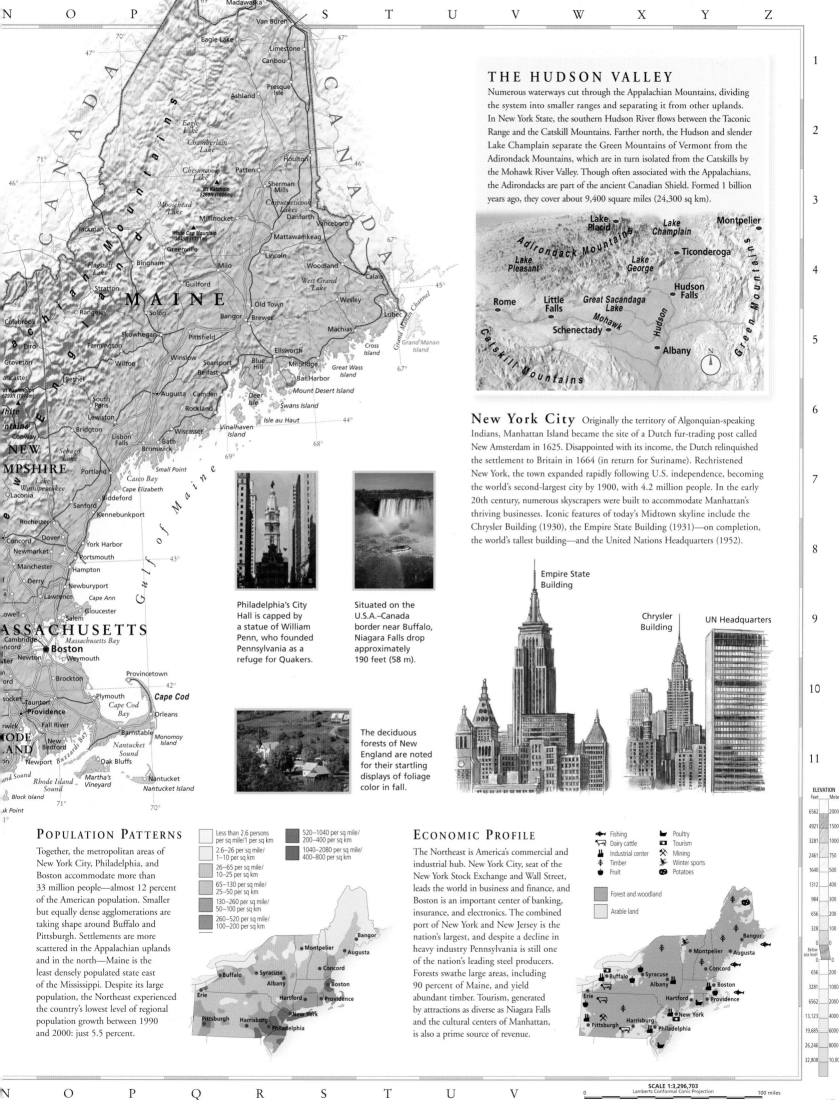

THE HUDSON VALLEY

Numerous waterways cut through the Appalachian Mountains, dividing the system into smaller ranges and separating it from other uplands. In New York State, the southern Hudson River flows between the Taconic Range and the Catskill Mountains. Farther north, the Hudson and slender Lake Champlain separate the Green Mountains of Vermont from the Adirondack Mountains, which are in turn isolated from the Catskills by the Mohawk River Valley. Though often associated with the Appalachians, the Adirondacks are part of the ancient Canadian Shield. Formed 1 billion years ago, they cover about 9,400 square miles (24,300 sq km).

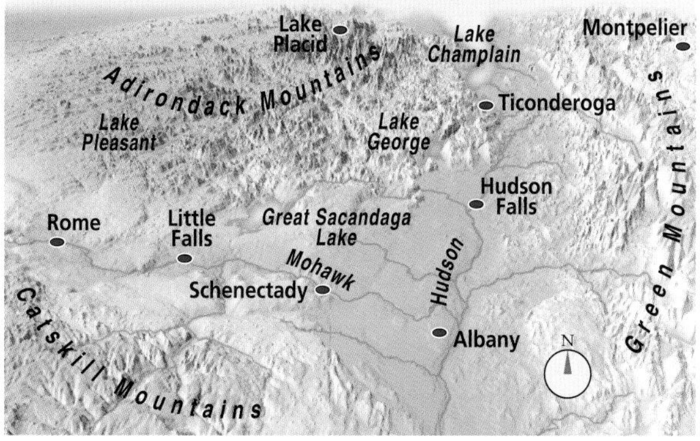
Lake Placid
Lake Champlain
Montpelier
Adirondack Mountains
Ticonderoga
Lake Pleasant
Lake George
Green Mountains
Hudson Falls
Rome
Little Falls
Great Sacandaga Lake
Mohawk
Hudson
Schenectady
Albany
Catskill Mountains
N

New York City Originally the territory of Algonquian-speaking Indians, Manhattan Island became the site of a Dutch fur-trading post called New Amsterdam in 1625. Disappointed with its income, the Dutch relinquished the settlement to Britain in 1664 (in return for Suriname). Rechristened New York, the town expanded rapidly following U.S. independence, becoming the world's second-largest city by 1900, with 4.2 million people. In the early 20th century, numerous skyscrapers were built to accommodate Manhattan's thriving businesses. Iconic features of today's Midtown skyline include the Chrysler Building (1930), the Empire State Building (1931)—on completion, the world's tallest building—and the United Nations Headquarters (1952).

Philadelphia's City Hall is capped by a statue of William Penn, who founded Pennsylvania as a refuge for Quakers.

Situated on the U.S.A.–Canada border near Buffalo, Niagara Falls drop approximately 190 feet (58 m).

The deciduous forests of New England are noted for their startling displays of foliage color in fall.

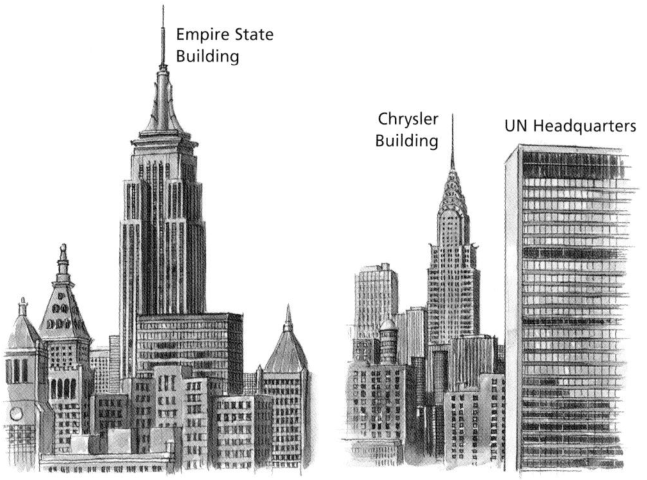
Empire State Building
Chrysler Building
UN Headquarters

POPULATION PATTERNS

Together, the metropolitan areas of New York City, Philadelphia, and Boston accommodate more than 33 million people—almost 12 percent of the American population. Smaller but equally dense agglomerations are taking shape around Buffalo and Pittsburgh. Settlements are more scattered in the Appalachian uplands and in the north—Maine is the least densely populated state east of the Mississippi. Despite its large population, the Northeast experienced the country's lowest level of regional population growth between 1990 and 2000: just 5.5 percent.

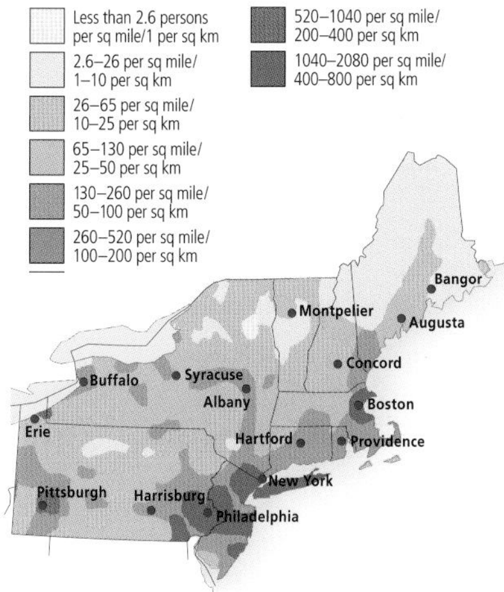
Less than 2.6 persons per sq mile/1 per sq km
2.6–26 per sq mile/ 1–10 per sq km
26–65 per sq mile/ 10–25 per sq km
65–130 per sq mile/ 25–50 per sq km
130–260 per sq mile/ 50–100 per sq km
260–520 per sq mile/ 100–200 per sq km
520–1040 per sq mile/ 200–400 per sq km
1040–2080 per sq mile/ 400–800 per sq km
Bangor
Montpelier
Augusta
Concord
Buffalo
Syracuse
Albany
Boston
Erie
Hartford
Providence
Pittsburgh
Harrisburg
New York
Philadelphia

ECONOMIC PROFILE

The Northeast is America's commercial and industrial hub. New York City, seat of the New York Stock Exchange and Wall Street, leads the world in business and finance, and Boston is an important center of banking, insurance, and electronics. The combined port of New York and New Jersey is the nation's largest, and despite a decline in heavy industry Pennsylvania is still one of the nation's leading steel producers. Forests swathe large areas, including 90 percent of Maine, and yield abundant timber. Tourism, generated by attractions as diverse as Niagara Falls and the cultural centers of Manhattan, is also a prime source of revenue.

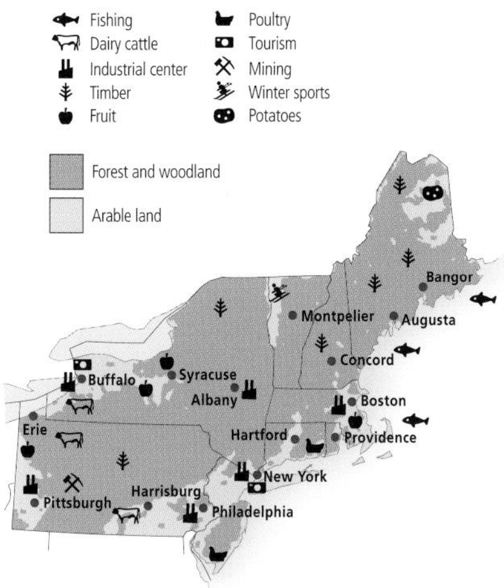
Fishing
Dairy cattle
Industrial center
Timber
Fruit
Poultry
Tourism
Mining
Winter sports
Potatoes
Forest and woodland
Arable land
Bangor
Montpelier
Augusta
Concord
Buffalo
Syracuse
Albany
Boston
Erie
Hartford
Providence
New York
Pittsburgh
Harrisburg
Philadelphia

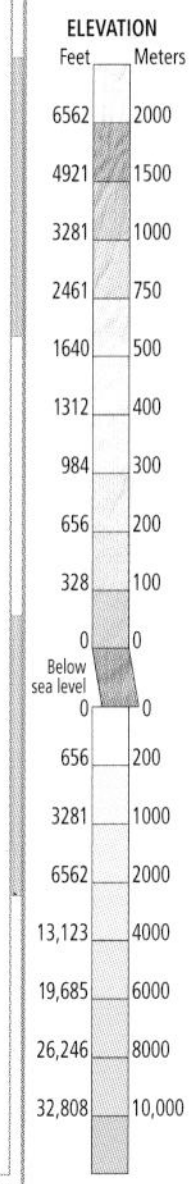
ELEVATION
Feet
Meters
6562 2000
4921 1500
3281 1000
2461 750
1640 500
1312 400
984 300
656 200
328 100
0 0
Below sea level
0 0
656 200
3281 1000
6562 2000
13,123 4000
19,685 6000
26,246 8000
32,808 10,000

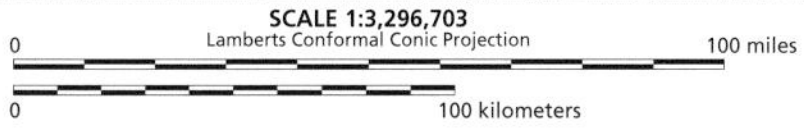
SCALE 1:3,296,703
Lamberts Conformal Conic Projection
0
100 miles
0
100 kilometers

South Atlantic U.S.A.

Delaware, District of Columbia, Kentucky, Maryland, North Carolina, South Carolina, Tennessee, Virginia, West Virginia

The northern perimeter of this region, formed by the Ohio River and the southern border of Pennsylvania—the so-called Mason and Dixon Line—is the traditional divide between North and South: prior to the Civil War it separated slave-owning states from abolitionists. History and terrain have created other regional distinctions. The thickly forested ridges of the Appalachian Mountains form a sparsely populated enclave of mining and timber towns. To the west lie the pastoral hills of central Tennessee and Kentucky's Bluegrass region, and the heavily cultivated lowlands of the Mississippi and Ohio rivers. In the east, the wooded Appalachian foothills, known as the Piedmont, descend to a broad coastal plain bordered by historic ports and barrier islands.

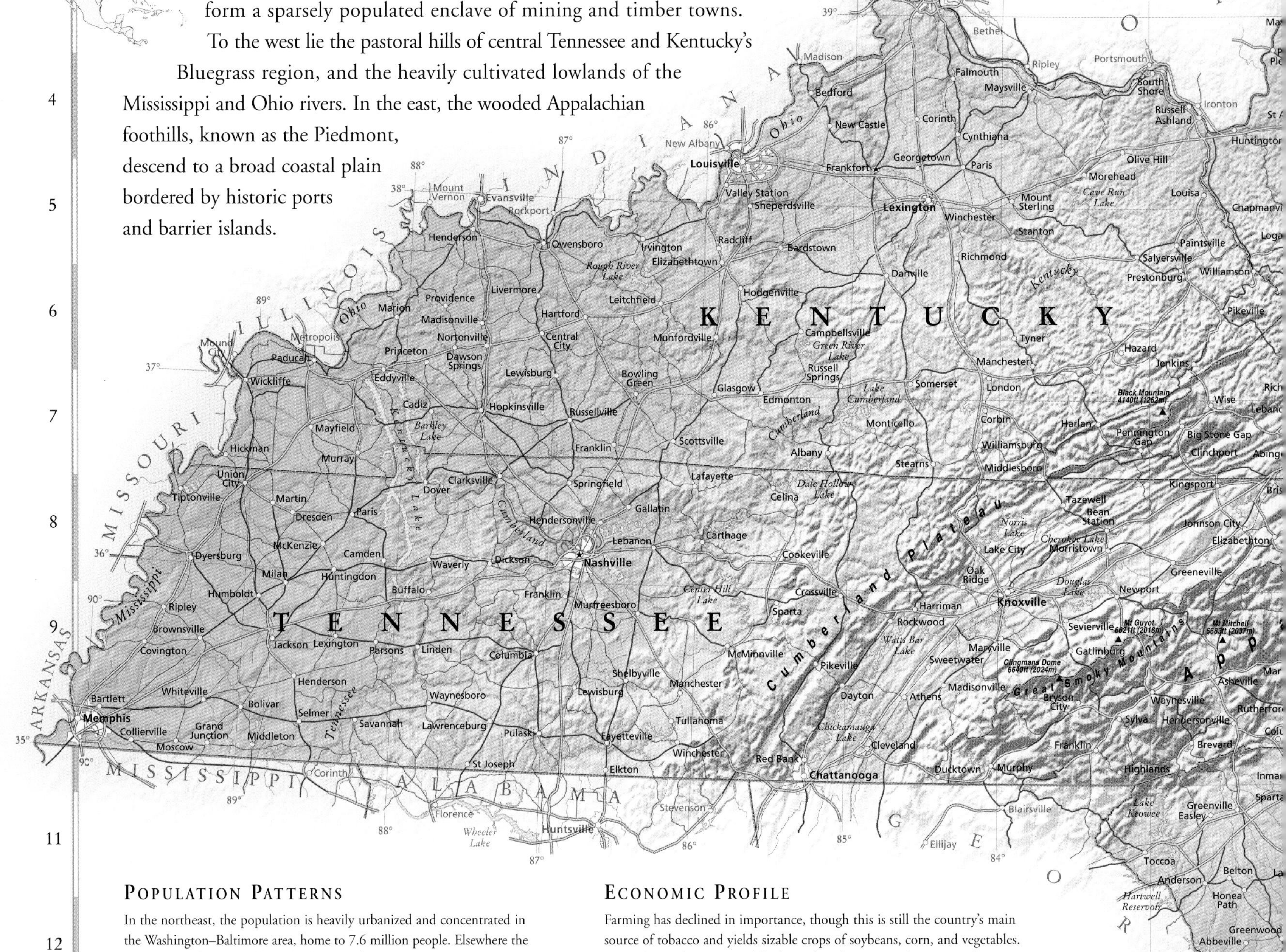

Population Patterns

In the northeast, the population is heavily urbanized and concentrated in the Washington–Baltimore area, home to 7.6 million people. Elsewhere the proportion of rural dwellers is high, rising from 27 percent in Virginia to 51 percent in West Virginia. In Virginia and the Carolinas, people cluster in the Piedmont, but the cities here are relatively small; the largest urban centers outside the northeast are Nashville and Memphis in Tennessee. Population growth between 1990 and 2000 varied markedly, from –5.7 percent in the District of Columbia to 21.4 percent in North Carolina.

Economic Profile

Farming has declined in importance, though this is still the country's main source of tobacco and yields sizable crops of soybeans, corn, and vegetables. Kentucky is also renowned for horse-breeding. Manufacturing industries include whiskey in Kentucky and Tennessee; chemicals in Tennessee, Virginia, and Delaware; and textiles and high-tech goods in North Carolina. Service industries predominate in the northeast, with the government being a major employer. Appalachia has some of America's most productive coal fields. Fishing, mainly of shellfish, remains important around Chesapeake Bay.

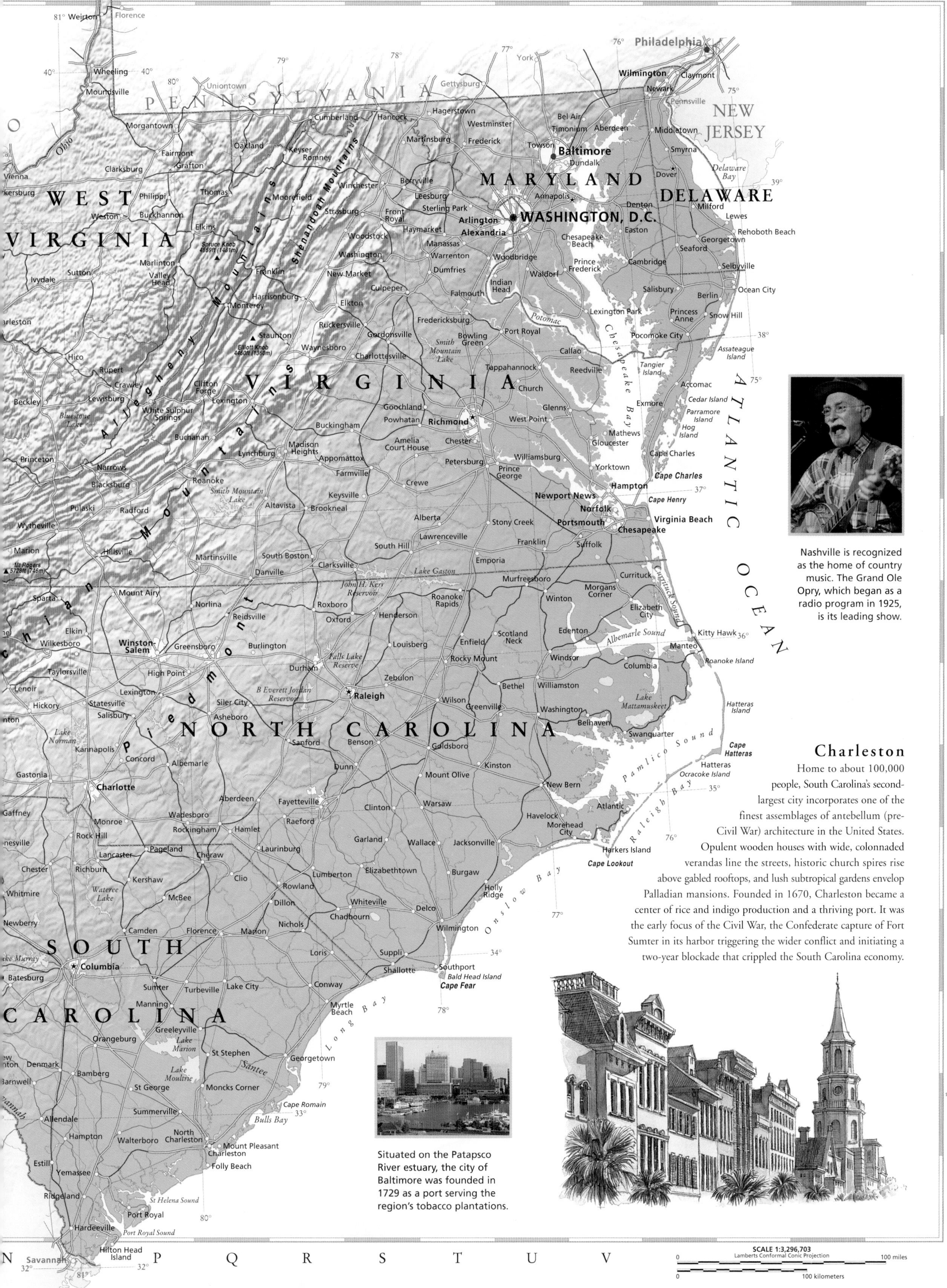

Nashville is recognized as the home of country music. The Grand Ole Opry, which began as a radio program in 1925, is its leading show.

Charleston

Home to about 100,000 people, South Carolina's second-largest city incorporates one of the finest assemblages of antebellum (pre-Civil War) architecture in the United States. Opulent wooden houses with wide, colonnaded verandas line the streets, historic church spires rise above gabled rooftops, and lush subtropical gardens envelop Palladian mansions. Founded in 1670, Charleston became a center of rice and indigo production and a thriving port. It was the early focus of the Civil War, the Confederate capture of Fort Sumter in its harbor triggering the wider conflict and initiating a two-year blockade that crippled the South Carolina economy.

Situated on the Patapsco River estuary, the city of Baltimore was founded in 1729 as a port serving the region's tobacco plantations.

A B C D E F G H I J K L M

SOUTHEASTERN U.S.A.

Alabama, Florida, Georgia, Louisiana, Mississippi

In the southeastern corner of the United States, rolling hills and low plateaus cover much of the interior, rising in northern Alabama and Georgia to the southern edge of the Appalachian Mountains and descending along a broad sweep to the alluvial plain of the Mississippi River, the Gulf and Atlantic coastal plains, and the broad, flat Florida Peninsula. In the 16th century, Spanish explorers became the first Europeans to visit this predominantly swampy coastline, then home to various Indian groups. The Spanish founded the settlement of St Augustine, Florida, in 1565, now the oldest city in the country. In the late 17th century, French traders took control of the Mississippi Basin, establishing a port at New Orleans. Under the Treaty of Paris of 1763, New Orleans and the western Mississippi Valley passed to Spain, while the land to the east of the Mississippi, including Spanish Florida, came under British control. After the Civil War, continuing discrimination against the African-American population made the Southeast the focus of civil-rights protests, which reached a peak in the 1960s with mass demonstrations in Montgomery and Birmingham, Alabama, and the 1963 March on Washington for Jobs and Freedom.

Hurricanes regularly strike the Southeast. In August 1992, Hurricane Andrew caused US$25 billion worth of damage and 23 deaths.

The distinctive architecture of New Orleans reflects the origins of its early inhabitants. Founded by the French in 1718, it was ceded to Spain in 1763.

POPULATION PATTERNS

The Southeast's inhabitants are fairly evenly spread, though coastal wetlands limit settlement in parts of the Gulf Coast (notably the Mississippi Delta) and Florida. Population density and urbanization are lower in the three western states, particularly in Mississippi. In contrast, Georgia and Florida have large urban populations, with settlement focused on cities such as Atlanta (home to half of Georgia's people), Tampa, and Miami. The populations of these two states are growing rapidly, with Florida's projected to reach 20 million by 2010, due in part to its popularity as a retirement destination.

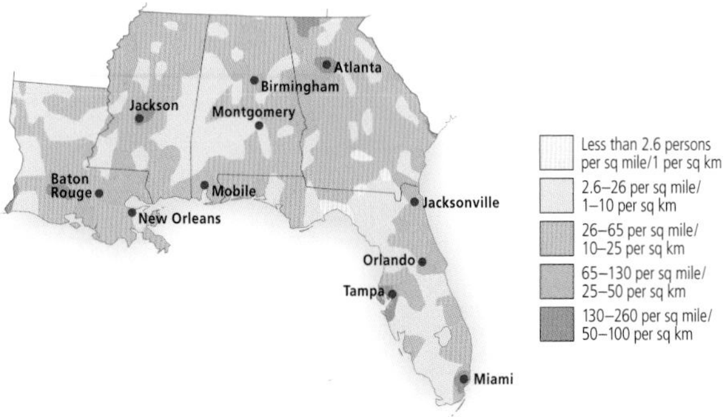

ECONOMIC PROFILE

Until the early 20th century, the Southeast was dependent on agriculture, especially the cultivation of cotton and tobacco. These crops remain significant, but farmers have diversified into soybeans, corn, peanuts, and, in Florida, citrus fruits. Extensive forests provide abundant timber, and the industrial sector has expanded to include textiles, transportation equipment, electronics, and the aerospace industry. Louisiana is one of the nation's leading producers of oil and gas, Georgia is home to major corporations—Atlanta is the headquarters of Coca-Cola and CNN (Cable News Network)—and Florida has a thriving tourist industry.

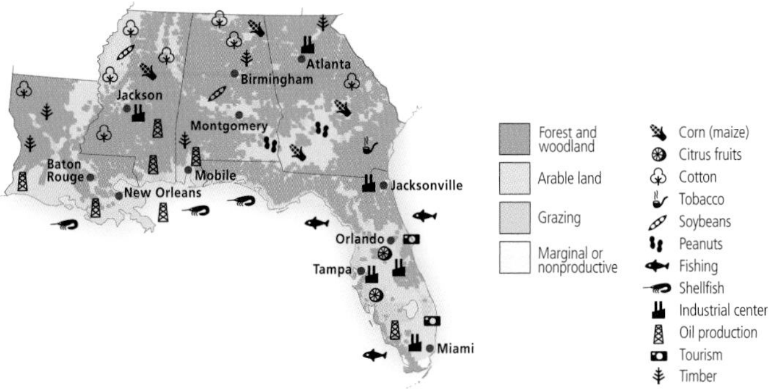

A B C D E F G H I J K L M

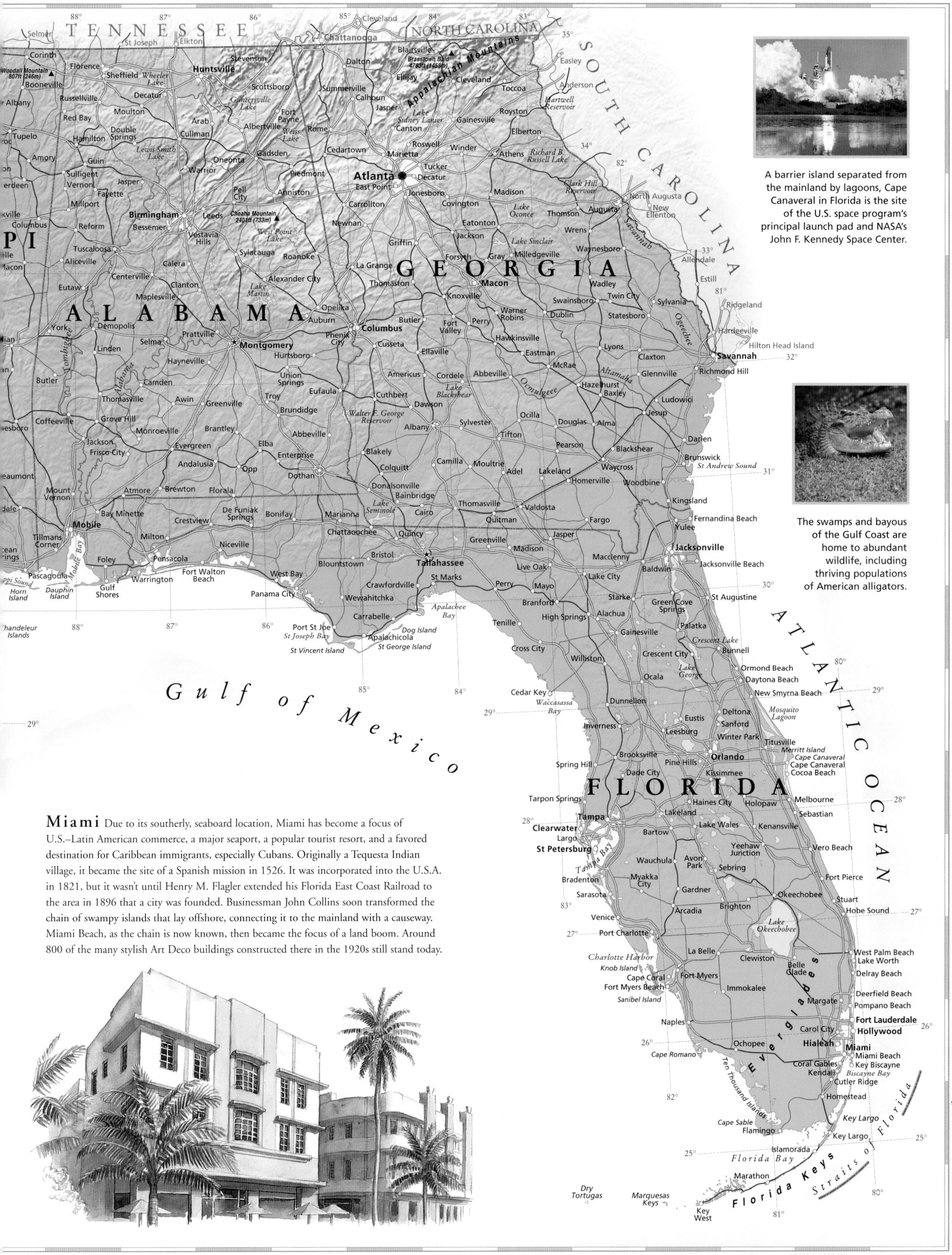

A barrier island separated from the mainland by lagoons, Cape Canaveral in Florida is the site of the U.S. space program's principal launch pad and NASA's John F. Kennedy Space Center.

The swamps and bayous of the Gulf Coast are home to abundant wildlife, including thriving populations of American alligators.

Miami Due to its southerly, seaboard location, Miami has become a focus of U.S.–Latin American commerce, a major seaport, a popular tourist resort, and a favored destination for Caribbean immigrants, especially Cubans. Originally a Tequesta Indian village, it became the site of a Spanish mission in 1526. It was incorporated into the U.S.A. in 1821, but it wasn't until Henry M. Flagler extended his Florida East Coast Railroad to the area in 1896 that a city was founded. Businessman John Collins soon transformed the chain of swampy islands that lay offshore, connecting it to the mainland with a causeway. Miami Beach, as the chain is now known, then became the focus of a land boom. Around 800 of the many stylish Art Deco buildings constructed there in the 1920s still stand today.

ELEVATION

Feet	Meters
6562	2000
4921	1500
3281	1000
2461	750
1640	500
1312	400
984	300
656	200
328	100
0	0
Below sea level	
0	0
656	200
3281	1000
6562	2000
13,123	4000
19,685	6000
26,246	8000
32,808	10,000

SCALE 1:4,395,604
Lamberts Conformal Conic Projection
0 120 miles
0 120 kilometers

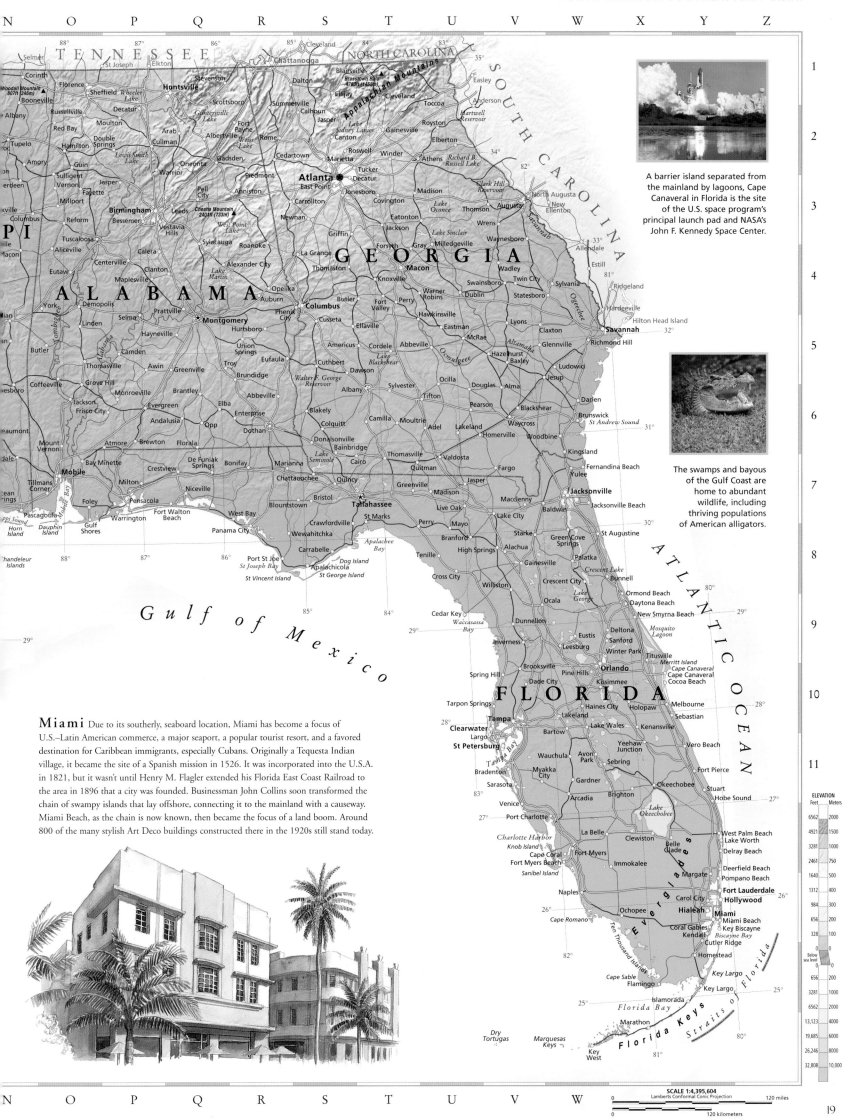

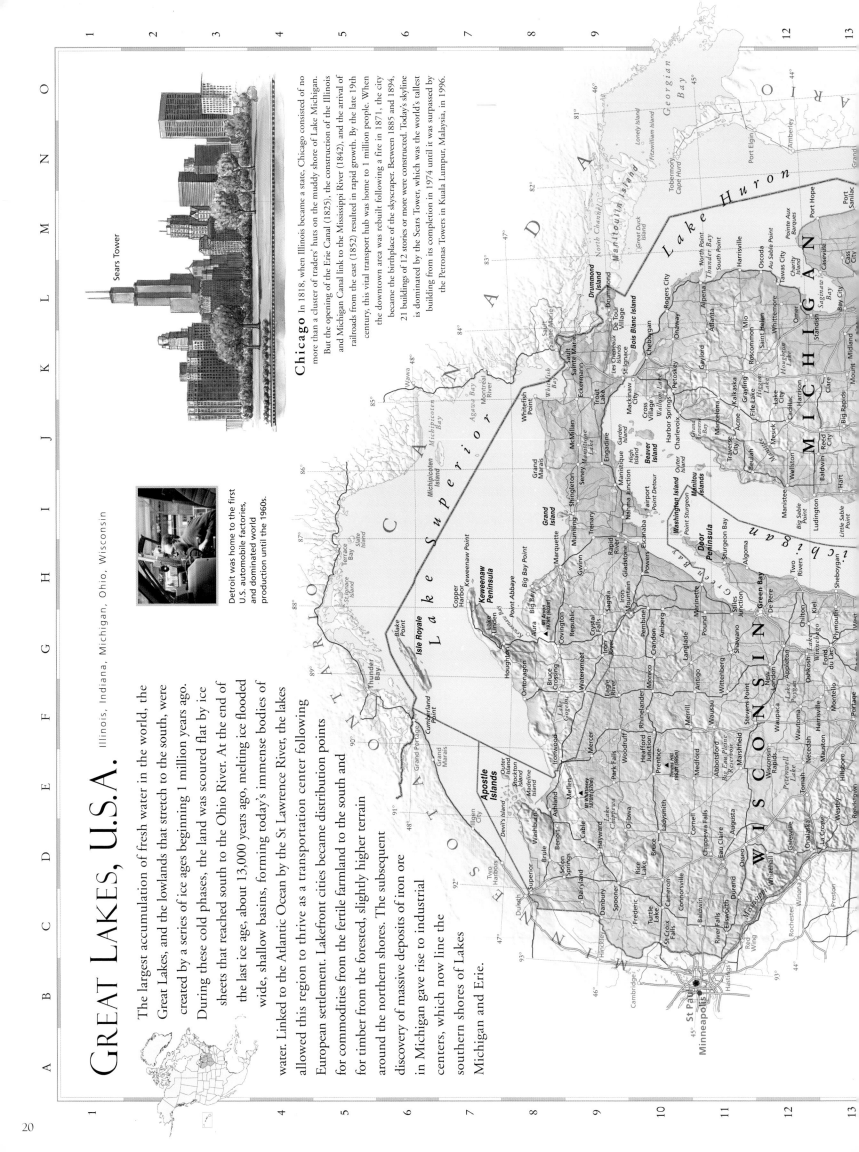

Great Lakes, U.S.A.

Illinois, Indiana, Michigan, Ohio, Wisconsin

The largest accumulation of fresh water in the world, the Great Lakes, and the lowlands that stretch to the south, were created by a series of ice ages beginning 1 million years ago. During these cold phases, the land was scoured flat by ice sheets that reached south to the Ohio River. At the end of the last ice age, about 13,000 years ago, melting ice flooded wide, shallow basins, forming today's immense bodies of water. Linked to the Atlantic Ocean by the St Lawrence River, the lakes allowed this region to thrive as a transportation center following European settlement. Lakefront cities became distribution points for commodities from the fertile farmland to the south and for timber from the forested, slightly higher terrain around the northern shores. The subsequent discovery of massive deposits of iron ore in Michigan gave rise to industrial centers, which now line the southern shores of Lakes Michigan and Erie.

Detroit was home to the first U.S. automobile factories, and dominated world production until the 1960s.

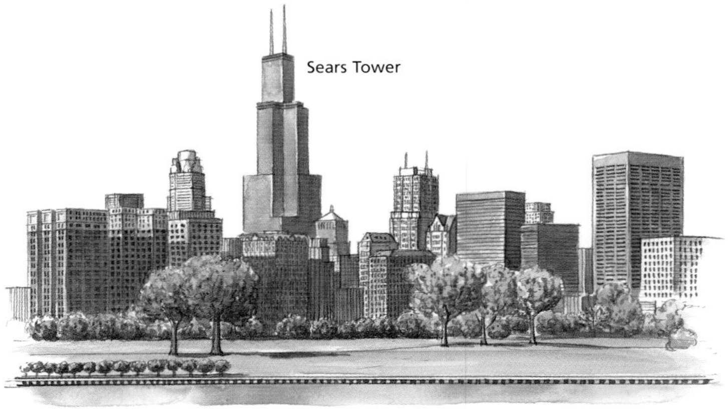

Chicago In 1818, when Illinois became a state, Chicago consisted of no more than a cluster of traders' huts on the muddy shore of Lake Michigan. But the opening of the Erie Canal (1825), the construction of the Illinois and Michigan Canal link to the Mississippi River (1842), and the arrival of railroads from the east (1852) resulted in rapid growth. By the late 19th century, this vital transport hub was home to 1 million people. When the downtown area was rebuilt following a fire in 1871, the city became the birthplace of the skyscraper. Between 1885 and 1894, 21 buildings of 12 stories or more were constructed. Today's skyline is dominated by the Sears Tower, which was the world's tallest building from its completion in 1974 until it was surpassed by the Petronas Towers in Kuala Lumpur, Malaysia, in 1996.

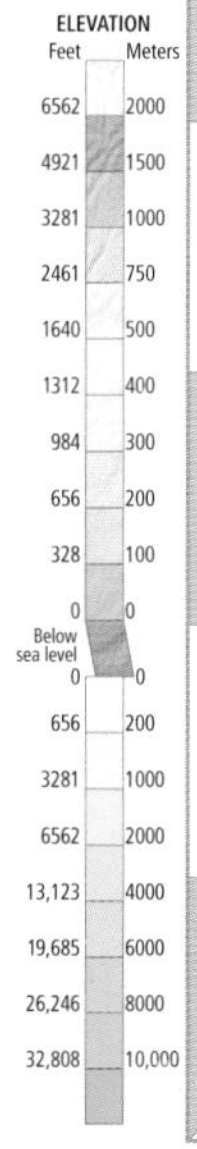

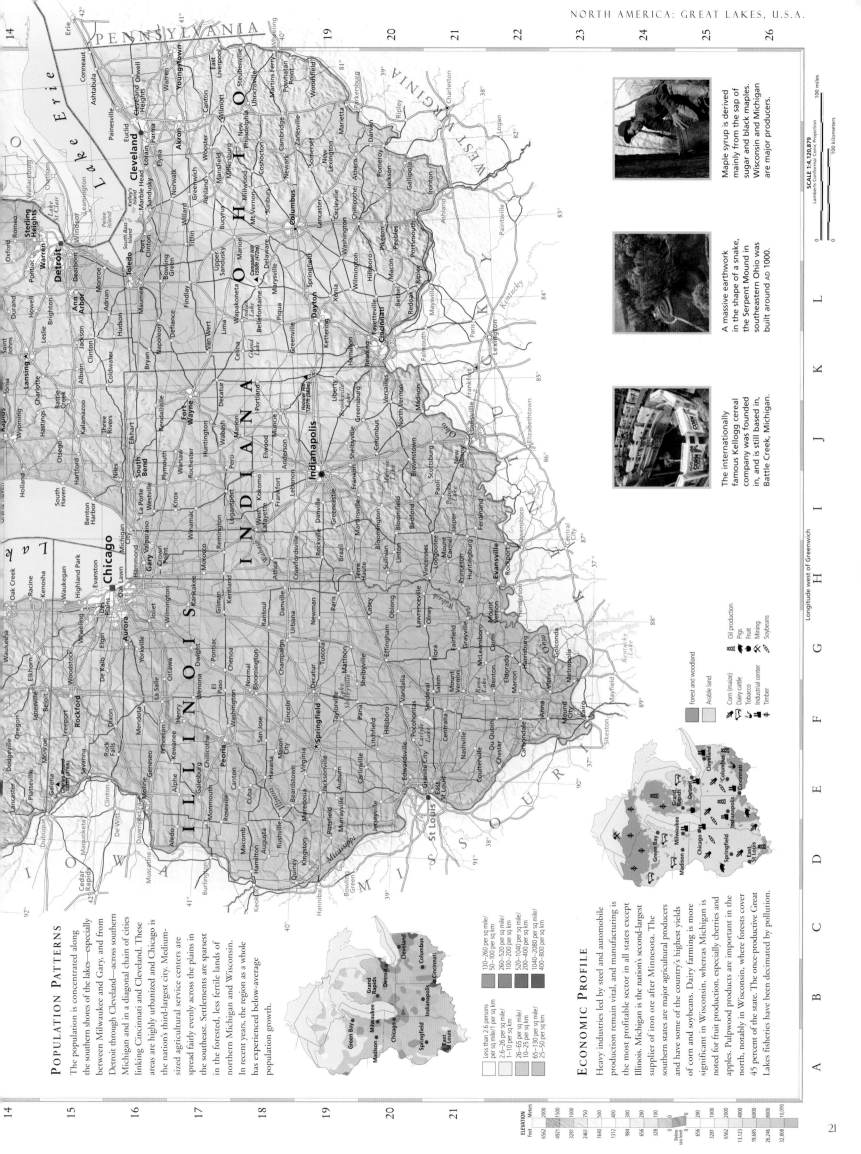

Population Patterns

The population is concentrated along the southern shores of the lakes—especially between Milwaukee and Gary, and from Detroit through Cleveland—across southern Michigan and in a diagonal chain of cities linking Cincinnati and Cleveland. These areas are highly urbanized and Chicago is the nation's third-largest city. Medium-sized agricultural service centers are spread fairly evenly across the plains in the southeast. Settlements are sparsest in the forested, less fertile lands of northern Michigan and Wisconsin. In recent years, the region as a whole has experienced below-average population growth.

Economic Profile

Heavy industries led by steel and automobile production remain vital, and manufacturing is the most profitable sector in all states except Illinois. Michigan is the nation's second-largest supplier of iron ore after Minnesota. The southern states are major agricultural producers and have some of the country's highest yields of corn and soybeans. Dairy farming is more significant in Wisconsin, whereas Michigan is noted for fruit production, especially cherries and apples. Pulpwood products are important in the north, notably in Wisconsin, where forests cover 45 percent of the state. The once-productive Great Lakes fisheries have been decimated by pollution.

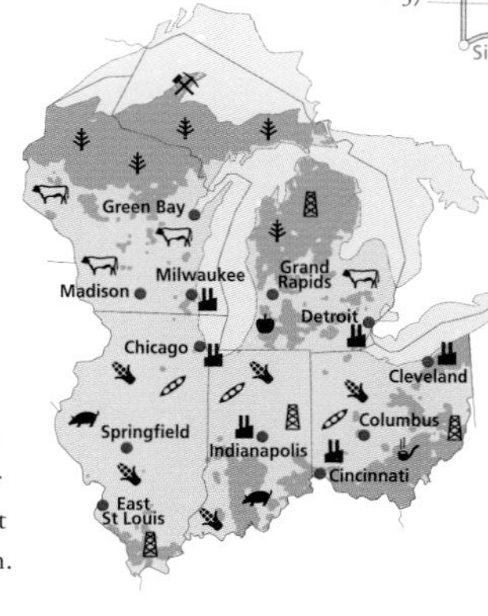

The internationally famous Kellogg cereal company was founded in, and is still based in, Battle Creek, Michigan.

A massive earthwork in the shape of a snake, the Serpent Mound in southeastern Ohio was built around AD 1000.

Maple syrup is derived mainly from the sap of sugar and black maples. Wisconsin and Michigan are major producers.

Upper Midwest, U.S.A.

Iowa, Minnesota, Nebraska, North Dakota, South Dakota

A seemingly boundless sea of crops is the image most strongly associated with the Upper Midwest, and indeed more than half of the land is used for cultivation and agriculture dominates the economy. Wheat fields swathe much of the Great Plains plateau on the western side of the region. Myriad streams and rivers follow the plateau's gentle eastward inclination, carving gullies and channels through hills and badlands, and feeding for the most part into the Missouri River. Undulating farmland—mainly fields of corn and soybeans—also covers most of Iowa and southern Minnesota. In the northeast, the plains are studded with lakes and marshes formed by the retreat of glaciers at the end of last ice age. The upper Mississippi and Missouri were vital transportation routes for Native Americans and early European explorers and trappers, but widespread intensive settlement did not take place until after the arrival of the railroads around 1870.

Population Patterns

The western part of this region is one of the most sparsely inhabited parts of the lower 48, and North and South Dakota are, respectively, the second and fourth least populous states. The east has larger settlements, especially along major rivers. The Upper Midwest generally experiences lower than average population growth: between 1990 and 2000, North Dakota had the country's lowest rate of growth, a mere 0.5 percent. The overall proportion of rural dwellers is significantly higher than average, reaching almost half in South Dakota.

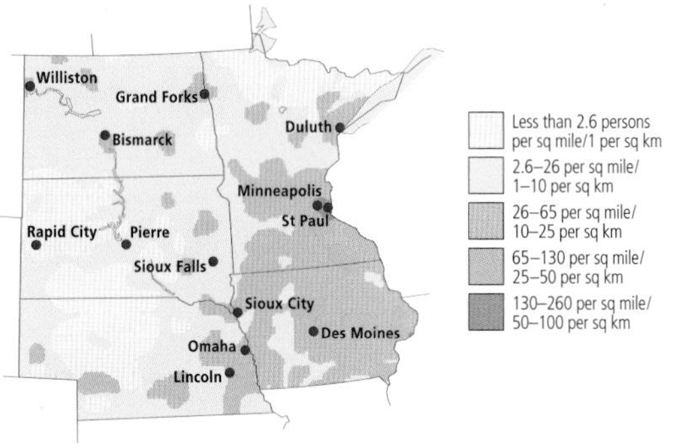

Economic Profile

These states are among the nation's largest agricultural producers. The west forms part of the Great Plains Wheat Belt; the so-called Corn Belt encompasses eastern Nebraska, Iowa, and southern Minnesota. Grazing of cattle and pigs occurs throughout the region. Minnesota is the nation's largest producer of iron ore, Nebraska and North Dakota have modest supplies of petroleum, and South Dakota's Black Hills are a prime source of gold. Farming is the basis of most manufacturing and services, though tourism and the insurance industry are also important.

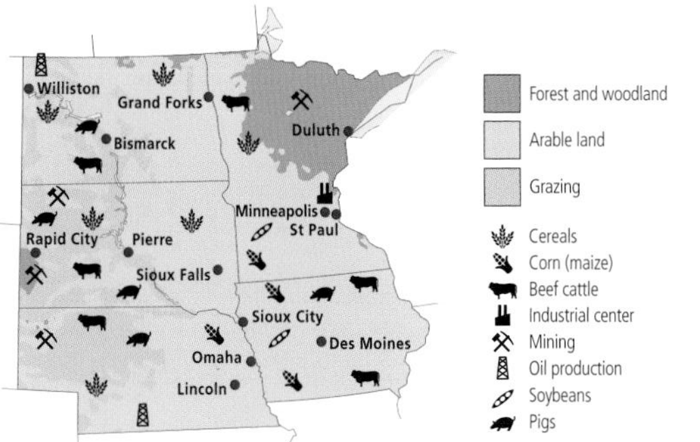

N O P R S T U V W X Y Z
1 2 3 4 5 6 7 8 9 10 11
CANADA
Lake of the Woods
Warroad
Baudette
Rainy Lake
International Falls
Namakan Lake
Lac la Croix
Saganaga Lake
Thunder Bay
Grand Portage
Basswood Lake
Grand Marais
Lake Superior
Karlstad
Red
Warren
Thief River Falls
Upper Red Lake
Lower Red Lake
Big Falls
Cook
Vermilion Lake
Grand Forks
Crookston
Erskine
Blackduck
Mesabi Range
Virginia
Hibbing
Silver Bay
Lake Winnibigoshish
Bemidji
Grand Rapids
Mahnomen
Lake Walker
Walker
Hill City
Duluth
Cloquet
Park Rapids
Fargo
Moorhead
Detroit Lakes
Pine River
Mississippi
Aitkin
Wadena
Brainerd
Mille Lacs
Sandstone
Fergus Falls
Wahpeton
MINNESOTA
Hinckley
Onamia
Little Falls
Alexandria
Sauk Centre
Milaca
Cambridge
North Branch
St Cloud
Elk River
Coon Rapids
Sisseton
Graceville
Morris
Belgrade
Paynesville
Ortonville
Benson
WISCONSIN
Milbank
Willmar
Minneapolis
St Paul
Hutchinson
Chaska
Hastings
Minnesota
Montevideo
Olivia
Bloomington
Watertown
Granite Falls
Canby
Redwood Falls
Le Sueur
Red Wing
Wabasha
Northfield
Faribault
Marshall
New Ulm
Brookings
Lake Benton
Owatonna
Rochester
Winona
Arlington
Springfield
Mankato
Stewartville
Madison
Pipestone
Preston
Windom
Austin
Albert Lea
Fairmont
Decorah
Sioux Falls
Luverne
Worthington
Estherville
Osage
Postville
Sibley
Clear Lake
Mason City
West Union
Freeman
Sheldon
Emmetsburg
Charles City
Spencer
Algona
Beresford
Guttenberg
Humboldt
Dubuque
Yankton
Cherokee
Cedar Falls
Waterloo
Vermillion
Le Mars
Storm Lake
Fort Dodge
Iowa Falls
Monticello
Holstein
Cedar
Maquoketa
Laurel
Dakota City
Sioux City
Ida Grove
Rockwell City
IOWA
Cedar Rapids
Marion
Clinton
Boone
Marshalltown
De Witt
Missouri Valley
Carroll
Ames
Jefferson
Norfolk
Decatur
Denison
Victor
Davenport
Moline
Des Moines
Newton
Iowa City
Muscatine
Dunlap
Ankeny
Oakland
Exira
De Soto
Humphrey
Blair
Indianola
Fremont
Neola
Atlantic
Winterset
Knoxville
Oskaloosa
Washington
Columbus
Mount Pleasant
Omaha
Council Bluffs
Bellevue
Creston
Lucas
Ottumwa
Chariton
Burlington
Stromsburg
Papillion
Glenwood
Villisca
Centerville
Bloomfield
York
Waverly
Shenandoah
Lincoln
Lancaster
Hamilton
Nebraska City
Hamburg
MISSOURI
ILLINOIS
Fairmont
Auburn
Maryville
Hebron
Beatrice
Falls City
KANSAS
96°
94°
92°
90°
48°
46°
44°
42°
40°
Longitude west of Greenwich
SCALE 1:3,846,154
Lamberts Conformal Conic Projection
0
100 miles
0
100 kilometers
ELEVATION
Feet
Meters
6562 2000
4921 1500
3281 1000
2461 750
1640 500
1312 400
984 300
656 200
328 100
0 0
Below sea level
0 0
656 200
3281 1000
6562 2000
13,123 4000
19,685 6000
26,246 8000
32,808 10,000

Between 1840 and 1890, the Sioux people waged a long campaign of resistance against white settlement.

St Paul Minnesota's capital was originally known as Pig's Eye, after the area's first European settler, Pierre "Pig's-Eye" Parrant. Its name was changed to St Paul in 1841 after the founding of a church dedicated to the saint, and the town became state capital when Minnesota acceded to the Union in 1858. Its strategically important position near the confluence of the Mississippi and Minnesota rivers, and subsequent rail links to the West Coast, allowed it to develop as a major transportation hub and commercial center. Together with Minneapolis, on the other side of the Mississippi, it now forms the Twin Cities metropolitan area, by far the largest urban center in the Upper Midwest. The city's cathedral, a successor to the original church of St Paul, was designed in a classical Renaissance style by Emmanuel Masquery and opened in 1915.

Carved by Gutzon Borglum, Mount Rushmore National Memorial in South Dakota was completed in 1941.

Increasing mechanization of farming has steadily reduced the number of workers employed in this sector.

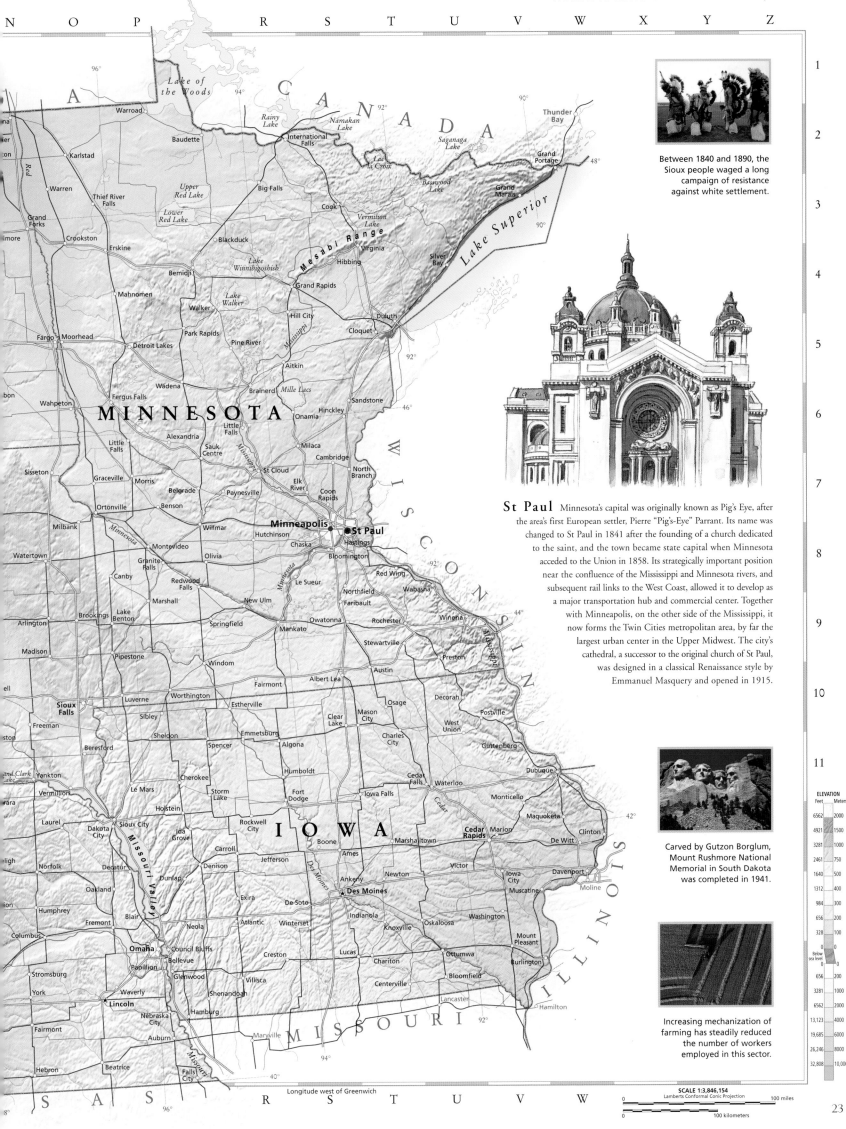

Lower Midwest, U.S.A.

Arkansas, Kansas, Missouri, Oklahoma

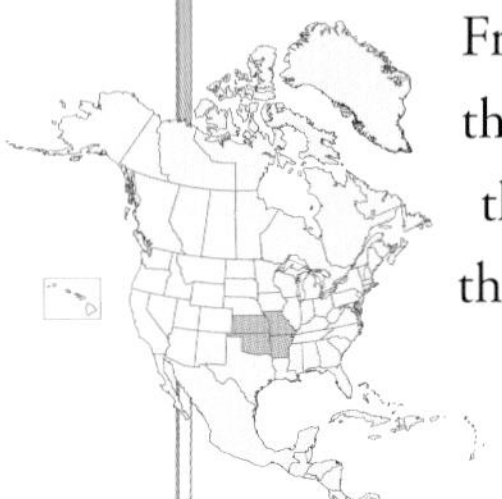

From the central Mississippi River, pioneers launched the great wave of westward expansion that began in the 1840s, turning this region into the "Gateway to the West." Most traveled along the Missouri River, over the hills of present-day Kansas and across the treeless plateau of the Great Plains. But the rugged, densely forested terrain of the Ozark Plateau and Ouachita Mountains in the east, the presence of large groups of displaced Native Americans in the so-called Indian Territory of the west, and early reports that the plains were a desert meant that the majority simply passed through. It wasn't until the end of the century that farmers turned the western plains into the major agricultural region that, despite occasional droughts such as those that created the Dust Bowl of the 1930s, it remains today.

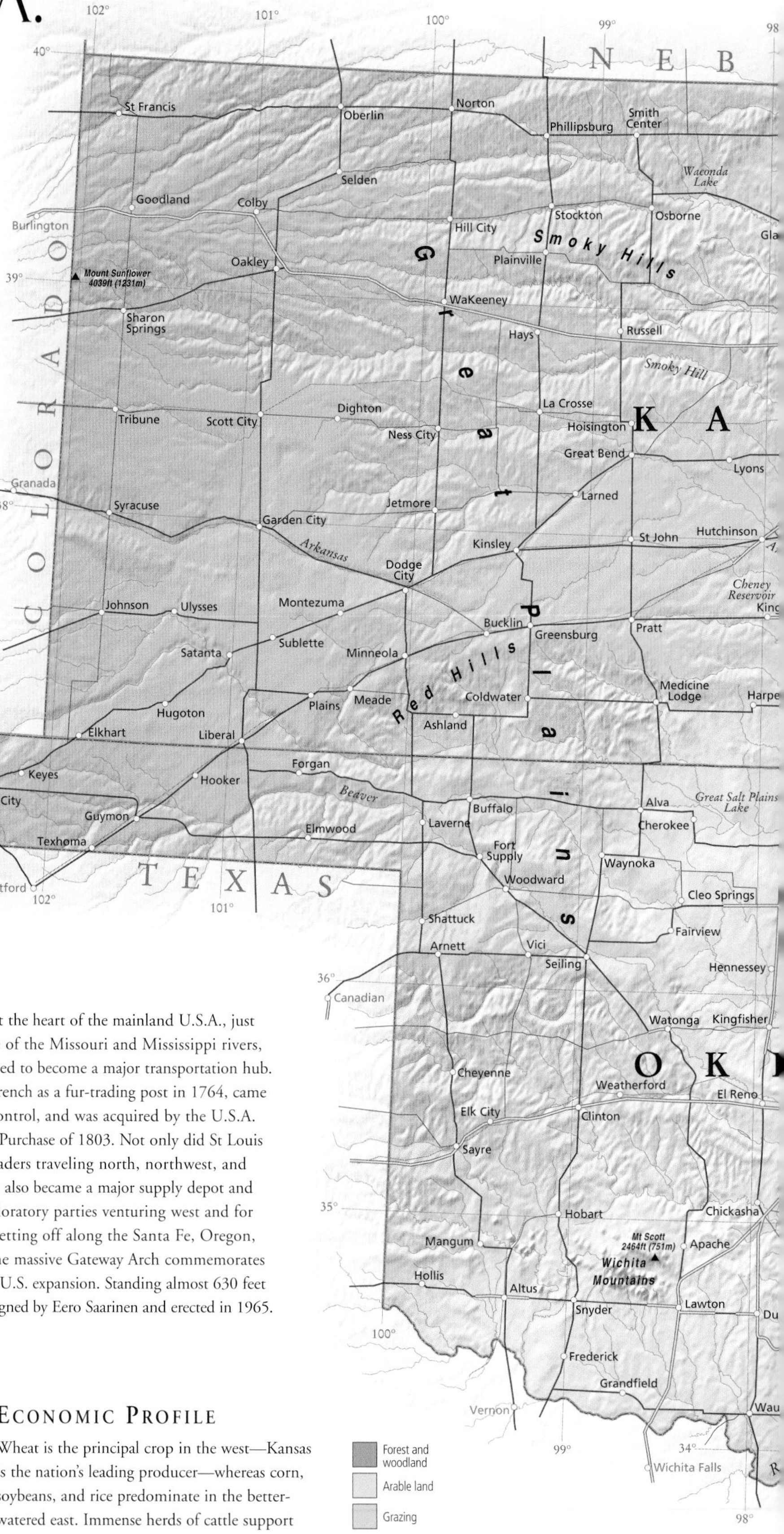

Thermal springs are among the attractions that have made the Ozark Plateau a popular tourist center.

St Louis Sited at the heart of the mainland U.S.A., just south of the confluence of the Missouri and Mississippi rivers, St Louis was ideally placed to become a major transportation hub. It was founded by the French as a fur-trading post in 1764, came briefly under Spanish control, and was acquired by the U.S.A. as part of the Louisiana Purchase of 1803. Not only did St Louis cater to trappers and traders traveling north, northwest, and south along the rivers, it also became a major supply depot and departure point for exploratory parties venturing west and for thousands of pioneers setting off along the Santa Fe, Oregon, and California trails. The massive Gateway Arch commemorates the city's historic role in U.S. expansion. Standing almost 630 feet (192 m) high, it was designed by Eero Saarinen and erected in 1965.

Population Patterns

The focus of early European settlement, the Mississippi and Missouri valleys are still the most densely populated areas, along with regional commercial and agricultural centers such as Oklahoma City and Wichita. Settlements are much more scattered on the western plains. More than a third of the region's inhabitants—including almost half of the population of Arkansas—live in rural areas. Limited economic diversity encourages migration to other areas, in turn keeping population growth well below the national average.

- 2.6–26 per sq mile/ 1–10 per sq km
- 26–65 per sq mile/ 10–25 per sq km
- 65–130 per sq mile/ 25–50 per sq km
- 130–260 per sq mile/ 50–100 per sq km

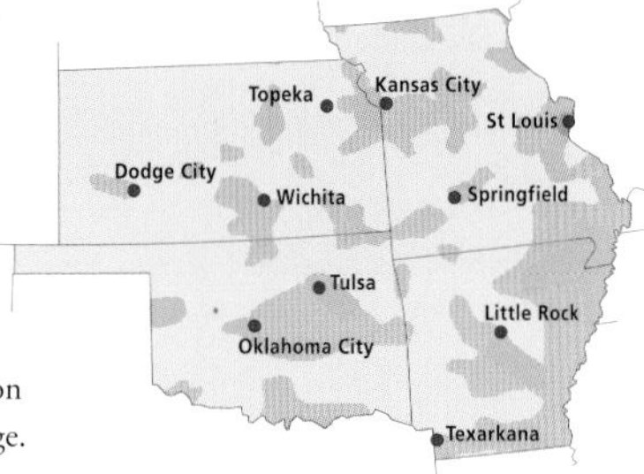

Economic Profile

Wheat is the principal crop in the west—Kansas is the nation's leading producer—whereas corn, soybeans, and rice predominate in the better-watered east. Immense herds of cattle support meat-packing and beef-processing industries. Sizable oil and gas reserves helped Kansas and Oklahoma recover from the Dust Bowl droughts and remain an important source of revenue. Missouri is the leading producer of lead and has large iron ore reserves. St Louis and Kansas City are centers of automobile and aerospace equipment production, and Wichita is one of the world's leading aircraft manufacturers.

- Forest and woodland
- Arable land
- Grazing

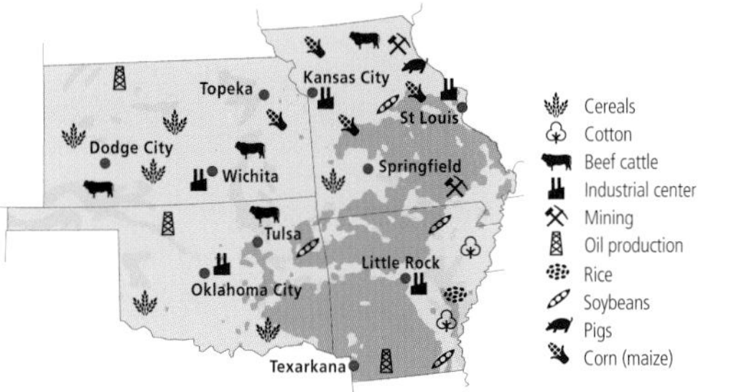

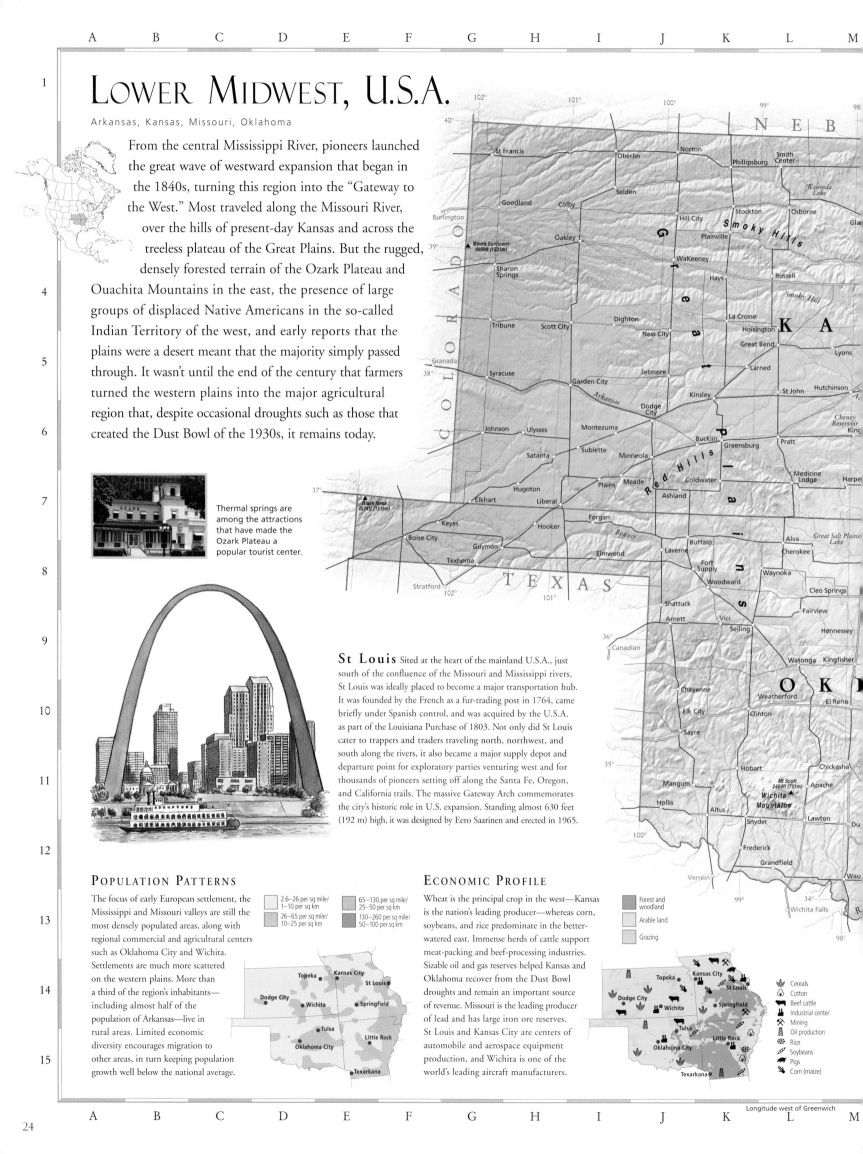

Longitude west of Greenwich

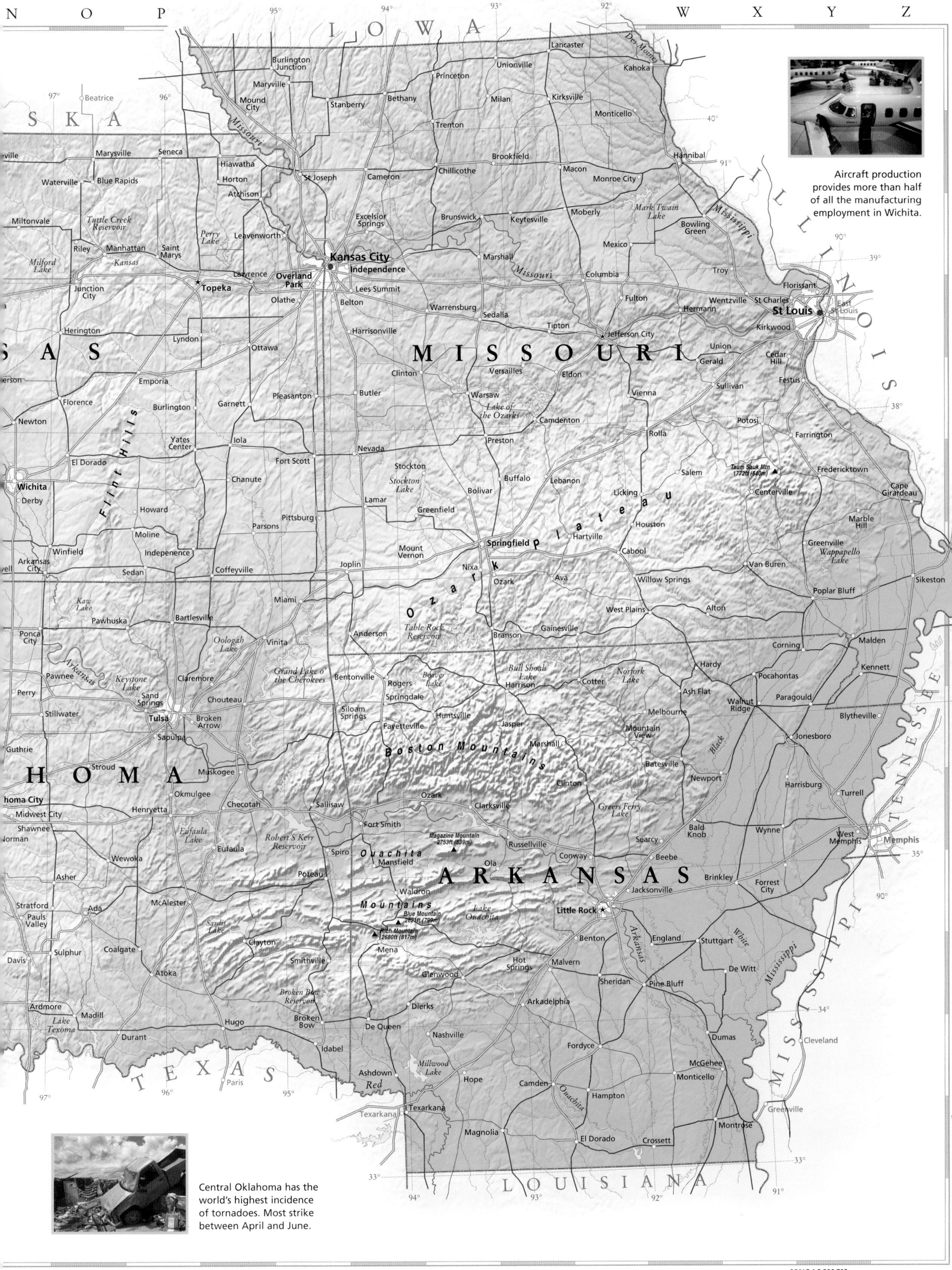

Aircraft production provides more than half of all the manufacturing employment in Wichita.

Central Oklahoma has the world's highest incidence of tornadoes. Most strike between April and June.

TEXAS, U.S.A.

The largest state by area in the lower 48, Texas spreads across 261,797 square miles (678,054 sq km) between the southern Rocky Mountains and the Gulf of Mexico. It is bounded in the northeast by the Red River and in the south by the Rio Grande, which forms part of the border with Mexico. The humid Gulf Coastal Plain covers the eastern two-fifths of the state; to the west, a series of escarpments climbs to the arid, dusty High Plains of the Panhandle, and the barren basins and ranges of the southwest. Texas had its origins in an Anglo-American colony founded in 1821, on Mexican territory. The colony declared itself an independent republic in 1836, but joined the U.S.A. as the 28th state nine years later. It then seceded, along with the rest of the South, in 1861, only to be readmitted in 1869. Having already become prosperous through farming of cotton and beef, Texas acquired even greater wealth following the discovery of oil deposits near Beaumont, east of Houston, in 1901.

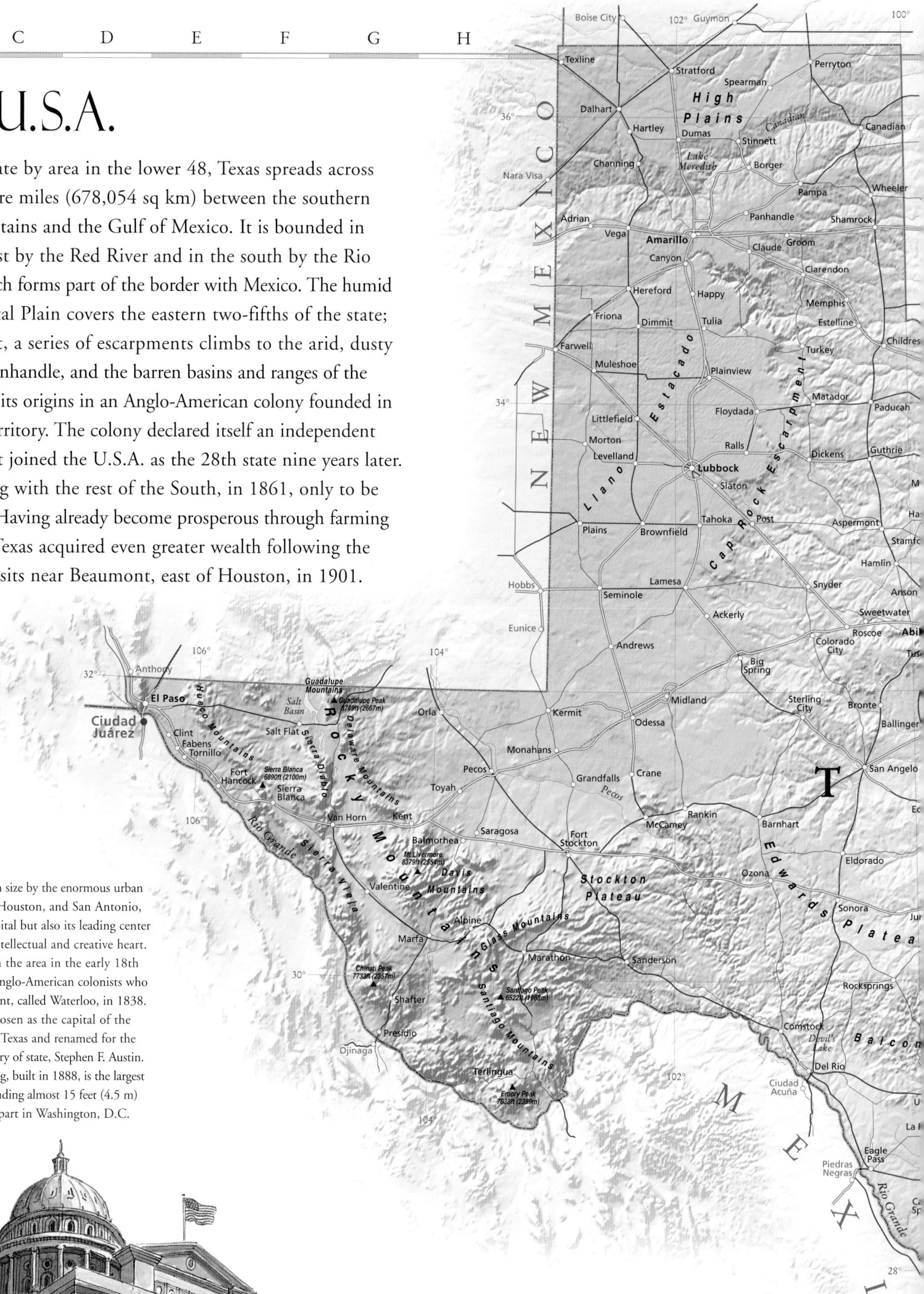

Austin Though dwarfed in size by the enormous urban centers of Dallas–Fort Worth, Houston, and San Antonio, Austin is not only the state's capital but also its leading center of high-tech industry and its intellectual and creative heart. Spanish missionaries worked in the area in the early 18th century, but it was a group of Anglo-American colonists who founded a fully fledged settlement, called Waterloo, in 1838. In the following year, it was chosen as the capital of the recently established Republic of Texas and renamed for the colony's founder and then secretary of state, Stephen F. Austin. The pink-granite Capitol Building, built in 1888, is the largest such building in the country, standing almost 15 feet (4.5 m) higher than its national counterpart in Washington, D.C.

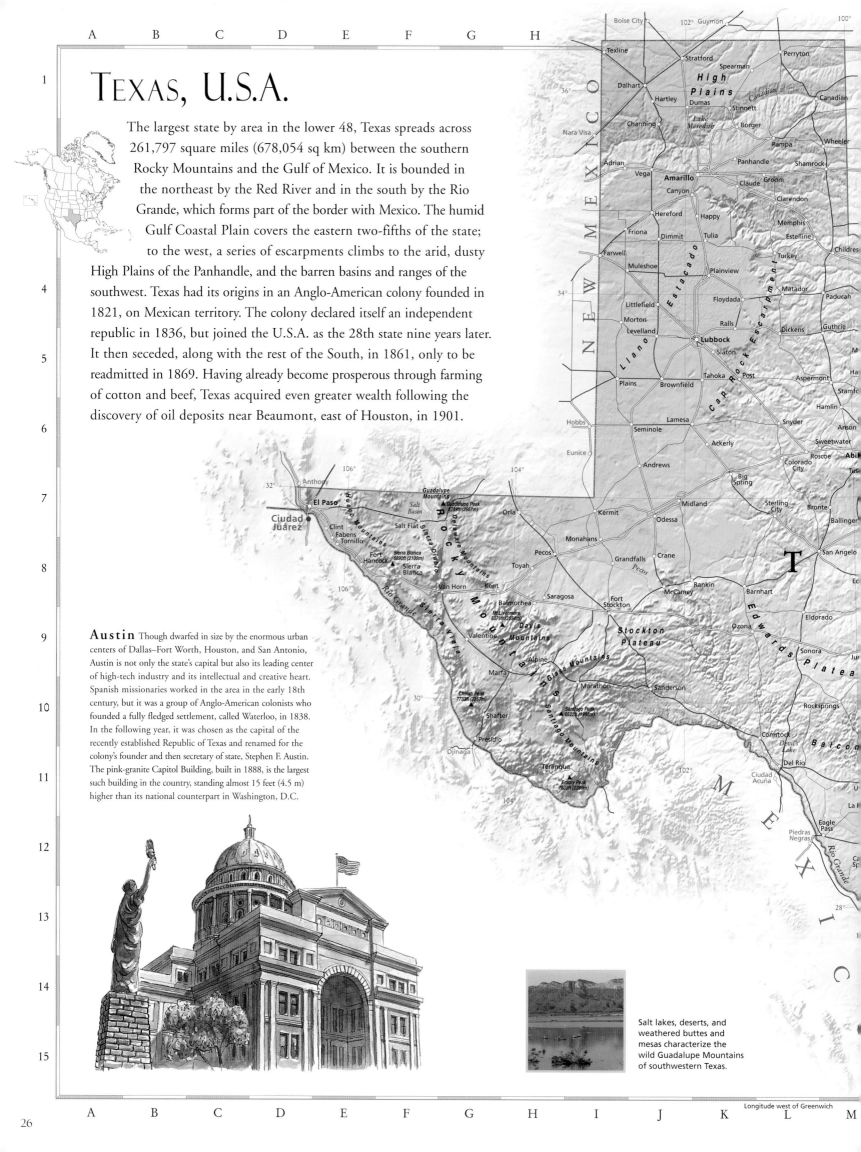

Salt lakes, deserts, and weathered buttes and mesas characterize the wild Guadalupe Mountains of southwestern Texas.

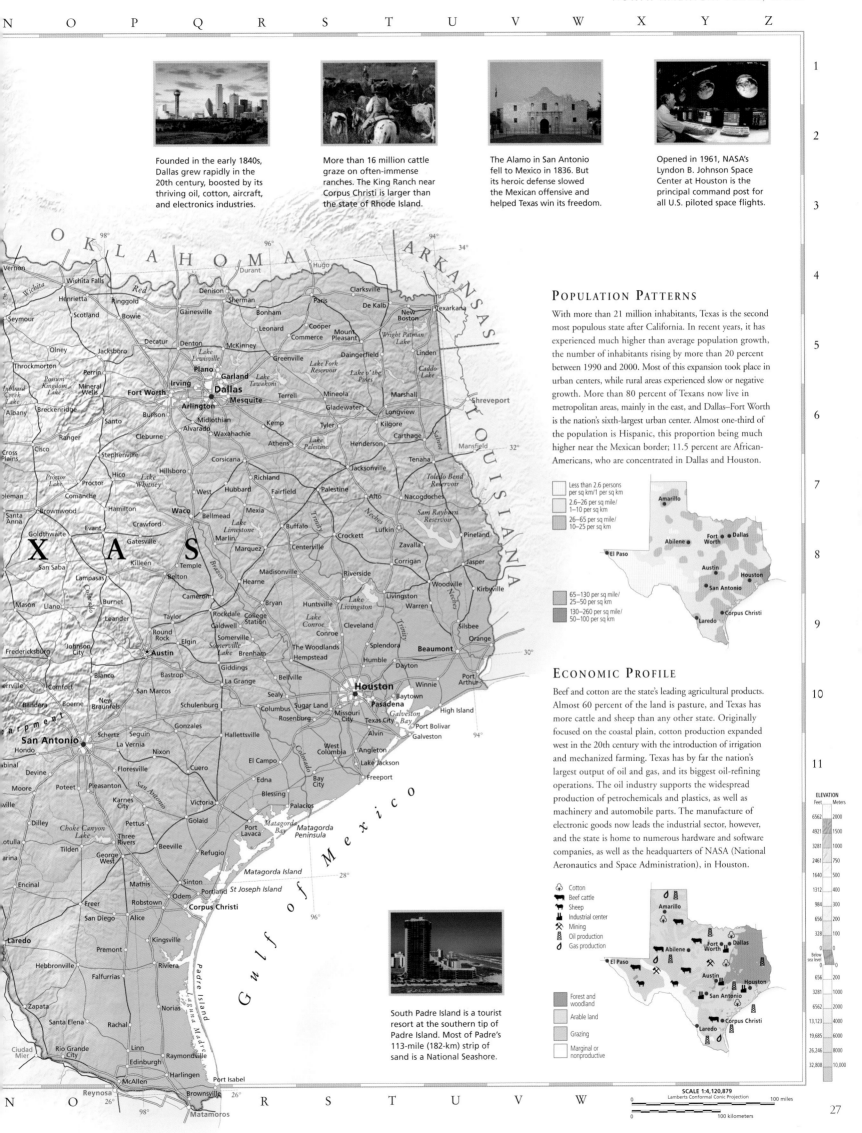

Founded in the early 1840s, Dallas grew rapidly in the 20th century, boosted by its thriving oil, cotton, aircraft, and electronics industries.

More than 16 million cattle graze on often-immense ranches. The King Ranch near Corpus Christi is larger than the state of Rhode Island.

The Alamo in San Antonio fell to Mexico in 1836. But its heroic defense slowed the Mexican offensive and helped Texas win its freedom.

Opened in 1961, NASA's Lyndon B. Johnson Space Center at Houston is the principal command post for all U.S. piloted space flights.

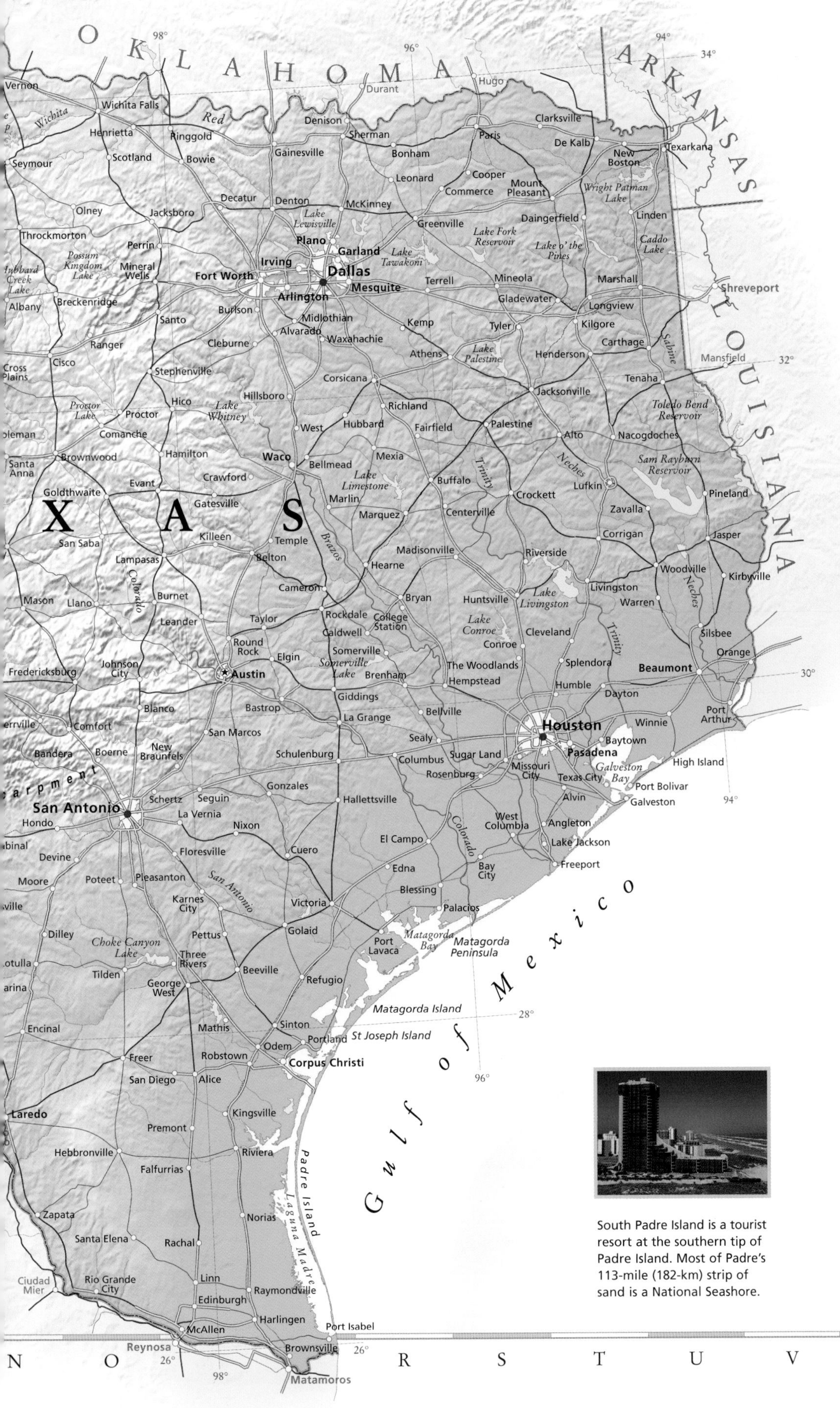

South Padre Island is a tourist resort at the southern tip of Padre Island. Most of Padre's 113-mile (182-km) strip of sand is a National Seashore.

SCALE 1:4,120,879
Lamberts Conformal Conic Projection
0 — 100 miles
0 — 100 kilometers

Population Patterns

With more than 21 million inhabitants, Texas is the second most populous state after California. In recent years, it has experienced much higher than average population growth, the number of inhabitants rising by more than 20 percent between 1990 and 2000. Most of this expansion took place in urban centers, while rural areas experienced slow or negative growth. More than 80 percent of Texans now live in metropolitan areas, mainly in the east, and Dallas–Fort Worth is the nation's sixth-largest urban center. Almost one-third of the population is Hispanic, this proportion being much higher near the Mexican border; 11.5 percent are African-Americans, who are concentrated in Dallas and Houston.

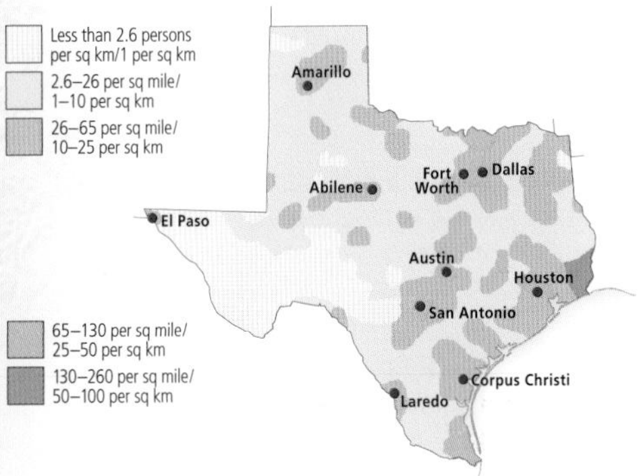

Economic Profile

Beef and cotton are the state's leading agricultural products. Almost 60 percent of the land is pasture, and Texas has more cattle and sheep than any other state. Originally focused on the coastal plain, cotton production expanded west in the 20th century with the introduction of irrigation and mechanized farming. Texas has by far the nation's largest output of oil and gas, and its biggest oil-refining operations. The oil industry supports the widespread production of petrochemicals and plastics, as well as machinery and automobile parts. The manufacture of electronic goods now leads the industrial sector, however, and the state is home to numerous hardware and software companies, as well as the headquarters of NASA (National Aeronautics and Space Administration), in Houston.

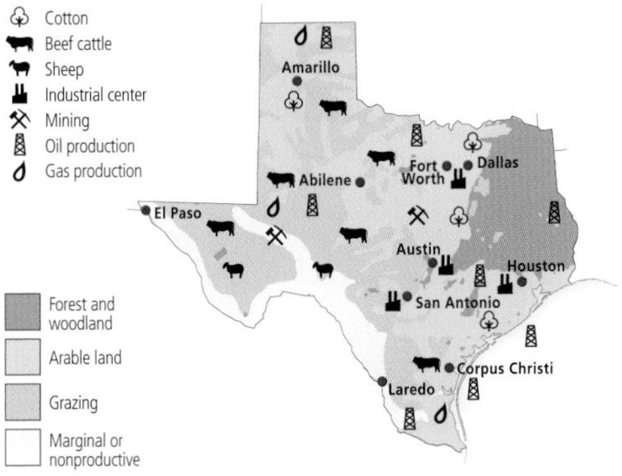

A B C D E F G H I J K L M

Northern Rockies, U.S.A.

Idaho, Montana, Wyoming

The Rocky Mountains form a broad diagonal band across northern Idaho and western Montana and Wyoming. In southern Idaho, the Columbia Plateau and Snake River Plain skirt the mountains. On their eastern flank, the Rockies level out on the Great Plains, an expanse of rolling pastures and wheat fields. Still little developed, the Northern Rockies are the traditional homeland of native peoples such as the Nez Perce, Shoshone, Cheyenne, and Sioux. The first Europeans to visit were Lewis and Clark, during their momentous expedition of 1804–06. Only a trickle of traders and trappers followed, until a gold rush in the early 1860s. Once the boom was over, prospectors turned their hands to mining other minerals, and to forestry and farming—still the foundations of the economy.

Old Faithful is one of 200 or so geysers in Yellowstone National Park, Wyoming. A major tourist destination, Yellowstone also encompasses 10,000 hot springs.

Population Patterns

Population density is low—Wyoming is the nation's least populous state, despite being the ninth biggest by area—and there are few large cities, with only Boise's population surpassing 100,000. Towns line the major river valleys, and half of Wyoming's population is concentrated in the southeastern quarter of the state. Wide open spaces separate settlements elsewhere. The population is overwhelmingly white, but includes a much higher than average proportion of Native Americans. In 1990–2000, Idaho was the fifth fastest-growing state and Boise was the nation's seventh fastest-growing metropolitan area.

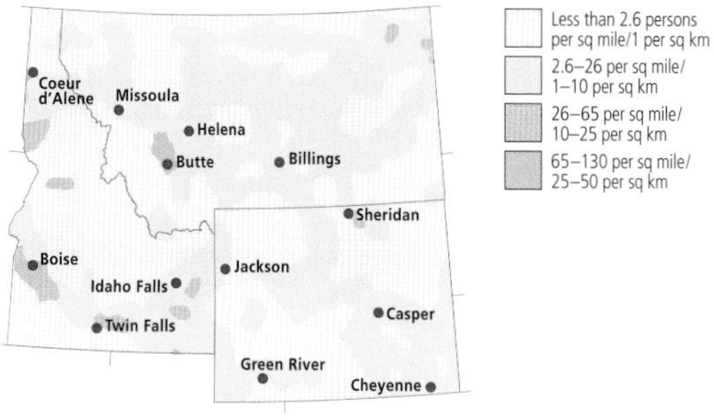

Economic Profile

Coal, oil, and gas are major sources of revenue in Montana and especially Wyoming (the nation's top coal producer), whereas mining in Idaho is focused on silver, lead, and molybdenum. Irrigation supports the cultivation of a range of crops, most notably potatoes in Idaho and wheat in the east. Huge numbers of cattle and sheep roam the plateaus and prairies. Forests are extensive, covering one-third of Idaho; timber is a vital resource there and in Montana. Most manufacturing involves the processing of raw materials. Tourism is a leading employer and revenue source.

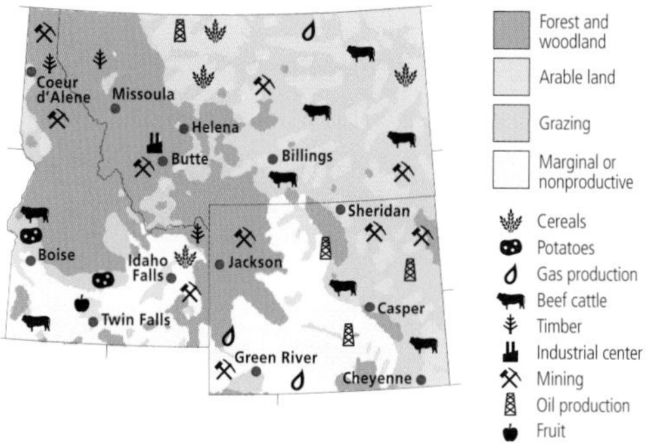

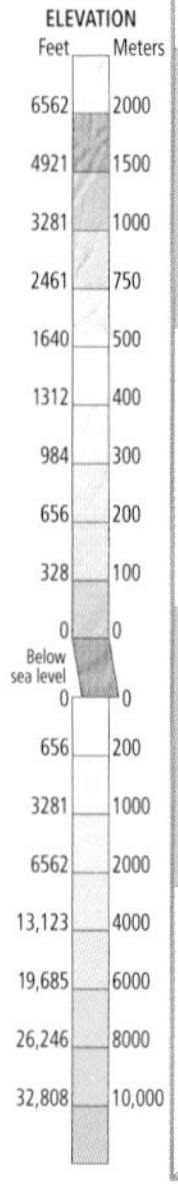

The Teton Range

Extending for 40 miles (64 km) across northwestern Wyoming, the Teton Range is one of the youngest and most imposing mountain ranges in the Rockies. Its jagged peaks began to form more than 1 million years ago when the land to the east dropped downward along a 50-mile (80-km) fault line. Today, 13,770-foot (4,197-m) Grand Teton, the highest peak in the range, rises 7,000 feet (2,135 m) above the valley of Jackson Hole.

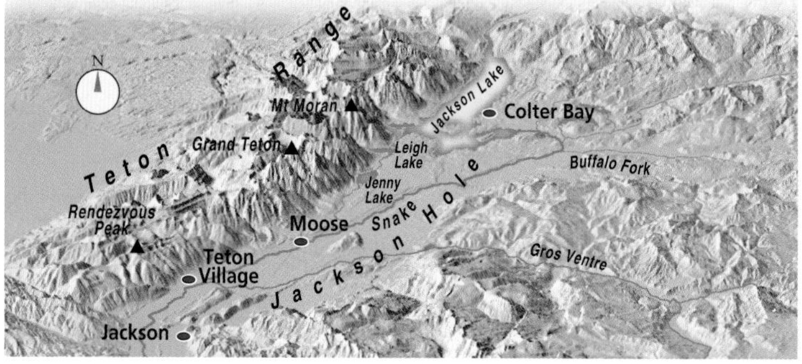

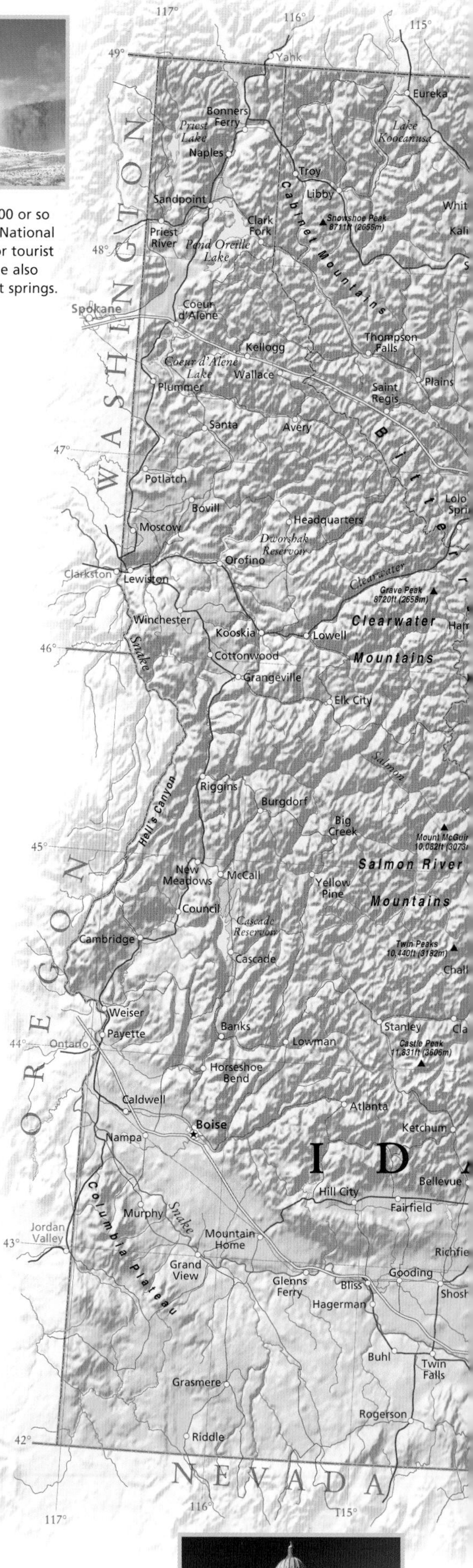

The Northern Rockies harbor the country's largest bison populations.

The Capitol Building in Boise was completed in 1920, 30 years after Idaho became a state.

A B C D E F G H I J K L M

CANADA
MONTANA
WYOMING
IDAHO
UTAH
COLORADO
NORTH DAKOTA
SOUTH DAKOTA
NEBRASKA
Great Plains
Rocky Mountains
Lewis Range
Big Belt Mountains
Crazy Mtns
Absaroka Range
Bighorn Mountains
Powder River Basin
Bighorn Basin
Wind River Range
Wyoming Range
Teton Range
Snake River Plain
Laramie Mountains
Great Divide Basin
Beaverhead Mountains
Missouri
Yellowstone
Musselshell
Bighorn
Little Bighorn
Powder
Cheyenne
North Platte
Snake
Green
Laramie
Fort Peck Reservoir
Tiber Reservoir
Canyon Ferry Lake
Hebgen Lake
Yellowstone Lake
Jackson Lake
Bighorn Lake
Palisades Reservoir
American Falls Reservoir
Blackfoot Reservoir
Bear Lake
Flaming Gorge Reservoir
Pathfinder Reservoir
Seminoe Reservoir
Glendo Reservoir
West Butte 6980ft (2128m)
Baldy Mountain 6621ft (2018m)
Rocky Mountain 9393ft (2863m)
Big Snow Mtn 8730ft (2661m)
Crow Peak 9413ft (2869m)
Granite Peak 12,800ft (3901m)
Trout Peak 12,244ft (3732m)
Needle Mountain 12,129ft (3697m)
Grand Teton 13,770ft (4197m)
Gannett Peak 13,786ft (4202m)
Devil's Tower 5112ft (1558m)
Babb
Sunburst
Cut Bank
Browning
Shelby
Chester
Simpson
Gildford
Havre
Chinook
Harlem
Dodson
Malta
Loring
Saco
Opheim
Scobey
Plentywood
Glasgow
Nashua
Wolf Point
Poplar
Culbertson
Fort Peck
Vida
Sidney
Dupuyer
Conrad
Big Sandy
Hays
Choteau
Fort Benton
Winifred
Augusta
Simms
Great Falls
Armington
Roy
Jordan
Circle
Glendive
Wibaux
Stanford
Lewistown
Grassrange
Winnett
Mosby
Moore
Rock Springs
Terry
Wolf Creek
Helena
Drummond
Garrison
White Sulphur Springs
Harlowton
Melstone
Ingomar
Roundup
Miles City
Baker
Philipsburg
Townsend
Ryegate
Lavina
Hysham
Forsyth
Anaconda
Ringling
Custer
Butte
Volborg
Ekalaka
Three Forks
Clyde Park
Big Timber
Billings
Divide
Bozeman
Livingston
Columbus
Laurel
Hardin
Crow Agency
Lame Deer
Broadus
Wisdom
Melrose
Twin Bridges
Boyd
Ennis
Bridger
Fort Smith
Lodge Grass
Virginia City
Red Lodge
Dillon
Biddle
Alzada
Wyola
Gardiner
Mammoth Hot Springs
Belle Fourche
Spotted Horse
Powell
Lovell
Sheridan
Spearfish
Lima
Canyon
West Yellowstone
Cody
Ucross
Sundance
Island Park
Greybull
Buffalo
Gillette
Spencer
Old Faithful
Basin
Four Corners
Dubois
Ashton
Meeteetse
Upton
Worland
Newcastle
Leslie
Rexburg
Moran
Kaycee
Wright
Terreton
Thermopolis
Mule Creek
Arco
Victor
Moose
Midwest
Edgemont
Idaho Falls
Jackson
Bill
Bondurant
Shoshoni
Blackfoot
Riverton
Powder River
Casper
Lusk
Harrison
Pocatello
Thayne
Daniel
Pinedale
Lander
Douglas
Orin
Minidoka
American Falls
McCammon
Soda Springs
Smoot
Jeffrey City
Alcova
Glendo
Marbleton
Downey
Muddy Gap
Guernsey
Montpelier
Malad City
Paris
La Barge
Torrington
Holbrook
Preston
Saint Charles
Farson
Medicine Bow
Hawk Springs
Strevell
Cokeville
Rawlins
Walcott
Chugwater
Kemmerer
Diamondville
Creston
Granger
Rock Springs
Green River
Laramie
Fort Bridger
Cheyenne
Evanston
Baggs
Manila
49°
48°
47°
46°
45°
44°
43°
42°
41°
113°
112°
111°
110°
109°
108°
107°
106°
105°
104°
SCALE 1:3,571,429
Lamberts Conformal Conic Projection
0
100 miles
0
100 kilometers

Southwestern U.S.A.

Arizona, Colorado, New Mexico, Utah

The immense Colorado Plateau constitutes the core of this arid region. Bounded to the west by basin and range country, to the north and east by the southern Rockies, and to the south by the Sonoran Desert, it is characterized by ancient, eroded landscapes where barren plateaus sit beneath forested, snow-capped peaks, and rivers have carved deep chasms between broad mesas and towering buttes. Scattered cliff-dwellings and pueblos testify to thousands of years of Native American habitation. Historic missions and adobe architecture recall Spanish occupation between the 16th and early 19th centuries, and subsequent Mexican rule over much of the Southwest until 1848. Today, the region's dry, sunny climate, thriving high-tech industries, and astounding scenery make it one of the most-visited and fastest-growing parts of the country.

The Grand Canyon

A deep gash in the southwestern corner of the Colorado Plateau, the Grand Canyon was carved over millennia by the Colorado River. Extending 277 miles (446 km) and measuring 15 miles (24 km) across at its widest point, it is up to 6,000 feet (1,800 m) deep. Erosion has exposed rocks at the bottom of the canyon that are about 2 billion years old. Now encompassed by the national park of the same name, the canyon attracts up to 5 million visitors annually.

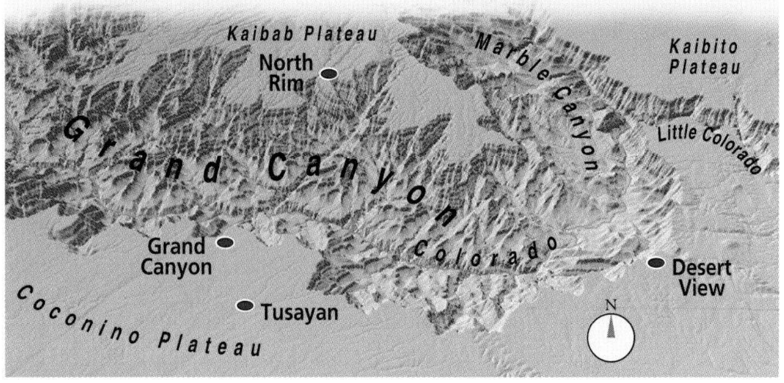

Salt Lake City In 1846, fleeing persecution in Illinois, 148 Mormons migrated more than 1,000 miles (1,600 km) to present-day Utah. Settling in the Valley of the Great Salt Lake in 1847, they founded a new settlement, initially called Great Salt Lake City. By the late 19th century, it had become, and remains, one of the most important commercial centers in the western U.S.A. Its focal point, and the heart of the Mormon faith, is Temple Square, site of the six-towered Mormon Temple, begun in 1853 and completed 40 years later.

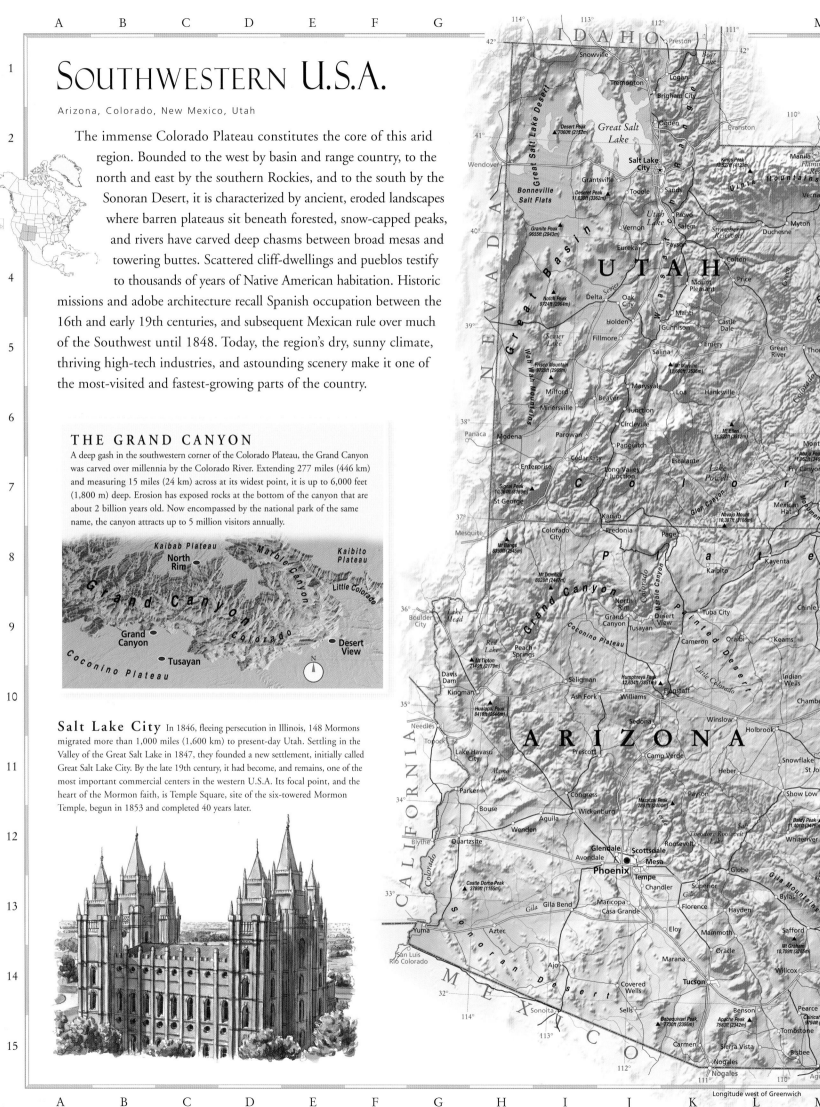

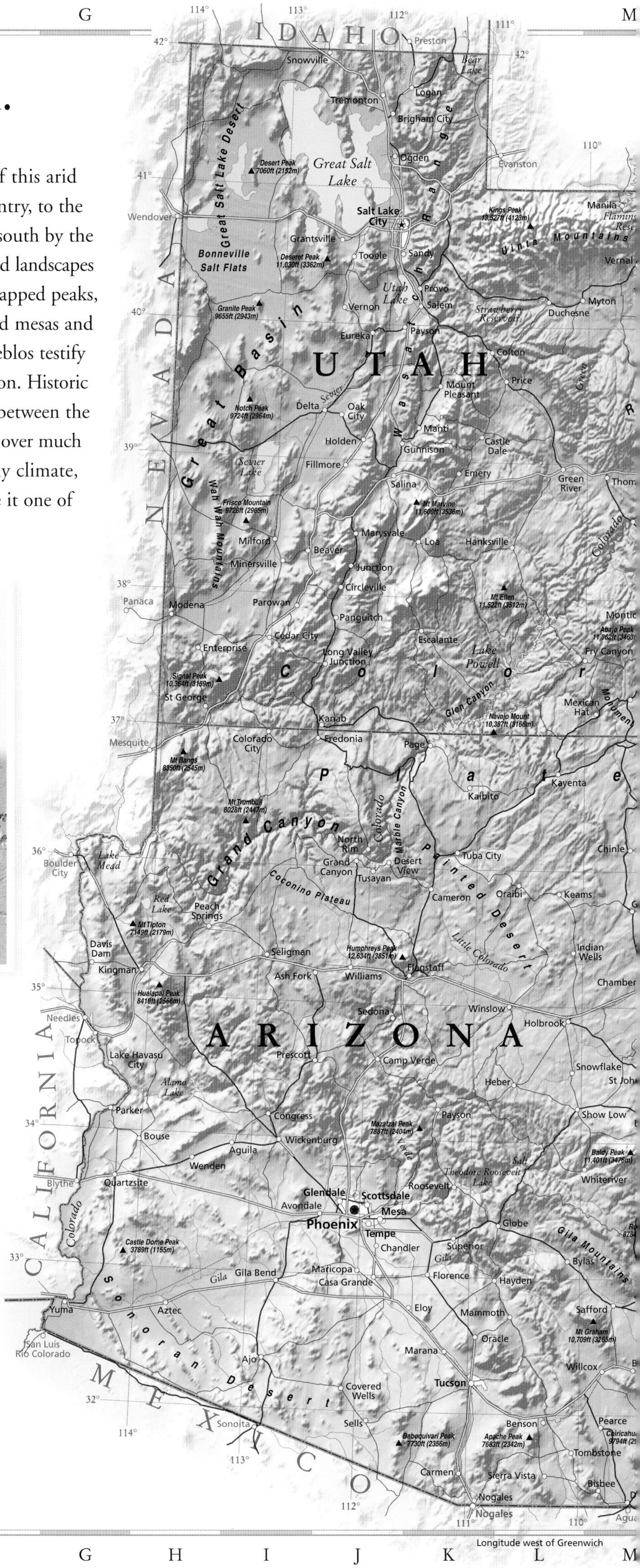

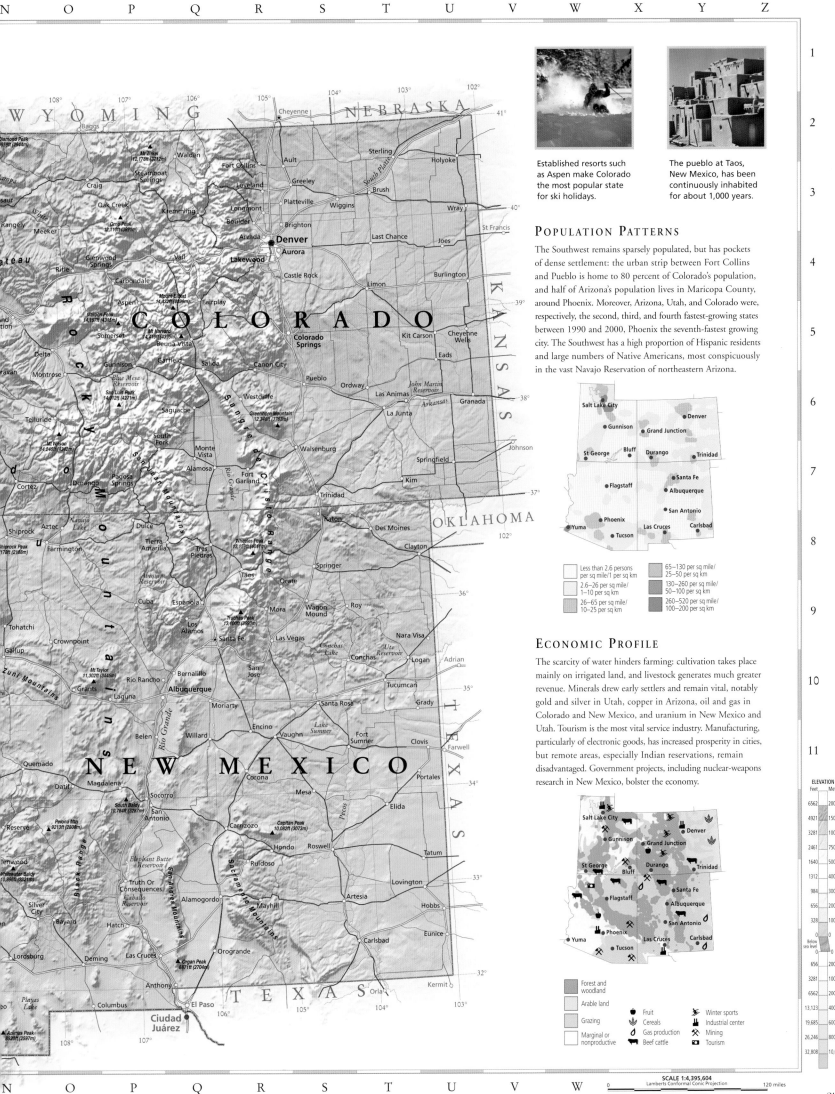

Established resorts such as Aspen make Colorado the most popular state for ski holidays.

The pueblo at Taos, New Mexico, has been continuously inhabited for about 1,000 years.

Population Patterns

The Southwest remains sparsely populated, but has pockets of dense settlement: the urban strip between Fort Collins and Pueblo is home to 80 percent of Colorado's population, and half of Arizona's population lives in Maricopa County, around Phoenix. Moreover, Arizona, Utah, and Colorado were, respectively, the second, third, and fourth fastest-growing states between 1990 and 2000, Phoenix the seventh-fastest growing city. The Southwest has a high proportion of Hispanic residents and large numbers of Native Americans, most conspicuously in the vast Navajo Reservation of northeastern Arizona.

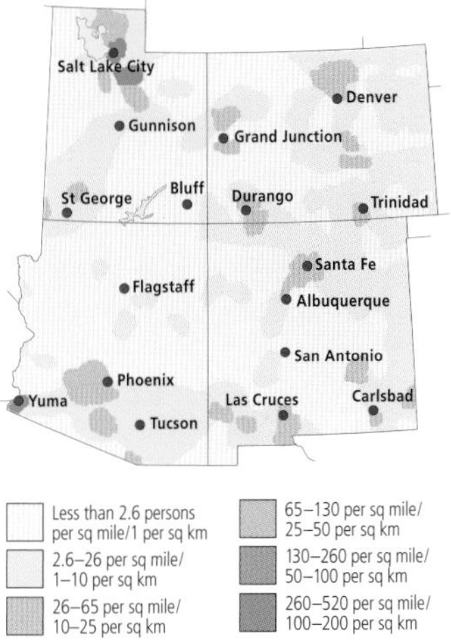

Economic Profile

The scarcity of water hinders farming: cultivation takes place mainly on irrigated land, and livestock generates much greater revenue. Minerals drew early settlers and remain vital, notably gold and silver in Utah, copper in Arizona, oil and gas in Colorado and New Mexico, and uranium in New Mexico and Utah. Tourism is the most vital service industry. Manufacturing, particularly of electronic goods, has increased prosperity in cities, but remote areas, especially Indian reservations, remain disadvantaged. Government projects, including nuclear-weapons research in New Mexico, bolster the economy.

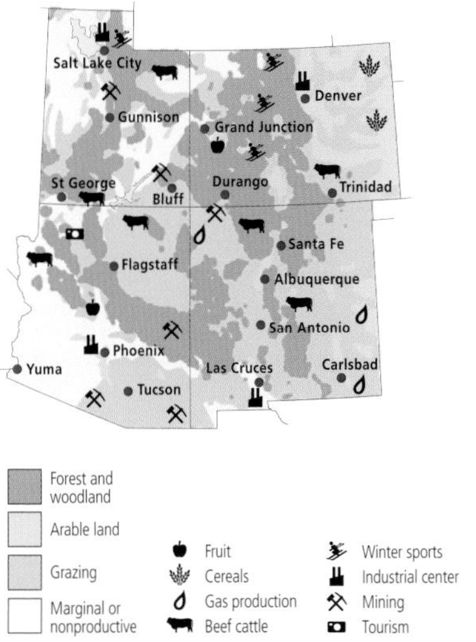

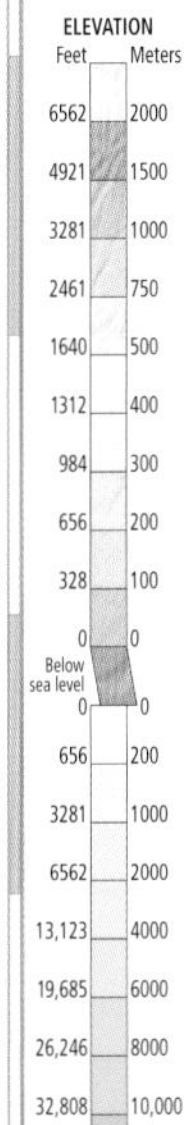

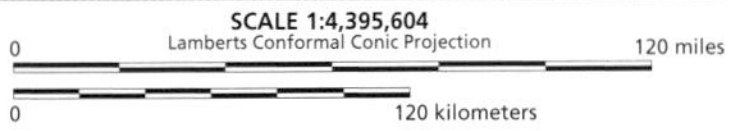

THE FAR WEST, U.S.A.

California, Nevada, Oregon, Washington

Geologically, the U.S. mainland's western fringe is its youngest and most active region. Plate movements here cause regular earthquakes in California and occasional volcanic eruptions in the Pacific Northwest. They have also given rise, over millions of years, to the two long mountain chains that parallel the shoreline. The Coast Ranges climb steeply from the sea, falling to sheltered lowlands, including the Central and Willamette valleys, which are enclosed in turn by the loftier peaks of the Cascade Range and Sierra Nevada. Farther east lies a jumble of arid landforms, including volcanic plateaus in the north, rows of north–south-trending basins and ranges in Nevada, and low-lying deserts in southeastern California. This intimidating terrain deterred early European immigrants, who clustered in coastal settlements and threaded their way along river valleys before being lured into the uplands by the discovery of gold and other minerals in the mid-19th century. In the 20th century, southern California's warm climate, available land, and thriving ports drew millions west, making it one of the nation's most populous regions.

POPULATION PATTERNS

California has the largest state population, of more than 34 million. More than 90 percent of these people live in urban areas, mainly around Los Angeles and San Diego, and San Francisco and Oakland. One-third of Californians are Hispanic or Latino. In the Pacific Northwest, densely populated areas include the shores of Puget Sound and Oregon's Willamette Valley. In the east, settlements are small and scattered; an exception is Las Vegas, a desert metropolis founded on gambling and tourism. Between 1990 and 2000, Nevada grew faster than any other state, increasing its population by 66 percent.

ECONOMIC PROFILE

The region has just a few pockets of arable land, most of which require irrigation, but they include California's productive Central Valley and its Napa Valley vineyards, and the fertile Columbia Basin. The Pacific Northwest has enormous stands of timber and abundant hydroelectric power—Washington generates one-third of U.S. supplies. Nevada benefits from reserves of gold and mercury, and hosts major military test sites—85 percent of the land is government-owned. Seattle and San Francisco's famed Silicon Valley are world leaders in new technologies, and Seattle is also a major aircraft manufacturer. As well as the Hollywood film industry, Los Angeles is home to major TV and music corporations. Tourism is a vital industry throughout the region.

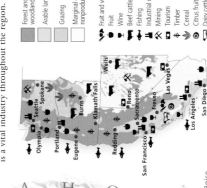

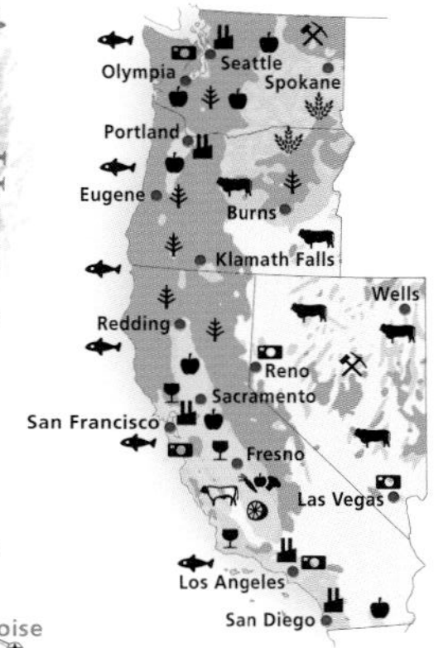

Washington's Mount Rainier is crowned by the largest glacier system in the lower 48 states.

Crater Lake, Oregon, fills a caldera that was once part of an enormous volcano, Mount Mazama.

Founded by Spanish settlers in 1781, Los Angeles became part of the U.S.A. in 1846. It is now its second-largest city.

In Death Valley, California, the land drops to 282 feet (86 m) below sea level, North America's lowest point.

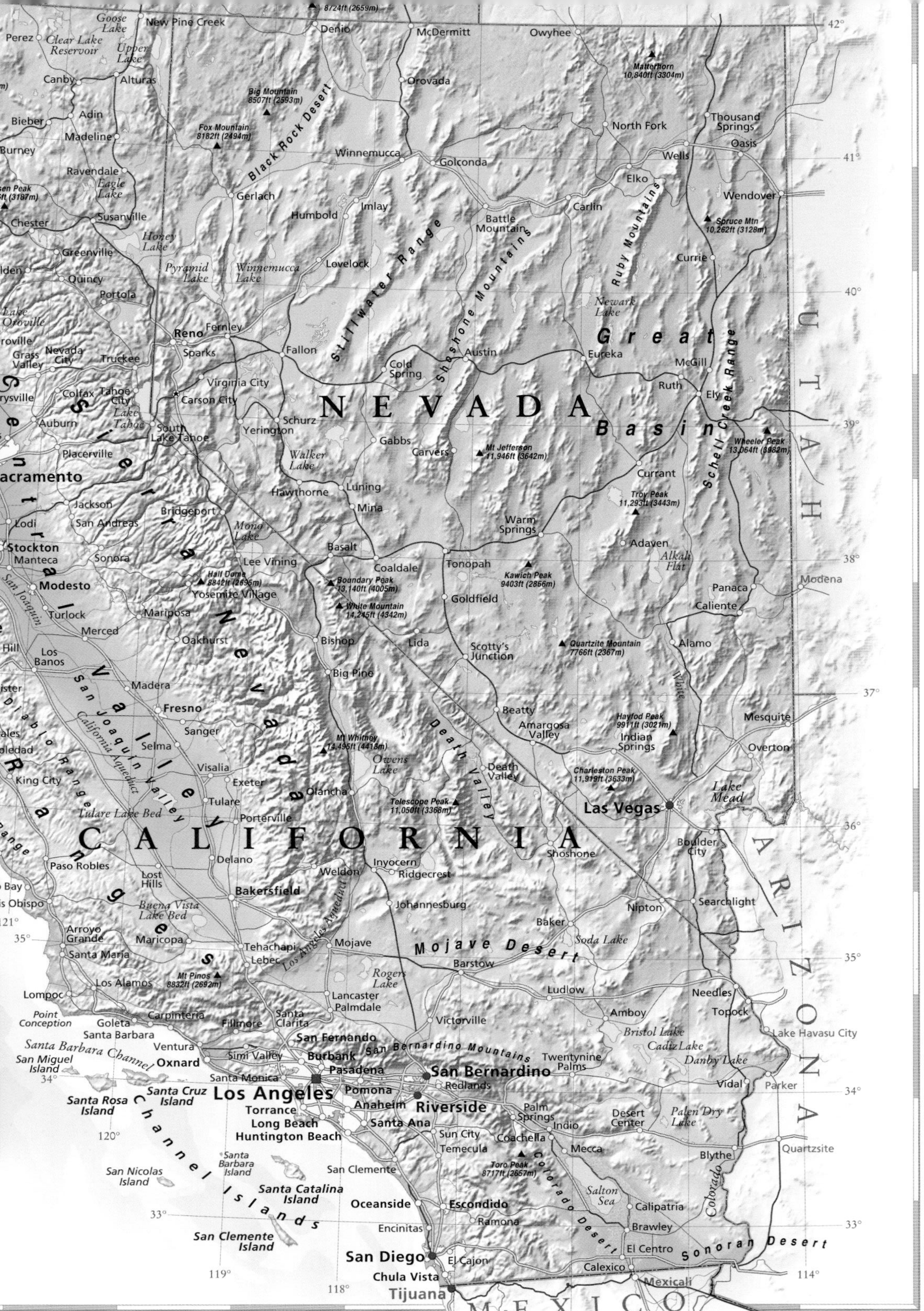

YOSEMITE VALLEY

The granite peaks of the Sierra Nevada were uplifted between 25 and 10 million years ago. Around 1 million years ago, during a major ice age, glaciers covered the highest slopes and snaked downward through valleys, grinding their walls smooth and steep. The results of this glaciation are visible throughout the range, but perhaps nowhere are they as dramatic as in Yosemite Valley. This U-shaped canyon's polished walls rise sheer from the valley floor, forming colossal cliffs surmounted by peaks such as 7,569-foot (2,346-m) El Capitan and 8,842-foot (2,695-m) Half Dome. Between the peaks, mountain streams tumble from hanging valleys, creating some of the world's tallest waterfalls.

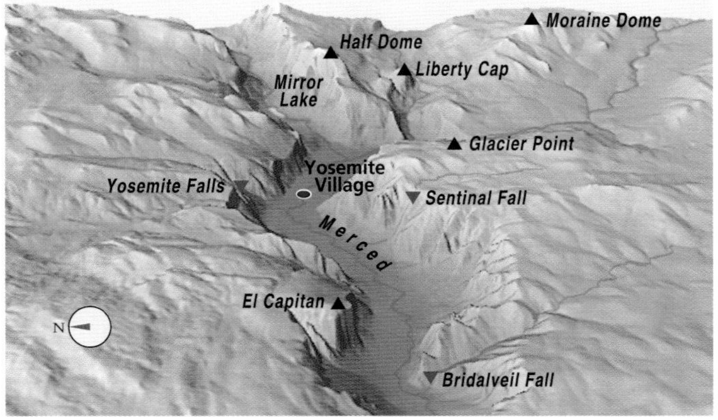

The construction of the Hoover Dam across the Colorado River created Lake Mead in Nevada.

1

ALASKA AND HAWAII, U.S.A.

Alaska and Hawaii are the only two states that are not part of the lower 48, and both became states—the 49th and 50th, respectively—in the same year, 1959. Their territories, however, could hardly be more different. Separated from the rest of the country by western Canada, Alaska is by far the largest state and about 95 times the size of Hawaii—though it has only half as many inhabitants. Its huge, oblong landmass is mountainous, little developed, and mostly inhospitable: winters are severe across most of the state and one-third of the land is barren tundra. Hawaii is a chain of 137 volcanic islands, measuring 1,500 miles (2,400 km) in length and including eight major islands, located in the middle of the Pacific Ocean, about 2,400 miles (3,860 km) west of San Francisco. Cloaked with tracts of tropical forest and fringed by golden beaches, the Hawaiian Islands have fertile soils and are warm and, for the most part, well-watered year-round.

4

5

In summer, herds of caribou migrate to Alaska's Arctic tundra to breed.

The Trans-Alaska Oil Pipeline extends from Prudhoe Bay to the port of Valdez.

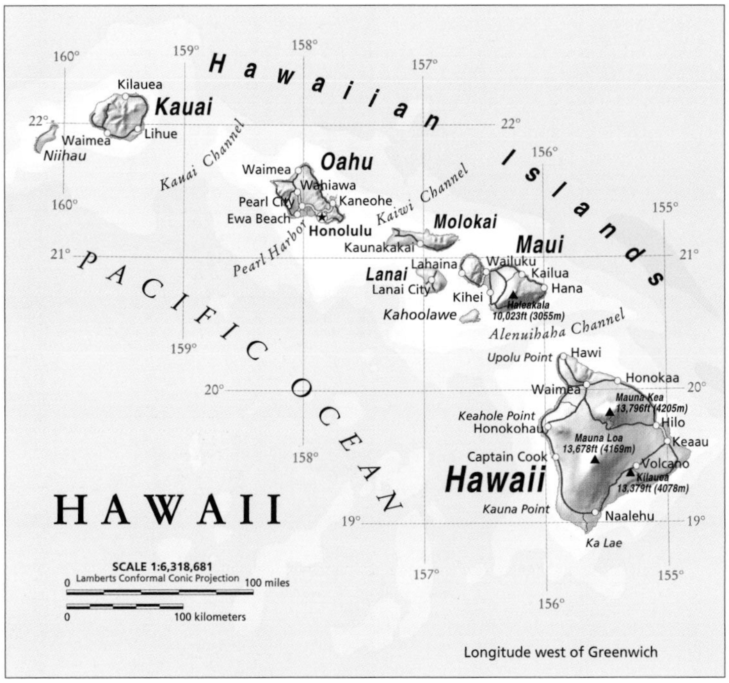

Hawaiian Islands
PACIFIC OCEAN
HAWAII
Kilauea
Kauai
Lihue
Waimea
Niihau
Kauai Channel
Oahu
Waimea
Wahiawa
Pearl City
Kaneohe
Ewa Beach
Honolulu
Pearl Harbor
Kaiwi Channel
Molokai
Kaunakakai
Maui
Lanai
Lanai City
Lahaina
Wailuku
Kailua
Hana
Kihei
Kahoolawe
Haleakala 10,023ft (3055m)
Alenuihaha Channel
Upolu Point
Hawi
Honokaa
Waimea
Mauna Kea 13,796ft (4205m)
Keahole Point
Honokohau
Hilo
Mauna Loa 13,678ft (4169m)
Keaau
Captain Cook
Volcano
Kilauea 13,379ft (4078m)
Hawaii
Kauna Point
Naalehu
Ka Lae
160° 159° 158° 157° 156° 155° 22° 21° 20° 19°
SCALE 1:6,318,681
Lamberts Conformal Conic Projection
0 100 miles
0 100 kilometers
Longitude west of Greenwich

Named Denali by local Native American people, Mount McKinley is the tallest peak in North America, rising to 20,321 feet (6,194 m).

Kilauea, on the island of Hawaii, is the world's largest active volcanic crater. Its regular eruptions generate extensive lava flows.

Chukchi Sea
Wevok
Point Hope
RUSSIAN FEDERATION
Arctic Circle
Kotz Sou
Shishmaref
Seward Peninsul
Bering Strait
Brevig Mission
Teller
Sinuk
Nome
Cape Nome
Northwest Cape
Savoonga
St Lawrence Island
Northeast Cape
Norton Sou
Bering Sea
Emmonak
Scammon Bay
Hooper Bay
Chevak
St Matthew Island
Etolin Strait
Cape Mohican
Nunivak Island
Tanunak
Chefornak
Kipnuk
Kwigillingok
Quinhaga
Kuskokwim Bay
Goodnew
Platinum
Cape Newenham
St Paul Island
Pribilof Islands
St George Island
175° 170° 65° 60°

11

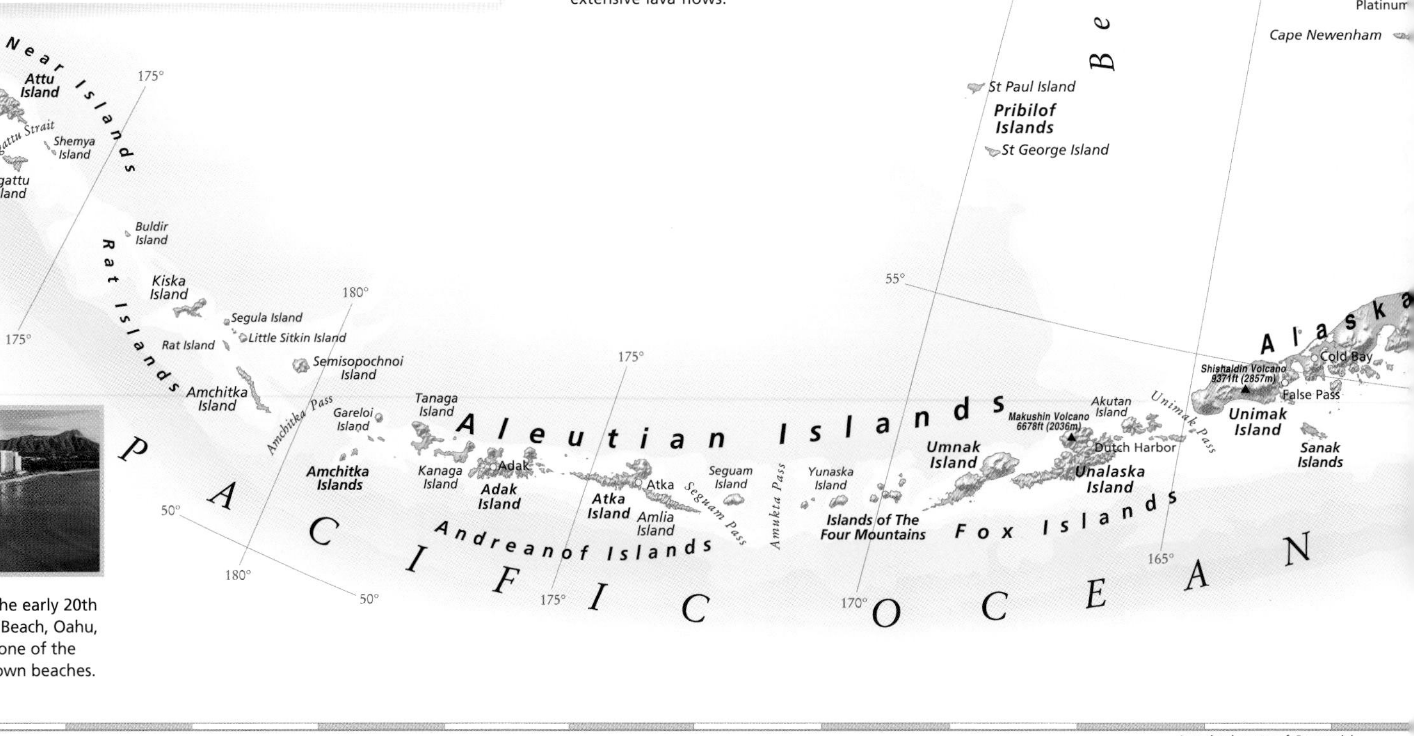

Near Islands
Attu Island
Agattu Strait
Shemya Island
Agattu Island
Buldir Island
Rat Islands
Kiska Island
Segula Island
Little Sitkin Island
Rat Island
Semisopochnoi Island
Amchitka Island
Amchitka Pass
Gareloi Island
Tanaga Island
Aleutian Islands
Amchitka Islands
Kanaga Island
Adak
Adak Island
Atka
Atka Island
Amlia Island
Seguam Island
Seguam Pass
Amukta Pass
Yunaska Island
Andreanof Islands
Islands of The Four Mountains
Umnak Island
Makushin Volcano 6678ft (2036m)
Akutan Island
Dutch Harbor
Unalaska Island
Fox Islands
Unimak Pass
Shishaldin Volcano 9371ft (2857m)
Cold Bay
False Pass
Unimak Island
Sanak Islands
Alaska
PACIFIC OCEAN
175° 180° 175° 170° 165° 55° 50°
Longitude west of Greenwich

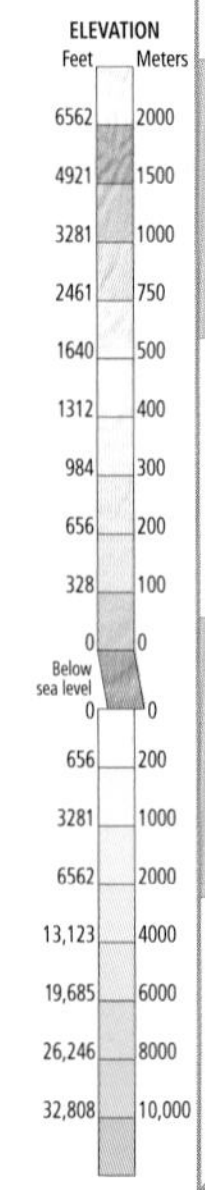

ELEVATION
Feet Meters
6562 2000
4921 1500
3281 1000
2461 750
1640 500
1312 400
984 300
656 200
328 100
0 0
Below sea level
0 0
656 200
3281 1000
6562 2000
13,123 4000
19,685 6000
26,246 8000
32,808 10,000

A swamp until the early 20th century, Waikiki Beach, Oahu, is Hawaii's, and one of the world's, best-known beaches.

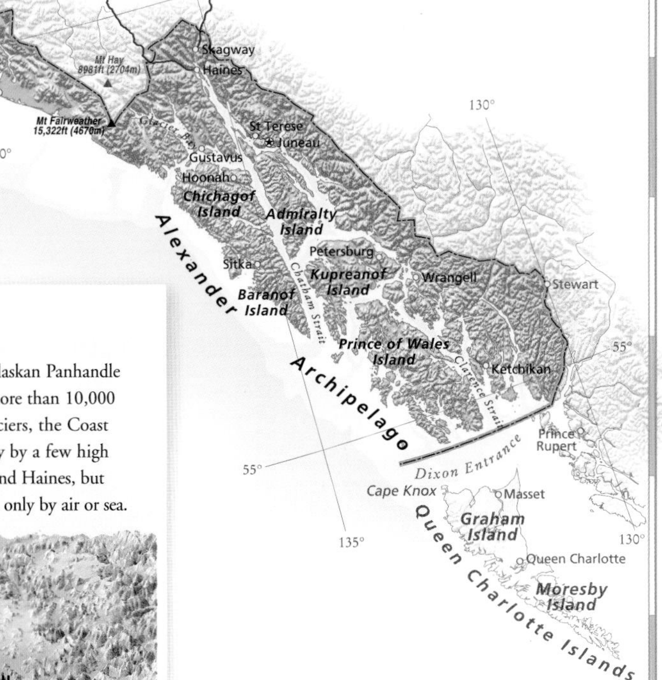

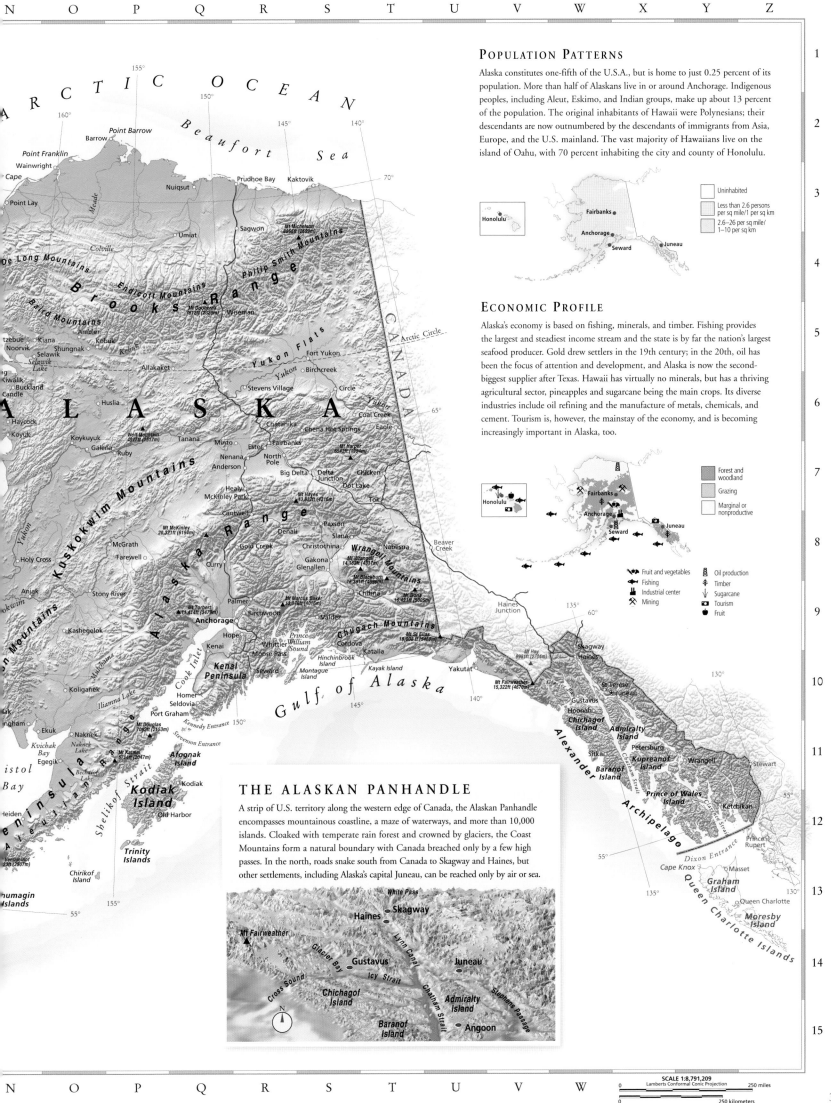

Population Patterns

Alaska constitutes one-fifth of the U.S.A., but is home to just 0.25 percent of its population. More than half of Alaskans live in or around Anchorage. Indigenous peoples, including Aleut, Eskimo, and Indian groups, make up about 13 percent of the population. The original inhabitants of Hawaii were Polynesians; their descendants are now outnumbered by the descendants of immigrants from Asia, Europe, and the U.S. mainland. The vast majority of Hawaiians live on the island of Oahu, with 70 percent inhabiting the city and county of Honolulu.

Economic Profile

Alaska's economy is based on fishing, minerals, and timber. Fishing provides the largest and steadiest income stream and the state is by far the nation's largest seafood producer. Gold drew settlers in the 19th century; in the 20th, oil has been the focus of attention and development, and Alaska is now the second-biggest supplier after Texas. Hawaii has virtually no minerals, but has a thriving agricultural sector, pineapples and sugarcane being the main crops. Its diverse industries include oil refining and the manufacture of metals, chemicals, and cement. Tourism is, however, the mainstay of the economy, and is becoming increasingly important in Alaska, too.

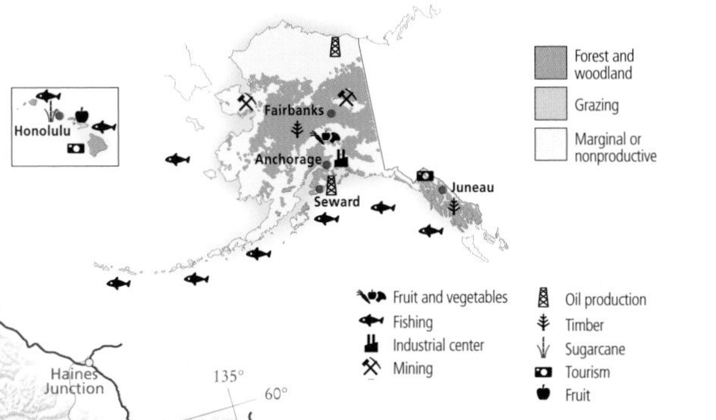

The Alaskan Panhandle

A strip of U.S. territory along the western edge of Canada, the Alaskan Panhandle encompasses mountainous coastline, a maze of waterways, and more than 10,000 islands. Cloaked with temperate rain forest and crowned by glaciers, the Coast Mountains form a natural boundary with Canada breached only by a few high passes. In the north, roads snake south from Canada to Skagway and Haines, but other settlements, including Alaska's capital Juneau, can be reached only by air or sea.

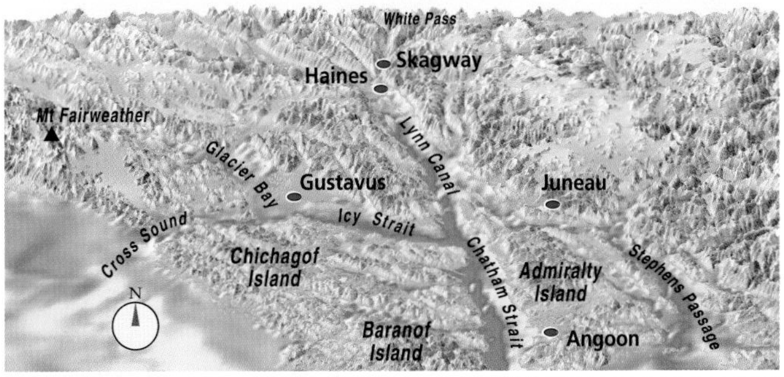

SCALE 1:8,791,209
Lamberts Conformal Conic Projection
0 250 miles
0 250 kilometers

CANADA

Occupying most of the northern third of North America, Canada is the world's second-largest country by area, but also one of its most sparsely inhabited. A band of western ranges, including the Coast and Rocky mountains, and a number of lower, much older mountain chains in the east, enclose the vast Canadian Shield, an ancient, low, bowl-shaped plateau. Originally home to scattered Indian and Inuit peoples, Canada was visited in the 11th century by Viking explorers, who founded a short-lived settlement in Newfoundland. The French laid claim to the St Lawrence River Valley in the 16th century, but by 1763 most of North America was under British control. The self-governing British dominion of Canada was created in 1867. Initially, it included only Ontario, Québec, New Brunswick, and Nova Scotia, but other areas were gradually absorbed into the confederation, which now consists of ten provinces and three territories.

Mostly uninhabited, mountainous Baffin Island is Canada's largest island.

Waterlogged boreal forest, of spruce, fir, and birch, spans the entire country.

Toronto Canada's most populous city, with around 5 million inhabitants, and its leading commercial and financial center, Toronto originated in the 17th century as a trading post founded at the intersection of several Indian trails (Toronto is a Huron word meaning "meeting place"). Despite being chosen as the site for the capital of Ontario in 1793, the settlement remained undeveloped until the arrival of the Grand Trunk and Great Western railways in the 1850s, after which its population rose to more than half a million by 1921. The modern skyline is dominated by the CN Tower, which rises to 1,815 feet (553 m) and is the world's tallest self-supporting structure.

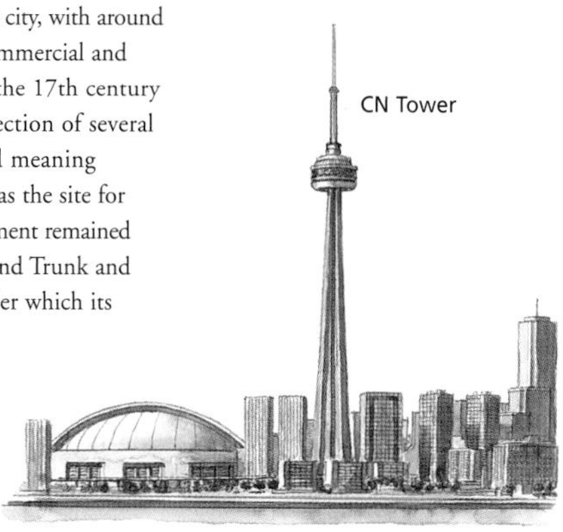
CN Tower

POPULATION PATTERNS

Vast areas of northern Canada are virtually uninhabited: Nunavut and the Yukon and Northwest territories encompass 41 percent of the land, but have just 0.3 percent of the population. Nunavut has no roads. About 80 percent of Canadians live in the temperate south, within 100 miles (160 km) of the U.S. border. The population is highly urbanized, with four-fifths living in towns and cities. It is also ethnically diverse, one-third of Canadians being of mixed descent. Most, however, are of European, especially British or French, origin. Indigenous peoples make up just 3 percent of the population. Both English and French are official languages and bilingualism is encouraged: 17 percent of Canadians can use both languages.

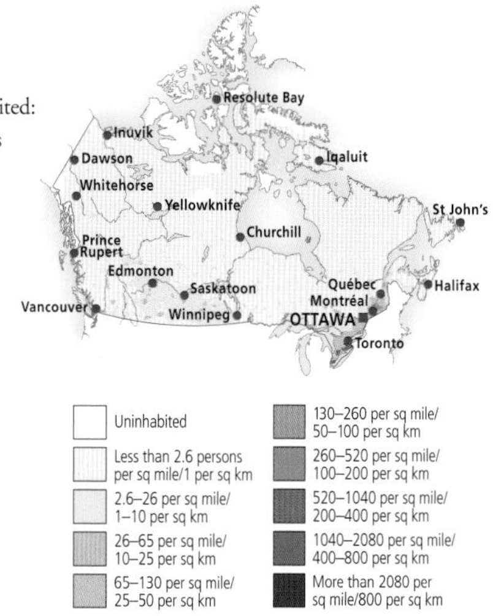
Resolute Bay
Inuvik
Dawson
Whitehorse
Iqaluit
Yellowknife
St John's
Churchill
Prince Rupert
Edmonton
Saskatoon
Québec
Halifax
Montréal
Vancouver
Winnipeg
OTTAWA
Toronto
Uninhabited
Less than 2.6 persons per sq mile/1 per sq km
2.6–26 per sq mile/ 1–10 per sq km
26–65 per sq mile/ 10–25 per sq km
65–130 per sq mile/ 25–50 per sq km
130–260 per sq mile/ 50–100 per sq km
260–520 per sq mile/ 100–200 per sq km
520–1040 per sq mile/ 200–400 per sq km
1040–2080 per sq mile/ 400–800 per sq km
More than 2080 per sq mile/800 per sq km

ECONOMIC PROFILE

Almost half of the country is forested and Canada is the world's leading producer of pulp, paper, and wood. Ample fresh water is harnessed by hydroelectric plants to provide 60 percent of energy needs. Canada is among the world's top sources of zinc, uranium, nickel, bauxite, copper, and gold, and produces far more oil and gas than it uses. Arable land is limited in extent, covering just 7 percent of the country, but productive. Manufacturing is led by transportation equipment, food, machinery, and wood products. Services employ three-quarters of Canadians and generate two-thirds of GDP.

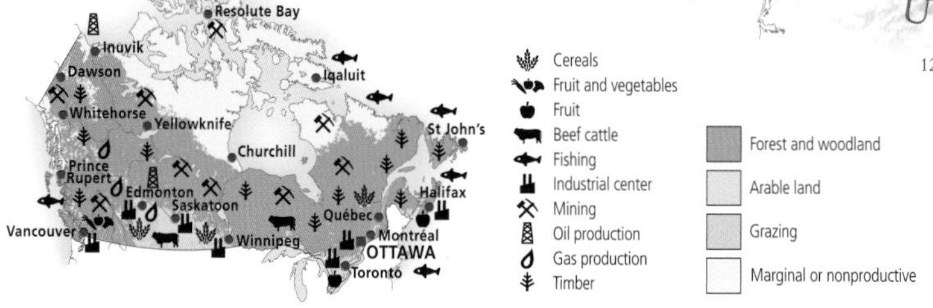
Resolute Bay
Inuvik
Dawson
Iqaluit
Whitehorse
Yellowknife
St John's
Churchill
Prince Rupert
Edmonton
Saskatoon
Halifax
Vancouver
Winnipeg
Québec
Montréal
OTTAWA
Toronto
Cereals
Fruit and vegetables
Fruit
Beef cattle
Fishing
Industrial center
Mining
Oil production
Gas production
Timber
Forest and woodland
Arable land
Grazing
Marginal or nonproductive

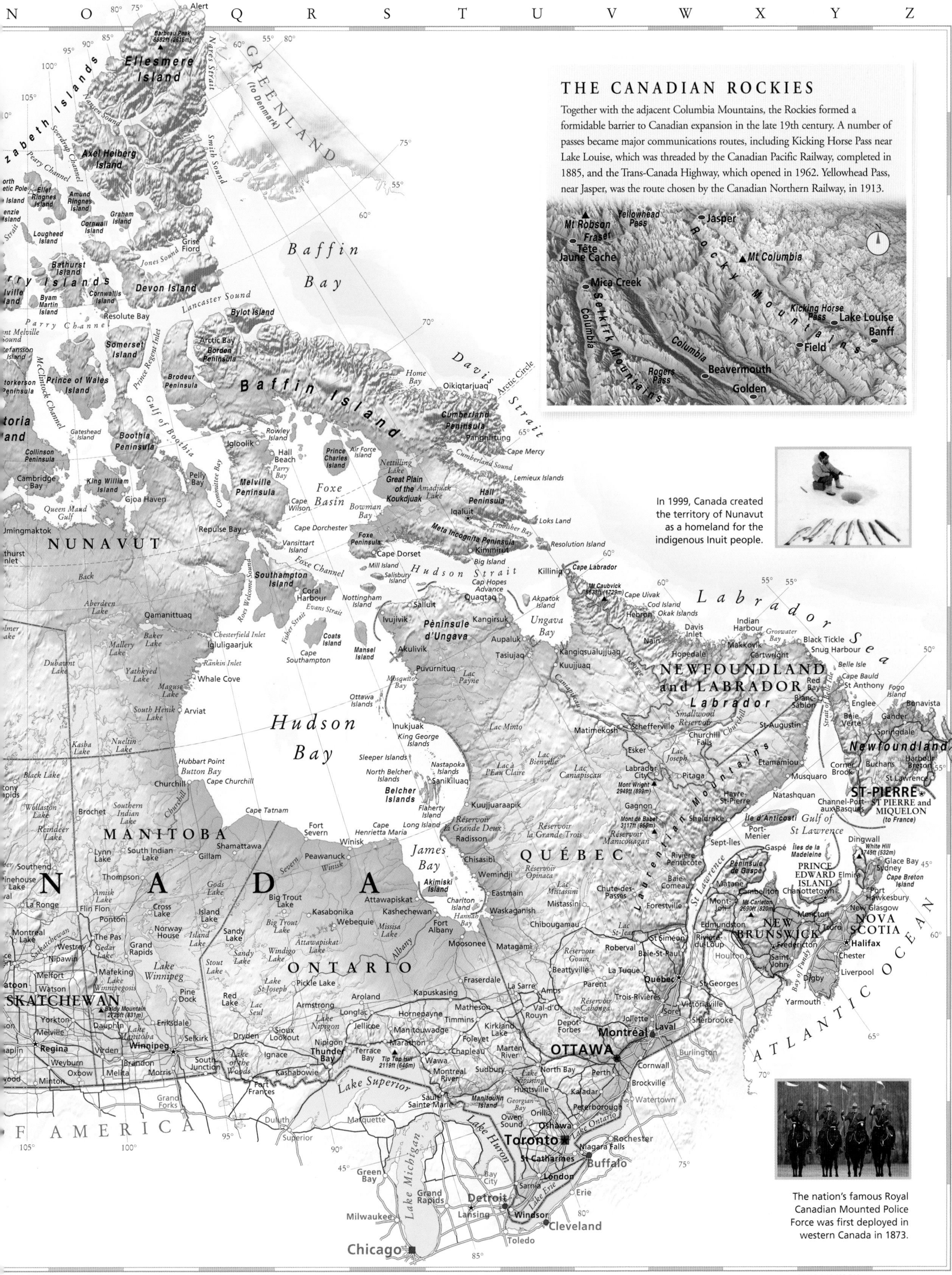

THE CANADIAN ROCKIES

Together with the adjacent Columbia Mountains, the Rockies formed a formidable barrier to Canadian expansion in the late 19th century. A number of passes became major communications routes, including Kicking Horse Pass near Lake Louise, which was threaded by the Canadian Pacific Railway, completed in 1885, and the Trans-Canada Highway, which opened in 1962. Yellowhead Pass, near Jasper, was the route chosen by the Canadian Northern Railway, in 1913.

In 1999, Canada created the territory of Nunavut as a homeland for the indigenous Inuit people.

The nation's famous Royal Canadian Mounted Police Force was first deployed in western Canada in 1873.

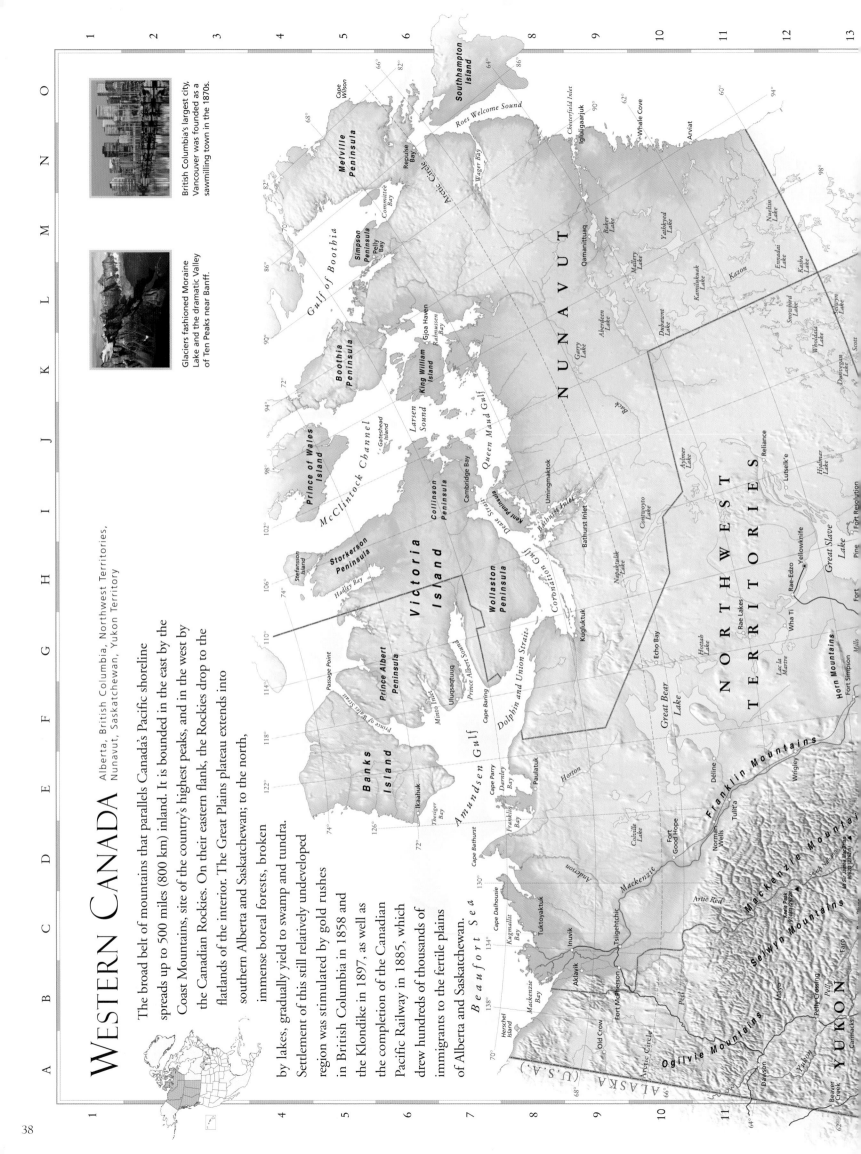

Western Canada

Alberta, British Columbia, Northwest Territories, Nunavut, Saskatchewan, Yukon Territory

The broad belt of mountains that parallels Canada's Pacific shoreline spreads up to 500 miles (800 km) inland. It is bounded in the east by the Coast Mountains, site of the country's highest peaks, and in the west by the Canadian Rockies. On their eastern flank, the Rockies drop to the flatlands of the interior. The Great Plains plateau extends into southern Alberta and Saskatchewan; to the north, immense boreal forests, broken by lakes, gradually yield to swamp and tundra. Settlement of this still relatively undeveloped region was stimulated by gold rushes in British Columbia in 1858 and the Klondike in 1897, as well as the completion of the Canadian Pacific Railway in 1885, which drew hundreds of thousands of immigrants to the fertile plains of Alberta and Saskatchewan.

Glaciers fashioned Moraine Lake and the dramatic Valley of Ten Peaks near Banff.

British Columbia's largest city, Vancouver was founded as a sawmilling town in the 1870s.

The Mackenzie River has North America's second-largest river basin.

Population Patterns

The largest settlements are to be found on the west coast and the prairies. British Columbia is the third most populous province and Vancouver has more than 2 million inhabitants—more than 20 times the number that lives in Nunavut and the Northwest and Yukon territories combined. In recent years, half of British Columbia's immigrants have come from Asia. Due in part to its thriving oil industry, Alberta has Canada's fastest-growing provincial population, which is concentrated in the Calgary–Edmonton corridor. Calgary is the nation's fastest-growing city.

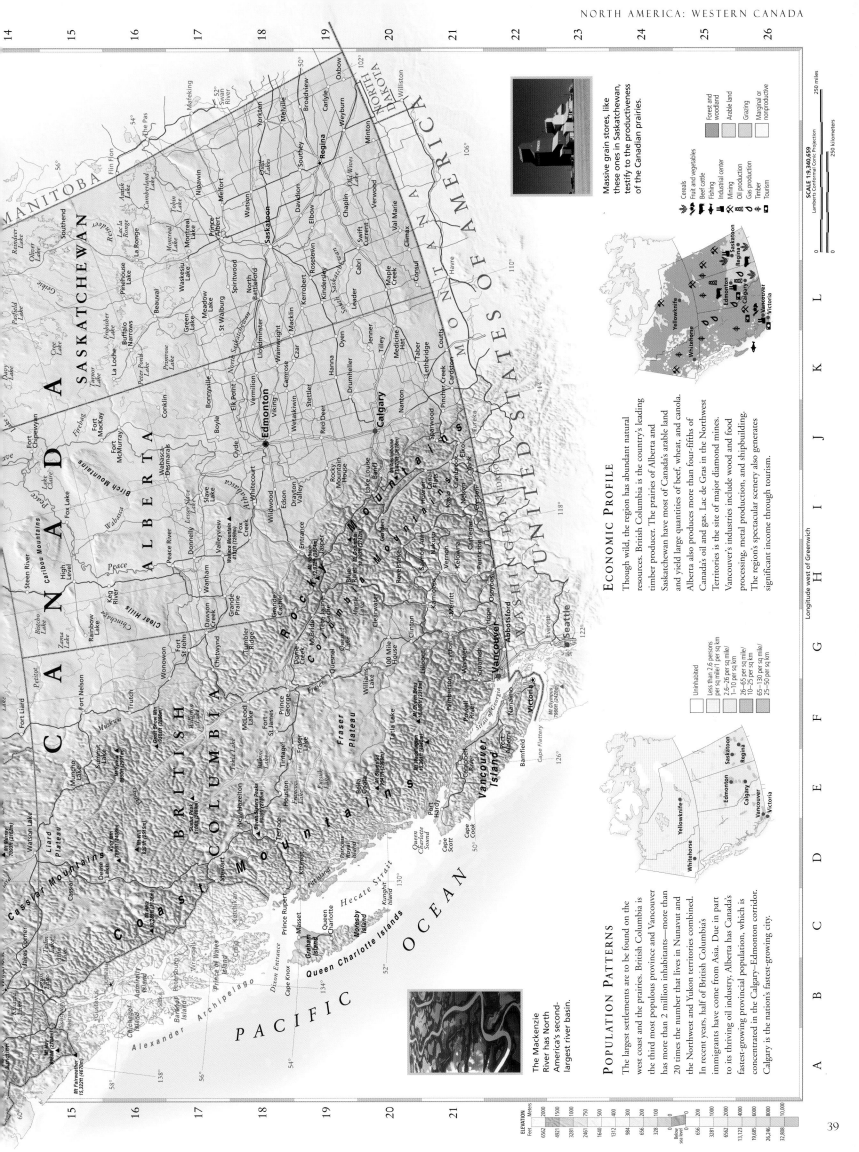

Economic Profile

Though wild, the region has abundant natural resources. British Columbia is the country's leading timber producer. The prairies of Alberta and Saskatchewan have most of Canada's arable land and yield large quantities of beef, wheat, and canola. Alberta also produces more than four-fifths of Canada's oil and gas. Lac de Gras in the Northwest Territories is the site of major diamond mines. Vancouver's industries include wood and food processing, metal production, and shipbuilding. The region's spectacular scenery also generates significant income through tourism.

Massive grain stores, like these ones in Saskatchewan, testify to the productiveness of the Canadian prairies.

Eastern Canada

Manitoba, New Brunswick, Newfoundland and Labrador, Nova Scotia, Nunavut, Ontario, Prince Edward Island, Québec, St Pierre and Miquelon

Underpinned by the ancient Canadian Shield, Eastern Canada consists of a horseshoe-shaped swathe of mostly low-lying land that curls around and inclines gently toward the shores of Hudson Bay. Mountains rise along the eastern fringes of the shield, on Baffin Island, and in Labrador, New Brunswick, and eastern Québec. North America's great belt of lake-studded boreal forest blankets much of Manitoba, Ontario, and Québec, separating the windswept northern tundra from a narrow temperate zone in the south that is home to most of Canada's cities, businesses, and industries, as well as its capital. Before coming under British control in the 18th century, this region was settled by groups of French immigrants. Many remained, and the province of Québec is still culturally distinct from the rest of Canada in that the vast majority of its inhabitants are of French descent and French-speaking. Its demands for greater autonomy constitute Canada's most problematic and potentially disruptive political issue.

In Hudson Bay, polar bears live onshore in summer but hunt seals across the pack ice throughout winter.

Founded in 1642 on an island in the St Lawrence River, Montréal is Canada's second-largest city.

Population Patterns

Six out of every ten Canadians live in the provinces of Ontario and Québec, which also encompass 15 of the country's 25 largest cities. Ontario has been the focus of recent immigration to Canada, absorbing half of all incomers in the 1990s. By far the densest settlement occurs along the Great Lakes–St Lawrence lowlands. In Manitoba, the population is concentrated in the productive southern prairies, but mechanization of agricultural processes has kept numbers low. Newfoundland and Labrador's population has dropped sharply in recent years, mainly as a result of migration to other provinces. The north is the site of far-flung indigenous communities and outposts founded on resource exploitation.

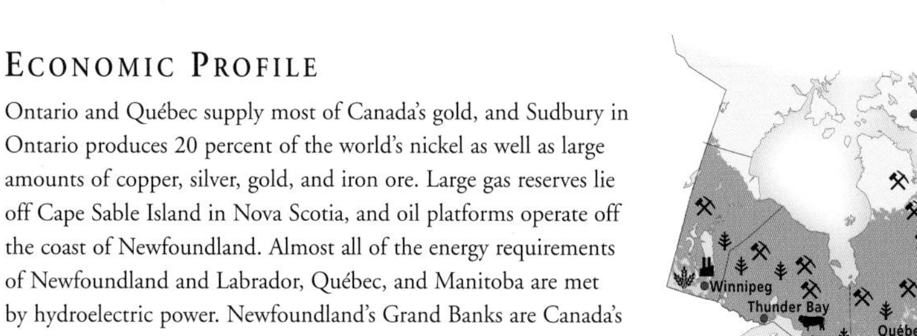

Economic Profile

Ontario and Québec supply most of Canada's gold, and Sudbury in Ontario produces 20 percent of the world's nickel as well as large amounts of copper, silver, gold, and iron ore. Large gas reserves lie off Cape Sable Island in Nova Scotia, and oil platforms operate off the coast of Newfoundland. Almost all of the energy requirements of Newfoundland and Labrador, Québec, and Manitoba are met by hydroelectric power. Newfoundland's Grand Banks are Canada's richest fisheries, although overfishing has significantly reduced catches since the mid-1970s. Southern Ontario and Québec form the country's industrial and commercial heartland.

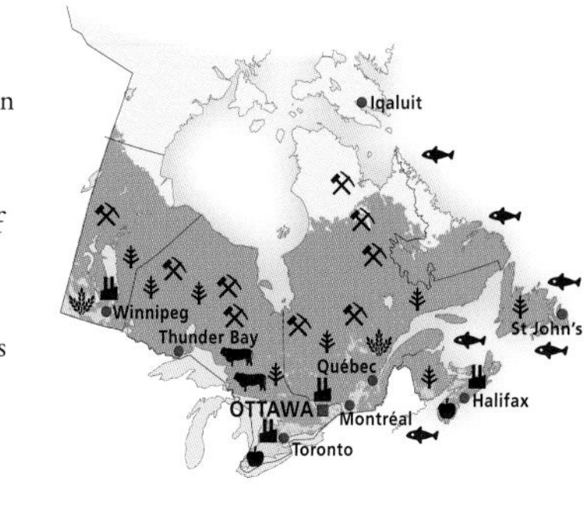

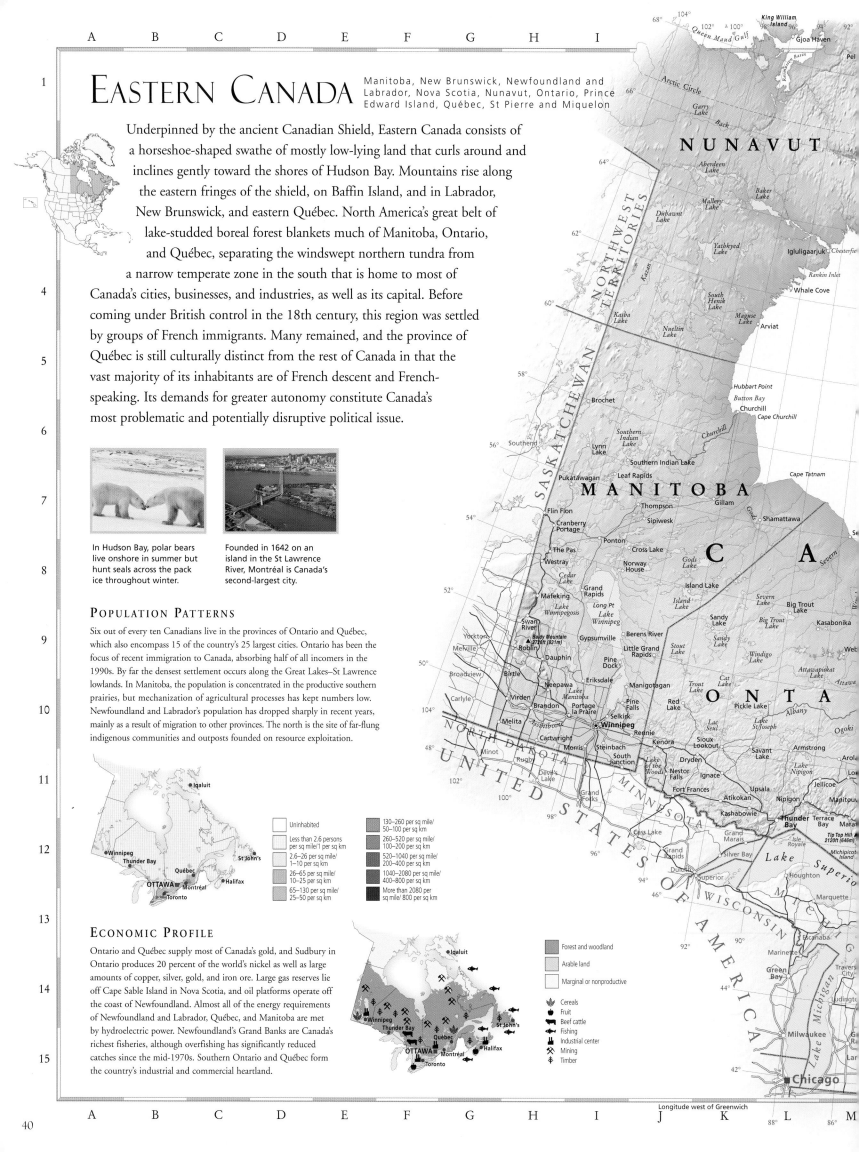

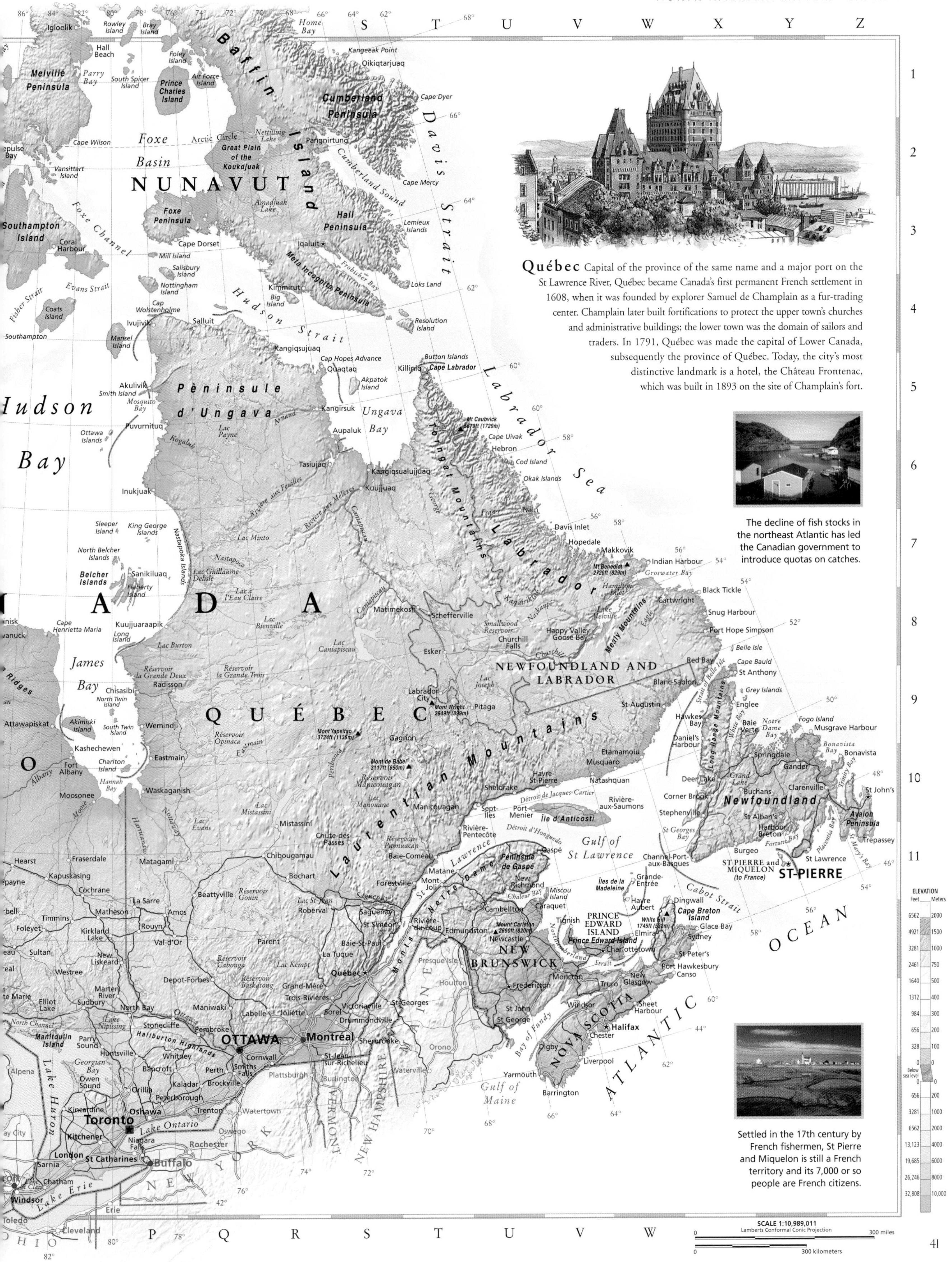

Québec Capital of the province of the same name and a major port on the St Lawrence River, Québec became Canada's first permanent French settlement in 1608, when it was founded by explorer Samuel de Champlain as a fur-trading center. Champlain later built fortifications to protect the upper town's churches and administrative buildings; the lower town was the domain of sailors and traders. In 1791, Québec was made the capital of Lower Canada, subsequently the province of Québec. Today, the city's most distinctive landmark is a hotel, the Château Frontenac, which was built in 1893 on the site of Champlain's fort.

The decline of fish stocks in the northeast Atlantic has led the Canadian government to introduce quotas on catches.

Settled in the 17th century by French fishermen, St Pierre and Miquelon is still a French territory and its 7,000 or so people are French citizens.

SCALE 1:10,989,011
Lamberts Conformal Conic Projection
0 300 miles
0 300 kilometers

Southeastern Canada

New Brunswick, Nova Scotia, Ontario, Prince Edward Island, Québec

Flowing northeast out of Lake Ontario, the St Lawrence River courses for almost 800 miles (1,300 km) to the wide Gulf of St Lawrence and the Atlantic Ocean. The river was the main entry point to the interior for early European adventurers, and in the 17th century the country's first ports were founded on its banks by French explorers. The temperate climate and fertile soils of the river valley and the northern shores of Lakes Ontario and Erie form a stark contrast to the cold, waterlogged plateaus to the north and the wet, precipitous terrain of the Appalachian Mountains to the south. Settlers consequently clustered on these lowlands, and today this is Canada's most populous region, the site of its largest cities, and the home of its national capital, Ottawa.

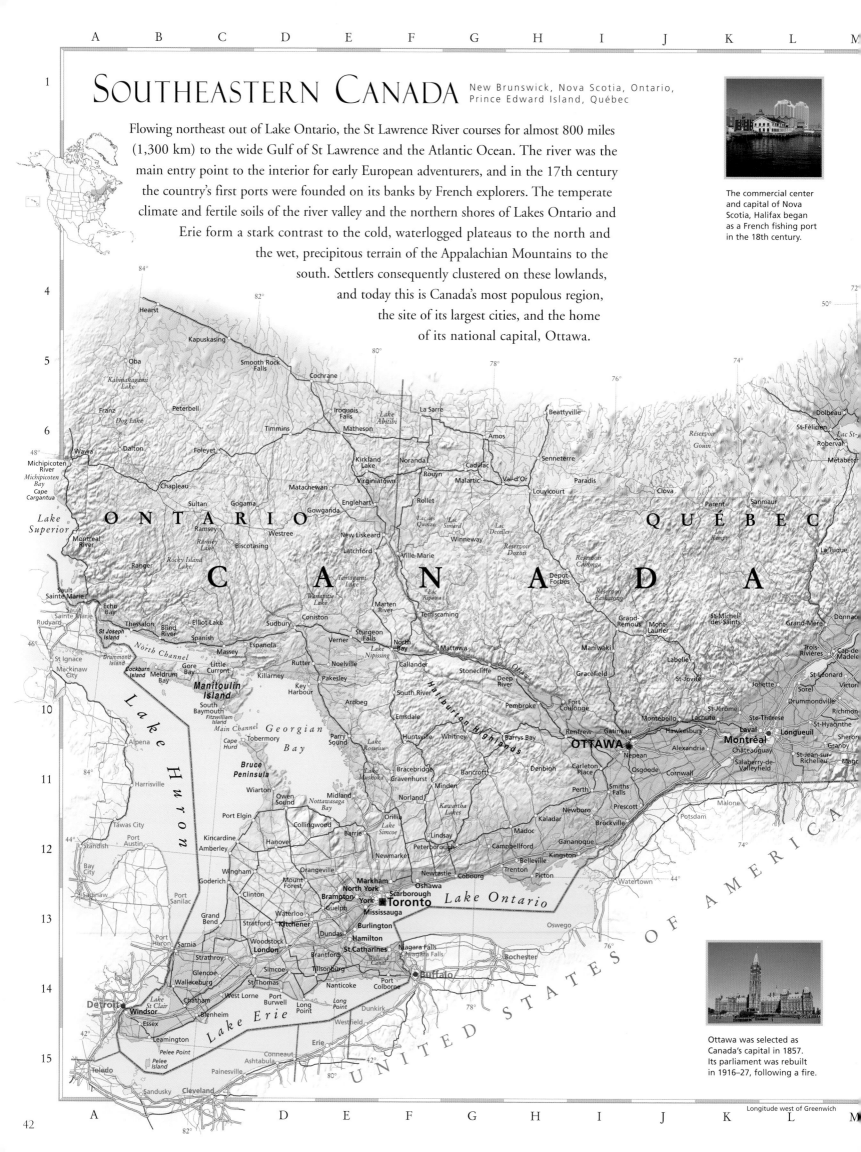

The commercial center and capital of Nova Scotia, Halifax began as a French fishing port in the 18th century.

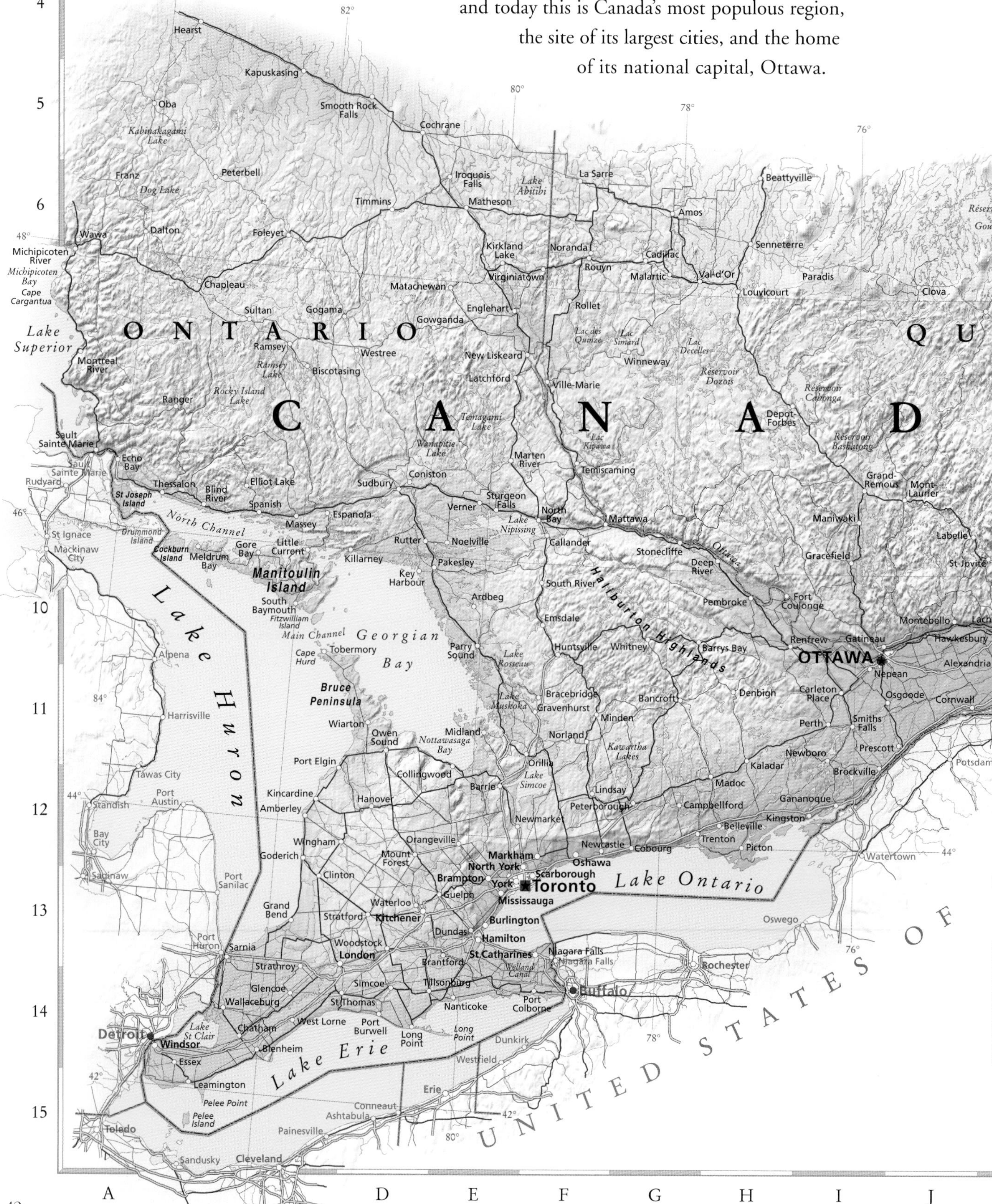

Ottawa was selected as Canada's capital in 1857. Its parliament was rebuilt in 1916–27, following a fire.

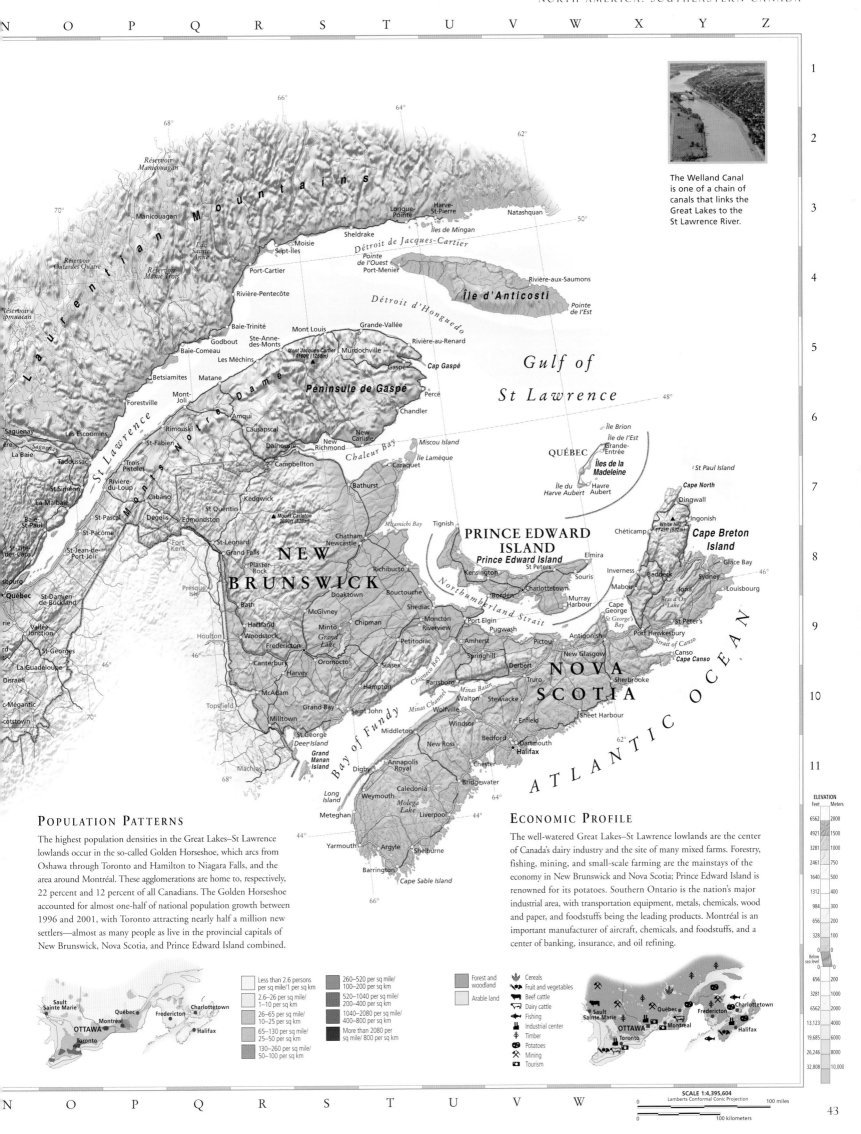

The Welland Canal is one of a chain of canals that links the Great Lakes to the St Lawrence River.

Population Patterns

The highest population densities in the Great Lakes–St Lawrence lowlands occur in the so-called Golden Horseshoe, which arcs from Oshawa through Toronto and Hamilton to Niagara Falls, and the area around Montréal. These agglomerations are home to, respectively, 22 percent and 12 percent of all Canadians. The Golden Horseshoe accounted for almost one-half of national population growth between 1996 and 2001, with Toronto attracting nearly half a million new settlers—almost as many people as live in the provincial capitals of New Brunswick, Nova Scotia, and Prince Edward Island combined.

Economic Profile

The well-watered Great Lakes–St Lawrence lowlands are the center of Canada's dairy industry and the site of many mixed farms. Forestry, fishing, mining, and small-scale farming are the mainstays of the economy in New Brunswick and Nova Scotia; Prince Edward Island is renowned for its potatoes. Southern Ontario is the nation's major industrial area, with transportation equipment, metals, chemicals, wood and paper, and foodstuffs being the leading products. Montréal is an important manufacturer of aircraft, chemicals, and foodstuffs, and a center of banking, insurance, and oil refining.

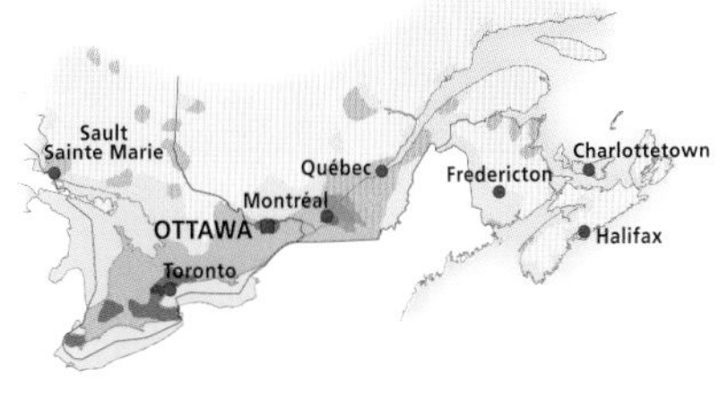

- Less than 2.6 persons per sq mile/1 per sq km
- 2.6–26 per sq mile/ 1–10 per sq km
- 26–65 per sq mile/ 10–25 per sq km
- 65–130 per sq mile/ 25–50 per sq km
- 130–260 per sq mile/ 50–100 per sq km
- 260–520 per sq mile/ 100–200 per sq km
- 520–1040 per sq mile/ 200–400 per sq km
- 1040–2080 per sq mile/ 400–800 per sq km
- More than 2080 per sq mile/ 800 per sq km

- Forest and woodland
- Arable land
- Cereals
- Fruit and vegetables
- Beef cattle
- Dairy cattle
- Fishing
- Industrial center
- Timber
- Potatoes
- Mining
- Tourism

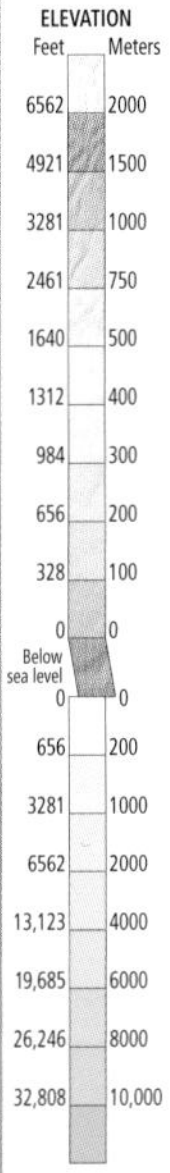

SCALE 1:4,395,604
Lamberts Conformal Conic Projection
0 100 miles
0 100 kilometers

Mexico

Mexico's interior is dominated by a vast, V-shaped plateau known as the Mesa Central. Extending from the U.S. border southward beyond Mexico City, it is edged by two major mountain ranges, the Sierra Madre Occidental and the Sierra Madre Oriental. A slender, broken coastal plain runs along the Pacific shore, converging in the far northwest with the long, rugged, and extremely arid arm of Baja California. At the southern end of the wide, humid east-coast lowlands, the Yucatan Peninsula, a flat, low swathe of limestone, juts into the Gulf of Mexico. In the early 16th century, Spain rapidly conquered the prosperous native civilizations of the Aztec and the Maya. Its subsequent colonization of the entire region resulted in the eradication of many Amerindian communities. Mexico shook off Spanish rule in 1821 and became a republic two years later, though it experienced revolutions and civil wars for the next 100 years. In the 20th century, explosive population growth limited the benefits of genuine social and economic progress.

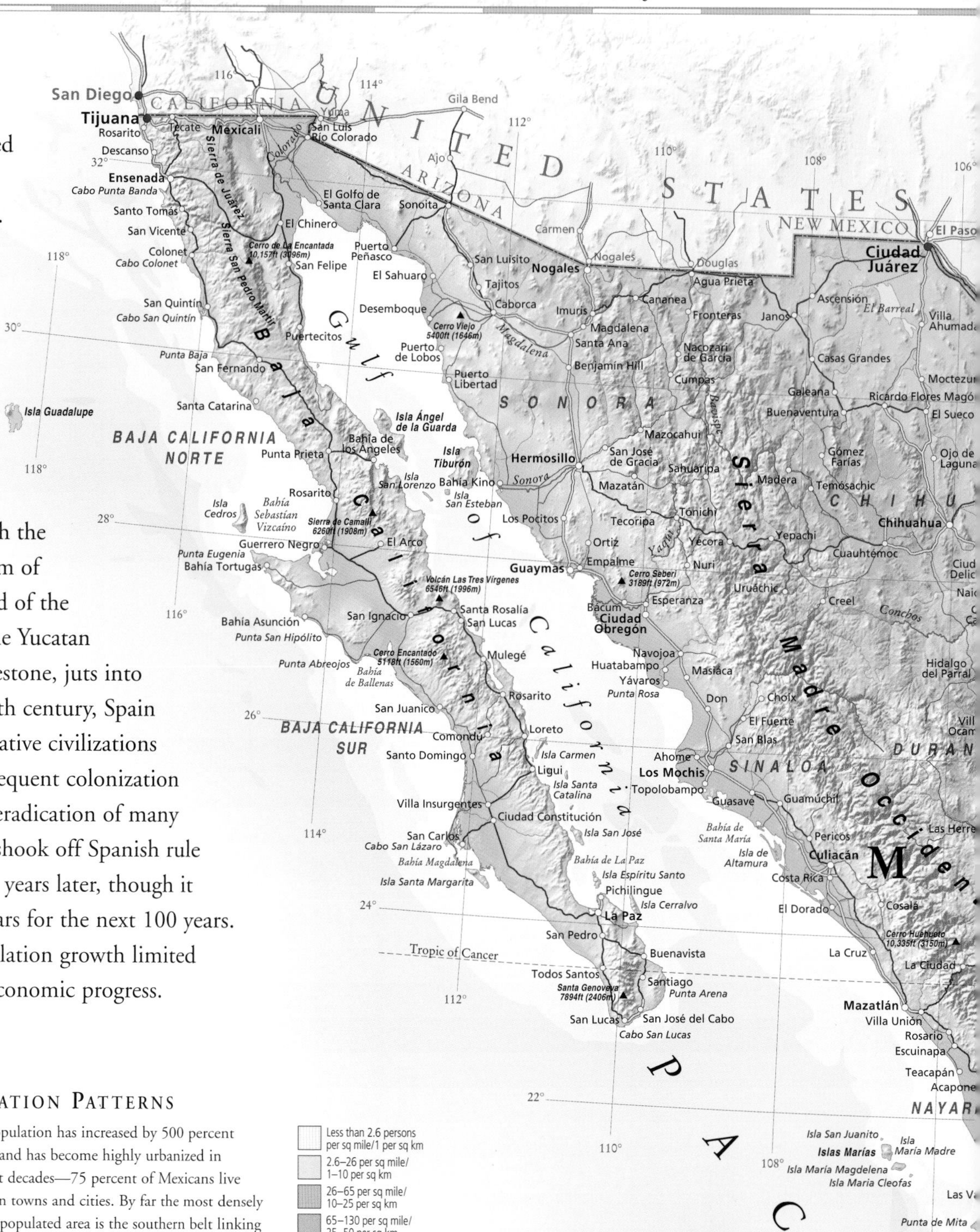

Population Patterns

Mexico's population has increased by 500 percent since 1915 and has become highly urbanized in recent decades—75 percent of Mexicans live in towns and cities. By far the most densely populated area is the southern belt linking Guadalajara, Mexico City, Puebla, and Veracruz. Fueled by U.S.-backed industrial expansion, the northern border towns are also growing rapidly. Population density is lowest in the arid north and in Chiapas and eastern Yucatan. About 60 percent of Mexicans are mestizos, 30 percent Amerindian, and 9 percent of European origin.

- Less than 2.6 persons per sq mile/1 per sq km
- 2.6–26 per sq mile/ 1–10 per sq km
- 26–65 per sq mile/ 10–25 per sq km
- 65–130 per sq mile/ 25–50 per sq km
- 130–260 per sq mile/ 50–100 per sq km
- 260–520 per sq mile/ 100–200 per sq km
- 520–1040 per sq mile/ 200–400 per sq km

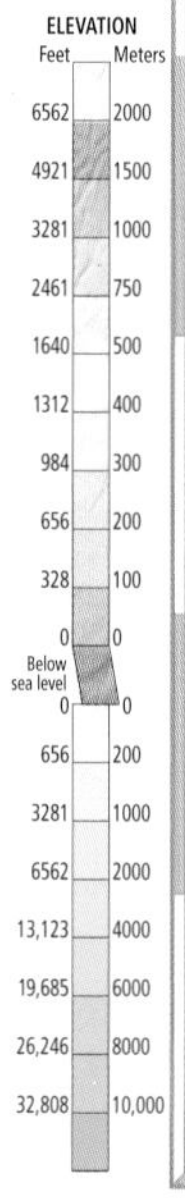

Economic Profile

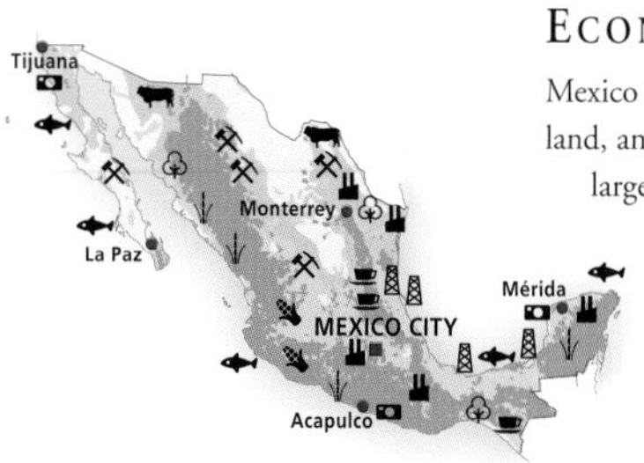

Mexico has enormous mineral resources, limited arable land, and expanding industries. It is one of the world's largest producers of oil—its main source of income—and the largest supplier of silver; it also has sizable gas and coal reserves. Industries, led by the processing of oil, food, and metals and the manufacture of machinery, chemicals, and textiles, are concentrated in Mexico City. Only about one-fifth of the country is arable; half of this area is given over to corn cultivation. Cattle ranching is the main agricultural activity in the arid north. Tourism is now the nation's second-biggest source of revenue.

- Forest and woodland
- Arable land
- Grazing
- Marginal or nonproductive

- Corn (maize)
- Cotton
- Coffee
- Sugarcane
- Industrial center
- Mining
- Oil production
- Fishing
- Beef cattle
- Tourism

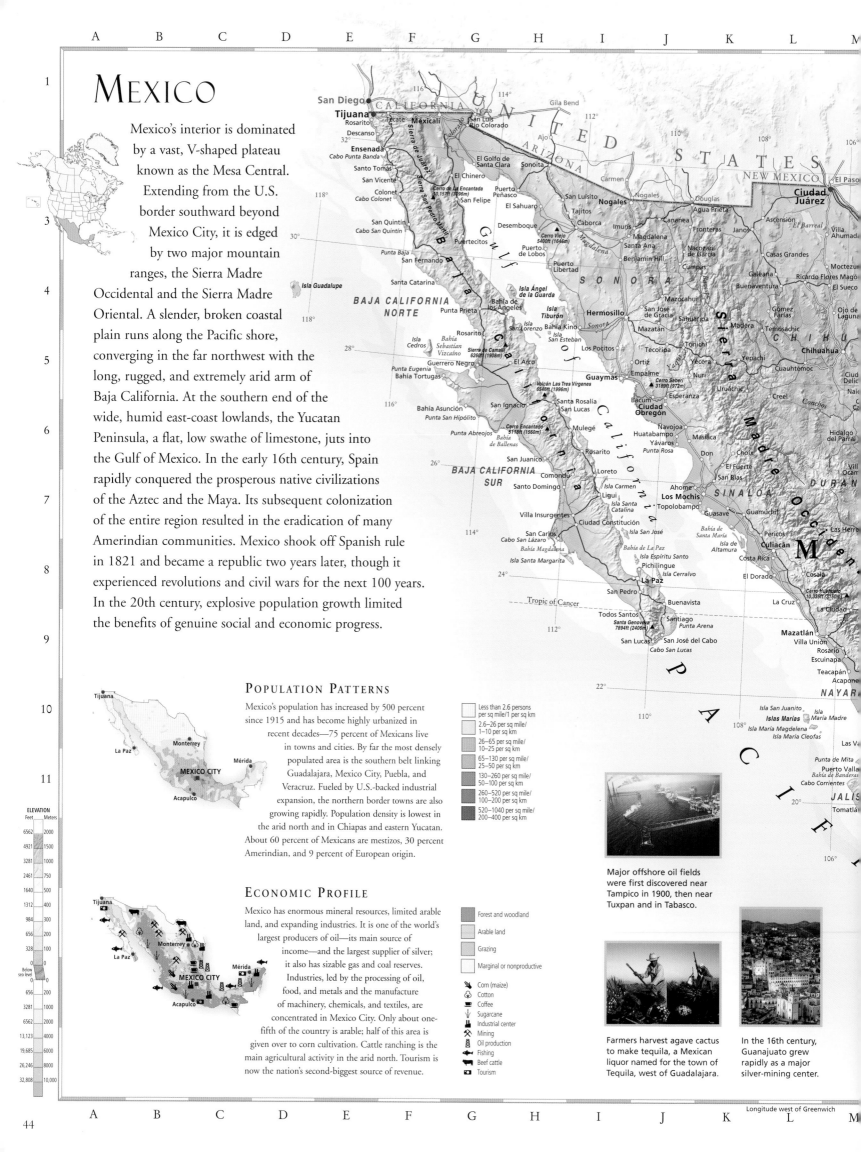

Major offshore oil fields were first discovered near Tampico in 1900, then near Tuxpan and in Tabasco.

Farmers harvest agave cactus to make tequila, a Mexican liquor named for the town of Tequila, west of Guadalajara.

In the 16th century, Guanajuato grew rapidly as a major silver-mining center.

Sited on a magnificent harbor, Acapulco is a vital Pacific port and popular tourist resort.

Around AD 1000, Chichén Itzá in Yucatán was the center of the Mayan civilization.

Mexico City The small band of Spanish conquistadors that reached the Aztec capital of Tenochtitlán in 1519 discovered a magnificent city of 250,000 people, built on an island surrounded by lakes and dominated by grand ceremonial structures. The centuries that followed saw the destruction of Tenochtitlán's buildings by the Spanish, the draining of the lakes to prevent flooding, and the growth of a new capital. Today, Mexico City is the third-largest and fastest-growing urban area in the world, with more than 19 million inhabitants. The heart of the city is the Zócalo (Plaza de la Constitución), site of the Metropolitan Cathedral, built in the 1520s over a razed Aztec temple.

THE CORDILLERA NEO-VOLCÁNICA

The mountain range known as the Cordillera Neo-Volcánica stretches west to east across the southern end of the Mesa Central, passing south of Mexico City and dropping steeply to the eastern coastal plains just north of Veracruz. It incorporates several towering volcanic peaks, including Popocatépetl, Iztaccíhuatl, and 18,405-foot (5,610-m) Pico de Orizaba, Mexico's highest mountain. Tectonic activity along the Pacific coast causes regular earthquakes here—a major tremor killed 9,500 people in Mexico City in 1985. In 1994 and 1996, it also gave rise to eruptions of Popocatépetl, which had previously been dormant for more than 50 years.

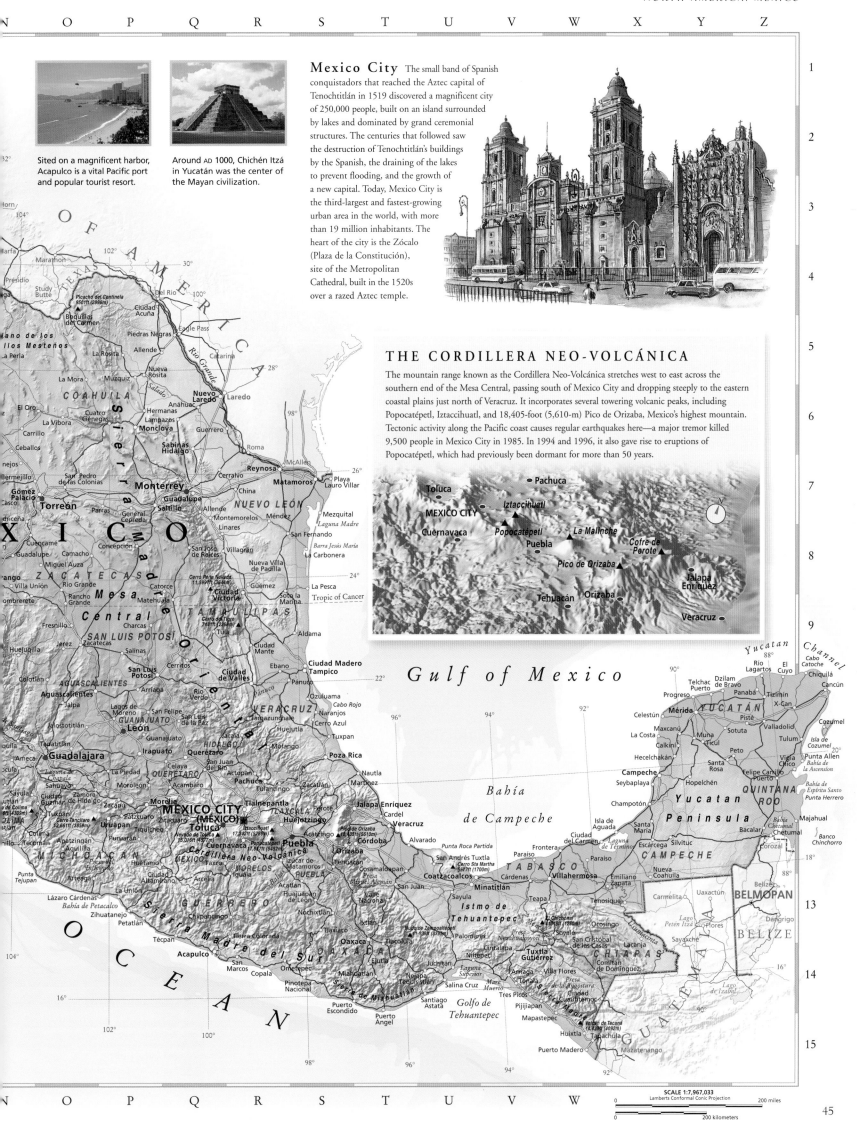

Central America

Belize, Costa Rica, El Salvador, Guatemala, Honduras, Nicaragua, Panama

From the Mexican border, Central America dog-legs and tapers southeastward, connecting with Colombia in South America at the eastern end of the Isthmus of Panama. Forested mountain ranges parallel the Pacific coast, spreading east across Honduras and northern Nicaragua, and covering four-fifths of the entire landmass. Narrow coastal plains line the Pacific shore; wider, swampy lowlands border the Caribbean Sea. With the exception of the former British colony of Belize, the nations of Central America share a predominantly Hispanic culture stemming from a long period of Spanish domination and shaped to varying degrees by other imported and indigenous cultures. Central America's recent history has been clouded by coups, periods of repressive military rule, and guerilla warfare, especially in the north. The southern nations of Costa Rica and Panama have the highest standards of living and have been more stable, although the U.S.A. invaded Panama in 1989 to remove a corrupt military regime.

Population Patterns

Most of the population is mestizo, though the ethnic makeup varies from country to country. Almost one-third of people in Belize are of African origin, and most Costa Ricans are of European descent. Indigenous peoples are in a small minority in most countries except Guatemala, where they form almost half of the population. Settlement has favored the west, especially the cool, fertile uplands, over the humid Caribbean plains, and the north is more populous—one-third of Central Americans live in Guatemala. Urbanization ranges from just over 40 percent in Guatemala to almost 66 percent in El Salvador.

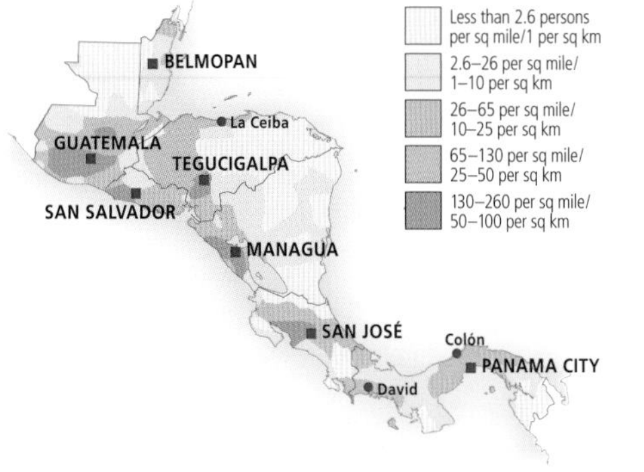

Economic Profile

Development is hampered by political unrest, poor infrastructure, and inequitable distribution of land. Many people grow corn, beans, squashes, and fruit for their own consumption, but much of the best farmland has been turned into large, often foreign-owned, cattle ranches and plantations producing sugar, bananas, and coffee. Mineral resources are, for the most part, scanty or undeveloped. Forests provide timber and chicle (used in chewing gum), but are not harvested sustainably. Industries are limited mainly to food processing and textiles. Services are most significant in Panama, where a free-trade zone is centered on Colón.

Wildlife-rich rain forests are among the attractions that draw over 1 million overseas visitors a year to Costa Rica.

Lake Nicaragua is the world's only freshwater lake that is home to saltwater fish such as sharks and swordfish.

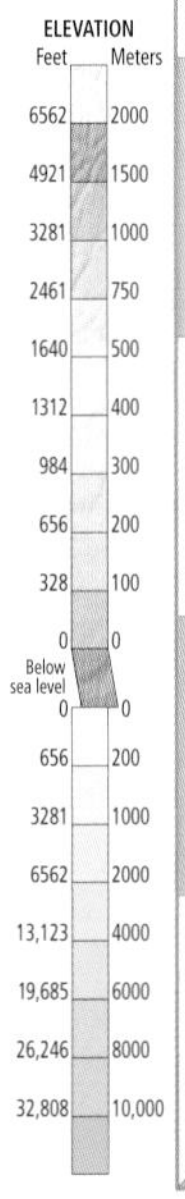

SCALE 1:4,395,604
Lamberts Conformal Conic Projection
0 100 miles
0 100 kilometers

Longitude west of Greenwich

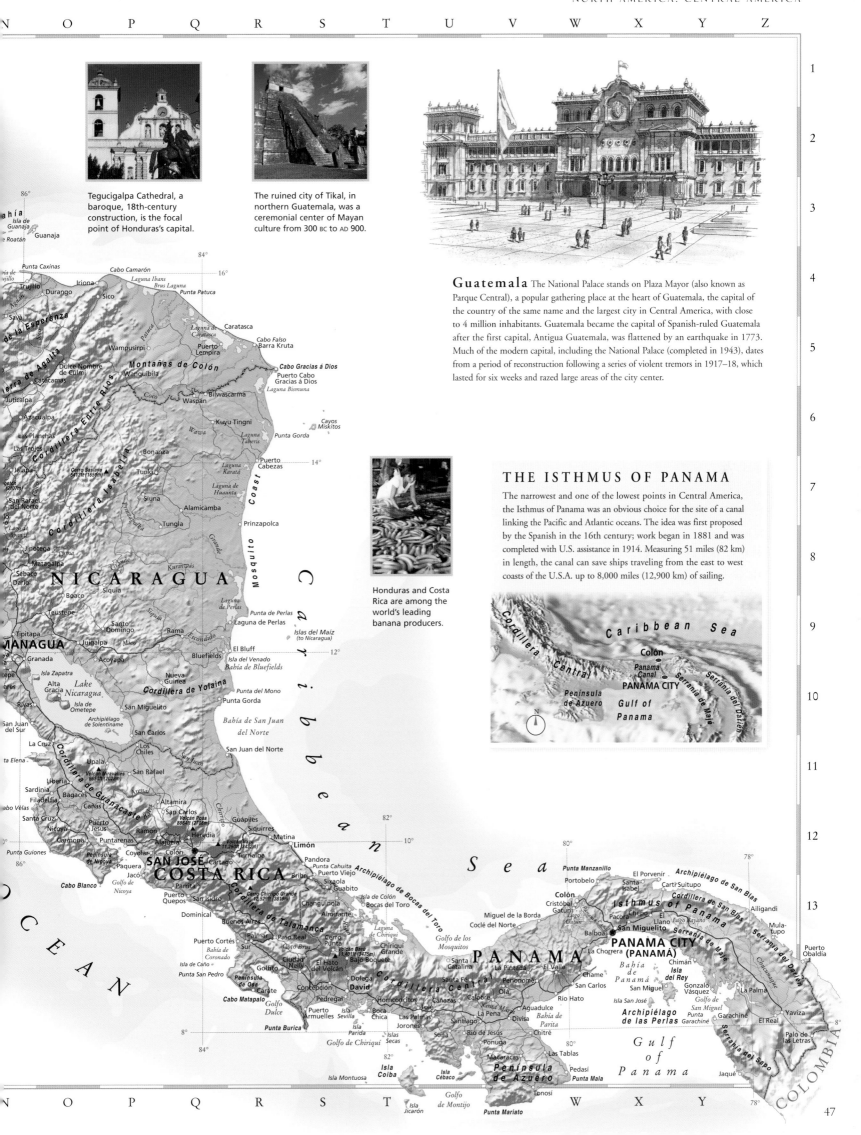

Tegucigalpa Cathedral, a baroque, 18th-century construction, is the focal point of Honduras's capital.

The ruined city of Tikal, in northern Guatemala, was a ceremonial center of Mayan culture from 300 BC to AD 900.

Guatemala The National Palace stands on Plaza Mayor (also known as Parque Central), a popular gathering place at the heart of Guatemala, the capital of the country of the same name and the largest city in Central America, with close to 4 million inhabitants. Guatemala became the capital of Spanish-ruled Guatemala after the first capital, Antigua Guatemala, was flattened by an earthquake in 1773. Much of the modern capital, including the National Palace (completed in 1943), dates from a period of reconstruction following a series of violent tremors in 1917–18, which lasted for six weeks and razed large areas of the city center.

Honduras and Costa Rica are among the world's leading banana producers.

THE ISTHMUS OF PANAMA

The narrowest and one of the lowest points in Central America, the Isthmus of Panama was an obvious choice for the site of a canal linking the Pacific and Atlantic oceans. The idea was first proposed by the Spanish in the 16th century; work began in 1881 and was completed with U.S. assistance in 1914. Measuring 51 miles (82 km) in length, the canal can save ships traveling from the east to west coasts of the U.S.A. up to 8,000 miles (12,900 km) of sailing.

The West Indies

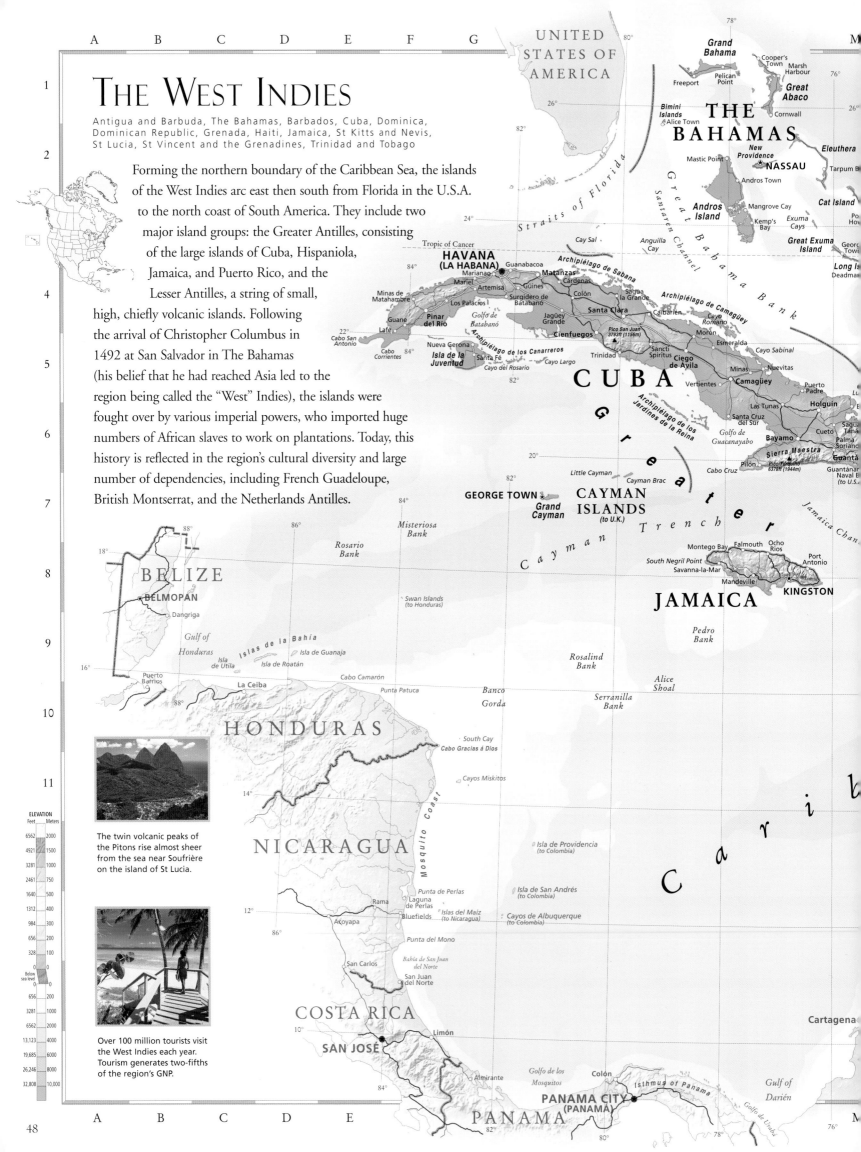

Antigua and Barbuda, The Bahamas, Barbados, Cuba, Dominica, Dominican Republic, Grenada, Haiti, Jamaica, St Kitts and Nevis, St Lucia, St Vincent and the Grenadines, Trinidad and Tobago

Forming the northern boundary of the Caribbean Sea, the islands of the West Indies arc east then south from Florida in the U.S.A. to the north coast of South America. They include two major island groups: the Greater Antilles, consisting of the large islands of Cuba, Hispaniola, Jamaica, and Puerto Rico, and the Lesser Antilles, a string of small, high, chiefly volcanic islands. Following the arrival of Christopher Columbus in 1492 at San Salvador in The Bahamas (his belief that he had reached Asia led to the region being called the "West" Indies), the islands were fought over by various imperial powers, who imported huge numbers of African slaves to work on plantations. Today, this history is reflected in the region's cultural diversity and large number of dependencies, including French Guadeloupe, British Montserrat, and the Netherlands Antilles.

A B C D E F G
1 2 4 5 6 7 8 9 10 11
UNITED STATES OF AMERICA
THE BAHAMAS
Grand Bahama
Freeport
Pelican Point
Cooper's Town
Marsh Harbour
Great Abaco
Cornwall
Bimini Islands
Alice Town
Eleuthera
Tarpum Bay
Mastic Point
New Providence
NASSAU
Andros Town
Andros Island
Mangrove Cay
Kemp's Bay
Exuma Cays
Cat Island
Great Exuma Island
Long Island
Straits of Florida
Santaren Channel
Great Bahama Bank
Cay Sal
Anguilla Cay
Tropic of Cancer
HAVANA (LA HABANA)
Guanabacoa
Marianao
Mariel
Matanzas
Artemisa
Güines
Cárdenas
Minas de Matahambre
Los Palacios
Surgidero de Batabanó
Colón
Sagua la Grande
Archipiélago de Sabana
Archipiélago de Camagüey
Guane
Pinar del Río
Golfo de Batabanó
Jagüey Grande
Santa Clara
Caibarién
Cayo Romano
Lafé
Cabo San Antonio
Cienfuegos
Pico San Juan 3793ft (1156m)
Morón
Cabo Corrientes
Nueva Gerona
Isla de la Juventud
Archipiélago de los Canarreros
Santa Fé
Cayo del Rosario
Cayo Largo
Trinidad
Sancti Spíritus
Ciego de Ávila
Esmeralda
Cayo Sabinal
CUBA
Minas
Nuevitas
Vertientes
Camagüey
Puerto Padre
Archipiélago de los Jardines de la Reina
Las Tunas
Holguín
Santa Cruz del Sur
Golfo de Guacanayabo
Bayamo
Cueto
Sierra Maestra
Pico Turquino 6378ft (1944m)
Pilón
Cabo Cruz
Guantánamo
Guantánamo Naval Base (to U.S.A.)
Greater Antilles
Little Cayman
Cayman Brac
GEORGE TOWN
Grand Cayman
CAYMAN ISLANDS (to U.K.)
Cayman Trench
Jamaica Channel
Misteriosa Bank
Rosario Bank
Montego Bay
Falmouth
Ocho Rios
Port Antonio
South Negril Point
Savanna-la-Mar
Mandeville
KINGSTON
JAMAICA
Pedro Bank
Rosalind Bank
Alice Shoal
Serranilla Bank
Banco Gorda
BELIZE
BELMOPAN
Dangriga
Swan Islands (to Honduras)
Gulf of Honduras
Islas de la Bahía
Isla de Guanaja
Isla de Utila
Isla de Roatán
Puerto Barrios
La Ceiba
Cabo Camarón
Punta Patuca
HONDURAS
South Cay
Cabo Gracias á Dios
Cayos Miskitos
Mosquito Coast
NICARAGUA
Isla de Providencia (to Colombia)
Isla de San Andrés (to Colombia)
Punta de Perlas
Rama
Laguna de Perlas
Bluefields
Islas del Maíz (to Nicaragua)
Cayos de Albuquerque (to Colombia)
Acoyapa
Punta del Mono
San Carlos
Bahía de San Juan del Norte
San Juan del Norte
COSTA RICA
Limón
SAN JOSÉ
Almirante
Golfo de los Mosquitos
Colón
Isthmus of Panama
PANAMA CITY (PANAMÁ)
PANAMA
Gulf of Darién
Golfo de Urabá
Cartagena
Caribbean
ELEVATION
Feet Meters
6562 2000
4921 1500
3281 1000
2461 750
1640 500
1312 400
984 300
656 200
328 100
0 0
Below sea level
0 0
656 200
3281 1000
6562 2000
13,123 4000
19,685 6000
26,246 8000
32,808 10,000

The twin volcanic peaks of the Pitons rise almost sheer from the sea near Soufrière on the island of St Lucia.

Over 100 million tourists visit the West Indies each year. Tourism generates two-fifths of the region's GNP.

Havana Occupying a deep, sheltered harbor on the northwest coast of Cuba, Havana was much prized by its Spanish founders, who began building the city in 1519. Among its many ornate buildings and structures is the 17th-century Plaza Vieja, or Old Square. In recent years, Old Havana has been carefully restored, and it is now a World Heritage site.

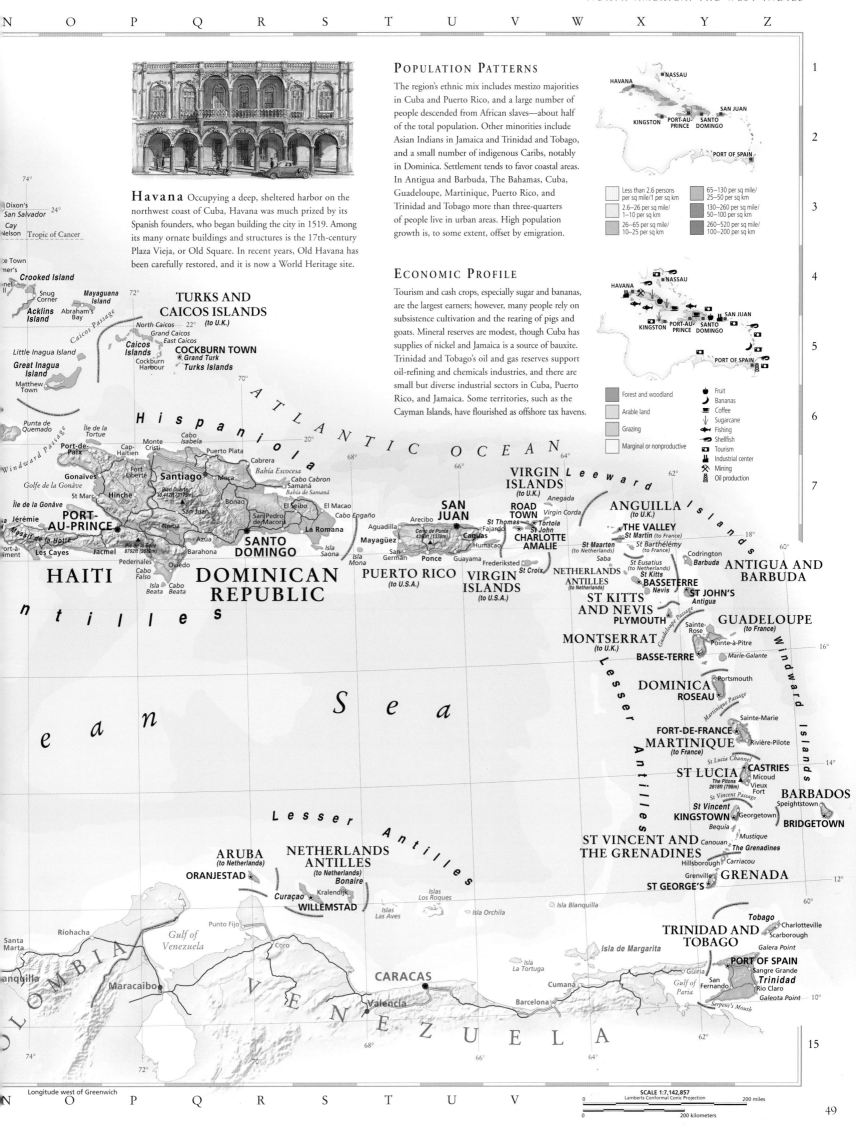

Population Patterns

The region's ethnic mix includes mestizo majorities in Cuba and Puerto Rico, and a large number of people descended from African slaves—about half of the total population. Other minorities include Asian Indians in Jamaica and Trinidad and Tobago, and a small number of indigenous Caribs, notably in Dominica. Settlement tends to favor coastal areas. In Antigua and Barbuda, The Bahamas, Cuba, Guadeloupe, Martinique, Puerto Rico, and Trinidad and Tobago more than three-quarters of people live in urban areas. High population growth is, to some extent, offset by emigration.

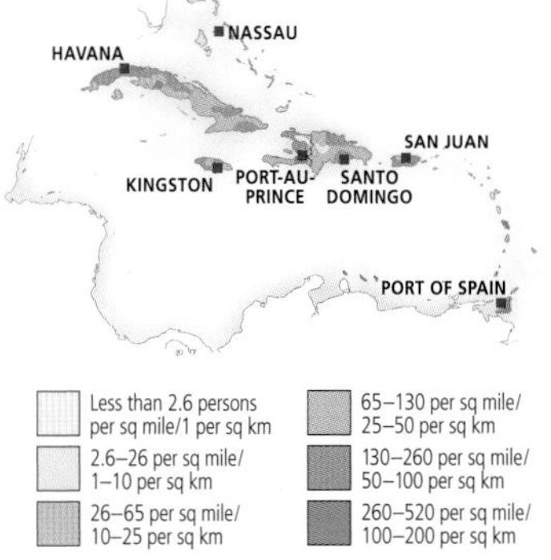

Economic Profile

Tourism and cash crops, especially sugar and bananas, are the largest earners; however, many people rely on subsistence cultivation and the rearing of pigs and goats. Mineral reserves are modest, though Cuba has supplies of nickel and Jamaica is a source of bauxite. Trinidad and Tobago's oil and gas reserves support oil-refining and chemicals industries, and there are small but diverse industrial sectors in Cuba, Puerto Rico, and Jamaica. Some territories, such as the Cayman Islands, have flourished as offshore tax havens.

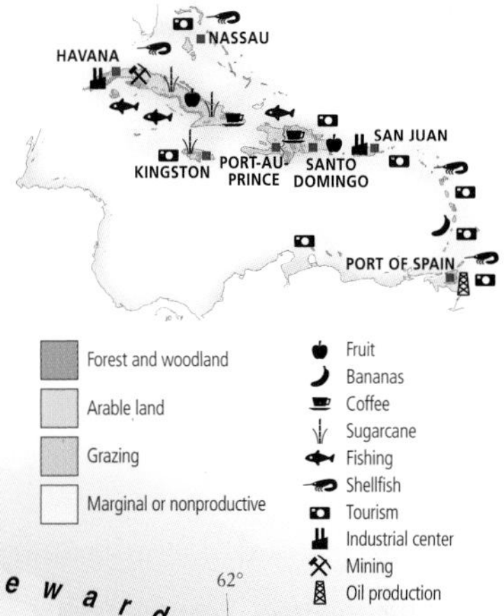

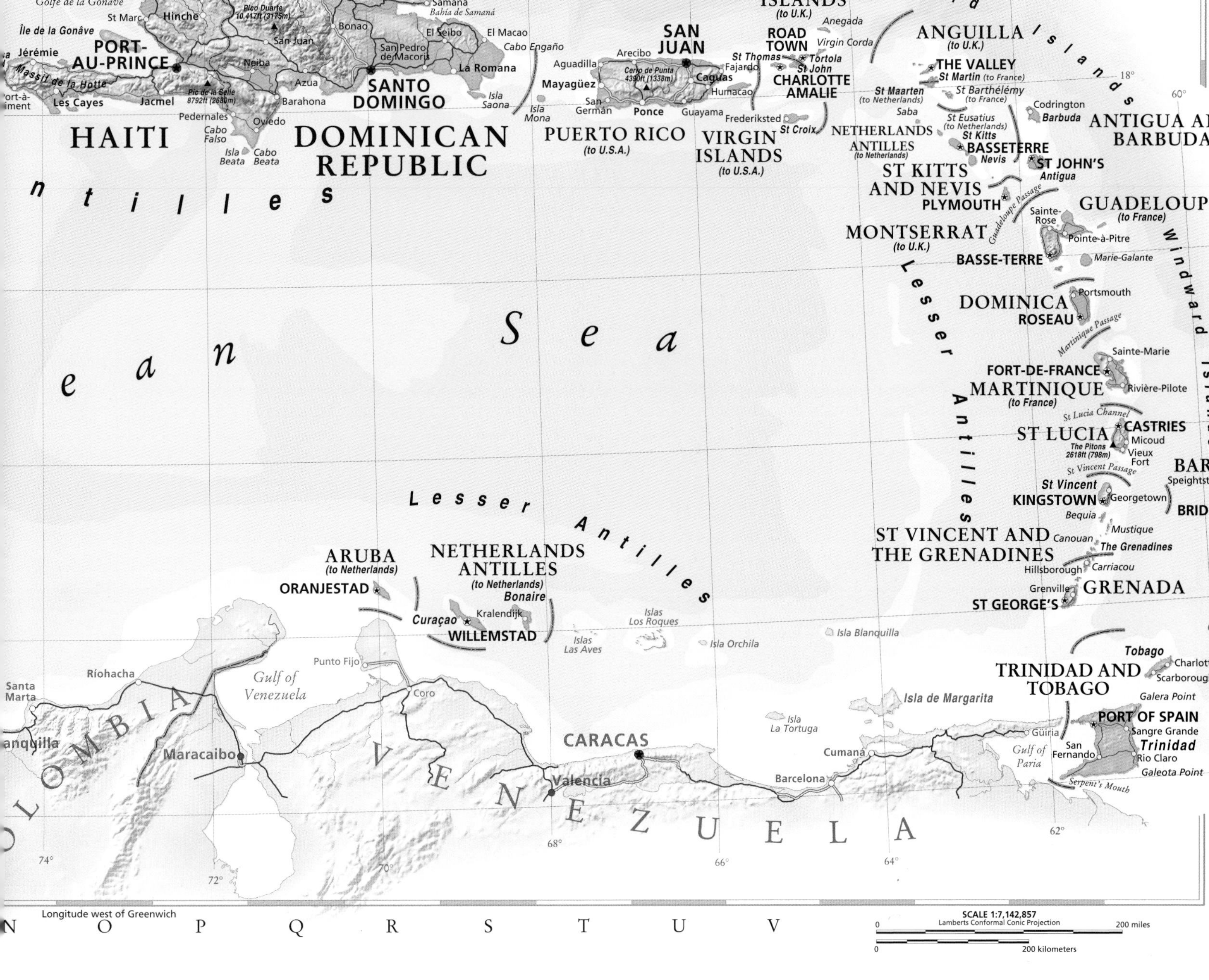

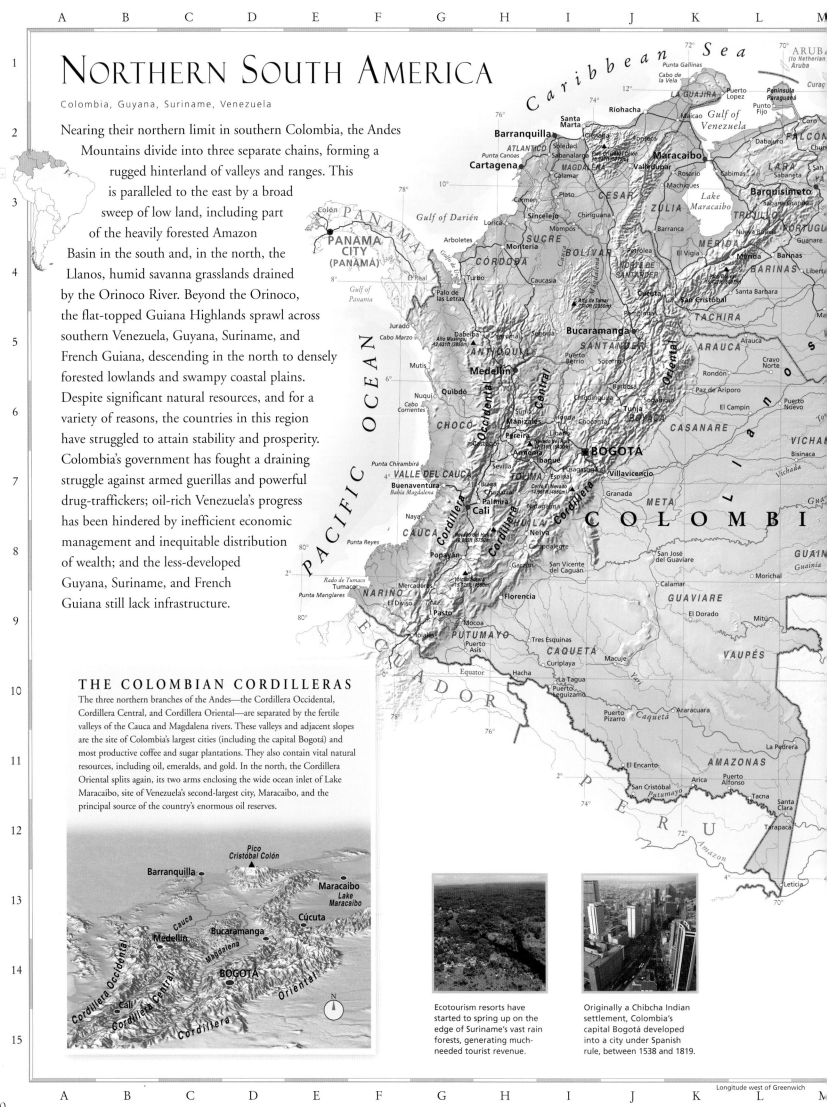

Northern South America

Colombia, Guyana, Suriname, Venezuela

Nearing their northern limit in southern Colombia, the Andes Mountains divide into three separate chains, forming a rugged hinterland of valleys and ranges. This is paralleled to the east by a broad sweep of low land, including part of the heavily forested Amazon Basin in the south and, in the north, the Llanos, humid savanna grasslands drained by the Orinoco River. Beyond the Orinoco, the flat-topped Guiana Highlands sprawl across southern Venezuela, Guyana, Suriname, and French Guiana, descending in the north to densely forested lowlands and swampy coastal plains. Despite significant natural resources, and for a variety of reasons, the countries in this region have struggled to attain stability and prosperity. Colombia's government has fought a draining struggle against armed guerillas and powerful drug-traffickers; oil-rich Venezuela's progress has been hindered by inefficient economic management and inequitable distribution of wealth; and the less-developed Guyana, Suriname, and French Guiana still lack infrastructure.

The Colombian Cordilleras

The three northern branches of the Andes—the Cordillera Occidental, Cordillera Central, and Cordillera Oriental—are separated by the fertile valleys of the Cauca and Magdalena rivers. These valleys and adjacent slopes are the site of Colombia's largest cities (including the capital Bogotá) and most productive coffee and sugar plantations. They also contain vital natural resources, including oil, emeralds, and gold. In the north, the Cordillera Oriental splits again, its two arms enclosing the wide ocean inlet of Lake Maracaibo, site of Venezuela's second-largest city, Maracaibo, and the principal source of the country's enormous oil reserves.

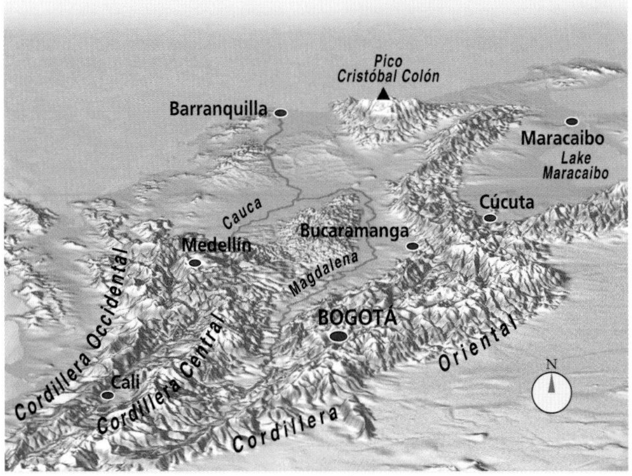

Ecotourism resorts have started to spring up on the edge of Suriname's vast rain forests, generating much-needed tourist revenue.

Originally a Chibcha Indian settlement, Colombia's capital Bogotá developed into a city under Spanish rule, between 1538 and 1819.

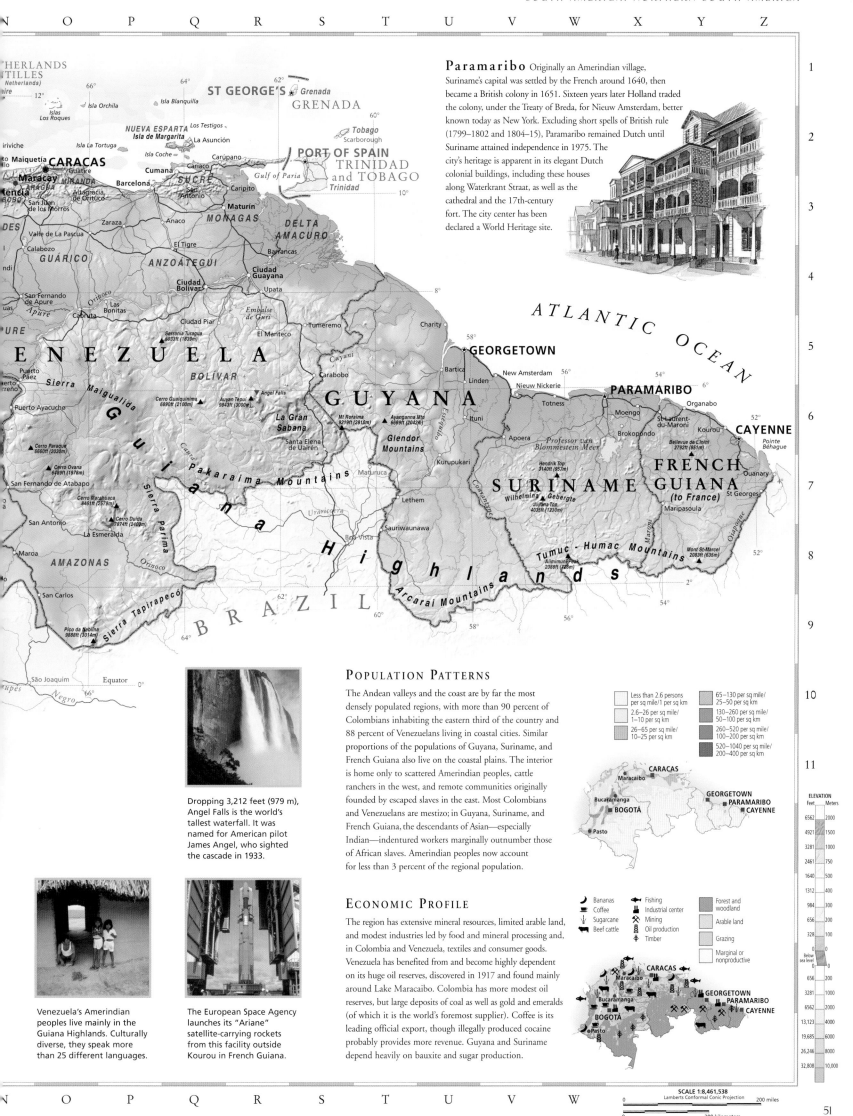

N O P Q R S T U V W X Y Z
1 2 3 4 5 6 7 8 9 10 11
NETHERLANDS ANTILLES (to Netherlands)
Islas Los Roques
Isla Orchila
Isla Blanquilla
ST GEORGE'S
Grenada
GRENADA
NUEVA ESPARTA
Los Testigos
Isla de Margarita
La Asunción
Isla La Tortuga
Isla Coche
Tobago
Scarborough
PORT OF SPAIN
TRINIDAD and TOBAGO
Trinidad
Gulf of Paria
Carúpano
Maiquetía
CARACAS
Guatire
Cumaná
Cariaco
Maracay
MIRANDA
Barcelona
SUCRE
Caripito
ARAGUA
Altagracia de Orituco
San Antonio
San Juan de los Morros
Maturín
Zaraza
Anaco
MONAGAS
DELTA AMACURO
Valle de La Pascua
El Tigre
Barrancas
Calabozo
GUÁRICO
ANZOÁTEGUI
Ciudad Guayana
Ciudad Bolívar
Upata
San Fernando de Apure
Orinoco
Apure
Las Bonitas
Caicara
Embalse de Guri
Ciudad Piar
Tumeremo
Charity
El Manteco
Serranía Turagua 6033ft (1839m)
VENEZUELA
BOLÍVAR
GEORGETOWN
Cuyuni
Bartica
Carabobo
Linden
New Amsterdam
Nieuw Nickerie
PARAMARIBO
Puerto Páez
Sierra Maigualida
Angel Falls
Cerro Guaiquinima 6890ft (2100m)
Auyan Tepui 9843ft (3000m)
GUYANA
Totness
Organabo
Puerto Ayacucho
La Gran Sabana
Mt Roraima 9219ft (2810m)
Ayanganna Mtn 6699ft (2042m)
Essequibo
Ituni
Moengo
St Laurent-du-Maroni
CAYENNE
Glendor Mountains
Apoera
Professor van Blommestein Meer
Brokopondo
Kourou
Santa Elena de Uairén
Bellevue de L'Inini 2792ft (851m)
Pointe Béhague
Cerro Paraque 6660ft (2030m)
Kurupukari
Hendrik Top 3140ft (957m)
FRENCH GUIANA (to France)
Cerro Ovana 6489ft (1978m)
Pakaraima Mountains
Maturuca
Ouanary
San Fernando de Atabapo
SURINAME
Wilhelmina Gebergte
Juliana Top 4035ft (1230m)
St Georges
Lethem
Cerro Marahuaca 8461ft (2579m)
Cerro Duida 7874ft (2400m)
Uraricoera
Corantijn
Maripasoula
San Antonio
Sierra Parima
Sauriwaunawa
Maroni
Oiapoque
La Esmeralda
Guiana Highlands
Boa Vista
Tumuc-Humac Mountains
Mont St-Marcel 2083ft (635m)
Maroa
Alimimuni Peak 2388ft (728m)
AMAZONAS
Orinoco
San Carlos
Acarai Mountains
Sierra Tapirapecó
BRAZIL
Pico da Neblina 9888ft (3014m)
ATLANTIC OCEAN
São Joaquim
Equator
Negro
Uaupés

Paramaribo

Originally an Amerindian village, Suriname's capital was settled by the French around 1640, then became a British colony in 1651. Sixteen years later Holland traded the colony, under the Treaty of Breda, for Nieuw Amsterdam, better known today as New York. Excluding short spells of British rule (1799–1802 and 1804–15), Paramaribo remained Dutch until Suriname attained independence in 1975. The city's heritage is apparent in its elegant Dutch colonial buildings, including these houses along Waterkrant Straat, as well as the cathedral and the 17th-century fort. The city center has been declared a World Heritage site.

Dropping 3,212 feet (979 m), Angel Falls is the world's tallest waterfall. It was named for American pilot James Angel, who sighted the cascade in 1933.

Population Patterns

The Andean valleys and the coast are by far the most densely populated regions, with more than 90 percent of Colombians inhabiting the eastern third of the country and 88 percent of Venezuelans living in coastal cities. Similar proportions of the populations of Guyana, Suriname, and French Guiana also live on the coastal plains. The interior is home only to scattered Amerindian peoples, cattle ranchers in the west, and remote communities originally founded by escaped slaves in the east. Most Colombians and Venezuelans are mestizo; in Guyana, Suriname, and French Guiana, the descendants of Asian—especially Indian—indentured workers marginally outnumber those of African slaves. Amerindian peoples now account for less than 3 percent of the regional population.

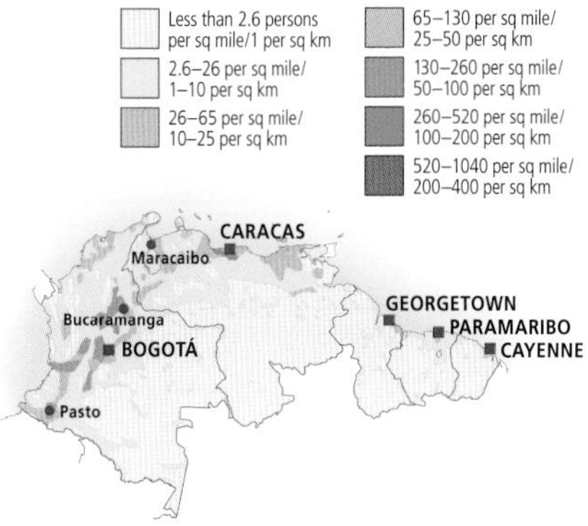
Less than 2.6 persons per sq mile/1 per sq km
2.6–26 per sq mile/ 1–10 per sq km
26–65 per sq mile/ 10–25 per sq km
65–130 per sq mile/ 25–50 per sq km
130–260 per sq mile/ 50–100 per sq km
260–520 per sq mile/ 100–200 per sq km
520–1040 per sq mile/ 200–400 per sq km
CARACAS
Maracaibo
Bucaramanga
BOGOTÁ
Pasto
GEORGETOWN
PARAMARIBO
CAYENNE

Venezuela's Amerindian peoples live mainly in the Guiana Highlands. Culturally diverse, they speak more than 25 different languages.

The European Space Agency launches its "Ariane" satellite-carrying rockets from this facility outside Kourou in French Guiana.

Economic Profile

The region has extensive mineral resources, limited arable land, and modest industries led by food and mineral processing and, in Colombia and Venezuela, textiles and consumer goods. Venezuela has benefited from and become highly dependent on its huge oil reserves, discovered in 1917 and found mainly around Lake Maracaibo. Colombia has more modest oil reserves, but large deposits of coal as well as gold and emeralds (of which it is the world's foremost supplier). Coffee is its leading official export, though illegally produced cocaine probably provides more revenue. Guyana and Suriname depend heavily on bauxite and sugar production.

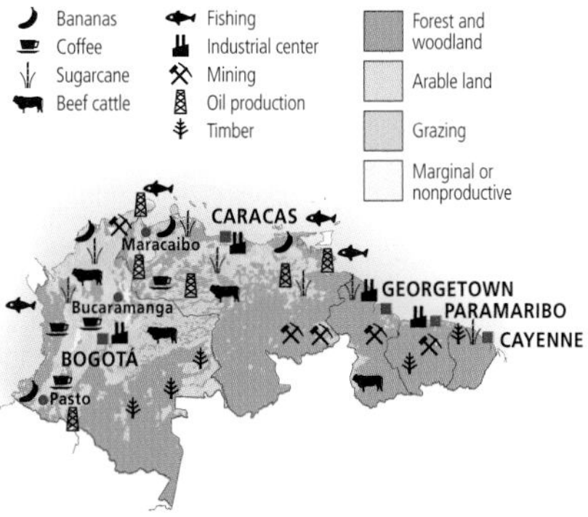
Bananas
Coffee
Sugarcane
Beef cattle
Fishing
Industrial center
Mining
Oil production
Timber
Forest and woodland
Arable land
Grazing
Marginal or nonproductive
CARACAS
Maracaibo
Bucaramanga
BOGOTÁ
Pasto
GEORGETOWN
PARAMARIBO
CAYENNE

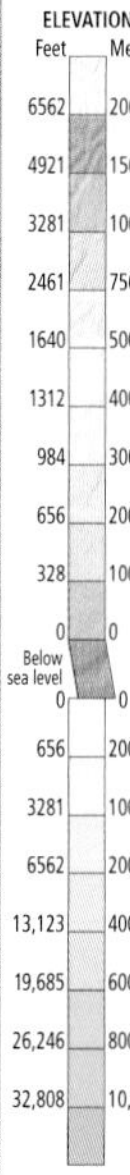
ELEVATION
Feet Meters
6562 2000
4921 1500
3281 1000
2461 750
1640 500
1312 400
984 300
656 200
328 100
0 0
Below sea level
0 0
656 200
3281 1000
6562 2000
13,123 4000
19,685 6000
26,246 8000
32,808 10,000

N O P Q R S T U V W

SCALE 1:8,461,538
Lamberts Conformal Conic Projection
0 200 miles
0 200 kilometers

WESTERN SOUTH AMERICA

Bolivia, Ecuador, Peru

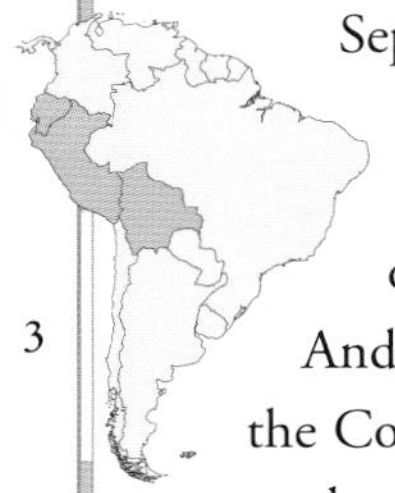

Separated from the Pacific Ocean by a slender coastal plain, the towering peaks of the Andes dominate the entire western side of this region, yielding in the east to well-watered, forest-cloaked lowlands, most of which drain into the vast Amazon Basin. Narrower in the north, the Andes broaden in southern Peru and Bolivia, splitting into two parallel chains, the Cordillera Occidental and the Cordillera Oriental. In the south, these ranges enclose an expansive, arid plateau known as the Altiplano. From around 1200 until shortly after the arrival of the Spanish conquistadors, Cuzco in the northern Altiplano was the capital of the Inca empire, which encompassed virtually the entire Andean sector of this region. Spanish rule left most of the region's wealth and resources in the hands of European-dominated elites. Dissatisfaction with this state of affairs has since fueled indigenous uprisings, labor unrest, Maoist guerilla activity in Peru, and repeated changes of government. In turn, this has hampered economic development, especially in Bolivia, South America's poorest nation.

In the 16th century, the silver-mining center of Potosí in Bolivia was the New World's largest city, with 120,000 inhabitants.

The Galapagos Islands' wildlife includes a host of species unique to the archipelago, including the land iguana.

Quito The world's second-highest capital city after La Paz in Bolivia, Ecuador's capital occupies a narrow valley on the slopes of spectacular Pichincha volcano in the Andes. Little trace remains of the Amerindian and Inca settlements that once stood here, but the city's rich array of buildings from the early period of Spanish settlement in the 16th and 17th centuries, including the elegant Monastery of San Francisco, Ecuador's oldest church, make it the best-preserved capital city in South America.

Less than 2.6 persons per sq mile/1 per sq km
2.6–26 per sq mile/ 1–10 per sq km
26–65 per sq mile/ 10–25 per sq km
65–130 per sq mile/ 25–50 per sq km
130–260 per sq mile/ 50–100 per sq km
QUITO
Guayaquil
Trujillo
LIMA
Arequipa
LA PAZ
Santa Cruz
SUCRE
Galapagos Islands

POPULATION PATTERNS

In Ecuador and Peru, the population is split evenly between coastal and mountain dwellers, with only a minority inhabiting the interior. One-third of Peruvians live in Lima. In Bolivia, the Altiplano is by far the most densely populated region, despite attempts in the late 20th century to encourage people to settle in the east. Relative to other South American nations, all three countries have high proportions of indigenous peoples—25 percent in Ecuador, 45 percent in Peru, and more than 50 percent in Bolivia. They live mainly in the Andean uplands.

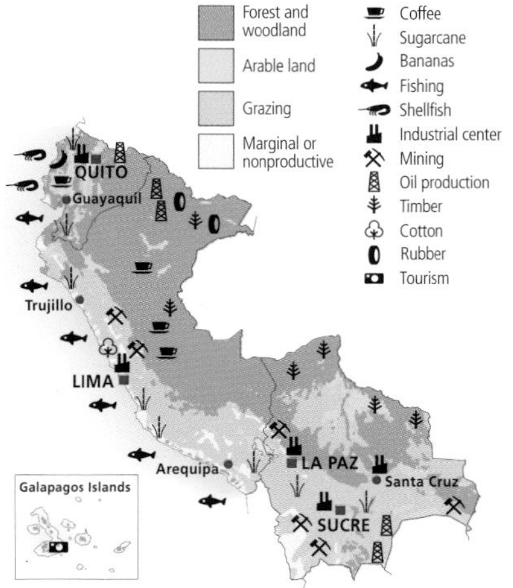
Forest and woodland
Arable land
Grazing
Marginal or nonproductive
Coffee
Sugarcane
Bananas
Fishing
Shellfish
Industrial center
Mining
Oil production
Timber
Cotton
Rubber
Tourism
QUITO
Guayaquil
Trujillo
LIMA
Arequipa
LA PAZ
Santa Cruz
SUCRE
Galapagos Islands

ECONOMIC PROFILE

Subsistence farming involving the cultivation of corn and potatoes and grazing of sheep and llamas takes place in the uplands. On the coast, Ecuador's fertile lowlands yield bananas (of which Ecuador is the world's largest exporter), coffee, and sugar; Peru's irrigated plains produce sugar, cotton, and rice. Peru and Bolivia are the leading producers of coca, the source of cocaine, an illegal but profitable crop. Metals, especially silver, copper, and tin, have long been mainstays of the economy; oil and gas have also become vital. Industries are mainly resource-based and include smelting, oil refining, food processing, and textiles.

COLOMBIA
ECUADOR
BRAZIL
Equator
QUITO
Guayaquil
Tumaco
Esmeraldas
San Lorenzo
Pasto
Mocoa
Nueva Loja
SUCUMBÍOS
Puerto Francisco de Orellana
Cabo Pantoja
Manta
Portoviejo
Ambato
Riobamba
Latacunga
Tena
Puyo
PASTAZA
Montalvo
Rio Tigre
Macas
MORONA-SANTIAGO
Cuenca
Machala
Loja
Tumbes
Zorritos
Talara
Sullana
Piura
PIURA
Chiclayo
Lambayeque
Jaén
Bagua
CAJAMARCA
Chachapoyas
Moyobamba
Tarapoto
SAN MARTÍN
Yurimaguas
LORETO
Iquitos
Nauta
Requena
Amazon
Leticia
Tabatinga
Caballococha
El Encanto
Pebas
Santa Clotilde
Puerto Socorro
Ipiranga
Elvira
Bolognesi
Monte Bello
AMAZONAS
Volcán Cotopaxi 19,344ft (5896m)
Chimborazo 20,702ft (6310m)
Volcán Sangay 17,159ft (5230m)
Cayambe 18,996ft (5790m)

PERU
BOLIVIA
BRAZIL
CHILE
ARGENTINA
PARAGUAY
PACIFIC OCEAN
LIMA
LA PAZ
SUCRE
Santa Cruz
Cochabamba
Oruro
Potosí
Arequipa
Cusco
Tacna
Arica
Iquique
Puno
Juliaca
Lake Titicaca
Cordillera Occidental
Cordillera Oriental
Altiplano
Andes
Salar de Uyuni
Galapagos Islands (to Ecuador)
Isla Isabela
Isla Fernandina
Isla Santa Cruz
Isla San Cristóbal
Isla San Salvador
SCALE 1:5,494,505
ELEVATION
Longitude west of Greenwich
SCALE 1:9,340,659
Lamberts Conformal Conic Projection
250 miles
250 kilometers

The mountaintop citadel of Machu Picchu, near Cuzco in southern Peru, was built by the Inca in the mid-15th century.

THE ALTIPLANO

Consisting of a series of basins located at around 12,000 feet (3,650 m) between the Cordillera Occidental and the Cordillera Oriental, the Altiplano extends for 600 miles (965 km) from southeastern Peru to southwestern Bolivia. Its northernmost basin, situated on the border between Peru and Bolivia, is the site of Lake Titicaca, at an altitude of 12,500 feet (3,810 m) the highest navigable body of water on Earth, and La Paz, the world's highest capital city, which climbs from 10,650 feet (3,250 m) to 13,250 feet (4,050 m). Many of the surrounding mountains, including Nevado de Illimani near La Paz and Bolivia's highest peak Nevado Sajama, rise above 20,000 feet (6,100 m). Just to the northwest of the Altiplano, in the Peruvian Andes, the Amazon River begins its long, transcontinental journey of over 4,000 miles (6,400 km) to the Atlantic Ocean.

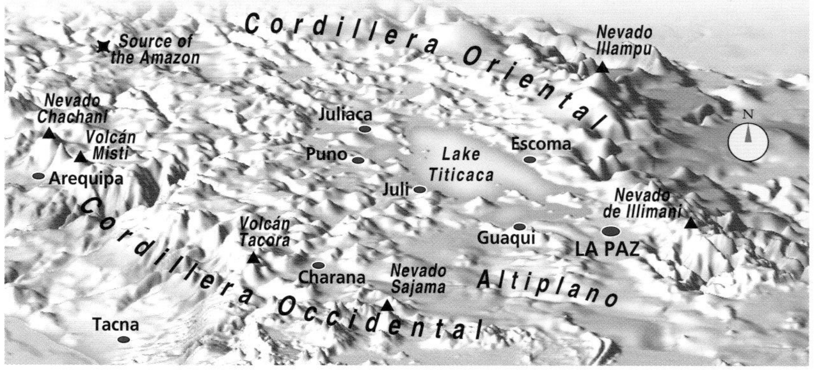
Cordillera Oriental
Cordillera Occidental
Source of the Amazon
Nevado Chachani
Volcán Misti
Arequipa
Juliaca
Puno
Juli
Lake Titicaca
Escoma
Nevado Illampu
Nevado de Illimani
Guaqui
LA PAZ
Volcán Tacora
Charana
Nevado Sajama
Altiplano
Tacna
N

La Paz (left) is Bolivia's administrative capital and seat of national government. Sucre is the constitutional capital and home of the supreme court.

The Aymara people are native to the Altiplano. Aymara women wear distinctive derby hats and woollen shawls.

Eastern South America Brazil, Paraguay

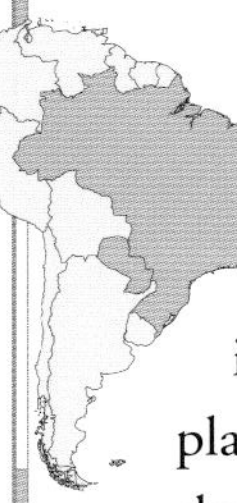

Encompassing more than 2.3 million square miles (6 million sq km) between the Andes and the eastern seaboard, the Amazon Basin is the world's largest drainage system. Cloaked with dense tropical rain forest embroidered by more than 1,000 tributaries, it dominates western and northern Brazil, its great river draining into the Atlantic Ocean near the town of Macapá. To the south rises the extensive plateau region of the Brazilian Highlands, which falls steeply to the coast in the east but descends more gently in the west to the swamps of the Pantanal, the low hills of eastern Paraguay, and the plains of Argentina. Here, the main drainage outlets are the Paraná River, which forms Paraguay's eastern boundary, and its major tributary, the Paraguay, which bisects the nation of the same name, dividing its eastern uplands from its semiarid western plains. Relatively small and landlocked, Paraguay has modest natural resources and a predominantly agricultural economy. In contrast, Brazil is South America's biggest and the world's fifth-largest country, with 5,400 miles (8,700 km) of coastline, the continent's largest population, and immense natural resources.

Population Patterns

Brazil's population is concentrated on the coast, especially around São Paulo and Rio de Janeiro. About half of Brazilians are of European origin, 6 percent are of African descent, and 38 percent are of mixed African-European or African-Amerindian descent (so-called mulatos or pardos). Just 0.1 percent are Amerindian. These diverse groups are united by the Portuguese language. In Spanish-speaking Paraguay, 95 percent of the population is mestizo. Many Paraguayans also speak the indigenous Guaraní language. Paraguay is sparsely inhabited, and only 5 percent of the population lives west of the Paraguay River.

Macapá
Manaus
Belém
Fortaleza
Recife
Salvador
BRASÍLIA
Campo Grande
Belo Horizonte
São Paulo
Rio de Janeiro
ASUNCIÓN
Curitiba
Porto Alegre
Less than 2.6 persons per sq mile/1 per sq km
2.6–26 per sq mile/ 1–10 per sq km
26–65 per sq mile/ 10–25 per sq km
65–130 per sq mile/ 25–50 per sq km
130–260 per sq mile/ 50–100 per sq km
260–520 per sq mile/ 100–200 per sq km

Economic Profile

Though hyperinflation, inequitable wealth distribution, and social problems have hampered development, Brazil has enormous economic potential. It is the world's second-largest iron-ore producer and third-biggest bauxite producer and it has the world's second-largest forests. Self-sufficient in food, it is the world's third-biggest meat producer and leading supplier of coffee, sugar, and oranges. Almost 90 percent of its energy comes from hydroelectric power. Industries include the manufacture of automobiles, petrochemicals, steel, shoes and textiles, and wood products. Paraguay generates all of its energy from hydroelectricity. It has a large "informal" or cash economy involving the resale of imported goods, often at street stalls.

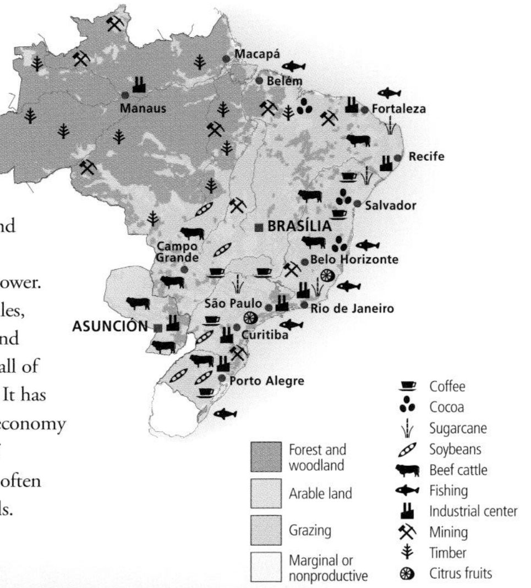

Macapá
Belém
Manaus
Fortaleza
Recife
Salvador
BRASÍLIA
Campo Grande
Belo Horizonte
São Paulo
Rio de Janeiro
ASUNCIÓN
Curitiba
Porto Alegre
Forest and woodland
Arable land
Grazing
Marginal or nonproductive
Coffee
Cocoa
Sugarcane
Soybeans
Beef cattle
Fishing
Industrial center
Mining
Timber
Citrus fruits

VENEZUELA
GUYANA
SURINAME
FRENCH GUIANA (to France)
COLOMBIA
PERU
ATLANTIC OCEAN
Guiana Highlands
Pakaraima Mountains
Tumuc-Humac Mountains
Acari Mountains
Mt Roraima 9219ft (2810m)
Pico da Neblina 9888ft (3014m)
Pico Tamacuari 7677ft (2340m)
Mitaraka 2264ft (690m)
Boa Vista
RORAIMA
AMAPÁ
Macapá
Mouths of the Amazon
Ilha de Marajó
Belém
Manaus
Santarém
Amazon Basin
AMAZONAS
PARÁ
MARANHÃO
CEARÁ
PIAUÍ
RIO GRANDE DO NORTE
PARAÍBA
PERNAMBUCO
ACRE
São Luís
Teresina
Fortaleza
Natal
João Pessoa
Recife
Porto Velho
Equator

Brazil's Iguaçu Falls stand 269 feet (82 m) high and span 1.7 miles (2.7 km)—three times the width of the U.S.A.'s Niagara Falls.

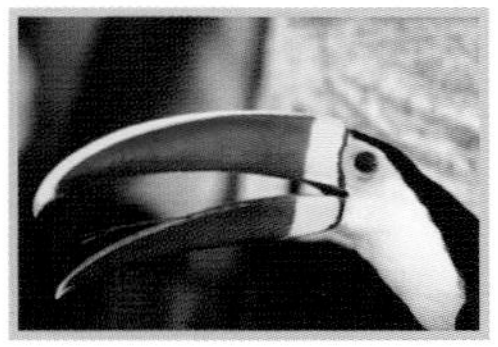

Toucans abound in the rain forests of the Amazon Basin, 4 square miles (10 sq km) of which may harbor more than 400 bird species.

Recife in northeastern Brazil was established in the 16th century by Portugal as a seaport serving the colonial sugar trade.

Brasília A proposal for a new capital city was first presented to the Brazilian government in 1823 and subsequently incorporated in the constitution of 1891. The site was selected in 1956, partly to entice new settlers to the then-sparsely populated interior. Designed by Brazilian architects Lucio Costa and Oscar Niemeyer in a monumental modernist style, Brasília became the national capital in 1960 and now has over 2 million inhabitants. Notable structures that helped it gain World Heritage status include its Cathedral and the National Congress—both designed by Niemeyer.

Cathedral

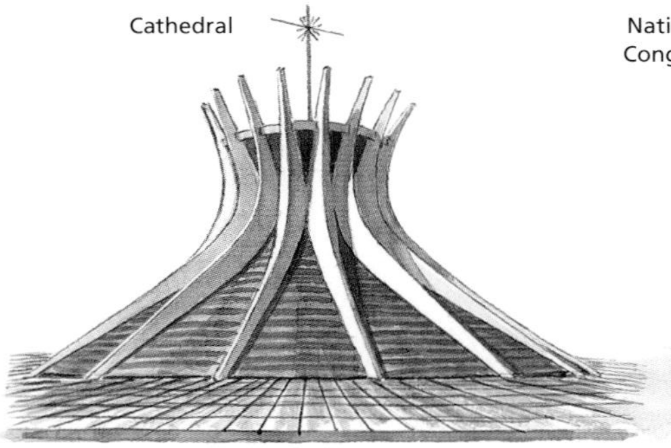

National Congress

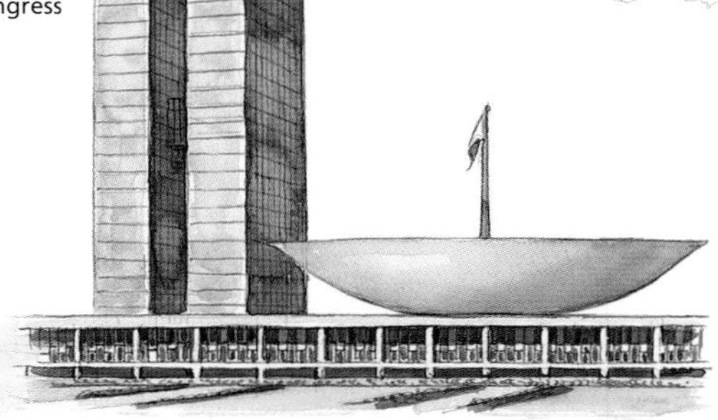

Western Paraguay is home to about 10,000 German-speaking Mennonites, whose forebears arrived in the 1920s from Eastern Europe.

Fortaleza in Brazil derives its name from a 17th-century Dutch (then Portuguese) fort around which the city grew.

THE PANTANAL

In western Brazil, the Planalto do Mato Grosso, an extension of the Brazilian Highlands, borders an immense plain known as the Pantanal. Tumbling down escarpments from the plateau, numerous rivers slow and meander across this plain. During the summer rainy season, the rivers overflow their banks, forming countless lakes and swamps and creating the world's largest freshwater wetland. Covering an area almost as big as Ohio, the Pantanal harbors an extraordinary diversity of wildlife. Though parts of the floodplain are protected by a national park, the ecosystem is threatened by poaching and pollution from mines and farms.

ELEVATION

Feet	Meters
6562	2000
4921	1500
3281	1000
2461	750
1640	500
1312	400
984	300
656	200
328	100
0	0
Below sea level	
0	0
656	200
3281	1000
6562	2000
13,123	4000
19,685	6000
26,246	8000
32,808	10,000

Longitude west of Greenwich

SCALE 1:15,384,615
Lamberts Conformal Conic Projection
0 — 400 miles
0 — 400 kilometers

SOUTHERN SOUTH AMERICA

Argentina, Chile, Uruguay

Below the Tropic of Capricorn, South America tapers and curls toward stormy Cape Horn, the continent's southern limit. In the west, the Andes form a great wall between Chile and Argentina, which is in turn separated from its eastern neighbor Uruguay by the Uruguay River and the estuary known as the River Plate. Twenty times as long as it is wide, Chile is divided into three climatically contrasting regions. The northern Atacama Desert is the driest place in the world. The center of the country, or Central Valley, roughly from Valparaíso to Temuco, experiences temperate weather and has rich, volcanic soils. In the south, thick, well-watered conifer forests climb steep Andean slopes. Arid plains spread eastward from the Andes across Argentina, merging with temperate grasslands that roll into low-lying Uruguay. In the 1970s, all three nations experienced military coups and periods of repressive government. A return to civilian rule in the late 1980s was followed by widespread economic reforms. Development was, however, hobbled by foreign debt and, especially in Argentina, crippling inflation.

Rainfall is almost nonexistent in the Atacama Desert of northern Chile, with localized showers occurring only a few times a century.

Founded in 1573, Córdoba became an important Spanish colonial center and is now Argentina's second city. Its cathedral dates from 1758.

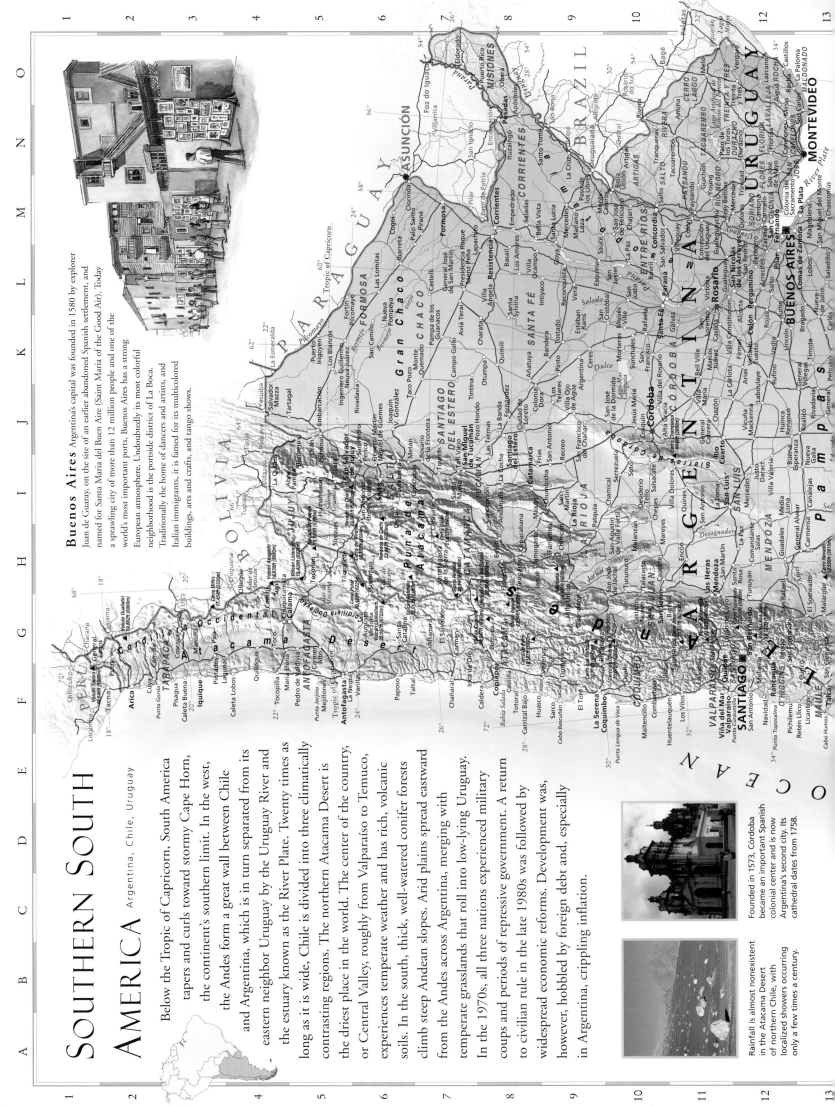

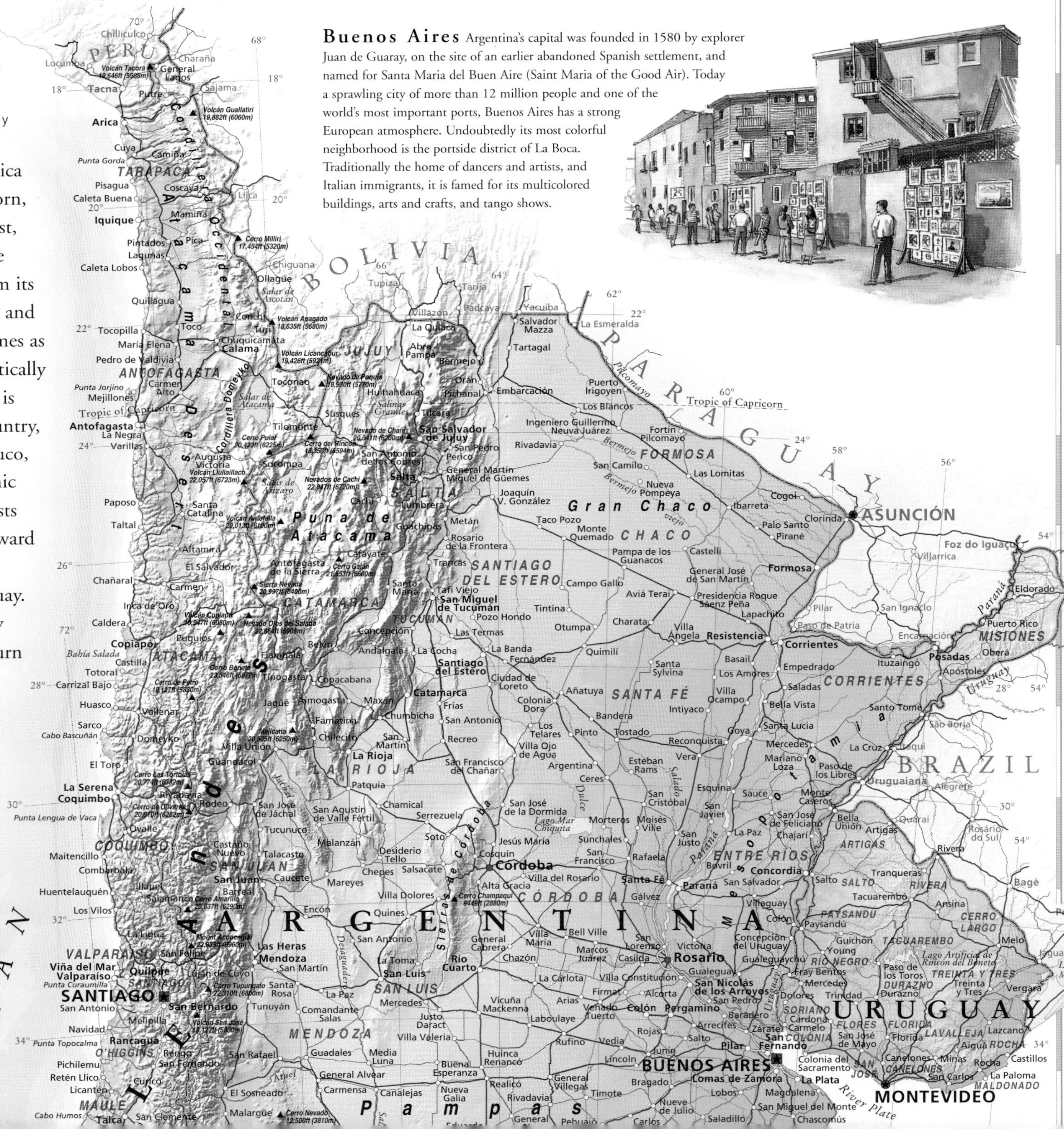

Buenos Aires Argentina's capital was founded in 1580 by explorer Juan de Guaray, on the site of an earlier abandoned Spanish settlement, and named for Santa Maria del Buen Aire (Saint Maria of the Good Air). Today a sprawling city of more than 12 million people and one of the world's most important ports, Buenos Aires has a strong European atmosphere. Undoubtedly its most colorful neighborhood is the portside district of La Boca. Traditionally the home of dancers and artists, and Italian immigrants, it is famed for its multicolored buildings, arts and crafts, and tango shows.

Population Patterns

Almost 90 percent of the region's inhabitants live in cities, mainly in the central temperate belt, in and around the cities of Santiago in Chile, Buenos Aires and Córdoba in Argentina, and Montevideo in Uruguay. Settlements are sparse on Andean peaks, and in the cold, wet southwest. Chile's population is predominantly mestizo, with a small residual population of mainly Mapuche Indians. Argentina and Uruguay have more varied cultures, influenced by the large numbers of Spanish, Italian, and German immigrants who arrived after 1870. Indigenous groups still inhabit remote parts of Argentina but have almost vanished from Uruguay.

- Uninhabited
- Less than 2.6 persons per sq mile/1 per sq km
- 2.6–26 per sq mile/ 1–10 per sq km
- 26–65 per sq mile/ 10–25 per sq km
- 65–130 per sq mile/ 25–50 per sq km
- 130–260 per sq mile/ 50–100 per sq km
- 260–520 per sq mile/ 100–200 per sq km

Economic Profile

All three countries are strong exporters of primary goods. Chile is the world's leading supplier of copper and in the top five fish producers. Its forests provide abundant timber and the Central Valley yields large quantities of wheat, rice, fruit, and vegetables. Beef and wool from livestock grazed on the Pampas are the traditional mainstays of the Argentine and Uruguayan economies. Uruguay has few mineral resources, but Argentina has sizable oil reserves. Chile and Argentina have thriving wine industries, and Argentina is now the world's fifth-largest producer. All three capital cities are important commercial centers. Leading industries include food processing, chemicals, and textiles.

- Forest and woodland
- Arable land
- Grazing
- Marginal or nonproductive
- Cereals
- Fruit
- Wine
- Beef cattle
- Sheep
- Fishing
- Industrial center
- Mining
- Timber
- Oil production

ELEVATION

Feet	Meters
6562	2000
4921	1500
3281	1000
2461	750
1640	500
1312	400
984	300
656	200
328	100
0	0
Below sea level	
0	0
656	200
3281	1000
6562	2000
13,123	4000
19,685	6000
26,246	8000
32,808	10,000

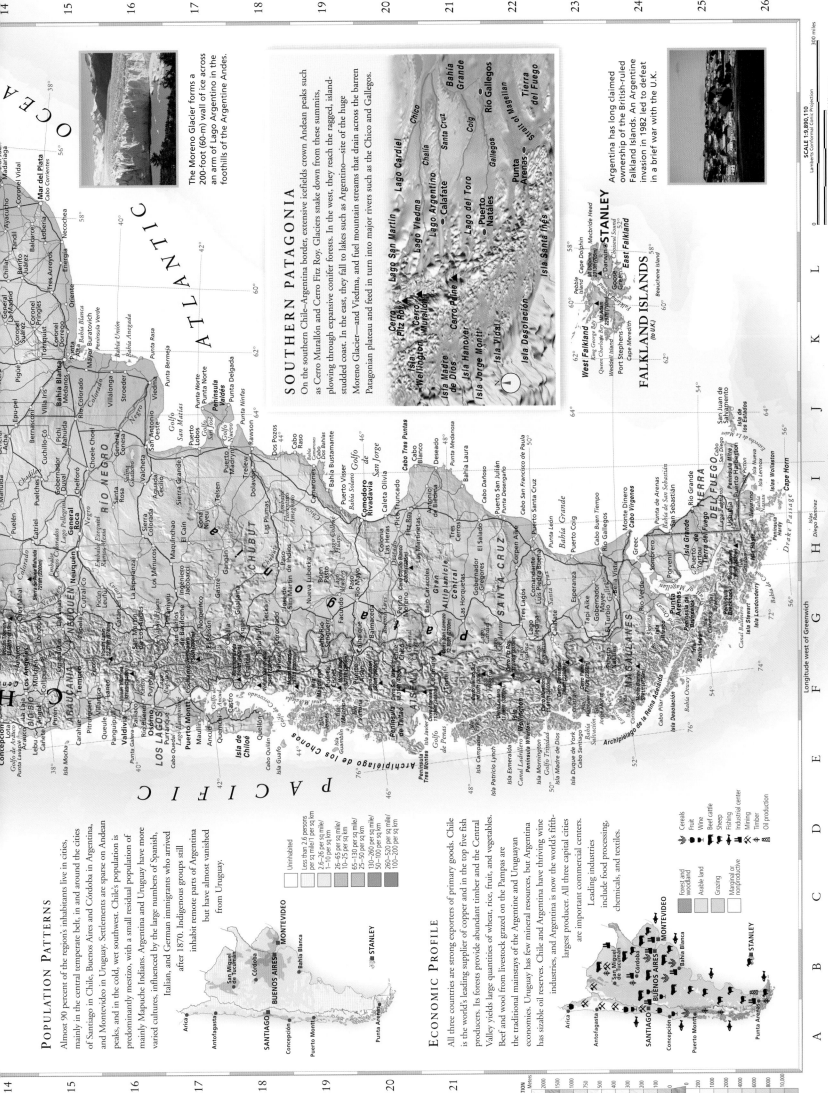

The Moreno Glacier forms a 200-foot (60-m) wall of ice across an arm of Lago Argentino in the foothills of the Argentine Andes.

Southern Patagonia

On the southern Chile–Argentina border, extensive icefields crown Andean peaks such as Cerro Murallón and Cerro Fitz Roy. Glaciers snake down from these summits, plowing through expansive conifer forests. In the west, they reach the ragged, island-studded coast. In the east, they fall to lakes such as Argentino—site of the huge Moreno Glacier—and Viedma, and fuel mountain streams that drain across the barren Patagonian plateau and feed in turn into major rivers such as the Chico and Gallegos.

Argentina has long claimed ownership of the British-ruled Falkland Islands. An Argentine invasion in 1982 led to defeat in a brief war with the U.K.

SCALE 1:9,890,110
Lamberts Conformal Conic Projection
0 300 miles
0 300 kilometers

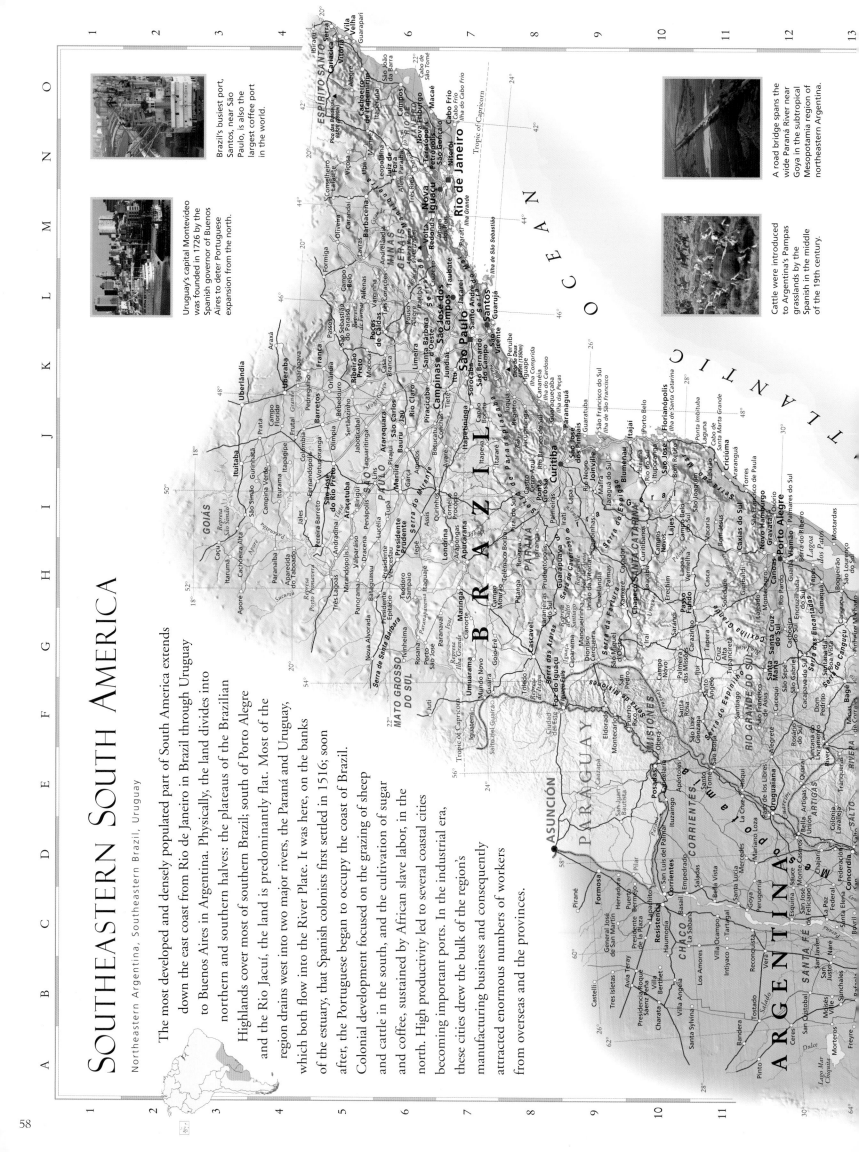

Southeastern South America

Northeastern Argentina, Southeastern Brazil, Uruguay

The most developed and densely populated part of South America extends down the east coast from Rio de Janeiro in Brazil through Uruguay to Buenos Aires in Argentina. Physically, the land divides into northern and southern halves: the plateaus of the Brazilian Highlands cover most of southern Brazil; south of Porto Alegre and the Rio Jacuí, the land is predominantly flat. Most of the region drains west into two major rivers, the Paraná and Uruguay, which both flow into the River Plate. It was here, on the banks of the estuary, that Spanish colonists first settled in 1516; soon after, the Portuguese began to occupy the coast of Brazil. Colonial development focused on the grazing of sheep and cattle in the south, and the cultivation of sugar and coffee, sustained by African slave labor, in the north. High productivity led to several coastal cities becoming important ports. In the industrial era, these cities drew the bulk of the region's manufacturing business and consequently attracted enormous numbers of workers from overseas and the provinces.

Uruguay's capital Montevideo was founded in 1726 by the Spanish governor of Buenos Aires to deter Portuguese expansion from the north.

Brazil's busiest port, Santos, near São Paulo, is also the largest coffee port in the world.

Cattle were introduced to Argentina's Pampas grasslands by the Spanish in the middle of the 19th century.

A road bridge spans the wide Paraná River near Goya in the subtropical Mesopotamia region of northeastern Argentina.

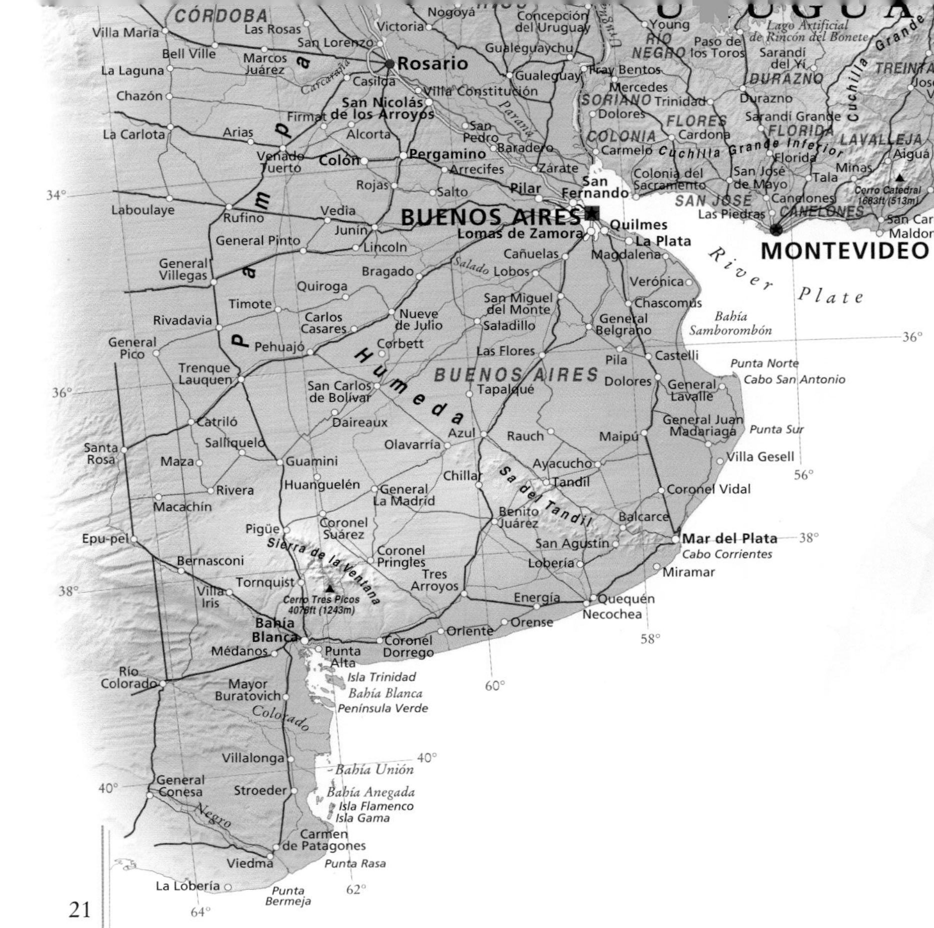

Population Patterns

The overwhelming majority of the region's inhabitants live in cities. Metropolitan Buenos Aires has more than 12 million people, almost one-third of the national population. Over 1.3 million Uruguayans, 40 percent of the country's inhabitants, live in Montevideo. Elsewhere, Uruguay is sparsely populated: the next largest city, Salto, is less than one-tenth the size of the capital. Southern Brazil includes the country's most populous urban centers, São Paulo and Rio de Janeiro (which accommodate about 17 percent of Brazil's huge population), as well as several other cities, including Curitiba and Porto Alegre. The state of São Paulo alone is home to 37 million people. Its capital's vast citizenry includes the biggest Japanese population outside Japan and South America's largest Jewish community.

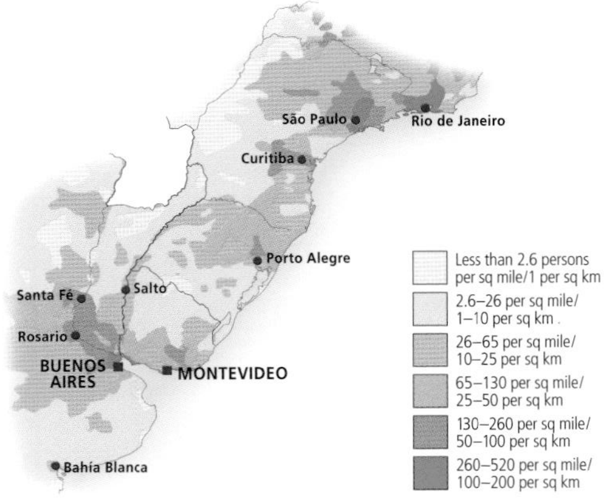

Economic Profile

The southern lowlands are used chiefly for raising beef cattle and sheep, though wheat is also cultivated on the Pampas. Fruit, including oranges and bananas, and rice are grown along the Brazilian coast; sugarcane, soybeans, and coffee are planted across the uplands. Livestock exports and food processing underpin the industrial sector in Montevideo and Buenos Aires, though the latter is also a center of automobile production, oil refining, and printing. São Paulo is South America's industrial powerhouse. It generates 40 percent of Brazil's GDP and its factories employ 15 percent of the national population. Its major industries are the manufacture of automobiles, textiles, chemicals, and metals, and oil refining. Services are more significant in Rio de Janeiro, the headquarters of many large businesses.

Uruguay has over 15 million sheep, and wool is one of the country's most valuable exports.

The Serra do Mar

On their eastern flank, the Brazilian Highlands abut the coast along a 1,600-mile (2,600-km) escarpment, the southern part of which is known as the Serra do Mar (Sea Range). Averaging 3,000 feet (1,000 m) in height, this range rises almost sheer from the sea at several points. The precipitous slopes provide a mountainous backdrop to Rio de Janeiro and other coastal cities. Associated outcrops have created islands, such as Ilha de São Sebastião and Ilha Grande, and other coastal formations including Rio's famous Sugar Loaf Mountain.

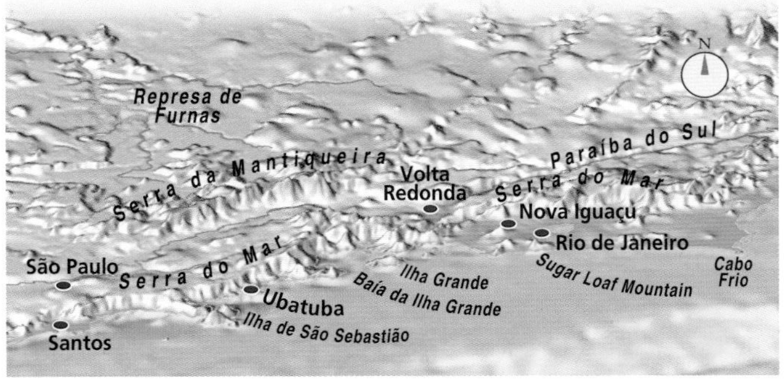

Rio de Janeiro One of the most distinctive landmarks in South America, the 100-foot (30-m) statue of Christ the Redeemer in Rio de Janeiro was built by engineer Heitor da Silva Costa and completed in 1931. From its site atop 2,428-foot (740-m) Mount Corcovado, it overlooks Guanabara Bay and the city of 11 million that spreads inland from the bay's northern and western shores. The name Rio de Janeiro, meaning "January River," was coined by the area's first Portuguese explorers: arriving in January, 1502, they assumed the bay was the mouth of a river. Portuguese settlers returned to occupy the bay in 1565, and a burgeoning sugar trade soon gave rise to a town. In 1763, Rio became the colonial capital, and in 1822, when Brazil achieved independence, it became the national capital, remaining so until 1960, when the country's seat of government was transferred to Brasília.

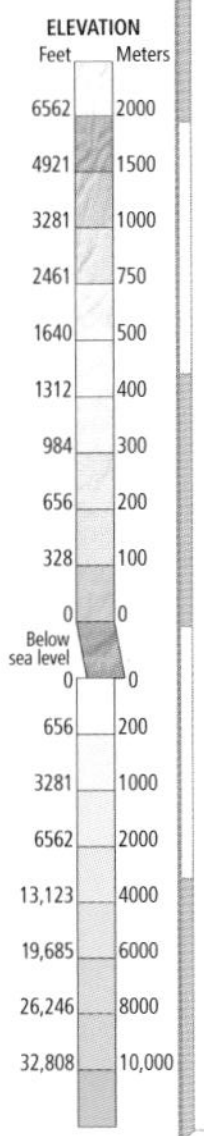

Longitude east of Greenwich

A B C D E F G H I J K L

14 15 16 17 18 19 20 21 22 23 24 25 26

21

SCALE 1:8,241,758
Lamberts Conformal Conic Projection
0 250 miles
0 250 kilometers

The British Isles

Republic of Ireland, United Kingdom

The British Isles consist of two large islands, Great Britain and Ireland, and numerous smaller islands located off the northwest coast of mainland Europe. Together with the troubled province of Northern Ireland, the once-independent nations of England, Scotland, and Wales make up the United Kingdom (U.K.). The southern part of the island of Ireland became self-governing in 1921. Most of southeastern Britain is low, gently undulating terrain, becoming almost entirely flat in the east-coast Fens region. To the north and west, the land is more rugged, with hills and mountains dominating central northern England, much of Wales, southern and northern Scotland, and parts of Northern Ireland. In southern Ireland, a well-watered central plain is studded with lakes and peat bogs and ringed by coastal uplands. Both the U.K. and Ireland have recently developed closer social and economic ties with other European nations, and a physical link between Britain and the rest of the continent was forged in 1994 with the completion of the Channel Tunnel.

Oxford, England, is a manufacturing center, noted for automobile production. But it is best known as the site of the U.K.'s oldest university, founded in the 12th century.

On the west coast of Ireland, uplands abut the Atlantic Ocean, forming dramatic coastal landforms such as the spectacular Cliffs of Moher, near Hag's Head.

Population Patterns

The U.K.'s highly urbanized population—about 90 percent inhabit towns and cities—is heavily concentrated in the southeast and around the industrial centers of Birmingham, Manchester, Leeds, Glasgow, and Belfast. The least densely populated areas are the Scottish Highlands, where sheep far outnumber people, and the uplands of northwest England and Wales. Ireland's population is more evenly distributed, with about 60 percent living in urban areas.

Economic Profile

The decline of the U.K.'s manufacturing industries has been paralleled by the growth in services, which now employ three-quarters of workers. Still-important industries include engineering, chemicals and chemical products, metals, and food and beverages. The nation's most abundant food crops are cereals (especially wheat and barley), potatoes, sugar beet, and oilseed rape. Ireland's farming sector is more dependent on livestock. Its industries experienced a boom in the late 20th century, led by textiles, chemicals, machinery, and computer hardware and software.

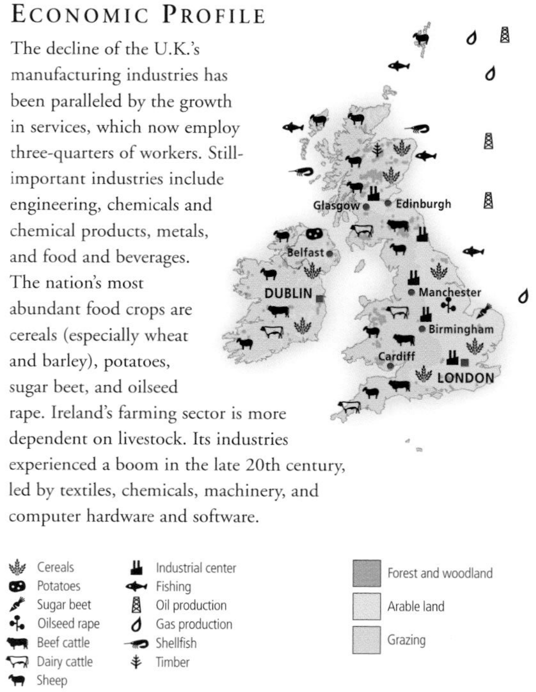

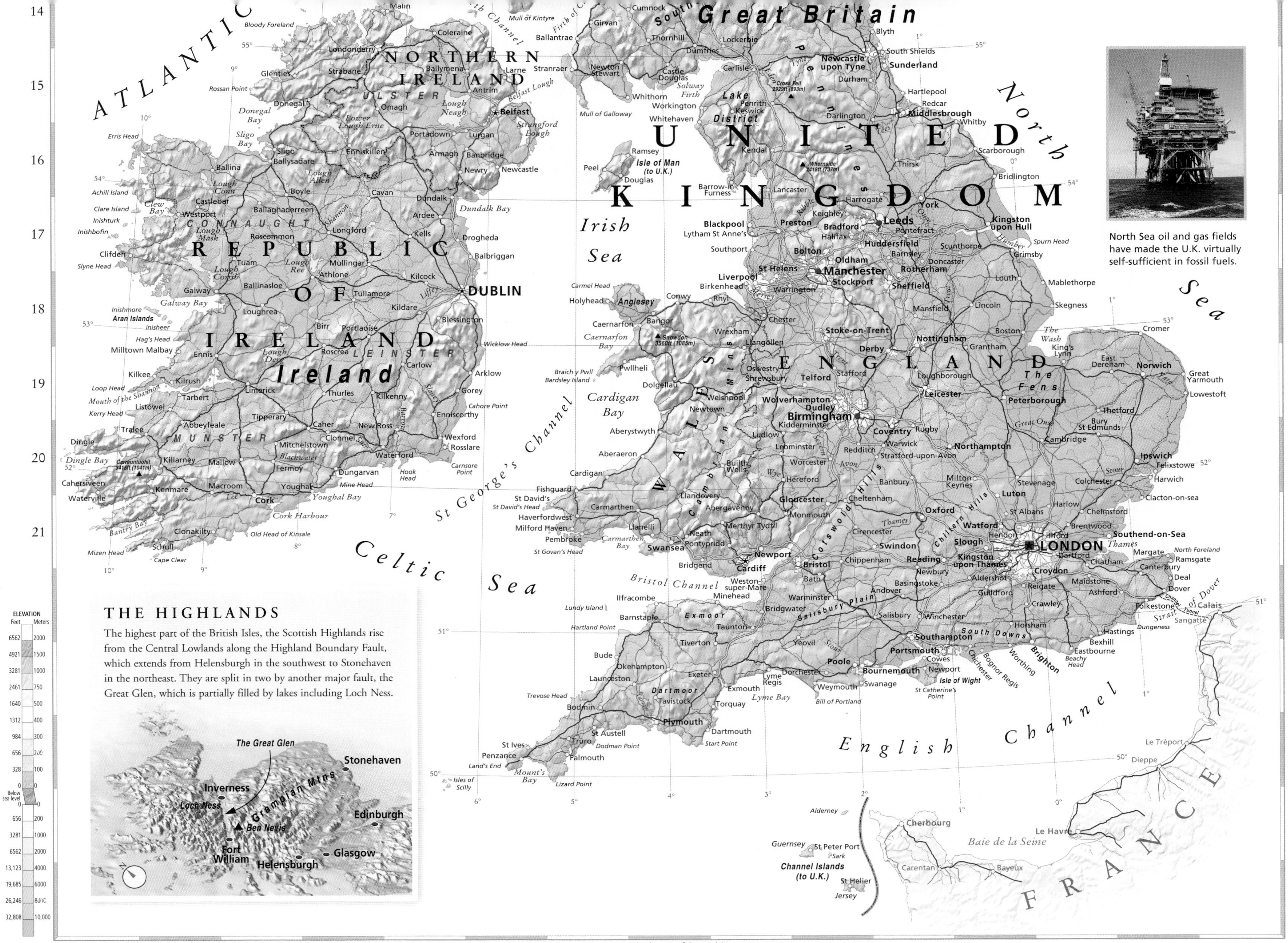
Great Britain
UNITED KINGDOM
NORTHERN IRELAND
REPUBLIC OF IRELAND
Ireland
ENGLAND
WALES
ULSTER
CONNAUGHT
LEINSTER
MUNSTER
ATLANTIC
North Sea
Irish Sea
Celtic Sea
St George's Channel
Bristol Channel
English Channel
FRANCE
LONDON
DUBLIN
Belfast
Cardiff
Birmingham
Manchester
Liverpool
Leeds
Sheffield
Bristol
Newcastle upon Tyne
Cork
Limerick
Galway
Waterford
Plymouth
Southampton
Norwich
Nottingham
Leicester
Coventry
Isle of Man (to U.K.)
Channel Islands (to U.K.)
Isle of Wight
Lake District
Pennines
Cambrian Mts
Cotswold Hills
Chiltern Hills
South Downs
Salisbury Plain
Exmoor
Dartmoor
The Fens
Snowdon 3560ft (1085m)
Cross Fell 2929ft (893m)
Whernside 2418ft (737m)
Carrauntuohil 3415ft (1041m)
ELEVATION
Feet Meters
6562 2000
4921 1500
3281 1000
2461 750
1640 500
1312 400
984 300
656 200
328 100
0 0
Below sea level
0 0
656 200
3281 1000
6562 2000
13,123 4000
19,685 6000
26,246 8000
32,808 10,000
Longitude west of Greenwich
SCALE 1:3,296,703
Lamberts Conformal Conic Projection
100 miles
100 kilometers
The Great Glen
Stonehaven
Inverness
Loch Ness
Grampian Mts
Edinburgh
Ben Nevis
Fort William
Glasgow
Helensburgh
N

North Sea oil and gas fields have made the U.K. virtually self-sufficient in fossil fuels.

THE HIGHLANDS

The highest part of the British Isles, the Scottish Highlands rise from the Central Lowlands along the Highland Boundary Fault, which extends from Helensburgh in the southwest to Stonehaven in the northeast. They are split in two by another major fault, the Great Glen, which is partially filled by lakes including Loch Ness.

Southern Great Britain

From the southern flanks of the Pennines, a broad belt of roads, towns, and cities runs southeastward through the low-lying heart of England, the region known as the Midlands, to London, the capital of the U.K. and its largest city. This corridor is by far the most developed part of the country, encompassing the majority of its industrial and commercial centers, the bulk of its freeways, and more than half of its population. The urban sprawl is, however, broken by sizable tracts of fertile farmland—most notably in the East Midlands—remnants of forests, and scenic ranges of hills, including the Cotswolds and the Chilterns. On the eastern and western fringes lie quieter, culturally and geographically distinctive areas. The Cambrian Mountains dominate the interior of the Celtic nation of Wales, descending to a long, heavily indented coastline. In the east, the formerly swampy Fens isolate the tranquil agricultural plains of East Anglia, and in the far southwest, a picturesque, rocky coastline bounds the narrow, traditionally Celtic enclave of Cornwall and the rolling pastures and moorlands of Devon.

Made of chalk, the famous white cliffs of Dover border the English Channel.

The Royal Liver Building, a Liverpool landmark, was completed in 1911.

Snowdon in northwest Wales has five peaks. The tallest, Yr Wyddfa, is the highest point in England and Wales.

Population Patterns

This region has more than two-thirds of the U.K. population, with the highest concentrations occurring in London (home to 7.6 million people), Birmingham, and the cluster of cities between Liverpool and Leeds. Population growth is relatively low and due mainly to natural increase. In the late 20th century, the demise of heavy industry and coal mining in the northwest, Wales, and Scotland accelerated migration to London. However, a concurrent trend saw many people and businesses move out of the capital to peripheral areas such as the East Midlands, East Anglia, and the southwest. One-quarter of people in Wales speak Welsh; the region's other Celtic language, Cornish, has all but died out.

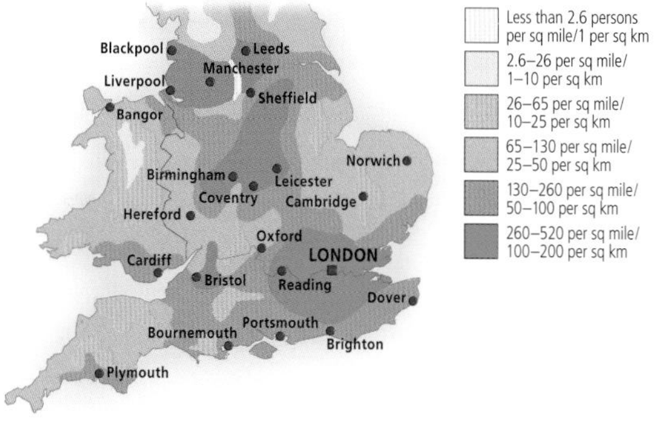
Blackpool
Leeds
Manchester
Liverpool
Sheffield
Bangor
Norwich
Birmingham
Leicester
Coventry
Cambridge
Hereford
Oxford
LONDON
Cardiff
Bristol
Reading
Dover
Portsmouth
Bournemouth
Brighton
Plymouth
Less than 2.6 persons per sq mile/1 per sq km
2.6–26 per sq mile/ 1–10 per sq km
26–65 per sq mile/ 10–25 per sq km
65–130 per sq mile/ 25–50 per sq km
130–260 per sq mile/ 50–100 per sq km
260–520 per sq mile/ 100–200 per sq km

Economic Profile

The economy is dominated by services, particularly finance, retailing, health care, and tourism. While the northwest and Wales have suffered due to the collapse of coal mining and heavy industries, the east and southeast have thrived due to the boom in services and success in attracting light, high-tech industries to areas such as Cambridge and Reading. Southern England has most of the U.K.'s best farmland. The highly mechanized cultivation of wheat, oilseed rape, and sugar beet takes place in the east; dairy and beef cattle are reared in the west; and market gardening (the small-scale cultivation of fruit and vegetables) predominates in the southeast.

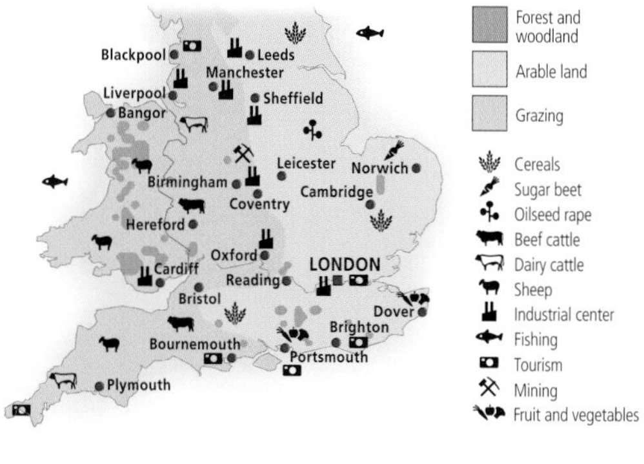
Blackpool
Leeds
Manchester
Liverpool
Sheffield
Bangor
Leicester
Norwich
Birmingham
Cambridge
Coventry
Hereford
Oxford
Cardiff
Reading
LONDON
Bristol
Dover
Brighton
Bournemouth
Portsmouth
Plymouth
Forest and woodland
Arable land
Grazing
Cereals
Sugar beet
Oilseed rape
Beef cattle
Dairy cattle
Sheep
Industrial center
Fishing
Tourism
Mining
Fruit and vegetables

London The Romans founded Londinium, as they named it, on the banks of the Thames in the first century AD. After being all but abandoned in the fifth century, the town flourished again under the Saxons and the Normans, whose king, William I (the Conqueror), built a fortress to control local trade. Known as the White Fort and later the Tower of London, it was expanded by several monarchs over the following centuries, becoming a royal residence and, notoriously, a prison and place of execution. The city grew with it, attaining a population of 1 million by 1800 and 6.5 million a century later. Now a popular tourist attraction, the tower still hosts a military garrison and is patrolled by guards, known as "beefeaters," who dress in distinctive Tudor uniforms.

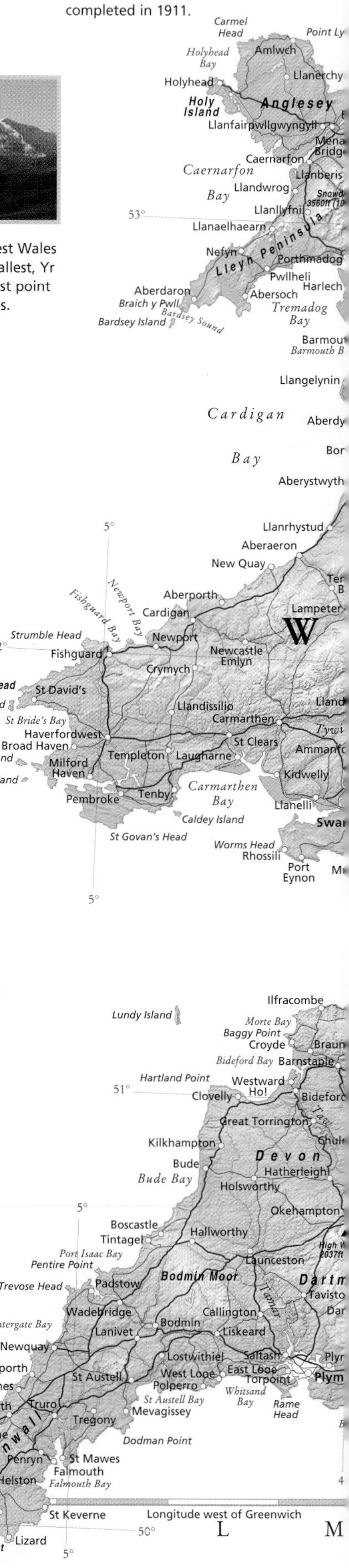
Carmel Head
Point Lynas
Holyhead Bay
Amlwch
Holyhead
Holy Island
Anglesey
Llanfairpwllgwyngyll
Menai Bridge
Caernarfon
Caernarfon Bay
Llanberis
Llandwrog
Llanllyfni
Llanaelhaearn
Nefyn
Lleyn Peninsula
Porthmadog
Pwllheli
Harlech
Aberdaron
Abersoch
Braich y Pwll
Bardsey Sound
Tremadog Bay
Bardsey Island
Barmouth
Barmouth Bay
Llangelynin
Cardigan Bay
Aberdyfi
Aberystwyth
Llanrhystud
Aberaeron
New Quay
Fishguard Bay
Newport Bay
Aberporth
Cardigan
Lampeter
Strumble Head
Newport
Newcastle Emlyn
Fishguard
Crymych
W
St David's Head
St David's
Ramsey Island
Llandissilio
Carmarthen
St Bride's Bay
Haverfordwest
Broad Haven
St Clears
Ammanford
Skomer Island
Milford Haven
Templeton
Laugharne
Kidwelly
Skokholm Island
Tenby
Carmarthen Bay
Pembroke
Llanelli
Caldey Island
St Govan's Head
Worms Head
Rhossili
Port Eynon
Lundy Island
Ilfracombe
Morte Bay
Baggy Point
Croyde
Braunton
Bideford Bay
Barnstaple
Hartland Point
Westward Ho!
Bideford
Clovelly
Great Torrington
Kilkhampton
Devon
Bude
Hatherleigh
Bude Bay
Holsworthy
Okehampton
Boscastle
Tintagel
Hallworthy
Port Isaac Bay
Pentire Point
Launceston
Trevose Head
Padstow
Bodmin Moor
Wadebridge
Callington
Watergate Bay
Bodmin
Lanivet
Liskeard
Newquay
Lostwithiel
Saltash
Perranporth
St Austell
West Looe
East Looe
St Agnes
Polperro
Torpoint
St Austell Bay
Whitsand Bay
Rame Head
Redruth
Truro
Mevagissey
St Ives Bay
St Ives
Zennor
Camborne
Tregony
Cornwall
Hayle
Dodman Point
Cape Cornwall
Penzance
Penryn
St Mawes
Sennen
Falmouth
Land's End
Mount's Bay
Helston
Falmouth Bay
Mullion
St Keverne
Lizard Point
Lizard
Longitude west of Greenwich

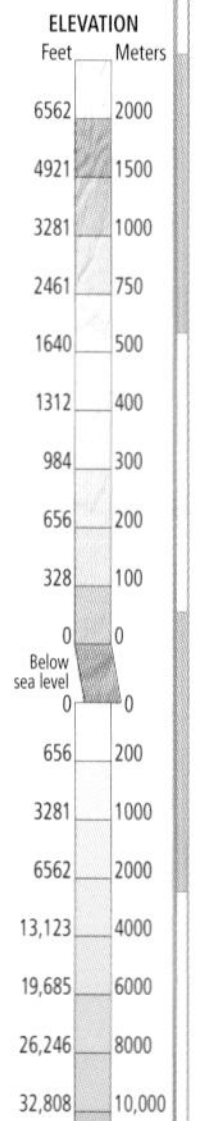
ELEVATION
Feet
Meters
6562
2000
4921
1500
3281
1000
2461
750
1640
500
1312
400
984
300
656
200
328
100
0
Below sea level
0
656
200
3281
1000
6562
2000
13,123
4000
19,685
6000
26,246
8000
32,808
10,000

SCALE 1:1,648,352
Lamberts Conformal Conic Projection
0 50 miles
0 50 kilometers

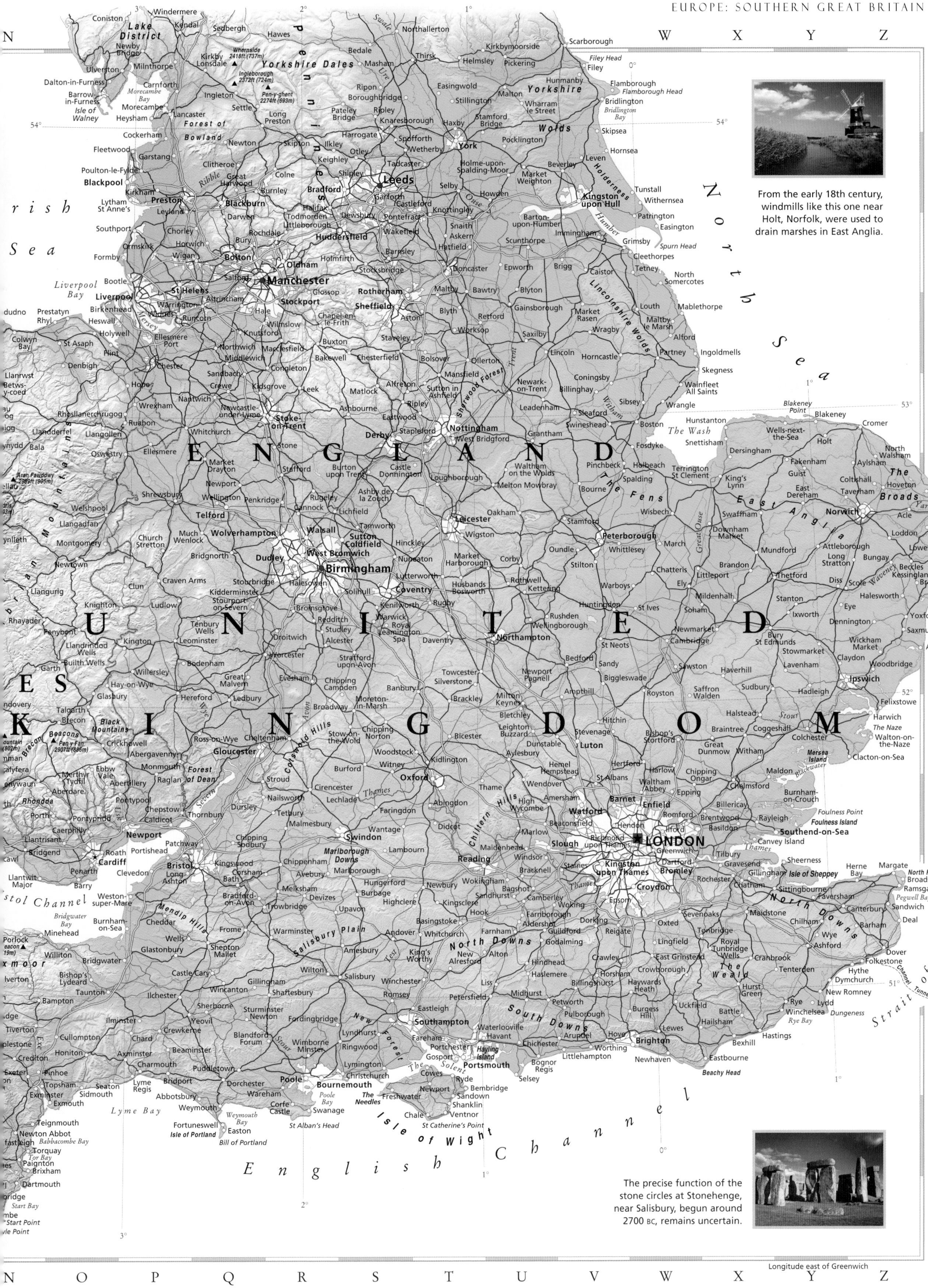

N W X Y Z
1 2 3 4 5 6 7 8 9 10 11 12 13 14 15
N O P Q R S T U V W X Y Z
Longitude east of Greenwich
Lake District
Yorkshire Dales
Pennines
Forest of Bowland
North York Moors
Yorkshire Wolds
Holderness
North Sea
Irish Sea
Liverpool Bay
Morecambe Bay
Lincolnshire Wolds
The Wash
The Fens
East Anglia
The Broads
Sherwood Forest
ENGLAND
UNITED KINGDOM
Cambrian Mountains
Black Mountains
Brecon Beacons
Cotswold Hills
Forest of Dean
Chiltern Hills
Mendip Hills
Salisbury Plain
North Downs
South Downs
The Weald
New Forest
Isle of Wight
The Solent
The Needles
English Channel
Bristol Channel
Lyme Bay
Strait of Dover
Channel Tunnel
Isle of Sheppey
Mersea Island
Foulness Island
Hayling Island
Isle of Portland
Isle of Walney
Spurn Head
Flamborough Head
Filey Head
Beachy Head
Dungeness
North Foreland
St Alban's Head
St Catherine's Point
Bill of Portland
Whernside 2418ft (737m)
Ingleborough 2372ft (724m)
Pen-y-ghent 2274ft (693m)
Aran Fawddwy 2969ft (905m)
Pen y Fan 2907ft (886m)
Thames
Trent
Severn
Wye
Humber
Ouse
Mersey
Ribble
Avon
Windermere
Kendal
Sedbergh
Hawes
Northallerton
Scarborough
Whitby
Helmsley
Pickering
Thirsk
Ripon
Harrogate
York
Leeds
Bradford
Halifax
Huddersfield
Wakefield
Sheffield
Rotherham
Doncaster
Kingston upon Hull
Grimsby
Lincoln
Manchester
Liverpool
Preston
Blackpool
Blackburn
Bolton
Oldham
Stockport
Stoke-on-Trent
Derby
Nottingham
Leicester
Birmingham
Wolverhampton
Coventry
Northampton
Peterborough
Norwich
Great Yarmouth
Ipswich
Cambridge
Oxford
Gloucester
Cheltenham
Worcester
Hereford
Shrewsbury
Telford
Chester
Bristol
Bath
Swindon
Reading
Newport
Cardiff
LONDON
Southampton
Portsmouth
Brighton
Bournemouth
Poole
Weymouth
Exeter
Torquay
Dover
Canterbury
Southend-on-Sea
Colchester
Chelmsford
Luton
Watford
Slough
Croydon
Bromley

From the early 18th century, windmills like this one near Holt, Norfolk, were used to drain marshes in East Anglia.

The precise function of the stone circles at Stonehenge, near Salisbury, begun around 2700 BC, remains uncertain.

FRANCE France, Monaco

Occupying a large area on the western edge of Europe, France is the only country that extends from the North European Plain to the Mediterranean. The north and west are characterized by broad lowlands traversed by major rivers, including the Seine, Loire, Dordogne, and Garonne. A wide plateau, the Massif Central, covers much of the southern interior, and in the southeast the land rises steeply to the high peaks of the Alps.

Along the southern border, the Pyrenees separate France from Spain. The tiny principality of Monaco—the second-smallest country in the world—occupies a coastal location within France, close to the border with Italy. France is a leading political, industrial, and agricultural force in Europe and has been at the forefront of European economic and social integration.

Paris France's largest city began as a small settlement on an island in the River Seine and became the national capital in AD 987. It is now home to over 9 million people, a major business and industrial center, and one of the world's top tourist destinations. Its splendid buildings include the cathedral of Notre-Dame, which dates from the 12th century, the 18th-century Panthéon, and France's most famous landmark, the Eiffel Tower, designed for the 1889 Paris Exposition.

Notre-Dame
Eiffel Tower

Population Patterns

The most sparsely inhabited parts of France are the high-mountain regions of the Alps, Pyrenees, and Massif Central. In rural areas, the population is fairly evenly spread, though slightly higher levels of settlement occur along major river valleys and parts of the coast. About 76 percent of the country's inhabitants live in urban areas, with one-fifth of the total population concentrated in the Paris region, the Île-de-France.

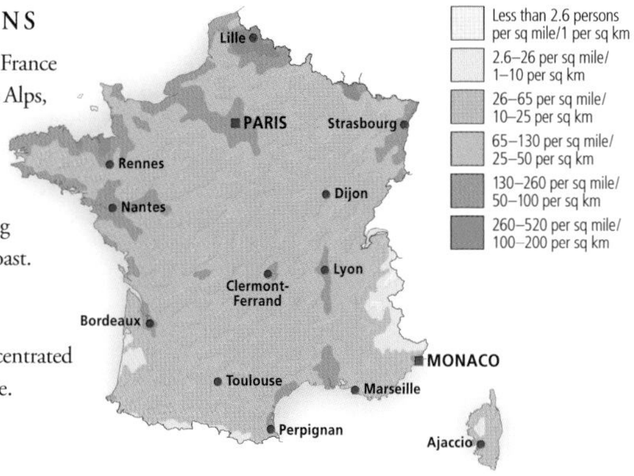

Lille
PARIS
Strasbourg
Rennes
Nantes
Dijon
Lyon
Clermont-Ferrand
Bordeaux
MONACO
Toulouse
Marseille
Perpignan
Ajaccio
Less than 2.6 persons per sq mile/1 per sq km
2.6–26 per sq mile/ 1–10 per sq km
26–65 per sq mile/ 10–25 per sq km
65–130 per sq mile/ 25–50 per sq km
130–260 per sq mile/ 50–100 per sq km
260–520 per sq mile/ 100–200 per sq km

Economic Profile

More than half of France is productive farmland, and the nation is one of the world's top exporters of agricultural produce. Important commodities include wheat, sugar beet, and wine (of which France is the world's largest producer). Metals, chemicals, cars, textiles, and aircraft are among the most vital manufactured goods. Services, including tourism, employ more than 70 percent of workers.

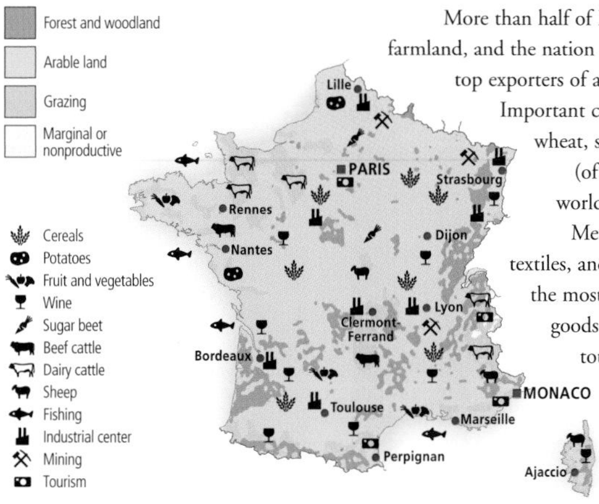

Forest and woodland
Arable land
Grazing
Marginal or nonproductive
Cereals
Potatoes
Fruit and vegetables
Wine
Sugar beet
Beef cattle
Dairy cattle
Sheep
Fishing
Industrial center
Mining
Tourism
Lille
PARIS
Strasbourg
Rennes
Nantes
Dijon
Lyon
Clermont-Ferrand
Bordeaux
MONACO
Toulouse
Marseille
Perpignan
Ajaccio

THE PYRENEES

Viewed from southern France, the Pyrenees rise like a great wall, forming a seemingly insurmountable barrier. Indeed, most of the range, which stretches for more than 270 miles (435 km) from the Atlantic Ocean to the Mediterranean Sea, is more than 9,000 feet (2,700 m) high and can be crossed only via passes above 6,000 feet (1,800 m). The highest peak, Aneto in Spain, rises to 11,168 feet (3,404 m).

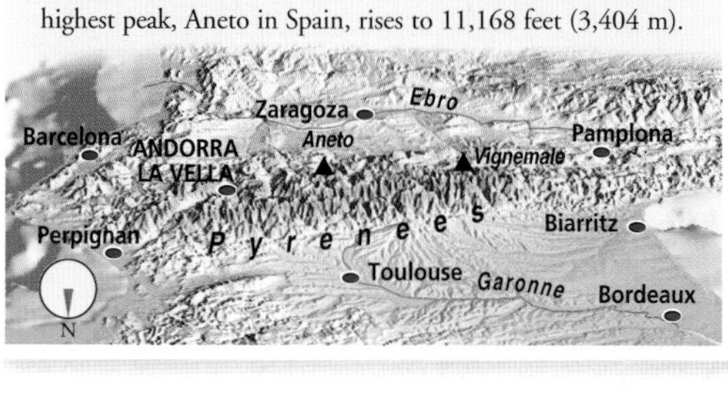

Zaragoza
Ebro
Barcelona
ANDORRA LA VELLA
Aneto
Vignemale
Pamplona
Perpignan
Pyrenees
Biarritz
Toulouse
Garonne
Bordeaux
N

A B C D E F G H I J K L M
1 2 4 5 6 7 8 9 10 11 12 13 14 15
UNITED KINGDOM
Exeter
Torquay
Plymouth
St Austell
Penzance
Newport
Isle of Wight
English Channel
Alderney
Guernsey
St Peter Port
Sark
Channel Islands (to U.K.)
Jersey
St Helier
Golfe de St-Malo
Cap de la Hague
Pointe de Barfleur
Cherbourg
Valognes
Baie de Seine
Carentan
BASSE-NORMANDIE
St-Lô
Coutances
Îles Chausey
Granville
Vire
Avranches
Le Mont-St-Michel
St-Malo
Cap Fréhel
Baie de St-Brieuc
Paimpol
Lannion
St-Pol-de-Léon
Ploudalmézeau
Île d'Ouessant
Morlaix
Guingamp
St-Brieuc
Brest
Pointe de St-Mathieu
Mer d'Iroise
Crozon
Carhaix-Plouguer
Lamballe
Dinan
Fougères
Ernée
Baie de Douarnenez
Châteaulin
Douarnenez
Pointe du Raz
Audierne
Baie de Audierne
BRETAGNE
Loudéac
Pontivy
Rennes
Vitré
Laval
Quimper
Quimperlé
Penmarch
Pointe de Penmarch
Îles de Glénan
Lorient
Ploërmel
Îls de Groix
Auray
Vannes
Châteaubriant
Segré
Muzillac
Quiberon
Nozay
PAYS DE
Pontchâteau
Belle-Île
Le Palais
La Baule-Escoublac
St-Nazaire
Ancenis
Loire
Nantes
Embouchure de la Loire
Pointe de St-Gildas
Pornic
Baie de Bourgneuf
Noirmoutier-en-l'Île
Île de Noirmoutier
Clisson
Cholet
Montaigu
St-Jean-de-Monts
Challans
Les Herbiers
Île d'Yeu
La Roche-sur-Yon
Chantonnay
Les Sables-d'Olonne
Luçon
St-Maxient-l'
ATLANTIC OCEAN
Bay of Biscay
Pertuis Breton
Île de Ré
La Rochelle
Pertuis d'Antioche
St-Pierre-d'Oléron
Île d'Oléron
Rochefort
Royan
Soulac-sur-Mer
Gironde
Lesparre-Médoc
Blaye
Lacanau
Bordeaux
Andernos-les-Bains
Arcachon
Sanguinet
AQUITAINE
Mimizan
Labouheyre
Sabres
Roquefort
Mont-de-Marsan
Léon
Dax
Aire-sur-l'Adour
Bayonne
Biarritz
Orthez
St-Jean-de-Luz
Bidache
St-Palais
Oloron-Ste-Marie
Pic d'Orhy 6617ft (2017m)
Etsaut
SPAIN
50°
48°
46°
44°
4°
2°
Longitude west of Greenwich

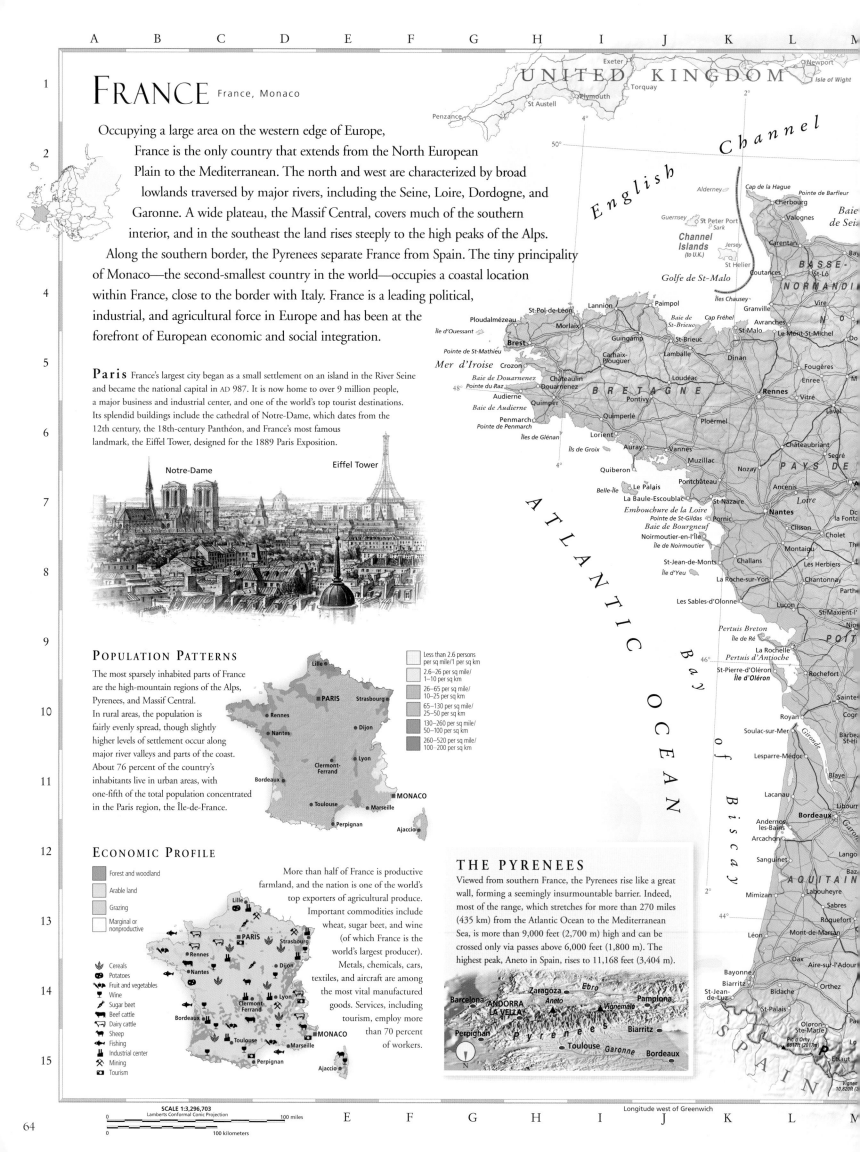

SCALE 1:3,296,703
Lamberts Conformal Conic Projection
0 100 miles
0 100 kilometers

The Arc de Triomphe in Paris was commissioned by Napoleon in 1806 to celebrate his military victories.

Located on the French–Italian border, Mont Blanc, at 15,771 feet (4,807 m), is the Alps' highest peak.

Monaco measures a mere 0.75 square miles (1.95 sq km). Its tourist facilities and casino are among its principal sources of revenue.

The mountainous island of Corsica was purchased by France from the city-state of Genoa in 1768.

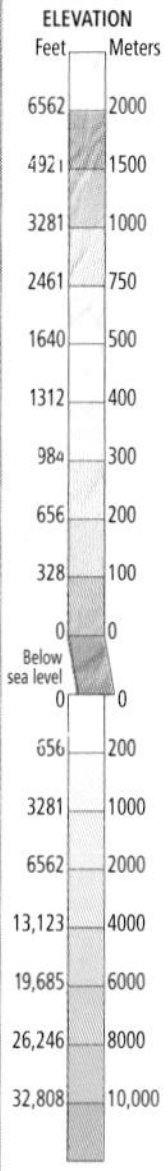

The Iberian Peninsula

Andorra, Portugal, Spain

Located at the southwestern edge of Europe, the wide, almost square-shaped Iberian Peninsula is flanked by the Atlantic Ocean to the west and by the Mediterranean Sea to the east. It is separated from France by the Pyrenees, and from Africa by the Strait of Gibraltar, which is just 8 miles (12.8 km) wide at its narrowest point. Spain occupies more than 80 percent of the landmass, Portugal almost all of the remainder; the tiny principality of Andorra nestles in the eastern Pyrenees. A large plateau, the Meseta, extends across much of the peninsula. It is bisected by the Sistema Central mountain chain and fringed by other ranges. Between the 15th and 17th centuries, Spain and Portugal ruled vast empires. But their 20th-century histories were marred by war and repressive regimes, and their economies are still recovering.

Completed in 1521, the Torre de Belém was built to protect the city of Lisbon.

In Spain's Castilla-La Mancha region, medieval windmills dot flat, semiarid plains.

Population Patterns

In Spain, rapid industrial growth in the late 20th century led to significant urbanization, with the result that 78 percent of the population now live in cities—17 percent in Madrid and Barcelona. The temperate coastal areas are generally more densely inhabited than the less fertile Meseta. In Portugal, the south is more sparsely populated than the north, with the exception of Lisbon and the crowded coastal region of the Algarve.

Economic Profile

Investment in agriculture is low relative to the European average and small farms are the norm. The region is renowned for its abundant fruit and vegetables; other major crops include cereals, wine grapes, and olives. About one-third of the land is forested, and Portugal is the world's foremost supplier of cork. Textiles and footwear, paper and paper products, chemicals, metals, wine, and tourism are the leading industries; automobile production is also important in Spain. Andorra relies heavily on tourism and its duty-free retail trade.

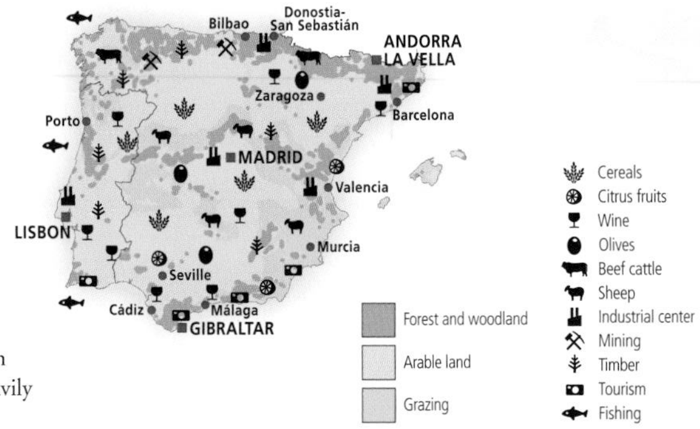

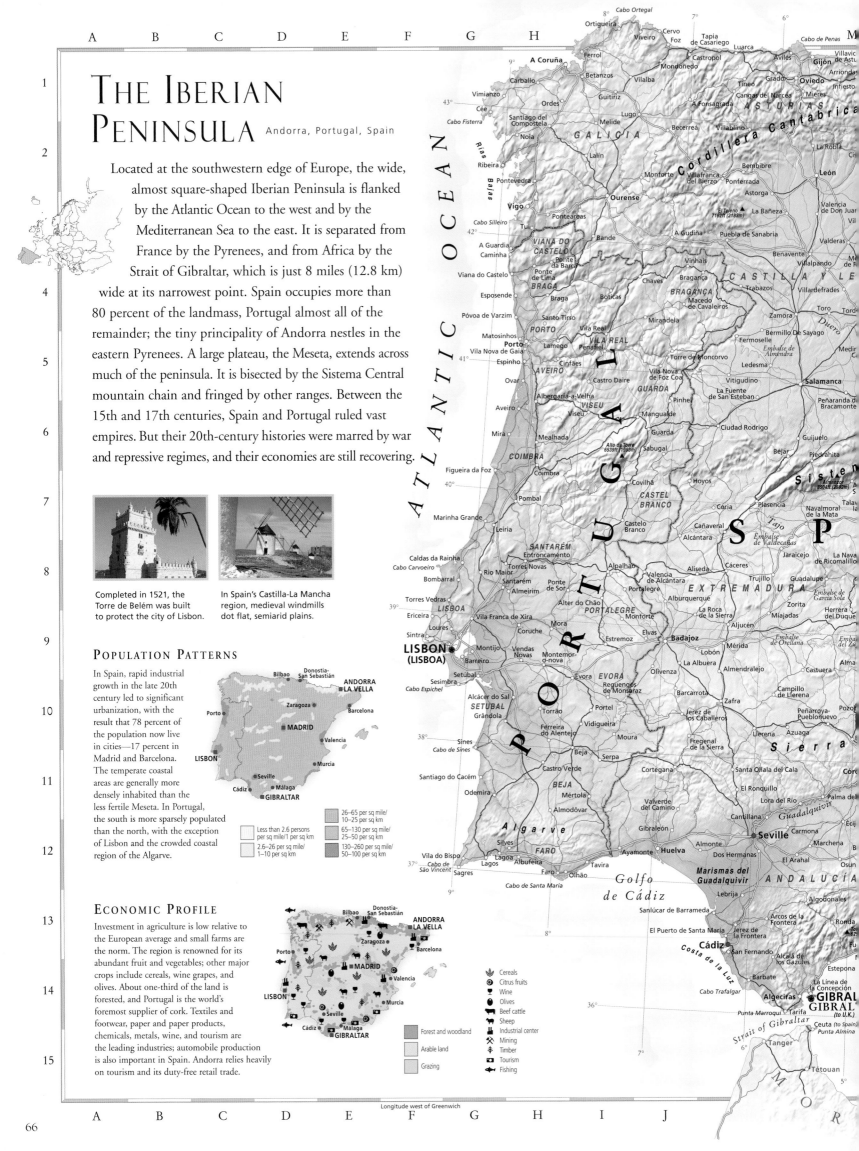

THE SISTEMAS BÉTICOS

In southeastern Spain, a mountain chain, known as the Sistemas Béticos or Baetic Cordillera, extends from Punta Marroquí on the Strait of Gibraltar to Cabo de la Nao on the Costa Blanca. Incorporating numerous small ranges, it rises to its highest point of 11,421 feet (3,481 m) at Mulhacén, northwest of Almería. East of Cabo de la Nao, the chain continues beneath the Mediterranean Sea—the Balearic Islands of Ibiza, Majorca, and Minorca are the summits of its submerged slopes.

The Low Countries

Belgium, Luxembourg, Netherlands

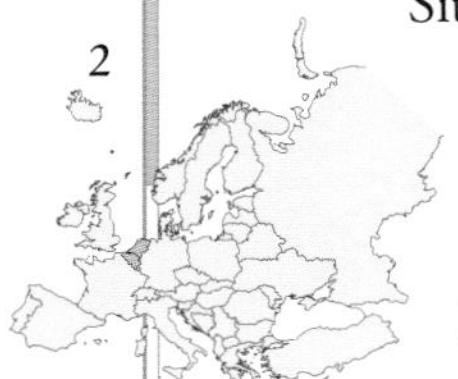

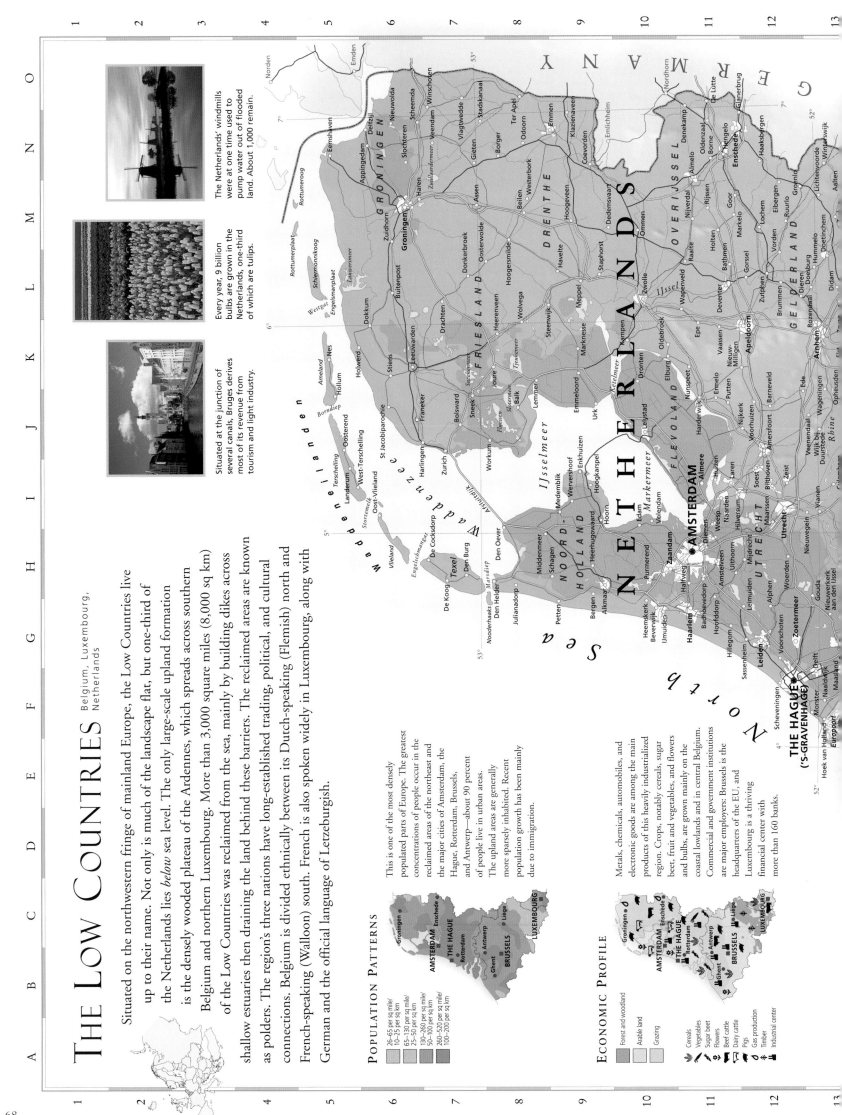

Situated on the northwestern fringe of mainland Europe, the Low Countries live up to their name. Not only is much of the landscape flat, but one-third of the Netherlands lies *below* sea level. The only large-scale upland formation is the densely wooded plateau of the Ardennes, which spreads across southern Belgium and northern Luxembourg. More than 3,000 square miles (8,000 sq km) of the Low Countries was reclaimed from the sea, mainly by building dikes across shallow estuaries then draining the land behind these barriers. The reclaimed areas are known as polders. The region's three nations have long-established trading, political, and cultural connections. Belgium is divided ethnically between its Dutch-speaking (Flemish) north and French-speaking (Walloon) south. French is also spoken widely in Luxembourg, along with German and the official language of Letzeburgish.

Situated at the junction of several canals, Bruges derives most of its revenue from tourism and light industry.

Every year, 9 billion bulbs are grown in the Netherlands, one-third of which are tulips.

The Netherlands' windmills were at one time used to pump water out of flooded land. About 1,000 remain.

Population Patterns

- 26–65 per sq mile/ 10–25 per sq km
- 65–130 per sq mile/ 25–50 per sq km
- 130–260 per sq mile/ 50–100 per sq km
- 260–520 per sq mile/ 100–200 per sq km

This is one of the most densely populated parts of Europe. The greatest concentrations of people occur in the reclaimed areas of the northeast and the major cities of Amsterdam, the Hague, Rotterdam, Brussels, and Antwerp—about 90 percent of people live in urban areas. The upland areas are generally more sparsely inhabited. Recent population growth has been mainly due to immigration.

Economic Profile

- Forest and woodland
- Arable land
- Grazing

- Cereals
- Vegetables
- Sugar beet
- Flowers
- Beef cattle
- Dairy cattle
- Pigs
- Gas production
- Timber
- Industrial center

Metals, chemicals, automobiles, and electronic goods are among the main products of this heavily industrialized region. Crops, notably cereals, sugar beet, fruit and vegetables, and flowers and bulbs, are grown mainly on the coastal lowlands and in central Belgium. Commercial and government institutions are major employers: Brussels is the headquarters of the EU, and Luxembourg is a thriving financial center with more than 160 banks.

The European Parliament meets at this building in Brussels, as well as others in Luxembourg and in Strasbourg, France.

Luxembourg's Grand Ducal Palace has been the home of the head of state (the Grand Duke) since the 1890s.

Amsterdam

In the 13th century, Amsterdam was a fishing village on the Amstel River. By the late 16th century, following an influx of people and funds from other parts of war-ravaged Europe, it had become the world's foremost financial and commercial center. Now one of the Netherlands' two capitals (the Hague is the seat of national government), Amsterdam spreads across 90 islands linked by more than 1,000 bridges. Elegant churches and gabled houses line the canals, which are plied by tourist boats and traditional wooden barges.

SCANDINAVIA Denmark, Finland, Iceland, Norway, Sweden

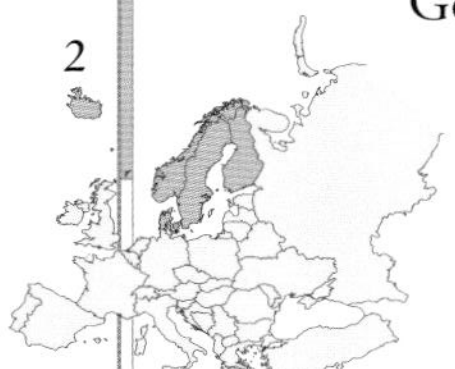

Geographically speaking, Scandinavia is the wide peninsula that divides the Norwegian Sea from the Baltic Sea and Gulf of Bothnia. Used in a broader context, however, the name encompasses all of the countries in this region, which share centuries-old historical, cultural, and linguistic ties. Occupied by Norway and Sweden, the Scandinavian Peninsula is dominated by a mountain chain that runs for almost its entire length. In the west, the peaks and plateaus drop steeply to the sea. To the east, they incline more gently toward Sweden's coastal and southern lowlands, and the flat, lake-studded terrain that covers most of Finland. Separated from Sweden by a sliver of sea, Denmark consists of fertile plains and low hills. In stark contrast, far-flung Iceland is a mountainous, mostly barren land that continues to be fashioned by earthquakes, volcanoes, and Europe's largest glaciers.

Population Patterns

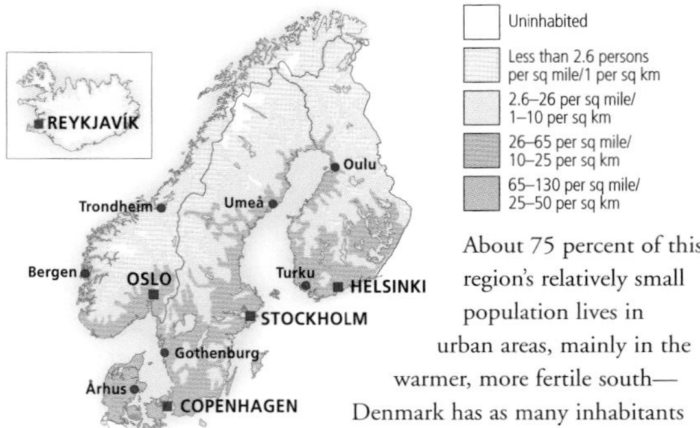

About 75 percent of this region's relatively small population lives in urban areas, mainly in the warmer, more fertile south—Denmark has as many inhabitants as either of the much larger countries of Norway and Finland. In the north and Iceland, inhospitable terrain, harsh climates, and a long winter (during which the sun may not rise for a week) have restricted human settlements to more temperate coastal areas and sheltered valleys.

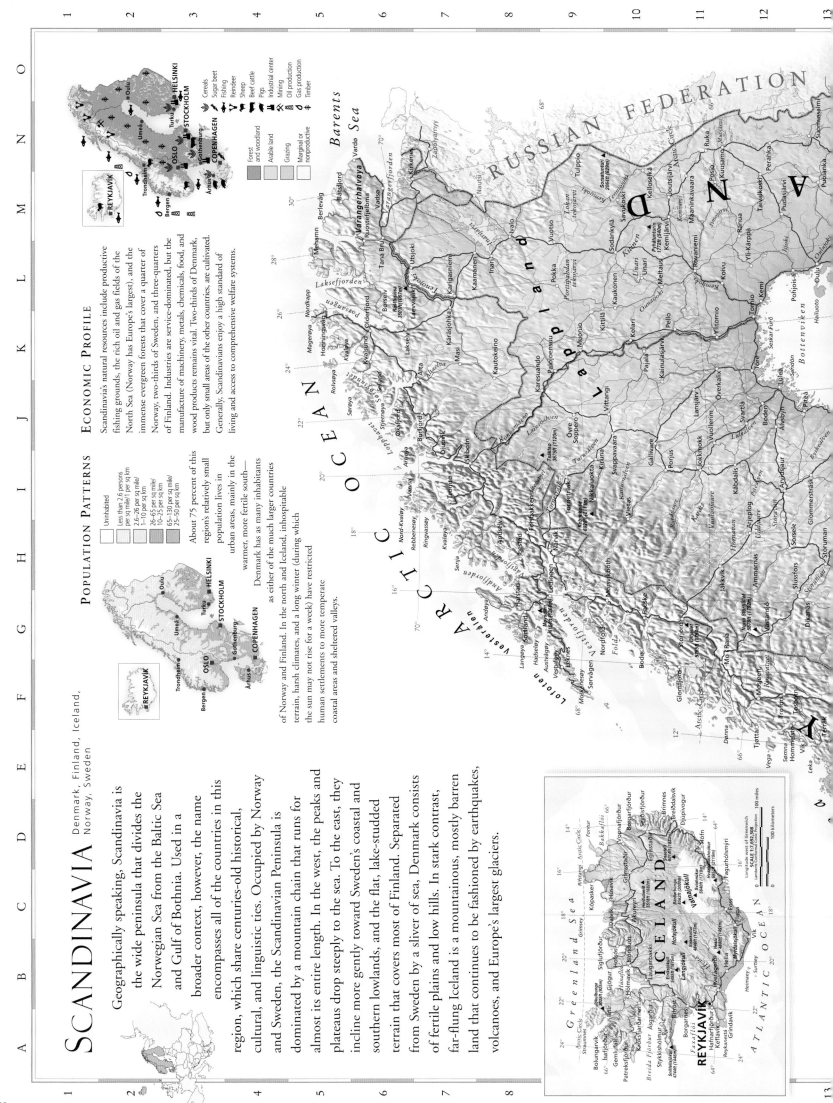

Economic Profile

Scandinavia's natural resources include productive fishing grounds, the rich oil and gas fields of the North Sea (Norway has Europe's largest), and the immense evergreen forests that cover a quarter of Norway, two-thirds of Sweden, and three-quarters of Finland. Industries are service-dominated, but the manufacture of machinery, metals, chemicals, food, and wood products remains vital. Two-thirds of Denmark, but only small areas of the other countries, are cultivated. Generally, Scandinavians enjoy a high standard of living and access to comprehensive welfare systems.

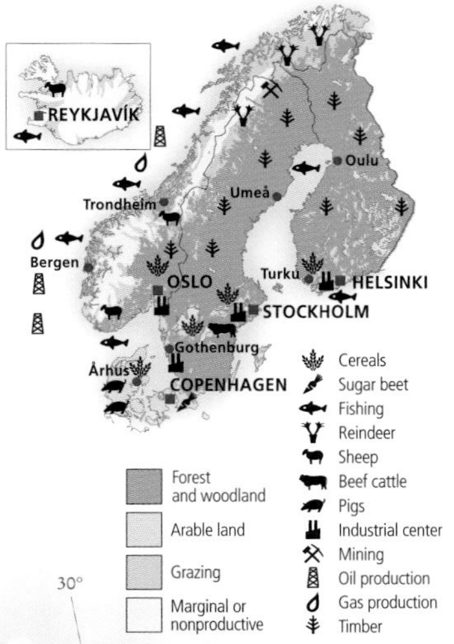

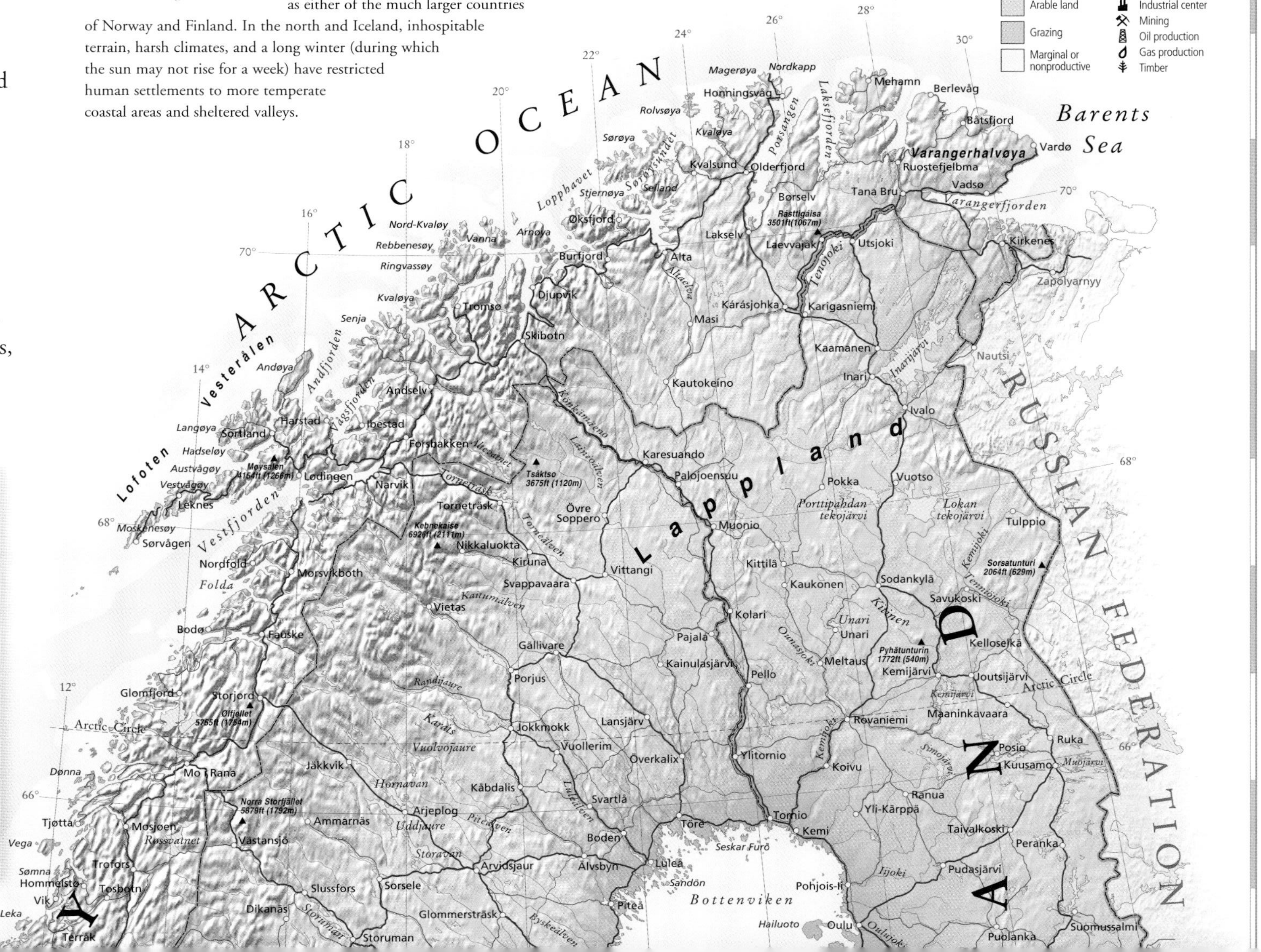

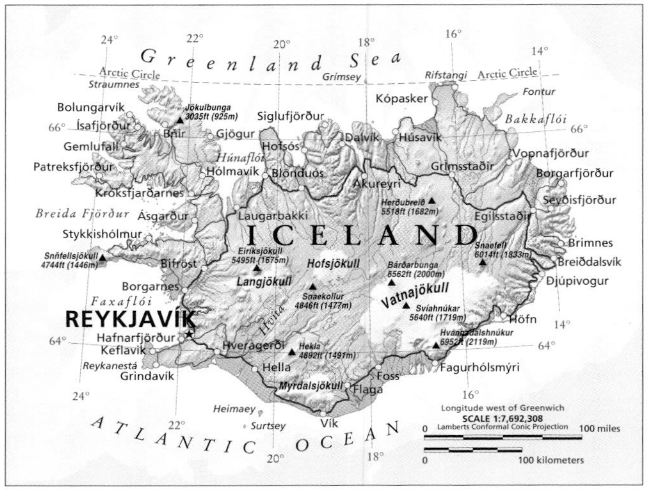

Historic boats and houses line the picturesque harbor in Copenhagen.

The Saami people inhabit northern Sweden, Norway, and Finland.

THE FJORDS OF NORWAY

During the last ice age, most of this region was blanketed by thick glaciers. On the western side of the Scandinavian Peninsula, rivers of ice cut deep into existing river valleys, forming U-shaped channels. As the climate warmed and the glaciers retreated, the rising sea filled coastal channels, creating the thousands of steep-sided inlets, or fjords, and the 150,000 islands that now line Norway's coast. The most deeply indented stretch of shoreline lies between Ålesund and Stavanger and includes several major fjords. The largest of these, Sognefjorden (Sogne Fjord), snakes 127 miles (204 km) inland, its walls rising as high as 4,291 feet (1,308 m).

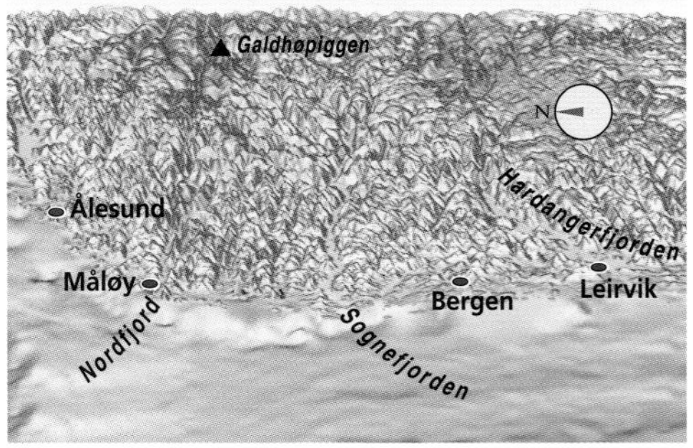

GERMANY

When East Germany and West Germany merged in October 1990, the reunified nation became the most populous country in Europe. More than 80 million people dwell in this broad land, which stretches south from the North and Baltic seas to the northern flank of the Alps. Germany can be divided into three main physical regions. In the northern lowlands, wide rivers, including the Elbe and Weser, meander seaward across expansive, sandy plains. A complex series of basins, partially wooded plateaus, and mountains extends across the center of the country. In the south, beyond the valley of the Main, stand the nation's highest ranges: the Black Forest, Swabian Alp, and Bavarian Alps. The great Rhine River, a historic artery of trade, defines the nation's southwestern boundaries. Continuing north, it cuts through the central uplands before veering westward across the plains to the Netherlands. Despite the economic and social challenges posed by reunification, Germany has retained its position as Europe's leading industrial power.

Population Patterns

Until the 19th century, Germany was divided into numerous small states with their own capitals and trading centers. As a result, its population is highly urbanized but fairly evenly distributed. Dense concentrations of inhabitants occur at the confluence of the Rhine and Ruhr rivers—the industrial heartland—and around Leipzig and Dresden in the east. Immigration has been the main contributor to recent population growth—10 million incomers settled in West Germany between 1950 and 1990.

Economic Profile

West Germany staged a remarkable economic recovery after the Second World War, and Germany is now the third-largest industrial power after the U.S.A. and Japan. The mainstays of manufacturing are machinery, automobiles, iron and steel, chemicals, electrical goods, and food and beverages. Two of the most significant agricultural products are wine and beer; cereals, potatoes, and sugar beet are also grown widely. The largest pastures are in the northwest, but dairying takes place throughout the country.

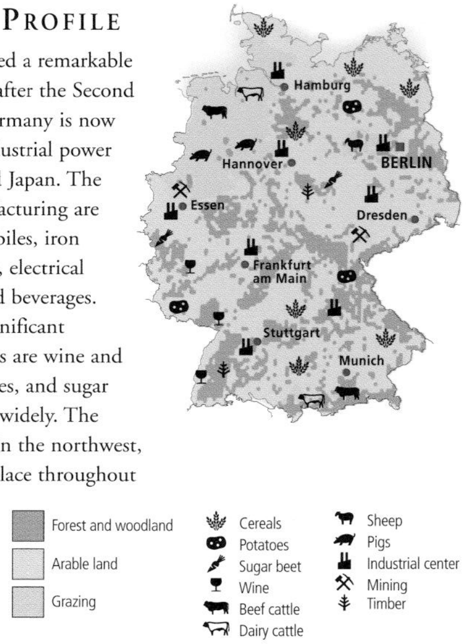

Construction of Cologne Cathedral, the largest Gothic church in Northern Europe, began in 1248 but was not completed until 1880.

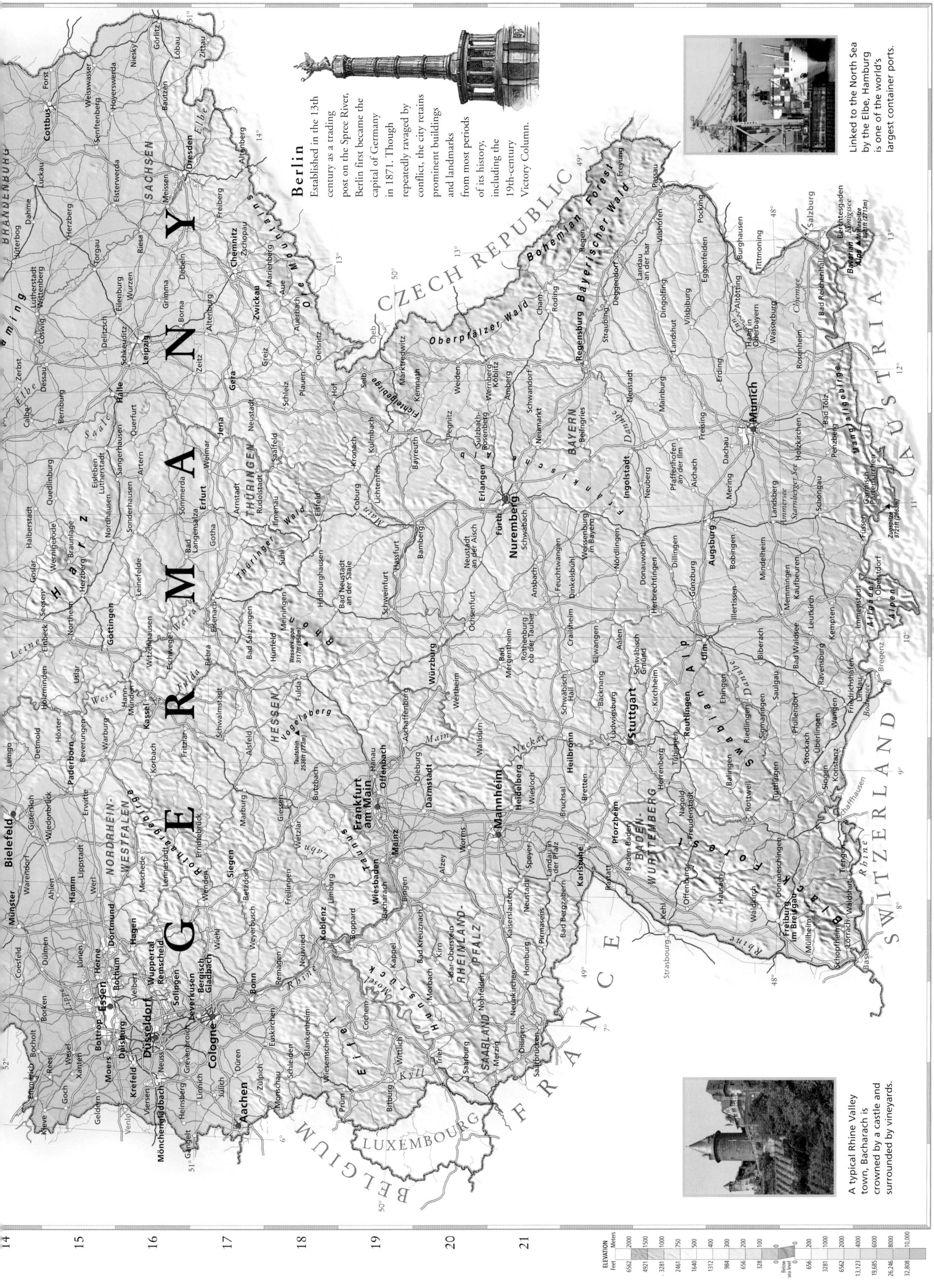
GERMANY
CZECH REPUBLIC
AUSTRIA
SWITZERLAND
FRANCE
LUXEMBOURG
BELGIUM
Berlin
Munich
Frankfurt am Main
Stuttgart
Nuremberg
Cologne
Düsseldorf
Dresden
Leipzig
Rhine
Danube
Main
Elbe
Black Forest
Bohemian Forest
Swabian Alb
Bavarian Alps
Longitude east of Greenwich
SCALE 1:2,472,527
Lamberts Conformal Conic Projection
0 60 miles
0 60 kilometers
ELEVATION
Feet Meters
6562 2000
4921 1500
3281 1000
2461 750
1640 500
1312 400
984 300
656 200
328 100
0 0
Below sea level
656 200
3281 1000
6562 2000
13,123 4000
19,685 6000
26,246 8000
32,808 10,000

Berlin
Established in the 13th century as a trading post on the Spree River, Berlin first became the capital of Germany in 1871. Though repeatedly ravaged by conflict, the city retains prominent buildings and landmarks from most periods of its history, including the 19th-century Victory Column.

Linked to the North Sea by the Elbe, Hamburg is one of the world's largest container ports.

A typical Rhine Valley town, Bacharach is crowned by a castle and surrounded by vineyards.

THE ALPINE NATIONS

Austria, Liechtenstein, Switzerland

Arcing northeastward from France, the countless peaks and valleys of the Alps sprawl across more than half of Switzerland, the tiny monarchy of Liechtenstein, and two-thirds of Austria. These nations occupy a continental crossroads, their mountain passes permitting the flow of people and goods between north and south, the Danube Valley forming a natural corridor between eastern and western Europe. Despite its strategic importance, Switzerland has remained politically neutral for almost 200 years. This, along with its prosperity and secretive banking practices, has made it a haven for international organizations, businesses, and funds. Austria's more tempestuous past includes periods as the heart of the powerful Holy Roman and Austro-Hungarian empires; its present boundaries were defined after the First World War. Liechtenstein established its independence, and neutrality, in 1866.

Millions of people visit the Alps each year to holiday at winter-sports resorts.

The spectacular Jet d'Eau, a 460-foot (140-m) fountain, is Geneva's best-known landmark.

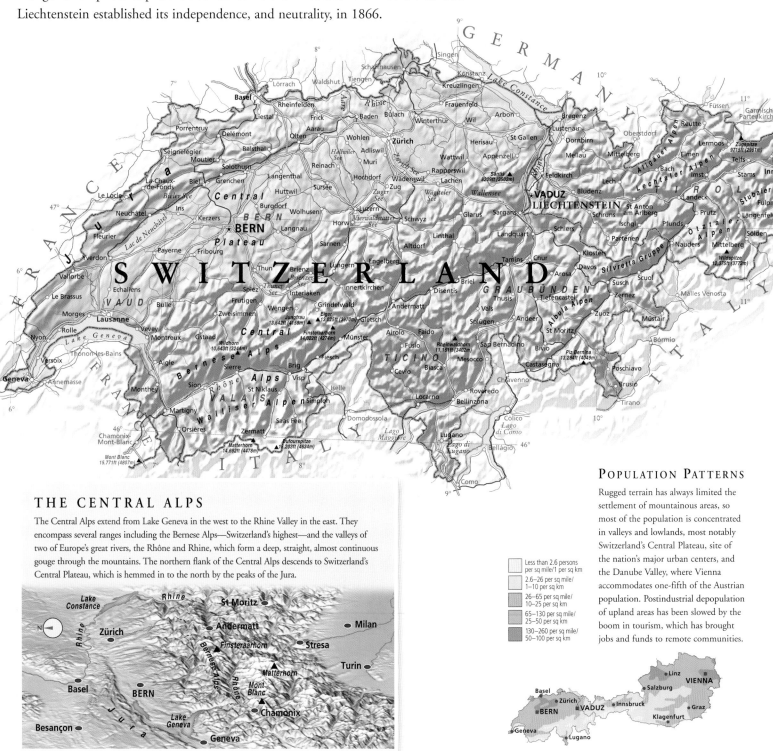

THE CENTRAL ALPS

The Central Alps extend from Lake Geneva in the west to the Rhine Valley in the east. They encompass several ranges including the Bernese Alps—Switzerland's highest—and the valleys of two of Europe's great rivers, the Rhône and Rhine, which form a deep, straight, almost continuous gouge through the mountains. The northern flank of the Central Alps descends to Switzerland's Central Plateau, which is hemmed in to the north by the peaks of the Jura.

POPULATION PATTERNS

Rugged terrain has always limited the settlement of mountainous areas, so most of the population is concentrated in valleys and lowlands, most notably Switzerland's Central Plateau, site of the nation's major urban centers, and the Danube Valley, where Vienna accommodates one-fifth of the Austrian population. Postindustrial depopulation of upland areas has been slowed by the boom in tourism, which has brought jobs and funds to remote communities.

- Less than 2.6 persons per sq mile/1 per sq km
- 2.6–26 per sq mile/ 1–10 per sq km
- 26–65 per sq mile/ 10–25 per sq km
- 65–130 per sq mile/ 25–50 per sq km
- 130–260 per sq mile/ 50–100 per sq km

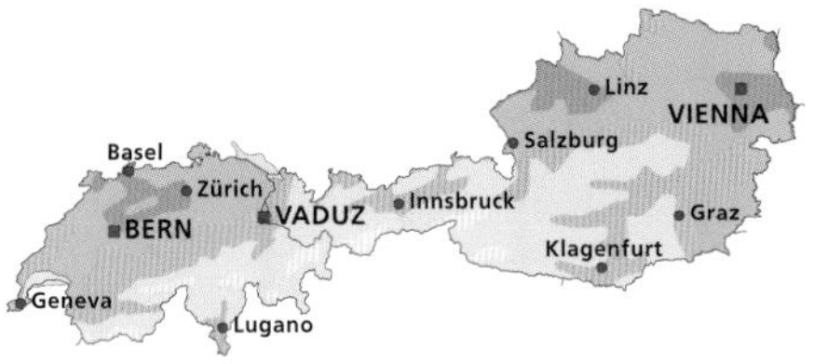

Longitude east of Greenwich

The Matterhorn's distinctive faceted peak was shaped by intersecting glaciers.

Economic Profile

The resources of this affluent region include the forests that cover a quarter of Switzerland and two-fifths of Austria; deposits of magnesite, iron, and coal in Austria; and water—hydroelectricity provides 60 percent of energy. Services dominate the economy, but the engineering, machinery, and chemicals industries are significant employers. Switzerland is renowned for precision instruments, especially clocks. Crops are grown mainly on the lowlands; dairy and beef cattle graze upland pastures.

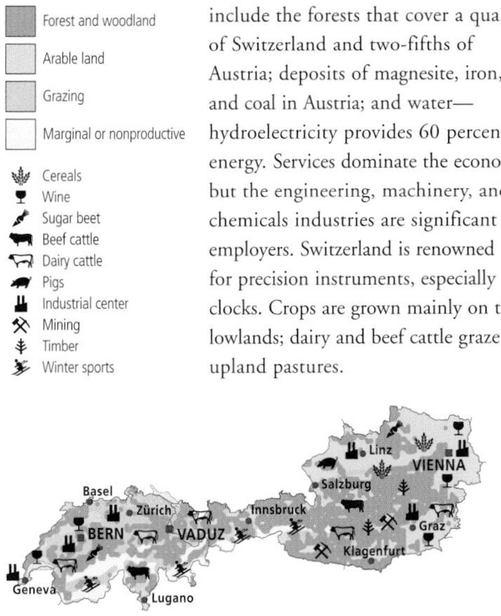

Vienna Renowned for its architecture and art collections, music and theater, cafés and parks, Austria's capital has a population of just over 2 million. Originally a Celtic stronghold, it was taken over by the Romans in the first century AD. It subsequently developed as a trading center under the House of Babenberg before being seized in 1278 by the Habsburgs, who remained in power for more than 600 years. During that time, Vienna became capital of the Holy Roman Empire (1558–1806) and then of the Austro-Hungarian Empire (1806–1918). Its many grand buildings include the early-18th-century St Peter's, the early-17th-century University Church, and the city's major landmark, the Gothic cathedral of St Stephen's, which dates from the 12th century but was entirely rebuilt between the 14th and mid-16th centuries.

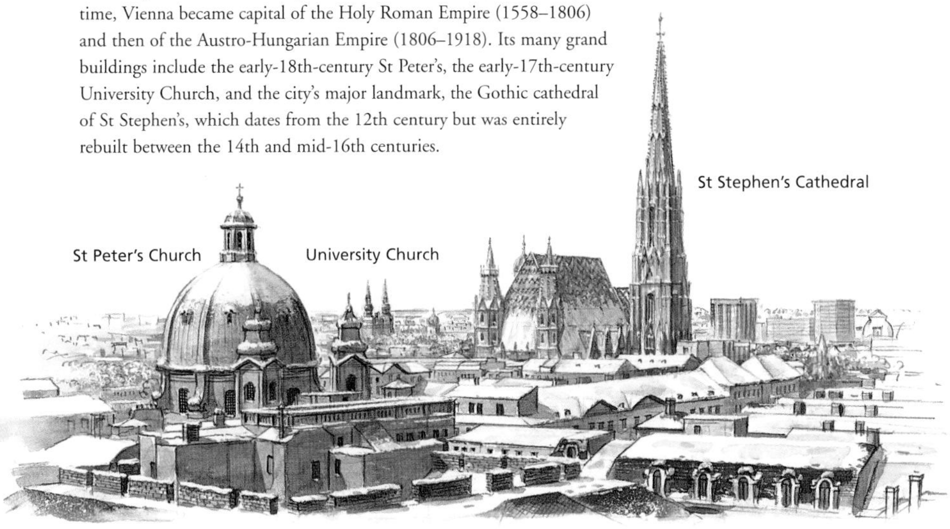

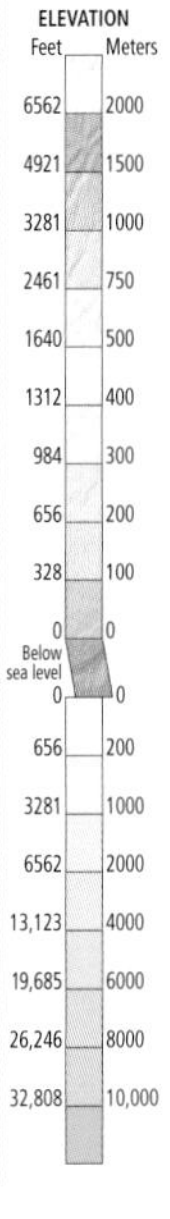

SCALE 1:1,923,077
Lamberts Conformal Conic Projection
0 50 miles
0 50 kilometers

Italy and Malta

Italy, Malta, San Marino, Vatican City

Resembling a high-heeled boot, Italy extends from the southern Alps to the middle of the Mediterranean Sea. Apart from the Northern Plain, much of the country is mountainous. Alpine peaks line the northern border, and the Apennines extend down the center of the country like a backbone. Two tiny nations lie within Italy: the Republic of San Marino and the Vatican City, the world's smallest state and the seat of the Roman Catholic Church. Situated 60 miles (100 km) south of Sicily, Malta is an independent republic with a distinctive culture and language.

Rome Many of Rome's most famous buildings date from the period when the city was the capital of the vast Roman Empire (27 BC–AD 330). Others, such as St Peter's Basilica, were erected by the Roman Catholic Church, which effectively controlled the city from the 8th century until the unification of Italy in 1870.

Population Patterns

During the preindustrial era, Italy's population was concentrated in ports, river valleys, and lowland plains. Following the Industrial Revolution and especially after the Second World War, many Italians from the less affluent south moved to the industrialized north, making this by far the most densely populated part of the country today.

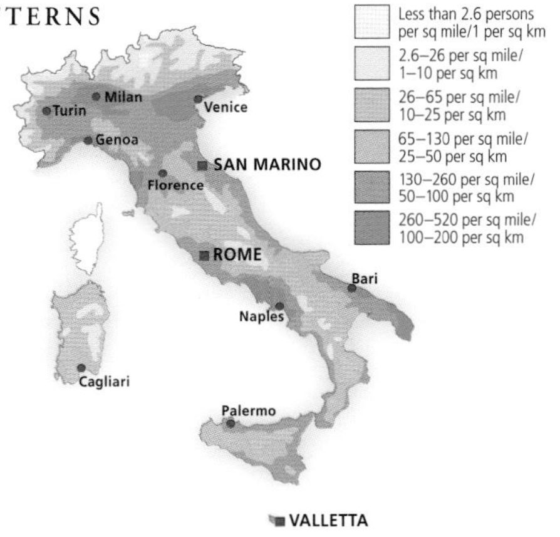

Economic Profile

Italy is a major producer of vegetables, cereals, citrus fruit, and olives, and is the world's second-largest manufacturer of wine. Most of its crops are grown on the Northern Plain and the coastal plains that flank the Apennines. Manufacturing is concentrated in the north, and automobiles, iron and steel, chemicals, and textiles are the most important products. Tourism is vital to all the countries in this region.

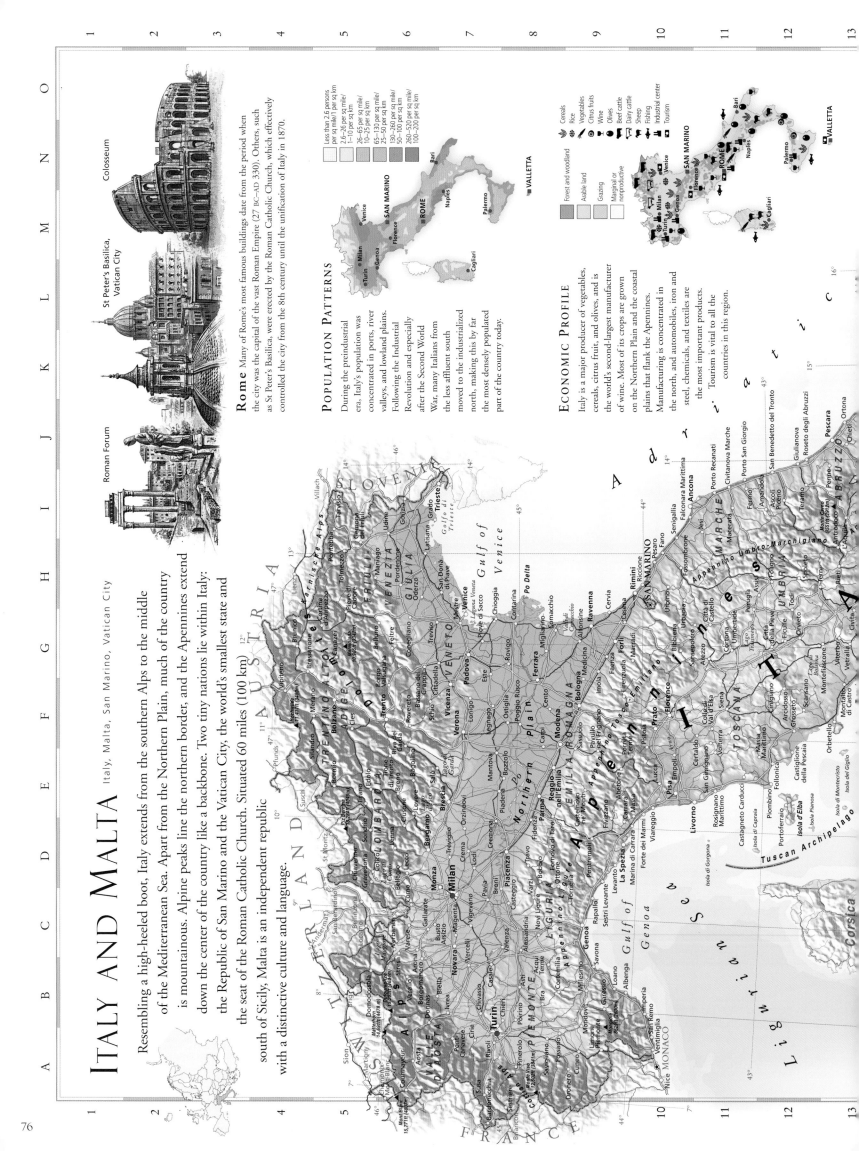

THE NORTHERN PLAIN

In northern Italy, between the Alps and the Apennines, lies a broad, flat region known as the Northern Plain or Po Valley. This is the site of Italy's most productive agricultural land as well as its largest manufacturing industries. The plain is drained by the Po River, the longest river in Italy, which rises in the western Alps then flows for 405 miles (652 km) to the Adriatic Sea. Most other rivers in northern Italy, as well as major lakes such as Maggiore and Garda, feed into the Po. Just before it reaches the sea, the Po slows and branches, forming a sprawling delta of marshes, streams, lagoons, and ponds.

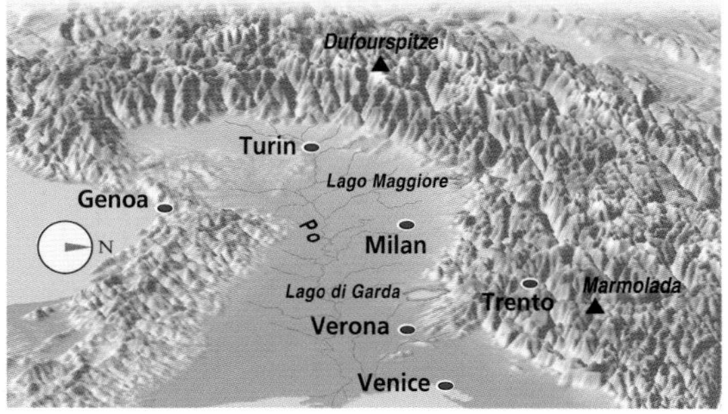

The spectacular Dolomites include 18 peaks above 10,000 feet (3,000 m).

Mount Etna in Sicily is Europe's most active volcano.

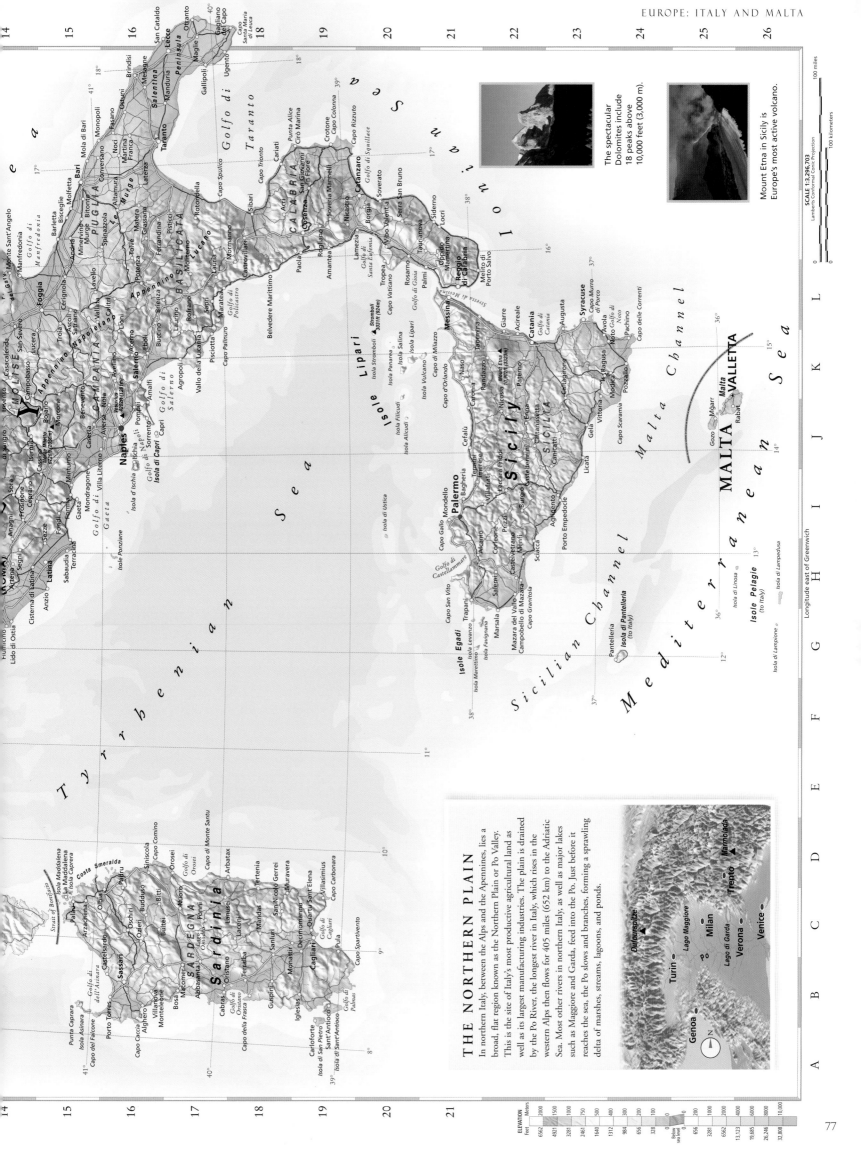

Northern Central Europe

Czech Republic, Hungary, Poland, Slovakia

The Bohemian Massif and the Carpathian Mountains bisect this region from west to east, separating the flatlands of the North European Plain from those of the Great Hungarian Plain in the south. A ring of mountain ranges around a broad central basin, the Bohemian Massif covers most of the Czech Republic. The heavily forested Carpathians—a continuation of the Alps—occupy northern and central Slovakia, giving way to plains in the south and east. Separated from these two nations by the peaks that line its southern border, Poland otherwise has little high land. Rivers meander across its central lowlands and lake-studded coastal plains, many, notably the Oder and Vistula, flowing all the way to the Baltic Sea. Hungary, too, is mostly flat, the Great Hungarian Plain spreading across more than half of its territory. All of these independent, democratic nations were part of the Eastern bloc until the collapse of communism in 1989. In 1992, Czechoslovakia split into two nations, the Czech Republic and Slovakia.

Population Patterns

About 65 percent of the region's inhabitants are urban dwellers, with the highest levels in the Czech Republic and the lowest in less-developed Slovakia (which has half the population of its northwestern neighbor). The most densely populated areas are Poland's industrialized south and its capital Warsaw, the northern Czech Republic, and the Budapest region, home to one-quarter of Hungary's people. Settlements are more scattered in the Slovakian mountains and on the windswept and relatively infertile Baltic Sea coast. More than 5 percent of Hungary's population are ethnic Roma (Gypsy) people.

Economic Profile

Significant natural resources in this region include Poland's rich Silesian coal fields, the more modest but vital mineral reserves of Slovakia's Ore Mountains, and Hungary's large swathes of arable land. Cereals and potatoes are the major crops, along with sugar beet in Poland and Hungary. Leading industries include engineering and the production of automobiles, chemicals, textiles, and food and beverages—the Czech Republic is renowned for its beer and Hungary has a thriving wine industry.

In the mid-18th century, Gdańsk was the largest city in Eastern Europe. Still Poland's main port, it is also a center of shipbuilding.

The jagged Tatra Mountains of northern Slovakia and southern Poland are a refuge for rare animals such as bears and wolves.

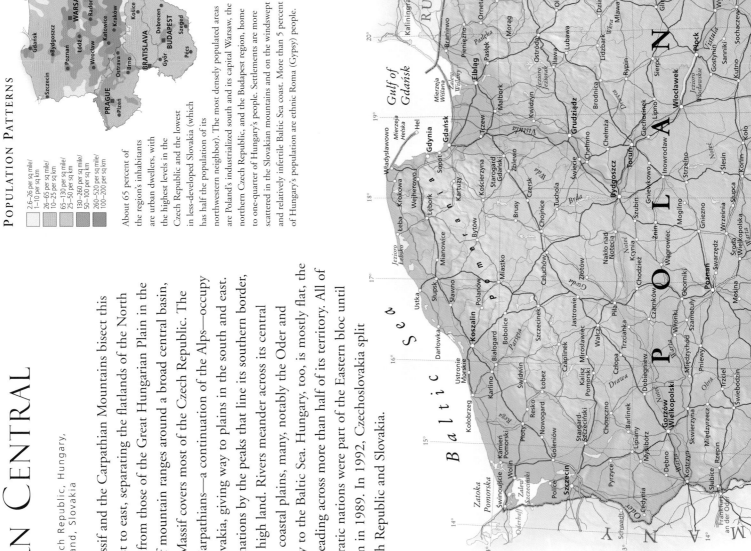

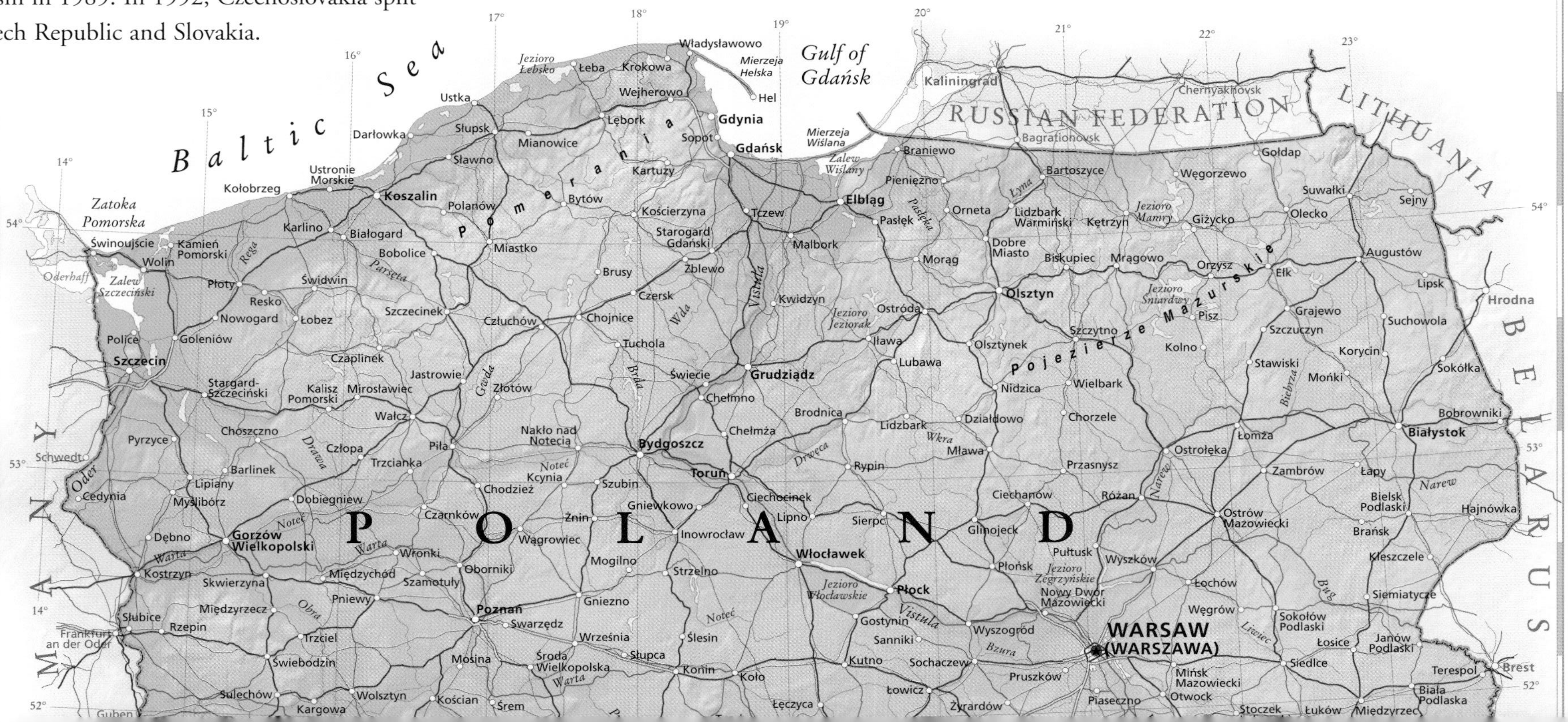

CZECH REPUBLIC
SLOVAKIA
HUNGARY
GERMANY
AUSTRIA
UKRAINE
ROMANIA
CROATIA
SLOVENIA
SERBIA and MONTENEGRO
PRAGUE (PRAHA)
BRATISLAVA
VIENNA (WIEN)
BUDAPEST
Ore Mountains
Bohemian Massif
Bohemian Forest
Sudeten
Silesia
Carpathian Mountains
Tatra Mountains
Slovak Ore Mountains
Great Hungarian Plain
Danube
Longitude east of Greenwich
SCALE 1:3,021,978
Lamberts Conformal Conic Projection
100 miles
100 kilometers
ELEVATION
Feet Meters
6562 2000
4921 1500
3281 1000
2461 750
1640 500
1312 400
984 300
656 200
328 100
0 0
Below sea level
0 0
656 200
3281 1000
6562 2000
13,123 4000
19,685 6000
26,246 8000
32,808 10,000
A B C D E F G H I J K

Prague Undoubtedly the most famous of the many bridges that cross the Vltava River in the city of Prague, the Charles Bridge dates from 1357. At that time, Prague was the capital of Bohemia and the Holy Roman Empire under Charles IV, and a major trading center. Merchants remained central to the development of the economy until the Industrial Revolution, and were responsible for commissioning many of the magnificent Gothic and Baroque buildings and monuments that today attract a steady influx of visitors. Prague became capital of the nation of Czechoslovakia in 1918 and capital of the newly formed Czech Republic in 1992.

Situated on the east bank of the Danube, Budapest's Parliament was completed in 1902.

Western Balkans

Albania, Bosnia and Herzegovina, Croatia, Serbia and Montenegro, Slovenia

Over the centuries, numerous peoples settled in the Balkans, giving rise to a patchwork of ethnically diverse communities. Until the 20th century, these communities remained relatively isolated from each other, partly as a result of the region's rugged terrain—mountains line the coast and spread across much of the interior, yielding to sizable lowlands only in the north. In the mid-20th century, all of the region's nations adopted communism and all but Albania were united as the Republic of Yugoslavia. The breakup of the republic in 1991 brought ethnic and religious rivalries to a head, resulting in a catastrophic civil war between Croats, Serbs, and Bosnian Muslims (Bosniaks). Peace was restored in 1995, but tensions remain high, especially in the culturally distinct and independently oriented provinces of Montenegro and Kosovo.

The Dinaric Alps

Stretching for 350 miles (560 km) along the coast from Slovenia to Albania and rising to 8,274 feet (2,522 m) at Durmitor, the Dinaric Alps form an almost impenetrable barrier between the Adriatic Sea and the Balkan hinterland. A single natural breach, the Neretva River valley, provides Bosnia and Herzegovina with its only coastal access; elsewhere, steep, arid slopes climb directly from the shoreline or narrow coastal plains. In the Dalmatia region of Croatia, the mountains have been partially submerged by the sea, giving rise to a series of long, parallel islands and slender, sheltered channels. The western slopes of the Dinaric Alps consist mainly of porous limestone; in places, the rock is honeycombed with underground channels and pools, and extensive cave systems.

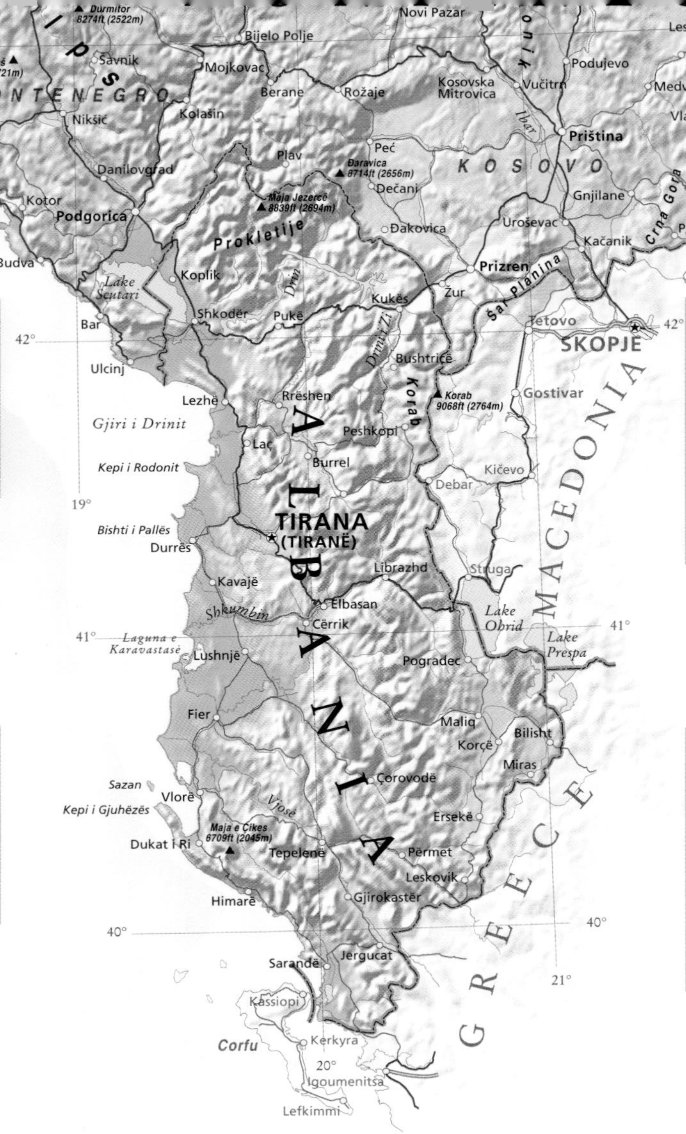

Dubrovnik A settlement existed on the site of Dubrovnik at least as far back as the sixth century AD, but the town came to prominence as a trading center only in the 13th century. By the 15th century, Dubrovnik was an independent republic and the most important port in the eastern Adriatic. After falling to Napoleon in 1808, the city became part of Croatia in 1815. During the recent civil war, Dubrovnik was devastated by Serb shelling. However, careful renovation has restored many historic buildings, and tourists are now beginning to return to the city in large numbers.

Mostar is the historical capital of Herzegovina. Its spectacular stone bridge, built in 1566, was destroyed by shelling in 1993.

Site of the pretty Church of St Maria and a dramatic clifftop castle, Lake Bled lies in the foothills of Slovenia's Julian Alps.

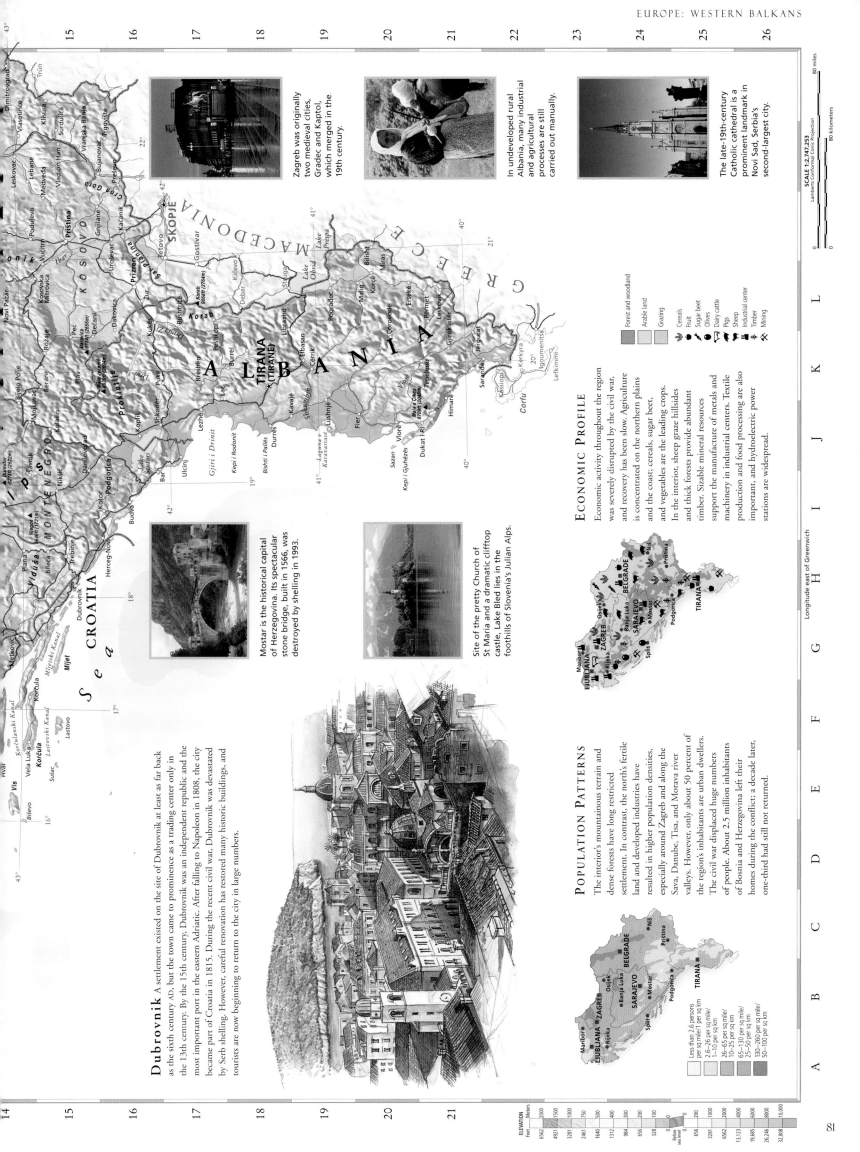

Zagreb was originally two medieval cities, Gradec and Kaptol, which merged in the 19th century.

In undeveloped rural Albania, many industrial and agricultural processes are still carried out manually.

The late-19th-century Catholic cathedral is a prominent landmark in Novi Sad, Serbia's second-largest city.

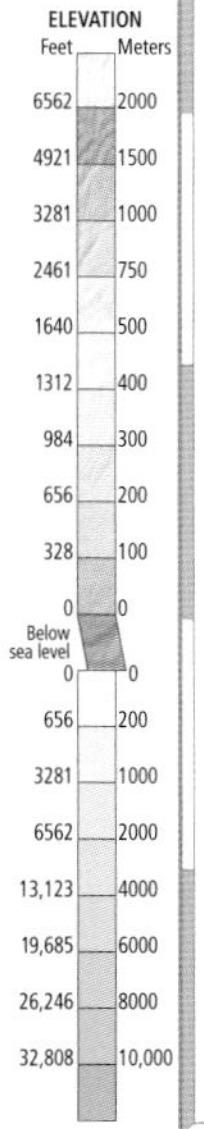

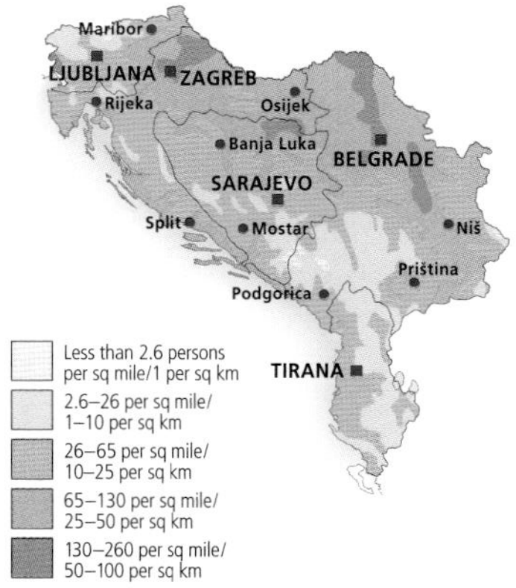

Population Patterns

The interior's mountainous terrain and dense forests have long restricted settlement. In contrast, the north's fertile land and developed industries have resulted in higher population densities, especially around Zagreb and along the Sava, Danube, Tisa, and Morava river valleys. However, only about 50 percent of the region's inhabitants are urban dwellers. The civil war displaced huge numbers of people. About 2.5 million inhabitants of Bosnia and Herzegovina left their homes during the conflict; a decade later, one-third had still not returned.

Economic Profile

Economic activity throughout the region was severely disrupted by the civil war, and recovery has been slow. Agriculture is concentrated on the northern plains and the coast; cereals, sugar beet, and vegetables are the leading crops. In the interior, sheep graze hillsides and thick forests provide abundant timber. Sizable mineral resources support the manufacture of metals and machinery in industrial centers. Textile production and food processing are also important, and hydroelectric power stations are widespread.

Forest and woodland
Arable land
Grazing
Cereals
Fruit
Sugar beet
Olives
Dairy cattle
Pigs
Sheep
Industrial center
Timber
Mining

Longitude east of Greenwich

SCALE 1:2,747,253
Lamberts Conformal Conic Projection
0 80 miles
0 80 kilometers

EASTERN BALKANS

Bulgaria, Greece, Macedonia

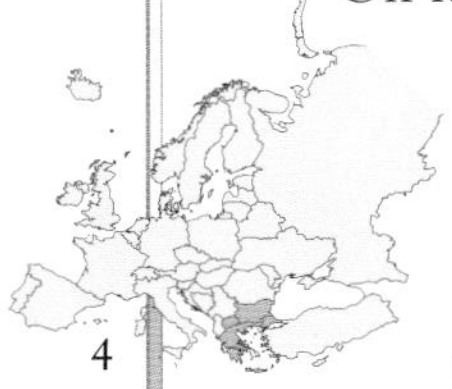

On its eastern side, the Balkan Peninsula is bounded by the Black and Aegean seas, and separated from Asia by the slender straits of the Bosporus and Dardanelles. The Former Yugoslav Republic of Macedonia occupies a high plateau in the interior of the peninsula. In neighboring Bulgaria (also a former communist country), the Balkan Mountains separate the wide plain of the Danube River from the southern lowlands, and the Rhodope Mountains form a natural boundary with Greece. Underpinned by the Pindus Mountains, central Greece stretches south from the Macedonian border, fraying into numerous narrow peninsulas and hundreds of widely scattered islands. Turkey's toehold on Europe is a legacy of that nation's long dominance over the entire Balkan Peninsula, which commenced in the 14th century and ended only in the early 20th century.

POPULATION PATTERNS

This region has a relatively low population density, with the highest concentrations occurring on the Bulgarian lowlands and in European Turkey. In Macedonia and Greece, rugged, arid terrain has restricted development. Since the mid-20th century, industrialization has led to a decline in natural population growth and an increase in urbanization. In Greece, more than 30 percent of the population now lives in Athens and many rural settlements have been abandoned.

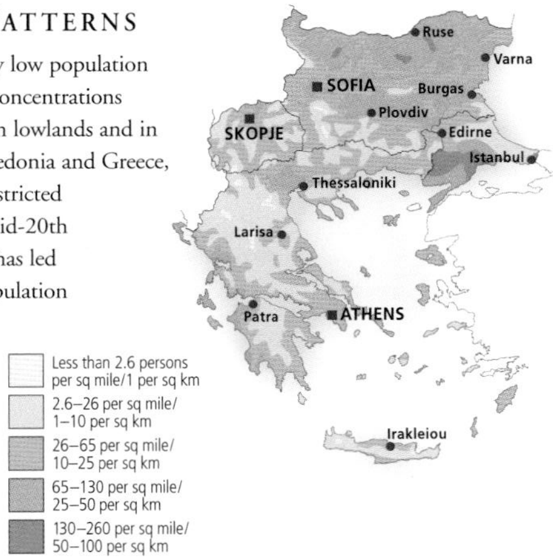

ECONOMIC PROFILE

Macedonia and Greece have little fertile farmland, few mineral resources, and undeveloped industrial sectors; consequently, Macedonia is one of Europe's poorest nations. Greece depends heavily on shipping and tourism. Bulgaria has had a difficult transition from a Soviet-style centralized economy to an open market. However, it possesses rich farmland, especially on the Danube floodplain, and sophisticated industries led by metals, chemicals, and textiles.

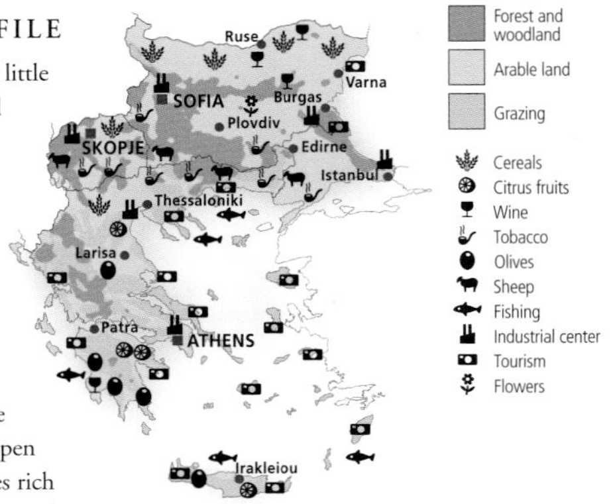

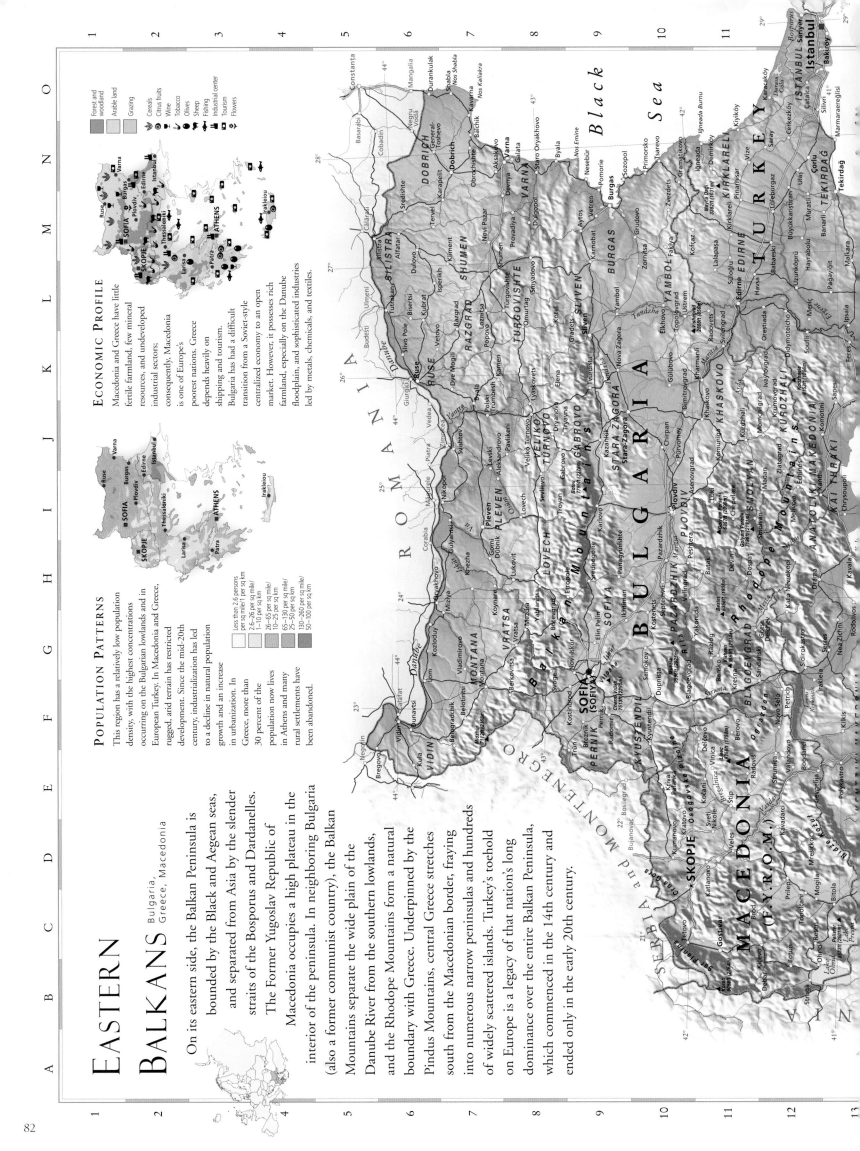

Built in 1882–93, the Corinth Canal links the Saronic Gulf and the Gulf of Corinth.

Bulgaria provides 80 percent of the world's attar of rose, an oil used in perfumes.

Athens Even after centuries of urban development, civil war, and foreign occupation, Greece's capital is still dominated—physically, economically, and culturally—by the remnants of its great classical civilization. The most prominent of these is the Parthenon, the fifth-century-BC temple to the goddess Athena, which crowns the citadel of the Acropolis.

A B C D E F G H I J K L M N O

Northeastern Europe
Belarus, Estonia, Latvia, Lithuania

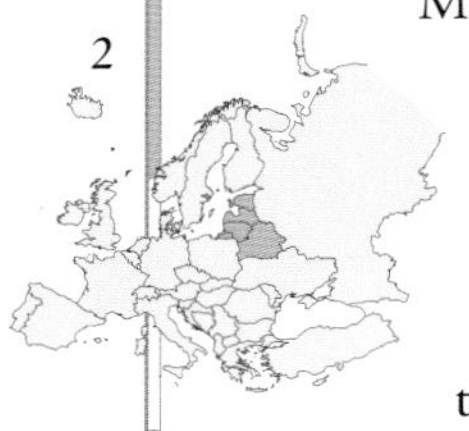

Much of Northeastern Europe's low-lying landscape was fashioned during the last ice age. Across the region, extensive plains, scoured flat by ice, are separated by hills and ridges originally deposited by the wide snouts of glaciers. Innumerable lakes fill hollows, and winding rivers have given rise to some of Europe's largest wetlands. Due to their proximity to the Baltic Sea, the nations of Estonia, Latvia, and Lithuania are often referred to as the Baltic States, even though the three countries are ethnically and linguistically distinct. In common with their southern neighbor Belarus, the Baltic States were, for long periods of their histories, controlled by more powerful nations, including Poland, Russia, Germany, Denmark, and Sweden. In the mid-20th century, all four countries became part of the Soviet Union, but all reasserted their independence soon after the collapse of the Eastern bloc in 1989. The Russian enclave around Kaliningrad is a remnant of the Soviet empire, and a vital Baltic port for the Russian Federation.

Population Patterns

Northeastern Europe's population is fairly evenly spread, though it thins out in northern Latvia and on Estonia's chilly Baltic coast—only 14 of Estonia's 1,541 islands are inhabited. About 60 percent of people in Latvia and 70 percent in the other countries are urban dwellers; in both Estonia and Latvia roughly one-third inhabit the capital city. People of Russian origin live throughout the region, but make up 30 percent of the population in Estonia and Latvia, the result of a Soviet policy of encouraging workers from the U.S.S.R. to settle in these states.

Economic Profile

These nations are still dealing with the transition to a market economy, and are still dependent to some extent (especially Belarus) on Russian raw materials and sales. Much of Belarus's arable land was contaminated by fallout from Chernobyl, but it remains a significant supplier of flax as well as potash (widely used for fertilizers), and peat (from its marshlands); its heavy industries produce machinery, tools, tractors, and trucks. Estonia's oil-shale provides much of the Baltic States' energy. The Baltic States are also noted for wood products and textiles, and Lithuania is a major source of amber.

RUSSIAN FEDERATION
KALININGRADSKAYA OBLAST'
Kaliningrad
Courland Lagoon
Vistula Lagoon
POLAND
UKRAINE
BELARUS
VILNIUS
MINSK
HRODZYENSKAYA VOBLASTS'
MINSKAYA VOBLASTS'
VITSYEBSKAYA VOBLASTS'
MAHILYOWSKAYA VOBLASTS'
HOMEL'SKAYA VOBLASTS'
BRESTSKAYA VOBLASTS'
Vitsyebsk
Mahilyow
Homyel'
Hrodna
Brest
Babruysk
Baranavichy
Barysaw
Orsha
Pinsk
Mazyr
Lida
Pripet Marshes
Dnieper
Pripet
Western Dvina
Neman
Dzyarzhynskaya Hara 1132ft (345m)
Juozapinės kalnas 958ft (292m)
ELEVATION
Feet Meters
6562 2000
4921 1500
3281 1000
2461 750
1640 500
1312 400
984 300
656 200
328 100
0 0
Below sea level
0 0
656 200
3281 1000
6562 2000
13,123 4000
19,685 6000
26,246 8000
32,808 10,000
Longitude east of Greenwich
SCALE 1:3,021,978
Lamberts Conformal Conic Projection
0 80 miles
0 80 kilometers

Situated on Lake Galve near Vilnius, Trakai Castle became the residence of the Grand Dukes of Lithuania in the 15th century.

Tallinn Estonia's capital has one of the best-preserved medieval town centers in northern Europe. The city took shape around a fort founded by Danes in 1219. Sold to the Teutonic Knights in 1346, it became a trading post of the Hanseatic League. Increasing affluence resulted in the construction of some majestic buildings, including St Olaf's Church (founded in the 12th century and the tallest church in medieval Europe), the magnificent Town Hall (the current building dates from the early 15th century) and its fine square, and the imposing 16th-century city ramparts.

St Olaf's Church
City ramparts

Workers in southern Belarus mark the harvest by wearing traditional dress. Many Belarusians work on large collective or state farms.

Latvia's capital and principal port, Riga, was founded in 1201. The adjacent Gulf of Riga usually freezes solid for much of winter.

Central Eastern Europe

Moldova, Romania, Ukraine

Three major rivers flow through Central Eastern Europe to the north shore of the Black Sea. The Danube courses along Romania's southern border, its vast floodplain contrasting with the mountains of the interior. The Dniester runs from the uplands of western Ukraine along the eastern edge of Moldova; in western Moldova, hundreds of other, mainly short, rivers have carved steep ravines and gorges amid low hills. Flowing first south, then east and west in a great S-shape, the Dnieper River snakes through the immense steppe grasslands that cover most of Ukraine. Formerly part of the Soviet Union, Ukraine is now Europe's largest country. Romania and Moldova share strong linguistic and ethnic links, and most of Moldova was incorporated into Romania from 1918 to 1940. In the mid-20th century, both nations were part of the Eastern bloc; like Ukraine, they are now independent fledgling democracies.

Population Patterns

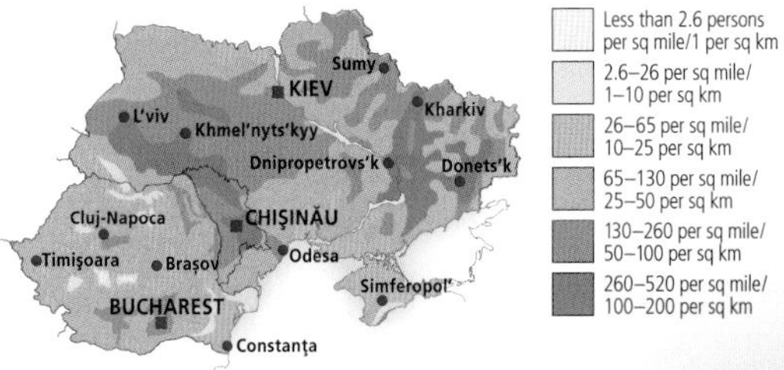

Moldova is the most densely populated of the former Soviet republics, yet the majority of its inhabitants still live in rural areas; one-third of the urban population dwells in the capital. More than half of Romanians and Ukrainians live in towns and cities. Romania has areas of low population density in the mountains and swampy Danube Delta; Ukraine's population is a little more evenly spread, with the highest concentrations in the industrial southeast—home to one-third of the population—and the fertile belt that runs eastward from the Dniester. Ukraine and Moldova have many inhabitants of Russian origin, whereas Romania's largest minorities are ethnic Roma (Gypsy) people and Hungarians.

Economic Profile

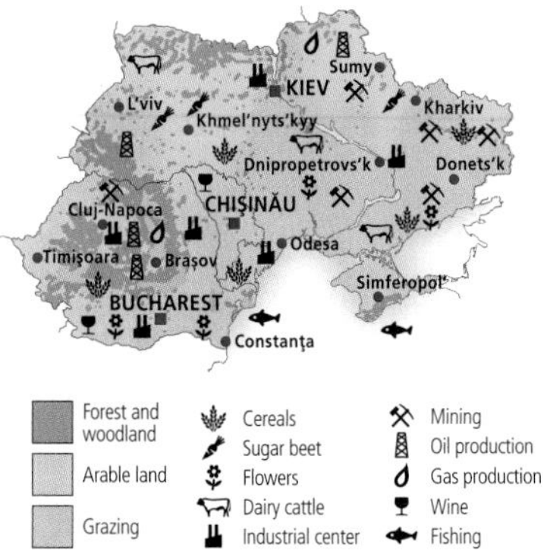

All three countries have productive farmland. Cereals are grown widely in lowland areas, especially on the fertile black-soil plains of Ukraine, formerly known as "the breadbasket of the Soviet Union." Sugar beet (Ukraine is the world's largest producer) and sunflowers are also vital crops, and Romania and Moldova are significant wine producers. Moldova has few mineral resources and remains dependent on agriculture. Romania and Ukraine's reserves of oil, coal, and gas support major industries including the manufacture of metals, machinery, and chemicals. Textiles and footwear are important in Romania. Despite some economic progress, these nations remain among Europe's poorest.

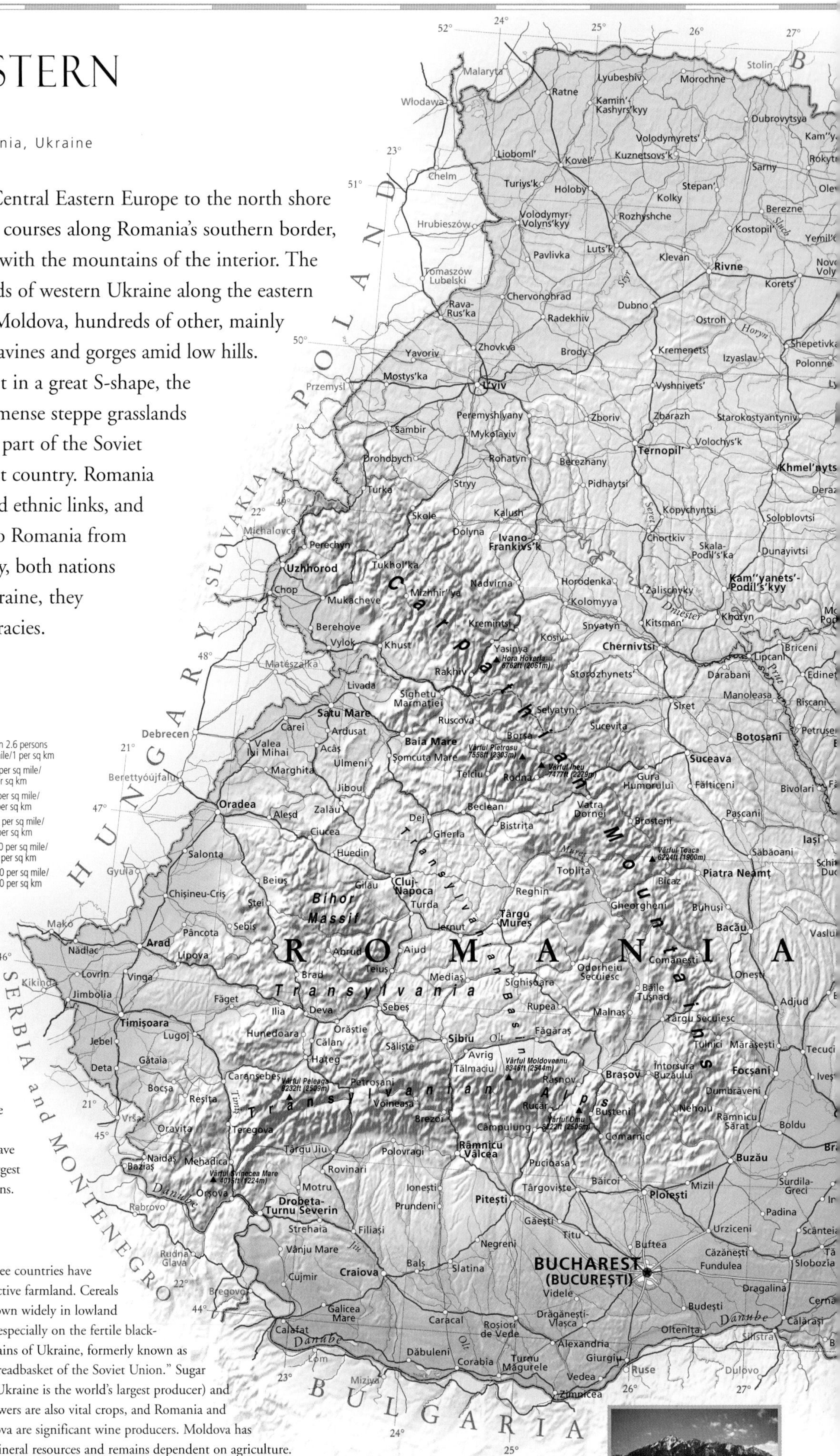

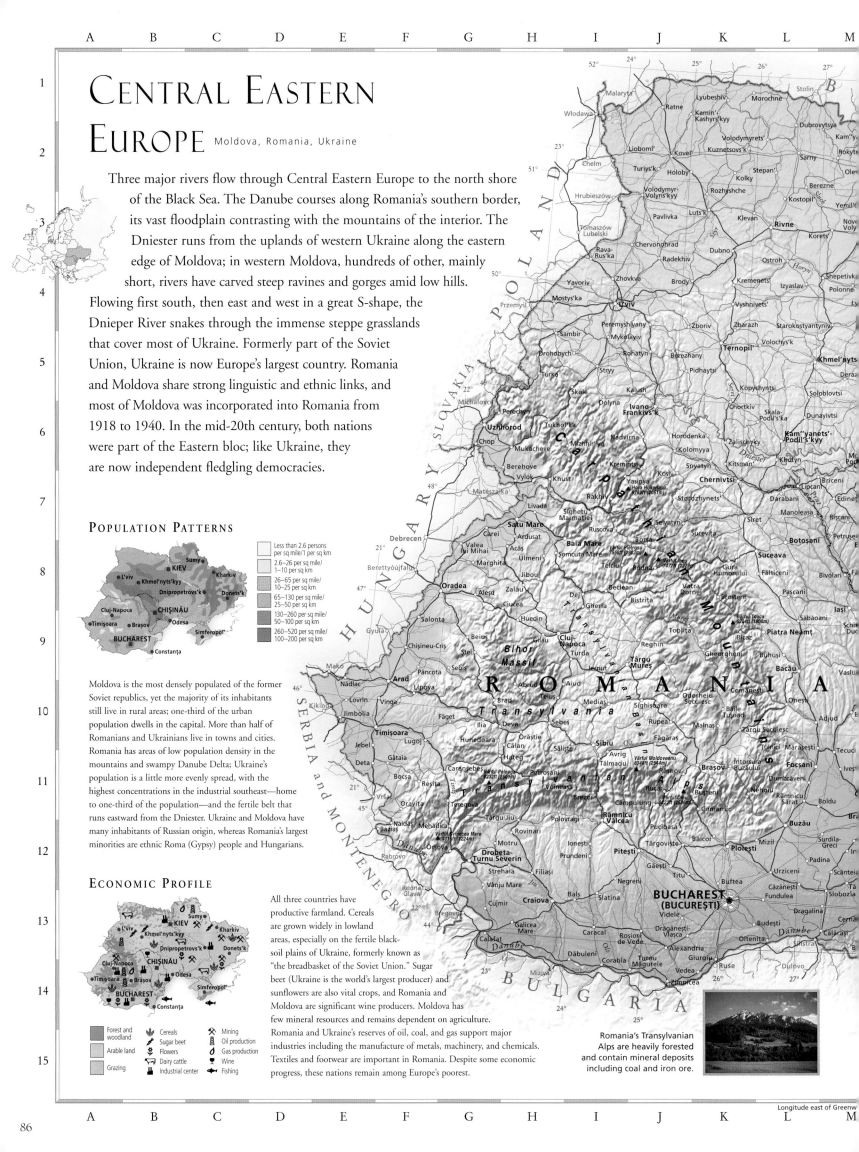

Romania's Transylvanian Alps are heavily forested and contain mineral deposits including coal and iron ore.

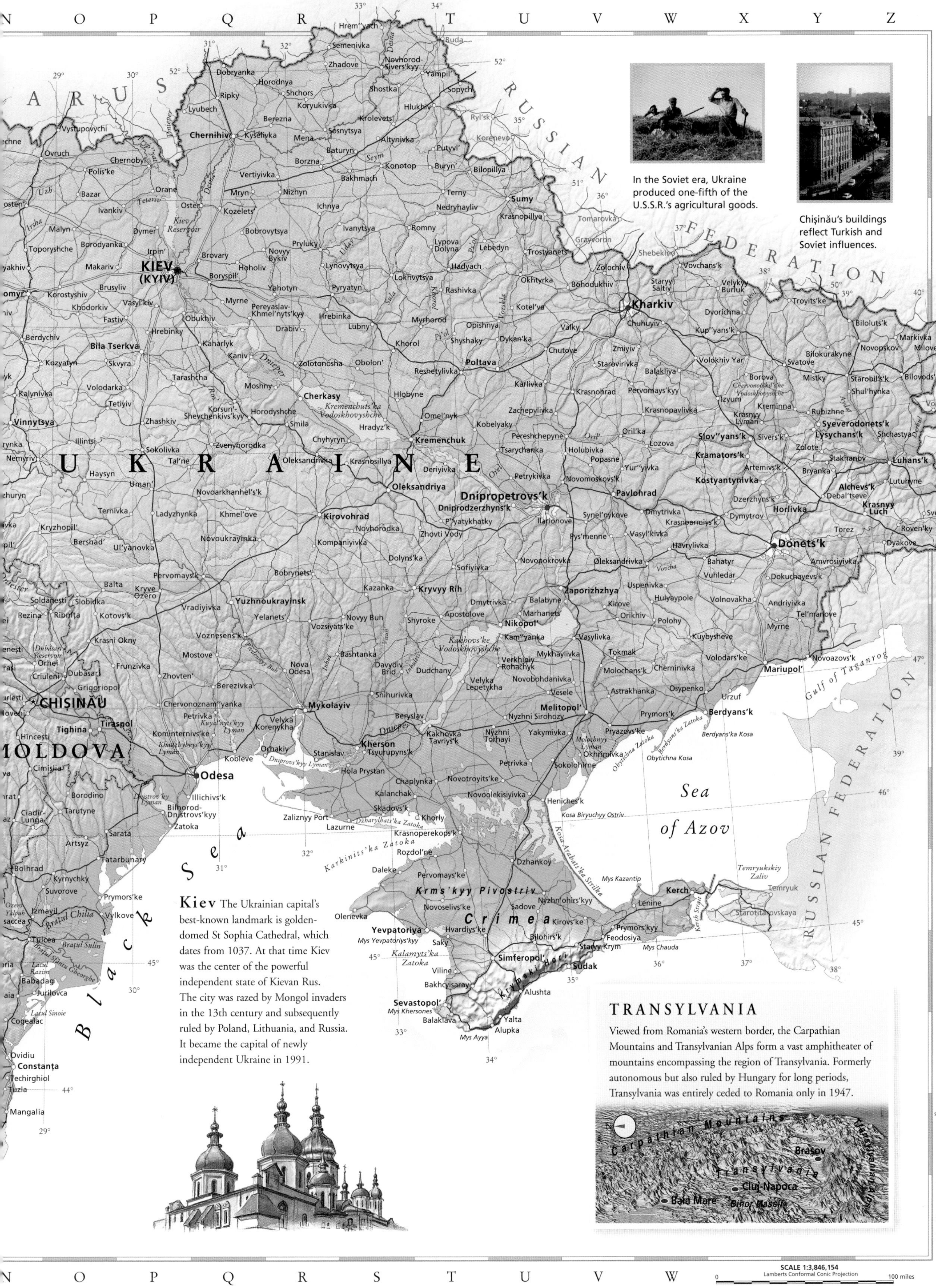

In the Soviet era, Ukraine produced one-fifth of the U.S.S.R.'s agricultural goods.

Chişinău's buildings reflect Turkish and Soviet influences.

Kiev The Ukrainian capital's best-known landmark is golden-domed St Sophia Cathedral, which dates from 1037. At that time Kiev was the center of the powerful independent state of Kievan Rus. The city was razed by Mongol invaders in the 13th century and subsequently ruled by Poland, Lithuania, and Russia. It became the capital of newly independent Ukraine in 1991.

TRANSYLVANIA

Viewed from Romania's western border, the Carpathian Mountains and Transylvanian Alps form a vast amphitheater of mountains encompassing the region of Transylvania. Formerly autonomous but also ruled by Hungary for long periods, Transylvania was entirely ceded to Romania only in 1947.

ELEVATION

Feet	Meters
6562	2000
4921	1500
3281	1000
2461	750
1640	500
1312	400
984	300
656	200
328	100
0	0
Below sea level	
0	0
656	200
3281	1000
6562	2000
13,123	4000
19,685	6000
26,246	8000
32,808	10,000

SCALE 1:3,846,154
Lamberts Conformal Conic Projection
0 100 miles
0 100 kilometers

The Russian Federation

Spanning 11 time zones and most of the Eastern Hemisphere, the Russian Federation is the largest country on Earth. It is divided into European Russia and Asian Russia, or Siberia, by the Ural Mountains, which stretch from the shore of the Kara Sea to Kazakhstan. In European Russia, the site of the nation's largest cities, major rivers divide plains and ranges of low, rolling hills. East of the Urals, an immense, swampy plain stretches to the Yenisey River, where the land climbs to the wide Central Siberian Plateau. High mountains line the Mongolian border and skirt the east coast. An almost unbroken band of boreal forest crosses the entire country, dividing the tundra of the far north from the woodlands and steppe grasslands of the south. In 1917, after a bloody revolution, Russia became a communist state known as the Soviet Union, or Union of Soviet Socialist Republics (U.S.S.R.). Following the collapse of communism in 1991, ten Soviet republics declared independence. The remainder of the union, about 75 percent of its land area, became the Russian Federation.

St Petersburg's Winter Palace is one of a series of buildings constructed in the mid-18th century by Peter the Great.

Local fishermen harvest more than 50 species of fish from Lake Baikal, the deepest lake in the world.

The Chukchi of northeastern Russia live mainly by herding reindeer, fishing, and hunting whales, seals, and walruses.

Moscow The focal point of Russia's capital city, Red Square, dates from the late 15th century and acquired its present name—the Russian word for "red" also means "beautiful"—in the 17th century. It is the site of some of the nation's most important buildings, including the Kremlin, Lenin's Tomb, and the 12-domed Cathedral of St Basil the Blessed (below). The cathedral was built between 1554 and 1560 by Ivan IV ("the Terrible") to celebrate his victory over the Mongols. Legend has it that Ivan then had the architect blinded to prevent him ever building anything to surpass this extraordinary work.

The Kamchatka Peninsula

Remote, cold, and desolate, the Kamchatka Peninsula extends for 750 miles (1,200 km) southwestward from the eastern edge of Russia, dividing the Sea of Okhotsk from the Bering Sea. Its forbidding landscape is characterized by forest-studded tundra, few towns or roads, hot springs, and more than 120 steep-sided volcanic peaks, including 15,584-foot (4,750-m) Sopka Klyuchevskaya, Siberia's highest mountain. No fewer than 22 of these volcanoes are still active.

St Petersburg
MOSCOW
Stavropol'
Anadyr'
Magadan
Novosibirsk
Irkutsk
Vladivostok
Uninhabited
Less than 2.6 persons per sq mile/1 per sq km
2.6–26 per sq mile/1–10 per sq km
26–65 per sq mile/10–25 per sq km
65–130 per sq mile/25–50 per sq km
130–260 per sq mile/50–100 per sq km
260–520 per sq mile/100–200 per sq km

Population Patterns

European Russia constitutes one-quarter of the country but is home to four-fifths of its inhabitants. Settlement is especially dense around Moscow, along the River Volga, and in the southwest. East of the Urals, Russians cluster around the industrial centers of Omsk and Novosibirsk, the towns strung along the Trans-Siberian railway, and far-flung northern ports and mining centers. Over the past century, Russians have steadily abandoned the countryside for cities; 73 percent now live in urban areas. More than four-fifths are ethnic Russians; the remainder consists of a large number of other ethnic groups, including Ukrainians, Tatars, and Bashkirs.

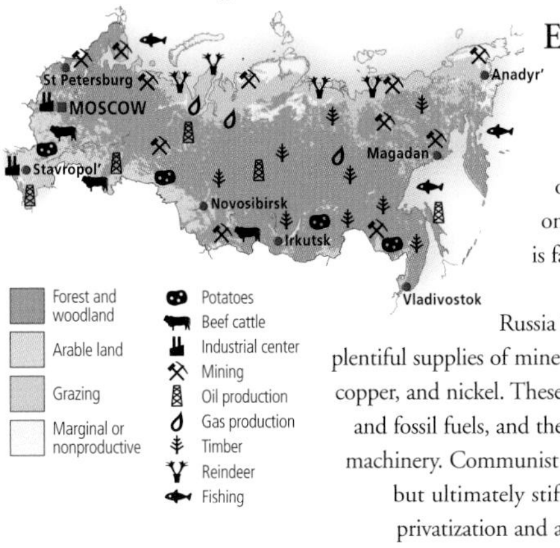
St Petersburg
MOSCOW
Stavropol'
Anadyr'
Magadan
Novosibirsk
Irkutsk
Vladivostok
Forest and woodland
Arable land
Grazing
Marginal or nonproductive
Potatoes
Beef cattle
Industrial center
Mining
Oil production
Gas production
Timber
Reindeer
Fishing

Economic Profile

Much of the Soviet Union's best arable land was located in the now-independent republics of Ukraine and Belarus. Less than one-sixth of the Russian Federation is farmland; wheat, barley, and sugar beet are among the major crops. Russia has the world's largest forests and plentiful supplies of minerals, including coal, oil, gas, gold, copper, and nickel. These support the processing of metals and fossil fuels, and the manufacturing of chemicals and machinery. Communist rule accelerated industrialization, but ultimately stifled development. A shift toward privatization and a more open market is under way.

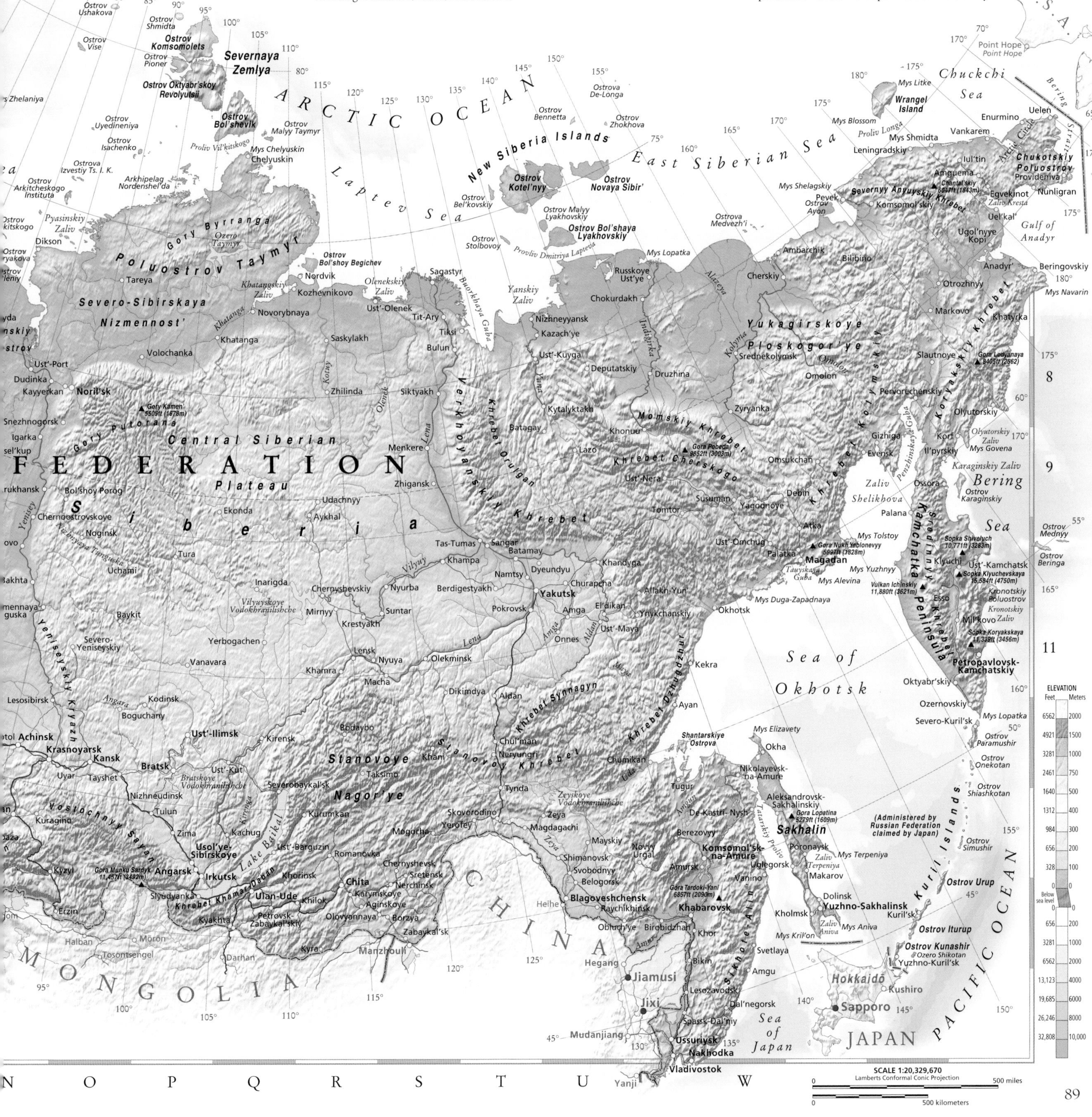
N O P Q R S T U V W X Y Z
ARCTIC OCEAN
Laptev Sea
East Siberian Sea
Chuckchi Sea
Bering Strait
Gulf of Anadyr
Bering Sea
Sea of Okhotsk
Sea of Japan
PACIFIC OCEAN
FEDERATION
Central Siberian Plateau
Siberia
Severnaya Zemlya
New Siberia Islands
Wrangel Island
Poluostrov Taymyr
Severo-Sibirskaya Nizmennost'
Yukagirskoye Ploskogor'ye
Verkhoyanskiy Khrebet
Khrebet Cherskogo
Stanovoye Nagor'ye
Kamchatka Peninsula
Sakhalin
Kuril Islands
Lake Baikal
CHINA
MONGOLIA
JAPAN
U.S.A.
Noril'sk
Dikson
Khatanga
Tiksi
Yakutsk
Magadan
Anadyr'
Petropavlovsk-Kamchatskiy
Okhotsk
Krasnoyarsk
Bratsk
Irkutsk
Ulan-Ude
Chita
Blagoveshchensk
Khabarovsk
Komsomol'sk-na-Amure
Vladivostok
Nakhodka
Yuzhno-Sakhalinsk
Sapporo
1
2
3
8
9
11
ELEVATION
Feet Meters
6562 2000
4921 1500
3281 1000
2461 750
1640 500
1312 400
984 300
656 200
328 100
0 0
Below sea level
13,123 4000
19,685 6000
26,246 8000
32,808 10,000
SCALE 1:20,329,670
Lamberts Conformal Conic Projection
500 miles
500 kilometers

NORTHERN EUROPEAN RUSSIA

The landscape of northwestern Russia was fashioned during the last ice age, when great sheets of ice advanced southward, planing the land flat and bulldozing piles of debris (moraines) to form low ranges of hills, then filling innumerable hollows with water as the ice melted and retreated north. Most of this terrain is now swathed by a belt of swampy coniferous forest, known as taiga, which dwindles to tundra along the shore of the Barents Sea and yields to wooded steppe in the south. The principal towns and cities are found mainly in this more temperate southern zone and along the northwest coast. Many developed as centers for processing and transporting the region's abundant natural resources. The largest center, St Petersburg, is Russia's second city and was its capital from 1712 to 1918. Linked to western Europe by the Gulf of Finland and Baltic Sea, it is also the nation's busiest port.

A B C D E F G H I J K L M
1 2 3 4 5 6 7 8 9 10 11 12 13 14 15
NORWAY
FINLAND
ESTONIA
LATVIA
BELARUS
RUSSIAN F
Barents
White Sea
Lake Ladoga
Lake Onega
Gulf of Finland
Lake Peipus
Lake Pskov
Kola Peninsula
Poluostrov Rybachiy
Murmanskiy Bereg
Terskiy Bereg
Kandalakshskiy Zaliv
Dvinskaya Guba
Onezhskaya Guba
Pomorskiy Bereg
Zimniy Bereg
Mezenskaya Guba
Arctic Circle
MURMANSKAYA OBLAST'
RESPUBLIKA KARELIYA
ARKHANGEL'SKAYA OBLAST'
LENINGRADSKAYA OBLAST'
VOLOGODSKAYA OBLAST'
NOVGORODSKAYA OBLAST'
PSKOVSKAYA OBLAST'
TVERSKAYA OBLAST'
YAROSLAVSKAYA OBLAST'
IVANOVSKAYA OBLAST'
KOSTROMSKAYA OBLAS
SMOLENSKAYA OBLAST
MOSKOVSKAYA OBLAST'
Murmansk
Severomorsk
Polyarnyy
Monchegorsk
Olenegorsk
Apatity
Kandalaksha
Kem'
Belomorsk
Severodvinsk
Arkhangel'sk
Onega
Petrozavodsk
Medvezh'yegorsk
Sortavala
Vyborg
Priozersk
St Petersburg
Kolpino
Gatchina
Kingisepp
Tikhvin
Volkhov
Kirishi
Velikiy Novgorod
Staraya Russa
Pskov
Velikiye Luki
Cherepovets
Vologda
Kotlas
Rybinsk
Yaroslavl'
Kostroma
Ivanovo
Tver'
Torzhok
Rzhev
Vyaz'ma
Smolensk
Kolomna
Serpukhov
Podol'sk
Zelenograd
Sergiyev Posad
Vladimir
Dzerzhinsk
Murom
MOSCOW (MOSKVA)
Volga
Rybinsk Reservoir
Northern Dvina
Longitude east of Greenwich

Forestry is by far the largest industry in the northeastern part of the region.

Velikiy Novgorod's domed cathedral, St Sophia, dates from the 11th century.

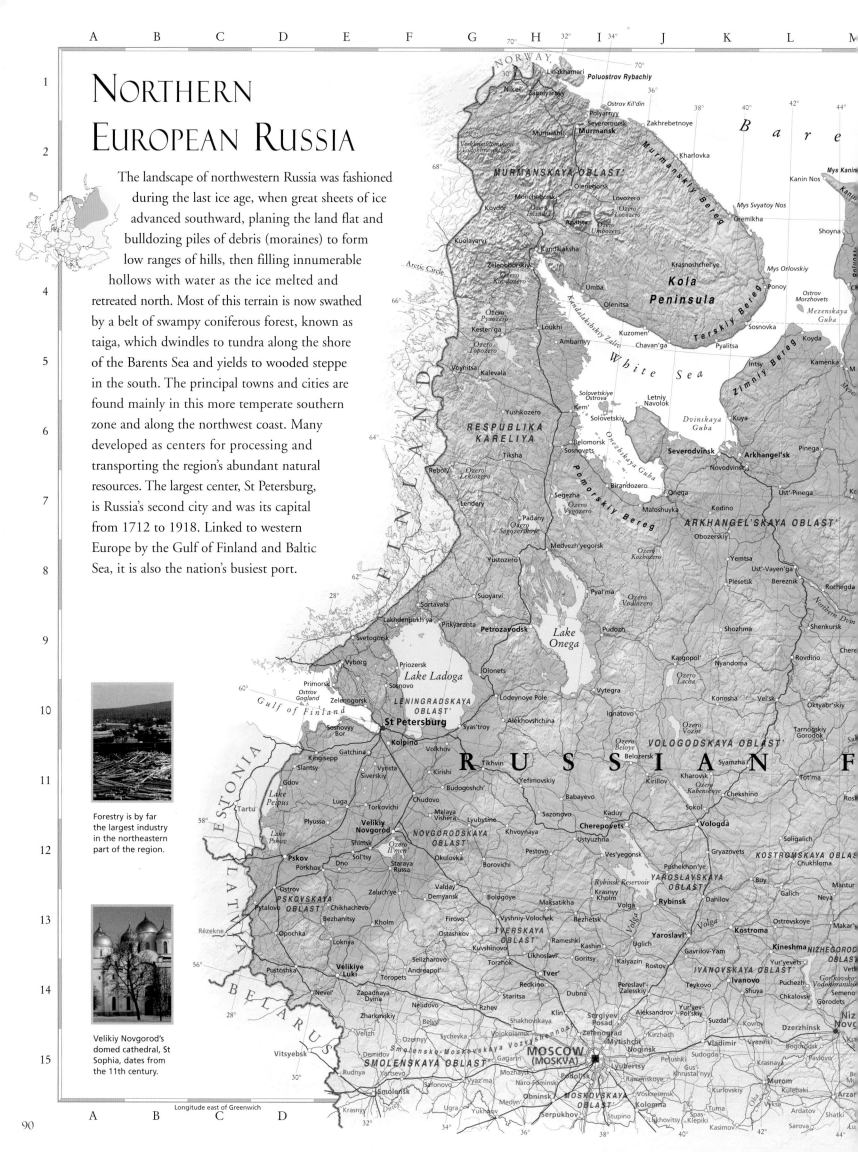

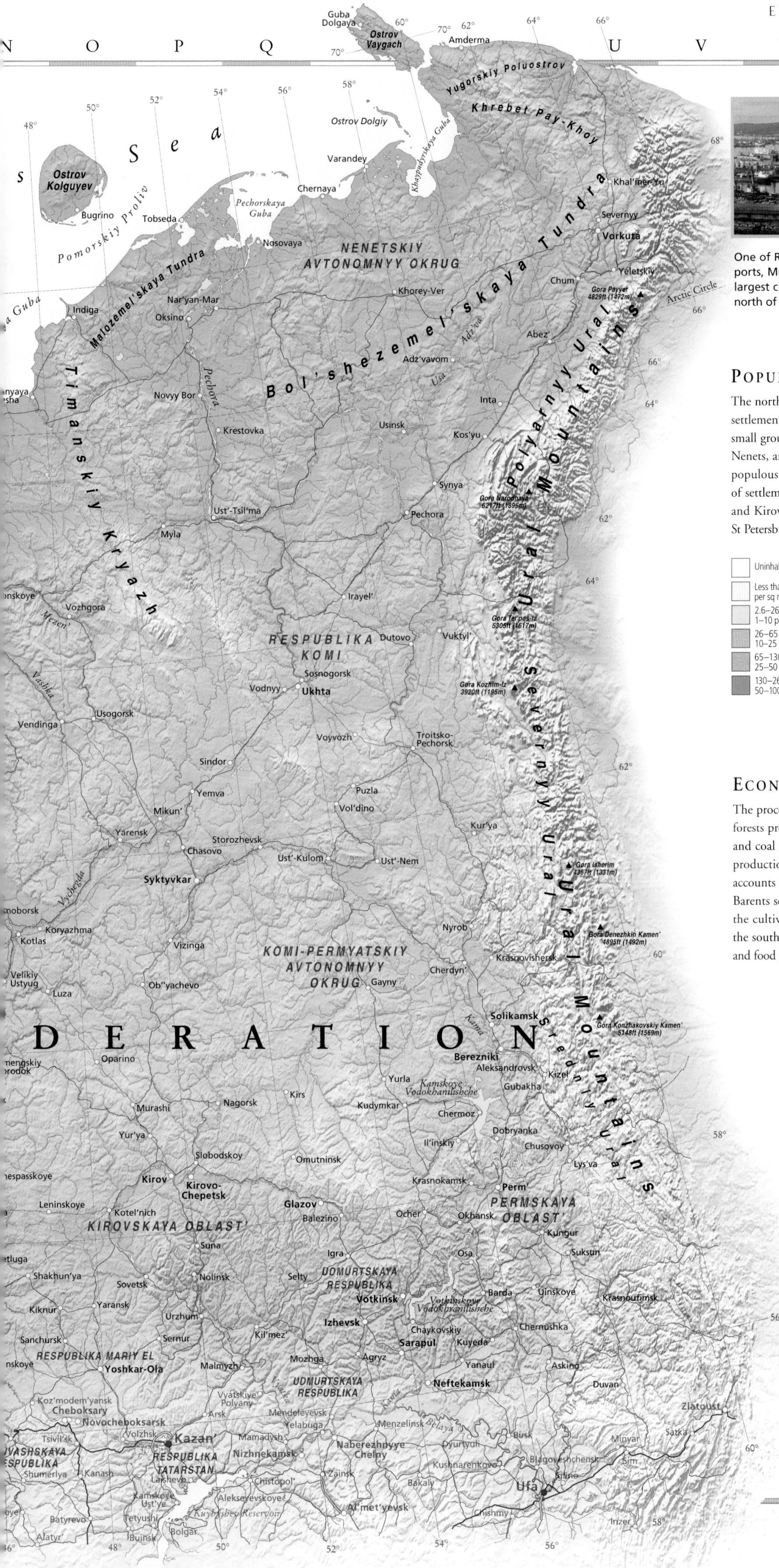
N
O
P
Q
U
V
W
X
Y
Z
1
2
3
4
5
6
7
8
9
10
11
Guba Dolgaya
Ostrov Vaygach
Amderma
Yugorskiy Poluostrov
Khrebet Pay-Khoy
Ostrov Dolgiy
Varandey
Khaypudyrskaya Guba
S e a
Ostrov Kolguyev
Bugrino
Pomorskiy Proliv
Tobseda
Pechorskaya Guba
Chernaya
Nosovaya
Khal'mer-Yu
Severnyy
Vorkuta
NENETSKIY AVTONOMNYY OKRUG
Bol'shezemel'skaya Tundra
Malozemel'skaya Tundra
Indiga
Nar'yan-Mar
Oksino
Khorey-Ver
Chum
Yeletskiy
Gora Payyer 4829ft (1472m)
Arctic Circle
Abez'
Adz'vavom
Adz'va
Usa
Timanskiy Kryazh
Novyy Bor
Pechora
Krestovka
Usinsk
Inta
Kos'yu
Polyarnyy Ural
Ural Mountains
Synya
Gora Narodnaya 6217ft (1895m)
Ust'-Tsil'ma
Pechora
Myla
Irayel'
Vozhgora
Mezen'
Gora Tel'pos-Iz 5305ft (1617m)
RESPUBLIKA KOMI
Dutovo
Vuktyl'
Sosnogorsk
Vodnyy
Ukhta
Gora Koz'mim-Iz 3920ft (1195m)
Severnyy Ural
Vashka
Usogorsk
Vendinga
Voyvozh
Troitsko-Pechorsk
Sindor
Yemva
Puzla
Vol'dino
Mikun'
Kur'ya
Yarensk
Storozhevsk
Chasovo
Ust'-Kulom
Ust'-Nem
Gora Isherim 4367ft (1331m)
Syktyvkar
Vychegda
Koryazhma
Kotlas
Vizinga
Nyrob
Gora Denezhkin Kamen' 4895ft (1492m)
KOMI-PERMYATSKIY AVTONOMNYY OKRUG
Krasnovishersk
Cherdyn'
Velikiy Ustyug
Ob"yachevo
Gayny
Luza
Solikamsk
Kama
Gora Konzhakovskiy Kamen' 5148ft (1569m)
D E R A T I O N
Srednyy Ural
Berezniki
Aleksandrovsk
Oparino
Yurla
Kamskoye Vodokhranilishche
Kizel
Gubakha
Murashi
Nagorsk
Kirs
Kudymkar
Chermoz
Yur'ya
Dobryanka
Il'inskiy
Chusovoy
Slobodskoy
Omutninsk
Lys'va
Kirov
Kirovo-Chepetsk
Krasnokamsk
Perm'
Leninskoye
Kotel'nich
Glazov
Balezino
Ocher
Okhansk
PERMSKAYA OBLAST'
KIROVSKAYA OBLAST'
Kungur
Suna
Igra
Osa
Suksun
Shakhun'ya
Nolinsk
Selty
UDMURTSKAYA RESPUBLIKA
Sovetsk
Votkinsk
Votkinskoye Vodokhranilishche
Barda
Uinskoye
Krasnoufimsk
Kiknur
Yaransk
Urzhum
Izhevsk
Chaykovskiy
Chernushka
Sanchursk
Sernur
Kil'mez'
Sarapul
Kuyeda
RESPUBLIKA MARIY EL
Yoshkar-Ola
Malmyzh
Mozhga
Agryz
Yanaul
Askino
UDMURTSKAYA RESPUBLIKA
Neftekamsk
Duvan
Koz'modem'yansk
Cheboksary
Novocheboksarsk
Vyatskiye Polyany
Mendeleyevsk
Yelabuga
Menzelinsk
Zlatoust
Satka
Kazan'
Tsivil'sk
Mamadysh
Naberezhnyye Chelny
Dyurtyuli
Birsk
Minyar
RESPUBLIKA TATARSTAN
Nizhnekamsk
Kushnarenkovo
Blagoveshchensk
Sim
Shumerlya
Kanash
Laishevo
Zainsk
Chistopol'
Bakaly
Ufa
Kamskoye Ust'ye
Alekseyevskoye
Al'met'yevsk
Batyrevo
Tetyushi
Kuybyshevskoye Reservoir
Chishmy
Inzer
Alatyr'
Buinsk
Bolgar
48°
50°
52°
54°
56°
58°
60°
62°
64°
66°
68°
70°

One of Russia's biggest ports, Murmansk is the largest city in the world north of the Arctic Circle.

These 18th-century churches lie on an island in Lake Onega, Europe's second-largest lake.

Population Patterns

The north's inhospitable subarctic climate has confined settlement to sheltered harbors and river valleys, though small groups of Arctic peoples, including the Komi and Nenets, are scattered across the northeast. By far the most populous area is the south, where the highest densities of settlement occur around the industrial centers of Perm' and Kirov in the east, and St Petersburg in the west. St Petersburg alone accommodates almost 4.5 million people.

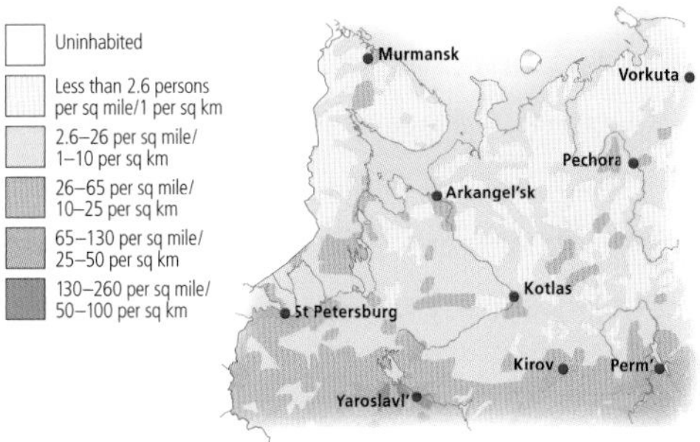
Uninhabited
Less than 2.6 persons per sq mile/1 per sq km
2.6–26 per sq mile/ 1–10 per sq km
26–65 per sq mile/ 10–25 per sq km
65–130 per sq mile/ 25–50 per sq km
130–260 per sq mile/ 50–100 per sq km
Murmansk
Vorkuta
Pechora
Arkangel'sk
St Petersburg
Kotlas
Kirov
Perm'
Yaroslavl'

Economic Profile

The processing of resources dominates the economy. Local forests provide one-third of Russia's wood products. Oil, gas, and coal reserves are exploited around Pechora, and metal production is also important, notably in Vologda, where it accounts for two-thirds of industrial output. The White and Barents seas yield one-quarter of Russia's fish. Dairying and the cultivation of fodder crops, oats, and rye take place in the southwest. Engineering, chemical production, printing, and food processing are the leading industries in St Petersburg.

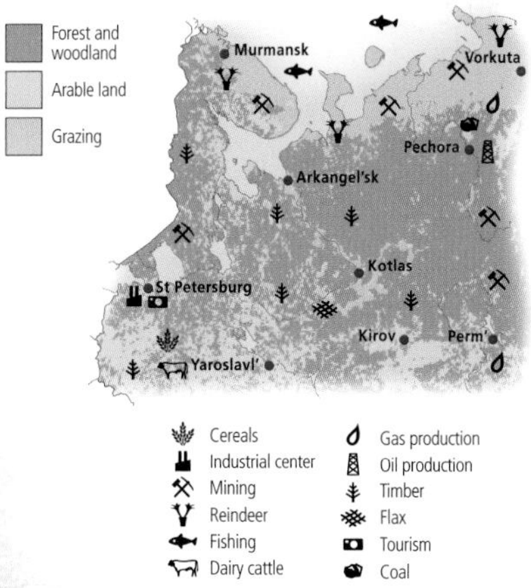
Forest and woodland
Arable land
Grazing
Murmansk
Vorkuta
Pechora
Arkangel'sk
Kotlas
St Petersburg
Kirov
Perm'
Yaroslavl'
Cereals
Industrial center
Mining
Reindeer
Fishing
Dairy cattle
Gas production
Oil production
Timber
Flax
Tourism
Coal

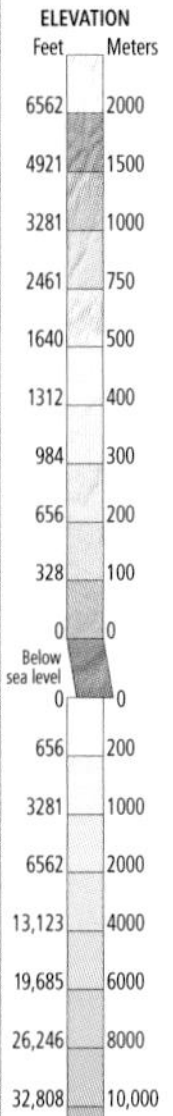
ELEVATION
Feet
Meters
6562
2000
4921
1500
3281
1000
2461
750
1640
500
1312
400
984
300
656
200
328
100
0
0
Below sea level
0
0
656
200
3281
1000
6562
2000
13,123
4000
19,685
6000
26,246
8000
32,808
10,000

Large quantities of crude oil from western Siberia are piped to Perm' for refining.

W

SCALE 1:6,043,956
Lamberts Conformal Conic Projection
0 — 150 miles
0 — 150 kilometers

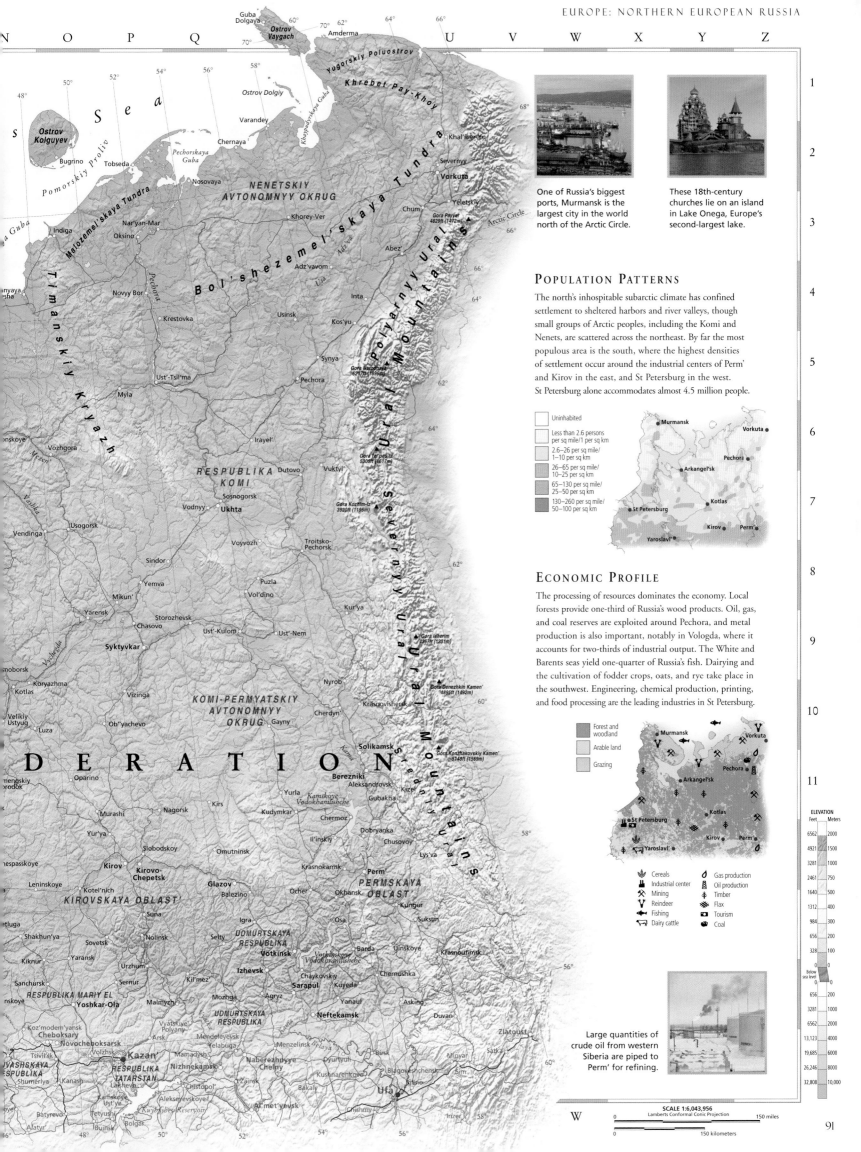

Southern European Russia

Europe's second-largest urban center, Moscow is not only the capital of the Russian Federation, but the heart of its most densely populated, developed, and productive region. The city lies on the wide valley of the Moskva River, a tributary of the Oka, which in turn flows east into the Volga, Europe's longest river. A chain of cities lines these waterways, running eastward and veering south with the Volga through Samara to Volgograd. West of the river, the Volga Hills roll down to the banks of the Don, Europe's fifth-longest waterway, which forms the eastern boundary of the Central Russian Uplands, a low plateau. Near Volgograd, the two rivers almost meet and are linked by the Volga–Don Canal. Turning away from each other, the Don and the Volga then drain across arid lowlands into, respectively, the Sea of Azov and the Caspian Sea. In the far south, where the mighty Caucasus range forms Russia's southern frontier and a natural boundary with Asia, a mere 200 miles (320 km) or so divides Europe's lowest point, in the Caspian Depression, from its highest, the towering summit of Elbrus.

A B C D E F G H I J K L M
1 2 3 4 5 6 7 8 9 10 11 12 13 14 15
MOSCOW (MOSKVA)
R U S S I A
B E L A R U S
U K R A I N E
Sea of Azov
Black Sea
Gulf of Taganrog
SMOLENSKAYA OBLAST'
KALUZHSKAYA OBLAST'
BRYANSKAYA OBLAST'
ORLOVSKAYA OBLAST'
KURSKAYA OBLAST'
BELGORODSKAYA OBLAST'
LIPETSKAYA OBLAST'
VORONEZHSKAYA OBLAST'
TUL'SKAYA OBLAST'
MOSKOVSKAYA OBLAST'
RYAZANSKAYA OBLAST'
ROSTOVSKAYA OBLAST'
KRASNODARSKIY KRAY
RESPUBLIKA ADYGEYA
KARACHAYEVO-CHERKESSKAYA RESPUBLIKA
Smolensko-Moskovskaya Vozvyshennost'
Sredne-Russkaya Vozvyshennost'
Vitsyebsk
Orsha
Homyel'
Kharkiv
Donets'k
Mariupol'
Kerch
Smolensk
Bryansk
Orel
Kursk
Belgorod
Voronezh
Lipetsk
Tula
Kaluga
Serpukhov
Obninsk
Zelenograd
Mytishchi
Lyubertsy
Podol'sk
Kolomna
Ryazan'
Novomoskovsk
Yelets
Michurinsk
Staryy Oskol
Novoshakhtinsk
Shakhty
Novocherkassk
Rostov-na-Donu
Taganrog
Bataysk
Yeysk
Krasnodar
Novorossiysk
Maykop
Sochi
Adler
Sokhumi
Tuapse
Anapa
Longitude east of Greenwich

The Caspian Depression

Covering 77,000 square miles (200,000 sq km), the Caspian Depression is a vast lowland on the northwestern edge of the Caspian Sea. Part of an immense downward fold caused by crumpling of Earth's crust, it descends to 92 feet (28 m) below sea level at the shoreline. In the north, the depression is traversed by the Volga River, which forms Russia's largest delta. Elsewhere, the depression is mainly barren, although beneath its surface lie large deposits of oil and salt.

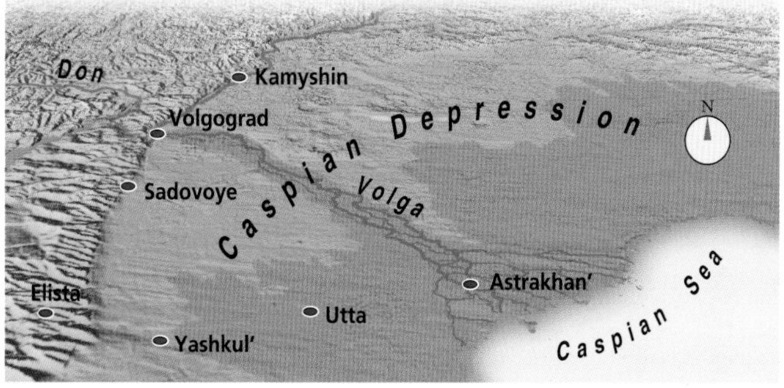

Don
Kamyshin
Volgograd
Depression
Sadovoye
Caspian
Volga
Elista
Utta
Astrakhan'
Yashkul'
Caspian Sea
N

A war between Russian forces and Chechen separatists that began in 1994 has ravaged Chechnya's capital Groznyy.

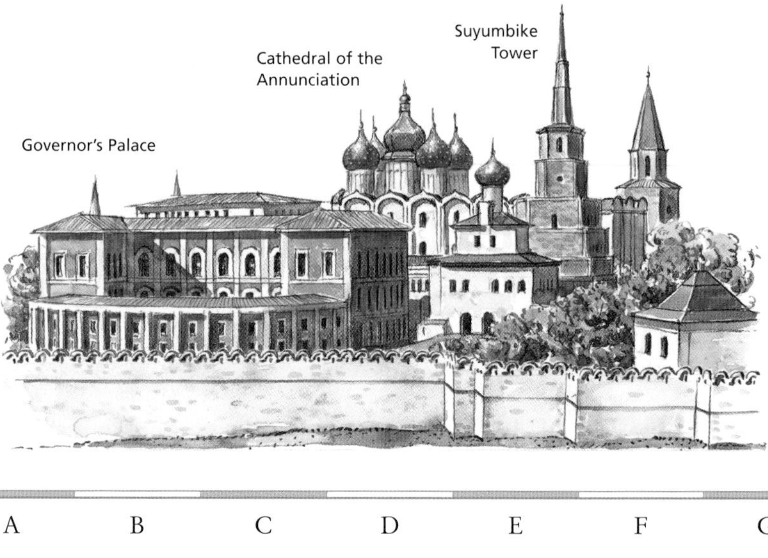

Suyumbike Tower
Cathedral of the Annunciation
Governor's Palace

Kazan' The westward expansion of the Mongol empire led to the founding of the city of Kazan' in the late 13th century. It became part of the Khanate of the Golden Horde and then an independent khanate. The city's founders, known in the West as Tatars, converted to Islam, creating the northernmost outpost of that religion. In 1552, following an extended siege, Ivan IV (the Terrible) of Russia captured the city, made it a Christian see, and constructed the vast white-walled fortress or kremlin that still stands. It now encompasses a remarkable cluster of historic buildings dating from the 16th to 19th centuries, as well as the remnants of earlier structures from the Tatar period. Kazan' remains a center of Tatar culture and about half of the population of the Republic of Tatarstan is of Tatar origin.

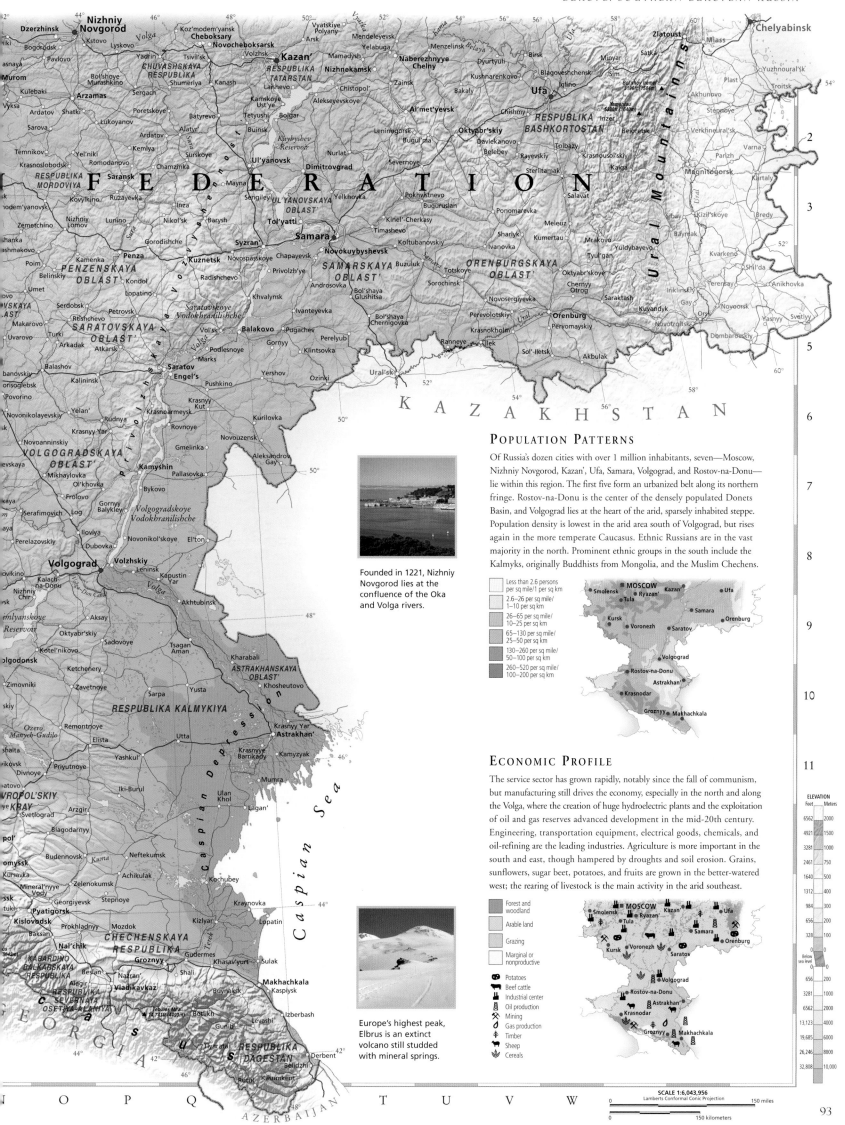

Founded in 1221, Nizhniy Novgorod lies at the confluence of the Oka and Volga rivers.

Population Patterns

Of Russia's dozen cities with over 1 million inhabitants, seven—Moscow, Nizhniy Novgorod, Kazan', Ufa, Samara, Volgograd, and Rostov-na-Donu—lie within this region. The first five form an urbanized belt along its northern fringe. Rostov-na-Donu is the center of the densely populated Donets Basin, and Volgograd lies at the heart of the arid, sparsely inhabited steppe. Population density is lowest in the arid area south of Volgograd, but rises again in the more temperate Caucasus. Ethnic Russians are in the vast majority in the north. Prominent ethnic groups in the south include the Kalmyks, originally Buddhists from Mongolia, and the Muslim Chechens.

Economic Profile

The service sector has grown rapidly, notably since the fall of communism, but manufacturing still drives the economy, especially in the north and along the Volga, where the creation of huge hydroelectric plants and the exploitation of oil and gas reserves advanced development in the mid-20th century. Engineering, transportation equipment, electrical goods, chemicals, and oil-refining are the leading industries. Agriculture is more important in the south and east, though hampered by droughts and soil erosion. Grains, sunflowers, sugar beet, potatoes, and fruits are grown in the better-watered west; the rearing of livestock is the main activity in the arid southeast.

Europe's highest peak, Elbrus is an extinct volcano still studded with mineral springs.

SCALE 1:6,043,956
Lamberts Conformal Conic Projection
0 150 miles
0 150 kilometers

TURKEY, CYPRUS, AND TRANSCAUCASIA

Armenia, Azerbaijan, Cyprus, Georgia, Turkey

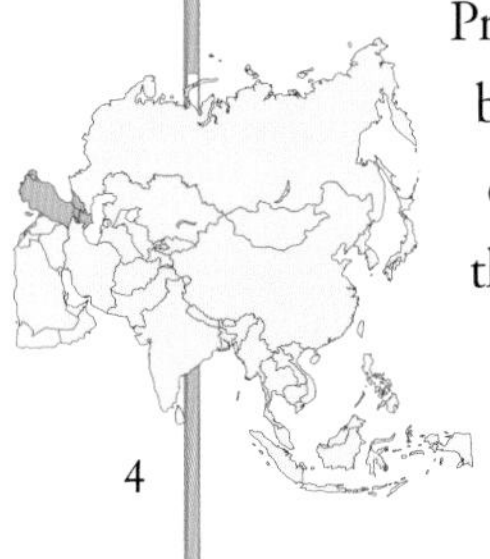

Projecting westward from the Middle East, Turkey forms a land bridge between Europe and Asia. Divided by the Bosporus, it straddles the two continents, its small region of Eastern Thrace lying within Europe and the remainder of the country, Anatolia, forming Asia's westernmost edge. An arid plateau covers much of Anatolia's interior, giving way in the east to a series of ranges that extends into Transcaucasia. Here, the towering Caucasus form another natural boundary between Asia and Europe. Three nations occupy Transcaucasia: Armenia, Azerbaijan, and Georgia. All became Soviet republics in the 20th century before attaining independence in 1991. Turkey was the heart of the Ottoman Empire, which endured from the 12th century to the early 20th century, and from 1573 to 1878 included the mainly Greek island of Cyprus.

THE CAUCASUS

The Caucasus and the associated Lesser Caucasus mountains isolate and define the region known as Transcaucasia. The much higher Caucasus peaks form a great wall that runs from the Black Sea to the shores of the Caspian Sea and reaches Europe's highest point of 18,510 feet (5,642 m) at Elbrus in Russia. The Lesser Caucasus spread to the south across Armenia, merging with the ranges of eastern Turkey. In-between are lowlands and major river valleys, including the Kür–Aras lowlands of Azerbaijan, parts of which lie below sea level.

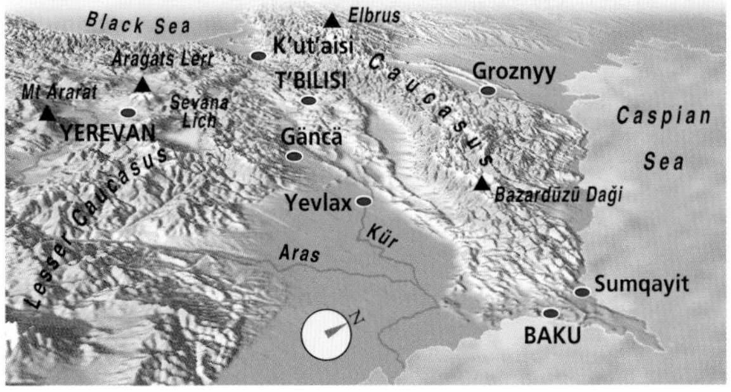

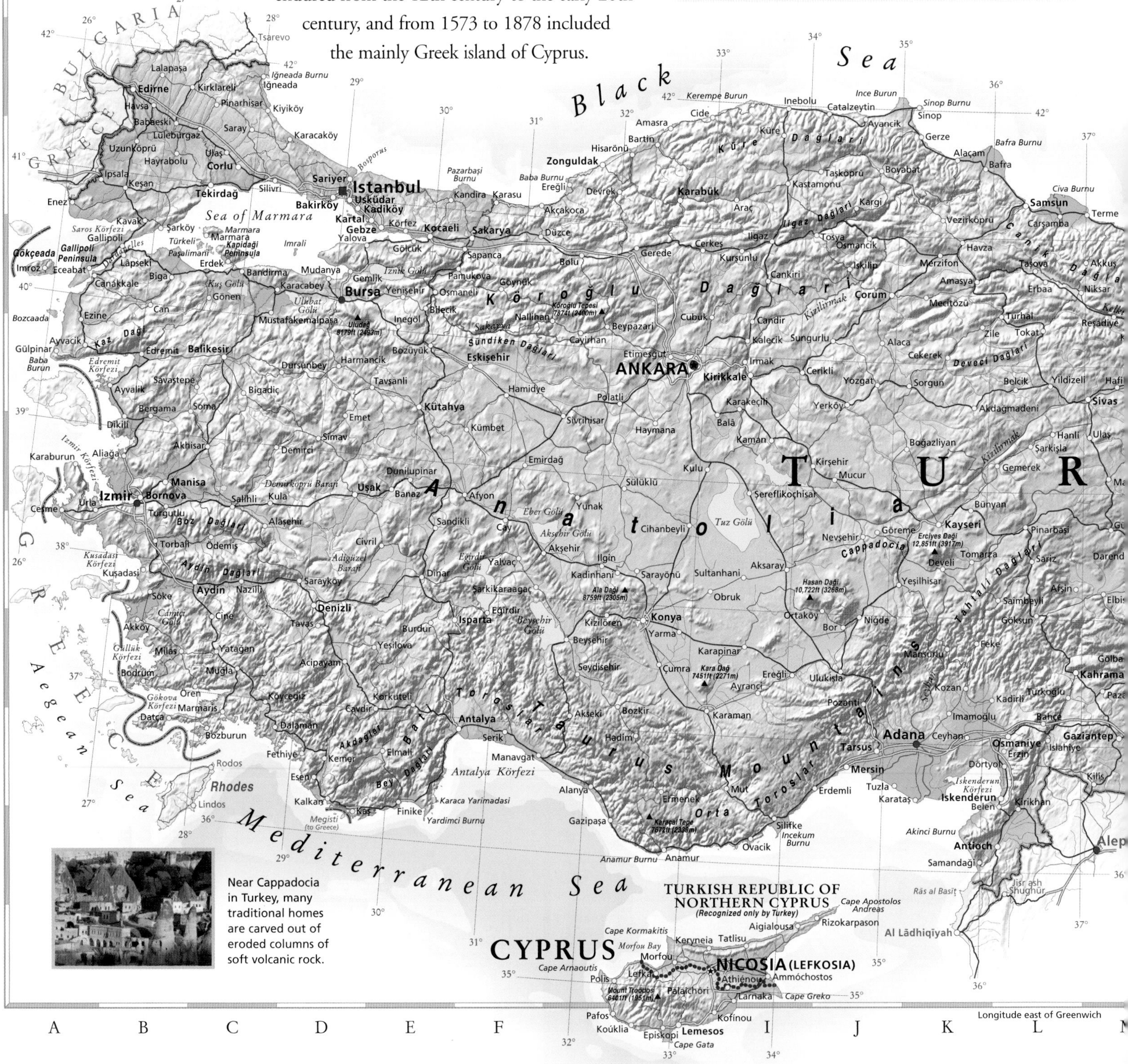

Near Cappadocia in Turkey, many traditional homes are carved out of eroded columns of soft volcanic rock.

N O P Q R S T U V W X Y Z

Population Patterns

In Turkey, the interior is less densely inhabited than the Black Sea and Aegean Sea coasts and European Turkey. Transcaucasia's inhabitants cluster on the Black Sea coast, along river valleys, and on foothills, shunning uplands and the Caspian lowlands. Cyprus is more densely populated in the south. Numerous peoples have fought over and settled in this region and ethnic diversity is high, with over 50 different groups in Transcaucasia alone. Turkey and Azerbaijan's populations are predominantly Muslim, whereas Christians are in the majority elsewhere.

Economic Profile

Metallic minerals, including chromium, manganese, mercury, and copper, are fairly widely distributed; the word Cyprus means "copper" in Greek and the island has long been renowned as a source of this metal. Oil reserves located in the Caspian Sea provide Azerbaijan with energy and valuable export revenue; the nation is also a major supplier of caviar. Traditional agriculture predominates in many areas, though industries and services have expanded rapidly in recent years, especially in Turkey. The production of textiles is important, along with metals, machinery, automobiles, food products, and some electronic goods in Transcaucausia.

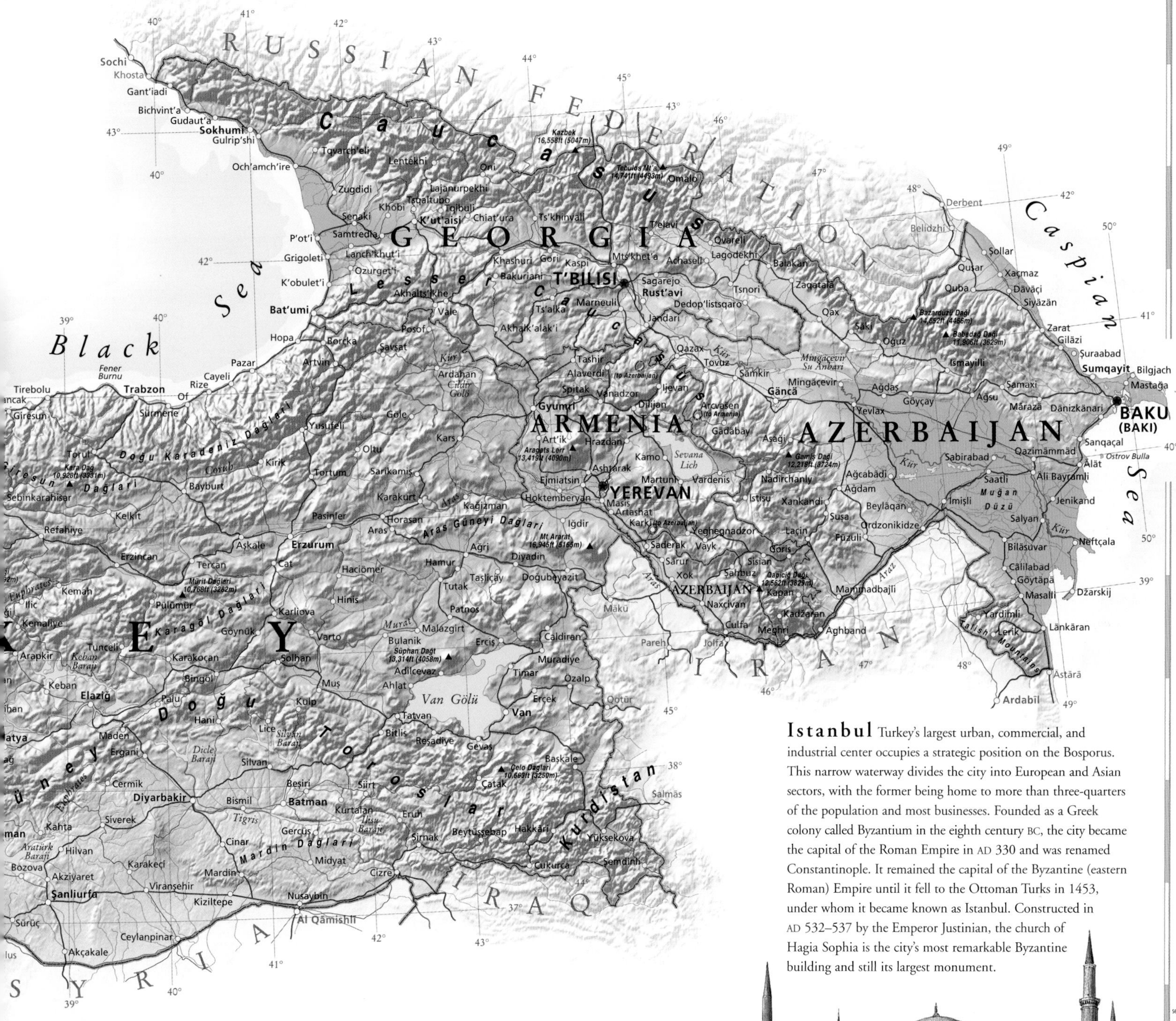

Istanbul Turkey's largest urban, commercial, and industrial center occupies a strategic position on the Bosporus. This narrow waterway divides the city into European and Asian sectors, with the former being home to more than three-quarters of the population and most businesses. Founded as a Greek colony called Byzantium in the eighth century BC, the city became the capital of the Roman Empire in AD 330 and was renamed Constantinople. It remained the capital of the Byzantine (eastern Roman) Empire until it fell to the Ottoman Turks in 1453, under whom it became known as Istanbul. Constructed in AD 532–537 by the Emperor Justinian, the church of Hagia Sophia is the city's most remarkable Byzantine building and still its largest monument.

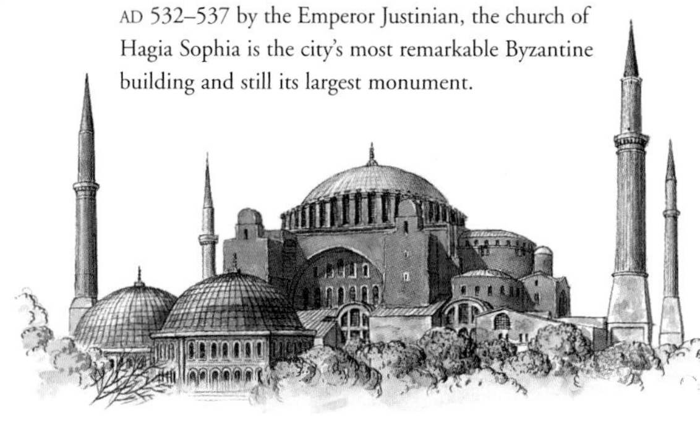

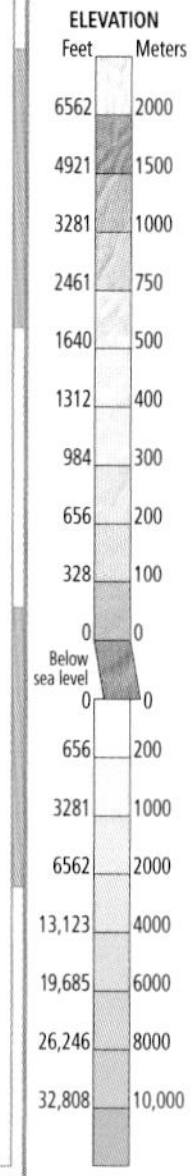

A Turkish invasion of Cyprus in 1974 led to the creation of Turkish and Greek sectors divided by a UN buffer zone.

Azerbaijan's oil is not as much in demand as it once was. Around 1900, Baku provided half the world's supplies.

SCALE 1:4,670,330
Lamberts Conformal Conic Projection
0 120 miles
0 120 kilometers

N O P Q R S T U V W

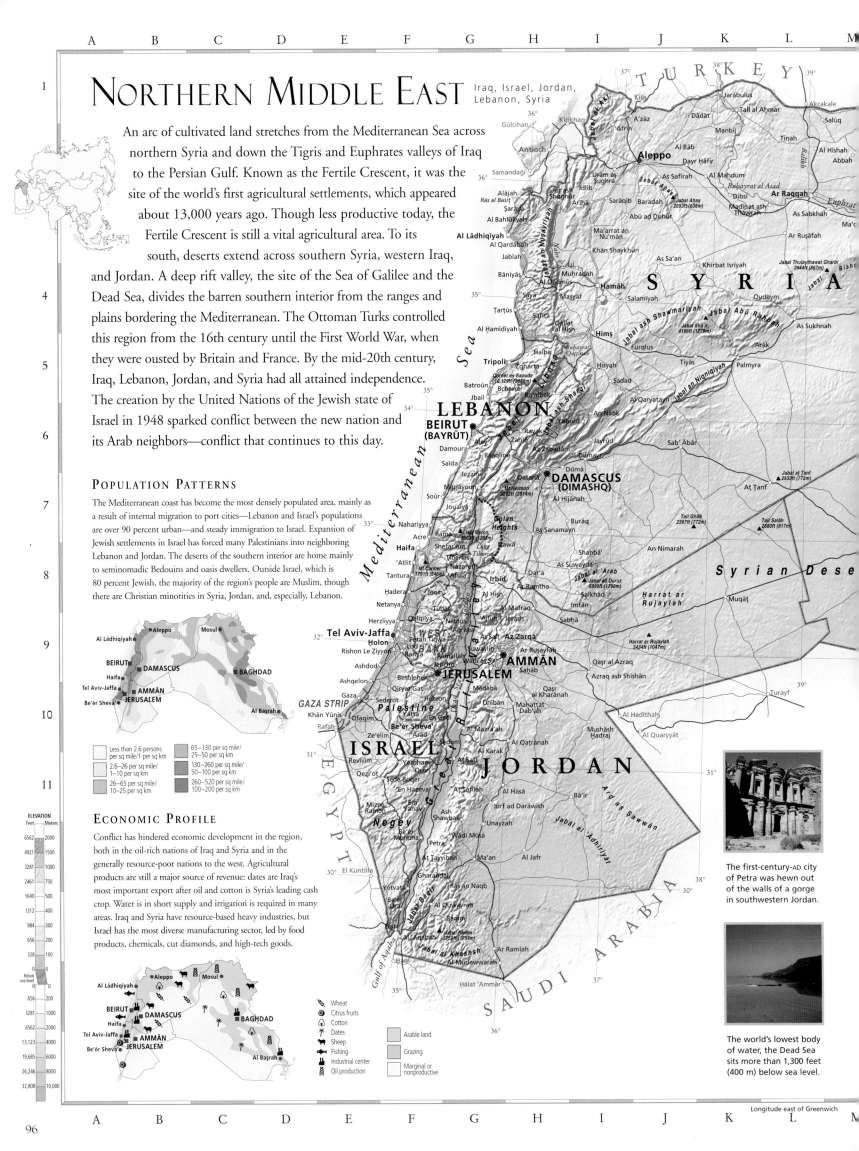

Northern Middle East

Iraq, Israel, Jordan, Lebanon, Syria

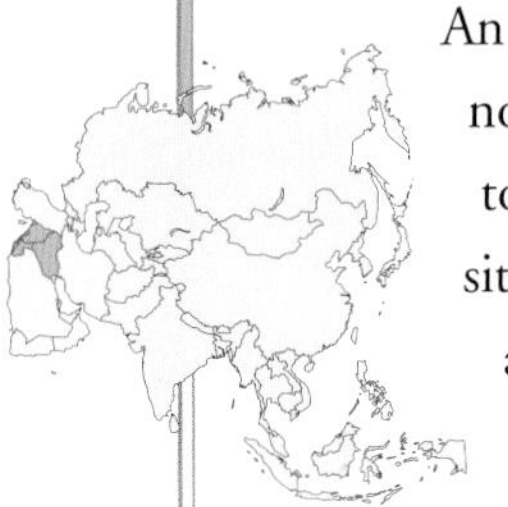

An arc of cultivated land stretches from the Mediterranean Sea across northern Syria and down the Tigris and Euphrates valleys of Iraq to the Persian Gulf. Known as the Fertile Crescent, it was the site of the world's first agricultural settlements, which appeared about 13,000 years ago. Though less productive today, the Fertile Crescent is still a vital agricultural area. To its south, deserts extend across southern Syria, western Iraq, and Jordan. A deep rift valley, the site of the Sea of Galilee and the Dead Sea, divides the barren southern interior from the ranges and plains bordering the Mediterranean. The Ottoman Turks controlled this region from the 16th century until the First World War, when they were ousted by Britain and France. By the mid-20th century, Iraq, Lebanon, Jordan, and Syria had all attained independence. The creation by the United Nations of the Jewish state of Israel in 1948 sparked conflict between the new nation and its Arab neighbors—conflict that continues to this day.

Population Patterns

The Mediterranean coast has become the most densely populated area, mainly as a result of internal migration to port cities—Lebanon and Israel's populations are over 90 percent urban—and steady immigration to Israel. Expansion of Jewish settlements in Israel has forced many Palestinians into neighboring Lebanon and Jordan. The deserts of the southern interior are home mainly to seminomadic Bedouins and oasis dwellers. Outside Israel, which is 80 percent Jewish, the majority of the region's people are Muslim, though there are Christian minorities in Syria, Jordan, and, especially, Lebanon.

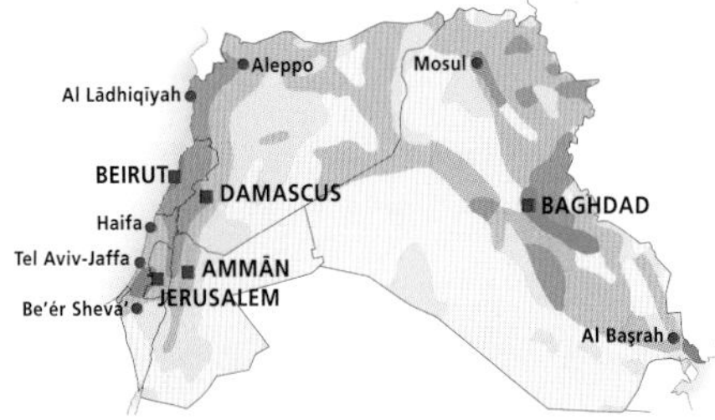

- Less than 2.6 persons per sq mile/1 per sq km
- 2.6–26 per sq mile/1–10 per sq km
- 26–65 per sq mile/10–25 per sq km
- 65–130 per sq mile/25–50 per sq km
- 130–260 per sq mile/50–100 per sq km
- 260–520 per sq mile/100–200 per sq km

Economic Profile

Conflict has hindered economic development in the region, both in the oil-rich nations of Iraq and Syria and in the generally resource-poor nations to the west. Agricultural products are still a major source of revenue: dates are Iraq's most important export after oil and cotton is Syria's leading cash crop. Water is in short supply and irrigation is required in many areas. Iraq and Syria have resource-based heavy industries, but Israel has the most diverse manufacturing sector, led by food products, chemicals, cut diamonds, and high-tech goods.

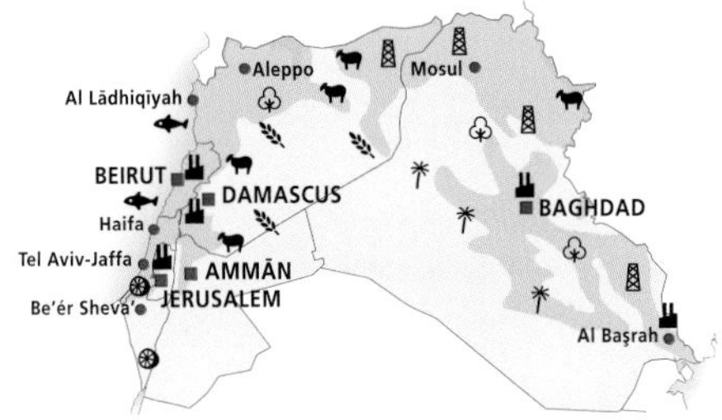

- Wheat
- Citrus fruits
- Cotton
- Dates
- Sheep
- Fishing
- Industrial center
- Oil production
- Arable land
- Grazing
- Marginal or nonproductive

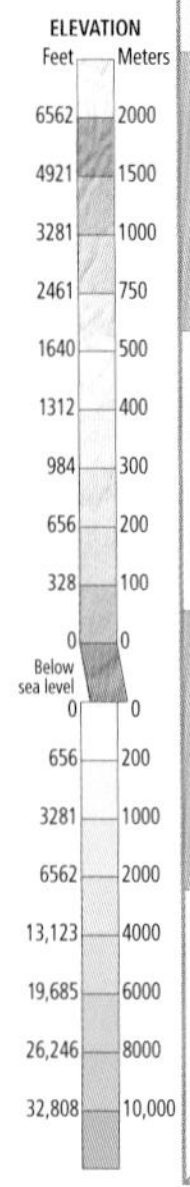

The first-century-AD city of Petra was hewn out of the walls of a gorge in southwestern Jordan.

The world's lowest body of water, the Dead Sea sits more than 1,300 feet (400 m) below sea level.

TURKEY
IRAN
IRAQ
KUWAIT
SAUDI ARABIA
Kurdistan
Al Jazīrah
BAGHDAD
(BAGHDĀD)
Mosul
Arbīl
Kirkūk
As Sulaymānīyah
Al Qāmishlī
Dayr az Zawr
Tikrīt
Sāmarrā'
Ar Ramādī
Al Fallūjah
Ba'qūbah
Al Muqdādīyah
Karbalā'
Al Ḩillah
An Najaf
Ad Dīwānīyah
Al Kūt
Al 'Amārah
An Nāşirīyah
As Samāwah
Al Başrah
Umm Qaşr
Az Zubayr
Khorramshahr
Ābādān
Al Fāw
Persian Gulf
Bubīyān Island
KUWAIT
(AL KUWAYT)
Ar Ruţbah
Hīt
'Ānah
Al Ḩadīthah
Abū Kamāl
Euphrates
Tigris
Great Zab
Little Zab
Jabal Ḩamrīn
Buḩayrat ath Tharthār
Hawr al Ḩabbānīyah
Buḩayrat ar Razāzah
Hawr al Ḩammār
Shaţţ al 'Arab
Ar Rihab
Ash Shāmīyah
Şaḩrā' al Ḩijārah
Z̧ahrat al Baţn
Al Haniyah
Wādī al Bāţin
Wādī Ḩawrān
Jabal Sinjār
Sar i Korawa 10,984ft (3351m)
Kūh-e Hājī Ebrāhīm 11,811ft (3600m)
Nişāb
Ash Shu'bah
Mehrān
Ilām
Qaşr-e Shīrīn
Sūsangerd
SCALE 1:3,571,429
Lamberts Conformal Conic Projection
100 miles
100 kilometers

Elat in Israel is a popular center for divers exploring the wonders of the Red Sea's extensive coral reefs.

The capital of Lebanon, Beirut was ravaged by civil war between 1975 and 1990, and is just starting to recover.

The Great Ziggurat of Ur is one of the best-preserved parts of the ancient city of Ur, near An Nāşirīyah in Iraq.

Jerusalem

Situated in a river valley linking the Mediterranean coast and the Dead Sea, the ancient city of Jerusalem is a place of pilgrimage for the adherents of three major faiths: Judaism, Christianity, and Islam. The Old City's many shrines reflect this diversity of beliefs, most notably around the Dome of the Rock. The oldest remaining Islamic temple and said to be the scene of Muhammad's ascension to heaven, it backs onto the Western Wall, the remains of a temple that constitute the most sacred site of Judaism. Nearby is the Church of the Holy Sepulchre, where Jesus is said to have been entombed before rising again.

Dome of the Rock

The Arabian Peninsula

Bahrain, Kuwait, Oman, Qatar, Saudi Arabia, United Arab Emirates, Yemen

Consisting of a broad plateau that slopes downward from a western coastal escarpment to low-lying eastern plains, the Arabian Peninsula is bounded by the Red Sea to the west, the Persian Gulf and Gulf of Oman to the northeast, and the Gulf of Aden and Arabian Sea to the south. Its interior is one of the most arid areas on Earth. Treeless, stony plains and vast sand deserts cover thousands of square miles. Rainfall is meager, and water flows only after seasonal showers along otherwise dry stream beds known as wadis. The Ottoman Turks occupied the western fringe of the peninsula from the 16th century until the early 20th century; by then Britain had established several protectorates on the east coast. An Islamic sect called the Wahhabis, led by the Saudi dynasty, held the interior from the 18th century, eventually founding Saudi Arabia in 1932. The discovery of oil has brought great wealth to that nation, as well as to the so-called Gulf States of Kuwait, Bahrain, Qatar, the United Arab Emirates, and, to a lesser extent, Oman.

Mecca The birthplace of the prophet Muhammad, Mecca is the most sacred site for Muslims, who are obliged by their faith to make at least one visit to the city, a pilgrimage known as the hajj. Two million pilgrims arrive each year, thronging the city and its temples, especially the Al-Haram Mosque. It encircles the Kaaba, a cubic stone shrine said to have been built originally by Abraham and Ishmael as a representation of God's house in heaven.

Population Patterns

The population is concentrated along the shoreline and in the marginally better-watered coastal ranges, with the fertile uplands of Yemen being the most densely inhabited zone. With the exception of the area around the Saudi capital of Riyadh, interior settlements are small and widely dispersed; most center on oases. The urban population is small in Yemen (26 percent) but large elsewhere, ranging from 78 percent in Oman to 96 percent in Kuwait. Culturally, the peninsula is homogenous, the vast majority of the inhabitants being Arab peoples who speak Arabic and follow Islam, which originated here.

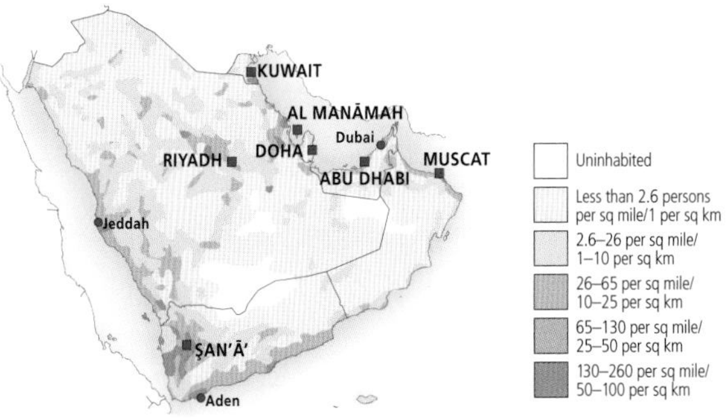

KUWAIT
AL MANĀMAH
Dubai
DOHA
RIYADH
MUSCAT
ABU DHABI
Jeddah
ṢAN'Ā'
Aden
Uninhabited
Less than 2.6 persons per sq mile/1 per sq km
2.6–26 per sq mile/ 1–10 per sq km
26–65 per sq mile/ 10–25 per sq km
65–130 per sq mile/ 25–50 per sq km
130–260 per sq mile/ 50–100 per sq km

Economic Profile

The Arabian Peninsula holds the world's largest petroleum reserves and enormous deposits of natural gas, and the oil and gas industries dominate the local economy. As well as a wide range of services including banking and printing, they support the manufacturing of metals, plastics, fertilizers, cement, and other products. Fossil fuels aside, however, the region is resource-poor. Only small pockets can be cultivated and many of these require irrigation. The major crops are dates and other fruits, coffee, and wheat. Sheep, goats, and camels are widely distributed, but have to graze over large areas to obtain sufficient food.

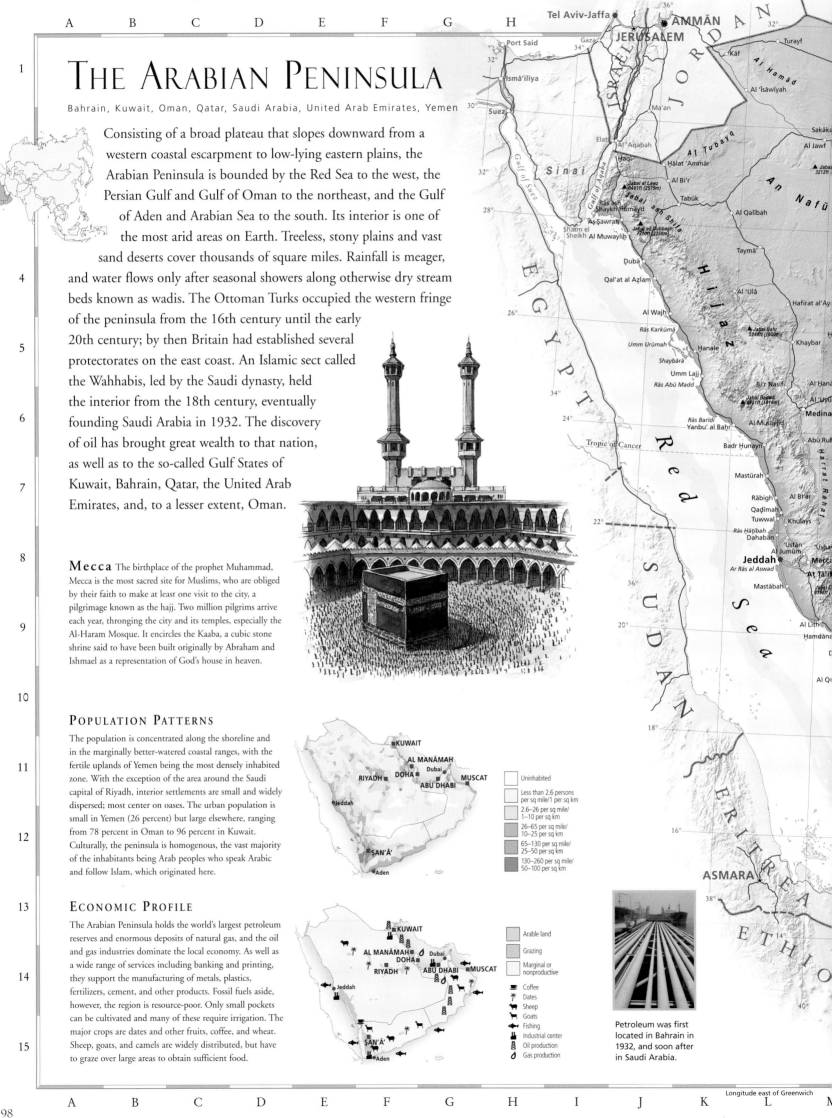

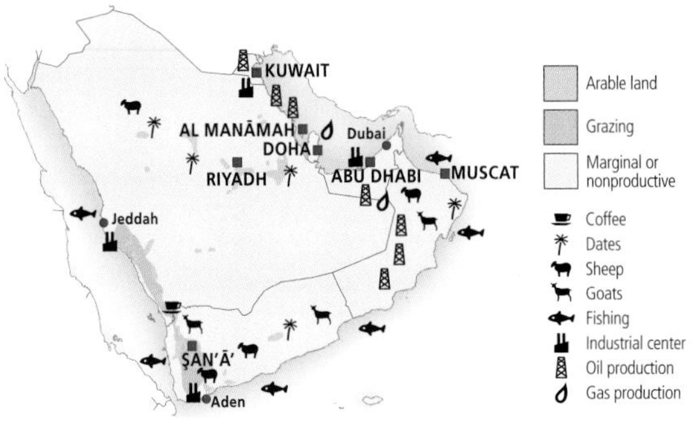

KUWAIT
AL MANĀMAH
Dubai
DOHA
RIYADH
ABU DHABI
MUSCAT
Jeddah
ṢAN'Ā'
Aden
Arable land
Grazing
Marginal or nonproductive
Coffee
Dates
Sheep
Goats
Fishing
Industrial center
Oil production
Gas production

Petroleum was first located in Bahrain in 1932, and soon after in Saudi Arabia.

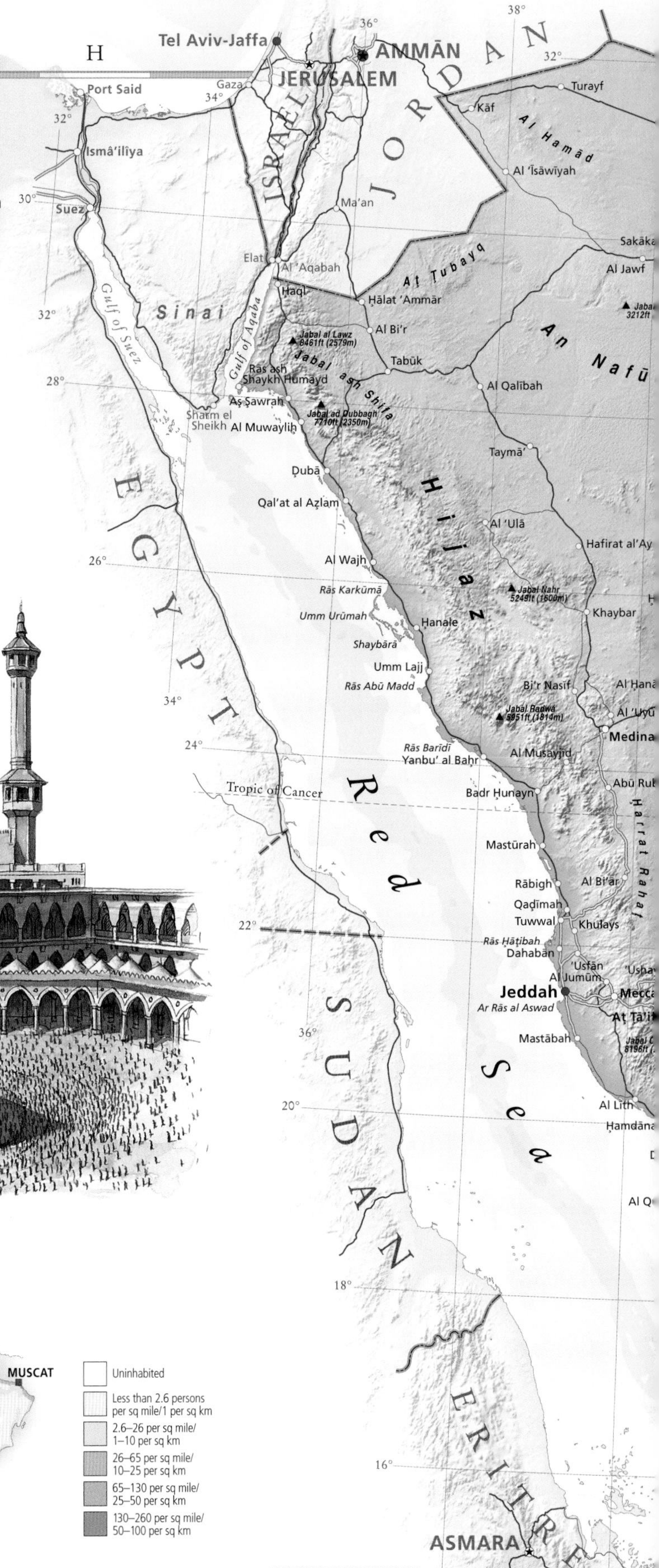

Tel Aviv-Jaffa
AMMĀN
JERUSALEM
JORDAN
ISRAEL
Port Said
Gaza
Ismâ'ilîya
Suez
Ma'an
Turayf
Kāf
Al Hamad
Al 'Isāwīyah
Sakākah
Al Jawf
Elat
Al 'Aqabah
Ḥaql
Sinai
Gulf of Suez
Gulf of Aqaba
Al Tubayq
Ḥālat 'Ammār
Al Bi'r
Tabūk
An Nafūd
Jabal al Lawz 8461ft (2579m)
Jabal ash Shifā
Rās ash Shaykh Ḥumayd
Aṣ Ṣawrah
Sharm el Sheikh
Al Muwayliḥ
Jabal ad Dubbagh 7710ft (2350m)
Al Qalībah
Taymā'
Ḍubā
Qal'at al Azlam
EGYPT
Hijaz
Al 'Ulā
Hafirat al Ay
Al Wajh
Rās Karkūmā
Umm Urūmah
Jabal Nahr 5249ft (1600m)
Khaybar
Ḥanale
Shaybārā
Umm Lajj
Rās Abū Madd
Bi'r Nasif
Jabal Radwa 5951ft (1814m)
Medina
Rās Barīdī
Yanbu' al Baḥr
Al Musayjīd
Badr Ḥunayn
Tropic of Cancer
Red Sea
Harrat Rahat
Mastūrah
Rābigh
Qaḍīmah
Tuwwal
Al Bi'ar
Khulays
Rās Ḥāṭibah
Dahabān
'Usfān
Al Jumūm
Jeddah
Ar Rās al Aswad
Mecca
Aṭ Ṭā'if
Mastābah
Al Līth
Ḥamdāna
SUDAN
Al Q
ERITREA
ASMARA
ETHIO
Longitude east of Greenwich

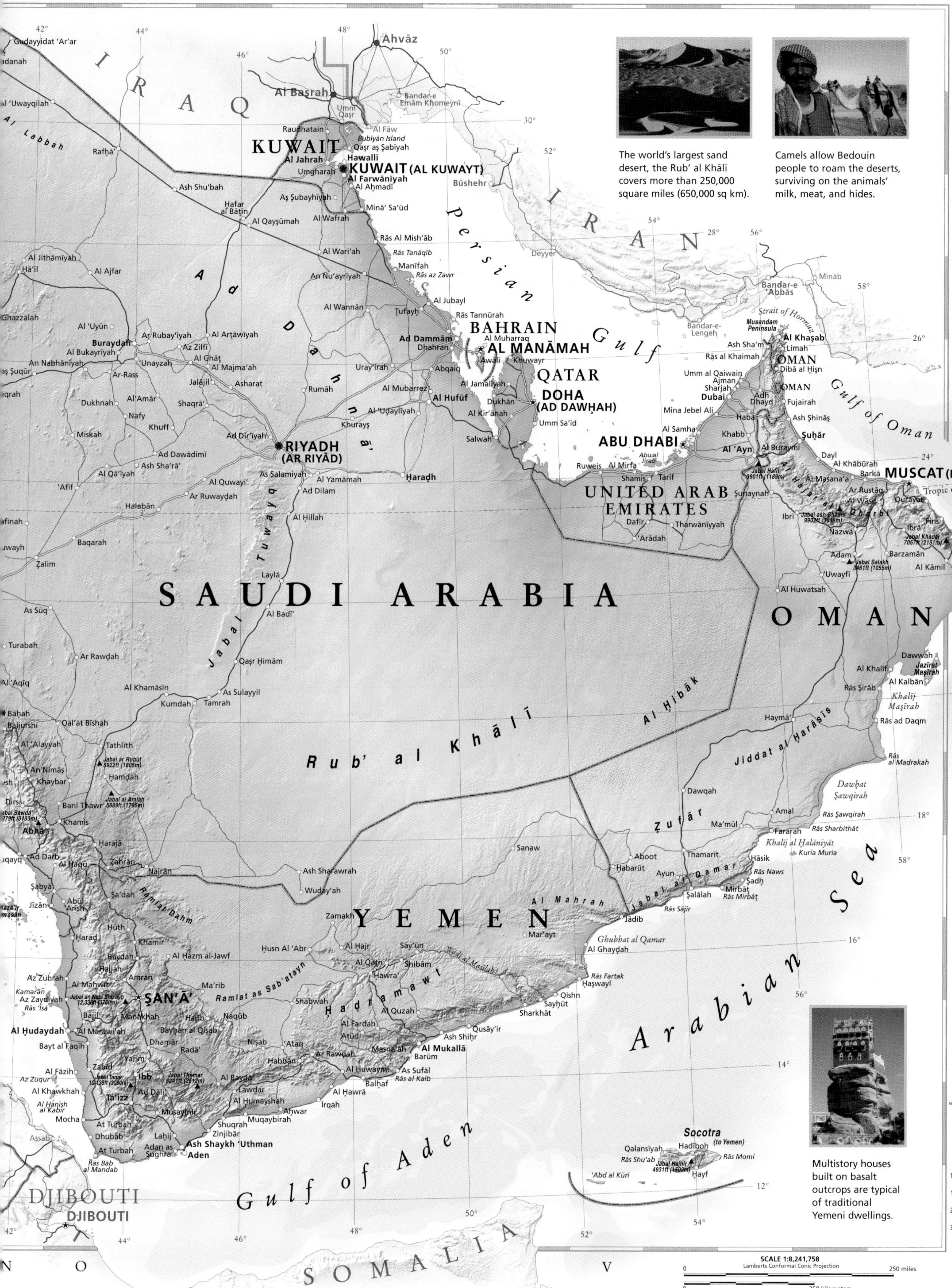

The world's largest sand desert, the Rub' al Khālī covers more than 250,000 square miles (650,000 sq km).

Camels allow Bedouin people to roam the deserts, surviving on the animals' milk, meat, and hides.

Multistory houses built on basalt outcrops are typical of traditional Yemeni dwellings.

SCALE 1:8,241,758
Lamberts Conformal Conic Projection
0 250 miles
0 250 kilometers

Afghanistan, Iran, and Pakistan

A high, mainly barren plateau dominates the western half of this region, occupying most of Iran and extending into Afghanistan and Pakistan. It is bounded in the northwest by the forested Elburz Mountains and in the west by the Zagros Mountains. In northeastern Afghanistan, it rises to the lofty summits of the Hindu Kush and the Karakorams, offshoots of the Himalaya; in Pakistan, its crumpled eastern fringe abuts the broad, low valley of the Indus River. More than 97 percent of the inhabitants of this rugged and mostly arid land are Muslims, and their religion has profoundly influenced the region's history. Pakistan was founded in 1947 as a home for India's Muslims; Iran has been ruled by Islamic clerics since a revolution in 1979; and in the late 1990s Afghanistan was run by the Taliban, a fundamentalist Islamic regime that was toppled by a U.S.-led invasion in 2001.

At 28,251 feet (8,611m), K2, in the Karakoram range, is the world's second-highest peak.

Thriving around 2500 BC, Mohenjo Daro, near Sukkur, Pakistan, was one of Indus Valley's first cities.

THE KHYBER PASS

One of just a few passes permitting travel between Central Asia and the Indian Subcontinent, the Khyber Pass has long been of strategic importance to locals and foreign powers, from the Persians, who used it to reach the Indus in the fifth century BC, to the British, who made it the focus of local operations in the late 19th century. Consisting of a narrow opening in the Safed Koh Range, the pass reaches its highest point of 3,543 feet (1,080 m) at Landi Kotal. Its road and rail links facilitate travel between Kabul in Afghanistan and Peshawar in Pakistan.

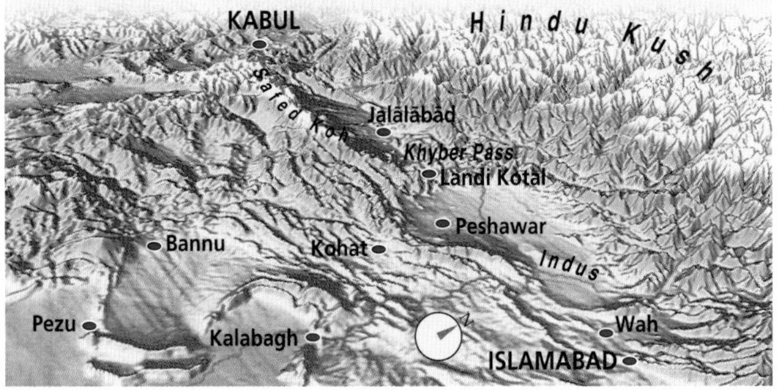

Iran's Dasht-e Kavīr is characterized by vast stony plains and low-lying salt pans (*kavirs*).

Iranian carpets, most of which are still woven by hand, are much in demand overseas.

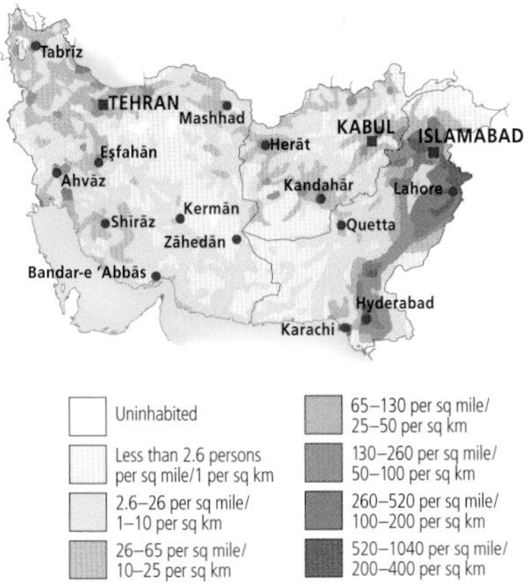

Population Patterns

Pakistan is the world's sixth most populous country, with over 150 million inhabitants—more than Afghanistan and Iran combined. Pakistanis cluster along the Indus River and especially in the Punjab, the country's heartland. Afghanistan has one of the world's fastest-growing populations; its major river valleys are the most densely inhabited areas, along with the string of towns between Kabul and Kandahār. The populations of Afghanistan and Pakistan are mainly rural; Iran, in contrast, is 67 percent urbanized, with one-fifth of its people living in or around Tehran.

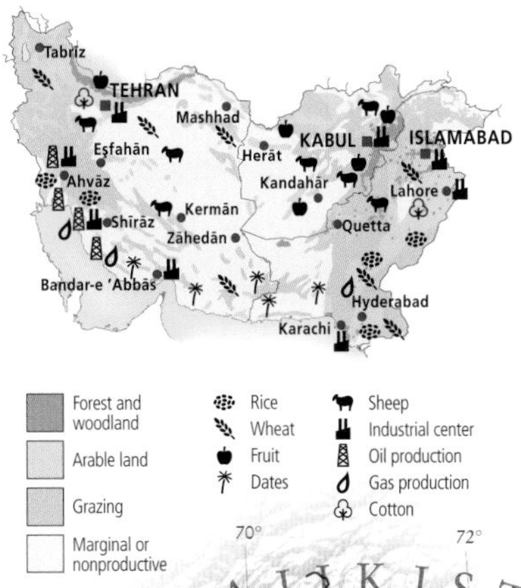

Economic Profile

An arid climate and poor soils confine intensive cultivation to the temperate uplands of northern Iran, the better-watered grasslands of northern Afghanistan, and Pakistan's heavily irrigated Indus Valley. Cotton, silk, and abundant sheep provide materials for widespread and varied textile production, especially carpet-weaving. Afghanistan has been ravaged by conflict and is one of the world's poorest nations. Pakistan is also impoverished, but Iran has derived significant wealth from its oil reserves. Both countries have diverse industrial sectors, including the manufacture of chemicals, steel, and machinery.

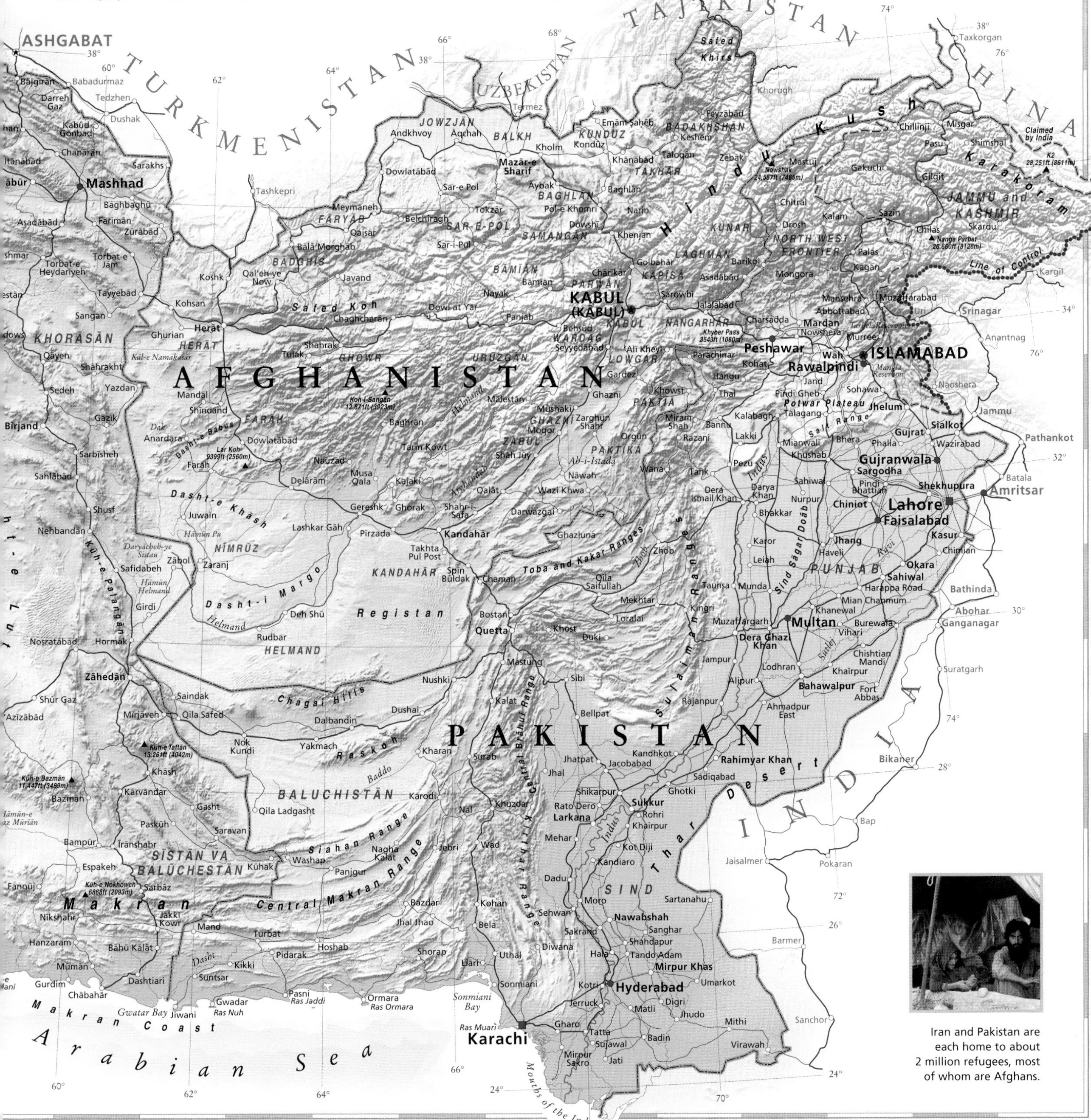

Iran and Pakistan are each home to about 2 million refugees, most of whom are Afghans.

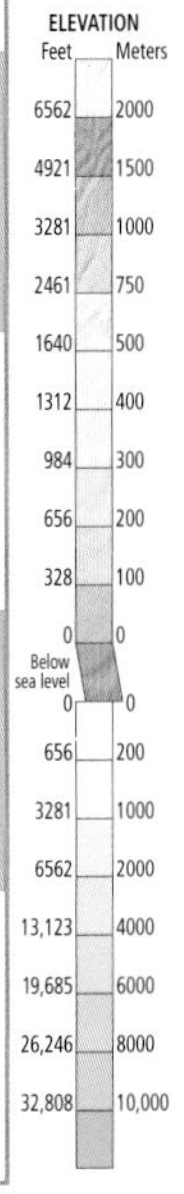

SCALE 1:7,692,308
Lamberts Conformal Conic Projection
0 — 250 miles
0 — 250 kilometers

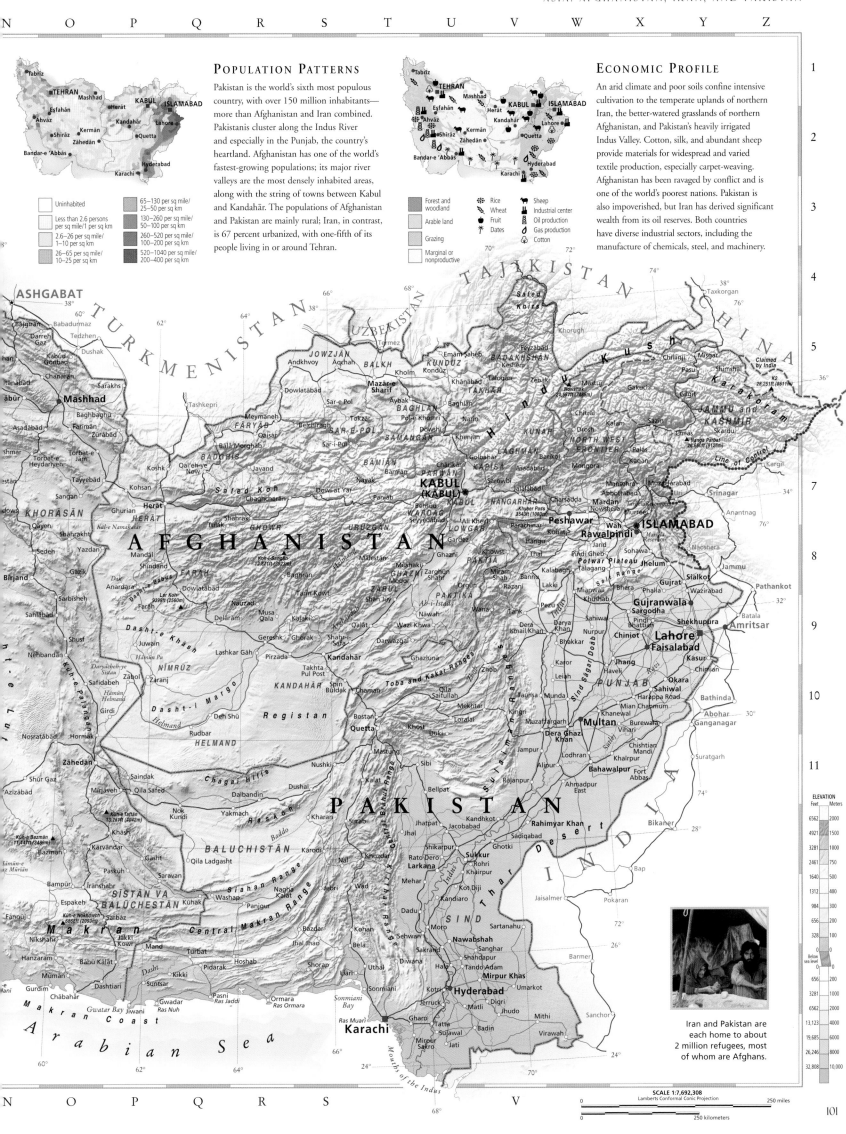

CENTRAL ASIA

Kazakhstan, Kyrgyzstan, Tajikistan, Turkmenistan, Uzbekistan

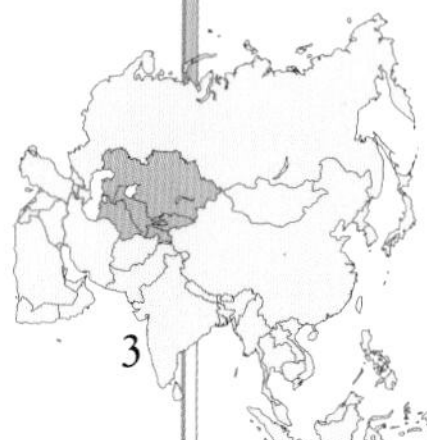

The peoples of Central Asia have long been linked by a shared Islamic religious and cultural heritage, traditionally pastoral and seminomadic lifestyles, and related, mainly Turkic languages. During the 19th century, they were brought even closer together when their lands were annexed by the Russian Empire. Subsequent Soviet control transformed an undeveloped region, rapidly industrializing farming, manufacturing, and mining, turning several villages into cities, and creating separate republics for each of the major ethnic groups—the Uzbeks, Kazaks, Tajiks, Turkmens, and Kyrgyz. After the fall of communism in 1991, all five republics became independent states. These nations occupy a wide, mainly arid and low-lying region. The grasslands of the Kazakh Steppe stretch across its northern third, spreading into Russia. South of the Aral Sea, deserts cover the Turan Lowland. In the east, a series of ranges climbs toward the Pamir and Tien Shan ranges, whose soaring peaks divide Central Asia from China.

Cotton is Turkmenistan's principal crop. Production centers on irrigated areas along the Amudar'ya River.

Russia's spacecraft-launching center is near Baykonur in Kazakhstan.

POPULATION PATTERNS

The scarcity of fresh water has restricted dense settlement to upland areas and the banks of major rivers, leaving the deserts and grasslands sparsely inhabited. During the Soviet era, Central Asia's population grew rapidly, due partly to an influx of Russians and Ukrainians and partly to improvements in medical services. Despite this, Central Asian society remains predominantly rural; indeed, with the departure of many Russians after the demise of the Soviet Union, the continuing focus on cotton production, and high birth rates in country areas, rural populations have grown recently, against the prevailing world trend.

Petropavlovsk
Ural'sk
Aktyubinsk
ASTANA
Ust'-Kamenogorsk
Kyzylorda
Dashkhovuz
TASHKENT
BISHKEK
ASHGABAT
DUSHANBE
Less than 2.6 persons per sq mile/1 per sq km
2.6–26 per sq mile/1–10 per sq km
26–65 per sq mile/10–25 per sq km
65–130 per sq mile/25–50 per sq km
130–260 per sq mile/50–100 per sq km
260–520 per sq mile/100–200 per sq km
520–1040 per sq mile/200–400 per sq km

ECONOMIC PROFILE

Central Asia's mineral reserves include oil and gas deposits near the Caspian Sea and supplies of coal, iron ore, and chromium in Kazakhstan; these support a variety of heavy industries. Three-fifths of the land is desert, and large areas are used for grazing. Crops can be grown only in fertile upland pockets and irrigated areas. Soviet emphasis on the production of coal and oil in Kazakhstan and cotton elsewhere not only created severe environmental problems, but left these nations dependent on just a few commodities. Recent expansion of the gas industry (Turkmenistan has the world's fifth-largest reserves) is part of an attempt to diversify produce and alleviate widespread poverty.

Petropavlovsk
Ural'sk
Aktyubinsk
ASTANA
Ust'-Kamenogorsk
Kyzylorda
Dashkhovuz
TASHKENT
BISHKEK
DUSHANBE
ASHGABAT
Cereals
Cotton
Beef cattle
Sheep
Fishing
Industrial center
Mining
Oil production
Gas production
Fruit and vegetables
Forest and woodland
Arable land
Grazing
Marginal or nonproductive

RUSSIAN FEDERATION
Ural'sk
ZAPADNYY KAZAKHSTAN
Aktyubinsk
AKTYUBINSK
Caspian Depression
Atyrau
ATYRAU
Astrakhan'
Fort-Shevchenko
Aktau
Caspian Sea
Aral Sea
Ustyurt Plateau
MANGISTAU
QORAQALPOGHISTON RESPUBLIKASI
Nukus
Dashkhovuz
DASHKHOVUZSKIY VELAYAT
TURKMENISTAN
Zaliv Kara-Bogaz-Gol
Turkmenbashi
BALKANSKIY VELAYAT
Turan Lowland
Karakum Desert
AKHALSKIY VELAYAT
ASHGABAT
IRAN
Mashhad
Longitude east of Greenwich

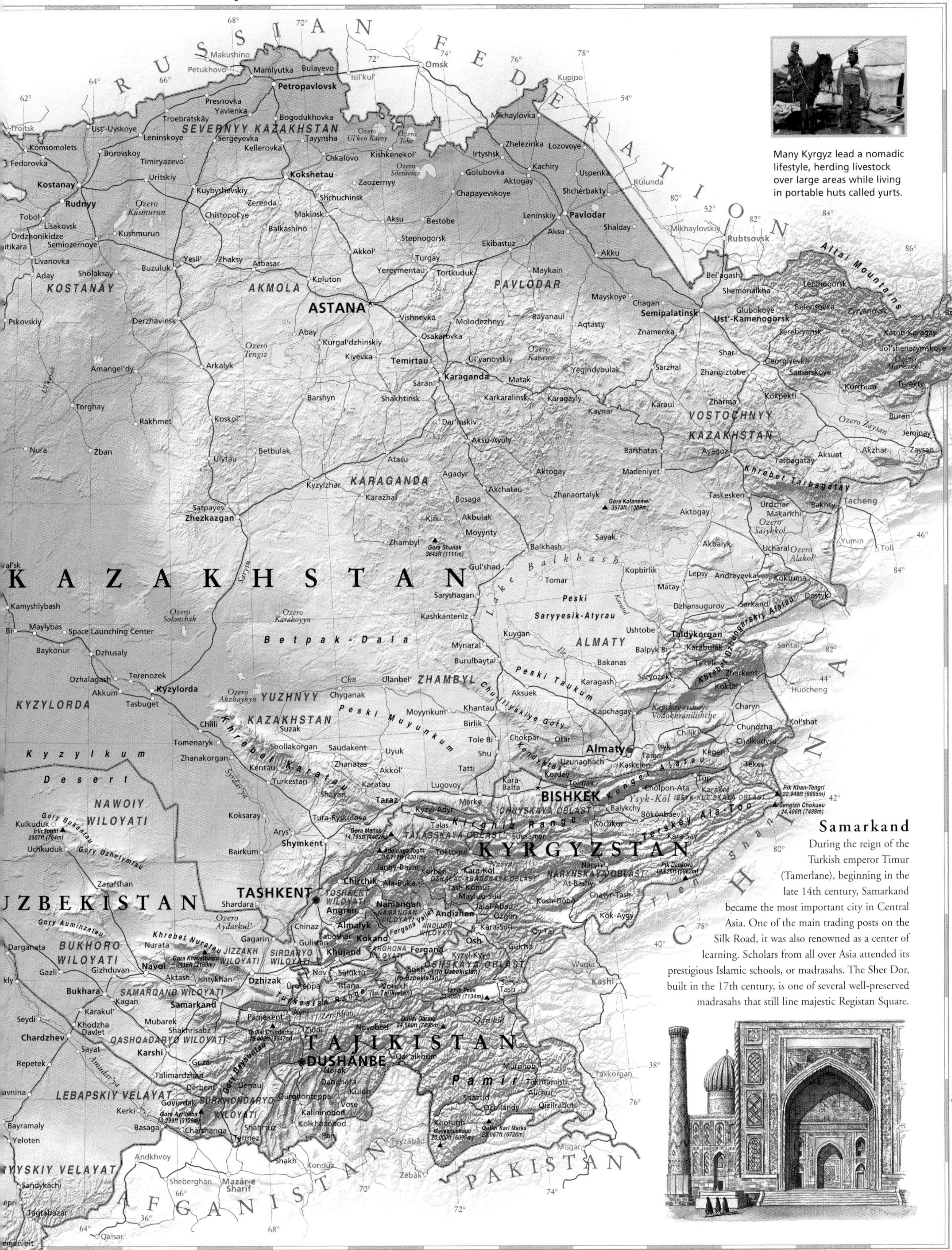

Many Kyrgyz lead a nomadic lifestyle, herding livestock over large areas while living in portable huts called yurts.

Samarkand

During the reign of the Turkish emperor Timur (Tamerlane), beginning in the late 14th century, Samarkand became the most important city in Central Asia. One of the main trading posts on the Silk Road, it was also renowned as a center of learning. Scholars from all over Asia attended its prestigious Islamic schools, or madrasahs. The Sher Dor, built in the 17th century, is one of several well-preserved madrasahs that still line majestic Registan Square.

SCALE 1:8,241,758
Lamberts Conformal Conic Projection
0 250 miles
0 250 kilometers

A B C D E F G H I J K L M N O

Southern Asia

Bangladesh, Bhutan, India, Maldives, Nepal, Sri Lanka

Sometimes referred to as the Subcontinent, this region is dominated by India, the world's seventh-largest and second-most populous country. It also includes the Himalayan kingdoms of Nepal and Bhutan, low-lying Bangladesh, and the island nations of Sri Lanka and the Maldives. From their dizzy heights, the mountains of the Himalaya drop steeply to the wide, low plain of the Ganges River. West of the Gangetic Plain, the Thar Desert spreads into Pakistan; to the south, the triangular Deccan Plateau occupies most of central and southern India. In the early 16th century, much of Southern Asia was united by the Muslim Mughal dynasty, which ruled until it was undermined by the rise of the Hindu Marathas in the 18th century. Britain controlled most of the region from the early 19th century until 1948; before withdrawing, it created the states of West Pakistan and East Pakistan, which later became Pakistan and Bangladesh, and granted independence to Ceylon, now Sri Lanka.

Population Patterns

More than one-sixth of the world's population lives in this region. India alone has more than 1 billion inhabitants and, given its growth rate—48,000 babies are born there every day—could surpass China as the world's most populous nation by 2050. High population densities occur on the Gangetic Plain and in the northeast—Bangladesh is one of the world's most densely populated countries—but only one-quarter of people live in cities. Most Indians and Nepalis are Hindu, whereas the majority of Bangladeshis are Muslim; Bhutan and Sri Lanka are predominantly Buddhist. Indigenous languages are many and varied, and English functions as a lingua franca.

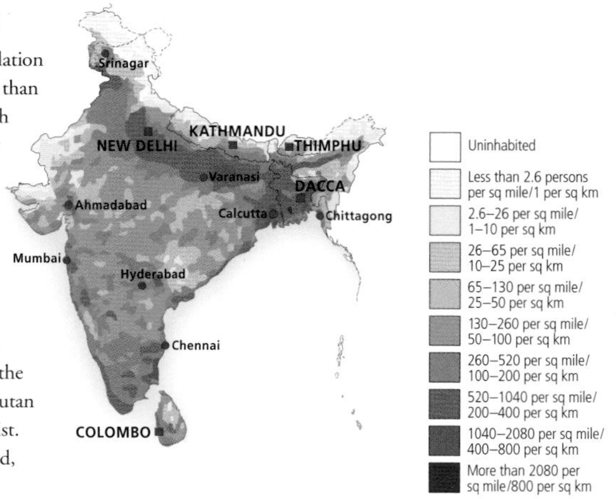

Economic Profile

The region's enormous population places great strain on its resources, which include large tracts of arable land (including 50 percent of India), forests, and minerals—India has the world's fourth-largest coal reserves, and oil and gas fields have been tapped in many areas. Most people are dependent on agriculture, yet output is insufficient to support the population: half of all Nepalis live below the poverty line and one-quarter of Indians are undernourished. The industrial sector is little developed in Bhutan, Bangladesh, and Nepal, but becoming increasingly sophisticated in India and Sri Lanka, where products include textiles, chemicals, computer software, and machinery.

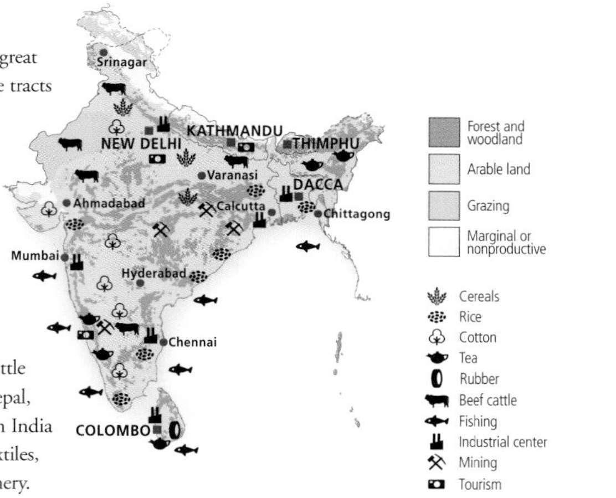

Tea is native to northeastern India. In the 19th century, the British greatly expanded its commercial cultivation.

In Sri Lanka, Tamil separatists have been waging war on the government since the 1980s.

The streets of Delhi are typical of India's densely populated urban centers.

SRI LANKA'S CENTRAL HIGHLANDS

On the island of Sri Lanka, low plains surround the country's mountainous core, an upland region known as the Central Highlands. Consisting of a series of plateaus, peaks, ridges, and basins cut by steep-sided gorges and cloaked with evergreen forest and grasses, the highlands reach their highest point of 8,281 feet (2,524 m) at Pidurutalagala. Much of the perimeter of the highlands is marked by massive cliffs, including one escarpment south of Nuwara Eliya called World's End, which plummets almost 4,000 feet (1,200 m) to the plains below.

The Himalaya and the Gangetic Plain

Bangladesh, Bhutan, Nepal, Northern India

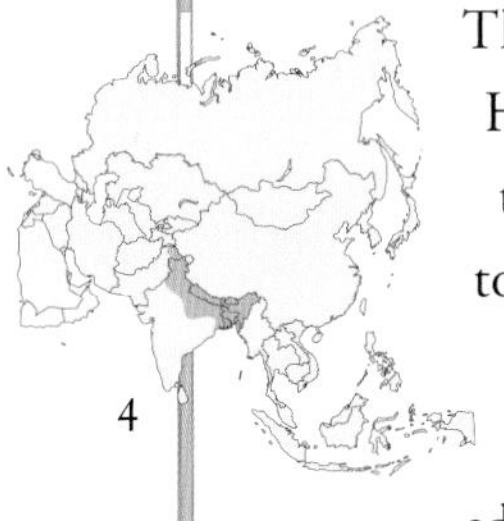

The world's tallest mountain range, the Himalaya forms a colossal barrier between the Subcontinent and Central Asia. Rising to the highest point on Earth, 29,035-foot (8,850-m) Mount Everest, it stretches for 1,550 miles (2,500 km) along the northern edge of India. Its southern flank yields abruptly to the densely populated and intensively farmed plain of the Ganges River. From its source in the western Himalaya, the Ganges flows south then east across northern India and into Bangladesh, branching repeatedly as it nears the Bay of Bengal to create one of the world's largest deltas. Cohesive states first took shape on the Gangetic Plain 3,000 years ago, and the valley was the heart of powerful Indian dynasties such as the Gupta (AD 300–550), the Mamluks (1206–1526), and the Mughals (1526–1761). Physical isolation helped preserve the autonomy of the kingdoms of Nepal, Sikkim, and Bhutan, though all were British protectorates during the 19th century, and in 1975 Sikkim acceded to India.

Up to 1,000 climbers a year now attempt an ascent of Mount Everest, which was first conquered in 1953.

Hindus view the Ganges as a holy river and visit places such as Varanasi to bathe in its waters.

The orchards of the fertile Kashmir Valley are one of India's most important sources of fruit and nuts.

Population Patterns

This region includes the Subcontinent's least and most crowded areas. Above 16,000 feet (5,000 m), the Himalaya is virtually uninhabited. In contrast, population densities are among the world's highest in Bangladesh, which averages 2,000 people per square mile (770 per sq km); in Calcutta, where up to 100,000 people occupy each square mile of the city (40,000 per sq km); and in irrigated parts of the Gangetic Plain. The majority of people live in rural areas—Bhutan had no towns until the 1960s—and population growth rates are high. The region's peoples are a mix of Indo-European and Tibeto-Burman groups, with the latter, who include the Newar and Sherpa, generally occupying the higher land.

- Uninhabited
- Less than 2.6 persons per sq mile/1 per sq km
- 2.6–26 per sq mile/1–10 per sq km
- 26–65 per sq mile/10–25 per sq km
- 65–130 per sq mile/25–50 per sq km
- 130–260 per sq mile/50–100 per sq km
- 260–520 per sq mile/100–200 per sq km
- 520–1040 per sq mile/200–400 per sq km
- 1040–2080 per sq mile/400–800 per sq km
- More than 2080 per sq mile/800 per sq km

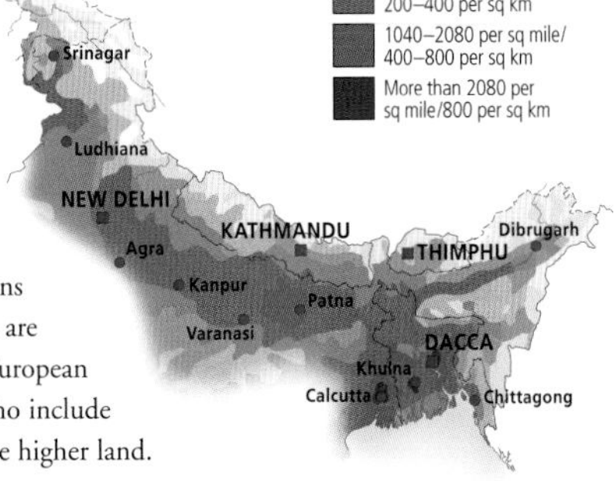

Economic Profile

The region includes many large cities, but is little developed and its people mainly poor. On the Gangetic Plain, irrigation is used to grow wheat, cotton, and sugar. In the wetter Brahmaputra Valley and Bangladesh, tea is cultivated on the hillsides, rice on the plains. Despite its rugged terrain, the Himalaya has extensive arable land—mainly in foothills, basins, and river valleys—which produces wheat, corn, millet, and potatoes. On the upper slopes, sheep, goats, and yaks are herded between seasonal pastures. Minerals, including gold, sapphires, copper, and iron ore, are widespread, though difficult to access. The Himalaya and cities such as Agra, Delhi, and Varanasi are major tourist attractions.

- Forest and woodland
- Arable land
- Grazing
- Marginal or nonproductive

- Cereals
- Rice
- Wheat
- Fruit
- Cotton
- Tea
- Dairy cattle
- Fishing
- Industrial center
- Tourism

Kathmandu Nepal's largest city, with a population of around 700,000, Kathmandu is the country's major commercial center and the hub of its transportation network and thriving tourist trade. It became the national capital following the unification of Nepal in 1769 and has been the seat of the ruling Shah dynasty ever since. Prior to unification, it was ruled for 500 years by the Malla kings. Most of the city's finest buildings date from this period, including the historic structures lining Durbar Square, the core of the old city. Prominent among these is the 16th-century Hanuman Dhoka, or Royal Palace, at the entrance to which stands the Jagannath Temple and a column topped by an image of King Pratap Malla, who built many of the surrounding temples.

THE HIMALAYAN RANGES

The Himalaya climbs from the Gangetic Plain in a series of great steps formed by parallel, increasingly elevated ranges. From the Tarai Plain in Nepal, for example, an escarpment ascends to the 4,000-foot (1,200-m) summits of the Churia Ghati Hills. To the north rise the yet-loftier Mahabharat Range and Lesser Himalaya, which enclose the Kathmandu and Pokhara valleys. The highest part of the system is the Great Himalayan Range, which in Nepal includes 9 of the world's 14 tallest peaks.

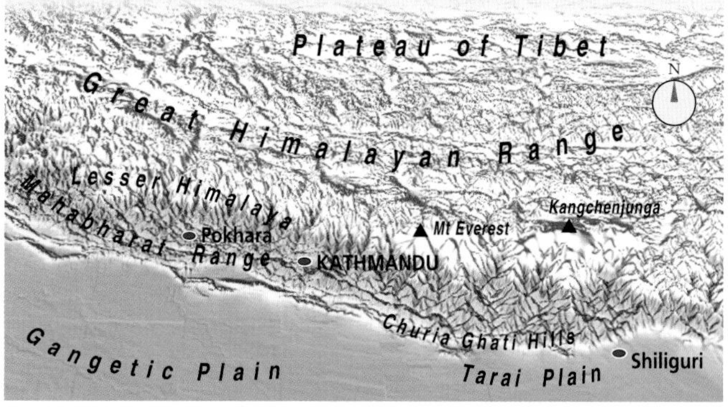

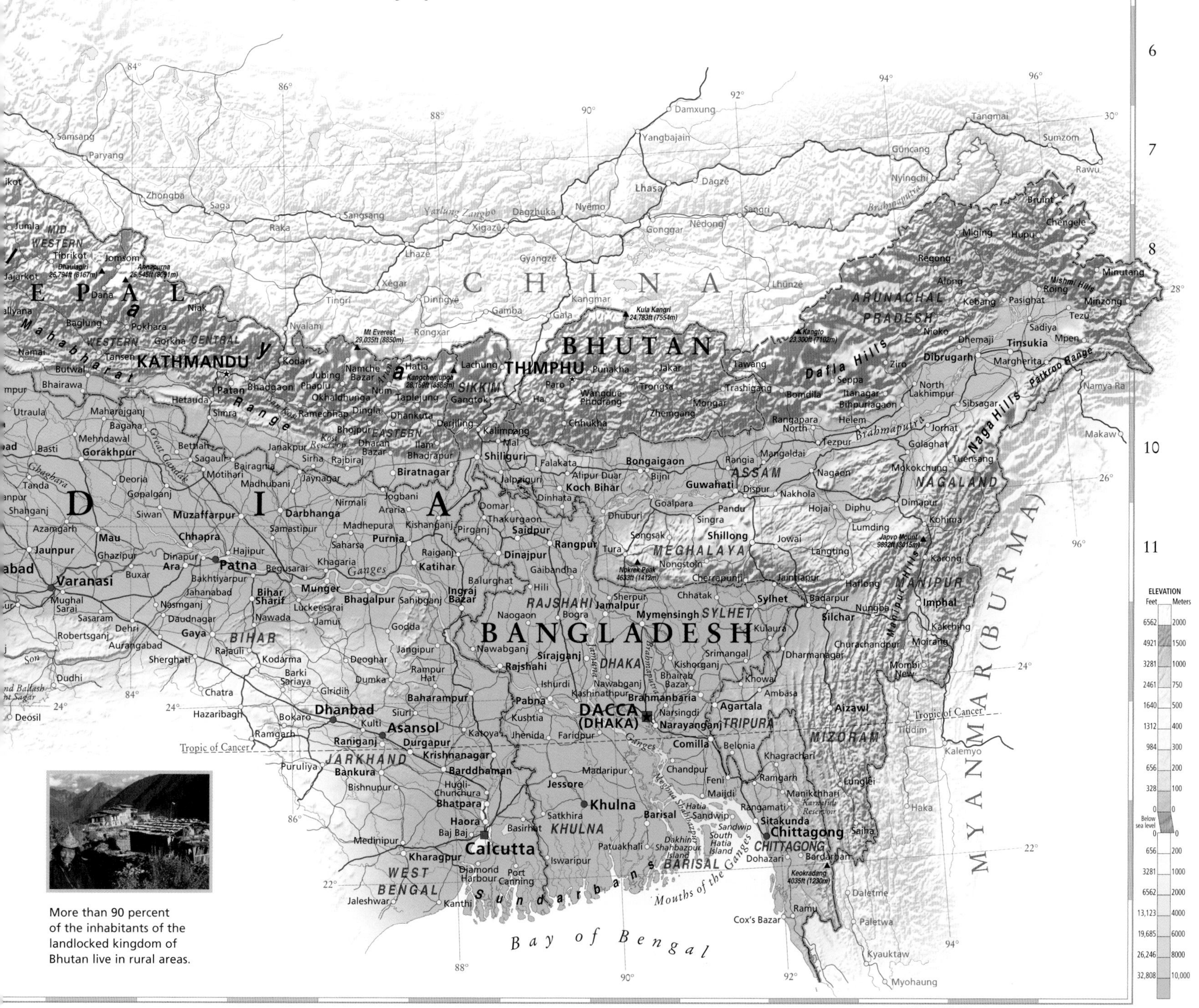

More than 90 percent of the inhabitants of the landlocked kingdom of Bhutan live in rural areas.

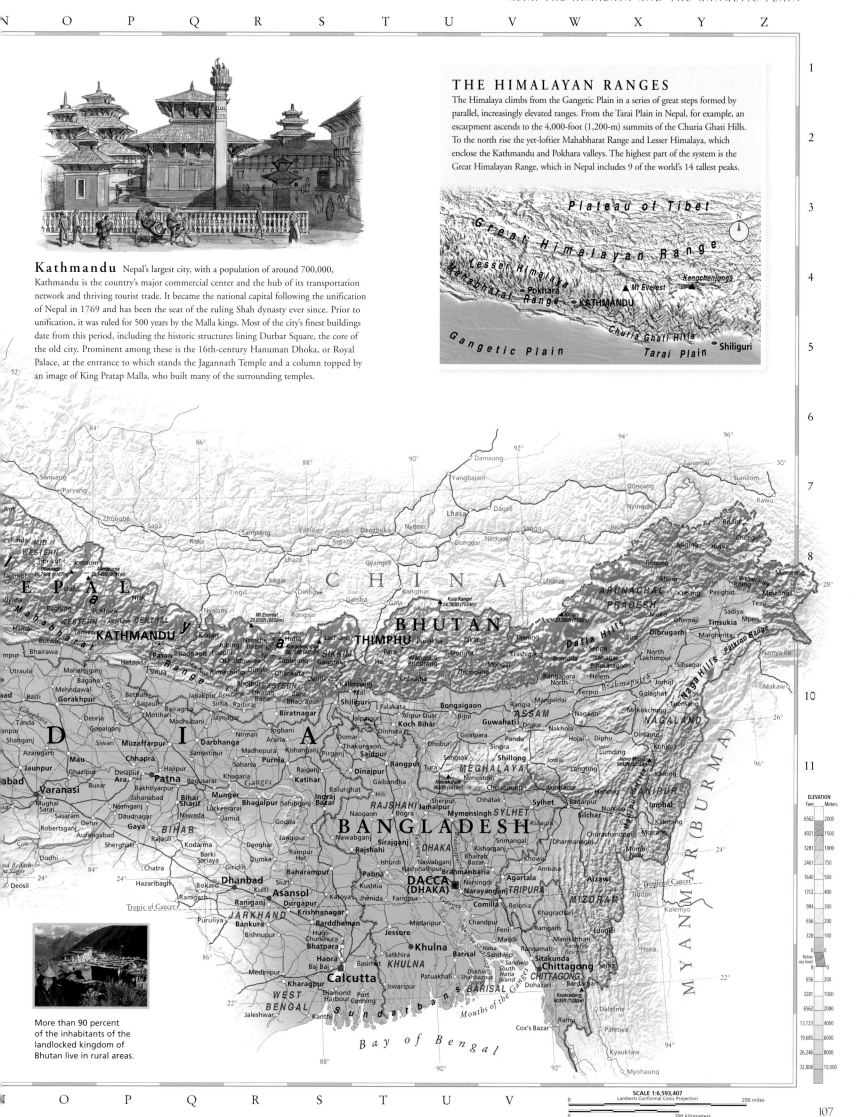

Eastern Asia

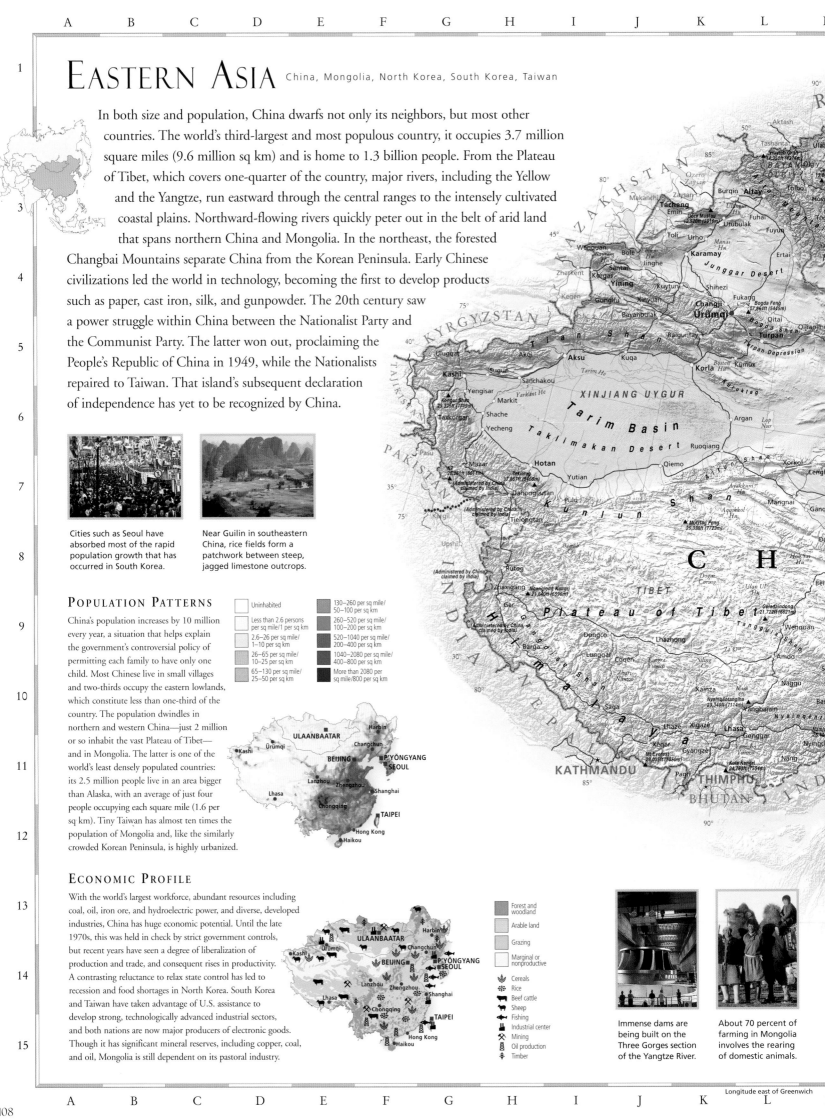

China, Mongolia, North Korea, South Korea, Taiwan

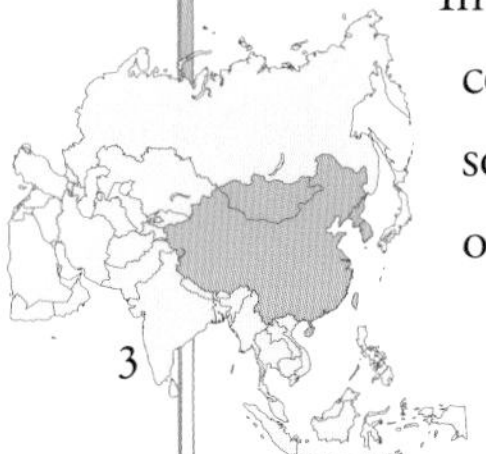

In both size and population, China dwarfs not only its neighbors, but most other countries. The world's third-largest and most populous country, it occupies 3.7 million square miles (9.6 million sq km) and is home to 1.3 billion people. From the Plateau of Tibet, which covers one-quarter of the country, major rivers, including the Yellow and the Yangtze, run eastward through the central ranges to the intensely cultivated coastal plains. Northward-flowing rivers quickly peter out in the belt of arid land that spans northern China and Mongolia. In the northeast, the forested Changbai Mountains separate China from the Korean Peninsula. Early Chinese civilizations led the world in technology, becoming the first to develop products such as paper, cast iron, silk, and gunpowder. The 20th century saw a power struggle within China between the Nationalist Party and the Communist Party. The latter won out, proclaiming the People's Republic of China in 1949, while the Nationalists repaired to Taiwan. That island's subsequent declaration of independence has yet to be recognized by China.

Cities such as Seoul have absorbed most of the rapid population growth that has occurred in South Korea.

Near Guilin in southeastern China, rice fields form a patchwork between steep, jagged limestone outcrops.

Population Patterns

China's population increases by 10 million every year, a situation that helps explain the government's controversial policy of permitting each family to have only one child. Most Chinese live in small villages and two-thirds occupy the eastern lowlands, which constitute less than one-third of the country. The population dwindles in northern and western China—just 2 million or so inhabit the vast Plateau of Tibet—and in Mongolia. The latter is one of the world's least densely populated countries: its 2.5 million people live in an area bigger than Alaska, with an average of just four people occupying each square mile (1.6 per sq km). Tiny Taiwan has almost ten times the population of Mongolia and, like the similarly crowded Korean Peninsula, is highly urbanized.

- Uninhabited
- Less than 2.6 persons per sq mile/1 per sq km
- 2.6–26 per sq mile/1–10 per sq km
- 26–65 per sq mile/10–25 per sq km
- 65–130 per sq mile/25–50 per sq km
- 130–260 per sq mile/50–100 per sq km
- 260–520 per sq mile/100–200 per sq km
- 520–1040 per sq mile/200–400 per sq km
- 1040–2080 per sq mile/400–800 per sq km
- More than 2080 per sq mile/800 per sq km

Economic Profile

With the world's largest workforce, abundant resources including coal, oil, iron ore, and hydroelectric power, and diverse, developed industries, China has huge economic potential. Until the late 1970s, this was held in check by strict government controls, but recent years have seen a degree of liberalization of production and trade, and consequent rises in productivity. A contrasting reluctance to relax state control has led to recession and food shortages in North Korea. South Korea and Taiwan have taken advantage of U.S. assistance to develop strong, technologically advanced industrial sectors, and both nations are now major producers of electronic goods. Though it has significant mineral reserves, including copper, coal, and oil, Mongolia is still dependent on its pastoral industry.

- Forest and woodland
- Arable land
- Grazing
- Marginal or nonproductive
- Cereals
- Rice
- Beef cattle
- Sheep
- Fishing
- Industrial center
- Mining
- Oil production
- Timber

Immense dams are being built on the Three Gorges section of the Yangtze River.

About 70 percent of farming in Mongolia involves the rearing of domestic animals.

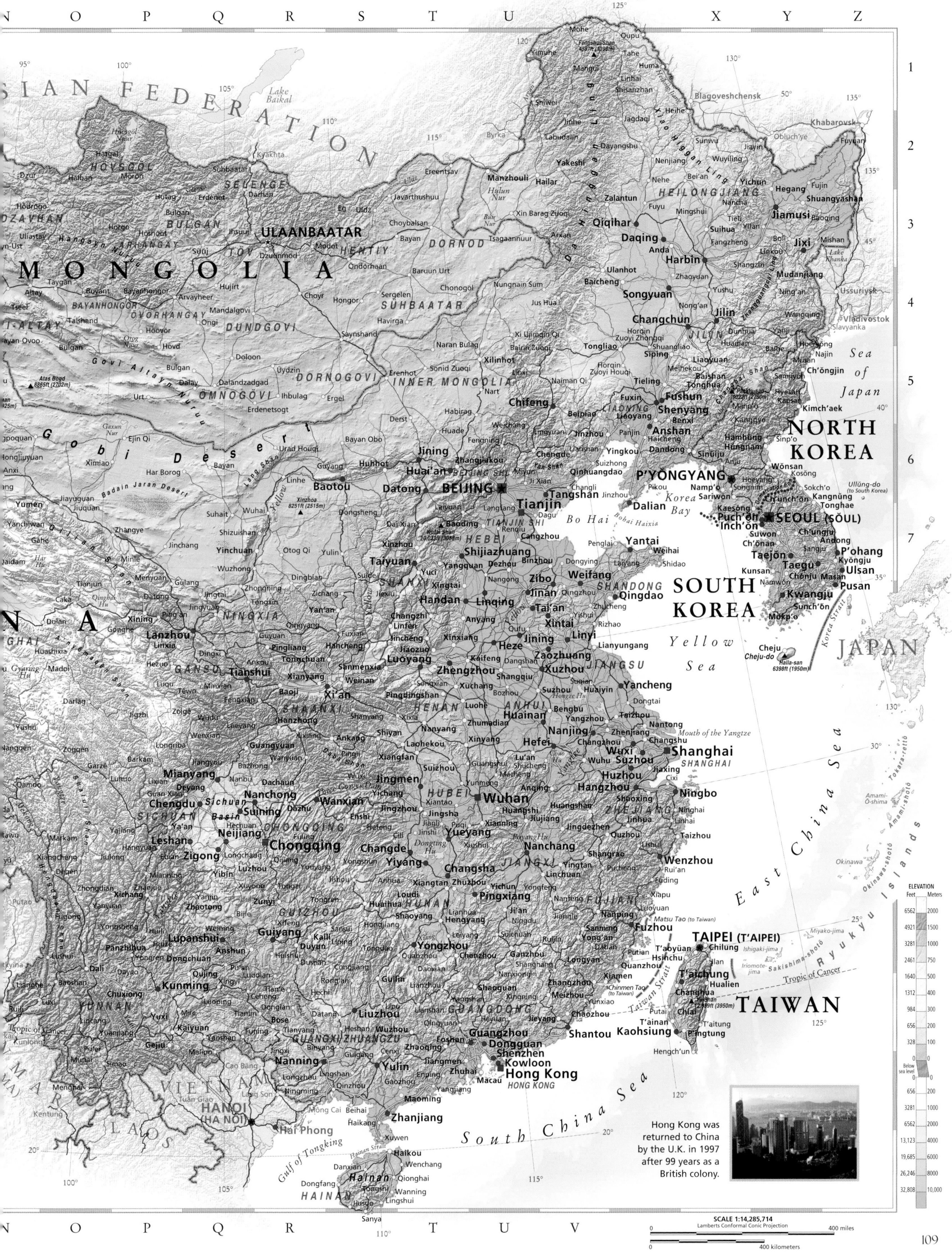

Hong Kong was returned to China by the U.K. in 1997 after 99 years as a British colony.

NORTHEASTERN CHINA AND KOREA

Northeastern China, North Korea, South Korea

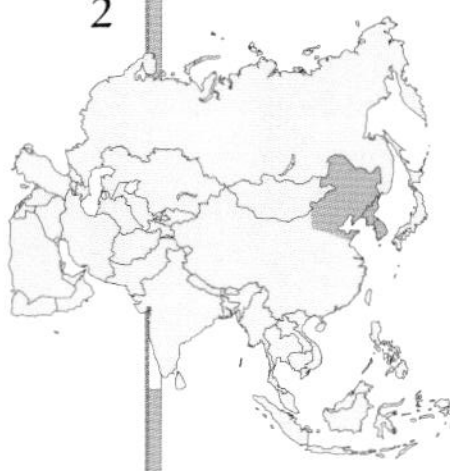

Northeastern China was formerly known as Manchuria and its major physical feature is the huge Manchurian Plain. This undulating lowland is bounded on three sides by mountains: the Da Hinggan Range in the west, which falls to the arid steppe of the interior; the Xiao Hinggan Range in the northeast, which lines the frontier with Russia; and a series of smaller ranges that extends into the Korean Peninsula. A narrow coastal strip links the southern end of the plain to China's populous eastern lowlands, site of the capital, Beijing. Manchuria was originally home to a distinctive people, the Manchus, and remained apart from early Chinese empires. Following the collapse of the Ming Dynasty in 1644, the Manchus took control of China, forming the Qing Dynasty. Its demise in the early 20th century allowed Japan to annex Korea and Manchuria before launching its offensive on the rest of Asia in 1941. The postwar division of Korea into Soviet- and U.S.-controlled sectors led to the Korean War of 1950–53 and the creation of communist North Korea and capitalist South Korea.

Monuments throughout North Korea mark the 46-year reign of Kim Il-Sung, who died in 1994.

The Great Wall of China stretches 4,500 miles (7,300 km) across the north of the country.

A major manufacturing center, Harbin is also the venue of China's best-known ice festival.

The 15th-century Forbidden City palace was so named because only the Ming emperor's court could enter.

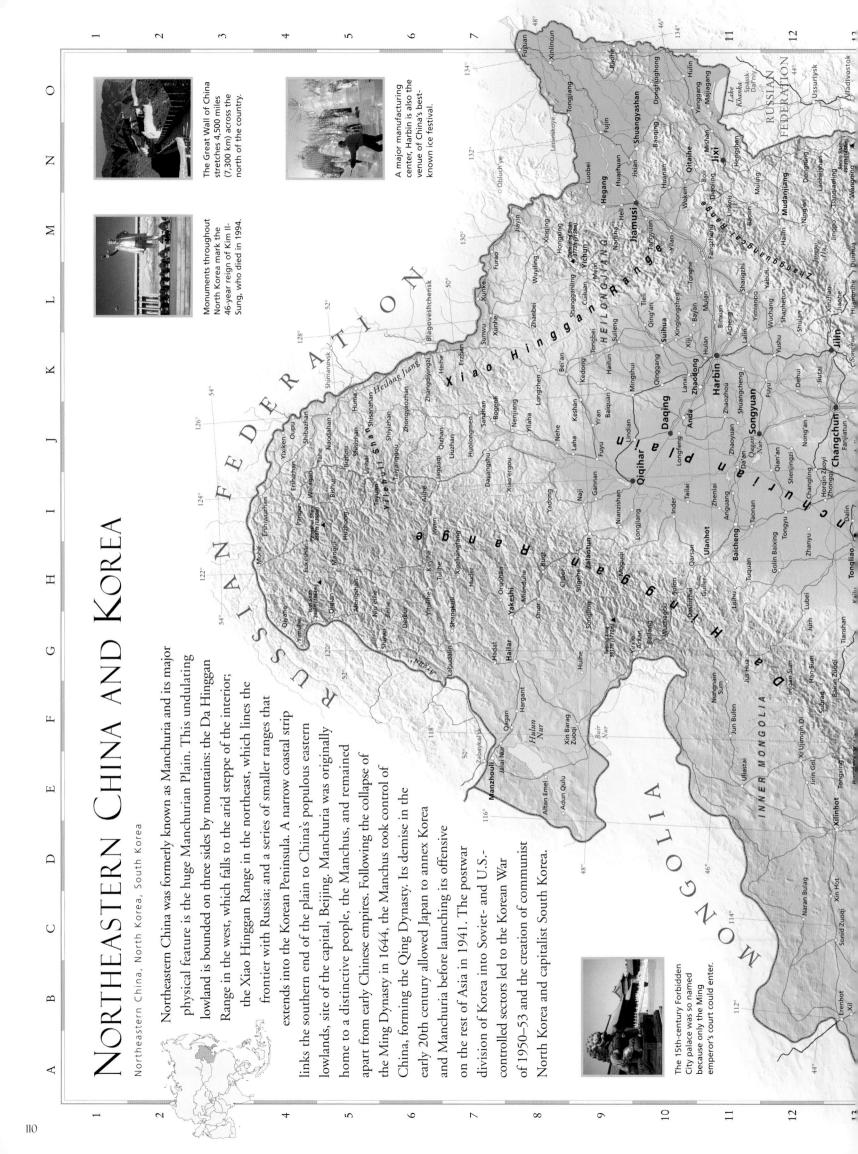

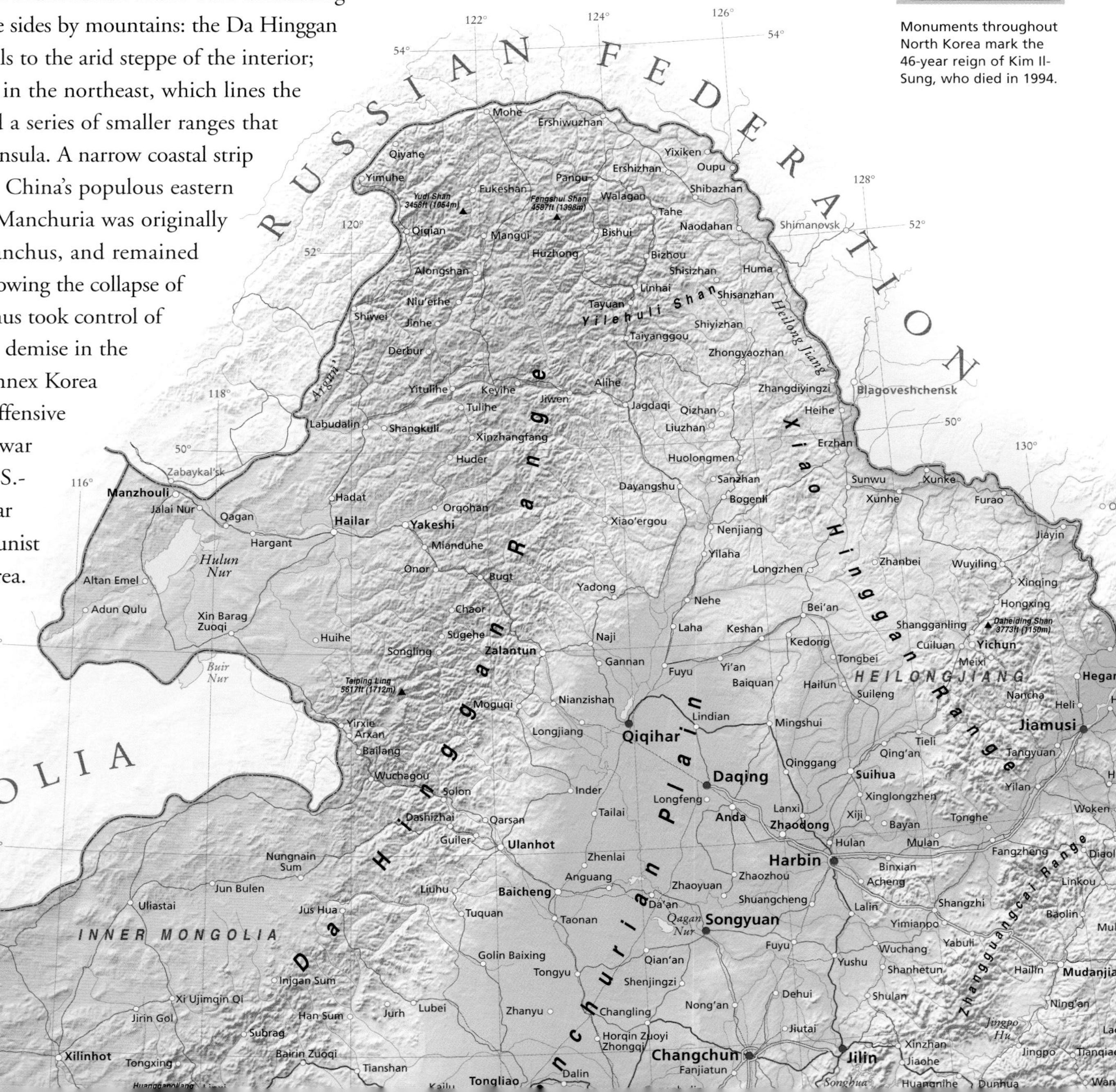

A B C D E F G H I J K L M N O
1 2 3 4 5 6 7 8 9 10 11 12

POPULATION PATTERNS

The region's inhabitants cluster on the highly developed and urbanized lowlands. In the north, Shenyang is the largest center, with 5 million inhabitants, and Harbin and Changchun both have populations of around 3 million. Yet even these cities are dwarfed by Beijing and Tianjin, which together accommodate more than 20 million people. In Korea, settlement favors the well-watered west coast; Seoul has close to 10 million inhabitants. Despite Manchuria's 250-year dominance of China, the Manchus have been almost totally assimilated by the Han (who now make up 90 percent of China's population), mainly as a result of Han migrations to underpopulated Manchuria throughout the Qing period.

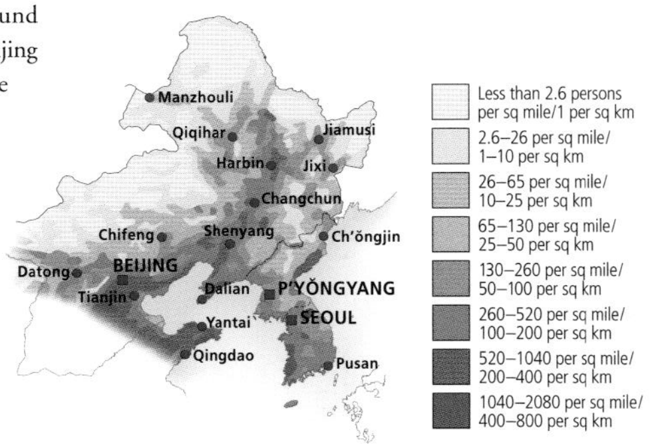

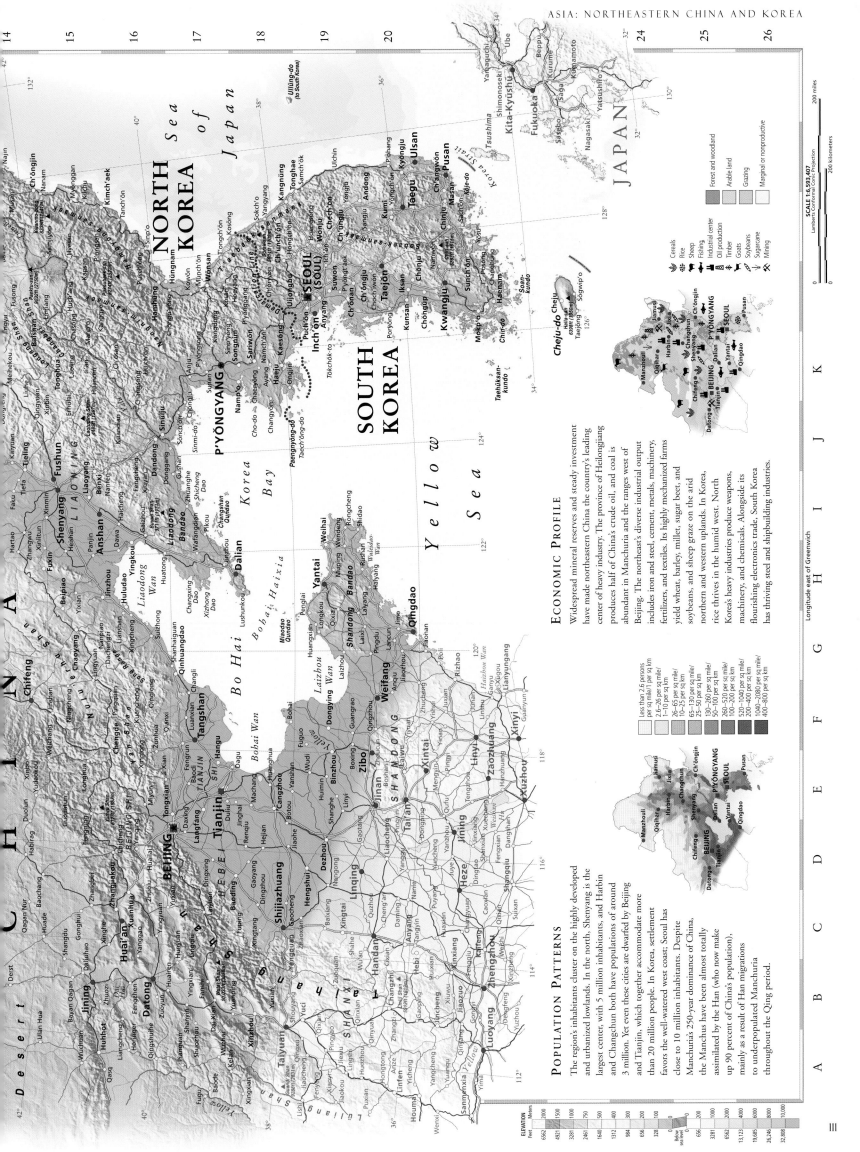

ECONOMIC PROFILE

Widespread mineral reserves and steady investment have made northeastern China the country's leading center of heavy industry. The province of Heilongjiang produces half of China's crude oil, and coal is abundant in Manchuria and the ranges west of Beijing. The northeast's diverse industrial output includes iron and steel, cement, metals, machinery, fertilizers, and textiles. Its highly mechanized farms yield wheat, barley, millet, sugar beet, and soybeans, and sheep graze on the arid northern and western uplands. In Korea, rice thrives in the humid west. North Korea's heavy industries produce weapons, machinery, and chemicals. Alongside its flourishing electronics trade, South Korea has thriving steel and shipbuilding industries.

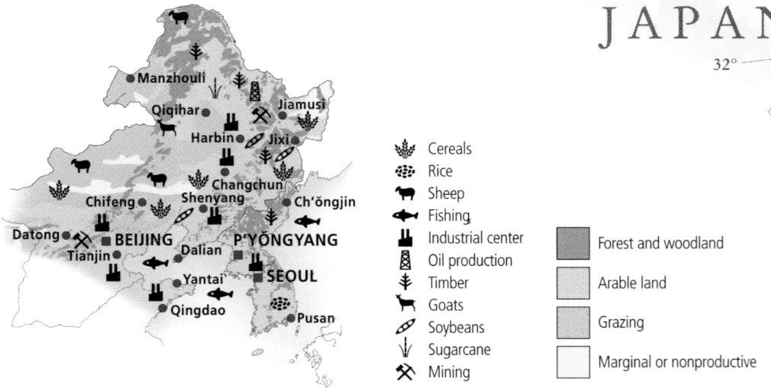

Southeastern China and Taiwan

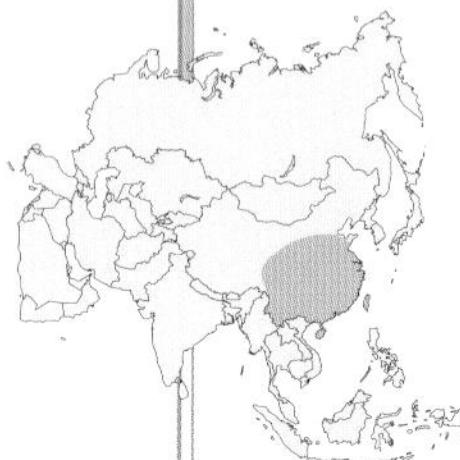

The valleys of the Yellow and Yangtze rivers were the cradles of Chinese civilization, giving rise to China's first agricultural societies, around 9,000 years ago, and its first urban society, the Shang Dynasty, around 1800 BC. They remained the center of development under the Han, who united most of this region in 221 BC. The Han gradually expanded their territory westward beyond the broad Sichuan Basin to the plateaus of modern-day Gansu and the deep valleys and steep slopes of Yunnan, and southward through the eroded limestone hills of present-day Guangdong to the humid lowlands lining the South China Sea. The Yellow and Yangtze valleys, and the plains that divide them, are still the cultural and economic heart of modern China, and were developed intensively by the communist government during the second half of the 20th century. Taiwan also underwent dramatic economic growth in the 20th century, initially under Japanese rule (1895–1943) and then under the leadership of the Chinese Nationalist Party, which controlled the island until 2000.

An ancient system of waterways dating from the 7th century, China's Grand Canal links Beijing with Hangzhou.

About 6,000 life-size terra-cotta warriors guard the tomb of Emperor Qin Shi Huang (259–210 BC), at Xi'an in Shaanxi province.

Population Patterns

The plains between the lower Yellow and Yangtze valleys now encompass 20 or so cities with more than 1 million inhabitants, including Shanghai, the nation's largest city, which has almost 13 million people. Other centers of population include the fertile Sichuan Basin, and the Pearl River Valley in the south. The Han are by far the largest ethnic group, but China's second-largest ethnic group, the Zhuang, cluster in the autonomous region of Guangxi Zhuangzu. Taiwan's mountainous terrain concentrates its large population on the northern and western coastal lowlands. Its indigenous Malayo-Polynesian inhabitants have, for the most part, been assimilated by Chinese immigrants, who began arriving in the 17th century.

Uninhabited
Less than 2.6 persons per sq mile/1 per sq km
2.6–26 per sq mile/1–10 per sq km
26–65 per sq mile/10–25 per sq km
65–130 per sq mile/25–50 per sq km
130–260 per sq mile/50–100 per sq km
260–520 per sq mile/100–200 per sq km
520–1040 per sq mile/200–400 per sq km
1040–2080 per sq mile/400–800 per sq km
More than 2080 per sq mile/800 per sq km

Economic Profile

The rich loess soils of the Yellow River have long provided wheat, millet, and cotton. Intensive farming of the fertile southeast and Sichuan Basin yields up to three crops a year, mainly of rice (of which China is the world's largest producer) and vegetables. Coal is abundant in Shanxi and Sichuan, which also has half of the nation's gas reserves; these resources underpin heavy industries in the interior. However, port cities such as Guangzhou and Shanghai have become the most prosperous centers, thanks to their long-established links with other Asian and Western trading partners and a recent influx of foreign investment. China is now the largest market for the exports—mainly electrical goods, metals, textiles, and plastics—that power Taiwan's thriving economy.

Forest and woodland
Arable land
Grazing
Marginal or nonproductive

Cereals
Rice
Beef cattle
Fishing
Industrial center
Mining
Oil production
Pigs
Gas production
Tea

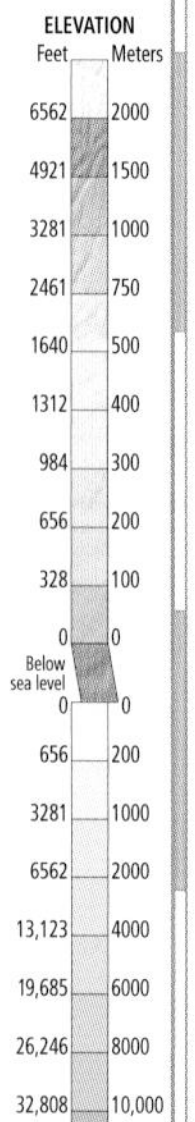

Though resource-rich, the island of Hainan remains relatively undeveloped. Most of its people live by farming and fishing.

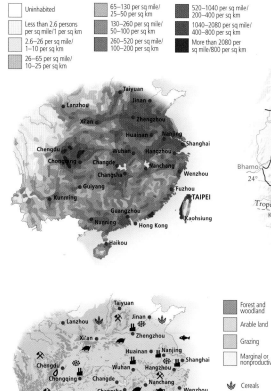

Longitude east of Greenwich

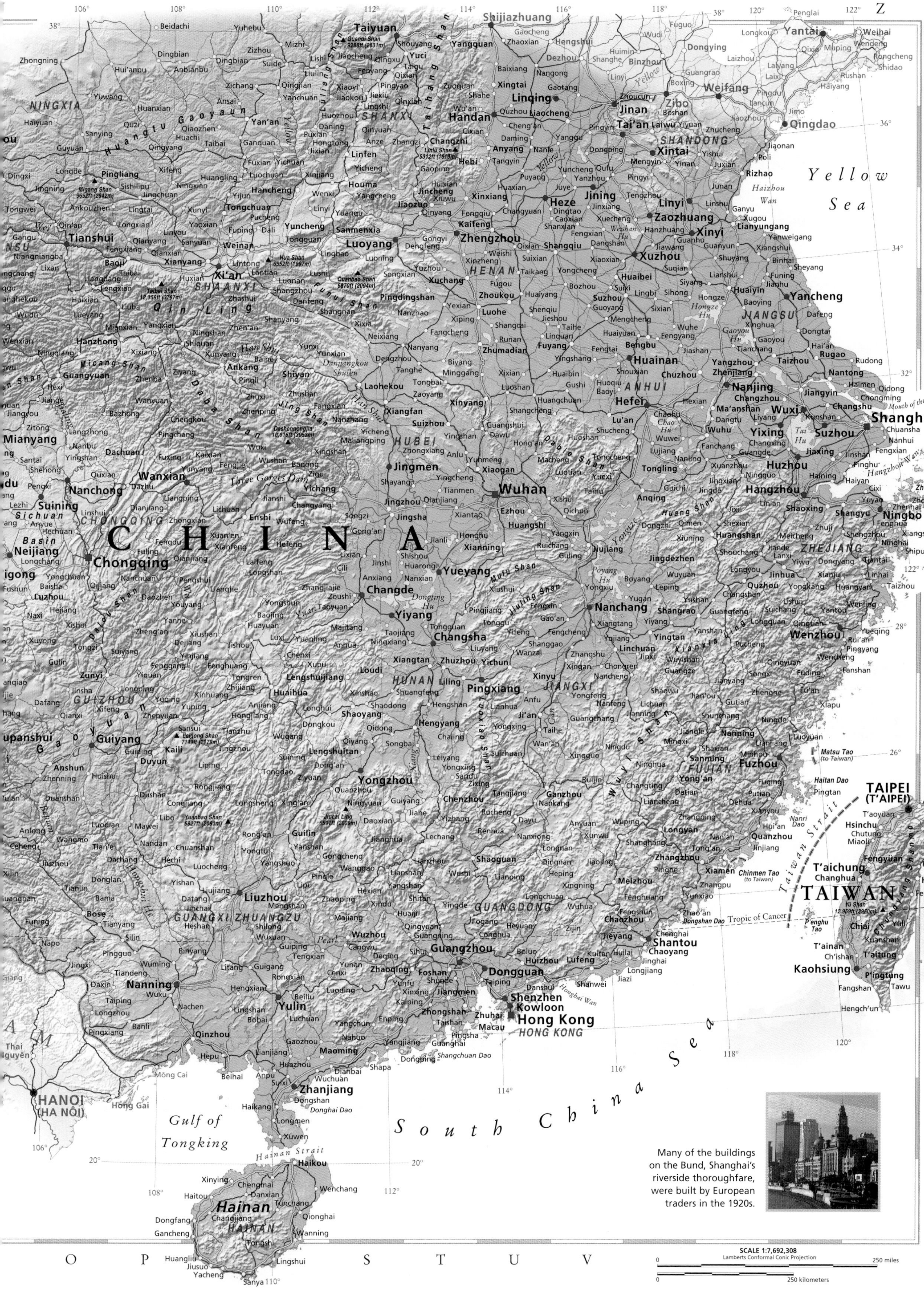

Many of the buildings on the Bund, Shanghai's riverside thoroughfare, were built by European traders in the 1920s.

Mainland Southeast Asia

Cambodia, Laos, Myanmar (Burma), Thailand, Vietnam

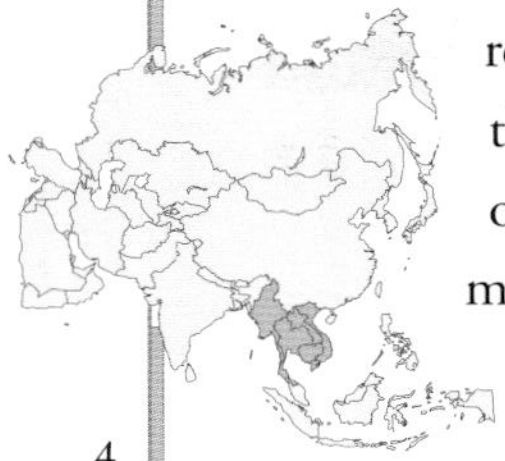

The Southeast Asian mainland consists of a broad peninsula—sometimes referred to as the Indochina Peninsula—that extends southeastward from the borders of Bangladesh, India, and China, as well as part of its narrow offshoot, the Malay Peninsula. From the Chinese Himalaya, a series of mountain ranges divided by rivers fans out over the north. On the southern lowlands, these rivers, which include the Irrawaddy and the Mekong, have formed wide alluvial plains and deltas. In the 16th century, towns along the coast became bases for European traders. By the late 19th century, Britain controlled Burma (now Myanmar) and France ruled Indochina (present-day Laos, Cambodia, and Vietnam). Post-World War II decolonization led to civil wars in Indochina, including the Vietnam War of 1964–75. Only Thailand resisted colonization throughout its history; its independence and political stability have helped it become the region's leading economic power.

Eastern Myanmar is the world's second-biggest source of illegal opium.

Most of the world's high-quality rubies come from mines in northern Myanmar.

Rice is the most widespread crop in Vietnam, covering approximately 80 percent of the country's arable land.

Population Patterns

Ethnically diverse, the inhabitants of Mainland Southeast Asia live mainly in rural villages. They are concentrated along the river valleys and especially the deltas of the Irrawaddy, Chao Phraya, Mekong, and Red rivers; they are sparsest in the heavily forested uplands of Cambodia, Laos, and the Myanmar–Thailand border. Though only about a quarter of the population is urban, the region has several large cities, most notably Bangkok (which is 20 times the size of Thailand's second city, Nonthaburi). Population growth is especially high in Laos and Cambodia; in contrast, Thailand has dramatically slowed its growth through social policies and education.

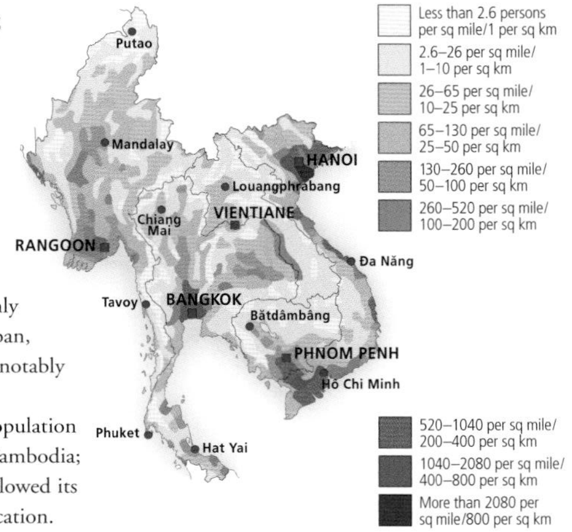

Putao
Mandalay
HANOI
Louangphrabang
VIENTIANE
Chiang Mai
RANGOON
Đa Nẵng
Tavoy
BANGKOK
Bătdâmbâng
PHNOM PENH
Hô Chi Minh
Phuket
Hat Yai
Less than 2.6 persons per sq mile/1 per sq km
2.6–26 per sq mile/ 1–10 per sq km
26–65 per sq mile/ 10–25 per sq km
65–130 per sq mile/ 25–50 per sq km
130–260 per sq mile/ 50–100 per sq km
260–520 per sq mile/ 100–200 per sq km
520–1040 per sq mile/ 200–400 per sq km
1040–2080 per sq mile/ 400–800 per sq km
More than 2080 per sq mile/800 per sq km

Economic Profile

Agriculture is still the principal source of employment and many people, especially in the poorer countries of Cambodia, Laos, Vietnam, and Myanmar, depend on subsistence cultivation, mainly of rice, corn, and vegetables. Cash crops including rubber, palm oil, sugar, and tropical fruits make up the bulk of exports, whereas most manufactured goods are imported. Industrial development is most advanced in Thailand, which produces textiles, foodstuffs, and electrical goods, and has a thriving tourist trade. Cambodia, Laos, and Myanmar continue to exploit their extensive forests for timber, whereas Thailand now limits harvesting following overexploitation. The area where Myanmar, Thailand, and Laos meet, known as the "Golden Triangle," is a major source of opium, from which heroin is derived.

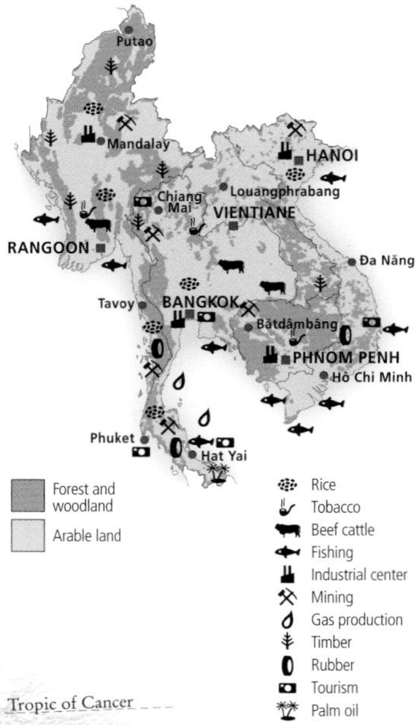

Putao
Mandalay
HANOI
Chiang Mai
Louangphrabang
VIENTIANE
RANGOON
Đa Nẵng
Tavoy
BANGKOK
Bătdâmbâng
PHNOM PENH
Hô Chi Minh
Phuket
Hat Yai
Forest and woodland
Arable land
Rice
Tobacco
Beef cattle
Fishing
Industrial center
Mining
Gas production
Timber
Rubber
Tourism
Palm oil

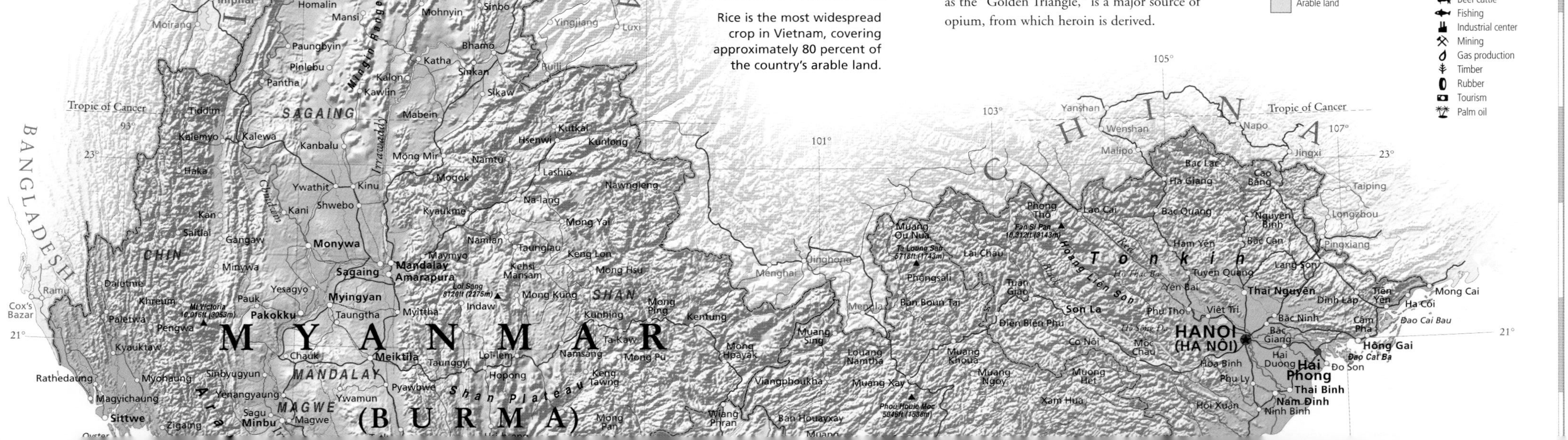

A
B
C
D
E
F
G
H
I
J
K
L
M
N
O
INDIA
CHINA
BANGLADESH
MYANMAR (BURMA)
Tropic of Cancer
KACHIN
SAGAING
CHIN
MANDALAY
MAGWE
SHAN
Shan Plateau
Hukawng Valley
The Triangle
Hkakabo Razi 19,296ft (5881m)
Saramati 12,552ft (3826m)
Fan Si Pan 10,312ft (3143m)
Hoang Lien Son
Tonkin
Putao
Myitkyina
Bhamo
Lashio
Mandalay
Amarapura
Sagaing
Monywa
Myingyan
Pakokku
Meiktila
Taunggyi
Sittwe
Minbu
Magwe
Kengtung
HANOI (HA NOI)
Hai Phong
Thai Nguyen
Nam Đinh
Thai Binh
Hong Gai
Viet Tri
Son La
Điên Biên Phu
Lao Cai
Mong Cai
Cox's Bazar

Cambodia, Laos, Myanmar (Burma), Thailand, Vietnam

Bangkok In 1782, Rama I, the King of Siam, as Thailand was then known, decided to relocate his royal court from the existing capital of Ayutthaya to a new site on the Chao Phraya River, 40 miles (64 km) to the south. The new capital, now called Bangkok, covered roughly 1.5 square miles (3.9 sq km), and at its heart, on the east bank of the Chao Phraya, lay the Grand Palace (below). In the second half of the 20th century, Bangkok expanded rapidly and its population grew sixfold. The well-preserved Grand Palace now sits amid a vast sea of modern buildings traversed by an enormous volume of slow-moving traffic and thronged by an evergrowing and increasingly cosmopolitan urban population.

Between the 9th and 15th centuries, Angkor, near Siem Reap, Cambodia, was the capital of the Khmer Empire.

Widely used as draft animals, elephants are also employed to transport tourists.

Maritime Southeast Asia

Brunei, East Timor, Indonesia, Malaysia, Philippines, Singapore

Scattered around the southeastern fringe of the Asian mainland are more than 20,000 islands. Ranging from the massive, rain-forest-cloaked landmass of Borneo—the world's third-largest island—to the tiny atolls of the Banda Sea, they form the largest island group on Earth, the Malay Archipelago. Divided mainly between the large countries of Malaysia (which includes the southern part of the Malay Peninsula), the Philippines, and Indonesia, it is also the site of the small states of Singapore, East Timor, and Brunei. Beginning in the 16th century, intense competition for control of the lucrative spice trade led various European powers to colonize large areas of the region. The Dutch seized most of present-day Indonesia, the British gradually gained control of Malaysia, the Portuguese established a foothold in Timor, and the Spanish occupied the Philippines (from where they were ousted by the U.S.A. in 1898). Since decolonization in the second half of the 20th century, Indonesia and Malaysia, in particular, have become major regional powers.

Java's Volcanoes

The islands of southern Indonesia formed as a result of subduction of the Indo-Australian Plate beneath the Eurasian Plate. This process continues to fuel the country's 76 volcanoes (more than any other nation), 22 of which are on Java. Sporadic and sometimes destructive volcanic activity takes place at Gunung Semeru in the east, Gunung Merapi near Yogyakarta, and Galunggung in the west. But the largest recorded eruption occurred on August 28, 1883, when Krakatau (Krakatoa) exploded, unleashing a tidal wave that killed 36,000 people.

Native to Borneo and Sumatra, the orangutan has become endangered due to habitat loss.

East Timor attained independence in 2002, following almost 25 years of Indonesian rule.

Controlled by the Dutch from 1619 to 1941, Jakarta became the capital of Indonesia in 1949.

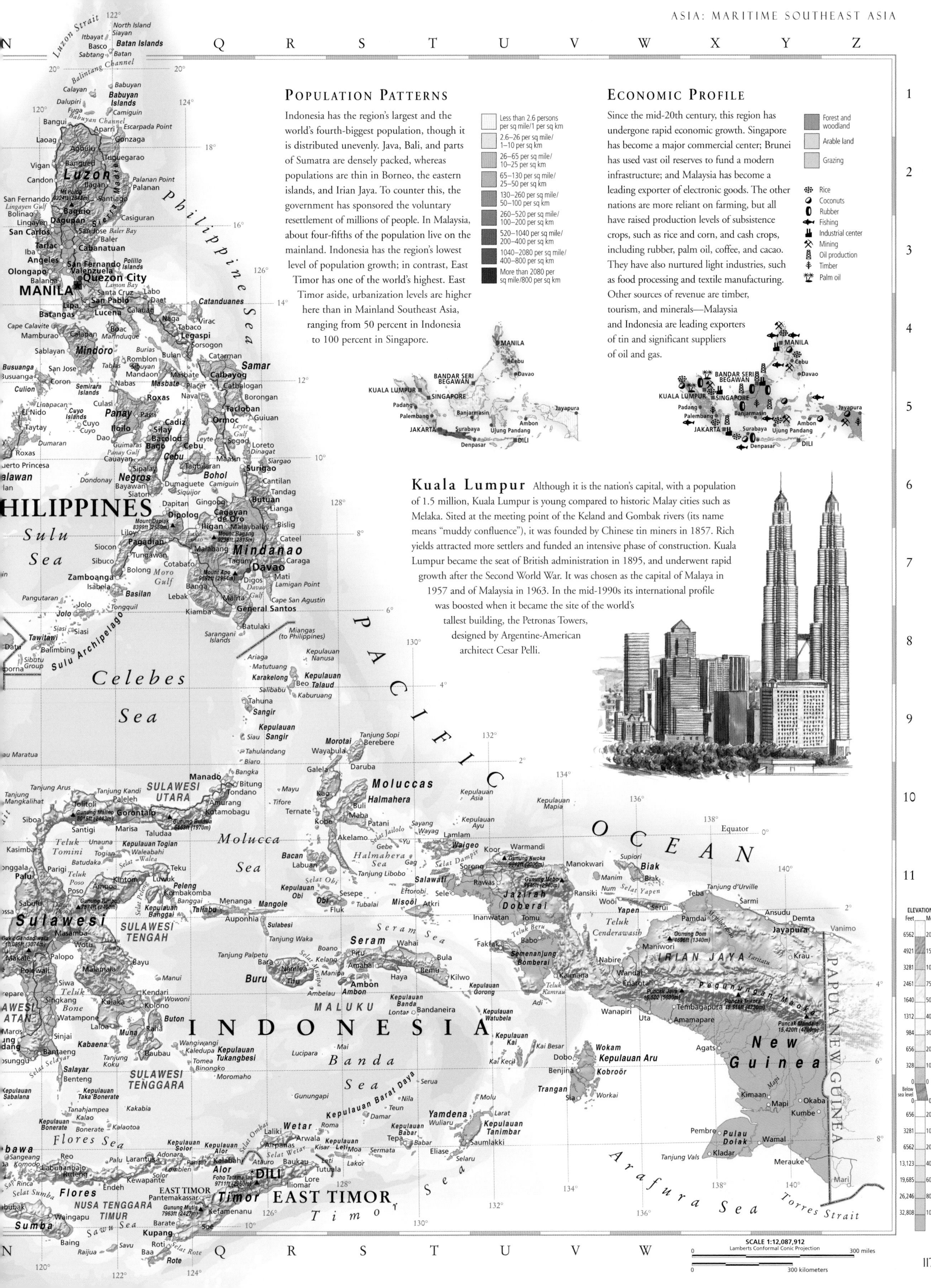

Population Patterns

Indonesia has the region's largest and the world's fourth-biggest population, though it is distributed unevenly. Java, Bali, and parts of Sumatra are densely packed, whereas populations are thin in Borneo, the eastern islands, and Irian Jaya. To counter this, the government has sponsored the voluntary resettlement of millions of people. In Malaysia, about four-fifths of the population live on the mainland. Indonesia has the region's lowest level of population growth; in contrast, East Timor has one of the world's highest. East Timor aside, urbanization levels are higher here than in Mainland Southeast Asia, ranging from 50 percent in Indonesia to 100 percent in Singapore.

Less than 2.6 persons per sq mile/1 per sq km
2.6–26 per sq mile/ 1–10 per sq km
26–65 per sq mile/ 10–25 per sq km
65–130 per sq mile/ 25–50 per sq km
130–260 per sq mile/ 50–100 per sq km
260–520 per sq mile/ 100–200 per sq km
520–1040 per sq mile/ 200–400 per sq km
1040–2080 per sq mile/ 400–800 per sq km
More than 2080 per sq mile/800 per sq km
MANILA
Cebu
Davao
BANDAR SERI BEGAWAN
KUALA LUMPUR
SINGAPORE
Padang
Palembang
Banjarmasin
Jayapura
Ambon
JAKARTA
Surabaya
Ujung Pandang
Denpasar
DILI

Economic Profile

Since the mid-20th century, this region has undergone rapid economic growth. Singapore has become a major commercial center; Brunei has used vast oil reserves to fund a modern infrastructure; and Malaysia has become a leading exporter of electronic goods. The other nations are more reliant on farming, but all have raised production levels of subsistence crops, such as rice and corn, and cash crops, including rubber, palm oil, coffee, and cacao. They have also nurtured light industries, such as food processing and textile manufacturing. Other sources of revenue are timber, tourism, and minerals—Malaysia and Indonesia are leading exporters of tin and significant suppliers of oil and gas.

Forest and woodland
Arable land
Grazing
Rice
Coconuts
Rubber
Fishing
Industrial center
Mining
Oil production
Timber
Palm oil
MANILA
Cebu
Davao
BANDAR SERI BEGAWAN
KUALA LUMPUR
SINGAPORE
Padang
Palembang
Banjarmasin
Jayapura
Ambon
JAKARTA
Surabaya
Ujung Pandang
Denpasar
DILI

Kuala Lumpur Although it is the nation's capital, with a population of 1.5 million, Kuala Lumpur is young compared to historic Malay cities such as Melaka. Sited at the meeting point of the Keland and Gombak rivers (its name means "muddy confluence"), it was founded by Chinese tin miners in 1857. Rich yields attracted more settlers and funded an intensive phase of construction. Kuala Lumpur became the seat of British administration in 1895, and underwent rapid growth after the Second World War. It was chosen as the capital of Malaya in 1957 and of Malaysia in 1963. In the mid-1990s its international profile was boosted when it became the site of the world's tallest building, the Petronas Towers, designed by Argentine-American architect Cesar Pelli.

Brunei, Malaysia, and Singapore

Malaysia comprises the southern third of the Malay Peninsula and the northern third of the island of Borneo. Divided by the South China Sea, these territories are known, respectively, as West (or Peninsular) Malaysia and East Malaysia (which is made up of the states of Sabah and Sarawak). Nestled on their fringes are two small independent states: Singapore, a tiny island republic on the southern tip of West Malaysia, and Brunei, a sultanate consisting of two enclaves on the north shore of East Malaysia. When the Portuguese arrived in the early 16th century, the Malay Peninsula and northern Borneo were divided into autonomous Islamic sultanates. In the 19th century, most of these states were brought under British control. Following Japanese occupation during the Second World War, the sultanates of the Malay Peninsula gained independence from Britain as Malaya in 1957; in 1963, they invited Singapore, Sabah, Sarawak, and Brunei to unite with them as Malaysia. All but Brunei accepted, though Singapore seceded peacefully in 1965. Today, these three states are among the most prosperous in Southeast Asia.

The jagged summit of Mount Kinabalu, Malaysia's highest peak, looms above a mosque near Kota Kinabalu.

Malaysia's largest port, George Town, occupies a sheltered position on the east side of the island of Pinang.

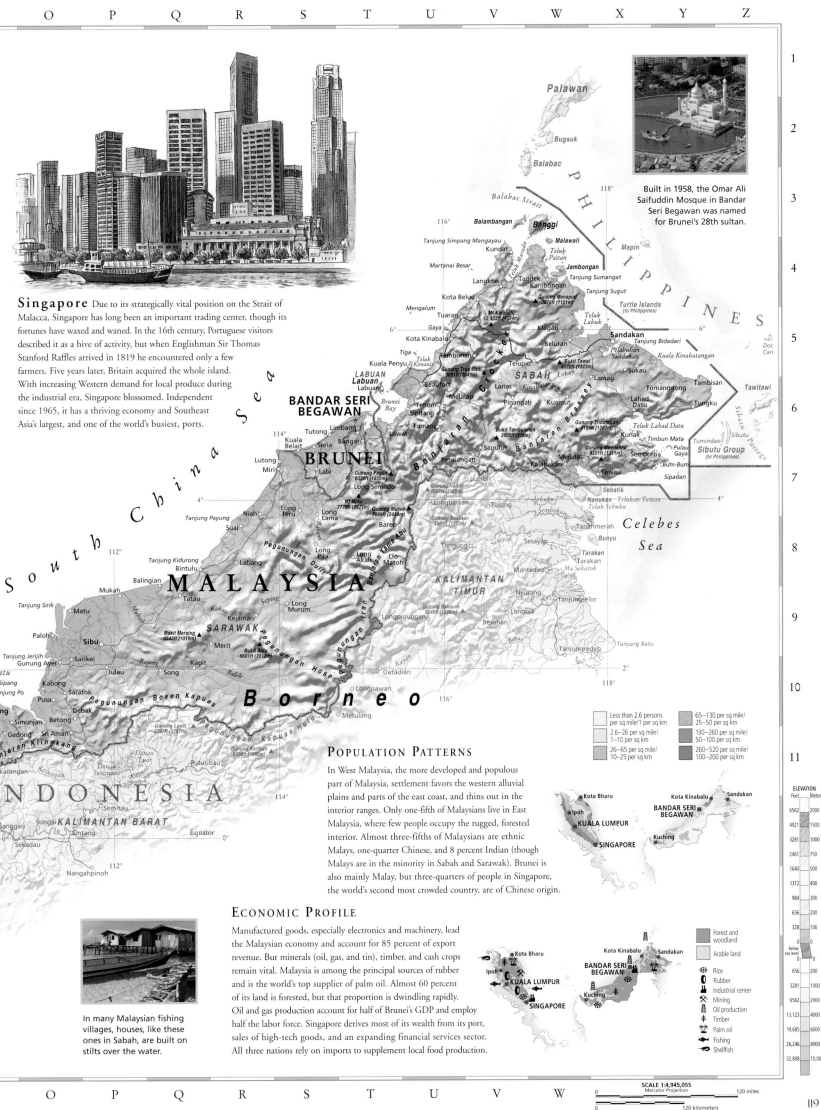

Singapore Due to its strategically vital position on the Strait of Malacca, Singapore has long been an important trading center, though its fortunes have waxed and waned. In the 16th century, Portuguese visitors described it as a hive of activity, but when Englishman Sir Thomas Stanford Raffles arrived in 1819 he encountered only a few farmers. Five years later, Britain acquired the whole island. With increasing Western demand for local produce during the industrial era, Singapore blossomed. Independent since 1965, it has a thriving economy and Southeast Asia's largest, and one of the world's busiest, ports.

Built in 1958, the Omar Ali Saifuddin Mosque in Bandar Seri Begawan was named for Brunei's 28th sultan.

Population Patterns

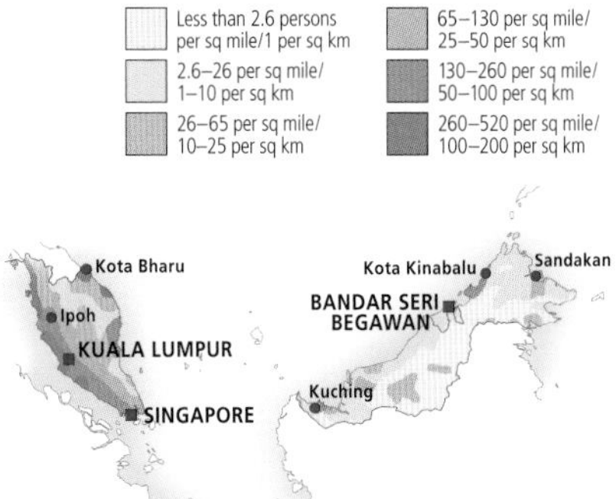

In West Malaysia, the more developed and populous part of Malaysia, settlement favors the western alluvial plains and parts of the east coast, and thins out in the interior ranges. Only one-fifth of Malaysians live in East Malaysia, where few people occupy the rugged, forested interior. Almost three-fifths of Malaysians are ethnic Malays, one-quarter Chinese, and 8 percent Indian (though Malays are in the minority in Sabah and Sarawak). Brunei is also mainly Malay, but three-quarters of people in Singapore, the world's second most crowded country, are of Chinese origin.

Economic Profile

Manufactured goods, especially electronics and machinery, lead the Malaysian economy and account for 85 percent of export revenue. But minerals (oil, gas, and tin), timber, and cash crops remain vital. Malaysia is among the principal sources of rubber and is the world's top supplier of palm oil. Almost 60 percent of its land is forested, but that proportion is dwindling rapidly. Oil and gas production account for half of Brunei's GDP and employ half the labor force. Singapore derives most of its wealth from its port, sales of high-tech goods, and an expanding financial services sector. All three nations rely on imports to supplement local food production.

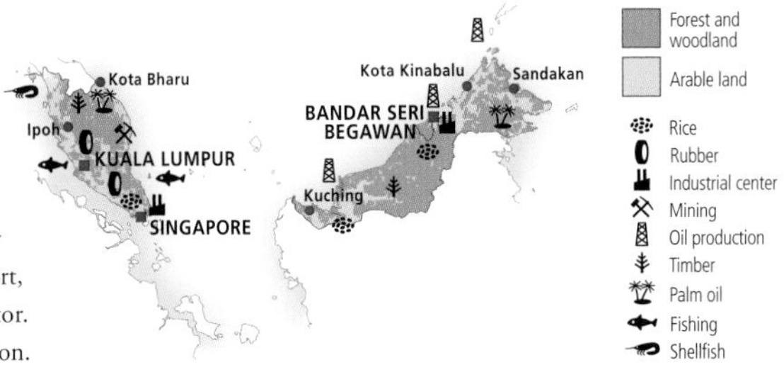

In many Malaysian fishing villages, houses, like these ones in Sabah, are built on stilts over the water.

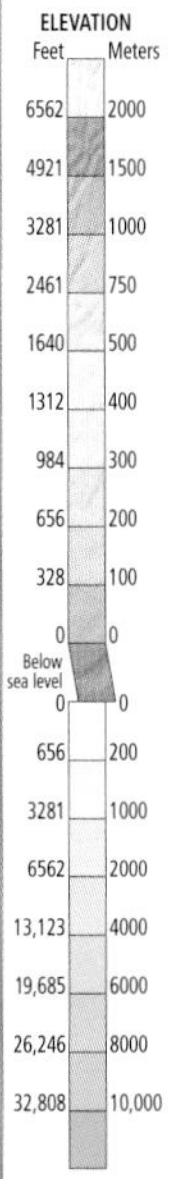

SCALE 1:4,945,055
Mercator Projection
0 120 miles
0 120 kilometers

The Philippines

A physically fractured country made up of more than 7,000 mainly volcanic islands, the Philippines encompasses 116,000 square miles (300,000 sq km) of land between China and Indonesia. Its two largest islands, Luzon in the north and Mindanao in the south, account for two-thirds of the country's area. Most of the islands are mountainous with narrow coastal plains. The indigenous inhabitants, the Filipinos, are of Malay origin, but modern Philippine society displays conspicuous colonial influences. Following Ferdinand Magellan's visit in 1521, Spain controlled the archipelago (naming it after its king, Philip II) from 1565 until 1898, when it was ceded to the U.S.A. Under Spanish rule, most of the population converted to Catholicism; under the Americans, English became the colony's lingua franca. The Second World War, during which Japan occupied the islands, delayed independence, which was achieved in 1946. In 1986, the repressive, 21-year rule of Ferdinand Marcos was ended by a popular uprising. A fragile democracy has since held, despite attempted coups, economic crises, and violence perpetrated by Muslim separatists, particularly on the islands of Mindanao and Basilan.

These rice terraces near Banaue, Luzon, were first built by the local Ifugao people 2,000 years ago.

Mayon in southeastern Luzon is a highly active volcano that poses a threat to nearby towns.

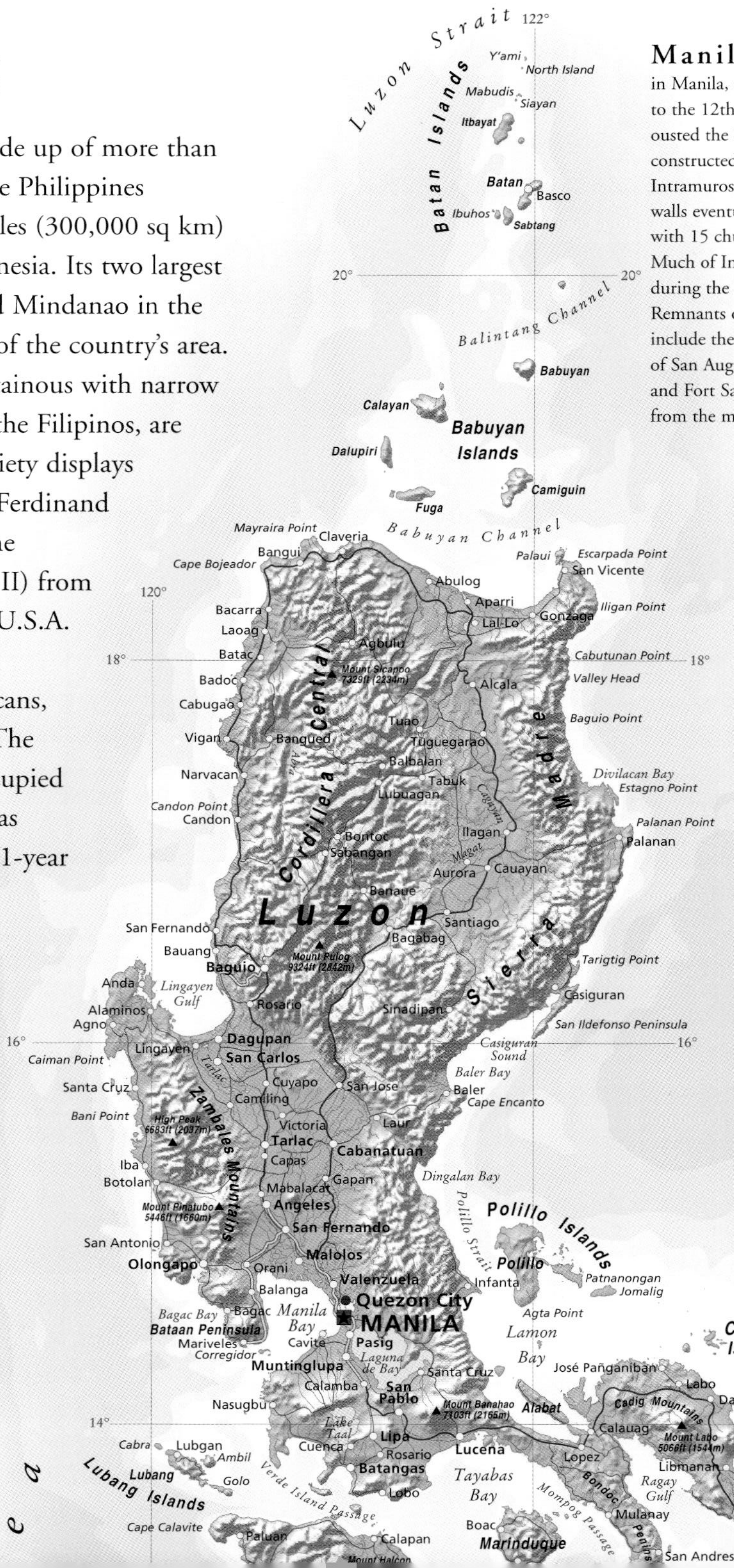

Luzon Strait
Batan Islands
Y'ami
North Island
Mabudis
Siayan
Itbayat
Batan
Basco
Ibuhos
Sabtang
Balintang Channel
Babuyan
Calayan
Babuyan Islands
Dalupiri
Camiguin
Fuga
Babuyan Channel
Luzon
Cordillera Central
Sierra Madre
Zambales Mountains
Cape Bojeador
Aparri
Tuguegarao
Baguio
Lingayen Gulf
Dagupan
San Carlos
Tarlac
Cabanatuan
Angeles
San Fernando
Olongapo
Bataan Peninsula
Manila Bay
Quezon City
MANILA
Laguna de Bay
Lamon Bay
Polillo Islands
Calagua Islands
Lubang Islands
Verde Island Passage
Tayabas Bay
Marinduque
Catanduanes
Naga
Lucena
Batangas
Lipa
San Pablo
Mount Pulog 9324ft (2842m)
Mount Banahao 7103ft (2165m)
Mount Isarog 6450ft (1966m)

Manila

Spanish forces arrived in Manila, a trading post dating back to the 12th century, in 1571. Having ousted the local Muslim ruler, they constructed a fortress called Intramuros, whose 20-foot (6-m) walls eventually enclosed a town with 15 churches and 6 monasteries. Much of Intramuros was obliterated during the Second World War. Remnants of the Spanish colony include the church and monastery of San Augustin, built in 1599, and Fort Santiago, which dates from the mid-17th century.

San Augustin Church

Fort Santiago

Population Patterns

The archipelago is densely though unevenly populated. The most developed area is central Luzon: Manila alone is home to 10 million people. Other areas, such as central Mindanao, Palawan, and northern Luzon, are sparsely inhabited. The population growth rate is high. Significant migration takes place, to the cities—urbanization has risen from 20 percent in 1900 to 63 percent in 2000—and overseas. More than 70 native languages are spoken; the official languages are Filipino (the Tagalog language of southern Luzon) and English.

Aparri
Dagupan
MANILA
Legaspi
Roxas
Cebu
Zamboanga
Davao

- Less than 2.6 persons per sq mile/1 per sq km
- 2.6–26 per sq mile/ 1–10 per sq km
- 26–65 per sq mile/ 10–25 per sq km
- 65–130 per sq mile/ 25–50 per sq km
- 130–260 per sq mile/ 50–100 per sq km
- 260–520 per sq mile/ 100–200 per sq km
- 520–1040 per sq mile/ 200–400 per sq km
- 1040–2080 per sq mile/ 400–800 per sq km

Economic Profile

About 20 percent of the land is arable and agriculture is the biggest employer. Rice and corn are the staple crops, sugar and coconuts the main exports. Fishing is also important. Abundant minerals include some of the world's largest deposits of nickel, copper, and chromite. Electronic goods, mainly assembled in foreign-owned factories using imported parts, account for over half of exports. Other industrial products include textiles, metals, chemicals, and foodstuffs. Substantial income is also derived from tourism.

Aparri
Dagupan
MANILA
Legaspi
Roxas
Cebu
Zamboanga
Davao

- Forest and woodland
- Arable land
- Grazing
- Rice
- Coconuts
- Fishing
- Industrial center
- Mining
- Oil production
- Timber
- Sugarcane

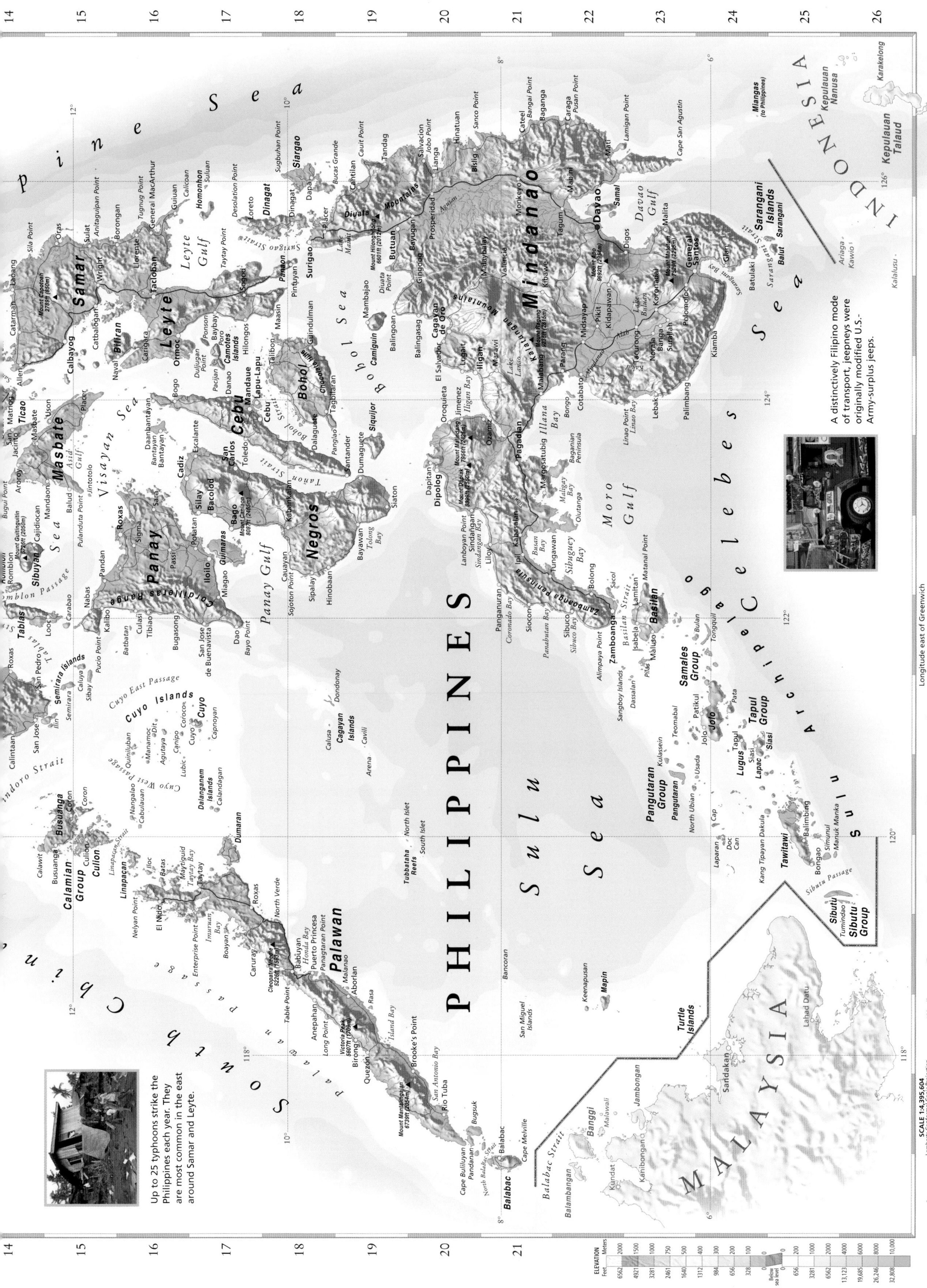
PHILIPPINES
MALAYSIA
INDONESIA
Philippine Sea
South China Sea
Sulu Sea
Celebes Sea
Sibuyan Sea
Visayan Sea
Camotes Sea
Bohol Sea
Moro Gulf
Davao Gulf
Leyte Gulf
Panay Gulf
Palawan Passage
Sulu Archipelago
Mindanao
Samar
Leyte
Cebu
Bohol
Negros
Panay
Masbate
Palawan
Basilan
Jolo
Tawitawi
Calamian Group
Cuyo Islands
Cagayan Islands
Turtle Islands
Samales Group
Tapul Group
Pangutaran Group
Sibutu Group
Sarangani Islands
Kepulauan Talaud
Kepulauan Nanusa
Dinagat
Siargao
Camiguin
Siquijor
Guimaras
Biliran
Ticao
Sibuyan
Tablas
Busuanga
Culion
Dumaran
Linapacan
Balabac
Banggi
Davao
Zamboanga
Cagayan de Oro
Iloilo
Bacolod
Tacloban
Butuan
General Santos
Puerto Princesa
Cotabato
Iligan
Surigao
Dipolog
Pagadian
Dumaguete
Roxas
Sandakan
Lahad Datu
Mount Apo 9692ft (2954m)
Mount Matutum 7519ft (2292m)
Mount Ragang 9236ft (2815m)
Mount Canlaon 8087ft (2465m)
Mount Malindang 7956ft (2425m)
Mount Dapiak 8865ft (2550m)
Mount Hilong-hilong 6601ft (2012m)
Mount Capotoan 2789ft (850m)
Mount Guiting-guiting 6726ft (2050m)
Cleopatra Needle 5226ft (1593m)
Victoria Peak 5607ft (1709m)
Mount Mantalingajan 6739ft (2054m)
Diwata Mountains
Kalatungan Mountains
Cordillera Range
Zamboanga Peninsula
Basilan Strait
Balabac Strait
Sibutu Passage
Cuyo East Passage
Cuyo West Passage
Mindoro Strait
Surigao Strait
Tañon Strait
Bohol Strait
Tubbataha Reefs
Longitude east of Greenwich
SCALE 1:4,395,604
Lamberts Conformal Conic Projection
120 miles
120 kilometers
ELEVATION
Feet Meters
6562 2000
4921 1500
3281 1000
2461 750
1640 500
1312 400
984 300
656 200
328 100
0 0
Below sea level
0 0
656 200
3281 1000
6562 2000
13,123 4000
19,685 6000
26,246 8000
32,808 10,000

Up to 25 typhoons strike the Philippines each year. They are most common in the east around Samar and Leyte.

A distinctively Filipino mode of transport, jeepneys were originally modified U.S. Army-surplus jeeps.

Japan

Although it occupies a strategically important position off the northeast coast of Asia, Japan remained isolated from outside influences for long periods of its history. It limited relations with its neighbors from the ninth century and adopted an official policy of isolation in 1639, soon after the arrival of the first Western missionaries and explorers. Only in the mid-19th century did it open up to foreign influences and trade.

Its subsequent attempts to expand its empire led to international conflicts and a devastating defeat in the Second World War. Yet the nation recovered spectacularly to become the world's second-strongest industrial power after the United States and wield an economic and political influence far out of proportion to its small size. Occupying a land area smaller than California, Japan consists of about 4,000 islands, dominated by the large islands of Hokkaidō, Honshū, Shikoku, and Kyūshū. In the interiors of these islands, mountain ranges are separated by river valleys and bounded by narrow coastal plains. Being situated on the Pacific Rim of Fire, the country experiences regular earthquakes and volcanic eruptions, which periodically wreak havoc on the land and its people.

Population Patterns

About 80 percent of Japan is mountainous and has low-to-moderate levels of population density; the other 20 percent, however—mainly valleys and coastal plains—supports the bulk of the population and includes some of the world's most densely inhabited areas. Urban dwellers account for 80 percent of the inhabitants and the capital, Tokyo, is the world's largest urban center. The population is ethnically homogenous, with 99 percent being Japanese. About 84% follow both Buddhist and Shinto traditions. In recent years, a declining birth rate and rapidly aging population have heightened concerns about labor shortages and the cost of maintaining social services.

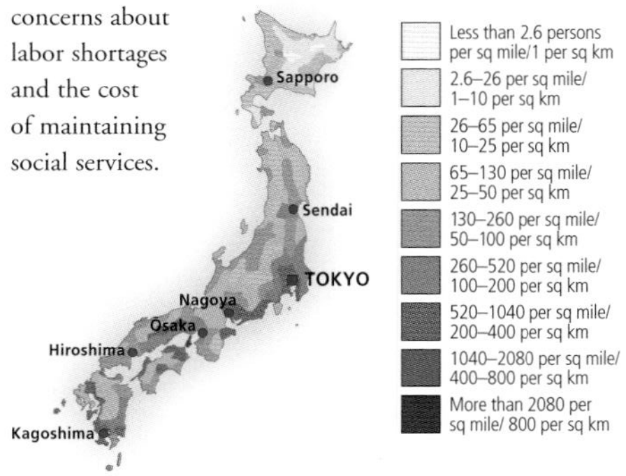

Sapporo
Sendai
TOKYO
Nagoya
Osaka
Hiroshima
Kagoshima
Less than 2.6 persons per sq mile/1 per sq km
2.6–26 per sq mile/ 1–10 per sq km
26–65 per sq mile/ 10–25 per sq km
65–130 per sq mile/ 25–50 per sq km
130–260 per sq mile/ 50–100 per sq km
260–520 per sq mile/ 100–200 per sq km
520–1040 per sq mile/ 200–400 per sq km
1040–2080 per sq mile/ 400–800 per sq km
More than 2080 per sq mile/ 800 per sq km

Economic Profile

Japan is an economic superpower despite having only a small area of cultivable land and modest mineral resources (small deposits of copper, coal, and iron ore and meager reserves of oil and gas). Its success is due mainly to government support and innovation: large subsidies and intensive farming practices have helped it become virtually self-sufficient in rice and produce large quantities of fruit and vegetables; heavy investment in education, research, and technology have created a sophisticated industrial sector renowned for machinery and electronic goods. Even the nation's impressive fish catches, accounting for 15 percent of world totals, are due in part to the use of technology-loaded, wide-ranging fishing boats. This industrial success has greatly increased export revenue; however, a recession in the late 1990s cast a shadow over the nation's economic future.

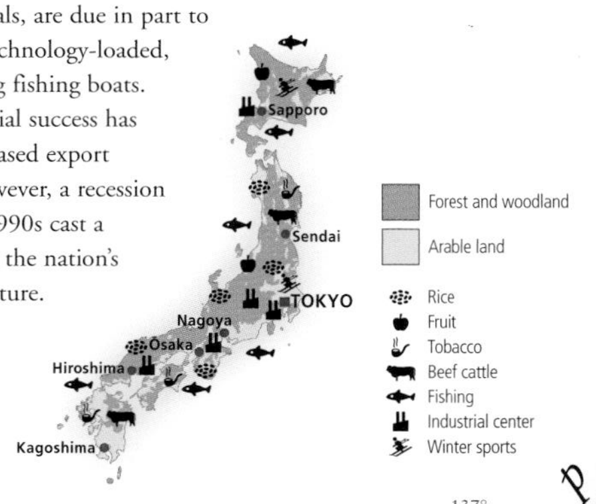

Sapporo
Sendai
TOKYO
Nagoya
Osaka
Hiroshima
Kagoshima
Forest and woodland
Arable land
Rice
Fruit
Tobacco
Beef cattle
Fishing
Industrial center
Winter sports

JAPAN
Hokkaidō
Sea of Okhotsk
PACIFIC OCEAN
Sea of Japan
RUSSIAN FEDERATION
Sakhalin
La Pérouse Strait
Kuril Islands
(Administered by Russian Federation claimed by Japan)
Sapporo
Asahikawa
Hakodate
Aomori
Morioka
Akita
Sendai
Niigata
ELEVATION
Feet Meters

In winter, mountain-dwelling macaque monkeys stay warm by sitting in pools fed by hot springs.

Bullet trains began operating in 1964. They now have a top speed of 160 mph (260 km/h).

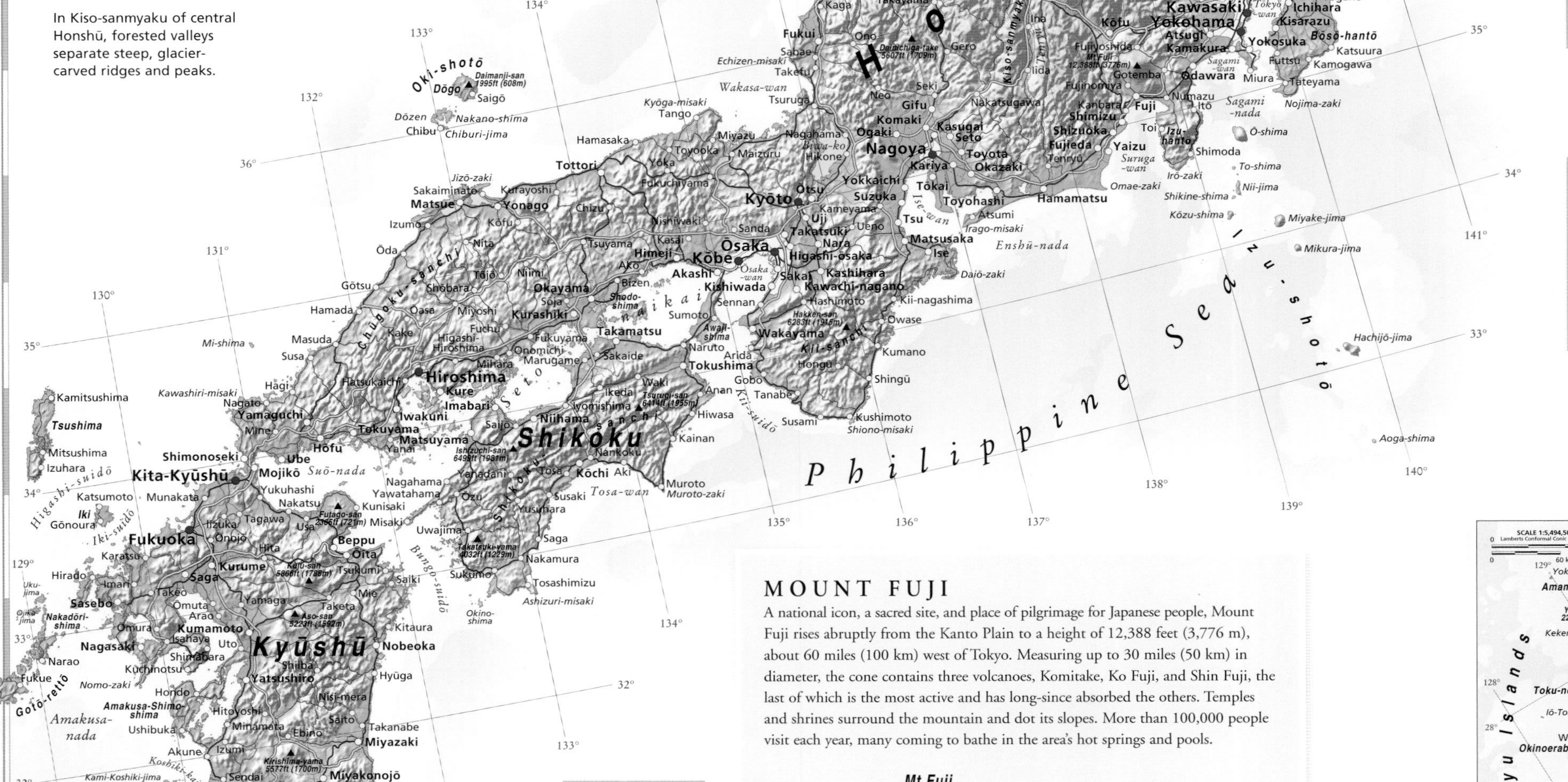
Sea of Japan
Philippine Sea
East China Sea
Honshū
Shikoku
Kyūshū
TOKYO
Yokohama
Kawasaki
Nagoya
Ōsaka
Kōbe
Kyōto
Hiroshima
Fukuoka
Kita-Kyūshū
Izu-shotō
Ōsumi-shotō
Tokara-rettō
Oki-shotō
Gotō-rettō
Seto naikai
Tsushima
Longitude east of Greenwich
SCALE 1:4,670,330
Lamberts Conformal Conic Projection
120 miles
120 kilometers

In Kiso-sanmyaku of central Honshū, forested valleys separate steep, glacier-carved ridges and peaks.

Tokyo's urban sprawl has swallowed up over 80 formerly separate towns.

The Ainu people of northern Japan have slowly been assimilated by the Japanese, and few true Ainu remain.

On January 17, 1995, an earthquake killed 5,000 people and toppled 150,000 buildings in Kōbe.

MOUNT FUJI

A national icon, a sacred site, and place of pilgrimage for Japanese people, Mount Fuji rises abruptly from the Kanto Plain to a height of 12,388 feet (3,776 m), about 60 miles (100 km) west of Tokyo. Measuring up to 30 miles (50 km) in diameter, the cone contains three volcanoes, Komitake, Ko Fuji, and Shin Fuji, the last of which is the most active and has long-since absorbed the others. Temples and shrines surround the mountain and dot its slopes. More than 100,000 people visit each year, many coming to bathe in the area's hot springs and pools.

Mt Fuji

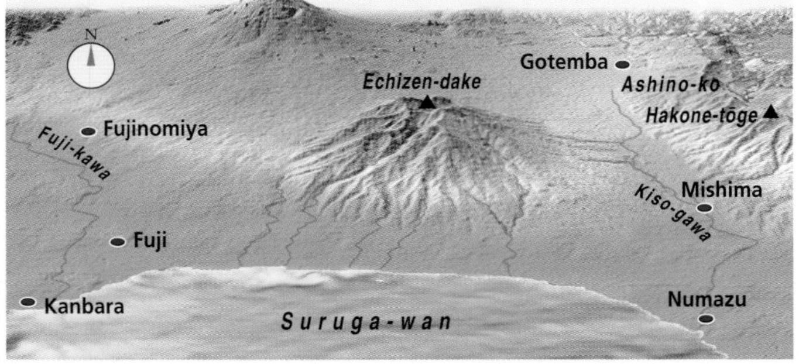
Echizen-dake
Gotemba
Ashino-ko
Hakone-tōge
Fujinomiya
Fuji-kawa
Mishima
Kiso-gawa
Fuji
Kanbara
Numazu
Suruga-wan

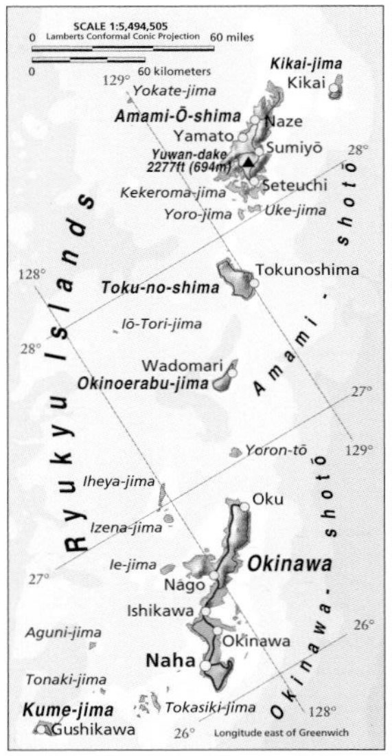
SCALE 1:5,494,505
Ryukyu Islands
Amami-shotō
Okinawa-shotō
Amami-Ō-shima
Toku-no-shima
Okinoerabu-jima
Okinawa
Naha
Kume-jima
Longitude east of Greenwich

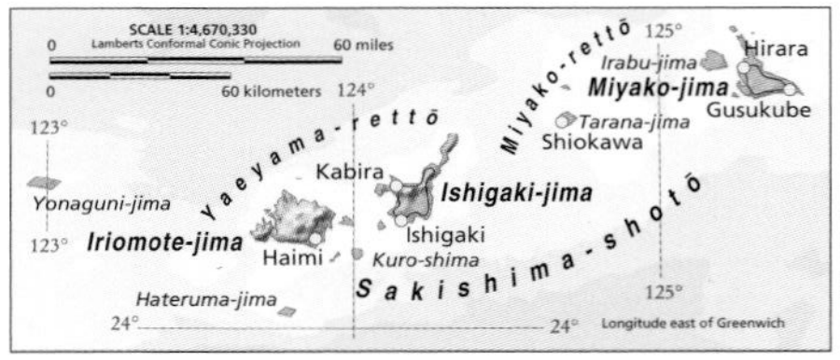
SCALE 1:4,670,330
Sakishima-shotō
Yaeyama-rettō
Miyako-rettō
Miyako-jima
Ishigaki-jima
Iriomote-jima
Yonaguni-jima
Hateruma-jima
Longitude east of Greenwich

Northwestern Africa

Algeria, Libya, Morocco, Tunisia

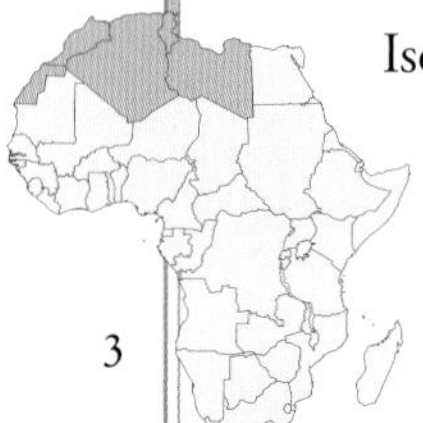

Isolated from the rest of the continent by the Sahara Desert, Northwestern Africa is a transitional zone, between sea and remote interior, Europe and Africa, the West and the Middle East. Its distinctive and relatively homogenous culture was flavored by classical European civilizations and its original, nomadic Berber inhabitants, but derives mainly from the Arab peoples who invaded and settled here in the seventh century AD. This Arabic, Islamic heritage not only withstood subsequent occupation by the Ottoman Empire (between the 16th and 19th centuries), European colonial rule, and a torrid phase of decolonization, but also permeated almost every part of a vast, inhospitable region. Bounded by the Atlas Mountains in the northwest, the Sahara Desert occupies more than 80 percent of the land, confining major population centers and communications routes, sedentary farming, and industries to a narrow coastal strip.

Population Patterns

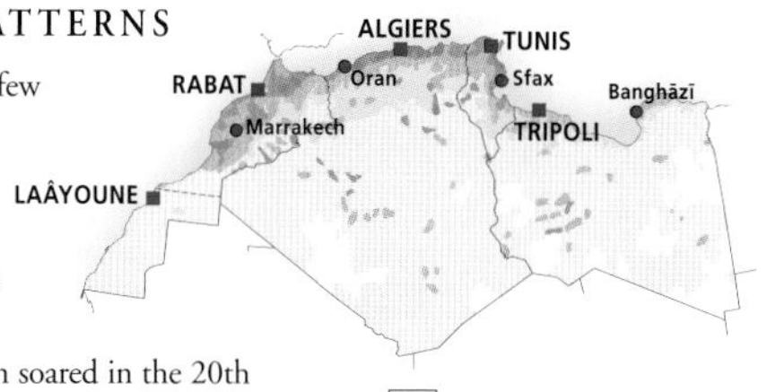

The Sahara contains just a few isolated towns, scattered oases, and groups of nomadic pastoralists; the vast majority of the region's inhabitants dwell on the north coast. The population soared in the 20th century (Algeria's population doubled between 1960 and 1990), due to improving health services and persistent high fertility (even today, each woman has an average of four children). Migration to cities began under European rule and accelerated with industrialization, making this the most urbanized part of Africa. Libya is distinctly underpopulated and has to import skilled workers, whereas there is a steady outward flow of migrants from the other countries.

- Uninhabited
- Less than 2.6 persons per sq mile/1 per sq km
- 2.6–26 per sq mile/ 1–10 per sq km
- 26–65 per sq mile/ 10–25 per sq km
- 65–130 per sq mile/ 25–50 per sq km
- 130–260 per sq mile/ 50–100 per sq km
- 260–520 per sq mile/ 100–200 per sq km

The seminomadic Tuareg people roam the desert lands of Algeria, Libya, Mali, and Niger.

The Atlas Mountains are home to large numbers of Berbers, the region's original inhabitants.

Tangier Befitting a port that has at various times been ruled by the Phoenicians, Romans, Arabs, Spanish, Portuguese, and British, Tangier was for much of the 20th century designated an international zone. Since it became part of Morocco in 1956, many foreign residents have departed, but the city retains a cosmopolitan atmosphere. Encircled by 15th-century ramparts and surmounted by the Great Mosque, its whitewashed buildings climb a craggy limestone outcrop.

Economic Profile

Relative to the rest of Africa, these nations are affluent. The discovery of oil and gas in the 1950s and 1960s brought unprecedented wealth to Libya and Algeria (and now generate more than 90 percent of their export revenue), and, to a lesser extent, Tunisia. Other valuable minerals include phosphates in Morocco (which has the world's largest reserves), Western Sahara, and Tunisia, and iron ore, especially in Algeria. Arable land is limited, water scarce; meager rises in agricultural production have been outstripped by population growth, resulting in an increased dependence on imports. Industries are based mainly on the processing of foods and minerals, though tourism is a major source of income in Morocco and Tunisia.

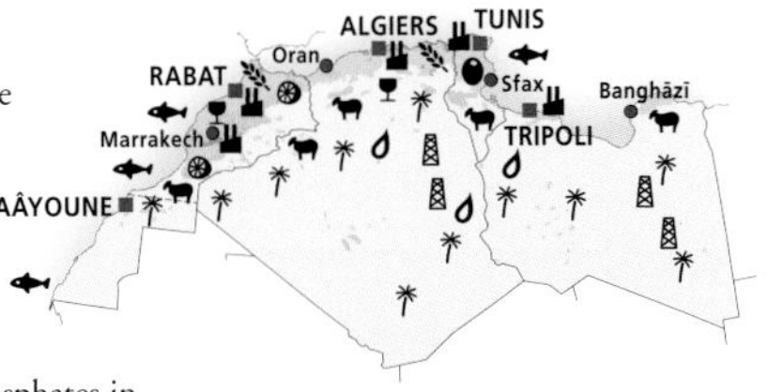

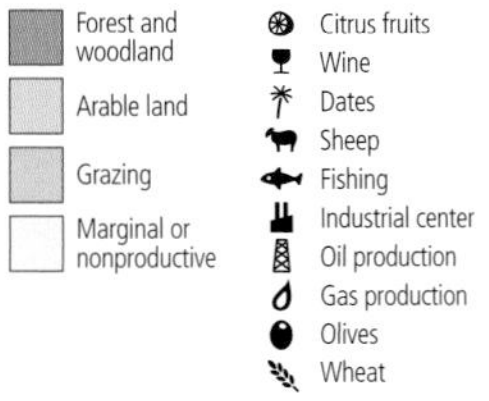

The High Atlas

The Atlas Mountains extend for 1,200 miles (2,000 km) from southwestern Morocco to eastern Tunisia. The highest part of the chain, known as the High Atlas, runs inland from the Moroccan port of Agadir, its sparsely forested slopes rising steeply to a cluster of snow-capped peaks crowned by 13,671-foot (4,167-m) Mount Toubkal. To the south, the range is paralleled by the lower Anti Atlas, which encloses the Oued Sous Basin, an important farming region. The much more arid southern flank of the Anti Atlas adjoins the northwestern edge of the Sahara Desert.

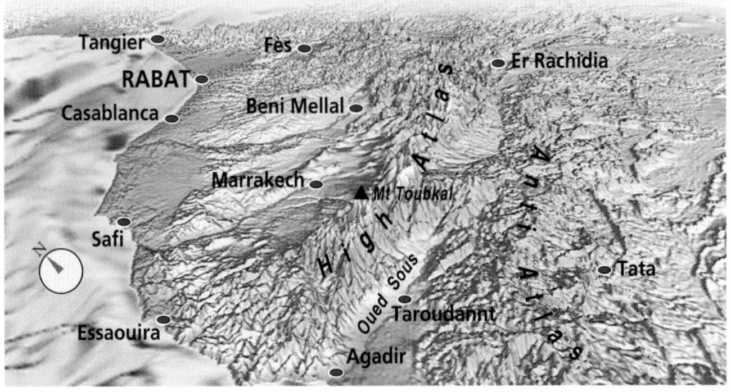

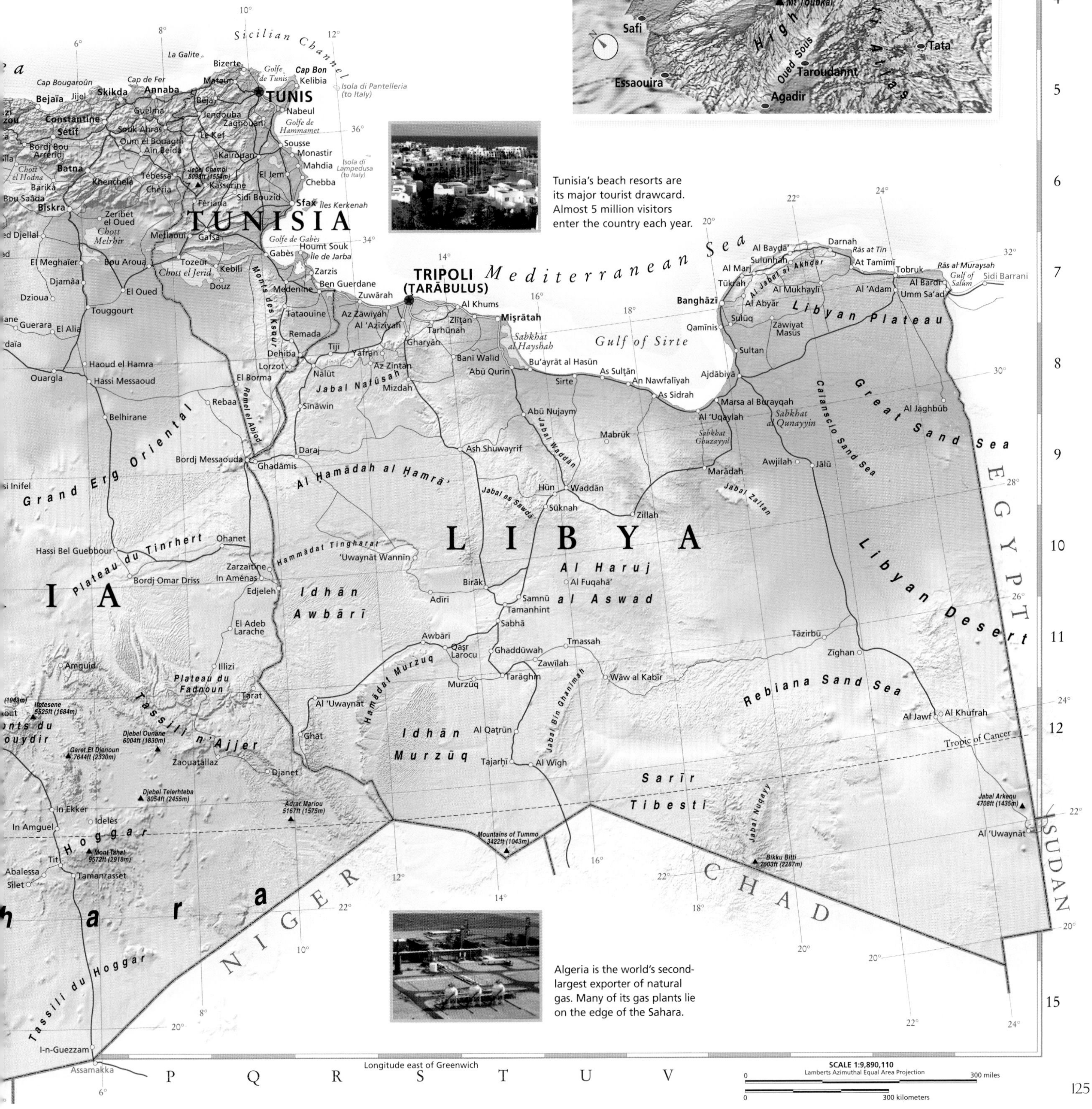

Tunisia's beach resorts are its major tourist drawcard. Almost 5 million visitors enter the country each year.

Algeria is the world's second-largest exporter of natural gas. Many of its gas plants lie on the edge of the Sahara.

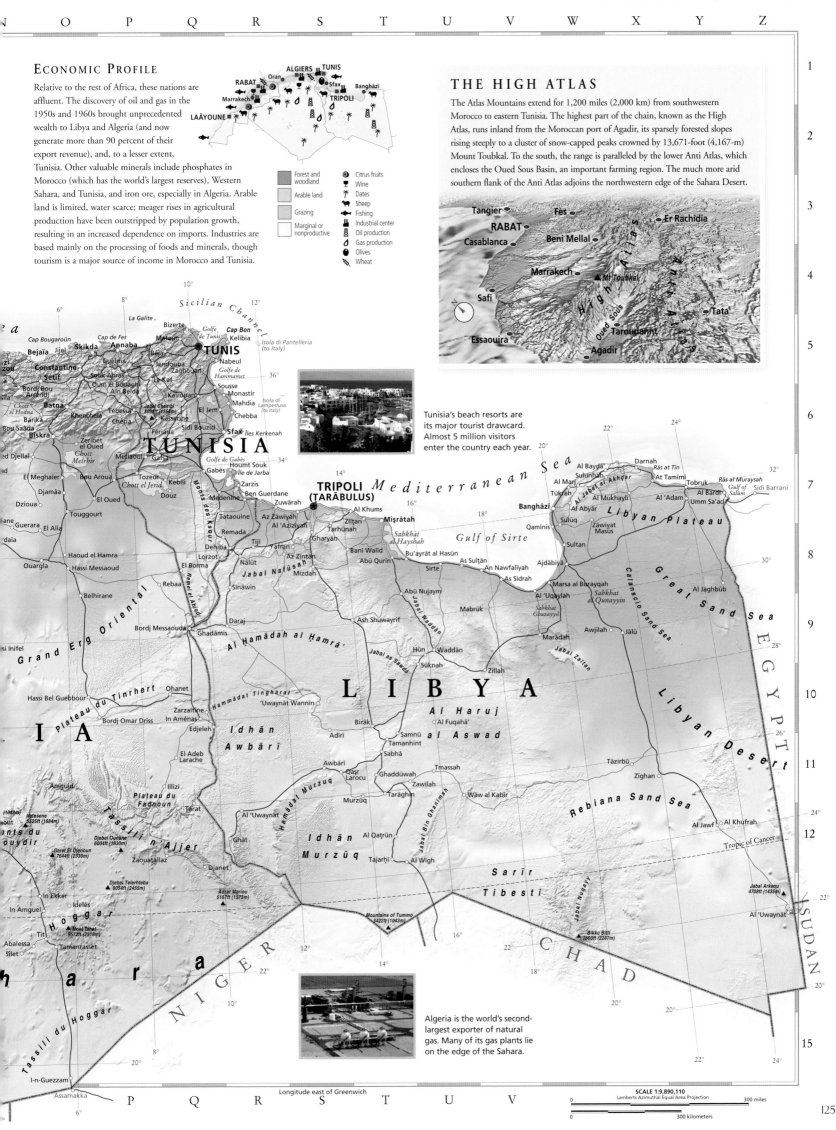

Northeastern Africa

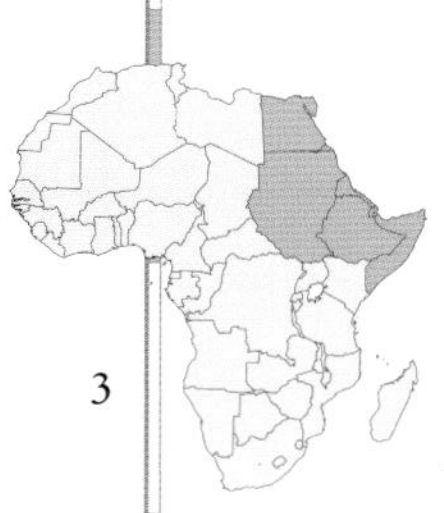

Djibouti, Egypt, Eritrea, Ethiopia, Somalia, Sudan

At the northern end of the Great Rift Valley, the Ethiopian Highlands divides the Horn of Africa in the east from the barren expanses of the Sahara in the west. Rivers that descend from the highlands, and from the East African Plateau to the south, are the lifeblood of this predominantly arid and impoverished land.

The Shebeli and Juba are the only permanent rivers in Somalia and supply most of the nation's water. From Lake Tana, the Blue Nile flows east then west to join the White Nile at Khartoum; continuing north, the Nile forms a riverine oasis that constitutes Egypt's only fertile zone. Since decolonization took place after the Second World War, the southern part of this region has been crippled by famines and political instability, including a long civil war that saw Eritrea secede from Ethiopia in 1993.

Population Patterns

The highest population densities occur in the fertile Ethiopian Highlands and along the major rivers—99 percent of Egyptians live in the Nile Valley, an area that constitutes just 3 percent of the country. The deserts of the eastern Sahara, northern Ethiopia, and Somalia, and the swamps of southern Sudan deter settlement. In semiarid zones, many people, including 70 percent of Somalians, maintain a nomadic lifestyle. The Sahara separates the mainly Arabic peoples of the north from the diverse African groups of the south; however, the Middle East has influenced the entire region and most inhabitants are adherents of Islam.

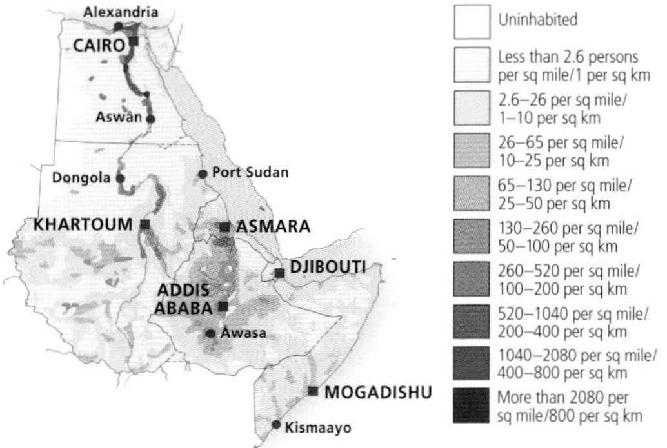

Economic Profile

The regional economy is undeveloped, and most people rely on subsistence farming of cereals, fruit and vegetables, sheep, cattle, goats, and camels—80 percent of Somalians are dependent on livestock. Cash crops include cotton and sugarcane, grown in the Nile Valley, and coffee from the Ethiopian Highlands (from whose Kaffa region the word "coffee" derives). Only Egypt has a developed industrial sector, based on engineering and the manufacture of metals and electronic goods. It also benefits from modest oil reserves, tourism, and revenue from the Suez Canal.

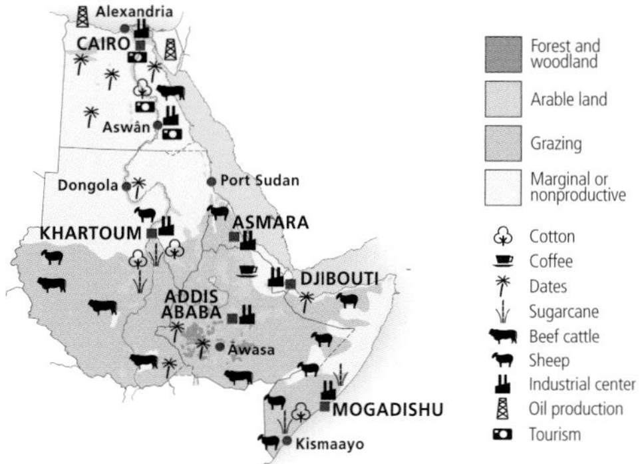

Completed in 1971, the Aswân Dam supplies half of Egypt's electricity.

The Ethiopian Highlands

An enormous plateau, the Ethiopian Highlands cover most of Ethiopia and are bisected by the Great Rift Valley. The western highlands encompass the region's highest peak, 14,872-foot (4,533-m) Rās Dashen, Lake Tana, and Ethiopia's capital Addis Ababa, which sits about 8,000 feet (2,500 m) above sea level. The eastern highlands are narrower but almost as high, reaching 14,176 feet (4,321 m) at Batu. South of Addis Ababa, lakes and volcanic peaks stud the floor of the Great Rift Valley; northeast of the capital, the valley widens, the western wall forming a great escarpment that runs north to the Red Sea, the eastern side arcing toward the Gulf of Aden.

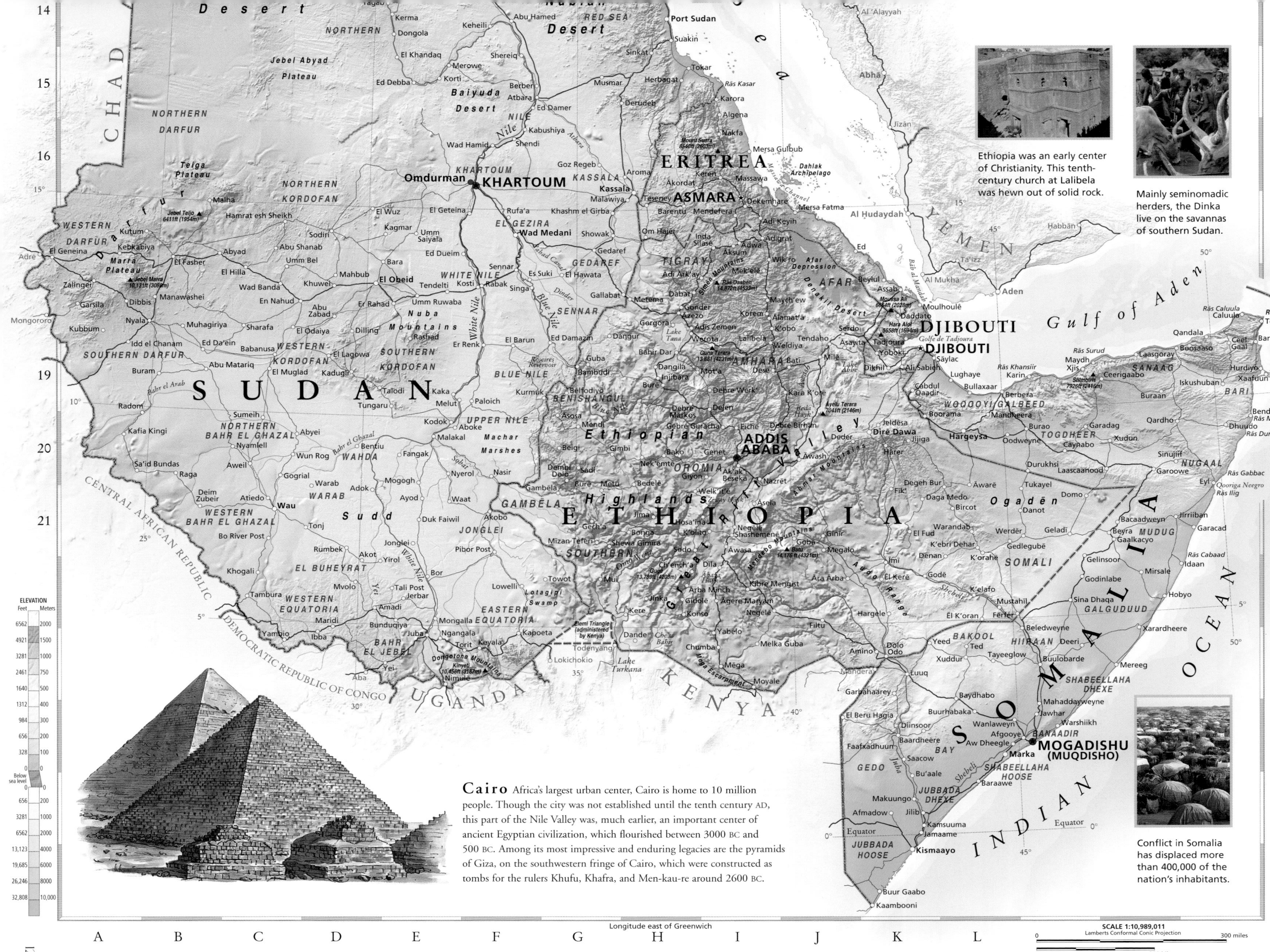

Ethiopia was an early center of Christianity. This tenth-century church at Lalibela was hewn out of solid rock.

Mainly seminomadic herders, the Dinka live on the savannas of southern Sudan.

Conflict in Somalia has displaced more than 400,000 of the nation's inhabitants.

Cairo Africa's largest urban center, Cairo is home to 10 million people. Though the city was not established until the tenth century AD, this part of the Nile Valley was, much earlier, an important center of ancient Egyptian civilization, which flourished between 3000 BC and 500 BC. Among its most impressive and enduring legacies are the pyramids of Giza, on the southwestern fringe of Cairo, which were constructed as tombs for the rulers Khufu, Khafra, and Men-kau-re around 2600 BC.

West Africa

Benin, Burkina Faso, Cameroon, Chad, Côte d'Ivoire, Equatorial Guinea, Gambia, Ghana, Guinea, Guinea-Bissau, Liberia, Mali, Mauritania, Niger, Nigeria, Senegal, Sierra Leone, Togo

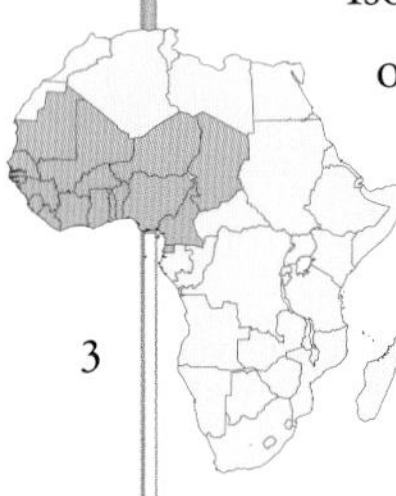

Isolated ranges and plateaus dot the West African landscape, but most of the terrain is low-lying. Distinctive environments and populations, however, divide the region into northern and southern sectors. Inhabited mainly by Muslim peoples, including Berbers and Arabs, the more arid northern two-thirds, sometimes called the Western Sudan, includes the western edge of the Sahara Desert, part of the scrubby Sahel, and wide savanna grasslands. The wetter southern third, the Guinea coast, is characterized by tropical rain forest and is home to diverse African peoples. In the Middle Ages, thriving trans-Saharan trade created prosperous kingdoms in the north. From the 16th century, the economic focus shifted to the coast with the arrival of European traders. European powers gradually took control of the region, relinquishing their hold only in the late 20th century.

Most inhabitants of the Sahel live near their livestock in traditional villages.

Djenné In the 14th century, Mali, located in the present-day country of the same name and centered on the cities of Djenné, Timbuktu, and Gao, was Africa's most powerful state. Larger than any contemporary state in Europe, it derived much of its wealth and power from its control of trans-Saharan trade in gold, salt, and slaves. Following its adoption of Islam, Mali became a center of Muslim scholarship and the site of several large mosques. The Great Mosque of Djenné was built in the 14th century, destroyed in 1896, and rebuilt in 1909. Made of sun-baked earth, it is the world's biggest mud-brick structure.

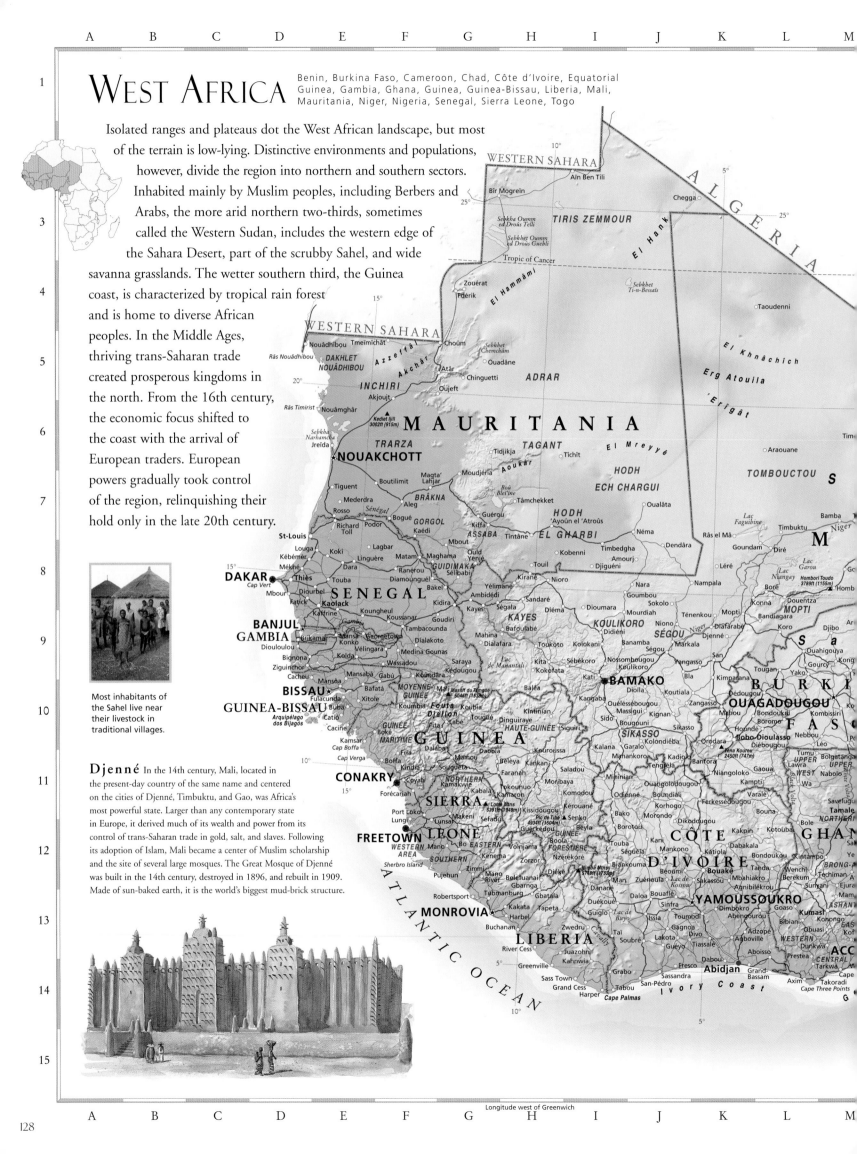

N O P Q R S T U V W X Y Z

Population Patterns

The peoples of the north, many of whom are nomadic, are fewer and more widely dispersed than those of the south, where settlement is focused on river valleys and coastal cities. Urbanization has occurred only recently, but rapidly, rising, for example, in Mauritania from 2 percent in 1950 to 64 percent today. The regional population is expanding quickly—Liberia and Sierra Leone have the world's fastest-growing populations.

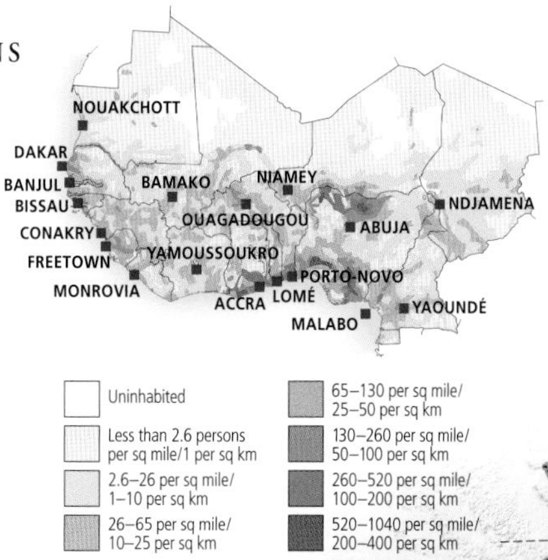

Economic Profile

Despite ample resources, most obviously its forests, West Africa has achieved limited development. Grazing predominates in the north. Cash crops include cotton and groundnuts in the interior, palm oil, coffee, and rubber in the south. Industries are mainly limited to food processing and textiles, but mineral resources, including oil (especially in Nigeria and Cameroon), iron ore (Liberia's main export), and bauxite (notably in Guinea), support production of metals, chemicals, and machinery.

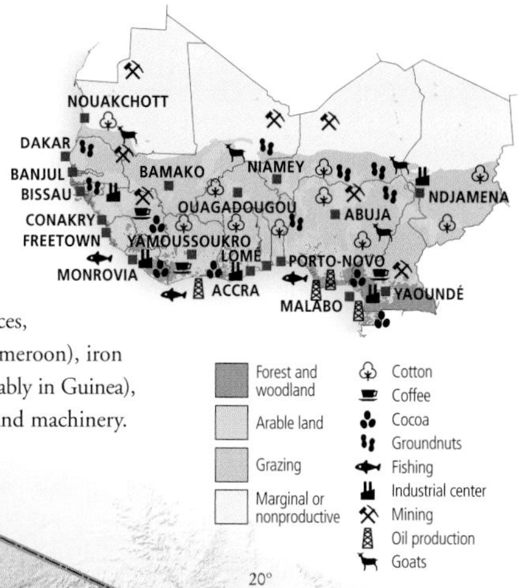

The Niger River is a vital source of fish, especially when coastal catches decline in the dry season.

N O P Q R S T U V W

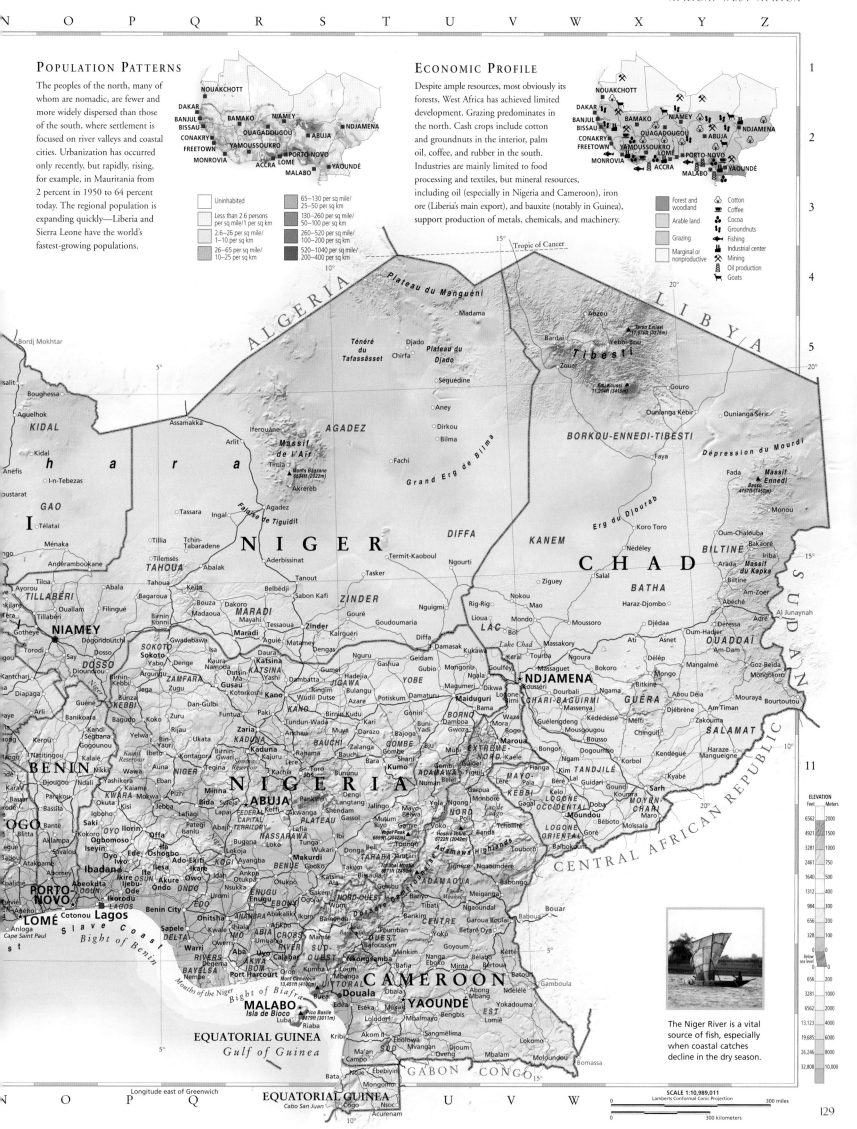

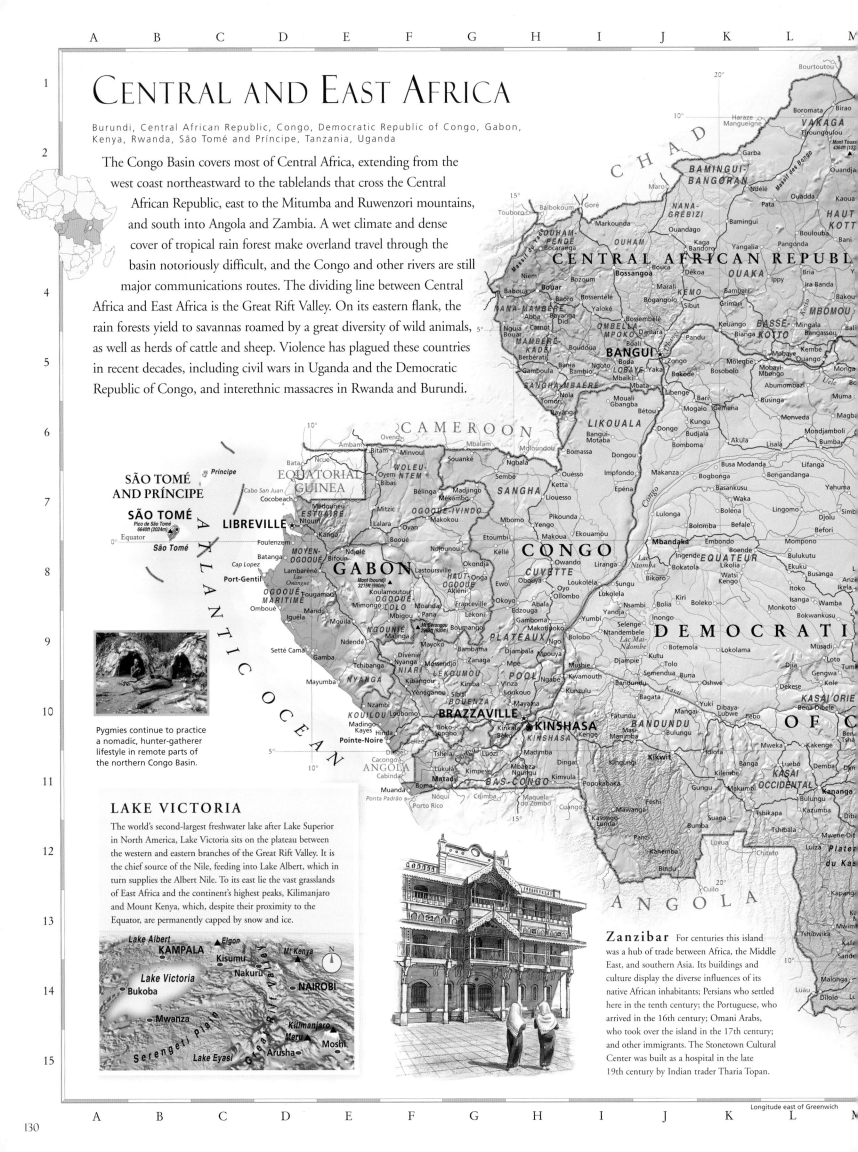

CENTRAL AND EAST AFRICA

Burundi, Central African Republic, Congo, Democratic Republic of Congo, Gabon, Kenya, Rwanda, São Tomé and Príncipe, Tanzania, Uganda

The Congo Basin covers most of Central Africa, extending from the west coast northeastward to the tablelands that cross the Central African Republic, east to the Mitumba and Ruwenzori mountains, and south into Angola and Zambia. A wet climate and dense cover of tropical rain forest make overland travel through the basin notoriously difficult, and the Congo and other rivers are still major communications routes. The dividing line between Central Africa and East Africa is the Great Rift Valley. On its eastern flank, the rain forests yield to savannas roamed by a great diversity of wild animals, as well as herds of cattle and sheep. Violence has plagued these countries in recent decades, including civil wars in Uganda and the Democratic Republic of Congo, and interethnic massacres in Rwanda and Burundi.

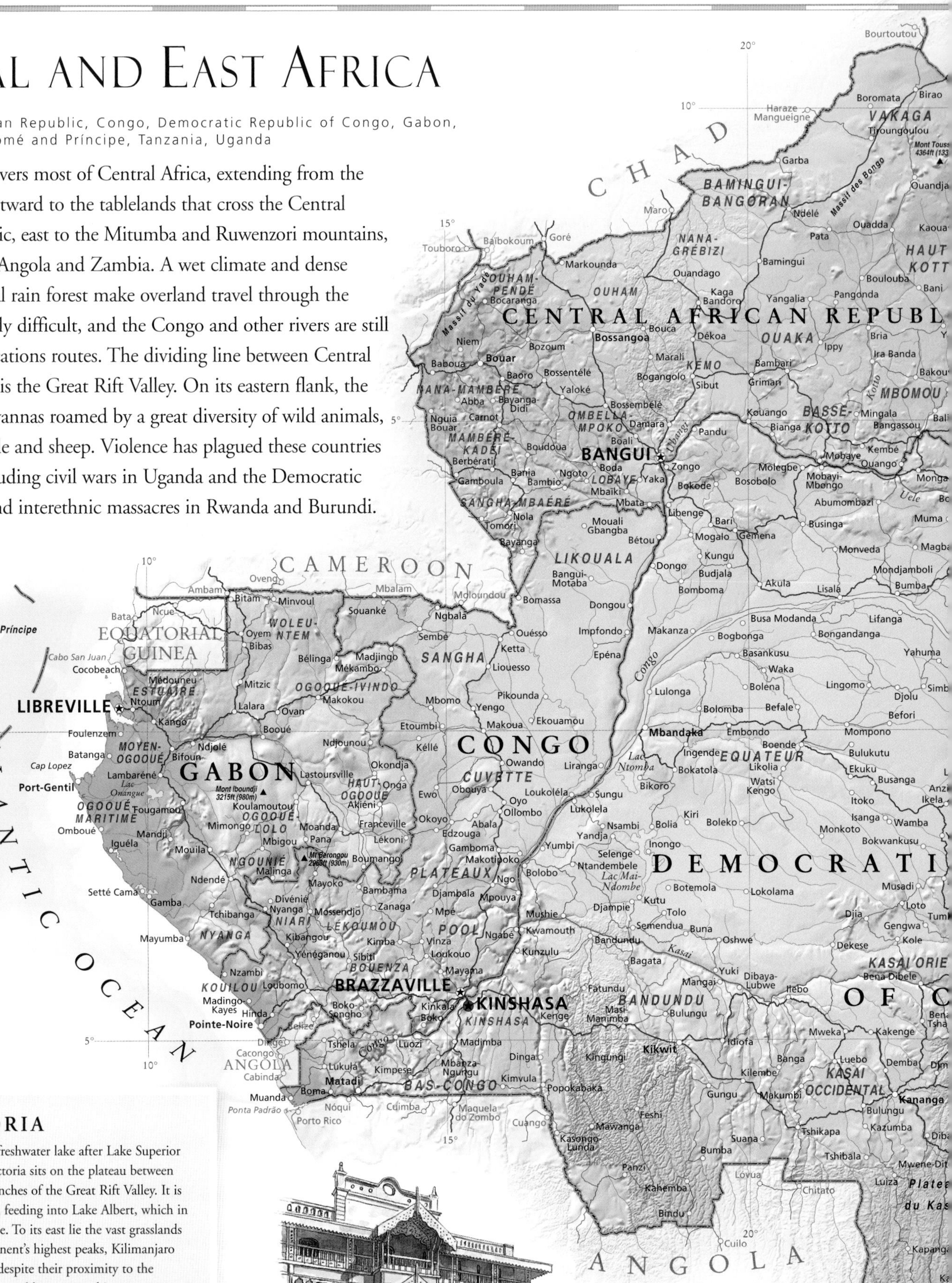

Pygmies continue to practice a nomadic, hunter-gatherer lifestyle in remote parts of the northern Congo Basin.

LAKE VICTORIA

The world's second-largest freshwater lake after Lake Superior in North America, Lake Victoria sits on the plateau between the western and eastern branches of the Great Rift Valley. It is the chief source of the Nile, feeding into Lake Albert, which in turn supplies the Albert Nile. To its east lie the vast grasslands of East Africa and the continent's highest peaks, Kilimanjaro and Mount Kenya, which, despite their proximity to the Equator, are permanently capped by snow and ice.

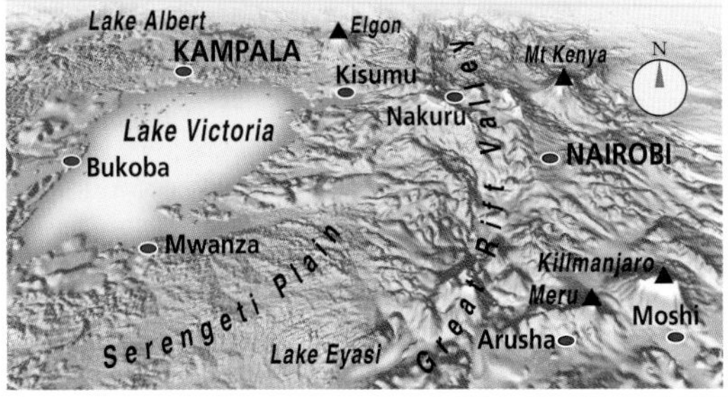

Zanzibar For centuries this island was a hub of trade between Africa, the Middle East, and southern Asia. Its buildings and culture display the diverse influences of its native African inhabitants; Persians who settled here in the tenth century; the Portuguese, who arrived in the 16th century; Omani Arabs, who took over the island in the 17th century; and other immigrants. The Stonetown Cultural Center was built as a hospital in the late 19th century by Indian trader Tharia Topan.

N O P Q R S T U V W X Y Z

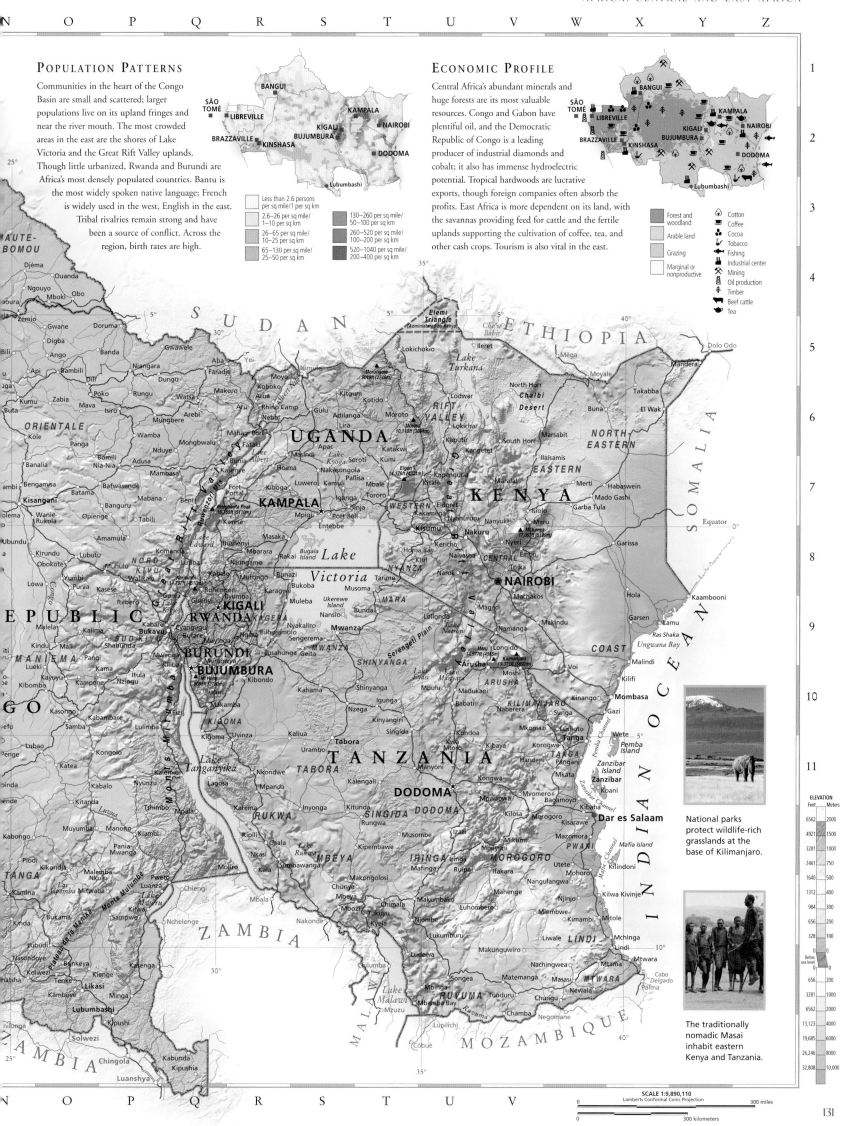

Population Patterns

Communities in the heart of the Congo Basin are small and scattered; larger populations live on its upland fringes and near the river mouth. The most crowded areas in the east are the shores of Lake Victoria and the Great Rift Valley uplands. Though little urbanized, Rwanda and Burundi are Africa's most densely populated countries. Bantu is the most widely spoken native language; French is widely used in the west, English in the east. Tribal rivalries remain strong and have been a source of conflict. Across the region, birth rates are high.

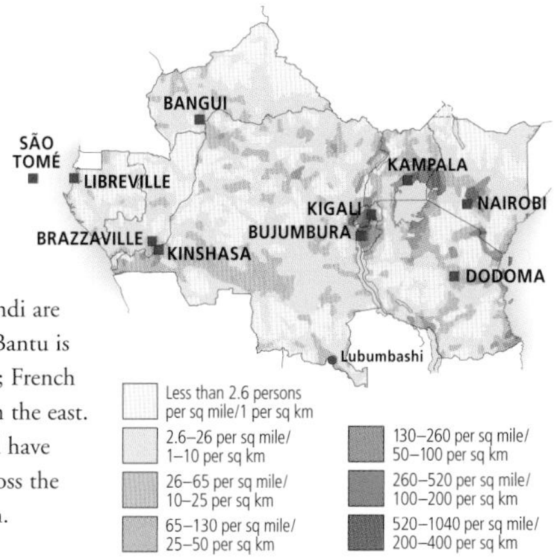
BANGUI
SÃO TOMÉ
LIBREVILLE
KAMPALA
KIGALI
NAIROBI
BUJUMBURA
BRAZZAVILLE
KINSHASA
DODOMA
Lubumbashi
Less than 2.6 persons per sq mile/1 per sq km
2.6–26 per sq mile/ 1–10 per sq km
26–65 per sq mile/ 10–25 per sq km
65–130 per sq mile/ 25–50 per sq km
130–260 per sq mile/ 50–100 per sq km
260–520 per sq mile/ 100–200 per sq km
520–1040 per sq mile/ 200–400 per sq km

Economic Profile

Central Africa's abundant minerals and huge forests are its most valuable resources. Congo and Gabon have plentiful oil, and the Democratic Republic of Congo is a leading producer of industrial diamonds and cobalt; it also has immense hydroelectric potential. Tropical hardwoods are lucrative exports, though foreign companies often absorb the profits. East Africa is more dependent on its land, with the savannas providing feed for cattle and the fertile uplands supporting the cultivation of coffee, tea, and other cash crops. Tourism is also vital in the east.

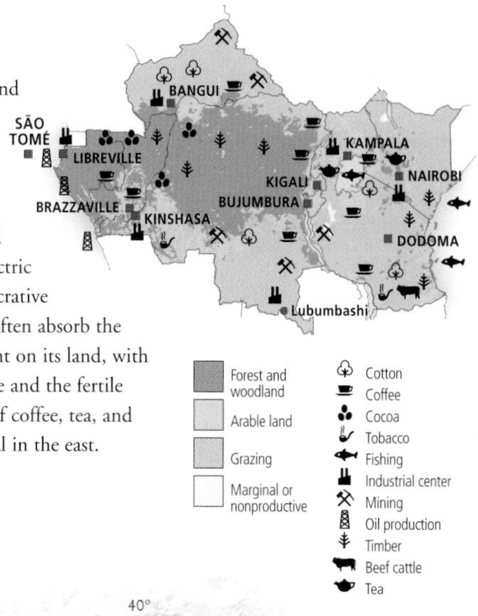
BANGUI
SÃO TOMÉ
LIBREVILLE
KAMPALA
KIGALI
NAIROBI
BUJUMBURA
BRAZZAVILLE
KINSHASA
DODOMA
Lubumbashi
Forest and woodland
Arable land
Grazing
Marginal or nonproductive
Cotton
Coffee
Cocoa
Tobacco
Fishing
Industrial center
Mining
Oil production
Timber
Beef cattle
Tea

SUDAN
ETHIOPIA
UGANDA
KENYA
SOMALIA
RWANDA
BURUNDI
TANZANIA
ZAMBIA
MALAWI
MOZAMBIQUE
INDIAN OCEAN
KAMPALA
NAIROBI
KIGALI
BUJUMBURA
DODOMA
Dar es Salaam
Mombasa
Lake Victoria
Lake Tanganyika
Lake Turkana
Lake Malawi
Elemi Triangle (Administered by Kenya)
Equator
ELEVATION
Feet Meters

National parks protect wildlife-rich grasslands at the base of Kilimanjaro.

The traditionally nomadic Masai inhabit eastern Kenya and Tanzania.

SCALE 1:9,890,110
Lamberts Conformal Conic Projection
0 300 miles
0 300 kilometers

Southern Africa

Angola, Botswana, Comoros, Lesotho, Madagascar, Malawi, Mozambique, Namibia, Republic of South Africa, Swaziland, Zambia, Zimbabwe

Consisting of an undulating tableland rimmed by escarpments and narrow coastal plains, the southern African mainland takes in contrasting environments, including the Namib and Kalahari deserts, the tropical forests of northern Mozambique, and the "Highveld" grasslands of South Africa. About 250 miles (400 km) off its east coast lie the culturally and ecologically distinct island of Madagascar and the small Comoros archipelago. As in other parts of Africa, colonialism left the region a legacy of instability and inequality. Portugal's efforts to retain Mozambique and Angola initiated devastating wars from the 1960s to the early 1990s. White-minority rule sparked conflict in postcolonial Zimbabwe, in Namibia, and in South Africa, where racial segregation was enshrined in law in 1948 as the system of apartheid, and formally abolished only in 1994.

Population Patterns

The east is more densely populated than the west, with heavy settlement occurring in southern Mozambique, central and southern Zimbabwe, and between Pretoria, Durban, and Port Elizabeth in South Africa. Few people live in the western deserts, and Namibia and Botswana are two of Africa's least densely populated countries. Urbanization remains between 30 and 50 percent in most countries, but reaches 60 percent in South Africa. Most southern Africans belong to Bantu-speaking groups, such as the Zulu, Swazi, and Ndebele (Matabele), but Madagascar's Malagasy peoples originated in Indonesia.

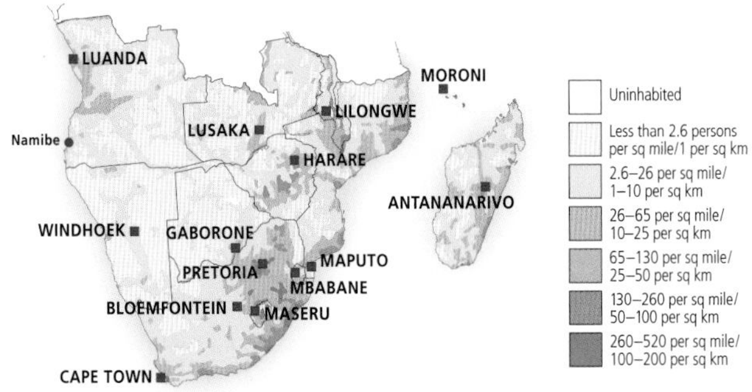

Economic Profile

South Africa has by far the most developed and diversified industrial sector in Africa. Led by iron and steel, transport equipment, and chemicals, it accounts for one-third of the continent's total manufacturing output. The country also has huge mineral reserves, including diamonds, gold (half of world reserves), uranium, and iron ore. Uranium and diamonds are also found in Namibia, gold in Zimbabwe. Angola has sizable oil reserves, Madagascar deposits of graphite. The best arable land lies in the east. Cash crops include tobacco, coffee, tea, and citrus fruits—South Africa is the world's largest producer of grapefruit.

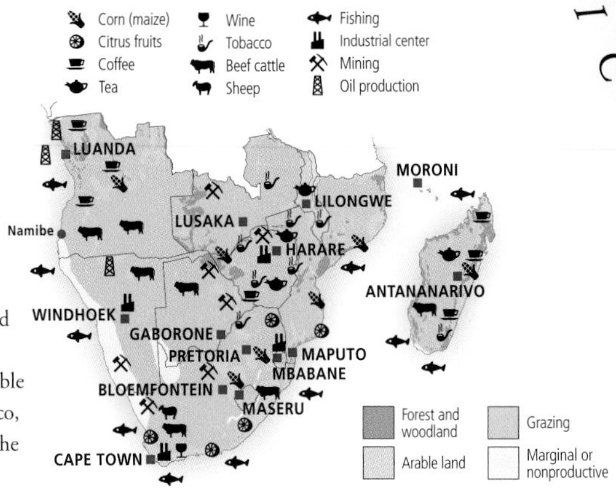

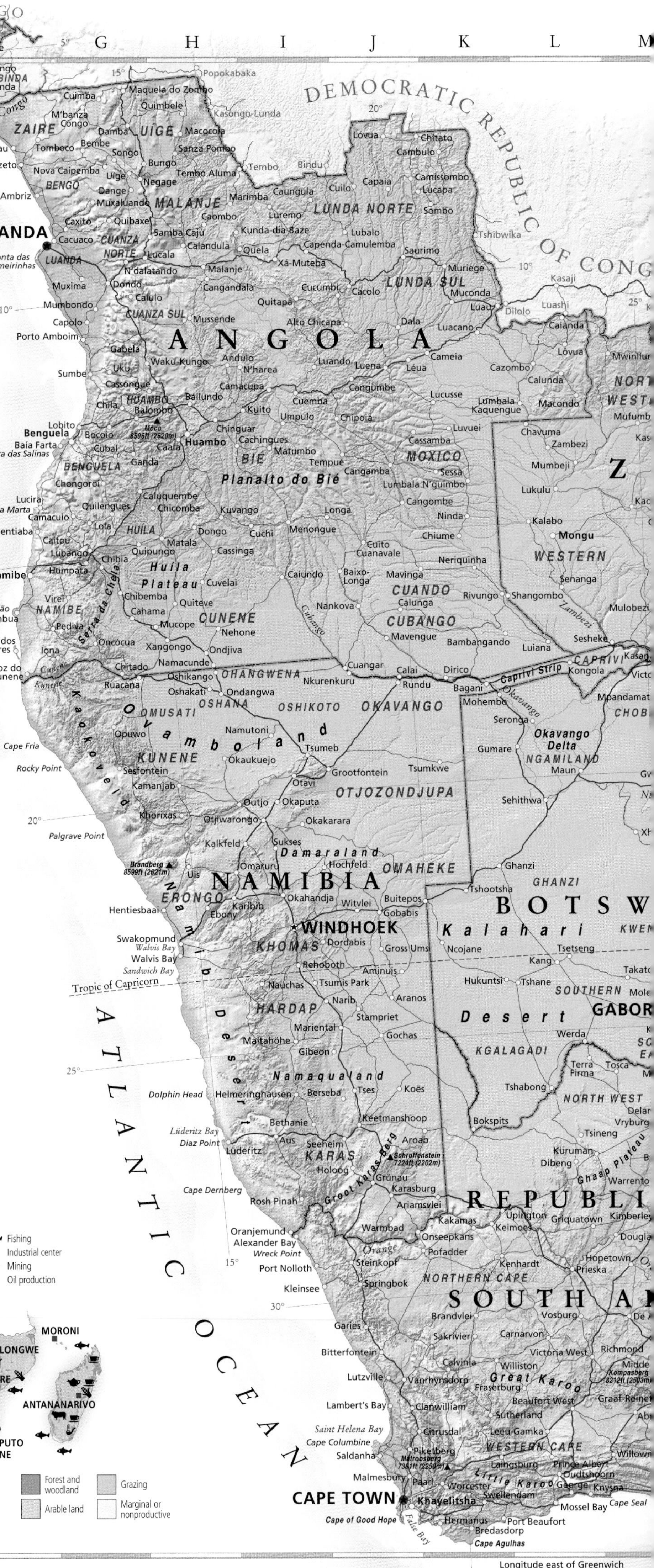

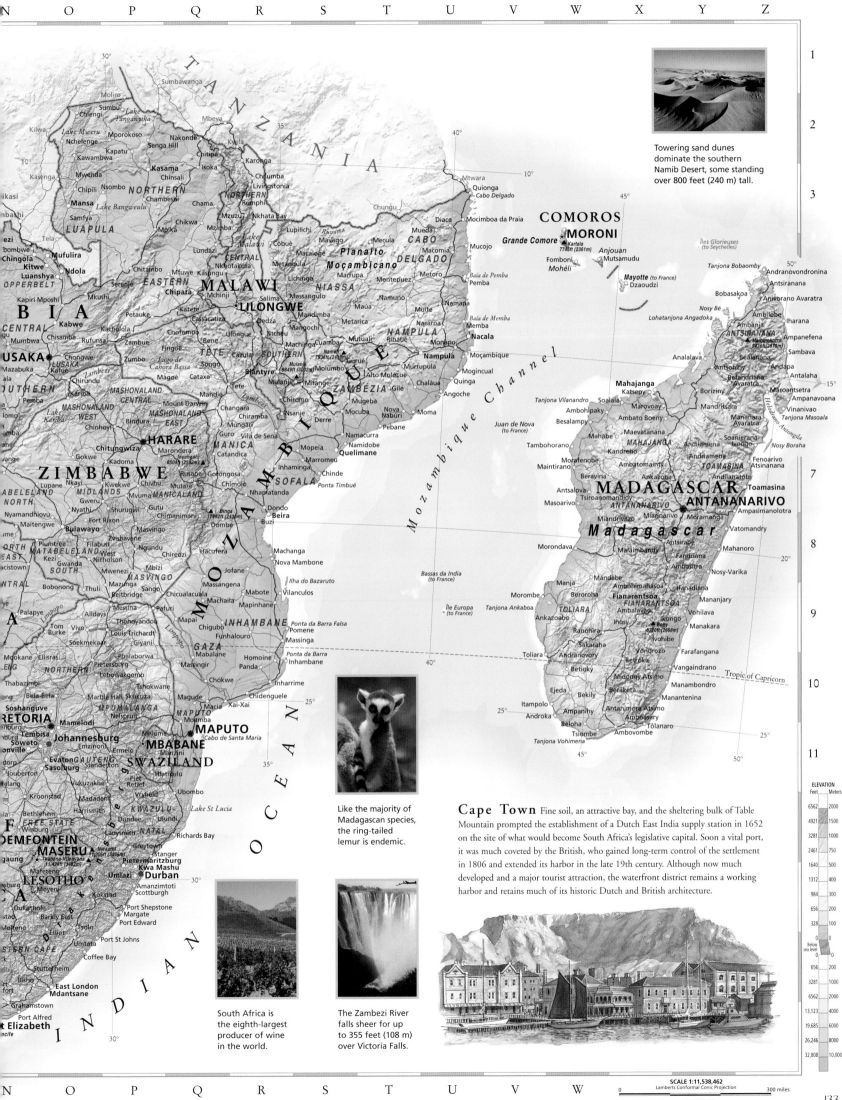

Towering sand dunes dominate the southern Namib Desert, some standing over 800 feet (240 m) tall.

Like the majority of Madagascan species, the ring-tailed lemur is endemic.

South Africa is the eighth-largest producer of wine in the world.

The Zambezi River falls sheer for up to 355 feet (108 m) over Victoria Falls.

Cape Town Fine soil, an attractive bay, and the sheltering bulk of Table Mountain prompted the establishment of a Dutch East India supply station in 1652 on the site of what would become South Africa's legislative capital. Soon a vital port, it was much coveted by the British, who gained long-term control of the settlement in 1806 and extended its harbor in the late 19th century. Although now much developed and a major tourist attraction, the waterfront district remains a working harbor and retains much of its historic Dutch and British architecture.

SCALE 1:11,538,462
Lamberts Conformal Conic Projection
0 — 300 miles
0 — 300 kilometers

Australia

The world's sixth-largest country by area, Australia constitutes an entire continent—the world's smallest, flattest, and (after Antarctica) driest. Its massive landmass consists of an ancient western plateau joined by broad sedimentary lowlands to heavily eroded eastern ranges. Known as the Great Dividing Range, the ranges parallel the Pacific coast, separating the better-watered eastern seaboard from the vast, arid interior or "outback." Despite the continent's poor soils and harsh climate, Aboriginal peoples lived off the land for 60,000 years, developing one of the world's most enduring societies. Europeans began arriving only in the late 18th century after the founding of a British penal colony at Port Jackson, now Sydney, in 1788. This and other British colonies drew increasing numbers of free settlers, especially after the discovery of gold in the southeast in the mid-19th century. In 1901, the colonies agreed to federation, resulting in the creation of the independent nation of Australia.

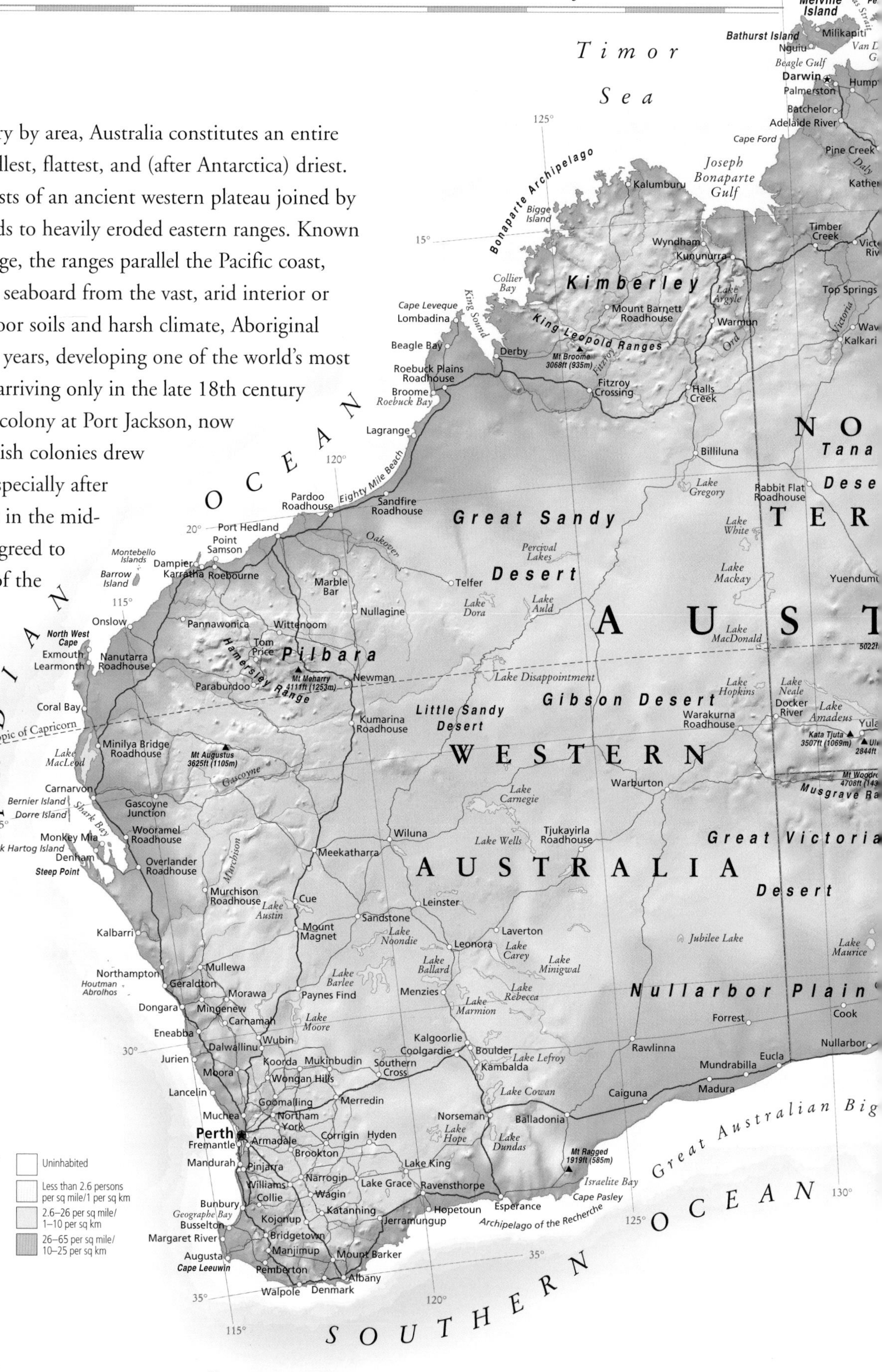

Population Patterns

Recent settlers have shunned the interior, clustering along the temperate east and southwest coasts, where 84 percent of Australians occupy one percent of the land. In the outback, vast areas are devoid of people. Although immigration from Asia has risen in the last 30 years, the majority of Australians are still of European, especially British, origin and English is the official language. Aboriginal and Torres Strait Islander peoples constitute just 2.4 percent of the population. Birth rates are low, and it is estimated that by 2035 immigration will be the country's only source of growth.

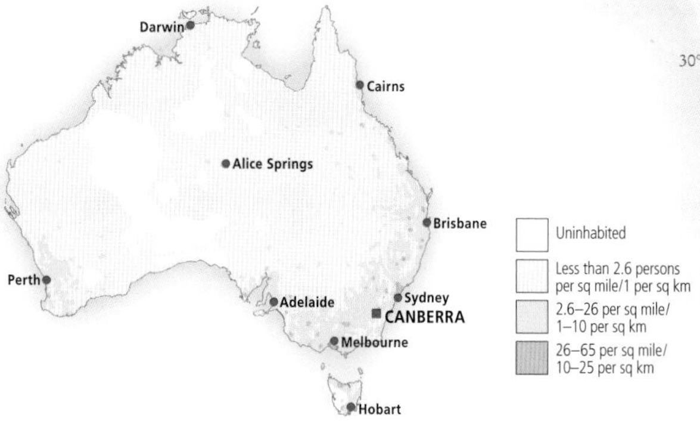

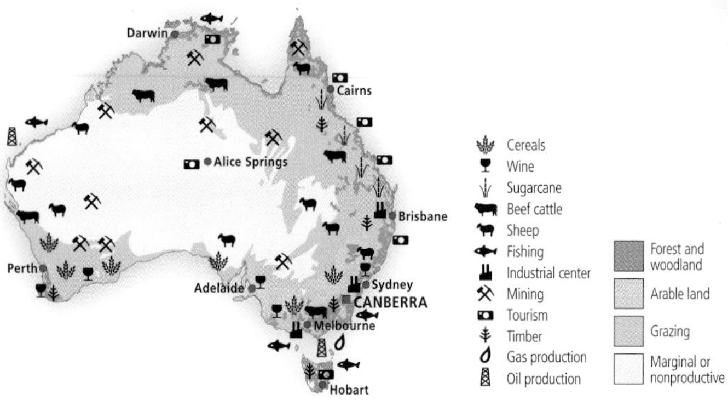

Economic Profile

Australia's economy was founded on agriculture, especially the wool industry, and mining. Arable land is limited to the temperate zones and irrigated areas along major rivers. Wheat is the largest crop and Australia is the world's third-largest exporter. The country is self-sufficient in natural gas and has the world's largest reserves of lead, uranium, silver, and zinc. It is also estimated to have 40 percent of world bauxite supplies and at least 20 percent of world coal, iron ore, and diamond reserves. These resources support heavy industries such as the manufacture of steel, machinery, cars, and chemicals, but services, including a thriving retail trade, banking, and tourism, employ 70 percent of the workforce.

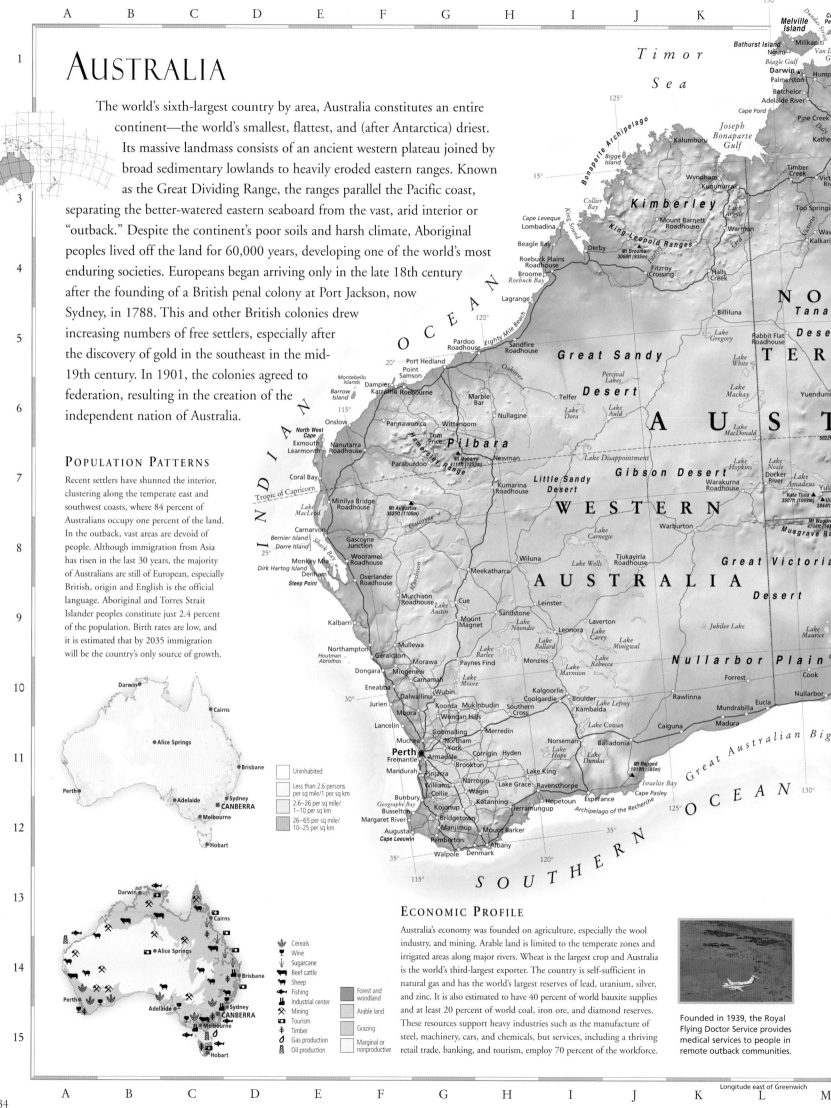

Founded in 1939, the Royal Flying Doctor Service provides medical services to people in remote outback communities.

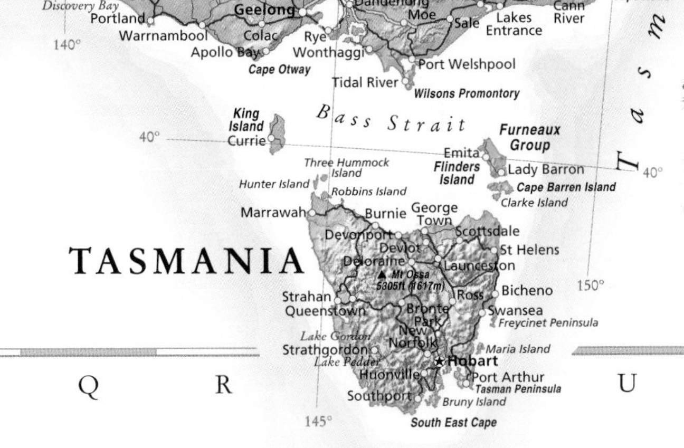

THE GREAT DIVIDING RANGE

More correctly called the Eastern Highlands, the Great Dividing Range stretches from Cape York in northeastern Australia to the island of Tasmania. Rather than a single range, it consists of a chain of eroded plateaus and peaks. The highest part of the range, known as the Australian Alps, lies between Canberra and southern Victoria. Capped by Mount Kosciuszko, the country's tallest peak, the Alps have winter snowfields as large as those of Switzerland, and are the source of the continent's longest waterway, the Murray–Darling.

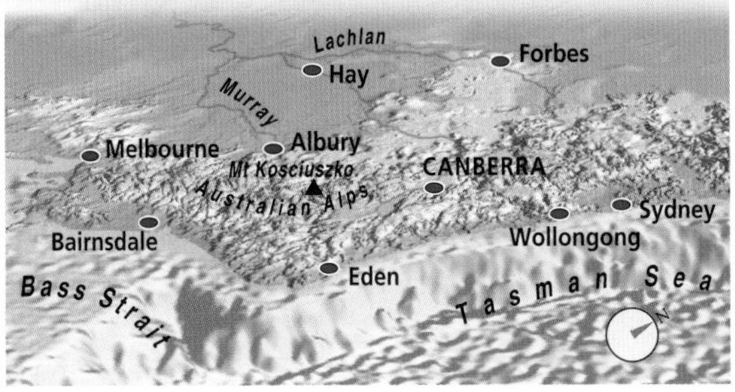

The rain forests of northern Queensland harbor 3,000 plant species, one-quarter of which grow nowhere else.

Introduced to Australia in 1915 from Hawaii, surfing has become an enormously popular recreational pastime.

Sydney The site of the first major European settlement in Australia, Sydney occupies a large, sheltered, and scenic harbor around which it has grown steadily over the past 200 years. Now home to more than 4 million people, it is Australia's largest urban center, sprawling across almost 4,000 square miles (10,000 sq km)—twice the area of New York City. Two highly distinctive landmarks constructed in the 20th century helped the city establish an international identity and have become national icons: the steel, single-span Sydney Harbour Bridge, completed in 1932, and the adjacent Sydney Opera House, designed by Danish architect Jørn Utzon, which opened in 1973.

The perpetuation of long-established rites and customs is an integral part of life in Aboriginal communities.

A B C D E F G H I J K L M N O

NEW ZEALAND

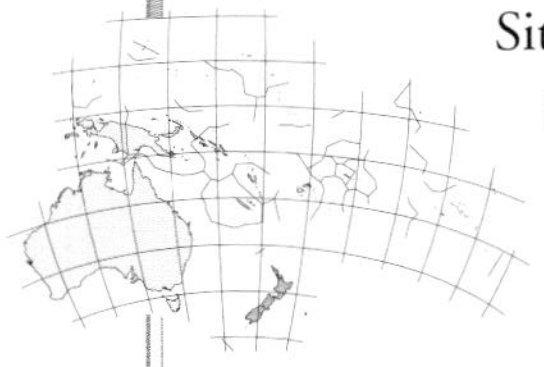

Situated 1,000 miles (1,600 km) southeast of Australia, its nearest neighbor, New Zealand consists of two large islands and several smaller ones. Both main islands straddle fault lines between the Indo-Australian and Pacific tectonic plates. Movement along these faults causes sporadic earthquakes and has formed active volcanoes and geysers in the North Island; over millions of years, it has also pushed up the steep-sided peaks of the Southern Alps, which form the backbone of the South Island. This rugged interior and the South Island's generally cold, wet climate concentrated the development of modern infrastructure in the North Island and along the drier, more fertile east coast of the South Island. Annexed by Britain in 1840, New Zealand became a self-governing colony in 1856 and a dominion in 1907, but did not achieve full independence until 1947. The descendants of British colonists now far outnumber the indigenous Maori, but Maori remains an official language and in recent years the government has made some reparations to Maori peoples for loss of traditional lands.

Wellington Though Auckland is by far the largest city in New Zealand, Wellington is the country's national capital and major business center. The city occupies a large sheltered harbor—the flooded crater of an ancient volcano—at the southern end of the North Island. Europeans arrived in 1840 and moved their seat of government here in 1865. The foreshore, much of it reclaimed land, is the site of the commercial district and major government buildings including the parliament, with its distinctive executive office building, widely known as the Beehive. Designed by British architect Sir Basil Spence, it was begun in 1969 and completed in 1980.

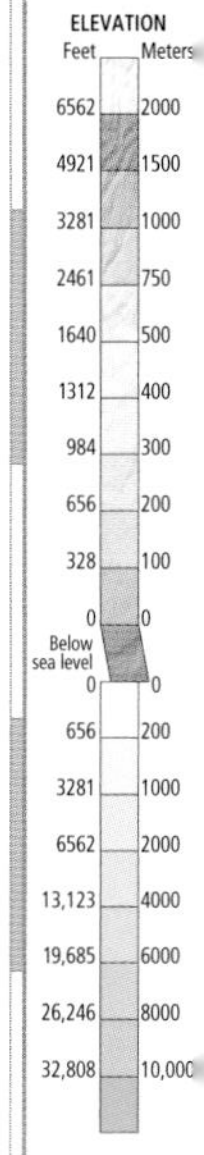

VOLCANO COUNTRY

Volcanic activity has fashioned the landscape of the North Island's central plateau and still has the potential to modify it further. Lake Taupo, the country's largest lake, occupies a crater formed by a massive volcanic explosion thought to have taken place in AD 186. To its south stretches a line of active volcanoes—Tongariro, Ngauruhoe, and Ruapehu—all of which erupted in the 20th century. In 1996, in the country's largest eruption in 400 years, Ruapehu spewed great clouds of steam and ash over the surrounding skifields; fortunately, there were no casualties. Farther west, the huge cone of Mount Taranaki (Mount Egmont) looms over the southwestern corner of the island. Now dormant, it last erupted in the 18th century.

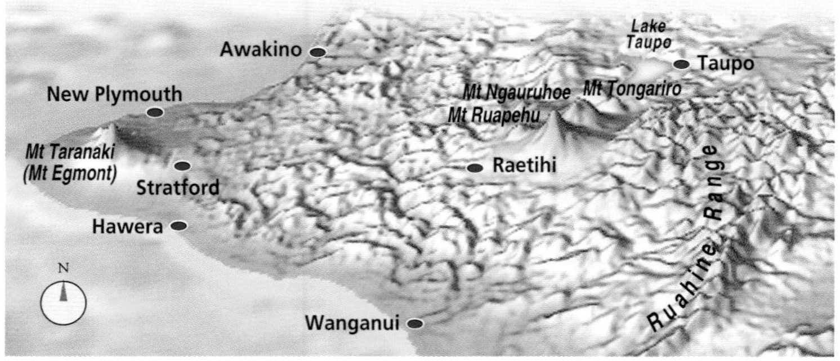

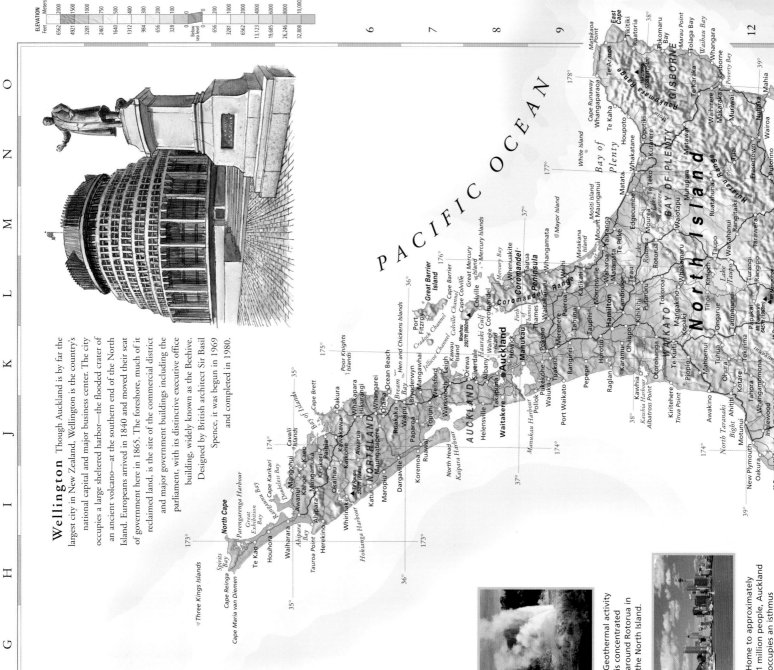

Geothermal activity is concentrated around Rotorua in the North Island.

Home to approximately 1 million people, Auckland occupies an isthmus between two broad harbors.

NEW ZEALAND

The traditional welcome dance, or powhiri, is still performed for visitors to Maori meeting houses.

In the western South Island, Franz Josef Glacier (above) and Fox Glacier descend as far as the coastal lowlands.

The southwest coast of the South Island is characterized by deep fjords, including spectacular Milford Sound.

Tasman Sea
PACIFIC OCEAN
South Island
Southern Alps
Stewart Island
Cook Strait
Foveaux Strait
Canterbury Bight
Tasman Bay
Golden Bay
Pegasus Bay
WELLINGTON
TASMAN
NELSON
MARLBOROUGH
WEST COAST
CANTERBURY
OTAGO
SOUTHLAND
Fiordland
Canterbury Plains
Christchurch
Dunedin
Invercargill
Queenstown
Nelson
Greymouth
Timaru
Oamaru
Mt Cook 12,316ft (3754m)
Banks Peninsula
Cape Farewell
Cape Palliser
West Cape
South West Cape
Longitude east of Greenwich
SCALE 1:3,571,429
Lamberts Conformal Conic Projection
100 miles
100 kilometers

Population Patterns

The North Island constitutes 42 percent of the country but is home to more than three-quarters of the population; indeed, more than 30 percent of New Zealanders live in the Auckland region. About 75 percent of inhabitants live in towns and cities. People of European extraction make up 80 percent of the population, and one in seven New Zealanders is Maori. Ethnic diversity is increasing. The number of residents of Asian origin, for example, climbed 140 percent between 1991 and 2001. Many Pacific Islander people have settled in New Zealand, and Auckland is recognized as the world's largest Polynesian city.

Cathedral Square is the heart of the South Island's largest city, Christchurch.

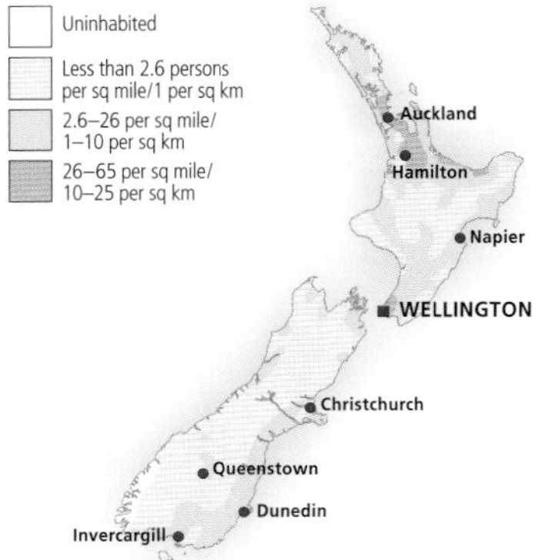
Uninhabited
Less than 2.6 persons per sq mile/1 per sq km
2.6–26 per sq mile/ 1–10 per sq km
26–65 per sq mile/ 10–25 per sq km
Auckland
Hamilton
Napier
WELLINGTON
Christchurch
Queenstown
Dunedin
Invercargill

Economic Profile

New Zealand has a long association with wool, which was the country's leading agricultural product until the late 1970s. But the sheep population has declined, and dairy products and meat are now the nation's most valuable exports. Forests cover 30 percent of the country and forest products, overwhelmingly from plantations, constitute the third most lucrative export. New Zealand is self-sufficient in all energy sources except oil; two-thirds of its electricity comes from hydroelectric power and over 6 percent from geothermal power. Leading industries include foods and beverages (notably wine), machinery, metals, and textiles. However, services employ 65 percent of workers, with tourism alone generating 10 percent of GDP and supporting one in ten jobs.

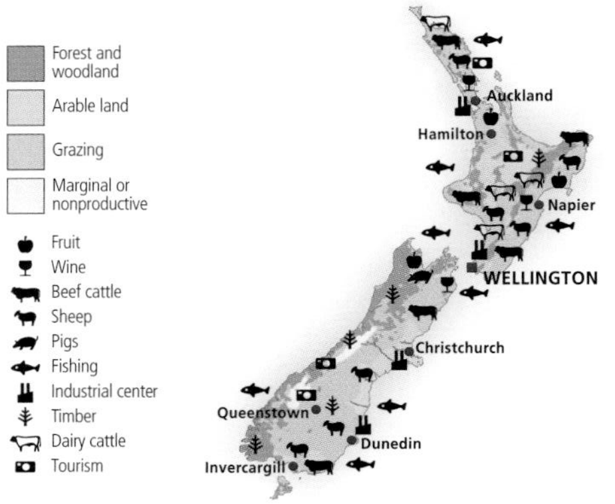
Forest and woodland
Arable land
Grazing
Marginal or nonproductive
Fruit
Wine
Beef cattle
Sheep
Pigs
Fishing
Industrial center
Timber
Dairy cattle
Tourism
Auckland
Hamilton
Napier
WELLINGTON
Christchurch
Queenstown
Dunedin
Invercargill

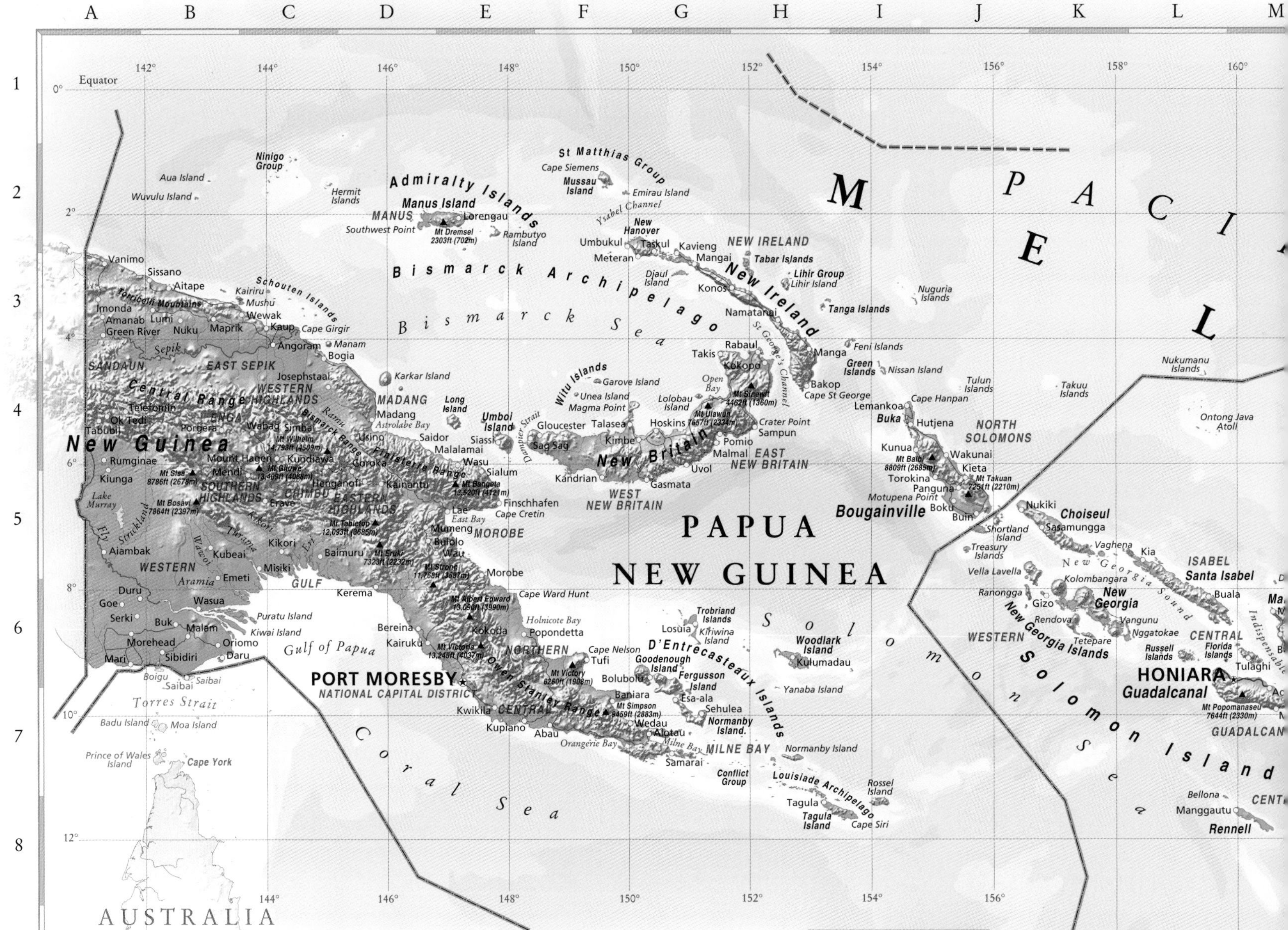

A B C D E F G H I J K L M
1 2 3 4 5 6 7 8 9
Equator
142° 144° 146° 148° 150° 152° 154° 156° 158° 160°
PAPUA
NEW GUINEA
New Guinea
Bismarck Archipelago
Bismarck Sea
Admiralty Islands
Manus Island
St Matthias Group
New Hanover
New Ireland
New Britain
WEST NEW BRITAIN
EAST NEW BRITAIN
NEW IRELAND
MANUS
MADANG
EAST SEPIK
SANDAUN
WESTERN HIGHLANDS
SOUTHERN HIGHLANDS
EASTERN HIGHLANDS
CHIMBU
ENGA
WESTERN
GULF
MOROBE
NORTHERN
CENTRAL
MILNE BAY
NORTH SOLOMONS
PORT MORESBY
NATIONAL CAPITAL DISTRICT
Gulf of Papua
Torres Strait
Coral Sea
Solomon Sea
Bougainville
Choiseul
Santa Isabel
New Georgia
Guadalcanal
HONIARA
Solomon Islands
Rennell
D'Entrecasteaux Islands
Louisiade Archipelago
Trobriand Islands
Woodlark Island
Cape York
AUSTRALIA
MELANESIA
PACIFIC
Longitude east of Greenwich

MELANESIA

Fiji, Papua New Guinea, Solomon Islands, Vanuatu

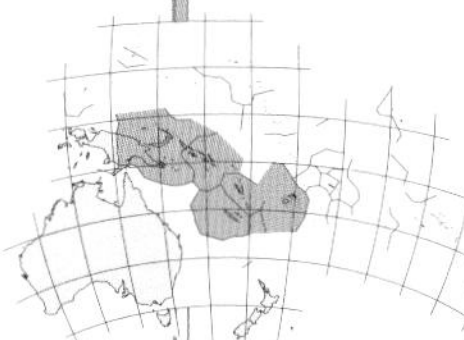

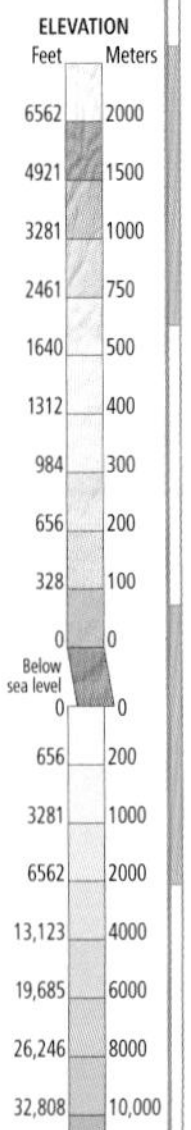

ELEVATION
Feet Meters
6562 2000
4921 1500
3281 1000
2461 750
1640 500
1312 400
984 300
656 200
328 100
0 0
Below sea level
0
656 200
3281 1000
6562 2000
13,123 4000
19,685 6000
26,246 8000
32,808 10,000

The islands of Melanesia arc around the northeast coast of Australia, extend south toward the Tropic of Capricorn and spread east to the edge of the Western Hemisphere. They lie close to the boundary between the Indo-Australian and Pacific plates and have been shaped by relatively recent tectonic activity. Most are mountainous and many have active volcanoes and dark volcanic soil—the word Melanesia derives from the Greek terms *melas* (meaning "black") and *nesoi* ("islands"). Almost all are blanketed with a dense covering of tropical rain forest, though parts of this forest have been cleared. Independence has been achieved by all of the island groups except New Caledonia, which chose to remain part of France. However, many parts of Melanesia have been politically volatile in recent years. In New Caledonia in the 1980s, indigenous Kanak people began a campaign for independence that led to sporadic violence. Coups took place in Fiji in 1987 and 2000, and in Bougainville an armed independence movement fought a war against the Papua New Guinea government from 1988 to 2001.

In the Papua New Guinea highlands, men attending festivals called sing-sings wear paint and headdresses.

Bougainville's giant Panguna copper mine was closed down during the secessionist war and has not reopened.

Fiji's picturesque islands and highly developed tourist facilities attract up to 400,000 visitors a year.

Villagers on the island of Tanna in Vanuatu perform a traditional dance in sight of Yasur, a highly active volcano.

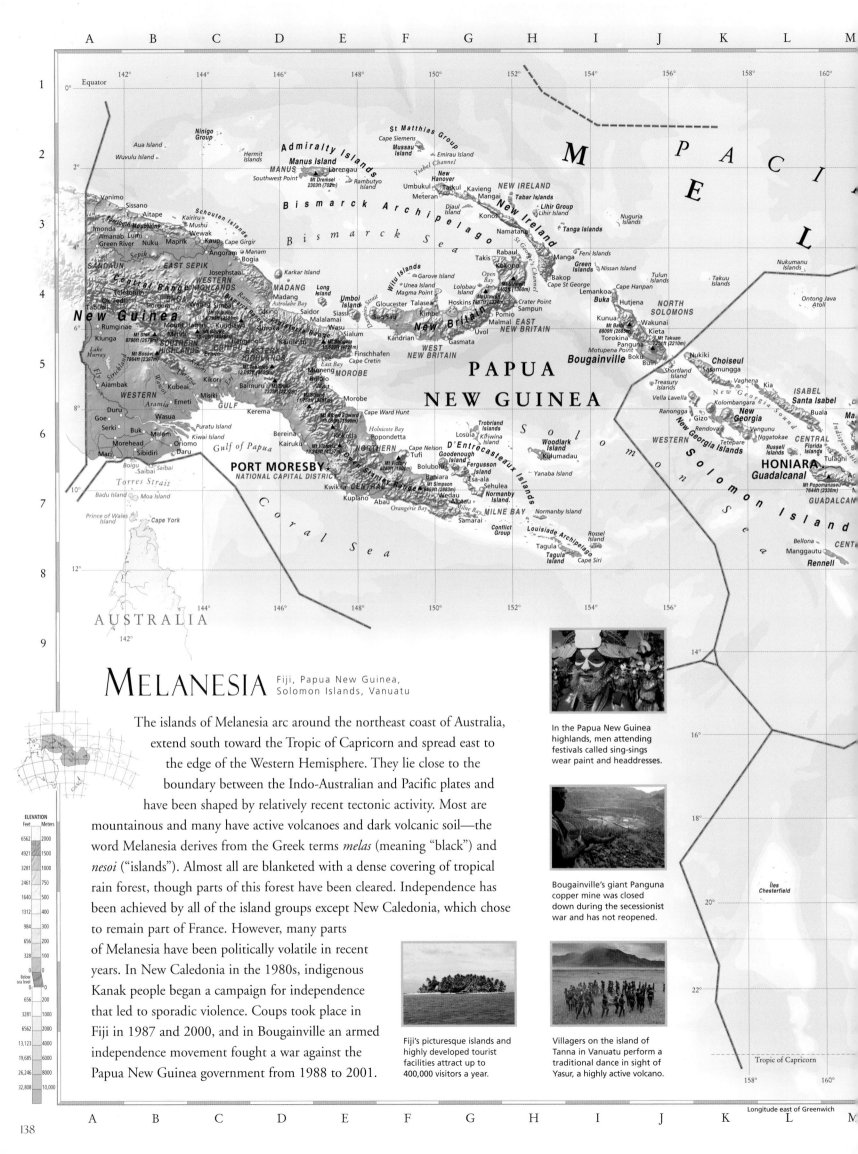

Population Patterns

Population density and growth rates are high in Melanesia, with steadily increasing numbers of people occupying relatively small islands. In the largest, most populous country, Papua New Guinea, the cooler highlands are the most crowded areas. Four-fifths of the inhabitants of New Caledonia live in the capital, Nouméa, but elsewhere urbanization remains low. An extraordinary variety of languages is spoken in Melanesia: over 700 are in use in Papua New Guinea, and over 100 in much smaller Vanuatu. Pidgin is used as a lingua franca in many areas and English is an official language everywhere except New Caledonia.

Economic Profile

The majority of people rely on fishing or subsistence farming of sweet potato, yams, taro, or cassava. Cash crops include cocoa, coffee, palm oil, coconuts and copra, tuna, and sugar in Fiji. Exceptionally, Vanuatu has a thriving beef industry. Minerals are abundant and widespread, including deposits of copper and gold in Papua New Guinea (Bougainville has the world's largest copper reserves), 40 percent of the world's nickel in New Caledonia, gold in Fiji, and phosphates in the Solomons. Industries are limited to resource (mainly food) processing, services are dominated by tourism. Vanuatu promotes itself as a tax haven, offering an offshore shipping registry and banking.

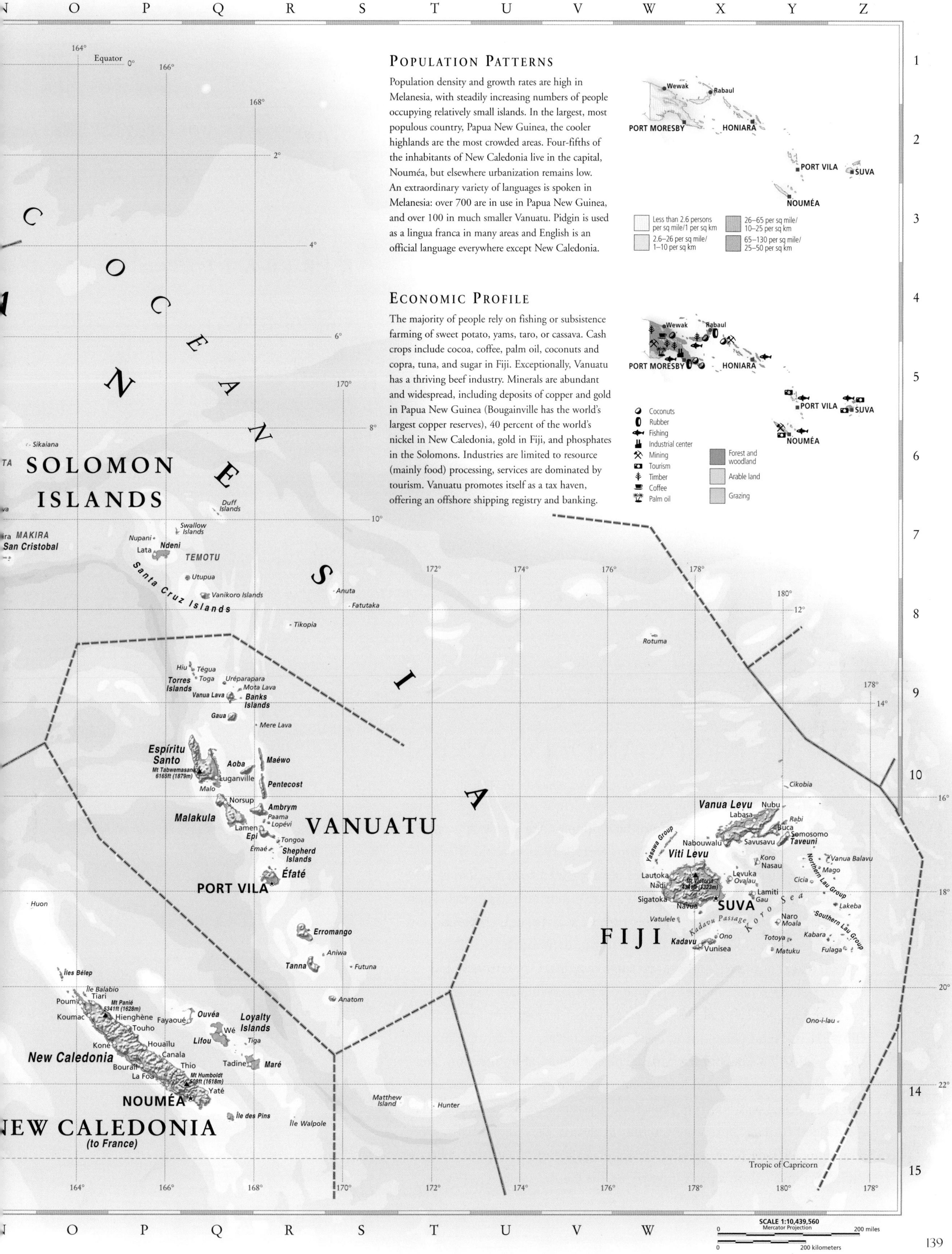
Wewak
Rabaul
PORT MORESBY
HONIARA
PORT VILA
SUVA
NOUMÉA
Less than 2.6 persons per sq mile/1 per sq km
2.6–26 per sq mile/ 1–10 per sq km
26–65 per sq mile/ 10–25 per sq km
65–130 per sq mile/ 25–50 per sq km
Coconuts
Rubber
Fishing
Industrial center
Mining
Tourism
Timber
Coffee
Palm oil
Forest and woodland
Arable land
Grazing
N O P Q R S T U V W X Y Z
1 2 3 4 5 6 7 8 9 10 14 15
Equator
OCEANIA
MELANESIA
SOLOMON ISLANDS
Sikaiana
MAKIRA
San Cristobal
Duff Islands
Swallow Islands
Nupani
Lata
Ndeni
TEMOTU
Santa Cruz Islands
Utupua
Vanikoro Islands
Anuta
Fatutaka
Tikopia
Hiu
Tégua
Torres Islands
Toga
Uréparapara
Mota Lava
Vanua Lava
Banks Islands
Gaua
Mere Lava
Espíritu Santo
Mt Tabwemasana 6165ft (1879m)
Aoba
Maéwo
Luganville
Pentecost
Malo
Norsup
Ambrym
Malakula
Paama
Lopévi
Lamen
Epi
Tongoa
Émaé
Shepherd Islands
Éfaté
VANUATU
PORT VILA
Erromango
Aniwa
Tanna
Futuna
Anatom
Huon
Îles Bélep
Île Balabio
Tiari
Poum
Mt Panié 5341ft (1628m)
Koumac
Hienghène
Fayaoué
Ouvéa
Loyalty Islands
Touho
Wé
Koné
Houaïlu
Lifou
Tiga
New Caledonia
Canala
Thio
Tadine
Maré
Bourail
La Foa
Mt Humboldt 5308ft (1618m)
Yaté
NOUMÉA
Île des Pins
NEW CALEDONIA
(to France)
Île Walpole
Matthew Island
Hunter
Rotuma
Cikobia
Vanua Levu
Nubu
Labasa
Rabi
Buca
Somosomo
Taveuni
Yasawa Group
Nabouwalu
Savusavu
Viti Levu
Koro
Nasau
Vanua Balavu
Northern Lau Group
Mago
Lautoka
Nadi
Mt Victoria 4341ft (1323m)
Levuka
Ovalau
Cicia
Lamiti
Gau
Sigatoka
Navua
SUVA
Koro Sea
Lakeba
Vatulele
Kadavu Passage
Naro
Moala
Southern Lau Group
FIJI
Kadavu
Ono
Vunisea
Totoya
Kabara
Matuku
Fulaga
Ono-i-lau
Tropic of Capricorn
SCALE 1:10,439,560
Mercator Projection
0 200 miles
0 200 kilometers

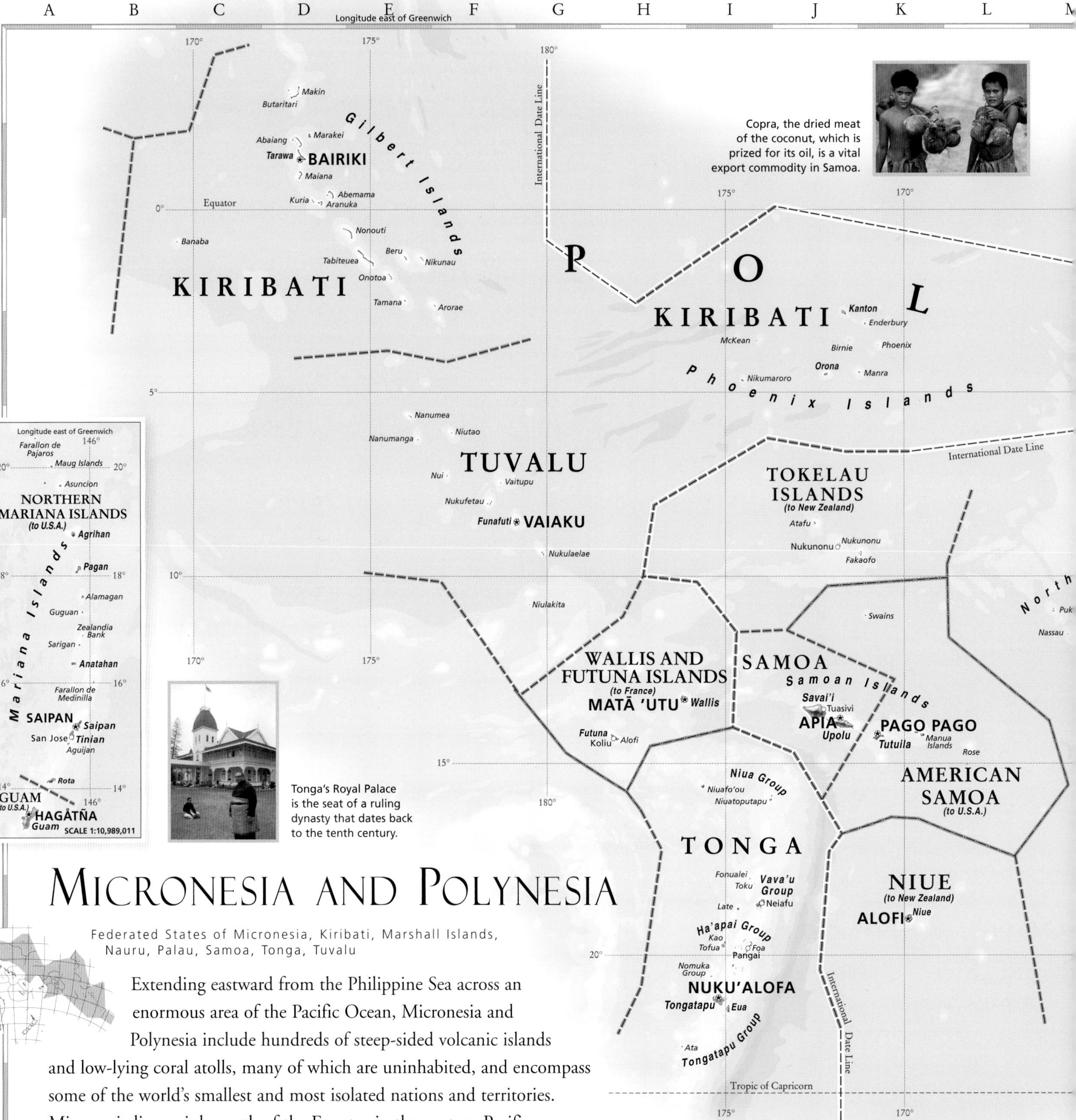
Longitude east of Greenwich
International Date Line
Equator
Gilbert Islands
Makin
Butaritari
Marakei
Abaiang
Tarawa
BAIRIKI
Maiana
Abemama
Kuria
Aranuka
Banaba
Nonouti
Beru
Tabiteuea
Nikunau
Onotoa
Tamana
Arorae
KIRIBATI
P O L
Kanton
Enderbury
McKean
Birnie
Phoenix
Orona
Manra
Nikumaroro
Phoenix Islands
Nanumea
Niutao
Nanumanga
TUVALU
Nui
Vaitupu
Nukufetau
Funafuti
VAIAKU
Nukulaelae
Niulakita
TOKELAU ISLANDS
(to New Zealand)
Atafu
Nukunonu
Fakaofo
Swains
North
Nassau
WALLIS AND FUTUNA ISLANDS
(to France)
MATĀ 'UTU
Wallis
Futuna
Koliu
Alofi
SAMOA
Samoan Islands
Savai'i
Tuasivi
APIA
Upolu
PAGO PAGO
Tutuila
Manua Islands
Rose
AMERICAN SAMOA
(to U.S.A.)
Niua Group
Niuafo'ou
Niuatoputapu
TONGA
Fonualei
Toku
Vava'u Group
Late
Neiafu
Ha'apai Group
Kao
Tofua
Foa
Pangai
Nomuka Group
NUKU'ALOFA
Tongatapu
Eua
Tongatapu Group
Ata
NIUE
(to New Zealand)
ALOFI
Niue
Tropic of Capricorn
Farallon de Pajaros
Maug Islands
Asuncion
NORTHERN MARIANA ISLANDS
(to U.S.A.)
Agrihan
Pagan
Alamagan
Guguan
Zealandia Bank
Sarigan
Anatahan
Mariana Islands
Farallon de Medinilla
SAIPAN
Saipan
San Jose
Tinian
Aguijan
Rota
GUAM
(to U.S.A.)
HAGÅTÑA
Guam
SCALE 1:10,989,011

Copra, the dried meat of the coconut, which is prized for its oil, is a vital export commodity in Samoa.

Tonga's Royal Palace is the seat of a ruling dynasty that dates back to the tenth century.

MICRONESIA AND POLYNESIA

Federated States of Micronesia, Kiribati, Marshall Islands, Nauru, Palau, Samoa, Tonga, Tuvalu

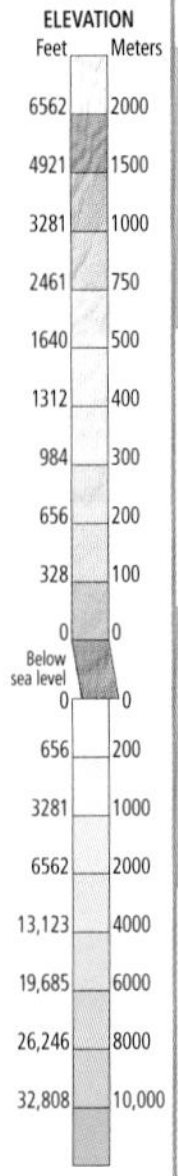
ELEVATION
Feet
Meters
6562 2000
4921 1500
3281 1000
2461 750
1640 500
1312 400
984 300
656 200
328 100
0 0
Below sea level
0 0
656 200
3281 1000
6562 2000
13,123 4000
19,685 6000
26,246 8000
32,808 10,000

Extending eastward from the Philippine Sea across an enormous area of the Pacific Ocean, Micronesia and Polynesia include hundreds of steep-sided volcanic islands and low-lying coral atolls, many of which are uninhabited, and encompass some of the world's smallest and most isolated nations and territories. Micronesia lies mainly north of the Equator in the western Pacific Ocean. Much of the region was, and some remains, U.S. territory, and the continuing American presence includes a major military base on the island of Guam. Polynesia, which spreads across the southern Pacific into the Western Hemisphere, incorporates mainly former and existing British, French, and New Zealand territories. The economies of both regions are based predominantly on subsistence cultivation (of coconuts, fruits, and cassava), fishing, and tourism. Phosphate deposits were once abundant on Nauru and Kiribati, but have been fully exploited. Less traditional sources of revenue include Niue's sales of local postage stamps to overseas collectors, and a lucrative cultured pearl industry on the Cook Islands.

The Rock Islands are an archipelago of 320 coralline limestone outcrops located east of Koror in Palau.

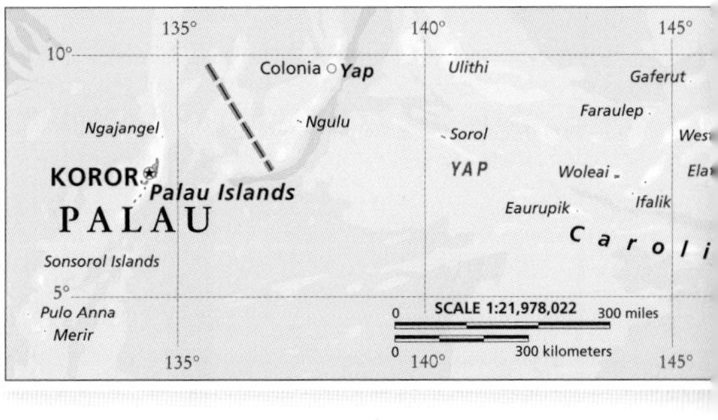
Colonia
Yap
Ulithi
Gaferut
Faraulep
Ngajangel
Ngulu
Sorol
YAP
Woleai
Ifalik
Eauripik
KOROR
Palau Islands
PALAU
Carol
Sonsorol Islands
Pulo Anna
Merir
SCALE 1:21,978,022
300 miles
300 kilometers

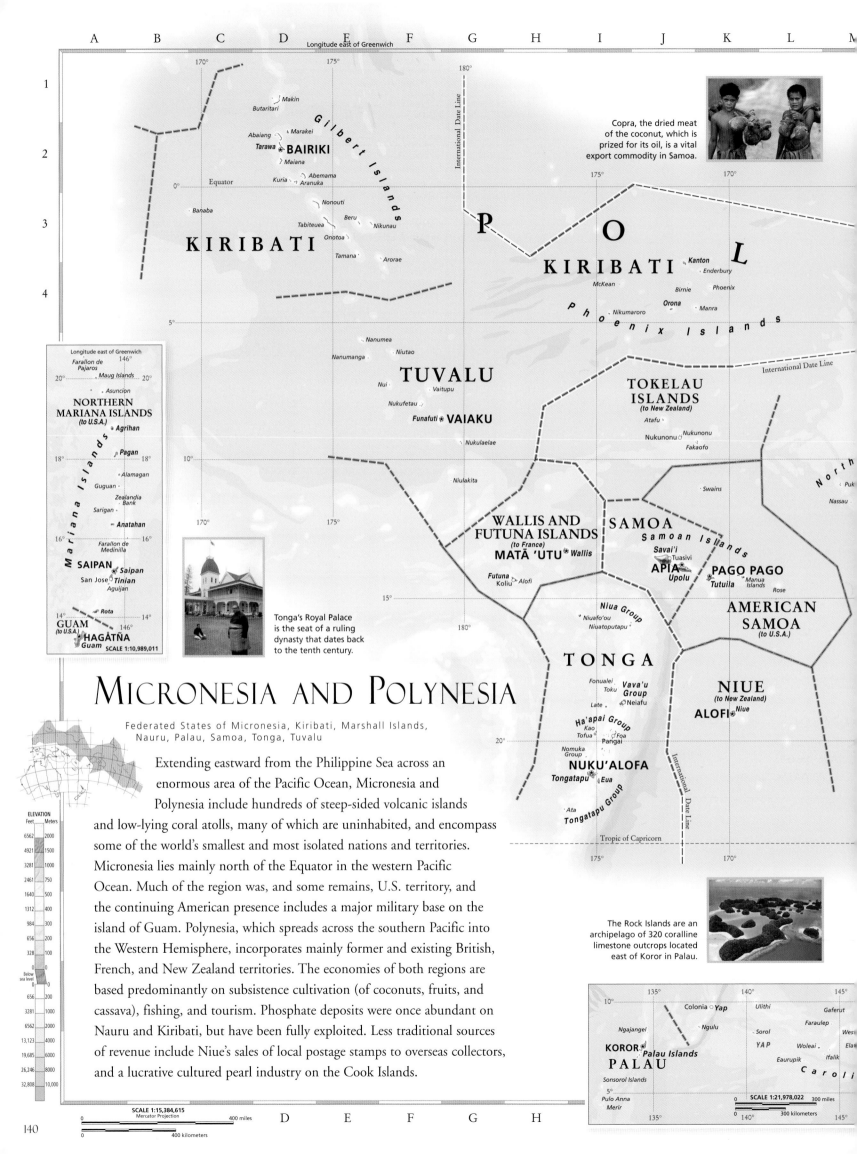

SCALE 1:15,384,615
Mercator Projection
0 400 miles
0 400 kilometers

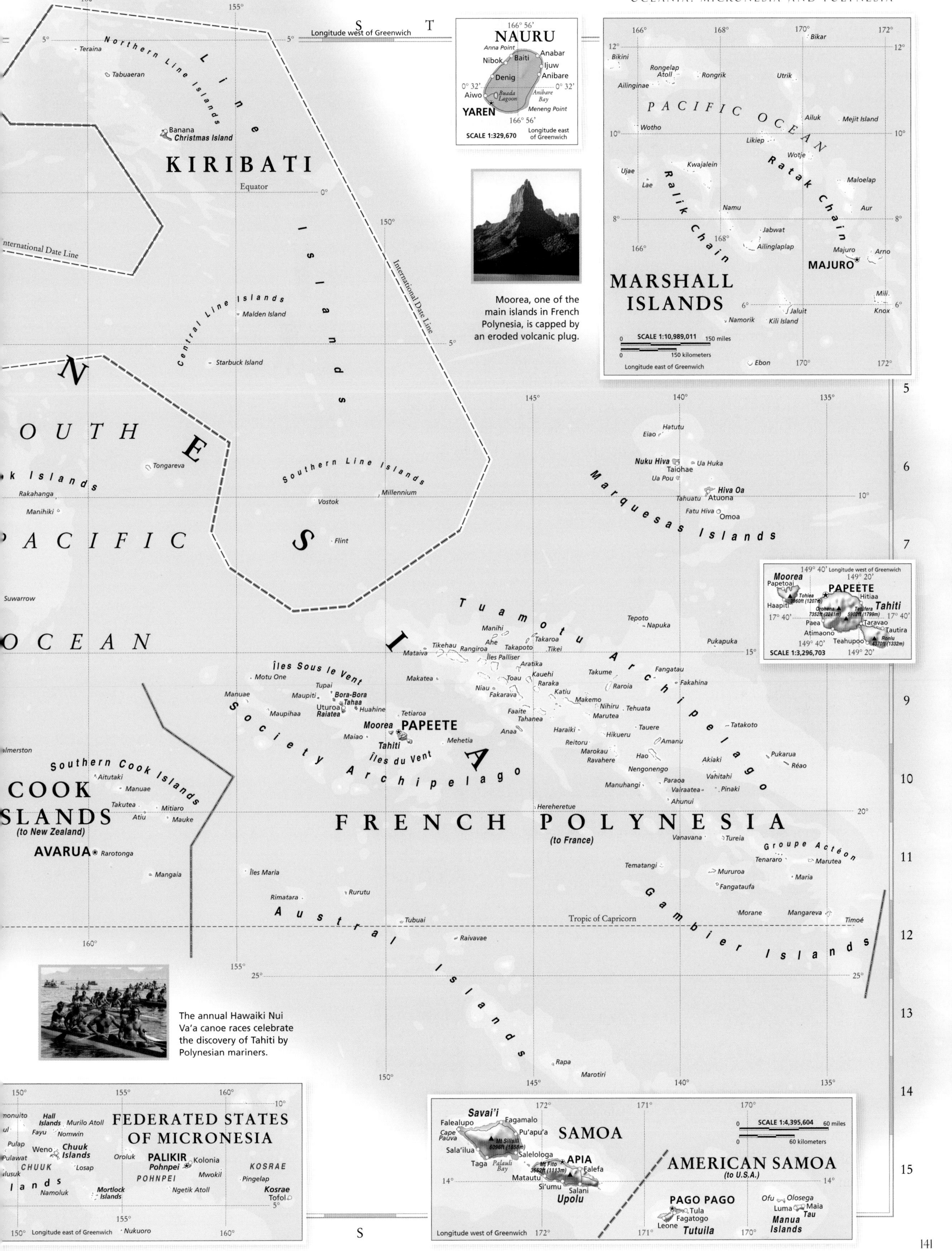

Moorea, one of the main islands in French Polynesia, is capped by an eroded volcanic plug.

The annual Hawaiki Nui Va'a canoe races celebrate the discovery of Tahiti by Polynesian mariners.

A B C D E F G H I J K L M

The Arctic

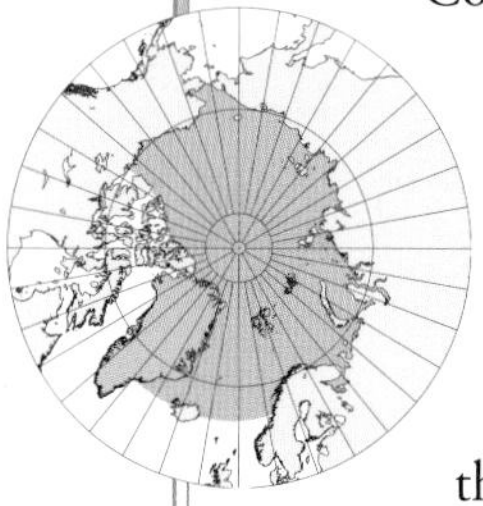

Covering 5.5 million square miles (14.1 million sq km), the Arctic Ocean is the world's smallest ocean. It is ringed by the continental fringes of North America, Europe, and Asia, as well as associated islands, including the largest island on Earth, Greenland. The ocean reaches depths of over 18,000 feet (5,500 m) and is divided into major basins by extensive undersea ranges, the largest of which, the Lomonosov Ridge, surpasses 10,000 feet (3,000 m) in height. Pack ice covers most of the sea surface year-round, expanding to reach most surrounding landmasses in winter. This shoreline has been inhabited by indigenous groups such as the North American Inuit, Asian Yakut, and European Saami for thousands of years. They have learned to cope with the Arctic's extreme climate, including months of darkness in winter, and exploit its restricted range of biological resources. Europeans first explored the Arctic Ocean in the 16th century, searching for a shortcut between Europe and Asia. More recently, outsiders have been lured here by the discovery of potentially vast undersea mineral reserves.

The polar ice pack is 10 feet (3 m) thick on average, but ridges form that may be up to three times that depth.

NORTH POLE
90N

Directly beneath the North Pole, the ocean is 13,410 feet (4,087 m) deep.

Natural Resources

The Arctic Ocean's pack ice blocks sunlight, inhibiting photosynthetic processes and limiting marine life, but rich fisheries exist in areas of open ocean such as the Barents, Greenland, and Bering seas. Seals and whales were long a valuable resource for native peoples and, from the late 17th century, the basis of lucrative commercial trades operated by Europeans. Whaling is now banned, but sealing still takes place in Newfoundland and the White Sea. Sparse grazing lands fringe the ocean, providing food for wild caribou in North America and about 3 million domesticated reindeer in Scandinavia and Russia. Huge reserves of oil, coal, and gas have been tapped in northern Siberia and Alaska; even larger supplies are thought to lie offshore, but so far remain inaccessible.

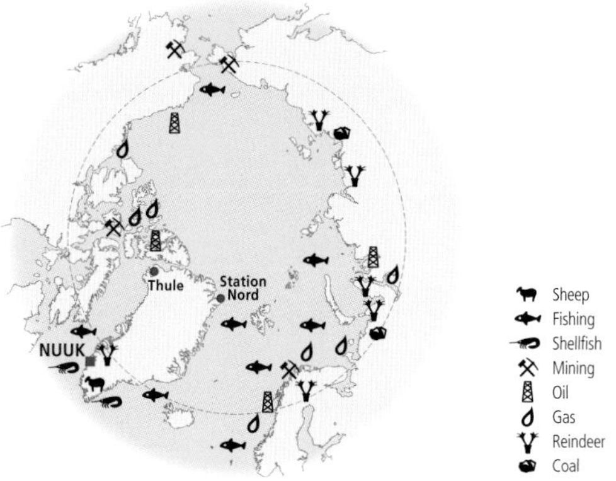
Thule
Station Nord
NUUK
Sheep
Fishing
Shellfish
Mining
Oil
Gas
Reindeer
Coal

Greenland and Iceland

At the boundary between the Arctic and Atlantic oceans, the narrow Denmark Strait divides Greenland from the much smaller island of Iceland. About two-thirds of Greenland lies within the Arctic Circle, and the northern tip of the island lies just 500 miles (800 km) from the North Pole. More than 80 percent of the landmass is blanketed by the world's second-largest ice sheet. Cupped within a basin encircled by coastal peaks, it has an average thickness of about 5,000 feet (1,500 m). Iceland sits astride the Reykjanes Ridge, part of the Mid-Atlantic Ridge. Divergence of tectonic plates along this boundary steadily tears the island apart, giving rise to great faults as well as volcanoes and geysers.

In winter, the Arctic fox grows a white coat to blend in with the snow.

Baffin Island
Davis Strait
Greenland
NUUK
Ammassalik
Ittoqqortoormiit
Denmark Strait
Iceland
Reykjanes Ridge

About 3,000 people live on Svalbard, working mainly in coal extraction.

Yakut hunters in the Siberian Arctic employ modern means to catch traditional prey, including seals and walruses.

NORTH AM
Great Slave Lake
Hudson Bay
Southampton Island
Coats Island
Mansel Island
Foxe Basin
Foxe Peninsula
Prince Charles Island
Melville Peninsula
King William Island
Queen Maud Gulf
Hudson Strait
Ungava Bay
Baffin Isl
Cape Chidley
Labrador Sea
Labrador Basin
NUUK
Ivittuut
Narsarsuaq
Nanortalik

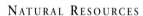

Ice cap
Ice shelf

ELEVATION Feet	Meters
6562	2000
4921	1500
3281	1000
2461	750
1640	500
1312	400
984	300
656	200
328	100
0	0
Below sea level 0	0

SCALE 1:21,978,022
Lamberts Azimuthal Equal Area Projection
0 — 600 miles
0 — 600 kilometers

E F G H I J K L M

X Y Z
Bering Sea
Gulf of Anadyr
St Lawrence Island
Norton Sound
Seward Peninsula
Bering Strait
Kotzebue Sound
Arctic Circle
Brooks Range
Proliv Longa
Wrangel Island
Yanskiy Zaliv
Kolyma
Indigirka
A S I A
Chukchi Sea
East Siberian Sea
Beaufort Sea
Northwind Plain
Chukchi Abyssal Plain
Chukchi Plateau
Canadian Abyssal Plain
Mendeleyev Ridge
Canada Basin
Limit of permanent ice cap
Ostrov Novaya Sibir'
Proliv Dmitriya Lapteva
Lyakhovskiye Ostrova
New Siberia Islands
Ostrov Kotel'nyy
Buorkhaya Guba
Yana
Lena
Wrangel Sea
Laptev Sea
Olenëk
Banks Island
Prince Patrick Island
McClure Strait
Melville Island
Viscount Melville Sound
Mackenzie King Island
Lougheed Island
Ellef Ringnes Island
Bathurst Island
Amund Ringnes Island
Parry Islands
Queen Elizabeth Islands
Axel Heiberg Island
Devon Island
Lancaster Sound
Ellesmere Island
ARCTIC OCEAN
Alpha Ridge
Makarov Basin
Lomonosov Ridge
North Pole
Pole Plain
Fram Basin
Nansen Cordillera
Nansen Basin
Khatangskiy Zaliv
Ozero Taymyr
Severnaya Zemlya
Proliv Vil'kitskogo
Ostrov Bol'shevik
Ostrov Oktyabr'skoy Revolyutsii
Kara Sea
Yenisey
Yeniseyskiy Zaliv
Taz
Cape Columbia
Nares Strait
Baffin Basin
Ummannaq
Thule
Knud Rasmussen Land
Kap Morris Jesup
Peary Land
Wandel Sea
Station Nord
Franz Josef Land
Ostrov Belyy
Obskaya Guba
Novaya Zemlya
Barents Plain
Baffin Bay
Nuussuaq
Tasiusaq
Sigguup Nunaa
Kangersuatsiaq
Nuugaatsiaq
Kong Frederik VIII Land
Ymer Nunatak 3596ft (1096m)
SVALBARD (to Norway)
Nordaustlandet
Spitsbergen
Longyearbyen
Edgeoya
Bjørnøya (to Norway)
Murmansk Rise
Barents Sea
Baydaratskaya Guba
Ostrov Vaygach
Proliv Karskiye Vorota
GREENLAND (to Denmark)
Ilulissat
Kong Frederik IX Land
Kangerlussuaq
Kong Wilhelm Land
Petermann Bjerg 9646ft (2940m)
Kong Christian X Land
Daneborg
Greenland Plain
Ostrov Kolguyev
Chesbskaya Guba
Kong Christian IX Land
Mont Forel 11,024ft (3360m)
Gunnbjørn Fjeld 12,139ft (3700m)
Greenland Sea
Barents Trough
Nordkapp
Ittoqqortoormiit
Mohns Ridge
Kap Brewster
Jan Mayen (to Norway)
Fugløya Bank
Kola Peninsula
White Sea
Ammassalik
Denmark Strait
Icelandic Plateau
Norwegian Sea
Reykjanes Basin
ICELAND
Arctic Circle
Voring Plateau
Norwegian Basin
Reykjanes Ridge
Faroe-Iceland Ridge
Iceland Basin
Faroe Islands (to Denmark)
Gulf of Bothnia
EUROPE
1 2 3 4 5 6 7 8 9 10 11 12 13 14 15

Antarctica

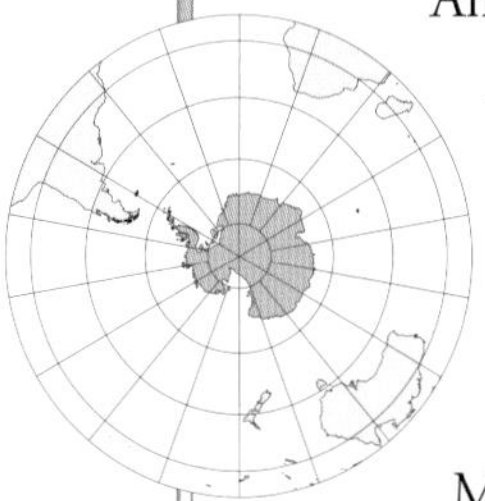

An almost circular landmass centered on the South Pole, Antarctica is the world's fifth-largest as well as its coldest, windiest, driest, and, on average, highest continent. A vast ice sheet covers 98 percent of the land. Among the few topographical features not totally obscured by the ice are the Transantarctic Mountains, which divide the continent into East and West Antarctica. In the east, the ice sheet hides a high plateau; to the west, it conceals a mountainous archipelago. Much of the surrounding ocean freezes in winter, effectively doubling the size of Antarctica, and for much of that season the sun does not rise. These severe conditions drastically restrict animal and plant distribution, and have prohibited permanent human occupation. Nevertheless, Antarctica is home to a fluctuating population of scientists and support staff based at a total of 42 research stations. Their numbers swell annually from around 1,000 in winter to approximately 4,000 in summer.

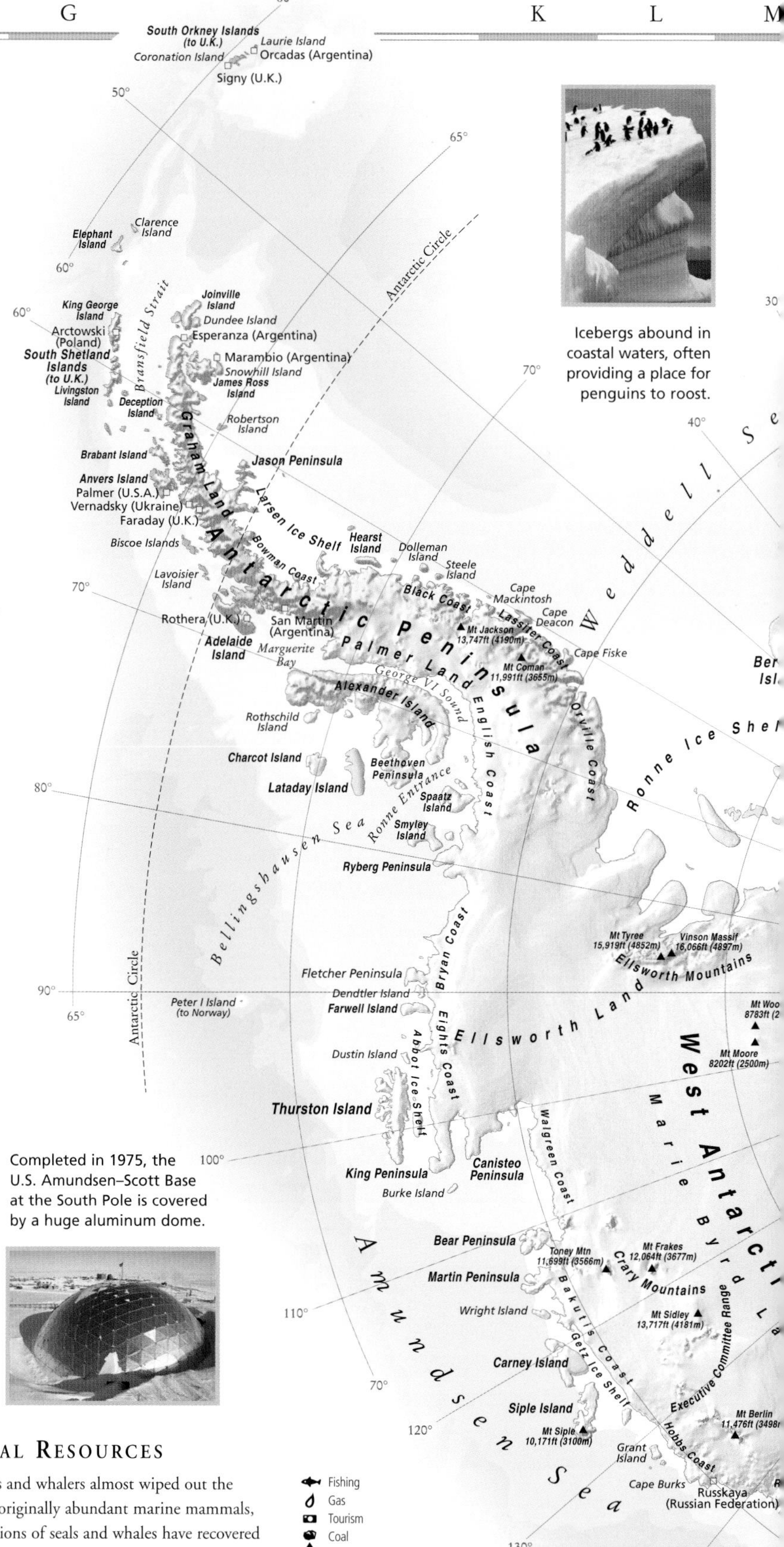

Icebergs abound in coastal waters, often providing a place for penguins to roost.

The Antarctic Peninsula

The roughly circular outline of Antarctica is interrupted by the narrow Antarctic Peninsula, which extends 800 miles (1,300 km) toward the southern tip of South America. The peninsula is mountainous—rising to 13,747 feet (4,190 m) at Mount Jackson—capped by ice sheets and glaciers, and fringed by numerous islands, slender channels, and ice shelves. Nevertheless, it experiences the continent's mildest conditions and includes most of its few patches of ice-free land. From the end of the peninsula, an undersea ridge known as the Scotia Arc runs east then west, forming a great loop that eventually connects with Cape Horn in South America.

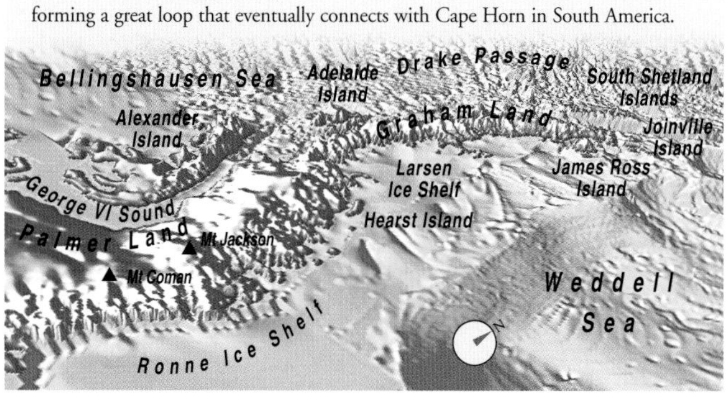

Completed in 1975, the U.S. Amundsen–Scott Base at the South Pole is covered by a huge aluminum dome.

The Antarctic Treaty

Seven countries—Argentina, Australia, Chile, France, New Zealand, Norway, and the United Kingdom—have at one time or other asserted sovereignty over parts of Antarctica. However, by becoming signatories to the Antarctic Treaty of 1959, they and 38 other nations have since agreed to suspend territorial claims and preserve the continent for nonmilitary scientific research. The Antarctic Treaty arose out of a worldwide scientific project called the International Geophysical Year, which began in 1957 and saw 12 nations establish numerous research stations across Antarctica.

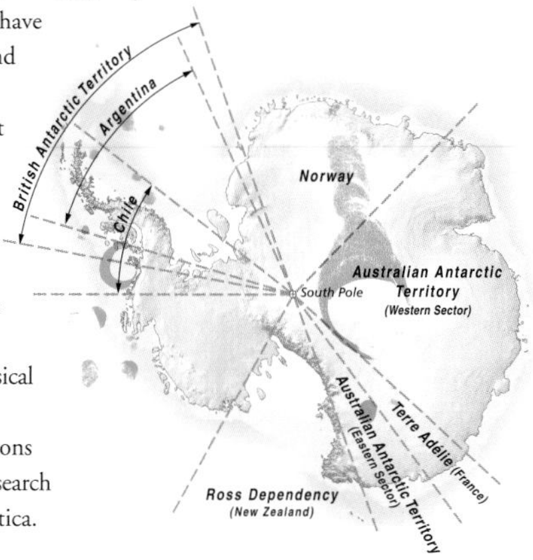

Natural Resources

Early sealers and whalers almost wiped out the continent's originally abundant marine mammals, but populations of seals and whales have recovered in recent years, especially since the International Whaling Commission declared most of the Southern Ocean a whale sanctuary in 1994. Although 23 countries have agreed to manage Antarctic fisheries for sustainability, illegal fishing is steadily depleting stocks of Antarctic cod, finfish, and toothfish. Geologists concur that Antarctica may harbor great mineral wealth, including copper, gold, platinum, and oil. No economically exploitable reserves have been found, however, and, in any case, mining is banned under the Antarctic Treaty. Tourism is proving a more viable economic activity, with visitor numbers rising steadily.

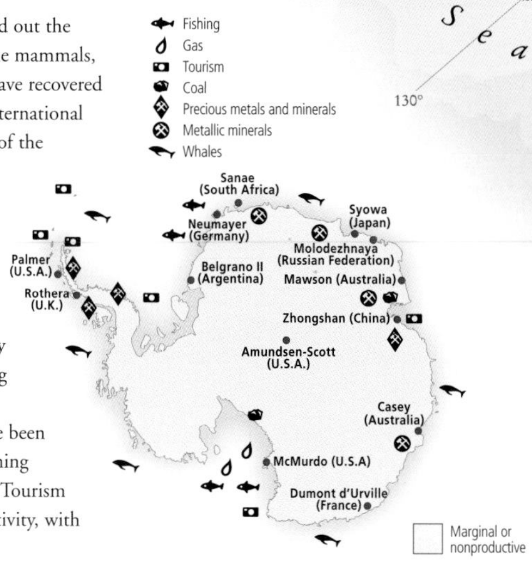

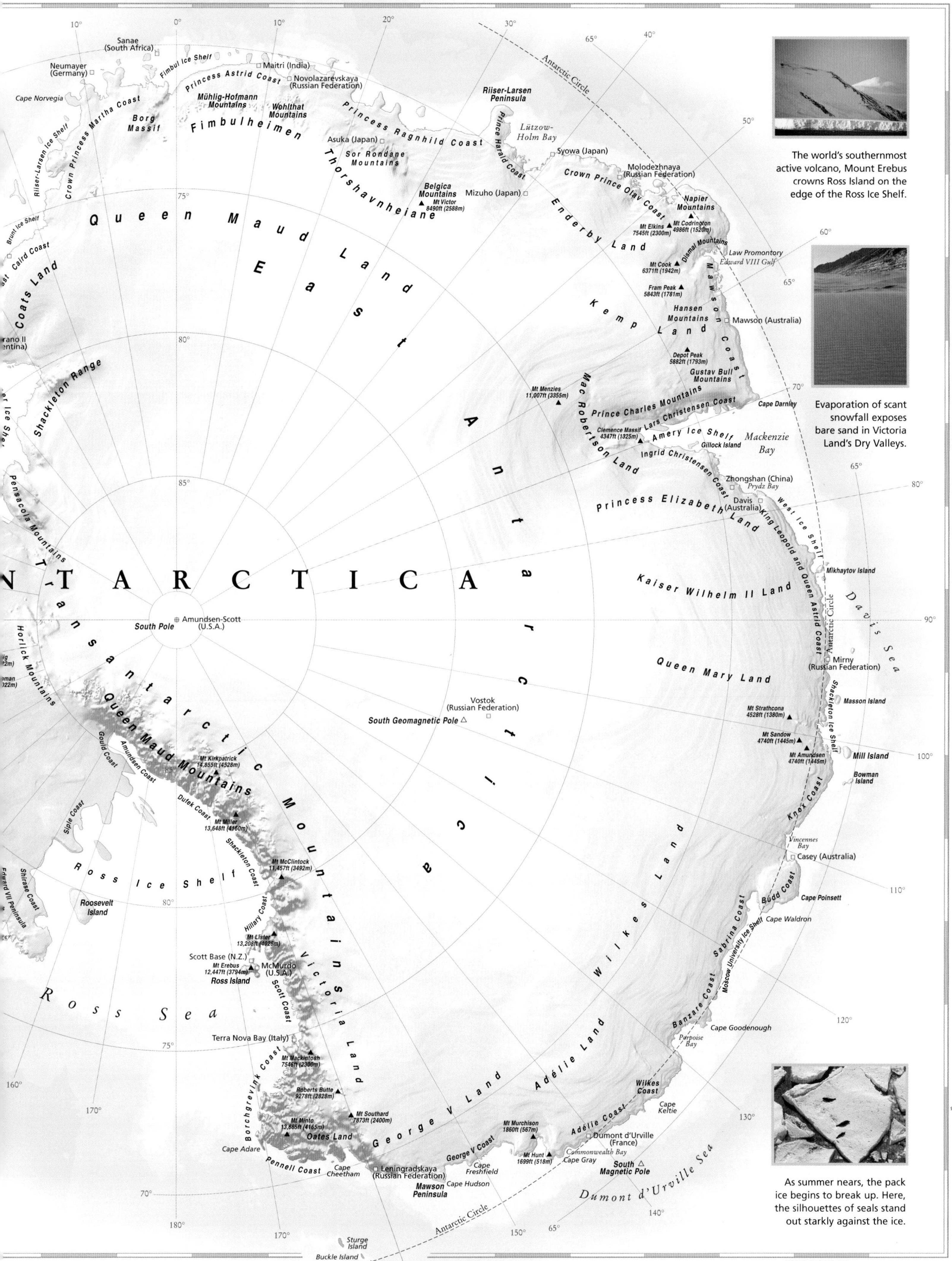

The world's southernmost active volcano, Mount Erebus crowns Ross Island on the edge of the Ross Ice Shelf.

Evaporation of scant snowfall exposes bare sand in Victoria Land's Dry Valleys.

As summer nears, the pack ice begins to break up. Here, the silhouettes of seals stand out starkly against the ice.

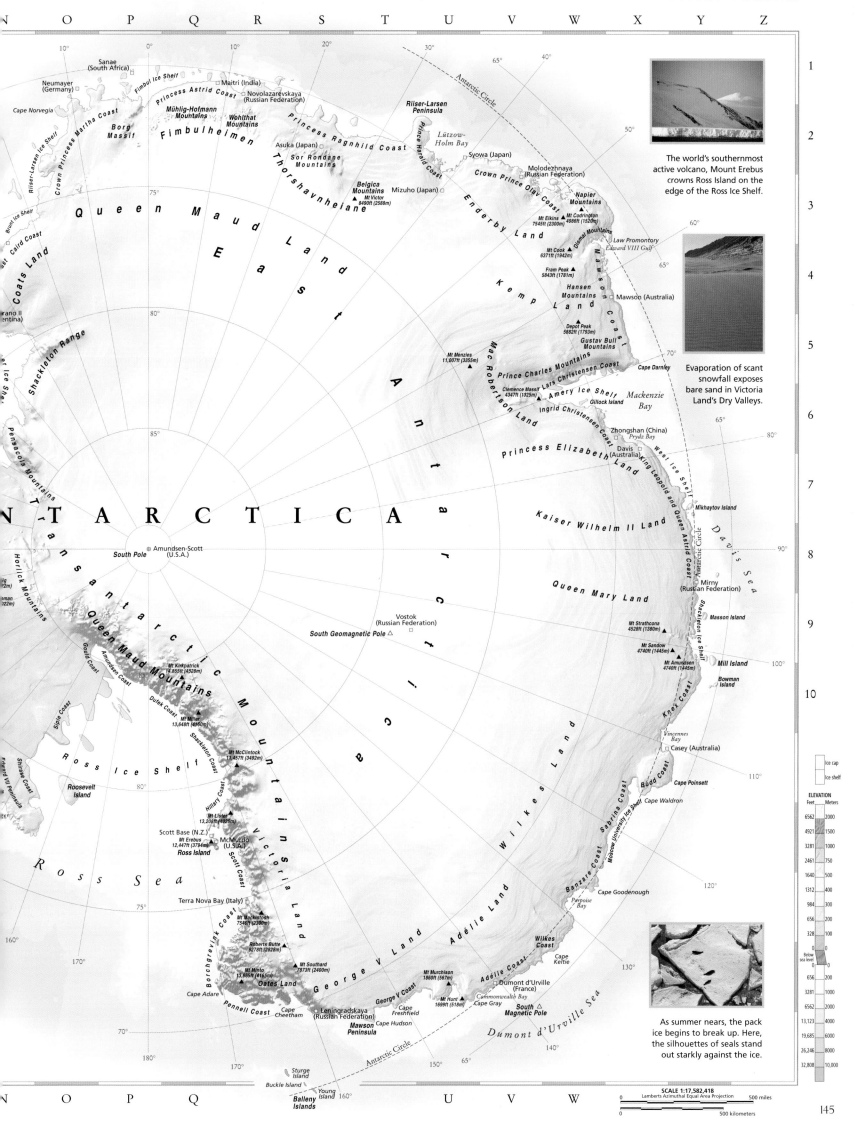

Abbreviations

United States of America

AL	Alabama
AK	Alaska
AZ	Arizona
AR	Arkansas
CA	California
CO	Colorado
CT	Connecticut
DE	Delaware
DC	District of Columbia
FL	Florida
GA	Georgia
HI	Hawaii
ID	Idaho
IL	Illinois
IN	Indiana
IA	Iowa
KS	Kansas
KY	Kentucky
LA	Louisiana
ME	Maine
MD	Maryland
MA	Massachusetts
MI	Michigan
MN	Minnesota
MS	Mississippi
MO	Missouri
MT	Montana
NE	Nebraska
NV	Nevada
NH	New Hampshire
NJ	New Jersey
NM	New Mexico
NY	New York
NC	North Carolina
ND	North Dakota
OH	Ohio
OK	Oklahoma
OR	Oregon
PA	Pennsylvania
RI	Rhode Island
SC	South Carolina
SD	South Dakota
TN	Tennessee
TX	Texas
UT	Utah
VT	Vermont
VA	Virginia
WA	Washington
WV	West Virginia
WI	Wisconsin
WY	Wyoming

Canada

AB	Alberta
BC	British Columbia
MB	Manitoba
NB	New Brunswick
NL	Newfoundland and Labrador
NT	Northwest Territories
NS	Nova Scotia
NU	Nunavut
ON	Ontario
PE	Prince Edward Island
QC	Québec
SK	Saskatchewan
YT	Yukon Territory

Australia

ACT	Australian Capital Territory
NSW	New South Wales
NT	Northern Territory
QLD	Queensland
SA	South Australia
TAS	Tasmania
VIC	Victoria
WA	Western Australia

1

39 G 20 **100 Mile House**, BC, Canada

A

66 H 1 **A Coruña**, Spain
66 J 1 **A Fonsagrada**, Spain
66 G 3 **A Guardia**, Spain
66 J 3 **A Gudiña**, Spain
73 B 17 **Aachen**, Germany
73 H 22 **Aalen**, Germany
69 J 16 **Aalst**, Netherlands
69 E 18 **Aalst**, Luxembourg
68 M 13 **Aalten**, Netherlands
69 D 17 **Aalter**, Belgium
74 F 6 **Aarau**, Switzerland
74 F 6 **Aare**, Switzerland 〰
69 H 18 **Aarschot**, Belgium
69 F 17 **Aartselaar**, Belgium
101 T 9 **Ab-i-Istada**, Afghanistan 🦢
112 L 4 **Aba**, China
129 R 14 **Aba**, Nigeria
131 Q 5 **Aba**, Democratic Republic of Congo
100 G 9 **Ābādān**, Iran
100 J 9 **Ābādeh**, Iran
124 J 8 **Abadla**, Algeria
140 D 2 **Abaiang**, Kiribati 🏝
129 R 12 **Abaji**, Nigeria
30 M 6 **Abajo Peak**, UT, U.S.A. ▲
129 R 13 **Abakaliki**, Nigeria
89 N 13 **Abakan**, Russian Federation
129 P 8 **Abala**, Niger
130 H 8 **Abala**, Congo
129 Q 8 **Abalak**, Niger
125 N 14 **Abalessa**, Algeria
53 F 17 **Abancay**, Peru
100 J 9 **Abarqū**, Iran
122 L 3 **Abashiri**, Japan
122 L 4 **Abashiri-ko**, Japan 🦢
138 F 7 **Abau**, Papua New Guinea
103 R 4 **Abay**, Kazakhstan
127 I 22 **Ābaya Hāyk'**, Ethiopia 🦢
89 N 13 **Abaza**, Russian Federation
130 H 4 **Abba**, Central African Republic
96 M 2 **Abbah**, Syria
77 B 17 **Abbasanta**, Italy
16 M 12 **Abbeville**, SC, U.S.A.
18 J 8 **Abbeville**, LA, U.S.A.
19 R 6 **Abbeville**, AL, U.S.A.
19 U 5 **Abbeville**, GA, U.S.A.
65 P 2 **Abbeville**, France
61 B 20 **Abbeyfeale**, Republic of Ireland
144 J 8 **Abbot Ice Shelf**, Antarctica ◇
63 P 14 **Abbotsbury**, U.K.
20 E 11 **Abbotsford**, WI, U.S.A.
39 G 22 **Abbotsford**, BC, Canada
101 X 7 **Abbottabad**, Pakistan
99 V 15 **'Abd al Kūrī**, Yemen 🏝
129 Y 9 **Abéché**, Chad
69 A 19 **Abele**, Belgium
140 D 2 **Abemama**, Kiribati 🏝
128 L 13 **Abengourou**, Côte d'Ivoire
71 B 26 **Åbenrå**, Denmark
129 P 13 **Abeokuta**, Nigeria
62 M 8 **Aberaeron**, U.K.
63 O 10 **Aberdare**, U.K.
62 L 6 **Aberdaron**, U.K.
17 V 2 **Aberdeen**, MD, U.S.A.
17 Q 10 **Aberdeen**, NC, U.S.A.
19 N 3 **Aberdeen**, MS, U.S.A.
22 M 7 **Aberdeen**, SD, U.S.A.
32 F 7 **Aberdeen**, WA, U.S.A.
60 J 10 **Aberdeen**, U.K.
132 M 14 **Aberdeen**, Republic of South Africa
40 K 2 **Aberdeen Lake**, NU, Canada 🦢
62 M 7 **Aberdyfi**, U.K.
63 P 9 **Abergavenny**, U.K.
62 L 8 **Aberporth**, U.K.
62 L 6 **Abersoch**, U.K.
63 O 10 **Abertillery**, U.K.
62 M 7 **Aberystwyth**, U.K.
76 E 9 **Abetone**, Italy
91 T 3 **Abez'**, Russian Federation
99 N 11 **Abhā**, Saudi Arabia
100 H 5 **Abhar**, Iran
129 R 13 **Abia**, Nigeria ⊡
128 K 14 **Abidjan**, Côte d'Ivoire
123 K 15 **Abiko**, Japan
26 M 6 **Abilene**, TX, U.S.A.
16 M 7 **Abingdon**, VA, U.S.A.
63 T 10 **Abingdon**, U.K.
14 I 13 **Abington**, PA, U.S.A.
31 P 8 **Abiquia Reservoir**, NM, U.S.A. 🦢
126 E 10 **Abnûb**, Egypt
106 G 7 **Abohar**, India
128 L 13 **Aboisso**, Côte d'Ivoire
127 E 20 **Aboke**, Sudan
129 O 13 **Abomey**, Benin
129 U 14 **Abong Mbang**, Cameroon
99 V 11 **Aboot**, Oman
121 C 19 **Aborlan**, Philippines
129 Y 10 **Abou Déia**, Chad
99 T 5 **Abqaiq**, Saudi Arabia
120 F 7 **Abra**, Philippines 〰
56 I 5 **Abra Pampa**, Argentina
49 O 4 **Abraham's Bay**, The Bahamas
126 D 13 **'Abri**, Sudan
86 H 10 **Abrud**, Romania
84 D 8 **Abruka**, Estonia 🏝
76 I 13 **Abruzzo**, Italy ⊡
12 K 6 **Absaroka Range**, MT/WY, U.S.A. ▲▲
75 R 6 **Abtenau**, Austria
96 I 3 **Abū aḑ Ḑuhūr**, Syria
97 R 7 **Abū al Jīr**, Iraq
99 W 6 **Abu al Jirab**, United Arab Emirates 🏝
99 O 11 **Abū 'Arīsh**, Saudi Arabia
99 W 6 **Abu Dhabi**, United Arab Emirates ⌂
126 D 8 **Abu Haggag**, Egypt
127 F 14 **Abu Hamed**, Sudan
97 O 5 **Abū Ḩardān**, Syria
97 O 5 **Abū Kamāl**, Syria
127 B 19 **Abu Matariq**, Sudan
100 K 13 **Abu Musa**, Iran 🏝
125 T 8 **Abū Nujaym**, Libya
125 T 8 **Abū Qurīn**, Libya
98 M 6 **Abū Rubayq**, Saudi Arabia
127 C 17 **Abu Shanab**, Sudan
126 E 12 **Abu Simbel**, Egypt
97 T 9 **Abū Şukhayr**, Iraq
127 D 18 **Abu Zabad**, Sudan
126 F 9 **Abu Zenîma**, Egypt
129 R 12 **Abuja**, Nigeria ⌂
120 G 5 **Abulog**, Philippines
130 L 5 **Abumombazi**, Democratic Republic of Congo
54 D 13 **Abunã**, Brazil
122 J 6 **Abuta**, Japan
127 C 17 **Abyad**, Sudan
127 C 20 **Abyei**, Sudan
54 K 11 **Açailândia**, Brazil
46 I 7 **Acajutla**, El Salvador
67 P 6 **Acalá de Henares**, Spain
45 Q 11 **Acambaro**, Mexico
44 M 10 **Acaponeta**, Mexico
45 Q 14 **Acapulco**, Mexico
54 K 10 **Acará**, Brazil
54 N 11 **Acaraú**, Brazil
54 F 9 **Acari Mountains**, Brazil ▲▲
50 M 3 **Acarigua**, Venezuela
86 H 8 **Acâş**, Romania
45 S 13 **Acatlan**, Mexico
45 S 12 **Acatzingo**, Mexico
17 W 5 **Accomac**, VA, U.S.A.
128 M 13 **Accra**, Ghana ⌂
116 B 8 **Aceh**, Indonesia ⊡
77 K 16 **Acerno**, Italy
51 N 4 **Achaguas**, Venezuela
105 E 16 **Achalpur**, India
95 U 6 **Achaseli**, Georgia
110 K 11 **Acheng**, China
75 N 6 **Achenkirch**, Austria
93 P 13 **Achikulak**, Russian Federation
61 A 16 **Achill Island**, Republic of Ireland 🏝
89 N 12 **Achinsk**, Russian Federation
92 J 11 **Achuyevo**, Russian Federation
94 D 12 **Acipayam**, Turkey
77 K 22 **Acireale**, Italy
26 K 6 **Ackerly**, TX, U.S.A.
49 N 4 **Acklins Island**, The Bahamas 🏝
63 Z 6 **Acle**, U.K.
20 J 11 **Acme**, MI, U.S.A.
47 P 9 **Acoyapa**, Nicaragua
76 C 8 **Acqui Terme**, Italy
54 B 13 **Acre**, Brazil ⊡
96 F 7 **Acre**, Israel
77 M 18 **Acri**, Italy
45 R 11 **Actopan**, Mexico
54 O 12 **Açu**, Brazil
129 T 15 **Acurenam**, Equatorial Guinea
99 N 7 **Ad Dafīnah**, Saudi Arabia
97 U 9 **Ad Daghgharah**, Iraq
99 P 4 **Ad Dahnā'**, Saudi Arabia ◇
124 B 12 **Ad Dakhla**, Western Sahara
99 P 14 **Aḑ Ḑāli'**, Yemen
99 T 5 **Ad Dammām**, Saudi Arabia
99 N 11 **Ad Darb**, Saudi Arabia
99 P 6 **Ad Dawādimī**, Saudi Arabia
97 S 5 **Ad Dawr**, Iraq
97 Y 11 **Ad Dayr**, Iraq
99 R 6 **Ad Dilam**, Saudi Arabia
99 Q 6 **Ad Dir'īyah**, Saudi Arabia
97 U 9 **Ad Dīwānīyah**, Iraq
97 T 6 **Ad Dujayl**, Iraq
25 O 11 **Ada**, OK, U.S.A.
80 K 8 **Ada**, Serbia and Montenegro
34 F 14 **Adak**, AK, U.S.A.
34 F 14 **Adak Island**, AK, U.S.A. 🏝
99 Y 7 **Adam**, Oman
129 U 13 **Adamaoua**, Cameroon ⊡
83 H 23 **Adamas**, Greece
129 U 11 **Adamawa**, Nigeria ⊡
129 U 12 **Adamawa Highlands**, Cameroon ▲▲
14 H 7 **Adams**, NY, U.S.A.
10 C 12 **Adamstown**, Pitcairn Island ⌂
99 P 14 **Adan as Sughra**, Yemen
94 K 13 **Adana**, Turkey
122 K 13 **Adatara-san**, Japan ▲
135 S 7 **Adavale**, QLD, Australia
33 M 19 **Adaven**, NV, U.S.A.
103 N 4 **Aday**, Kazakhstan
127 I 20 **Addis Ababa**, Ethiopia ⌂
105 L 20 **Addu Atoll**, Maldives 🏝
19 U 6 **Adel**, GA, U.S.A.
135 P 12 **Adelaide**, SA, Australia
144 H 5 **Adelaide Island**, Antarctica 🏝
134 M 2 **Adelaide River**, NT, Australia
145 U 14 **Adélie Coast**, Antarctica ◇
145 U 14 **Adélie Land**, Antarctica ◇
103 S 11 **Adelunga Toghi**, Uzbekistan ▲
67 S 7 **Ademuz**, Spain
99 P 14 **Aden**, Yemen
129 R 8 **Aderbissinat**, Niger
99 X 5 **Adh Dhayd**, United Arab Emirates
117 U 13 **Adi**, Indonesia 🏝
127 I 18 **Ādī Ārk'ay**, Ethiopia
127 I 17 **Adi Keyih**, Eritrea
127 I 17 **Ādīgrat**, Ethiopia
94 D 11 **Adigüzel Baraji**, Turkey 🦢
105 F 17 **Adilabad**, India
131 T 6 **Adilanga**, Uganda
95 S 10 **Adilcevaz**, Turkey
33 H 15 **Adin**, CA, U.S.A.
69 A 18 **Adinkerke**, Belgium
125 S 11 **Adīrī**, Libya
14 J 8 **Adirondack Mountains**, NY, U.S.A. ▲▲
127 H 18 **Ādīs Zemen**, Ethiopia
95 N 12 **Adiyaman**, Turkey
86 L 10 **Adjud**, Romania
92 L 14 **Adler**, Russian Federation
74 G 7 **Adliswil**, Switzerland
32 G 6 **Admiralty Inlet**, WA, U.S.A. ≈
35 X 11 **Admiralty Island**, AK, U.S.A. 🏝
138 D 2 **Admiralty Islands**, Papua New Guinea 🏝
129 Q 12 **Ado-Ekiti**, Nigeria
127 D 21 **Adok**, Sudan
117 P 15 **Adonara**, Indonesia 🏝
105 E 19 **Adoni**, India
67 P 13 **Adra**, Spain
124 K 11 **Adrar**, Algeria
128 H 5 **Adrar**, Mauritania ⊡
125 R 13 **Adrar Mariou**, Algeria ▲
124 B 14 **Adrar Souttouf**, Western Sahara ▲▲
129 Z 9 **Adré**, Chad
21 L 16 **Adrian**, MI, U.S.A.
26 I 2 **Adrian**, TX, U.S.A.
76 I 9 **Adriatic Sea**, Europe 🌊
110 E 8 **Adun Qulu**, China
131 P 7 **Adusa**, Democratic Republic of Congo
85 H 14 **Adutiškis**, Lithuania
127 I 17 **Ādwa**, Ethiopia
128 K 13 **Adzopé**, Côte d'Ivoire
91 S 4 **Adz'va**, Russian Federation 〰
91 S 4 **Adz'vavom**, Russian Federation
83 I 17 **Aegean Sea**, Greece 🌊
84 G 6 **Aegviidu**, Estonia
97 V 9 **'Afak**, Iraq
83 O 24 **Afantou**, Greece
127 J 18 **Afar**, Ethiopia ⊡
127 J 17 **Afar Depression**, Ethiopia ◇
101 R 8 **Afghanistan**, Asia □
127 M 24 **Afgooye**, Somalia
99 O 6 **'Afīf**, Saudi Arabia
129 R 13 **Afikpo**, Nigeria
124 M 7 **Aflou**, Algeria
127 K 25 **Afmadow**, Somalia
35 Q 11 **Afognak Island**, AK, U.S.A. 🏝
54 M 13 **Afrânio**, Brazil
96 J 2 **'Afrīn**, Syria
94 L 11 **Afşin**, Turkey
68 I 8 **Afsluitdijk**, Netherlands ◇
54 I 9 **Afuá**, Brazil
96 G 8 **'Afula**, Israel
94 F 10 **Afyon**, Turkey
129 R 7 **Agadez**, Niger
129 S 6 **Agadez**, Niger ⊡
124 F 9 **Agadir**, Morocco
103 T 6 **Agadyr'**, Kazakhstan
107 V 13 **Agartala**, India
83 M 21 **Agathonisi**, Greece 🏝
117 X 13 **Agats**, Indonesia
105 B 22 **Agatti**, India 🏝
34 B 12 **Agattu Island**, AK, U.S.A. 🏝
34 B 12 **Agattu Strait**, AK, U.S.A. ≈
128 K 13 **Agboville**, Côte d'Ivoire
120 G 6 **Agbulu**, Philippines
95 W 9 **Ağcabädi**, Azerbaijan
95 W 9 **Ağdam**, Azerbaijan
95 W 8 **Ağdaş**, Azerbaijan
65 R 14 **Agde**, France
65 N 13 **Agen**, France
127 I 22 **Āgere Maryam**, Ethiopia
95 W 10 **Aghband**, Azerbaijan
83 M 22 **Agia Marina**, Greece
83 K 17 **Agia Paraskevi**, Greece
89 R 14 **Aginskoye**, Russian Federation
83 F 16 **Agiokampos**, Greece
83 H 14 **Ágion Óros**, Greece ⊡
83 I 16 **Agios Efstratios**, Greece 🏝
83 H 21 **Agios Georgios**, Greece 🏝
83 E 22 **Ágios Ilías**, Greece ▲
83 L 21 **Agios Kirykos**, Greece
83 D 16 **Agnantero**, Greece
32 E 13 **Agness**, OR, U.S.A.
128 K 13 **Agnibilékrou**, Côte d'Ivoire
120 E 9 **Agno**, Philippines
106 J 10 **Agra**, India
67 R 4 **Ágreda**, Spain
95 S 9 **Ağri**, Turkey
77 I 23 **Agrigento**, Italy
140 B 6 **Agrihan**, Northern Mariana Islands 🏝
83 C 18 **Agrinio**, Greece
77 K 17 **Agropoli**, Italy
91 R 14 **Agryz**, Russian Federation
95 X 8 **Ağsu**, Azerbaijan
120 H 11 **Agta Point**, Philippines ▶
44 J 3 **Agua Prieta**, Mexico
57 I 16 **Aguada Cecilio**, Argentina
49 T 8 **Aguadilla**, Puerto Rico
47 V 14 **Aguadulce**, Panama
47 N 4 **Agúan**, Honduras 〰
45 O 10 **Aguascalientes**, Mexico
45 O 10 **Aguascalientes**, Mexico ⊡
58 J 6 **Agudos**, Brazil
129 N 6 **Aguelhok**, Mali
129 R 9 **Aguié**, Niger
140 B 8 **Aguijan**, Northern Mariana Islands 🏝
30 I 12 **Aguila**, AZ, U.S.A.
67 N 2 **Aguilar de Campóo**, Spain
46 I 7 **Aguilares**, El Salvador
67 R 12 **Águilas**, Spain
45 O 12 **Aguililla**, Mexico
58 M 6 **Agulhas Negras**, Brazil ▲
123 N 24 **Aguni-jima**, Japan 🏝
121 M 20 **Agusan**, Philippines 〰
121 G 16 **Agutaya**, Philippines 🏝
100 G 3 **Ahar**, Iran
137 G 18 **Ahaura**, New Zealand
73 C 14 **Ahaus**, Germany
136 I 5 **Ahipara**, New Zealand
136 I 5 **Ahipara Bay**, New Zealand ≈
136 J 12 **Ahititi**, New Zealand
35 O 13 **Ahklun Mountains**, AK, U.S.A. ▲▲
95 R 11 **Ahlat**, Turkey
73 E 15 **Ahlen**, Germany
105 C 14 **Ahmadabad**, India
105 C 17 **Ahmadnagar**, India
101 W 11 **Ahmadpur East**, Pakistan
127 J 21 **Ahmar Mountains**, Ethiopia ▲▲
44 J 7 **Ahome**, Mexico
100 G 9 **Āhū**, Iran
46 I 7 **Ahuachapán**, El Salvador
100 G 9 **Ahvāz**, Iran
105 C 16 **Ahwa**, India
99 R 14 **Aḩwar**, Yemen
115 N 17 **Ai Yin Young**, Vietnam
138 A 5 **Aiambak**, Papua New Guinea
73 J 23 **Aichach**, Germany
75 S 2 **Aigen**, Austria
94 I 15 **Aigialousa**, Cyprus
83 G 21 **Aigina**, Greece 🏝
83 G 20 **Aigina**, Greece
83 E 14 **Aiginio**, Greece
83 D 19 **Aigio**, Greece
74 C 10 **Aigle**, Switzerland
59 F 15 **Aiguá**, Uruguay
122 I 13 **Aikawa**, Japan
112 K 11 **Ailao Shan**, China ▲▲
135 N 6 **Aileron**, NT, Australia
47 Z 13 **Ailigandi**, Panama
141 W 1 **Ailinginae**, Marshall Islands 🏝
141 Y 3 **Ailinglaplap**, Marshall Islands 🏝
141 Y 2 **Ailuk**, Marshall Islands 🏝
56 H 8 **Aimogasta**, Argentina
125 P 6 **Aïn Beïda**, Algeria
128 I 2 **Aïn Ben Tili**, Mauritania
124 J 7 **Aïn Beni Mathar**, Morocco
124 M 5 **Aïn Defla**, Algeria
124 M 6 **Aïn Deheb**, Algeria
125 N 6 **Aïn el Hadjel**, Algeria
124 K 8 **Aïn Sefra**, Algeria
124 K 6 **Aïn Temouchent**, Algeria
84 F 9 **Ainaži**, Latvia
83 B 19 **Ainos**, Greece ▲
67 U 3 **Ainsa**, Spain
22 K 12 **Ainsworth**, NE, U.S.A.
53 K 20 **Aiquile**, Bolivia
116 G 9 **Air**, Indonesia 🏝
41 Q 1 **Air Force Island**, NU, Canada 🏝
116 D 10 **Airbangis**, Indonesia
64 M 14 **Aire-sur-l'Adour**, France
74 G 9 **Airolo**, Switzerland
117 R 14 **Airpanas**, Indonesia
57 F 20 **Aisén**, Chile ⊡
67 T 9 **Aitana**, Spain ▲
138 B 3 **Aitape**, Papua New Guinea
23 R 5 **Aitkin**, MN, U.S.A.
141 P 10 **Aitutaki**, Cook Islands 🏝
86 I 10 **Aiud**, Romania
84 H 11 **Aiviekste**, Latvia 〰
141 U 1 **Aiwo**, Nauru
65 U 14 **Aix-en-Provence**, France
65 V 10 **Aix-les-Bains**, France
107 W 13 **Aizawl**, India
84 G 11 **Aizkraukle**, Latvia
84 C 11 **Aizpute**, Latvia
122 K 13 **Aizu-Wakamatsu**, Japan
65 X 15 **Ajaccio**, France
106 L 12 **Ajaigarh**, India
105 D 16 **Ajanta**, India
105 D 16 **Ajanta Range**, India ▲▲
125 W 8 **Ajdābiyā**, Libya
80 A 7 **Ajdovščina**, Slovenia
96 G 9 **'Ajlūn**, Jordan
99 X 5 **Ajman**, United Arab Emirates
104 D 12 **Ajmer**, India
106 H 5 **Ajnala**, India
30 I 14 **Ajo**, AZ, U.S.A.
122 K 5 **Akabira**, Japan
124 L 11 **Akabli**, Algeria
127 I 20 **Āk'ak'ī**, Ethiopia
137 H 21 **Akaroa**, New Zealand
137 I 21 **Akaroa Harbour**, New Zealand ≈
97 N 6 **Akāshat**, Iraq
123 G 18 **Akashi**, Japan
103 W 7 **Akbalyk**, Kazakhstan
93 W 5 **Akbulak**, Russian Federation
103 T 7 **Akbulak**, Kazakhstan
95 N 11 **Akşşadağ**, Turkey
95 O 13 **Akşşakale**, Turkey
94 G 7 **Akşşakoca**, Turkey
128 F 5 **Akchâr**, Mauritania ▲▲
103 T 6 **Akchatau**, Kazakhstan
94 D 13 **Akdağlar**, Turkey
94 K 10 **Akdağmadeni**, Turkey
102 L 11 **Akdepe**, Turkmenistan
117 S 10 **Akelamo**, Indonesia
130 M 6 **Aketi**, Democratic Republic of Congo
95 S 7 **Akhalk'alak'i**, Georgia
102 L 13 **Akhalskiy Velayat**, Turkmenistan ⊡
95 S 7 **Akhalts'ikhe**, Georgia
94 C 10 **Akhisar**, Turkey
126 E 10 **Akhmim**, Egypt
106 H 4 **Akhnoor**, India
93 Q 9 **Akhtubinsk**, Russian Federation
123 F 20 **Aki**, Japan
130 G 8 **Akiéni**, Gabon
41 O 9 **Akimiski Island**, QC, Canada 🏝
94 K 14 **Akinci Burnu**, Turkey ▶
122 J 10 **Akita**, Japan
128 F 5 **Akjoujt**, Mauritania
124 G 9 **Akka**, Morocco
122 M 5 **Akkeshi**, Japan
122 M 5 **Akkeshi-wan**, Japan ≈
103 S 10 **Akkol'**, Kazakhstan
103 S 3 **Akkol'**, Kazakhstan
94 B 12 **Akköy**, Turkey
103 V 3 **Akku**, Kazakhstan
103 O 9 **Akkum**, Kazakhstan
94 M 8 **Akkuş**, Turkey
129 O 12 **Aklampa**, Benin
38 B 9 **Aklavik**, NT, Canada
103 R 4 **Akmola**, Kazakhstan ⊡
84 H 12 **Aknīste**, Latvia
123 F 18 **Akō**, Japan
127 F 21 **Akobo**, Sudan
105 E 14 **Akodia**, India
105 E 16 **Akola**, India
129 T 15 **Akom II**, Cameroon
127 H 16 **Akordat**, Eritrea
105 E 16 **Akot**, India
127 D 22 **Akot**, Sudan
41 S 5 **Akpatok Island**, NU, Canada 🏝
108 H 5 **Akqi**, China
83 K 26 **Akra Agios Ioannis**, Greece ▶
83 H 15 **Akra Akrathos**, Greece ▶
83 H 14 **Akra Arapis**, Greece ▶
83 C 19 **Akra Araxos**, Greece 🏝
83 H 15 **Akra Drepano**, Greece ▶
83 I 19 **Akra Kafireas**, Greece ▶
83 G 15 **Akra Kassandras**, Greece ▶
83 I 26 **Akra Lithino**, Greece ▶
83 F 23 **Akra Maleas**, Greece ▶
83 K 19 **Akra Meston**, Greece ▶
83 G 15 **Akra Paliouri**, Greece ▶
83 M 25 **Akra Paraspori**, Greece ▶
83 L 26 **Akra Sideros**, Greece ▶
83 K 17 **Akra Sigri**, Greece
83 G 25 **Akra Spatha**, Greece ▶
83 E 24 **Akra Tainaro**, Greece ▶
129 S 7 **Akrérèb**, Niger
21 N 17 **Akron**, OH, U.S.A.
106 L 3 **Aksai Chin**, India ⊡
82 N 7 **Aksakovo**, Bulgaria
94 I 11 **Aksaray**, Turkey
93 O 9 **Aksay**, Russian Federation
102 J 4 **Aksay**, Kazakhstan
94 G 11 **Akşehir**, Turkey
94 F 11 **Aksehir Gölü**, Turkey 🦢
94 G 13 **Akseki**, Turkey
103 S 3 **Aksu**, Kazakhstan
103 U 3 **Aksu**, Kazakhstan
108 I 5 **Aksu**, China
103 T 6 **Aksu-Ayuly**, Kazakhstan
103 Y 6 **Aksuat**, Kazakhstan
103 U 9 **Aksuek**, Kazakhstan
127 I 17 **Āksum**, Ethiopia
103 P 12 **Aktash**, Uzbekistan
102 H 9 **Aktau**, Kazakhstan
103 U 3 **Aktogay**, Kazakhstan
103 U 6 **Aktogay**, Kazakhstan
103 W 7 **Aktogay**, Kazakhstan
85 K 20 **Aktsyabrski**, Belarus
102 L 6 **Aktyubinsk**, Kazakhstan ⊡
102 L 5 **Aktyubinsk**, Kazakhstan
130 K 6 **Akula**, Democratic Republic of Congo
41 P 5 **Akulivik**, QC, Canada
123 B 23 **Akune**, Japan
129 Q 13 **Akure**, Nigeria
70 C 10 **Akureyri**, Iceland
123 B 26 **Akuseki-shima**, Japan 🏝
34 K 13 **Akutan Island**, AK, U.S.A. 🏝
129 R 14 **Akwa Ibom**, Nigeria ⊡
129 R 12 **Akwanga**, Nigeria
103 Y 6 **Akzhar**, Kazakhstan
95 O 12 **Akziyaret**, Turkey
125 W 7 **Al Abyār**, Libya
125 Y 7 **Al 'Adam**, Libya
99 S 3 **Al Aḩmadī**, Kuwait
99 O 4 **Al Ajfar**, Saudi Arabia
99 N 9 **Al 'Alayyah**, Saudi Arabia
97 S 1 **Al Amādīyah**, Iraq
97 Y 9 **Al 'Amārah**, Iraq
96 F 13 **Al 'Aqabah**, Jordan
99 N 9 **Al 'Aqīq**, Saudi Arabia
124 B 12 **Al Argoub**, Western Sahara
99 Q 4 **Al Arţāwīyah**, Saudi Arabia
97 O 4 **Al 'Ashārah**, Syria
99 X 6 **Al 'Ayn**, United Arab Emirates
97 U 8 **Al 'Azīzīyah**, Iraq
125 S 8 **Al 'Azīzīyah**, Libya
97 P 2 **Al Ba'āj**, Iraq
96 J 2 **Al Bāb**, Syria
97 P 3 **Al Bādī**, Iraq
99 Q 8 **Al Badī'**, Saudi Arabia
99 N 9 **Al Bāḩah**, Saudi Arabia
96 H 3 **Al Bahlūlīyah**, Syria
125 Y 7 **Al Bardī**, Libya
97 Z 11 **Al Başrah**, Iraq
99 Q 13 **Al Bayḑā'**, Yemen
125 W 7 **Al Bayḑā'**, Libya
98 M 7 **Al Bi'ār**, Saudi Arabia
98 K 3 **Al Bi'r**, Saudi Arabia
99 N 11 **Al Birk**, Saudi Arabia
99 O 5 **Al Bukayrīyah**, Saudi Arabia
99 X 6 **Al Buraymī**, Oman
97 N 4 **Al Buşayrah**, Syria
97 W 12 **Al Buşayyah**, Iraq
97 S 7 **Al Fallūjah**, Iraq
99 S 13 **Al Fardah**, Yemen
99 S 3 **Al Farwānīyah**, Kuwait
97 S 4 **Al Fatḩah**, Iraq
97 Z 12 **Al Fāw**, Iraq
99 O 13 **Al Fāzih**, Yemen
125 U 10 **Al Fuqahā'**, Libya
97 U 10 **Al Ghammās**, Iraq
99 P 5 **Al Ghāţ**, Saudi Arabia
99 V 12 **Al Ghayḑah**, Yemen
97 S 7 **Al Ḩabbānīyah**, Iraq
97 Q 6 **Al Ḩadīthah**, Iraq
97 R 3 **Al Ḩaḑr**, Iraq
124 E 10 **Al Haggounia**, Western Sahara
99 X 6 **Al Hajar'al Gharbī**, Oman ▲▲
99 R 12 **Al Ḩajr**, Yemen
97 Y 9 **Al Ḩalfāyah**, Iraq
98 L 1 **Al Hamād**, Saudi Arabia ◇
125 Q 9 **Al Ḩamādah al Ḩamrā'**, Libya ◇
96 H 4 **Al Ḩamīdīyah**, Syria
98 M 6 **Al Ḩanākīyah**, Saudi Arabia
99 O 14 **Al Ḩanīsh al Kabīr**, Yemen 🏝
97 W 14 **Al Haniyah**, Iraq ◇
99 O 11 **Al Haqū**, Saudi Arabia
125 U 10 **Al Haruj al Aswad**, Libya ◇
96 G 11 **Al Hāsā**, Jordan
97 O 2 **Al Ḩasakah**, Syria
97 U 9 **Al Hāshimīyah**, Iraq
97 O 2 **Al Hawl**, Syria
99 R 14 **Al Ḩawrā**, Yemen
97 W 9 **Al Ḩayy**, Iraq
99 P 12 **Al Ḩazm al-Jawf**, Yemen
99 V 9 **Al Ḩibāk**, Saudi Arabia ◇
96 H 7 **Al Ḩijānah**, Syria
97 T 8 **Al Ḩillah**, Iraq
99 R 7 **Al Ḩillah**, Saudi Arabia
97 T 8 **Al Hindīyah**, Iraq
96 L 2 **Al Hīshah**, Syria
96 G 8 **Al Ḩişn**, Jordan
124 J 6 **Al Hoceima**, Morocco
99 O 13 **Al Ḩudaydah**, Yemen
99 T 5 **Al Hufūf**, Saudi Arabia
99 Q 14 **Al Ḩumayshah**, Yemen
99 X 8 **Al Huwatsah**, Oman
99 S 13 **Al Ḩuwaymī**, Yemen
98 L 1 **Al 'Īsāwīyah**, Saudi Arabia
125 W 7 **Al Jabal al Akhḑar**, Libya ◇
96 H 12 **Al Jafr**, Jordan
125 Y 8 **Al Jaghbūb**, Libya
99 R 2 **Al Jahrah**, Kuwait
99 U 5 **Al Jamalīyah**, Qatar
98 M 2 **Al Jawf**, Saudi Arabia
125 Y 12 **Al Jawf**, Libya
97 N 2 **Al Jazīrah**, Syria ◇
99 N 4 **Al Jithāmīyah**, Saudi Arabia
99 T 4 **Al Jubayl**, Saudi Arabia
98 M 8 **Al Jumūm**, Saudi Arabia
99 Z 9 **Al Kalbān**, Oman
96 G 11 **Al Karak**, Jordan
126 F 11 **Al Karnak**, Egypt
99 Y 6 **Al Khābūrah**, Oman
99 Z 9 **Al Khalīf**, Oman
97 U 6 **Al Khāliş**, Iraq
99 P 9 **Al Khamāsīn**, Saudi Arabia
99 Y 5 **Al Khaşab**, Oman
99 O 14 **Al Khawkhah**, Yemen
97 V 10 **Al Khiḑr**, Iraq
125 Y 12 **Al Khufrah**, Libya
125 T 7 **Al Khums**, Libya
97 T 9 **Al Kifl**, Iraq
99 U 5 **Al Kir'ānah**, Qatar
97 T 9 **Al Kūfah**, Iraq
97 X 9 **Al Kumayt**, Iraq
97 W 8 **Al Kūt**, Iraq
99 N 2 **Al Labbah**, Saudi Arabia ◇
96 H 3 **Al Lādhiqīyah**, Syria
98 M 9 **Al Līth**, Saudi Arabia
97 R 11 **Al Ma'ānīyah**, Iraq
96 H 8 **Al Mafraq**, Jordan
124 F 10 **Al Mahbas**, Western Sahara
96 K 2 **Al Mahdum**, Syria
97 T 7 **Al Maḩmūdīyah**, Iraq
99 U 11 **Al Mahrah**, Yemen ◇
99 O 12 **Al Maḩwīt**, Yemen
99 Q 5 **Al Majma'ah**, Saudi Arabia
97 Q 1 **Al Mālikīyah**, Syria
99 T 5 **Al Manāmah**, Bahrain ⌂
97 Z 11 **Al Ma'qil**, Iraq
99 O 13 **Al Marāwi'ah**, Yemen
125 W 7 **Al Marj**, Libya
99 Y 6 **Al Masana'a**, Oman
97 N 4 **Al Mayādīn**, Syria
96 G 10 **Al Mazra'ah**, Jordan
99 V 6 **Al Mirfa**, United Arab Emirates
99 T 5 **Al Mubarrez**, Saudi Arabia
96 G 14 **Al Mudawwarah**, Jordan
99 T 5 **Al Muharraq**, Bahrain
99 T 13 **Al Mukallā**, Yemen
125 X 7 **Al Mukhaylī**, Libya
97 U 6 **Al Muqdādīyah**, Iraq
98 L 6 **Al Musayjīd**, Saudi Arabia
97 W 9 **Al Muwaffaqīyah**, Iraq
99 N 7 **Al Muwayh**, Saudi Arabia
98 J 3 **Al Muwayliḩ**, Saudi Arabia
97 Y 11 **Al Muzayri'ah**, Iraq
96 H 4 **Al Qadmūs**, Syria
97 P 5 **Al Qā'im**, Iraq
99 O 6 **Al Qā'īyah**, Saudi Arabia
98 L 3 **Al Qalībah**, Saudi Arabia
97 O 1 **Al Qāmishlī**, Syria
96 H 3 **Al Qardābah**, Syria
96 I 5 **Al Qaryatayn**, Syria
99 S 12 **Al Qaţn**, Yemen
96 H 10 **Al Qaţrānah**, Jordan
125 T 12 **Al Qaţrūn**, Libya
99 Q 3 **Al Qayşūmah**, Saudi Arabia
98 M 10 **Al Qunfidhah**, Saudi Arabia
97 Y 11 **Al Qurnah**, Iraq
97 W 11 **Al Qusayr**, Iraq
99 Q 6 **Al Quwayi'**, Saudi Arabia
96 F 13 **Al Quwayrah**, Jordan
99 S 13 **Al Quzah**, Yemen
99 W 6 **Al Samha**, United Arab Emirates
99 S 5 **Al 'Uḑaylīyah**, Saudi Arabia
98 L 4 **Al 'Ulā**, Saudi Arabia
125 V 9 **Al 'Uqaylah**, Libya
125 R 12 **Al 'Uwaynāt**, Libya
125 Z 13 **Al 'Uwaynāt**, Libya
99 O 2 **Al 'Uwayqīlah**, Saudi Arabia
98 M 6 **Al 'Uyūn**, Saudi Arabia
99 O 4 **Al 'Uyūn**, Saudi Arabia
97 Y 10 **Al 'Uzayr**, Iraq
99 S 3 **Al Wafrah**, Kuwait
98 J 4 **Al Wajh**, Saudi Arabia
99 S 4 **Al Wannān**, Saudi Arabia
99 R 3 **Al Warī'ah**, Saudi Arabia
99 Y 6 **Al Wāsiţ**, Oman
125 T 12 **Al Wīgh**, Libya
99 R 6 **Al Yamāmah**, Saudi Arabia
103 S 11 **Ala-Buka**, Kyrgyzstan
94 G 11 **Ala Dağl**, Turkey ▲
19 O 4 **Alabama**, U.S.A. ⊡
19 O 5 **Alabama**, AL, U.S.A. 〰
120 H 12 **Alabat**, Philippines 🏝
94 J 9 **Alaca**, Turkey
94 K 7 **Alaşşam**, Turkey
19 V 8 **Alachua**, FL, U.S.A.
93 O 14 **Alagir**, Russian Federation
54 O 13 **Alagoas**, Brazil ⊡
55 N 14 **Alagoinhas**, Brazil
67 S 4 **Alagón**, Spain
121 L 22 **Alah**, Philippines 〰

□ Country ⊡ Internal administrative region: State/Province/Territory/Dependent territory ⌂ Capital city ▲▲ Mountain range/Undersea ridge ▲ Mountain peak/Volcano/Seamount ◇ Geographic feature ▶ Headland/Point/Cape/Peninsula ◓ Desert 🏝 Island/Island group ⁙ Antarctic base Ⓞ Ocean 🌊 Sea ≈ Bay/Gulf/Channel/Strait 🦢 Lake ⚑ Salt pan/Dry/Intermittent lake 〰

H 3 **Alājah**, Syria
P 12 **Alajuela**, Costa Rica
B 7 **Alamagan**, Northern Mariana Islands ⁂
P 5 **Al'Amār**, Saudi Arabia
I 18 **Ālamat'ā**, Ethiopia
Q 7 **Alamicamba**, Nicaragua
E 9 **Alaminos**, Philippines
M 20 **Alamo**, NV, U.S.A.
H 11 **Alamo Lake**, AZ, U.S.A. ⊿
Q 13 **Alamogordo**, NM, U.S.A.
Q 7 **Alamosa**, CO, U.S.A.
I 19 **Åland**, Finland ⁂
I 19 **Ålands Hav**, Finland ≈
G 13 **Alanya**, Turkey
C 11 **Alaşehir**, Turkey
P 6 **Alaska**, U.S.A. ◘
P 9 **Alaska Range**, AK, U.S.A. ▲▲
L 13 **Alaskan Peninsula**, AK, U.S.A. ▶
Z 8 **Älät**, Azerbaijan
Q 2 **Alatyr'**, Russian Federation
B 10 **Alausí**, Ecuador
T 8 **Alaverdi**, Armenia
K 16 **Alavus**, Finland
V 7 **Alazeya**, Russian Federation ∫
R 9 **Albacete**, Spain
K 17 **Albania**, Europe ◘
K 9 **Albany**, NY, U.S.A.
H 7 **Albany**, KY, U.S.A.
S 6 **Albany**, GA, U.S.A.
N 6 **Albany**, TX, U.S.A.
G 10 **Albany**, OR, U.S.A.
L 10 **Albany**, ON, Canada ∫
H 12 **Albany**, WA, Australia
K 8 **Albany**, New Zealand
G 13 **Albasserdam**, Netherlands
R 1 **Albatross Bay**, QLD, Australia ≈
K 10 **Albatross Point**, New Zealand ▶
K 13 **Albay Gulf**, Philippines ≈
P 10 **Albemarle**, NC, U.S.A.
V 8 **Albemarle Sound**, NC, U.S.A. ≈
B 9 **Albenga**, Italy
G 20 **Alberdi**, Paraguay
O 8 **Alberga**, SA, Australia ∫
H 5 **Albergaria-a-Velha**, Portugal
Q 2 **Albert**, France
S 10 **Albert Lea**, MN, U.S.A.
R 6 **Albert Nile**, Uganda ∫
T 7 **Alberta**, VA, U.S.A.
I 16 **Alberta**, Canada ◘
J 23 **Albertirsa**, Hungary
R 2 **Albertville**, AL, U.S.A.
V 10 **Albertville**, France
Q 13 **Albi**, France
A 10 **Albion**, PA, U.S.A.
K 15 **Albion**, MI, U.S.A.
N 13 **Albion**, NE, U.S.A.
O 14 **Alboran Sea**, Africa/Spain ◢
C 23 **Ålborg**, Denmark
H 12 **Albufeira**, Portugal
I 9 **Albula Alpen**, Switzerland ▲▲
Q 10 **Albuquerque**, NM, U.S.A.
J 8 **Alburquerque**, Spain
T 12 **Albury**, NSW, Australia
H 10 **Alcácer do Sal**, Portugal
H 6 **Alcala**, Philippines
L 13 **Alcalá de los Gazules**, Spain
O 12 **Alcalá la Real**, Spain
H 22 **Alcamo**, Italy
T 5 **Alcañiz**, Spain
J 8 **Alcántara**, Spain
Q 10 **Alcaraz**, Spain
N 12 **Alcaudete**, Spain
P 8 **Alcázar de San Juan**, Spain
S 8 **Alcester**, U.K.
Y 6 **Alchevs'k**, Ukraine
T 6 **Alcorisa**, Spain
B 15 **Alcorta**, Argentina
U 7 **Alcossebre**, Spain
W 12 **Alcova**, WY, U.S.A.
T 9 **Alcoy**, Spain
Y 7 **Alcúdia**, Spain
S 9 **Aldama**, Mexico
U 11 **Aldan**, Russian Federation ∫
T 12 **Aldan**, Russian Federation
Z 8 **Aldeburgh**, U.K.
I 7 **Alder Creek**, NY, U.S.A.
J 25 **Alderney**, U.K. ⁂
U 11 **Aldershot**, U.K.
D 17 **Aledo**, IL, U.S.A.
F 7 **Aleg**, Mauritania
O 5 **Alegre**, Brazil
E 12 **Alegrete**, Brazil
H 10 **Alekhovshchina**, Russian Federation
J 14 **Aleksandrov**, Russian Federation
R 7 **Aleksandrov Gay**, Russian Federation
I 7 **Aleksandrovo**, Bulgaria
T 11 **Aleksandrovsk**, Russian Federation
X 13 **Aleksandrovsk-Sakhalinskiy**, Russian Federation
L 6 **Alekseyevka**, Russian Federation
N 7 **Alekseyevskaya**, Russian Federation
S 1 **Alekseyevskoye**, Russian Federation
K 2 **Aleksin**, Russian Federation
N 13 **Aleksinac**, Serbia and Montenegro
N 6 **Além Paraíba**, Brazil
N 5 **Alençon**, France
H 10 **Alenquer**, Brazil
D 8 **Alenuihaha Channel**, HI, U.S.A. ≈
J 2 **Aleppo**, Syria
Z 15 **Aléria**, France
P 1 **Alert**, NU, Canada
G 15 **Alerta**, Peru
S 13 **Alès**, France
G 8 **Aleşd**, Romania
C 8 **Alessandria**, Italy
B 16 **Ålesund**, Norway
E 13 **Aleutian Islands**, AK, U.S.A. ⁂
N 12 **Aleutian Range**, AK, U.S.A. ▲▲
W 11 **Alexander Archipelago**, AK, U.S.A. ⁂
I 12 **Alexander Bay**, Republic of South Africa
Q 4 **Alexander City**, AL, U.S.A.
I 6 **Alexander Island**, Antarctica ⁂
D 23 **Alexandra**, New Zealand
U 3 **Alexandria**, VA, U.S.A.
I 6 **Alexandria**, LA, U.S.A.
P 6 **Alexandria**, MN, U.S.A.
J 10 **Alexandria**, ON, Canada
J 13 **Alexandria**, Romania
D 7 **Alexandria**, Egypt
H 6 **Alexandria Bay**, NY, U.S.A.
K 13 **Alexandroupoli**, Greece
G 6 **'Aley**, Lebanon
L 13 **Aleysk**, Russian Federation
M 6 **Alfatar**, Bulgaria
L 5 **Alfenas**, Brazil
G 9 **Alfonsine**, Italy
63 W 4 **Alford**, U.K.
63 S 5 **Alfreton**, U.K.
102 I 4 **Algabas**, Kazakhstan
66 G 12 **Algarve**, Portugal ◇
66 L 14 **Algeciras**, Spain
127 I 15 **Algena**, Eritrea
124 K 11 **Algeria**, Africa ◘
77 A 16 **Alghero**, Italy
124 M 5 **Algiers**, Algeria ♜
67 T 9 **Alginet**, Spain
66 L 13 **Algodonales**, Spain
20 H 11 **Algoma**, WI, U.S.A.
23 R 11 **Algona**, IA, U.S.A.
97 V 8 **'Alī**, Iraq
97 X 8 **'Ali al Gharbī**, Iraq
95 Y 9 **Äli Bayramli**, Azerbaijan
101 V 7 **'Alī Kheyl**, Afghanistan
127 K 19 **Ali Sabieh**, Djibouti
94 B 10 **Aliağa**, Turkey
83 F 19 **Aliartos**, Greece
80 L 10 **Alibunar**, Serbia and Montenegro
67 T 10 **Alicante**, Spain
27 P 13 **Alice**, TX, U.S.A.
48 J 10 **Alice Shoal**, Jamaica ≈
135 O 6 **Alice Springs**, NT, Australia
48 J 2 **Alice Town**, The Bahamas
19 O 4 **Aliceville**, AL, U.S.A.
103 U 14 **Alichur**, Tajikistan
106 J 9 **Aligarh**, India
110 I 6 **Alihe**, China
83 N 24 **Alimia**, Greece ⁂
51 W 8 **Alimimuni Peak**, Suriname ▲
121 H 22 **Alimpaya Point**, Philippines ▶
101 W 11 **Alipur**, Pakistan
107 T 10 **Alipur Duar**, India
66 J 8 **Aliseda**, Spain
83 H 19 **Aliveri**, Greece
66 K 9 **Aljucén**, Spain
33 M 19 **Alkali Flat**, NV, U.S.A. ⊿
68 H 9 **Alkmaar**, Netherlands
107 N 11 **Allahabad**, India
35 Q 5 **Allakaket**, AK, U.S.A.
89 V 10 **Allakh-Yun'**, Russian Federation
133 O 9 **Alldays**, Republic of South Africa
14 E 10 **Allegeny Plateau**, NY, U.S.A. ◇
14 C 14 **Allegheny Mountains**, PA/WV, U.S.A. ▲▲
121 K 14 **Allen**, Philippines
17 O 14 **Allendale**, SC, U.S.A.
45 P 5 **Allende**, Mexico
45 Q 7 **Allende**, Mexico
14 H 13 **Allentown**, PA, U.S.A.
105 D 23 **Alleppey**, India
74 K 7 **Allgäuer Alpen**, Austria/Germany ▲▲
22 H 12 **Alliance**, NE, U.S.A.
105 E 23 **Allinagaram**, India
19 V 6 **Alma**, GA, U.S.A.
20 K 13 **Alma**, MI, U.S.A.
22 L 15 **Alma**, NE, U.S.A.
42 M 6 **Alma**, QC, Canada
67 U 4 **Almacelles**, Spain
66 M 9 **Almadén**, Spain
67 O 9 **Almagro**, Spain
103 S 12 **Almalyk**, Uzbekistan
67 S 9 **Almansa**, Spain
66 M 7 **Almanzor**, Spain ▲
55 K 14 **Almas**, Brazil
103 V 8 **Almaty**, Kazakhstan ◘
103 V 10 **Almaty**, Kazakhstan
67 Q 4 **Almazán**, Spain
54 I 10 **Almeirim**, Brazil
66 H 8 **Almeirim**, Portugal
68 N 11 **Almelo**, Netherlands
67 Q 4 **Almenar de Soria**, Spain
66 K 9 **Almendralejo**, Spain
68 I 11 **Almere**, Netherlands
67 Q 13 **Almería**, Spain
93 T 2 **Al'met'yevsk**, Russian Federation
71 F 24 **Älmhult**, Sweden
47 S 13 **Almirante**, Panama
66 H 11 **Almodôvar**, Portugal
66 J 12 **Almonte**, Spain
106 L 7 **Almora**, India
129 N 7 **Almoustarat**, Mali
67 O 13 **Almuñécar**, Spain
61 J 14 **Alnwick**, U.K.
140 J 10 **Alofi**, Niue ♜
140 H 8 **Alofi**, Wallis and Futuna Islands ⁂
84 G 9 **Aloja**, Latvia
107 X 8 **Along**, India
110 G 5 **Alongshan**, China
83 G 17 **Alonnisos**, Greece ⁂
117 Q 15 **Alor**, Indonesia ⁂
118 A 5 **Alor Setar**, Malaysia
138 G 7 **Alotau**, Papua New Guinea
66 I 8 **Alpalhao**, Portugal
20 L 11 **Alpena**, MI, U.S.A.
135 T 7 **Alpha**, QLD, Australia
143 R 7 **Alpha Ridge**, Arctic Ocean ▲▲
21 E 17 **Alphe**, IL, U.S.A.
68 G 12 **Alphen**, Netherlands
26 H 9 **Alpine**, TX, U.S.A.
30 M 12 **Alpine**, AZ, U.S.A.
76 A 6 **Alps**, Europe ▲▲
135 P 5 **Alpurrurulam**, NT, Australia
65 W 5 **Alsace**, France ◘
67 Q 2 **Alsasua**, Spain
73 G 17 **Alsfeld**, Germany
84 C 11 **Alsunga**, Latvia
70 K 7 **Alta**, Norway
47 O 10 **Alta Gracia**, Nicaragua
56 J 10 **Alta Gracia**, Argentina
70 K 7 **Altaelva**, Norway ∫
51 O 3 **Altagracia de Orituco**, Venezuela
108 L 2 **Altai Mountains**, Asia ▲▲
19 V 5 **Altamaha**, GA, U.S.A. ∫
47 P 11 **Altamira**, Costa Rica
54 I 10 **Altamira**, Brazil
56 G 7 **Altamira**, Chile
77 M 16 **Altamura**, Italy
110 E 8 **Altan Emel**, China
17 Q 7 **Altavista**, VA, U.S.A.
108 L 3 **Altay**, China
109 N 4 **Altay**, Mongolia
74 G 8 **Altdorf**, Switzerland
67 U 10 **Altea**, Spain
73 N 17 **Altenberg**, Germany
73 L 17 **Altenburg**, Germany
66 I 8 **Alter do Chão**, Portugal
70 I 8 **Altevatnet**, Norway ⊿
75 Q 4 **Altheim**, Austria
97 T 3 **Altin Köprü**, Iraq
53 H 20 **Altiplano**, Bolivia ◇
27 T 7 **Alto**, TX, U.S.A.
55 H 16 **Alto Araguaia**, Brazil
132 J 3 **Alto Chicapa**, Angola
46 F 4 **Alto Cuchumatanes**, Guatemala ▲▲
66 I 6 **Alto da Torre**, Portugal ▲
50 I 4 **Alto de Tamar**, Colombia ▲
55 H 16 **Alto Garças**, Brazil
133 T 6 **Alto Molócuè**, Mozambique
50 G 5 **Alto Musinga**, Colombia ▲
54 K 13 **Alto Parnaíba**, Brazil
53 G 15 **Alto Purús**, Peru ∫
57 G 19 **Alto Río Senguerr**, Argentina
25 W 8 **Alton**, MO, U.S.A.
63 U 12 **Alton**, U.K.
14 D 13 **Altoona**, PA, U.S.A.
73 L 24 **Altötting**, Germany
63 Q 4 **Altrincham**, U.K.
108 K 7 **Altun Shan**, China ▲▲
33 I 15 **Alturas**, CA, U.S.A.
24 K 11 **Altus**, OK, U.S.A.
87 S 2 **Altynivka**, Ukraine
84 I 10 **Alūksne**, Latvia
87 U 13 **Alupka**, Ukraine
105 E 19 **Alur**, India
87 U 12 **Alushta**, Ukraine
24 L 8 **Alva**, OK, U.S.A.
27 Q 6 **Alvarado**, TX, U.S.A.
45 T 12 **Alvarado**, Mexico
54 D 11 **Alvarães**, Brazil
71 D 17 **Alvdal**, Norway
71 E 18 **Alvdalen**, Sweden ∫
71 F 18 **Älvdalen**, Sweden
71 A 18 **Alvik**, Norway
27 T 11 **Alvin**, TX, U.S.A.
71 H 19 **Alvkarleby**, Sweden
70 J 12 **Älvsbyn**, Sweden
106 I 9 **Alwar**, India
85 F 16 **Alytus**, Lithuania
29 Z 8 **Alzada**, MT, U.S.A.
73 E 20 **Alzey**, Germany
129 Y 9 **Am-Dam**, Chad
129 Y 10 **Am Timan**, Chad
129 Z 8 **Am-Zoer**, Chad
127 D 22 **Amadi**, Sudan
97 S 1 **Amādīyah**, Iraq
41 Q 3 **Amadjuak Lake**, NU, Canada ⊿
117 S 12 **Amahai**, Indonesia
123 A 23 **Amakusa-nada**, Japan ≈
123 B 23 **Amakusa-Shimo-shima**, Japan ⁂
71 E 21 **Åmål**, Sweden
99 X 10 **Amal**, Oman
77 K 16 **Amalfi**, Italy
83 C 20 **Amaliada**, Greece
117 X 13 **Amamapare**, Indonesia
55 H 19 **Amambaí**, Brazil
123 N 21 **Amami-Ō-shima**, Japan ⁂
123 N 23 **Amami shotō**, Japan ⁂
131 P 8 **Amamula**, Democratic Republic of Congo
138 A 3 **Amanab**, Papua New Guinea
76 I 12 **Amandola**, Italy
103 P 5 **Amangel'dy**, Kazakhstan
77 M 19 **Amantea**, Italy
133 P 13 **Amanzimtoti**, Republic of South Africa
54 I 8 **Amapá**, Brazil
54 I 9 **Amapá**, Brazil ◘
114 D 11 **Amarapura**, Myanmar
33 L 21 **Amargosa Valley**, NV, U.S.A.
26 J 2 **Amarillo**, TX, U.S.A.
105 H 15 **Amarkantak**, India
94 H 7 **Amasra**, Turkey
94 K 8 **Amasya**, Turkey
54 C 11 **Amataurá**, Brazil
69 I 20 **Amay**, Belgium
54 F 11 **Amazon**, Brazil/Peru ∫
54 C 11 **Amazon Basin**, Brazil ◇
50 L 11 **Amazonas**, Colombia ◘
51 O 8 **Amazonas**, Venezuela ◘
52 C 11 **Amazonas**, Peru ◘
54 D 11 **Amazonas**, Brazil ◘
106 I 7 **Ambala**, India
133 X 9 **Ambalavao**, Madgascar
133 Z 5 **Ambanja**, Madgascar
89 W 7 **Ambarchik**, Russian Federation
90 H 5 **Ambarnyy**, Russian Federation
107 V 12 **Ambāsa**, India
52 B 9 **Ambato**, Ecuador
133 X 6 **Ambato Boeny**, Madgascar
133 X 7 **Ambatomainty**, Madgascar
117 R 12 **Ambelau**, Indonesia ⁂
20 G 10 **Amberg**, WI, U.S.A.
73 K 21 **Amberg**, Germany
46 L 1 **Ambergris Cay**, Belize ⁂
65 U 9 **Ambérieu-en-Bugey**, France
42 C 12 **Amberley**, ON, Canada
137 H 19 **Amberley**, New Zealand
128 G 8 **Ambidédi**, Mali
105 H 14 **Ambikapur**, India
120 F 12 **Ambil**, Philippines ⁂
133 Z 5 **Ambilobe**, Madgascar
35 O 5 **Ambler**, AK, U.S.A.
53 D 15 **Ambo**, Peru
133 X 10 **Amboasary**, Madgascar
133 X 9 **Ambohimahasoa**, Madgascar
133 W 6 **Ambohipaky**, Madgascar
117 S 12 **Ambon**, Indonesia
117 S 12 **Ambon**, Indonesia ⁂
133 X 8 **Ambositra**, Madgascar
133 X 11 **Ambovombe**, Madgascar
33 M 24 **Amboy**, CA, U.S.A.
132 F 2 **Ambriz**, Angola
139 R 10 **Ambrym**, Vanuatu ⁂
34 D 13 **Amchitka Island**, AK, U.S.A. ⁂
34 E 14 **Amchitka Islands**, AK, U.S.A. ⁂
34 D 14 **Amchitka Pass**, AK, U.S.A. ≈
91 S 1 **Amderma**, Russian Federation
108 L 9 **Amdo**, China
45 N 11 **Ameca**, Mexico
68 K 5 **Ameland**, Netherlands ⁂
17 S 6 **Amelia Court House**, VA, U.S.A.
29 O 12 **American Falls**, ID, U.S.A.
29 O 12 **American Falls Reservoir**, ID, U.S.A. ⊿
140 L 9 **American Samoa**, U.S.A. ◘
19 S 5 **Americus**, GA, U.S.A.
68 J 12 **Amersfoort**, Netherlands
63 V 10 **Amersham**, U.K.
145 W 6 **Amery Ice Shelf**, Antarctica ◇
23 S 12 **Ames**, IA, U.S.A.
63 S 12 **Amesbury**, U.K.
83 C 18 **Amfilochia**, Greece
83 E 19 **Amfissa**, Greece
89 T 11 **Amga**, Russian Federation ∫
89 U 11 **Amga**, Russian Federation
89 W 15 **Amgu**, Russian Federation
89 Z 6 **Amguema**, Russian Federation
125 O 11 **Amguid**, Algeria
89 V 13 **Amgun**, Russian Federation ∫
127 I 19 **Amhara**, Ethiopia ◘
14 M 9 **Amherst**, MA, U.S.A.
43 U 9 **Amherst**, NS, Canada
65 Q 2 **Amiens**, France
105 A 22 **Amindivi Islands**, India ⁂
105 B 22 **Amini**, India ⁂
127 K 23 **Amino**, Ethiopia
132 J 10 **Aminuis**, Namibia
39 N 16 **Amisk Lake**, SK, Canada ⊿
18 L 7 **Amite**, LA, U.S.A.
34 G 14 **Amlia Island**, AK, U.S.A. ⁂
62 L 4 **Amlwch**, U.K.
96 H 9 **Ammān**, Jordan ♜
62 M 9 **Ammanford**, U.K.
70 H 12 **Ammarnäs**, Sweden
143 N 13 **Ammassalik**, Greenland
73 J 25 **Ammersee**, Germany ⊿
94 I 15 **Ammóchostos**, Cyprus
115 L 17 **Amnat Charoen**, Thailand
105 C 15 **Amod**, India
100 J 5 **Amol**, Iran
67 Q 1 **Amorebieta**, Spain
83 K 23 **Amorgos**, Greece ⁂
19 N 2 **Amory**, MS, U.S.A.
42 G 6 **Amos**, QC, Canada
71 B 20 **Åmot**, Norway
128 J 8 **Amourj**, Mauritania
46 L 8 **Ampala**, Honduras
133 Z 6 **Ampanavoana**, Madgascar
133 Z 5 **Ampanefena**, Madgascar
133 W 10 **Ampanihy**, Madgascar
105 H 25 **Amparai**, Sri Lanka
133 Z 8 **Ampasimanolotra**, Madgascar
117 O 11 **Ampoa**, Indonesia
67 U 6 **Amposta**, Spain
63 V 8 **Ampthill**, U.K.
43 R 6 **Amqui**, QC, Canada
99 P 12 **Amrān**, Yemen
105 E 16 **Amravati**, India
106 H 5 **Amritsar**, India
72 E 7 **Amrum**, Germany ⁂
68 H 11 **Amstelveen**, Netherlands
68 H 11 **Amsterdam**, Netherlands ♜
75 U 4 **Amstetten**, Austria
103 O 13 **Amudar'ya**, Turkmenistan ∫
34 H 15 **Amukta Pass**, AK, U.S.A. ≈
37 O 3 **Amund Ringnes Island**, NU, Canada ⁂
143 P 8 **Amund Ringnes Island**, Canada ⁂
145 P 9 **Amundsen Coast**, Antarctica ◇
38 D 7 **Amundsen Gulf**, NT, Canada ≈
143 N 6 **Amundsen Gulf**, Arctic Ocean ≈
145 Q 8 **Amundsen-Scott**, Antarctica ⠿
144 I 9 **Amundsen Sea**, Antarctica ◢
116 L 12 **Amuntai**, Indonesia
89 U 14 **Amur**, Russian Federation ∫
117 Q 10 **Amurang**, Indonesia
67 P 2 **Amurrio**, Spain
89 V 13 **Amursk**, Russian Federation
83 B 17 **Amvrakikos Kolpos**, Greece ≈
87 Y 7 **Amvrosiyivka**, Ukraine
99 O 5 **An Nabhānīyah**, Saudi Arabia
96 I 6 **An Nabk**, Syria
98 L 2 **An Nafūd**, Saudi Arabia ◇
97 T 9 **An Najaf**, Iraq
97 W 11 **An Nāşirīyah**, Iraq
97 W 10 **An Naşr**, Iraq
125 V 8 **An Nawfalīyah**, Libya
96 J 8 **An Nimarah**, Syria
99 N 10 **An Nimāş**, Saudi Arabia
99 S 4 **An Nu'ayrīyah**, Saudi Arabia
97 Q 9 **An Nukhayb**, Iraq
97 U 8 **An Nu'mānīyah**, Iraq
97 V 8 **An Nu'mānīyah**, Iraq
141 V 1 **Anabar**, Nauru
51 Q 3 **Anaco**, Venezuela
29 O 6 **Anaconda**, MT, U.S.A.
89 Z 7 **Anadyr'**, Russian Federation
83 K 24 **Anafi**, Greece ⁂
55 M 15 **Anagé**, Brazil
77 I 14 **Anagni**, Italy
97 P 5 **'Ānah**, Iraq
33 K 25 **Anaheim**, CA, U.S.A.
45 Q 6 **Anáhuac**, Mexico
105 D 23 **Anai Mudi Peak**, India ▲
105 H 18 **Anakapalle**, India
133 Y 5 **Analalava**, Madgascar
54 E 11 **Anamã**, Brazil
129 R 13 **Anambra**, Nigeria ◘
94 H 14 **Anamur**, Turkey
94 H 14 **Anamur Burnu**, Turkey ▶
123 G 20 **Anan**, Japan
105 C 15 **Anand**, India
105 J 16 **Anandapur**, India
105 E 20 **Anantapur**, India
106 H 4 **Anantnag**, India
92 J 12 **Anapa**, Russian Federation
55 J 16 **Anápolis**, Brazil
100 K 10 **Anār**, Iran
100 K 8 **Anārak**, Iran
101 P 8 **Anardara**, Afghanistan
140 A 7 **Anatahan**, Northern Mariana Islands ⁂
94 D 10 **Anatolia**, Turkey ◇
82 I 12 **Anatoliki Makedonia Kai Thraki**, Greece ◘
139 S 13 **Anatom**, Vanuatu ⁂
56 K 8 **Añatuya**, Argentina
113 P 1 **Anbianbu**, China
53 C 14 **Ancash**, Peru ◘
64 L 7 **Ancenis**, France
129 R 11 **Anchau**, Nigeria
35 R 9 **Anchorage**, AK, U.S.A.
53 C 16 **Ancón**, Peru
76 I 11 **Ancona**, Italy
57 E 17 **Ancud**, Chile
110 J 10 **Anda**, China
120 E 8 **Anda**, Philippines
53 E 17 **Andahuaylas**, Peru
56 I 8 **Andalgalá**, Argentina
66 L 12 **Andalucía**, Spain ◘
19 Q 6 **Andalusia**, AL, U.S.A.
105 O 23 **Andaman and Nicobar Islands**, India ◘
105 O 21 **Andaman Islands**, India ⁂
115 D 18 **Andaman Sea**, Asia ◢
135 P 9 **Andamooka**, SA, Australia
133 Z 5 **Andapa**, Madgascar
74 I 9 **Andeer**, Switzerland
69 I 21 **Andenne**, Belgium
129 O 8 **Andéramboukane**, Mali
69 F 21 **Anderlues**, Belgium
74 G 9 **Andermatt**, Switzerland
64 L 12 **Andernos-les-Bains**, France
16 L 11 **Anderson**, SC, U.S.A.
21 J 18 **Anderson**, IN, U.S.A.
25 S 8 **Anderson**, MO, U.S.A.
35 R 7 **Anderson**, AK, U.S.A.
38 C 9 **Anderson**, NT, Canada ∫
56 G 13 **Andes**, South America ▲▲
70 G 8 **Andfjorden**, Norway ≈
105 F 19 **Andhra Pradesh**, India ◘
103 T 12 **Andijon Wiloyati**, Uzbekistan ◘
133 Y 7 **Andilamena**, Madgascar
133 Y 7 **Andilanatoby**, Madgascar
100 G 8 **Andīmeshk**, Iran
103 T 12 **Andizhan**, Uzbekistan
101 R 5 **Andkhvoy**, Afghanistan
52 D 10 **Andoas**, Peru
111 M 20 **Andong**, South Korea
67 W 2 **Andorra**, Europe ◘
67 W 2 **Andorra La Vella**, Andorra ♜
63 S 11 **Andover**, U.K.
70 G 8 **Andøya**, Norway ⁂
58 H 5 **Andradina**, Brazil
133 Z 4 **Andranovondronina**, Madgascar
133 W 10 **Andranovory**, Madgascar
67 X 8 **Andratx**, Spain
34 E 14 **Andreanof Islands**, AK, U.S.A. ⁂
90 F 14 **Andreapol'**, Russian Federation
58 M 6 **Andrelândia**, Brazil
26 J 6 **Andrews**, TX, U.S.A.
103 X 7 **Andreyevka**, Kazakhstan
77 M 15 **Andria**, Italy
133 Y 7 **Andriamena**, Madgascar
87 X 8 **Andriyivka**, Ukraine
133 W 10 **Androka**, Madgascar
83 I 20 **Andros**, Greece ⁂
48 K 3 **Andros Island**, The Bahamas ⁂
48 K 2 **Andros Town**, The Bahamas
93 S 4 **Androsovka**, Russian Federation
105 C 22 **Andrott**, India ⁂
70 I 8 **Andselv**, Norway
67 N 11 **Andújar**, Spain
132 H 4 **Andulo**, Angola
129 N 7 **Anéfis**, Mali
49 W 7 **Anegada**, Virgin Islands, U.K. ⁂
129 N 13 **Aného**, Togo
121 C 18 **Anepahan**, Philippines
67 U 2 **Aneto**, Spain ▲
129 U 6 **Aney**, Niger
113 U 9 **Anfu**, China
115 H 18 **Ang Thong**, Thailand
89 O 11 **Angara**, Russian Federation ∫
89 P 13 **Angarsk**, Russian Federation
71 G 16 **Ånge**, Sweden
51 R 6 **Angel Falls**, Venezuela ◇
120 F 10 **Angeles**, Philippines
71 E 24 **Ängelholm**, Sweden
72 N 12 **Angermünde**, Germany
64 M 7 **Angers**, France
71 J 15 **Ängesön**, Sweden ⁂
115 L 21 **Ângk Tasaôm**, Cambodia
62 L 4 **Anglesey**, U.K. ⁂
27 S 11 **Angleton**, TX, U.S.A.
131 O 5 **Ango**, Democratic Republic of Congo
133 U 6 **Angoche**, Mozambique
100 M 13 **Angohrān**, Iran
57 F 15 **Angol**, Chile
132 H 3 **Angola**, Africa ◘
138 C 3 **Angoram**, Papua New Guinea
65 N 10 **Angoulême**, France
58 M 7 **Angra dos Reis**, Brazil
103 S 11 **Angren**, Uzbekistan
131 N 5 **Angu**, Democratic Republic of Congo
110 I 11 **Anguang**, China
67 T 3 **Angüés**, Spain
49 X 7 **Anguilla**, U.K. ◘
48 J 3 **Anguilla Cay**, The Bahamas ⁂
71 D 24 **Anholt**, Denmark ⁂
113 S 8 **Anhua**, China
113 W 5 **Anhui**, China ◘
55 H 16 **Anhumas**, Brazil
122 J 10 **Ani**, Japan
35 N 9 **Aniak**, AK, U.S.A.
141 V 1 **Anibare**, Nauru
141 V 1 **Anibare Bay**, Nauru ≈
31 N 15 **Animas Peak**, NM, U.S.A. ▲
121 M 15 **Anitaguipan Point**, Philippines ▶
133 Z 4 **Anivorano Avaratra**, Madgascar
139 S 12 **Aniwa**, Vanuatu ⁂
113 R 9 **Anjiang**, China
133 W 4 **Anjouan**, Comoros ⁂
111 K 17 **Anju**, North Korea
97 O 5 **Anka**, Iraq
113 Q 5 **Ankang**, China
94 H 9 **Ankara**, Turkey ♜
133 V 9 **Ankazoabo**, Madgascar
133 Y 7 **Ankazobe**, Madgascar
23 S 13 **Ankeny**, IA, U.S.A.
72 M 9 **Anklam**, Germany
105 C 20 **Ankola**, India
109 R 9 **Ankou**, China
113 P 3 **Ankouzhen**, China
129 R 13 **Ankpa**, Nigeria
129 N 13 **Anloga**, Ghana
113 N 10 **Anlong**, China
113 T 6 **Anlu**, China
21 L 15 **Ann Arbor**, MI, U.S.A.
21 F 22 **Anna**, IL, U.S.A.
92 M 5 **Anna**, Russian Federation
141 U 1 **Anna Point**, Nauru ▶
125 P 5 **Annaba**, Algeria
115 M 15 **Annam**, Vietnam ◇
115 K 14 **Annam Highlands**, Laos ▲▲
17 V 3 **Annapolis**, MD, U.S.A.
43 T 11 **Annapolis Royal**, NS, Canada
107 P 8 **Annapurna**, Nepal ▲
65 V 9 **Annecy**, France
112 L 11 **Anning**, China
19 R 3 **Anniston**, AL, U.S.A.
65 T 11 **Annonay**, France
83 J 26 **Ano Viannos**, Greece
113 R 14 **Anpu**, China
113 W 6 **Anqing**, China
111 F 20 **Anqiu**, China
69 J 20 **Ans**, Belgium
113 Q 1 **Ansai**, China
73 I 21 **Ansbach**, Germany
111 H 16 **Anshan**, China
113 O 10 **Anshun**, China
58 F 13 **Ansina**, Uruguay
22 L 14 **Ansley**, NE, U.S.A.
26 M 6 **Anson**, TX, U.S.A.
129 N 8 **Ansongo**, Mali
117 Y 11 **Ansudu**, Indonesia
53 F 18 **Antabamba**, Peru
133 Z 6 **Antalaha**, Madgascar
94 F 13 **Antalya**, Turkey
94 F 13 **Antalya Körfezi**, Turkey ≈
133 Y 7 **Antananarivo**, Madgascar ♜
133 X 7 **Antananarivo**, Madgascar ◘
133 W 10 **Antanimora Atsimo**, Madgascar
144 H 4 **Antarctic Peninsula**, Antarctica ▶
145 Q 7 **Antarctica**, 0
67 N 13 **Antequera**, Spain
31 Q 14 **Anthony**, NM, U.S.A.
124 F 9 **Anti Atlas**, Morocco ▲▲
65 X 14 **Antibes**, France
20 F 11 **Antigo**, WI, U.S.A.
43 W 9 **Antigonish**, NS, Canada
46 H 6 **Antigua**, Guatemala
49 Y 9 **Antigua**, Antigua and Barbuda ⁂
49 Z 8 **Antigua and Barbuda**, North America ◘
83 F 25 **Antikythira**, Greece ⁂
83 H 23 **Antimilos**, Greece ⁂
94 L 14 **Antioch**, Turkey
50 H 5 **Antioquia**, Colombia ◘
83 I 22 **Antiparos**, Greece ⁂
83 A 17 **Antipaxoi**, Greece ⁂
88 M 8 **Antipayuta**, Russian Federation
56 F 5 **Antofagasta**, Chile
56 F 5 **Antofagasta**, Chile ◘
56 H 7 **Antofagasta de la Sierra**, Argentina
57 I 21 **Antonio de Biedma**, Argentina
61 F 15 **Antrim**, U.K.
76 H 13 **Antrodoco**, Italy
133 W 7 **Antsalova**, Madgascar
133 X 8 **Antsirabe**, Madgascar
133 Z 4 **Antsiranana**, Madgascar
133 Z 5 **Antsiranana**, Madgascar ◘
84 H 9 **Antsla**, Estonia
133 Y 5 **Antsohihy**, Madgascar
111 M 14 **Antu**, China
57 F 14 **Antuco**, Chile
69 G 17 **Antwerp**, Belgium
69 G 17 **Antwerpen**, Belgium ◘
105 I 16 **Anugul**, India
104 C 11 **Anupgarh**, India
105 G 24 **Anuradhapura**, Sri Lanka
139 S 8 **Anuta**, Solomon Islands ⁂
144 H 4 **Anvers Island**, Antarctica ⁂
109 N 6 **Anxi**, China
113 S 7 **Anxiang**, China
135 O 11 **Anxious Bay**, SA, Australia ≈
111 L 19 **Anyang**, South Korea
113 U 2 **Anyang**, China
83 K 23 **Anydro**, Greece ⁂
109 O 8 **A'nyêmaqên Shan**, China ▲▲
85 G 14 **Anykščiai**, Lithuania
113 V 10 **Anyuan**, China
113 N 7 **Anyue**, China
113 S 2 **Anze**, China
69 D 19 **Anzegem**, Belgium
130 M 8 **Anzi**, Democratic Republic of Congo
77 H 15 **Anzio**, Italy
51 Q 4 **Anzoátegui**, Venezuela ◘
115 G 23 **Ao Ban Don**, Thailand ≈
115 F 24 **Ao Luk**, Thailand
115 G 22 **Ao Sawi**, Thailand ≈
139 Q 10 **Aoba**, Vanuatu ⁂
123 L 20 **Aoga-shima**, Japan ⁂
138 M 7 **Aola**, Solomon Islands
122 J 9 **Aomori**, Japan
106 K 9 **Aonla**, India
76 A 6 **Aosta**, Italy
124 C 11 **Aoufist**, Western Sahara
128 G 7 **Aoukâr**, Mauritania ▲▲
124 L 11 **Aoulef**, Algeria
129 W 5 **Aozou**, Chad
131 S 6 **Apac**, Uganda
24 M 11 **Apache**, OK, U.S.A.
30 L 15 **Apache Peak**, AZ, U.S.A. ▲
19 T 8 **Apalachee Bay**, FL, U.S.A. ≈
19 S 8 **Apalachicola**, FL, U.S.A.
58 H 4 **Aparecida do Taboado**, Brazil
120 H 5 **Aparri**, Philippines
80 I 8 **Apatin**, Serbia and Montenegro
90 H 3 **Apatity**, Russian Federation
45 O 12 **Apatzingán**, Mexico
84 I 9 **Ape**, Latvia
68 L 12 **Apeldoorn**, Netherlands
76 D 9 **Apennines**, Italy ▲▲
106 M 7 **Api**, Nepal ▲
131 N 5 **Api**, Democratic Republic of Congo
140 J 8 **Apia**, Samoa ♜
53 F 19 **Aplao**, Peru
54 N 12 **Apodi**, Brazil
51 V 6 **Apoera**, Suriname
135 R 14 **Apollo Bay**, VIC, Australia
53 I 18 **Apolo**, Bolivia
58 H 3 **Aporé**, Brazil
58 H 4 **Aporé**, Brazil ∫
20 E 7 **Apostle Islands**, WI, U.S.A. ⁂
142 M 14 **Apostolens Tommefinger**, Greenland ▲
58 E 10 **Apóstoles**, Argentina
87 T 8 **Apostolove**, Ukraine
13 U 11 **Appalachian Mountains**, GA, U.S.A. ▲▲
76 I 13 **Appennino Abruzzese**, Italy ▲▲
76 B 9 **Appennino Ligure**, Italy ▲▲
77 L 16 **Appennino Lucano**, Italy ▲▲
77 K 15 **Appennino Napoletano**, Italy ▲▲
76 E 9 **Appennino Tosco-Emiliano**, Italy ▲▲
76 H 11 **Appennino Umbro-Marchigiano**, Italy ▲▲
74 I 7 **Appenzell**, Switzerland
68 N 6 **Appingedam**, Netherlands
20 G 12 **Appleton**, WI, U.S.A.
17 S 6 **Appomattox**, VA, U.S.A.
92 L 13 **Apsheronsk**, Russian Federation
65 U 13 **Apt**, France
58 H 7 **Apucarana**, Brazil
51 N 5 **Apure**, Venezuela ◘
51 N 4 **Apure**, Venezuela ∫
53 F 18 **Apurímac**, Peru ◘
53 E 16 **Apurímac**, Peru ∫
101 S 5 **Āqchah**, Afghanistan
100 K 8 **Āqdā**, Iran
108 K 7 **Aqqikkol Hu**, China ⊿
96 G 9 **'Aqraba**, Israel
97 S 1 **'Aqrah**, Iraq
103 V 4 **Aqtasty**, Kazakhstan
55 G 18 **Aquidauana**, Brazil
64 L 12 **Aquitaine**, France ◘
97 S 8 **Ar Raḩḩālīyah**, Iraq
97 S 7 **Ar Ramādī**, Iraq
96 G 13 **Ar Ramlah**, Jordan
96 H 8 **Ar Ramtha**, Jordan
96 L 3 **Ar Raqqah**, Syria
98 L 8 **Ar Rās al Aswad**, Saudi Arabia ▶
99 O 5 **Ar-Rass**, Saudi Arabia
99 O 8 **Ar Rawḑah**, Saudi Arabia
99 R 13 **Ar Rawḑah**, Yemen
97 W 10 **Ar Rifā'ī**, Iraq
97 V 10 **Ar Rihab**, Iraq ◇
99 P 5 **Ar Rubay'iyah**, Saudi Arabia
97 V 10 **Ar Rumaythah**, Iraq
96 L 3 **Ar Ruşāfah**, Syria
96 H 9 **Ar Ruşayfah**, Jordan
99 Z 6 **Ar Rustāq**, Oman
97 N 8 **Ar Ruţbah**, Iraq
99 P 6 **Ar Ruwayḑah**, Saudi Arabia

ountry ◘ Internal administrative region: State/Province/Territory/Dependent territory ♜ Capital city ▲▲ Mountain range/ Undersea ridge ▲ Mountain peak/ Volcano/Seamount ◇ Geographic feature ▶ Headland/Point/ Cape/Peninsula ◖ Desert ⁂ Island/Island group ⠿ Antarctic base ◎ Ocean ◢ Sea ≈ Bay/Gulf/Channel/Strait ⊿ Lake ▚ Salt pan/Dry/ Intermittent lake ∫ River

107 P 11 Ara, India
127 J 22 Āra Ārba, Ethiopia
19 Q 2 Arab, AL, U.S.A.
97 V 8 Arab Abdullah, Iraq
99 V 13 Arabian Sea, O ≈
94 I 7 Araş, Turkey
55 O 14 Aracaju, Brazil
54 O 11 Aracati, Brazil
58 I 5 Araçatuba, Brazil
86 F 10 Arad, Romania
96 F 10 'Arad, Israel
129 Y 8 Arada, Chad
97 Y 11 Aradah, Iraq
99 V 7 'Arādah, United Arab Emirates
117 V 14 Arafura Sea, Asia/Oceania ≈
95 T 8 Aragats Lerr, Armenia ▲
67 S 5 Aragón, Spain ▣
51 O 3 Aragua, Venezuela ▣
55 J 14 Araguaçu, Brazil
54 J 13 Araguaia, Brazil ∿
54 J 12 Araguaina, Brazil
55 J 17 Araguari, Brazil
123 I 14 Arai, Japan
56 L 5 Arak, Syria
100 H 7 Arāk, Iran
125 N 12 Arak, Algeria
114 B 13 Arakan, Myanmar ▣
114 B 12 Arakan Yoma, Myanmar ⛰
102 L 9 Aral Sea, Kazakhstan/Uzbekistan ≋
103 N 7 Aral'sk, Kazakhstan
135 S 6 Aramac, QLD, Australia
138 B 6 Aramia, Papua New Guinea ∿
63 N 6 Aran Fawddwy, U.K. ▲
64 A 18 Aran Islands, Republic of Ireland 🏝
67 O 4 Aranda de Duero, Spain
80 L 11 Arandelovac, Serbia and Montenegro
67 O 7 Aranjuez, Spain
132 J 10 Aranos, Namibia
140 D 2 Aranuka, Kiribati 🏝
115 J 19 Aranyaprathet, Thailand
123 B 22 Arao, Japan
128 L 6 Araouane, Mali
22 K 15 Arapahoe, NE, U.S.A.
137 J 16 Arapawa Island, New Zealand 🏝
54 O 13 Arapiraca, Brazil
95 N 10 Arapkir, Turkey
58 H 7 Arapongas, Brazil
99 N 1 'Ar'ar, Saudi Arabia
50 K 10 Araracuara, Colombia
58 I 11 Araranguá, Brazil
58 J 6 Araraquara, Brazil
54 H 12 Araras, Brazil
135 R 13 Ararat, VIC, Australia
107 R 11 Araria, India
95 R 9 Aras, Turkey
95 S 9 Aras, Azerbaijan/Turkey ∿
95 R 10 Aras Güneyi Dağlari, Turkey ⛰
95 N 12 Atatürk Baraji, Turkey ≋
50 K 5 Arauca, Colombia ▣
50 L 5 Arauca, Colombia
50 M 5 Arauca, Venezuela ∿
57 F 15 Araucanía, Chile ▣
57 E 14 Arauco, Chile
104 C 13 Aravalli Range, India ⛰
55 K 17 Araxá, Brazil
95 W 10 Araz, Azerbaijan ∿
127 H 22 Ārba Minch, Ethiopia
97 V 4 Arbat, Iraq
77 D 18 Arbatax, Italy
75 U 3 Arbesbach, Austria
97 T 2 Arbil, Iraq
71 G 20 Arboga, Sweden
50 G 4 Arboletes, Colombia
74 I 6 Arbon, Switzerland
60 I 12 Arbroath, U.K.
64 L 12 Arcachon, France
14 D 9 Arcade, NY, U.S.A.
18 I 4 Arcadia, LA, U.S.A.
19 W 11 Arcadia, FL, U.S.A.
51 T 8 Arcarai Mountains, Guyana ⛰
33 E 15 Arcata, CA, U.S.A.
45 Q 13 Arcelia, Mexico
134 I 12 Archipelago of the Recherche, WA, Australia 🏝
47 S 12 Archipiélago de Bocas del Toro, Panama 🏝
48 J 4 Archipiélago de Camagüey, Cuba 🏝
57 E 23 Archipiélago de la Reina Adelaida, Chile 🏝
47 X 15 Archipiélago de las Perlas, Panama 🏝
48 G 4 Archipiélago de los Canarreros, Cuba 🏝
48 J 5 Archipiélago de los Jardines de la Reina, Cuba 🏝
57 E 20 Archipiélago de los Chonos, Chile 🏝
48 H 3 Archipiélago de Sabana, Cuba 🏝
47 Y 12 Archipiélago de San Blas, Panama 🏝
47 P 10 Archipiélago de Solentiname, Nicaragua 🏝
76 F 12 Arcidosso, Italy
29 N 11 Arco, ID, U.S.A.
66 L 13 Arcos de la Frontera, Spain
37 Q 4 Arctic Bay, NU, Canada
143 Q 8 Arctic Ocean, O ◎
144 G 3 Arctowski, Antarctica ⁙
95 U 8 Arcvašen, Armenia
96 I 11 Arḍ aş Şawwān, Jordan ⛰
82 J 11 Arda, Bulgaria ∿
100 H 3 Ardabil, Iran
100 H 3 Ardabil, Iran ▣
95 S 8 Ardahan, Turkey
100 K 8 Ardakān, Iran
93 Q 2 Ardatov, Russian Federation
42 E 10 Ardbeg, ON, Canada
61 E 17 Ardee, Republic of Ireland
69 H 23 Ardennes, Belgium ◇
100 J 7 Ardestān, Iran
25 N 12 Ardmore, OK, U.S.A.
86 H 7 Ardud, Romania
71 F 15 Åre, Sweden
131 Q 6 Arebi, Democratic Republic of Congo
49 U 7 Arecibo, Puerto Rico
121 F 19 Arena, Philippines 🏝
47 P 11 Arenal, Costa Rica ∿
55 G 15 Arenápolis, Brazil
66 M 7 Arenas de San Pedro, Spain
71 B 21 Arendal, Norway
69 H 16 Arendonk, Belgium
83 E 23 Areopoli, Greece
53 G 19 Arequipa, Peru
53 F 20 Arequipa, Peru ▣
76 G 11 Arezzo, Italy
83 F 17 Argalasti, Greece
108 L 6 Argan, China
67 O 7 Arganda, Spain
65 N 4 Argentan, France
56 J 11 Argentina, South America ■
56 J 9 Argentina, Argentina
101 S 9 Arghandab, Afghanistan ∿
83 E 21 Argolikos Kolpos, Greece ≃
83 E 21 Argos, Greece
83 C 14 Argos Orestiko, Greece
83 B 19 Argostoli, Greece
110 G 6 Argun', China ∿
129 P 10 Argungu, Nigeria
43 T 12 Argyle, NS, Canada
109 P 3 Arhangay, Mongolia ▣
71 C 24 Århus, Denmark
105 L 18 Ari Atoll, Maldives 🏝
117 Q 8 Ariaga, Indonesia 🏝
132 J 12 Ariamsvlei, Namibia
59 B 15 Arias, Argentina
128 M 9 Aribinda, Burkina Faso
50 K 11 Arica, Colombia
52 D 9 Arica, Peru
56 F 2 Arica, Chile
123 G 19 Arida, Japan
96 I 3 Arīḥā, Syria
80 K 13 Arilje, Serbia and Montenegro
55 G 14 Arinos, Brazil ∿
54 F 12 Aripuanã, Brazil ∿
54 E 13 Ariquemes, Brazil
51 N 4 Arismendi, Venezuela
105 K 18 Ariyaddu Channel, Maldives ≃
67 Q 5 Ariza, Spain
30 H 11 Arizona, U.S.A. ▣
71 E 20 Årjäng, Sweden
70 H 12 Arjeplog, Sweden
93 O 5 Arkadak, Russian Federation
25 U 12 Arkadelphia, AR, U.S.A.
103 Q 5 Arkalyk, Kazakhstan
25 T 11 Arkansas, U.S.A. ▣
25 O 8 Arkansas, U.S.A., U.S.A. ∿
25 N 7 Arkansas City, KS, U.S.A.
90 K 6 Arkhangel'sk, Russian Federation
90 L 7 Arkhangel'skaya Oblast', Russian Federation ▣
89 P 6 Arkhipelag Nordenshel'da, Russian Federation 🏝
83 F 18 Arkitsa, Greece
61 F 19 Arklow, Republic of Ireland
65 T 14 Arles, France
129 N 10 Arli, Burkina Faso
17 U 3 Arlington, DC, U.S.A.
23 O 9 Arlington, SD, U.S.A.
27 Q 6 Arlington, TX, U.S.A.
129 Q 6 Arlit, Niger
69 K 25 Arlon, Belgium
134 G 11 Armadale, WA, Australia
61 E 16 Armagh, U.K.
126 F 11 Armant, Egypt
83 M 26 Armathia, Greece 🏝
92 M 12 Armavir, Russian Federation
50 H 7 Armenia, Colombia
95 T 8 Armenia, Asia ■
135 V 10 Armidale, NSW, Australia
29 Q 4 Armington, MT, U.S.A.
40 L 10 Armstrong, ON, Canada
83 G 14 Arnaia, Greece
41 R 5 Arnaud, QC, Canada ∿
69 D 15 Arnemuiden, Netherlands
24 J 9 Arnett, OK, U.S.A.
68 K 13 Arnhem, Netherlands
82 D 13 Arnissa, Greece
76 E 10 Arno, Italy ∿
73 Z 3 Arno, Marshall Islands 🏝
70 I 6 Arnøya, Norway 🏝
73 I 17 Arnstadt, Germany
132 K 11 Aroab, Namibia
40 M 11 Aroland, ON, Canada
127 H 16 Aroma, Sudan
76 C 6 Arona, Italy
140 F 3 Arorae, Kiribati 🏝
121 J 14 Aroroy, Philippines
74 I 8 Arosa, Switzerland
128 D 10 Arquipélago dos Bijagós, Guinea-Bissau 🏝
60 G 13 Arran, U.K. 🏝
65 Q 2 Arras, France
65 N 15 Arreau, France
59 C 15 Arrecifes, Argentina
45 P 10 Arriaga, Mexico
45 V 14 Arriaga, Mexico
66 M 1 Arriondas, Spain
59 G 14 Arroio Grande, Brazil
33 H 23 Arroyo Grande, CA, U.S.A.
71 C 23 Års, Denmark
93 S 1 Arsk, Russian Federation
67 Z 8 Artà, Spain
83 C 17 Arta, Greece
95 U 9 Artashat, Armenia
45 O 13 Arteaga, Mexico
48 G 4 Artemisa, Cuba
87 X 6 Artemivs'k, Ukraine
77 H 14 Artena, Italy
73 J 16 Artern, Germany
67 V 4 Artesa de Segre, Spain
31 S 13 Artesia, NM, U.S.A.
22 I 13 Arthur, NE, U.S.A.
137 G 19 Arthur's Pass, New Zealand
38 C 10 Artic Red, NT, Canada ∿
58 E 12 Artigas, Uruguay
58 E 12 Artigas, Uruguay ▣
95 T 8 Art'ik, Armenia
87 O 10 Artsyz, Ukraine
95 Q 7 Artvin, Turkey
131 R 6 Aru, Democratic Republic of Congo
131 R 6 Arua, Uganda
55 I 15 Aruanã, Brazil
49 R 12 Aruba, The Netherlands, The Netherlands ▣
54 E 11 Arumã, Brazil
107 R 9 Arun, Nepal ∿
107 X 8 Arunachal Pradesh, India ▣
63 V 13 Arundel, U.K.
131 V 10 Arusha, Tanzania ▣
131 V 10 Arusha, Tanzania
31 R 4 Arvada, CO, U.S.A.
109 P 4 Arvayheer, Mongolia
38 N 11 Arviat, NU, Canada
40 L 4 Arviat, NU, Canada
70 I 12 Arvidsjaur, Sweden
71 E 20 Arvika, Sweden
117 R 14 Arwala, Indonesia
110 G 10 Arxan, China
103 R 11 Arys', Kazakhstan
77 C 15 Arzachena, Italy
93 O 1 Arzamas, Russian Federation
124 L 6 Arzew, Algeria
92 O 12 Arzgir, Russian Federation
96 J 3 As Sa'an, Syria
96 M 3 As Sabkhah, Syria
96 G 11 Aş Şafī, Jordan
97 N 1 Aş Şafīh, Syria
96 J 2 As Safirah, Syria
99 R 6 As Salamiyah, Saudi Arabia
97 U 12 As Salmān, Iraq
96 G 9 As Salt, Jordan
97 V 10 As Samāwah, Iraq
96 H 7 Aş Şanamayn, Syria
98 J 3 Aş Şawrah, Saudi Arabia
97 O 5 As Sayyāl, Syria
125 V 8 As Sidrah, Libya
99 R 3 Aş Şubayhiyah, Kuwait
99 S 13 As Sufāl, Yemen
96 L 4 As Sukhnah, Syria
97 U 3 As Sulaymānīyah, Iraq
99 Q 9 As Sulayyil, Saudi Arabia
125 U 8 As Sulţān, Libya
99 O 8 As Sūq, Saudi Arabia
97 O 3 Aş Şuwār, Syria
96 H 8 As Suwaydā', Syria
97 T 8 As Suwayrah, Iraq
100 G 6 Asadābād, Iran
101 O 6 Asadābād, Iran
101 V 7 Asadābād, Afghanistan
95 V 8 Asağı, Azerbaijan
122 K 4 Asahi-dake, Japan ▲
122 K 4 Asahikawa, Japan
100 H 4 Asālem, Iran
107 R 13 Asansol, India
127 J 19 Āsayita, Ethiopia
14 J 13 Asbury Park, NJ, U.S.A.
10 L 10 Ascension, U.K. ▣
44 L 3 Ascensión, Mexico
73 F 19 Aschaffenburg, Germany
76 I 12 Ascoli Piceno, Italy
77 L 15 Ascoli Satriano, Italy
127 I 21 Āsela, Ethiopia
71 H 14 Åsele, Sweden
82 I 10 Asenovgrad, Bulgaria
70 B 10 Ásgarður, Iceland
25 W 9 Ash Flat, AR, U.S.A.
30 I 18 Ash Fork, AZ, U.S.A.
97 S 11 Ash Shabakah, Iraq
97 O 2 Ash Shaddādah, Syria
99 X 5 Ash Sha'm, United Arab Emirates
97 V 12 Ash Shāmiyah, Iraq ◇
97 U 10 Ash Shanāfiyah, Iraq
99 P 6 Ash Sha'rā', Saudi Arabia
99 R 11 Ash Sharawrah, Saudi Arabia
97 S 3 Ash Sharqāţ, Iraq
97 W 10 Ash Shaţrah, Iraq
96 G 11 Ash Shawbak, Jordan
99 W 12 Ash Shaykh 'Uthman, Yemen
99 T 13 Ash Shiḥr, Yemen
99 X 5 Ash Shināş, Oman
99 P 3 Ash Shu'bah, Saudi Arabia
99 N 11 Ash Shuqayq, Saudi Arabia
125 T 9 Ash Shuwayrif, Libya
128 M 13 Ashanti, Ghana ▣
99 Q 5 Asharat, Saudi Arabia
63 S 5 Ashbourne, U.K.
137 G 21 Ashburton, New Zealand
63 S 6 Ashby de la Zouch, U.K.
96 E 9 Ashdod, Israel
25 S 13 Ashdown, AR, U.S.A.
17 Q 9 Asheboro, NC, U.S.A.
25 O 11 Asher, OK, U.S.A.
16 M 9 Asheville, NC, U.S.A.
63 Y 12 Ashford, U.K.
102 L 14 Ashgabat, Turkmenistan ♜
122 K 5 Ashibetsu, Japan
123 J 15 Ashikaga, Japan
123 K 20 Ashiro, Japan
123 E 22 Ashizuri-misaki, Japan ▶
15 R 1 Ashland, ME, U.S.A.
16 L 4 Ashland, KY, U.S.A.
20 E 8 Ashland, WI, U.S.A.
21 N 17 Ashland, OH, U.S.A.
24 J 7 Ashland, KS, U.S.A.
33 G 14 Ashland, OR, U.S.A.
22 L 6 Ashley, ND, U.S.A.
85 H 16 Ashmyany, Belarus
122 L 5 Ashoro, Japan
96 E 10 Ashqelon, Israel
21 O 15 Ashtabula, OH, U.S.A.
95 T 8 Ashtarak, Armenia
29 Q 10 Ashton, ID, U.S.A.
121 J 15 Asid Gulf, Philippines ≃
105 F 17 Asifabad, India
105 I 17 Asika, India
124 I 6 Asilah, Morocco
88 M 12 Asino, Russian Federation
85 K 18 Asipovichy, Belarus
95 P 9 Aşkale, Turkey
63 T 3 Askern, U.K.
71 D 20 Askim, Norway
91 T 14 Askino, Russian Federation
71 A 18 Askøy, Norway 🏝
100 G 2 Aşlāndūz, Iran
127 I 17 Asmara, Eritrea ♜
71 F 24 Åsnen, Sweden ≋
129 X 9 Asnet, Chad
123 C 22 Aso-san, Japan ▲
83 F 23 Asopos, Greece
127 G 20 Āsosa, Ethiopia
75 X 5 Aspang-Markt, Austria
31 P 5 Aspen, CO, U.S.A.
26 M 5 Aspermont, TX, U.S.A.
127 K 18 Assab, Eritrea
128 G 7 Assaba, Mauritania ▣
107 V 10 Assam, India ▣
129 Q 6 Assamakka, Niger
17 X 5 Assateague Island, VA, U.S.A. 🏝
69 F 18 Asse, Belgium
68 M 7 Assen, Netherlands
69 I 21 Assesse, Belgium
40 H 10 Assiniboine, MB, Canada ∿
58 I 6 Assis, Brazil
55 B 14 Assis Brasil, Brazil
76 H 12 Assisi, Italy
71 D 18 Åsta, Norway ∿
83 M 25 Astakida, Greece 🏝
83 C 18 Astakos, Greece
103 R 4 Astana, Kazakhstan ♜
100 H 3 Āstārā, Iran
69 K 16 Asten, Netherlands
76 B 8 Asti, Italy
53 H 17 Astillero, Peru
63 T 4 Aston, U.K.
66 L 3 Astorga, Spain
32 F 8 Astoria, OR, U.S.A.
93 R 11 Astrakhan', Russian Federation
87 V 9 Astrakhanka, Ukraine
93 R 10 Astrakhanskaya Oblast', Russian Federation ▣
138 D 4 Astrolabe Bay, Papua New Guinea ≃
83 E 21 Astros, Greece
85 F 18 Astryna, Belarus
66 L 1 Asturias, Spain ▣
83 L 23 Astypalaia, Greece 🏝
145 S 2 Asuka, Antarctica ⁙
53 I 16 Asunción, Bolivia
55 G 20 Asunción, Paraguay ♜
140 A 5 Asuncion, Northern Mariana Islands 🏝
46 I 6 Asunción Mita, Guatemala
84 J 13 Asvyeya, Belarus
126 F 12 Aswân, Egypt
126 E 10 Asyût, Egypt
103 U 11 At-Bashy, Kyrgyzstan
96 G 11 Aţ Ţafīlah, Jordan
98 M 8 Aţ Ţā'if, Saudi Arabia
125 X 7 At Tamīmi, Libya
96 L 7 Aţ Ţanf, Syria
97 T 9 Aţ Ţaqţaqānah, Iraq
96 G 12 Aţ Ţayyibah, Jordan
97 N 3 At Tibnī, Syria
98 K 2 Aţ Ţubayq, Saudi Arabia ◇
99 O 14 At Turbah, Yemen
99 P 14 At Turbah, Yemen
140 H 11 Ata, Tonga 🏝
56 F 8 Atacama, Chile ▣
56 F 2 Atacama Desert, Chile ◇
140 J 6 Atafu, Tokelau Islands 🏝
129 N 12 Atakpamé, Togo
53 E 15 Atalaya, Peru
99 R 13 'Ataq, Yemen
128 G 5 Atâr, Mauritania
109 O 5 Atas Bogd, Mongolia ▲
103 S 6 Atasu, Kazakhstan
117 Q 15 Atauro, Indonesia 🏝
127 F 15 Atbara, Sudan
127 G 16 Atbara, Sudan ∿
103 Q 4 Atbasar, Kazakhstan
18 J 9 Atchafalaya Bay, LA, U.S.A. ≃
25 Q 3 Atchison, KS, U.S.A.
128 M 12 Atebubu, Ghana
69 E 20 Ath, Belgium
39 I 18 Athabasca, AB, Canada ∿
16 I 10 Athens, TN, U.S.A.
19 U 2 Athens, GA, U.S.A.
21 N 19 Athens, OH, U.S.A.
27 R 6 Athens, TX, U.S.A.
83 G 20 Athens, Greece ♜
94 H 15 Athienou, Cyprus
61 D 18 Athlone, Republic of Ireland
14 M 9 Athol, MA, U.S.A.
83 H 15 Athos, Greece ▲
129 X 9 Ati, Chad
53 E 19 Atico, Peru
127 C 21 Atiedo, Sudan
67 P 5 Atienza, Spain
40 K 11 Atikokan, ON, Canada
46 I 7 Atiquizaya, El Salvador
46 G 6 Atitlán, Guatemala
141 P 10 Atiu, Cook Islands 🏝
34 G 14 Atka, AK, U.S.A.
89 X 10 Atka, Russian Federation
34 G 14 Atka Island, AK, U.S.A. 🏝
93 P 5 Atkarsk, Russian Federation
117 T 11 Atkri, Indonesia
19 S 3 Atlanta, GA, U.S.A.
20 K 11 Atlanta, MI, U.S.A.
28 L 10 Atlanta, ID, U.S.A.
17 V 10 Atlantic, NC, U.S.A.
23 R 13 Atlantic, IA, U.S.A.
14 J 15 Atlantic City, NJ, U.S.A.
8 K 9 Atlantic Ocean, O ◎
50 H 2 Atlántico, Colombia ▣
124 H 9 Atlas Mountains, Morocco ⛰
124 L 7 Atlas Saharien, Algeria ⛰
39 B 15 Atlin Lake, BC, Canada ≋
96 F 8 'Atlit, Israel
19 P 6 Atmore, AL, U.S.A.
53 J 22 Atocha, Bolivia
25 P 12 Atoka, OK, U.S.A.
115 N 17 Atouat, Laos ▲
100 M 4 Atrak, Iran ∿
123 K 16 Atsugi, Japan
122 J 12 Atsumi, Japan
123 I 18 Atsumi, Japan
122 J 5 Atsuta, Japan
115 N 18 Attapu, Laos
83 O 24 Attavyros, Greece ▲
40 M 10 Attawapiskat, ON, Canada ∿
41 O 9 Attawapiskat, ON, Canada
40 L 9 Attawapiskat Lake, ON, Canada ≋
75 R 5 Attersee, Austria ≋
69 K 25 Attert, Belgium
14 D 8 Attica, NY, U.S.A.
21 H 18 Attica, IN, U.S.A.
83 G 22 Attiki, Greece ▣
63 Y 7 Attleborough, U.K.
34 B 11 Attu Island, AK, U.S.A. 🏝
99 S 13 Atūd, Yemen
57 H 14 Atuel, Argentina ∿
102 I 7 Atyrau, Kazakhstan ▣
102 I 7 Atyrau, Kazakhstan
20 L 12 Au Sable Point, MI, U.S.A. ▶
138 B 2 Aua Island, Papua New Guinea 🏝
69 K 26 Aubange, Belgium
65 S 12 Aubenas, France
65 Q 7 Aubigny-sur-Nère, France
65 Q 12 Aubin, France
14 G 8 Auburn, NY, U.S.A.
15 N 10 Auburn, MA, U.S.A.
19 R 4 Auburn, AL, U.S.A.
21 E 19 Auburn, IL, U.S.A.
23 Q 15 Auburn, NE, U.S.A.
32 G 7 Auburn, WA, U.S.A.
33 H 18 Auburn, CA, U.S.A.
65 Q 9 Aubusson, France
84 G 12 Auce, Latvia
65 N 14 Auch, France
136 K 8 Auckland, New Zealand
136 J 8 Auckland, New Zealand ▣
64 H 5 Audierne, France
127 J 22 Audo Range, Ethiopia ⛰
73 L 18 Aue, Germany
73 L 18 Auerbach, Germany
135 T 7 Augathella, QLD, Australia
73 I 24 Augsburg, Germany
84 H 13 Augšzemes Augstiene, Latvia ⛰
15 P 6 Augusta, ME, U.S.A.
19 V 3 Augusta, GA, U.S.A.
20 D 11 Augusta, WI, U.S.A.
21 D 18 Augusta, IL, U.S.A.
29 P 4 Augusta, MT, U.S.A.
77 L 23 Augusta, Italy
134 F 12 Augusta, WA, Australia
56 G 6 Augusta Victoria, Chile
78 N 9 Augustów, Poland
138 M 6 Auki, Solomon Islands
31 R 2 Ault, CO, U.S.A.
129 P 11 Auna, Nigeria
41 S 6 Aupaluk, QC, Canada
117 R 12 Auponhia, Indonesia
116 F 9 Aur, Malaysia 🏝
141 Z 3 Aur, Marshall Islands 🏝
20 G 8 Aura, MI, U.S.A.
106 L 10 Auraiya, India
107 P 12 Aurangabad, India
64 J 6 Auray, France
72 D 10 Aurich, Germany
65 Q 11 Aurillac, France
71 B 18 Aurlandsvangen, Norway
21 G 16 Aurora, IL, U.S.A.
31 R 4 Aurora, CO, U.S.A.
120 H 8 Aurora, Philippines
54 K 10 Aurora do Pará, Brazil
135 R 2 Aurukun, QLD, Australia
132 I 11 Aus, Namibia
23 T 10 Austin, MN, U.S.A.
27 P 9 Austin, TX, U.S.A.
33 L 17 Austin, NV, U.S.A.
135 N 6 Australia, Oceania ■
135 U 12 Australian Capital Territory, Australia ▣
75 P 7 Austria, Europe ■
70 G 9 Austvågøy, Norway 🏝
54 F 11 Autazes, Brazil
45 N 11 Autlán, Mexico
65 S 8 Autun, France
65 Q 10 Auvergne, France ▣
65 R 6 Auxerre, France
51 R 6 Auyan Tepui, Venezuela ▲
25 U 7 Ava, MO, U.S.A.
65 S 7 Avallon, France
14 I 15 Avalon, NJ, U.S.A.
41 Z 10 Avalon Peninsula, NL, Canada ▶
58 J 7 Avaré, Brazil
141 N 11 Avarua, Cook Islands ♜
63 R 11 Avebury, U.K.
54 H 11 Aveiro, Brazil
66 H 5 Aveiro, Portugal ▣
66 H 6 Aveiro, Portugal
77 K 16 Avellino, Italy
77 J 16 Aversa, Italy
28 K 4 Avery, ID, U.S.A.
65 S 2 Avesnes-sur-Helpe, France
71 G 19 Avesta, Sweden
56 L 7 Aviá Terai, Argentina
58 C 10 Avia Teray, Argentina
60 H 10 Aviemore, U.K.
65 T 13 Avignon, France
67 N 6 Ávila, Spain
66 L 1 Avilés, Spain
84 I 6 Avinurme, Estonia
83 G 19 Avlida, Greece
77 K 23 Avola, Italy
14 E 8 Avon, NY, U.S.A.
63 R 9 Avon, U.K. ∿
19 W 11 Avon Park, FL, U.S.A.
30 I 12 Avondale, AZ, U.S.A.
64 L 4 Avranches, France
86 I 11 Avrig, Romania
127 L 24 Aw Dheegle, Somalia
122 J 12 Awa-shima, Japan 🏝
123 G 19 Awaji-shima, Japan 🏝
136 K 11 Awakino, New Zealand
99 T 5 Awālī, Bahrain
136 I 5 Awanui, New Zealand
127 J 21 Āwarē, Ethiopia
136 J 6 Awarua, New Zealand
137 B 23 Awarua Point, New Zealand ▶
127 I 21 Āwasa, Ethiopia
127 J 20 Āwash, Ethiopia
127 J 19 Āwash, Ethiopia ∿
137 F 17 Awatere, New Zealand ∿
125 S 11 Awbārī, Libya
127 C 20 Aweil, Sudan
19 P 5 Awin, AL, U.S.A.
125 X 9 Awjilah, Libya
124 C 13 Awserd, Western Sahara
37 O 2 Axel Heiberg Island, NU, Canada 🏝
128 L 14 Axim, Ghana
82 E 13 Axios, Greece ∿
63 O 13 Axminster, U.K.
53 E 17 Ayacucho, Peru
53 E 18 Ayacucho, Peru ▣
59 D 18 Ayacucho, Argentina
103 X 6 Ayagoz, Kazakhstan
108 L 7 Ayakkum Hu, China ≋
66 I 12 Ayamonte, Spain
89 V 12 Ayan, Russian Federation
94 J 7 Ayancık, Turkey
111 K 18 Ayang, North Korea
51 T 6 Ayanganna Mountain, Guyana ▲
129 R 12 Ayangba, Nigeria
53 G 18 Ayaviri, Peru
101 T 6 Āybak, Afghanistan
87 Y 5 Aydar, Ukraine ∿
94 C 11 Aydın, Turkey
94 B 11 Aydın Dağlari, Turkey ⛰
127 J 19 Āyelu Terara, Ethiopia ▲
118 E 10 Ayer Hitam, Malaysia
67 S 3 Ayerbe, Spain
89 R 10 Aykhal, Russian Federation
63 U 9 Aylesbury, U.K.
137 H 20 Aylesbury, New Zealand
67 P 5 Ayllón, Spain
38 J 10 Aylmer Lake, NT, Canada ≋
63 Z 6 Aylsham, U.K.
103 R 13 Ayni, Tajikistan
127 E 21 Ayod, Sudan
67 S 9 Ayora, Spain
129 N 8 Ayorou, Niger
128 H 7 'Ayoûn el 'Atroûs, Mauritania
61 G 14 Ayr, U.K.
135 U 5 Ayr, QLD, Australia
94 I 12 Ayranci, Turkey
103 N 8 Ayteke Bi, Kazakhstan
82 M 9 Aytos, Bulgaria
99 W 11 Ayun, Oman
115 H 18 Ayutthaya, Thailand
94 A 9 Ayvacık, Turkey
94 B 9 Ayvalık, Turkey
96 H 6 Az Zabadānī, Syria
96 H 9 Az Zarqā', Jordan
125 S 7 Az Zāwiyah, Libya
99 V 13 Az Zaydiyah, Yemen
99 P 5 Az Zilfī, Saudi Arabia
125 R 8 Az Zintān, Libya
97 Z 12 Az Zubayr, Iraq
99 O 12 Az Zuhrah, Yemen
99 O 14 Az Zuqur, Yemen 🏝
47 N 6 Azacualpa, Honduras
32 F 13 Azalea, OR, U.S.A.
107 O 11 Azamgarh, India
100 F 4 Āzarbāyjān-e Gharbī, Iran ▣
100 G 3 Āzarbāyjān-e Sharqī, Iran ▣
129 S 10 Azare, Nigeria
85 L 20 Azarychy, Belarus
96 J 1 A'zāz, Syria
124 G 7 Azemmour, Morocco
95 V 10 Azerbaijan, Asia ■
127 H 18 Āzezo, Ethiopia
124 H 8 Azilal, Morocco
101 N 11 'Azīzābād, Iran
10 K 6 Azores, Portugal ▣
92 L 10 Azov, Russian Federation
96 I 9 Azraq ash Shishān, Jordan
124 I 7 Azrou, Morocco
30 H 13 Aztec, AZ, U.S.A.
31 O 8 Aztec, NM, U.S.A.
49 Q 8 Azua, Dominican Republic
66 L 10 Azuaga, Spain
52 B 10 Azuay, Ecuador ▣
59 C 17 Azul, Argentina
128 E 5 Azzeffâl, Mauritania ⛰

B

17 R 9 B. Everett Jordan Reservoir, NC, U.S.A. ≋
115 N 19 Bâ Kêv, Cambodia
117 P 15 Baa, Indonesia
96 H 5 Ba'albek, Lebanon
96 G 6 Baaqline, Lebanon
127 L 24 Baardheere, Somalia
127 K 17 Bāb al Mandab, Africa/Asia ≃
94 G 7 Baba Burnu, Turkey ▶
94 A 9 Baba Burun, Turkey ▶
87 N 12 Babadag, Romania
95 X 7 Babadağ Dağl, Azerbaijan ▲
102 L 14 Babadurmaz, Turkmenistan
94 B 7 Babaeski, Turkey
127 C 19 Babanusa, Sudan
117 T 14 Babar, Indonesia 🏝
131 U 10 Babati, Tanzania
90 I 11 Babayevo, Russian Federation
29 O 2 Babb, MT, U.S.A.
63 N 14 Babbacombe Bay, U.K. ≃
118 F 9 Babi Besar, Malaysia 🏝
39 E 18 Babine Lake, BC, Canada ≋
117 U 12 Babo, Indonesia
100 J 5 Bābol, Iran
129 V 13 Babongo, Cameroon
30 K 15 Baboquivari Peak, AZ, U.S.A. ▲
130 G 4 Baboua, Central African Republic
85 L 19 Babruysk, Belarus
120 H 6 Babuyan, Philippines
121 D 18 Babuyan, Philippines
120 G 5 Babuyan Channel, Philippines ≃
120 H 4 Babuyan Islands, Philippines 🏝
114 M 11 Bắc Can, Vietnam
114 M 12 Bắc Giang, Vietnam
114 L 10 Bac Lac, Vietnam
115 M 23 Bac Liêu, Vietnam
114 M 12 Bắc Ninh, Vietnam
114 L 11 Bắc Quang, Vietnam
127 N 21 Bacaadweyn, Somalia
54 L 11 Bacabal, Brazil
54 I 11 Bacajá, Brazil ∿
45 Z 12 Bacalar, Mexico
117 R 11 Bacan, Indonesia 🏝
120 F 6 Bacarra, Philippines
86 L 9 Bacău, Romania
65 V 5 Baccarat, France
74 K 7 Bach, Austria
73 D 19 Bacharach, Germany
40 K 1 Back, NU, Canada ∿
80 J 9 Bačka Palanka, Serbia and Montenegro
80 J 8 Bačka Topola, Serbia and Montenegro
73 G 22 Backnang, Germany
121 J 17 Bacolod, Philippines
44 J 6 Bácum, Mexico
75 S 6 Bad Aussee, Austria
73 D 22 Bad Bergzabern, Germany
72 H 9 Bad Bramstedt, Germany
72 N 12 Bad Freienwalde, Germany
75 R 6 Bad Goisern, Austria
75 Q 7 Bad Hofgastein, Austria
73 E 14 Bad Iburg, Germany
75 R 5 Bad Ischl, Austria
75 S 8 Bad Kleinkirchheim, Austria
73 D 20 Bad Kreuznach, Germany
73 I 17 Bad Langensalza, Germany
75 T 3 Bad Leonfelden, Austria
73 H 21 Bad Mergentheim, Germany
73 H 19 Bad Neustadt an der Saale, Germany
72 H 10 Bad Oldesloe, Germany
75 X 8 Bad Radkersburg, Austria
73 L 25 Bad Reichenhall, Germany
73 H 17 Bad Salzungen, Germany
72 H 9 Bad Segeberg, Germany
75 U 7 Bad St Leonhard, Austria
73 J 25 Bad Tölz, Germany
73 G 25 Bad Waldsee, Germany
115 F 22 Bada, Myanmar 🏝
105 D 22 Badagara, India
113 N 11 Badahe, China
109 O 7 Badain Jaran Desert, China ◇
66 J 9 Badajoz, Spain
101 V 5 Badakhshān, Afghanistan ▣
99 N 1 Badanah, Saudi Arabia
104 F 9 Badarinath Peaks, India ▲
107 W 11 Badarpur, India
43 X 8 Baddeck, NS, Canada
101 R 12 Baddo, Pakistan ∿
75 X 4 Baden, Austria
73 E 22 Baden Baden, Germany
73 E 23 Baden-wurttemberg, Germany ▣
75 Q 7 Badgastein, Austria
101 Q 7 Bādghīs, Afghanistan ▣
68 H 11 Badhoevedorp, Netherlands
67 Z 7 Badia d'Alcúdia, Spain ≃
67 X 8 Badia de Palma, Spain ≃
101 U 15 Badin, Pakistan
22 G 6 Badlands, ND, U.S.A. ◇
120 F 6 Badoc, Philippines
113 R 6 Badong, China
129 N 12 Badou, Togo
98 L 6 Badr Ḥunayn, Saudi Arabia
97 W 7 Badrah, Iraq
106 L 6 Badrinath Peaks, India ▲
135 R 1 Badu Island, QLD, Australia 🏝
105 G 25 Badulla, Sri Lanka
67 N 12 Baena, Spain
67 O 11 Baeza, Spain
128 E 10 Bafatá, Guinea-Bissau
143 O 9 Baffin Basin, Arctic Ocean ◇
143 N 10 Baffin Bay, Arctic Ocean ≃
41 Q 1 Baffin Island, NU, Canada 🏝
129 T 14 Bafia, Cameroon

■ Country ▣ Internal administrative region: State/Province/Territory/Dependent territory ♜ Capital city ⛰ Mountain range/Undersea ridge ▲ Mountain peak/Volcano/Seamount ◇ Geographic feature ▶ Headland/Point/Cape/Peninsula ◓ Desert 🏝 Island/Island group ⁙ Antarctic base ◎ Ocean ≈ Sea ≃ Bay/Gulf/Channel/Strait ≋ Lake ⊠ Salt pan/Dry/Intermittent lake ∿

H 9 **Bafoulabé**, Mali
T 14 **Bafoussam**, Cameroon
L 9 **Bāfq**, Iran
K 7 **Bafra**, Turkey
L 7 **Bafra Burnu**, Turkey ▶
P 7 **Bafwasende**, Democratic Republic of Congo
G 8 **Bagabag**, Philippines
F 11 **Bagac**, Philippines
F 11 **Bagac Bay**, Philippines ≈
O 11 **Bagaces**, Costa Rica
O 10 **Bagaha**, India
D 19 **Bagalkot**, India
W 11 **Bagamoyo**, Tanzania
N 21 **Baganga**, Philippines
K 7 **Bagani**, Namibia
J 22 **Baganian Peninsula**, Philippines ▶
D 9 **Bagansiapiapi**, Indonesia
P 9 **Bagaroua**, Niger
J 10 **Bagata**, Democratic Republic of Congo
F 13 **Bagé**, Brazil
L 7 **Bageshwar**, India
V 15 **Baggs**, WY, U.S.A.
M 12 **Baggy Point**, U.K. ▶
O 6 **Baghbaghū**, Iran
T 7 **Baghdad**, Iraq ▙
I 21 **Bagheria**, Italy
L 10 **Bāghīn**, Iran
T 6 **Baghlān**, Afghanistan ▣
U 6 **Baghlān**, Afghanistan
R 8 **Baghrān**, Afghanistan
O 9 **Baglung**, Nepal
I 17 **Bago**, Philippines
E 6 **Bagolino**, Italy
B 16 **Bagrationovsk**, Russian Federation
J 10 **Bagre**, Brazil
W 8 **Bagsaya**, Iraq
U 11 **Bagshot**, U.K.
B 12 **Bagua**, Peru
P 10 **Bagudo**, Nigeria
F 8 **Baguio**, Philippines
H 6 **Baguio Point**, Philippines ▶
K 1 **Bahamas, The**, North America □
R 13 **Baharampur**, India
D 9 **Bahariya Oasis**, Egypt ◇
W 7 **Bahatyr**, Ukraine
D 9 **Bahau**, Malaysia
W 11 **Bahawalpur**, Pakistan
L 13 **Bahşşe**, Turkey
M 14 **Bahia**, Brazil ▣
K 16 **Bahía Anegada**, Argentina ≈
G 6 **Bahía Asunción**, Mexico
B 19 **Bahía Blanca**, Argentina ≈
B 19 **Bahía Blanca**, Argentina
I 19 **Bahía Bustamante**, Argentina
I 19 **Bahía Camarones**, Argentina ≈
Z 12 **Bahía Chetumal**, Mexico ≈
J 4 **Bahía de Amatique**, Guatemala ≈
B 7 **Bahía de Ancón de Sardinas**, Ecuador ≈
G 6 **Bahía de Ballenas**, Mexico ≈
M 11 **Bahía de Banderas**, Mexico ≈
R 10 **Bahía de Bluefields**, Nicaragua ≈
V 11 **Bahía de Campeche**, Mexico ≈
A 9 **Bahía de Caráquez**, Ecuador ≈
L 1 **Bahía de Chetumal**, Belize ≈
G 26 **Bahía de Cook**, Chile ≈
Q 14 **Bahía de Coronado**, Costa Rica ≈
Z 11 **Bahía de Espíritu Santo**, Mexico ≈
K 8 **Bahía de Jiquilisco**, El Salvador ≈
Z 11 **Bahía de la Ascension**, Mexico ≈
I 8 **Bahía de La Paz**, Mexico ≈
G 4 **Bahía de los Ángeles**, Mexico
A 9 **Bahía de Mania**, Ecuador ≈
X 14 **Bahía de Panamá**, Panama ≈
W 15 **Bahía de Parita**, Panama ≈
P 13 **Bahía de Petacalco**, Mexico ≈
R 7 **Bahía de Samaná**, Dominican Republic ≈
R 10 **Bahía de San Juan del Norte**, Nicaragua ≈
H 24 **Bahía de San Sebastián**, Argentina ≈
A 9 **Bahía de Santa Elena**, Ecuador ≈
K 7 **Bahía de Santa María**, Mexico ≈
A 12 **Bahía de Sechura**, Peru ≈
N 4 **Bahía de Trujillo**, Honduras ≈
R 7 **Bahía Escocesa**, Dominican Republic ≈
H 23 **Bahía Grande**, Argentina ≈
I 4 **Bahía Kino**, Mexico
I 21 **Bahía Laura**, Argentina
H 8 **Bahía Magdalena**, Mexico ≈
G 7 **Bahía Magdalena**, Colombia ≈
I 26 **Bahía Nassau**, Chile ≈
G 18 **Bahía Negra**, Paraguay
F 25 **Bahía Otway**, Chile ≈
F 8 **Bahía Salada**, Chile ≈
E 23 **Bahía Salvación**, Chile ≈
E 16 **Bahía Samborombón**, Argentina ≈
E 18 **Bahía San Nicolás**, Peru ≈
G 5 **Bahía Sebastían Vizcaíno**, Mexico ≈
I 19 **Bahía Solano**, Argentina ≈
F 5 **Bahía Tortugas**, Mexico
B 20 **Bahía Unión**, Argentina ≈
H 19 **Bahir Dar**, Ethiopia
A 19 **Bahr el Arab**, Sudan ∫
D 20 **Bahr el Ghazal**, Sudan ∫
E 23 **Bahr el Jebel**, Sudan ▣
M 9 **Bahraich**, India
U 4 **Bahrain**, Asia □
P 14 **Bāhū Kālāt**, Iran
M 15 **Bahushewsk**, Belarus
L 13 **Bai Thurong**, Vietnam
N 12 **Baia**, Romania
J 10 **Baía de Marajó**, Brazil ≈
U 5 **Baía de Memba**, Mozambique ≈
U 4 **Baía de Pemba**, Mozambique ≈
L 10 **Baía de São Marcos**, Brazil ≈
F 6 **Baía dos Tigres**, Angola
F 4 **Baía Farta**, Angola
I 8 **Baia Mare**, Romania
J 10 **Baião**, Brazil
L 8 **Baiazeh**, Iran
W 12 **Baïbokoum**, Chad
H 11 **Baicheng**, China
K 12 **Băicoi**, Romania
Q 5 **Baie-Comeau**, QC, Canada
H 6 **Baie de Audierne**, France ≈
K 7 **Baie de Bourgneuf**, France ≈
H 5 **Baie de Douarnenez**, France ≈
M 3 **Baie de Seine**, France ≈
J 4 **Baie de St-Brieuc**, France ≈
N 7 **Baie-St-Paul**, QC, Canada
R 5 **Baie-Trinité**, QC, Canada
X 9 **Baie Verte**, NL, Canada
M 14 **Baihe**, China
R 5 **Baihe**, China
G 10 **Bailang**, China
86 K 10 **Băile Tuşnad**, Romania
67 O 11 **Bailén**, Spain
54 J 9 **Bailique**, Brazil
69 J 22 **Baillonville**, Belgium
132 H 4 **Bailundo**, Angola
112 K 4 **Baima**, China
138 C 5 **Baimuru**, Papua New Guinea
19 S 6 **Bainbridge**, GA, U.S.A.
117 O 15 **Baing**, Indonesia
110 K 9 **Baiquan**, China
96 I 11 **Bā'ir**, Jordan
108 I 8 **Bairab Co**, China ∽
107 Q 10 **Bairagnia**, India
35 O 5 **Baird Mountains**, AK, U.S.A. ⛰
140 D 2 **Bairiki**, Kiribati ▙
110 F 13 **Bairin Qiao**, China
110 F 13 **Bairin Zuoqi**, China
103 Q 11 **Bairkum**, Kazakhstan
135 T 13 **Bairnsdale**, VIC, Australia
113 O 7 **Baisha**, China
111 K 14 **Baishan**, China
111 L 14 **Baishan**, China
106 M 8 **Baitadi**, Nepal
112 I 4 **Baitang**, China
141 U 1 **Baiti**, Nauru
113 U 1 **Baixiang**, China
132 J 6 **Baixo-Longa**, Angola
112 J 5 **Baiyü**, China
127 F 15 **Baiyuda Desert**, Sudan ◇
107 S 14 **Baj Baj**, India
79 I 25 **Baja**, Hungary
44 F 2 **Baja California**, Mexico ▶
44 F 4 **Baja California Norte**, Mexico ▣
44 G 7 **Baja California Sur**, Mexico ▣
106 M 8 **Bajang**, Nepal
116 G 9 **Bajau**, Indonesia ⁂
101 N 7 **Bajestān**, Iran
101 O 5 **Bājgīrān**, Iran
99 O 13 **Bājil**, Yemen
47 S 14 **Bajo Boquete**, Panama
57 G 21 **Bajo Caracoles**, Argentina
129 T 11 **Bajoga**, Nigeria
93 U 1 **Bakaly**, Russian Federation
103 V 8 **Bakanas**, Kazakhstan
129 Z 8 **Bakaoré**, Chad
128 G 8 **Bakel**, Senegal
29 Z 6 **Baker**, MT, U.S.A.
32 K 11 **Baker**, OR, U.S.A.
33 L 23 **Baker**, CA, U.S.A.
40 K 3 **Baker Lake**, NU, Canada ∽
33 J 23 **Bakersfield**, CA, U.S.A.
63 S 4 **Bakewell**, U.K.
102 L 13 **Bakhardok**, Turkmenistan
87 T 12 **Bakhcyisaray**, Ukraine
102 K 13 **Bakherden**, Turkmenistan
87 S 2 **Bakhmach**, Ukraine
89 N 10 **Bakhta**, Russian Federation
107 Q 11 **Bakhtiyarpur**, India
103 Y 7 **Bakhty**, Kazakhstan
94 D 7 **Bakirköy**, Turkey
82 O 13 **Bakiröy**, Turkey
70 D 10 **Bakkaflói**, Iceland ≈
106 H 5 **Bakloh**, India
127 H 20 **Bako**, Ethiopia
128 I 11 **Bako**, Côte d'Ivoire
79 G 24 **Bakony**, Hungary ⛰
127 L 23 **Bakool**, Somalia ▣
138 H 4 **Bakop**, Papua New Guinea
130 M 4 **Bakouma**, Central African Republic
93 O 13 **Baksan**, Russian Federation
95 Z 8 **Baku**, Azerbaijan ▙
95 S 7 **Bakuriani**, Georgia
144 K 10 **Bakutis Coast**, Antarctica ◇
63 N 5 **Bala**, U.K.
94 H 10 **Balâ**, Turkey
101 Q 6 **Bālā Morghāb**, Afghanistan
121 B 21 **Balabac**, Philippines
121 A 21 **Balabac**, Philippines ⁂
121 A 21 **Balabac Strait**, Philippines ≈
87 U 7 **Balabyne**, Ukraine
97 T 6 **Balad**, Iraq
97 U 6 **Balad Rūz**, Iraq
105 G 15 **Balaghat**, India
105 D 17 **Balaghat Range**, India ⛰
67 V 4 **Balaguer**, Spain
95 V 6 **Balakän**, Azerbaijan
87 T 13 **Balaklava**, Ukraine
87 W 5 **Balakliya**, Ukraine
93 R 5 **Balakovo**, Russian Federation
119 V 3 **Balambangan**, Malaysia ⁂
120 F 11 **Balanga**, Philippines
105 H 16 **Balangir**, India
93 O 5 **Balashov**, Russian Federation
79 J 21 **Balassagyarmat**, Hungary
79 G 24 **Balaton**, Hungary ∽
120 G 7 **Balbalan**, Philippines
54 F 10 **Balbina**, Brazil
47 W 13 **Balboa**, Panama
61 F 17 **Balbriggan**, Republic of Ireland
59 D 18 **Balcarce**, Argentina
82 N 7 **Balchik**, Bulgaria
137 E 25 **Balclutha**, New Zealand
26 N 10 **Balcones Escarpment**, TX, U.S.A. ⛰
17 T 12 **Bald Head Island**, NC, U.S.A. ⁂
25 W 10 **Bald Knob**, AR, U.S.A.
19 W 7 **Baldwin**, FL, U.S.A.
20 C 11 **Baldwin**, WI, U.S.A.
20 J 13 **Baldwin**, MI, U.S.A.
14 G 8 **Baldwinsville**, NY, U.S.A.
29 S 3 **Baldy Mountain**, MT, U.S.A. ▲
40 H 9 **Baldy Mountain**, MB, Canada ▲
30 M 12 **Baldy Peak**, AZ, U.S.A. ▲
128 H 10 **Baléa**, Mali
67 V 9 **Balearic Islands**, Spain ⁂
119 R 10 **Baleh**, Malaysia ∫
120 H 9 **Baler**, Philippines
120 H 9 **Baler Bay**, Philippines ≈
105 K 16 **Baleshwar**, India
91 Q 13 **Balezino**, Russian Federation
108 K 5 **Balguntay**, China
99 S 14 **Balḩaf**, Yemen
104 C 13 **Bali**, India
116 L 14 **Bali**, Indonesia ⁂
116 L 15 **Bali**, Indonesia ▣
116 K 14 **Bali Sea**, Indonesia ◒
116 D 9 **Balige**, Indonesia
94 C 9 **Balikesir**, Turkey
96 L 2 **Balīkh**, Syria ∫
116 M 11 **Balikpapan**, Indonesia
121 E 25 **Balimbing**, Philippines
121 L 20 **Balingasag**, Philippines
73 F 24 **Balingen**, Germany
119 P 8 **Balingian**, Malaysia
121 L 19 **Balingoan**, Philippines
120 G 3 **Balintang Channel**, Philippines ≈
130 M 5 **Balitondo**, Central African Republic
99 N 9 **Baljurshi**, Saudi Arabia
68 J 8 **Balk**, Netherlands
82 F 8 **Balkan Mountains**, Bulgaria ⛰
102 J 12 **Balkanskiy Velayat**, Turkmenistan ▣
103 Q 3 **Balkashino**, Kazakhstan
101 T 5 **Balkh**, Afghanistan ▣
103 U 7 **Balkhash**, Kazakhstan
60 G 11 **Ballachulish**, U.K.
134 J 11 **Balladonia**, WA, Australia
61 C 17 **Ballaghaderreen**, Republic of Ireland
105 F 17 **Ballalpur**, India
61 G 14 **Ballantrae**, U.K.
135 R 13 **Ballarat**, VIC, Australia
145 S 15 **Balleny Islands**, Antarctica ⁂
61 B 16 **Ballina**, Republic of Ireland
135 W 9 **Ballina**, NSW, Australia
61 C 18 **Ballinasloe**, Republic of Ireland
26 M 7 **Ballinger**, TX, U.S.A.
61 F 15 **Ballymena**, U.K.
61 C 16 **Ballysadare**, Republic of Ireland
57 G 20 **Balmaceda**, Chile
26 H 8 **Balmorhea**, TX, U.S.A.
132 G 4 **Balombo**, Angola
104 B 13 **Balotra**, India
103 W 8 **Balpyk Bi**, Kazakhstan
107 N 9 **Balrampur**, India
135 R 11 **Balranald**, NSW, Australia
86 I 13 **Balş**, Romania
47 P 12 **Balsa**, Costa Rica ∫
45 R 13 **Balsas**, Mexico ∫
52 C 13 **Balsas**, Peru
54 K 12 **Balsas**, Brazil
74 E 7 **Balsthal**, Switzerland
87 O 7 **Balta**, Ukraine
80 O 13 **Balta Berilovac**, Serbia and Montenegro
86 M 8 **Bălţi**, Moldova
71 G 26 **Baltic Sea**, Europe ◒
17 U 2 **Baltimore**, MD, U.S.A.
85 A 15 **Baltiysk**, Russian Federation
101 R 12 **Baluchistān**, Pakistan ▣
121 J 15 **Balud**, Philippines
107 S 11 **Balurghat**, India
121 M 25 **Balut**, Philippines ⁂
84 I 10 **Balvi**, Latvia
103 V 10 **Balykchy**, Kyrgyzstan
102 I 7 **Balykshi**, Kazakhstan
101 N 11 **Bam**, Iran
113 P 11 **Bama**, China
129 U 10 **Bama**, Nigeria
135 R 1 **Bamaga**, QLD, Australia
128 J 10 **Bamako**, Mali ▙
128 M 7 **Bamba**, Mali
130 G 9 **Bambama**, Congo
132 K 6 **Bambangando**, Angola
130 K 4 **Bambari**, Central African Republic
17 O 14 **Bamberg**, SC, U.S.A.
73 I 20 **Bamberg**, Germany
131 O 5 **Bambili**, Democratic Republic of Congo
130 I 5 **Bambio**, Central African Republic
127 G 19 **Bambudi**, Ethiopia
55 K 17 **Bambuí**, Brazil
112 I 6 **Bamda**, China
129 S 13 **Bamenda**, Cameroon
39 F 22 **Bamfield**, BC, Canada
102 K 13 **Bami**, Turkmenistan
101 T 7 **Bāmīān**, Afghanistan ▣
101 T 7 **Bāmīān**, Afghanistan
110 J 13 **Bamiancheng**, China
130 K 3 **Bamingui**, Central African Republic
130 K 2 **Bamingui-Bangoran**, Central African Republic ▣
115 K 20 **Bâmnak**, Cambodia
63 N 12 **Bampton**, U.K.
101 O 13 **Bampūr**, Iran
114 K 13 **Ban Ban**, Laos
114 I 12 **Ban Boun Tai**, Laos
115 I 17 **Ban Bua Chum**, Thailand
115 J 21 **Ban Hat Lek**, Thailand
114 H 13 **Ban Houayxay**, Laos
115 G 21 **Ban Huai Yang**, Thailand
115 H 17 **Ban Khao Sai**, Thailand
115 E 24 **Ban Khok Kloi**, Thailand
115 G 24 **Ban Na San**, Thailand
115 I 14 **Ban Nalè**, Laos
115 L 15 **Ban Napè**, Laos
115 H 15 **Ban Pak Pat**, Thailand
115 K 15 **Ban Phaeng**, Laos
115 J 17 **Ban Phai**, Thailand
115 M 17 **Ban Phon**, Laos
115 J 15 **Ban Phu**, Thailand
115 G 19 **Ban Pong**, Thailand
115 G 18 **Ban Rai**, Thailand
115 F 15 **Ban Tha Song Yang**, Thailand
115 J 15 **Ban Thabôk**, Laos
115 M 17 **Ban Tôp**, Laos
115 K 14 **Ban Vang-An**, Laos
115 M 18 **Ban Xepian**, Laos
127 M 24 **Banaadir**, Somalia ▣
140 C 3 **Banaba**, Kiribati ⁂
131 N 7 **Banalia**, Democratic Republic of Congo
128 I 9 **Banamba**, Mali
141 P 2 **Banana**, Kiribati
105 O 25 **Bananga**, India
82 M 13 **Banarli**, Turkey
104 D 13 **Banas**, India ∫
120 G 8 **Banaue**, Philippines
94 E 10 **Banaz**, Turkey
108 M 10 **Banbar**, China
61 F 16 **Banbridge**, U.K.
63 S 8 **Banbury**, U.K.
45 Z 12 **Banco Chinchorro**, Mexico ⁂
48 G 10 **Banco Gorda**, Jamaica ≈
121 D 21 **Bancoran**, Philippines ⁂
42 G 11 **Bancroft**, ON, Canada
106 L 11 **Banda**, India
129 U 12 **Banda**, Cameroon
131 P 5 **Banda**, Democratic Republic of Congo
116 B 8 **Banda Aceh**, Indonesia
117 S 13 **Banda Sea**, Indonesia ◒
117 T 13 **Bandaneira**, Indonesia
100 L 12 **Bandar-e 'Abbās**, Iran
100 H 4 **Bandar-e Anzalī**, Iran
100 G 9 **Bandar-e Emām Khomeynī**, Iran
100 K 13 **Bandar-e Lengeh**, Iran
100 J 13 **Bandar-e Moghūyeh**, Iran
116 G 13 **Bandar Lampung**, Indonesia
119 S 6 **Bandar Seri Begawan**, Brunei ▙
66 I 3 **Bande**, Spain
27 N 10 **Bandera**, TX, U.S.A.
56 K 9 **Bandera**, Argentina
128 L 9 **Bandiagara**, Mali
106 H 3 **Bandipur**, India
94 C 8 **Bandirma**, Turkey
32 E 12 **Bandon**, OR, U.S.A.
130 J 10 **Bandundu**, Democratic Republic of Congo ▣
130 I 10 **Bandundu**, Democratic Republic of Congo
116 H 14 **Bandung**, Indonesia
86 M 13 **Băneasa**, Romania
48 M 6 **Banes**, Cuba
39 I 20 **Banff**, AB, Canada
60 I 9 **Banff**, U.K.
128 K 11 **Banfora**, Burkina Faso
121 L 23 **Banga**, Philippines
130 K 11 **Banga**, Democratic Republic of Congo
121 N 21 **Bangai Point**, Philippines ▶
105 D 21 **Bangalore**, India
119 T 6 **Bangar**, Malaysia
130 M 5 **Bangassou**, Central African Republic
117 P 11 **Banggai**, Indonesia ⁂
119 W 3 **Banggi**, Malaysia ⁂
125 W 7 **Banghāzī**, Libya
116 G 11 **Bangka**, Indonesia ⁂
117 Q 10 **Bangka**, Indonesia ⁂
116 K 14 **Bangkalan**, Indonesia
116 D 10 **Bangkinang**, Indonesia
116 F 11 **Bangko**, Indonesia
115 I 19 **Bangkok**, Thailand ▙
107 U 12 **Bangladesh**, Asia □
15 R 5 **Bangor**, ME, U.S.A.
62 M 4 **Bangor**, U.K.
120 F 7 **Bangued**, Philippines
120 F 5 **Bangui**, Philippines
130 J 5 **Bangui**, Central African Republic ▙
130 I 6 **Bangui-Motaba**, Congo
131 P 7 **Banguru**, Democratic Republic of Congo
130 M 3 **Bani**, Central African Republic
120 E 10 **Bani Point**, Philippines ▶
99 O 10 **Banī Thawr**, Saudi Arabia
125 S 8 **Banī Walīd**, Libya
130 H 5 **Bania**, Central African Republic
138 G 7 **Baniara**, Papua New Guinea
129 O 10 **Banikoara**, Benin
96 H 4 **Bāniyās**, Syria
80 G 10 **Banja Luka**, Bosnia and Herzegovina
119 V 7 **Banjaran Brassey**, Malaysia ⛰
119 U 7 **Banjaran Crocker**, Malaysia ⛰
119 N 11 **Banjaran Klingkang**, Malaysia ⛰
119 T 9 **Banjaran Tama Abu**, Malaysia ⛰
116 L 12 **Banjarmasin**, Indonesia
128 D 9 **Banjul**, Gambia ▙
129 N 9 **Bankilaré**, Niger
129 T 13 **Bankim**, Cameroon
28 K 9 **Banks**, ID, U.S.A.
38 E 5 **Banks Island**, NT, Canada ⁂
139 R 9 **Banks Islands**, Vanuatu ⁂
32 J 6 **Banks Lake**, WA, U.S.A. ∽
137 I 20 **Banks Peninsula**, New Zealand ▶
107 R 13 **Bankura**, India
113 P 13 **Banli**, China
101 V 8 **Bannu**, Pakistan
113 N 9 **Banqiao**, China
79 J 20 **Banská Bystrica**, Slovakia
82 G 11 **Bansko**, Bulgaria
105 C 14 **Banswara**, India
117 O 13 **Bantaeng**, Indonesia
121 K 16 **Bantayan**, Philippines
121 J 16 **Bantayan**, Philippines ⁂
129 O 12 **Bantè**, Benin
61 A 21 **Bantry Bay**, Republic of Ireland ≈
129 U 13 **Banyo**, Cameroon
116 K 14 **Banyuwangi**, Indonesia
145 W 13 **Banzare Coast**, Antarctica ◇
115 N 21 **Bao Lôc**, Vietnam
111 C 15 **Baochang**, China
111 A 17 **Baode**, China
111 E 17 **Baodi**, China
111 D 18 **Baoding**, China
113 P 3 **Baoji**, China
113 R 8 **Baojing**, China
110 M 11 **Baolin**, China
110 O 10 **Baoqing**, China
130 H 4 **Baoro**, Central African Republic
112 J 10 **Baoshan**, China
109 S 6 **Baotou**, China
113 V 5 **Baoyi**, China
113 X 4 **Baoying**, China
104 C 12 **Bap**, India
99 O 7 **Baqarah**, Saudi Arabia
97 U 6 **Ba'qūbah**, Iraq
81 I 17 **Bar**, Serbia and Montenegro
86 M 6 **Bar**, Ukraine
15 S 6 **Bar Harbor**, ME, U.S.A.
65 T 4 **Bar-le-Duc**, France
117 R 12 **Bara**, Indonesia
127 E 17 **Bara**, Sudan
129 T 11 **Bara**, Nigeria
106 M 10 **Bara Banki**, India
127 L 25 **Baraawe**, Somalia
96 J 3 **Baradah**, Syria
59 C 15 **Baradero**, Argentina
49 Q 8 **Barahona**, Dominican Republic
105 I 15 **Barakot**, India
119 S 7 **Baram**, Malaysia ∫
105 C 18 **Baramati**, India
106 H 3 **Baramula**, India
85 H 19 **Baranavichy**, Belarus
35 W 11 **Baranof Island**, AK, U.S.A. ⁂
69 J 22 **Baraque de Fraiture**, Belgium ▲
117 P 15 **Barate**, Indonesia
55 L 18 **Barbacena**, Brazil
58 M 5 **Barbacena**, Brazil
49 Z 11 **Barbados**, North America □
67 U 3 **Barbastro**, Spain
66 K 14 **Barbate**, Spain
37 P 1 **Barbeau Peak**, NU, Canada ▲
64 M 10 **Barbezieux-St-Hilaire**, France
50 J 6 **Barbosa**, Colombia
49 Y 8 **Barbuda**, Antigua and Barbuda ⁂
135 S 6 **Barcaldine**, QLD, Australia
66 J 10 **Barcarrota**, Spain
51 P 3 **Barcelona**, Venezuela
67 X 5 **Barcelona**, Spain
54 E 10 **Barcelos**, Brazil
79 G 26 **Barcs**, Hungary
91 T 13 **Barda**, Russian Federation
129 W 5 **Bardai**, Chad
107 W 14 **Bardarban**, Bangladesh
70 C 11 **Bárðarbunga**, Iceland ▲
56 G 13 **Bardas Blancas**, Argentina
107 S 13 **Barddhaman**, India
79 L 19 **Bardejov**, Slovakia
76 A 7 **Bardonecchia**, Italy
62 K 6 **Bardsey Island**, U.K. ⁂
62 K 6 **Bardsey Sound**, U.K. ≈
61 G 19 **Bardsley Island**, U.K. ⁂
16 H 5 **Bardstown**, KY, U.S.A.
106 L 9 **Bareilly**, India
143 T 10 **Barents Plain**, Arctic Ocean ◇
70 N 5 **Barents Sea**, Europe ◒
143 U 13 **Barents Trough**, Arctic Ocean ◇
127 H 17 **Barentu**, Eritrea
119 T 8 **Bareo**, Malaysia
108 H 9 **Barga**, China
127 O 19 **Bargaal**, Somalia
105 I 16 **Bargarh**, India
63 Z 11 **Barham**, U.K.
77 N 15 **Bari**, Italy
127 O 19 **Bari**, Somalia ▣
130 K 6 **Bari**, Democratic Republic of Congo
125 O 6 **Barika**, Algeria
101 W 7 **Barikoì**, Afghanistan
50 L 4 **Barinas**, Venezuela ▣
50 L 4 **Barinas**, Venezuela
126 E 11 **Bârîs**, Egypt
107 U 14 **Barisal**, Bangladesh
107 V 14 **Barisal**, Bangladesh ▣
116 L 11 **Barito**, Indonesia ∫
99 Y 6 **Barkā**, Oman
112 L 5 **Barkam**, China
84 I 11 **Barkava**, Latvia
107 Q 12 **Barki Sariaya**, India
16 D 7 **Barkley Lake**, KY, U.S.A. ∽
133 O 13 **Barkly East**, Republic of South Africa
135 P 5 **Barkly Homestead Roadhouse**, NT, Australia
135 O 3 **Barkly Tableland**, NT, Australia ◇
108 M 5 **Barkol**, China
86 M 10 **Bârlad**, Romania
77 M 15 **Barletta**, Italy
78 E 11 **Barlinek**, Poland
104 B 13 **Barmer**, India
62 M 6 **Barmouth**, U.K.
62 M 6 **Barmouth Bay**, U.K. ≈
88 M 13 **Barnaul**, Russian Federation
63 V 10 **Barnet**, U.K.
68 J 12 **Barneveld**, Netherlands
26 K 8 **Barnhart**, TX, U.S.A.
63 S 3 **Barnsley**, U.K.
15 P 11 **Barnstable**, MA, U.S.A.
62 M 12 **Barnstaple**, U.K.
17 N 14 **Barnwell**, SC, U.S.A.
50 L 3 **Barquisimeto**, Venezuela
55 L 14 **Barra**, Brazil
60 D 11 **Barra**, U.K. ⁂
54 G 12 **Barra de São Manuel**, Brazil
55 G 15 **Barra do Bugres**, Brazil
54 L 12 **Barra do Corda**, Brazil
55 I 16 **Barra do Garças**, Brazil
58 H 12 **Barra do Ribeiro**, Brazil
45 S 8 **Barra Jesús María**, Mexico ≈
47 S 5 **Barra Kruta**, Honduras
54 L 13 **Barragem de Sobradinho**, Brazil ∽
55 J 17 **Barragen de São Simão**, Brazil ∽
50 J 3 **Barranca**, Venezuela
53 C 15 **Barranca**, Peru
51 R 4 **Barrancas**, Venezuela
50 I 2 **Barranquilla**, Colombia
14 M 9 **Barre**, MA, U.S.A.
56 G 11 **Barreal**, Argentina
55 L 14 **Barreiras**, Brazil
54 E 12 **Barreirinha do Baeta**, Brazil
66 G 9 **Barreiro**, Portugal
105 O 21 **Barren Island**, India ⁂
58 K 5 **Barretos**, Brazil
42 E 12 **Barrie**, ON, Canada
43 T 12 **Barrington**, NS, Canada
135 S 9 **Barringun**, NSW, Australia
35 O 2 **Barrow**, AK, U.S.A.
61 E 19 **Barrow**, Republic of Ireland ∫
135 N 5 **Barrow Creek**, NT, Australia
63 O 1 **Barrow-in-Furness**, U.K.
134 E 6 **Barrow Island**, WA, Australia ⁂
63 O 11 **Barry**, U.K.
42 H 10 **Barrys Bay**, ON, Canada
103 W 6 **Barshatas**, Kazakhstan
103 R 5 **Barshyn**, Kazakhstan
33 L 23 **Barstow**, CA, U.S.A.
84 C 12 **Bārta**, Latvia
72 L 8 **Barth**, Germany
51 U 5 **Bartica**, Guyana
94 H 7 **Bartin**, Turkey
135 T 3 **Bartle Frere**, QLD, Australia ▲
25 P 8 **Bartlesville**, OK, U.S.A.
16 A 10 **Bartlett**, TN, U.S.A.
22 M 13 **Bartlett**, NE, U.S.A.
14 M 5 **Barton**, VT, U.S.A.
63 U 3 **Barton-upon-Humber**, U.K.
78 K 8 **Bartoszyce**, Poland
19 W 11 **Bartow**, FL, U.S.A.
99 S 13 **Barūm**, Yemen
116 M 10 **Barung**, Indonesia
116 K 15 **Barung**, Indonesia ⁂
116 C 9 **Barus**, Indonesia
109 T 4 **Baruun Urt**, Mongolia
105 C 15 **Barwani**, India
79 F 14 **Barycz**, Poland ∫
85 K 16 **Barysaw**, Belarus
93 Q 3 **Barysh**, Russian Federation
99 Z 7 **Barzamān**, Oman
130 H 11 **Bas-Congo**, Democratic Republic of Congo ▣
103 P 14 **Basaga**, Turkmenistan
56 L 8 **Basail**, Argentina
33 J 19 **Basalt**, NV, U.S.A.
130 K 7 **Basankusu**, Democratic Republic of Congo
120 H 2 **Basco**, Philippines
73 D 26 **Basel**, Germany
74 D 6 **Basel**, Switzerland
93 O 4 **Bashmakovo**, Russian Federation
100 H 10 **Bāsht**, Iran
87 S 8 **Bashtanka**, Ukraine
121 H 23 **Basilan**, Philippines ⁂
121 H 23 **Basilan Strait**, Philippines ≈
63 X 10 **Basildon**, U.K.
77 M 17 **Basilicata**, Italy ▣
29 U 9 **Basin**, WY, U.S.A.
63 T 11 **Basingstoke**, U.K.
107 T 14 **Basirhat**, India
80 C 10 **Baška**, Croatia
95 T 11 **Başkale**, Turkey
130 M 7 **Basoko**, Democratic Republic of Congo
33 K 14 **Basque**, OR, U.S.A.
135 S 14 **Bass Strait**, TAS, Australia ≈
76 G 6 **Bassano del Grappa**, Italy
129 N 11 **Bassar**, Togo
133 U 8 **Bassas da India**, France ⁂
130 L 4 **Basse-Kotto**, Central African Republic ▣
64 L 4 **Basse-Normandie**, France ▣
49 Y 9 **Basse-Terre**, Guadeloupe ▙
115 C 16 **Bassein**, Myanmar
67 V 3 **Bassella**, Spain
49 X 8 **Basseterre**, St Kitts and Nevis ▙
22 L 12 **Bassett**, NE, U.S.A.
129 O 12 **Bassila**, Benin
129 Z 7 **Basso**, Chad ▲
23 U 3 **Basswood Lake**, MN, U.S.A. ∽
100 K 12 **Bastak**, Iran
100 G 3 **Bastānābād**, Iran
107 N 10 **Basti**, India
65 Z 14 **Bastia**, France
69 K 23 **Bastogne**, Belgium
18 J 4 **Bastrop**, LA, U.S.A.
27 Q 10 **Bastrop**, TX, U.S.A.
129 S 15 **Bata**, Equatorial Guinea
120 F 11 **Bataan Peninsula**, Philippines ▶
120 F 6 **Batac**, Philippines
89 T 9 **Batagay**, Russian Federation
58 H 5 **Bataguassu**, Brazil
82 H 11 **Batak**, Bulgaria
116 L 13 **Batakan**, Indonesia
106 H 5 **Batala**, India
116 F 10 **Batam**, Indonesia ⁂
131 O 7 **Batama**, Democratic Republic of Congo
89 T 10 **Batamay**, Russian Federation
120 H 2 **Batan**, Philippines ⁂
120 K 13 **Batan**, Philippines ⁂
120 H 3 **Batan Islands**, Philippines ⁂
112 J 7 **Batang**, China
130 D 8 **Batanga**, Gabon
120 G 12 **Batangas**, Philippines
121 E 16 **Batas**, Philippines ⁂
14 D 8 **Batavia**, NY, U.S.A.
92 L 10 **Bataysk**, Russian Federation
121 H 16 **Batbatan**, Philippines ⁂
134 M 1 **Batchelor**, NT, Australia
115 J 20 **Bătdâmbâng**, Cambodia
135 U 12 **Batemans Bay**, NSW, Australia
17 N 12 **Batesburg**, SC, U.S.A.
18 M 2 **Batesville**, MS, U.S.A.
25 W 9 **Batesville**, AR, U.S.A.
27 N 12 **Batesville**, TX, U.S.A.
14 F 9 **Bath**, NY, U.S.A.
15 P 6 **Bath**, ME, U.S.A.
43 R 9 **Bath**, NB, Canada
63 Q 11 **Bath**, U.K.
129 X 8 **Batha**, Chad ▣
106 H 7 **Bathinda**, India
68 L 11 **Bathmen**, Netherlands
43 S 7 **Bathurst**, NB, Canada
135 U 11 **Bathurst**, NSW, Australia
143 O 7 **Bathurst Island**, Canada ⁂
38 H 9 **Bathurst Inlet**, NU, Canada
38 I 8 **Bathurst Inlet**, NU, Canada ≈
37 O 3 **Bathurst Island**, NU, Canada ⁂
134 L 1 **Bathurst Island**, NT, Australia ⁂
127 J 19 **Batī**, Ethiopia
94 E 13 **Bati Toroslar**, Turkey ⛰
95 Q 12 **Batman**, Turkey
125 O 6 **Batna**, Algeria
80 L 12 **Batočina**, Serbia and Montenegro
18 K 7 **Baton Rouge**, LA, U.S.A.
106 H 4 **Batote**, India
129 V 14 **Batouri**, Cameroon
96 G 5 **Batroûn**, Lebanon
70 M 5 **Båtsfjord**, Norway
105 N 24 **Batti Malv**, India ⁂
105 G 24 **Batticaloa**, Sri Lanka
63 X 12 **Battle**, U.K.
21 J 15 **Battle Creek**, MI, U.S.A.
33 L 16 **Battle Mountain**, NV, U.S.A.
127 J 21 **Batu**, Ethiopia ▲
118 B 7 **Batu Gajah**, Malaysia
118 D 10 **Batu Pahat**, Malaysia
117 O 11 **Batudaka**, Indonesia ⁂
121 M 24 **Batulaki**, Philippines
95 Q 7 **Bat'umi**, Georgia
116 F 13 **Baturaja**, Indonesia
87 R 2 **Baturyn**, Ukraine
93 Q 2 **Batyrevo**, Russian Federation
119 N 10 **Bau**, Malaysia
120 F 8 **Bauang**, Philippines
117 P 13 **Baubau**, Indonesia
129 S 11 **Bauchi**, Nigeria
129 S 11 **Bauchi**, Nigeria ▣
23 Q 2 **Baudette**, MN, U.S.A.
117 R 15 **Baukau**, East Timor
138 M 6 **Baunani**, Solomon Islands
58 J 6 **Bauru**, Brazil
55 H 17 **Baús**, Brazil
84 F 12 **Bauska**, Latvia
73 O 16 **Bautzen**, Germany
73 L 25 **Bavarian Alps**, Germany ⛰
44 K 4 **Bavispe**, Mexico ∫
116 I 12 **Bawal**, Indonesia ⁂
116 K 13 **Bawean**, Indonesia ⁂
126 D 9 **Bawiti**, Egypt
63 T 3 **Bawtry**, U.K.
19 V 5 **Baxley**, GA, U.S.A.
127 L 24 **Bay**, Somalia ▣
20 L 13 **Bay City**, MI, U.S.A.
27 S 11 **Bay City**, TX, U.S.A.
19 P 7 **Bay Minette**, AL, U.S.A.
107 S 15 **Bay of Bengal**, Asia ≈
64 I 7 **Bay of Biscay**, France ≈
43 S 11 **Bay of Fundy**, NS, Canada ≈
136 J 5 **Bay of Islands**, New Zealand ≈
136 N 10 **Bay of Plenty**, New Zealand ≈
136 N 11 **Bay of Plenty**, New Zealand ▣
18 M 5 **Bay Springs**, MS, U.S.A.
136 N 13 **Bay View**, New Zealand
48 L 6 **Bayamo**, Cuba
109 T 3 **Bayan**, Mongolia
110 L 11 **Bayan**, China
112 J 3 **Bayan Har Shan**, China ⛰
109 S 6 **Bayan Obo**, China
108 L 2 **Bayan-Ölgiy**, Mongolia ▣
109 N 4 **Bayan-Ovoo**, Mongolia
111 B 15 **Bayan Qagan**, China
103 U 4 **Bayanaul**, Kazakhstan
108 J 5 **Bayanbulak**, China
130 H 6 **Bayanga**, Central African Republic
130 H 4 **Bayanga-Didi**, Central African Republic
109 O 4 **Bayanhongor**, Mongolia ▣
109 P 4 **Bayanhongor**, Mongolia
31 O 13 **Bayard**, NM, U.S.A.
121 I 19 **Bayawan**, Philippines
100 L 10 **Bayāz**, Iran
121 L 17 **Baybay**, Philippines
95 P 9 **Bayburt**, Turkey
88 L 7 **Baydaratskaya Guba**, Russian Federation ≈
143 X 10 **Baydaratskåya Guba**, Arctic Ocean ≈
127 L 23 **Baydhabo**, Somalia
129 Q 14 **Bayelsa**, Nigeria ▣
73 L 22 **Bayerischer Wald**, Germany ◇
73 J 22 **Bayern**, Germany ▣
64 M 3 **Bayeux**, France
102 K 6 **Bayganin**, Kazakhstan
99 Q 13 **Bayḩan al Qişab**, Yemen

ountry ▣ Internal administrative region: State/Province/Territory/Dependent territory ▙ Capital city ⛰ Mountain range/ Undersea ridge ▲ Mountain peak/ Volcano/Seamount ◇ Geographic feature ▶ Headland/Point/ Cape/Peninsula ◖ Desert ⁂ Island/Island group ⊞ Antarctic base ◎ Ocean ◒ Sea ≈ Bay/Gulf/Channel/Strait ∽ Lake ⚑ Salt pan/Dry/ Intermittent lake ∫ River

Country · Internal administrative region: State/Province/Territory/Dependent territory · Capital city · Mountain range/Undersea ridge · Mountain peak/Volcano/Seamount · Geographic feature · Headland/Point/Cape/Peninsula · Desert · Island/Island group · Antarctic base · Ocean · Sea · Bay/Gulf/Channel/Strait · Lake · Salt pan/Dry/Intermittent lake

	J 17	**Blenheim**, New Zealand
	R 11	**Blessing**, TX, U.S.A.
	E 18	**Blessington**, Republic of Ireland
	U 9	**Bletchley**, U.K.
	M 5	**Blida**, Algeria
	A 22	**Bligh Sound**, New Zealand ≈
	B 9	**Blind River**, ON, Canada
	L 12	**Bliss**, ID, U.S.A.
	J 15	**Blitar**, Indonesia
	N 12	**Blitta**, Togo
	N 12	**Block Island**, RI, U.S.A. 🏝
	N 11	**Block Island Sound**, RI, U.S.A. ≈
	N 12	**Bloemfontein**, Republic of South Africa ■
	M 12	**Bloemhof**, Republic of South Africa
	O 7	**Blois**, France
	B 10	**Blönduós**, Iceland
	C 14	**Bloody Foreland**, Republic of Ireland ◗
	I 20	**Bloomfield**, IN, U.S.A.
	U 14	**Bloomfield**, IA, U.S.A.
	F 18	**Bloomington**, IL, U.S.A.
	I 20	**Bloomington**, IN, U.S.A.
	T 8	**Bloomington**, MN, U.S.A.
	R 7	**Blountstown**, FL, U.S.A.
	J 7	**Bludenz**, Austria
	R 5	**Blue Hill**, ME, U.S.A.
	P 6	**Blue Mesa Reservoir**, CO, U.S.A. ◣
	J 7	**Blue Mountain**, NY, U.S.A. ▲
	S 11	**Blue Mountain**, AR, U.S.A. ▲
	J 11	**Blue Mountains**, OR, U.S.A. ⛰
	O 2	**Blue Mud Bay**, NT, Australia ≈
	G 19	**Blue Nile**, Ethiopia/Sudan ∫
	F 19	**Blue Nile**, Sudan ▣
	O 2	**Blue Rapids**, KS, U.S.A.
	H 19	**Blue River**, BC, Canada
	Q 9	**Bluefields**, Nicaragua
	O 6	**Bluestone Lake**, WV, U.S.A. ◣
	M 7	**Bluff**, UT, U.S.A.
	C 26	**Bluff**, New Zealand
	J 9	**Blumenau**, Brazil
	K 9	**Blunt**, SD, U.S.A.
	T 4	**Blyth**, U.K.
	N 25	**Blythe**, CA, U.S.A.
	Z 9	**Blytheville**, AR, U.S.A.
	U 3	**Blyton**, U.K.
	G 12	**Bo**, Sierra Leone
	F 18	**Bo Hai**, China ≈
	C 21	**Bo River Post**, Sudan
	E 8	**Boa Vista**, Brazil
	H 13	**Boac**, Philippines
	O 9	**Boaco**, Nicaragua
	J 5	**Boali**, Central African Republic
	R 12	**Boano**, Indonesia 🏝
	D 17	**Boayan**, Philippines 🏝
	R 13	**Bobai**, China
	Z 4	**Bobasakoa**, Madgascar
	D 8	**Bobbio**, Italy
	I 24	**Bobingen**, Germany
	L 10	**Bobo-Dioulasso**, Burkina Faso
	F 9	**Bobolice**, Poland
	O 9	**Bobonong**, Botswana
	E 15	**Bóbr**, Poland ∫
	L 16	**Bobr**, Belarus
	M 6	**Bobrov**, Russian Federation
	Q 3	**Bobrovytsya**, Ukraine
	O 10	**Bobrowniki**, Poland
	R 7	**Bobrynets'**, Ukraine
	M 4	**Bobso**, China
	X 9	**Boby**, Madgascar ▲
	L 1	**Boca Bacalar Chico**, Belize 🏝
	T 14	**Boca Chica**, Panama
	C 13	**Boca do Acre**, Brazil
	H 3	**Bocaranga**, Central African Republic
	T 13	**Bocas del Toro**, Panama
	R 11	**Bochart**, QC, Canada
	C 14	**Bocholt**, Germany
	C 16	**Bochum**, Germany
	G 4	**Bocoio**, Angola
	F 11	**Bocşa**, Romania
	H 23	**Böda**, Sweden
	I 5	**Boda**, Central African Republic
	R 12	**Bodaybo**, Russian Federation
	J 12	**Boden**, Sweden
	P 8	**Bodenham**, U.K.
	G 26	**Bodensee**, Germany ◣
	L 14	**Bodmin**, U.K.
	L 14	**Bodmin Moor**, U.K. ◇
	G 10	**Bodø**, Norway
	B 12	**Bodrum**, Turkey
	K 8	**Boende**, Democratic Republic of Congo
	O 10	**Boerne**, TX, U.S.A.
	F 11	**Boffa**, Guinea
	D 17	**Bogale**, Myanmar
	M 7	**Bogalusa**, LA, U.S.A.
	J 4	**Bogangolo**, Central African Republic
	K 10	**Boğazliyan**, Turkey
	K 7	**Bogbonga**, Democratic Republic of Congo
	L 4	**Bogda Feng**, China ▲
	L 4	**Bogda Shan**, China ⛰
	E 12	**Bogdanci**, Macedonia (F.Y.R.O.M.)
	J 7	**Bogenli**, China
	C 3	**Bogia**, Papua New Guinea
	U 13	**Bognor Regis**, U.K.
	K 16	**Bogo**, Philippines
	V 10	**Bogo**, Cameroon
	R 2	**Bogodukhovka**, Kazakhstan
	H 14	**Bogor**, Indonesia
	O 1	**Bogorodsk**, Russian Federation
	I 7	**Bogotá**, Colombia ■
	N 12	**Bogotol**, Russian Federation
	T 12	**Bogra**, Bangladesh
	O 12	**Boguchany**, Russian Federation
	M 7	**Boguchar**, Russian Federation
	F 7	**Bogué**, Mauritania
	F 18	**Bohai**, China
	G 18	**Bohai Haixia**, China ≈
	E 18	**Bohai Wan**, China ≈
	B 18	**Bohemia**, Czech Republic ◇
	A 18	**Bohemian Forest**, Czech Republic/Germany ◇
	D 19	**Bohemian Massif**, Czech Republic ⛰
	E 13	**Bohmte**, Germany
	V 4	**Bohodukhiv**, Ukraine
	K 18	**Bohol**, Philippines 🏝
	K 19	**Bohol Sea**, Philippines ◒
	J 18	**Bohol Strait**, Philippines ≈
	L 10	**Bois Blanc Island**, MI, U.S.A. 🏝
	K 10	**Boise**, ID, U.S.A.
	F 7	**Boise City**, OK, U.S.A.
	H 11	**Boizenburg**, Germany
	J 15	**Bojano**, Italy
	M 5	**Bojnūrd**, Iran
	Q 13	**Bokaro**, India
	J 8	**Bokatola**, Democratic Republic of Congo
	F 10	**Boké**, Guinea
71	A 20	**Boknafjorden**, Norway ≈
130	G 10	**Boko**, Congo
130	G 10	**Boko-Songho**, Congo
130	J 5	**Bokode**, Democratic Republic of Congo
103	V 10	**Bökönbaev**, Kyrgyzstan
129	W 10	**Bokoro**, Chad
93	N 8	**Bokovskaya**, Russian Federation
132	K 11	**Bokspits**, Botswana
138	J 5	**Boku**, Papua New Guinea
130	M 9	**Bokwankusu**, Democratic Republic of Congo
129	V 9	**Bol**, Chad
131	N 9	**Bolaiti**, Democratic Republic of Congo
65	N 3	**Bolbec**, France
86	L 11	**Boldu**, Romania
102	M 11	**Boldumsaz**, Turkmenistan
108	J 4	**Bole**, China
128	L 12	**Bole**, Ghana
130	K 8	**Boleko**, Democratic Republic of Congo
130	K 7	**Bolena**, Democratic Republic of Congo
79	E 15	**Bolesławiec**, Poland
93	R 2	**Bolgar**, Russian Federation
128	M 11	**Bolgatanga**, Ghana
87	N 11	**Bolhrad**, Ukraine
110	N 11	**Boli**, China
130	J 8	**Bolia**, Democratic Republic of Congo
117	N 3	**Bolinao**, Philippines
16	B 10	**Bolivar**, TN, U.S.A.
25	T 6	**Bolivar**, MO, U.S.A.
50	I 4	**Bolívar**, Colombia ▣
51	Q 5	**Bolívar**, Venezuela ▣
52	B 9	**Bolívar**, Ecuador ▣
53	J 19	**Bolivia**, South America □
80	N 12	**Boljevac**, Serbia and Montenegro
92	J 3	**Bolkhov**, Russian Federation
65	T 13	**Bollene**, France
71	G 18	**Bollnäs**, Sweden
135	T 8	**Bollon**, QLD, Australia
71	H 16	**Bollstabruk**, Sweden
71	E 24	**Bolmen**, Sweden ◣
130	I 9	**Bolobo**, Democratic Republic of Congo
76	F 9	**Bologna**, Italy
52	F 13	**Bolognesi**, Peru
53	E 15	**Bolognesi**, Peru
90	G 13	**Bologoye**, Russian Federation
130	J 7	**Bolomba**, Democratic Republic of Congo
121	I 22	**Bolong**, Philippines
85	C 15	**Bol'shakovo**, Russian Federation
93	T 5	**Bol'shaya Chernigovka**, Russian Federation
93	T 4	**Bol'shaya Glushitsa**, Russian Federation
103	Z 5	**Bol'shenarymskoye**, Kazakhstan
91	P 4	**Bol'shezemel'skaya Tundra**, Russian Federation ◇
93	X 1	**Bol'shoy Iremel'**, Russian Federation ▲
89	O 9	**Bol'shoy Porog**, Russian Federation
93	P 1	**Bol'shoye Murashkino**, Russian Federation
63	T 4	**Bolsover**, U.K.
68	J 7	**Bolsward**, Netherlands
67	T 3	**Boltaña**, Spain
63	Q 3	**Bolton**, U.K.
94	G 8	**Bolu**, Turkey
138	G 6	**Bolubolu**, Papua New Guinea
70	A 9	**Bolungarvík**, Iceland
113	U 12	**Boluo**, China
76	F 5	**Bolzano**, Italy
58	I 11	**Bom Jesus**, Brazil
55	L 15	**Bom Jesus da Lapa**, Brazil
58	I 10	**Bom Retiro**, Brazil
130	F 11	**Boma**, Democratic Republic of Congo
130	H 6	**Bomassa**, Congo
135	U 13	**Bombala**, NSW, Australia
66	G 8	**Bombarral**, Portugal
130	J 6	**Bomboma**, Democratic Republic of Congo
107	W 9	**Bomdila**, India
131	O 7	**Bomili**, Democratic Republic of Congo
71	A 19	**Bømlo**, Norway 🏝
100	F 4	**Bonāb**, Iran
49	S 13	**Bonaire**, Netherlands Antilles 🏝
47	P 6	**Bonanza**, Nicaragua
49	Q 7	**Bonao**, Dominican Republic
134	I 3	**Bonaparte Archipelago**, WA, Australia 🏝
41	Z 10	**Bonavista**, NL, Canada
41	Y 10	**Bonavista Bay**, NL, Canada ≈
130	M 5	**Bondo**, Democratic Republic of Congo
120	H 12	**Bondoc Peninsula**, Philippines ◗
128	L 12	**Bondoukou**, Côte d'Ivoire
128	L 10	**Bondoukui**, Burkina Faso
29	R 11	**Bondurant**, WY, U.S.A.
117	O 14	**Bonerate**, Indonesia 🏝
115	O 18	**Bông Son**, Vietnam
127	H 21	**Bonga**, Ethiopia
121	H 14	**Bongabong**, Philippines
107	U 10	**Bongaigaon**, India
130	L 7	**Bongandanga**, Democratic Republic of Congo
121	E 25	**Bongao**, Philippines
121	K 22	**Bongo**, Philippines 🏝
129	V 11	**Bongor**, Chad
27	R 4	**Bonham**, TX, U.S.A.
65	Y 15	**Bonifacio**, France
19	Q 7	**Bonifay**, FL, U.S.A.
55	G 18	**Bonito**, Brazil
73	C 17	**Bonn**, Germany
65	P 9	**Bonnat**, France
28	K 2	**Bonners Ferry**, ID, U.S.A.
65	V 9	**Bonneville**, France
30	I 3	**Bonneville Salt Flats**, UT, U.S.A. ◇
39	K 17	**Bonnyville**, AB, Canada
123	B 24	**Bōno-misaki**, Japan ◗
115	O 21	**Bonom Mhai**, Vietnam ▲
135	V 9	**Bonshaw**, NSW, Australia
116	M 11	**Bontang**, Indonesia
120	G 7	**Bontoc**, Philippines
117	N 13	**Bontosunggu**, Indonesia
79	I 25	**Bonyhád**, Hungary
128	I 12	**Boola**, Guinea
17	N 8	**Boone**, NC, U.S.A.
23	S 12	**Boone**, IA, U.S.A.
19	N 1	**Booneville**, MS, U.S.A.
127	K 20	**Boorama**, Somalia
69	G 18	**Boortmeerbeek**, Belgium
127	O 19	**Boosaaso**, Somalia
38	K 5	**Boothia Peninsula**, NU, Canada ◗
63	O 3	**Bootle**, U.K.
130	F 8	**Booué**, Gabon
73	D 19	**Boppard**, Germany
58	H 13	**Boqueirão**, Brazil
45	O 5	**Boquillas del Carmen**, Mexico
79	A 18	**Bor**, Czech Republic
80	N 12	**Bor**, Serbia and Montenegro
94	J 12	**Bor**, Turkey
127	E 22	**Bor**, Sudan
108	M 4	**Bor- Üdzüür**, Mongolia
29	N 10	**Borah Peak**, ID, U.S.A. ▲
71	E 22	**Borås**, Sweden
100	H 10	**Borāzjān**, Iran
54	F 11	**Borba**, Brazil
145	Q 14	**Borchgrevink Coast**, Antarctica ◇
95	Q 7	**Borşşka**, Turkey
64	M 11	**Bordeaux**, France
43	V 9	**Borden**, PE, Canada
37	N 3	**Borden Island**, NT, Canada 🏝
37	Q 4	**Borden Peninsula**, NU, Canada ◗
135	Q 12	**Bordertown**, SA, Australia
125	O 6	**Bordj Bou Arréridj**, Algeria
125	Q 9	**Bordj Messaouda**, Algeria
124	L 14	**Bordj Mokhtar**, Algeria
125	P 10	**Bordj Omar Driss**, Algeria
128	L 8	**Boré**, Mali
145	P 2	**Borg Massif**, Antarctica ⛰
70	D 10	**Borgarfjörður**, Iceland
70	A 11	**Borgarnes**, Iceland
26	K 2	**Borger**, TX, U.S.A.
68	N 8	**Borger**, Netherlands
71	H 24	**Borgholm**, Sweden
77	M 20	**Borgia**, Italy
76	F 6	**Borgo Valsugana**, Italy
76	B 6	**Borgomanero**, Italy
93	N 6	**Borisoglebsk**, Russian Federation
133	Y 6	**Boriziny**, Madgascar
52	C 11	**Borja**, Peru
67	R 4	**Borja**, Spain
84	J 13	**Borkavichy**, Belarus
73	C 15	**Borken**, Germany
129	X 6	**Borkou-Ennedi-Tibesti**, Chad ▣
72	C 10	**Borkum**, Germany 🏝
71	G 19	**Borlänge**, Sweden
76	E 5	**Bormio**, Italy
73	L 16	**Borna**, Germany
68	J 5	**Borndiep**, Netherlands ≈
68	N 11	**Borne**, Netherlands
116	J 10	**Borneo**, Indonesia 🏝
71	F 26	**Bornholm**, Denmark 🏝
129	U 10	**Borno**, Nigeria ▣
94	B 10	**Bornova**, Turkey
87	O 10	**Borodino**, Ukraine
87	O 3	**Borodyanka**, Ukraine
130	L 1	**Boromata**, Central African Republic
128	L 10	**Boromo**, Burkina Faso
121	M 16	**Borongan**, Philippines
128	I 12	**Borotou**, Côte d'Ivoire
63	S 1	**Boroughbridge**, U.K.
87	X 5	**Borova**, Ukraine
90	G 12	**Borovichi**, Russian Federation
103	O 2	**Borovskoy**, Kazakhstan
135	O 3	**Borroloola**, NT, Australia
86	J 8	**Borşa**, Romania
70	K 6	**Børselv**, Norway
62	M 7	**Borth**, U.K.
100	G 7	**Borūjerd**, Iran
87	Q 3	**Boryspil'**, Ukraine
87	R 2	**Borzna**, Ukraine
89	S 14	**Borzya**, Russian Federation
77	B 17	**Bosa**, Italy
103	T 6	**Bosaga**, Kazakhstan
80	F 9	**Bosanska Dubica**, Bosnia and Herzegovina
80	F 9	**Bosanska Gradiška**, Bosnia and Herzegovina
80	E 11	**Bosanski Petrovac**, Bosnia and Herzegovina
62	K 13	**Boscastle**, U.K.
113	O 12	**Bose**, China
113	W 2	**Boshan**, China
80	H 10	**Bosna**, Bosnia and Herzegovina ∫
80	G 11	**Bosnia and Herzegovina**, Europe □
123	L 16	**Bōsō-hantō**, Japan ◗
130	K 5	**Bosobolo**, Democratic Republic of Congo
94	D 7	**Bosporus**, Turkey ≈
130	I 4	**Bossangoa**, Central African Republic
130	I 4	**Bossembélé**, Central African Republic
130	I 4	**Bossentélé**, Central African Republic
18	H 4	**Bossier City**, LA, U.S.A.
101	T 10	**Bostan**, Pakistan
108	K 5	**Bosten Hu**, China ◣
15	O 9	**Boston**, MA, U.S.A.
63	W 5	**Boston**, U.K.
25	S 9	**Boston Mountains**, AR, U.S.A. ⛰
14	C 13	**Boswell**, PA, U.S.A.
105	B 15	**Botad**, India
135	V 12	**Botany Bay**, NSW, Australia ≈
130	J 9	**Botemola**, Democratic Republic of Congo
82	I 9	**Botev**, Bulgaria ▲
82	G 8	**Botevgrad**, Bulgaria
66	I 4	**Boticas**, Portugal
93	Q 15	**Botlikh**, Russian Federation
120	E 10	**Botolan**, Philippines
86	L 8	**Botoşani**, Romania
111	E 18	**Botou**, China
71	I 14	**Botsmark**, Sweden
132	K 9	**Botswana**, Africa □
70	K 13	**Bottenviken**, Sweden ≈
73	C 15	**Bottrop**, Germany
58	J 6	**Botucatu**, Brazil
82	B 12	**Botun**, Macedonia (F.Y.R.O.M.)
125	P 7	**Bou Aroua**, Algeria
128	H 7	**Boû Bleï'îne**, Mauritania ◣
124	F 9	**Bou Izakarn**, Morocco
125	N 6	**Bou Saâda**, Algeria
128	J 13	**Bouaflé**, Côte d'Ivoire
128	K 12	**Bouaké**, Côte d'Ivoire
130	H 4	**Bouar**, Central African Republic
124	K 8	**Bouârfa**, Morocco
130	J 4	**Bouca**, Central African Republic
43	U 8	**Bouctouche**, NB, Canada
130	I 5	**Boudoua**, Central African Republic
130	G 10	**Bouenza**, Congo ▣
138	I 5	**Bougainville**, Papua New Guinea 🏝
129	O 6	**Boughessa**, Mali
128	I 10	**Bougouni**, Mali
124	L 7	**Bougtob**, Algeria
69	I 24	**Bouillon**, Belgium
125	N 5	**Bouira**, Algeria
124	C 11	**Boujdour**, Western Sahara
124	D 11	**Boukra**, Western Sahara
31	R 3	**Boulder**, CO, U.S.A.
134	I 10	**Boulder**, WA, Australia
33	N 22	**Boulder City**, NV, U.S.A.
124	I 7	**Boulemane**, Morocco
135	Q 6	**Boulia**, QLD, Australia
65	O 1	**Boulogne-sur-Mer**, France
130	L 3	**Boulouba**, Central African Republic
124	H 8	**Boumalne Dadès**, Morocco
130	G 9	**Boumango**, Gabon
128	L 11	**Bouna**, Côte d'Ivoire
33	J 19	**Boundary Peak**, NV, U.S.A. ▲
128	J 11	**Boundiali**, Côte d'Ivoire
139	P 14	**Bourail**, New Caledonia
65	U 9	**Bourg-en-Bresse**, France
65	W 10	**Bourg-St-Maurice**, France
65	P 10	**Bourganeuf**, France
65	Q 7	**Bourges**, France
65	R 7	**Bourgogne**, France ▣
65	T 10	**Bourgoin-Jallieu**, France
135	S 9	**Bourke**, NSW, Australia
63	V 6	**Bourne**, U.K.
63	R 13	**Bournemouth**, U.K.
69	L 24	**Bourscheid**, Luxembourg
129	Z 10	**Bourtoutou**, Chad
30	H 12	**Bouse**, AZ, U.S.A.
129	W 11	**Bousso**, Chad
69	H 19	**Boutersem**, Belgium
128	F 7	**Boutilimit**, Mauritania
129	Q 9	**Bouza**, Niger
63	N 14	**Bovey Tracey**, U.K.
28	K 5	**Bovill**, ID, U.S.A.
58	C 13	**Bovril**, Argentina
22	I 2	**Bowbells**, ND, U.S.A.
135	U 5	**Bowen**, QLD, Australia
27	P 5	**Bowie**, TX, U.S.A.
30	M 14	**Bowie**, AZ, U.S.A.
16	F 7	**Bowling Green**, KY, U.S.A.
17	T 5	**Bowling Green**, VA, U.S.A.
21	L 17	**Bowling Green**, OH, U.S.A.
25	W 3	**Bowling Green**, MO, U.S.A.
22	G 6	**Bowman**, ND, U.S.A.
37	S 6	**Bowman Bay**, NU, Canada ≈
144	H 4	**Bowman Coast**, Antarctica ◇
145	Y 10	**Bowman Island**, Antarctica 🏝
135	U 12	**Bowral**, NSW, Australia
111	F 19	**Boxing**, China
69	K 15	**Boxmeer**, Netherlands
69	I 15	**Boxtel**, Netherlands
94	J 7	**Boyabat**, Turkey
50	J 6	**Boyaca**, Colombia ▣
113	W 7	**Boyang**, China
18	I 6	**Boyce**, LA, U.S.A.
29	T 7	**Boyd**, MT, U.S.A.
39	J 17	**Boyle**, AB, Canada
61	C 16	**Boyle**, Republic of Ireland
53	L 22	**Boyuibe**, Bolivia
94	B 11	**Boz Dağlari**, Turkey
94	C 13	**Bozburun**, Turkey
94	A 9	**Bozcaada**, Turkey 🏝
29	Q 7	**Bozeman**, MT, U.S.A.
113	V 4	**Bozhou**, China
94	G 13	**Bozkir**, Turkey
130	I 4	**Bozoum**, Central African Republic
95	N 12	**Bozova**, Turkey
94	E 9	**Bozüyük**, Turkey
76	E 8	**Bozzolo**, Italy
76	B 8	**Bra**, Italy
144	H 4	**Brabant Island**, Antarctica 🏝
69	F 19	**Brabant Wallon**, Belgium ▣
80	E 13	**Brač**, Croatia 🏝
42	F 11	**Bracebridge**, ON, Canada
63	T 9	**Brackley**, U.K.
63	U 11	**Bracknell**, U.K.
86	G 10	**Brad**, Romania
19	V 11	**Bradenton**, FL, U.S.A.
63	S 2	**Bradford**, U.K.
63	Q 11	**Bradford-on-Avon**, U.K.
27	N 8	**Brady**, TX, U.S.A.
60	J 4	**Brae**, U.K.
60	I 11	**Braemar**, U.K.
66	H 4	**Braga**, Portugal ▣
66	H 4	**Braga**, Portugal
59	C 16	**Bragado**, Argentina
54	K 10	**Bragança**, Brazil
66	J 4	**Bragança**, Portugal ▣
66	K 4	**Bragança**, Portugal
85	M 21	**Brahin**, Belarus
107	V 13	**Brahmanbaria**, Bangladesh
105	I 17	**Brahmapur**, India
107	W 10	**Brahmaputra**, India ∫
62	K 6	**Braich y Pwll**, U.K. ◗
86	M 11	**Brăila**, Romania
69	F 20	**Braine-l'Alleud**, Belgium
23	R 6	**Brainerd**, MN, U.S.A.
63	X 9	**Braintree**, U.K.
72	E 11	**Brake**, Germany
128	F 7	**Brâkna**, Mauritania ▣
42	E 13	**Brampton**, ON, Canada
63	Z 7	**Brampton**, U.K.
72	E 13	**Bramsche**, Germany
54	E 9	**Branco**, Brazil ∫
132	G 9	**Brandberg**, Namibia ▲
71	D 19	**Brandbu**, Norway
72	L 13	**Brandenburg**, Germany
73	M 14	**Brandenburg**, Germany ▣
40	H 10	**Brandon**, MB, Canada
63	X 7	**Brandon**, U.K.
132	K 13	**Brandvlei**, Republic of South Africa
19	U 8	**Branford**, FL, U.S.A.
78	J 8	**Braniewo**, Poland
144	H 3	**Bransfield Strait**, Antarctica ≈
78	N 11	**Brańsk**, Poland
25	T 8	**Branson**, MO, U.S.A.
42	E 13	**Brantford**, ON, Canada
19	Q 6	**Brantley**, AL, U.S.A.
43	Y 9	**Bras d'Or Lake**, NS, Canada ◣
54	A 11	**Brasil**, Brazil
55	C 14	**Brasiléia**, Brazil
55	J 16	**Brasília**, Brazil ■
85	I 14	**Braslaw**, Belarus
86	K 11	**Braşov**, Romania
69	G 17	**Brasschaat**, Belgium
19	T 1	**Brasstown Bald**, GA, U.S.A. ▲
79	G 21	**Bratislava**, Slovakia ■
89	P 12	**Bratsk**, Russian Federation
89	P 12	**Bratskoye Vodokhranilishche**, Russian Federation ◣
14	M 9	**Brattleboro**, VT, U.S.A.
87	O 11	**Braţul Chilia**, Romania ∫
87	N 12	**Braţul Sfântu Gheorghe**, Romania ∫
87	O 12	**Braţul Sulina**, Romania ∫
75	Q 4	**Braunau am Inn**, Austria
73	I 15	**Braunlage**, Germany
72	I 13	**Braunschweig**, Germany
62	M 12	**Braunton**, U.K.
33	M 26	**Brawley**, CA, U.S.A.
41	P 1	**Bray Island**, NU, Canada 🏝
21	H 19	**Brazil**, IN, U.S.A.
54	H 13	**Brazil**, South America □
55	K 16	**Brazilian Highlands**, Brazil ⛰
27	Q 7	**Brazos**, TX, U.S.A. ∫
130	H 10	**Brazzaville**, Congo ■
80	I 10	**Brčko**, Bosnia and Herzegovina
78	H 10	**Brda**, Poland ∫
137	A 24	**Breaksea Island**, New Zealand 🏝
136	K 6	**Bream Bay**, New Zealand ≈
69	G 16	**Brecht**, Belgium
27	N 6	**Breckenridge**, TX, U.S.A.
79	F 20	**Břeclav**, Czech Republic
63	O 9	**Brecon**, U.K.
63	N 9	**Brecon Beacons**, U.K. ⛰
69	H 15	**Breda**, Netherlands
132	K 15	**Bredasdorp**, Republic of South Africa
72	F 7	**Bredstedt**, Germany
69	J 17	**Bree**, Belgium
82	E 11	**Bregalnica**, Macedonia (F.Y.R.O.M.) ∫
73	G 26	**Bregenz**, Germany
74	J 6	**Bregenz**, Austria
82	E 6	**Bregovo**, Bulgaria
70	A 10	**Breida Fjörður**, Iceland ≈
70	D 11	**Breiðdalsvík**, Iceland
22	J 6	**Breien**, ND, U.S.A.
54	M 11	**Brejo**, Brazil
72	F 11	**Bremen**, Germany ▣
72	F 11	**Bremen**, Germany
72	F 10	**Bremerhaven**, Germany
32	G 7	**Bremerton**, WA, U.S.A.
72	G 10	**Bremervörde**, Germany
27	R 9	**Brenham**, TX, U.S.A.
74	M 8	**Brenner**, Austria
76	E 6	**Breno**, Italy
63	W 10	**Brentwood**, U.K.
76	E 7	**Brescia**, Italy
69	D 16	**Breskens**, Netherlands
76	G 4	**Bressanone**, Italy
60	K 5	**Bressay**, U.K. 🏝
64	M 8	**Bressuire**, France
64	H 5	**Brest**, France
85	E 21	**Brest**, Belarus
85	G 20	**Brestskaya Voblasts'**, Belarus ▣
64	I 5	**Bretagne**, France ▣
65	Q 3	**Breteuil**, France
18	M 8	**Breton Sound**, LA, U.S.A. ≈
73	F 22	**Bretten**, Germany
16	L 10	**Brevard**, NC, U.S.A.
54	J 10	**Breves**, Brazil
34	L 6	**Brevig Mission**, AK, U.S.A.
135	T 9	**Brewarrina**, NSW, Australia
15	R 5	**Brewer**, ME, U.S.A.
32	J 6	**Brewster**, WA, U.S.A.
19	P 6	**Brewton**, AL, U.S.A.
82	F 9	**Breznik**, Bulgaria
86	I 11	**Brezoi**, Romania
130	L 4	**Bria**, Central African Republic
65	W 11	**Briançon**, France
47	S 13	**Bribri**, Costa Rica
86	M 7	**Briceni**, Moldova
63	N 10	**Bridgend**, U.K.
14	L 12	**Bridgeport**, CT, U.S.A.
22	G 13	**Bridgeport**, NE, U.S.A.
33	I 19	**Bridgeport**, CA, U.S.A.
29	T 8	**Bridger**, MT, U.S.A.
14	I 15	**Bridgeton**, NJ, U.S.A.
49	Z 12	**Bridgetown**, Barbados ■
134	G 12	**Bridgetown**, WA, Australia
43	U 11	**Bridgewater**, NS, Canada
63	P 7	**Bridgnorth**, U.K.
15	O 6	**Bridgton**, ME, U.S.A.
63	P 12	**Bridgwater**, U.K.
63	O 11	**Bridgwater Bay**, U.K. ≈
63	V 1	**Bridlington**, U.K.
63	V 1	**Bridlington Bay**, U.K. ≈
63	P 13	**Bridport**, U.K.
74	H 8	**Briel**, Switzerland
65	T 5	**Brienne-le-Château**, France
74	F 8	**Brienz**, Switzerland
77	L 16	**Brienza**, Italy
74	E 8	**Brienzer See**, Switzerland ◣
74	E 10	**Brig**, Switzerland
63	V 3	**Brigg**, U.K.
30	J 1	**Brigham City**, UT, U.S.A.
135	S 13	**Bright**, VIC, Australia
19	X 11	**Brighton**, FL, U.S.A.
21	L 15	**Brighton**, MI, U.S.A.
31	R 3	**Brighton**, CO, U.S.A.
63	W 13	**Brighton**, U.K.
137	E 25	**Brighton**, New Zealand
128	D 9	**Brikama**, Gambia
70	D 10	**Brimnes**, Iceland
77	O 16	**Brindisi**, Italy
25	X 11	**Brinkley**, AR, U.S.A.
65	R 11	**Brioude**, France
135	W 9	**Brisbane**, QLD, Australia
16	M 8	**Bristol**, TN, U.S.A.
19	S 7	**Bristol**, FL, U.S.A.
63	P 11	**Bristol**, U.K.
35	N 11	**Bristol Bay**, AK, U.S.A. ≈
62	M 11	**Bristol Channel**, U.K. ≈
33	M 24	**Bristol Lake**, CA, U.S.A. ◣
39	E 17	**British Columbia**, Canada ▣
65	P 11	**Brive-la-Gaillarde**, France
67	P 2	**Briviesca**, Spain
63	N 14	**Brixham**, U.K.
79	F 19	**Brno**, Czech Republic
62	J 9	**Broad Haven**, U.K.
60	F 10	**Broadford**, U.K.
63	Z 11	**Broadstairs**, U.K.
29	X 7	**Broadus**, MT, U.S.A.
39	O 19	**Broadview**, SK, Canada
63	R 9	**Broadway**, U.K.
40	I 6	**Brochet**, MB, Canada
15	O 10	**Brockton**, MA, U.S.A.
42	I 12	**Brockville**, ON, Canada
14	D 11	**Brockway**, PA, U.S.A.
82	C 11	**Brod**, Macedonia (F.Y.R.O.M.)
37	P 5	**Brodeur Peninsula**, NU, Canada ◗
78	J 10	**Brodnica**, Poland
86	J 4	**Brody**, Ukraine
32	K 11	**Brogan**, OR, U.S.A.
25	Q 9	**Broken Arrow**, OK, U.S.A.
25	R 13	**Broken Bow**, OK, U.S.A.
25	R 12	**Broken Bow Reservoir**, OK, U.S.A. ◣
135	R 10	**Broken Hill**, NSW, Australia
51	X 6	**Brokopondo**, Suriname
63	W 11	**Bromley**, U.K.
63	R 7	**Bromsgrove**, U.K.
71	C 23	**Brønderslev**, Denmark
128	M 12	**Brong-Ahafo**, Ghana ▣
76	C 7	**Broni**, Italy
26	M 7	**Bronte**, TX, U.S.A.
135	T 15	**Bronte Park**, TAS, Australia
121	C 20	**Brooke's Point**, Philippines
25	T 2	**Brookfield**, MO, U.S.A.
18	L 6	**Brookhaven**, MS, U.S.A.
23	P 9	**Brookings**, SD, U.S.A.
33	E 14	**Brookings**, OR, U.S.A.
17	R 7	**Brookneal**, VA, U.S.A.
35	O 4	**Brooks Range**, AK, U.S.A. ⛰
19	V 10	**Brooksville**, FL, U.S.A.
134	G 11	**Brookton**, WA, Australia
21	K 19	**Brookville Lake**, IN, U.S.A. ◣
134	I 4	**Broome**, WA, Australia
86	K 8	**Broşteni**, Romania
105	N 22	**Brothers**, India 🏝
65	O 5	**Brou**, France
87	Q 3	**Brovary**, Ukraine
26	K 5	**Brownfield**, TX, U.S.A.
29	O 2	**Browning**, MT, U.S.A.
21	I 20	**Brownstown**, IN, U.S.A.
16	A 9	**Brownsville**, TN, U.S.A.
27	Q 15	**Brownsville**, TX, U.S.A.
27	N 7	**Brownwood**, TX, U.S.A.
85	L 19	**Brozha**, Belarus
18	M 2	**Bruce**, MS, U.S.A.
20	D 10	**Bruce**, WI, U.S.A.
20	G 8	**Bruce Crossing**, MI, U.S.A.
42	C 11	**Bruce Peninsula**, ON, Canada ◗
73	F 22	**Bruchsal**, Germany
75	Q 7	**Bruck**, Austria
75	Y 4	**Bruck an der Leitha**, Austria
75	V 6	**Bruck an der Mur**, Austria
116	A 8	**Brueuh**, Indonesia 🏝
69	C 17	**Bruges**, Belgium
107	Z 7	**Bruint**, India
20	D 8	**Brule**, WI, U.S.A.
69	G 24	**Brûly**, Belgium
55	M 15	**Brumado**, Brazil
68	L 12	**Brummen**, Netherlands
19	R 5	**Brundidge**, AL, U.S.A.
119	T 7	**Brunei**, Asia □
119	T 6	**Brunei Bay**, Malaysia ≈
76	G 4	**Brunico**, Italy
72	F 9	**Brunsbüttel**, Germany
15	P 7	**Brunswick**, ME, U.S.A.
19	W 6	**Brunswick**, GA, U.S.A.
25	T 3	**Brunswick**, MO, U.S.A.
145	N 3	**Brunt Ice Shelf**, Antarctica ◇
79	G 17	**Bruntál**, Czech Republic
135	T 15	**Bruny Island**, TAS, Australia 🏝
80	M 13	**Brus**, Serbia and Montenegro
47	P 4	**Brus Laguna**, Honduras ◣
31	T 3	**Brush**, CO, U.S.A.
74	K 10	**Brusio**, Switzerland
69	E 19	**Brussels**, Belgium ■
78	H 9	**Brusy**, Poland
87	O 4	**Brusyliv**, Ukraine
21	K 16	**Bryan**, OH, U.S.A.
27	R 9	**Bryan**, TX, U.S.A.
144	J 8	**Bryan Coast**, Antarctica ◇
87	Y 6	**Bryanka**, Ukraine
92	I 3	**Bryansk**, Russian Federation
92	H 4	**Bryanskaya Oblast'**, Russian Federation ▣
63	N 9	**Brynamman**, U.K.
136	J 7	**Brynderwyn**, New Zealand
16	K 10	**Bryson City**, NC, U.S.A.
80	O 11	**Brza**, Serbia and Montenegro
79	G 15	**Brzeg**, Poland
127	K 25	**Bu'aale**, Somalia
141	U 1	**Buada Lagoon**, Nauru ◣
138	L 6	**Buala**, Solomon Islands
125	T 8	**Bu'ayrāt al Hasūn**, Libya
128	E 10	**Buba**, Guinea-Bissau
99	S 2	**Bubīyān Island**, Kuwait 🏝
139	Y 11	**Buca**, Fiji
50	J 5	**Bucaramanga**, Colombia
121	N 19	**Bucas Grande**, Philippines 🏝
77	K 16	**Buccino**, Italy
60	J 10	**Buchan Ness**, U.K. ◗
17	Q 6	**Buchanan**, VA, U.S.A.
128	H 13	**Buchanan**, Liberia
41	X 10	**Buchans**, NL, Canada
86	J 13	**Bucharest**, Romania ■
63	N 14	**Buckfastleigh**, U.K.
17	P 3	**Buckhannon**, WV, U.S.A.
17	S 6	**Buckingham**, VA, U.S.A.
35	N 6	**Buckland**, AK, U.S.A.
145	S 15	**Buckle Island**, Antarctica 🏝
24	K 6	**Bucklin**, KS, U.S.A.
79	G 19	**Bučovice**, Czech Republic
21	M 17	**Bucyrus**, OH, U.S.A.
85	M 20	**Buda-Kashelyova**, Belarus
79	I 23	**Budapest**, Hungary ■
106	K 9	**Budaun**, India
145	X 11	**Budd Coast**, Antarctica ◇
77	C 16	**Buddusò**, Italy
18	K 6	**Bude**, MS, U.S.A.
62	L 13	**Bude**, U.K.
62	K 13	**Bude Bay**, U.K. ≈
69	J 17	**Budel**, Netherlands
93	O 12	**Budennovsk**, Russian Federation
86	L 13	**Budeşti**, Romania
130	K 6	**Budjala**, Democratic Republic of Congo
90	G 11	**Budogoshch'**, Russian Federation
81	I 16	**Budva**, Serbia and Montenegro
129	S 14	**Buea**, Cameroon
57	H 19	**Buen Pasto**, Argentina
56	I 12	**Buena Esperanza**, Argentina
33	I 23	**Buena Vista Lake Bed**, CA, U.S.A. ◣
44	L 4	**Buenaventura**, Mexico
50	G 7	**Buenaventura**, Colombia
44	J 8	**Buenavista**, Mexico
120	H 13	**Buenavista**, Philippines
47	R 13	**Buenos Aires**, Costa Rica
59	D 16	**Buenos Aires**, Argentina ■
59	C 17	**Buenos Aires**, Argentina ▣
44	M 6	**Búfalo**, Mexico
14	D 8	**Buffalo**, NY, U.S.A.
16	D 9	**Buffalo**, TN, U.S.A.
22	G 7	**Buffalo**, SD, U.S.A.
24	J 8	**Buffalo**, OK, U.S.A.
25	U 6	**Buffalo**, MO, U.S.A.
27	R 8	**Buffalo**, TX, U.S.A.
29	W 9	**Buffalo**, WY, U.S.A.
39	K 16	**Buffalo Narrows**, SK, Canada
86	K 12	**Buftea**, Romania
78	N 12	**Bug**, Poland ∫
50	H 7	**Buga**, Colombia
131	S 8	**Bugala Island**, Uganda 🏝
129	R 12	**Bugana**, Nigeria
121	H 16	**Bugasong**, Philippines
102	I 13	**Bugdayli**, Turkmenistan
91	O 2	**Bugrino**, Russian Federation
121	B 20	**Bugsuk**, Philippines 🏝
110	H 8	**Bugt**, China
121	J 14	**Bugui Point**, Philippines ◗
93	U 2	**Bugul'ma**, Russian Federation
93	U 3	**Buguruslan**, Russian Federation
96	K 2	**Buḩayrat al Asad**, Syria ◣
97	S 8	**Buḩayrat ar Razāzah**, Iraq ◣
97	S 6	**Buḩayrat ath Tharthār**, Iraq ◣
96	I 5	**Buḩayrat Qaţţīnah**, Syria ◣
28	L 12	**Buhl**, ID, U.S.A.
86	L 9	**Buhuşi**, Romania
63	O 8	**Builth Wells**, U.K.
138	J 5	**Buin**, Papua New Guinea
93	R 2	**Buinsk**, Russian Federation
109	U 3	**Buir Nur**, China ◣
68	L 6	**Buitenpost**, Netherlands
132	K 9	**Buitepos**, Namibia

□ Country ▣ Internal administrative region: State/Province/Territory/Dependent territory ■ Capital city ⛰ Mountain range/Undersea ridge ▲ Mountain peak/Volcano/Seamount ◇ Geographic feature ◗ Headland/Point/Cape/Peninsula ◭ Desert 🏝 Island/Island group ⁙ Antarctic base ◎ Ocean ◒ Sea ≈ Bay/Gulf/Channel/Strait ◣ Lake ⚑ Salt pan/Dry/Intermittent lake ∫ River

81	N 15	**Bujanovac**, Serbia and Montenegro
67	T 4	**Bujaraloz**, Spain
131	Q 10	**Bujumbura**, Burundi ♜
138	B 6	**Buk**, Papua New Guinea
138	I 4	**Buka**, Papua New Guinea ♣
131	O 13	**Bukama**, Democratic Republic of Congo
131	Q 9	**Bukavu**, Democratic Republic of Congo
103	O 12	**Bukhara**, Uzbekistan
103	O 12	**Bukhoro Wiloyati**, Uzbekistan ▣
119	R 9	**Bukit Batu**, Malaysia ▲
117	N 12	**Bukit Gandadiwata**, Indonesia ▲
118	A 14	**Bukit Gombak**, Singapore ▲
116	L 10	**Bukit Liangpran**, Indonesia ▲
116	E 12	**Bukit Masurai**, Indonesia ▲
118	A 6	**Bukit Merah**, Malaysia
119	Q 9	**Bukit Mersing**, Malaysia ▲
118	A 14	**Bukit Panjang**, Singapore
116	K 11	**Bukit Raya**, Indonesia ▲
119	V 6	**Bukit Tambulanan**, Malaysia ▲
119	W 5	**Bukit Tawai**, Malaysia ▲
116	D 11	**Bukittinggi**, Indonesia
131	S 8	**Bukoba**, Tanzania
118	A 15	**Bukum**, Singapore ♣
118	A 15	**Bukum Kechil**, Singapore ♣
117	T 12	**Bula**, Indonesia
74	G 6	**Bülach**, Switzerland
121	K 14	**Bulan**, Philippines
121	H 24	**Bulan**, Philippines ♣
95	N 8	**Bulancak**, Turkey
129	S 10	**Bulangu**, Nigeria
95	R 10	**Bulanik**, Turkey
126	E 11	**Bûlâq**, Egypt
133	O 8	**Bulawayo**, Zimbabwe
103	R 1	**Bulayevo**, Kazakhstan
105	D 16	**Buldana**, India
34	C 12	**Buldir Island**, AK, U.S.A. ♣
109	P 3	**Bulgan**, Mongolia ▣
109	O 5	**Bulgan**, Mongolia
109	P 3	**Bulgan**, Mongolia
109	Q 5	**Bulgan**, Mongolia
82	G 10	**Bulgaria**, Europe □
117	S 10	**Buli**, Indonesia
25	U 8	**Bull Shoals Lake**, AR, U.S.A. ⬊
127	L 19	**Bullaxaar**, Somalia
74	C 9	**Bulle**, Switzerland
137	G 17	**Buller**, New Zealand ∫
137	K 14	**Bulls**, New Zealand
17	Q 14	**Bulls Bay**, SC, U.S.A. ≃
138	D 5	**Bulolo**, Papua New Guinea
77	C 17	**Bultei**, Italy
130	L 8	**Bulukutu**, Democratic Republic of Congo
89	S 8	**Bulun**, Russian Federation
130	J 10	**Bulungu**, Democratic Republic of Congo
130	L 11	**Bulungu**, Democratic Republic of Congo
121	K 14	**Bulusan**, Philippines
119	Y 7	**Bum-Bum**, Malaysia ♣
130	J 12	**Bumba**, Democratic Republic of Congo
130	L 6	**Bumba**, Democratic Republic of Congo
130	J 9	**Buna**, Democratic Republic of Congo
131	W 6	**Buna**, Kenya
131	R 8	**Bunazi**, Tanzania
134	G 12	**Bunbury**, WA, Australia
131	T 9	**Bunda**, Tanzania
135	W 7	**Bundaberg**, QLD, Australia
104	D 13	**Bundi**, India
127	D 22	**Bunduqiya**, Sudan
63	Z 7	**Bungay**, U.K.
132	H 2	**Bungo**, Angola
123	D 21	**Bungo-suidō**, Japan ≃
129	T 10	**Buni-Yadi**, Nigeria
131	R 7	**Bunia**, Democratic Republic of Congo
131	O 14	**Bunkeya**, Democratic Republic of Congo
18	J 6	**Bunkie**, LA, U.S.A.
19	X 8	**Bunnell**, FL, U.S.A.
129	S 11	**Bununu**, Nigeria
94	K 10	**Bünyan**, Turkey
129	P 10	**Bunza**, Nigeria
115	N 20	**Buôn Mê Thuột**, Vietnam
89	S 7	**Buorkhaya Guba**, Russian Federation ≃
126	G 10	**Bûr Safâga**, Egypt
127	N 19	**Buraan**, Somalia
127	B 19	**Buram**, Sudan
103	Z 5	**Buran**, Kazakhstan
127	M 20	**Burao**, Somalia
96	I 7	**Burāq**, Syria
99	P 5	**Buraydah**, Saudi Arabia
63	S 11	**Burbage**, U.K.
33	J 24	**Burbank**, CA, U.S.A.
135	T 4	**Burdekin**, QLD, Australia ∫
69	I 20	**Burdinne**, Belgium
94	E 12	**Burdur**, Turkey
127	G 21	**Burē**, Ethiopia
127	H 19	**Burē**, Ethiopia
101	X 10	**Burewala**, Pakistan
70	J 7	**Burfjord**, Norway
63	S 9	**Burford**, U.K.
72	K 13	**Burg**, Germany
82	M 9	**Burgas**, Bulgaria ▣
82	M 9	**Burgas**, Bulgaria
17	T 11	**Burgaw**, NC, U.S.A.
28	K 8	**Burgdorf**, ID, U.S.A.
74	E 7	**Burgdorf**, Switzerland
75	X 8	**Burgenland**, Austria ▣
41	X 11	**Burgeo**, NL, Canada
63	W 12	**Burgess Hill**, U.K.
69	D 14	**Burgh-Haamstede**, Netherlands
73	L 24	**Burghausen**, Germany
77	I 22	**Burgio**, Italy
67	O 3	**Burgos**, Spain
71	I 23	**Burgsvik**, Sweden
105	E 16	**Burhanpur**, India
120	I 13	**Burias**, Philippines ♣
115	J 18	**Buriram**, Thailand
135	R 4	**Burke and Wills Roadhouse**, QLD, Australia
144	J 9	**Burke Island**, Antarctica ♣
135	Q 4	**Burketown**, QLD, Australia
128	M10	**Burkina Faso**, Africa □
29	N 12	**Burley**, ID, U.S.A.
102	I 4	**Burlin**, Kazakhstan
14	L 6	**Burlington**, VT, U.S.A.
17	Q 8	**Burlington**, NC, U.S.A.
23	V 14	**Burlington**, IA, U.S.A.
25	P 5	**Burlington**, KS, U.S.A.
31	U 4	**Burlington**, CO, U.S.A.
42	F 13	**Burlington**, ON, Canada
25	R 1	**Burlington Junction**, MO, U.S.A.
27	P 6	**Burlson**, TX, U.S.A.
137	H 17	**Burnbrae**, New Zealand
27	O 9	**Burnet**, TX, U.S.A.
33	G 15	**Burney**, CA, U.S.A.
63	Y 10	**Burnham-on-Crouch**, U.K.
63	O 11	**Burnham-on-Sea**, U.K.
135	S 15	**Burnie**, TAS, Australia
63	Q 2	**Burnley**, U.K.
32	J 12	**Burns**, OR, U.S.A.
32	K 13	**Burns Junction**, OR, U.S.A.
108	L 3	**Burqin**, China
135	P 11	**Burra**, SA, Australia
81	K 18	**Burrel**, Albania
67	T 7	**Burriana**, Spain
67	U 6	**Burriana**, Spain
94	D 8	**Bursa**, Turkey
63	S 6	**Burton upon Trent**, U.K.
117	Q 12	**Buru**, Indonesia ♣
103	T 8	**Burulbaytal**, Kazakhstan
131	Q 9	**Burundi**, Africa □
131	Q 10	**Bururi**, Burundi
63	Q 3	**Bury**, U.K.
63	Y 8	**Bury St Edmunds**, U.K.
87	T 2	**Buryn'**, Ukraine
130	K 6	**Busa Modanda**, Democratic Republic of Congo
121	I 21	**Busan Bay**, Philippines ≃
130	L 8	**Busanga**, Democratic Republic of Congo
100	I 11	**Būshehr**, Iran ▣
100	H 11	**Būshehr**, Iran
131	Q 8	**Bushenyi**, Uganda
81	L 17	**Bushtricë**, Albania
130	L 6	**Businga**, Democratic Republic of Congo
79	K 16	**Busko-Zdrój**, Poland
134	F 12	**Busselton**, WA, Australia
86	K 11	**Buşteni**, Romania
76	C 7	**Busto Arsizio**, Italy
121	E 15	**Busuanga**, Philippines
121	F 15	**Busuanga**, Philippines ♣
72	F 9	**Büsum**, Germany
131	N 6	**Buta**, Democratic Republic of Congo
115	G 26	**Butang Group**, Thailand ♣
131	Q 9	**Butare**, Rwanda
140	D 1	**Butaritari**, Kiribati ♣
14	B 12	**Butler**, PA, U.S.A.
19	O 5	**Butler**, AL, U.S.A.
19	S 4	**Butler**, GA, U.S.A.
25	S 5	**Butler**, MO, U.S.A.
117	P 13	**Buton**, Indonesia ♣
60	F 8	**Butt of Lewis**, U.K. ▶
29	O 6	**Butte**, MT, U.S.A.
118	A 6	**Butterworth**, Malaysia
40	K 5	**Button Bay**, MB, Canada ≃
41	T 5	**Button Islands**, NU, Canada ♣
121	M 19	**Butuan**, Philippines
112	L 8	**Butuo**, China
92	M 6	**Buturlinovka**, Russian Federation
107	O 9	**Butwal**, Nepal
73	F 18	**Butzbach**, Germany
127	M 23	**Buulobarde**, Somalia
127	K 26	**Buur Gaabo**, Somalia
127	L 24	**Buurhabaka**, Somalia
107	O 11	**Buxar**, India
32	G 9	**Buxton**, OR, U.S.A.
63	R 4	**Buxton**, U.K.
90	K 12	**Buy**, Russian Federation
109	O 4	**Buyant**, Mongolia
93	R 14	**Buynaksk**, Russian Federation
85	K 21	**Buynavichy**, Belarus
82	M 12	**Büyükkarıştiran**, Turkey
111	I 16	**Buyun Shan**, China ▲
86	L 12	**Buzău**, Romania
133	R 8	**Buzi**, Mozambique
93	U 4	**Buzuluk**, Russian Federation
103	P 4	**Buzuluk**, Kazakhstan
15	O 11	**Buzzards Bay**, MA, U.S.A. ≃
85	J 15	**Byahoml'**, Belarus
82	J 7	**Byala**, Bulgaria
82	N 8	**Byala**, Bulgaria
85	L 17	**Byalynichy**, Belarus
37	N 4	**Byam Martin Island**, NU, Canada ♣
85	L 19	**Byarezina**, Belarus ∫
85	G 20	**Byaroza**, Belarus
79	N 15	**Bychawa**, Poland
78	H 11	**Bydgoszcz**, Poland
85	J 15	**Byerazino**, Belarus
85	K 17	**Byerazino**, Belarus
85	L 15	**Byeshankovichy**, Belarus
71	J 14	**Bygdeå**, Sweden
71	B 21	**Bygland**, Norway
85	M 18	**Bykhaw**, Belarus
71	B 20	**Bykle**, Norway
93	P 7	**Bykovo**, Russian Federation
30	L 13	**Bylas**, AZ, U.S.A.
37	Q 4	**Bylot Island**, NU, Canada ♣
70	I 13	**Byskeälven**, Sweden ∫
79	J 19	**Bystra**, Slovakia ▲
79	I 17	**Bytom**, Poland
78	G 8	**Bytów**, Poland
131	Q 9	**Byumba**, Rwanda
78	K 12	**Bzura**, Poland ∫

C

115	L 23	**Ca Mau**, Vietnam
132	H 4	**Caala**, Angola
55	G 20	**Caazapá**, Paraguay
53	D 18	**Caballas**, Peru
31	P 13	**Caballo Reservoir**, NM, U.S.A. ⬊
52	H 11	**Caballococha**, Peru
120	G 10	**Cabanatuan**, Philippines
43	P 7	**Cabano**, QC, Canada
80	C 8	**Čabar**, Croatia
127	K 19	**Cabdul Qaadir**, Somalia
53	L 21	**Cabezas**, Bolivia
50	K 3	**Cabimas**, Venezuela
132	F 1	**Cabinda**, Angola
132	F 1	**Cabinda**, Angola ▣
28	K 2	**Cabinet Mountains**, MT, U.S.A. ▲▲
20	D 9	**Cable**, WI, U.S.A.
56	F 9	**Cabo Bascuñán**, Chile ▶
49	Q 8	**Cabo Beata**, Dominican Republic ▶
47	O 13	**Cabo Blanco**, Costa Rica ▶
57	I 20	**Cabo Blanco**, Argentina
57	H 23	**Cabo Buen Tiempo**, Argentina ▶
49	R 7	**Cabo Cabron**, Dominican Republic ▶
47	P 4	**Cabo Camarón**, Honduras ▶
66	F 8	**Cabo Carvoeiro**, Portugal ▶
45	Z 9	**Cabo Catoche**, Mexico ▶
44	F 3	**Cabo Colonet**, Mexico ▶
44	M 11	**Cabo Corrientes**, Mexico ▶
48	F 5	**Cabo Corrientes**, Cuba ▶
59	E 18	**Cabo Corrientes**, Argentina ▶
48	K 7	**Cabo Cruz**, Cuba ▶
57	I 22	**Cabo Dañoso**, Argentina ▶
67	U 9	**Cabo de la Nao**, Spain ▶
50	J 1	**Cabo de la Vela**, Colombia ▶
67	T 11	**Cabo de Palos**, Spain ▶
66	L 1	**Cabo de Penas**, Spain ▶
67	U 9	**Cabo de San Antonio**, Spain ▶
66	H 12	**Cabo de Santa Maria**, Portugal ▶
133	Q 11	**Cabo de Santa Maria**, Mozambique ▶
132	F 5	**Cabo de Santa Marta**, Angola ▶
58	J 11	**Cabo de Santa Marta Grande**, Brazil ▶
54	O 13	**Cabo de Santo Agostinho**, Brazil
55	M 18	**Cabo de São Tomé**, Brazil ▶
66	G 12	**Cabo de São Vincent**, Portugal ▶
66	G 11	**Cabo de Sines**, Portugal ▶
133	U 3	**Cabo Delgado**, Mozambique ▶
133	U 4	**Cabo Delgado**, Mozambique ▣
57	I 19	**Cabo Dos Bahías**, Argentina ▶
49	S 7	**Cabo Engaño**, Dominican Republic ▶
66	G 10	**Cabo Espichel**, Portugal ▶
47	R 5	**Cabo Falso**, Honduras ▶
49	P 8	**Cabo Falso**, Dominican Republic ▶
66	G 2	**Cabo Fisterra**, Spain ▶
58	N 7	**Cabo Frio**, Brazil
58	O 7	**Cabo Frio**, Brazil ▶
47	R 5	**Cabo Gracias á Dios**, Nicaragua/Honduras ▶
67	T 10	**Cabo Huertas**, Spain ▶
56	F 13	**Cabo Humos**, Chile ▶
49	Q 6	**Cabo Isabela**, Dominican Republic ▶
48	M 5	**Cabo Lucrecia**, Cuba ▶
67	P 1	**Cabo Machichaco**, Spain ▶
50	G 5	**Cabo Marzo**, Colombia ▶
47	R 14	**Cabo Matapalo**, Costa Rica ▶
67	O 1	**Cabo Mayor**, Spain ▶
54	J 8	**Cabo Norte**, Brazil ▶
54	I 7	**Cabo Orange**, Brazil ▶
66	I 1	**Cabo Ortegal**, Spain ▶
52	E 9	**Cabo Pantoja**, Peru
57	F 24	**Cabo Pilar**, Chile ▶
44	E 2	**Cabo Punta Banda**, Mexico ▶
57	E 17	**Cabo Quedal**, Chile ▶
57	E 18	**Cabo Quilán**, Chile ▶
57	J 19	**Cabo Raso**, Argentina
45	S 10	**Cabo Rojo**, Mexico ▶
67	O 13	**Cabo Sacratif**, Spain ▶
48	E 5	**Cabo San Antonio**, Cuba ▶
59	E 17	**Cabo San Antonio**, Argentina ▶
57	I 25	**Cabo San Diego**, Argentina ▶
57	H 22	**Cabo San Francisco de Paula**, Argentina ▶
129	S 15	**Cabo San Juan**, Equatorial Guinea ▶
44	H 8	**Cabo San Lázaro**, Mexico ▶
44	J 9	**Cabo San Lucas**, Mexico ▶
44	F 3	**Cabo San Quintín**, Mexico ▶
47	N 11	**Cabo Santa Elena**, Costa Rica ▶
59	G 16	**Cabo Santa Maria**, Uruguay ▶
57	E 23	**Cabo Santiago**, Chile ▶
66	H 3	**Cabo Silleiro**, Spain ▶
66	K 14	**Cabo Trafalgar**, Spain ▶
57	I 20	**Cabo Tres Puntas**, Argentina ▶
47	N 12	**Cabo Vèlas**, Costa Rica ▶
57	H 24	**Cabo Vírgenes**, Argentina ▶
25	V 7	**Cabool**, MO, U.S.A.
135	W 8	**Caboolture**, QLD, Australia
44	I 3	**Caborca**, Mexico
41	W 11	**Cabot Strait**, NS, Canada ≃
120	E 12	**Cabra**, Philippines ♣
77	B 17	**Cabras**, Italy
49	R 7	**Cabrera**, Dominican Republic
67	Y 9	**Cabrera**, Spain ♣
39	L 20	**Cabri**, SK, Canada
54	N 13	**Cabrobó**, Brazil
51	O 5	**Cabruta**, Venezuela
120	F 6	**Cabugao**, Philippines
121	F 16	**Cabulauan**, Philippines ♣
120	H 6	**Cabutunan Point**, Philippines ▶
58	H 9	**Caçador**, Brazil
80	K 12	**Čačak**, Serbia and Montenegro
58	G 12	**Cacapava do Sul**, Brazil
58	F 12	**Cacequi**, Brazil
55	G 16	**Cáceres**, Brazil
66	K 8	**Cáceres**, Spain
128	D 9	**Cacheu**, Guinea-Bissau
56	I 6	**Cachi**, Argentina
54	H 13	**Cachimbo**, Brazil
132	I 4	**Cachingues**, Angola
58	I 3	**Cachoeira Alta**, Brazil
58	G 12	**Cachoeira do Sul**, Brazil
54	H 11	**Cachoeirinha**, Brazil
58	O 5	**Cachoeiro de Itapemirim**, Brazil
53	J 15	**Cachuela Esperanza**, Bolivia
128	E 10	**Cacine**, Guinea-Bissau
132	J 3	**Cacolo**, Angola
132	F 1	**Cacongo**, Angola
55	I 17	**Caçu**, Brazil
132	G 2	**Cacuaco**, Angola
63	N 6	**Cadair Idris**, U.K. ▲
67	Y 3	**Cadaqués**, Spain
27	U 5	**Caddo Lake**, TX, U.S.A. ⬊
120	I 12	**Cadig Mountains**, Philippines ▲▲
20	K 12	**Cadillac**, MI, U.S.A.
42	G 6	**Cadillac**, QC, Canada
16	D 7	**Cadiz**, KY, U.S.A.
66	K 13	**Cádiz**, Spain
121	J 16	**Cadiz**, Philippines
33	M 24	**Cadiz Lake**, CA, U.S.A. ⬊
64	M 4	**Caen**, France
62	M 4	**Caernarfon**, U.K.
62	L 5	**Caernarfon Bay**, U.K. ≃
63	O 10	**Caerphilly**, U.K.
55	M 15	**Caetité**, Brazil
56	I 7	**Cafayate**, Argentina
120	H 7	**Cagayan**, Philippines ∫
121	L 20	**Cagayan de Oro**, Philippines
121	G 19	**Cagayan Islands**, Philippines ♣
77	B 19	**Cagliari**, Italy
49	U 8	**Caguas**, Puerto Rico
132	G 6	**Cahama**, Angola
61	D 20	**Caher**, Republic of Ireland
61	A 20	**Cahersiveen**, Republic of Ireland
61	F 19	**Cahore Point**, Republic of Ireland ▶
65	P 12	**Cahors**, France
52	C 12	**Cahuapanas**, Peru
87	N 10	**Cahul**, Moldova
115	L 24	**Cai Nuoc**, Vietnam
132	L 3	**Caianda**, Angola
55	I 16	**Caiapônia**, Brazil
48	J 4	**Caibarién**, Cuba
54	O 12	**Caicó**, Brazil
49	P 5	**Caicos Islands**, Turks and Caicos Islands ♣
49	O 5	**Caicos Passage**, The Bahamas ≃
134	K 10	**Caiguna**, WA, Australia
54	H 11	**Caima**, Brazil
120	E 9	**Caiman Point**, Philippines ▶
112	L 5	**Cainnyigoin**, China
145	N 4	**Caird Coast**, Antarctica ◇
135	T 3	**Cairns**, QLD, Australia
19	S 7	**Cairo**, GA, U.S.A.
21	F 23	**Cairo**, IL, U.S.A.
126	F 8	**Cairo**, Egypt ♜
63	V 3	**Caistor**, U.K.
132	G 5	**Caitou**, Angola
132	I 6	**Caiundo**, Angola
52	B 13	**Cajamarca**, Peru
52	B 12	**Cajamarca**, Peru ▣
54	N 12	**Cajazeiras**, Brazil
80	K 12	**Čajetina**, Serbia and Montenegro
121	I 14	**Cajidiocan**, Philippines
109	O 8	**Caka**, China
80	E 6	**Čakovec**, Croatia
129	R 14	**Calabar**, Nigeria
51	N 4	**Calabozo**, Venezuela
77	M 19	**Calabria**, Italy ▣
53	I 20	**Calacoto**, Bolivia
86	G 13	**Calafat**, Romania
57	G 23	**Calafate**, Argentina
120	J 11	**Calagua Islands**, Philippines ♣
67	R 3	**Calahorra**, Spain
132	J 7	**Calai**, Angola
15	T 4	**Calais**, ME, U.S.A.
65	P 1	**Calais**, France
54	E 13	**Calama**, Brazil
56	G 5	**Calama**, Chile
50	I 3	**Calamar**, Colombia
50	J 8	**Calamar**, Colombia
120	G 12	**Calamba**, Philippines
121	E 15	**Calamian Group**, Philippines ♣
86	H 10	**Călan**, Romania
121	F 17	**Calandagan**, Philippines ♣
132	H 2	**Calandula**, Angola
116	B 8	**Calang**, Indonesia
125	X 8	**Calanscio Sand Sea**, Libya ◇
120	G 13	**Calapan**, Philippines
86	M 13	**Călăraşi**, Romania
87	N 8	**Călăraşi**, Moldova
67	R 5	**Calatayud**, Spain
120	I 12	**Calauag**, Philippines
121	E 14	**Calawit**, Philippines ♣
120	G 4	**Calayan**, Philippines ♣
121	K 15	**Calbayog**, Philippines
73	J 14	**Calbe**, Germany
18	H 8	**Calcasieu Lake**, LA, U.S.A. ⬊
54	I 8	**Calçoene**, Brazil
54	I 9	**Calçoene**, Brazil ∫
107	S 14	**Calcutta**, India
66	G 8	**Caldas da Rainha**, Portugal
56	F 8	**Caldera**, Chile
62	L 10	**Caldey Island**, U.K. ♣
63	P 10	**Caldicot**, U.K.
95	T 10	**Caldiran**, Turkey
25	N 7	**Caldwell**, KS, U.S.A.
27	R 9	**Caldwell**, TX, U.S.A.
28	J 10	**Caldwell**, ID, U.S.A.
43	U 11	**Caledonia**, NS, Canada
19	P 4	**Calera**, AL, U.S.A.
56	F 3	**Caleta Buena**, Chile
56	F 4	**Caleta Lobos**, Chile
57	I 20	**Caleta Olivia**, Argentina
33	M 26	**Calexico**, CA, U.S.A.
39	J 20	**Calgary**, AB, Canada
19	S 2	**Calhoun**, GA, U.S.A.
50	G 7	**Cali**, Colombia
121	M 16	**Calicoan**, Philippines ♣
105	D 22	**Calicut**, India
33	N 20	**Caliente**, NV, U.S.A.
33	H 22	**California**, U.S.A., U.S.A. ▣
33	H 21	**California Aqueduct**, CA, U.S.A. ∫
95	Y 9	**Cälilabad**, Azerbaijan
121	G 14	**Calintaan**, Philippines
33	M 26	**Calipatria**, CA, U.S.A.
33	F 18	**Calistoga**, CA, U.S.A.
77	L 16	**Calitri**, Italy
45	Y 11	**Calkiní**, Mexico
42	F 9	**Callander**, ON, Canada
17	V 5	**Callao**, VA, U.S.A.
53	C 16	**Callao**, Peru
62	L 14	**Callington**, U.K.
47	V 14	**Calobre**, Panama
135	W 8	**Caloundra**, QLD, Australia
77	K 23	**Caltagirone**, Italy
77	J 22	**Caltanissetta**, Italy
132	G 3	**Calulo**, Angola
132	L 4	**Calunda**, Angola
132	J 6	**Calunga**, Angola
132	G 5	**Caluquembe**, Angola
121	G 18	**Calusa**, Philippines ♣
127	O 18	**Caluula**, Somalia
121	H 15	**Caluya**, Philippines ♣
65	Y 14	**Calvi**, France
132	K 14	**Calvinia**, Republic of South Africa
114	N 12	**Câm Pha**, Vietnam
115	O 20	**Cam Ranh**, Vietnam
55	N 15	**Camaçari**, Brazil
45	O 8	**Camacho**, Mexico
132	F 5	**Camacuio**, Angola
132	I 4	**Camacupa**, Angola
48	K 5	**Camagüey**, Cuba
55	N 15	**Camamu**, Brazil
53	F 19	**Camaná**, Peru
55	H 17	**Camapuã**, Brazil
58	H 13	**Camaquã**, Brazil
57	I 19	**Camarones**, Argentina
41	U 12	**Cambellton**, NB, Canada
63	U 11	**Camberley**, U.K.
115	K 20	**Cambodia**, Asia □
62	J 15	**Camborne**, U.K.
65	R 2	**Cambrai**, France
62	M 9	**Cambrian Mountains**, U.K. ▲▲
15	N 9	**Cambridge**, MA, U.S.A.
17	V 4	**Cambridge**, MD, U.S.A.
21	O 18	**Cambridge**, OH, U.S.A.
23	S 7	**Cambridge**, MN, U.S.A.
28	J 9	**Cambridge**, ID, U.S.A.
63	W 8	**Cambridge**, U.K.
136	L 10	**Cambridge**, New Zealand
38	I 7	**Cambridge Bay**, NU, Canada
132	K 1	**Cambulo**, Angola
14	H 8	**Camden**, NY, U.S.A.
15	Q 6	**Camden**, ME, U.S.A.
16	D 8	**Camden**, TN, U.S.A.
17	P 12	**Camden**, SC, U.S.A.
19	P 5	**Camden**, AL, U.S.A.
25	U 13	**Camden**, AR, U.S.A.
135	U 12	**Camden**, NSW, Australia
25	U 5	**Camdenton**, MO, U.S.A.
132	K 3	**Cameia**, Angola
18	H 8	**Cameron**, LA, U.S.A.
20	C 10	**Cameron**, WI, U.S.A.
25	S 2	**Cameron**, MO, U.S.A.
27	Q 9	**Cameron**, TX, U.S.A.
30	K 9	**Cameron**, AZ, U.S.A.
118	B 7	**Cameron Highlands**, Malaysia
118	B 7	**Cameron Highlands**, Malaysia ▲▲
137	A 25	**Cameron Mountains**, New Zealand ▲▲
129	T 14	**Cameroon**, Africa □
54	J 10	**Cametá**, Brazil
94	B 12	**Camişşi Gölü**, Turkey ⬊
120	H 5	**Camiguin**, Philippines ♣
121	L 19	**Camiguin**, Philippines ♣
120	F 9	**Camiling**, Philippines
19	T 6	**Camilla**, GA, U.S.A.
56	F 2	**Camiña**, Chile
66	H 3	**Caminha**, Portugal
53	L 22	**Camiri**, Bolivia
132	K 2	**Camissombo**, Angola
54	M 10	**Camocim**, Brazil
135	P 5	**Camooweal**, QLD, Australia
105	O 24	**Camorta**, India ♣
121	L 17	**Camotes Islands**, Philippines ♣
30	J 11	**Camp Verde**, AZ, U.S.A.
46	M 6	**Campamento**, Honduras
77	K 15	**Campania**, Italy ▣
21	M 18	**Campbell Hill**, OH, U.S.A. ▲
115	F 22	**Campbell Island**, Myanmar ♣
39	E 21	**Campbell River**, BC, Canada
42	G 12	**Campbellford**, ON, Canada
16	H 6	**Campbellsville**, KY, U.S.A.
43	R 7	**Campbellton**, NB, Canada
61	F 14	**Campbeltown**, U.K.
45	X 11	**Campeche**, Mexico
45	Y 12	**Campeche**, Mexico ▣
66	L 10	**Campillo de Llerena**, Spain
54	O 12	**Campina Grande**, Brazil
58	I 4	**Campina Verde**, Brazil
55	K 19	**Campinas**, Brazil
58	K 7	**Campinas**, Brazil
129	T 15	**Campo**, Cameroon
58	L 5	**Campo Belo**, Brazil
58	I 10	**Campo Belo do Sul**, Brazil
58	J 4	**Campo Florido**, Brazil
55	M 14	**Campo Formoso**, Brazil
56	K 7	**Campo Gallo**, Argentina
55	H 18	**Campo Grande**, Brazil
58	H 7	**Campo Mourão**, Brazil
58	G 10	**Campo Novo**, Brazil
55	G 15	**Campo Novo de Parecis**, Brazil
51	N 6	**Campo Troco**, Colombia
50	H 8	**Campoalegre**, Colombia
77	J 14	**Campobasso**, Italy
77	H 22	**Campobello di Mazara**, Italy
58	O 6	**Campos**, Brazil
55	K 15	**Campos Belos**, Brazil
58	H 10	**Campos Novos**, Brazil
86	J 11	**Câmpulung**, Romania
39	K 18	**Camrose**, AB, Canada
94	B 8	**Can**, Turkey
115	M 23	**Cân Tho**, Vietnam
37	O 11	**Canada**, North America □
143	O 4	**Canada Basin**, Arctic Ocean ◇
26	L 1	**Canadian**, TX, U.S.A.
26	K 2	**Canadian**, TX, U.S.A. ∫
143	P 4	**Canadian Abyssal Plain**, Arctic Ocean ◇
83	K 14	**Çanakkale**, Turkey ▣
94	A 8	**Canakkale**, Turkey
57	G 26	**Canal Ballenero**, Chile ≃
54	I 9	**Canal do Norte**, Brazil ∫
39	I 21	**Canal Flats**, BC, Canada
53	A 18	**Canal Isabela**, Ecuador ≃
57	E 22	**Canal Ladrillero**, Chile ≃
57	F 19	**Canal Moraleda**, Chile ≃
139	P 14	**Canala**, New Caledonia
56	I 13	**Canalejas**, Argentina
44	J 3	**Cananea**, Mexico
58	K 8	**Cananéia**, Brazil
52	B 10	**Cañar**, Ecuador
52	B 10	**Cañar**, Ecuador ▣
10	L 7	**Canary Islands**, Spain ▣
47	P 12	**Cañas**, Costa Rica
45	N 8	**Canatlán**, Mexico
66	K 7	**Cañaveral**, Spain
55	N 16	**Canavieiras**, Brazil
47	U 14	**Cañazas**, Panama
76	G 5	**Canazei**, Italy
135	U 12	**Canberra**, ACT, Australia ♜
23	P 8	**Canby**, MN, U.S.A.
33	H 15	**Canby**, CA, U.S.A.
45	Z 10	**Cancún**, Mexico
46	J 6	**Candelaria**, Honduras
58	E 10	**Candelaria**, Argentina
94	I 9	**Candir**, Turkey
35	N 6	**Candle**, AK, U.S.A.
22	L 2	**Cando**, ND, U.S.A.
120	F 7	**Candon**, Philippines
120	F 7	**Candon Point**, Philippines ▶
59	E 15	**Canelones**, Uruguay
59	F 16	**Canelones**, Uruguay ▣
57	E 15	**Cañete**, Chile
67	R 7	**Cañete**, Spain
53	E 17	**Cangallo**, Peru
132	J 5	**Cangamba**, Angola
132	H 3	**Cangandala**, Angola
66	K 1	**Cangas del Narcea**, Spain
132	J 5	**Cangombe**, Angola
58	G 13	**Canguçu**, Brazil
132	J 4	**Cangumbe**, Angola
113	S 12	**Cangwu**, China
112	J 12	**Cangyuan**, China
111	E 18	**Cangzhou**, China
41	S 8	**Caniapiscau**, QC, Canada ∫
77	J 23	**Canicatti**, Italy
94	K 7	**Canik Dağlari**, Turkey ▲▲
54	N 11	**Canindé**, Brazil
121	G 16	**Canipo**, Philippines ♣
144	K 9	**Canisteo Peninsula**, Antarctica ▶
94	I 8	**Cankiri**, Turkey
135	U 13	**Cann River**, VIC, Australia
60	E 11	**Canna**, U.K. ♣
105	D 22	**Cannanore**, India
105	B 23	**Cannanore Islands**, India ♣
65	W 14	**Cannes**, France
63	R 6	**Cannock**, U.K.
32	F 9	**Cannon Beach**, OR, U.S.A.
22	I 6	**Cannonball**, ND, U.S.A. ∫
51	N 8	**Caño Colorado**, Colombia
58	H 12	**Canoas**, Brazil
58	I 10	**Canoas**, Brazil ∫
58	I 9	**Canoinhas**, Brazil
31	R 5	**Canon City**, CO, U.S.A.
49	Y 12	**Canouan**, St Vincent and the Grenadines ♣
43	Y 9	**Canso**, NS, Canada
53	D 16	**Canta**, Peru
67	O 1	**Cantabria**, Spain ▣
54	F 11	**Cantagalo**, Brazil
43	R 9	**Canterbury**, NB, Canada
63	Y 11	**Canterbury**, U.K.
137	G 20	**Canterbury**, New Zealand ▣
137	H 21	**Canterbury Bight**, New Zealand ≃
137	G 20	**Canterbury Plains**, New Zealand ◇
121	N 19	**Cantilan**, Philippines
66	L 12	**Cantillana**, Spain
54	M 13	**Canto do Buriti**, Brazil
14	F 11	**Canton**, PA, U.S.A.
14	H 5	**Canton**, NY, U.S.A.
18	L 4	**Canton**, MS, U.S.A.
19	S 2	**Canton**, GA, U.S.A.
21	E 18	**Canton**, IL, U.S.A.
21	O 17	**Canton**, OH, U.S.A.
35	R 8	**Cantwell**, AK, U.S.A.
59	D 16	**Cañuelas**, Argentina
54	F 11	**Canumã**, Brazil
54	D 12	**Canutama**, Brazil
63	X 10	**Canvey Island**, U.K.
26	J 3	**Canyon**, TX, U.S.A.
29	R 9	**Canyon**, WY, U.S.A.
29	Q 6	**Canyon Ferry Lake**, MT, U.S.A. ⬊
32	F 13	**Canyonville**, OR, U.S.A.
114	M 10	**Cao Băng**, Vietnam
112	J 10	**Caojian**, China
132	H 2	**Caombo**, Angola
113	V 3	**Caoxian**, China
121	F 24	**Cap**, Philippines ♣
124	B 13	**Cap Barbas**, Western Sahara ▶
128	E 11	**Cap Boffa**, Guinea ▶
125	R 5	**Cap Bon**, Tunisia ▶
125	O 5	**Cap Bougaroûn**, Algeria ▶
125	O 5	**Cap de Fer**, Algeria ▶
67	Y 7	**Cap de Formentor**, Spain ▶
64	K 2	**Cap de la Hague**, France ▶
42	M 9	**Cap-de-la-Madeleine**, QC, Canada
67	Y 8	**Cap de ses Salines**, Spain ▶
67	Z 7	**Cap des Freu**, Spain ▶
124	E 10	**Cap Draâ**, Morocco ▶
64	K 4	**Cap Fréhel**, France ▶
43	U 5	**Cap Gaspé**, QC, Canada ▶
49	P 6	**Cap-Haïtien**, Haiti
41	R 5	**Cap Hopes Advance**, QC, Canada ▶
124	D 10	**Cap Juby**, Morocco ▶
130	D 8	**Cap Lopez**, Gabon ▶
124	F 8	**Cap Rhir**, Morocco ▶
26	J 6	**Cap Rock Escarpment**, TX, U.S.A. ▲▲
128	E 11	**Cap Verga**, Guinea ▶
128	D 8	**Cap Vert**, Senegal ▶
41	P 4	**Cap Wolstenholme**, QC, Canada ▶
132	J 2	**Capaia**, Angola
58	G 9	**Capanema**, Brazil
58	J 7	**Capão Bonito**, Brazil
120	F 10	**Capas**, Philippines
145	Q 14	**Cape Adare**, Antarctica ▶
132	K 15	**Cape Agulhas**, Republic of South Africa ▶
15	O 9	**Cape Ann**, MA, U.S.A. ▶
94	J 15	**Cape Apostolos Andreas**, Cyprus ▶
94	G 15	**Cape Arnaoutis**, Cyprus ▶
135	P 1	**Cape Arnhem**, NT, Australia ▶
38	F 7	**Cape Baring**, NT, Canada ▶
135	T 14	**Cape Barren Island**, TAS, Australia ♣
136	L 7	**Cape Barrier**, New Zealand ▶
38	D 7	**Cape Bathurst**, NT, Canada ▶
41	X 8	**Cape Bauld**, NL, Canada ▶
32	E 13	**Cape Blanco**, OR, U.S.A. ▶
120	F 5	**Cape Bojeador**, Philippines ▶
43	Y 8	**Cape Breton Island**, NS, Canada ♣
136	J 5	**Cape Brett**, New Zealand ▶
121	B 20	**Cape Buliluyan**, Philippines ▶
144	L 12	**Cape Burks**, Antarctica ▶
135	W 9	**Cape Byron**, NSW, Australia ▶
120	F 13	**Cape Calavite**, Philippines ▶
137	J 17	**Cape Campbell**, New Zealand ▶
19	X 10	**Cape Canaveral**, FL, U.S.A.
19	Y 10	**Cape Canaveral**, FL, U.S.A. ▶
43	Y 9	**Cape Canso**, NS, Canada ▶
42	A 7	**Cape Cargantua**, ON, Canada ▶
135	O 12	**Cape Catastrophe**, SA, Australia ▶
17	W 6	**Cape Charles**, VA, U.S.A.
17	W 6	**Cape Charles**, VA, U.S.A. ▶
145	R 14	**Cape Cheetham**, Antarctica ▶
142	L 12	**Cape Chidley**, Arctic Ocean ▶
105	G 19	**Cape Chirala**, India ▶
40	L 6	**Cape Churchill**, MB, Canada ▶
61	B 21	**Cape Clear**, Republic of Ireland ▶
128	M 14	**Cape Coast**, Ghana
15	P 10	**Cape Cod**, MA, U.S.A. ▶
15	P 10	**Cape Cod Bay**, MA, U.S.A. ≃
143	Q 9	**Cape Columbia**, Arctic Ocean ▶
132	J 14	**Cape Columbine**, Republic of South Africa ▶
136	L 7	**Cape Colville**, New Zealand ▶
105	E 24	**Cape Comorin**, India ▶
39	D 21	**Cape Cook**, BC, Canada ▶
19	W 12	**Cape Coral**, FL, U.S.A.
62	I 15	**Cape Cornwall**, U.K. ▶
135	O 3	**Cape Crawford**, NT, Australia
138	E 5	**Cape Cretin**, Papua New Guinea ▶
38	D 7	**Cape Dalhousie**, NT, Canada ▶
145	X 5	**Cape Darnley**, Antarctica ▶
144	K 5	**Cape Deacon**, Antarctica ▶
132	I 12	**Cape Dernberg**, Namibia ▶
32	F 8	**Cape Disappointment**, WA, U.S.A. ▶
57	L 23	**Cape Dolphin**, Falkland Islands ▶
37	R 7	**Cape Dorchester**, NU, Canada ▶
41	P 3	**Cape Dorset**, NU, Canada
41	T 1	**Cape Dyer**, NU, Canada ▶
15	P 7	**Cape Elizabeth**, ME, U.S.A. ▶
120	H 9	**Cape Encanto**, Philippines ▶
137	H 15	**Cape Farewell**, New Zealand ▶
17	T 12	**Cape Fear**, NC, U.S.A. ▶
144	K 5	**Cape Fiske**, Antarctica ▶
32	F 5	**Cape Flattery**, WA, U.S.A. ▶
135	T 2	**Cape Flattery**, QLD, Australia ▶
134	L 2	**Cape Ford**, NT, Australia ▶
137	F 17	**Cape Foulwind**, New Zealand ▶
145	T 14	**Cape Freshfield**, Antarctica ▶
132	F 7	**Cape Fria**, Namibia ▶
94	H 15	**Cape Gata**, Cyprus ▶
43	X 9	**Cape George**, NS, Canada
25	Z 6	**Cape Girardeau**, MO, U.S.A.
138	C 3	**Cape Girgir**, Papua New Guinea ▶
145	X 13	**Cape Goodenough**, Antarctica ▶
145	U 14	**Cape Gray**, Antarctica ▶
94	I 15	**Cape Greko**, Cyprus ▶
135	S 1	**Cape Grenville**, QLD, Australia ▶
138	I 4	**Cape Hanpan**, Papua New Guinea ▶
17	X 10	**Cape Hatteras**, NC, U.S.A. ▶
41	O 8	**Cape Henrietta Maria**, ON, Canada ▶
17	W 7	**Cape Henry**, VA, U.S.A. ▶
57	I 26	**Cape Horn**, Chile ▶
135	U 13	**Cape Howe**, NSW, Australia ▶

□ Country ▣ Internal administrative region: State/Province/Territory/Dependent territory ♜ Capital city ▲▲ Mountain range/Undersea ridge ▲ Mountain peak/Volcano/Seamount ◇ Geographic feature ▶ Headland/Point/Cape/Peninsula ◭ Desert ♣ Island/Island group ⁂ Antarctic base ∿ Ocean ≈ Sea ≃ Bay/Gulf/Channel/Strait ⬊ Lake ⊏ Salt pan/Dry/Intermittent lake ∫ Ri

T 15 Cape Hudson, Antarctica ▶
C 10 Cape Hurd, ON, Canada ▶
Q 13 Cape Jaffa, SA, Australia ▶
I 4 Cape Karikari, New Zealand ▶
W 14 Cape Keltie, Antarctica ▶
N 13 Cape Kidnappers, New Zealand ▶
B 18 Cape Knox, BC, Canada ▶
H 15 Cape Kormakitis, Cyprus ▶
T 5 Cape Labrador, NL, Canada ▶
G 12 Cape Leeuwin, WA, Australia ▶
I 3 Cape Leveque, WA, Australia ▶
V 11 Cape Lookout, NC, U.S.A. ▶
K 5 Cape Mackintosh, Antarctica ▶
H 4 Cape Maria van Diemen, New Zealand ▶
I 15 Cape May, NJ, U.S.A. ▶
I 15 Cape May, NJ, U.S.A.
A 21 Cape Melville, Philippines ▶
S 2 Cape Melville, QLD, Australia ▶
E 16 Cape Mendocino, CA, U.S.A. ▶
T 2 Cape Mercy, NU, Canada ▶
K 24 Cape Meredith, Falkland Islands ▶
K 9 Cape Mohican, AK, U.S.A. ▶
F 6 Cape Nelson, Papua New Guinea ▶
M 11 Cape Newenham, AK, U.S.A. ▶
M 7 Cape Nome, AK, U.S.A. ▶
Y 7 Cape North, NS, Canada ▶
O 2 Cape Norvegia, Antarctica ▶
J 15 Cape of Good Hope, Republic of South Africa ▶
R 14 Cape Otway, VIC, Australia ▶
L 17 Cape Palliser, New Zealand ▶
I 14 Cape Palmas, Côte d'Ivoire ▶
E 7 Cape Parry, NT, Canada ▶
J 11 Cape Pasley, WA, Australia ▶
Y 11 Cape Poinsett, Antarctica ▶
L 4 Cape Prince Alfred, NT, Canada ▶
A 25 Cape Providence, New Zealand ▶
N 15 Cape Recife, Republic of South Africa ▶
H 4 Cape Reinga, New Zealand ▶
R 14 Cape Romain, SC, U.S.A. ▶
W 13 Cape Romano, FL, U.S.A. ▶
O 10 Cape Runaway, New Zealand ▶
X 14 Cape Sable, FL, U.S.A. ▶
T 13 Cape Sable Island, NS, Canada ▶
N 13 Cape Saint Paul, Ghana ▶
N 23 Cape San Agustin, Philippines ▶
D 21 Cape Scott, BC, Canada ▶
M 15 Cape Seal, Republic of South Africa ▶
O 1 Cape Shield, NT, Australia ▶
F 2 Cape Siemens, Papua New Guinea ▶
I 8 Cape Siri, Papua New Guinea ▶
N 4 Cape Southampton, NU, Canada ▶
P 12 Cape Spencer, SA, Australia ▶
H 4 Cape St George, Papua New Guinea ▶
J 15 Cape Stephens, New Zealand ▶
L 7 Cape Tatnam, MB, Canada ▶
J 16 Cape Terawhiti, New Zealand ▶
L 14 Cape Three Points, Ghana ▶
J 15 Cape Town, Republic of South Africa ▙
M 15 Cape Turnagain, New Zealand ▶
U 6 Cape Uivak, NL, Canada ▶
K 8 Cape Verde, Atlantic Ocean ◘
X 12 Cape Waldron, Antarctica ▶
E 6 Cape Ward Hunt, Papua New Guinea ▶
O 1 Cape Wessel, NT, Australia ▶
O 2 Cape Wilson, NU, Canada ▶
G 8 Cape Wrath, U.K. ▶
R 1 Cape York, QLD, Australia ▶
R 1 Cape York Peninsula, QLD, Australia ▶
M 16 Capelinha, Brazil
U 6 Capella, QLD, Australia
G 13 Capelle aan den IJssel, Netherlands
L 25 Capellen, Luxembourg
I 2 Capenda-Camulemba, Angola
I 13 Capestrano, Italy
R 12 Capitan Peak, NM, U.S.A. ▲
G 17 Capnoyan, Philippines 🏝
A 16 Capo Caccia, Italy ▶
C 19 Capo Carbonara, Italy ▶
N 19 Capo Colonna, Italy ▶
D 16 Capo Comino, Italy ▶
B 15 Capo del Falcone, Italy ▶
B 18 Capo della Frasca, Italy ▶
K 24 Capo delle Correnti, Italy ▶
K 21 Capo di Milazzo, Italy ▶
D 17 Capo di Monte Santu, Italy ▶
K 21 Capo d'Orlando, Italy ▶
I 21 Capo Gallo, Italy ▶
L 23 Capo Murro di Porco, Italy ▶
L 17 Capo Palinuro, Italy ▶
N 20 Capo Rizzuto, Italy ▶
H 21 Capo San Vito, Italy ▶
O 18 Capo Santa Maria di Leuca, Italy ▶
J 24 Capo Scaramia, Italy ▶
B 20 Capo Spartivento, Italy ▶
N 17 Capo Spulico, Italy ▶
N 18 Capo Trionto, Italy ▶
L 20 Capo Vaticano, Italy ▶
G 3 Capolo, Angola
J 11 Cappadocia, Turkey ◇
J 16 Capri, Italy
L 7 Caprivi, Namibia ◘
K 7 Caprivi Strip, Namibia ◇
D 9 Captain Cook, HI, U.S.A.
I 9 Caquetá, Colombia ◘
J 10 Caquetá, Colombia ∫
N 23 Car Nicobar, India 🏝
H 15 Carabao, Philippines 🏝
N 3 Carabobo, Venezuela ◘
S 5 Carabobo, Venezuela
I 13 Caracal, Romania
E 8 Caracaraí, Brazil
O 2 Caracas, Venezuela ▙
L 13 Caracol, Brazil
I 20 Caracollo, Bolivia
N 22 Caraga, Philippines
F 15 Carahue, Chile
J 12 Caramoan Peninsula, Philippines ▶
M 5 Carandaí, Brazil
G 11 Caransebeș, Romania
T 7 Caraquet, NB, Canada
A 9 Caráquez, Ecuador
Q 5 Caratasca, Honduras
R 14 Carate, Costa Rica
C 11 Carauari, Brazil
R 11 Caravaca de la Cruz, Spain
N 17 Caravelas, Brazil
G 11 Carazinho, Brazil
H 1 Carballo, Spain
H 11 Carbondale, PA, U.S.A.
F 22 Carbondale, IL, U.S.A.
P 4 Carbondale, CO, U.S.A.
67 R 13 Carboneras, Spain
67 R 7 Carboneras de Guadazaón, Spain
59 B 15 Carcaraña, Argentina ∫
65 Q 14 Carcassonne, France
52 B 8 Carchi, Ecuador ◘
105 E 22 Cardamom Hills, India ⛰
45 T 12 Cardel, Mexico
67 N 10 Cárdena, Spain
45 V 13 Cárdenas, Mexico
48 H 4 Cárdenas, Cuba
63 O 11 Cardiff, U.K.
62 K 8 Cardigan, U.K.
62 L 7 Cardigan Bay, U.K. ≈
115 J 21 Cardomom Range, Cambodia ⛰
59 E 15 Cardona, Uruguay
137 D 23 Cardrona, New Zealand
39 K 21 Cardston, AB, Canada
135 T 4 Cardwell, QLD, Australia
86 G 7 Carei, Romania
64 L 3 Carentan, France
28 M 11 Carey, ID, U.S.A.
64 I 5 Carhaix-Plouguer, France
58 O 5 Cariacica, Brazil
51 Q 2 Cariaco, Venezuela
52 B 11 Cariamanga, Ecuador
77 N 18 Cariati, Italy
48 I 13 Caribbean Sea, North America ◒
15 R 1 Caribou, ME, U.S.A.
39 H 15 Caribou Mountains, AB, Canada ⛰
121 L 16 Carigara, Philippines
67 S 5 Cariñena, Spain
55 L 15 Carinhanha, Brazil
51 R 3 Caripito, Venezuela
42 I 11 Carleton Place, ON, Canada
133 N 11 Carletonville, Republic of South Africa
33 M 16 Carlin, NV, U.S.A.
21 E 20 Carlinville, IL, U.S.A.
14 F 13 Carlisle, PA, U.S.A.
61 I 15 Carlisle, U.K.
77 B 19 Carloforte, Italy
59 B 16 Carlos Casares, Argentina
61 E 19 Carlow, Republic of Ireland
31 T 14 Carlsbad, NM, U.S.A.
39 O 19 Carlyle, SK, Canada
21 F 21 Carlyle Lake, IL, U.S.A. ◡
38 B 13 Carmacks, YT, Canada
62 L 9 Carmarthen, U.K.
62 L 10 Carmarthen Bay, U.K. ≈
65 P 13 Carmaux, France
62 L 3 Carmel Head, U.K. ▶
46 I 2 Carmelita, Guatemala
59 D 15 Carmelo, Uruguay
30 K 15 Carmen, AZ, U.S.A.
50 I 3 Carmen, Colombia
56 G 7 Carmen, Chile
56 G 5 Carmen Alto, Chile
59 B 20 Carmen de Patagones, Argentina
56 H 13 Carmensa, Argentina
21 G 22 Carmi, IL, U.S.A.
47 O 12 Carmona, Costa Rica
66 L 12 Carmona, Spain
60 G 10 Carn Eighe, U.K. ▲
134 G 10 Carnamah, WA, Australia
132 L 13 Carnarvon, Republic of South Africa
134 E 8 Carnarvon, WA, Australia
144 K 11 Carney Island, Antarctica 🏝
63 P 1 Carnforth, U.K.
130 H 4 Carnot, Central African Republic
60 I 12 Carnoustie, U.K.
61 F 20 Carnsore Point, Republic of Ireland ▶
19 Y 13 Carol City, FL, U.S.A.
54 K 12 Carolina, Brazil
140 L 15 Caroline Islands, Federated States of Micronesia 🏝
77 J 21 Caronia, Italy
79 J 18 Carpathian Mountains, Europe ⛰
65 T 13 Carpentras, France
76 F 8 Carpi, Italy
33 I 24 Carpinteria, CA, U.S.A.
19 S 8 Carrabelle, FL, U.S.A.
76 D 9 Carrara, Italy
67 P 7 Carrascosa del Campo, Spain
61 A 20 Carrauntuohil, Republic of Ireland ▲
49 Y 12 Carriacou, Grenada 🏝
45 N 6 Carrillo, Mexico
22 L 4 Carrington, ND, U.S.A.
56 F 8 Carrizal Bajo, Chile
26 M 12 Carrizo Springs, TX, U.S.A.
31 R 12 Carrizozo, NM, U.S.A.
23 R 12 Carroll, IA, U.S.A.
19 S 3 Carrollton, GA, U.S.A.
94 L 8 Çarşamba, Turkey
76 I 13 Carsoli, Italy
33 I 18 Carson City, NV, U.S.A.
50 H 2 Cartagena, Colombia
67 S 12 Cartagena, Spain
47 Q 12 Cartago, Costa Rica
50 H 6 Cartago, Colombia
16 G 8 Carthage, TN, U.S.A.
18 M 4 Carthage, MS, U.S.A.
27 T 6 Carthage, TX, U.S.A.
47 X 13 Carti Suitupo, Panama
40 H 10 Cartwright, MB, Canada
41 W 8 Cartwright, NL, Canada
54 O 13 Caruarú, Brazil
51 Q 2 Carúpano, Venezuela
121 D 17 Caruray, Philippines
54 K 10 Carutapera, Brazil
33 K 18 Carvers, NV, U.S.A.
58 K 6 Casa Branca, Brazil
30 J 13 Casa Grande, AZ, U.S.A.
124 H 7 Casablanca, Morocco
77 K 14 Casacalenda, Italy
76 B 7 Casale, Italy
50 K 6 Casanare, Colombia ◘
47 N 10 Casares, Nicaragua
44 L 3 Casas Grandes, Mexico
67 R 9 Casas Ibáñez, Spain
58 H 11 Casca, Brazil
28 K 9 Cascade, ID, U.S.A.
137 C 21 Cascade Point, New Zealand ▶
32 G 13 Cascade Range, Canada/U.S.A. ⛰
28 K 9 Cascade Reservoir, ID, U.S.A. ◡
54 N 11 Cascavel, Brazil
58 G 8 Cascavel, Brazil
15 P 7 Casco Bay, ME, U.S.A. ≈
77 J 15 Caserta, Italy
20 L 13 Caseville, MI, U.S.A.
21 G 20 Casey, IL, U.S.A.
145 Y 11 Casey, Antarctica ⁙
120 I 9 Casiguran, Philippines
120 H 9 Casiguran Sound, Philippines ≈
59 B 15 Casilda, Argentina
135 W 9 Casino, NSW, Australia
53 B 15 Casma, Peru
67 T 5 Caspe, Spain
29 W 12 Casper, WY, U.S.A.
102 G 6 Caspian Depression, Kazakhstan/Russian Federation ◇
93 S 14 Caspian Sea, Asia/Europe ◒
20 M 13 Cass City, MI, U.S.A.
133 Q 5 Cassacatiza, Mozambique
132 J 4 Cassamba, Angola
39 D 15 Cassiar, BC, Canada
39 C 14 Cassiar Mountains, YT, Canada ⛰
55 I 17 Cassilândia, Brazil
132 H 5 Cassinga, Angola
77 I 15 Cassino, Italy
132 H 4 Cassongue, Angola
108 M 2 Cast Uul, Mongolia ▲
76 D 11 Castagneto Carducci, Italy
54 F 12 Castanha, Brazil
54 K 10 Castanhal, Brazil
56 G 10 Castaño, Argentina
74 I 10 Castasegna, Switzerland
76 C 8 Casteggio, Italy
66 J 7 Castel Branco, Portugal ◘
77 J 14 Castél di Sangro, Italy
65 V 13 Castellane, France
56 L 7 Castelli, Argentina
59 D 17 Castelli, Argentina
67 U 7 Castelló de la Plana, Spain
65 P 14 Castelnaudary, France
76 E 9 Castelnovo ne' Monti, Italy
66 I 7 Castelo Branco, Portugal
77 B 16 Castelsardo, Italy
77 I 22 Casteltermini, Italy
77 H 22 Castelvetrano, Italy
135 Q 13 Casterton, VIC, Australia
76 E 12 Castiglione della Pescaia, Italy
56 F 8 Castilla, Chile
67 Q 8 Castilla-La Mancha, Spain ◘
66 K 4 Castilla Y Leōn, Spain ◘
59 G 15 Castillos, Uruguay
63 P 12 Castle Cary, U.K.
30 L 5 Castle Dale, UT, U.S.A.
30 H 13 Castle Dome Peak, AZ, U.S.A. ▲
63 S 6 Castle Donnington, U.K.
61 H 15 Castle Douglas, U.K.
28 M 10 Castle Peak, ID, U.S.A. ▲
31 R 4 Castle Rock, CO, U.S.A.
61 B 17 Castlebar, Republic of Ireland
63 T 2 Castleford, U.K.
39 I 21 Castlegar, BC, Canada
65 Q 14 Castres, France
49 Z 11 Castries, St Lucia ▙
57 F 18 Castro, Chile
58 I 8 Castro, Brazil
66 I 5 Castro Daire, Portugal
66 H 11 Castro Verde, Portugal
66 J 1 Castropol, Spain
77 M 18 Castrovillari, Italy
66 L 9 Castuera, Spain
137 A 23 Caswell Sound, New Zealand ≈
95 Q 9 Cat, Turkey
48 L 3 Cat Island, The Bahamas 🏝
40 K 10 Cat Lake, ON, Canada ◡
47 N 5 Catacamas, Honduras
18 J 6 Catahoula Lake, LA, U.S.A. ◡
95 S 12 Çatak, Turkey
55 J 17 Catalão, Brazil
82 O 12 Çatalca, Turkey
67 W 4 Cataluña, Spain ◘
94 J 6 Catalzeytin, Turkey
56 I 8 Catamarca, Argentina
56 H 7 Catamarca, Argentina ◘
57 G 16 Catán Lil, Argentina
133 Q 7 Catandica, Mozambique
120 L 12 Catanduanes, Philippines 🏝
77 K 22 Catania, Italy
77 M 20 Catanzaro, Italy
27 N 12 Catarina, TX, U.S.A.
121 L 14 Catarman, Philippines
133 Q 6 Cataxa, Mozambique
121 L 15 Catbalogan, Philippines
121 N 21 Cateel, Philippines
128 E 10 Catió, Guinea-Bissau
137 D 25 Catlins, New Zealand ⛰
45 Q 8 Catorce, Mexico
57 H 15 Catriel, Argentina
56 J 13 Catriló, Argentina
14 K 10 Catskill, NY, U.S.A.
14 I 10 Catskill Mountains, NY, U.S.A. ⛰
120 H 8 Cauayan, Philippines
121 I 18 Cauayan, Philippines
50 G 8 Cauca, Colombia ◘
50 I 4 Cauca, Colombia ∫
50 H 4 Caucasia, Colombia
92 L 13 Caucasus, Russian Federation ⛰
95 Q 5 Caucasus, Georgia ⛰
56 H 10 Caucete, Argentina
121 N 19 Cauit Point, Philippines ▶
132 I 2 Caungula, Angola
56 F 13 Cauquenes, Chile
51 Q 6 Caura, Venezuela ∫
43 R 6 Causapscal, QC, Canada
23 N 2 Cavalier, ND, U.S.A.
136 J 5 Cavalli Islands, New Zealand 🏝
128 I 13 Cavally, Liberia ∫
61 D 16 Cavan, Republic of Ireland
94 E 13 Cavdir, Turkey
137 F 21 Cave, New Zealand
16 K 5 Cave Run Lake, KY, U.S.A. ◡
121 G 19 Cavili, Philippines 🏝
120 G 11 Cavite, Philippines
54 L 11 Caxias, Brazil
58 H 11 Caxias do Sul, Brazil
132 G 2 Caxito, Angola
94 F 11 Çay, Turkey
48 I 3 Cay Sal, The Bahamas 🏝
52 C 8 Cayambe, Ecuador ▲
95 P 8 Cayeli, Turkey
51 Z 6 Cayenne, French Guiana ▙
94 G 9 Cayirhan, Turkey
48 I 7 Cayman Brac, Cayman Islands 🏝
48 I 7 Cayman Islands, U.K. ◘
48 H 8 Cayman Trench, Cayman Islands ≈
127 M 20 Caynabo, Somalia
48 G 5 Cayo del Rosario, Cuba 🏝
48 H 5 Cayo Largo, Cuba 🏝
48 K 4 Cayo Romano, Cuba 🏝
48 K 5 Cayo Sabinal, Cuba 🏝
47 S 6 Cayos Miskitos, Nicaragua 🏝
86 L 12 Căzănești, Romania
65 O 14 Cazères, France
132 L 4 Cazombo, Angola
133 R 5 Cazula, Mozambique
54 N 12 Ceará, Brazil ◘
45 N 6 Ceballos, Mexico
67 P 4 Cebollera, Spain ▲
121 K 18 Cebu, Philippines
121 K 17 Cebu, Philippines 🏝
79 I 24 Cece, Hungary
23 T 11 Cedar, IA, U.S.A. ∫
30 I 7 Cedar City, UT, U.S.A.
23 T 11 Cedar Falls, IA, U.S.A.
25 X 4 Cedar Hill, MO, U.S.A.
17 W 5 Cedar Island, VA, U.S.A. 🏝
19 U 9 Cedar Key, FL, U.S.A.
40 H 8 Cedar Lake, MB, Canada ◡
23 U 12 Cedar Rapids, IA, U.S.A.
19 S 2 Cedartown, GA, U.S.A.
46 L 8 Cedeño, Honduras
135 N 10 Ceduna, SA, Australia
78 D 11 Cedynia, Poland
66 G 1 Cée, Spain
127 O 19 Ceel Gaal, Somalia
127 N 19 Ceerigaabo, Somalia
77 J 21 Cefalù, Italy
79 J 23 Cegléd, Hungary
113 O 11 Ceheng, China
94 K 9 Cekerek, Turkey
45 Q 11 Celaya, Mexico
117 P 8 Celebes Sea, Asia ◒
45 X 10 Celestún, Mexico
16 H 8 Celina, TN, U.S.A.
21 K 18 Celina, OH, U.S.A.
80 D 7 Celje, Slovenia
72 H 13 Celle, Germany
69 D 20 Celles, Belgium
95 T 11 Çelo Daglari, Turkey ▲
61 D 21 Celtic Sea, Republic of Ireland ◒
16 G 9 Center Hill Lake, TN, U.S.A. ◡
19 P 4 Centerville, AL, U.S.A.
23 T 14 Centerville, IA, U.S.A.
25 X 6 Centerville, MO, U.S.A.
27 R 8 Centerville, TX, U.S.A.
76 F 8 Cento, Italy
105 G 24 Central, Sri Lanka ◘
107 P 9 Central, Nepal ◘
128 M 14 Central, Ghana ◘
131 V 8 Central, Kenya ◘
133 N 5 Central, Zambia ◘
133 N 9 Central, Botswana ◘
133 Q 4 Central, Malawi ◘
138 E 7 Central, Papua New Guinea ◘
138 L 6 Central, Solomon Islands ◘
138 M 8 Central, Solomon Islands ◘
130 H 4 Central African Republic, Africa ◘
74 E 9 Central Alps, Switzerland ◇
101 T 12 Central Brāhui Range, Pakistan ⛰
16 F 6 Central City, KY, U.S.A.
84 H 11 Central Highlands of Vidzemes, Latvia ⛰
141 Q 5 Central Line Islands, Kiribati 🏝
101 Q 13 Central Makran Range, Pakistan ⛰
74 D 7 Central Plateau, Switzerland ◇
138 A 4 Central Range, Papua New Guinea ⛰
89 Q 9 Central Siberian Plateau, Russian Federation ◇
33 H 16 Central Valley, CA, U.S.A. ◇
57 F 14 Central Valley, Chile ◇
21 F 21 Centralia, IL, U.S.A.
32 G 8 Centralia, WA, U.S.A.
65 P 7 Centre, France ◘
129 U 13 Centre, Cameroon ◘
137 B 25 Centre Island, New Zealand 🏝
113 R 12 Cenxi, China
80 I 8 Čepin, Croatia
77 I 14 Ceprano, Italy
56 K 9 Ceres, Argentina
77 L 15 Cerignola, Italy
94 I 9 Cerikli, Turkey
94 H 8 Cerkeș, Turkey
82 N 12 Cerkezköy, Turkey
80 B 8 Cerknica, Slovenia
95 O 12 Cermik, Turkey
87 N 12 Cerna, Romania
86 M 13 Cernavodă, Romania
45 Q 7 Cerralvo, Mexico
81 K 19 Cërrik, Albania
45 Q 10 Cerritos, Mexico
56 G 11 Cerro Amarillo, Argentina ▲
57 F 21 Cerro Arenales, Chile ▲
53 A 19 Cerro Azol, Ecuador ▲
45 S 10 Cerro Azul, Mexico
58 J 8 Cerro Azul, Brazil
53 J 23 Cerro Bonete, Bolivia ▲
56 G 8 Cerro Bonete, Argentina ▲
59 F 15 Cerro Catedral, Uruguay ▲
57 F 23 Cerro Cervantes, Argentina ▲
56 J 11 Cerro Champaqui, Argentina ▲
47 R 13 Cerro Chirripó Grande, Costa Rica ▲
57 H 20 Cerro Cojudo Blanco, Argentina ▲
44 F 2 Cerro de La Encantada, Mexico ▲
56 G 10 Cerro de Olivares, Chile ▲
53 D 15 Cerro de Pasco, Peru
56 G 8 Cerro de Petro, Chile ▲
49 U 8 Cerro de Punta, Puerto Rico ▲
56 H 6 Cerro del Rincón, Argentina ▲
45 R 9 Cerro del Tigre, Mexico ▲
51 P 7 Cerro Duida, Venezuela ▲
50 I 7 Cerro El Nevado, Colombia ▲
44 H 6 Cerro Encantado, Mexico ▲
57 F 22 Cerro Fitz Roy, Argentina ▲
56 H 7 Cerro Galán, Argentina ▲
51 Q 6 Cerro Guaiquinima, Venezuela ▲
57 F 20 Cerro Hudson, Chile ▲
44 L 8 Cerro Huehueto, Mexico ▲
58 F 13 Cerro Largo, Uruguay ◘
46 K 6 Cerro Las Minas, Honduras ▲
56 F 9 Cerro Las Tórtolas, Chile ▲
57 F 22 Cerro Lautaro, Chile ▲
51 O 7 Cerro Marahuaca, Venezuela ▲
57 F 21 Cerro Mellizo Sur, Chile ▲
53 I 22 Cerro Milliri, Bolivia/Chile ▲
57 F 22 Cerro Murallón, Chile ▲
56 H 13 Cerro Nevado, Argentina ▲
51 O 7 Cerro Ovana, Venezuela ▲
57 F 23 Cerro Paine, Chile ▲
51 O 6 Cerro Paraque, Venezuela ▲
57 H 14 Cerro Payún, Argentina ▲
45 R 8 Cerro Peña Nevada, Mexico ▲
56 H 6 Cerro Pular, Chile ▲
47 S 13 Cerro Punta, Panama
57 F 21 Cerro San Lorenzo, Argentina ▲
55 G 20 Cerro San Rafael, Paraguay ▲
57 F 20 Cerro San Valentín, Chile ▲
47 O 7 Cerro Saslaya, Nicaragua ▲
44 J 5 Cerro Seberi, Mexico ▲
45 U 12 Cerro Sta Martha, Mexico ▲
45 O 12 Cerro Tancitaro, Mexico ▲
59 B 19 Cerro Tres Picos, Argentina ▲
56 G 12 Cerro Tupungato, Argentina ▲
44 H 3 Cerro Viejo, Mexico ▲
53 C 15 Cerro Yerupaja, Peru ▲
76 F 11 Certaldo, Italy
67 V 4 Cervera, Spain
76 H 9 Cervia, Italy
66 J 1 Cervo, Spain
50 J 3 Cesar, Colombia ◘
76 G 9 Cesena, Italy
84 G 10 Cēsis, Latvia
79 D 16 Česká Lípa, Czech Republic
79 F 17 Česká Třebová, Czech Republic
79 C 19 České Budějovice, Czech Republic
79 C 20 Český Krumlov, Czech Republic
80 F 8 Česma, Croatia ∫
94 A 11 Çeşme, Turkey
135 V 11 Cessnock, NSW, Australia
84 H 11 Cesvaine, Latvia
66 L 14 Ceuta, Spain
74 G 10 Cevio, Switzerland
94 K 13 Ceyhan, Turkey
95 P 13 Ceylanpinar, Turkey
101 O 14 Chābahār, Iran
52 C 12 Chachapoyas, Peru
85 N 19 Chachersk, Belarus
56 K 7 Chaco, Argentina ◘
129 W 8 Chad, Africa ◘
17 R 12 Chadbourn, NC, U.S.A.
57 I 14 Chadileo, Argentina ∫
22 H 11 Chadron, NE, U.S.A.
111 K 18 Chaeryŏng, North Korea
101 P 11 Chagai Hills, Pakistan ⛰
103 W 4 Chagan, Kazakhstan
101 R 7 Chaghcharān, Afghanistan
100 I 8 Chahār Mahall Va Bakhtīārī, Iran ◘
105 J 15 Chaibasa, India
115 H 18 Chainat, Thailand
57 F 18 Chaitén, Chile
115 I 17 Chaiyaphum, Thailand
58 D 13 Chajarí, Argentina
105 J 15 Chakradharpur, India
106 J 6 Chakrata, India
53 E 19 Chala, Peru
131 R 12 Chala, Tanzania
65 N 11 Chalais, France
46 J 6 Chalatenango, El Salvador
133 T 6 Chaláua, Mozambique
131 V 6 Chalbi Desert, Kenya ◇
63 T 14 Chale, U.K.
43 S 7 Chaleur Bay, NB, Canada ≈
113 T 9 Chaling, China
83 N 24 Chalki, Greece 🏝
83 G 19 Chalkida, Greece
103 X 9 Chalkudysu, Kazakhstan
64 K 8 Challans, France
53 J 21 Challapata, Bolivia
28 M 9 Challis, ID, U.S.A.
65 T 8 Chalon-sur-Saône, France
65 S 4 Châlons-en-Champagne, France
100 I 5 Chālūs, Iran
73 L 21 Cham, Germany
133 Q 3 Chama, Zambia
101 S 10 Chaman, Pakistan
106 I 5 Chamba, India
131 V 15 Chamba, Tanzania
22 L 10 Chamberlain, SD, U.S.A.
15 Q 2 Chamberlain Lake, ME, U.S.A. ◡
30 M 10 Chambers, AZ, U.S.A.
14 E 14 Chambersburg, PA, U.S.A.
65 V 10 Chambéry, France
133 P 3 Chambeshi, Zambia
97 U 3 Chamchamāl, Iraq
47 W 14 Chame, Panama
46 J 5 Chamelec, Honduras ∫
56 I 10 Chamical, Argentina
106 L 7 Chamoli, India
65 W 9 Chamonix-Mont-Blanc, France
105 H 15 Champa, India
65 T 4 Champagne-Ardenne, France ◘
21 G 18 Champaign, IL, U.S.A.
115 L 18 Champasak, Laos
14 K 5 Champlain, NY, U.S.A.
45 X 12 Champotón, Mexico
105 D 22 Chamrajnagar, India
93 P 2 Chamzinka, Russian Federation
56 F 7 Chañaral, Chile
101 O 5 Chanārān, Iran
56 F 13 Chanco, Chile
106 K 8 Chandausi, India
105 J 16 Chandbali, India
19 N 8 Chandeleur Islands, MS, U.S.A. 🏝
19 N 8 Chandeleur Sound, MS, U.S.A. ≈
104 E 13 Chanderi, India
106 J 6 Chandigarh, India
30 J 13 Chandler, AZ, U.S.A.
43 T 6 Chandler, QC, Canada
107 U 13 Chandpur, Bangladesh
105 F 17 Chandrapur, India
133 Q 6 Changara, Mozambique
111 K 15 Changbai Shan, China ⛰
110 J 13 Changchun, China
113 S 8 Changde, China
113 Z 11 Changhua, Taiwan
111 L 22 Changhŭng, South Korea
118 C 14 Changi, Singapore
108 K 4 Changji, China
113 Q 15 Changjiang, China
111 F 17 Changli, China
110 I 12 Changling, China
113 T 8 Changsha, China
113 X 8 Changshan, China
111 I 17 Changshan Qundao, China 🏝
113 Y 5 Changshu, China
111 J 16 Changsong, North Korea
113 W 10 Changting, China
111 J 14 Changtu, China
47 S 13 Changuinola, Panama
111 N 21 Ch'angwŏn, South Korea
113 Y 6 Changxing, China
111 H 17 Changxing Dao, China 🏝
113 S 6 Changyang, China
111 J 18 Changyŏn, North Korea
113 U 3 Changyuan, China
113 T 2 Changzhi, China
113 Y 5 Changzhou, China
83 H 26 Chania, Greece
33 I 24 Channel Islands, CA, U.S.A. 🏝
61 J 26 Channel Islands, U.K. 🏝
41 X 11 Channel-Port-aux-Basques, NL, Canada
63 Z 12 Channel Tunnel, France/United Kingdom ◇
26 J 2 Channing, TX, U.S.A.
89 Z 6 Chantal'skiy, Russian Federation ▲
115 I 20 Chanthaburi, Thailand
64 L 8 Chantonnay, France
105 N 24 Chanumla, India
25 Q 6 Chanute, KS, U.S.A.
53 B 14 Chao, Peru
113 W 5 Chao Hu, China ◡
115 G 17 Chao Phraya, Thailand ∫
113 W 5 Chaohu, China
110 H 8 Chaor, China
124 I 6 Chaouèn, Morocco
111 G 15 Chaoyang, China
113 W 12 Chaoyang, China
113 W 12 Chaozhou, China
50 H 7 Chaparral, Colombia
102 I 4 Chapayevo, Kazakhstan
93 S 4 Chapayevsk, Russian Federation
103 T 3 Chapayevskoye, Kazakhstan
58 G 10 Chapecó, Brazil
63 R 4 Chapel-en-le-Frith, U.K.
42 B 7 Chapleau, ON, Canada
39 M 19 Chaplin, SK, Canada
92 M 4 Chaplygin, Russian Federation
87 T 10 Chaplynka, Ukraine
16 M 5 Chapmanville, WV, U.S.A.
53 L 22 Charagua, Bolivia
53 H 20 Charana, Bolivia
56 K 8 Charata, Argentina
45 P 9 Charcas, Mexico
144 I 6 Charcot Island, Antarctica 🏝
63 P 13 Chard, U.K.
103 O 13 Chardzhev, Turkmenistan
129 W 10 Chari-Baguirmi, Chad ◘
101 U 7 Chārīkār, Afghanistan
23 T 14 Chariton, IA, U.S.A.
51 U 5 Charity, Guyana
20 L 12 Charity Island, MI, U.S.A. 🏝
106 I 8 Charkhi Dadri, India
69 G 21 Charleroi, Belgium
23 T 11 Charles City, IA, U.S.A.
21 E 15 Charles Mound, IL, U.S.A. ▲
43 N 8 Charlesbourg, QC, Canada
17 Q 15 Charleston, SC, U.S.A.
17 N 4 Charleston, WV, U.S.A.
137 F 17 Charleston, New Zealand
33 M 21 Charleston Peak, NV, U.S.A. ▲
135 T 8 Charleville, QLD, Australia
65 S 3 Charleville-Mézières, France
20 J 10 Charlevoix, MI, U.S.A.
17 O 10 Charlotte, NC, U.S.A.
21 K 14 Charlotte, MI, U.S.A.
49 V 8 Charlotte Amalie, Virgin Islands, U.S.A. ▙
19 W 12 Charlotte Harbor, FL, U.S.A. ≈
17 S 5 Charlottesville, VA, U.S.A.
43 V 8 Charlottetown, PE, Canada
49 Z 13 Charlotteville, Trinidad and Tobago
135 R 12 Charlton, VIC, Australia
37 T 11 Charlton Island, NU, Canada 🏝
65 V 5 Charmes, France
63 P 13 Charmouth, U.K.
101 W 7 Charsadda, Pakistan
103 P 14 Charshanga, Turkmenistan
135 T 5 Charters Towers, QLD, Australia
65 P 5 Chartres, France
103 X 9 Charyn, Kazakhstan
59 D 16 Chascomús, Argentina
85 K 15 Chashniki, Belarus
23 S 8 Chaska, MN, U.S.A.
111 K 15 Chasŏng, North Korea
91 P 9 Chasovo, Russian Federation
35 S 6 Chatanika, AK, U.S.A.
65 S 7 Château-Chinon, France
65 N 6 Château-du-Loir, France
65 R 4 Château-Thierry, France
64 L 6 Châteaubriant, France
65 O 6 Châteaudun, France
42 L 11 Châteauguay, QC, Canada
64 H 5 Châteaulin, France
65 P 8 Châteauroux, France
65 N 8 Châtellerault, France
42 B 14 Chatham, ON, Canada
43 T 8 Chatham, NB, Canada
63 X 11 Chatham, U.K.
35 X 11 Chatham Strait, AK, U.S.A. ≈
65 O 8 Châtillon-sur-Indre, France
65 T 6 Châtillon-sur-Seine, France
107 P 12 Chatra, India
16 H 10 Chattanooga, TN, U.S.A.
19 S 7 Chattaoochee, FL, U.S.A.
63 W 7 Chatteris, U.K.
115 I 17 Chatturat, Thailand
103 V 11 Chatyr-Tash, Kyrgyzstan
115 L 22 Châu Đốc, Vietnam
114 C 12 Chauk, Myanmar
106 L 9 Chauka, India ∫
65 T 5 Chaumont, France
105 G 23 Chavakachcheri, Sri Lanka
90 J 5 Chavan'ga, Russian Federation
54 J 9 Chaves, Brazil
66 J 4 Chaves, Portugal
132 L 4 Chavuma, Zambia
85 N 17 Chavusy, Belarus
91 S 14 Chaykovskiy, Russian Federation
56 J 11 Chazón, Argentina
19 Q 3 Cheaha Mountain, AL, U.S.A. ▲
79 A 17 Cheb, Czech Republic
125 R 6 Chebba, Tunisia
93 R 1 Cheboksary, Russian Federation
20 K 10 Cheboygan, MI, U.S.A.
93 P 13 Chechenskaya Respublika, Russian Federation ◘
111 M 19 Chech'ŏn, South Korea
79 K 16 Chęciny, Poland
25 Q 10 Checotah, OK, U.S.A.
63 P 11 Cheddar, U.K.
115 B 14 Cheduba Island, Myanmar 🏝
34 L 9 Chefornak, AK, U.S.A.
128 K 3 Chegga, Mauritania
32 G 8 Chehalis, WA, U.S.A.
111 L 23 Cheju, South Korea
111 L 23 Cheju-do, South Korea 🏝
90 K 11 Chekshino, Russian Federation
102 I 12 Cheleken, Turkmenistan
57 I 15 Chelforó, Argentina
102 M 7 Chelkar, Kazakhstan
79 O 15 Chełm, Poland
78 I 10 Chełmno, Poland
63 X 10 Chelmsford, U.K.
78 I 11 Chełmża, Poland
63 Q 9 Cheltenham, U.K.

ountry ◘ Internal administrative region: State/Province/Territory/Dependent territory ▙ Capital city ⛰ Mountain range/Undersea ridge ▲ Mountain peak/Volcano/Seamount ◇ Geographic feature ▶ Headland/Point/Cape/Peninsula ◠ Desert 🏝 Island/Island group ⁙ Antarctic base ◎ Ocean ◒ Sea ≈ Bay/Gulf/Channel/Strait ◡ Lake ⚑ Salt pan/Dry/Intermittent lake ∫ River

137 L 14 **Cheltenham**, New Zealand
67 S 8 **Chelva**, Spain
105 G 18 **Chelvai**, India
88 I 11 **Chelyabinsk**, Russian Federation
89 Q 6 **Chelyuskin**, Russian Federation
124 G 8 **Chemaïa**, Morocco
103 N 15 **Chemenibit**, Turkmenistan
73 L 17 **Chemnitz**, Germany
32 H 12 **Chemult**, OR, U.S.A.
35 S 6 **Chena Hot Springs**, AK, U.S.A.
124 I 11 **Chenachane**, Algeria
127 H 22 **Ch'ench'a**, Ethiopia
24 M 6 **Cheney Reservoir**, KS, U.S.A. ◢
113 U 2 **Cheng'an**, China
111 E 16 **Chengde**, China
113 N 6 **Chengdu**, China
107 Z 8 **Chengele**, India
113 W 12 **Chenghai**, China
113 Q 5 **Chengkou**, China
113 R 15 **Chengmai**, China
105 G 21 **Chennai**, India
21 G 18 **Chenoa**, IL, U.S.A.
113 R 8 **Chenxi**, China
113 T 10 **Chenzhou**, China
82 I 11 **Chepelare**, Bulgaria
52 B 13 **Chepén**, Peru
56 I 10 **Chepes**, Argentina
47 X 13 **Chepo**, Panama
63 P 10 **Chepstow**, U.K.
17 Q 11 **Cheraw**, SC, U.S.A.
64 L 3 **Cherbourg**, France
91 S 10 **Cherdyn'**, Russian Federation
88 M 12 **Cherepanovo**, Russian Federation
90 I 12 **Cherepovets**, Russian Federation
90 M 9 **Cherevkovo**, Russian Federation
125 P 6 **Chéria**, Algeria
105 C 23 **Cheriyam**, India 🏝
87 R 5 **Cherkasy**, Ukraine
93 N 13 **Cherkessk**, Russian Federation
88 K 12 **Cherlak**, Russian Federation
91 S 12 **Chermoz**, Russian Federation
91 Q 2 **Chernaya**, Russian Federation
82 F 9 **Cherni Vrŭkh**, Bulgaria ▲
87 Q 2 **Chernihiv**, Ukraine
87 W 8 **Cherninivka**, Ukraine
86 K 7 **Chernivtsi**, Ukraine
87 P 2 **Chernobyl**, Ukraine
89 N 10 **Chernoostrovskoye**, Russian Federation
91 T 14 **Chernushka**, Russian Federation
87 N 3 **Chernyakhiv**, Ukraine
85 C 16 **Chernyakhovsk**, Russian Federation
89 S 13 **Chernyshevsk**, Russian Federation
89 R 10 **Chernyshevskiy**, Russian Federation
93 W 4 **Chernyy Otrog**, Russian Federation
23 Q 11 **Cherokee**, IA, U.S.A.
24 L 8 **Cherokee**, OK, U.S.A.
16 K 8 **Cherokee Lake**, TN, U.S.A. ◢
107 V 11 **Cherrapunji**, India
14 I 14 **Cherry Hill**, NJ, U.S.A.
89 W 7 **Cherskiy**, Russian Federation
86 J 3 **Chervonohrad**, Ukraine
87 Y 5 **Chervonooskil's'ke Vodoskhovyshche**, Ukraine ◢
87 P 9 **Chervonoznam"yanka**, Ukraine
85 K 18 **Chervyen'**, Belarus
85 N 18 **Cherykaw**, Belarus
21 L 14 **Chesaning**, MI, U.S.A.
17 V 7 **Chesapeake**, VA, U.S.A.
17 V 4 **Chesapeake Bay**, MD, U.S.A. ≈
17 V 3 **Chesapeake Beach**, MD, U.S.A.
91 N 4 **Cheshskaya Guba**, Russian Federation ≈
17 O 11 **Chester**, SC, U.S.A.
17 T 6 **Chester**, VA, U.S.A.
21 E 22 **Chester**, IL, U.S.A.
29 Q 2 **Chester**, MT, U.S.A.
33 H 16 **Chester**, CA, U.S.A.
43 U 11 **Chester**, NS, Canada
63 P 4 **Chester**, U.K.
63 S 4 **Chesterfield**, U.K.
40 M 3 **Chesterfield Inlet**, NU, Canada ≈
15 Q 3 **Chesuncook Lake**, ME, U.S.A. ◢
43 X 8 **Chéticamp**, NS, Canada
105 B 22 **Chetlat**, India 🏝
45 Z 12 **Chetumal**, Mexico
137 J 15 **Chetwode Islands**, New Zealand 🏝
39 G 17 **Chetwynd**, BC, Canada
34 L 9 **Chevak**, AK, U.S.A.
137 I 19 **Cheviot**, New Zealand
127 H 23 **Che'w Bahir**, Ethiopia ◢
32 K 6 **Chewelah**, WA, U.S.A.
24 J 10 **Cheyenne**, OK, U.S.A.
29 Z 14 **Cheyenne**, WY, U.S.A.
29 Y 11 **Cheyenne**, WY/UT, U.S.A. ∫
31 U 5 **Cheyenne Wells**, CO, U.S.A.
107 P 11 **Chhapra**, India
107 V 11 **Chhatak**, Bangladesh
106 L 12 **Chhatarpur**, India
105 I 17 **Chhatrapur**, India
105 F 15 **Chhindwara**, India
107 T 10 **Chhukha**, Bhutan
113 Z 12 **Chiai**, Taiwan
115 I 15 **Chiang Khan**, Thailand
115 G 14 **Chiang Mai**, Thailand
114 H 13 **Chiang Rai**, Thailand
45 X 14 **Chiapas**, Mexico ▣
95 S 6 **Chiat'ura**, Georgia
76 D 5 **Chiavenno**, Italy
123 L 16 **Chiba**, Japan
132 G 6 **Chibemba**, Angola
132 G 6 **Chibia**, Angola
41 R 11 **Chibougamau**, QC, Canada
123 D 17 **Chibu**, Japan
123 D 17 **Chiburi-jima**, Japan 🏝
21 H 16 **Chicago**, IL, U.S.A.
35 W 11 **Chichagof Island**, AK, U.S.A. 🏝
124 G 8 **Chichaoua**, Morocco
46 G 5 **Chiché**, Guatemala
111 D 16 **Chicheng**, China
63 U 13 **Chichester**, U.K.
51 N 2 **Chichiriviche**, Venezuela
16 I 10 **Chickamauga Lake**, TN, U.S.A. ◢
24 L 11 **Chickasha**, OK, U.S.A.
35 T 7 **Chicken**, AK, U.S.A.
52 B 13 **Chiclayo**, Peru
33 G 17 **Chico**, CA, U.S.A.
57 H 19 **Chico**, Argentina ∫
132 H 5 **Chicomba**, Angola
133 Q 9 **Chicualacuala**, Mozambique
133 R 10 **Chidenguele**, Mozambique
73 L 25 **Chiemsee**, Germany ◢
133 O 2 **Chiengi**, Zambia
115 F 23 **Chieo Lan Reservoir**, Thailand ◢
76 B 8 **Chieri**, Italy
76 J 13 **Chieti**, Italy
111 F 14 **Chifeng**, China
43 T 10 **Chigneco Bay**, NB, Canada ≈
53 I 22 **Chiguana**, Bolivia
133 Q 9 **Chigubo**, Mozambique
44 M 5 **Chihuahua**, Mexico
44 M 5 **Chihuahua**, Mexico ▣
103 Q 9 **Chiili**, Kazakhstan
90 E 13 **Chikhachevo**, Russian Federation
105 C 21 **Chikmagalur**, India
105 C 19 **Chikodi**, India
133 Q 3 **Chikwa**, Zambia
122 J 7 **Chikyū-misaki**, Japan ▶
132 G 4 **Chila**, Angola
101 Y 6 **Chilas**, Pakistan
106 H 2 **Chilas**, India
105 F 24 **Chilaw**, Sri Lanka
135 V 7 **Childers**, QLD, Australia
26 M 3 **Childress**, TX, U.S.A.
57 F 15 **Chile**, South America □
57 G 20 **Chile Chico**, Chile
56 H 9 **Chilecito**, Argentina
63 Y 11 **Chilham**, U.K.
103 W 9 **Chilik**, Kazakhstan
133 N 4 **Chililabombwe**, Zambia
135 S 3 **Chillagoe**, QLD, Australia
57 F 14 **Chillán**, Chile
59 C 18 **Chillar**, Argentina
21 F 17 **Chillicothe**, IL, U.S.A.
21 M 19 **Chillicothe**, OH, U.S.A.
25 T 2 **Chillicothe**, MO, U.S.A.
53 H 20 **Chilliculco**, Peru
101 Y 5 **Chillinji**, Pakistan
32 G 13 **Chiloquin**, OR, U.S.A.
45 R 13 **Chilpancingo**, Mexico
63 T 10 **Chiltern Hills**, U.K. ▲▲
20 G 12 **Chilton**, WI, U.S.A.
133 R 3 **Chilumba**, Malawi
113 Z 10 **Chilung**, Taiwan
131 T 13 **Chimala**, Tanzania
46 G 6 **Chimaltenango**, Guatemala
47 X 14 **Chimán**, Panama
133 Q 8 **Chimanimani**, Zimbabwe
69 F 23 **Chimay**, Belgium
52 B 9 **Chimborazo**, Ecuador ▲
52 B 9 **Chimborazo**, Ecuador ▣
53 B 14 **Chimbote**, Peru
138 C 5 **Chimbu**, Papua New Guinea ▣
101 Y 10 **Chimian**, Pakistan
133 Q 7 **Chimoio**, Mozambique
114 B 11 **Chin**, Myanmar ▣
111 L 22 **Chin-do**, South Korea 🏝
45 R 7 **China**, Mexico
111 E 14 **China**, Asia □
46 H 4 **Chinajá**, Guatemala
46 M 8 **Chinandega**, Nicaragua
26 G 10 **Chinati Peak**, TX, U.S.A. ▲
103 R 12 **Chinaz**, Uzbekistan
53 D 17 **Chincha Alta**, Peru
39 G 16 **Chinchaga**, AB, Canada ∫
135 V 8 **Chinchilla**, QLD, Australia
133 S 7 **Chinde**, Mozambique
112 H 4 **Chindu**, China
114 C 8 **Chindwin**, Myanmar ∫
102 J 4 **Chingirlau**, Kazakhstan
133 N 4 **Chingola**, Zambia
132 H 4 **Chinguar**, Angola
128 G 5 **Chinguetti**, Mauritania
129 X 11 **Chinguil**, Chad
133 P 6 **Chinhoyi**, Zimbabwe
101 X 9 **Chiniot**, Pakistan
111 M 21 **Chinju**, South Korea
102 J 11 **Chink Kaplankyr**, Uzbekistan ▲▲
30 M 9 **Chinle**, AZ, U.S.A.
113 X 11 **Chinmen Tao**, Taiwan 🏝
105 F 17 **Chinnur**, India
123 I 16 **Chino**, Japan
65 N 7 **Chinon**, France
29 S 2 **Chinook**, MT, U.S.A.
133 Q 3 **Chinsali**, Zambia
105 E 21 **Chintamani**, India
76 G 7 **Chioggia**, Italy
83 K 19 **Chios**, Greece
83 K 19 **Chios**, Greece 🏝
133 Q 4 **Chipata**, Zambia
133 O 3 **Chipili**, Zambia
43 S 9 **Chipman**, NB, Canada
132 J 4 **Chipoia**, Angola
63 R 11 **Chippenham**, U.K.
20 D 11 **Chippewa Falls**, WI, U.S.A.
63 S 8 **Chipping Campden**, U.K.
63 S 9 **Chipping Norton**, U.K.
63 W 9 **Chipping Ongar**, U.K.
63 Q 10 **Chipping Sodbury**, U.K.
15 R 3 **Chiputneticook Lakes**, ME, U.S.A. ◢
53 D 15 **Chiquian**, Peru
45 Z 10 **Chiquilá**, Mexico
46 I 5 **Chiquimula**, Guatemala
50 I 6 **Chiquinquira**, Colombia
93 N 8 **Chir**, Russian Federation ∫
105 G 19 **Chirala**, India
133 R 6 **Chiramba**, Mozambique
106 I 8 **Chirawa**, India
103 R 11 **Chirchik**, Uzbekistan
133 P 8 **Chiredzi**, Zimbabwe
129 T 5 **Chirfa**, Niger
111 M 21 **Chiri-san**, South Korea ▲
30 M 15 **Chiricahua Peak**, AZ, U.S.A. ▲
50 J 3 **Chiriguana**, Colombia
35 O 13 **Chirikof Island**, AK, U.S.A. 🏝
47 T 14 **Chiriquí Grande**, Panama
105 H 15 **Chirmiri**, India
133 R 6 **Chiromo**, Mozambique
82 J 10 **Chirpan**, Bulgaria
47 Q 11 **Chirripo**, Costa Rica ∫
133 O 6 **Chirundu**, Zambia
100 J 13 **Chīrūyeh**, Iran
133 O 5 **Chisamba**, Zambia
41 P 9 **Chisasibi**, QC, Canada
46 H 4 **Chisec**, Guatemala
113 Z 12 **Ch'ishan**, Taiwan
93 V 2 **Chishmy**, Russian Federation
101 X 11 **Chishtian Mandi**, Pakistan
87 O 9 **Chişinău**, Moldova ⌂
86 F 9 **Chişineu-Criş**, Romania
93 S 1 **Chistopol'**, Russian Federation
103 Q 3 **Chistopol'ye**, Kazakhstan
89 R 14 **Chita**, Russian Federation
132 G 7 **Chitado**, Angola
133 P 4 **Chitambo**, Zambia
132 K 1 **Chitato**, Angola
35 S 9 **Chitina**, AK, U.S.A.
133 Q 2 **Chitipa**, Malawi
122 K 6 **Chitose**, Japan
105 D 20 **Chitradurga**, India
101 W 6 **Chitral**, Pakistan
47 V 15 **Chitré**, Panama
107 W 14 **Chittagong**, Bangladesh
107 W 14 **Chittagong**, Bangladesh ▣
104 D 13 **Chittaurgarh**, India
105 F 21 **Chittoor**, India
133 O 7 **Chitungwiza**, Zimbabwe
132 K 5 **Chiume**, Angola
76 B 7 **Chivasso**, Italy
133 P 7 **Chivhu**, Zimbabwe
46 G 4 **Chixoy**, Guatemala ∫
90 M 4 **Chizha**, Russian Federation
123 F 18 **Chizu**, Japan
103 R 2 **Chkalovo**, Kazakhstan
90 L 14 **Chkalovsk**, Russian Federation
79 L 16 **Chmielnik**, Poland
111 J 18 **Cho-do**, North Korea 🏝
115 L 18 **Chŏâm Khsant**, Cambodia
132 M 7 **Chobe**, Botswana ▣
111 L 20 **Choch'iwŏn**, South Korea
50 G 6 **Chocó**, Colombia ▣
121 K 18 **Chocolate Hills**, Philippines ▲▲
50 J 6 **Chocontá**, Colombia
78 G 11 **Chodzież**, Poland
57 I 15 **Choele Choel**, Argentina
133 Q 5 **Chofombo**, Mozambique
138 K 5 **Choiseul**, Solomon Islands 🏝
57 L 24 **Choiseul Sound**, Falkland Islands ≈
44 K 6 **Choix**, Mexico
78 H 10 **Chojnice**, Poland
122 K 11 **Chōkai-san**, Japan ▲
27 O 12 **Choke Canyon Lake**, TX, U.S.A. ◢
103 U 9 **Chokpar**, Kazakhstan
89 V 7 **Chokurdakh**, Russian Federation
133 Q 10 **Chókwe**, Mozambique
64 M 7 **Cholet**, France
57 G 18 **Cholila**, Argentina
103 V 10 **Cholpon-Ata**, Kyrgyzstan
46 M 8 **Choluteca**, Honduras
115 G 15 **Chom Thong**, Thailand
133 N 6 **Choma**, Zambia
79 B 16 **Chomutov**, Czech Republic
115 H 19 **Chon Buri**, Thailand
115 N 21 **Chon Thanh**, Vietnam
111 L 19 **Ch'ŏnan**, South Korea
52 A 9 **Chone**, Ecuador
111 N 14 **Ch'ŏngjin**, North Korea
111 L 20 **Ch'ŏngju**, South Korea
111 J 17 **Chŏngju**, North Korea
113 Z 5 **Chongming**, China
132 F 5 **Chongoroi**, Angola
111 K 17 **Chŏngp'yŏng**, North Korea
113 O 7 **Chongqing**, China
113 P 7 **Chongqing**, China ▣
113 V 8 **Chongren**, China
111 L 21 **Chŏngŭp**, South Korea
133 O 5 **Chongwe**, Zambia
111 L 21 **Chŏnju**, South Korea
109 T 4 **Chonogol**, Mongolia
86 G 6 **Chop**, Ukraine
63 P 3 **Chorley**, U.K.
86 K 6 **Chortkiv**, Ukraine
105 A 15 **Chorwad**, India
111 L 18 **Ch'ŏrwŏn**, South Korea
78 L 10 **Chorzele**, Poland
57 G 14 **Chos Malal**, Argentina
111 K 16 **Ch'osan**, North Korea
123 L 16 **Chōshi**, Japan
78 E 11 **Choszczno**, Poland
52 B 13 **Chota**, Peru
105 I 14 **Chota Nagpur**, India ▲▲
29 P 4 **Choteau**, MT, U.S.A.
124 L 6 **Chott ech Chergui**, Algeria ◢
125 N 6 **Chott el Hodna**, Algeria ◢
125 P 7 **Chott el Jerid**, Tunisia ◢
125 O 7 **Chott Melrhir**, Algeria ◢
128 G 5 **Choûm**, Mauritania
25 Q 9 **Chouteau**, OK, U.S.A.
109 S 3 **Choybalsan**, Mongolia
109 R 4 **Choyr**, Mongolia
63 S 13 **Christchurch**, U.K.
137 H 20 **Christchurch**, New Zealand
116 G 15 **Christmas Island**, Australia 🏝
141 P 2 **Christmas Island**, Kiribati 🏝
35 S 8 **Christochina**, AK, U.S.A.
83 K 21 **Christos**, Greece
79 E 17 **Chrudim**, Czech Republic
82 I 13 **Chrysoupoli**, Greece
79 J 17 **Chrzanów**, Poland
103 R 9 **Chu**, Kazakhstan ∫
103 T 9 **Chu-Iliyskiye Gory**, Kazakhstan ▲▲
115 O 20 **Chu Yang Sin**, Vietnam ▲
113 Z 6 **Chuansha**, China
113 P 11 **Chuanshan**, China
112 J 7 **Chubalung**, China
57 H 18 **Chubut**, Argentina ▣
57 H 18 **Chubut**, Argentina ∫
89 Z 5 **Chuckchi Sea**, Russian Federation/U.S.A. 🌊
47 Z 14 **Chucunaque**, Panama ∫
87 N 4 **Chudniv**, Ukraine
90 F 11 **Chudovo**, Russian Federation
85 I 20 **Chudzin**, Belarus
35 S 9 **Chugach Mountains**, AK, U.S.A. ▲▲
123 D 19 **Chūgoku-sanchi**, Japan ▲▲
29 Z 13 **Chugwater**, WY, U.S.A.
87 W 4 **Chuhuyiv**, Ukraine
112 I 7 **Chuka**, China
143 S 4 **Chukchi Abyssal Plain**, Arctic Ocean ◇
143 R 5 **Chukchi Plateau**, Arctic Ocean ◇
34 J 3 **Chukchi Sea**, Russian Federation/U.S.A. 🌊
90 L 12 **Chukhloma**, Russian Federation
89 Z 6 **Chukotskiy Poluostrov**, Russian Federation ▶
33 K 26 **Chula Vista**, CA, U.S.A.
89 T 12 **Chul'man**, Russian Federation
62 M 13 **Chulmleigh**, U.K.
88 L 12 **Chulym**, Russian Federation
91 T 3 **Chum**, Russian Federation
115 I 16 **Chum Phae**, Thailand
106 K 4 **Chumatang**, India
127 I 23 **Chumba**, Ethiopia
56 I 9 **Chumbicha**, Argentina
112 I 4 **Chumda**, China
89 V 12 **Chumikan**, Russian Federation
115 G 22 **Chumphon**, Thailand
115 H 17 **Chumsaeng**, Thailand
111 M 18 **Ch'unch'ŏn**, South Korea
103 X 9 **Chundzha**, Kazakhstan
132 M 5 **Chunga**, Zambia
111 M 19 **Ch'ungju**, South Korea
131 W 14 **Chungu**, Tanzania
113 Z 12 **Chungyang Shanmo**, Taiwan ▲▲
131 S 13 **Chunya**, Tanzania
115 K 21 **Chuŏr Phnum Dâmrei**, Cambodia ▲▲
115 K 18 **Chuŏr Phnum Dângrek**, Thailand ▲▲
56 G 4 **Chuquicamata**, Chile
53 K 22 **Chuquisaca**, Bolivia ▣
74 I 8 **Chur**, Switzerland
107 X 12 **Churachandpur**, India
89 U 10 **Churapcha**, Russian Federation
17 U 5 **Church**, VA, U.S.A.
63 P 7 **Church Stretton**, U.K.
37 P 10 **Churchill**, Canada ∫
40 K 6 **Churchill**, MB, Canada
41 U 8 **Churchill Falls**, NL, Canada
106 H 8 **Churu**, India
50 M 2 **Churuguara**, Venezuela
122 L 6 **Chūrui**, Japan
106 K 4 **Chushul**, India
91 T 12 **Chusovoy**, Russian Federation
41 S 11 **Chute-des-Passes**, QC, Canada
87 U 4 **Chutove**, Ukraine
113 Z 11 **Chutung**, Taiwan
141 O 15 **Chuuk**, Federated States of Micronesia ▣
141 O 15 **Chuuk Islands**, Federated States of Micronesia 🏝
93 Q 1 **Chuvashskaya Respublika**, Russian Federation ▣
112 K 10 **Chuxiong**, China
103 U 10 **Chuyskaya Oblast'**, Kyrgyzstan ▣
113 W 5 **Chuzhou**, China
103 R 9 **Chyganak**, Kazakhstan
87 S 5 **Chyhyryn**, Ukraine
87 N 10 **Ciadîr-Lunga**, Moldova
116 H 14 **Ciamis**, Indonesia
116 H 14 **Cianjur**, Indonesia
58 G 7 **Cianorte**, Brazil
80 M 12 **Ćićevac**, Serbia and Montenegro
139 Y 11 **Cicia**, Fiji 🏝
94 H 7 **Cide**, Turkey
78 K 11 **Ciechanów**, Poland
78 I 11 **Ciechocinek**, Poland
48 J 5 **Ciego de Ávila**, Cuba
50 I 2 **Ciénaga**, Colombia
48 I 5 **Cienfuegos**, Cuba
79 O 16 **Cieszanów**, Poland
79 I 18 **Cieszyn**, Poland
67 R 10 **Cieza**, Spain
94 H 11 **Cihanbeyli**, Turkey
45 N 12 **Cihuatlán**, Mexico
139 Y 10 **Cikobia**, Fiji 🏝
116 I 14 **Cilacap**, Indonesia
95 S 8 **Cildir Gölö**, Turkey ◢
113 S 7 **Cili**, China
67 O 2 **Cilleruelo de Bezana**, Spain
95 Z 8 **Ciloy Adasi**, Azerbaijan 🏝
87 N 10 **Cimişlia**, Moldova
95 P 12 **Cinar**, Turkey
80 F 12 **Cincar**, Bosnia and Herzegovina ▲
21 K 20 **Cincinnati**, OH, U.S.A.
94 C 12 **Cine**, Turkey
69 I 22 **Ciney**, Belgium
66 H 5 **Cinfães**, Portugal
76 F 12 **Cinigiano**, Italy
45 V 14 **Cintalapa**, Mexico
67 R 3 **Cintruénigo**, Spain
55 N 14 **Cipó**, Brazil
29 X 4 **Circle**, MT, U.S.A.
35 S 6 **Circle**, AK, U.S.A.
21 M 19 **Circleville**, OH, U.S.A.
30 J 6 **Circleville**, UT, U.S.A.
116 H 14 **Cirebon**, Indonesia
63 R 10 **Cirencester**, U.K.
76 A 7 **Cirie**, Italy
77 N 19 **Cirò Marina**, Italy
27 N 6 **Cisco**, TX, U.S.A.
79 N 19 **Cisna**, Poland
77 H 14 **Cisterna di Latina**, Italy
66 M 2 **Cistierna**, Spain
33 G 18 **Citrus Heights**, CA, U.S.A.
132 K 14 **Citrusdal**, Republic of South Africa
76 G 12 **Città della Pieve**, Italy
76 G 11 **Città di Castello**, Italy
76 F 6 **Cittadella**, Italy
86 H 8 **Ciucea**, Romania
45 P 4 **Ciudad Acuña**, Mexico
45 P 13 **Ciudad Altamirano**, Mexico
51 Q 4 **Ciudad Bolívar**, Venezuela
44 M 6 **Ciudad Camargo**, Mexico
44 I 7 **Ciudad Constitución**, Mexico
45 W 14 **Ciudad Cuauhtémoc**, Mexico
56 J 8 **Ciudad de Loreto**, Argentina
45 R 10 **Ciudad de Valles**, Mexico
45 W 12 **Ciudad del Carmen**, Mexico
44 M 5 **Ciudad Delicias**, Mexico
51 R 4 **Ciudad Guayana**, Venezuela
45 O 11 **Ciudad Guzmán**, Mexico
44 L 3 **Ciudad Juárez**, Mexico
45 S 10 **Ciudad Madero**, Mexico
45 R 9 **Ciudad Mante**, Mexico
47 S 14 **Ciudad Neily**, Costa Rica
44 J 6 **Ciudad Obregón**, Mexico
51 Q 5 **Ciudad Piar**, Venezuela
67 N 9 **Ciudad Real**, Spain
66 K 6 **Ciudad Rodrigo**, Spain
45 Q 8 **Ciudad Victoria**, Mexico
67 Z 7 **Ciutadella de Menorca**, Spain
94 L 7 **Civa Burnu**, Turkey ▶
76 G 13 **Civita Castellana**, Italy
76 I 11 **Civitanova Marche**, Italy
76 G 13 **Civitavecchia**, Italy
65 N 9 **Civray**, France
94 E 11 **Civril**, Turkey
113 Z 6 **Cixi**, China
113 U 2 **Cixian**, China
95 R 12 **Cizre**, Turkey
63 Z 9 **Clacton-on-Sea**, U.K.
65 R 7 **Clamecy**, France
19 Q 4 **Clanton**, AL, U.S.A.
132 J 14 **Clanwilliam**, Republic of South Africa
115 F 22 **Clara Island**, Myanmar 🏝
20 K 13 **Clare**, MI, U.S.A.
61 A 17 **Clare Island**, Republic of Ireland 🏝
14 M 7 **Claremont**, NH, U.S.A.
25 Q 8 **Claremore**, OK, U.S.A.
137 J 18 **Clarence**, New Zealand
137 I 18 **Clarence**, New Zealand ∫
144 H 2 **Clarence Island**, Antarctica 🏝
35 Y 12 **Clarence Strait**, AK, U.S.A. ≈
49 N 4 **Clarence Town**, The Bahamas
26 L 3 **Clarendon**, TX, U.S.A.
41 Y 10 **Clarenville**, NL, Canada
14 C 11 **Clarion**, PA, U.S.A.
28 K 3 **Clark Fork**, ID, U.S.A.
16 M 13 **Clark Hill Reservoir**, SC, U.S.A. ◢
19 V 3 **Clark Hill Reservoir**, GA, U.S.A. ◢
135 T 15 **Clarke Island**, TAS, Australia 🏝
17 P 3 **Clarksburg**, WV, U.S.A.
18 L 2 **Clarksdale**, MS, U.S.A.
32 K 8 **Clarkston**, WA, U.S.A.
16 E 8 **Clarksville**, TN, U.S.A.
17 S 7 **Clarksville**, VA, U.S.A.
25 T 10 **Clarksville**, AR, U.S.A.
27 S 4 **Clarksville**, TX, U.S.A.
137 E 25 **Clarksville**, New Zealand
26 K 2 **Claude**, TX, U.S.A.
120 G 5 **Claveria**, Philippines
19 V 5 **Claxton**, GA, U.S.A.
63 Y 8 **Claydon**, U.K.
17 W 1 **Claymont**, DE, U.S.A.
18 J 5 **Clayton**, LA, U.S.A.
25 Q 12 **Clayton**, OK, U.S.A.
28 M 9 **Clayton**, ID, U.S.A.
31 T 8 **Clayton**, NM, U.S.A.
39 G 16 **Clear Hills**, AB, Canada ▲▲
23 S 10 **Clear Lake**, IA, U.S.A.
33 F 18 **Clear Lake**, CA, U.S.A. ◢
33 H 14 **Clear Lake Reservoir**, CA, U.S.A. ◢
14 D 12 **Clearfield**, PA, U.S.A.
19 V 10 **Clearwater**, FL, U.S.A.
28 L 6 **Clearwater**, ID, U.S.A. ∫
39 H 20 **Clearwater**, BC, Canada
28 L 6 **Clearwater Mountains**, ID, U.S.A. ▲▲
27 P 6 **Cleburne**, TX, U.S.A.
63 W 3 **Cleethorpes**, U.K.
145 V 6 **Clemence Massif**, Antarctica ▲
118 A 14 **Clementi**, Singapore
24 L 8 **Cleo Springs**, OK, U.S.A.
121 D 18 **Cleopatra Needle**, Philippines ▲
65 Q 3 **Clermont**, France
135 U 6 **Clermont**, QLD, Australia
65 R 10 **Clermont-Ferrand**, France
69 L 23 **Clervaux**, Luxembourg
76 F 5 **Cles**, Italy
63 P 11 **Clevedon**, U.K.
16 I 10 **Cleveland**, TN, U.S.A.
18 L 3 **Cleveland**, MS, U.S.A.
19 T 1 **Cleveland**, GA, U.S.A.
21 N 16 **Cleveland**, OH, U.S.A.
27 S 9 **Cleveland**, TX, U.S.A.
21 O 16 **Cleveland Heights**, OH, U.S.A.
58 H 9 **Clevelândia**, Brazil
61 B 17 **Clew Bay**, Republic of Ireland ≈
19 X 12 **Clewiston**, FL, U.S.A.
61 A 17 **Clifden**, Republic of Ireland
137 J 17 **Clifford Bay**, New Zealand ≈
17 Q 5 **Clifton Forge**, VA, U.S.A.
39 M 20 **Climax**, SK, Canada
16 L 7 **Clinchport**, VA, U.S.A.
16 J 9 **Clingmans Dome**, NC, U.S.A. ▲
26 E 7 **Clint**, TX, U.S.A.
14 M 11 **Clinton**, CT, U.S.A.
16 M 11 **Clinton**, SC, U.S.A.
17 S 10 **Clinton**, NC, U.S.A.
18 K 6 **Clinton**, LA, U.S.A.
18 L 5 **Clinton**, MS, U.S.A.
21 K 15 **Clinton**, MI, U.S.A.
23 W 12 **Clinton**, IA, U.S.A.
24 K 10 **Clinton**, OK, U.S.A.
25 S 5 **Clinton**, MO, U.S.A.
25 V 10 **Clinton**, AR, U.S.A.
39 G 20 **Clinton**, BC, Canada
42 C 13 **Clinton**, ON, Canada
17 Q 11 **Clio**, SC, U.S.A.
64 L 7 **Clisson**, France
63 Q 2 **Clitheroe**, U.K.
61 B 21 **Clonakilty**, Republic of Ireland
135 Q 5 **Cloncurry**, QLD, Australia
61 D 20 **Clonmel**, Republic of Ireland
72 D 12 **Cloppenburg**, Germany
23 T 5 **Cloquet**, MN, U.S.A.
56 M 6 **Clorinda**, Argentina
137 J 16 **Cloudy Bay**, New Zealand ≈
42 J 7 **Clova**, QC, Canada
62 L 12 **Clovelly**, U.K.
33 F 18 **Cloverdale**, CA, U.S.A.
31 U 11 **Clovis**, NM, U.S.A.
86 H 9 **Cluj-Napoca**, Romania
63 P 7 **Clun**, U.K.
65 S 9 **Cluny**, France
65 W 9 **Cluses**, France
76 D 6 **Clusone**, Italy
137 D 24 **Clutha**, New Zealand ∫
39 J 18 **Clyde**, AB, Canada
60 H 13 **Clyde**, U.K. ∫
29 R 7 **Clyde Park**, MT, U.S.A.
137 D 25 **Clydevale**, New Zealand
114 K 12 **Co Nôi**, Vietnam
33 L 25 **Coachella**, CA, U.S.A.
45 O 6 **Coahuila**, Mexico ▣
35 S 6 **Coal Creek**, AK, U.S.A.
33 K 19 **Coaldale**, NV, U.S.A.
25 P 12 **Coalgate**, OK, U.S.A.
54 E 11 **Coari**, Brazil
54 D 12 **Coari**, Brazil ∫
131 X 9 **Coast**, Kenya ▣
39 C 16 **Coast Mountains**, BC, Canada ▲▲
33 E 15 **Coast Ranges**, U.S.A., U.S.A. ▲▲
46 F 5 **Coatepeque**, Guatemala
41 O 4 **Coats Island**, NU, Canada 🏝
145 N 4 **Coats Land**, Antarctica ◇
45 U 13 **Coatzacoalcos**, Mexico
46 H 5 **Cobán**, Guatemala
135 S 10 **Cobar**, NSW, Australia
53 I 16 **Cobija**, Bolivia
14 J 9 **Cobleskill**, NY, U.S.A.
42 G 12 **Cobourg**, ON, Canada
134 M 1 **Cobourg Peninsula**, NT, Australia ▶
133 R 4 **Cóbuè**, Mozambique
73 I 19 **Coburg**, Germany
53 G 20 **Cocachacra**, Peru
55 I 15 **Cocalinho**, Brazil
53 J 20 **Cochabamba**, Bolivia
53 J 19 **Cochabamba**, Bolivia ▣
57 F 17 **Cochamó**, Chile
73 C 19 **Cochem**, Germany
105 D 23 **Cochin**, India
115 M 23 **Cochin**, Vietnam ◇
42 D 5 **Cochrane**, ON, Canada
57 F 21 **Cochrane**, Chile
135 Q 10 **Cockburn**, SA, Australia
49 P 5 **Cockburn Harbour**, Turks and Caicos Islands
42 B 9 **Cockburn Island**, ON, Canada 🏝
49 Q 5 **Cockburn Town**, Turks and Caicos Islands ⌂
63 P 2 **Cockerham**, U.K.
47 V 13 **Coclé del Norte**, Panama
47 P 6 **Coco**, Nicaragua/Honduras ∫
105 N 20 **Coco Channel**, India ≈
19 X 10 **Cocoa Beach**, FL, U.S.A.
130 D 7 **Cocobeach**, Gabon
30 I 9 **Coconino Plateau**, AZ, U.S.A. ◇
55 L 15 **Cocos**, Brazil
11 T 11 **Cocos Islands**, Australia ▣
45 N 11 **Cocula**, Mexico
41 U 6 **Cod Island**, NL, Canada 🏝
54 E 11 **Codajás**, Brazil
137 B 26 **Codfish Island**, New Zealand 🏝
54 L 11 **Codó**, Brazil
49 Y 8 **Codrington**, Antigua and Barbuda
29 T 9 **Cody**, WY, U.S.A.
135 S 2 **Coen**, QLD, Australia
73 D 14 **Coesfeld**, Germany
28 K 3 **Coeur**, ID, U.S.A.
28 K 4 **Coeur d'Alene Lake**, ID, U.S.A. ◢
68 N 9 **Coevorden**, Netherlands
133 O 14 **Coffee Bay**, Republic of South Africa
19 N 6 **Coffeeville**, AL, U.S.A.
25 Q 7 **Coffeyville**, KS, U.S.A.
135 O 11 **Coffin Bay**, SA, Australia ≈
135 O 12 **Coffin Bay**, SA, Australia
135 O 11 **Coffin Bay Peninsula**, SA, Australia ▶
135 W 10 **Coffs Harbour**, NSW, Australia
46 K 5 **Cofradiá**, Honduras
87 N 13 **Cogealac**, Romania
63 X 9 **Coggeshall**, U.K.
64 M 10 **Cognac**, France
129 T 15 **Cogo**, Equatorial Guinea
56 M 6 **Cogoi**, Argentina
57 F 20 **Coihaique**, Chile
105 E 22 **Coimbatore**, India
66 H 6 **Coimbra**, Portugal ▣
66 H 7 **Coimbra**, Portugal
51 N 3 **Cojedes**, Venezuela ▣
46 J 7 **Cojutepeque**, El Salvador
29 Q 13 **Cokeville**, WY, U.S.A.
135 R 13 **Colac**, VIC, Australia
137 B 25 **Colac**, New Zealand
55 M 17 **Colatina**, Brazil
24 H 3 **Colby**, KS, U.S.A.
63 Y 9 **Colchester**, U.K.
34 L 13 **Cold Bay**, AK, U.S.A.
33 K 17 **Cold Spring**, NV, U.S.A.
21 K 16 **Coldwater**, MI, U.S.A.
24 K 7 **Coldwater**, KS, U.S.A.
15 N 5 **Colebrook**, NH, U.S.A.
27 N 7 **Coleman**, TX, U.S.A.
61 E 14 **Coleraine**, U.K.
18 I 6 **Colfax**, LA, U.S.A.
32 L 8 **Colfax**, WA, U.S.A.
33 H 18 **Colfax**, CA, U.S.A.
76 D 6 **Colico**, Italy
69 E 15 **Colijnsplaat**, Netherlands
45 N 12 **Colima**, Mexico
45 N 12 **Colima**, Mexico ▣
54 L 12 **Colinas**, Brazil
60 E 11 **Coll**, U.K. 🏝
67 O 6 **Collado Villalba**, Spain
76 F 11 **Colle di Val d'Elsa**, Italy
27 R 9 **College Station**, TX, U.S.A.
134 G 11 **Collie**, WA, Australia
134 I 3 **Collier Bay**, WA, Australia ≈
16 A 10 **Collierville**, TN, U.S.A.
42 E 12 **Collingwood**, ON, Canada
137 I 15 **Collingwood**, New Zealand
18 M 6 **Collins**, MS, U.S.A.
38 I 6 **Collinson Peninsula**, NU, Canada ▶
135 U 5 **Collinsville**, QLD, Australia
57 F 15 **Collipulli**, Chile
65 W 5 **Colmar**, France
63 R 2 **Colne**, U.K.
73 C 17 **Cologne**, Germany
50 I 8 **Colombia**, Colombia □
58 J 4 **Colômbia**, Brazil
105 F 25 **Colombo**, Sri Lanka ⌂
47 Q 12 **Colón**, Costa Rica
47 W 13 **Colón**, Panama
48 I 4 **Colón**, Cuba
59 B 15 **Colón**, Argentina
59 D 14 **Colón**, Argentina
49 N 4 **Colonel Hill**, The Bahamas
44 F 3 **Colonet**, Mexico
59 D 15 **Colonia**, Uruguay ▣
140 K 14 **Colonia**, Federated States of Micrones
59 D 15 **Colonia del Sacramento**, Uruguay
56 J 8 **Colonia Dora**, Argentina
57 H 20 **Colonia Las Heras**, Argentina
58 E 13 **Colonia Lavalleja**, Uruguay
60 F 13 **Colonsay**, U.K. 🏝
30 M 6 **Colorado**, UT/AZ, U.S.A. ∫
31 P 5 **Colorado**, U.S.A. ▣
44 F 2 **Colorado**, Mexico ∫
57 H 14 **Colorado**, Argentina ∫
26 L 6 **Colorado City**, TX, U.S.A.
30 I 8 **Colorado City**, AZ, U.S.A.
33 L 25 **Colorado Desert**, CA, U.S.A. ◇
30 L 7 **Colorado Plateau**, UT, U.S.A. ◇
31 S 5 **Colorado Springs**, CO, U.S.A.
45 O 10 **Colotlán**, Mexico
19 S 6 **Colquitt**, GA, U.S.A.
63 Z 6 **Coltishall**, U.K.
30 L 4 **Colton**, UT, U.S.A.
16 E 9 **Columbia**, TN, U.S.A.
17 V 9 **Columbia**, NC, U.S.A.
17 O 12 **Columbia**, SC, U.S.A.
18 I 5 **Columbia**, LA, U.S.A.
18 M 6 **Columbia**, MS, U.S.A.
25 V 4 **Columbia**, MO, U.S.A.
32 I 9 **Columbia**, U.S.A., U.S.A. ∫
32 K 8 **Columbia Basin**, WA, U.S.A. ◇
29 N 3 **Columbia Falls**, MT, U.S.A.
39 G 19 **Columbia Mountains**, BC, Canada ▲▲
28 J 11 **Columbia Plateau**, ID, U.S.A. ◇
16 M 10 **Columbus**, NC, U.S.A.
19 S 4 **Columbus**, GA, U.S.A.
19 N 3 **Columbus**, MS, U.S.A.
20 F 13 **Columbus**, WI, U.S.A.
21 M 18 **Columbus**, OH, U.S.A.
21 J 20 **Columbus**, IN, U.S.A.
23 N 13 **Columbus**, NE, U.S.A.
27 R 10 **Columbus**, TX, U.S.A.
29 S 7 **Columbus**, MT, U.S.A.
31 O 15 **Columbus**, NM, U.S.A.
32 K 6 **Colville**, WA, U.S.A.
35 O 4 **Colville**, AK, U.S.A. ∫
136 L 8 **Colville**, New Zealand
136 K 7 **Colville Channel**, New Zealand ≈
38 D 10 **Colville Lake**, NT, Canada ◢
63 N 4 **Colwyn Bay**, U.K.
76 G 8 **Comacchio**, Italy

□ Country ▣ Internal administrative region: State/Province/Territory/Dependent territory ⌂ Capital city ▲▲ Mountain range/ Undersea ridge ▲ Mountain peak/ Volcano/Seamount ◇ Geographic feature ▶ Headland/Point/ Cape/Peninsula ◠ Desert 🏝 Island/Island group ⁙ Antarctic base ◎ Ocean 🌊 Sea ≈ Bay/Gulf/Channel/Strait ◢ Lake ⚑ Salt pan/Dry/ Intermittent lake ∫ R

O 7 **Comanche**, TX, U.S.A.
H 22 **Comandante Luis Piedra Buena**, Argentina
H 12 **Comandante Salas**, Argentina
L 10 **Comănești**, Romania
K 11 **Comarnic**, Romania
L 6 **Comayagua**, Honduras
F 10 **Combarbalá**, Chile
B 13 **Combermere Bay**, Myanmar ≈
O 10 **Comfort**, TX, U.S.A.
V 13 **Comilla**, Bangladesh
N 1 **Comillas**, Spain
W 14 **Comitán de Domínguez**, Mexico
R 5 **Commerce**, TX, U.S.A.
N 1 **Committee Bay**, NU, Canada ≈
V 14 **Commonwealth Bay**, Antarctica ≈
C 6 **Como**, Italy
I 20 **Comodoro Rivadavia**, Argentina
I 7 **Comondú**, Mexico
V 3 **Comoros**, Africa □
Q 3 **Compiègne**, France
N 10 **Comrat**, Moldova
L 10 **Comstock**, TX, U.S.A.
M 24 **Côn Đao**, Vietnam
M 24 **Côn Son**, Vietnam ✱
H 17 **Cona Niyeu**, Argentina
F 11 **Conakry**, Guinea ■
M 17 **Conceição da Barra**, Brazil
J 12 **Conceição do Araguaia**, Brazil
P 8 **Concepción**, Mexico
S 14 **Concepción**, Panama
J 16 **Concepción**, Bolivia
G 19 **Concepción**, Paraguay
I 8 **Concepción**, Argentina
E 14 **Concepción**, Chile
D 14 **Concepción del Uruguay**, Argentina
S 10 **Conchas**, NM, U.S.A.
J 7 **Conchas**, Brazil
S 9 **Conchas Lake**, NM, U.S.A. ∽
O 4 **Conches-en-Ouche**, France
G 4 **Conchi**, Chile
L 6 **Conchos**, Mexico ∫
N 8 **Concord**, NH, U.S.A.
N 9 **Concord**, MA, U.S.A.
P 10 **Concord**, NC, U.S.A.
G 19 **Concord**, CA, U.S.A.
E 11 **Concordia**, Peru
D 13 **Concordia**, Argentina
Q 11 **Condat**, France
T 11 **Condobolin**, NSW, Australia
N 13 **Condom**, France
I 10 **Condon**, OR, U.S.A.
G 6 **Conegliano**, Italy
N 7 **Conejos**, Mexico
H 7 **Conflict Group**, Papua New Guinea ✱
N 10 **Congaz**, Moldova
U 12 **Conghua**, China
Q 10 **Congjiang**, China
R 4 **Congleton**, U.K.
H 8 **Congo**, Africa □
J 7 **Congo**, Democratic Republic of Congo/Angola ∫
I 11 **Congress**, AZ, U.S.A.
V 5 **Coningsby**, U.K.
D 9 **Coniston**, ON, Canada
O 1 **Coniston**, U.K.
J 17 **Conklin**, AB, Canada
B 17 **Connaught**, Republic of Ireland ▣
O 15 **Conneaut**, OH, U.S.A.
K 11 **Connecticut**, U.S.A. ▣
L 11 **Connecticut**, CT, U.S.A. ∫
J 8 **Connell**, WA, U.S.A.
C 10 **Connorsville**, WI, U.S.A.
P 3 **Conrad**, MT, U.S.A.
S 9 **Conroe**, TX, U.S.A.
K 1 **Consejo**, Belize
N 5 **Conselheiro Lafaiete**, Brazil
N 13 **Constanța**, Romania
O 5 **Constantine**, Algeria
O 8 **Consuegra**, Spain
L 20 **Consul**, SK, Canada
G 8 **Contarina**, Italy
B 13 **Contumazá**, Peru
I 10 **Contwoyto Lake**, NU, Canada ∽
N 16 **Conversano**, Italy
N 6 **Conway**, NH, U.S.A.
R 12 **Conway**, SC, U.S.A.
V 11 **Conway**, AR, U.S.A.
N 4 **Conwy**, U.K.
N 9 **Coober Pedy**, SA, Australia
S 3 **Cook**, MN, U.S.A.
M 10 **Cook**, SA, Australia
P 10 **Cook Inlet**, AK, U.S.A. ≈
O 1 **Cook Inlet**, Arctic Ocean ≈
O 10 **Cook Islands**, New Zealand ▣
J 15 **Cook Strait**, New Zealand ≈
H 8 **Cookeville**, TN, U.S.A.
T 3 **Cooktown**, QLD, Australia
W 9 **Coolangatta**, QLD, Australia
I 10 **Coolgardie**, WA, Australia
U 12 **Cooma**, NSW, Australia
Q 11 **Coombah**, NSW, Australia
S 7 **Coon Rapids**, MN, U.S.A.
T 10 **Coonabarabran**, NSW, Australia
U 10 **Coonamble**, NSW, Australia
C 20 **Coondapoor**, India
D 22 **Coonoor**, India
S 5 **Cooper**, TX, U.S.A.
P 9 **Cooper**, SA, Australia ∫
L 1 **Cooper's Town**, The Bahamas
E 12 **Coos Bay**, OR, U.S.A.
H 8 **Copacabana**, Argentina
R 14 **Copala**, Mexico
D 25 **Copenhagen**, Denmark ■
F 8 **Copiapó**, Chile
H 7 **Copper Harbor**, MI, U.S.A.
N 4 **Copperbelt**, Zambia ▣
N 13 **Copplestone**, U.K.
J 9 **Coqên**, China
F 10 **Coquimbo**, Chile
F 10 **Coquimbo**, Chile ▣
I 14 **Corabia**, Romania
E 18 **Coracora**, Peru
E 7 **Coral Bay**, WA, Australia
Y 13 **Coral Gables**, FL, U.S.A.
O 3 **Coral Harbour**, NU, Canada
C 6 **Coral Sea**, Oceania ≋
B 17 **Corbett**, Argentina
J 7 **Corbin**, KY, U.S.A.
U 7 **Corby**, U.K.
G 18 **Corcovado**, Argentina
T 5 **Cordele**, GA, U.S.A.
J 2 **Cordillera Cantabrica**, Spain ▲▲
47 T 14 **Cordillera Central**, Panama ▲▲
50 H 8 **Cordillera Central**, Colombia ▲▲
120 F 8 **Cordillera Central**, Philippines ▲▲
47 O 11 **Cordillera de Guanacaste**, Costa Rica ▲▲
47 Y 13 **Cordillera de San Blas**, Panama ▲▲
47 R 13 **Cordillera de Talamanca**, Costa Rica ▲▲
47 P 10 **Cordillera de Yolaina**, Nicaragua ▲▲
56 G 6 **Cordillera Domeyko**, Chile ▲▲
47 N 7 **Cordillera Entre Rios**, Honduras ▲▲
47 O 8 **Cordillera Isabelia**, Nicaragua ▲▲
45 Q 12 **Cordillera Neo-Volcánica**, Mexico ▲▲
53 C 14 **Cordillera Occidental**, South America ▲▲
53 D 15 **Cordillera Oriental**, South AmericanF817 ▲▲
121 H 17 **Cordilleras Range**, Philippines ▲▲
45 T 12 **Córdoba**, Mexico
50 H 4 **Córdoba**, Colombia ▣
56 K 11 **Córdoba**, Argentina ▣
56 J 10 **Córdoba**, Argentina
66 M 11 **Córdoba**, Spain
35 S 9 **Cordova**, AK, U.S.A.
63 R 14 **Corfe Castle**, U.K.
83 A 16 **Corfu**, Greece ✱
66 K 7 **Coria**, Spain
16 I 4 **Corinth**, KY, U.S.A.
19 N 1 **Corinth**, MS, U.S.A.
83 F 20 **Corinth Canal**, Greece ≈
46 M 9 **Corinto**, Nicaragua
55 F 16 **Corixa Grande**, Brazil ∫
61 C 21 **Cork**, Republic of Ireland
61 C 21 **Cork Harbour**, Republic of Ireland ≈
77 I 22 **Corleone**, Italy
82 N 12 **Çorlu**, Turkey
94 C 7 **Corlu**, Turkey
58 I 7 **Cornélio Procópio**, Brazil
20 D 11 **Cornell**, WI, U.S.A.
41 X 10 **Corner Brook**, NL, Canada
14 F 10 **Corning**, NY, U.S.A.
25 Y 8 **Corning**, AR, U.S.A.
33 G 17 **Corning**, CA, U.S.A.
42 J 11 **Cornwall**, ON, Canada
48 L 1 **Cornwall**, The Bahamas
37 O 3 **Cornwall Island**, NU, Canada ✱
37 O 4 **Cornwallis Island**, NU, Canada ✱
50 M 2 **Coro**, Venezuela
121 G 16 **Coroco**, Philippines ✱
53 I 19 **Coroico**, Bolivia
136 L 8 **Coromandel**, New Zealand
105 G 20 **Coromandel Coast**, India ◇
136 L 8 **Coromandel Peninsula**, New Zealand ▶
136 L 8 **Coromandel Range**, New Zealand ▲▲
121 F 15 **Coron**, Philippines
121 F 15 **Coron**, Philippines ✱
31 R 11 **Corona**, NM, U.S.A.
121 H 21 **Coronado Bay**, Philippines ≈
38 H 8 **Coronation Gulf**, NU, Canada ≈
144 H 1 **Coronation Island**, South Orkney Islands ✱
59 B 14 **Coronda**, Argentina
59 C 19 **Coronel Dorrego**, Argentina
55 H 20 **Coronel Oviedo**, Paraguay
59 B 18 **Coronel Pringles**, Argentina
55 H 19 **Coronel Sapucaia**, Brazil
59 B 18 **Coronel Suárez**, Argentina
59 E 18 **Coronel Vidal**, Argentina
137 C 23 **Coronet Peak**, New Zealand ▲
81 K 20 **Çorovodë**, Albania
135 S 12 **Corowa**, NSW, Australia
46 K 1 **Corozal**, Belize
57 H 22 **Corpen Aike**, Argentina
27 Q 13 **Corpus Christi**, TX, U.S.A.
53 I 21 **Corque**, Bolivia
120 F 11 **Corregidor**, Philippines ✱
55 L 14 **Corrente**, Brazil
55 H 16 **Correntes**, Brazil
55 L 15 **Correntina**, Brazil
58 C 10 **Corrientes**, Argentina
58 D 11 **Corrientes**, Argentina ▣
27 T 8 **Corrigan**, TX, U.S.A.
134 G 11 **Corrigin**, WA, Australia
63 Q 11 **Corsham**, U.K.
65 X 14 **Corsica**, France ✱
27 R 7 **Corsicana**, TX, U.S.A.
66 J 11 **Cortegana**, Spain
76 B 8 **Cortemilia**, Italy
31 N 7 **Cortez**, CO, U.S.A.
76 H 5 **Cortina d'Ampezzo**, Italy
14 G 9 **Cortland**, NY, U.S.A.
76 G 11 **Cortona**, Italy
66 H 9 **Coruche**, Portugal
95 P 9 **Coruh**, Turkey ∫
94 J 8 **Çorum**, Turkey
55 G 17 **Corumbá**, Brazil
55 O 14 **Coruripe**, Brazil
32 F 11 **Corvallis**, OR, U.S.A.
44 L 8 **Cosalá**, Mexico
45 T 12 **Cosamaloapan**, Mexico
56 G 3 **Coscaya**, Chile
77 M 19 **Cosenza**, Italy
21 N 18 **Coshocton**, OH, U.S.A.
65 R 7 **Cosne-cours-sur-Loire**, France
56 J 10 **Cosquín**, Argentina
67 T 11 **Costa Blanca**, Spain ◇
67 X 4 **Costa Brava**, Spain ◇
66 J 13 **Costa de la Luz**, Spain ◇
67 T 8 **Costa del Azahar**, Spain ◇
67 N 14 **Costa del Sol**, Spain ◇
67 V 6 **Costa Dorada**, Spain ◇
55 D 14 **Costa Marques**, Brazil
44 L 8 **Costa Rica**, Mexico
47 Q 13 **Costa Rica**, North America □
77 D 15 **Costa Smeralda**, Italy ◇
67 N 1 **Costa Verde**, Spain ◇
73 K 15 **Coswig**, Germany
121 K 22 **Cotabato**, Philippines
53 J 22 **Cotagaita**, Bolivia
53 F 18 **Cotahuasi**, Peru
65 W 15 **Côte d'Azur**, France ◇
128 K 12 **Côte d'Ivoire**, Africa □
47 R 14 **Coto Brus**, Costa Rica ∫
129 O 13 **Cotonou**, Benin
52 B 9 **Cotopaxi**, Ecuador ▣
63 R 10 **Cotswold Hills**, U.K. ▲▲
73 N 15 **Cottbus**, Germany
25 V 8 **Cotter**, AR, U.S.A.
76 A 8 **Cottian Alps**, Italy ▲▲
28 K 6 **Cottonwood**, ID, U.S.A.
33 G 16 **Cottonwood**, CA, U.S.A.
27 N 12 **Cotulla**, TX, U.S.A.
14 E 10 **Coudersport**, PA, U.S.A.
32 J 7 **Coulee City**, WA, U.S.A.
65 Q 4 **Coulommiers**, France
21 F 21 **Coulterville**, IL, U.S.A.
28 J 8 **Council**, ID, U.S.A.
34 M 6 **Council**, AK, U.S.A.
23 Q 14 **Council Bluffs**, IA, U.S.A.
51 U 7 **Courantyne**, Suriname ∫
69 F 21 **Courcelles**, Belgium
85 B 15 **Courland Lagoon**, Russian Federation ∽
76 A 6 **Courmayeur**, Italy
18 H 5 **Coushatta**, LA, U.S.A.
64 L 4 **Coutances**, France
39 K 21 **Coutts**, AB, Canada
69 G 23 **Couvin**, Belgium
63 S 7 **Coventry**, U.K.
30 J 14 **Covered Wells**, AZ, U.S.A.
66 J 7 **Covilhã**, Portugal
16 A 9 **Covington**, TN, U.S.A.
18 L 7 **Covington**, LA, U.S.A.
19 T 3 **Covington**, GA, U.S.A.
20 G 8 **Covington**, MI, U.S.A.
135 P 11 **Cowell**, SA, Australia
63 T 13 **Cowes**, U.K.
135 T 11 **Cowra**, NSW, Australia
58 G 12 **Coxilha Grande**, Brazil ▲▲
55 H 17 **Coxim**, Brazil
107 W 15 **Cox's Bazar**, Bangladesh
128 F 11 **Coyah**, Guinea
47 P 12 **Coyolar**, Costa Rica
45 Z 10 **Cozumel**, Mexico
133 N 14 **Cradock**, Republic of South Africa
136 K 7 **Cradock Channel**, New Zealand ≈
31 O 3 **Craig**, CO, U.S.A.
73 H 22 **Crailsheim**, Germany
86 H 13 **Craiova**, Romania
40 H 7 **Cranberry Portage**, MB, Canada
39 I 21 **Cranbrook**, BC, Canada
63 X 12 **Cranbrook**, U.K.
20 G 10 **Crandon**, WI, U.S.A.
26 J 8 **Crane**, TX, U.S.A.
32 J 12 **Crane**, OR, U.S.A.
144 L 10 **Crary Mountains**, Antarctica ▲▲
32 G 13 **Crater Lake**, OR, U.S.A. ∽
138 H 4 **Crater Point**, Papua New Guinea ▶
54 M 11 **Crateús**, Brazil
63 P 7 **Craven Arms**, U.K.
50 L 5 **Cravo Norte**, Colombia
22 G 12 **Crawford**, NE, U.S.A.
27 P 8 **Crawford**, TX, U.S.A.
21 I 19 **Crawfordsville**, IN, U.S.A.
19 S 8 **Crawfordville**, FL, U.S.A.
17 O 5 **Crawley**, WV, U.S.A.
63 V 12 **Crawley**, U.K.
29 R 6 **Crazy Mtns**, MT, U.S.A. ▲▲
63 N 13 **Crediton**, U.K.
39 K 15 **Cree Lake**, SK, Canada ∽
44 L 5 **Creel**, Mexico
76 D 7 **Crema**, Italy
76 D 7 **Cremona**, Italy
18 L 2 **Crenshaw**, MS, U.S.A.
80 B 10 **Cres**, Croatia ✱
32 H 12 **Crescent**, OR, U.S.A.
19 W 8 **Crescent City**, FL, U.S.A.
33 E 14 **Crescent City**, CA, U.S.A.
19 W 8 **Crescent Lake**, FL, U.S.A. ∽
32 G 12 **Crescent Lake**, OR, U.S.A.
59 C 14 **Crespo**, Argentina
65 T 12 **Crest**, France
23 R 14 **Creston**, IA, U.S.A.
29 V 14 **Creston**, WY, U.S.A.
39 I 21 **Creston**, BC, Canada
19 Q 7 **Crestview**, FL, U.S.A.
83 I 26 **Crete**, Greece ✱
17 S 6 **Crewe**, VA, U.S.A.
63 Q 5 **Crewe**, U.K.
63 P 13 **Crewkerne**, U.K.
58 J 11 **Criciúma**, Brazil
63 O 9 **Crickhowell**, U.K.
60 H 12 **Crieff**, U.K.
80 C 9 **Crikvenica**, Croatia
87 U 11 **Crimea**, Ukraine ◇
54 L 13 **Cristino Castro**, Brazil
47 W 13 **Cristóbal**, Panama
87 O 8 **Criuleni**, Moldova
55 J 15 **Crixás**, Brazil
81 M 16 **Crna Gora**, Macedonia (F.Y.R.O.M.)/Serbia and Montenegro ▲▲
80 G 9 **Croatia**, Europe □
27 S 8 **Crockett**, TX, U.S.A.
63 Z 5 **Cromer**, U.K.
137 D 23 **Cromwell**, New Zealand
49 N 4 **Crooked Island**, The Bahamas ✱
23 O 3 **Crookston**, MN, U.S.A.
19 U 8 **Cross City**, FL, U.S.A.
61 J 15 **Cross Fell**, U.K. ▲
15 T 5 **Cross Island**, ME, U.S.A. ✱
40 J 8 **Cross Lake**, MB, Canada
27 N 6 **Cross Plains**, TX, U.S.A.
129 R 13 **Cross River**, Nigeria ▣
20 J 10 **Cross Village**, MI, U.S.A.
25 V 14 **Crossett**, AR, U.S.A.
16 H 9 **Crossville**, TN, U.S.A.
20 M 13 **Croswell**, MI, U.S.A.
77 N 19 **Crotone**, Italy
29 V 7 **Crow Agency**, MT, U.S.A.
29 P 6 **Crow Peak**, MT, U.S.A. ▲
63 W 12 **Crowborough**, U.K.
18 I 7 **Crowley**, LA, U.S.A.
21 H 16 **Crown Point**, IN, U.S.A.
145 U 3 **Crown Prince Olav Coast**, Antarctica ◇
145 O 3 **Crown Princess Martha Coast**, Antarctica ◇
31 O 9 **Crownpoint**, NM, U.S.A.
62 M 12 **Croyde**, U.K.
63 W 11 **Croydon**, U.K.
135 R 4 **Croydon**, QLD, Australia
64 H 5 **Crozon**, France
58 G 11 **Cruz Alta**, Brazil
58 L 6 **Cruzeiro**, Brazil
54 A 13 **Cruzeiro do Sul**, Brazil
62 L 9 **Crymych**, U.K.
20 G 9 **Crystal Falls**, MI, U.S.A.
79 N 22 **Csenger**, Hungary
79 G 22 **Csorna**, Hungary
79 I 22 **Csóványos**, Hungary ▲
115 O 17 **Cu Lao Cham**, Vietnam ✱
115 O 17 **Cu Lao Re**, Vietnam ✱
115 O 22 **Cu Lao Thu**, Vietnam ✱
133 S 5 **Cuamba**, Mozambique
132 K 6 **Cuando Cubango**, Angola ▣
132 J 7 **Cuangar**, Angola
132 G 2 **Cuanza Norte**, Angola ▣
132 H 3 **Cuanza Sul**, Angola ▣
58 E 12 **Cuareim**, Brazil ∫
45 O 6 **Cuatro Ciénegas**, Mexico
44 L 5 **Cuauhtémoc**, Mexico
21 E 18 **Cuba**, IL, U.S.A.
31 P 9 **Cuba**, NM, U.S.A.
48 I 5 **Cuba**, North America □
132 G 4 **Cubal**, Angola
132 I 6 **Cubango**, Angola ∫
94 H 9 **Cubuk**, Turkey
46 H 5 **Cubulco**, Guatemala
132 I 5 **Cuchi**, Angola
59 F 15 **Cuchilla Grande**, Uruguay ▲▲
59 D 15 **Cuchilla Grande Inferior**, Uruguay ▲▲
57 I 15 **Cuchillo-Có**, Argentina
54 C 9 **Cucuí**, Brazil
132 J 3 **Cucumbi**, Angola
50 J 4 **Cúcuta**, Colombia
105 F 22 **Cuddalore**, India
105 F 20 **Cuddapah**, India
134 G 9 **Cue**, WA, Australia
67 N 5 **Cuéllar**, Spain
132 I 4 **Cuemba**, Angola
52 B 10 **Cuenca**, Ecuador
67 Q 7 **Cuenca**, Spain
120 G 12 **Cuenca**, Philippines
45 N 8 **Cuencamé**, Mexico
45 R 12 **Cuernavaca**, Mexico
27 Q 11 **Cuero**, TX, U.S.A.
48 M 6 **Cueto**, Cuba
54 F 12 **Cuiaba**, Brazil
55 G 16 **Cuiabá**, Brazil
46 H 6 **Cuilapa**, Guatemala
46 F 4 **Cuilco**, Guatemala ∫
132 J 2 **Cuilo**, Angola
110 L 9 **Cuiluan**, China
132 G 1 **Cuimba**, Angola
132 J 5 **Cuito Cuanavale**, Angola
86 G 13 **Cujmir**, Romania
118 E 7 **Cukai**, Malaysia
95 T 12 **Cukurca**, Turkey
121 H 16 **Culasi**, Philippines
29 Y 3 **Culbertson**, MT, U.S.A.
53 C 15 **Culebras**, Peru
68 I 13 **Culemborg**, Netherlands
95 V 10 **Culfa**, Azerbaijan
44 L 8 **Culiacán**, Mexico
121 E 15 **Culion**, Philippines
121 E 15 **Culion**, Philippines ✱
67 Q 12 **Cúllar-Baza**, Spain
67 T 9 **Cullera**, Spain
19 Q 2 **Cullman**, AL, U.S.A.
63 O 13 **Cullompton**, U.K.
17 S 4 **Culpeper**, VA, U.S.A.
51 Q 2 **Cumaná**, Venezuela
16 E 8 **Cumberland**, TN/KY, U.S.A. ∫
17 R 2 **Cumberland**, MD, U.S.A.
39 N 16 **Cumberland Lake**, SK, Canada ∽
41 S 1 **Cumberland Peninsula**, NU, Canada ▶
16 G 10 **Cumberland Plateau**, TN, U.S.A. ◇
20 F 6 **Cumberland Point**, MI, U.S.A. ▶
41 S 2 **Cumberland Sound**, NU, Canada ≈
54 H 9 **Cuminapanema**, Brazil ∫
61 H 14 **Cumnock**, U.K.
44 J 4 **Cumpas**, Mexico
94 H 12 **Çumra**, Turkey
46 G 5 **Cunén**, Guatemala
132 H 6 **Cunene**, Angola ▣
132 F 7 **Cunene**, Angola ∫
76 A 9 **Cuneo**, Italy
115 O 19 **Cung Son**, Vietnam
135 T 9 **Cunnamulla**, QLD, Australia
54 N 13 **Curaçá**, Brazil
54 A 12 **Curaçá**, Brazil ∫
49 R 13 **Curaçao**, Netherlands Antilles ✱
57 F 15 **Curacautín**, Chile
52 E 9 **Curaray**, Peru/Ecuador ∫
56 F 13 **Curicó**, Chile
50 I 10 **Curiplaya**, Colombia
58 J 8 **Curitiba**, Brazil
58 I 10 **Curitibanos**, Brazil
33 M 18 **Currant**, NV, U.S.A.
33 N 16 **Currie**, NV, U.S.A.
135 R 14 **Currie**, TAS, Australia
17 W 7 **Currituck**, NC, U.S.A.
17 W 7 **Currituck Sound**, NC, U.S.A. ≈
35 Q 8 **Curry**, AK, U.S.A.
32 F 12 **Curtin**, OR, U.S.A.
135 V 7 **Curtis Island**, QLD, Australia ✱
54 H 9 **Curuá**, Brazil ∫
54 I 10 **Curumu**, Brazil
53 G 17 **Cusco**, Peru ▣
19 S 5 **Cusseta**, GA, U.S.A.
22 G 10 **Custer**, SD, U.S.A.
29 V 6 **Custer**, MT, U.S.A.
29 P 2 **Cut Bank**, MT, U.S.A.
18 L 8 **Cut Off**, LA, U.S.A.
19 S 5 **Cuthbert**, GA, U.S.A.
19 Y 14 **Cutler Ridge**, FL, U.S.A.
57 G 15 **Cutral-Co**, Argentina
105 J 16 **Cuttack**, India
132 H 6 **Cuvelai**, Angola
130 H 8 **Cuvette**, Congo ▣
72 F 9 **Cuxhaven**, Germany
56 F 2 **Cuya**, Chile
120 F 9 **Cuyapo**, Philippines
121 G 17 **Cuyo**, Philippines
121 G 17 **Cuyo**, Philippines ✱
121 G 15 **Cuyo East Passage**, Philippines ≈
121 G 15 **Cuyo Islands**, Philippines ✱
121 F 16 **Cuyo West Passage**, Philippines ≈
51 S 5 **Cuyuni**, Guyana ∫
53 G 17 **Cuzco**, Peru
131 Q 9 **Cyangugu**, Rwanda
83 I 22 **Cyclades**, Greece ✱
16 J 4 **Cynthiana**, KY, U.S.A.
50 G 6 **Cabo Corrientes**, Colombia ▶
94 G 15 **Cyprus**, Asia □
94 I 14 **Cyprus (Turkish Republic Of Northern Cyprus)**, Asia □
78 F 10 **Czaplinek**, Poland
39 K 19 **Czar**, AB, Canada
78 F 11 **Czarnków**, Poland
79 C 18 **Czech Republic**, Europe □
78 H 9 **Czersk**, Poland
79 I 16 **Częstochowa**, Poland
78 F 11 **Człopa**, Poland
78 G 10 **Człuchów**, Poland

D

109 V 3 **Da Hinggan Ling**, China ▲▲
110 G 11 **Da Hinggan Range**, China ▲▲
108 M 8 **Da Juh**, China
115 O 21 **Đa Lat**, Vietnam
115 O 17 **Đa Năng**, Vietnam
109 N 7 **Da Qaidam**, China
110 J 11 **Da'an**, China
121 K 16 **Daanbantayan**, Philippines
113 Q 5 **Daba Shan**, China ▲▲
50 L 2 **Dabajuro**, Venezuela
128 K 12 **Dabakala**, Côte d'Ivoire
110 F 13 **Daban**, China
79 J 23 **Dabas**, Hungary
127 H 18 **Dabat**, Ethiopia
50 G 5 **Dabeiba**, Colombia
105 C 18 **Dabhol**, India
113 U 6 **Dabie Shan**, China ▲▲
128 G 11 **Dabola**, Guinea
128 K 14 **Dabou**, Côte d'Ivoire
79 J 17 **Dąbrowa Górnicza**, Poland
86 I 13 **Dăbuleni**, Romania
107 U 13 **Dacca**, Bangladesh ■
113 P 11 **Dachang**, China
73 J 24 **Dachau**, Germany
109 R 10 **Dachaun**, China
111 G 16 **Dachengzi**, China
113 P 6 **Dachuan**, China
137 C 25 **Dacre**, New Zealand
96 K 1 **Dādāt**, Syria
127 K 18 **Daddato**, Djibouti
19 V 10 **Dade City**, FL, U.S.A.
105 C 16 **Dadra and Nagar Haveli**, India ▣
101 T 13 **Dadu**, Pakistan
120 J 12 **Daet**, Philippines
113 N 9 **Dafang**, China
113 Y 4 **Dafeng**, China
99 V 7 **Dafīr**, United Arab Emirates
107 W 9 **Dafla Hills**, India ▲▲
127 L 21 **Daga Medo**, Ethiopia
84 I 13 **Dagda**, Latvia
111 E 18 **Dagu**, China
112 M 8 **Daguan**, China
120 F 9 **Dagupan**, Philippines
98 L 8 **Dahabān**, Saudi Arabia
105 B 16 **Dahanu**, India
110 M 9 **Daheiding Shan**, China ▲
127 J 16 **Dahlak Archipelago**, Eritrea ✱
73 M 14 **Dahme**, Germany
108 H 7 **Dahongliutan**, China
97 R 1 **Dahūk**, Iraq
138 M 6 **Dai**, Solomon Islands ✱
111 B 16 **Dai Hai**, China ∽
111 B 17 **Dai Xian**, China
115 E 15 **Daik-u**, Myanmar
123 E 17 **Daimanji-san**, Japan ▲
67 O 9 **Daimiel**, Spain
27 T 5 **Daingerfield**, TX, U.S.A.
123 H 16 **Dainichiga-take**, Japan ▲
112 I 4 **Dainkog**, China
123 I 18 **Daiō-zaki**, Japan ▶
59 B 17 **Daireaux**, Argentina
126 E 9 **Dairût**, Egypt
20 C 9 **Dairyland**, WI, U.S.A.
135 Q 5 **Dajarra**, QLD, Australia
101 P 8 **Dak**, Afghanistan ∽
115 N 18 **Dak Kon**, Vietnam
128 D 8 **Dakar**, Senegal ■
107 U 14 **Dakhin Shahbazpur Island**, Bangladesh ✱
126 D 11 **Dakhla Oasis**, Egypt ◇
128 E 5 **Dakhlet Nouâdhibou**, Mauritania ▣
105 O 25 **Dakoank**, India
105 C 15 **Dakor**, India
129 Q 9 **Dakoro**, Niger
23 O 12 **Dakota City**, NE, U.S.A.
81 L 16 **Đakovica**, Serbia and Montenegro
80 H 9 **Đakovo**, Croatia
132 J 3 **Dala**, Angola
128 G 11 **Dalaba**, Guinea
121 J 18 **Dalaguete**, Philippines
110 E 13 **Dalai Nur**, China ∽
94 D 13 **Dalaman**, Turkey
109 Q 5 **Dalandzadgad**, Mongolia
121 F 17 **Dalanganem Islands**, Philippines ✱
109 P 5 **Dalay**, Mongolia
101 R 11 **Dalbandin**, Pakistan
135 V 8 **Dalby**, QLD, Australia
16 H 8 **Dale Hollow Lake**, TN, U.S.A. ∽
87 S 11 **Daleke**, Ukraine
114 B 11 **Daletme**, Myanmar
26 I 1 **Dalhart**, TX, U.S.A.
43 S 6 **Dalhousie**, QC, Canada
112 J 10 **Dali**, China
113 R 3 **Dali**, China
111 H 18 **Dalian**, China
110 I 13 **Dalin**, China
111 B 15 **Daliuhao**, China
27 Q 6 **Dallas**, TX, U.S.A.
32 F 10 **Dallas**, OR, U.S.A.
80 D 12 **Dalmatia**, Croatia ▲▲
89 W 15 **Dal'negorsk**, Russian Federation
128 J 13 **Daloa**, Côte d'Ivoire
113 O 8 **Dalou Shan**, China ▲▲
105 I 14 **Daltenganj**, India
19 S 1 **Dalton**, GA, U.S.A.
42 A 6 **Dalton**, ON, Canada
63 O 1 **Dalton-in-Furness**, U.K.
120 G 4 **Dalupiri**, Philippines ✱
70 C 10 **Dalvík**, Iceland
134 G 10 **Dalwallinu**, WA, Australia
134 M 2 **Daly**, NT, Australia ∫
135 N 3 **Daly Waters**, NT, Australia
105 B 16 **Daman**, India
105 B 16 **Daman and Diu**, India ▣
126 E 7 **Damanhûr**, Egypt
117 S 14 **Damar**, Indonesia ✱
130 J 5 **Damara**, Central African Republic
132 J 8 **Damaraland**, Namibia ◇
129 U 9 **Damasak**, Nigeria
96 H 7 **Damascus**, Syria ■
129 T 10 **Damaturu**, Nigeria
132 G 1 **Damba**, Angola
129 R 10 **Dambatta**, Nigeria
129 U 10 **Damboa**, Nigeria
105 G 24 **Dambulla**, Sri Lanka
100 K 6 **Damghan**, Iran
113 U 2 **Daming**, China
105 F 14 **Damoh**, India
96 G 6 **Damour**, Lebanon
134 F 6 **Dampier**, WA, Australia
138 E 4 **Dampier Strait**, Papua New Guinea ≈
129 Q 10 **Dan-Gulbi**, Nigeria
107 O 8 **Dana**, Nepal
128 I 13 **Danané**, Côte d'Ivoire
121 K 17 **Danao**, Philippines
102 J 13 **Danata**, Turkmenistan
116 K 10 **Danau Luar**, Indonesia ∽
117 O 11 **Danau Poso**, Indonesia ∽
116 F 13 **Danau Ranau**, Indonesia ∽
116 L 10 **Danau Semayang**, Indonesia ∽
116 J 12 **Danau Sembulu**, Indonesia ∽
116 C 9 **Danau Toba**, Indonesia ∽
117 O 12 **Danau Towuti**, Indonesia ∽
112 L 6 **Danba**, China
14 K 11 **Danbury**, CT, U.S.A.
20 C 9 **Danbury**, WI, U.S.A.
33 M 24 **Danby Lake**, CA, U.S.A. ∽
127 H 23 **Dande**, Ethiopia
105 C 19 **Dandeli**, India
135 S 13 **Dandenong**, VIC, Australia
111 J 16 **Dandong**, China
143 Q 12 **Daneborg**, Greenland
113 R 4 **Danfeng**, China
15 S 3 **Danforth**, ME, U.S.A.
113 N 4 **Dangchang**, China
132 G 2 **Dange**, Angola
103 R 14 **Danghara**, Tajikistan
127 H 19 **Dangila**, Ethiopia
46 K 3 **Dangriga**, Belize
113 V 3 **Dangshan**, China
113 X 5 **Dangtu**, China
127 G 19 **Dangur**, Ethiopia
29 R 12 **Daniel**, WY, U.S.A.
41 X 9 **Daniel's Harbour**, NL, Canada
90 K 13 **Danilov**, Russian Federation
81 I 15 **Danilovgrad**, Serbia and Montenegro
113 R 2 **Daning**, China
95 Z 8 **Dänizkänari**, Azerbaijan
113 S 5 **Danjiangkou Shuiku**, China ∽
123 A 23 **Danjo-guntō**, Japan ✱
92 L 3 **Dankov**, Russian Federation
72 I 11 **Dannenberg**, Germany
127 M 21 **Danot**, Ethiopia
113 U 12 **Danshui**, China
14 E 9 **Dansville**, NY, U.S.A.
73 G 24 **Danube**, Europe ∫
115 D 16 **Danubyu**, Myanmar
16 I 6 **Danville**, KY, U.S.A.
17 Q 7 **Danville**, VA, U.S.A.
21 G 18 **Danville**, IL, U.S.A.
21 I 19 **Danville**, IN, U.S.A.
113 Q 15 **Danxian**, China
121 H 17 **Dao**, Philippines
114 N 12 **Đao Cai Bau**, Vietnam ✱
114 M 12 **Đao Cat Ba**, Vietnam ✱
115 K 22 **Đao Phu Quôc**, Vietnam ✱
115 K 23 **Đao Thô Chur**, Vietnam ✱
115 J 23 **Đao Vây**, Vietnam ✱
113 S 10 **Daoxian**, China
113 P 8 **Daozhen**, China
121 M 18 **Dapa**, Philippines
129 N 11 **Dapaong**, Togo
121 J 20 **Dapitan**, Philippines
110 J 10 **Daqing**, China
97 T 4 **Dāqūq**, Iraq
131 W 12 **Dar Es Salaam**, Tanzania
96 H 8 **Dar'a**, Syria
128 E 8 **Dara**, Senegal
100 K 11 **Dārāb**, Iran
86 L 7 **Darabani**, Romania
120 J 13 **Daraga**, Philippines
125 R 9 **Daraj**, Libya
100 H 8 **Dārān**, Iran
81 K 15 **Đaravica**, Serbia and Montenegro ▲
126 F 11 **Daraw**, Egypt
129 T 10 **Darazo**, Nigeria
100 M 9 **Darband**, Iran
107 Q 11 **Darbhanga**, India
28 M 6 **Darby**, MT, U.S.A.
94 B 8 **Dardanelles**, Turkey ≈
94 M 11 **Darende**, Turkey
127 A 18 **Darfur**, Sudan ◇
103 N 12 **Darganata**, Turkmenistan
136 J 7 **Dargaville**, New Zealand
109 Q 3 **Darhan**, Mongolia
19 W 6 **Darien**, GA, U.S.A.
103 T 6 **Dar'inskiv**, Kazakhstan
47 N 8 **Darío**, Nicaragua
107 S 10 **Darjiling**, India
112 K 4 **Darlag**, China
135 S 10 **Darling**, NSW, Australia ∫
61 J 15 **Darlington**, U.K.
78 F 8 **Darłowka**, Poland
73 F 20 **Darmstadt**, Germany
125 X 7 **Darnah**, Libya
38 E 8 **Darnley Bay**, NT, Canada ≈
67 R 5 **Daroca**, Spain
101 O 5 **Darreh Gaz**, Iran
72 K 8 **Darss**, Germany ✱
102 H 12 **Darta**, Turkmenistan
63 W 11 **Dartford**, U.K.
62 M 14 **Dartmeet**, U.K.
62 M 14 **Dartmoor**, U.K. ◇
43 V 11 **Dartmouth**, NS, Canada
63 N 15 **Dartmouth**, U.K.
138 B 6 **Daru**, Papua New Guinea
117 S 10 **Daruba**, Indonesia
102 K 12 **Darvaza**, Turkmenistan
101 T 9 **Darwazgai**, Afghanistan
63 Q 3 **Darwen**, U.K.
105 E 16 **Darwha**, India
21 N 20 **Darwin**, OH, U.S.A.
57 L 23 **Darwin**, Falkland Islands
134 L 1 **Darwin**, NT, Australia
101 W 9 **Darya Khan**, Pakistan
100 J 11 **Daryācheh-ye Bakhtegan**, Iran ∽
100 J 6 **Daryācheh-ye Namak**, Iran ∽
101 P 10 **Daryācheh-ye Sistau**, Iran ∽
100 J 10 **Daryācheh-ye Tashk**, Iran ∽
100 M 11 **Dārzīn**, Iran
113 R 6 **Dashennongjia**, China ▲
110 H 10 **Dashizhai**, China
102 M 11 **Dashkhovuz**, Turkmenistan
102 L 11 **Dashkhovuzskiy Velayat**, Turkmenistan ▣
100 M 5 **Dasht**, Iran
101 P 14 **Dasht**, Pakistan ∫
101 P 9 **Dasht-e Babus**, Afghanistan ◇
100 J 7 **Dasht-e Kavīr**, Iran ◇
101 O 9 **Dasht-e Khāsh**, Afghanistan ◇
100 M 8 **Dasht-e Lut**, Iran ◇
101 P 10 **Dasht-i Margo**, Afghanistan ◇
101 O 14 **Dashtiari**, Iran
112 M 9 **Dashuijing**, China
121 G 23 **Dassalan**, Philippines ✱
106 H 1 **Dastegil Sar**, India ▲
113 Q 11 **Datang**, China
94 B 13 **Datşşa**, Turkey
122 J 7 **Date**, Japan
113 X 10 **Datian**, China
31 O 11 **Datil**, NM, U.S.A.
109 P 8 **Datong**, China
111 B 16 **Datong**, China

ountry ▣ Internal administrative region: State/Province/Territory/Dependent territory ■ Capital city ▲▲ Mountain range/Undersea ridge ▲ Mountain peak/Volcano/Seamount ◇ Geographic feature ▶ Headland/Point/Cape/Peninsula ◓ Desert ✱ Island/Island group ⁘ Antarctic base ◎ Ocean ≋ Sea ≈ Bay/Gulf/Channel/Strait ∽ Lake ⚑ Salt pan/Dry/Intermittent lake ∫ River

107 P 12 Daudnagar, India
85 F 16 Daugai, Lithuania
84 H 13 Daugavpils, Latvia
105 C 17 Daund, India
115 F 20 Daung Kyun, Myanmar
40 H 9 Dauphin, MB, Canada
19 O 8 Dauphin Island, AL, U.S.A.
129 R 9 Daura, Nigeria
95 Y 7 Däväşşi, Azerbaijan
105 D 20 Davangere, India
121 N 22 Davao, Philippines
117 R 7 Davao Gulf, Philippines
23 W 13 Davenport, IA, U.S.A.
32 K 7 Davenport, WA, U.S.A.
63 T 8 Daventry, U.K.
47 S 14 David, Panama
39 M 19 Davidson, SK, Canada
25 N 12 Davis, OK, U.S.A.
33 G 18 Davis, CA, U.S.A.
145 X 6 Davis, Antarctica
30 G 10 Davis Dam, AZ, U.S.A.
41 V 7 Davis Inlet, NL, Canada
26 H 9 Davis Mountains, TX, U.S.A.
145 Y 8 Davis Sea, Antarctica
41 T 1 Davis Strait, NU, Canada
93 U 2 Davlekanovo, Russian Federation
74 J 8 Davos, Switzerland
39 K 14 Davy Lake, SK, Canada
87 S 8 Davydiv Brid, Ukraine
111 H 16 Dawa, China
99 Y 10 Dawḩat Şawqirah, Oman
85 I 16 Dawhinava, Belarus
98 M 9 Dawqah, Saudi Arabia
99 W 10 Dawqah, Oman
124 D 10 Dawra, Western Sahara
19 S 5 Dawson, GA, U.S.A.
22 K 5 Dawson, ND, U.S.A.
38 A 12 Dawson, YT, Canada
39 G 17 Dawson Creek, BC, Canada
16 E 6 Dawson Springs, KY, U.S.A.
112 K 6 Dawu, China
113 U 6 Dawu, China
99 Z 8 Dawwah, Oman
64 L 13 Dax, France
113 P 12 Daxin, China
111 D 17 Daxing, China
112 L 6 Daxue Shan, China
118 A 5 Dayang Bunting, Malaysia
109 W 2 Dayangshu, China
110 J 7 Dayangshu, China
112 K 10 Dayao, China
112 M 6 Dayi, China
99 Y 6 Dayl, Oman
97 N 4 Dayr az Zawr, Syria
96 J 2 Dayr Ḩāfir, Syria
16 H 10 Dayton, TN, U.S.A.
21 L 19 Dayton, OH, U.S.A.
27 T 10 Dayton, TX, U.S.A.
32 K 9 Dayton, WA, U.S.A.
19 X 9 Daytona Beach, FL, U.S.A.
113 U 10 Dayu, China
32 J 11 Dayville, OR, U.S.A.
113 P 6 Dazhu, China
132 M 13 De Aar, Republic of South Africa
68 H 7 De Cocksdorp, Netherlands
19 Q 7 De Funiak Springs, FL, U.S.A.
69 B 16 De Haan, Belgium
21 G 16 De Kalb, IL, U.S.A.
27 T 4 De Kalb, TX, U.S.A.
89 W 13 De-Kastri-Nysh, Russian Federation
68 H 7 De Koog, Netherlands
35 N 4 De Long Mountains, AK, U.S.A.
68 O 11 De Lutte, Netherlands
69 A 17 De Panne, Belgium
20 G 12 De Pere, WI, U.S.A.
25 S 13 De Queen, AR, U.S.A.
18 H 7 De Ridder, LA, U.S.A.
23 S 13 De Soto, IA, U.S.A.
20 L 9 De Tour Village, MI, U.S.A.
23 W 12 De Witt, IA, U.S.A.
25 X 12 De Witt, AR, U.S.A.
96 G 10 Dead Sea, Israel
48 M 4 Deadman's Cay, The Bahamas
63 Z 11 Deal, U.K.
21 M 15 Dearborn, MI, U.S.A.
39 D 16 Dease Lake, BC, Canada
38 I 8 Dease Strait, NU, Canada
33 L 21 Death Valley, CA, U.S.A.
33 K 21 Death Valley, CA, U.S.A.
119 O 10 Debak, Malaysia
87 Y 6 Debal'tseve, Ukraine
82 B 12 Debar, Macedonia (F.Y.R.O.M.)
79 L 17 Dębica, Poland
89 X 9 Debin, Russian Federation
79 M 14 Dęblin, Poland
78 D 11 Dębno, Poland
127 I 20 Debre Birhan, Ethiopia
127 H 19 Debre Markos, Ethiopia
127 I 19 Debre Werk', Ethiopia
79 M 22 Debrecen, Hungary
81 K 15 Dečani, Serbia and Montenegro
19 P 2 Decatur, AL, U.S.A.
19 S 3 Decatur, GA, U.S.A.
21 F 19 Decatur, IL, U.S.A.
21 K 17 Decatur, IN, U.S.A.
23 P 12 Decatur, NE, U.S.A.
27 P 5 Decatur, TX, U.S.A.
105 E 18 Deccan Plateau, India
144 H 3 Deception Island, Antarctica
77 C 19 Decimomannu, Italy
65 R 8 Decize, France
23 U 10 Decorah, IA, U.S.A.
68 M 9 Dedemsvaart, Netherlands
127 J 20 Deder, Ethiopia
58 K 8 Dedo de Deus, Brazil
95 V 7 Dedop'listsqaro, Georgia
128 L 10 Dédougou, Burkina Faso
133 R 5 Dedza, Malawi
60 I 11 Dee, U.K.
42 H 10 Deep River, ON, Canada
43 S 11 Deer Island, NB, Canada
15 R 6 Deer Isle, ME, U.S.A.
41 X 10 Deer Lake, NL, Canada
32 K 6 Deer Park, WA, U.S.A.
19 Y 12 Deerfield Beach, FL, U.S.A.
127 M 23 Deeri, Somalia
35 N 6 Deering, AK, U.S.A.
21 K 17 Defiance, OH, U.S.A.
112 I 5 Dêgê, China
127 L 21 Degeh Bur, Ethiopia
43 P 7 Dégelis, QC, Canada
129 R 14 Degema, Nigeria
73 L 22 Deggendorf, Germany
92 M 8 Degtevo, Russian Federation
100 J 10 Deh Bīd, Iran
101 Q 10 Deh Shū, Afghanistan
125 Q 8 Dehiba, Tunisia
100 F 7 Dehlorān, Iran
106 J 7 Dehra Dun, India
107 O 12 Dehri, India
113 X 10 Dehua, China
110 K 12 Dehui, China
127 B 21 Deim Zubeir, Sudan
69 D 18 Deinze, Belgium
86 I 8 Dej, Romania
127 I 19 Dejen, Ethiopia
113 P 8 Dejiang, China
127 I 17 Dekemhare, Eritrea
130 L 10 Dekese, Democratic Republic of Congo
130 J 4 Dékoa, Central African Republic
26 L 11 Del Rio, TX, U.S.A.
33 I 22 Delano, CA, U.S.A.
101 Q 9 Delārām, Afghanistan
132 M 11 Delareyville, Republic of South Africa
14 I 10 Delaware, NY, U.S.A.
17 W 3 Delaware, U.S.A.
21 M 18 Delaware, OH, U.S.A.
17 X 2 Delaware Bay, DE, U.S.A.
26 G 7 Delaware Mountains, TX, U.S.A.
82 E 11 Delčevo, Macedonia (F.Y.R.O.M.)
17 S 12 Delco, NC, U.S.A.
74 D 6 Delémont, Switzerland
129 X 9 Délép, Chad
68 F 13 Delft, Netherlands
68 N 6 Delfzijl, Netherlands
127 E 14 Delgo, Sudan
106 J 8 Delhi, India
106 J 8 Delhi, India
100 I 7 Delījān, Iran
38 E 11 Déline, NT, Canada
73 K 15 Delitzsch, Germany
125 N 5 Dellys, Algeria
72 E 12 Delmenhorst, Germany
80 C 9 Delnice, Croatia
135 S 15 Deloraine, TAS, Australia
83 J 21 Delos, Greece
19 Y 12 Delray Beach, FL, U.S.A.
30 J 4 Delta, UT, U.S.A.
31 O 5 Delta, CO, U.S.A.
129 Q 13 Delta, Nigeria
51 S 3 Delta Amacuro, Venezuela
35 S 7 Delta Junction, AK, U.S.A.
19 X 9 Deltona, FL, U.S.A.
105 B 16 Delvada, India
130 L 11 Demba, Democratic Republic of Congo
127 G 20 Dembī Dolo, Ethiopia
131 N 5 Dembia, Central African Republic
92 H 1 Demidov, Russian Federation
31 O 14 Deming, NM, U.S.A.
94 D 10 Demirci, Turkey
94 C 10 Demirköprü Baraji, Turkey
82 N 11 Demirköy, Turkey
72 L 9 Demmin, Germany
130 M 9 Democratic Republic Of Congo, Africa
19 O 4 Demopolis, AL, U.S.A.
117 Y 12 Demta, Indonesia
90 F 13 Demyansk, Russian Federation
68 H 7 Den Burg, Netherlands
115 H 15 Den Chai, Thailand
68 H 8 Den Helder, Netherlands
68 I 8 Den Oever, Netherlands
127 J 18 Denakil Desert, Ethiopia
35 R 8 Denali, AK, U.S.A.
127 L 22 Denan, Ethiopia
103 Q 14 Denau, Uzbekistan
42 H 11 Denbigh, ON, Canada
63 O 4 Denbigh, U.K.
116 H 12 Dendang, Indonesia
128 J 8 Dendâra, Mauritania
69 E 19 Denderleeuw, Belgium
69 F 18 Dendermonde, Belgium
144 J 8 Dendtler Island, Antarctica
68 N 11 Denekamp, Netherlands
129 S 9 Dengas, Niger
129 Q 10 Denge, Nigeria
113 T 3 Dengfeng, China
129 S 11 Dengi, Nigeria
113 S 5 Dengzhou, China
134 E 8 Denham, WA, Australia
67 U 9 Denia, Spain
141 U 1 Denig, Nauru
135 S 12 Deniliquin, NSW, Australia
33 J 14 Denio, NV, U.S.A.
23 Q 12 Denison, IA, U.S.A.
27 Q 4 Denison, TX, U.S.A.
94 D 12 Denizli, Turkey
17 N 13 Denmark, SC, U.S.A.
71 C 25 Denmark, Europe
134 G 12 Denmark, WA, Australia
143 O 14 Denmark Strait, Arctic Ocean
63 Z 8 Dennington, U.K.
116 L 15 Denpasar, Indonesia
17 V 3 Denton, MD, U.S.A.
27 Q 5 Denton, TX, U.S.A.
138 G 6 D'Entrecasteaux Islands, Papua New Guinea
31 R 4 Denver, CO, U.S.A.
104 C 13 Deogarh, India
107 R 12 Deoghar, India
105 F 16 Deoli, India
105 F 14 Deori, India
107 P 10 Deoria, India
107 N 13 Deosil, India
42 H 8 Depot-Forbes, QC, Canada
145 W 5 Depot Peak, Antarctica
129 Y 6 Dépression Du Mourdi, Chad
89 U 8 Deputatskiy, Russian Federation
112 J 8 Dêqên, China
113 S 12 Deqing, China
101 W 11 Dera Ghazi Khan, Pakistan
101 V 9 Dera Ismail Khan, Pakistan
86 M 5 Derazhnya, Ukraine
93 S 15 Derbent, Russian Federation
103 Q 14 Derbent, Uzbekistan
43 V 10 Derbert, NS, Canada
110 H 6 Derbur, China
25 N 6 Derby, KS, U.S.A.
63 S 5 Derby, U.K.
134 I 4 Derby, WA, Australia
129 Y 9 Déréssa, Chad
87 T 6 Deriyivka, Ukraine
87 Z 6 Derkul, Ukraine
112 J 8 Dêrong, China
133 S 6 Derre, Mozambique
15 N 8 Derry, NH, U.S.A.
63 X 6 Dersingham, U.K.
111 B 14 Derst, China
127 H 15 Derudeb, Sudan
80 H 10 Derventa, Bosnia and Herzegovina
103 P 4 Derzhavinsk, Kazakhstan
21 H 16 Des Plains, IL, U.S.A.
23 S 13 Des Moines, IA, U.S.A.
23 S 12 Des Moines, IA/MO, U.S.A.
31 T 8 Des Moines, NM, U.S.A.
56 H 11 Desaguadero, Argentina
44 E 2 Descanso, Mexico
127 I 19 Desē, Ethiopia
57 I 21 Deseado, Argentina
57 H 20 Deseado, Argentina
44 H 3 Desemboque, Mexico
30 I 3 Deseret Peak, UT, U.S.A.
33 M 25 Desert Center, CA, U.S.A.
30 I 2 Desert Peak, UT, U.S.A.
30 K 9 Desert View, AZ, U.S.A.
56 I 10 Desiderio Tello, Argentina
83 D 15 Deskati, Greece
87 Q 3 Desna, Ukraine
121 M 17 Desolation Point, Philippines
80 M 12 Despotovac, Serbia and Montenegro
73 K 15 Dessau, Germany
69 E 18 Destelbergen, Belgium
86 E 11 Deta, Romania
133 N 7 Dete, Zimbabwe
73 F 14 Detmold, Germany
21 M 15 Detroit, MI, U.S.A.
43 S 4 Détroit de Jacques-Cartier, QC, Canada
43 T 4 Détroit d'Honguedo, QC, Canada
23 P 5 Detroit Lakes, MN, U.S.A.
69 K 16 Deurne, Netherlands
75 Y 5 Deutschkreutz, Austria
75 V 8 Deutschlandsberg, Austria
86 H 10 Deva, Romania
94 K 9 Deveci Dağlari, Turkey
94 K 11 Develi, Turkey
68 L 11 Deventer, Netherlands
104 B 12 Devikot, India
137 H 15 Devil River Peak, New Zealand
20 D 8 Devil's Island, WI, U.S.A.
22 L 3 Devil's Lake, ND, U.S.A.
22 L 3 Devil's Lake, ND, U.S.A.
29 Y 8 Devil's Tower, WY, U.S.A.
82 H 11 Devin, Bulgaria
27 O 11 Devine, TX, U.S.A.
135 S 15 Deviot, TAS, Australia
63 R 11 Devizes, U.K.
82 M 8 Devnya, Bulgaria
37 P 4 Devon Island, NU, Canada
135 S 15 Devonport, TAS, Australia
94 G 7 Devrek, Turkey
105 E 15 Dewas, India
63 S 3 Dewsbury, U.K.
113 N 6 Deyang, China
100 M 8 Deyhuk, Iran
100 I 12 Deyyer, Iran
100 G 8 Dezfūl, Iran
111 D 19 Dezhou, China
99 T 5 Dhahran, Saudi Arabia
107 U 12 Dhaka, Bangladesh
99 P 13 Dhamār, Yemen
105 G 16 Dhamtari, India
107 R 13 Dhanbad, India
106 M 8 Dhangadhi, Nepal
107 R 10 Dhankuta, Nepal
105 D 15 Dhar, India
107 R 10 Dharan Bazar, Nepal
107 W 12 Dharmanagar, India
105 C 19 Dharwad, India
107 O 8 Dhaulagiri, Nepal
107 Y 9 Dhemaji, India
96 G 10 Dhībān, Jordan
99 O 14 Dhubāb, Yemen
107 U 11 Dhuburi, India
105 D 16 Dhule, India
127 O 20 Dhuudo, Somalia
115 O 21 Di Linh, Vietnam
83 J 26 Dia, Greece
33 G 21 Diablo Range, CA, U.S.A.
133 U 3 Diaca, Mozambique
128 K 9 Diafarabé, Mali
128 G 9 Dialafara, Mali
128 F 9 Dialakoto, Senegal
59 C 14 Diamante, Argentina
135 Q 7 Diamantina, QLD, Australia
107 S 14 Diamond Harbour, India
31 N 2 Diamond Peak, CO, U.S.A.
29 R 14 Diamondville, WY, U.S.A.
128 F 8 Diamounguél, Senegal
113 S 13 Dianbai, China
112 K 10 Diancang Shan, China
113 P 6 Dianjiang, China
110 M 11 Diaoling, China
129 O 10 Diapaga, Burkina Faso
132 H 11 Diaz Point, Namibia
99 X 5 Dibā al Ḩişn, Oman
130 M 11 Dibaya, Democratic Republic of Congo
130 K 10 Dibaya-Lubwe, Democratic Republic of Congo
127 A 18 Dibbis, Sudan
132 L 12 Dibeng, Republic of South Africa
107 X 9 Dibrugarh, India
96 K 3 Dibsī, Syria
26 L 5 Dickens, TX, U.S.A.
22 H 5 Dickinson, ND, U.S.A.
16 E 8 Dickson, TN, U.S.A.
95 P 11 Dicle Baraji, Turkey
68 L 13 Didam, Netherlands
63 T 10 Didcot, U.K.
128 I 9 Didiéni, Mali
104 D 12 Didwana, India
82 L 12 Didymoteicho, Greece
65 U 12 Die, France
128 L 10 Diébougou, Burkina Faso
73 F 20 Dieburg, Germany
128 H 12 Diéké, Guinea
69 K 23 Diekirch, Luxembourg
69 L 24 Diekirch, Luxembourg
128 I 9 Diéma, Mali
68 H 11 Diemen, Netherlands
114 J 12 Điên Biên Phu, Vietnam
115 L 14 Diên Châu, Vietnam
84 G 12 Dienvidsusēja, Latvia
72 E 13 Diepholz, Germany
65 O 2 Dieppe, France
68 L 12 Dieren, Netherlands
25 S 12 Dierks, AR, U.S.A.
69 I 18 Diest, Belgium
129 U 9 Diffa, Niger
129 U 8 Diffa, Niger
131 O 5 Digba, Democratic Republic of Congo
43 T 11 Digby, NS, Canada
24 I 4 Dighton, KS, U.S.A.
65 V 13 Digne-les-Baines, France
65 S 9 Digoin, France
121 M 23 Digos, Philippines
101 V 14 Digri, Pakistan
127 K 24 Diinsoor, Somalia
65 T 7 Dijon, France
70 G 13 Dikanäs, Sweden
127 K 19 Dikhil, Djibouti
94 B 10 Dikili, Turkey
89 S 11 Dikimdya, Russian Federation
128 J 12 Dikodougou, Côte d'Ivoire
69 B 18 Diksmuide, Belgium
89 N 6 Dikson, Russian Federation
129 V 10 Dikwa, Nigeria
127 I 22 Dīla, Ethiopia
117 Q 15 Dili, East Timor
131 O 5 Dili, Democratic Republic of Congo
95 U 8 Dilijan, Armenia
27 N 12 Dilley, TX, U.S.A.
73 C 21 Dilligen, Germany
127 D 18 Dilling, Sudan
73 I 23 Dillingen, Germany
35 N 11 Dillingham, AK, U.S.A.
17 R 11 Dillon, SC, U.S.A.
29 O 8 Dillon, MT, U.S.A.
130 L 14 Dilolo, Democratic Republic of Congo
69 K 18 Dilsen, Belgium
97 T 6 Diltāwa, Iraq
107 X 11 Dimapur, India
130 M 11 Dimbelenge, Democratic Republic of Congo
128 K 13 Dimbokro, Côte d'Ivoire
81 O 14 Dimitrovgrad, Serbia and Montenegro
82 J 10 Dimitrovgrad, Bulgaria
93 S 2 Dimitrovgrad, Russian Federation
26 J 3 Dimmit, TX, U.S.A.
121 M 18 Dinagat, Philippines
121 M 18 Dinagat, Philippines
107 T 11 Dinajpur, Bangladesh
64 K 5 Dinan, France
69 H 22 Dinant, Belgium
107 P 11 Dinapur, India
94 E 11 Dinar, Turkey
80 E 12 Dinara, Croatia
80 E 11 Dinaric Alps, Bosnia and Herzegovina
127 G 18 Dinder, Sudan
105 E 23 Dindigul, India
105 G 15 Dindori, India
130 I 11 Dinga, Democratic Republic of Congo
120 G 10 Dingalan Bay, Philippines
113 P 1 Dingbian, China
113 Q 1 Dingbian, China
132 F 1 Dinge, Angola
107 R 10 Dingla, Nepal
61 A 20 Dingle, Republic of Ireland
61 A 20 Dingle Bay, Republic of Ireland
14 I 11 Dingmans Ferry, PA, U.S.A.
113 U 11 Dingnan, China
73 L 23 Dingolfing, Germany
113 V 3 Dingtao, China
128 G 10 Dinguiraye, Guinea
43 Y 7 Dingwall, NS, Canada
113 N 2 Dingxi, China
111 D 17 Dingxing, China
111 C 18 Dingzhou, China
114 N 12 Dinh Lâp, Vietnam
107 T 10 Dinhata, India
73 H 22 Dinkelsbühl, Germany
31 N 3 Dinosaur, CO, U.S.A.
69 F 15 Dinteloord, Netherlands
68 M 13 Dinxperlo, Netherlands
128 J 10 Dioïla, Mali
58 G 9 Dionísio Cerqueira, Brazil
55 I 20 Dioníso Cerqueira, Brazil
128 D 9 Diouloulou, Senegal
128 I 8 Dioumara, Mali
129 P 10 Dioundiou, Niger
128 E 8 Diourbel, Senegal
106 M 8 Dipayal, Nepal
107 W 11 Diphu, India
121 J 20 Dipolog, Philippines
69 L 25 Dippach, Luxembourg
128 L 8 Diré, Mali
127 K 20 Dirē Dawa, Ethiopia
47 N 9 Diriamba, Nicaragua
132 K 7 Dirico, Angola
134 E 8 Dirk Hartog Island, WA, Australia
129 U 6 Dirkou, Niger
135 U 9 Dirranbandi, QLD, Australia
99 N 10 Ḑirs, Saudi Arabia
135 Q 13 Discovery Bay, SA, Australia
74 H 9 Disentis, Switzerland
143 N 11 Disko, Greenland
145 W 4 Dismal Mountains, Antarctica
107 V 10 Dispur, India
43 N 10 Disraëli, QC, Canada
63 Y 7 Diss, U.K.
17 U 3 District of Columbia, U.S.A.
121 G 16 Dit, Philippines
105 A 16 Diu, India
121 M 19 Diuata Mountains, Philippines
121 L 19 Diuata Point, Philippines
100 G 5 Dīvān Derreh, Iran
130 F 9 Divénié, Congo
29 O 7 Divide, MT, U.S.A.
120 I 7 Divilacan Bay, Philippines
55 K 18 Divinópolis, Brazil
47 V 15 Divisa, Panama
93 N 11 Divnoye, Russian Federation
128 J 13 Divo, Côte d'Ivoire
95 N 10 Divriği, Turkey
101 T 14 Diwana, Pakistan
21 F 16 Dixon, IL, U.S.A.
39 B 18 Dixon Entrance, BC, Canada
49 N 3 Dixon's, The Bahamas
95 S 9 Diyadin, Turkey
95 P 12 Diyarbakir, Turkey
129 T 5 Djado, Niger
125 O 7 Djamâa, Algeria
130 H 9 Djambala, Congo
130 J 9 Djampie, Democratic Republic of Congo
125 Q 12 Djanet, Algeria
138 G 3 Djaul Island, Papua New Guinea
124 L 7 Djebel Aïssa, Algeria
125 P 12 Djebel Ounane, Algeria
125 P 13 Djebel Telerhteba, Algeria
125 N 12 Djebr, Algeria
129 X 10 Djébrène, Chad
129 X 9 Djédaa, Chad
124 K 11 Djedid, Algeria
124 M 6 Djelfa, Algeria
131 N 4 Djéma, Central African Republic
128 K 9 Djenné, Mali
130 L 9 Djia, Democratic Republic of Congo
128 M 9 Djibo, Burkina Faso
127 K 19 Djibouti, Djibouti
127 L 18 Djibouti, Africa
128 I 8 Djiguéni, Mauritania
130 L 7 Djolu, Democratic Republic of Congo
129 O 11 Djougou, Benin
129 U 15 Djoum, Cameroon
70 D 11 Djúpivogur, Iceland
70 I 7 Djupvik, Norway
87 U 7 Dmytrivka, Ukraine
87 W 6 Dmytrivka, Ukraine
87 Q 4 Dnieper, Europe
86 K 6 Dniester, Moldova/Ukraine
87 U 6 Dniprodzerzhyns'k, Ukraine
87 U 6 Dnipropetrovs'k, Ukraine
87 Q 9 Dniprovs'kyy Lyman, Ukraine
87 P 10 Dnistrov'ky Lyman, Ukraine
90 E 12 Dno, Russian Federation
85 F 21 Dnyaprowski Buhski Kanal, Belarus
115 L 14 Đô Luong, Vietnam
114 M 12 Đo Son, Vietnam
43 S 8 Doaktown, NB, Canada
116 M 13 Doangdoangan Kecil, Indonesia
129 W 12 Doba, Chad
85 L 19 Dobasna, Belarus
84 E 11 Dobele, Latvia
73 L 16 Döbeln, Germany
75 V 1 Dobersberg, Austria
78 E 11 Dobiegniew, Poland
117 V 13 Dobo, Indonesia
80 H 10 Doboj, Bosnia and Herzegovina
78 K 9 Dobre Miasto, Poland
82 N 6 Dobrich, Bulgaria
82 N 7 Dobrich, Bulgaria
92 M 5 Dobrinka, Russian Federation
85 D 15 Dobrovol'sk, Russian Federation
85 N 20 Dobrush, Belarus
87 Q 1 Dobryanka, Ukraine
91 T 12 Dobryanka, Russian Federation
121 E 24 Doc Can, Philippines
134 L 7 Docker River, NT, Australia
106 I 4 Doda, India
105 D 22 Dodda Betta, India
83 L 21 Dodecanese, Greece
24 J 6 Dodge City, KS, U.S.A.
21 E 14 Dodgeville, WI, U.S.A.
62 K 15 Dodman Point, U.K.
131 U 11 Dodoma, Tanzania
131 U 12 Dodoma, Tanzania
29 U 2 Dodson, MT, U.S.A.
68 L 13 Doesburg, Netherlands
68 L 13 Doetinchem, Netherlands
19 S 8 Dog Island, FL, U.S.A.
42 B 6 Dog Lake, ON, Canada
108 K 8 Dogai Coring, China
123 D 17 Dōgo, Japan
129 P 9 Dogondoutchi, Niger
129 W 11 Dogoumbo, Chad
95 O 8 Doğu Karadeniz Dağlari, Turkey
95 T 10 Doğubeyazit, Turkey
99 U 5 Doha, Qatar
107 W 14 Dohazari, Bangladesh
115 F 14 Doi Inthanon, Thailand
71 D 18 Dokka, Norway
68 K 6 Dokkum, Netherlands
85 J 15 Dokshytsy, Belarus
87 X 7 Dokuchayevs'k, Ukraine
57 I 18 Dolavón, Argentina
42 M 6 Dolbeau, QC, Canada
65 U 7 Dôle, France
47 S 14 Dolega, Panama
63 N 6 Dolgellau, U.K.
89 X 14 Dolinsk, Russian Federation
81 N 14 Doljevac, Serbia and Montenegro
72 D 11 Dollart, Germany
72 J 13 Dolle, Germany
144 J 4 Dolleman Island, Antarctica
79 J 19 Dolný Kubín, Slovakia
127 K 23 Dolo Odo, Ethiopia
76 F 5 Dolomites, Italy
109 Q 5 Doloon, Mongolia
46 J 3 Dolores, Guatemala
59 D 15 Dolores, Uruguay
59 D 17 Dolores, Argentina
38 F 8 Dolphin and Union Strait, NU, Canada
132 H 11 Dolphin Head, Namibia
86 I 6 Dolyna, Ukraine
87 S 7 Dolyns'ka, Ukraine
58 F 13 Dom Pedrito, Brazil
107 T 11 Domar, Bangladesh
79 M 18 Domaradz, Poland
79 B 18 Domažlice, Czech Republic
71 C 17 Dombås, Norway
133 Q 8 Dombe, Mozambique
79 H 25 Dombóvár, Hungary
39 G 19 Dome Creek, BC, Canada
56 F 9 Domeyko, Chile
64 M 5 Domfront, France
49 Y 10 Dominica, North America
47 Q 13 Dominical, Costa Rica
49 R 8 Dominican Republic, North America
127 M 21 Domo, Ethiopia
76 B 5 Domodossola, Italy
83 E 17 Domokos, Greece
117 N 15 Dompu, Indonesia
80 C 7 Domžale, Slovenia
44 K 6 Don, Mexico
60 I 10 Don, U.K.
92 M 9 Don, Russian Federation
18 K 8 Donaldsonville, LA, U.S.A.
19 S 6 Donalsonville, GA, U.S.A.
73 E 25 Donaueschingen, Germany
73 I 23 Donauwörth, Germany
63 T 3 Doncaster, U.K.
132 G 3 Dondo, Angola
133 R 7 Dondo, Mozambique
121 G 19 Dondonay, Philippines
61 D 15 Donegal, Republic of Ireland
61 C 15 Donegal Bay, Republic of Ireland
87 X 7 Donets'k, Ukraine
115 N 16 Đông Ha, Vietnam
115 M 15 Đông Hôi, Vietnam
129 S 12 Donga, Nigeria
113 R 10 Dong'an, China
134 F 10 Dongara, WA, Australia
112 M 10 Dongchuan, China
108 J 9 Dongco, China
113 Q 15 Dongfang, China
110 O 10 Dongfanghong, China
111 K 14 Dongfeng, China
117 N 11 Donggala, Indonesia
111 J 17 Donggang, China
113 U 12 Dongguan, China
113 R 14 Donghai Dao, China
113 R 9 Dongkou, China
113 P 11 Donglan, China
110 N 12 Dongning, China
112 K 8 Dongnyi, China
130 J 6 Dongo, Democratic Republic of Cong
132 H 5 Dongo, Angola
127 E 14 Dongola, Sudan
127 E 23 Dongotona Mountains, Sudan
130 J 6 Dongou, Congo
113 S 13 Dongping, China
113 V 2 Dongping, China
113 R 14 Dongshan, China
113 W 12 Dongshan Dao, China
109 S 7 Dongsheng, China
113 Y 4 Dongtai, China
113 T 8 Dongting Hu, China
113 Y 7 Dongyang, China
111 F 19 Dongying, China
113 W 7 Dongzhi, China
68 L 7 Donkerbroek, Netherlands
70 F 11 Dønna, Norway
42 M 9 Donnacona, QC, Canada
76 B 6 Donnas, Italy
39 H 17 Donnelly, AB, Canada
75 T 6 Donnersbach, Austria
67 Q 1 Donostia-San Sebastián, Spain
83 K 22 Donoussa, Greece
93 N 12 Donskoye, Russian Federation
121 J 14 Donsol, Philippines
20 H 11 Door Peninsula, WI, U.S.A.
63 Q 13 Dorchester, U.K.
132 I 9 Dordabis, Namibia
65 N 12 Dordogne, France
69 G 14 Dordrecht, Netherlands
129 N 9 Dori, Burkina Faso
63 V 11 Dorking, U.K.
74 J 6 Dornbirn, Austria
60 H 9 Dornoch Firth, U.K.
109 T 3 Dornod, Mongolia
109 R 5 Dornogovi, Mongolia
128 M 8 Doro, Mali
79 I 22 Dorog, Hungary
71 H 14 Dorotea, Sweden
134 E 8 Dorre Island, WA, Australia
135 V 10 Dorrigo, NSW, Australia
129 S 13 Dorsale Camerounaise, Cameroon
73 D 15 Dortmund, Germany
94 L 13 Dörtyol, Turkey
131 P 5 Doruma, Democratic Republic of Con
100 M 7 Dorūneh, Iran
66 K 12 Dos Hermanas, Spain
46 I 1 Dos Lagunos, Guatemala
57 I 18 Dos Pozos, Argentina
82 H 11 Dospat, Bulgaria
129 O 9 Dosso, Niger
129 O 10 Dosso, Niger
102 I 6 Dossor, Kazakhstan
103 Y 8 Dostyk, Kazakhstan
35 S 7 Dot Lake, AK, U.S.A.
19 R 6 Dothan, AL, U.S.A.
65 R 2 Douai, France
129 S 14 Douala, Cameroon
64 H 5 Douarnenez, France
137 D 23 Double Cone, New Zealand
19 P 2 Double Springs, AL, U.S.A.
137 A 23 Doubtful Sound, New Zealand
136 I 5 Doubtless Bay, New Zealand
64 M 7 Doué-la Fontaine, France
128 L 8 Douentza, Mali
19 U 6 Douglas, GA, U.S.A.
29 Y 12 Douglas, WY, U.S.A.
30 M 15 Douglas, AZ, U.S.A.
61 G 16 Douglas, U.K.
132 M 12 Douglas, Republic of South Africa
16 K 9 Douglas Lake, TN, U.S.A.
65 Q 2 Doullens, France
55 H 18 Dourados, Brazil
129 W 10 Dourbali, Chad
125 P 7 Douz, Tunisia
14 J 12 Dover, NJ, U.S.A.
15 O 8 Dover, NH, U.S.A.
16 D 8 Dover, TN, U.S.A.
17 W 2 Dover, DE, U.S.A.
63 Z 12 Dover, U.K.
100 H 7 Dow Rūd, Iran
101 S 7 Dowl at Yār, Afghanistan
101 Q 8 Dowlatābād, Afghanistan
101 R 6 Dowlatābād, Afghanistan
29 P 13 Downey, ID, U.S.A.
63 X 6 Downham Market, U.K.
14 I 10 Downsville, NY, U.S.A.
101 U 6 Dowshī, Afghanistan
85 M 19 Dowsk, Belarus
123 D 17 Dōzen, Japan
87 R 4 Drabiv, Ukraine
58 H 5 Dracena, Brazil
68 L 7 Drachten, Netherlands
86 M 13 Dragalina, Romania
86 J 13 Drăgănești-Vlașca, Romania
83 K 26 Dragonada, Greece
85 G 21 Drahichyn, Belarus
57 G 26 Drake Passage, Chile
133 N 14 Drakensberg, Republic of South Africa
82 H 12 Drama, Greece
71 D 20 Drammen, Norway
79 F 25 Dráva, Hungary
80 F 7 Drava, Croatia
80 C 6 Dravograd, Slovenia
78 E 10 Drawa, Poland
39 I 19 Drayton Valley, AB, Canada
68 M 9 Drenthe, Netherlands
16 C 8 Dresden, TN, U.S.A.
73 N 17 Dresden, Germany
84 K 13 Dretun', Belarus
65 O 4 Dreux, France
71 E 17 Drevsjø, Norway
32 K 12 Drewsey, OR, U.S.A.
137 L 15 Dreyers Rock, New Zealand
81 K 16 Drin, Albania
80 I 11 Drina, Bosnia and Herzegovina
81 K 17 Drini i Zi, Albania
18 I 5 Driskill Mountain, LA, U.S.A.
80 E 12 Drniš, Croatia
86 G 12 Drobeta-Turnu Severin, Romania
61 E 17 Drogheda, Republic of Ireland

Country · Internal administrative region: State/Province/Territory/Dependent territory · Capital city · Mountain range/Undersea ridge · Mountain peak/Volcano/Seamount · Geographic feature · Headland/Point/Cape/Peninsula · Desert · Island/Island group · Antarctic base · Ocean · Sea · Bay/Gulf/Channel/Strait · Lake · Salt pan/Dry/Intermittent lake

I 5 Drohobych, Ukraine
R 8 Droitwich, U.K.
A 9 Dronero, Italy
N 12 Dronning Ingrid Land, Greenland
K 10 Dronten, Netherlands
V 2 Drosendorf, Austria
W 6 Drosh, Pakistan
K 19 Drumheller, AB, Canada
L 9 Drummond, MI, U.S.A.
N 5 Drummond, MT, U.S.A.
L 9 Drummond Island, MI, U.S.A.
M 10 Drummondville, QC, Canada
E 17 Druskininkai, Lithuania
L 17 Druts', Belarus
I 13 Druya, Belarus
V 8 Druzhina, Russian Federation
I 11 Drwęca, Poland
V 15 Dry Tortugas, FL, U.S.A.
R 8 Dryanovo, Bulgaria
J 11 Dryden, ON, Canada
K 13 Drysa, Belarus
C 12 Du Bois, PA, U.S.A.
F 12 Du Quoin, IL, U.S.A.
O 10 Duanshan, China
U 7 Duaringa, QLD, Australia
J 4 Ḑubā, Saudi Arabia
X 5 Dubai, United Arab Emirates
O 8 Dubăsari, Moldova
O 8 Dubăsari Reservoir, Moldova
J 3 Dubawnt Lake, NU, Canada
U 11 Dubbo, NSW, Australia
U 4 Dublin, GA, U.S.A.
F 18 Dublin, Republic of Ireland
I 14 Dubna, Russian Federation
K 3 Dubno, Ukraine
P 10 Dubois, ID, U.S.A.
S 11 Dubois, WY, U.S.A.
P 8 Dubovka, Russian Federation
H 15 Dubrovnik, Croatia
L 2 Dubrovytsya, Ukraine
M 16 Dubrowna, Belarus
W 11 Dubuque, IA, U.S.A.
O 18 Đuc Pho, Vietnam
O 21 Đuc Trong, Vietnam
L 3 Duchesne, UT, U.S.A.
Q 5 Duchess, QLD, Australia
I 10 Ducktown, TN, U.S.A.
T 8 Dudchany, Ukraine
L 26 Dudelange, Luxembourg
E 18 Dudhani, India
O 12 Dudhi, India
N 8 Dudinka, Russian Federation
R 7 Dudley, U.K.
I 13 Duékoué, Côte d'Ivoire
N 4 Dueñas, Spain
L 4 Duero, Spain
P 10 Dufek Coast, Antarctica
Q 7 Duff Islands, Solomon Islands
B 6 Dufourspitze, Italy/Switzerland
C 13 Dugi Otok, Croatia
C 16 Duisburg, Germany
E 21 Duk Faiwil, Sudan
J 21 Dukat i Ri, Albania
N 13 Dukathole, Republic of South Africa
U 5 Dukhān, Qatar
O 5 Dukhnah, Saudi Arabia
U 11 Duki, Pakistan
H 14 Dūkštas, Lithuania
O 8 Dulan, China
P 8 Dulce, NM, U.S.A.
K 9 Dulce, Argentina
O 5 Dulce Nombre de Culmí, Honduras
M 8 Dŭlgopol, Bulgaria
E 18 Duliu, China
K 17 Duljugan Point, Philippines
D 15 Dülmen, Germany
M 6 Dulovo, Bulgaria
V 7 Dululu, QLD, Australia
T 5 Duluth, MN, U.S.A.
N 12 Dulverton, U.K.
H 6 Dūmā, Syria
J 19 Dumaguete, Philippines
E 10 Dumai, Indonesia
E 17 Dumaran, Philippines
W 13 Dumas, AR, U.S.A.
J 1 Dumas, TX, U.S.A.
I 6 Ḑumayr, Syria
G 13 Dumbarton, U.K.
L 11 Dumbrăveni, Romania
K 4 Dumchele, India
T 4 Dumfries, VA, U.S.A.
H 15 Dumfries, U.K.
R 12 Dumka, India
U 7 Dumont d'Urville, Antarctica
U 15 Dumont d'Urville Sea, Antarctica
F 7 Dumyāt, Egypt
H 22 Dunajská Streda, Slovakia
I 26 Dunaszekcső, Hungary
I 24 Dunaújváros, Hungary
F 6 Dunavtsi, Bulgaria
L 6 Dunayivtsi, Ukraine
M 12 Duncan, OK, U.S.A.
N 13 Duncan, AZ, U.S.A.
N 22 Duncan Passage, India
J 7 Duncansby Head, U.K.
D 9 Dundaga, Latvia
U 2 Dundalk, MD, U.S.A.
E 17 Dundalk, Republic of Ireland
E 17 Dundalk Bay, Republic of Ireland
E 13 Dundas, ON, Canada
M 1 Dundas Strait, NT, Australia
I 12 Dundee, U.K.
P 12 Dundee, Republic of South Africa
H 3 Dundee Island, Antarctica
Q 4 Dundgovi, Mongolia
E 24 Dunedin, New Zealand
C 14 Dungarpur, India
D 20 Dungarvan, Republic of Ireland
Y 13 Dungeness, U.K.
P 5 Dungu, Democratic Republic of Congo
E 6 Dungun, Malaysia
H 13 Dungunab, Sudan
L 13 Dunhua, China
N 6 Dunhuang, China
E 10 Dunilupinar, Turkey
Q 1 Dunkerque, France
N 12 Dunkery Beacon, U.K.
C 9 Dunkirk, NY, U.S.A.
M 13 Dunkwa, Ghana
Q 13 Dunlap, IA, U.S.A.
N 3 Dunmarra, NT, Australia
H 11 Dunmore, PA, U.S.A.
R 10 Dunn, NC, U.S.A.

19 V 9 Dunnellon, FL, U.S.A.
22 K 13 Dunning, NE, U.S.A.
137 D 24 Dunrobin, New Zealand
22 K 2 Dunseith, ND, U.S.A.
33 G 15 Dunsmuir, CA, U.S.A.
63 U 9 Dunstable, U.K.
137 D 23 Dunstan Mountains, New Zealand
84 F 10 Dunte, Latvia
38 K 13 Dunvegan Lake, NT, Canada
111 E 14 Duolun, China
82 F 10 Dupnista, Bulgaria
22 I 8 Dupree, SD, U.S.A.
29 O 3 Dupuyer, MT, U.S.A.
20 C 11 Durand, WI, U.S.A.
21 L 14 Durand, MI, U.S.A.
31 O 7 Durango, CO, U.S.A.
44 M 7 Durango, Mexico
45 N 8 Durango, Mexico
47 O 4 Durango, Honduras
67 P 1 Durango, Spain
82 O 6 Durankulak, Bulgaria
25 O 13 Durant, OK, U.S.A.
59 E 15 Durazno, Uruguay
59 E 15 Durazno, Uruguay
133 P 13 Durban, Republic of South Africa
67 O 13 Dúrcal, Spain
73 B 17 Düren, Germany
105 G 16 Durg, India
107 R 13 Durgapur, India
17 R 9 Durham, NC, U.S.A.
61 J 15 Durham, U.K.
116 E 10 Duri, Indonesia
87 N 9 Durlești, Moldova
81 J 14 Durmitor, Serbia and Montenegro
60 G 8 Durness, U.K.
75 Y 3 Dürnkrut, Austria
81 J 18 Durrës, Albania
63 Q 10 Dursley, U.K.
94 D 9 Dursunbey, Turkey
138 A 6 Duru, Papua New Guinea
127 M 20 Durukhsi, Somalia
82 O 12 Durusu Gölü, Turkey
137 I 15 D'Urville Island, New Zealand
101 S 11 Dushai, Pakistan
102 M 14 Dushak, Turkmenistan
113 P 10 Dushan, China
103 R 13 Dushanbe, Tajikistan
14 G 11 Dushore, PA, U.S.A.
137 A 24 Dusky Sound, New Zealand
73 C 16 Düsseldorf, Germany
144 J 8 Dustin Island, Antarctica
116 F 11 Dusunmudo, Indonesia
34 K 14 Dutch Harbor, AK, U.S.A.
91 S 7 Dutovo, Russian Federation
129 S 10 Dutse, Nigeria
129 R 10 Dutsin-Ma, Nigeria
105 F 20 Duttaluru, India
91 U 14 Duvan, Russian Federation
135 R 1 Duyfken Point, QLD, Australia
113 P 10 Duyun, China
79 M 15 Duża, Poland
94 G 8 Düzce, Turkey
82 K 7 Dve Mogili, Bulgaria
90 K 6 Dvinskaya Guba, Russian Federation
87 X 4 Dvorichna, Ukraine
105 A 15 Dwarka, India
21 G 17 Dwight, IL, U.S.A.
28 K 5 Dworshak Reservoir, ID, U.S.A.
87 Z 7 Dyakove, Ukraine
16 B 8 Dyersburg, TN, U.S.A.
89 T 10 Dyeundyu, Russian Federation
87 U 4 Dykan'ka, Ukraine
63 Y 12 Dymchurch, U.K.
87 P 3 Dymer, Ukraine
87 X 6 Dymytrov, Ukraine
79 M 18 Dynów, Poland
135 U 6 Dysart, QLD, Australia
83 D 20 Dytiki Ellas, Greece
83 D 14 Dytiki Makedonia, Greece
93 V 1 Dyurtyuli, Russian Federation
133 X 4 Dzaoudzi, France
95 Z 10 Dżarskij, Azerbaijan
109 N 3 Dzavhan, Mongolia
93 O 1 Dzerzhinsk, Russian Federation
87 X 6 Dzerzhyns'k, Ukraine
103 O 9 Dzhalagash, Kazakhstan
103 T 11 Dzhalal-Abadskaya Oblast', Kyrgyzstan
102 H 5 Dzhangala, Kazakhstan
87 U 11 Dzhankoy, Ukraine
103 X 8 Dzhansugurov, Kazakhstan
102 F 5 Dzhanybek, Kazakhstan
87 S 10 Dzharylhats'ka Zatoka, Ukraine
102 I 12 Dzhebel, Turkmenistan
103 T 14 Dzhilandy, Tajikistan
103 Q 12 Dzhizak, Uzbekistan
92 K 13 Dzhubga, Russian Federation
87 N 6 Dzhuryn, Ukraine
103 O 8 Dzhusaly, Kazakhstan
78 K 10 Działdowo, Poland
45 Y 10 Dzilam de Bravo, Mexico
125 O 7 Dzioua, Algeria
85 J 14 Dzisna, Belarus
85 F 21 Dzivin, Belarus
109 N 2 Dzur, Mongolia
109 R 3 Dzuunmod, Mongolia
85 I 18 Dzyarzhynsk, Belarus
85 J 22 Dzyarzhynsk, Belarus
85 I 17 Dzyarzhynskaya Hara, Belarus

E

115 O 19 Ea Hleo, Vietnam
31 U 5 Eads, CO, U.S.A.
30 M 11 Eagar, AZ, U.S.A.
35 T 6 Eagle, AK, U.S.A.
41 W 8 Eagle, NL, Canada
15 Q 2 Eagle Lake, ME, U.S.A.
15 R 1 Eagle Lake, ME, U.S.A.
33 H 16 Eagle Lake, CA, U.S.A.
26 M 12 Eagle Pass, TX, U.S.A.
20 F 9 Eagle River, WI, U.S.A.
63 W 3 Easington, U.K.
63 T 1 Easingwold, U.K.
16 L 11 Easley, SC, U.S.A.
63 X 6 East Anglia, U.K.
145 R 4 East Antarctica, Antarctica
14 D 9 East Aurora, NY, U.S.A.
18 M 9 East Bay, LA, U.S.A.
138 E 5 East Bay, Papua New Guinea
49 Q 5 East Caicos, Turks and Caicos Islands
136 O 10 East Cape, New Zealand
109 X 12 East China Sea, China/Japan
63 Y 6 East Dereham, U.K.

57 L 24 East Falkland, Falkland Islands
63 W 12 East Grinstead, U.K.
14 M 12 East Hampton, NY, U.S.A.
60 H 13 East Kilbride, U.K.
21 O 17 East Liverpool, OH, U.S.A.
133 O 14 East London, Republic of South Africa
62 L 14 East Looe, U.K.
138 H 4 East New Britain, Papua New Guinea
19 S 3 East Point, GA, U.S.A.
138 C 4 East Sepik, Papua New Guinea
89 V 5 East Siberian Sea, Russian Federation
21 E 21 East St Louis, IL, U.S.A.
117 R 15 East Timor, Asia
63 X 13 Eastbourne, U.K.
10 E 12 Easter Island, Chile
105 G 24 Eastern, Sri Lanka
107 R 10 Eastern, Nepal
128 G 12 Eastern, Sierra Leone
128 M 13 Eastern, Ghana
131 W 7 Eastern, Kenya
133 P 4 Eastern, Zambia
133 N 14 Eastern Cape, Republic of South Africa
126 F 9 Eastern Desert, Egypt
127 F 22 Eastern Equatoria, Sudan
105 F 20 Eastern Ghats, India
138 D 5 Eastern Highlands, Papua New Guinea
63 T 12 Eastleigh, U.K.
41 Q 10 Eastmain, QC, Canada
41 P 10 Eastmain, QC, Canada
19 U 5 Eastman, GA, U.S.A.
14 I 12 Easton, PA, U.S.A.
17 V 3 Easton, MD, U.S.A.
63 Q 14 Easton, U.K.
63 T 5 Eastwood, U.K.
19 T 3 Eatonton, GA, U.S.A.
20 D 11 Eau Claire, WI, U.S.A.
140 L 15 Eaurupik, Federated States of Micronesia
129 P 11 Eban, Nigeria
45 R 10 Ebano, Mexico
63 O 9 Ebbw Vale, U.K.
129 T 15 Ebebiyin, Equatorial Guinea
75 S 5 Ebensee, Austria
94 G 11 Eber Gölü, Turkey
72 M 12 Eberswalde-Finow, Germany
122 J 5 Ebetsu, Japan
112 M 7 Ebian, China
123 C 23 Ebino, Japan
108 J 4 Ebinur Hu, China
77 K 16 Eboli, Italy
129 T 15 Ebolowa, Cameroon
140 Y 5 Ebon, Marshall Islands
132 H 9 Ebony, Namibia
129 R 13 Ebonyi, Nigeria
67 T 5 Ebro, Spain
94 A 8 Eceabat, Turkey
124 L 6 Ech Chélif, Algeria
74 B 9 Echallens, Switzerland
82 I 12 Echinos, Greece
123 G 16 Echizen-misaki, Japan
32 J 9 Echo, OR, U.S.A.
38 G 10 Echo Bay, NT, Canada
42 A 8 Echo Bay, ON, Canada
69 K 17 Echt, Netherlands
69 M 24 Echternach, Luxembourg
135 S 12 Echuca, VIC, Australia
66 M 12 Écija, Spain
20 K 9 Eckermann, MI, U.S.A.
72 H 8 Eckernförde, Germany
52 A 9 Ecuador, South America
127 J 17 Ed, Eritrea
127 B 19 Ed Da'ein, Sudan
127 G 19 Ed Damazin, Sudan
127 F 15 Ed Damer, Sudan
127 E 15 Ed Debba, Sudan
127 E 17 Ed Dueim, Sudan
68 I 10 Edam, Netherlands
60 I 7 Eday, U.K.
16 D 7 Eddyville, KY, U.S.A.
68 K 13 Ede, Netherlands
129 P 12 Ede, Nigeria
129 S 14 Edéa, Cameroon
26 M 8 Eden, TX, U.S.A.
61 I 15 Eden, U.K.
135 U 13 Eden, NSW, Australia
137 C 25 Edendale, New Zealand
17 V 8 Edenton, NC, U.S.A.
82 D 13 Edessa, Greece
136 M 10 Edgecumbe, New Zealand
22 M 6 Edgeley, ND, U.S.A.
22 G 11 Edgemont, SD, U.S.A.
143 U 11 Edgeøya, Svalbard
27 P 15 Edinburg, TX, U.S.A.
60 I 13 Edinburgh, U.K.
86 M 7 Edineț, Moldova
82 M 11 Edirne, Turkey
94 B 6 Edirne, Turkey
125 Q 10 Edjeleh, Algeria
16 H 7 Edmonton, KY, U.S.A.
39 J 18 Edmonton, AB, Canada
43 Q 7 Edmundston, NB, Canada
27 R 11 Edna, TX, U.S.A.
129 Q 13 Edo, Nigeria
76 E 5 Edolo, Italy
94 B 9 Edremit, Turkey
94 A 9 Edremit Körfezi, Turkey
39 I 18 Edson, AB, Canada
56 J 13 Eduardo Castex, Argentina
145 N 11 Edward VII Peninsula, Antarctica
145 X 4 Edward VIII Gulf, Antarctica
26 K 8 Edwards Plateau, TX, U.S.A.
21 F 20 Edwardsville, IL, U.S.A.
130 H 9 Edzouga, Congo
34 M 10 Eek, AK, U.S.A.
69 D 17 Eeklo, Belgium
68 N 5 Eemshaven, Netherlands
139 R 11 Éfaté, Vanuatu
75 S 3 Eferding, Austria
21 G 20 Effingham, IL, U.S.A.
117 T 11 Eftorobi, Indonesia
109 S 3 Eg, Mongolia
35 N 11 Egegik, AK, U.S.A.
79 K 22 Eger, Hungary
75 W 2 Eggenburg, Austria
73 L 24 Eggenfelden, Germany
69 H 20 Eghezée, Belgium
70 D 10 Egilsstaðir, Iceland
94 F 12 Eğirdir, Turkey
94 F 11 Eğirdir Gölü, Turkey
65 P 10 Égletons, France
36 M 3 Eglinton Island, NT, Canada
89 Z 6 Egvekinot, Russian Federation

126 C 10 Egypt, Africa
73 G 24 Ehingen, Germany
123 C 24 Ei, Japan
68 M 12 Eibergen, Netherlands
75 V 8 Eibiswald, Austria
71 B 19 Eidfjord, Norway
73 B 19 Eifel, Germany
74 F 9 Eiger, Switzerland
60 F 11 Eigg, U.K.
105 B 25 Eight Degree Channel, Maldives
144 J 8 Eights Coast, Antarctica
134 H 5 Eighty Mile Beach, WA, Australia
73 L 16 Eilenburg, Germany
96 F 11 Ein Yahav, Israel
135 S 4 Einasleigh, QLD, Australia
73 H 15 Einbeck, Germany
69 J 16 Eindhoven, Netherlands
70 B 11 Eiríksjökull, Iceland
54 B 12 Eirunepé, Brazil
73 H 17 Eisenach, Germany
75 U 6 Eisenerz, Austria
75 U 9 Eisenkappel, Austria
75 Y 5 Eisenstadt, Austria
73 I 18 Eisfeld, Germany
85 F 17 Eišiškės, Lithuania
73 J 15 Eisleben Lutherstadt, Germany
67 W 9 Eivissa, Spain
67 S 3 Ejea de los Caballeros, Spain
133 W 10 Ejeda, Madgascar
109 P 6 Ejin Qi, China
95 T 9 Ejmiatsin, Armenia
128 M 12 Ejura, Ghana
45 T 14 Ejutla, Mexico
29 Y 6 Ekalaka, MT, U.S.A.
137 K 15 Eketahuna, New Zealand
103 U 3 Ekibastuz, Kazakhstan
89 Q 9 Ekonda, Russian Federation
130 I 7 Ekouamou, Congo
71 F 23 Eksjö, Sweden
35 O 11 Ekuk, AK, U.S.A.
130 L 8 Ekuku, Democratic Republic of Congo
41 N 9 Ekwan, ON, Canada
125 Q 11 El Adeb Larache, Algeria
126 D 8 El 'Alamein, Egypt
125 O 8 El Alia, Algeria
66 L 12 El Arahal, Spain
44 H 5 El Arco, Mexico
124 K 7 El Aricha, Algeria
126 G 7 El 'Arîsh, Egypt
126 F 10 El Balyana, Egypt
44 L 3 El Barreal, Mexico
127 F 19 El Barun, Sudan
51 N 4 El Baúl, Venezuela
124 L 7 El Bayadh, Algeria
127 J 24 El Beru Hagia, Somalia
47 R 9 El Bluff, Nicaragua
57 G 17 El Bolsón, Argentina
125 Q 8 El Borma, Tunisia
127 D 22 El Buheyrat, Sudan
57 H 17 El Cain, Argentina
33 K 26 El Cajon, CA, U.S.A.
50 K 6 El Campin, Colombia
27 R 11 El Campo, TX, U.S.A.
52 B 8 El Carmen, Ecuador
53 L 18 El Carmen, Bolivia
45 N 7 El Casco, Mexico
33 M 26 El Centro, CA, U.S.A.
53 M 20 El Cerro, Bolivia
45 W 13 El Chichónal, Mexico
44 G 2 El Chinero, Mexico
45 Z 10 El Cuyo, Mexico
50 F 9 El Diviso, Colombia
25 O 6 El Dorado, KS, U.S.A.
25 V 14 El Dorado, AR, U.S.A.
44 L 8 El Dorado, Mexico
50 K 9 El Dorado, Colombia
50 J 11 El Encanto, Colombia
46 J 4 El Estor, Guatemala
126 E 9 El Faiyûm, Egypt
127 B 17 El Fasher, Sudan
126 E 9 El Fashn, Egypt
127 K 21 El Fud, Ethiopia
44 K 6 El Fuerte, Mexico
127 A 17 El Geneina, Sudan
127 F 17 El Geteina, Sudan
127 F 17 El Gezira, Sudan
126 E 8 El Gîza, Egypt
124 M 9 El Goléa, Algeria
46 J 4 El Golfete, Guatemala
44 G 2 El Golfo de Santa Clara, Mexico
128 G 4 El Hammâmi, Mauritania
128 J 4 El Hank, Mauritania
47 S 14 El Hato del Volcán, Panama
127 G 18 El Hawata, Sudan
127 C 18 El Hilla, Sudan
127 H 18 El Homr, Algeria
124 G 7 El Jadida, Morocco
125 Q 6 El Jem, Tunisia
124 G 8 El Kelaâ des Srarhna, Morocco
127 K 22 Ēl Kerē, Ethiopia
127 E 15 El Khandaq, Sudan
126 E 11 El Khârga, Egypt
128 K 5 El Khnâchich, Mali
127 K 22 Ēl K'oran, Ethiopia
127 D 19 El Lagowa, Sudan
47 X 13 El Llano, Panama
49 S 7 El Macao, Dominican Republic
126 E 8 El Mansûra, Egypt
51 R 5 El Manteco, Venezuela
125 O 7 El Meghaïer, Algeria
126 E 9 El Minya, Egypt
67 O 6 El Molar, Spain
128 I 6 El Mreyyé, Mauritania
127 C 19 El Muglad, Sudan
46 L 5 El Negrito, Honduras
121 E 16 El Nido, Philippines
127 D 18 El Obeid, Sudan
127 C 18 El Odaiya, Sudan
45 O 6 El Oro, Mexico
52 A 11 El Oro, Ecuador
125 O 7 El Oued, Algeria
21 F 17 El Paso, IL, U.S.A.
26 E 7 El Paso, TX, U.S.A.
67 U 6 El Perelló, Spain
47 X 13 El Porvenir, Panama
46 I 5 El Progreso, Guatemala
46 I 6 El Progreso, Guatemala
46 M 8 El Puente, Nicaragua
53 L 19 El Puente, Bolivia
66 K 13 El Puerto de Santa Maria, Spain
126 D 11 El Qasr, Egypt
47 Z 15 El Real, Panama
24 M 10 El Reno, OK, U.S.A.

126 F 11 El Ridisiya Bahari, Egypt
66 K 11 El Ronquillo, Spain
126 E 8 El Saff, Egypt
44 H 3 El Sahuaro, Mexico
57 H 21 El Salado, Argentina
44 M 8 El Salto, Mexico
46 J 7 El Salvador, North America
56 G 7 El Salvador, Chile
121 L 20 El Salvador, Philippines
49 S 7 El Seibo, Dominican Republic
56 G 13 El Sosneado, Argentina
44 M 4 El Sueco, Mexico
66 K 3 El Teleno, Spain
51 Q 4 El Tigre, Venezuela
56 F 9 El Toro, Chile
59 B 14 El Trebol, Argentina
126 F 9 El Tûr, Egypt
57 G 24 El Turbio, Argentina
47 W 14 El Valle, Panama
67 W 5 El Vendrell, Spain
46 M 8 El Viejo, Nicaragua
50 K 4 El Vigia, Venezuela
131 X 6 El Wak, Kenya
127 D 17 El Wuz, Sudan
83 F 23 Elafonisos, Greece
83 L 26 Elasa, Greece
83 E 15 Elassona, Greece
96 F 13 Elat, Israel
140 M 15 Elato, Federated States of Micronesia
95 O 10 Elazığ, Turkey
19 Q 6 Elba, AL, U.S.A.
81 K 19 Elbasan, Albania
32 H 8 Elbe, WA, U.S.A.
72 I 11 Elbe, Czech Republic/Germany
19 U 2 Elberton, GA, U.S.A.
94 M 11 Elbistan, Turkey
78 J 8 Elbląg, Poland
39 M 19 Elbow, SK, Canada
93 N 14 Elbrus, Russian Federation
68 K 10 Elburg, Netherlands
100 I 5 Elburz Mountains, Iran
67 S 10 Elche, Spain
67 R 10 Elche de la Sierra, Spain
67 S 10 Elda, Spain
89 U 11 El'dikan, Russian Federation
25 U 5 Eldon, MO, U.S.A.
21 G 22 Eldorado, IL, U.S.A.
26 L 9 Eldorado, TX, U.S.A.
58 F 9 Eldorado, Argentina
54 J 12 Eldorado dos Carajás, Brazil
131 U 7 Eldoret, Kenya
83 G 20 Elefsina, Greece
84 E 12 Eleja, Latvia
131 U 4 Elemi Triangle, Kenya
82 K 8 Elena, Bulgaria
31 P 13 Elephant Butte Reservoir, NM, U.S.A.
144 G 2 Elephant Island, Antarctica
48 L 2 Eleuthera, The Bahamas
21 G 16 Elgin, IL, U.S.A.
22 I 6 Elgin, ND, U.S.A.
27 Q 9 Elgin, TX, U.S.A.
32 K 10 Elgin, OR, U.S.A.
60 I 9 Elgin, U.K.
131 T 7 Elgon, Kenya
117 T 15 Eliase, Indonesia
31 T 12 Elida, NM, U.S.A.
82 G 9 Elin Pelin, Bulgaria
131 N 8 Elipa, Democratic Republic of Congo
54 L 13 Eliseu Martins, Brazil
93 O 11 Elista, Russian Federation
14 J 13 Elizabeth, NJ, U.S.A.
17 W 8 Elizabeth City, NC, U.S.A.
16 L 8 Elizabethton, TN, U.S.A.
16 G 6 Elizabethtown, KY, U.S.A.
17 S 11 Elizabethtown, NC, U.S.A.
78 M 9 Ełk, Poland
24 J 10 Elk City, OK, U.S.A.
28 L 7 Elk City, ID, U.S.A.
39 K 18 Elk Point, AB, Canada
23 S 7 Elk River, MN, U.S.A.
21 J 16 Elkhart, IN, U.S.A.
24 G 7 Elkhart, KS, U.S.A.
21 G 14 Elkhorn, WI, U.S.A.
82 L 10 Elkhovo, Bulgaria
17 O 8 Elkin, NC, U.S.A.
17 P 3 Elkins, WV, U.S.A.
33 M 16 Elko, NV, U.S.A.
39 J 21 Elko, BC, Canada
16 F 10 Elkton, TN, U.S.A.
17 R 4 Elkton, VA, U.S.A.
19 S 5 Ellaville, GA, U.S.A.
37 N 2 Ellef Ringnes Island, NU, Canada
22 M 6 Ellendale, ND, U.S.A.
32 I 8 Ellensburg, WA, U.S.A.
63 P 6 Ellesmere, U.K.
37 P 1 Ellesmere Island, NU, Canada
63 P 4 Ellesmere Port, U.K.
19 S 1 Ellijay, GA, U.S.A.
133 O 14 Elliot, Republic of South Africa
42 C 9 Elliot Lake, ON, Canada
135 N 3 Elliott, NT, Australia
17 Q 5 Elliott Knob, VA, U.S.A.
133 N 10 Ellisras, Republic of South Africa
135 O 11 Elliston, SA, Australia
60 J 10 Ellon, U.K.
15 R 5 Ellsworth, ME, U.S.A.
20 C 11 Ellsworth, WI, U.S.A.
144 J 8 Ellsworth Land, Antarctica
144 L 8 Ellsworth Mountains, Antarctica
73 H 22 Ellwangen, Germany
32 G 7 Elma, WA, U.S.A.
94 E 13 Elmalı, Turkey
74 K 7 Elmen, Austria
14 F 10 Elmira, NY, U.S.A.
43 W 8 Elmira, PE, Canada
72 G 10 Elmshorn, Germany
24 I 8 Elmwood, OK, U.S.A.
30 K 13 Eloy, AZ, U.S.A.
68 K 13 Elst, Netherlands
73 M 16 Elsterwerda, Germany
136 J 13 Eltham, New Zealand
93 Q 8 El'ton, Russian Federation
105 G 19 Eluru, India
84 H 8 Elva, Estonia
66 J 9 Elvas, Portugal
71 E 18 Elverum, Norway
54 A 12 Elvira, Brazil
21 J 18 Elwood, IN, U.S.A.
33 N 18 Ely, NV, U.S.A.
63 W 7 Ely, U.K.
21 N 16 Elyria, OH, U.S.A.
73 G 14 Elze, Germany
139 R 11 Émaé, Vanuatu

101 U 5 Emām Ṣaḥēb, Afghanistan
102 K 7 Emba, Kazakhstan
102 L 6 Emba, Kazakhstan
46 J 7 Embalse Cerrón Grande, El Salvador
57 H 15 Embalse Cerros Colorados, Argentina
46 H 5 Embalse Chixoy, Guatemala
67 Q 8 Embalse de Alarcón, Spain
66 L 5 Embalse de Almendra, Spain
67 Q 6 Embalse de Buendia, Spain
66 M 8 Embalse de Cíjara, Spain
66 M 8 Embalse de García Sola, Spain
51 R 4 Embalse de Guri, Venezuela
67 N 12 Embalse de Iznajar, Spain
66 L 9 Embalse de Orellana, Spain
66 K 8 Embalse de Valdecañas, Spain
66 M 9 Embalse del Zújar, Spain
57 H 15 Embalse Ezequiel Ramos Mexía, Argentina
57 H 18 Embalse Florentino Ameghino, Argentina
56 J 5 Embarcación, Argentina
130 K 8 Embondo, Democratic Republic of Congo
64 K 7 Embouchure de la Loire, France
131 V 8 Embu, Kenya
72 D 10 Emden, Germany
112 M 7 Emei, China
135 U 6 Emerald, QLD, Australia
30 K 5 Emery, UT, U.S.A.
94 D 10 Emet, Turkey
138 B 6 Emeti, Papua New Guinea
129 X 6 Emi Koussi, Chad
76 F 9 Emilia-Romagna, Italy
45 X 13 Emiliano Zapata, Mexico
108 J 3 Emin, China
138 F 2 Emirau Island, Papua New Guinea
94 F 10 Emirdağ, Turkey
135 T 14 Emita, TAS, Australia
72 C 13 Emlichheim, Germany
84 D 7 Emmaste, Estonia
68 K 9 Emmeloord, Netherlands
68 N 9 Emmen, Netherlands
73 B 14 Emmerich, Germany
135 S 7 Emmet, QLD, Australia
23 R 11 Emmetsburg, IA, U.S.A.
34 L 8 Emmonak, AK, U.S.A.
26 I 11 Emory Peak, TX, U.S.A.
44 I 5 Empalme, Mexico
58 C 10 Empedrado, Argentina
76 E 10 Empoli, Italy
17 T 7 Emporia, VA, U.S.A.
25 P 5 Emporia, KS, U.S.A.
14 D 11 Emporium, PA, U.S.A.
72 D 12 Ems, Germany
42 F 10 Emsdale, ON, Canada
133 P 11 Emzinoni, Republic of South Africa
96 F 10 En Gedi, Israel
96 F 11 'En Hazeva, Israel
127 C 18 En Nahud, Sudan
117 W 12 Enarotali, Indonesia
59 G 20 Encarnación, Paraguay
27 N 13 Encinal, TX, U.S.A.
33 K 26 Encinitas, CA, U.S.A.
31 R 11 Encino, NM, U.S.A.
56 H 11 Encón, Argentina
58 H 12 Encruzilhada do Sul, Brazil
79 L 21 Encs, Hungary
118 E 9 Endau, Malaysia
117 O 15 Endeh, Indonesia
140 K 4 Enderbury, Kiribati
145 U 3 Enderby Land, Antarctica
14 H 10 Endicott, NY, U.S.A.
35 P 4 Endicott Mountains, AK, U.S.A.
134 F 10 Eneabba, WA, Australia
59 D 19 Energía, Argentina
82 K 13 Enez, Turkey
94 A 7 Enez, Turkey
14 L 10 Enfield, CT, U.S.A.
17 T 8 Enfield, NC, U.S.A.
43 V 10 Enfield, NS, Canada
63 W 10 Enfield, U.K.
138 B 4 Enga, Papua New Guinea
20 J 9 Engadine, MI, U.S.A.
71 C 15 Engan, Norway
122 L 4 Engaru, Japan
74 G 8 Engelberg, Switzerland
75 R 3 Engelhartszell, Austria
93 Q 5 Engel's, Russian Federation
68 H 6 Engelschmangat, Netherlands
68 L 5 Engelsmanplaat, Netherlands
116 E 13 Enggano, Indonesia
69 E 20 Enghien, Belgium
25 W 12 England, AR, U.S.A.
61 I 19 England, U.K.
41 X 9 Englee, NL, Canada
42 E 7 Englehart, ON, Canada
63 Q 14 English Channel, France/United Kingdom
144 J 6 English Coast, Antarctica
84 E 10 Engure, Latvia
84 E 10 Engures ezers, Latvia
24 M 8 Enid, OK, U.S.A.
122 J 6 Eniwa, Japan
68 I 9 Enkhuizen, Netherlands
77 J 22 Enna, Italy
38 L 12 Ennadai Lake, NU, Canada
29 P 8 Ennis, MT, U.S.A.
61 B 19 Ennis, Republic of Ireland
61 E 19 Enniscorthy, Republic of Ireland
61 D 16 Enniskillen, U.K.
75 T 4 Enns, Austria
113 S 13 Enping, China
64 L 5 Enree, France
68 N 11 Enschede, Netherlands
44 F 2 Ensenada, Mexico
113 Q 7 Enshi, China
123 I 18 Enshū-nada, Japan
131 S 8 Entebbe, Uganda
19 R 6 Enterprise, AL, U.S.A.
30 H 7 Enterprise, UT, U.S.A.
32 L 10 Enterprise, OR, U.S.A.
39 H 14 Enterprise, NT, Canada
121 D 17 Enterprise Point, Philippines
39 H 19 Entrance, AB, Canada
59 C 14 Entre Ríos, Argentina
66 H 8 Entroncamento, Portugal
129 R 13 Enugu, Nigeria
129 R 13 Enugu, Nigeria
89 Z 5 Enurmino, Russian Federation
54 B 12 Envira, Brazil
66 K 11 Epe, Netherlands
130 I 7 Epéna, Congo
65 S 4 Épernay, France
14 G 13 Ephrata, PA, U.S.A.
32 J 7 Ephrata, WA, U.S.A.

Country | Internal administrative region: State/Province/Territory/Dependent territory | Capital city | Mountain range/Undersea ridge | Mountain peak/Volcano/Seamount | Geographic feature | Headland/Point/Cape/Peninsula | Desert | Island/Island group | Antarctic base | Ocean | Sea | Bay/Gulf/Channel/Strait | Lake | Salt pan/Dry/Intermittent lake | River

139 R 11 Epi, Vanuatu ♣
65 V 5 Épinal, France
94 H 15 Episkopi, Cyprus
63 W 10 Epping, U.K.
63 V 11 Epsom, U.K.
57 J 14 Epu-pel, Argentina
63 U 3 Epworth, U.K.
130 K 8 Equateur, Democratic Republic of Congo ▣
105 L 20 Equatorial Channel, Maldives ≈
129 R 15 Equatorial Guinea, Africa □
124 I 8 Er Rachidia, Morocco
127 E 18 Er Rahad, Sudan
124 J 9 Er Raoui, Algeria ◇
127 F 19 Er Renk, Sudan
138 C 5 Erave, Papua New Guinea
94 L 8 Erbaa, Turkey
95 T 11 Erşşek, Turkey
95 S 10 Erciş, Turkey
94 K 11 Erciyes Dağl, Turkey ▲
79 I 23 Érd, Hungary
94 C 8 Erdek, Turkey
94 J 13 Erdemli, Turkey
109 Q 3 Erdenet, Mongolia
109 Q 5 Erdenetsogt, Mongolia
73 K 24 Erding, Germany
58 H 10 Erechim, Brazil
109 T 2 Ereentsav, Mongolia
94 I 12 Ereğli, Turkey
94 G 7 Ereğli, Turkey
110 B 13 Erenhot, China
124 I 8 Erfoud, Morocco
73 I 17 Erfurt, Germany
128 K 5 Erg Atouila, Mali ◇
124 H 13 'Erg Chech, Algeria ◇
129 W 8 Erg du Djourab, Chad ◇
124 I 10 Erg labès, Algeria ◇
124 G 11 Erg Iguidi, Algeria ◇
95 O 11 Ergani, Turkey
109 S 5 Ergel, Mongolia
82 L 13 Ergene, Turkey ʃ
84 G 11 Ērgļi, Latvia
111 J 15 Erhulai, China
138 C 5 Eri, Papua New Guinea ʃ
66 F 9 Ericeira, Portugal
14 B 10 Erie, PA, U.S.A.
83 A 15 Eriekoussa, Greece ♣
128 K 5 'Erîgât, Mali ◇
40 I 10 Eriksdale, MB, Canada
122 L 6 Erimo, Japan
122 L 7 Erimo-misaki, Japan ▶
60 E 11 Eriskay, U.K. ♣
127 H 16 Eritrea, Africa □
72 M 13 Erkner, Germany
73 I 20 Erlangen, Germany
135 N 7 Erldunda, NT, Australia
68 J 11 Ermelo, Netherlands
133 P 11 Ermelo, Republic of South Africa
94 H 13 Ermenek, Turkey
83 F 21 Ermioni, Greece
83 I 21 Ermoupoli, Greece
73 E 17 Erndtebrück, Germany
75 X 3 Ernstbrunn, Austria
105 E 22 Erode, India
135 R 8 Eromanga, QLD, Australia
132 H 9 Erongo, Namibia ▣
69 F 22 Erquelinnes, Belgium
61 B 16 Erris Head, Republic of Ireland ▶
15 N 5 Errol, NH, U.S.A.
139 R 12 Erromango, Vanuatu ♣
81 L 20 Ersekë, Albania
110 I 4 Ershiwuzhan, China
110 J 4 Ershizhan, China
23 P 4 Erskine, MN, U.S.A.
108 L 4 Ertai, China
95 R 12 Eruh, Turkey
58 G 13 Erval, Brazil
73 F 15 Erwitte, Germany
83 F 19 Erythres, Greece
112 J 10 Eryuan, China
110 K 7 Erzhan, China
89 O 14 Erzin, Russian Federation
94 L 13 Erzin, Turkey
95 O 9 Erzincan, Turkey
95 Q 9 Erzurum, Turkey
85 D 14 Eržvilkas, Lithuania
124 E 11 Es Semara, Western Sahara
127 F 18 Es Suki, Sudan
138 G 7 Esa-ala, Papua New Guinea
122 J 7 Esan-misaki, Japan ▶
122 I 8 Esashi, Japan
122 K 3 Esashi, Japan
71 B 25 Esbjerg, Denmark
30 K 7 Escalante, UT, U.S.A.
121 J 17 Escalante, Philippines
45 N 6 Escalón, Mexico
20 H 10 Escanaba, MI, U.S.A.
45 X 12 Escárcega, Mexico
120 I 5 Escarpada Point, Philippines ▶
69 F 16 Escaut, Belgium ʃ
69 K 26 Esch-sur-Alzette, Luxembourg
73 H 16 Eschwege, Germany
53 H 19 Escoma, Bolivia
33 K 26 Escondido, CA, U.S.A.
47 Q 9 Escondido, Nicaragua ʃ
44 M 9 Escuinapa, Mexico
46 H 6 Escuintla, Guatemala
129 T 14 Eséka, Cameroon
94 D 13 Esen, Turkey
102 I 14 Esenguly, Turkmenistan
100 J 7 Eşfahān, Iran ▣
100 I 8 Eşfahān, Iran
100 M 5 Esfarāyen, Iran
41 T 8 Esker, NL, Canada
71 G 21 Eskilstuna, Sweden
94 F 9 Eskişehir, Turkey
100 F 6 Eslāmābād-e Gharb, Iran
48 K 5 Esmeralda, Cuba
52 B 7 Esmeraldas, Ecuador
52 A 8 Esmeraldas, Ecuador ▣
101 O 13 Espakeh, Iran
65 Q 12 Espalion, France
31 Q 9 Espanola, NM, U.S.A.
42 C 9 Espanola, ON, Canada
72 F 13 Espelkamp, Germany
134 I 12 Esperance, WA, Australia
44 J 5 Esperanza, Mexico
53 G 15 Esperanza, Peru
57 G 23 Esperanza, Argentina
144 H 3 Esperanza, Antarctica ⁙
66 M 10 Espiel, Spain
50 I 7 Espinal, Colombia
66 G 5 Espinho, Portugal
55 M 17 Espírito Santo, Brazil ▣
139 P 10 Espíritu Santo, Vanuatu ♣
55 N 14 Esplanada, Brazil
71 L 19 Espoo, Finland
66 H 4 Esposende, Portugal
57 G 18 Esquel, Argentina
58 C 12 Esquina, Argentina
124 F 8 Essaouira, Morocco
73 C 15 Essen, Germany
51 U 6 Essequibo, Guyana ʃ
42 B 14 Essex, ON, Canada
89 Y 10 Esso, Russian Federation
129 V 15 Est, Cameroon ▣
120 I 7 Estagno Point, Philippines ▶
55 N 14 Estância, Brazil
76 G 7 Este, Italy
56 K 9 Esteban Rams, Argentina
47 N 8 Estelí, Nicaragua
67 Q 2 Estella, Spain
26 L 3 Estelline, TX, U.S.A.
66 M 14 Estepona, Spain
35 R 7 Ester, AK, U.S.A.
23 Q 10 Estherville, IA, U.S.A.
17 N 15 Estill, SC, U.S.A.
84 F 7 Estonia, Europe □
57 I 26 Estrecho de Le Maire, Argentina ≈
57 E 24 Estrecho Nelson, Chile ≈
66 I 9 Estremoz, Portugal
130 D 7 Estuaire, Gabon ▣
106 K 9 Etah, India
65 U 3 Étain, France
37 Y 9 Etamamiou, QC, Canada
41 W 10 Etamamoiu, QC, Canada
65 P 5 Étampes, France
106 K 10 Etawah, India
127 G 21 Ethiopia, Africa □
127 G 20 Ethiopian Highlands, Ethiopia ▲▲
94 H 9 Etimesğut, Turkey
34 K 9 Etolin Strait, AK, U.S.A. ≈
130 H 7 Etoumbi, Congo
65 N 3 Étretat, France
82 H 9 Etropole, Bulgaria
64 M 15 Etsaut, France
69 L 24 Ettelbruck, Luxembourg
140 I 11 Eua, Tonga ♣
134 L 10 Eucla, WA, Australia
21 N 16 Euclid, OH, U.S.A.
19 R 5 Eufaula, AL, U.S.A.
25 Q 11 Eufaula, OK, U.S.A.
25 P 10 Eufaula Lake, OK, U.S.A. ∽
32 F 11 Eugene, OR, U.S.A.
135 S 9 Eulo, QLD, Australia
18 J 7 Eunice, LA, U.S.A.
31 U 14 Eunice, NM, U.S.A.
69 L 20 Eupen, Belgium
96 L 3 Euphrates, Syria/Iraq ʃ
18 M 3 Eupora, MS, U.S.A.
28 M 2 Eureka, MT, U.S.A.
30 J 4 Eureka, UT, U.S.A.
33 E 15 Eureka, CA, U.S.A.
33 M 17 Eureka, NV, U.S.A.
68 F 13 Europoort, Netherlands ◇
73 C 18 Euskirchen, Germany
19 W 9 Eustis, FL, U.S.A.
19 O 4 Eutaw, AL, U.S.A.
39 E 19 Eutsuk Lake, BC, Canada ∽
41 O 4 Evans Strait, NU, Canada ≈
21 H 15 Evanston, IL, U.S.A.
29 Q 15 Evanston, WY, U.S.A.
21 H 22 Evansville, IN, U.S.A.
27 O 8 Evant, TX, U.S.A.
133 O 11 Evaton, Republic of South Africa
100 J 12 Evaz, Iran
89 Y 9 Evensk, Russian Federation
14 D 13 Everett, PA, U.S.A.
32 H 6 Everett, WA, U.S.A.
19 X 14 Everglades, FL, U.S.A. ◇
19 P 6 Evergreen, AL, U.S.A.
63 R 8 Evesham, U.K.
71 K 15 Evijärvi, Finland ∽
71 B 21 Evje, Norway
66 I 10 Evora, Portugal ▣
66 I 9 Évora, Portugal
65 O 4 Évreux, France
82 K 13 Evros, Greece ʃ
83 H 19 Evvoia, Greece ♣
34 B 7 Ewa Beach, HI, U.S.A.
130 G 8 Ewo, Congo
25 S 3 Excelsior Springs, MO, U.S.A.
63 N 13 Exe, U.K. ʃ
144 L 11 Executive Committee Range, Antarctica ▲▲
33 J 21 Exeter, CA, U.S.A.
63 N 13 Exeter, U.K.
23 R 13 Exira, IA, U.S.A.
63 O 14 Exminster, U.K.
63 N 12 Exmoor, U.K. ◇
17 W 5 Exmore, VA, U.S.A.
63 O 14 Exmouth, U.K.
134 E 6 Exmouth, WA, Australia
14 H 14 Exton, PA, U.S.A.
66 K 8 Extremadura, Spain ▣
129 V 11 Extrême-Nord, Cameroon ▣
48 L 3 Exuma Cays, The Bahamas ♣
63 Y 7 Eye, U.K.
127 O 21 Eyl, Somalia
65 P 10 Eymoutiers, France
135 O 11 Eyre Peninsula, SA, Australia ▶
137 H 20 Eyreton, New Zealand
84 J 12 Ezernieki, Latvia
113 U 7 Ezhou, China
94 A 9 Ezine, Turkey

F

105 L 17 Faadhippolhu Atoll, Maldives ♣
127 J 24 Faafxadhuun, Somalia
26 E 7 Fabens, TX, U.S.A.
129 T 7 Fachi, Niger
57 G 19 Facundo, Argentina
129 Y 7 Fada, Chad
129 N 10 Fada-Ngourma, Burkina Faso
76 G 9 Faenza, Italy
86 J 10 Făgăraş, Romania
71 G 20 Fagersta, Sweden
86 G 10 Făget, Romania
70 C 11 Fagurhólsmýri, Iceland
74 G 9 Faido, Switzerland
60 J 6 Fair Isle, U.K. ♣
35 R 7 Fairbanks, AK, U.S.A.
21 G 21 Fairfield, IL, U.S.A.
27 R 7 Fairfield, TX, U.S.A.
28 L 11 Fairfield, ID, U.S.A.
33 G 19 Fairfield, CA, U.S.A.
137 F 21 Fairlie, New Zealand
17 P 2 Fairmont, WV, U.S.A.
23 N 15 Fairmont, NE, U.S.A.
23 R 10 Fairmont, MN, U.S.A.
31 Q 5 Fairplay, CO, U.S.A.
20 I 10 Fairport, MI, U.S.A.
24 L 9 Fairview, OK, U.S.A.
101 X 9 Faisalabad, Pakistan
22 I 8 Faith, SD, U.S.A.
107 N 10 Faizabad, India
49 U 8 Fajardo, Puerto Rico
97 W 9 Fajir, Iraq
140 J 6 Fakaofo, Tokelau Islands ♣
63 Y 6 Fakenham, U.K.
117 U 12 Fakfak, Indonesia
82 M 10 Fakiya, Bulgaria
71 D 26 Fakse Bugt, Denmark ≈
111 I 14 Faku, China
64 M 4 Falaise, France
129 R 7 Falaise de Tiguidit, Niger ▲▲
107 T 10 Falakata, India
50 M 2 Falcón, Venezuela ▣
76 I 10 Falconara Marittima, Italy
86 M 8 Făleşti, Moldova
27 P 14 Falfurrias, TX, U.S.A.
72 L 13 Falkensee, Germany
60 H 13 Falkirk, U.K.
57 J 24 Falkland Islands, U.K. ▣
57 K 24 Falkland Sound, Falkland Islands ≈
83 G 23 Falkonera, Greece ♣
71 E 22 Falköping, Sweden
15 O 11 Fall River, MA, U.S.A.
33 J 17 Fallon, NV, U.S.A.
23 Q 15 Falls City, NE, U.S.A.
17 S 8 Falls Lake Reserve, NC, U.S.A. ∽
16 J 4 Falmouth, KY, U.S.A.
17 T 4 Falmouth, VA, U.S.A.
48 K 8 Falmouth, Jamaica
62 J 15 Falmouth, U.K.
62 J 15 Falmouth Bay, U.K. ≈
132 J 15 False Bay, Republic of South Africa ≈
34 L 13 False Pass, AK, U.S.A.
105 J 16 False Point, India ▶
71 D 26 Falster, Denmark ♣
86 L 8 Fălticeni, Romania
71 G 19 Falun, Sweden
56 H 9 Famatina, Argentina
100 H 6 Famenin, Iran
114 J 11 Fan Si Pan, Vietnam ▲
113 X 6 Fanchang, China
133 Y 8 Fandriana, Madgascar
114 G 13 Fang, Thailand
127 E 20 Fangak, Sudan
113 T 4 Fangcheng, China
113 Z 12 Fangshan, Taiwan
113 R 5 Fangxian, China
110 M 11 Fangzheng, China
110 J 13 Fanjiatun, China
101 N 13 Fannūj, Iran
71 B 25 Fanø, Denmark ♣
76 H 10 Fano, Italy
113 Y 8 Fanshan, China
111 B 17 Fanshi, China
106 M 8 Far Western, Nepal ▣
144 H 4 Faraday, Antarctica ⁙
131 Q 5 Faradje, Democratic Republic of Congo
133 Y 10 Farafangana, Madgascar
101 Q 8 Farāh, Afghanistan ▣
101 P 9 Farāh, Afghanistan
140 A 8 Farallon de Medinilla, Northern Mariana Islands ♣
140 A 5 Farallon de Pajaros, Northern Mariana Islands ♣
128 H 11 Faranah, Guinea
99 X 10 Fararah, Oman
140 M 14 Faraulep, Federated States of Micronesia ♣
63 T 13 Fareham, U.K.
35 P 8 Farewell, AK, U.S.A.
137 H 15 Farewell Spit, New Zealand ▶
103 S 12 Farghona Wiloyati, Uzbekistan ▣
19 V 7 Fargo, GA, U.S.A.
23 O 5 Fargo, ND, U.S.A.
23 S 9 Faribault, MN, U.S.A.
106 J 9 Faridabad, India
106 H 6 Faridkot, India
107 T 13 Faridpur, Bangladesh
101 O 6 Farīmān, Iran
63 S 10 Faringdon, U.K.
71 G 24 Färjestaden, Sweden
15 P 5 Farmington, ME, U.S.A.
31 O 8 Farmington, NM, U.S.A.
17 R 6 Farmville, VA, U.S.A.
63 U 11 Farnborough, U.K.
63 T 11 Farnham, U.K.
38 C 13 Faro, YT, Canada
66 H 12 Faro, Portugal ▣
66 H 12 Faro, Portugal
143 R 15 Faroe Islands, Denmark ♣
143 Q 15 FaroeŠIceland Ridge, Arctic Ocean ▲▲
71 I 22 Fårösund, Sweden ♣
71 I 22 Fårösund, Sweden
25 X 5 Farrington, MO, U.S.A.
100 J 10 Fārs, Iran ▣
83 E 17 Farsala, Greece
29 S 13 Farson, WY, U.S.A.
26 I 3 Farwell, TX, U.S.A.
144 J 8 Farwell Island, Antarctica ♣
101 R 6 Fāryāb, Afghanistan ▣
100 J 11 Fasā, Iran
77 N 16 Fasano, Italy
87 P 4 Fastiv, Ukraine
131 R 6 Fataki, Democratic Republic of Congo
106 I 7 Fatehabad, India
106 L 9 Fatehgarh, India
106 M 11 Fatehpur, India
92 J 4 Fatezh, Russian Federation
128 D 8 Fatick, Senegal
130 I 10 Fatundu, Democratic Republic of Congo
139 S 8 Fatutaka, Solomon Islands ♣
70 G 10 Fauske, Norway
63 Y 11 Faversham, U.K.
70 A 11 Faxaflói, Iceland ≈
129 X 7 Faya, Chad
139 Q 13 Fayaoué, New Caledonia
18 K 5 Fayette, MS, U.S.A.
19 O 3 Fayette, AL, U.S.A.
16 F 10 Fayetteville, TN, U.S.A.
17 R 10 Fayetteville, NC, U.S.A.
21 L 20 Fayetteville, OH, U.S.A.
25 S 9 Fayetteville, AR, U.S.A.
141 N 14 Fayu, Federated States of Micronesia ♣
128 G 4 Fdérik, Mauritania
65 N 3 Fécamp, France
80 H 13 Federacija Bosna Hercegovina, Bosnia and Herzegovina ▣
58 D 13 Federación, Argentina
58 D 13 Federal, Argentina
129 R 12 Federal Capital Territory, Nigeria ▣
141 Q 14 Federated States of Micronesia, Oceania □
97 O 3 Fedghāmī, Syria
103 O 2 Fedorovka, Kazakhstan
72 I 8 Fehmarn, Germany ♣
72 I 7 Fehmarnbelt, Germany ≈
75 X 8 Fehring, Austria
54 B 13 Feijó, Brazil
55 N 14 Feira de Santana, Brazil
94 K 12 Feke, Turkey
67 Y 8 Felanitx, Spain
75 X 8 Feldbach, Austria
74 I 7 Feldkirch, Austria
75 S 8 Feldkirchen in Kärnten, Austria
105 L 18 Felidhu Atoll, Maldives ♣
45 Z 11 Felipe Carrillo Puerto, Mexico
63 Z 9 Felixstowe, U.K.
76 G 6 Feltre, Italy
71 E 17 Femunden, Norway ∽
95 O 8 Fener Burnu, Turkey ▶
83 J 14 Fengari, Greece ▲
111 I 16 Fengcheng, China
113 U 8 Fengcheng, China
113 P 7 Fengdu, China
113 P 8 Fenggang, China
113 Z 7 Fenghua, China
113 Q 8 Fenghuang, China
113 W 11 Fenghuang, China
113 Q 6 Fengjie, China
113 Z 11 Fenglin, Taiwan
111 E 15 Fengning, China
112 J 11 Fengqing, China
113 U 3 Fengqiu, China
111 F 17 Fengrun, China
110 I 4 Fengshui Shan, China ▲
113 V 11 Fengshun, China
113 V 5 Fengtai, China
113 O 4 Fengxian, China
113 V 3 Fengxian, China
113 Z 6 Fengxian, China
113 P 3 Fengxiang, China
113 V 8 Fengxin, China
113 W 4 Fengyang, China
113 Z 11 Fengyüan, Taiwan
111 B 16 Fengzhen, China
107 V 13 Feni, Bangladesh
138 I 3 Feni Islands, Papua New Guinea ♣
21 E 14 Fennimore, WI, U.S.A.
133 Z 7 Fenoarivo Atsinanana, Madgascar
113 S 1 Fenyang, China
87 V 12 Feodosiya, Ukraine
21 I 21 Ferdinand, IN, U.S.A.
101 N 7 Ferdows, Iran
82 K 13 Feres, Greece
127 L 22 Fērfēr, Ethiopia
103 T 12 Fergana, Uzbekistan
103 S 12 Fergana Valley, Uzbekistan ◇
23 P 6 Fergus Falls, MN, U.S.A.
138 G 6 Fergusson Island, Papua New Guinea ♣
125 P 6 Fériana, Tunisia
128 K 11 Ferkessédougou, Côte d'Ivoire
76 I 11 Fermo, Italy
66 K 5 Fermoselle, Spain
61 C 20 Fermoy, Republic of Ireland
56 J 8 Fernández, Argentina
19 W 7 Fernandina Beach, FL, U.S.A.
58 I 4 Fernandópolis, Brazil
33 I 17 Fernley, NV, U.S.A.
77 M 16 Ferrandina, Italy
76 G 8 Ferrara, Italy
66 H 10 Ferreira do Alentejo, Portugal
18 K 6 Ferriday, LA, U.S.A.
66 I 1 Ferrol, Spain
124 I 7 Fès, Morocco
130 J 11 Feshi, Democratic Republic of Congo
22 K 4 Fessenden, ND, U.S.A.
25 Y 5 Festus, MO, U.S.A.
86 M 13 Feteşti-Gara, Romania
94 D 13 Fethiye, Turkey
102 I 10 Fetisovo, Kazakhstan
60 K 4 Fetlar, U.K. ♣
73 H 22 Feuchtwangen, Germany
65 S 10 Feurs, France
101 V 5 Feyzābād, Afghanistan
63 N 5 Ffestiniog, U.K.
56 H 8 Fiambalá, Argentina
133 X 9 Fianarantsoa, Madgascar
133 X 9 Fianarantsoa, Madgascar ▣
129 V 11 Fianga, Chad
127 I 20 Fichē, Ethiopia
73 J 20 Fichtelgebirge, Germany ▲▲
76 G 12 Ficulle, Italy
76 E 8 Fidenza, Italy
81 J 20 Fier, Albania
74 F 10 Fiesch, Switzerland
20 J 12 Fife Lake, MI, U.S.A.
60 I 12 Fife Ness, U.K. ▶
65 P 12 Figeac, France
66 G 7 Figueira da Foz, Portugal
67 Y 3 Figueres, Spain
124 K 8 Figuig, Morocco
129 V 11 Figuil, Cameroon
139 W 12 Fiji, Oceania □
127 K 21 Fik', Ethiopia
133 O 8 Filabusi, Zimbabwe
47 O 10 Filadelfia, Costa Rica
55 F 18 Filadélfia, Paraguay
79 K 21 Filakovo, Slovakia
145 N 5 Filchner Ice Shelf, Antarctica ◇
63 V 1 Filey, U.K.
63 V 1 Filey Head, U.K. ▶
86 H 12 Filiaşi, Romania
83 C 22 Filiatra, Greece
129 P 9 Filingué, Niger
83 B 17 Filippiada, Greece
30 I 5 Fillmore, UT, U.S.A.
33 J 24 Fillmore, CA, U.S.A.
127 J 23 Filtu, Ethiopia
145 P 1 Fimbul Ice Shelf, Antarctica ◇
145 P 2 Fimbulheimen, Antarctica ▲▲
67 P 12 Fiñana, Spain
21 L 17 Findlay, OH, U.S.A.
14 F 9 Finger Lakes, NY, U.S.A. ∽
133 P 5 Fingoè, Mozambique
94 E 14 Finike, Turkey
138 D 4 Finisterre Range, Papua New Guinea ▲▲
135 O 7 Finke, NT, Australia
71 L 18 Finland, Europe □
39 E 16 Finlay, BC, Canada ʃ
23 N 4 Finley, ND, U.S.A.
135 S 12 Finley, NSW, Australia
99 Z 7 Fins, Oman
138 E 5 Finschhafen, Papua New Guinea
74 F 9 Finsteraarhorn, Switzerland ▲
137 A 25 Fiordland, New Zealand ◇
39 J 15 Firebag, AB, Canada ʃ
76 F 9 Firenzuola, Italy
59 B 15 Firmat, Argentina
65 S 11 Firminy, France
90 G 13 Firovo, Russian Federation
106 K 10 Firozabad, India
106 H 6 Firozpur, India
61 G 14 Firth of Clyde, U.K. ≈
60 I 12 Firth of Forth, U.K. ≈
60 F 12 Firth of Lorn, U.K. ≈
136 L 8 Firth of Thames, New Zealand ≈
100 J 11 Fīrūzābād, Iran
100 J 6 Fīrūzkūh, Iran
41 N 4 Fisher Strait, NU, Canada ≈
62 K 9 Fishguard, U.K.
62 J 8 Fishguard Bay, U.K. ≈
65 R 3 Fismes, France
60 J 5 Fitful Head, U.K. ▶
57 H 20 Fitz Roy, Argentina
53 F 16 Fitzcarrald, Peru
134 J 4 Fitzroy, WA, Australia ʃ
134 J 4 Fitzroy Crossing, WA, Australia
42 C 10 Fitzwilliam Island, ON, Canada ♣
77 G 14 Fiumicino, Italy
76 D 9 Fivizzano, Italy
131 Q 10 Fizi, Democratic Republic of Congo
71 C 19 Flå, Norway
70 C 12 Flaga, Iceland
30 K 10 Flagstaff, AZ, U.S.A.
15 O 4 Flagstaff Lake, ME, U.S.A. ∽
41 P 8 Flaherty Island, ON, Canada ♣
63 V 1 Flamborough, U.K.
63 V 1 Flamborough Head, U.K. ▶
73 K 14 Fläming, Germany ▲▲
30 M 2 Flaming Gorge Reservoir, UT/WY, U.S.A. ∽
19 X 14 Flamingo, FL, U.S.A.
69 C 19 Flanders, Belgium ◇
71 G 14 Flåsjön, Sweden ∽
29 N 3 Flathead Lake, MT, U.S.A. ∽
75 S 8 Flattnitz, Austria
63 O 2 Fleetwood, U.K.
71 A 21 Flekkefjord, Norway
71 B 26 Flensburg, Denmark
72 G 7 Flensburg, Germany
64 M 4 Flers, France
144 I 8 Fletcher Peninsula, Antarctica ▶
74 B 8 Fleurier, Switzerland
68 I 10 Flevoland, Netherlands ▣
40 H 7 Flin Flon, MB, Canada
135 R 5 Flinders, QLD, Australia ʃ
135 T 14 Flinders Island, TAS, Australia ♣
135 P 10 Flinders Ranges, SA, Australia ▲▲
21 L 14 Flint, MI, U.S.A.
63 O 4 Flint, U.K.
141 S 7 Flint, Kiribati ♣
25 O 7 Flint Hills, KS, U.S.A. ◇
71 E 18 Flisa, Norway ʃ
71 E 19 Flisa, Norway
21 G 21 Flora, IL, U.S.A.
65 S 12 Florac, France
19 Q 6 Florala, AL, U.S.A.
14 A 13 Florence, PA, U.S.A.
17 P 12 Florence, SC, U.S.A.
19 O 1 Florence, AL, U.S.A.
25 O 5 Florence, KS, U.S.A.
30 K 13 Florence, AZ, U.S.A.
32 F 11 Florence, OR, U.S.A.
76 F 10 Florence, Italy
50 H 9 Florencia, Colombia
69 G 22 Florennes, Belgium
69 J 25 Florenville, Belgium
46 I 3 Flores, Guatemala
59 E 15 Flores, Uruguay ▣
117 O 15 Flores, Indonesia ♣
117 N 15 Flores Sea, Indonesia ◒
54 N 13 Floresta, Brazil
87 N 7 Floreşti, Moldova
27 P 11 Floresville, TX, U.S.A.
54 L 12 Floriano, Brazil
58 J 10 Florianópolis, Brazil
19 W 10 Florida, U.S.A. ▣
59 E 15 Florida, Uruguay
59 E 15 Florida, Uruguay ▣
19 X 14 Florida Bay, FL, U.S.A. ≈
138 L 6 Florida Islands, Solomon Islands ♣
19 W 15 Florida Keys, FL, U.S.A. ♣
82 C 13 Florina, Greece
25 Y 4 Florissant, MO, U.S.A.
71 A 17 Florø, Norway
26 K 4 Floydada, TX, U.S.A.
68 J 8 Fluessen, Netherlands ∽
117 S 11 Fluk, Indonesia
138 A 5 Fly, Papua New Guinea ʃ
140 I 10 Foa, Tonga ♣
80 I 13 Foča, Bosnia and Herzegovina
86 L 11 Focşani, Romania
130 M 4 Fodé, Central African Republic
113 T 12 Fogang, China
124 M 11 Foggâret ez Zoûa, Algeria
77 L 15 Foggia, Italy
41 Y 9 Fogo Island, NL, Canada ♣
117 Q 15 Foho Tatamailau, East Timor ▲
72 F 7 Föhr, Germany ♣
65 P 15 Foix, France
70 G 10 Folda, Norway ≈
83 I 23 Folegandros, Greece ♣
19 O 7 Foley, AL, U.S.A.
41 P 1 Foley Island, NU, Canada ♣
42 C 6 Foleyet, ON, Canada
76 H 12 Foligno, Italy
63 Z 12 Folkestone, U.K.
76 E 12 Follonica, Italy
17 Q 15 Folly Beach, SC, U.S.A.
133 W 4 Fomboni, Comoros
20 G 13 Fond du Lac, WI, U.S.A.
77 I 15 Fondi, Italy
77 C 17 Fonni, Italy
50 J 2 Fonseca, Colombia
69 F 21 Fontaine-l'Eveque, Belgium
65 Q 5 Fontainebleau, France
54 D 10 Fonte Boa, Brazil
65 Q 4 Fontenay-Trésigny, France
70 D 9 Fontur, Iceland ▶
140 I 10 Fonualei, Tonga ♣
79 G 24 Fonyód, Hungary
135 T 11 Forbes, NSW, Australia
71 A 17 Førde, Norway
71 A 19 Førde, Norway
63 R 13 Fordingbridge, U.K.
14 J 13 Fords, NJ, U.S.A.
25 V 13 Fordyce, AR, U.S.A.
128 F 11 Forécariah, Guinea
18 M 5 Forest, MS, U.S.A.
63 Q 1 Forest of Bowland, U.K. ◇
63 Q 9 Forest of Dean, U.K. ◇
43 P 6 Forestville, QC, Canada
60 I 11 Forfar, U.K.
24 I 7 Forgan, OK, U.S.A.
32 F 6 Forks, WA, U.S.A.
76 G 9 Forli, Italy
63 O 3 Formby, U.K.
67 W 9 Formentera, Spain ♣
77 I 15 Formia, Italy
55 K 18 Formiga, Brazil
55 K 16 Formosa, Brazil
56 M 7 Formosa, Argentina
56 L 6 Formosa, Argentina ▣
55 K 14 Formosa do Rio Preto, Brazil
67 Z 7 Fornells, Spain
76 D 8 Fornovo di Taro, Italy
71 D 16 Forolshogna, Norway ▲
134 K 10 Forrest, WA, Australia
25 X 11 Forrest City, AR, U.S.A.
135 S 4 Forsayth, QLD, Australia
70 H 8 Forsbakken, Norway
71 L 18 Forssa, Finland
73 O 15 Forst, Germany
135 V 11 Forster, NSW, Australia
19 T 4 Forsyth, GA, U.S.A.
29 W 6 Forsyth, MT, U.S.A.
101 X 11 Fort Abbas, Pakistan
41 O 10 Fort Albany, ON, Canada
60 G 10 Fort Augustus, U.K.
133 N 14 Fort Beaufort, Republic of South Afri
29 R 4 Fort Benton, MT, U.S.A.
33 E 17 Fort Bragg, CA, U.S.A.
29 R 14 Fort Bridger, WY, U.S.A.
39 J 14 Fort Chipewyan, AB, Canada
31 R 3 Fort Collins, CO, U.S.A.
42 I 10 Fort Coulonge, QC, Canada
49 Y 11 Fort-de-France, Martinique ▙
23 S 11 Fort Dodge, IA, U.S.A.
40 J 11 Fort Frances, ON, Canada
31 R 7 Fort Garland, CO, U.S.A.
38 D 10 Fort Good Hope, NT, Canada
26 E 8 Fort Hancock, TX, U.S.A.
19 Y 13 Fort Lauderdale, FL, U.S.A.
39 F 14 Fort Liard, NT, Canada
49 P 7 Fort Liberté, Haiti
39 J 15 Fort MacKay, AB, Canada
39 J 16 Fort McMurray, AB, Canada
38 B 9 Fort McPherson, NT, Canada
19 W 12 Fort Myers, FL, U.S.A.
19 W 12 Fort Myers Beach, FL, U.S.A.
39 F 15 Fort Nelson, BC, Canada
19 R 2 Fort Payne, AL, U.S.A.
29 W 3 Fort Peck, MT, U.S.A.
29 W 4 Fort Peck Reservoir, MT, U.S.A. ∽
19 Y 11 Fort Pierce, FL, U.S.A.
131 R 7 Fort Portal, Uganda
38 H 13 Fort Providence, NT, Canada
38 I 13 Fort Resolution, NT, Canada
133 O 8 Fort Rixon, Zimbabwe
25 R 6 Fort Scott, KS, U.S.A.
40 M 7 Fort Severn, ON, Canada
102 G 8 Fort-Shevchenko, Kazakhstan
38 F 13 Fort Simpson, NT, Canada
25 S 10 Fort Smith, AR, U.S.A.
29 U 8 Fort Smith, MT, U.S.A.
39 I 14 Fort Smith, NT, Canada
39 F 18 Fort St James, BC, Canada
39 G 17 Fort St John, BC, Canada
26 I 8 Fort Stockton, TX, U.S.A.
31 T 11 Fort Sumner, NM, U.S.A.
24 K 8 Fort Supply, OK, U.S.A.
19 T 4 Fort Valley, GA, U.S.A.
19 Q 7 Fort Walton Beach, FL, U.S.A.
21 J 17 Fort Wayne, IN, U.S.A.
60 G 11 Fort William, U.K.
27 P 6 Fort Worth, TX, U.S.A.
35 S 5 Fort Yukon, AK, U.S.A.
54 N 11 Fortaleza, Brazil
53 O 22 Forte Coimbra, Bolivia
76 E 10 Forte dei Marmi, Italy
60 H 12 Forth, U.K. ʃ
53 N 21 Fortín, Bolivia
55 F 18 Fortín Carlos Antonio López, Paragua
55 E 18 Fortín Coronel Eugenio Garay, Paragu
55 F 17 Fortín Galpón, Paraguay
55 E 18 Fortín Infante Rivarola, Paraguay
55 F 18 Fortín Madrejón, Paraguay
56 L 5 Fortín Pilcomayo, Argentina
53 M 21 Fortín Ravelo, Bolivia
137 D 26 Fortrose, New Zealand
22 G 2 Fortuna, ND, U.S.A.
33 E 16 Fortuna, CA, U.S.A.
41 Y 11 Fortune Bay, NL, Canada ≈
63 Q 14 Fortuneswell, U.K.
100 J 13 Forūr, Iran ♣
65 T 14 Fos-sur-Mer, France
63 W 5 Fosdyke, U.K.
113 T 12 Foshan, China
70 C 12 Foss, Iceland
76 A 8 Fossano, Italy
69 G 21 Fosses-la-Ville, Belgium
76 H 10 Fossombrone, Italy
130 E 8 Fougamou, Gabon
64 L 5 Fougères, France
126 G 12 Foul Bay, Egypt ≈
60 J 5 Foula, U.K. ♣
130 D 8 Foulenzem, Gabon
63 Y 10 Foulness Island, U.K. ♣
63 Y 10 Foulness Point, U.K. ▶
124 H 9 Foum Zguid, Morocco
129 T 13 Foumban, Cameroon
29 Z 9 Four Corners, WY, U.S.A.
83 L 21 Fournoi, Greece ♣
128 G 10 Fouta Djallon, Guinea ▲▲
137 B 26 Foveaux Strait, New Zealand ≈
135 N 10 Fowlers Bay, SA, Australia
39 I 18 Fox Creek, AB, Canada
137 D 20 Fox Glacier, New Zealand
34 I 14 Fox Islands, AK, U.S.A. ♣
39 I 15 Fox Lake, AB, Canada
33 I 15 Fox Mountain, NV, U.S.A. ▲
137 F 20 Fox Peak, New Zealand ▲
41 P 2 Foxe Basin, NU, Canada ≈
41 O 2 Foxe Channel, NU, Canada ≈

□ Country ▣ Internal administrative region: State/Province/Territory/Dependent territory ▙ Capital city ▲▲ Mountain range/Undersea ridge ▲ Mountain peak/Volcano/Seamount ◇ Geographic feature ▶ Headland/Point/Cape/Peninsula ◢ Desert ♣ Island/Island group ⁙ Antarctic base ◎ Ocean ◒ Sea ≈ Bay/Gulf/Channel/Strait ∽ Lake ◩ Salt pan/Dry/Intermittent lake ʃ

P 3 **Foxe Peninsula**, NU, Canada ▶
D 20 **Foxen**, Sweden ◣
K 15 **Foxton**, New Zealand
J 1 **Foz**, Spain
F 7 **Foz do Cunene**, Angola
F 8 **Foz do Iguaçu**, Brazil
U 4 **Fraga**, Spain
G 22 **Fraire**, Belgium
S 9 **Fram Basin**, Arctic Ocean ◇
W 4 **Fram Peak**, Antarctica ▲
K 5 **Franca**, Brazil
M 9 **France**, Europe □
G 8 **Franceville**, Gabon
U 7 **Franche-Comté**, France ▣
F 10 **Francisco de Orellana**, Peru
N 8 **Francistown**, Botswana
E 19 **Francois Lake**, BC, Canada ◣
J 7 **Franeker**, Netherlands
I 5 **Frankfort**, KY, U.S.A.
I 18 **Frankfort**, IN, U.S.A.
F 19 **Frankfurt am Main**, Germany
N 13 **Frankfurt an der Oder**, Germany
I 23 **Fränkische Alb**, Germany ◇
B 11 **Franklin**, PA, U.S.A.
F 7 **Franklin**, KY, U.S.A.
K 10 **Franklin**, NC, U.S.A.
F 9 **Franklin**, TN, U.S.A.
U 7 **Franklin**, VA, U.S.A.
Q 4 **Franklin**, WV, U.S.A.
K 8 **Franklin**, LA, U.S.A.
J 19 **Franklin**, IN, U.S.A.
D 8 **Franklin Bay**, NT, Canada ≈
K 6 **Franklin D. Roosevelt Lake**, WA, U.S.A. ◣
D 11 **Franklin Mountains**, NT, Canada ▲▲
A 6 **Franz**, ON, Canada
E 20 **Franz Josef Glacier**, New Zealand
N 3 **Franz Josef Land**, Russian Federation ⛱
F 19 **Fraser**, BC/NL, Canada ∿
W 8 **Fraser Island**, QLD, Australia ⛱
F 19 **Fraser Lake**, BC, Canada
F 19 **Fraser Plateau**, BC, Canada ◇
K 14 **Fraserburg**, Republic of South Africa
J 9 **Fraserburgh**, U.K.
O 11 **Fraserdale**, ON, Canada
N 12 **Frasertown**, New Zealand
D 20 **Frasnes-lez-Buissenal**, Belgium
H 6 **Frauenfeld**, Switzerland
D 14 **Fray Bentos**, Uruguay
C 10 **Frederic**, WI, U.S.A.
B 25 **Fredericia**, Denmark
T 2 **Frederick**, MD, U.S.A.
K 12 **Frederick**, OK, U.S.A.
T 4 **Fredericksburg**, VA, U.S.A.
O 9 **Fredericksburg**, TX, U.S.A.
Y 6 **Fredericktown**, MO, U.S.A.
S 9 **Fredericton**, NB, Canada
C 23 **Frederikshavn**, Denmark
V 8 **Frederiksted**, Virgin Islands, U.S.A.
J 8 **Fredonia**, AZ, U.S.A.
I 14 **Fredrika**, Sweden
N 12 **Free State**, Republic of South Africa ▣
J 13 **Freehold**, NJ, U.S.A.
N 10 **Freeman**, SD, U.S.A.
F 15 **Freeport**, IL, U.S.A.
T 11 **Freeport**, TX, U.S.A.
K 1 **Freeport**, The Bahamas
O 13 **Freer**, TX, U.S.A.
F 12 **Freetown**, Sierra Leone ♜
J 10 **Fregenal de la Sierra**, Spain
M 17 **Freiberg**, Germany
D 25 **Freiburg im Breisgau**, Germany
D 18 **Freilingen**, Germany
K 23 **Freising**, Germany
T 3 **Freistadt**, Austria
G 11 **Fremantle**, WA, Australia
J 13 **Fremont**, MI, U.S.A.
P 13 **Fremont**, NE, U.S.A.
G 20 **Fremont**, CA, U.S.A.
X 7 **French Guiana**, French Guiana ▣
L 6 **Frenda**, Algeria
J 14 **Fresco**, Côte d'Ivoire
S 14 **Freshwater**, U.K.
O 9 **Fresnillo**, Mexico
I 21 **Fresno**, CA, U.S.A.
E 23 **Freudenstadt**, Germany
T 15 **Freycinet Peninsula**, TAS, Australia ▶
V 4 **Freyming-Merlebach**, France
B 13 **Freyre**, Argentina
M 22 **Freyung**, Germany
F 11 **Fria**, Guinea
I 9 **Frías**, Argentina
D 8 **Fribourg**, Switzerland
F 6 **Frick**, Switzerland
X 6 **Friedberg**, Austria
G 25 **Friedrichshafen**, Germany
T 8 **Friesach**, Austria
K 7 **Friesland**, Netherlands ▣
I 3 **Friona**, TX, U.S.A.
P 6 **Frisco City**, AL, U.S.A.
I 5 **Frisco Mountain**, UT, U.S.A. ▲
G 16 **Fritzlar**, Germany
H 5 **Friuli-Venezia Giulia**, Italy ▣
S 3 **Frobisher Bay**, NU, Canada ≈
K 16 **Frobisher Lake**, SK, Canada ◣
D 14 **Frohavet**, Norway ≈
V 7 **Frohnleiten**, Austria
O 7 **Frolovo**, Russian Federation
Q 11 **Frome**, U.K.
S 3 **Front Royal**, VA, U.S.A.
W 12 **Frontera**, Mexico
J 3 **Fronteras**, Mexico
I 14 **Frosinone**, Italy
C 14 **Frøya**, Norway ⛱
O 8 **Frunzivka**, Ukraine
J 9 **Fruška Gora**, Serbia and Montenegro ▲▲
J 4 **Frutal**, Brazil
E 9 **Frutigen**, Switzerland
M 7 **Fry Canyon**, UT, U.S.A.
L 20 **Fua Mulaku Island**, Maldives ⛱
Y 9 **Fu'an**, China
E 19 **Fuchu**, Japan
Y 9 **Fuding**, China
M 13 **Fuengirola**, Spain
G 5 **Fuga**, Philippines ⛱
T 13 **Fugløya Bank**, Arctic Ocean ◇
J 9 **Fugong**, China
U 4 **Fugou**, China
A 17 **Fugu**, China
F 19 **Fuguo**, China
L 3 **Fuhai**, China
Q 6 **Fuḩaymī**, Iraq
X 5 **Fujairah**, United Arab Emirates

123 J 17 **Fuji**, Japan
113 X 10 **Fujian**, China ▣
123 J 17 **Fujieda**, Japan
110 N 9 **Fujin**, China
123 J 17 **Fujinomiya**, Japan
123 J 16 **Fujiyoshida**, Japan
122 J 5 **Fukagawa**, Japan
108 K 4 **Fukang**, China
122 J 9 **Fukaura**, Japan
110 H 4 **Fukeshan**, China
123 G 18 **Fukuchiyama**, Japan
123 A 22 **Fukue**, Japan
123 A 22 **Fukue-jima**, Japan ⛱
123 G 16 **Fukui**, Japan
123 B 21 **Fukuoka**, Japan
122 K 13 **Fukushima**, Japan
123 E 19 **Fukuyama**, Japan
128 D 10 **Fulacunda**, Guinea-Bissau
139 Z 12 **Fulaga**, Fiji ⛱
73 G 16 **Fulda**, Germany ∿
73 G 18 **Fulda**, Germany
105 L 18 **Fulidhu Channel**, Maldives ≈
113 P 7 **Fuling**, China
74 M 7 **Fulpmes**, Austria
14 G 8 **Fulton**, NY, U.S.A.
25 V 4 **Fulton**, MO, U.S.A.
65 O 12 **Fumel**, France
123 K 16 **Funabashi**, Japan
140 F 6 **Funafuti**, Tuvalu ⛱
71 E 16 **Funäsdalen**, Sweden
86 L 13 **Fundulea**, Romania
133 R 9 **Funhalouro**, Mozambique
113 N 12 **Funing**, China
113 Y 4 **Funing**, China
129 Q 10 **Funtua**, Nigeria
113 R 4 **Funui Shan**, China ▲▲
111 C 18 **Fuping**, China
113 Q 3 **Fuping**, China
113 Y 10 **Fuqing**, China
122 K 5 **Furano**, Japan
110 M 7 **Furao**, China
135 T 14 **Furneaux Group**, TAS, Australia ⛱
96 J 5 **Furqlus**, Syria
75 X 7 **Fürstenfeld**, Austria
72 N 13 **Fürstenwalde**, Germany
73 I 21 **Fürth**, Germany
122 K 12 **Furukawa**, Japan
50 I 7 **Fusagasugá**, Colombia
111 I 15 **Fushun**, China
113 N 7 **Fushun**, China
74 G 9 **Fusio**, Switzerland
111 L 14 **Fusong**, China
73 I 26 **Füssen**, Germany
123 C 21 **Futago-san**, Japan ▲
57 F 18 **Futaleufú**, Chile
80 J 9 **Futog**, Serbia and Montenegro
123 K 16 **Futtsu**, Japan
139 S 12 **Futuna**, Vanuatu ⛱
140 H 8 **Futuna**, Wallis and Futuna Islands ⛱
113 Q 2 **Fuxian**, China
111 H 15 **Fuxin**, China
113 P 6 **Fuxing**, China
122 J 12 **Fuya**, Japan
113 U 4 **Fuyang**, China
110 J 9 **Fuyu**, China
110 K 12 **Fuyu**, China
110 O 8 **Fuyuan**, China
112 M 10 **Fuyuan**, China
108 L 3 **Fuyun**, China
79 L 22 **Füzesabony**, Hungary
113 X 10 **Fuzhou**, China
95 W 9 **Füzuli**, Azerbaijan
71 C 25 **Fyn**, Denmark ⛱
83 C 18 **Fyteies**, Greece

G

127 N 21 **Gaalkacyo**, Somalia
33 K 18 **Gabbs**, NV, U.S.A.
132 G 3 **Gabela**, Angola
125 Q 7 **Gabès**, Tunisia
130 E 8 **Gabon**, Africa □
132 M 10 **Gaborone**, Botswana ♜
82 J 9 **Gabrovo**, Bulgaria ▣
82 J 8 **Gabrovo**, Bulgaria
128 F 9 **Gabú**, Guinea-Bissau
81 H 14 **Gacko**, Bosnia and Herzegovina
95 V 8 **Gädäbäy**, Azerbaijan
105 D 19 **Gadag**, India
105 F 15 **Gadarwara**, India
105 A 16 **Gadhra**, India
19 R 2 **Gadsden**, AL, U.S.A.
105 E 19 **Gadwal**, India
86 J 12 **Găeşti**, Romania
77 I 15 **Gaeta**, Italy
140 M 14 **Gaferut**, Federated States of Micronesia ⛱
17 N 10 **Gaffney**, SC, U.S.A.
125 P 7 **Gafsa**, Tunisia
117 T 11 **Gag**, Indonesia ⛱
129 V 12 **Gagal**, Chad
92 J 1 **Gagarin**, Russian Federation
103 Q 12 **Gagarin**, Uzbekistan
77 O 17 **Gagliano del Capo**, Italy
128 J 13 **Gagnoa**, Côte d'Ivoire
41 T 9 **Gagnon**, QC, Canada
109 O 7 **Gahe**, China
107 T 11 **Gaibandha**, Bangladesh
65 P 13 **Gaillac**, France
19 T 2 **Gainesville**, GA, U.S.A.
19 V 8 **Gainesville**, FL, U.S.A.
25 V 8 **Gainesville**, MO, U.S.A.
27 Q 4 **Gainesville**, TX, U.S.A.
63 U 4 **Gainsborough**, U.K.
111 I 16 **Gaizhou**, China
84 G 11 **Gaiziņkalns**, Latvia ▲
123 B 26 **Gaja-jima**, Japan ⛱
129 S 13 **Gakem**, Nigeria
35 S 8 **Gakona**, AK, U.S.A.
101 X 6 **Gakuch**, Pakistan
53 A 17 **Galapagos Islands**, Ecuador ⛱
60 I 13 **Galashiels**, U.K.
82 N 8 **Galata**, Bulgaria
86 M 11 **Galaţi**, Romania
83 F 14 **Galatista**, Greece
71 C 17 **Galdhøpiggen**, Norway ▲
44 L 4 **Galeana**, Mexico
117 S 10 **Galela**, Indonesia
21 E 15 **Galena**, IL, U.S.A.
35 O 7 **Galena**, AK, U.S.A.
49 Z 14 **Galeota Point**, Trinidad and Tobago ▶
49 Z 14 **Galera Point**, Trinidad and Tobago ▶
21 E 17 **Galesburg**, IL, U.S.A.
20 D 12 **Galesville**, WI, U.S.A.
14 E 10 **Galeton**, PA, U.S.A.
127 N 22 **Galguduud**, Somalia ▣
86 H 13 **Galicea Mare**, Romania
90 L 13 **Galich**, Russian Federation
66 I 2 **Galicia**, Spain ▣
127 H 18 **Gallabat**, Sudan
76 C 6 **Gallarate**, Italy
16 F 8 **Gallatin**, TN, U.S.A.
105 F 25 **Galle**, Sri Lanka
57 G 24 **Gallegos**, Argentina ∿
77 O 17 **Gallipoli**, Italy
94 B 8 **Gallipoli**, Turkey
94 A 8 **Gallipoli Peninsula**, Turkey ▶
21 N 20 **Gallipolis**, OH, U.S.A.
70 J 10 **Gällivare**, Sweden
31 N 9 **Gallup**, NM, U.S.A.
124 D 12 **Galtat Zemmour**, Western Sahara
27 T 11 **Galveston**, TX, U.S.A.
27 T 10 **Galveston Bay**, TX, U.S.A. ≈
56 K 11 **Gálvez**, Argentina
107 N 7 **Galwa**, Nepal
61 B 18 **Galway**, Republic of Ireland
61 B 18 **Galway Bay**, Republic of Ireland ≈
130 D 9 **Gamba**, Gabon
118 D 8 **Gambang**, Malaysia
127 G 21 **Gambēla**, Ethiopia
127 F 21 **Gambēla**, Ethiopia ▣
128 D 9 **Gambia**, Africa □
128 E 9 **Gambia**, Gambia ∿
130 H 9 **Gamboma**, Congo
130 H 5 **Gamboula**, Central African Republic
95 W 8 **Gamiş Dağl**, Azerbaijan ▲
112 J 5 **Gamtog**, China
113 V 9 **Gan**, China ∿
112 K 5 **Gana**, China
30 M 9 **Ganado**, AZ, U.S.A.
42 I 12 **Gananoque**, ON, Canada
100 H 10 **Ganāveh**, Iran
95 V 8 **Gäncä**, Azerbaijan
113 Q 15 **Gancheng**, China
132 G 5 **Ganda**, Angola
41 Y 10 **Gander**, NL, Canada
67 U 5 **Gandesa**, Spain
105 A 14 **Gandhidham**, India
105 C 14 **Gandhinagar**, India
67 T 9 **Gandía**, Spain
57 H 17 **Gangán**, Argentina
106 G 7 **Ganganagar**, India
104 E 12 **Gangapur**, India
114 C 11 **Gangaw**, Myanmar
108 H 9 **Gangdise Shan**, China ▲▲
73 B 17 **Gangelt**, Germany
65 S 13 **Ganges**, France
106 K 9 **Ganges**, India/Bangladesh ∿
104 G 12 **Gangetic Plain**, India ◇
107 S 10 **Gangtok**, India
113 O 3 **Gangu**, China
112 L 7 **Ganluo**, China
110 I 9 **Gannan**, China
65 R 9 **Gannat**, France
29 S 11 **Gannett Peak**, WY, U.S.A. ▲
108 M 7 **Ganq**, China
113 Q 2 **Ganquan**, China
75 Y 3 **Gänserndorf**, Austria
113 N 3 **Gansu**, China
113 N 3 **Gansu**, China ▣
95 P 5 **Gant'iadi**, Georgia
129 T 12 **Ganye**, Nigeria
113 X 3 **Ganyu**, China
102 G 7 **Ganyushkino**, Kazakhstan
113 U 10 **Ganzhou**, China
129 N 8 **Gao**, Mali
129 O 7 **Gao**, Mali ▣
113 V 8 **Gao'an**, China
111 C 18 **Gaocheng**, China
113 T 2 **Gaoping**, China
113 V 1 **Gaotang**, China
128 L 11 **Gaoua**, Burkina Faso
113 N 8 **Gaoxian**, China
111 D 18 **Gaoyang**, China
113 X 4 **Gaoyou**, China
113 X 4 **Gaoyou Hu**, China ◣
113 R 13 **Gaozhou**, China
65 V 12 **Gap**, France
120 G 10 **Gapan**, Philippines
108 H 9 **Gar**, China
127 O 21 **Garacad**, Somalia
47 Y 15 **Garachiné**, Panama
127 M 20 **Garadag**, Somalia
128 I 10 **Garalo**, Mali
54 O 13 **Garanhuns**, Brazil
130 K 2 **Garba**, Central African Republic
131 W 7 **Garba Tula**, Kenya
127 K 23 **Garbahaarey**, Somalia
33 E 16 **Garberville**, CA, U.S.A.
72 G 13 **Garbsen**, Germany
58 I 6 **Garça**, Brazil
72 J 13 **Gardelegen**, Germany
24 I 5 **Garden City**, KS, U.S.A.
20 J 9 **Garden Island**, MI, U.S.A. ⛱
101 U 8 **Gardez**, Afghanistan
29 R 8 **Gardiner**, MT, U.S.A.
19 W 11 **Gardner**, FL, U.S.A.
34 E 13 **Gareloi Island**, AK, U.S.A. ⛱
76 B 9 **Garessio**, Italy
125 O 12 **Garet El Djenoun**, Algeria ▲
31 Q 5 **Garfield**, CO, U.S.A.
63 S 2 **Garforth**, U.K.
84 B 13 **Gargždai**, Lithuania
105 G 16 **Garhchiroli**, India
58 H 11 **Garibaldi**, Brazil
132 J 13 **Garies**, Republic of South Africa
131 X 8 **Garissa**, Kenya
17 S 11 **Garland**, NC, U.S.A.
27 Q 5 **Garland**, TX, U.S.A.
85 E 15 **Garliava**, Lithuania
100 H 3 **Garmī**, Iran
73 I 26 **Garmisch-Partenkirchen**, Germany
100 J 6 **Garmsār**, Iran
25 Q 5 **Garnett**, KS, U.S.A.
135 R 11 **Garnpung Lake**, NSW, Australia ◣
64 M 11 **Garonne**, France ∿
127 N 20 **Garoowe**, Somalia
129 U 11 **Garoua**, Cameroon
129 V 13 **Garoua Boulai**, Cameroon
138 F 4 **Garove Island**, Papua New Guinea ⛱
29 O 6 **Garrison**, MT, U.S.A.
40 K 1 **Garry Lake**, NU, Canada ◣
131 X 9 **Garsen**, Kenya
127 A 18 **Garsila**, Sudan
63 P 2 **Garstang**, U.K.
63 O 8 **Garth**, U.K.
116 H 14 **Garut**, Indonesia
137 C 24 **Garvie Mountains**, New Zealand ▲▲
105 I 14 **Garwa**, India
78 M 13 **Garwolin**, Poland
21 H 16 **Gary**, IN, U.S.A.
112 K 5 **Garzê**, China
50 H 8 **Garzón**, Colombia
64 M 13 **Gascony**, France ◇
134 F 8 **Gascoyne**, WA, Australia ∿
134 F 8 **Gascoyne Junction**, WA, Australia
101 P 12 **Gasht**, Iran
129 T 10 **Gashua**, Nigeria
138 G 5 **Gasmata**, Papua New Guinea
43 T 5 **Gaspé**, QC, Canada
122 K 12 **Gassan**, Japan ▲
129 T 12 **Gassol**, Nigeria
17 O 10 **Gastonia**, NC, U.S.A.
83 C 20 **Gastouni**, Greece
57 G 17 **Gastre**, Argentina
86 F 11 **Gătaia**, Romania
90 E 11 **Gatchina**, Russian Federation
38 J 6 **Gateshead Island**, NU, Canada ⛱
27 P 8 **Gatesville**, TX, U.S.A.
42 I 10 **Gatineau**, QC, Canada
16 K 9 **Gatlinburg**, TN, U.S.A.
47 W 13 **Gatún**, Panama
139 Y 12 **Gau**, Fiji ⛱
139 Q 9 **Gaua**, Vanuatu ⛱
84 G 9 **Gauja**, Latvia ∿
105 E 21 **Gauribidanur**, India
71 C 19 **Gausta**, Norway ▲
133 O 11 **Gauteng**, Republic of South Africa ▣
100 I 12 **Gāvbandī**, Iran
83 H 26 **Gavdopoula**, Greece ⛱
83 H 26 **Gavdos**, Greece ⛱
54 C 12 **Gaviãozinho**, Brazil
71 H 19 **Gävle**, Sweden
90 J 13 **Gavrilov-Yam**, Russian Federation
135 P 11 **Gawler**, SA, Australia
109 P 6 **Gaxun Nur**, China ◣
107 P 12 **Gaya**, India
119 U 5 **Gaya**, Malaysia ⛱
20 K 11 **Gaylord**, MI, U.S.A.
91 R 10 **Gayny**, Russian Federation
96 E 10 **Gaza**, Israel
133 Q 9 **Gaza**, Mozambique ▣
96 E 10 **Gaza Strip**, Israel ◇
102 J 13 **Gazandzhyk**, Turkmenistan
131 X 10 **Gazi**, Kenya
94 M 13 **Gaziantep**, Turkey
101 O 8 **Gazīk**, Iran
94 G 14 **Gazipaşa**, Turkey
103 O 12 **Gazli**, Uzbekistan
128 H 12 **Gbarnga**, Liberia
128 H 13 **Gbatala**, Liberia
129 S 12 **Gboko**, Nigeria
78 I 8 **Gdańsk**, Poland
90 D 11 **Gdov**, Russian Federation
78 I 8 **Gdynia**, Poland
117 S 11 **Gebe**, Indonesia ⛱
126 G 11 **Gebel Hamâta**, Egypt ▲
126 F 9 **Gebel Katherîna**, Egypt ▲
127 I 20 **Gebre Guracha**, Ethiopia
94 E 8 **Gebze**, Turkey
127 G 21 **Gech'a**, Ethiopia
127 G 17 **Gedaref**, Sudan
127 G 18 **Gedaref**, Sudan ▣
127 L 21 **Gedlegubē**, Ethiopia
127 K 24 **Gedo**, Somalia ▣
119 N 11 **Gedong**, Malaysia
71 D 26 **Gedser**, Denmark
69 H 17 **Geel**, Belgium
135 S 13 **Geelong**, VIC, Australia
129 T 9 **Geidam**, Nigeria
39 L 15 **Geikie**, SK, Canada ∿
71 C 18 **Geilo**, Norway
131 S 9 **Geita**, Tanzania
112 L 12 **Gejiu**, China
77 J 23 **Gela**, Italy
108 L 9 **Geladaindong**, China ▲
127 M 21 **Geladī**, Ethiopia
68 K 12 **Gelderland**, Netherlands ▣
73 B 15 **Geldern**, Germany
69 J 16 **Geldrop**, Netherlands
69 K 18 **Geleen**, Netherlands
92 K 12 **Gelendzhik**, Russian Federation
127 M 22 **Gelinsoor**, Somalia
118 C 9 **Gemas**, Malaysia
69 G 20 **Gembloux**, Belgium
129 T 13 **Gembu**, Nigeria
130 K 6 **Gemena**, Democratic Republic of Congo
94 L 10 **Gemerek**, Turkey
94 D 8 **Gemlik**, Turkey
70 A 10 **Gemlufall**, Iceland
76 I 5 **Gemona del Friuli**, Italy
126 F 10 **Gemsa**, Egypt
57 J 14 **General Acha**, Argentina
56 H 13 **General Alvear**, Argentina
59 D 16 **General Belgrano**, Argentina
56 J 11 **General Cabrera**, Argentina
45 P 7 **General Cepeda**, Mexico
59 A 20 **General Conesa**, Argentina
58 C 9 **General José de San Martín**, Argentina
59 E 17 **General Juan Madariaga**, Argentina
59 C 18 **General La Madrid**, Argentina
56 G 1 **General Lagos**, Chile
59 E 17 **General Lavalle**, Argentina
121 M 16 **General MacArthur**, Philippines
56 I 6 **General Martín Miguel de Güemes**, Argentina
59 A 17 **General Pico**, Argentina
59 B 16 **General Pinto**, Argentina
57 H 15 **General Roca**, Argentina
121 M 23 **General Santos**, Philippines
82 N 6 **General-Toshevo**, Bulgaria
59 A 16 **General Villegas**, Argentina
21 E 16 **Geneseo**, IL, U.S.A.
127 I 20 **Genet**, Ethiopia
14 F 8 **Geneva**, NY, U.S.A.
74 A 10 **Geneva**, Switzerland
112 J 11 **Gengma**, China
130 M 9 **Gengwa**, Democratic Republic of Congo
69 J 18 **Genk**, Belgium
76 C 9 **Genoa**, Italy
116 G 14 **Genteng**, Indonesia
72 K 13 **Genthin**, Germany
118 C 8 **Genting Highlands**, Malaysia
134 G 12 **Geographe Bay**, WA, Australia ≈
41 T 6 **George**, QC, Canada ∿
132 L 15 **George**, Republic of South Africa
137 A 23 **George Sound**, New Zealand ≈
48 H 7 **George Town**, Cayman Islands ♜
48 M 3 **George Town**, The Bahamas
118 A 6 **George Town**, Malaysia
135 T 15 **George Town**, TAS, Australia
145 T 14 **George V Coast**, Antarctica ◇
145 S 14 **George V Land**, Antarctica ◇
144 I 5 **George VI Sound**, Antarctica ≈
27 P 12 **George West**, TX, U.S.A.
16 I 5 **Georgetown**, KY, U.S.A.
17 W 3 **Georgetown**, DE, U.S.A.
17 R 13 **Georgetown**, SC, U.S.A.
49 Z 12 **Georgetown**, St Vincent and the Grenadines
51 U 5 **Georgetown**, Guyana ♜
128 E 9 **Georgetown**, Gambia
135 S 4 **Georgetown**, QLD, Australia
19 S 4 **Georgia**, U.S.A. ▣
95 T 6 **Georgia**, Asia □
42 D 10 **Georgian Bay**, ON, Canada ≈
135 P 5 **Georgina**, QLD, Australia ∿
103 X 5 **Georgiyevka**, Kazakhstan
93 O 13 **Georgiyevsk**, Russian Federation
72 D 10 **Georgsheil**, Germany
73 K 17 **Gera**, Germany
69 E 19 **Geraardsbergen**, Belgium
83 E 22 **Geraki**, Greece
25 X 5 **Gerald**, MO, U.S.A.
134 F 10 **Geraldton**, WA, Australia
95 Q 12 **Gercüş**, Turkey
94 H 8 **Gerede**, Turkey
101 R 9 **Gereshk**, Afghanistan
67 Q 12 **Gérgal**, Spain
33 J 16 **Gerlach**, NV, U.S.A.
79 K 19 **Gerlachovský štít**, Slovakia ▲
73 H 17 **Germany**, Europe □
123 I 16 **Gero**, Japan
94 K 7 **Gerze**, Turkey
71 I 19 **Geta**, Finland
67 O 7 **Getafe**, Spain
14 F 14 **Gettysburg**, PA, U.S.A.
22 K 8 **Gettysburg**, SD, U.S.A.
144 K 10 **Getz Ice Shelf Range**, Antarctica ◇
95 S 11 **Gevaş**, Turkey
82 E 12 **Gevgelija**, Macedonia (F.Y.R.O.M.)
105 D 17 **Gevrai**, India
118 B 14 **Geylang**, Singapore
75 V 3 **Gföhl**, Austria
132 L 12 **Ghaap Plateau**, Republic of South Africa ◇
125 Q 9 **Ghadāmis**, Libya
125 T 11 **Ghaddūwah**, Libya
107 N 10 **Ghaghara**, India ∿
128 M12 **Ghana**, Africa □
132 K 9 **Ghanzi**, Botswana
132 L 9 **Ghanzi**, Botswana ▣
96 F 12 **Gharandal**, Jordan
125 N 8 **Ghardaïa**, Algeria
101 T 15 **Gharo**, Pakistan
125 S 8 **Gharyān**, Libya
125 R 12 **Ghāt**, Libya
124 K 6 **Ghazaouet**, Algeria
106 J 8 **Ghaziabad**, India
107 O 11 **Ghazipur**, India
101 T 9 **Ghazluna**, Pakistan
101 U 8 **Ghaznī**, Afghanistan
101 T 8 **Ghaznī**, Afghanistan ▣
99 N 4 **Ghazzālah**, Saudi Arabia
69 D 18 **Ghent**, Belgium
86 K 9 **Gheorgheni**, Romania
86 I 8 **Gherla**, Romania
101 R 9 **Ghorak**, Afghanistan
101 V 12 **Ghotki**, Pakistan
101 R 8 **Ghowr**, Afghanistan ▣
99 V 12 **Ghubbat al Qamar**, Yemen ≈
97 O 2 **Ghūnā**, Syria
101 P 7 **Ghurian**, Afghanistan
115 N 22 **Gia Đinh**, Vietnam
115 L 23 **Gia Rai**, Vietnam
82 E 13 **Giannitsa**, Greece
77 L 22 **Giarre**, Italy
29 N 7 **Gibbonsville**, ID, U.S.A.
132 I 10 **Gibeon**, Namibia
66 J 12 **Gibraleón**, Spain
66 L 14 **Gibraltar**, Gibraltar ♜
66 L 14 **Gibraltar**, U.K. ▣
134 J 7 **Gibson Desert**, WA, Australia ◇
27 Q 10 **Giddings**, TX, U.S.A.
71 H 14 **Gideälven**, Sweden ∿
127 H 22 **Gīdolē**, Ethiopia
65 Q 6 **Gien**, France
73 F 18 **Giessen**, Germany
68 N 7 **Gieten**, Netherlands
32 K 6 **Gifford**, WA, U.S.A.
72 H 13 **Gifhorn**, Germany
123 H 17 **Gifu**, Japan
66 L 1 **Gijón**, Spain
30 K 13 **Gila**, AZ, U.S.A. ∿
30 I 13 **Gila Bend**, AZ, U.S.A.
30 L 12 **Gila Mountains**, AZ, U.S.A. ▲▲
100 H 4 **Gīlān**, Iran ▣
86 H 9 **Gilău**, Romania
95 Y 7 **Giläzi**, Azerbaijan
140 D 1 **Gilbert Islands**, Kiribati ⛱
54 K 13 **Gilbués**, Brazil
29 R 2 **Gildford**, MT, U.S.A.
133 T 6 **Gilé**, Mozambique
126 B 12 **Gilf Kebir Plateau**, Egypt ◇
135 U 10 **Gilgandra**, NSW, Australia
101 Y 6 **Gilgit**, Pakistan
106 H 2 **Gilgit**, India
40 K 7 **Gillam**, MB, Canada
29 X 9 **Gillette**, WY, U.S.A.
63 Q 12 **Gillingham**, U.K.
63 X 11 **Gillingham**, U.K.
145 W 6 **Gillock Island**, Antarctica ⛱
21 G 17 **Gilman**, IL, U.S.A.
33 G 20 **Gilroy**, CA, U.S.A.
127 G 20 **Gīmbī**, Ethiopia
121 L 20 **Gingoog**, Philippines
127 J 21 **Gīnīr**, Ethiopia
83 H 17 **Gioura**, Greece ⛱
101 P 10 **Girdi**, Iran
60 J 11 **Girdle Ness**, U.K. ▶
95 N 8 **Giresun**, Turkey
94 M 8 **Giresun Dağlari**, Turkey ▲▲
126 F 10 **Girga**, Egypt
107 R 12 **Giridih**, India
67 Y 3 **Girona**, Spain
64 L 10 **Gironde**, France ∿
61 G 14 **Girvan**, U.K.
136 O 12 **Gisborne**, New Zealand
136 O 11 **Gisborne**, New Zealand ▣
131 Q 9 **Gisenyi**, Rwanda
71 E 23 **Gislaved**, Sweden
65 P 3 **Gisors**, France
69 B 17 **Gistel**, Belgium
76 J 12 **Giulianova**, Italy
86 K 14 **Giurgiu**, Romania
69 E 21 **Givry**, Belgium
133 P 9 **Giyani**, Republic of South Africa
127 I 20 **Giyon**, Ethiopia
103 P 12 **Gizhduvan**, Uzbekistan
89 Y 9 **Gizhiga**, Russian Federation
138 K 6 **Gizo**, Solomon Islands
78 M 9 **Giżycko**, Poland
81 I 17 **Gjiri i Drinit**, Albania ≈
81 K 21 **Gjirokastër**, Albania
40 L 1 **Gjoa Haven**, NU, Canada
70 B 10 **Gjögur**, Iceland
71 D 18 **Gjøvik**, Norway
43 Y 8 **Glace Bay**, NS, Canada
35 V 10 **Glacier Bay**, AK, U.S.A. ≈
27 T 6 **Gladewater**, TX, U.S.A.
20 H 9 **Gladstone**, MI, U.S.A.
135 V 7 **Gladstone**, QLD, Australia
135 P 11 **Gladstone**, SA, Australia
71 D 18 **Glåma**, Norway ∿
121 M 24 **Glan**, Philippines
68 O 12 **Glanerbrug**, Netherlands
74 H 7 **Glarus**, Switzerland
63 P 9 **Glasbury**, U.K.
24 M 3 **Glasco**, KS, U.S.A.
16 G 7 **Glasgow**, KY, U.S.A.
29 W 3 **Glasgow**, MT, U.S.A.
60 H 13 **Glasgow**, U.K.
26 H 10 **Glass Mountains**, TX, U.S.A. ▲▲
63 P 12 **Glastonbury**, U.K.
91 R 12 **Glazov**, Russian Federation
92 J 4 **Glazunovka**, Russian Federation
75 W 7 **Gleisdorf**, Austria
30 K 7 **Glen Canyon**, UT, U.S.A. ◇
135 V 10 **Glen Innes**, NSW, Australia
35 S 8 **Glenallen**, AK, U.S.A.
137 F 23 **Glenavy**, New Zealand
42 C 14 **Glencoe**, ON, Canada
30 I 12 **Glendale**, AZ, U.S.A.
135 O 10 **Glendambo**, SA, Australia
135 U 5 **Glenden**, QLD, Australia
29 Y 4 **Glendive**, MT, U.S.A.
29 Y 12 **Glendo**, WY, U.S.A.
29 Z 12 **Glendo Reservoir**, WY, U.S.A. ◣
51 T 6 **Glendor Mountains**, Guyana ▲▲
17 U 5 **Glenns**, VA, U.S.A.
28 K 12 **Glenns Ferry**, ID, U.S.A.
19 V 5 **Glennville**, GA, U.S.A.
137 C 22 **Glenorchy**, New Zealand
14 K 8 **Glens Falls**, NY, U.S.A.
61 C 15 **Glenties**, Republic of Ireland
23 Q 14 **Glenwood**, IA, U.S.A.
25 T 12 **Glenwood**, AR, U.S.A.
31 N 13 **Glenwood**, NM, U.S.A.
31 P 4 **Glenwood Springs**, CO, U.S.A.
74 F 9 **Gletsch**, Switzerland
78 K 11 **Glinojeck**, Poland
79 I 17 **Gliwice**, Poland
30 L 12 **Globe**, AZ, U.S.A.
75 X 5 **Gloggnitz**, Austria
79 F 14 **Głogów**, Poland
70 F 11 **Glomfjord**, Norway
70 I 13 **Glommersträsk**, Sweden
63 R 4 **Glossop**, U.K.
15 O 9 **Gloucester**, MA, U.S.A.
17 V 6 **Gloucester**, VA, U.S.A.
63 Q 9 **Gloucester**, U.K.
138 F 4 **Gloucester**, Papua New Guinea
92 M 8 **Glubokiy**, Russian Federation
103 X 4 **Glubokoye**, Kazakhstan
93 Q 6 **Gmelinka**, Russian Federation
75 R 8 **Gmünd**, Austria
75 U 2 **Gmünd**, Austria
75 S 5 **Gmunden**, Austria
78 H 11 **Gniewkowo**, Poland
78 H 12 **Gniezno**, Poland
81 M 15 **Gnjilane**, Serbia and Montenegro
115 N 22 **Go Công**, Vietnam
105 C 20 **Goa**, India ▣
107 U 11 **Goalpara**, India
128 L 13 **Goaso**, Ghana
127 J 21 **Goba**, Ethiopia
132 J 9 **Gobabis**, Namibia
57 I 15 **Gobernador Duval**, Argentina
57 H 21 **Gobernador Gregores**, Argentina
57 G 23 **Gobernador Mayer**, Argentina
111 A 14 **Gobi Desert**, China ◇
123 G 19 **Gobo**, Japan
73 B 15 **Goch**, Germany
132 J 10 **Gochas**, Namibia
63 U 12 **Godalming**, U.K.
105 F 17 **Godavari**, India ∿
43 Q 5 **Godbout**, QC, Canada
107 R 12 **Godda**, India
127 K 22 **Godē**, Ethiopia
42 C 12 **Goderich**, ON, Canada
127 M 22 **Godinlabe**, Somalia
79 J 22 **Gödöllő**, Hungary
40 K 7 **Gods**, MB, Canada ∿
40 J 8 **Gods Lake**, MB, Canada ◣
138 A 6 **Goe**, Papua New Guinea
69 E 15 **Goes**, Netherlands
75 V 2 **Göfritz**, Austria
42 C 7 **Gogama**, ON, Canada
129 O 11 **Gogounou**, Benin
127 C 20 **Gogrial**, Sudan
106 K 10 **Gohad**, India
55 J 16 **Goiânia**, Brazil
55 J 16 **Goiás**, Brazil
55 J 16 **Goiás**, Brazil ▣
58 G 7 **Goio-Erê**, Brazil
69 I 15 **Goirle**, Netherlands
94 A 8 **Gökçeada**, Turkey ⛱
94 B 12 **Gökova Körfezi**, Turkey ≈
94 L 12 **Göksun**, Turkey
133 O 7 **Gokwe**, Zimbabwe
71 C 18 **Gol**, Norway
106 L 9 **Gola**, India
27 Q 12 **Golaid**, TX, U.S.A.
96 G 7 **Golan Heights**, Israel ◇
101 U 7 **Golbahār**, Afghanistan
94 M 12 **Gölbasi**, Turkey
21 G 23 **Golconda**, IL, U.S.A.
33 K 15 **Golconda**, NV, U.S.A.
94 E 8 **Gölcük**, Turkey
32 E 13 **Gold Beach**, OR, U.S.A.
128 M 14 **Gold Coast**, Ghana ◇
135 W 9 **Gold Coast**, QLD, Australia ◇
35 R 8 **Gold Creek**, AK, U.S.A.
78 M 8 **Gołdap**, Poland
39 I 20 **Golden**, BC, Canada
137 H 15 **Golden Bay**, New Zealand ≈

[Country] ▣ Internal administrative region: State/Province/Territory/Dependent territory ♜ Capital city ▲▲ Mountain range/Undersea ridge ▲ Mountain peak/Volcano/Seamount ◇ Geographic feature ▶ Headland/Point/Cape/Peninsula ◗ Desert ⛱ Island/Island group ⌗ Antarctic base ◌ Ocean ◒ Sea ≈ Bay/Gulf/Channel/Strait ◣ Lake ◤ Salt pan/Dry/Intermittent lake ∿ River

18 L 9 **Golden Meadow**, LA, U.S.A.
32 I 9 **Goldendale**, WA, U.S.A.
33 K 20 **Goldfield**, NV, U.S.A.
17 T 10 **Goldsboro**, NC, U.S.A.
27 O 8 **Goldthwaite**, TX, U.S.A.
95 R 8 **Göle**, Turkey
78 D 10 **Goleniów**, Poland
100 L 4 **Golestān**, Iran ▣
33 I 24 **Goleta**, CA, U.S.A.
67 W 5 **Golf de Sant Jordi**, Spain ≈
125 Q 7 **Golfe de Gabès**, Tunisia ≈
125 R 5 **Golfe de Hammamet**, Tunisia ≈
49 O 7 **Golfe de la Gonâve**, Haiti ≈
64 J 4 **Golfe de St-Malo**, France ≈
127 L 19 **Golfe de Tadjoura**, Djibouti ≈
125 Q 5 **Golfe de Tunis**, Tunisia ≈
47 R 14 **Golfito**, Costa Rica
67 Q 13 **Golfo de Almería**, Spain ≈
57 F 17 **Golfo de Ancud**, Chile ≈
57 E 14 **Golfo de Arauco**, Chile ≈
48 G 4 **Golfo de Batabanó**, Cuba ≈
66 J 12 **Golfo de Cádiz**, Portugal/Spain ≈
47 T 15 **Golfo de Chiriquí**, Panama ≈
57 E 18 **Golfo de Corcovado**, Chile ≈
46 L 8 **Golfo de Fonseca**, Honduras ≈
48 K 6 **Golfo de Guacanayabo**, Cuba ≈
47 U 13 **Golfo de los Mosquitos**, Panama ≈
67 S 12 **Golfo de Mazarrón**, Spain ≈
47 U 15 **Golfo de Montijo**, Panama ≈
47 P 13 **Golfo de Nicoya**, Costa Rica ≈
57 E 21 **Golfo de Penas**, Chile ≈
57 I 20 **Golfo de San Jorge**, Argentina ≈
47 Y 14 **Golfo de San Miguel**, Panama ≈
45 U 14 **Golfo de Tehuantepec**, Mexico ≈
50 G 4 **Golfo de Urabá**, Colombia ≈
67 U 8 **Golfo de Valencia**, Spain ≈
77 C 19 **Golfo di Cagliari**, Italy ≈
77 H 21 **Golfo di Castellammare**, Italy ≈
77 L 22 **Golfo di Catania**, Italy ≈
77 B 15 **Golfo di dell'Asinara**, Italy ≈
77 I 15 **Golfo di Gaeta**, Italy ≈
77 L 20 **Golfo di Gioia**, Italy ≈
77 M 14 **Golfo di Manfredonia**, Italy ≈
77 I 16 **Golfo di Napoli**, Italy ≈
77 L 24 **Golfo di Noto**, Italy ≈
77 B 18 **Golfo di Oristano**, Italy ≈
77 D 17 **Golfo di Orosei**, Italy ≈
77 B 19 **Golfo di Palmas**, Italy ≈
77 L 18 **Golfo di Policastro**, Italy ≈
77 K 17 **Golfo di Salerno**, Italy ≈
77 M 20 **Golfo di Santa Eufemia**, Italy ≈
77 N 20 **Golfo di Squillace**, Italy ≈
77 N 18 **Golfo di Taranto**, Italy ≈
76 I 7 **Golfo di Trieste**, Italy ≈
47 R 14 **Golfo Dulce**, Costa Rica ≈
57 J 17 **Golfo Nuevo**, Argentina ≈
57 J 17 **Golfo San José**, Argentina ≈
57 J 17 **Golfo San Matías**, Argentina ≈
57 E 23 **Golfo Trinidad**, Chile ≈
110 H 12 **Golin Baixing**, China
109 N 8 **Golmud**, China
120 F 12 **Golo**, Philippines ⁂
100 H 7 **Golpāyegān**, Iran
60 H 9 **Golspie**, U.K.
103 T 3 **Golubovka**, Kazakhstan
82 H 11 **Golyam Perelik**, Bulgaria ▲
82 I 11 **Golyam Persenk**, Bulgaria ▲
131 Q 9 **Goma**, Democratic Republic of Congo
104 G 12 **Gomati**, India ∫
129 T 11 **Gombe**, Nigeria
129 T 11 **Gombe**, Nigeria ▣
129 U 11 **Gombi**, Nigeria
44 L 4 **Gómez Farías**, Mexico
45 N 7 **Gómez Palacio**, Mexico
49 O 7 **Gonaïves**, Haiti
100 L 5 **Gonbad-e Kavus**, Iran
107 N 10 **Gonda**, India
127 H 18 **Gonder**, Ethiopia
105 F 15 **Gondia**, India
113 S 7 **Gong'an**, China
113 R 11 **Gongcheng**, China
112 L 7 **Gongga Shan**, China ▲
108 L 11 **Gonggar**, China
109 P 8 **Gonghe**, China
111 C 15 **Gonghui**, China
108 J 4 **Gongliu**, China
109 N 6 **Gongpoquan**, China
113 T 3 **Gongyi**, China
110 J 13 **Gongzhuling**, China
129 T 10 **Goniri**, Nigeria
123 A 21 **Gōnoura**, Japan
120 H 6 **Gonzaga**, Philippines
27 Q 10 **Gonzales**, TX, U.S.A.
33 G 21 **Gonzales**, CA, U.S.A.
47 Y 14 **Gonzalo Vásquez**, Panama
17 T 5 **Goochland**, VA, U.S.A.
138 G 6 **Goodenough Island**, Papua New Guinea ⁂
28 L 12 **Gooding**, ID, U.S.A.
24 G 3 **Goodland**, KS, U.S.A.
34 M 10 **Goodnews**, AK, U.S.A.
135 S 11 **Goolgowi**, NSW, Australia
134 G 11 **Goomalling**, WA, Australia
135 U 9 **Goondiwindi**, QLD, Australia
68 M 11 **Goor**, Netherlands
57 L 24 **Goose Green**, Falkland Islands
33 I 14 **Goose Lake**, CA, U.S.A. ↘
107 P 10 **Gopalganj**, India
106 K 7 **Gopeshwar**, India
79 F 14 **Góra**, Poland
102 J 12 **Gora Arlang**, Turkmenistan ▲
103 P 14 **Gora Ayribaba**, Turkmenistan ▲
88 M 14 **Gora Belukha**, Russian Federation ▲
102 I 9 **Gora Besshoky**, Kazakhstan ▲
91 U 10 **Gora Denezhkin Kamen'**, Russian Federation ▲
91 U 9 **Gora Isherim**, Russian Federation ▲
102 J 13 **Gora Khasardag**, Turkmenistan ▲
103 P 12 **Gora Khayatbashi**, Uzbekistan ▲
91 U 11 **Gora Konzhakovskiy Kamen'**, Russian Federation ▲
103 V 7 **Gora Kotanemel'**, Kazakhstan ▲
91 S 7 **Gora Kozhim-Iz**, Russian Federation ▲
89 Z 8 **Gora Ledyanaya**, Russian Federation ▲
89 X 13 **Gora Lopatina**, Russian Federation ▲
103 S 10 **Gora Manas**, Kyrgyzstan ▲
89 O 13 **Gora Munku Sardyk**, Russian Federation ▲
108 K 3 **Gora Mustau**, China ▲
91 T 5 **Gora Narodnaya**, Russian Federation ▲
89 X 10 **Gora Nukh Yablonevyy**, Russian Federation ▲
91 U 3 **Gora Payyer**, Russian Federation ▲
89 W 9 **Gora Pobeda**, Russian Federation ▲
103 T 7 **Gora Shunak**, Kazakhstan ▲
102 K 13 **Gora Tagarev**, Turkmenistan ▲
89 V 14 **Gora Tardoki-Yani**, Russian Federation ▲
91 T 6 **Gora Tel'pos-Iz**, Russian Federation ▲
88 J 8 **Gora Telposiz**, Russian Federation ▲
107 O 10 **Gorakhpur**, India
80 I 13 **Goražde**, Bosnia and Herzegovina
17 S 5 **Gordonsville**, VA, U.S.A.
129 W 12 **Goré**, Chad
137 D 25 **Gore**, New Zealand
42 B 9 **Gore Bay**, ON, Canada
14 M 5 **Gore Mountain**, VT, U.S.A. ▲
94 J 11 **Göreme**, Turkey
61 E 19 **Gorey**, Republic of Ireland
100 K 5 **Gorgān**, Iran
137 D 23 **Gorge Creek**, New Zealand
128 F 7 **Gorgol**, Mauritania ▣
127 H 18 **Gorgora**, Ethiopia
95 T 6 **Gori**, Georgia
69 H 14 **Gorinchem**, Netherlands
95 V 9 **Goris**, Armenia
90 I 14 **Goritsy**, Russian Federation
76 I 6 **Gorizia**, Italy
107 P 9 **Gorkha**, Nepal
90 M 14 **Gor'kovskoye Vodokhranilishche**, Russian Federation ↘
79 L 18 **Gorlice**, Poland
73 O 16 **Görlitz**, Germany
82 H 7 **Gorni Dŭbnik**, Bulgaria
80 L 12 **Gornji Milanovac**, Serbia and Montenegro
88 M 13 **Gorno Altaysk**, Russian Federation
88 L 13 **Gornyak**, Russian Federation
93 R 5 **Gornyy**, Russian Federation
93 P 7 **Gornyy Balykley**, Russian Federation
90 L 14 **Gorodets**, Russian Federation
93 P 3 **Gorodishche**, Russian Federation
93 N 11 **Gorodovikovsk**, Russian Federation
138 D 4 **Goroka**, Papua New Guinea
133 R 7 **Gorongosa**, Mozambique
117 P 10 **Gorontalo**, Indonesia
68 L 12 **Gorssel**, Netherlands
102 I 11 **Gory Akkyr**, Turkmenistan ▲▲
103 N 12 **Gory Auminzatau**, Uzbekistan ▲▲
103 Q 14 **Gory Baysuntau**, Uzbekistan ▲▲
103 N 10 **Gory Bukantau**, Uzbekistan ▲▲
89 P 7 **Gory Byrranga**, Russian Federation ▲▲
103 O 11 **Gory Dzhetymtau**, Uzbekistan ▲▲
89 P 8 **Gory Kamen'**, Russian Federation ▲
102 J 11 **Gory Koymatdag**, Turkmenistan ▲▲
102 L 7 **Gory Mugodzhary**, Kazakhstan ▲▲
89 O 9 **Gory Putorana**, Russian Federation ▲▲
79 K 15 **Góry Świętokrzyskie**, Poland ▲▲
78 E 11 **Gorzów Wielkopolski**, Poland
135 V 11 **Gosford**, NSW, Australia
122 J 9 **Goshogawara**, Japan
73 H 14 **Goslar**, Germany
80 D 11 **Gospić**, Croatia
63 T 13 **Gosport**, U.K.
69 G 21 **Gosselies**, Belgium
71 B 15 **Gossen**, Norway ⁂
128 M 8 **Gossi**, Mali
82 C 11 **Gostivar**, Macedonia (F.Y.R.O.M.)
78 G 13 **Gostyń**, Poland
78 J 12 **Gostynin**, Poland
123 J 17 **Gotemba**, Japan
73 I 17 **Gotha**, Germany
22 K 14 **Gothenburg**, NE, U.S.A.
71 D 22 **Gothenburg**, Sweden
129 O 9 **Gothèye**, Niger
71 I 23 **Gotland**, Sweden ⁂
123 A 23 **Gotō-rettō**, Japan ⁂
82 G 12 **Gotse Delchev**, Bulgaria
71 I 22 **Gotska Sandön**, Sweden ⁂
123 D 19 **Gōtsu**, Japan
73 H 15 **Göttingen**, Germany
68 G 13 **Gouda**, Netherlands
128 F 9 **Goudiri**, Senegal
129 T 9 **Goudoumaria**, Niger
135 U 12 **Goulburn**, NSW, Australia
135 N 1 **Goulburn Islands**, NT, Australia ⁂
145 O 9 **Gould Coast**, Antarctica ◇
129 V 10 **Goulféy**, Cameroon
128 I 8 **Goumbou**, Mali
128 L 8 **Goundam**, Mali
129 X 11 **Goundi**, Chad
128 L 9 **Gourcy**, Burkina Faso
129 S 9 **Gouré**, Niger
65 P 3 **Gournay-en-Bray**, France
129 Y 6 **Gouro**, Chad
14 H 6 **Gouverneur**, NY, U.S.A.
55 M 17 **Governador Valadares**, Brazil
109 N 4 **Govi-Altay**, Mongolia ▣
109 O 5 **Govi Altayn Nuruu**, Mongolia ▲▲
107 N 12 **Govind Ballash Pant Sagar**, India ↘
103 P 14 **Govurdak**, Turkmenistan
14 C 9 **Gowanda**, NY, U.S.A.
42 D 7 **Gowganda**, ON, Canada
58 C 11 **Goya**, Argentina
95 X 8 **Göyşşay**, Azerbaijan
94 F 8 **Göynük**, Turkey
95 Q 10 **Göynük**, Turkey
129 U 14 **Goyoum**, Cameroon
95 Y 10 **Göytäpä**, Azerbaijan
129 Z 10 **Goz-Beïda**, Chad
127 G 16 **Goz Regeb**, Sudan
108 I 8 **Gozha Co**, China ↘
77 J 25 **Gozo**, Malta ⁂
132 M 14 **Graaf-Reinet**, Republic of South Africa
128 I 14 **Grabo**, Côte d'Ivoire
80 D 11 **Gračac**, Croatia
42 I 9 **Gracefield**, QC, Canada
23 O 7 **Graceville**, MN, U.S.A.
46 K 6 **Gracias**, Honduras
80 H 10 **Gradačac**, Bosnia and Herzegovina
82 L 9 **Gradets**, Bulgaria
66 L 1 **Grado**, Spain
76 I 6 **Grado**, Italy
31 T 10 **Grady**, NM, U.S.A.
17 P 2 **Grafton**, WV, U.S.A.
23 N 2 **Grafton**, ND, U.S.A.
135 W 10 **Grafton**, NSW, Australia
37 O 3 **Graham Island**, NU, Canada ⁂
39 C 19 **Graham Island**, BC, Canada ⁂
144 H 3 **Graham Land**, Antarctica ◇
133 N 15 **Grahamstown**, Republic of South Africa
54 K 12 **Grajaú**, Brazil
78 M 9 **Grajewo**, Poland
82 N 10 **Gramatikovo**, Bulgaria
60 H 11 **Grampian Mtns**, U.K. ▲▲
72 N 11 **Gramzow**, Germany
57 G 21 **Gran Altiplanicie Central**, Argentina ▲▲
56 K 6 **Gran Chaco**, Argentina/Paraguay ◇
53 E 15 **Gran Pajonal**, Peru ◇
31 U 6 **Granada**, CO, U.S.A.
47 N 9 **Granada**, Nicaragua
50 J 7 **Granada**, Colombia
67 O 12 **Granada**, Spain
42 M 10 **Granby**, QC, Canada
22 H 7 **Grand**, SD, U.S.A. ∫
48 K 1 **Grand Bahama**, The Bahamas ⁂
128 K 14 **Grand-Bassam**, Côte d'Ivoire
43 S 10 **Grand Bay**, NB, Canada
42 C 13 **Grand Bend**, ON, Canada
49 P 5 **Grand Caicos**, Turks and Caicos Islands ⁂
30 J 9 **Grand Canyon**, AZ, U.S.A.
30 H 9 **Grand Canyon**, AZ, U.S.A. ◇
48 H 7 **Grand Cayman**, Cayman Islands ⁂
128 I 14 **Grand Cess**, Liberia
32 J 6 **Grand Coulee**, WA, U.S.A.
129 T 7 **Grand Erg de Bilma**, Niger ◇
124 J 9 **Grand Erg Occidental**, Algeria ◇
125 N 10 **Grand Erg Oriental**, Algeria ◇
43 Q 8 **Grand Falls**, NB, Canada
23 N 3 **Grand Forks**, ND, U.S.A.
21 I 14 **Grand Haven**, MI, U.S.A.
20 I 8 **Grand Island**, MI, U.S.A. ⁂
22 M 14 **Grand Island**, NE, U.S.A.
16 B 10 **Grand Junction**, TN, U.S.A.
31 N 5 **Grand Junction**, CO, U.S.A.
18 I 8 **Grand Lake**, LA, U.S.A. ↘
21 K 18 **Grand Lake**, OH, U.S.A. ↘
41 X 10 **Grand Lake**, NL, Canada ↘
43 S 9 **Grand Lake**, NB, Canada ↘
25 R 8 **Grand Lake o' the Cherokees**, OK, U.S.A. ↘
15 T 5 **Grand Manan Channel**, ME, U.S.A. ≈
43 S 11 **Grand Manan Island**, NB, Canada ⁂
20 J 8 **Grand Marais**, MI, U.S.A.
23 V 3 **Grand Marais**, MN, U.S.A.
42 L 9 **Grand-Mère**, QC, Canada
23 V 2 **Grand Portage**, MN, U.S.A.
21 J 14 **Grand Rapids**, MI, U.S.A.
23 R 4 **Grand Rapids**, MN, U.S.A.
40 I 8 **Grand Rapids**, MB, Canada
42 I 9 **Grand-Remous**, QC, Canada
29 R 10 **Grand Teton**, WY, U.S.A. ▲
20 J 11 **Grand Traverse Bay**, MI, U.S.A. ≈
49 Q 5 **Grand Turk**, Turks and Caicos Islands ⁂
28 J 11 **Grand View**, ID, U.S.A.
47 Q 8 **Grande**, Nicaragua ∫
53 L 21 **Grande**, Bolivia/Brazil ∫
39 H 18 **Grande Cache**, AB, Canada
133 W 4 **Grande Comore**, Comoros ⁂
43 W 6 **Grande-Entrée**, QC, Canada
39 H 18 **Grande Prairie**, AB, Canada
43 T 5 **Grande-Vallée**, QC, Canada
26 J 8 **Grandfalls**, TX, U.S.A.
24 L 12 **Grandfield**, OK, U.S.A.
66 G 10 **Grândola**, Portugal
32 I 9 **Grandview**, WA, U.S.A.
29 S 14 **Granger**, WY, U.S.A.
28 K 6 **Grangeville**, ID, U.S.A.
21 E 21 **Granite City**, IL, U.S.A.
23 P 8 **Granite Falls**, MN, U.S.A.
29 S 7 **Granite Peak**, MT, U.S.A. ▲
30 I 3 **Granite Peak**, UT, U.S.A. ▲
22 I 14 **Grant**, NE, U.S.A.
144 L 11 **Grant Island**, Antarctica ⁂
63 U 5 **Grantham**, U.K.
31 O 10 **Grants**, NM, U.S.A.
32 F 13 **Grants Pass**, OR, U.S.A.
30 J 3 **Grantsville**, UT, U.S.A.
64 L 4 **Granville**, France
28 J 12 **Grasmere**, ID, U.S.A.
71 I 19 **Gräsö**, Sweden ⁂
33 H 17 **Grass Valley**, CA, U.S.A.
77 M 16 **Grassano**, Italy
65 W 13 **Grasse**, France
29 S 5 **Grassrange**, MT, U.S.A.
22 G 4 **Grassy Butte**, ND, U.S.A.
74 H 9 **Graubünden**, Switzerland ▣
67 U 3 **Graus**, Spain
58 H 12 **Gravataí**, Brazil
69 K 14 **Grave**, Netherlands
28 L 6 **Grave Peak**, ID, U.S.A. ▲
76 D 5 **Gravedona**, Italy
42 F 11 **Gravenhurst**, ON, Canada
63 X 11 **Gravesend**, U.K.
19 T 4 **Gray**, GA, U.S.A.
65 U 7 **Gray**, France
20 K 11 **Grayling**, MI, U.S.A.
21 G 21 **Grayville**, IL, U.S.A.
92 I 6 **Grayvoron**, Russian Federation
75 W 7 **Graz**, Austria
48 L 1 **Great Abaco**, The Bahamas ⁂
134 K 11 **Great Australian Bight**, WA, Australia ≈
48 J 2 **Great Bahama Bank**, The Bahamas ≈
136 L 7 **Great Barrier Island**, New Zealand ⁂
135 S 1 **Great Barrier Reef**, QLD, Australia ◇
14 L 10 **Great Barrington**, MA, U.S.A.
33 M 17 **Great Basin**, NV/UT, U.S.A. ◇
38 F 10 **Great Bear Lake**, NT, Canada ↘
24 L 5 **Great Bend**, KS, U.S.A.
61 J 14 **Great Britain**, U.K. ⁂
105 N 25 **Great Channel**, India ≈
115 B 19 **Great Coco Island**, Myanmar ⁂
29 U 13 **Great Divide Basin**, WY, U.S.A. ◇
135 T 13 **Great Dividing Range**, VIC, Australia ▲▲
63 X 9 **Great Dunmow**, U.K.
136 I 4 **Great Exhibition Bay**, New Zealand ≈
48 L 3 **Great Exuma Island**, The Bahamas ⁂
29 Q 4 **Great Falls**, MT, U.S.A.
107 P 10 **Great Gandak**, India ∫
63 Q 2 **Great Harwood**, U.K.
79 L 24 **Great Hungarian Plain**, Hungary ◇
49 N 5 **Great Inagua Island**, The Bahamas ⁂
132 K 14 **Great Karoo**, Republic of South Africa ▲▲
63 Q 8 **Great Malvern**, U.K.
136 L 8 **Great Mercury Island**, New Zealand ⁂
105 O 25 **Great Nicobar**, India ⁂
63 X 7 **Great Ouse**, U.K. ∫
41 Q 2 **Great Plain of the Koukdjuak**, NU, Canada ◇
12 M 5 **Great Plains**, U.S.A., U.S.A. ◇
96 F 12 **Great Rift Valley**, Jordan ◇
127 H 22 **Great Rift Valley**, Africa ◇
14 J 8 **Great Sacandaga Lake**, NY, U.S.A. ↘
30 J 2 **Great Salt Lake**, UT, U.S.A. ↘
30 I 3 **Great Salt Lake Desert**, UT, U.S.A. ◇
24 M 7 **Great Salt Plains Lake**, OK, U.S.A. ↘
126 B 9 **Great Sand Sea**, Egypt/Libya ◇
134 J 5 **Great Sandy Desert**, WA, Australia ◇
38 H 13 **Great Slave Lake**, NT, Canada ↘
16 J 10 **Great Smoky Mountains**, NC, U.S.A. ▲▲
39 F 16 **Great Snow Mountain**, BC, Canada ▲
62 M 12 **Great Torrington**, U.K.
134 L 8 **Great Victoria Desert**, WA, Australia ◇
15 S 5 **Great Wass Island**, ME, U.S.A. ⁂
115 E 21 **Great West Torres Islands**, Myanmar ⁂
63 Z 6 **Great Yarmouth**, U.K.
97 S 2 **Great Zab**, Iraq ∫
129 N 13 **Greater Accra**, Ghana ▣
48 I 5 **Greater Antilles**, Cuba ⁂
57 H 24 **Greec**, Chile
14 E 8 **Greece**, NY, U.S.A.
83 C 17 **Greece**, Europe □
31 S 3 **Greeley**, CO, U.S.A.
17 P 13 **Greeleyville**, SC, U.S.A.
30 L 4 **Green**, UT, U.S.A. ∫
20 H 11 **Green Bay**, WI, U.S.A. ≈
20 H 12 **Green Bay**, WI, U.S.A.
19 W 8 **Green Cove Springs**, FL, U.S.A.
138 I 4 **Green Islands**, Papua New Guinea ⁂
39 L 17 **Green Lake**, SK, Canada
14 L 8 **Green Mountains**, VT, U.S.A. ▲▲
30 L 5 **Green River**, UT/WY, U.S.A.
138 A 3 **Green River**, Papua New Guinea
16 H 6 **Green River Lake**, KY, U.S.A. ↘
21 I 19 **Greencastle**, IN, U.S.A.
16 L 8 **Greeneville**, TN, U.S.A.
14 L 9 **Greenfield**, MA, U.S.A.
25 S 6 **Greenfield**, MO, U.S.A.
31 R 6 **Greenhorn Mountain**, CO, U.S.A. ▲
143 P 11 **Greenland**, Denmark ▣
143 S 12 **Greenland Plain**, Arctic Ocean ◇
143 R 13 **Greenland Sea**, Arctic Ocean ◒
14 M 12 **Greenport**, NY, U.S.A.
17 P 8 **Greensboro**, NC, U.S.A.
14 B 13 **Greensburg**, PA, U.S.A.
18 L 7 **Greensburg**, LA, U.S.A.
21 J 20 **Greensburg**, IN, U.S.A.
24 K 6 **Greensburg**, KS, U.S.A.
14 A 11 **Greenville**, PA, U.S.A.
15 Q 4 **Greenville**, ME, U.S.A.
16 M 11 **Greenville**, SC, U.S.A.
17 T 9 **Greenville**, NC, U.S.A.
18 K 3 **Greenville**, MS, U.S.A.
19 Q 5 **Greenville**, AL, U.S.A.
19 T 7 **Greenville**, FL, U.S.A.
21 K 18 **Greenville**, OH, U.S.A.
25 Y 7 **Greenville**, MO, U.S.A.
27 R 5 **Greenville**, TX, U.S.A.
33 H 16 **Greenville**, CA, U.S.A.
128 H 14 **Greenville**, Liberia
21 N 17 **Greenwich**, OH, U.S.A.
63 W 10 **Greenwich**, U.K.
16 M 12 **Greenwood**, SC, U.S.A.
18 H 4 **Greenwood**, LA, U.S.A.
18 M 3 **Greenwood**, MS, U.S.A.
25 V 10 **Greers Ferry Lake**, AR, U.S.A. ↘
22 L 11 **Gregory**, SD, U.S.A.
135 R 4 **Gregory Range**, QLD, Australia ▲▲
72 M 9 **Greifswald**, Germany
72 M 8 **Greifswalder Bodden**, Germany ≈
75 U 4 **Grein**, Austria
73 K 18 **Greiz**, Germany
90 K 3 **Gremikha**, Russian Federation
71 D 24 **Grenå**, Denmark
18 M 3 **Grenada**, MS, U.S.A.
49 Y 13 **Grenada**, North America □
18 M 2 **Grenada Lake**, MS, U.S.A. ↘
74 D 7 **Grenchen**, Switzerland
65 U 11 **Grenoble**, France
49 Y 13 **Grenville**, Grenada
69 E 14 **Grevelingen**, Netherlands ≈
73 D 14 **Greven**, Germany
83 C 15 **Grevena**, Greece
73 B 16 **Grevenbroich**, Germany
69 L 24 **Grevenmacher**, Luxembourg ▣
69 M 25 **Grevenmacher**, Luxembourg
72 I 9 **Grevesmühlen**, Germany
137 F 18 **Grey**, New Zealand ∫
41 X 9 **Grey Islands**, NL, Canada ⁂
29 V 9 **Greybull**, WY, U.S.A.
137 F 18 **Greymouth**, New Zealand
133 P 12 **Greytown**, Republic of South Africa
137 L 16 **Greytown**, New Zealand
93 N 5 **Gribanovskiy**, Russian Federation
75 S 4 **Grieskirchen**, Austria
19 S 3 **Griffin**, GA, U.S.A.
135 S 11 **Griffith**, NSW, Australia
95 Q 6 **Grigoleti**, Georgia
87 O 9 **Grigoriopol**, Moldova
130 K 4 **Grimari**, Central African Republic
73 L 16 **Grimma**, Germany
72 L 9 **Grimmen**, Germany
63 V 3 **Grimsby**, U.K.
70 C 9 **Grímsey**, Iceland ⁂
70 C 10 **Grímsstaðir**, Iceland
70 A 12 **Grindavík**, Iceland
74 F 9 **Grindelwald**, Switzerland
80 C 6 **Grintovec**, Slovenia ▲
132 L 12 **Griquatown**, Republic of South Africa
37 P 3 **Grise Fiord**, NU, Canada
80 E 10 **Grmeč**, Bosnia and Herzegovina ▲▲
69 H 17 **Grobbendonk**, Belgium
84 B 11 **Grobiņa**, Latvia
75 S 6 **Gröbming**, Austria
79 G 16 **Grodków**, Poland
68 M 12 **Groenlo**, Netherlands
78 L 13 **Grójec**, Poland
71 E 14 **Grong**, Norway
68 M 6 **Groningen**, Netherlands ▣
68 M 6 **Groningen**, Netherlands
26 L 2 **Groom**, TX, U.S.A.
132 I 12 **Groot Karas Berg**, Namibia ▲▲
135 P 2 **Groote Eylandt**, NT, Australia ⁂
132 J 8 **Grootfontein**, Namibia
132 J 9 **Gross Ums**, Namibia
76 F 12 **Grosseto**, Italy
75 P 7 **Grossglockner**, Austria ▲
41 W 7 **Groswater Bay**, NL, Canada ≈
14 B 11 **Grove City**, PA, U.S.A.
19 O 6 **Grove Hill**, AL, U.S.A.
15 N 5 **Groveton**, NH, U.S.A.
93 Q 14 **Groznyy**, Russian Federation
82 M 10 **Grudovo**, Bulgaria
78 I 10 **Grudziądz**, Poland
132 J 12 **Grünau**, Namibia
84 E 12 **Gruzdžiai**, Lithuania
92 M 4 **Gryazi**, Russian Federation
90 K 12 **Gryazovets**, Russian Federation
74 D 9 **Gstaad**, Switzerland
118 C 6 **Gua Musang**, Malaysia
47 S 13 **Guabito**, Panama
56 I 7 **Guachipas**, Argentina
45 O 11 **Guadalajara**, Mexico
67 P 6 **Guadalajara**, Spain
138 K 7 **Guadalcanal**, Solomon Islands ⁂
138 M 7 **Guadalcanal**, Solomon Islands ▣
56 H 12 **Guadales**, Argentina
66 L 12 **Guadalquivir**, Spain ∫
45 Q 7 **Guadalupe**, Mexico
45 N 8 **Guadalupe**, Mexico
66 M 8 **Guadalupe**, Spain
26 F 7 **Guadalupe Mountains**, TX, U.S.A. ▲▲
26 G 7 **Guadalupe Peak**, TX, U.S.A. ▲
49 Y 9 **Guadeloupe**, France ▣
49 X 9 **Guadeloupe Passage**, Montserrat ≈
67 N 9 **Guadiana**, Spain ∫
67 P 12 **Guadix**, Spain
58 H 12 **Guaíba**, Brazil
50 M 8 **Guainía**, Colombia ▣
50 M 8 **Guainía**, Colombia ∫
58 F 7 **Guaíra**, Brazil
55 D 14 **Guajará-Mirim**, Brazil
58 C 13 **Gualeguay**, Argentina ∫
59 C 15 **Gualeguay**, Argentina
56 L 11 **Gualeguaychú**, Argentina
59 D 14 **Gualeguaychu**, Argentina
57 G 18 **Gualjaina**, Argentina
140 A 9 **Guam**, Guam ⁂
140 A 9 **Guam**, U.S.A. ▣
59 B 18 **Guamini**, Argentina
44 K 7 **Guamúchil**, Mexico
112 M 6 **Guan Xian**, China
48 H 4 **Guanabacoa**, Cuba
47 N 3 **Guanaja**, Honduras
45 P 11 **Guanajuato**, Mexico
45 P 10 **Guanajuato**, Mexico ▣
55 L 15 **Guanambi**, Brazil
50 M 4 **Guanare**, Venezuela
56 G 9 **Guandacol**, Argentina
113 S 1 **Guandi Shan**, China ▲
48 F 4 **Guane**, Cuba
113 V 9 **Guangchang**, China
113 X 6 **Guangde**, China
113 U 11 **Guangdong**, China ▣
113 X 8 **Guangfeng**, China
113 T 13 **Guanghai**, China
112 K 9 **Guangmao Shan**, China ▲
113 N 11 **Guangnan**, China
113 T 12 **Guangning**, China
111 F 19 **Guangrao**, China
113 U 5 **Guangshui**, China
113 Q 12 **Guangxi Zhuangzu**, China ▣
113 O 5 **Guangyuan**, China
113 W 9 **Guangze**, China
113 T 12 **Guangzhou**, China
113 W 3 **Guanhu**, China
48 M 6 **Guantánamo**, Cuba
48 M 6 **Guantánamo Bay Naval Base**, U.S.A., U.S.A.
113 X 3 **Guanyun**, China
47 R 12 **Guápiles**, Costa Rica
55 E 15 **Guaporé**, Brazil ∫
53 H 19 **Guaqui**, Bolivia
58 O 5 **Guarapari**, Brazil
58 H 8 **Guarapuava**, Brazil
58 J 8 **Guaraqueçaba**, Brazil
58 J 9 **Guaratuba**, Brazil
53 I 17 **Guarayos**, Bolivia
66 J 5 **Guarda**, Portugal ▣
66 J 6 **Guarda**, Portugal
51 O 4 **Guárico**, Venezuela ▣
58 L 7 **Guarujá**, Brazil
44 K 7 **Guasave**, Mexico
46 H 6 **Guatemala**, Guatemala ♜
46 I 4 **Guatemala**, North America □
51 O 2 **Guatire**, Venezuela
50 K 9 **Guaviare**, Colombia ▣
50 M 7 **Guaviare**, Colombia ∫
49 U 8 **Guayama**, Puerto Rico
52 A 10 **Guayaquil**, Ecuador
53 K 15 **Guayaramerin**, Bolivia
52 A 10 **Guayas**, Ecuador ▣
44 I 5 **Guaymas**, Mexico
46 H 6 **Guazacapán**, Guatemala
88 M 8 **Guba**, Russian Federation ≈
127 G 19 **Guba**, Ethiopia
91 R 1 **Guba Dolgaya**, Russian Federation
91 T 11 **Gubakha**, Russian Federation
78 D 13 **Gubin**, Poland
129 U 10 **Gubio**, Nigeria
95 P 5 **Gudaut'a**, Georgia
99 O 1 **Gudayyidat 'Ar'ar**, Saudi Arabia
93 Q 14 **Gudermes**, Russian Federation
105 G 19 **Gudivada**, India
105 F 20 **Gudur**, India
128 H 12 **Guéckédou**, Guinea
129 V 10 **Guélengdeng**, Chad
125 P 5 **Guelma**, Algeria
124 F 9 **Guelmine**, Morocco
42 E 13 **Guelph**, ON, Canada
45 R 8 **Güémez**, Mexico
129 O 10 **Guéné**, Benin
129 X 10 **Guéra**, Chad ▣
125 N 8 **Guerara**, Algeria
124 J 7 **Guercif**, Morocco
65 P 9 **Guéret**, France
29 Z 12 **Guernsey**, WY, U.S.A.
61 J 25 **Guernsey**, U.K. ▣
128 G 7 **Guérou**, Mauritania
45 Q 6 **Guerrero**, Mexico
45 Q 13 **Guerrero**, Mexico ▣
44 G 5 **Guerrero Negro**, Mexico
128 J 13 **Guéyo**, Côte d'Ivoire
127 H 22 **Gugē**, Ethiopia ▲
140 A 7 **Guguan**, Northern Mariana Islands ⁂
51 O 6 **Guiana Highlands**, South America ▲▲
113 W 6 **Guichi**, China
59 E 14 **Guichón**, Uruguay
129 W 11 **Guidari**, Chad
129 V 11 **Guider**, Cameroon
128 G 8 **Guidimaka**, Mauritania ▣
113 P 10 **Guiding**, China
113 Q 12 **Guigang**, China
128 I 13 **Guiglo**, Côte d'Ivoire
66 L 6 **Guijuelo**, Spain
63 U 11 **Guildford**, U.K.
110 H 11 **Guiler**, China
15 Q 4 **Guilford**, ME, U.S.A.
113 R 11 **Guilin**, China
65 W 12 **Guillestre**, France
121 I 17 **Guimaras**, Philippines ⁂
19 O 2 **Guin**, AL, U.S.A.
121 L 18 **Guindulman**, Philippines
128 F 10 **Guinea**, Africa □
128 E 10 **Guinea-Bissau**, Africa □
128 I 12 **Guinée-Forestière**, Guinea ▣
128 F 10 **Guinée-Maritime**, Guinea ▣
48 H 4 **Güines**, Cuba
64 J 5 **Guingamp**, France
113 R 12 **Guiping**, China
63 Y 6 **Guist**, U.K.
66 I 1 **Guitiriz**, Spain
121 M 16 **Guiuan**, Philippines
113 O 9 **Guiyang**, China
113 T 10 **Guiyang**, China
113 O 9 **Guizhou**, China ▣
105 B 14 **Gujarat**, India ▣
101 Y 9 **Gujranwala**, Pakistan
101 Y 8 **Gujrat**, Pakistan
109 P 8 **Gulang**, China
105 E 18 **Gulbarga**, India
84 I 10 **Gulbene**, Latvia
103 U 12 **Gülchö**, Kyrgyzstan
138 C 6 **Gulf**, Papua New Guinea ▣
115 I 22 **Gulf of Thailand**, Thailand ≈
127 M 18 **Gulf of Aden**, Africa/Asia ≈
35 Q 11 **Gulf of Alaska**, AK, U.S.A. ≈
89 Z 6 **Gulf of Anadyr**, Russian Federation ≈
98 I 3 **Gulf of Aqaba**, Asia ≈
38 L 4 **Gulf of Boothia**, NU, Canada ≈
71 I 19 **Gulf of Bothnia**, Sweden ≈
44 G 3 **Gulf of California**, Mexico ≈
135 Q 2 **Gulf of Carpentaria**, QLD, Australia ≈
83 E 19 **Gulf of Corinth**, Greece ≈
50 G 3 **Gulf of Darién**, Colombia ≈
71 L 20 **Gulf of Finland**, Europe ≈
78 J 7 **Gulf of Gdańsk**, Europe ≈
76 C 10 **Gulf of Genoa**, Italy ≈
52 A 10 **Gulf of Guayaquil**, Ecuador ≈
129 R 15 **Gulf of Guinea**, Africa ≈
46 M 3 **Gulf of Honduras**, Honduras ≈
105 A 14 **Gulf of Kachchh**, India ≈
105 B 16 **Gulf of Khambhat**, India ≈
15 P 9 **Gulf of Maine**, ME, U.S.A. ≈
105 F 24 **Gulf of Mannar**, Sri Lanka ≈
115 E 17 **Gulf of Martaban**, Myanmar ≈
13 R 15 **Gulf of Mexico**, North America ≈
99 Y 5 **Gulf of Oman**, Asia ≈
47 X 15 **Gulf of Panama**, Panama ≈
138 C 6 **Gulf of Papua**, Papua New Guinea ≈
51 R 3 **Gulf of Paria**, Venezuela ≈
84 E 9 **Gulf of Riga**, Estonia/Latvia ≈
126 C 7 **Gulf of Salûm**, Egypt/Libya ≈
125 V 8 **Gulf of Sirte**, Libya ≈
43 W 5 **Gulf of St Lawrence**, QC, Canada ≈
126 F 8 **Gulf of Suez**, Egypt ≈
87 Y 9 **Gulf of Taganrog**, Russian Federation/Ukraine ≈
113 Q 14 **Gulf of Tongking**, China ≈
80 A 8 **Gulf of Trieste**, Slovenia ≈
50 K 2 **Gulf of Venezuela**, Venezuela ≈
76 H 7 **Gulf of Venice**, Italy ≈
19 O 8 **Gulf Shores**, AL, U.S.A.
135 P 12 **Gulf St Vincent**, SA, Australia ≈
13 T 13 **Gulfport**, MS, U.S.A.
113 O 8 **Gulin**, China/Vietnam
113 V 7 **Guling**, China
103 R 12 **Gulistan**, Uzbekistan
94 B 12 **Güllük Körfezi**, Turkey ≈
94 A 9 **Gülpinar**, Turkey
95 Q 5 **Gulrip'shi**, Georgia
103 U 7 **Gul'shad**, Kazakhstan
131 S 6 **Gulu**, Uganda
82 K 10 **Gŭlŭbovo**, Bulgaria
82 I 7 **Gulyantsi**, Bulgaria
132 L 7 **Gumare**, Botswana
102 I 13 **Gumdag**, Turkmenistan
129 S 10 **Gumel**, Nigeria
105 I 15 **Gumla**, India
104 E 13 **Guna**, India
127 I 19 **Guna Terara**, Ethiopia ▲
75 Q 4 **Gundertshausen**, Austria
94 L 12 **Güney Doğu Toroslar**, Turkey ▲▲
130 J 11 **Gungu**, Democratic Republic of Cong
93 R 15 **Gunib**, Russian Federation
80 I 10 **Gunja**, Croatia
143 P 13 **Gunnbjørn Fjeld**, Greenland ▲
135 U 10 **Gunnedah**, NSW, Australia
30 K 5 **Gunnison**, UT, U.S.A.
31 P 5 **Gunnison**, CO, U.S.A.
105 E 19 **Guntakal**, India
19 Q 2 **Guntersville Lake**, AL, U.S.A. ↘
105 G 19 **Guntur**, India
116 B 8 **Gunung Abongabong**, Indonesia ▲
119 O 10 **Gunung Ayer**, Malaysia
118 C 7 **Gunung Batu Puteh**, Malaysia ▲
118 E 10 **Gunung Belumut**, Malaysia ▲
118 C 7 **Gunung Benum**, Malaysia ▲
118 A 6 **Gunung Bintang**, Malaysia ▲
117 Q 10 **Gunung Bulawa**, Indonesia ▲
118 C 6 **Gunung Camah**, Malaysia ▲
117 W 12 **Gunung Dom**, Indonesia ▲
116 D 11 **Gunung Kerinci**, Indonesia ▲
117 U 11 **Gunung Kwoka**, Indonesia ▲
118 D 5 **Gunung Lawit**, Malaysia ▲
118 D 9 **Gunung Ledang**, Malaysia ▲
118 C 7 **Gunung Liang Timur**, Malaysia ▲
119 X 7 **Gunung Magdaline**, Malaysia ▲
117 O 10 **Gunung Malino**, Indonesia ▲
118 D 6 **Gunung Mandi Angin**, Malaysia ▲
117 V 11 **Gunung Mebo**, Indonesia ▲
119 W 4 **Gunung Menapod**, Malaysia ▲
119 T 7 **Gunung Murud**, Malaysia ▲
117 Q 15 **Gunung Mutis**, Indonesia ▲
118 C 5 **Gunung Noring**, Malaysia ▲
119 T 7 **Gunung Pagon**, Malaysia ▲
116 K 15 **Gunung Semeru**, Indonesia ▲
116 I 14 **Gunung Slamet**, Indonesia ▲
118 D 6 **Gunung Tahan**, Malaysia ▲
118 D 7 **Gunung Tapis**, Malaysia ▲
119 X 6 **Gunung Tribulation**, Malaysia ▲
119 U 5 **Gunung Trus Madi**, Malaysia ▲
117 P 11 **Gunung Tumpu**, Indonesia ▲
117 R 14 **Gunungapi**, Indonesia ⁂
116 C 10 **Gunungsitoli**, Indonesia
105 I 17 **Gunupur**, India
73 H 23 **Günzburg**, Germany
111 E 15 **Guojiatun**, China
113 V 4 **Guoyang**, China
86 K 8 **Gura Humorului**, Romania
106 H 3 **Gurais**, India
110 A 13 **Gurban Obo**, China
101 O 14 **Gurdim**, Iran
104 B 13 **Gurha**, India
58 I 4 **Gurinhatã**, Brazil
75 T 8 **Gurk**, Austria
133 Q 6 **Guro**, Mozambique
133 S 5 **Gurué**, Mozambique
94 M 11 **Gürün**, Turkey

□ Country ▣ Internal administrative region: State/Province/Territory/Dependent territory ♜ Capital city ▲▲ Mountain range/ Undersea ridge ▲ Mountain peak/ Volcano/Seamount ◇ Geographic feature ▶ Headland/Point/ Cape/Peninsula ◭ Desert ⁂ Island/Island group ⁙ Antarctic base ◎ Ocean ◒ Sea ≈ Bay/Gulf/Channel/Strait ↘ Lake ⊠ Salt pan/Dry/ Intermittent lake ∫

I 10 Gurupá, Brazil
J 14 Gurupi, Brazil
M 1 Gus'-Khrustal'nyy, Russian Federation
Q 10 Gusau, Nigeria
C 16 Gusev, Russian Federation
I 17 Gushan, China
V 5 Gushi, China
M 25 Gushikawa, Japan
B 18 Guspini, Italy
X 7 Güssing, Austria
V 5 Gusswerk, Austria
W 5 Gustav Bull Mountains, Antarctica
W 10 Gustavus, AK, U.S.A.
O 26 Gusukube, Japan
E 14 Gütersloh, Germany
N 9 Guthrie, OK, U.S.A.
M 4 Guthrie, TX, U.S.A.
M 13 Guthrie, AZ, U.S.A.
X 9 Gutian, China
V 11 Guttenberg, IA, U.S.A.
P 7 Gutu, Zimbabwe
V 10 Guwahati, India
S 2 Guwēr, Iraq
S 6 Guyana, South America
R 6 Guyang, China
G 8 Guymon, OK, U.S.A.
O 2 Guyuan, China
P 13 Guzar, Uzbekistan
B 16 Gvardeysk, Russian Federation
C 15 Gwa, Myanmar
Q 9 Gwadabawa, Nigeria
P 14 Gwadar, Pakistan
J 11 Gwalior, India
O 8 Gwanda, Zimbabwe
O 5 Gwane, Democratic Republic of Congo
P 14 Gwatar Bay, Iran
Q 5 Gwawele, Democratic Republic of Congo
G 10 Gwda, Poland
O 7 Gweru, Zimbabwe
M 8 Gweta, Botswana
H 9 Gwinn, MI, U.S.A.
U 10 Gwoza, Nigeria
M 23 Gyali, Greece
K 11 Gyangzê, China
N 9 Gyaring Hu, China
I 21 Gyaros, Greece
K 7 Gyawa, China
N 7 Gyda, Russian Federation
N 7 Gydanskiy Poluostrov, Russian Federation
I 6 Gyitang, China
W 8 Gympie, QLD, Australia
L 24 Gyomaendrőd, Hungary
K 22 Gyöngyös, Hungary
H 22 Győr, Hungary
I 9 Gypsumville, MB, Canada
E 23 Gytheio, Greece
L 24 Gyula, Hungary
T 8 Gyumri, Armenia
J 13 Gyzylarbat, Turkmenistan
I 14 Gyzyletrek, Turkmenistan

T 9 Ha, Bhutan
N 12 Ha Côi, Vietnam
L 10 Ha Giang, Vietnam
L 22 Ha Tiên, Vietnam
M 15 Ha Tinh, Vietnam
F 8 Häädemeeste, Estonia
K 24 Haag in Oberbayern, Germany
N 12 Haaksbergen, Netherlands
I 10 Ha'apai Group, Tonga
L 15 Haapajärvi, Finland
E 7 Haapsalu, Estonia
G 11 Haarlem, Netherlands
D 21 Haast, New Zealand
X 5 Haba, United Arab Emirates
V 11 Ḩabarūt, Oman
X 7 Habaswein, Kenya
J 25 Habay-la-Neuve, Belgium
R 13 Ḩabbān, Yemen
D 14 Habirag, China
H 10 Hacha, Colombia
L 19 Hachijō-jima, Japan
K 9 Hachinohe, Japan
R 9 Hacıömer, Turkey
J 12 Hackensack, NJ, U.S.A.
Q 8 Hacufera, Mozambique
G 7 Hadat, China
S 10 Hadejia, Nigeria
F 8 Hadera, Israel
B 26 Haderslev, Denmark
E 17 Hadgaon, India
L 19 Hadhdhunmathi Atoll, Maldives
W 14 Hadīboh, Yemen
H 13 Hadim, Turkey
Y 8 Hadleigh, U.K.
H 5 Hadley Bay, NU, Canada
R 13 Ḩadramawt, Yemen
G 8 Hadseløy, Norway
C 24 Hadsund, Denmark
T 3 Hadyach, Ukraine
K 18 Haeju, North Korea
L 22 Haenam, South Korea
Q 3 Ḩafar al Bāţin, Saudi Arabia
M 9 Hafik, Turkey
L 4 Hafirat al'Aydā, Saudi Arabia
W 11 Haflong, India
A 11 Hafnarfjörður, Iceland
A 9 Hagåtña, Guam
D 16 Hagen, Germany
L 12 Hagerman, ID, U.S.A.
T 2 Hagerstown, MD, U.S.A.
F 20 Hagfors, Sweden
C 20 Hagi, Japan
B 18 Hag's Head, Republic of Ireland
X 4 Haguenau, France
M 12 Hai Duong, Vietnam
M 12 Hai Phong, Vietnam
Y 4 Hai'an, China
I 16 Haicheng, China
F 8 Haifa, Israel
R 14 Haikang, China
R 15 Haikou, China
N 4 Ḩā'il, Saudi Arabia
G 8 Hailar, China
M 12 Hailin, China
W 13 Hailsham, U.K.
K 9 Hailun, China
I 10 Hailuoto, Finland
Z 5 Haimen, China
M 26 Haimi, Japan
Q 15 Hainan, China

113 Q 15 Hainan, China
113 Q 15 Hainan Strait, China
69 E 21 Hainaut, Belgium
75 Z 4 Hainburg an der Donau, Austria
35 W 10 Haines, AK, U.S.A.
19 W 10 Haines City, FL, U.S.A.
39 A 14 Haines Junction, YT, Canada
75 W 4 Hainfeld, Austria
113 Y 6 Haining, China
113 Y 10 Haitan Dao, China
49 O 8 Haiti, North America
113 Q 15 Haitou, China
113 Z 6 Haiyan, China
111 H 20 Haiyang, China
113 O 2 Haiyuan, China
113 X 3 Haizhou Wan, China
79 M 22 Hajdúböszörmény, Hungary
79 M 23 Hajdúszoboszló, Hungary
97 V 8 Hājī Muḩsin, Iraq
122 I 13 Hajiki-zaki, Japan
107 Q 11 Hajipur, India
99 O 12 Ḩajjah, Yemen
100 L 12 Ḩājjīābād, Iran
78 O 11 Hajnówka, Poland
114 B 10 Haka, Myanmar
95 T 12 Hakkâri, Turkey
123 G 19 Hakken-san, Japan
122 K 5 Hakkōda-san, Japan
122 K 3 Hako-dake, Japan
122 J 8 Hakodate, Japan
123 H 15 Hakui, Japan
101 U 14 Hala, Pakistan
99 P 7 Ḩalabān, Saudi Arabia
97 V 4 Halabja, Iraq
126 H 13 Halaib, Sudan
126 G 12 Halaib Triangle, Sudan
98 J 2 Ḩālat 'Ammār, Saudi Arabia
96 H 5 Halba, Lebanon
109 O 2 Halban, Mongolia
73 I 14 Halberstadt, Germany
71 D 20 Halden, Norway
106 L 8 Haldwani, India
63 Q 4 Hale, U.K.
34 D 8 Haleakala, HI, U.S.A.
63 R 7 Halesowen, U.K.
63 Z 7 Halesworth, U.K.
33 I 19 Half Dome, CA, U.S.A.
95 N 13 Halfeti, Turkey
137 C 26 Halfmoon Bay, New Zealand
68 H 11 Halfweg, Netherlands
42 G 10 Haliburton Highlands, ON, Canada
43 V 11 Halifax, NS, Canada
63 R 2 Halifax, U.K.
41 O 1 Hall Beach, NU, Canada
75 N 7 Hall in Tirol, Austria
141 O 14 Hall Islands, Federated States of Micronesia
41 S 3 Hall Peninsula, NU, Canada
111 L 23 Halla-san, South Korea
69 F 19 Halle, Belgium
73 K 16 Halle, Germany
75 Q 6 Hallein, Austria
27 Q 11 Hallettsville, TX, U.S.A.
145 N 3 Halley, Antarctica
22 H4 Halliday, ND, U.S.A.
134 K 4 Halls Creek, WA, Australia
75 R 6 Hallstatt, Austria
74 F 7 Hallwiler See, Switzerland
62 L 13 Hallworthy, U.K.
117 S 10 Halmahera, Indonesia
117 S 11 Halmahera Sea, Indonesia
71 E 24 Halmstad, Sweden
63 X 9 Halstead, U.K.
69 F 15 Halsteren, Netherlands
63 N 15 Halwell, U.K.
114 L 11 Ham Yên, Vietnam
123 C 19 Hamada, Japan
100 G 6 Hamadān, Iran
100 G 6 Hamadān, Iran
125 R 12 Hamādat Murzuq, Libya
124 J 9 Hamaguir, Algeria
96 I 4 Ḩamāh, Syria
123 I 18 Hamamatsu, Japan
71 D 18 Hamar, Norway
123 F 17 Hamasaka, Japan
122 J 3 Hamatonbetsu, Japan
105 G 26 Hambantota, Sri Lanka
14 C 9 Hamburg, NY, U.S.A.
23 Q 15 Hamburg, IA, U.S.A.
72 H 10 Hamburg, Germany
99 O 10 Ḩamḑah, Saudi Arabia
98 M 9 Hamdānah, Saudi Arabia
71 L 18 Hämeenlinna, Finland
73 G 14 Hameln, Germany
134 F 6 Hamersley Range, WA, Australia
111 L 16 Hamgyŏng-sanmaek, North Korea
111 L 16 Hamhŭng, North Korea
108 M 5 Hami, China
94 F 9 Hamidiye, Turkey
19 O 2 Hamilton, AL, U.S.A.
21 D 18 Hamilton, IL, U.S.A.
17 K 19 Hamilton, OH, U.S.A.
27 P 7 Hamilton, TX, U.S.A.
28 M 6 Hamilton, MT, U.S.A.
42 E 13 Hamilton, ON, Canada
60 H 13 Hamilton, U.K.
135 R 13 Hamilton, VIC, Australia
136 K 10 Hamilton, New Zealand
41 W 8 Hamilton Inlet, NL, Canada
71 N 19 Hamina, Finland
106 I 5 Hamirpur, India
17 Q 11 Hamlet, NC, U.S.A.
27 N 6 Hamlin, TX, U.S.A.
73 D 15 Hamm, Germany
124 G 10 Hammada du Drâa, Algeria
125 Q 10 Hammâdat Tingharat, Libya
97 R 2 Ḩammān al 'Alīl, Iraq
71 G 16 Hammarstrand, Sweden
69 H 19 Hamme-Mille, Belgium
71 G 15 Hammerdal, Sweden
18 L 7 Hammond, LA, U.S.A.
21 H 16 Hammond, IN, U.S.A.
14 I 14 Hammonton, NJ, U.S.A.
69 I 22 Hamois, Belgium
137 F 23 Hampden, New Zealand
15 O 8 Hampton, NH, U.S.A.
17 O 14 Hampton, SC, U.S.A.
17 V 6 Hampton, VA, U.S.A.
25 V 14 Hampton, AR, U.S.A.
32 I 12 Hampton, OR, U.S.A.
43 T 10 Hampton, NB, Canada
127 C 17 Hamrat esh Sheikh, Sudan
101 N 12 Hāmūn-e Jaz Mūrīān, Iran

101 P 10 Hāmūn Helmand, Iran
101 P 9 Hāmūn Pu, Afghanistan
95 S 9 Hamur, Turkey
113 Q 5 Han Shui, China
110 G 12 Han Sum, China
34 D 8 Hana, HI, U.S.A.
98 K 5 Ḩanale, Saudi Arabia
122 K 10 Hanamaki, Japan
73 F 16 Hanau, Germany
113 R 3 Hancheng, China
14 I 10 Hancock, NY, U.S.A.
17 S 2 Hancock, MD, U.S.A.
113 U 2 Handan, China
131 W 11 Handeni, Tanzania
79 I 20 Handlová, Slovakia
71 D 17 Hanestad, Norway
109 O 3 Hangayn Nuruu, Mongolia
101 V 8 Hangu, Pakistan
111 E 17 Hangu, China
109 P 11 Hangyuan, China
113 Y 6 Hangzhou, China
113 Z 6 Hangzhou Wan, China
95 P 11 Hani, Turkey
71 K 20 Hanko, Finland
30 L 6 Hanksville, UT, U.S.A.
106 K 5 Hanle, India
94 L 10 Hanlı, Turkey
137 H 18 Hanmer Springs, New Zealand
73 G 16 Hann-Münden, Germany
39 K 19 Hanna, AB, Canada
41 O 10 Hannah Bay, ON, Canada
25 W 2 Hannibal, MO, U.S.A.
72 G 13 Hannover, Germany
69 I 20 Hannut, Belgium
71 F 25 Hanöbukten, Sweden
114 L 12 Hanoi, Vietnam
42 D 12 Hanover, ON, Canada
145 W 4 Hansen Mountains, Antarctica
106 H 8 Hansi, India
85 H 20 Hantsavichy, Belarus
71 B 23 Hantsholm, Denmark
106 G 7 Hanumangarh, India
101 O 14 Hanzaram, Iran
113 O 4 Hanzhong, China
113 W 3 Hanzhuang, China
107 S 14 Haora, India
125 O 8 Haoud el Hamra, Algeria
124 E 10 Haouza, Western Sahara
26 K 3 Happy, TX, U.S.A.
33 F 14 Happy Camp, CA, U.S.A.
41 V 8 Happy Valley Goose Bay, NL, Canada
98 J 2 Ḩaql, Saudi Arabia
109 P 6 Har Borog, China
109 N 7 Har Hu, China
96 G 7 Har Meron, Israel
109 N 3 Har Nuur, Mongolia
108 M 3 Har Us Nuur, Mongolia
127 K 18 Hara Alol, Djibouti
99 O 12 Ḩaraḑ, Yemen
99 S 6 Ḩaraḑh, Saudi Arabia
85 L 14 Haradok, Belarus
85 H 18 Haradzyeya, Belarus
99 O 11 Ḩarajā, Saudi Arabia
122 L 13 Haramachi, Japan
101 X 10 Harappa Road, Pakistan
133 P 6 Harare, Zimbabwe
129 X 9 Haraz-Djombo, Chad
129 Y 11 Haraze Mangueigne, Chad
128 H 13 Harbel, Liberia
111 K 11 Harbin, China
20 K 10 Harbor Springs, MI, U.S.A.
41 Y 11 Harbour Breton, NL, Canada
105 E 15 Harda Khas, India
71 A 19 Hardangerfjorden, Norway
132 I 10 Hardap, Namibia
17 O 15 Hardeeville, SC, U.S.A.
68 J 11 Harderwijk, Netherlands
29 V 7 Hardin, MT, U.S.A.
106 L 9 Hardoi, India
25 W 8 Hardy, AR, U.S.A.
69 C 19 Harelbeke, Belgium
68 M 6 Haren, Netherlands
127 K 20 Hārer, Ethiopia
110 F 8 Hargant, China
127 K 22 Hargele, Ethiopia
127 L 20 Hargeysa, Somalia
84 H 9 Hargla, Estonia
99 Q 13 Harib, Yemen
106 K 7 Haridwar, India
105 D 20 Harihar, India
137 E 19 Harihari, New Zealand
69 F 14 Haringvliet, Netherlands
105 E 14 Harisal, India
17 V 11 Harkers Island, NC, U.S.A.
16 K 7 Harlan, KY, U.S.A.
62 M 6 Harlech, U.K.
29 T 2 Harlem, MT, U.S.A.
27 Q 15 Harlingen, TX, U.S.A.
68 J 7 Harlingen, Netherlands
63 W 9 Harlow, U.K.
29 S 6 Harlowton, MT, U.S.A.
94 D 9 Harmancik, Turkey
32 I 12 Harney Basin, OR, U.S.A.
32 J 12 Harney Lake, OR, U.S.A.
71 H 16 Härnösand, Sweden
67 P 2 Haro, Spain
24 M 7 Harper, KS, U.S.A.
32 K 12 Harper, OR, U.S.A.
128 I 14 Harper, Liberia
96 J 8 Ḩarrat ar Rujaylah, Jordan
96 J 9 Harrat ar Rujaylah, Jordan
98 M 6 Ḩarrat Rahaţ, Saudi Arabia
41 P 10 Harricanaw, QC, Canada
16 J 9 Harriman, TN, U.S.A.
60 E 9 Harris, U.K.
14 F 13 Harrisburg, PA, U.S.A.
21 G 22 Harrisburg, IL, U.S.A.
25 X 10 Harrisburg, AR, U.S.A.
133 O 12 Harrismith, Republic of South Africa
20 K 12 Harrison, MI, U.S.A.
22 F 12 Harrison, NE, U.S.A.
25 U 9 Harrison, AR, U.S.A.
17 R 4 Harrisonburg, VA, U.S.A.
25 S 4 Harrisonville, MO, U.S.A.
20 F 13 Harrisville, WI, U.S.A.
20 L 11 Harrisville, MI, U.S.A.
63 S 2 Harrogate, U.K.
100 G 6 Harsin, Iran
70 H 8 Harstad, Norway
20 I 13 Hart, MI, U.S.A.
111 H 14 Hartao, China
75 X 6 Hartberg, Austria
71 B 19 Hårteigen, Norway

14 L 10 Hartford, CT, U.S.A.
16 E 6 Hartford, KY, U.S.A.
21 J 15 Hartford, MI, U.S.A.
43 R 9 Hartland, NB, Canada
62 L 12 Hartland Point, U.K.
61 K 15 Hartlepool, U.K.
26 J 1 Hartley, TX, U.S.A.
135 O 6 Harts Range, NT, Australia
25 U 7 Hartville, MO, U.S.A.
19 U 2 Hartwell Reservoir, GA/SC, U.S.A.
43 U 3 Harve-St-Pierre, QC, Canada
22 K 4 Harvey, ND, U.S.A.
43 R 10 Harvey, NB, Canada
63 Z 9 Harwich, U.K.
106 H 7 Haryana, India
73 H 15 Harz, Germany
94 J 11 Hasan Daği, Turkey
100 L 12 Ḩasan Langī, Iran
72 D 12 Haselünne, Germany
123 G 19 Hashimoto, Japan
100 I 5 Hashtgerd, Iran
99 X 11 Ḩāsik, Oman
26 M 5 Haskell, TX, U.S.A.
63 U 12 Haslemere, U.K.
105 D 21 Hassan, India
69 J 18 Hasselt, Belgium
73 I 19 Hassfurt, Germany
125 O 10 Hassi Bel Guebbour, Algeria
125 N 9 Hassi Inifel, Algeria
125 O 8 Hassi Messaoud, Algeria
71 E 25 Hässleholm, Sweden
21 J 15 Hastings, MI, U.S.A.
22 M 15 Hastings, NE, U.S.A.
23 T 8 Hastings, MN, U.S.A.
63 X 13 Hastings, U.K.
136 N 13 Hastings, New Zealand
99 V 12 Ḩaswayl, Yemen
115 H 26 Hat Yai, Thailand
31 P 13 Hatch, NM, U.S.A.
86 H 11 Haţeg, Romania
123 M 26 Hateruma-jima, Japan
63 T 3 Hatfield, U.K.
109 P 2 Hatgal, Mongolia
62 M 13 Hatherleigh, U.K.
106 J 9 Hathras, India
107 R 9 Hatia, Nepal
107 V 14 Hatia, Bangladesh
123 D 19 Hatsukaichi, Japan
105 F 14 Hatta, India
17 W 10 Hatteras, NC, U.S.A.
17 X 9 Hatteras Island, NC, U.S.A.
18 M 6 Hattiesburg, MS, U.S.A.
137 M 14 Hatuma, New Zealand
79 J 22 Hatvan, Hungary
71 A 20 Haugesund, Norway
75 X 2 Haugsdorf, Austria
71 B 19 Haukeligrend, Norway
71 N 16 Haukivesi, Finland
58 C 10 Haumonia, Argentina
136 K 8 Hauraki Gulf, New Zealand
73 D 24 Hausach, Germany
130 G 8 Haut-Ogooué, Gabon
128 H 10 Haute-Guinée, Guinea
130 M 3 Haute-Kotto, Central African Republic
131 N 3 Haute-Mbomou, Central African Republic
65 O 3 Haute-Normandie, France
124 J 7 Hauts Plateaux, Morocco
21 E 18 Havana, IL, U.S.A.
48 G 3 Havana, Cuba
63 U 13 Havant, U.K.
72 L 13 Havel, Germany
69 I 21 Havelange, Belgium
101 W 10 Haveli, Pakistan
17 U 10 Havelock, NC, U.S.A.
137 I 16 Havelock, New Zealand
105 N 21 Havelock Island, India
68 L 9 Havelte, Netherlands
62 K 9 Haverfordwest, U.K.
63 X 8 Haverhill, U.K.
69 I 22 Haversin, Belgium
109 T 4 Havirga, Mongolia
79 E 18 Havlíčkův Brod, Czech Republic
29 S 2 Havre, MT, U.S.A.
41 W 12 Havre Aubert, QC, Canada
41 U 10 Havre-St-Pierre, QC, Canada
87 W 7 Havrylivka, Ukraine
94 B 6 Havsa, Turkey
94 K 8 Havza, Turkey
34 D 9 Hawaii, HI, U.S.A.
34 A 9 Hawaii, U.S.A.
34 A 6 Hawaiian Islands, HI, U.S.A.
99 S 2 Ḩawallī, Kuwait
136 J 13 Hawera, New Zealand
63 R 1 Hawes, U.K.
34 E 8 Hawi, HI, U.S.A.
61 I 14 Hawick, U.K.
29 Z 13 Hawk Springs, WY, U.S.A.
136 N 13 Hawke Bay, New Zealand
135 P 10 Hawker, SA, Australia
41 X 9 Hawkes Bay, NL, Canada
136 M 13 Hawke's Bay, New Zealand
42 K 10 Hawkesbury, ON, Canada
19 T 5 Hawkinsville, GA, U.S.A.
137 I 19 Hawkswood, New Zealand
97 S 7 Hawr al Ḩabbānīyah, Iraq
97 Y 11 Hawr al Ḩammār, Iraq
97 W 9 Hawr as Sa'dīyah, Iraq
99 S 12 Ḩawra', Yemen
33 J 19 Hawthorne, NV, U.S.A.
63 T 1 Haxby, U.K.
135 S 12 Hay, NSW, Australia
63 O 8 Hay-on-Wye, U.K.
38 H 13 Hay River, NT, Canada
22 H 12 Hay Springs, NE, U.S.A.
117 S 12 Haya, Indonesia
122 L 10 Hayachine-san, Japan
35 N 6 Haycock, AK, U.S.A.
100 F 4 Haydarābād, Iran
30 L 13 Hayden, AZ, U.S.A.
22 J 9 Hayes, SD, U.S.A.
99 W 15 Ḩayf, Yemen
33 M 21 Hayford Peak, NV, U.S.A.
62 J 15 Hayle, U.K.
63 T 13 Hayling Island, U.K.
99 X 9 Haymā', Oman
94 H 10 Haymana, Turkey
17 T 3 Haymarket, VA, U.S.A.
18 I 4 Haynesville, LA, U.S.A.
19 Q 5 Hayneville, AL, U.S.A.
94 C 7 Hayrabolu, Turkey
24 K 4 Hays, KS, U.S.A.

29 T 3 Hays, MT, U.S.A.
87 O 6 Haysyn, Ukraine
20 D 9 Hayward, WI, U.S.A.
33 G 19 Hayward, CA, U.S.A.
63 W 12 Haywards Heath, U.K.
16 K 6 Hazard, KY, U.S.A.
105 I 14 Hazaribag, India
107 P 13 Hazaribagh, India
19 V 5 Hazelhurst, GA, U.S.A.
37 N 3 Hazen Strait, NU, Canada
18 L 5 Hazlehurst, MS, U.S.A.
28 K 5 Headquarters, ID, U.S.A.
20 F 10 Heafford Junction, WI, U.S.A.
33 F 18 Healdsburg, CA, U.S.A.
35 R 7 Healy, AK, U.S.A.
27 R 8 Hearne, TX, U.S.A.
42 B 4 Hearst, ON, Canada
144 J 4 Hearst Island, Antarctica
27 N 14 Hebbronville, TX, U.S.A.
111 C 17 Hebei, China
135 T 9 Hebel, QLD, Australia
30 L 11 Heber, AZ, U.S.A.
29 Q 9 Hebgen Lake, MT, U.S.A.
113 T 2 Hebi, China
22 I 5 Hebron, ND, U.S.A.
23 N 15 Hebron, NE, U.S.A.
41 U 6 Hebron, NL, Canada
96 F 10 Hebron, Israel
39 C 19 Hecate Strait, BC, Canada
45 Y 11 Hecelchakán, Mexico
113 P 11 Hechi, China
69 J 17 Hechtel, Belgium
113 O 7 Hechuan, China
71 F 16 Hede, Sweden
69 I 14 Hedel, Netherlands
68 G 10 Heemskerk, Netherlands
68 K 8 Heerenveen, Netherlands
68 H 9 Heerhugowaard, Netherlands
69 L 19 Heerlen, Netherlands
69 I 19 Heers, Belgium
69 J 14 Heesh, Netherlands
113 V 5 Hefei, China
113 R 7 Hefeng, China
110 M 9 Hegang, China
72 F 8 Heide, Germany
73 F 21 Heidelberg, Germany
75 U 2 Heidenreichstein, Austria
110 K 7 Heihe, China
73 G 22 Heilbronn, Germany
75 Q 7 Heiligenblut, Austria
75 X 7 Heiligenkreuz, Austria
110 K 5 Heilong Jiang, China
110 K 9 Heilongjiang, China
70 B 12 Heimaey, Iceland
71 M 18 Heinola, Finland
73 B 16 Heinsberg, Germany
111 H 15 Heishan, China
69 H 18 Heist-op-den-Berg, Belgium
111 D 18 Hejian, China
113 O 8 Hejiang, China
95 N 11 Hekimhan, Turkey
70 B 11 Hekla, Iceland
78 I 8 Hel, Poland
107 X 10 Helem, India
29 P 5 Helena, MT, U.S.A.
60 G 13 Helensburgh, U.K.
136 J 8 Helensville, New Zealand
72 E 9 Helgoländer Bucht, Germany
110 M 9 Heli, China
70 B 11 Hella, Iceland
71 A 21 Helleland, Norway
69 F 14 Hellevoetsluis, Netherlands
67 R 10 Hellín, Spain
12 H 6 Hells Canyon, ID/OR, U.S.A.
101 Q 10 Helmand, Afghanistan
101 P 10 Helmand, Afghanistan
132 H 11 Helmeringhausen, Namibia
69 J 15 Helmond, Netherlands
60 H 9 Helmsdale, U.K.
63 T 1 Helmsley, U.K.
133 Z 6 Helodrano Antongila, Madgascar
111 M 14 Helong, China
71 E 25 Helsingborg, Sweden
71 M 19 Helsinki, Finland
62 J 15 Helston, U.K.
126 E 8 Helwân, Egypt
63 V 9 Hemel Hempstead, U.K.
22 H 12 Hemingford, NE, U.S.A.
72 G 10 Hemmoor, Germany
27 R 9 Hempstead, TX, U.S.A.
71 H 18 Hemränge, Sweden
63 Z 6 Hemsby, U.K.
136 K 7 Hen and Chickens Islands, New Zealand
113 T 4 Henan, China
122 J 9 Henashi-zaki, Japan
16 E 5 Henderson, KY, U.S.A.
16 C 9 Henderson, TN, U.S.A.
17 S 8 Henderson, NC, U.S.A.
27 T 6 Henderson, TX, U.S.A.
16 L 10 Hendersonville, NC, U.S.A.
16 F 8 Hendersonville, TN, U.S.A.
63 W 10 Hendon, U.K.
100 J 13 Hendorābī, Iran
51 W 7 Hendrik Top, Suriname
138 C 5 Henganofi, Papua New Guinea
113 Z 13 Hengch'un, Taiwan
112 I 7 Hengduan Shan, China
68 N 11 Hengelo, Netherlands
110 N 11 Hengshan, China
113 T 9 Hengshan, China
111 C 19 Hengshui, China
113 Q 12 Hengxian, China
113 T 9 Hengyang, China
87 U 10 Heniches'k, Ukraine
24 M 9 Hennessey, OK, U.S.A.
72 L 12 Hennigsdorf, Germany
27 O 4 Henrietta, TX, U.S.A.
21 F 17 Henry, IL, U.S.A.
25 P 10 Henryetta, OK, U.S.A.
132 H 9 Hentiesbaai, Namibia
109 S 3 Hentiy, Mongolia
115 D 15 Henzada, Myanmar
113 U 11 Heping, China
32 J 10 Heppner, OR, U.S.A.
113 Q 13 Hepu, China
101 P 7 Herāt, Afghanistan
101 P 7 Herāt, Afghanistan
127 H 15 Herbagat, Sudan
73 H 23 Herbrechtingen, Germany
81 I 16 Herceg-Novi, Serbia and Montenegro
70 C 10 Herðubreið, Iceland
47 Q 12 Heredia, Costa Rica

26 J 3 Hereford, TX, U.S.A.
63 P 9 Hereford, U.K.
136 I 5 Herekino, New Zealand
67 O 8 Herencia, Spain
69 H 17 Herentals, Belgium
73 F 14 Herford, Germany
25 O 4 Herington, KS, U.S.A.
74 H 6 Herisau, Switzerland
60 K 3 Herma Ness, U.K.
75 R 9 Hermagor, Austria
45 P 6 Hermanas, Mexico
25 W 4 Hermann, MO, U.S.A.
135 N 7 Hermannsburg, NT, Australia
132 K 15 Hermanus, Republic of South Africa
32 J 9 Hermiston, OR, U.S.A.
138 C 2 Hermit Islands, Papua New Guinea
44 I 4 Hermosillo, Mexico
18 M 1 Hernando, MS, U.S.A.
73 D 15 Herne, Germany
63 Z 11 Herne Bay, U.K.
71 B 24 Herning, Denmark
58 C 9 Herradura, Argentina
73 F 23 Herrenberg, Germany
67 N 2 Herrera de Pisuerga, Spain
66 M 9 Herrera del Duque, Spain
38 A 8 Herschel Island, YT, Canada
63 V 9 Hertford, U.K.
69 K 20 Herve, Belgium
135 W 7 Hervey Bay, QLD, Australia
135 W 8 Hervey Bay, QLD, Australia
73 H 15 Herzberg, Germany
73 M 15 Herzberg, Germany
96 F 9 Herzliyya, Israel
65 P 2 Hesdin, France
72 D 11 Hesel, Germany
113 Q 12 Heshan, China
73 G 18 Hessen, Germany
63 O 4 Heswall, U.K.
107 P 10 Hetauda, Nepal
22 H 6 Hettinger, ND, U.S.A.
79 K 22 Heves, Hungary
112 L 8 Hexi, China
113 O 5 Hexi, China
113 S 11 Hexian, China
113 X 5 Hexian, China
63 P 1 Heysham, U.K.
113 U 12 Heyuan, China
113 U 3 Heze, China
113 N 9 Hezhang, China
109 P 9 Hezuo, China
19 Y 13 Hialeah, FL, U.S.A.
25 Q 2 Hiawatha, KS, U.S.A.
23 T 4 Hibbing, MN, U.S.A.
16 B 7 Hickman, KY, U.S.A.
17 N 9 Hickory, NC, U.S.A.
46 K 1 Hicks Cay, Belize
17 O 5 Hico, WV, U.S.A.
27 P 7 Hico, TX, U.S.A.
122 K 6 Hidaka, Japan
122 K 6 Hidaka-sanmyaku, Japan
45 Q 11 Hidalgo, Mexico
44 M 6 Hidalgo del Parral, Mexico
72 L 7 Hiddensee, Germany
75 U 6 Hieflau, Austria
139 P 13 Hienghène, New Caledonia
123 D 19 Higashi-Hiroshima, Japan
123 G 18 Higashi-ōsaka, Japan
123 A 21 Higashi-suidō, Japan
20 K 12 Higgins Lake, MI, U.S.A.
124 H 8 High Atlas, Morocco
20 J 10 High Island, MI, U.S.A.
27 U 10 High Island, TX, U.S.A.
39 H 15 High Level, AB, Canada
120 F 10 High Peak, Philippines
26 K 1 High Plains, TX, U.S.A.
14 J 11 High Point, NJ, U.S.A.
17 P 9 High Point, NC, U.S.A.
19 V 8 High Springs, FL, U.S.A.
62 M 13 High Willhays, U.K.
63 U 10 High Wycombe, U.K.
63 T 11 Highclere, U.K.
21 H 15 Highland Park, IL, U.S.A.
16 K 10 Highlands, NC, U.S.A.
22 L 9 Highmore, SD, U.S.A.
127 M 23 Hiiraan, Somalia
84 D 6 Hiiumaa, Estonia
98 K 3 Hijaz, Saudi Arabia
123 H 17 Hikone, Japan
136 J 6 Hikurangi, New Zealand
136 O 10 Hikurangi, New Zealand
73 I 18 Hildburghausen, Germany
73 H 14 Hildesheim, Germany
107 T 11 Hili, Bangladesh
46 K 2 Hill Bank, Belize
23 R 5 Hill City, MN, U.S.A.
24 J 3 Hill City, KS, U.S.A.
28 L 11 Hill City, ID, U.S.A.
145 Q 12 Hillary Coast, Antarctica
68 G 11 Hillegom, Netherlands
71 D 25 Hillerød, Denmark
14 M 8 Hillsboro, NH, U.S.A.
20 E 13 Hillsboro, WI, U.S.A.
21 F 20 Hillsboro, IL, U.S.A.
21 L 20 Hillsboro, OH, U.S.A.
27 Q 7 Hillsboro, TX, U.S.A.
49 Y 12 Hillsborough, Grenada
135 S 11 Hillston, NSW, Australia
17 P 7 Hillsville, VA, U.S.A.
34 E 8 Hilo, HI, U.S.A.
121 L 17 Hilongos, Philippines
17 O 15 Hilton Head Island, SC, U.S.A.
95 O 12 Hilvan, Turkey
68 I 11 Hilversum, Netherlands
106 J 5 Himachal Pradesh, India
106 I 4 Himalaya, India
81 K 21 Himarë, Albania
137 K 14 Himatangi, New Zealand
105 C 14 Himatnagar, India
123 F 18 Himeji, Japan
123 H 15 Himi, Japan
96 I 5 Ḩimş, Syria
121 N 20 Hinatuan, Philippines
87 N 9 Hinceşti, Moldova
49 P 7 Hinche, Haiti
35 Q 10 Hinchinbrook Island, AK, U.S.A.
135 T 4 Hinchinbrook Island, QLD, Australia
23 S 6 Hinckley, MN, U.S.A.
63 S 7 Hinckley, U.K.
130 F 10 Hinda, Congo
104 E 12 Hindaun, India
63 U 12 Hindhead, U.K.
137 G 21 Hinds, New Zealand
101 U 6 Hindu Kush, Afghanistan

untry | Internal administrative region: State/Province/Territory/Dependent territory | Capital city | Mountain range/Undersea ridge | Mountain peak/Volcano/Seamount | Geographic feature | Headland/Point/Cape/Peninsula | Desert | Island/Island group | Antarctic base | Ocean | Sea | Bay/Gulf/Channel/Strait | Lake | Salt pan/Dry/Intermittent lake | River

105	E 20	**Hindupur**, India
105	F 16	**Hinganghat**, India
95	R 10	**Hinis**, Turkey
121	I 18	**Hinobaan**, Philippines
75	N 7	**Hintertux**, Austria
123	A 21	**Hirado**, Japan
105	H 15	**Hirakud Reservoir**, India ∽
123	O 26	**Hirara**, Japan
105	E 20	**Hiriyur**, India
122	L 6	**Hiroo**, Japan
122	J 9	**Hirosaki**, Japan
123	D 19	**Hiroshima**, Japan
65	S 2	**Hirson**, France
106	H 8	**Hisar**, India
94	G 7	**Hisarönü**, Turkey
49	O 6	**Hispaniola**, Dominican Republic ≛
96	I 5	**Ḥisyah**, Syria
97	R 6	**Hīt**, Iraq
123	C 21	**Hita**, Japan
123	L 14	**Hitachi**, Japan
105	L 20	**Hitaddu**, Maldives
63	V 9	**Hitchin**, U.K.
123	C 23	**Hitoyoshi**, Japan
71	C 15	**Hitra**, Norway ≛
139	P 9	**Hiu**, Vanuatu ≛
123	J 14	**Hiuchiga-take**, Japan ▲
123	F 20	**Hiwasa**, Japan
38	I 13	**Hjalmar Lake**, NT, Canada ∽
71	G 21	**Hjälmaren**, Sweden ∽
71	C 23	**Hjørring**, Denmark
114	F 5	**Hkakabo Razi**, Myanmar ▲
133	P 11	**Hlatikulu**, Swaziland
87	S 5	**Hlobyne**, Ukraine
79	H 21	**Hlohovec**, Slovakia
87	T 1	**Hlukhiv**, Ukraine
85	K 19	**Hlusk**, Belarus
85	J 15	**Hlybokaye**, Belarus
129	N 13	**Ho**, Ghana
115	M 22	**Hô Chi Minh**, Vietnam
114	K 12	**Hô Sông Đa**, Vietnam ∽
114	K 11	**Hô Thac Ba**, Vietnam ∽
114	L 12	**Hoa Binh**, Vietnam
114	K 11	**Hoang Liên Son**, Vietnam ▲▲
24	K 11	**Hobart**, OK, U.S.A.
135	T 15	**Hobart**, TAS, Australia
31	U 13	**Hobbs**, NM, U.S.A.
144	L 11	**Hobbs Coast**, Antarctica ◇
19	Y 11	**Hobe Sound**, FL, U.S.A.
71	C 24	**Hobro**, Denmark
127	N 22	**Hobyo**, Somalia
75	R 8	**Hochalmspitze**, Austria ▲
74	F 7	**Hochdorf**, Switzerland
132	I 9	**Hochfeld**, Namibia
75	T 6	**Hochreichart**, Austria ▲
75	U 5	**Hochschwab**, Austria ▲▲
76	F 4	**Hochwilde**, Austria/Italy ▲
123	H 15	**Hodaka-dake**, Japan ▲
16	G 6	**Hodgenville**, KY, U.S.A.
128	I 7	**Hodh Ech Chargui**, Mauritania ▣
128	I 7	**Hodh El Gharbi**, Mauritania ▣
79	K 25	**Hódmezővásárhely**, Hungary
79	G 20	**Hodonín**, Czech Republic
109	O 3	**Hödrögö**, Mongolia
68	F 13	**Hoek van Holland**, Netherlands
111	M 19	**Hoengsŏng**, South Korea
69	K 18	**Hoensbroek**, Netherlands
111	N 14	**Hoeryŏng**, North Korea
111	L 18	**Hoeyang**, North Korea
73	K 18	**Hof**, Germany
70	D 11	**Höfn**, Iceland
70	C 11	**Hofsjökull**, Iceland ◇
70	B 10	**Hofsós**, Iceland
123	C 20	**Hōfu**, Japan
17	W 6	**Hog Island**, VA, U.S.A. ≛
22	G 13	**Hogback Mountain**, NE, U.S.A. ▲
125	O 14	**Hoggar**, Algeria ▲▲
71	G 23	**Högsby**, Sweden
108	M 8	**Hoh Sai Hu**, China ∽
75	O 7	**Hohe Tauern**, Austria ▲▲
75	Y 2	**Hohenau an der March**, Austria
75	S 6	**Hoher Dachstein**, Austria ▲
129	N 13	**Hohoe**, Ghana
87	Q 3	**Hoholiv**, Ukraine
115	O 17	**Hôi An**, Vietnam
114	L 13	**Hôi Xuân**, Vietnam
131	R 7	**Hoima**, Uganda
24	L 5	**Hoisington**, KS, U.S.A.
107	W 11	**Hojai**, India
136	H 6	**Hokianga Harbour**, New Zealand ≈
137	F 19	**Hokitika**, New Zealand
122	K 5	**Hokkaidō**, Japan ≛
123	L 15	**Hokota**, Japan
95	T 9	**Hoktemberyan**, Armenia
131	X 9	**Hola**, Kenya
87	S 10	**Hola Prystan**, Ukraine
105	D 20	**Holalkere**, India
53	K 18	**Holanda**, Bolivia
63	W 6	**Holbeach**, U.K.
29	O 13	**Holbrook**, ID, U.S.A.
30	L 10	**Holbrook**, AZ, U.S.A.
30	J 5	**Holden**, UT, U.S.A.
63	V 2	**Holderness**, U.K. ◇
22	L 15	**Holdrege**, NE, U.S.A.
48	L 6	**Holguín**, Cuba
79	G 20	**Holíč**, Slovakia
71	E 18	**Höljes**, Sweden
75	X 2	**Hollabrunn**, Austria
21	I 14	**Holland**, MI, U.S.A.
69	G 14	**Hollands Diep**, Netherlands ≈
69	K 24	**Hollange**, Belgium
14	D 13	**Hollidaysburg**, PA, U.S.A.
24	J 11	**Hollis**, OK, U.S.A.
33	G 21	**Hollister**, CA, U.S.A.
68	J 5	**Hollum**, Netherlands
17	T 11	**Holly Ridge**, NC, U.S.A.
18	L 1	**Holly Springs**, MS, U.S.A.
19	Y 13	**Hollywood**, FL, U.S.A.
70	B 10	**Hólmavík**, Iceland
63	T 2	**Holme-upon-Spalding-Moor**, U.K.
63	R 3	**Holmfirth**, U.K.
138	E 6	**Holnicote Bay**, Papua New Guinea ≈
86	J 2	**Holoby**, Ukraine
96	F 9	**Ḥolon**, Israel
132	J 12	**Holoog**, Namibia
19	X 10	**Holopaw**, FL, U.S.A.
71	B 24	**Holstebro**, Denmark
23	Q 12	**Holstein**, IA, U.S.A.
62	L 13	**Holsworthy**, U.K.
63	Y 5	**Holt**, U.K.
68	L 11	**Holten**, Netherlands
87	V 6	**Holubivka**, Ukraine
68	K 6	**Holwerd**, Netherlands
35	N 8	**Holy Cross**, AK, U.S.A.
62	L 4	**Holy Island**, U.K. ≛
62	L 4	**Holyhead**, U.K.
62	L 4	**Holyhead Bay**, U.K. ≈
14	L 10	**Holyoke**, MA, U.S.A.
31	U 3	**Holyoke**, CO, U.S.A.
63	O 4	**Holywell**, U.K.
73	J 25	**Holzkirchen**, Germany
73	G 15	**Holzminden**, Germany
131	T 8	**Homa Bay**, Kenya
114	C 8	**Homalin**, Myanmar
128	M 8	**Hombori**, Mali
128	L 8	**Hombori Toudo**, Mali ▲
73	D 21	**Homburg**, Germany
41	R 1	**Home Bay**, NU, Canada ≈
85	L 20	**Homel'skaya Voblasts'**, Belarus ▣
18	I 4	**Homer**, LA, U.S.A.
35	Q 10	**Homer**, AK, U.S.A.
19	U 6	**Homerville**, GA, U.S.A.
19	Y 14	**Homestead**, FL, U.S.A.
70	F 12	**Hommelstø**, Norway
105	E 18	**Homnabad**, India
133	R 10	**Homoine**, Mozambique
121	M 17	**Homonhon**, Philippines ≛
85	N 20	**Homyel'**, Belarus
115	L 24	**Hon Khoai**, Vietnam ≛
115	L 23	**Hon Rai**, Vietnam ≛
50	I 6	**Honda**, Colombia
121	D 18	**Honda Bay**, Philippines ≈
27	N 11	**Hondo**, TX, U.S.A.
31	R 12	**Hondo**, NM, U.S.A.
46	J 1	**Hondo**, Belize ≀
123	B 22	**Hondo**, Japan
46	L 5	**Honduras**, North America □
16	L 12	**Honea Path**, SC, U.S.A.
71	D 19	**Hønefoss**, Norway
33	I 16	**Honey Lake**, CA, U.S.A. ∽
114	N 12	**Hông Gai**, Vietnam
113	U 13	**Hong Kong**, China
113	U 13	**Hong Kong**, China ▣
113	U 6	**Hong'an**, China
111	M 18	**Hongch'ŏn**, South Korea
113	V 12	**Honghai Wan**, China ≈
113	T 7	**Honghu**, China
113	R 9	**Hongjiang**, China
109	N 6	**Hongliuyuan**, China
109	S 4	**Hongor**, Mongolia
113	P 11	**Hongshui He**, China ≀
113	S 2	**Hongtong**, China
123	H 19	**Hongū**, Japan
110	M 8	**Hongxing**, China
112	M 7	**Hongya**, China
112	M 5	**Hongyuan**, China
113	X 4	**Hongze**, China
113	X 4	**Hongze Hu**, China ∽
138	L 6	**Honiara**, Solomon Islands ■
63	O 13	**Honiton**, U.K.
122	J 11	**Honjō**, Japan
70	K 5	**Honningsvåg**, Norway
34	E 8	**Honokaa**, HI, U.S.A.
34	D 9	**Honokohau**, HI, U.S.A.
34	C 7	**Honolulu**, HI, U.S.A.
123	H 17	**Honshū**, Japan ≛
68	G 11	**Hoofddorp**, Netherlands
72	F 7	**Hooge**, Germany ≛
68	M 8	**Hoogersmilde**, Netherlands
68	M 9	**Hoogeveen**, Netherlands
68	I 9	**Hoogkarspel**, Netherlands
63	T 11	**Hook**, U.K.
61	E 20	**Hook Head**, Republic of Ireland ▶
24	H 7	**Hooker**, OK, U.S.A.
35	W 10	**Hoonah**, AK, U.S.A.
34	L 8	**Hooper Bay**, AK, U.S.A.
68	I 9	**Hoorn**, Netherlands
21	K 19	**Hoosier Hill**, IN, U.S.A. ▲
109	P 4	**Höövör**, Mongolia
95	Q 7	**Hopa**, Turkey
25	T 13	**Hope**, AR, U.S.A.
35	R 9	**Hope**, AK, U.S.A.
39	G 22	**Hope**, BC, Canada
63	P 5	**Hope**, U.K.
18	M 8	**Hopedale**, LA, U.S.A.
41	V 7	**Hopedale**, NL, Canada
45	Y 11	**Hopelchén**, Mexico
134	I 12	**Hopetoun**, WA, Australia
135	R 12	**Hopetoun**, VIC, Australia
132	M 13	**Hopetown**, Republic of South Africa
114	E 8	**Hopin**, Myanmar
16	E 7	**Hopkinsville**, KY, U.S.A.
114	E 12	**Hopong**, Myanmar
32	F 7	**Hoquiam**, WA, U.S.A.
86	J 7	**Hora Hoverla**, Ukraine ▲
95	R 9	**Horasan**, Turkey
67	N 8	**Horcajo de los Montes**, Spain
109	O 3	**Horgo**, Mongolia
87	N 12	**Horia**, Romania
111	A 16	**Horinger**, China
85	N 16	**Horki**, Belarus
145	N 8	**Horlick Mountains**, Antarctica ▲▲
87	X 6	**Horlivka**, Ukraine
101	O 11	**Hormak**, Iran
100	L 13	**Hormoz**, Iran ≛
100	L 12	**Hormozgān**, Iran ▣
75	W 2	**Horn**, Austria
19	N 8	**Horn Island**, MS, U.S.A. ≛
135	R 1	**Horn Island**, QLD, Australia ≛
38	F 13	**Horn Mountains**, NT, Canada ▲▲
70	H 12	**Hornavan**, Sweden ∽
33	G 14	**Hornbrook**, CA, U.S.A.
63	V 4	**Horncastle**, U.K.
47	T 14	**Hornconcitos**, Panama
14	E 9	**Hornell**, NY, U.S.A.
41	N 11	**Hornepayne**, ON, Canada
63	V 2	**Hornsea**, U.K.
86	K 6	**Horodenka**, Ukraine
87	Q 1	**Horodnya**, Ukraine
87	Q 5	**Horodyshche**, Ukraine
122	J 3	**Horonobe**, Japan
122	K 6	**Horoshiri-dake**, Japan ▲
136	K 10	**Horotiu**, New Zealand
109	W 4	**Horqin Zouyi Zhongqi**, China
111	H 14	**Horqin Zuoyi Houqi**, China
110	I 13	**Horqin Zuoyi Zhongqi**, China
105	L 17	**Horsburgh Atoll**, Maldives ≛
71	C 25	**Horsens**, Denmark
28	K 10	**Horseshoe Bend**, ID, U.S.A.
63	V 12	**Horsham**, U.K.
135	R 13	**Horsham**, VIC, Australia
69	L 16	**Horst**, Netherlands
25	Q 2	**Horton**, KS, U.S.A.
38	E 8	**Horton**, NT, Canada ≀
74	F 8	**Horw**, Switzerland
63	Q 3	**Horwich**, U.K.
86	L 4	**Horyn**, Ukraine ≀
127	I 21	**Hosa'ina**, Ethiopia
105	D 21	**Hosdrug**, India
129	U 12	**Hoséré Vokre**, Cameroon ▲
101	R 14	**Hoshab**, Pakistan
105	E 15	**Hoshangabad**, India
106	I 6	**Hoshiarpur**, India
109	P 3	**Höshööt**, Mongolia
69	L 23	**Hosingen**, Luxembourg
138	G 4	**Hoskins**, Papua New Guinea
105	D 19	**Hospet**, India
22	G 10	**Hot Springs**, SD, U.S.A.
25	U 12	**Hot Springs**, AR, U.S.A.
71	F 14	**Hotagen**, Sweden ∽
108	H 7	**Hotan**, China
71	G 14	**Hoting**, Sweden
38	G 11	**Hottah Lake**, NT, Canada ∽
139	P 13	**Houaïlu**, New Caledonia
69	K 23	**Houffalize**, Belgium
118	B 14	**Hougang**, Singapore
20	G 8	**Houghton**, MI, U.S.A.
20	K 12	**Houghton Lake**, MI, U.S.A. ∽
136	I 4	**Houhora**, New Zealand
15	S 2	**Houlton**, ME, U.S.A.
18	K 8	**Houma**, LA, U.S.A.
113	S 3	**Houma**, China
125	R 7	**Houmt Souk**, Tunisia
128	K 10	**Houndé**, Burkina Faso
136	N 10	**Houpoto**, New Zealand
19	N 2	**Houston**, MS, U.S.A.
25	V 7	**Houston**, MO, U.S.A.
27	T 10	**Houston**, TX, U.S.A.
39	E 18	**Houston**, BC, Canada
69	J 18	**Houthalen**, Belgium
134	E 9	**Houtman Abrolhos**, WA, Australia ≛
108	M 4	**Hovd**, Mongolia ▣
108	M 3	**Hovd**, Mongolia
109	P 5	**Hovd**, Mongolia
63	V 13	**Hove**, U.K.
63	Z 6	**Hoveton**, U.K.
109	O 2	**Hövsgöl**, Mongolia ▣
109	P 2	**Hövsgöl Nuur**, Mongolia ∽
25	P 6	**Howard**, KS, U.S.A.
63	T 2	**Howden**, U.K.
21	L 14	**Howell**, MI, U.S.A.
22	I 9	**Howes**, SD, U.S.A.
136	K 8	**Howick**, New Zealand
39	I 21	**Howser**, BC, Canada
73	G 15	**Höxter**, Germany
60	H 7	**Hoy**, U.K. ≛
73	N 15	**Hoyerswerda**, Germany
66	J 7	**Hoyos**, Spain
71	O 15	**Höytiäinen**, Finland ∽
79	E 17	**Hradec Králové**, Czech Republic
87	S 5	**Hradyz'k**, Ukraine
85	K 18	**Hradzyanka**, Belarus
80	H 12	**Hrasnica**, Bosnia and Herzegovina
95	U 8	**Hrazdan**, Armenia
87	R 4	**Hrebinka**, Ukraine
87	P 4	**Hrebinky**, Ukraine
85	E 18	**Hrodna**, Belarus
85	G 18	**Hrodzyenskaya Voblasts'**, Belarus ▣
79	O 15	**Hrubieszów**, Poland
114	F 10	**Hsenwi**, Myanmar
114	E 13	**Hsi-hseng**, Myanmar
113	Z 11	**Hsinch'eng**, Taiwan
113	Z 10	**Hsinchu**, Taiwan
115	H 20	**Hua Hin**, Thailand
113	R 3	**Hua Shan**, China ▲
113	P 2	**Huachi**, China
53	C 16	**Huacho**, Peru
110	N 9	**Huachuan**, China
53	C 14	**Huacrachuco**, Peru
111	C 15	**Huade**, China
111	K 14	**Huadian**, China
111	C 16	**Huai'an**, China
113	V 4	**Huaibei**, China
113	V 5	**Huaibin**, China
113	R 9	**Huaihua**, China
113	S 12	**Huaiji**, China
111	D 16	**Huailai**, China
113	W 5	**Huainan**, China
111	B 17	**Huairen**, China
113	U 4	**Huaiyang**, China
113	X 4	**Huaiyin**, China
113	V 4	**Huaiyuan**, China
45	S 13	**Huajuápan de León**, Mexico
30	H 10	**Hualapai Peak**, AZ, U.S.A. ▲
113	Z 11	**Hualien**, Taiwan
53	D 14	**Huallaga**, Peru ≀
52	C 13	**Huamachuco**, Peru
132	H 4	**Huambo**, Angola
132	G 4	**Huambo**, Angola ▣
110	N 10	**Huanan**, China
53	E 17	**Huancavelica**, Peru
53	E 17	**Huancavelica**, Peru ▣
53	E 16	**Huancayo**, Peru
113	W 7	**Huang Shan**, China ▲▲
113	U 5	**Huangchuan**, China
110	E 13	**Huanggangliang**, China ▲
111	E 18	**Huanghua**, China
113	Q 2	**Huangling**, China
113	Q 15	**Huangliu**, China
110	L 13	**Huangnihe**, China
113	X 7	**Huangshan**, China
113	U 7	**Huangshi**, China
113	O 2	**Huangtu Gaoyaun**, China ◇
59	B 18	**Huanguelén**, Argentina
111	G 19	**Huangxian**, China
113	Y 7	**Huangyan**, China
111	K 15	**Huanren**, China
53	E 17	**Huanta**, Peru
53	D 15	**Huánuco**, Peru
53	D 15	**Huánuco**, Peru ▣
53	J 20	**Huanuni**, Bolivia
113	P 2	**Huanxian**, China
53	C 15	**Huaráz**, Peru
53	C 15	**Huari**, Peru
53	C 15	**Huarmey**, Peru
113	T 7	**Huarong**, China
56	F 9	**Huasco**, Chile
109	N 8	**Huashixia**, China
44	J 6	**Huatabampo**, Mexico
111	H 16	**Huatong**, China
113	U 3	**Huaxian**, China
53	C 14	**Huaylas**, Peru
113	Q 8	**Huayuan**, China
113	R 13	**Huazhou**, China
27	Q 7	**Hubbard**, TX, U.S.A.
27	N 6	**Hubbard Creek Lake**, TX, U.S.A. ∽
40	K 5	**Hubbart Point**, MB, Canada ▶
113	T 6	**Hubei**, China ▣
105	D 19	**Hubli**, India
111	L 15	**Huch'ang**, North Korea
61	J 17	**Huddersfield**, U.K.
63	S 3	**Huddersfield**, U.K.
110	H 7	**Huder**, China
71	H 17	**Hudiksvall**, Sweden
14	K 9	**Hudson**, NY, U.S.A. ≀
21	K 16	**Hudson**, MI, U.S.A.
41	N 5	**Hudson Bay**, QC, Canada ≈
14	K 8	**Hudson Falls**, NY, U.S.A.
41	Q 4	**Hudson Strait**, NU, Canada ≈
115	N 16	**Huê**, Vietnam
26	E 7	**Hueco Mountains**, TX, U.S.A. ▲▲
86	H 9	**Huedin**, Romania
46	G 5	**Huehuetenango**, Guatemala
45	R 12	**Huejotzingo**, Mexico
45	N 9	**Huejuqilla**, Mexico
45	R 10	**Huejutla**, Mexico
67	O 11	**Huelma**, Spain
66	J 12	**Huelva**, Spain
56	F 11	**Huentelauquén**, Chile
67	Q 12	**Huércal-Overa**, Spain
67	T 3	**Huesca**, Spain
67	Q 11	**Huéscar**, Spain
45	P 12	**Huétamo**, Mexico
135	S 5	**Hughenden**, QLD, Australia
107	S 13	**Hugli-Chunchura**, India
25	Q 13	**Hugo**, OK, U.S.A.
24	H 7	**Hugoton**, KS, U.S.A.
111	A 16	**Huhhot**, China
113	X 10	**Hui'an**, China
113	P 1	**Hui'anpu**, China
136	M 12	**Huiarau Range**, New Zealand ▲▲
111	K 16	**Huich'ŏn**, North Korea
112	L 9	**Huidong**, China
110	G 9	**Huihe**, China
50	H 8	**Huila**, Colombia ▣
132	G 5	**Huíla**, Angola ▣
132	H 6	**Huíla Plateau**, Angola ◇
113	V 12	**Huilai**, China
112	L 9	**Huili**, China
111	E 19	**Huimin**, China
56	I 5	**Huinahuaca**, Argentina
111	K 14	**Huinan**, China
56	J 12	**Huinca Renancó**, Argentina
113	O 10	**Huishui**, China
71	K 18	**Huittinen**, Finland
113	O 4	**Huixian**, China
113	T 2	**Huixian**, China
45	W 15	**Huixtla**, Mexico
112	M 10	**Huize**, China
68	I 11	**Huizen**, Netherlands
113	U 12	**Huizhou**, China
109	Q 4	**Hujirt**, Mongolia
114	D 6	**Hukawng Valley**, Myanmar ◇
132	K 10	**Hukuntsi**, Botswana
110	K 11	**Hulan**, China
98	M 5	**Ḥulayfah**, Saudi Arabia
110	O 10	**Hulin**, China
105	D 21	**Huliyar**, India
69	E 17	**Hulst**, Netherlands
111	H 16	**Huludao**, China
110	F 8	**Hulun Nur**, China ∽
87	W 7	**Hulyaypole**, Ukraine
110	K 5	**Huma**, China
49	U 8	**Humacao**, Puerto Rico
54	E 12	**Humaitá**, Brazil
63	V 3	**Humber**, U.K. ≀
27	T 9	**Humble**, TX, U.S.A.
33	J 16	**Humbold**, NV, U.S.A.
12	H 8	**Humboldt**, NV, U.S.A. ≀
16	B 9	**Humboldt**, TN, U.S.A.
23	R 11	**Humboldt**, IA, U.S.A.
59	B 17	**Humeda**, Argentina ◇
79	M 19	**Humenné**, Slovakia
68	L 13	**Hummelo**, Netherlands
132	F 6	**Humpata**, Angola
23	N 13	**Humphrey**, NE, U.S.A.
30	J 10	**Humphreys Peak**, AZ, U.S.A. ▲
134	M 1	**Humpty Doo**, NT, Australia
46	L 5	**Humuya**, Honduras ≀
125	U 9	**Hūn**, Libya
70	B 10	**Húnaflói**, Iceland ≈
113	T 9	**Hunan**, China ▣
110	N 13	**Hunchun**, China
86	G 10	**Hunedoara**, Romania
73	G 18	**Hünfeld**, Germany
79	H 24	**Hungary**, Europe □
63	S 11	**Hungerford**, U.K.
135	S 9	**Hungerford**, QLD, Australia
111	L 17	**Hŭngnam**, North Korea
63	U 1	**Hunmanby**, U.K.
73	C 20	**Hunsrück**, Germany ▲▲
63	X 5	**Hunstanton**, U.K.
139	T 14	**Hunter**, 0 ≛
135	S 14	**Hunter Island**, TAS, Australia ≛
21	I 21	**Huntingburg**, IN, U.S.A.
16	C 8	**Huntingdon**, TN, U.S.A.
63	V 7	**Huntingdon**, U.K.
16	M 4	**Huntington**, WV, U.S.A.
21	J 17	**Huntington**, IN, U.S.A.
33	J 25	**Huntington Beach**, CA, U.S.A.
60	I 10	**Huntly**, U.K.
19	P 1	**Huntsville**, AL, U.S.A.
25	T 9	**Huntsville**, AR, U.S.A.
27	S 9	**Huntsville**, TX, U.S.A.
42	F 10	**Huntsville**, ON, Canada
111	C 17	**Hunyuan**, China
110	J 7	**Huolongmen**, China
139	N 12	**Huon**, New Caledonia ≛
115	M 15	**Huong Khê**, Vietnam
135	S 15	**Huonville**, TAS, Australia
113	V 5	**Huoqiu**, China
113	V 6	**Huoshan**, China
113	S 2	**Huozhou**, China
107	Y 8	**Hupu**, India
79	H 22	**Hurbanovo**, Slovakia
127	O 19	**Hurdiyo**, Somalia
111	H 14	**Hure**, China
126	F 10	**Hurghada**, Egypt
22	M 9	**Huron**, SD, U.S.A.
63	X 12	**Hurst Green**, U.K.
19	R 5	**Hurtsboro**, AL, U.S.A.
70	C 10	**Húsavík**, Iceland
97	U 7	**Ḥusayn al Ghafūs**, Iraq
63	T 7	**Husbands Bosworth**, U.K.
86	M 9	**Huși**, Romania
71	F 22	**Huskvarna**, Sweden
35	O 6	**Huslia**, AK, U.S.A.
99	Q 12	**Ḥusn Al 'Abr**, Yemen
72	F 8	**Husum**, Germany
109	P 3	**Hutag**, Mongolia
23	R 8	**Hutchinson**, MN, U.S.A.
24	M 5	**Hutchinson**, KS, U.S.A.
99	P 12	**Ḥūth**, Yemen
138	I 4	**Hutjena**, Papua New Guinea
74	E 7	**Huttwil**, Switzerland
113	Q 4	**Huxian**, China
69	I 21	**Huy**, Belgium
108	L 2	**Huyten Orgil**, Mongolia ▲
110	I 5	**Huzhong**, China
113	Y 6	**Huzhou**, China
70	C 11	**Hvannadalshnúkur**, Iceland ▲
81	E 14	**Hvar**, Croatia
81	F 14	**Hvar**, Croatia ≛
87	T 12	**Hvardiys'ke**, Ukraine
70	B 11	**Hveragerði**, Iceland
70	B 11	**Hvíta**, Iceland ≀
133	N 7	**Hwange**, Zimbabwe
22	I 13	**Hyannis**, NE, U.S.A.
109	N 3	**Hyargus Nuur**, Mongolia ∽
134	H 11	**Hyden**, WA, Australia
101	U 14	**Hyderabad**, Pakistan
105	F 18	**Hyderabad**, India
65	V 15	**Hyères**, France
111	M 15	**Hyesan**, North Korea
29	V 6	**Hysham**, MT, U.S.A.
63	Z 12	**Hythe**, U.K.
123	D 22	**Hyūga**, Japan

I

125	O 15	**I-n-Guezzam**, Algeria
129	O 7	**I-n-Tebezas**, Mali
55	M 15	**Iaçu**, Brazil
87	N 9	**Ialoveni**, Moldova
86	M 9	**Iași**, Romania
54	B 9	**Iauaretê**, Brazil
120	E 10	**Iba**, Philippines
129	P 12	**Ibadan**, Nigeria
50	I 7	**Ibagué**, Colombia
81	L 15	**Ibar**, Serbia and Montenegro ≀
52	C 8	**Ibarra**, Ecuador
56	L 6	**Ibarreta**, Argentina
99	P 13	**Ibb**, Yemen
127	D 23	**Ibba**, Sudan
72	D 13	**Ibbenbüren**, Germany
52	E 12	**Iberia**, Peru
70	H 8	**Ibestad**, Norway
129	Q 11	**Ibeto**, Nigeria
67	T 10	**Ibi**, Spain
129	S 12	**Ibi**, Nigeria
58	O 5	**Ibiraçu**, Brazil
58	I 10	**Ibirama**, Brazil
67	W 9	**Ibiza**, Spain ≛
55	L 14	**Ibotirama**, Brazil
99	Z 7	**Ibrā'**, Oman
99	X 7	**Ibrī**, Oman
120	H 2	**Ibuhos**, Philippines ≛
53	D 18	**Ica**, Perú
53	D 18	**Ica**, Peru ▣
54	B 10	**Içá**, Brazil ≀
54	C 9	**Içana**, Brazil
54	C 9	**Içana**, Brazil ≀
70	C 10	**Iceland**, Europe □
143	Q 14	**Icelandic Plateau**, Arctic Ocean ◇
105	D 19	**Ichalkaranji**, India
123	L 16	**Ichihara**, Japan
122	K 11	**Ichinoseki**, Japan
87	R 3	**Ichnya**, Ukraine
111	M 19	**Ich'ŏn**, South Korea
69	B 17	**Ichtegem**, Belgium
54	N 12	**Icó**, Brazil
35	N 3	**Icy Cape**, AK, U.S.A. ▶
23	Q 12	**Ida Grove**, IA, U.S.A.
127	O 22	**Idaan**, Somalia
25	R 13	**Idabel**, OK, U.S.A.
137	E 23	**Idaburn**, New Zealand
129	Q 13	**Idah**, Nigeria
28	L 10	**Idaho**, U.S.A. ▣
29	P 11	**Idaho Falls**, ID, U.S.A.
73	D 20	**Idar-Oberstein**, Germany
127	A 19	**Idd el Chanam**, Sudan
125	O 13	**Idelès**, Algeria
126	F 11	**Idfu**, Egypt
125	R 10	**Idhān Awbārī**, Libya ◇
125	S 12	**Idhān Murzūq**, Libya ◇
130	K 11	**Idiofa**, Democratic Republic of Congo
96	I 2	**Idlib**, Syria
123	N 24	**Ie-jima**, Japan ≛
84	F 12	**Iecava**, Latvia
58	H 6	**Iepê**, Brazil
69	B 19	**Ieper**, Belgium
83	K 26	**Ierapetra**, Greece
86	I 9	**Iernut**, Romania
131	V 12	**Ifakara**, Tanzania
140	M 15	**Ifalik**, Federated States of Micronesia ≛
133	Y 9	**Ifanadiana**, Madgascar
129	P 13	**Ife**, Nigeria
129	R 6	**Iferouâne**, Niger
125	N 12	**Ifetesene**, Algeria ▲
79	H 25	**Igal**, Hungary
131	T 7	**Iganga**, Uganda
58	K 4	**Igarapava**, Brazil
89	N 9	**Igarka**, Russian Federation
129	P 12	**Igboho**, Nigeria
95	T 9	**Iğdir**, Turkey
77	B 19	**Iglesias**, Italy
93	W 1	**Iglino**, Russian Federation
41	O 1	**Igloolik**, NU, Canada
40	M 3	**Igluligaarjuk**, NU, Canada
40	K 11	**Ignace**, ON, Canada
85	H 14	**Ignalina**, Lithuania
90	I 10	**Ignatovo**, Russian Federation
94	C 6	**Iğneada**, Turkey
94	C 6	**Iğneada Burnu**, Turkey ▶
105	N 22	**Ignoitijala**, India
83	A 16	**Igoumenitsa**, Greece
91	R 13	**Igra**, Russian Federation
88	K 9	**Igrim**, Russian Federation
58	I 9	**Iguaçu**, Brazil ≀
58	F 9	**Iguaçu Falls**, Brazil ◇
45	R 13	**Iguala**, Mexico
58	K 8	**Iguape**, Brazil
58	F 7	**Iguatemi**, Brazil
54	N 12	**Iguatu**, Brazil
130	D 9	**Iguéla**, Gabon
131	T 10	**Igunga**, Tanzania
133	Z 5	**Iharana**, Madgascar
105	L 16	**Ihavandhippolhu Atoll**, Maldives ≛
109	R 5	**Ihbulag**, Mongolia
123	N 24	**Iheya-jima**, Japan ≛
129	R 13	**Ihiala**, Nigeria
133	X 9	**Ihosy**, Madgascar
109	Q 3	**Ihsuuj**, Mongolia
123	I 17	**Iida**, Japan
70	L 12	**Iijoki**, Finland ≀
71	M 15	**Iisalmi**, Finland
123	B 21	**Iizuka**, Japan
129	P 13	**Ijebu-Ode**, Nigeria
95	U 8	**Ijevan**, Armenia
68	G 10	**IJmuiden**, Netherlands
68	L 10	**IJssel**, Netherlands ≀
68	I 8	**IJsselmeer**, Netherlands ≈
58	G 11	**Ijuí**, Brazil
141	V 1	**Ijuw**, Nauru
69	B 17	**IJzer**, Belgium ≀
38	E 6	**Ikaahuk**, NT, Canada
137	G 18	**Ikamatua**, New Zealand
129	Q 12	**Ikare**, Nigeria
83	K 21	**Ikaria**, Greece ≛
137	F 23	**Ikawai**, New Zealand
122	L 5	**Ikeda**, Japan
123	F 20	**Ikeda**, Japan
130	M 8	**Ikela**, Democratic Republic of Congo
82	G 9	**Ikhtiman**, Bulgaria
123	A 21	**Iki**, Japan ≛
93	P 11	**Iki-Burul**, Russian Federation
123	A 21	**Iki-suidō**, Japan ≈
129	P 13	**Ikire**, Nigeria
129	S 13	**Ikom**, Nigeria
133	X 9	**Ikongo**, Madgascar
129	P 13	**Ikorodu**, Nigeria
111	L 20	**Iksan**, South Korea
129	P 12	**Ila**, Nigeria
120	H 7	**Ilagan**, Philippines
131	V 7	**Ilaisamis**, Kenya
100	F 7	**Īlām**, Iran ▣
100	F 7	**Īlām**, Iran
107	S 10	**Ilam**, Nepal
113	Z 10	**Ilan**, Taiwan
87	V 6	**Ilarionove**, Ukraine
78	J 10	**Iława**, Poland
63	P 12	**Ilchester**, U.K.
103	U 8	**Ile**, Kazakhstan ≀
139	O 13	**Île Balabio**, New Caledonia ≛
43	X 6	**Île Brion**, QC, Canada ≛
43	V 4	**Île d'Anticosti**, QC, Canada ≛
65	P 5	**Île-de-France**, France ▣
125	R 7	**Île de Jarba**, Tunisia ≛
49	N 7	**Île de la Gonâve**, Haiti ≛
49	O 6	**Île de la Tortue**, Haiti ≛
43	W 6	**Île de l'Est**, QC, Canada ≛
64	K 8	**Île de Noirmoutier**, France ≛
65	V 15	**Île de Porquerolles**, France ≛
64	K 9	**Île de Ré**, France ≛
139	Q 14	**Île des Pins**, New Caledonia ≛
64	L 9	**Île d'Oléron**, France ≛
64	G 5	**Île d'Ouessant**, France ≛
43	W 7	**Île du Harve Aubert**, QC, Canada ≛
64	J 8	**Île d'Yeu**, France ≛
133	U 9	**Île Europa**, France ≛
43	T 7	**Île Lamèque**, NB, Canada ≛
139	R 14	**Île Walpole**, New Caledonia ≛
130	K 10	**Ilebo**, Democratic Republic of Congo
93	V 5	**Ilek**, Russian Federation
102	J 4	**Ilek**, Kazakhstan
131	U 5	**Ileret**, Kenya
139	O 13	**Îles Bélep**, New Caledonia ≛
64	K 4	**Îles Chausey**, France ≛
138	L 12	**Îles Chesterfield**, New Caledonia ≛
64	H 6	**Îles de Glénan**, France ≛
65	W 15	**Îles de Hyères**, France ≛
43	X 7	**Îles de la Madeleine**, QC, Canada ≛
43	U 3	**Îles de Mingan**, QC, Canada ≛
133	Y 4	**Îles Glorieuses**, Seychelles ≛
125	R 6	**Îles Kerkenah**, Tunisia ≛
129	P 12	**Ilesa**, Nigeria
63	W 10	**Ilford**, U.K.
62	M 11	**Ilfracombe**, U.K.
94	I 8	**Ilgaz**, Turkey
94	I 8	**Ilgaz Dağlari**, Turkey
94	G 11	**Ilgin**, Turkey
54	J 9	**Ilha Caviana**, Brazil ≛
58	K 8	**Ilha Comprida**, Brazil ≛
54	J 9	**Ilha Curuá**, Brazil ≛
58	J 8	**Ilha das Peças**, Brazil ≛
54	J 8	**Ilha de Maracá**, Brazil ≛
54	J 9	**Ilha de Marajó**, Brazil ≛
58	J 10	**Ilha de Santa Catarina**, Brazil ≛
58	J 9	**Ilha de São Francisco**, Brazil ≛
58	L 7	**Ilha de São Sebastião**, Brazil ≛
133	R 8	**Ilha do Bazaruto**, Mozambique ≛
58	O 7	**Ilha do Cabo Frio**, Brazil ≛
58	K 8	**Ilha do Cardoso**, Brazil ≛
58	M 7	**Ilha Grande**, Brazil ≛
54	J 9	**Ilha Janaucu**, Brazil ≛
54	J 9	**Ilha Mexiana**, Brazil ≛
55	N 15	**Ilhéus**, Brazil
86	G 10	**Ilia**, Romania
35	O 10	**Iliamna Lake**, AK, U.S.A. ∽
95	N 10	**Ilic**, Turkey
121	K 21	**Iligan**, Philippines
121	K 20	**Iligan Bay**, Philippines ≈
120	I 5	**Iligan Point**, Philippines ▶
121	G 15	**Ilin**, Philippines ≛
91	S 12	**Il'inskiy**, Russian Federation
117	R 15	**Iliomar**, East Timor
95	R 12	**Ilisu Baraji**, Turkey ∽
63	R 2	**Ilkley**, U.K.
121	K 21	**Illana Bay**, Philippines ≈
56	F 10	**Illapel**, Chile
73	H 24	**Illertissen**, Germany
87	Q 10	**Illichivs'k**, Ukraine
21	D 17	**Illinois**, U.S.A. ▣
21	E 18	**Illinois**, IL, U.S.A. ≀
87	O 6	**Illintsi**, Ukraine
125	Q 11	**Illizi**, Algeria
73	I 18	**Ilmenau**, Germany
63	P 13	**Ilminster**, U.K.
53	G 20	**Ilo**, Peru
121	E 16	**Iloc**, Philippines ≛
121	I 17	**Iloilo**, Philippines
129	P 12	**Ilorin**, Nigeria
80	B 11	**Ilovik**, Croatia ≛
93	O 8	**Ilovlya**, Russian Federation
79	E 14	**Iłowa**, Poland
89	Y 9	**Il'pyrskiy**, Russian Federation
64	I 6	**Îls de Groix**, France ≛
84	H 13	**Ilūkste**, Latvia
143	N 12	**Ilulissat**, Greenland
85	I 16	**Il'ya**, Belarus
123	D 20	**Imabari**, Japan
122	J 8	**Imabetsu**, Japan
97	U 9	**Imām al Hamzah**, Iraq
97	U 7	**Imām Ḥamid**, Iraq
94	K 13	**Imamoğlu**, Turkey
123	B 21	**Imari**, Japan
53	G 19	**Imata**, Peru
71	O 18	**Imatra**, Finland
52	B 8	**Imbabura**, Ecuador ▣
127	K 22	**Īmī**, Ethiopia

□ Country ▣ Internal administrative region: State/Province/Territory/Dependent territory ■ Capital city ▲▲ Mountain range/Undersea ridge ▲ Mountain peak/Volcano/Seamount ◇ Geographic feature ▶ Headland/Point/Cape/Peninsula ● Desert ≛ Island/Island group ∷ Antarctic base ⊚ Ocean ◣ Sea ≈ Bay/Gulf/Channel/Strait ∽ Lake ▚ Salt pan/Dry/Intermittent lake ≀

G 8 Imi-n-Tanoute, Morocco
X 9 Imişli, Azerbaijan
K 16 Imlay, NV, U.S.A.
B 12 Imlili, Western Sahara
H 26 Immenstadt, Germany
V 3 Immingham, U.K.
X 12 Immokalee, FL, U.S.A.
R 13 Imo, Nigeria
G 9 Imola, Italy
A 3 Imonda, Papua New Guinea
K 11 Imperatriz, Brazil
B 10 Imperia, Italy
I 15 Imperial, NE, U.S.A.
D 17 Imperial, Peru
J 7 Impfondo, Congo
X 12 Imphal, India
D 8 Imrali, Turkey
A 8 Imroz, Turkey
L 7 Imst, Austria
I 8 Imtān, Syria
I 3 Imuris, Mexico
D 17 Imuruan Bay, Philippines
Q 10 In Aménas, Algeria
O 13 In Amguel, Algeria
O 13 In Ekker, Algeria
M 11 In Salah, Algeria
I 16 Ina, Japan
G 17 Inangahua Junction, New Zealand
U 12 Inanwatan, Indonesia
H 16 Iñapari, Peru
L 8 Inari, Finland
Q 10 Inarigda, Russian Federation
M 8 Inarijärvi, Finland
J 13 Inawashiro-ko, Japan
G 7 Inca de Oro, Chile
J 6 Ince Burun, Turkey
I 14 Incekum Burnu, Turkey
F 5 Inchiri, Mauritania
L 19 Inch'ŏn, South Korea
H 20 Incourt, Belgium
F 11 Inčukalns, Latvia
I 17 Inda Silasē, Ethiopia
F 15 Indalsälven, Sweden
E 12 Indaw, Myanmar
S 3 Independence, MO, U.S.A.
R 10 Independence Fjord, Greenland
P 7 Indepenence, KS, U.S.A.
I 10 Inder, China
I 6 Inderborskiy, Kazakhstan
O 11 India, Asia
W 7 Indian Harbour, NL, Canada
U 4 Indian Head, MD, U.S.A.
L 18 Indian Lake, OH, U.S.A.
S 11 Indian Ocean, 0
M 21 Indian Springs, NV, U.S.A.
M 10 Indian Wells, AZ, U.S.A.
C 12 Indiana, PA, U.S.A.
H 18 Indiana, U.S.A.
I 19 Indianapolis, IN, U.S.A.
L 3 Indianola, MS, U.S.A.
S 13 Indianola, IA, U.S.A.
O 3 Indiga, Russian Federation
U 7 Indigirka, Russian Federation
L 25 Indio, CA, U.S.A.
M 6 Indispensable Strait, Solomon Islands
M 19 Indochina Peninsula, Cambodia
H 13 Indonesia, Asia
D 15 Indore, India
G 17 Indravati, India
E 18 Indura, Belarus
W 9 Indus, India/Pakistan
I 6 Inebolu, Turkey
E 9 Inegöl, Turkey
H 11 Infanta, Philippines
M 1 Infiesto, Spain
Q 7 Ingal, Niger
J 8 Ingende, Democratic Republic of Congo
K 5 Ingeniero Guillermo Neuva Juárez, Argentina
G 17 Ingeniero Jacobacci, Argentina
T 4 Ingham, QLD, Australia
Q 1 Ingleborough, U.K.
Q 1 Ingleton, U.K.
J 12 Inglewood, New Zealand
W 4 Ingoldmells, U.K.
J 22 Ingolstadt, Germany
V 5 Ingomar, MT, U.S.A.
Y 7 Ingonish, NS, Canada
S 11 Ingraj Bazar, India
W 6 Ingrid Christensen Coast, Antarctica
R 10 Inhambane, Mozambique
Q 9 Inhambane, Mozambique
R 7 Inhaminga, Mozambique
R 10 Inharrime, Mozambique
R 8 Inhul, Ukraine
S 8 Inhulets, Ukraine
A 17 Inishbofin, Republic of Ireland
B 18 Inisheer, Republic of Ireland
B 18 Inishmore, Republic of Ireland
A 17 Inishturk, Republic of Ireland
F 12 Injgan Sum, China
H 19 Injibara, Ethiopia
U 8 Injune, QLD, Australia
I 18 Inland Kaikoura Range, New Zealand
M 10 Inman, SC, U.S.A.
K 24 Inn, Germany
Q 8 Innamincka, SA, Australia
E 13 Inner Hebrides, U.K.
E 12 Inner Mongolia, China
F 9 Innertkirchen, Switzerland
T 4 Innisfail, QLD, Australia
M 7 Innsbruck, Austria
J 9 Inongo, Democratic Republic of Congo
H 11 Inowrocław, Poland
J 20 Inquisivi, Bolivia
C 7 Ins, Switzerland
M 12 Insurăţei, Romania
T 4 Inta, Russian Federation
E 9 Interlaken, Switzerland
S 2 International Falls, MN, U.S.A.
N 21 Interview Island, India
C 11 Intiyaco, Argentina
K 11 Întorsura Buzăului, Romania
K 5 Intsy, Russian Federation
E 10 Intutu, Peru
L 15 Inubō-zaki, Japan
P 6 Inukjuak, QC, Canada
C 9 Inuvik, NT, Canada
G 12 Inveraray, U.K.
C 25 Invercargill, New Zealand
V 10 Inverell, NSW, Australia
V 9 Inverness, FL, U.S.A.
X 8 Inverness, NS, Canada
60 H 10 Inverness, U.K.
88 M 13 Inya, Russian Federation
133 Q 7 Inyangani, Zimbabwe
33 K 22 Inyocern, CA, U.S.A.
131 S 12 Inyonga, Tanzania
93 Q 3 Inza, Russian Federation
93 X 2 Inzer, Russian Federation
123 C 25 Iō-jima, Japan
123 N 23 Iō-Tori-jima, Japan
83 B 16 Ioannina, Greece
25 Q 6 Iola, KS, U.S.A.
43 Y 8 Iona, NS, Canada
60 E 12 Iona, U.K.
132 G 6 Iona, Angola
86 I 12 Ioneşti, Romania
21 K 14 Ionia, MI, U.S.A.
83 A 17 Ionian Islands, Greece
83 B 17 Ionioi Nisoi, Greece
83 J 23 Ios, Greece
18 I 7 Iowa, LA, U.S.A.
23 R 12 Iowa, U.S.A.
23 V 13 Iowa City, IA, U.S.A.
23 T 11 Iowa Falls, IA, U.S.A.
46 I 6 Ipala, Guatemala
55 L 17 Ipatinga, Brazil
93 N 11 Ipatovo, Russian Federation
83 B 16 Ipeiros, Greece
79 I 21 Ipel, Slovakia
50 G 9 Ipiales, Colombia
121 I 21 Ipil, Philippines
58 I 8 Ipiranga, Brazil
54 A 13 Ipixuna, Brazil
118 B 7 Ipoh, Malaysia
130 L 4 Ippy, Central African Republic
94 B 7 Ipsala, Turkey
63 Z 8 Ipswich, U.K.
135 W 9 Ipswich, QLD, Australia
54 M 11 Ipu, Brazil
41 R 3 Iqaluit, NU, Canada
109 N 7 Iqe, China
53 F 19 Iquipi, Peru
56 F 3 Iquique, Chile
52 F 11 Iquitos, Peru
130 L 4 Ira Banda, Central African Republic
123 N 26 Irabu-jima, Japan
123 I 18 Irago-misaki, Japan
58 G 10 Iraí, Brazil
82 F 13 Irakleia, Greece
83 J 23 Irakleia, Greece
83 J 26 Irakleiou, Greece
55 M 15 Iramaia, Brazil
100 K 7 Iran, Asia
100 K 9 Iranian Plateau, Iran
101 O 13 Īrānshahr, Iran
45 P 11 Irapuato, Mexico
97 R 8 Iraq, Asia
58 I 9 Irati, Brazil
91 R 6 Irayel', Russian Federation
84 C 9 Irbe Strait, Estonia/Latvia
96 H 8 Irbid, Jordan
55 M 14 Irecê, Brazil
61 D 17 Ireland, Republic of, Europe
103 N 6 Irgiz, Kazakhstan
124 H 8 Irhil M'Goun, Morocco
100 F 4 Īrī Dāgh, Iran
117 W 12 Irian Jaya, Indonesia
129 Z 8 Iriba, Chad
120 J 13 Iriga, Philippines
131 U 12 Iringa, Tanzania
131 U 12 Iringa, Tanzania
123 M 26 Iriomote-jima, Japan
47 O 4 Iriona, Honduras
54 H 11 Iriri, Brazil
61 G 17 Irish Sea, Republic of Ireland/United Kingdom
54 K 10 Irituia, Brazil
89 P 14 Irkutsk, Russian Federation
103 N 10 Irlir Toghi, Uzbekistan
94 I 9 Irmak, Turkey
123 J 18 Irō-zaki, Japan
20 H 9 Iron Mountain, MI, U.S.A.
20 G 9 Iron River, MI, U.S.A.
21 M 21 Ironton, OH, U.S.A.
20 E 8 Ironwood, MI, U.S.A.
42 E 6 Iroquois Falls, ON, Canada
87 P 3 Irpin', Ukraine
99 R 14 Irqah, Yemen
114 C 13 Irrawaddy, Myanmar
115 C 17 Irrawaddy, Myanmar
87 N 3 Irsha, Ukraine
88 K 10 Irtysh, Russian Federation
103 U 2 Irtyshsk, Kazakhstan
123 K 16 Iruma, Japan
53 I 19 Irupana, Bolivia
27 Q 5 Irving, TX, U.S.A.
16 F 5 Irvington, KY, U.S.A.
137 G 20 Irwell, New Zealand
129 Q 9 Isa, Nigeria
22 I 7 Isabel, SD, U.S.A.
138 L 5 Isabel, Solomon Islands
121 H 23 Isabela, Philippines
87 N 11 Isaccea, Romania
70 A 10 Ísafjörður, Iceland
123 B 22 Isahaya, Japan
130 L 8 Isanga, Democratic Republic of Congo
129 Q 12 Isanlu, Nigeria
74 K 8 Ischgl, Austria
77 J 16 Ischia, Italy
123 H 18 Ise, Japan
123 H 18 Ise-wan, Japan
131 N 7 Isengi, Democratic Republic of Congo
77 J 14 Isernia, Italy
129 P 12 Iseyin, Nigeria
103 R 12 Isfana, Kyrgyzstan
97 U 9 Ishaq, Iraq
123 N 26 Ishigaki, Japan
123 N 26 Ishigaki-jima, Japan
122 J 5 Ishikari-wan, Japan
123 N 24 Ishikawa, Japan
88 K 11 Ishim, Russian Federation
122 L 12 Ishinomaki, Japan
123 E 20 Ishizuchi-san, Japan
103 Q 12 Ishtykhan, Uzbekistan
107 T 12 Ishurdi, Bangladesh
88 K 11 Isil'kul', Russian Federation
131 V 7 Isiolo, Kenya
131 P 6 Isiro, Democratic Republic of Congo
135 S 7 Isisford, QLD, Australia
94 L 13 Iskenderun, Turkey
94 K 13 Iskenderun Körfezi, Turkey
94 J 8 Iskilip, Turkey
82 H 7 Iskŭr, Bulgaria
127 O 19 Iskushuban, Somalia
44 H 4 Isla Ángel de la Guarda, Mexico
57 G 25 Isla Aracena, Chile
53 B 18 Isla Baltra, Ecuador
49 P 8 Isla Beata, Dominican Republic
51 P 1 Isla Blanquilla, Venezuela
57 E 21 Isla Campana, Chile
44 I 7 Isla Carmen, Mexico
44 F 5 Isla Cedros, Mexico
44 J 8 Isla Cerralvo, Mexico
57 F 23 Isla Chatham, Chile
57 G 25 Isla Clarence, Chile
51 Q 2 Isla Coche, Venezuela
47 T 15 Isla Coiba, Panama
57 F 24 Isla Contreras, Chile
45 W 12 Isla de Aguada, Mexico
67 P 15 Isla de Alborán, Spain
44 K 8 Isla de Altamura, Mexico
129 R 15 Isla de Bioco, Equatorial Guinea
47 Q 14 Isla de Caño, Costa Rica
57 E 18 Isla de Chiloé, Chile
47 T 13 Isla de Colón, Panama
45 Z 11 Isla de Cozumel, Mexico
47 N 3 Isla de Guanaja, Honduras
48 G 5 Isla de la Juventud, Cuba
57 J 26 Isla de los Estados, Argentina
51 Q 2 Isla de Margarita, Venezuela
47 O 10 Isla de Ometepe, Nicaragua
47 N 3 Isla de Roatán, Honduras
46 M 4 Isla de Utila, Honduras
47 Y 14 Isla del Rey, Panama
47 R 9 Isla del Venado, Nicaragua
57 F 25 Isla Desolación, Chile
57 E 23 Isla Duque de York, Chile
57 E 22 Isla Esmeralda, Chile
53 C 19 Isla Española, Ecuador
44 J 8 Isla Espíritu Santo, Mexico
53 A 19 Isla Fernandina, Ecuador
59 B 20 Isla Flamenco, Argentina
59 B 20 Isla Gama, Argentina
53 C 18 Isla Genovesa, Ecuador
57 H 26 Isla Gordon, Chile
57 H 25 Isla Grande de Tierra del Fuego, Chile
44 E 4 Isla Guadalupe, Mexico
57 E 18 Isla Guafo, Chile
57 E 19 Isla Guamblin, Chile
57 F 23 Isla Hanover, Chile
57 H 26 Isla Hoste, Chile
53 A 19 Isla Isabela, Ecuador
57 F 19 Isla James, Chile
57 F 21 Isla Javier, Chile
47 T 15 Isla Jicarón, Panama
57 F 23 Isla Jorge Montt, Chile
51 P 2 Isla La Tortuga, Venezuela
57 I 26 Isla Lennox, Chile
57 G 26 Isla Londonderry, Chile
57 E 23 Isla Madre de Dios, Chile
57 F 19 Isla Magdalena, Chile
53 A 18 Isla Marchena, Ecuador
44 L 10 Isla María Cleofas, Mexico
44 L 10 Isla María Madre, Mexico
44 L 10 Isla María Magdelena, Mexico
57 F 19 Isla Melchor, Chile
57 E 15 Isla Mocha, Chile
49 T 8 Isla Mona, Puerto Rico
47 T 15 Isla Montuosa, Panama
57 E 22 Isla Mornington, Chile
57 H 26 Isla Navarino, Chile
57 I 26 Isla Nueva, Chile
51 O 2 Isla Orchila, Venezuela
47 T 15 Isla Parida, Panama
57 E 22 Isla Patricio Lynch, Chile
57 I 26 Isla Picton, Chile
53 B 17 Isla Pinta, Ecuador
57 E 21 Isla Prat, Chile
52 A 10 Isla Puná, Ecuador
57 G 24 Isla Riesco, Chile
53 C 19 Isla San Cristóbal, Ecuador
44 H 5 Isla San Esteban, Mexico
44 I 7 Isla San José, Mexico
47 X 14 Isla San José, Panama
44 L 10 Isla San Juanito, Mexico
44 H 4 Isla San Lorenzo, Mexico
53 B 18 Isla San Salvador, Ecuador
44 I 7 Isla Santa Catalina, Mexico
53 B 18 Isla Santa Cruz, Ecuador
53 B 19 Isla Santa Fé, Ecuador
57 G 25 Isla Santa Inés, Chile
44 H 8 Isla Santa Margarita, Mexico
53 B 19 Isla Santa Maria, Ecuador
49 S 8 Isla Saona, Dominican Republic
47 S 14 Isla Sevilla, Panama
57 G 26 Isla Stewart, Chile
44 H 4 Isla Tiburón, Mexico
59 B 19 Isla Trinidad, Argentina
57 F 20 Isla Victoria, Chile
57 F 24 Isla Vidal, Chile
57 F 22 Isla Wellington, Chile
47 O 10 Isla Zapatra, Nicaragua
94 L 13 Islahiye, Turkey
101 Y 8 Islamabad, Pakistan
19 Y 14 Islamorada, FL, U.S.A.
121 C 19 Island Bay, Philippines
40 J 8 Island Lake, MB, Canada
40 J 8 Island Lake, MB, Canada
29 Q 9 Island Park, ID, U.S.A.
34 I 14 Islands of The Four Mountains, AK, U.S.A.
67 V 7 Islas Columbretes, Spain
46 M 4 Islas de la Bahía, Honduras
47 S 9 Islas del Maíz, Nicaragua
57 H 26 Islas Diego Ramirez, Chile
51 O 2 Islas Los Roques, Venezuela
44 L 10 Islas Marías, Mexico
47 T 15 Islas Secas, Panama
57 I 26 Islas Wollaston, Chile
60 E 13 Islay, U.K.
15 R 6 Isle au Haut, ME, U.S.A.
60 E 8 Isle of Lewis, U.K.
61 H 16 Isle of Man, U.K.
63 Q 14 Isle of Portland, U.K.
63 Y 11 Isle of Sheppey, U.K.
63 O 1 Isle of Walney, U.K.
63 S 14 Isle of Wight, U.K.
20 G 6 Isle Royale, MI, U.S.A.
18 K 9 Isles Dernieres, LA, U.S.A.
61 E 24 Isles of Scilly, U.K.
126 F 8 Ismâ'ilîya, Egypt
95 X 7 Ismayilli, Azerbaijan
126 F 11 Isna, Egypt
133 Q 3 Isoka, Zambia
77 J 20 Isola Alicudi, Italy
77 B 15 Isola Asinara, Italy
77 C 15 Isola Caprera, Italy
76 D 12 Isola d'Elba, Italy
77 I 16 Isola d'Ischia, Italy
76 E 13 Isola del Giglio, Italy
76 D 12 Isola di Capraia, Italy
77 J 16 Isola di Capri, Italy
76 D 11 Isola di Gorgona, Italy
77 H 26 Isola di Lampedusa, Italy
77 G 26 Isola di Lampione, Italy
77 H 26 Isola di Linosa, Italy
76 E 13 Isola di Montecristo, Italy
77 G 24 Isola di Pantelleria, Italy
77 B 19 Isola di San Pietro, Italy
77 B 19 Isola di Sant'Antioco, Italy
77 I 20 Isola di Ustica, Italy
77 G 22 Isola Favignana, Italy
77 J 20 Isola Filicudi, Italy
77 G 21 Isola Levanzo, Italy
77 K 20 Isola Lipari, Italy
77 C 15 Isola Maddalena, Italy
77 G 21 Isola Marettimo, Italy
77 K 20 Isola Panarea, Italy
76 D 12 Isola Pianosa, Italy
77 K 20 Isola Salina, Italy
77 K 20 Isola Stromboli, Italy
77 K 21 Isola Vulcano, Italy
77 F 21 Isole Egadi, Italy
77 G 26 Isole Pelagie, Italy
76 L 13 Isole Pianosa, Italy
77 H 16 Isole Ponziane, Italy
76 L 13 Isole San Domino, Italy
76 L 13 Isole Tremiti, Italy
94 F 12 Isparta, Turkey
82 L 7 Isperikh, Bulgaria
96 F 11 Israel, Asia
134 J 11 Israelite Bay, WA, Australia
128 J 13 Issia, Côte d'Ivoire
103 W 10 Issyk-Kul'skaya Oblast', Kyrgyzstan
79 K 21 Istállós-kő, Hungary
82 O 12 Istanbul, Turkey
94 D 7 Istanbul, Turkey
100 H 7 Īstgāh-e Eznā, Iran
115 F 23 Isthmus of Kra, Thailand
47 W 13 Isthmus of Panama, Panama
83 F 18 Istiaia, Greece
95 V 9 Istisu, Azerbaijan
45 V 13 Istmo de Tehuantepec, Mexico
80 A 9 Istra, Croatia
107 T 14 Iswaripur, Bangladesh
103 W 9 Isyk, Kazakhstan
55 N 15 Itabuna, Brazil
54 F 10 Itacoatiara, Brazil
58 H 6 Itaguajé, Brazil
55 K 15 Itaguari, Brazil
54 G 11 Itaituba, Brazil
58 J 10 Itajaí, Brazil
58 L 6 Itajubá, Brazil
76 F 10 Italy, Europe
133 W 10 Itampolo, Madgascar
107 X 9 Itanagar, India
55 M 16 Itaobím, Brazil
58 I 4 Itapagipe, Brazil
55 N 16 Itapebi, Brazil
54 L 11 Itapecuru Mirim, Brazil
58 O 6 Itaperuna, Brazil
58 J 7 Itapetininga, Brazil
58 J 7 Itapeva, Brazil
54 B 12 Itaquai, Brazil
58 E 11 Itaqui, Brazil
58 J 7 Itararé, Brazil
105 E 15 Itarsi, India
58 H 3 Itarumã, Brazil
54 I 9 Itaupã, Brazil
120 H 2 Itbayat, Philippines
53 G 20 Ite, Peru
83 E 19 Itea, Greece
131 P 9 Itebero, Democratic Republic of Congo
14 G 9 Ithaca, NY, U.S.A.
83 B 19 Ithaki, Greece
83 B 19 Ithaki, Greece
55 M 16 Itinga, Brazil
55 G 16 Itiquira, Brazil
123 K 17 Itō, Japan
123 I 15 Itoigawa, Japan
130 L 8 Itoko, Democratic Republic of Congo
143 Q 13 Ittoqqortoormiit, Greenland
58 K 7 Itu, Brazil
54 B 11 Ituí, Brazil
58 J 3 Ituitaba, Brazil
55 J 17 Ituiutaba, Brazil
131 P 10 Itula, Democratic Republic of Congo
55 J 17 Itumbiara, Brazil
51 U 6 Ituni, Guyana
58 I 10 Ituporanga, Brazil
58 I 4 Iturama, Brazil
56 N 8 Ituzaingó, Argentina
58 E 10 Ituzaingo, Argentina
72 G 9 Itzehoe, Germany
89 Z 6 Iul'tin, Russian Federation
58 G 7 Ivaí, Brazil
70 M 8 Ivalo, Finland
85 G 21 Ivanava, Belarus
80 E 7 Ivanec, Croatia
135 S 11 Ivanhoe, NSW, Australia
80 E 8 Ivanić Grad, Croatia
80 K 13 Ivanjica, Serbia and Montenegro
80 F 10 Ivanjska, Bosnia and Herzegovina
87 P 3 Ivankiv, Ukraine
86 J 6 Ivano-Frankivs'k, Ukraine
93 V 4 Ivanovka, Russian Federation
90 K 14 Ivanovo, Russian Federation
90 K 14 Ivanovskaya Oblast', Russian Federation
93 S 4 Ivanteyevka, Russian Federation
87 S 3 Ivanytsya, Ukraine
85 G 20 Ivatsevichy, Belarus
82 K 12 Ivaylovgrad, Bulgaria
88 J 9 Ivdel', Russian Federation
86 M 11 Iveşti, Romania
58 G 6 Ivinheima, Brazil
142 L 13 Ivittuut, Greenland
133 X 9 Ivohibe, Madgascar
128 J 14 Ivory Coast, Côte d'Ivoire
76 B 7 Ivrea, Italy
41 P 4 Ivujivik, QC, Canada
85 I 17 Ivyanyets, Belarus
17 O 4 Ivydale, WV, U.S.A.
122 L 10 Iwaizumi, Japan
123 L 14 Iwaki, Japan
122 J 9 Iwaki-san, Japan
123 D 20 Iwakuni, Japan
122 J 5 Iwamizawa, Japan
122 I 6 Iwanai, Japan
122 K 10 Iwate-san, Japan
129 P 12 Iwo, Nigeria
85 G 17 Iwye, Belarus
53 I 17 Ixiamas, Bolivia
45 N 10 Ixtlán, Mexico
45 T 13 Ixtlán, Mexico
63 Y 8 Ixworth, U.K.
123 E 20 Iyomishima, Japan
131 U 12 Izazi, Tanzania
93 R 15 Izberbash, Russian Federation
69 C 18 Izegem, Belgium
123 N 24 Izena-jima, Japan
91 R 14 Izhevsk, Russian Federation
87 N 11 Izmayil, Ukraine
94 B 10 Izmir, Turkey
94 A 10 Izmir Körfezi, Turkey
94 E 8 Iznik Gölü, Turkey
92 M 12 Izobil'nyy, Russian Federation
45 R 12 Iztaccíhuatl, Mexico
46 H 7 Iztapa, Guatemala
123 K 17 Izu-hantō, Japan
123 K 18 Izu-shotō, Japan
45 R 12 Izúcar de Matamoros, Mexico
123 A 20 Izuhara, Japan
123 B 23 Izumi, Japan
123 D 18 Izumo, Japan
86 L 4 Izyaslav, Ukraine
87 X 5 Izyum, Ukraine

J

142 M 13 J.A.D. Jenson Nunatakker, Greenland
97 N 2 Jabal 'Abd al 'Azīz, Syria
97 N 2 Jabal Abd al Azīz, Syria
96 K 4 Jabal Abū Raḩbah, Syria
98 J 3 Jabal ad Dubbagh, Saudi Arabia
96 I 8 Jabal ad Duruz, Syria
96 J 3 Jabal Aḩaş, Syria
96 H 11 Jabāl al 'Ādhiriyāt, Jordan
96 I 2 Jabal al Akr, Syria
99 P 10 Jabal al Amlaḩ, Saudi Arabia
96 I 8 Jabal al 'Arab, Syria
96 F 13 Jabal al Khashsh, Jordan
98 J 3 Jabal al Lawz, Saudi Arabia
99 V 11 Jabal al Qamar, Oman
99 O 13 Jabal an Nabī Shu'ayb, Yemen
96 J 6 Jabal an Niqniqīyah, Syria
96 H 4 Jabal an Nuşayrīyah, Syria
99 P 10 Jabal ar Rubūţ, Saudi Arabia
125 Z 13 Jabal Arkenu, Libya
125 S 9 Jabal as Sawdā', Libya
99 Y 7 Jabal ash Shāms, Oman
96 H 6 Jabal ash Sharqī, Lebanon
96 I 5 Jabal ash Shawmarīyah, Syria
98 J 3 Jabal ash Shifa, Saudi Arabia
96 L 7 Jabal aţ Ţanf, Syria
96 F 13 Jabal Bāqir, Jordan
125 U 13 Jabal Bin Ghanīmah, Libya
96 L 4 Jabal Bishrī, Syria
99 X 6 Jabal Ḩafīt, United Arab Emirates
99 W 15 Jabal Ḩajhir, Yemen
97 S 4 Jabal Hamrin, Iraq
99 Z 7 Jabal Khadar, Oman
125 R 8 Jabal Nafūsah, Libya
98 L 5 Jabal Nahr, Saudi Arabia
125 W 14 Jabal Nuqayy, Libya
98 M 8 Jabal Qarnayţ, Saudi Arabia
98 L 6 Jabal Raḑwá, Saudi Arabia
98 M 2 Jabal Rāf, Saudi Arabia
96 G 13 Jabal Ramm, Jordan
99 Z 7 Jabal Salakh, Oman
99 N 10 Jabal Sawdá', Saudi Arabia
96 K 4 Jabal Shā'īr, Syria
97 O 2 Jabal Sinjār, Iraq
99 O 13 Jabal Taqar, Yemen
99 P 13 Jabal Thamar, Yemen
96 L 4 Jabal Thulaythawat Gharbi, Syria
99 Q 9 Jabal Tuwayq, Saudi Arabia
125 U 8 Jabal Waddān, Libya
125 V 9 Jabal Zaltan, Libya
105 G 15 Jabalpur, India
69 B 17 Jabbeke, Belgium
135 N 1 Jabiru, NT, Australia
96 H 3 Jablah, Syria
80 G 13 Jablanica, Bosnia and Herzegovina
79 E 16 Jablonec nad Nisou, Czech Republic
58 J 5 Jaboticabal, Brazil
141 Y 3 Jabwat, Marshall Islands
67 T 2 Jaca, Spain
45 R 11 Jacala, Mexico
46 F 4 Jacaltenango, Guatemala
54 G 12 Jacareacanga, Brazil
58 L 7 Jacareí, Brazil
56 H 9 Jáchal, Argentina
54 D 13 Jaciparaná, Brazil
15 P 3 Jackman, ME, U.S.A.
27 O 5 Jacksboro, TX, U.S.A.
16 C 9 Jackson, TN, U.S.A.
18 L 5 Jackson, MS, U.S.A.
19 O 6 Jackson, AL, U.S.A.
19 T 3 Jackson, GA, U.S.A.
21 K 15 Jackson, MI, U.S.A.
21 N 20 Jackson, OH, U.S.A.
29 R 11 Jackson, WY, U.S.A.
33 H 19 Jackson, CA, U.S.A.
137 C 21 Jackson Bay, New Zealand
137 C 21 Jackson Bay, New Zealand
29 R 10 Jackson Lake, WY, U.S.A.
137 G 19 Jacksons, New Zealand
17 T 11 Jacksonville, NC, U.S.A.
19 W 7 Jacksonville, FL, U.S.A.
21 E 19 Jacksonville, IL, U.S.A.
25 V 11 Jacksonville, AR, U.S.A.
27 S 7 Jacksonville, TX, U.S.A.
19 W 7 Jacksonville Beach, FL, U.S.A.
49 P 8 Jacmel, Haiti
47 P 13 Jacó, Costa Rica
101 U 12 Jacobabad, Pakistan
54 J 11 Jacunda, Brazil
58 J 8 Jacupiranga, Brazil
72 E 10 Jadebusen, Germany
99 V 12 Jādib, Yemen
67 P 6 Jadraque, Spain
52 B 12 Jaén, Peru
67 O 11 Jaén, Spain
105 F 23 Jaffna, Sri Lanka
14 M 9 Jaffrey, NH, U.S.A.
105 H 17 Jagdalpur, India
110 I 6 Jagdaqi, China
97 O 1 Jāghir Bāzār, Syria
80 M 12 Jagodina, Serbia and Montenegro
106 H 6 Jagraon, India
105 F 17 Jagtial, India
59 G 14 Jaguarão, Brazil
59 G 14 Jaguarão, Uruguay
56 H 8 Jagüé, Argentina
48 H 4 Jagüey Grande, Cuba
107 P 11 Jahanabad, India
100 J 11 Jahrom, Iran
54 M 12 Jaicós, Brazil
107 W 11 Jaintiapur, Bangladesh
104 D 12 Jaipur, India
104 B 12 Jaisalmer, India
107 N 8 Jajarkot, Nepal
80 G 11 Jajce, Bosnia and Herzegovina
107 U 9 Jakar, Bhutan
116 H 13 Jakarta, Indonesia
116 H 13 Jakarta Raya, Indonesia
39 B 14 Jakes Corner, YT, Canada
101 P 13 Jakkī, Iran
70 H 11 Jäkkvik, Sweden
71 K 15 Jakobstad, Finland
110 E 7 Jalai Nur, China
99 Q 5 Jalājil, Saudi Arabia
103 T 11 Jalal-Abad, Kyrgyzstan
101 V 7 Jalālābād, Afghanistan
106 I 6 Jalandhar, India
46 I 6 Jalapa, Guatemala
47 N 7 Jalapa, Nicaragua
45 T 12 Jalapa Enríquez, Mexico
106 K 11 Jalaun, India
97 U 5 Jalawlā, Iraq
58 I 4 Jales, Brazil
107 R 15 Jaleshwar, India
105 D 16 Jalgaon, India
97 X 11 Jalībah, Iraq
129 T 12 Jalingo, Nigeria
44 M 11 Jalisco, Mexico
105 D 17 Jalna, India
104 C 13 Jalor, India
45 O 10 Jalostotitlån, Mexico
45 O 10 Jalpa, Mexico
107 S 10 Jalpaiguri, India
125 X 9 Jālū, Libya
141 Y 4 Jaluit, Marshall Islands
127 K 25 Jamaame, Somalia
48 K 8 Jamaica, North America
48 L 7 Jamaica Channel, Jamaica
107 U 12 Jamalpur, Bangladesh
116 F 9 Jamaluang, Malaysia
116 F 11 Jambi, Indonesia
116 E 11 Jambi, Indonesia
119 W 4 Jambongan, Malaysia
22 M 5 James, ND/SD, U.S.A.
37 T 10 James Bay, NU, Canada
144 H 3 James Ross Island, Antarctica
14 C 10 Jamestown, NY, U.S.A.
22 M 5 Jamestown, ND, U.S.A.
106 H 4 Jammu, India
106 I 3 Jammu and Kashmir, India/Pakistan
105 A 15 Jamnagar, India
69 J 25 Jamoigne, Belgium
101 V 11 Jampur, Pakistan
71 L 17 Jämsä, Finland
105 J 15 Jamshedpur, India
129 T 12 Jamtari, Nigeria
107 Q 12 Jamui, India
107 T 12 Jamuna, Bangladesh
143 R 13 Jan Mayen, Norway
107 Q 10 Janakpur, Nepal
55 L 16 Janaúba, Brazil
101 W 8 Jand, Pakistan
100 K 7 Jandaq, Iran
95 U 7 Jandari, Georgia
21 F 14 Janesville, WI, U.S.A.
116 M 12 Jangeru, Indonesia
107 R 12 Jangipur, India
103 S 11 Jangy-Bazar, Kyrgyzstan
44 K 3 Janos, Mexico
79 N 15 Janów Lubelski, Poland
78 N 12 Janów Podlaski, Poland
55 L 16 Januária, Brazil
122 I 11 Japan, Asia
72 E 7 Japsand, Germany
54 B 10 Japurá, Brazil
107 X 11 Japvo Mount, India
47 Z 15 Jaqué, Panama
96 K 1 Jarābulus, Syria
58 J 9 Jaraguá do Sul, Brazil
66 L 8 Jaraicejo, Spain
96 H 9 Jarash, Jordan
55 G 18 Jardim, Brazil
54 H 9 Jari, Brazil
107 R 13 Jarkhand, India
78 G 13 Jarocin, Poland
79 N 17 Jarosław, Poland
105 I 15 Jashpurnagar, India
85 G 16 Jâšiūnai, Lithuania
100 M 14 Jāsk, Iran
79 M 18 Jasło, Poland
144 I 4 Jason Peninsula, Antarctica
19 P 3 Jasper, AL, U.S.A.
19 S 2 Jasper, GA, U.S.A.
19 U 7 Jasper, FL, U.S.A.
21 I 21 Jasper, IN, U.S.A.
25 U 9 Jasper, AR, U.S.A.
27 U 8 Jasper, TX, U.S.A.
39 H 19 Jasper, AB, Canada
97 W 7 Jaşşān, Iraq
78 G 10 Jastrowie, Poland
79 I 18 Jastrzębie-Zdrój, Poland
79 K 23 Jászberény, Hungary
55 I 17 Jataí, Brazil
54 F 9 Jatapu, Brazil
101 U 15 Jati, Pakistan
58 J 6 Jaú, Brazil
53 D 16 Jauja, Peru
84 G 12 Jaunjelgava, Latvia
84 H 10 Jaunpiebalga, Latvia
84 D 11 Jaunpils, Latvia
107 N 11 Jaunpur, India
116 H 15 Java, Indonesia
116 I 13 Java Sea, Indonesia
101 R 7 Javand, Afghanistan
109 S 3 Javarthushuu, Mongolia
79 E 19 Javořice, Czech Republic
79 H 19 Javorníky, Slovakia
116 G 14 Jawa Barat, Indonesia
116 I 14 Jawa Tengah, Indonesia
116 K 15 Jawa Timur, Indonesia
127 M 24 Jawhar, Somalia
52 B 13 Jayanca, Peru
117 Y 12 Jayapura, Indonesia
107 Q 10 Jaynagar, India
105 H 17 Jaypur, India
96 I 6 Jayrūd, Syria
99 N 11 Jazā'ir Farasān, Saudi Arabia

Country · Internal administrative region: State/Province/Territory/Dependent territory · Capital city · Mountain range/Undersea ridge · Mountain peak/Volcano/Seamount · Geographic feature · Headland/Point/Cape/Peninsula · Desert · Island/Island group · Antarctic base · Ocean · Sea · Bay/Gulf/Channel/Strait · Lake · Salt pan/Dry/Intermittent lake · River

117	U 11	**Jazirah Doberai**, Indonesia ▶
99	Z 8	**Jazirat Maşīrah**, Oman ⛱
97	N 3	**Jazrah**, Syria
96	G 5	**Jbail**, Lebanon
124	J 7	**Jbel Bou Naceur**, Morocco ▲
124	F 10	**Jdiriya**, Western Sahara
96	J 2	**Jebal Aḩaş**, Syria ⛰
129	P 12	**Jebba**, Nigeria
86	E 10	**Jebel**, Romania
127	C 15	**Jebel Abyad Plateau**, Sudan ◇
125	P 6	**Jebel Chambi**, Tunisia ▲
96	G 6	**Jebel Libnan**, Lebanon ⛰
127	B 18	**Jebel Marra**, Sudan ▲
127	H 14	**Jebel Oda**, Sudan ▲
127	B 17	**Jebel Teljo**, Sudan ▲
127	B 13	**Jebel Uweinat**, Sudan ▲
101	S 13	**Jebri**, Pakistan
98	L 8	**Jeddah**, Saudi Arabia
79	K 16	**Jędrzejów**, Poland
23	R 12	**Jefferson**, IA, U.S.A.
25	V 4	**Jefferson City**, MO, U.S.A.
29	U 12	**Jeffrey City**, WY, U.S.A.
132	M 15	**Jeffrey's Bay**, Republic of South Africa
129	P 10	**Jega**, Nigeria
84	H 12	**Jēkabpils**, Latvia
127	K 20	**Jeldēsa**, Ethiopia
79	E 15	**Jelenia Góra**, Poland
84	E 11	**Jelgava**, Latvia
118	C 5	**Jeli**, Malaysia
40	L 11	**Jellicoe**, ON, Canada
136	K 7	**Jellicoe Channel**, New Zealand ≈
116	G 9	**Jemaja**, Indonesia ⛱
116	K 15	**Jember**, Indonesia
69	G 21	**Jemeppe**, Belgium
103	Z 6	**Jeminay**, Kazakhstan
18	J 6	**Jena**, LA, U.S.A.
73	J 17	**Jena**, Germany
125	P 5	**Jendouba**, Tunisia
103	Y 10	**Jengish Chokusu**, Kyrgyzstan ▲
95	Y 9	**Jenikand**, Azerbaijan
96	G 8	**Jenin**, Israel
16	L 6	**Jenkins**, KY, U.S.A.
39	K 20	**Jenner**, AB, Canada
18	I 8	**Jennings**, LA, U.S.A.
30	M 3	**Jensen**, UT, U.S.A.
116	I 13	**Jepara**, Indonesia
55	M 15	**Jequié**, Brazil
127	E 22	**Jerbar**, Sudan
49	N 7	**Jérémie**, Haiti
45	O 9	**Jerez**, Mexico
66	K 13	**Jerez de la Frontera**, Spain
66	J 10	**Jerez de los Caballeros**, Spain
81	L 21	**Jergucat**, Albania
96	G 9	**Jericho**, Israel
135	T 6	**Jericho**, QLD, Australia
135	S 12	**Jerilderie**, NSW, Australia
134	H 12	**Jerramungup**, WA, Australia
101	U 14	**Jerruck**, Pakistan
61	J 26	**Jersey**, U.K. ▣
14	J 13	**Jersey City**, NJ, U.S.A.
21	E 20	**Jerseyville**, IL, U.S.A.
96	G 9	**Jerusalem**, Israel ⌂
76	I 11	**Jesi**, Italy
107	T 13	**Jessore**, Bangladesh
19	W 5	**Jesup**, GA, U.S.A.
56	J 10	**Jesús María**, Argentina
24	J 5	**Jetmore**, KS, U.S.A.
72	E 10	**Jever**, Germany
78	J 9	**Jezioro Jeziorak**, Poland ◣
78	G 7	**Jezioro Łebsko**, Poland ◣
78	L 9	**Jezioro Mamry**, Poland ◣
78	L 9	**Jezioro Sniardwy**, Poland ◣
78	J 12	**Jezioro Włocławskie**, Poland ◣
78	L 12	**Jezioro Zegrzyńskie**, Poland ◣
96	G 7	**Jezzine**, Lebanon
105	D 15	**Jhabua**, India
101	T 12	**Jhal**, Pakistan
101	R 14	**Jhal Jhao**, Pakistan
101	X 9	**Jhang**, Pakistan
104	F 13	**Jhansi**, India
105	I 15	**Jharkhand**, India ▣
105	I 15	**Jharsuguda**, India
101	U 12	**Jhatpat**, Pakistan
101	X 8	**Jhelum**, Pakistan
107	T 13	**Jhenida**, Bangladesh
101	V 14	**Jhudo**, Pakistan
55	E 14	**Ji-Paraná**, Brazil
111	E 17	**Ji Xian**, China
113	T 10	**Jiahe**, China
113	O 5	**Jialing**, China ∫
110	M 10	**Jiamusi**, China
111	K 15	**Ji'an**, China
113	U 9	**Ji'an**, China
112	J 9	**Jianchuan**, China
113	X 7	**Jiande**, China
113	O 5	**Jiange**, China
113	S 11	**Jianghua**, China
113	W 9	**Jiangle**, China
113	T 12	**Jiangmen**, China
113	X 4	**Jiangsu**, China ▣
113	V 9	**Jiangxi**, China ▣
113	Y 5	**Jiangyin**, China
113	N 5	**Jiangyou**, China
113	X 4	**Jianhu**, China
113	T 7	**Jianli**, China
113	W 9	**Jianning**, China
113	X 9	**Jian'ou**, China
113	R 6	**Jianshi**, China
112	L 12	**Jianshui**, China
113	N 6	**Jianyang**, China
113	X 9	**Jianyang**, China
113	S 1	**Jiaocheng**, China
110	L 13	**Jiaohe**, China
111	D 19	**Jiaohe**, China
113	S 1	**Jiaokou**, China
113	V 11	**Jiaoling**, China
111	G 21	**Jiaonan**, China
113	X 2	**Jiaonan**, China
111	F 20	**Jiaozhou**, China
113	T 3	**Jiaozuo**, China
112	K 11	**Jiasa**, China
113	W 5	**Jiashan**, China
113	W 3	**Jiawang**, China
113	Y 6	**Jiaxing**, China
110	M 8	**Jiayin**, China
109	O 6	**Jiayuguan**, China
113	V 12	**Jiazi**, China
86	H 8	**Jibou**, Romania
99	X 10	**Jiddat al Ḩarāsīs**, Oman ◇
113	U 4	**Jieshou**, China
113	S 1	**Jiexiu**, China
113	W 12	**Jieyang**, China
85	F 16	**Jieznas**, Lithuania
129	S 10	**Jigawa**, Nigeria ▣
112	L 4	**Jigzhi**, China
79	E 19	**Jihlava**, Czech Republic
125	O 5	**Jijel**, Algeria
127	K 20	**Jijiga**, Ethiopia
127	K 25	**Jilib**, Somalia
110	K 13	**Jilin**, China
110	L 13	**Jilin**, China ▣
127	H 21	**Jīma**, Ethiopia
86	E 10	**Jimbolia**, Romania
45	N 6	**Jiménez**, Mexico
121	K 20	**Jimenez**, Philippines
111	G 20	**Jimo**, China
113	V 2	**Jinan**, China
113	Q 11	**Jinchai**, China
109	P 7	**Jinchang**, China
113	T 3	**Jincheng**, China
112	L 5	**Jinchuan**, China
106	I 8	**Jind**, India
135	T 13	**Jindabyne**, NSW, Australia
79	D 19	**Jindřichův Hradec**, Czech Republic
113	R 5	**Jing Shan**, China ⛰
113	P 3	**Jingchuan**, China
113	X 6	**Jingde**, China
113	W 7	**Jingdezhen**, China
112	J 12	**Jinggu**, China
111	D 18	**Jinghai**, China
113	W 12	**Jinghai**, China
108	J 4	**Jinghe**, China
112	K 13	**Jinghong**, China
113	T 6	**Jingmen**, China
113	O 3	**Jingning**, China
110	E 13	**Jingpeng**, China
110	M 13	**Jingpo**, China
110	M 12	**Jingpo Hu**, China ◣
113	S 7	**Jingsha**, China
109	Q 8	**Jingtai**, China
113	O 12	**Jingxi**, China
113	X 6	**Jingxian**, China
111	K 14	**Jingyu**, China
109	Q 8	**Jingyuan**, China
113	T 6	**Jingzhou**, China
113	Q 9	**Jingzhou**, China
110	H 6	**Jinhe**, China
113	X 7	**Jinhua**, China
111	B 15	**Jining**, China
113	V 3	**Jining**, China
131	S 7	**Jinja**, Uganda
112	K 10	**Jinjiang**, China
113	X 11	**Jinjiang**, China
127	H 22	**Jinka**, Ethiopia
112	L 7	**Jinkouhe**, China
47	N 8	**Jinotega**, Nicaragua
47	N 10	**Jinotepe**, Nicaragua
113	O 9	**Jinsha**, China
111	F 15	**Jinshan**, China
113	Z 6	**Jinshan**, China
113	S 7	**Jinshi**, China
113	N 6	**Jintang**, China
121	J 15	**Jintotolo**, Philippines ⛱
113	W 8	**Jinxi**, China
113	V 3	**Jinxiang**, China
111	H 16	**Jinzhou**, China
111	I 17	**Jinzhou**, China
52	A 9	**Jipijapa**, Ecuador
110	E 12	**Jirin Gol**, China
100	M 11	**Jīroft**, Iran
127	N 21	**Jirriiban**, Somalia
113	Q 8	**Jishou**, China
96	H 2	**Jisr Ash Shughūr**, Syria
118	A 5	**Jitra**, Malaysia
86	H 12	**Jiu**, Romania ∫
113	S 10	**Jiucai Ling**, China ▲
113	V 7	**Jiujiang**, China
113	U 8	**Jiuling Shan**, China ⛰
112	L 7	**Jiulong**, China
109	O 7	**Jiuquan**, China
113	Q 15	**Jiusuo**, China
110	K 12	**Jiutai**, China
113	O 11	**Jiuzhou**, China
101	P 14	**Jiwani**, Pakistan
110	I 6	**Jiwen**, China
110	N 11	**Jixi**, China
113	X 7	**Jixi**, China
110	N 10	**Jixian**, China
113	R 2	**Jixian**, China
99	O 11	**Jīzān**, Saudi Arabia
123	E 18	**Jizō-zaki**, Japan ▶
103	Q 12	**Jizzakh Wiloyati**, Uzbekistan ▣
58	H 10	**Joaçaba**, Brazil
54	O 12	**João Pessoa**, Brazil
55	K 17	**João Pinheiro**, Brazil
56	J 6	**Joaquín V. González**, Argentina
121	N 20	**Jobo Point**, Philippines ▶
104	C 12	**Jodhpur**, India
71	O 16	**Joensuu**, Finland
31	U 4	**Joes**, CO, U.S.A.
123	I 14	**Jōetsu**, Japan
133	R 8	**Jofane**, Mozambique
107	R 10	**Jogbani**, India
106	L 8	**Jogbura**, Nepal
84	H 7	**Jõgeva**, Estonia
84	I 6	**Jõgua**, Estonia
33	K 23	**Johannesburg**, CA, U.S.A.
133	O 11	**Johannesburg**, Republic of South Africa
32	J 11	**John Day**, OR, U.S.A.
17	S 8	**John H. Kerr Reservoir**, NC, U.S.A. ◣
31	U 6	**John Martin Reservoir**, CO, U.S.A. ◣
60	I 8	**John o'Groats**, U.K.
24	G 6	**Johnson**, KS, U.S.A.
16	M 8	**Johnson City**, TN, U.S.A.
27	O 9	**Johnson City**, TX, U.S.A.
118	E 10	**Johor**, Malaysia ∫
118	E 9	**Johor**, Malaysia ▣
118	E 10	**Johor Bahru**, Malaysia
84	I 6	**Jõhvi**, Estonia
58	J 9	**Joinville**, Brazil
65	T 5	**Joinville**, France
144	H 2	**Joinville Island**, Antarctica ⛱
70	I 11	**Jokkmokk**, Sweden
70	B 9	**Jökulbunga**, Iceland ▲
100	F 3	**Jolfa**, Iran
21	G 16	**Joliet**, IL, U.S.A.
42	L 10	**Joliette**, QC, Canada
121	G 24	**Jolo**, Philippines
121	G 24	**Jolo**, Philippines ⛱
120	I 11	**Jomalig**, Philippines ⛱
107	O 8	**Jomsom**, Nepal
46	K 3	**Jonathán Point**, Belize ▶
85	F 15	**Jonava**, Lithuania
37	P 3	**Jones Sound**, NU, Canada ≈
18	I 5	**Jonesboro**, LA, U.S.A.
19	S 3	**Jonesboro**, GA, U.S.A.
25	X 9	**Jonesboro**, AR, U.S.A.
17	N 11	**Jonesville**, SC, U.S.A.
18	J 6	**Jonesville**, LA, U.S.A.
127	E 21	**Jonglei**, Sudan
127	F 21	**Jonglei**, Sudan ▣
84	E 12	**Joniškis**, Lithuania
71	F 22	**Jönköping**, Sweden
43	N 6	**Jonquière**, QC, Canada
25	R 7	**Joplin**, MO, U.S.A.
104	E 12	**Jora**, India
29	V 4	**Jordan**, MT, U.S.A.
96	H 11	**Jordan**, Asia □
96	G 9	**Jordan**, Israel ∫
32	L 13	**Jordan Valley**, OR, U.S.A.
107	X 10	**Jorhat**, India
47	U 15	**Jorones**, Panama
129	S 11	**Jos**, Nigeria
53	J 17	**José Agustín Palacios**, Bolivia
57	G 18	**José de San Martin**, Argentina
120	I 12	**José Pañganiban**, Philippines
59	G 15	**José Pedro Varela**, Uruguay
134	L 2	**Joseph Bonaparte Gulf**, WA, Australia ≈
138	C 4	**Josephstaal**, Papua New Guinea
96	G 7	**Jouaiya**, Lebanon
133	N 11	**Jouberton**, Republic of South Africa
68	K 8	**Joure**, Netherlands
70	M 11	**Joutsijärvi**, Finland
107	W 11	**Jowai**, India
101	S 5	**Jowzjān**, Afghanistan ▣
32	F 6	**Joyce**, WA, U.S.A.
128	E 6	**Jreïda**, Mauritania
32	E 5	**Juan de Fuca Strait**, WA, U.S.A. ≈
133	V 6	**Juan de Nova**, France ⛱
10	G 12	**Juan Fernández Islands**, Chile ▣
52	D 13	**Juanjuí**, Peru
54	M 13	**Juàzeiro**, Brazil
54	N 12	**Juázeiro do Norte**, Brazil
128	I 13	**Juazohn**, Liberia
127	E 23	**Juba**, Sudan
127	K 24	**Juba**, Somalia ∫
127	K 25	**Jubbada Dhexe**, Somalia ▣
127	K 26	**Jubbada Hoose**, Somalia ▣
134	K 9	**Jubilee Lake**, WA, Australia ◣
107	R 9	**Jubing**, Nepal
67	Q 8	**Júcar**, Spain ∫
45	U 14	**Juchitán**, Mexico
45	N 11	**Juchitlán**, Mexico
97	P 10	**Judaidat al Hamir**, Iraq
75	U 7	**Judenburg**, Austria
112	J 9	**Judian**, China
47	O 9	**Juigalpa**, Nicaragua
55	F 14	**Juína**, Brazil
72	C 10	**Juist**, Germany ⛱
58	N 6	**Juiz de Fora**, Brazil
56	I 5	**Jujuy**, Argentina ▣
53	I 22	**Julaca**, Bolivia
119	P 10	**Julau**, Malaysia
53	H 19	**Juli**, Peru
135	R 5	**Julia Creek**, QLD, Australia
53	H 19	**Juliaca**, Peru
80	A 6	**Julian Alps**, Slovenia ⛰
51	W 7	**Juliana Top**, Suriname ▲
68	H 8	**Julianadorp**, Netherlands
73	B 17	**Jülich**, Germany
67	S 10	**Jumilla**, Spain
107	N 8	**Jumla**, Nepal
110	F 11	**Jun Bulen**, China
105	A 15	**Junagadh**, India
105	H 17	**Junagarh**, India
113	X 3	**Junan**, China
26	M 9	**Junction**, TX, U.S.A.
30	J 6	**Junction**, UT, U.S.A.
18	I 4	**Junction City**, LA, U.S.A.
25	O 4	**Junction City**, KS, U.S.A.
32	F 11	**Junction City**, OR, U.S.A.
135	R 7	**Jundah**, QLD, Australia
58	K 7	**Jundiaí**, Brazil
35	X 10	**Juneau**, AK, U.S.A.
74	F 9	**Jungfrau**, Switzerland ▲
108	K 4	**Junggar Desert**, China ◇
53	D 16	**Junín**, Peru ▣
59	B 16	**Junín**, Argentina
113	N 8	**Junlian**, China
71	H 15	**Junsele**, Sweden
32	K 12	**Juntura**, OR, U.S.A.
85	G 16	**Juozapinės kalnas**, Lithuania ▲
58	K 8	**Juquiá**, Brazil
58	K 8	**Juquiá**, Brazil ∫
60	F 12	**Jura**, U.K. ⛱
65	U 9	**Jura**, France/Switzerland ⛰
50	F 5	**Juradó**, Colombia
85	D 15	**Jurbarkas**, Lithuania
96	G 11	**Jurf ad Darāwīsh**, Jordan
110	G 12	**Jurh**, China
134	F 10	**Jurien**, WA, Australia
87	N 12	**Jurilovca**, Romania
84	E 11	**Jūrmala**, Latvia
118	A 14	**Jurong**, Singapore
118	A 14	**Jurong Island**, Singapore ⛱
54	C 11	**Juruá**, Brazil
54	C 11	**Juruá**, Brazil ∫
54	F 13	**Juruena**, Brazil ∫
110	F 11	**Jus Hua**, China
56	I 12	**Justo Daract**, Argentina
54	C 10	**Jutaí**, Brazil
54	C 11	**Jutaí**, Brazil ∫
73	L 14	**Jüterbog**, Germany
58	F 6	**Juti**, Brazil
46	I 6	**Jutiapa**, Guatemala
47	N 4	**Jutiapa**, Honduras
47	N 6	**Juticalpa**, Honduras
71	N 17	**Juva**, Finland
101	P 9	**Juwain**, Afghanistan
113	X 2	**Juxian**, China
113	V 3	**Juye**, China
100	J 12	**Jūyom**, Iran
71	C 24	**Jylland**, Denmark ◇
71	M 16	**Jyväskylä**, Finland

K

101	Z 5	**K2**, Pakistan ▲
34	E 9	**Ka Lae**, HI, U.S.A. ▶
70	L 8	**Kaamanen**, Finland
127	K 26	**Kaambooni**, Somalia
131	Y 9	**Kaambooni**, Kenya
117	O 13	**Kabaena**, Indonesia ⛱
103	N 12	**Kabakly**, Turkmenistan
128	G 11	**Kabala**, Sierra Leone
131	Q 8	**Kabale**, Uganda
131	O 11	**Kabalo**, Democratic Republic of Congo
131	P 10	**Kabambare**, Democratic Republic of Congo
116	C 9	**Kabanjahe**, Indonesia
121	I 18	**Kabankalan**, Philippines
139	Y 12	**Kabara**, Fiji ⛱
93	O 14	**Kabardino Balkarskaya Respublika**, Russian Federation ▣
131	P 9	**Kabare**, Democratic Republic of Congo
121	I 21	**Kabasalan**, Philippines
70	I 12	**Kåbdalis**, Sweden
115	I 19	**Kabin Buri**, Thailand
42	B 5	**Kabinakagami Lake**, ON, Canada ◣
131	N 11	**Kabinda**, Democratic Republic of Congo
123	M 26	**Kabira**, Japan
119	O 10	**Kabong**, Malaysia
131	N 12	**Kabongo**, Democratic Republic of Congo
115	F 20	**Kabosa Island**, Myanmar ⛱
101	O 5	**Kabūd Gonbad**, Iran
100	G 6	**Kabūd Rāhang**, Iran
101	U 7	**Kābul**, Afghanistan ▣
101	U 7	**Kabul**, Afghanistan ⌂
131	Q 15	**Kabunda**, Democratic Republic of Congo
117	R 9	**Kaburuang**, Indonesia ⛱
127	F 16	**Kabushiya**, Sudan
133	O 5	**Kabwe**, Zambia
81	M 16	**Kačanik**, Serbia and Montenegro
129	R 11	**Kachia**, Nigeria
114	E 8	**Kachin**, Myanmar ▣
103	U 2	**Kachiry**, Kazakhstan
133	P 5	**Kacholola**, Zambia
89	Q 13	**Kachug**, Russian Federation
115	F 20	**Kadan Kyun**, Myanmar ⛱
139	W 12	**Kadavu**, Fiji ⛱
139	W 12	**Kadavu Passage**, Fiji ≈
97	T 7	**Kādhimain**, Iraq
94	D 7	**Kadiköy**, Turkey
94	G 11	**Kadinhani**, Turkey
128	J 11	**Kadiolo**, Mali
105	E 20	**Kadiri**, India
94	L 12	**Kadirli**, Turkey
105	B 22	**Kadmat**, India ⛱
22	I 10	**Kadoka**, SD, U.S.A.
133	P 7	**Kadoma**, Zimbabwe
127	D 19	**Kadugli**, Sudan
129	R 11	**Kaduna**, Nigeria
129	R 11	**Kaduna**, Nigeria ▣
90	I 11	**Kaduy**, Russian Federation
95	V 10	**Kadžaran**, Armenia
128	F 7	**Kaédi**, Mauritania
129	V 11	**Kaélé**, Cameroon
136	J 5	**Kaeo**, New Zealand
111	K 18	**Kaesŏng**, North Korea
98	K 1	**Kāf**, Saudi Arabia
130	M 13	**Kafakumba**, Democratic Republic of Congo
128	E 9	**Kaffrine**, Senegal
127	A 20	**Kafia Kingi**, Sudan
133	O 5	**Kafue**, Zambia
123	H 16	**Kaga**, Japan
130	K 3	**Kaga Bandoro**, Central African Republic
101	X 7	**Kagan**, Pakistan
103	O 13	**Kagan**, Uzbekistan
131	R 9	**Kagera**, Tanzania ▣
95	S 9	**Kağizman**, Turkey
127	E 17	**Kagmar**, Sudan
123	C 24	**Kagoshima**, Japan
100	M 5	**Kāhak**, Iran
131	S 10	**Kahama**, Tanzania
87	Q 4	**Kaharlyk**, Ukraine
130	J 12	**Kahemba**, Democratic Republic of Congo
100	M 12	**Kahnūj**, Iran
128	I 14	**Kahnwia**, Liberia
136	I 5	**Kahoe**, New Zealand
25	V 1	**Kahoka**, MO, U.S.A.
34	C 8	**Kahoolawe**, HI, U.S.A. ⛱
94	L 12	**Kahramanmaraş**, Turkey
95	N 12	**Kahta**, Turkey
117	U 13	**Kai Besar**, Indonesia ⛱
117	U 13	**Kai Kecil**, Indonesia ⛱
129	P 11	**Kaiama**, Nigeria
137	H 20	**Kaiapoi**, New Zealand
30	K 8	**Kaibito**, AZ, U.S.A.
113	T 3	**Kaifeng**, China
136	J 6	**Kaikohe**, New Zealand
137	I 18	**Kaikoura**, New Zealand
137	I 18	**Kaikoura Peninsula**, New Zealand ▶
113	P 9	**Kaili**, China
110	H 13	**Kailu**, China
34	D 7	**Kailua**, HI, U.S.A.
117	V 12	**Kaimana**, Indonesia
84	D 7	**Käina**, Estonia
123	F 20	**Kainan**, Japan
138	D 5	**Kainantu**, Papua New Guinea
75	X 7	**Kaindorf**, Austria
129	P 11	**Kainji Reservoir**, Nigeria ◣
70	K 10	**Kainulasjärvi**, Sweden
136	I 7	**Kaipara Harbour**, New Zealand ≈
113	S 13	**Kaiping**, China
137	N 14	**Kairakau Beach**, New Zealand
138	B 3	**Kairiru**, Papua New Guinea ⛱
125	Q 6	**Kairouan**, Tunisia
138	D 6	**Kairuku**, Papua New Guinea
145	W 7	**Kaiser Wilhelm II Land**, Antarctica ◇
73	D 21	**Kaiserslautern**, Germany
85	F 15	**Kaišiadorys**, Lithuania
137	E 25	**Kaitangata**, New Zealand
70	I 10	**Kaitumälven**, Sweden ∫
34	C 7	**Kaiwi Channel**, HI, U.S.A. ≈
113	Q 6	**Kaixian**, China
111	J 14	**Kaiyuan**, China
112	M 11	**Kaiyuan**, China
71	M 14	**Kajaani**, Finland
135	Q 5	**Kajabbi**, QLD, Australia
101	R 9	**Kajaki**, Afghanistan
118	C 8	**Kajang**, Malaysia
129	R 11	**Kajuru**, Nigeria
127	E 19	**Kaka**, Sudan
137	E 25	**Kaka Point**, New Zealand
117	P 14	**Kakabia**, Indonesia ⛱
121	K 23	**Kakal**, Philippines ∫
132	K 12	**Kakamas**, Republic of South Africa
131	T 7	**Kakamega**, Kenya
105	N 23	**Kakana**, India
136	K 13	**Kakaramea**, New Zealand
128	H 13	**Kakata**, Liberia
136	K 13	**Kakatahi**, New Zealand
107	X 12	**Kakching**, India
123	D 19	**Kake**, Japan
130	L 10	**Kakenge**, Democratic Republic of Congo
87	T 9	**Kakhovka Tavriys'k**, Ukraine
87	T 8	**Kakhovs'ke Vodoskhovyshche**, Ukraine ◣
100	I 11	**Kākī**, Iran
105	H 18	**Kakinada**, India
128	K 12	**Kakpin**, Côte d'Ivoire
35	S 3	**Kaktovik**, AK, U.S.A.
122	K 12	**Kakuda**, Japan
119	Q 9	**Kakus**, Malaysia ∫
101	O 8	**Kāl-e Namakasār**, Afghanistan ◣
131	R 12	**Kala**, Tanzania
101	V 8	**Kalabagh**, Pakistan
117	Q 15	**Kalabahi**, Indonesia
119	W 7	**Kalabakan**, Malaysia
132	L 5	**Kalabo**, Zambia
92	M 7	**Kalach**, Russian Federation
93	O 8	**Kalach-na-Donu**, Russian Federation
42	H 12	**Kaladar**, ON, Canada
132	K 9	**Kalahari Desert**, Botswana ◇
71	L 14	**Kalajoki**, Finland ∫
71	K 14	**Kalajoki**, Finland
129	P 11	**Kalalé**, Benin
101	W 6	**Kalam**, Pakistan
83	F 14	**Kalamaria**, Greece
83	D 22	**Kalamata**, Greece
21	J 15	**Kalamazoo**, MI, U.S.A.
105	E 17	**Kalamnuri**, India
83	B 18	**Kalamos**, Greece ⛱
83	D 16	**Kalampaka**, Greece
87	T 12	**Kalamyts'ka Zatoka**, Ukraine ≈
128	I 10	**Kalana**, Mali
87	S 10	**Kalanchak**, Ukraine
131	T 11	**Kalangali**, Tanzania
117	O 14	**Kalao**, Indonesia ⛱
117	O 14	**Kalaotoa**, Indonesia ⛱
97	V 5	**Kalār**, Iraq
115	K 16	**Kalasin**, Thailand
101	T 11	**Kalat**, Pakistan
121	K 21	**Kalatungan Mountains**, Philippines ⛰
83	D 20	**Kalavryta**, Greece
134	F 9	**Kalbarri**, WA, Australia
94	I 9	**Kalecik**, Turkey
117	Q 13	**Kaledupa**, Indonesia ⛱
131	N 10	**Kalema**, Democratic Republic of Congo
131	Q 11	**Kalémié**, Democratic Republic of Congo
114	C 10	**Kalemyo**, Myanmar
90	G 5	**Kalevala**, Russian Federation
114	C 10	**Kalewa**, Myanmar
93	X 2	**Kalga**, Russian Federation
134	I 10	**Kalgoorlie**, WA, Australia
121	H 15	**Kalibo**, Philippines
131	O 9	**Kalima**, Democratic Republic of Congo
116	I 11	**Kalimantan Barat**, Indonesia ▣
116	M 12	**Kalimantan Selatan**, Indonesia ▣
116	J 12	**Kalimantan Tengah**, Indonesia ▣
116	L 10	**Kalimantan Timur**, Indonesia ▣
107	S 10	**Kalimpang**, India
105	I 16	**Kalinga**, India
85	B 15	**Kaliningrad**, Russian Federation
85	B 15	**Kaliningradskaya Oblast'**, Russian Federation ▣
103	R 14	**Kalininobod**, Tajikistan
93	O 5	**Kalininsk**, Russian Federation
85	L 21	**Kalinkavichy**, Belarus
28	M 3	**Kalispell**, MT, U.S.A.
79	H 14	**Kalisz**, Poland
78	F 10	**Kalisz Pomorski**, Poland
131	R 11	**Kaliua**, Tanzania
94	D 13	**Kalkan**, Turkey
134	M 4	**Kalkarindji**, NT, Australia
20	J 11	**Kalkaska**, MI, U.S.A.
132	I 8	**Kalkfeld**, Namibia
71	F 15	**Kallsjön**, Sweden ◣
71	G 24	**Kalmar**, Sweden
84	F 11	**Kalnciems**, Latvia
79	I 25	**Kalocsa**, Hungary
133	N 6	**Kalomo**, Zambia
114	D 9	**Kalon**, Myanmar
106	K 6	**Kalpa**, India
105	C 23	**Kalpeni**, India ⛱
106	L 11	**Kalpi**, India
129	S 9	**Kalrguéri**, Niger
85	H 14	**Kaltanėnai**, Lithuania
92	J 2	**Kaluga**, Russian Federation
134	K 2	**Kalumburu**, WA, Australia
71	D 25	**Kalundborg**, Denmark
86	I 5	**Kalush**, Ukraine
105	F 25	**Kalutara**, Sri Lanka
92	I 2	**Kaluzhskaya Oblast'**, Russian Federation ▣
85	E 16	**Kalvarija**, Lithuania
90	I 14	**Kalyazin**, Russian Federation
83	M 22	**Kalymnos**, Greece ⛱
83	M 22	**Kalymnos**, Greece
87	N 5	**Kalynivka**, Ukraine
91	S 10	**Kama**, Russian Federation ∫
115	C 14	**Kama**, Myanmar
131	O 10	**Kama**, Democratic Republic of Congo
122	L 10	**Kamaishi**, Japan
123	J 16	**Kamakura**, Japan
128	G 11	**Kamakwie**, Sierra Leone
94	I 10	**Kaman**, Turkey
132	G 8	**Kamanjab**, Namibia
99	O 12	**Kamarān**, Yemen ⛱
128	G 11	**Kamaron**, Sierra Leone
134	I 10	**Kambalda**, WA, Australia
131	O 14	**Kambove**, Democratic Republic of Congo
89	Y 9	**Kamchatka Peninsula**, Russian Federation ▶
82	K 7	**Kamen**, Bulgaria
88	M 12	**Kamen'-na-Obi**, Russian Federation
131	N 11	**Kamende**, Democratic Republic of Congo
90	M 5	**Kamenka**, Russian Federation
93	O 4	**Kamenka**, Russian Federation
102	H 4	**Kamenka**, Kazakhstan
92	L 13	**Kamennomostskiy**, Russian Federation
92	L 9	**Kamenolomni**, Russian Federation
92	M 8	**Kamensk-Shakhtinskiy**, Russian Federation
88	J 10	**Kamensk-Ural'skiy**, Russian Federation
123	H 18	**Kameyama**, Japan
123	B 23	**Kami-Koshiki-jima**, Japan ⛱
78	D 9	**Kamień Pomorski**, Poland
79	J 15	**Kamieńsk**, Poland
122	K 4	**Kamikawa**, Japan
38	L 11	**Kamilukuak Lake**, NU, Canada ◣
86	K 1	**Kamin'-Kashyrs'kyy**, Ukraine
131	N 13	**Kamina**, Democratic Republic of Congo
123	H 16	**Kamioka**, Japan
123	A 20	**Kamitsushima**, Japan
39	H 21	**Kamloops**, BC, Canada
95	U 8	**Kamo**, Armenia
123	L 16	**Kamogawa**, Japan
131	S 7	**Kampala**, Uganda ⌂
116	E 8	**Kampar**, Malaysia
68	K 10	**Kampen**, Netherlands
131	O 10	**Kampene**, Democratic Republic of Congo
115	G 16	**Kamphaeng Phet**, Thailand
115	M 20	**Kâmpóng Cham**, Cambodia
115	L 20	**Kâmpóng Chhnăng**, Cambodia
115	K 19	**Kâmpóng Khleăng**, Cambodia
115	K 22	**Kâmpóng Saôm**, Cambodia
118	F 10	**Kampong Sedili Kechil**, Malaysia
115	K 21	**Kâmpóng Spoe**, Cambodia
115	L 20	**Kâmpóng Thum**, Cambodia
115	K 22	**Kâmpôt**, Cambodia
128	L 11	**Kampti**, Burkina Faso
118	A 7	**Kampung Koh**, Malaysia
128	E 10	**Kamsar**, Guinea
93	R 1	**Kamskoye Ust'ye**, Russian Federation
91	S 11	**Kamskoye Vodokhanilishche**, Russian Federation ◣
127	K 25	**Kamsuuma**, Somalia
122	L 6	**Kamui-dake**, Japan ▲
122	I 6	**Kamui-misaki**, Japan ▶
131	S 7	**Kamuli**, Uganda
86	M 2	**Kam"yane**, Ukraine
86	L 6	**Kam"yanets'-Podil's'kyy**, Ukraine
87	U 8	**Kam"yanka**, Ukraine
85	E 20	**Kamyanyets**, Belarus
100	F 6	**Kāmyārān**, Iran
85	K 15	**Kamyen'**, Belarus
93	P 7	**Kamyshin**, Russian Federation
103	N 8	**Kamyshlybash**, Kazakhstan
93	R 11	**Kamyzyak**, Russian Federation
114	C 11	**Kan**, Myanmar
30	J 7	**Kanab**, UT, U.S.A.
34	E 14	**Kanaga Island**, AK, U.S.A. ⛱
41	U 8	**Kanairiktoktok**, NL, Canada ∫
83	B 17	**Kanallaki**, Greece
130	L 11	**Kananga**, Democratic Republic of Con[go]
93	Q 1	**Kanash**, Russian Federation
123	H 15	**Kanazawa**, Japan
114	D 10	**Kanbalu**, Myanmar
123	J 17	**Kanbara**, Japan
115	G 19	**Kanchanaburi**, Thailand
105	F 21	**Kanchipuram**, India
101	S 10	**Kandahār**, Afghanistan ▣
101	S 9	**Kandahār**, Afghanistan
90	H 3	**Kandalaksha**, Russian Federation
90	H 4	**Kandalakshskiy Zaliv**, Russian Federation ≈
129	N 11	**Kandé**, Togo
101	V 12	**Kandhkot**, Pakistan
129	O 10	**Kandi**, Benin
101	U 13	**Kandiaro**, Pakistan
83	B 18	**Kandila**, Greece
94	F 7	**Kandira**, Turkey
105	A 14	**Kandla**, India
133	W 7	**Kandreho**, Madgascar
138	F 5	**Kandrian**, Papua New Guinea
105	G 25	**Kandy**, Sri Lanka
102	L 5	**Kandyagash**, Kazakhstan
14	C 11	**Kane**, PA, U.S.A.
129	W 8	**Kanem**, Chad ▣
34	C 7	**Kaneohe**, HI, U.S.A.
84	I 9	**Kanepi**, Estonia
132	L 10	**Kang**, Botswana
121	F 24	**Kang Tipayan Dakula**, Philippines ⛱
142	M 12	**Kangaamiut**, Greenland
128	I 10	**Kangaba**, Mali
94	M 10	**Kangal**, Turkey
100	M 14	**Kangān**, Iran
118	A 4	**Kangar**, Malaysia
135	P 12	**Kangaroo Island**, SA, Australia ⛱
71	M 17	**Kangasniemi**, Finland
107	S 9	**Kangchenjunga**, India/Nepal ▲
112	L 6	**Kangding**, China
111	K 17	**Kangdong**, North Korea
41	S 1	**Kangeeak Point**, NU, Canada ▶
143	N 12	**Kangerlussaq**, Greenland
143	O 11	**Kangersuatsiaq**, Greenland
131	U 6	**Kangetet**, Kenya
111	L 16	**Kanggye**, North Korea
41	T 6	**Kangiqsualujjuaq**, QC, Canada
41	R 4	**Kangiqsujuaq**, QC, Canada
41	R 5	**Kangirsuk**, QC, Canada
111	M 18	**Kangnŭng**, South Korea
130	E 7	**Kango**, Gabon
111	I 14	**Kangping**, China
106	I 5	**Kangra**, India
107	W 9	**Kangto**, India ▲
115	C 16	**Kangyidaung**, Myanmar
114	C 11	**Kani**, Myanmar
128	J 12	**Kani**, Côte d'Ivoire
119	W 4	**Kanibongan**, Malaysia
90	M 2	**Kanin Kamen'**, Russian Federation ◇
90	L 2	**Kanin Nos**, Russian Federation
87	Q 4	**Kaniv**, Ukraine
105	F 15	**Kaniwara**, India
80	K 7	**Kanjiža**, Serbia and Montenegro
21	H 17	**Kankakee**, IL, U.S.A.
128	H 11	**Kankan**, Guinea
105	G 16	**Kanker**, India
115	F 21	**Kanmaw Kyun**, Myanmar ⛱
17	O 10	**Kannapolis**, NC, U.S.A.
106	K 10	**Kannauj**, India
129	R 10	**Kano**, Nigeria
129	S 10	**Kano**, Nigeria ▣
123	C 24	**Kanoya**, Japan
106	M 10	**Kanpur**, India
24	L 5	**Kansas**, U.S.A. ▣
25	O 3	**Kansas**, KS, U.S.A. ∫
25	R 3	**Kansas City**, MO, U.S.A.
89	O 12	**Kansk**, Russian Federation
115	G 25	**Kantang**, Thailand
129	N 10	**Kantchari**, Burkina Faso
92	L 7	**Kantemirovka**, Russian Federation
107	S 15	**Kanthi**, India
140	J 4	**Kanton**, Kiribati ⛱
123	K 15	**Kanuma**, Japan
106	H 9	**Kanwat**, India
132	M 10	**Kanye**, Botswana
117	S 10	**Kao**, Indonesia
140	I 10	**Kao**, Tonga ⛱
115	J 21	**Kaôh Kŏng**, Cambodia ⛱
115	J 22	**Kaôh Rŭng**, Cambodia ⛱
113	Z 12	**Kaohsiung**, Taiwan
132	G 7	**Kaokoveld**, Namibia ◇
128	E 8	**Kaolack**, Senegal
132	M 5	**Kaoma**, Zambia
130	M 3	**Kaouadja**, Central African Republic
72	M 7	**Kap Arkona**, Germany ▶
143	Q 13	**Kap Brewster**, Greenland ▶
142	M 14	**Kap Farvel**, Greenland ▶
143	R 9	**Kap Morris Jesup**, Greenland ▶
95	V 10	**Kapan**, Armenia
130	M 13	**Kapanga**, Democratic Republic of Co[ngo]
133	P 2	**Kapatu**, Zambia
103	V 9	**Kapchagay**, Kazakhstan
103	W 9	**Kapchagayskoye Vodokhranilishche**, Kazakhstan ◣
69	E 16	**Kapelle**, Netherlands
69	G 16	**Kapellen**, Belgium
71	I 20	**Kapellskär**, Sweden

□ Country ▣ Internal administrative region: State/Province/Territory/Dependent territory ⌂ Capital city ⛰ Mountain range/ Undersea ridge ▲ Mountain peak/ Volcano/Seamount ◇ Geographic feature ▶ Headland/Point/ Cape/Peninsula ◠ Desert ⛱ Island/Island group ⁂ Antarctic base ◎ Ocean ◓ Sea ≈ Bay/Gulf/Channel/Strait ◣ Lake ⚑ Salt pan/Dry/ Intermittent lake ∫ F

U 7 **Kapenguria**, Kenya
V 6 **Kapfenberg**, Austria
C 8 **Kapidaği Peninsula**, Turkey ▶
O 4 **Kapiri Mposhi**, Zambia
V 7 **Kāpīsā**, Afghanistan ◘
Q 10 **Kapit**, Malaysia
K 15 **Kapiti Island**, New Zealand ⁂
F 23 **Kapoe**, Thailand
F 23 **Kapoeta**, Sudan
H 25 **Kaposvár**, Hungary
D 19 **Kappel**, Germany
H 7 **Kappeln**, Germany
M 15 **Kapsan**, North Korea
I 11 **Kapuas**, Indonesia ∫
C 5 **Kapuskasing**, ON, Canada
Q 8 **Kapustin Yar**, Russian Federation
U 6 **Kaputir**, Kenya
G 23 **Kapuvár**, Hungary
I 19 **Kapyl'**, Belarus
N 11 **Kara**, Togo
U 10 **Kara-Balta**, Kyrgyzstan
H 12 **Kara Dağ**, Turkey ▲
O 8 **Kara Dağ**, Turkey ▲
T 11 **Kara-Köl**, Kyrgyzstan
J 19 **Kara K'orē**, Ethiopia
W 11 **Kara-Say**, Kyrgyzstan
M 6 **Kara Sea**, Russian Federation ∽
T 12 **Kara-Suu**, Kyrgyzstan
I 11 **Karabogazkel'**, Turkmenistan
H 7 **Karabük**, Turkey
W 8 **Karabulak**, Kazakhstan
A 10 **Karaburun**, Turkey
M 5 **Karabutak**, Kazakhstan
E 13 **Karaca Yarimadasi**, Turkey ▶
D 8 **Karacabey**, Turkey
D 7 **Karacaköy**, Turkey
H 14 **Karaçal Tepe**, Turkey ▲
M 13 **Karachayevo Cherkesskaya Respublika**, Russian Federation ◘
M 13 **Karachayevsk**, Russian Federation
I 3 **Karachev**, Russian Federation
T 15 **Karachi**, Pakistan
C 18 **Karad**, India
S 6 **Karaganda**, Kazakhstan ◘
T 5 **Karaganda**, Kazakhstan
V 9 **Karagash**, Kazakhstan
U 5 **Karagayly**, Kazakhstan
Z 9 **Karaginskiy Zaliv**, Russian Federation ≈
O 10 **Karagöl Dağlari**, Turkey ▲▲
R 8 **Karagwe**, Tanzania
F 22 **Karaikal**, India
F 23 **Karaikkudi**, India
I 6 **Karaj**, Iran
C 8 **Karak**, Malaysia
K 9 **Karakalpakiya**, Uzbekistan
O 12 **Karakeşşi**, Turkey
I 9 **Karakeşşili**, Turkey
R 8 **Karakelong**, Indonesia ⁂
P 10 **Karakoşşan**, Turkey
W 10 **Karakol**, Kyrgyzstan
Y 5 **Karakoram**, Pakistan ▲▲
D 6 **Karakoram Range**, India ▲▲
O 13 **Karakul'**, Uzbekistan
L 13 **Karakum Desert**, Turkmenistan ◇
R 9 **Karakurt**, Turkey
V 9 **Karal**, Chad
C 8 **Karala**, Estonia
H 13 **Karaman**, Turkey
K 4 **Karamay**, China
G 16 **Karamea**, New Zealand
G 17 **Karamea Bight**, New Zealand ≈
L 13 **Karamian**, Indonesia ⁂
K 10 **Karamu**, New Zealand
E 16 **Karanji**, India
M 7 **Karapelit**, Bulgaria
I 12 **Karapinar**, Turkey
I 12 **Karas**, Namibia ◘
J 12 **Karasburg**, Namibia
L 7 **Kárásjohka**, Norway
F 7 **Karasu**, Turkey
L 12 **Karasuk**, Russian Federation
K 13 **Karataş**, Turkey
S 10 **Karatau**, Kazakhstan
J 5 **Karatobe**, Kazakhstan
V 8 **Karatol**, Kazakhstan ∫
I 7 **Karaton**, Kazakhstan
I 11 **Karats**, Sweden ◣
B 21 **Karatsu**, Japan
W 5 **Karaul**, Kazakhstan
S 9 **Karawanken**, Austria ▲▲
S 6 **Karazhal**, Kazakhstan
T 8 **Karbalā'**, Iraq
G 17 **Kårböle**, Sweden
L 23 **Karcag**, Hungary
D 17 **Karditsa**, Greece
L 17 **Kardiva Channel**, Maldives ≈
D 6 **Kärdla**, Estonia
F 15 **Kareli**, India
H 18 **Karelichy**, Belarus
R 12 **Karema**, Tanzania
F 16 **Karen**, Myanmar ◘
E 13 **Karera**, India
J 8 **Karesuando**, Finland
M 11 **Kargasok**, Russian Federation
J 7 **Kargi**, Turkey
I 3 **Kargil**, India
J 9 **Kargopol'**, Russian Federation
E 13 **Kargowa**, Poland
T 10 **Kari**, Nigeria
O 6 **Kariba**, Zimbabwe
H 9 **Karibib**, Namibia
L 7 **Karigasniemi**, Finland
I 11 **Karimata**, Indonesia ⁂
F 18 **Karimnagar**, India
M 19 **Karin**, Somalia
Q 8 **Karisimbi**, Democratic Republic of Congo/Rwanda ▲
I 17 **Kariya**, Japan
D 4 **Karkar Island**, Papua New Guinea ⁂
U 5 **Karkaralinsk**, Kazakhstan
U 9 **Karki**, Azerbaijan
R 11 **Karkinits'ka Zatoka**, Ukraine ≈
G 8 **Karksi-Nuia**, Estonia
N 5 **Karlik Shan**, China ▲
E 9 **Karlino**, Poland
Q 10 **Karliova**, Turkey
U 5 **Karlivka**, Ukraine
D 8 **Karlovac**, Croatia
I 9 **Karlovo**, Bulgaria
B 17 **Karlovy Vary**, Czech Republic
F 25 **Karlshamn**, Sweden
F 20 **Karlskoga**, Sweden
G 25 **Karlskrona**, Sweden

73 E 22 **Karlsruhe**, Germany
23 O 2 **Karlstad**, MN, U.S.A.
71 F 20 **Karlstad**, Sweden
75 U 2 **Karlstift**, Austria
85 N 19 **Karma**, Belarus
107 W 14 **Karnafuli Reservoir**, Bangladesh ◣
106 J 7 **Karnal**, India
106 M 8 **Karnali**, Nepal ∫
105 D 20 **Karnataka**, India ◘
27 P 11 **Karnes City**, TX, U.S.A.
75 P 9 **Karnische Alpen**, Austria ▲▲
76 G 5 **Karnische Alps**, Austria/Italy ▲▲
82 M 9 **Karnobat**, Bulgaria
75 S 9 **Kärnten**, Austria ◘
101 S 12 **Karodi**, Pakistan
107 X 11 **Karong**, India
133 R 2 **Karonga**, Malawi
101 W 9 **Karor**, Pakistan
127 I 15 **Karora**, Eritrea
117 N 11 **Karossa**, Indonesia
83 L 22 **Karpáthio Pélagos**, Greece ∽
83 M 26 **Karpathos**, Greece
83 M 25 **Karpathos**, Greece ⁂
83 D 18 **Karpenisi**, Greece
90 M 7 **Karpogory**, Russian Federation
134 F 6 **Karratha**, WA, Australia
95 S 8 **Kars**, Turkey
71 L 14 **Kärsämäki**, Finland
84 J 11 **Kārsava**, Latvia
102 I 11 **Karshi**, Turkmenistan
103 P 13 **Karshi**, Uzbekistan
94 E 8 **Kartal**, Turkey
133 W 4 **Kartala**, Comoros ▲
88 I 11 **Kartaly**, Russian Federation
78 H 8 **Kartuzy**, Poland
135 Q 3 **Karumba**, QLD, Australia
101 O 12 **Kārvāndar**, Iran
105 C 20 **Karwar**, India
74 M 7 **Karwendelgebirge**, Austria ▲▲
83 B 18 **Karya**, Greece
89 R 14 **Karymskoye**, Russian Federation
83 H 20 **Karystos**, Greece
94 D 13 **Kaş**, Turkey
40 L 9 **Kasabonika**, ON, Canada
123 F 18 **Kasai**, Japan
130 J 10 **Kasai**, Democratic Republic of Congo ∫
130 L 11 **Kasai Occidental**, Democratic Republic of Congo ◘
130 M 10 **Kasai Oriental**, Democratic Republic of Congo ◘
130 M 14 **Kasaji**, Democratic Republic of Congo
133 P 3 **Kasama**, Zambia
132 M 7 **Kasane**, Botswana
105 C 21 **Kasaragod**, India
37 O 9 **Kasba Lake**, NU, Canada ◣
124 H 7 **Kasba Tadla**, Morocco
132 M 4 **Kasempa**, Zambia
131 P 14 **Kasenga**, Democratic Republic of Congo
131 Q 7 **Kasenye**, Democratic Republic of Congo
131 O 8 **Kasese**, Democratic Republic of Congo
131 Q 7 **Kasese**, Uganda
115 K 17 **Kaset Wisai**, Thailand
106 K 9 **Kasganj**, India
40 L 11 **Kashabowie**, ON, Canada
100 I 7 **Kāshān**, Iran
92 M 8 **Kashary**, Russian Federation
37 T 11 **Kashechewan**, ON, Canada
41 P 10 **Kashechewen**, ON, Canada
35 O 9 **Kashegelok**, AK, U.S.A.
108 G 5 **Kashi**, China
123 H 18 **Kashihara**, Japan
123 L 14 **Kashima-nada**, Japan ≈
90 I 13 **Kashin**, Russian Federation
107 T 12 **Kashinathpur**, Bangladesh
106 K 8 **Kashipur**, India
92 L 2 **Kashira**, Russian Federation
123 I 14 **Kashiwazaki**, Japan
103 T 8 **Kashkanteniz**, Kazakhstan
101 N 6 **Kāshmar**, Iran
106 H 3 **Kashmir Valley**, India ◇
117 N 11 **Kasimbar**, Indonesia
93 N 2 **Kasimov**, Russian Federation
103 V 10 **Kaskelen**, Kazakhstan
88 I 10 **Kasli**, Russian Federation
39 I 21 **Kaslo**, BC, Canada
131 O 10 **Kasongo**, Democratic Republic of Congo
130 I 12 **Kasongo-Lunda**, Democratic Republic of Congo
83 M 26 **Kasos**, Greece ⁂
95 T 6 **Kaspi**, Georgia
93 R 14 **Kaspiysk**, Russian Federation
127 H 16 **Kassala**, Sudan
127 G 16 **Kassala**, Sudan ◘
83 G 15 **Kassandreia**, Greece
73 G 16 **Kassel**, Germany
125 P 6 **Kasserine**, Tunisia
83 A 16 **Kassiopi**, Greece
94 I 7 **Kastamonu**, Turkey
83 G 26 **Kastelli**, Greece
83 J 26 **Kastelli**, Greece
69 H 17 **Kasterlee**, Belgium
83 C 14 **Kastoria**, Greece
92 K 5 **Kastornoye**, Russian Federation
83 B 18 **Kastos**, Greece ⁂
85 O 18 **Kastsyukovichy**, Belarus
123 I 17 **Kasugai**, Japan
123 L 15 **Kasumiga-ura**, Japan ◣
93 S 15 **Kasumkent**, Russian Federation
133 Q 4 **Kasungu**, Malawi
101 Y 9 **Kasur**, Pakistan
134 M 7 **Kata Tjuta**, NT, Australia ▲
106 K 2 **Kataklik**, India
131 N 10 **Katako-Kombe**, Democratic Republic of Congo
131 T 6 **Katakwi**, Uganda
35 T 10 **Katalla**, AK, U.S.A.
131 N 13 **Katanga**, Democratic Republic of Congo ◘
134 H 12 **Katanning**, WA, Australia
83 B 20 **Katastari**, Greece
105 O 24 **Katchall**, India ⁂
131 O 11 **Katea**, Democratic Republic of Congo
83 E 15 **Katerini**, Greece
133 Q 5 **Katete**, Zambia
114 E 9 **Katha**, Myanmar
134 M 2 **Katherine**, NT, Australia
105 A 15 **Kathiawar Peninsula**, India ▶
107 Q 9 **Kathmandu**, Nepal ▙
128 I 9 **Kati**, Mali
107 S 11 **Katihar**, India
136 L 9 **Katikati**, New Zealand
128 K 12 **Katiola**, Côte d'Ivoire
82 D 11 **Katlanovo**, Macedonia (F.Y.R.O.M.)
83 D 20 **Kato Achaïa**, Greece

82 H 12 **Kato Nevrokopi**, Greece
83 E 18 **Kato Tithorea**, Greece
103 Z 4 **Katon-Karagay**, Kazakhstan
118 B 14 **Katong**, Singapore
135 U 11 **Katoomba**, NSW, Australia
79 I 17 **Katowice**, Poland
107 S 13 **Katoya**, India
71 G 21 **Katrineholm**, Sweden
133 X 6 **Katsepy**, Madgascar
129 R 9 **Katsina**, Nigeria
129 R 10 **Katsina**, Nigeria ◘
129 S 13 **Katsina-Ala**, Nigeria
123 A 21 **Katsumoto**, Japan
123 L 16 **Katsuura**, Japan
83 N 24 **Kattavia**, Greece
71 D 23 **Kattegat**, Denmark ≈
70 H 13 **Kattisavan**, Sweden
136 I 6 **Katui**, New Zealand
115 F 22 **Kau-ye Kyun**, Myanmar ⁂
34 A 6 **Kauai**, HI, U.S.A. ⁂
34 A 7 **Kauai Channel**, HI, U.S.A. ≈
73 I 25 **Kaufbeuren**, Germany
71 K 17 **Kauhajoki**, Finland
70 L 10 **Kaukonen**, Finland
84 I 6 **Kauksi**, Estonia
34 D 9 **Kauna Point**, HI, U.S.A. ▶
34 C 7 **Kaunakakai**, HI, U.S.A.
85 E 15 **Kaunas**, Lithuania
138 C 3 **Kaup**, Papua New Guinea
71 B 17 **Kaupanger**, Norway
129 Q 9 **Kaura-Namoda**, Nigeria
71 K 15 **Kaustinen**, Finland
70 K 8 **Kautokeino**, Norway
137 L 14 **Kauwhata**, New Zealand
82 D 12 **Kavadarci**, Macedonia (F.Y.R.O.M.)
81 J 19 **Kavajë**, Albania
94 B 8 **Kavak**, Turkey
82 H 13 **Kavala**, Greece
105 G 20 **Kavali**, India
100 I 11 **Kavār**, Iran
105 B 22 **Kavaratti**, India ⁂
105 B 22 **Kavaratti**, India
82 O 7 **Kavarna**, Bulgaria
138 G 2 **Kavieng**, Papua New Guinea
25 O 7 **Kaw Lake**, OK, U.S.A. ◣
123 G 19 **Kawachi-nagano**, Japan
136 J 6 **Kawakawa**, New Zealand
133 O 2 **Kawambwa**, Zambia
105 G 15 **Kawardha**, India
42 G 11 **Kawartha Lakes**, ON, Canada ◣
123 K 16 **Kawasaki**, Japan
123 B 20 **Kawashiri-misaki**, Japan ▶
136 K 7 **Kawau Island**, New Zealand ⁂
136 M 12 **Kaweka**, New Zealand ▲
136 J 10 **Kawhia**, New Zealand
136 J 10 **Kawhia Harbour**, New Zealand ≈
33 L 19 **Kawich Peak**, NV, U.S.A. ▲
114 D 9 **Kawlin**, Myanmar
128 M 9 **Kaya**, Burkina Faso
116 E 13 **Kayaapu**, Indonesia
115 E 14 **Kayah**, Myanmar ◘
35 T 10 **Kayak Island**, AK, U.S.A. ⁂
105 D 23 **Kayankulam**, India
29 W 10 **Kaycee**, WY, U.S.A.
130 M 13 **Kayembe-Mukulu**, Democratic Republic of Congo
30 L 8 **Kayenta**, AZ, U.S.A.
128 G 9 **Kayes**, Mali
128 H 9 **Kayes**, Mali ◘
103 V 5 **Kaynar**, Kazakhstan
94 K 11 **Kayseri**, Turkey
116 G 12 **Kayuagung**, Indonesia
131 O 10 **Kayuyu**, Democratic Republic of Congo
89 O 8 **Kayyerkan**, Russian Federation
94 A 9 **Kaz Daği**, Turkey
89 T 7 **Kazach'ye**, Russian Federation
102 H 10 **Kazakhskiy Zaliv**, Kazakhstan ≈
103 Q 8 **Kazakhstan**, Asia ◘
40 J 4 **Kazan**, NU, Canada ∫
93 R 1 **Kazan'**, Russian Federation
87 S 7 **Kazanka**, Ukraine
82 J 9 **Kazanlŭk**, Bulgaria
95 T 5 **Kazbek**, Georgia ▲
100 I 10 **Kāzerūn**, Iran
79 K 21 **Kazincbarcika**, Hungary
85 E 15 **Kazlu Rūda**, Lithuania
123 K 15 **Kazo**, Japan
38 L 11 **Kazon**, NU, Canada ∫
102 G 5 **Kaztalovka**, Kazakhstan
130 L 11 **Kazumba**, Democratic Republic of Congo
78 G 11 **Kcynia**, Poland
83 H 21 **Kea**, Greece ⁂
34 E 9 **Keaau**, HI, U.S.A.
34 D 8 **Keahole Point**, HI, U.S.A. ▶
30 L 9 **Keams**, AZ, U.S.A.
22 L 15 **Kearney**, NE, U.S.A.
95 N 11 **Keban**, Turkey
95 O 10 **Keban Baraji**, Turkey ◣
107 Y 9 **Kebang**, India
129 P 10 **Kebbi**, Nigeria ◘
128 D 8 **Kébémèr**, Senegal
125 Q 7 **Kebili**, Tunisia
127 A 17 **Kebkabiya**, Sudan
70 I 9 **Kebnekaise**, Sweden ▲
127 L 21 **K'ebrī Dehar**, Ethiopia
79 J 24 **Kecskemét**, Hungary
118 A 5 **Kedah**, Malaysia ◘
85 E 14 **Kėdainiai**, Lithuania
129 W 10 **Kédédéssé**, Chad
43 R 7 **Kedgwick**, NB, Canada
128 F 6 **Kediet Ijill**, Mauritania ▲
116 J 14 **Kediri**, Indonesia
110 K 9 **Kedong**, China
128 G 9 **Kédougou**, Senegal
79 H 17 **Kędzierzyn-Koźle**, Poland
38 C 12 **Keele Peak**, YT, Canada ▲
121 C 22 **Keenapusan**, Philippines ⁂
14 M 8 **Keene**, NH, U.S.A.
132 J 11 **Keetmanshoop**, Namibia
83 A 19 **Kefallonia**, Greece ⁂
83 M 23 **Kefalos**, Greece
117 Q 15 **Kefamenanu**, Indonesia
129 R 12 **Keffi**, Nigeria
70 A 11 **Keflavik**, Iceland
39 H 16 **Keg River**, AB, Canada
103 X 10 **Kegen**, Kazakhstan
127 F 14 **Keheili**, Sudan
73 D 23 **Kehl**, Germany
84 G 6 **Kehra**, Estonia
114 F 11 **Kehsi Mansam**, Myanmar
63 R 2 **Keighley**, U.K.
84 F 6 **Keila**, Estonia
132 K 12 **Keimoes**, Republic of South Africa

129 Q 8 **Keïta**, Niger
71 M 16 **Keitele**, Finland ◣
135 Q 12 **Keith**, SA, Australia
119 R 9 **Kejaman**, Malaysia
137 J 17 **Kekerengu**, New Zealand
123 N 22 **Kekeroma-jima**, Japan ⁂
79 K 22 **Kékes**, Hungary ▲
89 V 11 **Kekra**, Russian Federation
127 L 22 **K'elafo**, Ethiopia
111 A 18 **Kelan**, China
117 R 12 **Kelang**, Indonesia ⁂
118 B 8 **Kelang**, Malaysia
118 C 5 **Kelantan**, Malaysia ∫
118 C 6 **Kelantan**, Malaysia ◘
125 R 5 **Kelibia**, Tunisia
94 M 8 **Kelkit**, Turkey ∫
95 O 9 **Kelkit**, Turkey
130 G 8 **Kéllé**, Congo
103 R 2 **Kellerovka**, Kazakhstan
21 M 16 **Kelley's Island**, OH, U.S.A. ⁂
28 K 4 **Kellogg**, ID, U.S.A.
70 N 10 **Kelloselkä**, Finland
61 E 17 **Kells**, Republic of Ireland
84 D 13 **Kelmė**, Lithuania
69 L 20 **Kelmis**, Belgium
129 W 11 **Kelo**, Chad
39 H 21 **Kelowna**, BC, Canada
32 G 9 **Kelso**, WA, U.S.A.
118 E 10 **Keluang**, Malaysia
116 F 11 **Kelume**, Indonesia
90 I 6 **Kem'**, Russian Federation
95 O 10 **Kemah**, Turkey
95 N 10 **Kemaliye**, Turkey
130 L 5 **Kembé**, Central African Republic
94 D 13 **Kemer**, Turkey
88 M 12 **Kemerovo**, Russian Federation
70 L 12 **Kemi**, Finland
70 M 11 **Kemijärvi**, Finland ◣
70 M 11 **Kemijärvi**, Finland
70 M 10 **Kemijoki**, Finland ∫
93 P 2 **Kemlya**, Russian Federation
29 R 14 **Kemmerer**, WY, U.S.A.
73 K 20 **Kemnath**, Germany
130 J 4 **Kémo**, Central African Republic ◘
27 R 6 **Kemp**, TX, U.S.A.
145 U 4 **Kemp Land**, Antarctica ◇
48 L 3 **Kemp's Bay**, The Bahamas
135 V 10 **Kempsey**, NSW, Australia
73 H 25 **Kempten**, Germany
35 Q 9 **Kenai**, AK, U.S.A.
35 Q 10 **Kenai Peninsula**, AK, U.S.A. ▶
19 X 10 **Kenansville**, FL, U.S.A.
63 P 1 **Kendal**, U.K.
19 Y 13 **Kendall**, FL, U.S.A.
21 K 16 **Kendallville**, IN, U.S.A.
117 P 12 **Kendari**, Indonesia
116 I 12 **Kendawangan**, Indonesia
129 X 11 **Kendégué**, Chad
105 J 16 **Kendraparha**, India
103 U 9 **Kendyktas**, Kazakhstan ▲▲
128 H 12 **Kenema**, Sierra Leone
102 L 11 **Keneurgench**, Turkmenistan
114 F 11 **Keng Lon**, Myanmar
114 F 12 **Keng Tawng**, Myanmar
130 I 10 **Kenge**, Democratic Republic of Congo
132 K 13 **Kenhardt**, Republic of South Africa
63 S 7 **Kenilworth**, U.K.
124 H 6 **Kénitra**, Morocco
22 I 2 **Kenmare**, ND, U.S.A.
61 B 20 **Kenmare**, Republic of Ireland
15 O 7 **Kennebunkport**, ME, U.S.A.
35 Q 10 **Kennedy Entrance**, AK, U.S.A. ≈
18 L 8 **Kenner**, LA, U.S.A.
25 Y 8 **Kennett**, MO, U.S.A.
32 J 9 **Kennewick**, WA, U.S.A.
40 J 10 **Kenora**, ON, Canada
21 H 15 **Kenosha**, WI, U.S.A.
43 V 8 **Kensington**, PE, Canada
26 G 8 **Kent**, TX, U.S.A.
38 I 8 **Kent Peninsula**, NU, Canada ▶
103 R 10 **Kentau**, Kazakhstan
21 H 17 **Kentland**, IN, U.S.A.
82 F 13 **Kentriki Makedonia**, Greece ◘
16 I 6 **Kentucky**, U.S.A. ◘
16 K 6 **Kentucky**, KY, U.S.A. ∫
16 D 7 **Kentucky Lake**, KY, U.S.A. ◣
114 G 12 **Kentung**, Myanmar
131 U 7 **Kenya**, Africa ◘
107 W 14 **Keokradang**, Bangladesh ▲
105 J 15 **Keonjhar**, India
116 F 12 **Kepahiang**, Indonesia
81 J 20 **Kepi i Gjuhëzës**, Albania ▶
81 J 18 **Kepi i Rodonit**, Albania ▶
79 H 15 **Kępno**, Poland
117 Q 14 **Kepulauan Alor**, Indonesia ⁂
116 G 9 **Kepulauan Anambas**, Indonesia ⁂
117 V 13 **Kepulauan Aru**, Indonesia ⁂
117 U 10 **Kepulauan Asia**, Indonesia ⁂
117 U 10 **Kepulauan Ayu**, Indonesia ⁂
117 T 14 **Kepulauan Babar**, Indonesia ⁂
117 T 13 **Kepulauan Banda**, Indonesia ⁂
117 P 11 **Kepulauan Banggai**, Indonesia ⁂
116 C 9 **Kepulauan Banyak**, Indonesia ⁂
117 R 14 **Kepulauan Barat Daya**, Indonesia ⁂
116 C 11 **Kepulauan Batu**, Indonesia ⁂
117 O 14 **Kepulauan Bonerate**, Indonesia ⁂
117 U 12 **Kepulauan Gorong**, Indonesia ⁂
117 U 13 **Kepulauan Kai**, Indonesia ⁂
116 L 14 **Kepulauan Kangean**, Indonesia ⁂
116 J 13 **Kepulauan Karimunjawa**, Indonesia ⁂
116 L 13 **Kepulauan Laut Kecil**, Indonesia ⁂
117 S 14 **Kepulauan Leti**, Indonesia ⁂
116 G 11 **Kepulauan Lingga**, Indonesia ⁂
117 V 10 **Kepulauan Mapia**, Indonesia ⁂
117 R 8 **Kepulauan Nanusa**, Indonesia ⁂
116 H 8 **Kepulauan Natuna**, Indonesia ⁂
117 R 11 **Kepulauan Obi**, Indonesia ⁂
117 N 14 **Kepulauan Sabalana**, Indonesia ⁂
117 R 9 **Kepulauan Sangir**, Indonesia ⁂
117 P 14 **Kepulauan Solor**, Indonesia ⁂
117 O 14 **Kepulauan Taka'Bonerate**, Indonesia ⁂
117 R 8 **Kepulauan Talaud**, Indonesia ⁂
116 H 10 **Kepulauan Tambelan**, Indonesia ⁂
117 U 14 **Kepulauan Tanimbar**, Indonesia ⁂
116 M 14 **Kepulauan Tengah**, Indonesia ⁂
117 P 11 **Kepulauan Togian**, Indonesia ⁂
117 Q 13 **Kepulauan Tukangbesi**, Indonesia ⁂
117 U 13 **Kepulauan Watubela**, Indonesia ⁂
105 D 23 **Kerala**, India ◘
135 R 12 **Kerang**, VIC, Australia
83 H 20 **Keratea**, Greece
103 S 11 **Kerben**, Kyrgyzstan
87 W 11 **Kerch**, Ukraine

87 W 12 **Kerch Strait**, Ukraine ≈
127 H 22 **Kere**, Ethiopia
138 C 6 **Kerema**, Papua New Guinea
94 I 6 **Kerempe Burun**, Turkey ▶
127 I 16 **Keren**, Eritrea
131 U 8 **Kericho**, Kenya
136 J 5 **Kerikeri**, New Zealand
103 P 14 **Kerki**, Turkmenistan
83 A 16 **Kerkyra**, Greece
127 E 14 **Kerma**, Sudan
100 M 11 **Kermān**, Iran ◘
100 M 10 **Kermān**, Iran
100 F 6 **Kermānshāh**, Iran ◘
100 F 6 **Kermānshāh**, Iran
26 I 7 **Kermit**, TX, U.S.A.
83 K 22 **Keros**, Greece ⁂
129 O 11 **Kérou**, Benin
128 H 11 **Kérouané**, Guinea
39 L 19 **Kerrobert**, SK, Canada
27 N 10 **Kerrville**, TX, U.S.A.
61 A 19 **Kerry Head**, Republic of Ireland ▶
17 P 11 **Kershaw**, SC, U.S.A.
116 I 11 **Kertamulia**, Indonesia
94 H 15 **Keryneia**, Cyprus
124 K 9 **Kerzaz**, Algeria
74 D 8 **Kerzers**, Switzerland
94 B 7 **Keşan**, Turkey
110 K 9 **Keshan**, China
101 V 5 **Keshem**, Afghanistan
69 L 16 **Kessel**, Netherlands
90 G 5 **Kesten'ga**, Russian Federation
61 I 15 **Keswick**, U.K.
79 G 24 **Keszthely**, Hungary
88 M 11 **Ket'**, Russian Federation ∫
116 I 11 **Ketapang**, Indonesia
93 O 10 **Ketchenery**, Russian Federation
35 Y 12 **Ketchikan**, AK, U.S.A.
28 M 10 **Ketchum**, ID, U.S.A.
68 J 10 **Ketelmeer**, Netherlands ≈
78 L 9 **Kętrzyn**, Poland
130 H 7 **Ketta**, Congo
129 V 14 **Kétté**, Cameroon
21 L 19 **Kettering**, OH, U.S.A.
63 U 7 **Kettering**, U.K.
32 K 5 **Kettle Falls**, WA, U.S.A.
71 L 16 **Keuruu**, Finland
21 E 17 **Kewanee**, IL, U.S.A.
117 P 15 **Kewapante**, Indonesia
20 G 8 **Keweenaw Bay**, MI, U.S.A. ≈
20 H 7 **Keweenaw Peninsula**, MI, U.S.A. ▶
20 H 7 **Keweenaw Point**, MI, U.S.A. ▶
19 Y 13 **Key Biscayne**, FL, U.S.A.
42 D 10 **Key Harbour**, ON, Canada
19 Y 14 **Key Largo**, FL, U.S.A.
19 Y 14 **Key Largo**, FL, U.S.A. ⁂
19 W 15 **Key West**, FL, U.S.A.
127 F 23 **Keyala**, Sudan
24 G 7 **Keyes**, OK, U.S.A.
110 H 6 **Keyihe**, China
17 R 2 **Keyser**, WV, U.S.A.
25 P 8 **Keystone Lake**, OK, U.S.A. ◣
17 S 6 **Keysville**, VA, U.S.A.
25 U 3 **Keytesville**, MO, U.S.A.
133 O 8 **Kezi**, Zimbabwe
79 K 19 **Kežmarok**, Slovakia
132 K 10 **Kgalagadi**, Botswana ◘
133 N 10 **Kgatleng**, Botswana ◘
89 V 14 **Khabarovsk**, Russian Federation
99 X 6 **Khabb**, United Arab Emirates
92 L 12 **Khadyzhensk**, Russian Federation
87 P 9 **Khadzhybeys'kyy Lyman**, Ukraine ◣
107 Q 11 **Khagaria**, India
107 V 13 **Khagrachari**, Bangladesh
101 U 12 **Khairpur**, Pakistan
101 X 11 **Khaïrpur**, Pakistan
126 D 7 **Khalîg el 'Arab**, Egypt ≈
99 Y 11 **Khalīj al Ḥalāniyāt**, Oman ≈
99 Z 9 **Khalīj Maşīrah**, Oman ≈
105 I 17 **Khallikot**, India
91 U 2 **Khal'mer-Yu**, Russian Federation
85 K 16 **Khalopyenichy**, Belarus
115 K 15 **Kham Ta Kla**, Thailand
105 D 16 **Khamgaon**, India
99 P 12 **Khamir**, Yemen
100 K 13 **Khamīr**, Iran
99 O 10 **Khamis**, Saudi Arabia
115 K 15 **Khamkkeut**, Laos
105 G 18 **Khammam**, India
89 S 10 **Khampa**, Russian Federation
89 R 11 **Khamra**, Russian Federation
97 Q 6 **Khān al Baghdādī**, Iraq
97 T 8 **Khan al Maḥāwīl**, Iraq
97 T 7 **Khān al Mashāhidah**, Iraq
97 T 9 **Khān al Muşallá**, Iraq
97 T 10 **Khān ar Rahbah**, Iraq
97 P 2 **Khān as Sūr**, Iraq
97 U 9 **Khān Jadwal**, Iraq
96 I 3 **Khān Shaykhūn**, Syria
96 E 10 **Khān Yūnis**, Israel
101 U 5 **Khānābād**, Afghanistan
97 V 5 **Khānaqīn**, Iraq
105 E 15 **Khandwa**, India
89 U 10 **Khandyga**, Russian Federation
101 W 10 **Khanewal**, Pakistan
115 O 20 **Khanh Duong**, Vietnam
89 S 12 **Khani**, Russian Federation
106 I 6 **Khanna**, India
103 T 9 **Khantau**, Kazakhstan
88 K 10 **Khanty-Mansiysk**, Russian Federation
115 H 24 **Khao Chum Thong**, Thailand
115 I 18 **Khao Khiaw**, Thailand ▲
115 G 17 **Khao Laem Reservoir**, Thailand ◣
115 I 20 **Khao Sai Dao Tai**, Thailand ▲
106 I 2 **Khapalu**, India
93 R 9 **Kharabali**, Russian Federation
107 S 14 **Kharagpur**, India
101 S 12 **Kharan**, Pakistan
106 G 8 **Kharbara**, India
97 X 11 **Kharfiyah**, Iraq
100 H 10 **Khārg Islands**, Iran ⁂
105 D 15 **Khargon**, India
105 H 16 **Khariar**, India
87 V 4 **Kharkiv**, Ukraine
90 J 2 **Kharlovka**, Russian Federation
82 K 11 **Kharmanli**, Bulgaria
90 K 11 **Kharovsk**, Russian Federation
127 F 16 **Khartoum**, Sudan ▙
127 F 16 **Khartoum**, Sudan ◘
93 Q 14 **Khasav'yurt**, Russian Federation
101 P 12 **Khāsh**, Iran
88 L 8 **Khashgort**, Russian Federation
127 G 17 **Khashm el Girba**, Sudan
95 S 6 **Khashuri**, Georgia

82 K 11 **Khaskovo**, Bulgaria ◘
82 J 11 **Khaskovo**, Bulgaria
89 P 8 **Khatanga**, Russian Federation ∫
89 Q 8 **Khatanga**, Russian Federation
89 Q 7 **Khatangskiy Zaliv**, Russian Federation ≈
89 Z 7 **Khatyrka**, Russian Federation
105 A 14 **Khavda**, India
115 F 18 **Khawsa**, Myanmar
99 N 10 **Khawsh**, Saudi Arabia
98 L 5 **Khaybar**, Saudi Arabia
99 O 10 **Khaybar**, Saudi Arabia
132 K 15 **Khayelitsha**, Republic of South Africa
91 S 2 **Khaypudyrskaya Guba**, Russian Federation ≈
115 K 14 **Khê Bo**, Vietnam
115 N 16 **Khe Sanh**, Vietnam
106 M 7 **Khela**, India
124 I 7 **Khemisset**, Morocco
115 L 17 **Khemmarat**, Thailand
125 P 6 **Khenchela**, Algeria
124 I 7 **Khenifra**, Morocco
101 U 6 **Khenjan**, Afghanistan
87 S 9 **Kherson**, Ukraine
100 J 5 **Khezerābād**, Iran
89 R 14 **Khilok**, Russian Federation
96 K 4 **Khirbat Isrīyah**, Syria
115 G 17 **Khlong Khlung**, Thailand
86 M 5 **Khmel'nyts'kyy**, Ukraine
87 Q 6 **Khmel'ove**, Ukraine
87 N 5 **Khmil'nyk**, Ukraine
102 K 5 **Khobda**, Kazakhstan
95 R 6 **Khobi**, Georgia
87 O 4 **Khodorkiv**, Ukraine
103 O 13 **Khodzha Davlet**, Uzbekistan
127 C 22 **Khogali**, Sudan
115 H 18 **Khok Samrong**, Thailand
90 E 13 **Kholm**, Russian Federation
101 T 5 **Kholm**, Afghanistan
89 X 14 **Kholmsk**, Russian Federation
85 M 21 **Kholmyech**, Belarus
132 I 9 **Khomas**, Namibia ◘
100 H 7 **Khomeyn**, Iran
100 I 8 **Khomeynīshahr**, Iran
115 J 16 **Khon Kaen**, Thailand
100 J 12 **Khonj**, Iran
89 V 9 **Khonuu**, Russian Federation
89 V 14 **Khor**, Russian Federation
101 O 7 **Khorāsān**, Iran ◘
115 J 16 **Khorat Plateau**, Thailand ◇
91 S 3 **Khorey-Ver**, Russian Federation
89 Q 13 **Khorinsk**, Russian Federation
132 H 8 **Khorixas**, Namibia
87 T 10 **Khorly**, Ukraine
87 T 3 **Khorol**, Ukraine ∫
87 S 4 **Khorol**, Ukraine
100 G 7 **Khorramābād**, Iran
100 F 9 **Khorramshahr**, Iran
103 T 14 **Khorugh**, Tajikistan
93 R 10 **Khosheutovo**, Russian Federation
101 T 10 **Khost**, Pakistan
86 L 6 **Khotyn**, Ukraine
124 H 7 **Khouribga**, Morocco
107 V 12 **Khowai**, India
100 H 11 **Khowr-e Soltānī**, Iran ≈
101 V 8 **Khowst**, Afghanistan
85 M 21 **Khoyniki**, Belarus
89 U 9 **Khrebet Cherskogo**, Russian Federation ▲▲
89 U 12 **Khrebet Dzhugdzhur**, Russian Federation ▲▲
103 W 9 **Khrebet Dzhungarskiy Alatau**, Kazakhstan ▲▲
103 Q 9 **Khrebet Karatau**, Kazakhstan ◇
89 P 14 **Khrebet Khamar-Daban**, Russian Federation ▲▲
89 X 10 **Khrebet Kolymskiy**, Russian Federation ▲▲
103 P 12 **Khrebet Nuratau**, Uzbekistan ▲▲
89 T 8 **Khrebet Orulgan**, Russian Federation ▲▲
91 S 1 **Khrebet Pay-Khoy**, Russian Federation ▲▲
89 T 12 **Khrebet Synnagyn**, Russian Federation ▲▲
103 X 6 **Khrebet Tarbagatay**, Kazakhstan ▲▲
114 B 12 **Khreum**, Myanmar
102 L 5 **Khromtau**, Kazakhstan
115 K 18 **Khu Khan**, Thailand
99 P 6 **Khuff**, Saudi Arabia
103 R 12 **Khŭjand**, Tajikistan
98 L 7 **Khulays**, Saudi Arabia
107 T 14 **Khulna**, Bangladesh
107 T 14 **Khulna**, Bangladesh ◘
115 F 14 **Khun Yuam**, Thailand
105 J 14 **Khunti**, India
99 R 6 **Khurayş**, Saudi Arabia
106 J 9 **Khurja**, India
101 W 9 **Khushab**, Pakistan
86 H 7 **Khust**, Ukraine
99 U 5 **Khuwayr**, Qatar
127 D 18 **Khuwei**, Sudan
101 T 12 **Khuzdar**, Pakistan
100 G 9 **Khūzestān**, Iran ◘
93 R 4 **Khvalynsk**, Russian Federation
100 L 7 **Khvor**, Iran
100 I 11 **Khvormūj**, Iran
100 F 3 **Khvoy**, Iran
90 H 12 **Khvoynaya**, Russian Federation
101 V 7 **Khyber Pass**, Afghanistan ▲
138 L 5 **Kia**, Solomon Islands
135 U 12 **Kiama**, NSW, Australia
121 L 24 **Kiamba**, Philippines
131 P 12 **Kiambi**, Democratic Republic of Congo
35 N 5 **Kiana**, AK, U.S.A.
135 T 12 **Kiandra**, NSW, Australia
131 W 12 **Kibaha**, Tanzania
130 F 10 **Kibangou**, Congo
121 L 21 **Kibawe**, Philippines
131 V 11 **Kibaya**, Tanzania
131 R 7 **Kiboga**, Uganda
131 O 10 **Kibombo**, Democratic Republic of Congo
131 R 10 **Kibondo**, Tanzania
127 I 22 **Kibre Mengist**, Ethiopia
82 C 12 **Kičevo**, Macedonia (F.Y.R.O.M.)
91 N 11 **Kichmengskiy Gorodok**, Russian Federation
129 N 7 **Kidal**, Mali
129 O 6 **Kidal**, Mali ◘
121 L 22 **Kidapawan**, Philippines
63 Q 7 **Kidderminster**, U.K.
128 G 8 **Kidira**, Senegal
63 T 9 **Kidlington**, U.K.
63 R 5 **Kidsgrove**, U.K.
62 M 10 **Kidwelly**, U.K.
20 G 12 **Kiel**, WI, U.S.A.

Country ◘ Internal administrative region: State/Province/Territory/Dependent territory ▙ Capital city ▲▲ Mountain range/Undersea ridge ▲ Mountain peak/Volcano/Seamount ◇ Geographic feature ▶ Headland/Point/Cape/Peninsula ◠ Desert ⁂ Island/Island group ⁙ Antarctic base ≋ Ocean ∽ Sea ≈ Bay/Gulf/Channel/Strait ◣ Lake ⚑ Salt pan/Dry/Intermittent lake ∫ River

72 H 8 **Kiel**, Germany
79 K 15 **Kielce**, Poland
72 H 8 **Kieler Bucht**, Germany ≈
131 P 14 **Kienge**, Democratic Republic of Congo
138 J 5 **Kieta**, Papua New Guinea
87 P 3 **Kiev**, Ukraine ▟
87 P 3 **Kiev Reservoir**, Ukraine ∽
128 G 7 **Kiffa**, Mauritania
81 H 14 **Kifino Selo**, Bosnia and Herzegovina
83 G 20 **Kifisia**, Greece
83 E 18 **Kifisos**, Greece ∫
97 U 5 **Kifrī**, Iraq
131 Q 9 **Kigali**, Rwanda ▟
128 J 10 **Kignan**, Mali
131 Q 10 **Kigoma**, Tanzania ▣
131 Q 11 **Kigoma**, Tanzania
34 D 8 **Kihei**, HI, U.S.A.
136 L 10 **Kihikihi**, New Zealand
84 F 8 **Kihnu**, Estonia ⛱
123 H 19 **Kii-nagashima**, Japan
123 G 19 **Kii-sanchi**, Japan ⛰
123 G 19 **Kii-suidō**, Japan ≈
103 T 7 **Kiik**, Kazakhstan
123 O 21 **Kikai**, Japan
123 O 21 **Kikai-jima**, Japan ⛱
80 L 8 **Kikinda**, Serbia and Montenegro
101 Q 14 **Kikki**, Pakistan
91 O 14 **Kiknur**, Russian Federation
131 O 12 **Kikondja**, Democratic Republic of Congo
138 C 5 **Kikori**, Papua New Guinea
138 C 5 **Kikori**, Papua New Guinea ∫
130 J 11 **Kikwit**, Democratic Republic of Congo
34 A 6 **Kilauea**, HI, U.S.A.
34 E 9 **Kilauea**, HI, U.S.A. ▲
111 M 15 **Kilchu**, North Korea
61 E 18 **Kilcock**, Republic of Ireland
61 E 18 **Kildare**, Republic of Ireland
130 K 11 **Kilembe**, Democratic Republic of Congo
27 T 6 **Kilgore**, TX, U.S.A.
141 Y 4 **Kili Island**, Marshall Islands ⛱
131 Q 10 **Kiliba**, Democratic Republic of Congo
131 X 10 **Kilifi**, Kenya
131 V 9 **Kilimanjaro**, Tanzania ▲
131 V 10 **Kilimanjaro**, Tanzania ▣
131 X 12 **Kilindoni**, Tanzania
84 F 8 **Kilingi-Nõmme**, Estonia
94 M 13 **Kilis**, Turkey
96 J 1 **Kilis**, Syria
61 B 19 **Kilkee**, Republic of Ireland
61 D 19 **Kilkenny**, Republic of Ireland
62 K 13 **Kilkhampton**, U.K.
82 F 13 **Kilkis**, Greece
42 D 9 **Killarney**, ON, Canada
61 B 20 **Killarney**, Republic of Ireland
22 H 4 **Killdeer**, ND, U.S.A.
27 P 8 **Killeen**, TX, U.S.A.
41 T 5 **Killiniq**, QC, Canada
60 G 13 **Kilmarnock**, U.K.
91 Q 14 **Kil'mez'**, Russian Federation
131 V 12 **Kilosa**, Tanzania
61 B 19 **Kilrush**, Republic of Ireland
105 B 22 **Kilttan**, India ⛱
131 P 13 **Kilwa**, Democratic Republic of Congo
131 W 13 **Kilwa Kivinje**, Tanzania
117 T 12 **Kilwo**, Indonesia
31 T 7 **Kim**, CO, U.S.A.
129 W 11 **Kim**, Chad
117 X 14 **Kimaan**, Indonesia
131 W 13 **Kimambi**, Tanzania
130 G 10 **Kimba**, Congo
135 O 11 **Kimba**, SA, Australia
22 G 14 **Kimball**, NE, U.S.A.
138 G 4 **Kimbe**, Papua New Guinea
132 M 12 **Kimberley**, Republic of South Africa
134 K 3 **Kimberley**, WA, Australia ◇
111 M 16 **Kimch'aek**, North Korea
41 R 4 **Kimmirut**, NU, Canada
83 I 23 **Kimolos**, Greece ⛱
128 K 10 **Kimparana**, Mali
130 G 11 **Kimpese**, Democratic Republic of Congo
122 I 13 **Kimpoku-san**, Japan ▲
130 H 11 **Kimvula**, Democratic Republic of Congo
119 V 6 **Kinabatangan**, Malaysia ∫
131 W 10 **Kinango**, Kenya
83 L 22 **Kinaros**, Greece ⛱
42 C 12 **Kincardine**, ON, Canada
131 N 13 **Kinda**, Democratic Republic of Congo
18 I 7 **Kinder**, LA, U.S.A.
39 L 19 **Kindersley**, SK, Canada
128 F 11 **Kindia**, Guinea
131 O 9 **Kindu**, Democratic Republic of Congo
93 T 3 **Kinel'-Cherkasy**, Russian Federation
90 L 13 **Kineshma**, Russian Federation
33 H 21 **King City**, CA, U.S.A.
57 K 23 **King George Bay**, Falkland Islands ≈
144 G 3 **King George Island**, Antarctica ⛱
37 S 9 **King George Islands**, NU, Canada ⛱
135 R 14 **King Island**, TAS, Australia ⛱
145 X 7 **King Leopold and Queen Astrid Coast**, Antarctica ◇
134 I 3 **King Leopold Ranges**, WA, Australia ⛰
39 D 16 **King Mountain**, BC, Canada ▲
144 J 9 **King Peninsula**, Antarctica ▶
134 I 3 **King Sound**, WA, Australia ≈
40 L 1 **King William Island**, NU, Canada ⛱
135 W 8 **Kingaroy**, QLD, Australia
24 M 9 **Kingfisher**, OK, U.S.A.
90 D 11 **Kingisepp**, Russian Federation
24 M 6 **Kingman**, KS, U.S.A.
30 G 10 **Kingman**, AZ, U.S.A.
101 V 10 **Kingri**, Pakistan
61 M 19 **King's**, U.K.
63 X 6 **King's Lynn**, U.K.
14 L 12 **Kings Park**, NY, U.S.A.
30 L 2 **Kings Peak**, UT, U.S.A. ▲
63 T 12 **King's Worthy**, U.K.
63 N 15 **Kingsbridge**, U.K.
63 T 11 **Kingsclere**, U.K.
135 P 12 **Kingscote**, SA, Australia
19 W 6 **Kingsland**, GA, U.S.A.
16 L 8 **Kingsport**, TN, U.S.A.
14 J 10 **Kingston**, NY, U.S.A.
15 N 11 **Kingston**, RI, U.S.A.
21 D 19 **Kingston**, IL, U.S.A.
42 I 12 **Kingston**, ON, Canada
48 L 8 **Kingston**, Jamaica ▟
137 C 23 **Kingston**, New Zealand
135 Q 13 **Kingston S.E.**, SA, Australia
63 V 2 **Kingston upon Hull**, U.K.
63 V 11 **Kingston upon Thames**, U.K.
49 Y 12 **Kingstown**, St Vincent and the Grenadines ▟
27 P 13 **Kingsville**, TX, U.S.A.
63 Q 11 **Kingswood**, U.K.
63 P 8 **Kington**, U.K.
130 J 11 **Kingungi**, Democratic Republic of Congo
122 L 12 **Kinka-san**, Japan ▶
130 G 10 **Kinkala**, Congo
136 L 11 **Kinloch**, New Zealand
71 E 23 **Kinna**, Sweden
69 K 17 **Kinrooi**, Belgium
130 H 10 **Kinshasa**, Democratic Republic of Congo ▟
130 H 10 **Kinshasa**, Democratic Republic of Congo ▣
24 K 5 **Kinsley**, KS, U.S.A.
17 T 10 **Kinston**, NC, U.S.A.
128 M 12 **Kintampo**, Ghana
128 H 10 **Kintinian**, Guinea
117 P 11 **Kintom**, Indonesia
116 L 12 **Kintop**, Indonesia
61 F 14 **Kintyre**, U.K. ⛱
114 D 10 **Kinu**, Myanmar
131 T 10 **Kinyangiri**, Tanzania
127 F 23 **Kinyeti**, Sudan ▲
131 T 12 **Kipembawe**, Tanzania
131 R 12 **Kipili**, Tanzania
34 L 10 **Kipnuk**, AK, U.S.A.
131 P 15 **Kipushi**, Democratic Republic of Congo
131 Q 15 **Kipushia**, Democratic Republic of Congo
139 N 7 **Kirakira**, Solomon Islands
105 G 17 **Kirandul**, India
128 H 8 **Kirané**, Mali
105 F 23 **Kiranur**, India
85 L 18 **Kirawsk**, Belarus
27 U 8 **Kirbyville**, TX, U.S.A.
75 T 5 **Kirchdorf**, Austria
73 G 23 **Kirchheim**, Germany
89 Q 13 **Kirenga**, Russian Federation ∫
89 Q 12 **Kirensk**, Russian Federation
103 T 10 **Kirghiz Range**, Kyrgyzstan ⛰
130 J 8 **Kiri**, Democratic Republic of Congo
140 I 4 **Kiribati**, Oceania □
95 Q 8 **Kirik**, Turkey
94 L 13 **Kirikhan**, Turkey
94 I 9 **Kirikkale**, Turkey
90 J 11 **Kirillov**, Russian Federation
90 F 11 **Kirishi**, Russian Federation
123 C 23 **Kirishima-yama**, Japan ▲
136 K 11 **Kiritehere**, New Zealand
138 G 6 **Kiriwina Island**, Papua New Guinea ⛱
63 Q 1 **Kirkby Lonsdale**, U.K.
63 U 1 **Kirkbymoorside**, U.K.
60 I 12 **Kirkcaldy**, U.K.
70 M 6 **Kirkenes**, Norway
63 P 2 **Kirkham**, U.K.
71 L 19 **Kirkkonummi**, Finland
42 E 6 **Kirkland Lake**, ON, Canada
82 M 11 **Kirklareli**, Turkey
94 C 6 **Kirklareli**, Turkey
25 U 1 **Kirksville**, MO, U.S.A.
97 T 3 **Kirkūk**, Iraq
60 I 7 **Kirkwall**, U.K.
25 X 4 **Kirkwood**, MO, U.S.A.
73 D 20 **Kirn**, Germany
91 P 12 **Kirov**, Russian Federation
92 I 2 **Kirov**, Russian Federation
87 V 8 **Kirove**, Ukraine
91 P 12 **Kirovo-Chepetsk**, Russian Federation
87 R 6 **Kirovohrad**, Ukraine
91 P 13 **Kirovskaya Oblast'**, Russian Federation ▣
87 V 11 **Kirovs'ke**, Ukraine
91 Q 11 **Kirs**, Russian Federation
94 J 10 **Kirşehir**, Turkey
101 T 12 **Kirthar Range**, Pakistan ⛰
70 I 9 **Kiruna**, Sweden
131 N 8 **Kirundu**, Democratic Republic of Congo
92 L 1 **Kirzhach**, Russian Federation
71 G 22 **Kisa**, Sweden
131 N 7 **Kisangani**, Democratic Republic of Congo
117 R 14 **Kisar**, Indonesia ⛱
131 W 12 **Kisarawe**, Tanzania
123 K 16 **Kisarazu**, Japan
88 M 12 **Kiselevsk**, Russian Federation
80 H 12 **Kiseljak**, Bosnia and Herzegovina
107 R 11 **Kishanganj**, India
123 C 24 **Kishika-zaki**, Japan ▶
123 G 19 **Kishiwada**, Japan
103 S 2 **Kishkenekol'**, Kazakhstan
107 U 12 **Kishorganj**, Bangladesh
106 I 4 **Kishtwar**, India
129 P 12 **Kisi**, Nigeria
131 T 8 **Kisii**, Kenya
34 C 12 **Kiska Island**, AK, U.S.A. ⛱
79 J 25 **Kiskőrös**, Hungary
79 K 24 **Kiskunfélegyháza**, Hungary
79 J 25 **Kiskunhalas**, Hungary
93 O 13 **Kislovodsk**, Russian Federation
127 K 26 **Kismaayo**, Somalia
123 I 17 **Kiso-sanmyaku**, Japan ⛰
128 H 11 **Kissidougou**, Guinea
19 W 10 **Kissimmee**, FL, U.S.A.
131 T 8 **Kisumu**, Kenya
79 N 21 **Kisvárda**, Hungary
31 U 5 **Kit Carson**, CO, U.S.A.
128 H 9 **Kita**, Mali
123 B 20 **Kita-Kyūshū**, Japan
123 L 14 **Kitaibaraki**, Japan
122 K 11 **Kitakami**, Japan
122 K 13 **Kitakata**, Japan
131 U 7 **Kitale**, Kenya
122 L 4 **Kitami**, Japan
122 J 3 **Kitami-sanchi**, Japan ⛰
131 O 11 **Kitanda**, Democratic Republic of Congo
123 D 22 **Kitaura**, Japan
42 D 13 **Kitchener**, ON, Canada
131 S 6 **Kitgum**, Uganda
39 D 19 **Kitimat**, BC, Canada
70 L 10 **Kitinen**, Finland ∫
83 E 14 **Kitros**, Greece
86 K 6 **Kitsman'**, Ukraine
14 B 12 **Kittanning**, PA, U.S.A.
70 K 10 **Kittilä**, Finland
17 W 8 **Kitty Hawk**, NC, U.S.A.
131 S 12 **Kitunda**, Tanzania
133 O 4 **Kitwe**, Zambia
75 P 6 **Kitzbühel**, Austria
75 O 7 **Kitzbüheler Alpen**, Austria ⛰
138 A 5 **Kiunga**, Papua New Guinea
71 L 15 **Kivijärvi**, Finland ∽
84 I 6 **Kiviõli**, Estonia
138 C 6 **Kiwai Island**, Papua New Guinea ⛱
35 N 6 **Kiwalik**, AK, U.S.A.
103 S 5 **Kiyevka**, Kazakhstan
94 C 6 **Kiyiköy**, Turkey
91 T 11 **Kizel**, Russian Federation
90 M 10 **Kizema**, Russian Federation
94 I 9 **Kizilirmak**, Turkey ∫
94 G 12 **Kizilören**, Turkey
95 P 13 **Kiziltepe**, Turkey
93 Q 13 **Kizlyar**, Russian Federation
69 G 14 **Klaaswaal**, Netherlands
117 X 15 **Kladar**, Indonesia
79 C 17 **Kladno**, Czech Republic
80 O 10 **Kladovo**, Serbia and Montenegro
115 I 20 **Klaeng**, Thailand
119 W 5 **Klagan**, Malaysia
75 T 9 **Klagenfurt**, Austria
84 B 13 **Klaipėda**, Lithuania
33 E 14 **Klamath**, CA, U.S.A.
33 H 14 **Klamath Falls**, OR, U.S.A.
79 B 18 **Klatovy**, Czech Republic
68 N 9 **Klazienaveen**, Netherlands
132 I 13 **Kleinsee**, Republic of South Africa
80 E 11 **Klekovača**, Bosnia and Herzegovina ▲
87 N 7 **Klembivka**, Ukraine
133 N 11 **Klerksdorp**, Republic of South Africa
78 N 12 **Kleszczele**, Poland
92 H 3 **Kletnya**, Russian Federation
86 L 3 **Klevan**, Ukraine
73 B 15 **Kleve**, Germany
85 L 18 **Klichaw**, Belarus
85 O 17 **Klimavichy**, Belarus
82 L 7 **Kliment**, Bulgaria
90 H 14 **Klin**, Russian Federation
71 H 23 **Klintehamn**, Sweden
93 S 5 **Klintsovka**, Russian Federation
92 G 3 **Klintsy**, Russian Federation
81 O 15 **Klisura**, Serbia and Montenegro
80 F 11 **Ključ**, Bosnia and Herzegovina
79 I 15 **Kłobuck**, Poland
79 F 17 **Kłodzko**, Poland
71 D 19 **Kløfta**, Norway
69 E 16 **Kloosterzande**, Netherlands
74 J 8 **Klosters**, Switzerland
79 H 15 **Kluczbork**, Poland
85 I 19 **Klyetsk**, Belarus
89 Y 10 **Klyuchi**, Russian Federation
63 S 1 **Knaresborough**, U.K.
71 A 18 **Knarvik**, Norway
82 H 7 **Knezha**, Bulgaria
80 L 12 **Knić**, Serbia and Montenegro
63 O 7 **Knighton**, U.K.
80 E 12 **Knin**, Croatia
75 U 7 **Knittelfeld**, Austria
19 V 12 **Knob Island**, FL, U.S.A. ⛱
69 C 16 **Knokke-Heist**, Belgium
63 T 2 **Knottingley**, U.K.
21 I 17 **Knox**, IN, U.S.A.
141 Z 4 **Knox**, Marshall Islands ⛱
145 X 10 **Knox Coast**, Antarctica ◇
16 J 9 **Knoxville**, TN, U.S.A.
19 T 4 **Knoxville**, GA, U.S.A.
23 T 13 **Knoxville**, IA, U.S.A.
143 P 10 **Knud Rasmussen Land**, Greenland ◇
63 Q 4 **Knutsford**, U.K.
132 L 15 **Knysna**, Republic of South Africa
115 F 23 **Ko Chan**, Thailand ⛱
115 J 21 **Ko Chang**, Thailand ⛱
122 I 8 **Ko-jima**, Japan ⛱
115 J 21 **Ko Kut**, Thailand ⛱
115 F 25 **Ko Lanta**, Thailand ⛱
115 G 25 **Ko Lanta**, Thailand
115 G 25 **Ko Libong**, Thailand ⛱
115 H 23 **Ko Phangan**, Thailand ⛱
115 F 23 **Ko Phra Thong**, Thailand ⛱
115 F 25 **Ko Phuket**, Thailand ⛱
115 H 23 **Ko Samui**, Thailand ⛱
115 G 23 **Ko Tao**, Thailand ⛱
115 G 25 **Ko Yao Yai**, Thailand ⛱
131 W 11 **Koani**, Tanzania
116 G 12 **Koba**, Indonesia
80 A 7 **Kobarid**, Slovenia
117 R 10 **Kobe**, Indonesia
123 F 18 **Kōbe**, Japan
87 T 5 **Kobelyaky**, Ukraine
128 H 8 **Kobenni**, Mauritania
73 D 18 **Koblenz**, Germany
87 Q 9 **Kobleve**, Ukraine
127 I 18 **K'obo**, Ethiopia
131 R 6 **Koboko**, Uganda
117 V 13 **Kobroör**, Indonesia ⛱
85 F 21 **Kobryn**, Belarus
35 O 5 **Kobuk**, AK, U.S.A.
35 O 5 **Kobuk**, AK, U.S.A. ∫
95 Q 7 **K'obulet'i**, Georgia
94 E 8 **Kocaeli**, Turkey
82 E 11 **Kočani**, Macedonia (F.Y.R.O.M.)
80 K 11 **Koceljevo**, Serbia and Montenegro
80 C 8 **Kočevje**, Slovenia
107 T 10 **Koch Bihar**, India
123 E 20 **Kōchi**, Japan
103 V 10 **Kochkor**, Kyrgyzstan
93 R 13 **Kochubey**, Russian Federation
79 N 14 **Kock**, Poland
123 B 26 **Kodakara-jima**, Japan ⛱
107 Q 9 **Kodari**, Nepal
107 Q 12 **Kodarma**, India
35 Q 11 **Kodiak**, AK, U.S.A.
35 P 12 **Kodiak Island**, AK, U.S.A. ⛱
105 A 16 **Kodinar**, India
90 K 7 **Kodino**, Russian Federation
89 P 12 **Kodinsk**, Russian Federation
127 E 20 **Kodok**, Sudan
122 J 8 **Kodomari-misaki**, Japan ▶
82 K 12 **Kodzhaele**, Greece ▲
132 J 11 **Koës**, Namibia
82 M 11 **Kofşşaz**, Turkey
94 H 15 **Kofínou**, Cyprus
75 V 7 **Köflach**, Austria
128 M 13 **Koforidua**, Ghana
123 J 16 **Kōfu**, Japan
123 E 18 **Kōfu**, Japan
41 P 6 **Kogaluk**, QC, Canada ∫
88 L 10 **Kogalym**, Russian Federation
71 D 25 **Køge**, Denmark
129 Q 12 **Kogi**, Nigeria ▣
101 R 8 **Koh-i-Sangān**, Afghanistan ▲
101 S 13 **Kohan**, Pakistan
101 W 8 **Kohat**, Pakistan
84 G 6 **Kohila**, Estonia
107 X 11 **Kohima**, India
100 H 9 **Kohkīlūyeh Va Būyeraḩmadī**, Iran ▣
101 P 7 **Kohsan**, Afghanistan
84 I 5 **Kohtla-Järve**, Estonia
97 T 2 **Koi Sanjaq**, Iraq
70 L 11 **Koivu**, Finland
111 N 21 **Kōje-do**, South Korea ⛱
134 G 12 **Kojonup**, WA, Australia
103 V 12 **Kök-Aygy**, Kyrgyzstan
103 S 12 **Kokand**, Uzbekistan
128 E 8 **Koki**, Senegal
71 K 14 **Kokkola**, Finland
129 P 10 **Koko**, Nigeria
138 E 6 **Kokoda**, Papua New Guinea
128 H 9 **Kokofata**, Mali
21 I 18 **Kokomo**, IN, U.S.A.
137 E 23 **Kokonga**, New Zealand
138 H 4 **Kokopo**, Papua New Guinea
129 O 12 **Kokoro**, Benin
103 X 5 **Kokpekti**, Kazakhstan
103 Q 10 **Koksaray**, Kazakhstan
103 R 3 **Kokshetau**, Kazakhstan
69 A 17 **Koksijde**, Belgium
133 O 13 **Kokstad**, Republic of South Africa
103 X 9 **Koktal**, Kazakhstan
103 Y 7 **Koktuma**, Kazakhstan
123 C 23 **Kokubu**, Japan
90 J 4 **Kola Peninsula**, Russian Federation ▶
117 O 13 **Kolaka**, Indonesia
105 E 21 **Kolar**, India
104 E 13 **Kolaras**, India
70 K 10 **Kolari**, Finland
81 J 15 **Kolašin**, Serbia and Montenegro
104 C 11 **Kolayat**, India
128 E 9 **Kolda**, Senegal
130 M 10 **Kole**, Democratic Republic of Congo
131 N 6 **Kole**, Democratic Republic of Congo
84 H 7 **Kolga-Jaani**, Estonia
84 G 5 **Kolga laht**, Estonia ≈
105 C 18 **Kolhapur**, India
105 L 19 **Kolhumadulu Atoll**, Maldives ⛱
35 O 10 **Koliganek**, AK, U.S.A.
71 O 15 **Kolin**, Finland ▲
79 E 17 **Kolín**, Czech Republic
127 I 21 **K'olīto**, Ethiopia
140 H 8 **Koliu**, Wallis and Futuna Islands
84 D 9 **Kolkasrags**, Latvia ▶
103 R 14 **Kolkhozobod**, Tajikistan
86 K 2 **Kolky**, Ukraine
75 S 3 **Kollerschlag**, Austria
78 M 10 **Kolno**, Poland
78 I 13 **Koło**, Poland
78 E 8 **Kołobrzeg**, Poland
128 I 9 **Kolokani**, Mali
138 K 6 **Kolombangara**, Solomon Islands ⛱
92 L 2 **Kolomna**, Russian Federation
86 J 6 **Kolomyya**, Ukraine
128 J 10 **Kolondiéba**, Mali
141 Q 15 **Kolonia**, Federated States of Micronesia
117 P 13 **Kolono**, Indonesia
88 M 11 **Kolpashevo**, Russian Federation
90 F 10 **Kolpino**, Russian Federation
83 H 15 **Kolpos Agiou Orous**, Greece ≈
83 H 25 **Kolpos Chanion**, Greece ≈
83 G 14 **Kolpos Ierissou**, Greece ≈
83 G 15 **Kolpos Kassandras**, Greece ≈
82 H 13 **Kolpos Kavalas**, Greece ≈
83 G 25 **Kolpos Kissamou**, Greece ≈
103 X 9 **Kol'shat**, Kazakhstan
93 T 3 **Koltubanovskiy**, Russian Federation
103 R 4 **Koluton**, Kazakhstan
131 N 14 **Kolwezi**, Democratic Republic of Congo
85 M 22 **Kolyban**, Belarus
89 W 8 **Kolyma**, Russian Federation ∫
126 F 11 **Kôm Ombo**, Egypt
123 H 17 **Komaki**, Japan
131 Q 8 **Komanda**, Democratic Republic of Congo
79 H 22 **Komárno**, Slovakia
123 H 16 **Komatsu**, Japan
117 P 11 **Kombakomba**, Indonesia
128 M 10 **Kombissiri**, Burkina Faso
91 R 10 **Komi-Permyatskiy Avtonomnyy Okrug**, Russian Federation ▣
87 Q 9 **Kominternivs'ke**, Ukraine
79 H 25 **Komló**, Hungary
117 N 15 **Komodo**, Indonesia ⛱
128 H 11 **Komodou**, Guinea
123 J 15 **Komoro**, Japan
83 J 13 **Komotini**, Greece
87 R 7 **Kompaniyivka**, Ukraine
132 M 14 **Kompasberg**, Republic of South Africa ▲
103 N 2 **Komsomolets**, Kazakhstan
89 W 13 **Komsomol'sk-na-Amure**, Russian Federation
89 Y 6 **Komsomol'skiy**, Russian Federation
102 M 5 **Komsomol'skoye**, Kazakhstan
82 J 11 **Komuniga**, Bulgaria
115 O 18 **Kon Plong**, Vietnam
115 O 18 **Kon Tum**, Vietnam
105 J 17 **Konarka**, India
106 K 11 **Konch**, India
105 H 17 **Kondagaon**, India
131 U 11 **Kondoa**, Tanzania
93 P 4 **Kondol**, Russian Federation
101 U 5 **Kondūz**, Afghanistan
139 P 13 **Koné**, New Caledonia
143 O 13 **Kong Christian IX Land**, Greenland ◇
143 P 12 **Kong Christian X Land**, Greenland ◇
143 N 12 **Kong Frederik IX Land**, Greenland ◇
143 Q 11 **Kong Frederik VIII Land**, Greenland ◇
143 Q 12 **Kong Wilhelm Land**, Greenland ◇
132 L 7 **Kongola**, Namibia
131 O 11 **Kongolo**, Democratic Republic of Congo
128 M 9 **Kongoussi**, Burkina Faso
71 D 20 **Kongsberg**, Norway
71 E 19 **Kongsvinger**, Norway
108 G 6 **Kongur Shan**, China ▲
131 U 11 **Kongwa**, Tanzania
73 M 25 **Königssee**, Germany ∽
78 H 13 **Konin**, Poland
137 L 15 **Konini**, New Zealand
83 B 15 **Konitsa**, Greece
80 H 13 **Konjic**, Bosnia and Herzegovina
70 J 8 **Könkämäeno**, Finland ∫
128 K 8 **Konna**, Mali
128 M 13 **Konongo**, Ghana
138 G 3 **Konos**, Papua New Guinea
90 K 10 **Konosha**, Russian Federation
87 S 2 **Konotop**, Ukraine
79 K 15 **Końskie**, Poland
127 H 22 **Konso**, Ethiopia
73 F 25 **Konstanz**, Germany
105 G 18 **Konta**, India
129 Q 11 **Kontagora**, Nigeria
71 N 14 **Kontiomäki**, Finland
94 H 12 **Konya**, Turkey
117 U 11 **Koor**, Indonesia
134 G 10 **Koorda**, WA, Australia
28 K 6 **Kooskia**, ID, U.S.A.
136 K 11 **Kopaki**, New Zealand
81 L 14 **Kopaonik**, Serbia and Montenegro ⛰
70 C 9 **Kópasker**, Iceland
103 V 7 **Kopbirlik**, Kazakhstan
80 A 8 **Koper**, Slovenia
102 J 13 **Kopet Dag**, Turkmenistan ⛰
81 J 16 **Koplik**, Albania
105 D 21 **Koppa**, India
71 D 17 **Koppang**, Norway
80 F 7 **Koprivnica**, Croatia
86 L 5 **Kopychyntsi**, Ukraine
81 L 17 **Korab**, Albania ▲
81 L 17 **Korab**, Albania ⛰
92 M 3 **Korablino**, Russian Federation
127 L 22 **K'orahē**, Ethiopia
105 E 18 **Korangal**, India
105 H 15 **Korba**, India
73 F 16 **Korbach**, Germany
129 X 11 **Korbol**, Chad
81 L 20 **Korşşë**, Albania
81 F 15 **Korčula**, Croatia
81 E 15 **Korčula**, Croatia ⛱
81 E 14 **Korčulanski Kanal**, Croatia ≈
103 U 10 **Korday**, Kazakhstan
100 F 5 **Kordestān**, Iran ▣
111 I 18 **Korea Bay**, China/North Korea ≈
111 M 22 **Korea Strait**, Japan/South Korea ≈
127 I 18 **Korem**, Ethiopia
136 J 7 **Koremoa**, New Zealand
92 I 5 **Korenevo**, Russian Federation
92 L 11 **Korenovsk**, Russian Federation
86 L 3 **Korets'**, Ukraine
89 Z 9 **Korf**, Russian Federation
94 E 8 **Körfez**, Turkey
108 I 4 **Korgas**, China
128 J 11 **Korhogo**, Côte d'Ivoire
83 F 20 **Korinthos**, Greece
79 H 23 **Kőris-hegy**, Hungary ▲
122 K 13 **Kōriyama**, Japan
94 E 12 **Korkuteli**, Turkey
108 K 5 **Korla**, China
79 F 24 **Körmend**, Hungary
80 C 12 **Kornat**, Croatia ⛱
75 X 3 **Korneuburg**, Austria
128 L 9 **Koro**, Mali
139 Y 11 **Koro**, Fiji ⛱
139 X 12 **Koro Sea**, Fiji ◒
129 X 8 **Koro Toro**, Chad
94 F 8 **Köroğlu Dağlari**, Turkey ⛰
94 G 8 **Köroğlu Tepesi**, Turkey ▲
131 W 11 **Korogwe**, Tanzania
121 L 23 **Koronadal**, Philippines
83 D 23 **Koroni**, Greece
140 I 15 **Koror**, Palau ▟
79 K 24 **Körös**, Hungary ∫
87 N 3 **Korosten'**, Ukraine
87 O 4 **Korostyshiv**, Ukraine
71 M 17 **Korpilahti**, Finland
87 Q 5 **Korsun'-Shevchenkivs'kyy**, Ukraine
69 B 18 **Kortemark**, Belgium
127 E 15 **Korti**, Sudan
69 C 19 **Kortrijk**, Belgium
89 Y 9 **Koryakskiy Khrebet**, Russian Federation ⛰
91 N 10 **Koryazhma**, Russian Federation
78 N 10 **Korycin**, Poland
87 R 1 **Koryukivka**, Ukraine
83 M 22 **Kos**, Greece
83 M 23 **Kos**, Greece ⛱
87 U 10 **Kosa Arabats'ka Strilka**, Ukraine ≈
87 V 10 **Kosa Biryuchyy Ostriv**, Ukraine ▶
111 L 17 **Kosan**, North Korea
78 F 13 **Kościan**, Poland
78 H 9 **Kościerzyna**, Poland
18 M 4 **Kosciusko**, MS, U.S.A.
84 G 6 **Kose**, Estonia
88 M 14 **Kosh-Agach**, Russian Federation
103 U 11 **Kosh-Döbö**, Kyrgyzstan
123 B 23 **Koshiki-kaikyō**, Japan ≈
123 A 23 **Koshikijima-rettō**, Japan ⛱
101 P 7 **Koshk**, Afghanistan
107 R 10 **Kosi Reservoir**, Nepal ∽
79 L 20 **Košice**, Slovakia
86 J 7 **Kosiv**, Ukraine
80 K 12 **Kosjerić**, Serbia and Montenegro
103 Q 5 **Koskol'**, Kazakhstan
111 M 18 **Kosŏng**, North Korea
81 L 15 **Kosovo**, Serbia and Montenegro ▣
81 L 15 **Kosovska Mitrovica**, Serbia and Montenegro
141 R 15 **Kosrae**, Federated States of Micronesia ⛱
141 R 15 **Kosrae**, Federated States of Micronesia ▣
75 P 6 **Kössen**, Austria
103 O 4 **Kostanay**, Kazakhstan ▣
103 O 3 **Kostanay**, Kazakhstan
82 H 10 **Kostenets**, Bulgaria
127 F 18 **Kosti**, Sudan
82 F 9 **Kostinbrod**, Bulgaria
86 L 3 **Kostopil'**, Ukraine
90 K 13 **Kostroma**, Russian Federation
90 L 12 **Kostromskaya Oblast'**, Russian Federation ▣
78 D 12 **Kostrzyn**, Poland
87 X 6 **Kostyantynivka**, Ukraine
91 S 4 **Kos'yu**, Russian Federation
78 F 8 **Koszalin**, Poland
79 K 17 **Koszyce**, Poland
101 U 13 **Kot Diji**, Pakistan
106 I 9 **Kot Putli**, India
104 D 13 **Kota**, India
119 V 4 **Kota Belud**, Malaysia
118 C 5 **Kota Bharu**, Malaysia
119 U 5 **Kota Kinabalu**, Malaysia
118 F 10 **Kota Tinggi**, Malaysia
116 F 13 **Kotaagung**, Indonesia
116 M 12 **Kotabaru**, Indonesia
116 F 13 **Kotabumi**, Indonesia
117 Q 10 **Kotamobagu**, Indonesia
116 D 10 **Kotapinang**, Indonesia
136 K 12 **Kotare**, New Zealand
82 L 8 **Kotel**, Bulgaria
91 O 13 **Kotel'nich**, Russian Federation
93 O 9 **Kotel'nikovo**, Russian Federation
87 U 4 **Kotel'va**, Ukraine
131 T 6 **Kotido**, Uganda
71 N 18 **Kotka**, Finland
91 N 10 **Kotlas**, Russian Federation
106 G 4 **Kotli**, India
81 I 16 **Kotor**, Serbia and Montenegro
80 G 10 **Kotor Varoš**, Bosnia and Herzegovina
129 R 10 **Kotorkoshi**, Nigeria
128 L 12 **Kotouba**, Côte d'Ivoire
87 O 8 **Kotovs'k**, Ukraine
85 F 18 **Kotra**, Belarus ∫
101 U 14 **Kotri**, Pakistan
75 Q 9 **Kötschach**, Austria
105 G 18 **Kottagudem**, India
105 G 19 **Kottapatnam**, India
130 L 4 **Kotto**, Central African Republic ∫
89 R 8 **Kotuy**, Russian Federation ∫
35 N 5 **Kotzebue**, AK, U.S.A.
34 M 5 **Kotzebue Sound**, AK, U.S.A. ≈
130 K 4 **Kouango**, Central African Republic
128 G 10 **Koubia**, Guinea
130 E 10 **Kouilou**, Congo ▣
94 G 15 **Koúklia**, Cyprus
130 E 8 **Koulamoutou**, Gabon
128 I 9 **Koulikoro**, Mali
128 I 9 **Koulikoro**, Mali ▣
139 O 13 **Koumac**, New Caledonia
128 F 10 **Koumbia**, Guinea
129 X 11 **Koumra**, Chad
128 F 9 **Koûndâra**, Guinea
128 E 9 **Koungheul**, Senegal
128 M 10 **Koupéla**, Burkina Faso
51 Y 6 **Kourou**, French Guiana
128 H 11 **Kouroussa**, Guinea
128 F 9 **Koussanar**, Senegal
129 V 10 **Kousséri**, Chad
128 J 10 **Koutiala**, Mali
83 D 16 **Koutsochero**, Greece
71 N 18 **Kouvola**, Finland
90 G 3 **Kovdor**, Russian Federation
86 J 2 **Kovel'**, Ukraine
93 N 1 **Kovrov**, Russian Federation
93 O 3 **Kovylkino**, Russian Federation
135 R 3 **Kowanyama**, QLD, Australia
113 U 13 **Kowloon**, China
111 L 17 **Kowŏn**, North Korea
94 C 12 **Köycegiz**, Turkey
90 L 5 **Koyda**, Russian Federation
35 O 6 **Koykuyuk**, AK, U.S.A.
105 C 18 **Koyna Reservoir**, India ∽
82 G 7 **Koynare**, Bulgaria
35 N 6 **Koyuk**, AK, U.S.A.
94 M 9 **Koyulhisar**, Turkey
94 K 12 **Kozan**, Turkey
83 D 15 **Kozani**, Greece
80 F 9 **Kozara**, Bosnia and Herzegovina ⛰
87 Q 3 **Kozelets'**, Ukraine
92 J 3 **Kozel'sk**, Russian Federation
89 R 7 **Kozhevnikovo**, Russian Federation
79 L 14 **Kozienice**, Poland
82 G 6 **Kozloduy**, Bulgaria
93 Q 1 **Koz'modem'yansk**, Russian Federation
123 K 18 **Kōzu-shima**, Japan ⛱
87 O 5 **Kozyatyn**, Ukraine
129 N 13 **Kpalimé**, Togo
115 F 22 **Kra Buri**, Thailand
115 G 25 **Krabi**, Thailand
115 M 20 **Krâchéh**, Cambodia
80 L 12 **Kragujevac**, Serbia and Montenegro
116 G 14 **Krakatau**, Indonesia ▲
79 K 17 **Kraków**, Poland
115 K 19 **Krâlănh**, Cambodia
49 S 13 **Kralendijk**, Netherlands Antilles
80 B 9 **Kraljevića**, Croatia
80 L 12 **Kraljevo**, Serbia and Montenegro
79 B 17 **Kralovice**, Czech Republic
87 X 6 **Kramators'k**, Ukraine
69 F 15 **Krammer**, Netherlands ≈
83 F 21 **Kranidi**, Greece
80 B 7 **Kranj**, Slovenia
118 A 13 **Kranji Reservoir**, Singapore ∽
102 K 4 **Kransoyar**, Kazakhstan
80 D 7 **Krapina**, Croatia
79 H 16 **Krapkowice**, Poland
88 K 6 **Krasino**, Russian Federation
84 I 13 **Krāslava**, Latvia
85 N 18 **Krasnapollye**, Belarus
93 N 1 **Krasnaya**, Russian Federation
92 L 13 **Krasnaya Polyana**, Russian Federation
85 I 19 **Krasnaya Slabada**, Belarus
87 O 8 **Krasni Okny**, Ukraine
79 M 15 **Kraśnik**, Poland
93 Q 6 **Krasnoarmeysk**, Russian Federation
87 X 7 **Krasnoarmiys'k**, Ukraine
91 N 9 **Krasnoborsk**, Russian Federation
92 K 12 **Krasnodar**, Russian Federation
92 L 11 **Krasnodarskiy Kray**, Russian Federation ▣
92 M 11 **Krasnogvardeyskoye**, Russian Federation
87 V 5 **Krasnohrad**, Ukraine
91 S 12 **Krasnokamsk**, Russian Federation
93 U 5 **Krasnokholm**, Russian Federation
87 W 5 **Krasnopavlivka**, Ukraine
87 T 10 **Krasnoperekops'k**, Ukraine
87 U 3 **Krasnopillya**, Ukraine
89 N 9 **Krasnosel'kup**, Russian Federation
90 J 4 **Krasnoshchel'ye**, Russian Federation
87 S 6 **Krasnosillya**, Ukraine
93 O 2 **Krasnoslobodsk**, Russian Federation
91 U 13 **Krasnoufimsk**, Russian Federation
93 W 2 **Krasnousol'skiy**, Russian Federation
91 T 10 **Krasnovishersk**, Russian Federation
102 H 12 **Krasnovodskiy Zaliv**, Turkmenistan ≈
89 N 12 **Krasnoyarsk**, Russian Federation
92 H 2 **Krasnoye**, Russian Federation
79 O 15 **Krasnystaw**, Poland
92 G 2 **Krasnyy**, Russian Federation
90 I 13 **Krasnyy Kholm**, Russian Federation
93 Q 6 **Krasnyy Kut**, Russian Federation
87 Z 6 **Krasnyy Luch**, Ukraine
87 X 5 **Krasnyy Lyman**, Ukraine
93 P 6 **Krasnyy Yar**, Russian Federation
93 S 10 **Krasnyy Yar**, Russian Federation
93 R 11 **Krasnyye Barrikady**, Russian Federation
82 E 10 **Kratovo**, Macedonia (F.Y.R.O.M.)
117 Y 12 **Krau**, Indonesia
93 R 13 **Kraynovka**, Russian Federation
73 B 16 **Krefeld**, Germany
87 T 6 **Kremenchuk**, Ukraine
87 S 5 **Kremenchuts'ka Vodoskhovyshche**, Ukraine ∽
86 K 4 **Kremenets'**, Ukraine
87 Y 5 **Kreminna**, Ukraine
86 J 6 **Kremintsi**, Ukraine
31 Q 3 **Kremmling**, CO, U.S.A.
75 V 3 **Krems an der Donau**, Austria
82 F 11 **Kresna**, Bulgaria
83 D 21 **Krestena**, Greece
91 Q 4 **Krestovka**, Russian Federation
89 R 11 **Krestyakh**, Russian Federation
84 B 13 **Kretinga**, Lithuania
75 Q 8 **Kreuzeck**, Austria ▲
74 H 6 **Kreuzlingen**, Switzerland

□ Country ▣ Internal administrative region: State/Province/Territory/Dependent territory ▟ Capital city ⛰ Mountain range/ Undersea ridge ▲ Mountain peak/ Volcano/Seamount ◇ Geographic feature ▶ Headland/Point/ Cape/Peninsula ▲ Desert ⛱ Island/Island group ⁙ Antarctic base ◎ Ocean ◒ Sea ≈ Bay/Gulf/Channel/Strait ∽ Lake ⚑ Salt pan/Dry/ Intermittent lake ∫ R

S 15 **Kribi**, Cameroon
W 6 **Krieglach**, Austria
C 18 **Krikellos**, Greece
O 7 **Krimml**, Austria
E 19 **Krishna**, India
E 21 **Krishnagiri**, India
S 13 **Krishnanagar**, India
D 21 **Krishnaraja Sagara**, India
B 22 **Kristiansand**, Norway
F 25 **Kristianstad**, Sweden
C 15 **Kristiansund**, Norway
J 17 **Kristinestad**, Finland
J 26 **Kríti**, Greece
E 10 **Kriva Palanka**, Macedonia (F.Y.R.O.M.)
F 7 **Križevci**, Croatia
B 9 **Krk**, Croatia
B 9 **Krk**, Croatia
E 12 **Krka**, Croatia
U 11 **Krms'kyy Pivostriv**, Ukraine
H 7 **Krokowa**, Poland
B 10 **Króksfjarðarnes**, Iceland
S 2 **Krolevets'**, Ukraine
J 4 **Kromy**, Russian Federation
J 19 **Kronach**, Germany
J 21 **Krŏng Kaôh Kŏng**, Cambodia
Z 10 **Kronotskiy Poluostrov**, Russian Federation
Z 11 **Kronotskiy Zaliv**, Russian Federation
N 12 **Kroonstad**, Republic of South Africa
L 11 **Kropotkin**, Russian Federation
M 18 **Krosno**, Poland
G 14 **Krotoszyn**, Poland
J 7 **Krotz Springs**, LA, U.S.A.
D 7 **Krško**, Slovenia
J 12 **Krumovgrad**, Bulgaria
J 11 **Krupanj**, Serbia and Montenegro
I 21 **Krupina**, Slovakia
M 13 **Kruševac**, Serbia and Montenegro
N 17 **Kryichaw**, Belarus
J 12 **Krymsk**, Russian Federation
T 13 **Krymski Hori**, Ukraine
L 18 **Krynica**, Poland
P 7 **Kryve Ozero**, Ukraine
T 7 **Kryvyy Rih**, Ukraine
N 7 **Kryzhopil'**, Ukraine
I 15 **Krzepice**, Poland
K 10 **Ksabi**, Algeria
M 6 **Ksar Chellala**, Algeria
M 6 **Ksar el Boukhari**, Algeria
I 6 **Ksar el Kebir**, Morocco
O 1 **Kstovo**, Russian Federation
S 6 **Kuala Belait**, Brunei
B 6 **Kuala Kangsar**, Malaysia
C 5 **Kuala Kerai**, Malaysia
Y 5 **Kuala Kinabatangan**, Malaysia
C 7 **Kuala Lipis**, Malaysia
C 8 **Kuala Lumpur**, Malaysia
C 8 **Kuala Lumpur**, Malaysia
U 5 **Kuala Penyu**, Malaysia
B 8 **Kuala Selangor**, Malaysia
E 6 **Kuala Terengganu**, Malaysia
K 11 **Kualakurun**, Indonesia
W 6 **Kuamut**, Malaysia
F 16 **Kuancheng**, China
J 16 **Kuandian**, China
Z 12 **Kuanshan**, Taiwan
E 8 **Kuantan**, Malaysia
O 1 **Kubaybāt**, Syria
R 7 **Kubaysah**, Iraq
A 18 **Kubbum**, Sudan
B 5 **Kubeai**, Papua New Guinea
L 6 **Kubrat**, Bulgaria
M 11 **Kučevo**, Serbia and Montenegro
J 15 **Kuchaiburi**, India
N 10 **Kuching**, Malaysia
B 25 **Kuchino-Erabu-shima**, Japan
B 26 **Kuchino-shima**, Japan
B 22 **Kuchinotsu**, Japan
L 19 **Kuda Huvadu Channel**, Maldives
C 19 **Kudal**, India
N 10 **Kudayd**, Saudi Arabia
F 16 **Kudowa-Zdrój**, Poland
J 14 **Kudus**, Indonesia
S 11 **Kudymkar**, Russian Federation
O 6 **Kufstein**, Austria
G 9 **Kugluktuk**, NU, Canada
C 8 **Kugmallit Bay**, NT, Canada
N 12 **Kūh-e Bazmān**, Iran
F 5 **Kūh-e Chehel Chashmeh**, Iran
L 12 **Kūh-e Fūrgun**, Iran
H 8 **Kūh-e Garbosh**, Iran
T 2 **Kūh-e Ḩājī Ebrāhīm**, Iraq
F 5 **Kūh-e-Haji Ebrahim**, Iran
K 12 **Kūh-e Hormoz**, Iran
L 11 **Kūh-e Ilazārān**, Iran
M 8 **Kūh-e Nāy Band**, Iran
O 13 **Kūh-e Nokhowch**, Iran
O 9 **Kūh-e Palangān**, Iran
I 11 **Kūh-e Shīb**, Iran
P 12 **Kūh-e Taftān**, Iran
Q 13 **Kūhak**, Iran
H 3 **Kuhha-ye Sabalan**, Iran
N 14 **Kuhmo**, Finland
V 12 **Kuitan**, China
I 4 **Kuito**, Angola
L 9 **Kuji**, Japan
K 14 **Kuji**, Japan
C 21 **Kujū-san**, Japan
U 9 **Kukawa**, Nigeria
L 16 **Kukës**, Albania
E 10 **Kukup**, Malaysia
J 8 **Kula**, Serbia and Montenegro
E 6 **Kula**, Bulgaria
C 10 **Kula**, Turkey
K 11 **Kula Kangri**, China
F 23 **Kulassein**, Philippines
V 12 **Kulaura**, Bangladesh
C 11 **Kuldīga**, Latvia
N 1 **Kulebaki**, Russian Federation
N 7 **Kulgera**, NT, Australia
O 10 **Kulkuduk**, Uzbekistan
J 5 **Kullu**, India
J 19 **Kulmbach**, Germany
S 14 **Kŭlob**, Tajikistan
Q 11 **Kulp**, Turkey
J 7 **Kul'sary**, Kazakhstan
R 13 **Kulti**, India
H 10 **Kulu**, Turkey
H 6 **Kulumadau**, Papua New Guinea
L 12 **Kulunda**, Russian Federation
O 12 **Kuma**, Russian Federation
K 15 **Kumagaya**, Japan
I 7 **Kumaishi**, Japan
123 C 22 **Kumamoto**, Japan
123 H 19 **Kumano**, Japan
82 D 10 **Kumanovo**, Macedonia (F.Y.R.O.M.)
137 E 18 **Kumara Junction**, New Zealand
134 H 7 **Kumarina Roadhouse**, WA, Australia
128 L 13 **Kumasi**, Ghana
129 S 14 **Kumba**, Cameroon
105 F 22 **Kumbakonam**, India
117 Y 14 **Kumbe**, Indonesia
94 F 10 **Kümbet**, Turkey
99 P 9 **Kumdah**, Saudi Arabia
123 M 25 **Kume-jima**, Japan
93 W 3 **Kumertau**, Russian Federation
111 M 20 **Kumi**, South Korea
131 T 7 **Kumi**, Uganda
71 G 21 **Kumla**, Sweden
72 L 9 **Kummerower See**, Germany
129 T 11 **Kumo**, Nigeria
115 J 16 **Kumphawapi**, Thailand
105 C 20 **Kumta**, India
131 N 6 **Kumu**, Democratic Republic of Congo
108 L 5 **Kümüx**, China
119 X 6 **Kunak**, Malaysia
101 V 6 **Kunar**, Afghanistan
84 H 5 **Kunda**, Estonia
106 M 11 **Kunda**, India
132 I 2 **Kunda-dia-Baze**, Angola
119 V 4 **Kundat**, Malaysia
138 C 4 **Kundiawa**, Papua New Guinea
116 F 10 **Kundur**, Indonesia
101 U 5 **Kunduz**, Afghanistan
132 G 8 **Kunene**, Namibia
132 F 7 **Kunene**, Namibia
103 V 10 **Kungei Alatau**, Kyrgyzstan
39 C 20 **Kunghit Island**, BC, Canada
102 L 10 **Kungrad**, Uzbekistan
71 D 23 **Kungsbacka**, Sweden
130 J 6 **Kungu**, Democratic Republic of Congo
91 T 13 **Kungur**, Russian Federation
114 F 12 **Kunhing**, Myanmar
123 D 21 **Kunisaki**, Japan
114 F 10 **Kunlong**, Myanmar
108 H 7 **Kunlun Shan**, China
112 L 11 **Kunming**, China
111 L 20 **Kunsan**, South Korea
113 Y 5 **Kunshan**, China
79 K 24 **Kunszentmárton**, Hungary
138 I 4 **Kunua**, Papua New Guinea
134 K 3 **Kununurra**, WA, Australia
130 H 10 **Kunzulu**, Democratic Republic of Congo
90 G 3 **Kuolayarvi**, Russian Federation
71 N 15 **Kuopio**, Finland
117 P 15 **Kupang**, Indonesia
138 E 7 **Kupiano**, Papua New Guinea
84 G 13 **Kupiškis**, Lithuania
35 X 11 **Kupreanof Island**, AK, U.S.A.
87 X 4 **Kup"yans'k**, Ukraine
108 J 5 **Kuqa**, China
95 V 7 **Kür**, Azerbaijan/Turkey
89 N 13 **Kuragino**, Russian Federation
123 E 19 **Kurashiki**, Japan
123 E 18 **Kurayoshi**, Japan
103 Y 5 **Kurchum**, Kazakhstan
100 E 2 **Kurdistan**, Iran
82 J 12 **Kŭrdzhali**, Bulgaria
82 J 11 **Kŭrdzhali**, Bulgaria
94 I 7 **Küre**, Turkey
123 D 20 **Kure**, Japan
94 H 7 **Küre Dağlari**, Turkey
84 D 8 **Kuressaare**, Estonia
103 R 5 **Kurgal'dzhinskiy**, Kazakhstan
88 J 11 **Kurgan**, Russian Federation
92 M 12 **Kurganinsk**, Russian Federation
140 D 2 **Kuria**, Kiribati
99 Y 11 **Kuria Muria**, Oman
71 K 16 **Kurikka**, Finland
89 Y 14 **Kuril Islands**, Russian Federation
93 R 6 **Kurilovka**, Russian Federation
89 Y 14 **Kuril'sk**, Russian Federation
47 Q 8 **Kurinwás**, Nicaragua
92 M 1 **Kurlovskiy**, Russian Federation
127 G 19 **Kurmuk**, Sudan
105 E 19 **Kurnool**, India
123 N 26 **Kuro-shima**, Japan
123 H 15 **Kurobe**, Japan
123 K 14 **Kuroiso**, Japan
79 M 14 **Kurów**, Poland
137 E 22 **Kurow**, New Zealand
93 N 13 **Kursavka**, Russian Federation
84 E 13 **Kuršėnai**, Lithuania
84 D 12 **Kursīši**, Latvia
92 J 5 **Kursk**, Russian Federation
85 B 15 **Kurskaya Kosa**, Russian Federation
92 I 5 **Kurskaya Oblast'**, Russian Federation
94 H 8 **Kurşunlu**, Turkey
95 R 12 **Kurtalan**, Turkey
108 K 5 **Kuruktag**, China
132 L 11 **Kuruman**, Republic of South Africa
123 B 21 **Kurume**, Japan
89 R 13 **Kurumkan**, Russian Federation
105 F 25 **Kurunegala**, Sri Lanka
51 U 7 **Kurupukari**, Guyana
91 S 8 **Kur'ya**, Russian Federation
102 H 10 **Kuryk**, Kazakhstan
94 C 8 **Kuş Gölü**, Turkey
94 B 11 **Kuşadasi**, Turkey
83 M 20 **Kuşadasi Körfezi**, Greece
94 B 11 **Kusadasi Körfezi**, Turkey
39 B 14 **Kusawa Lake**, YT, Canada
92 L 10 **Kushchevskaya**, Russian Federation
123 C 24 **Kushima**, Japan
123 H 20 **Kushimoto**, Japan
122 M 5 **Kushiro**, Japan
103 O 3 **Kushmurun**, Kazakhstan
93 V 1 **Kushnarenkovo**, Russian Federation
105 D 19 **Kushtagi**, India
107 T 13 **Kushtia**, Bangladesh
102 I 4 **Kushum**, Kazakhstan
34 M 9 **Kuskokwim**, AK, U.S.A.
34 L 10 **Kuskokwim Bay**, AK, U.S.A.
35 O 10 **Kuskokwim Mountains**, AK, U.S.A.
122 M 4 **Kussharo-ko**, Japan
94 E 9 **Kütahya**, Turkey
95 R 6 **K'ut'aisi**, Georgia
136 N 10 **Kutarere**, New Zealand
122 J 6 **Kutchan**, Japan
80 F 8 **Kutina**, Croatia
114 F 10 **Kutkai**, Myanmar
78 J 13 **Kutno**, Poland
130 J 9 **Kutu**, Democratic Republic of Congo
127 B 17 **Kutum**, Sudan
41 S 6 **Kuujjuaq**, QC, Canada
41 P 8 **Kuujjuaraapik**, QC, Canada
84 G 5 **Kuusalu**, Estonia
70 N 11 **Kuusamo**, Finland
93 Y 4 **Kuvandyk**, Russian Federation
132 H 5 **Kuvango**, Angola
90 G 13 **Kuvshinovo**, Russian Federation
99 S 3 **Kuwait**, Kuwait
99 R 2 **Kuwait**, Asia
90 K 6 **Kuya**, Russian Federation
87 Q 9 **Kuyal'nyts'kyy Lyman**, Ukraine
88 L 12 **Kuybyshev**, Russian Federation
93 S 2 **Kuybyshev Reservoir**, Russian Federation
87 W 8 **Kuybysheve**, Ukraine
103 Q 3 **Kuybyshevskiy**, Kazakhstan
91 T 14 **Kuyeda**, Russian Federation
103 U 8 **Kuygan**, Kazakhstan
108 K 4 **Kuytun**, China
47 Q 6 **Kuyu Tingni**, Nicaragua
93 Q 4 **Kuznetsk**, Russian Federation
86 K 2 **Kuznetsovs'k**, Ukraine
90 J 5 **Kuzomen'**, Russian Federation
122 K 10 **Kuzumaki**, Japan
70 H 7 **Kvaløya**, Norway
70 K 5 **Kvaløya**, Norway
70 K 6 **Kvalsund**, Norway
80 B 10 **Kvarner**, Croatia
80 B 10 **Kvarnerić**, Croatia
35 O 11 **Kvichak Bay**, AK, U.S.A.
133 P 13 **Kwa Mashu**, Republic of South Africa
131 U 11 **Kwa Mtoro**, Tanzania
115 F 18 **Kwai**, Thailand
141 X 2 **Kwajalein**, Marshall Islands
129 Q 13 **Kwale**, Nigeria
130 H 9 **Kwamouth**, Democratic Republic of Congo
111 L 21 **Kwangju**, South Korea
111 M 14 **Kwanmo-bong**, North Korea
129 P 11 **Kwara**, Nigeria
133 P 12 **Kwazulu-Natal**, Republic of South Africa
133 P 7 **Kwekwe**, Zimbabwe
132 M 9 **Kweneng**, Botswana
78 I 9 **Kwidzyn**, Poland
34 M 10 **Kwigillingok**, AK, U.S.A.
138 E 7 **Kwikila**, Papua New Guinea
129 X 11 **Kyabé**, Chad
115 E 16 **Kyaikto**, Myanmar
89 P 14 **Kyakhta**, Russian Federation
135 N 11 **Kyancutta**, SA, Australia
115 C 15 **Kyangin**, Myanmar
114 E 11 **Kyaukme**, Myanmar
115 F 20 **Kyaukpya**, Myanmar
114 B 12 **Kyauktaw**, Myanmar
115 C 15 **Kyeintali**, Myanmar
131 T 13 **Kyela**, Tanzania
60 F 10 **Kyle of Lochalsh**, U.K.
73 B 19 **Kyll**, Germany
83 E 20 **Kyllini**, Greece
83 H 18 **Kymi**, Greece
135 R 5 **Kynuna**, QLD, Australia
123 G 17 **Kyōga-misaki**, Japan
111 N 20 **Kyŏngju**, South Korea
123 G 18 **Kyōto**, Japan
122 J 10 **Kyowa**, Japan
83 C 21 **Kyparissia**, Greece
83 C 21 **Kyparissiakos Kolpos**, Greece
89 R 14 **Kyra**, Russian Federation
83 H 17 **Kyra Panagia**, Greece
103 V 11 **Kyrgyzstan**, Asia
72 K 12 **Kyritz**, Germany
87 O 11 **Kyrnychky**, Ukraine
87 Q 2 **Kyselivka**, Ukraine
89 U 8 **Kytalyktakh**, Russian Federation
83 F 24 **Kythira**, Greece
83 F 24 **Kythira**, Greece
83 H 21 **Kythnos**, Greece
115 F 22 **Kyun Pila**, Myanmar
102 K 8 **Kyushe**, Kazakhstan
123 C 22 **Kyūshū**, Japan
82 F 10 **Kyustendil**, Bulgaria
82 F 10 **Kyustendil**, Bulgaria
71 L 15 **Kyyjärvi**, Finland
89 O 13 **Kyzyl**, Russian Federation
103 S 10 **Kyzyl-Adyr**, Kyrgyzstan
103 T 12 **Kyzyl-Kyya**, Kyrgyzstan
103 O 10 **Kyzylkum Desert**, Kazakhstan
103 O 9 **Kyzylorda**, Kazakhstan
103 P 9 **Kyzylorda**, Kazakhstan
102 I 9 **Kyzylsay**, Kazakhstan
103 R 6 **Kyzylzhar**, Kazakhstan

L

66 J 9 **La Albuera**, Spain
67 S 4 **La Almunia de Doña Godina**, Spain
51 Q 2 **La Asunción**, Venezuela
43 N 6 **La Baie**, QC, Canada
56 J 8 **La Banda**, Argentina
66 L 3 **La Bañeza**, Spain
29 R 13 **La Barge**, WY, U.S.A.
64 J 7 **La Baule-Escoublac**, France
19 W 12 **La Belle**, FL, U.S.A.
65 Q 10 **La Bourboule**, France
45 S 8 **La Carbonera**, Mexico
59 A 15 **La Carlota**, Argentina
67 O 10 **La Carolina**, Spain
46 M 4 **La Ceiba**, Honduras
65 R 7 **La Charité-sur-Loire**, France
65 P 8 **La Châtre**, France
74 C 7 **La-Chaux-de-Fonds**, Switzerland
47 W 14 **La Chorrera**, Panama
44 M 8 **La Ciudad**, Mexico
56 I 8 **La Cocha**, Argentina
45 X 11 **La Costa**, Mexico
20 D 13 **La Crosse**, WI, U.S.A.
24 K 4 **La Crosse**, KS, U.S.A.
44 L 8 **La Cruz**, Mexico
47 N 11 **La Cruz**, Costa Rica
58 E 11 **La Cruz**, Argentina
46 G 6 **La Democracia**, Guatemala
51 O 8 **La Esmeralda**, Venezuela
53 L 23 **La Esmeralda**, Bolivia
46 K 6 **La Esperanza**, Honduras
57 G 16 **La Esperanza**, Argentina
53 L 19 **La Estrella**, Bolivia
65 N 6 **La Flèche**, France
139 P 14 **La Foa**, New Caledonia
66 K 5 **La Fuente de San Esteban**, Spain
125 P 5 **La Galite**, Tunisia
51 S 6 **La Gran Sabana**, Venezuela
32 K 10 **La Grande**, OR, U.S.A.
19 S 4 **La Grange**, GA, U.S.A.
27 Q 10 **La Grange**, TX, U.S.A.
43 N 10 **La Guadeloupe**, QC, Canada
50 K 1 **La Guajira**, Colombia
31 T 6 **La Junta**, CO, U.S.A.
59 A 14 **La Laguna**, Argentina
57 F 14 **La Laja**, Chile
46 I 3 **La Libertad**, Guatemala
46 L 6 **La Libertad**, Honduras
46 I 7 **La Libertad**, El Salvador
52 B 13 **La Libertad**, Peru
56 G 11 **La Ligua**, Chile
46 L 5 **La Lima**, Honduras
66 M 14 **La Línea de la Concepción**, Spain
59 A 21 **La Lobería**, Argentina
39 K 16 **La Loche**, SK, Canada
69 F 21 **La Louviére**, Belgium
77 D 15 **La Maddalena**, Italy
43 O 7 **La Malbaie**, QC, Canada
53 E 17 **La Mejorada**, Peru
53 E 16 **La Merced**, Peru
45 O 5 **La Mora**, Mexico
65 V 11 **La Mure**, France
66 M 8 **La Nava de Ricomalillo**, Spain
56 F 6 **La Negra**, Chile
53 D 16 **La Oroya**, Peru
46 I 2 **La Palma**, Guatemala
47 Z 14 **La Palma**, Panama
59 G 15 **La Paloma**, Uruguay
57 I 14 **La Pampa**, Argentina
44 J 8 **La Paz**, Mexico
46 L 6 **La Paz**, Honduras
46 M 9 **La Paz**, Nicaragua
53 I 19 **La Paz**, Bolivia
53 H 18 **La Paz**, Bolivia
56 H 12 **La Paz**, Argentina
58 C 13 **La Paz**, Argentina
50 M 11 **La Pedrera**, Colombia
47 U 15 **La Pena**, Panama
45 N 5 **La Perla**, Mexico
122 I 2 **La Pérouse Strait**, Japan
45 S 8 **La Pesca**, Mexico
45 P 11 **La Piedad**, Mexico
32 H 12 **La Pine**, OR, U.S.A.
47 V 14 **La Pintada**, Panama
22 J 8 **La Plant**, SD, U.S.A.
59 D 16 **La Plata**, Argentina
21 I 16 **La Porte**, IN, U.S.A.
26 M 11 **La Pryor**, TX, U.S.A.
56 I 4 **La Quiaca**, Argentina
56 H 9 **La Rioja**, Argentina
56 I 9 **La Rioja**, Argentina
67 Q 3 **La Rioja**, Spain
66 L 2 **La Robla**, Spain
66 K 9 **La Roca de la Sierra**, Spain
69 J 22 **La Roche-en-Ardenne**, Belgium
64 L 8 **La Roche-sur-Yon**, France
64 L 9 **La Rochelle**, France
67 Q 9 **La Roda**, Spain
49 S 8 **La Romana**, Dominican Republic
39 M 16 **La Ronge**, SK, Canada
45 P 5 **La Rosita**, Mexico
58 C 11 **La Sabana**, Argentina
21 F 16 **La Salle**, IL, U.S.A.
42 F 6 **La Sarre**, QC, Canada
56 F 9 **La Serena**, Chile
67 W 3 **La Seu d'Urgell**, Spain
67 P 9 **La Solana**, Spain
76 D 9 **La Spezia**, Italy
50 I 10 **La Tagua**, Colombia
56 I 11 **La Toma**, Argentina
42 L 8 **La Tuque**, QC, Canada
45 P 13 **La Unión**, Mexico
46 L 8 **La Unión**, El Salvador
53 M 19 **La Unión**, Bolivia
67 S 12 **La Unión**, Spain
27 P 11 **La Vernia**, TX, U.S.A.
45 O 6 **La Vibora**, Mexico
53 G 20 **La Yarada**, Peru
75 X 2 **Laa an der Thaya**, Austria
72 K 9 **Laage**, Germany
127 N 20 **Laascaanood**, Somalia
127 N 19 **Laasgoray**, Somalia
124 D 10 **Laâyoune**, Western Sahara
119 R 8 **Labang**, Malaysia
139 X 11 **Labasa**, Fiji
128 G 10 **Labé**, Guinea
42 J 9 **Labelle**, QC, Canada
119 S 7 **Labi**, Brunei
80 B 9 **Labin**, Croatia
92 M 12 **Labinsk**, Russian Federation
118 D 9 **Labis**, Malaysia
120 I 12 **Labo**, Philippines
64 L 13 **Labouheyre**, France
59 A 16 **Laboulaye**, Argentina
41 U 7 **Labrador**, NL, Canada
142 L 13 **Labrador Basin**, Arctic Ocean
41 T 9 **Labrador City**, NL, Canada
142 L 12 **Labrador Sea**, Arctic Ocean
54 D 12 **Lábrea**, Brazil
116 F 11 **Labu**, Indonesia
119 T 6 **Labuan**, Malaysia
110 G 7 **Labudalin**, China
117 N 15 **Labuhanbajo**, Indonesia
116 D 9 **Labuhanbilik**, Indonesia
116 B 9 **Labuhanhaji**, Indonesia
116 G 13 **Labuhanmeringgai**, Indonesia
88 L 8 **Labytnangi**, Russian Federation
81 K 17 **Laş**, Albania
129 V 9 **Lac**, Chad
41 Q 8 **Lac à l'Eau Claire**, QC, Canada
41 R 8 **Lac Bienville**, QC, Canada
41 P 8 **Lac Burton**, QC, Canada
41 S 8 **Lac Caniapiscau**, QC, Canada
129 T 13 **Lac de Bamendjing**, Cameroon
128 I 13 **Lac de Buyo**, Côte d'Ivoire
128 J 12 **Lac de Kossou**, Côte d'Ivoire
129 V 12 **Lac de Ladgo**, Cameroon
128 H 9 **Lac de Manantali**, Mali
129 U 13 **Lac de Mbakaou**, Cameroon
74 C 8 **Lac de Neuchâtel**, Switzerland
42 G 7 **Lac Decelles**, QC, Canada
42 F 7 **Lac des Quinze**, QC, Canada
41 Q 10 **Lac Evans**, QC, Canada
128 K 7 **Lac Faguibine**, Mali
128 L 8 **Lac Garou**, Mali
41 Q 7 **Lac Guillaume-Delisle**, QC, Canada
41 U 9 **Lac Joseph**, NL, Canada
42 K 7 **Lac Kempt**, QC, Canada
42 F 8 **Lac Kipawa**, QC, Canada
23 T 2 **Lac la Croix**, MN, U.S.A.
38 G 12 **Lac la Martre**, NT, Canada
39 M 16 **Lac la Ronge**, SK, Canada
130 J 9 **Lac Mai- Ndombe**, Democratic Republic of Congo
41 S 10 **Lac Manouane**, QC, Canada
43 N 10 **Lac-Mégantic**, QC, Canada
41 Q 7 **Lac Minto**, QC, Canada
41 Q 10 **Lac Mistassini**, QC, Canada
128 L 8 **Lac Niangay**, Mali
130 J 8 **Lac Ntomba**, Democratic Republic of Congo
130 D 8 **Lac Onangue**, Gabon
41 Q 5 **Lac Payne**, QC, Canada
43 Q 3 **Lac Sainte Anne**, QC, Canada
40 K 10 **Lac Seul**, ON, Canada
42 G 7 **Lac Simàrd**, QC, Canada
42 M 6 **Lac St-Jean**, QC, Canada
115 O 20 **Lac Thiên**, Vietnam
131 O 13 **Lac Upemba**, Democratic Republic of Congo
64 L 11 **Lacanau**, France
45 X 14 **Lacanja**, Mexico
80 J 10 **Lacarak**, Serbia and Montenegro
65 Q 14 **Lacaune**, France
105 A 22 **Laccadive Islands**, India
74 H 7 **Lachen**, Switzerland
135 S 11 **Lachlan**, NSW, Australia
107 S 9 **Lachung**, India
42 K 10 **Lachute**, QC, Canada
95 W 9 **Laşşin**, Azerbaijan
14 D 8 **Lackawanna**, NY, U.S.A.
77 C 18 **Laconi**, Italy
15 N 7 **Laconia**, NH, U.S.A.
87 N 12 **Lacul Razim**, Romania
87 N 13 **Lacul Sinoie**, Romania
106 I 3 **Ladakh Range**, India
85 A 16 **Ladushkin**, Russian Federation
135 T 14 **Lady Barron**, TAS, Australia
20 D 10 **Ladysmith**, WI, U.S.A.
133 P 12 **Ladysmith**, Republic of South Africa
87 P 6 **Ladyzhynka**, Ukraine
138 E 5 **Lae**, Papua New Guinea
141 W 2 **Lae**, Marshall Islands
71 D 23 **Laesø**, Denmark
70 L 7 **Laevvajåk**, Norway
16 G 8 **Lafayette**, TN, U.S.A.
18 J 7 **Lafayette**, LA, U.S.A.
48 F 4 **Lafé**, Cuba
129 S 12 **Lafia**, Nigeria
129 Q 12 **Lafiagi**, Nigeria
93 R 12 **Lagan'**, Russian Federation
128 E 8 **Lagbar**, Senegal
71 C 17 **Lågen**, Norway
101 V 6 **Laghmān**, Afghanistan
124 M 7 **Laghouat**, Algeria
82 F 13 **Lagkadas**, Greece
57 F 22 **Lago Argentino**, Argentina
59 F 14 **Lago Artificial de Rincón del Bonete**, Uruguay
47 Y 13 **Lago Bayano**, Panama
57 G 20 **Lago Buenos Aires**, Argentina
57 G 22 **Lago Cardiel**, Argentina
46 I 7 **Lago Coatepeque**, El Salvador
57 H 19 **Lago Colhué Huapi**, Argentina
46 H 6 **Lago de Amatitlán**, Guatemala
47 N 8 **Lago de Apanás**, Nicaragua
46 G 6 **Lago de Atitlán**, Guatemala
133 Q 5 **Lago de Cahora Bassa**, Mozambique
46 I 6 **Lago de Guija**, El Salvador
46 J 4 **Lago de Izabal**, Guatemala
46 L 4 **Lago de Los Micos**, Honduras
47 N 9 **Lago de Managua**, Nicaragua
53 I 21 **Lago de Poopó**, Bolivia
76 G 12 **Lago di Bolsena**, Italy
76 H 13 **Lago di Bracciano**, Italy
76 D 6 **Lago di Como**, Italy
76 E 7 **Lago di Garda**, Italy
77 L 14 **Lago di Lesina**, Italy
74 H 11 **Lago di Lugano**, Switzerland
77 L 14 **Lago di Varano**, Italy
76 E 6 **Lago d'Iseo**, Italy
57 H 25 **Lago Fagnano**, Argentina
47 W 13 **Lago Gatún**, Panama
57 G 20 **Lago General Carrera**, Chile
46 J 7 **Lago Ilopango**, El Salvador
57 E 17 **Lago Llanquihué**, Chile
76 C 6 **Lago Maggiore**, Italy
59 G 14 **Lago Mangueira**, Brazil
58 A 13 **Lago Mar Chiquita**, Argentina
57 H 19 **Lago Musters**, Argentina
57 F 16 **Lago Nahuel Huapi**, Argentina
57 F 22 **Lago O'Higgins**, Chile
77 C 17 **Lago Omodeo**, Italy
57 H 15 **Lago Pellegrini**, Argentina
46 I 3 **Lago Petén Itzá**, Guatemala
57 F 16 **Lago Ranco**, Chile
57 F 16 **Lago Rupanco**, Chile
57 F 22 **Lago San Martin**, Argentina
76 G 11 **Lago Trasimeno**, Italy
57 G 22 **Lago Viedma**, Argentina
57 F 22 **Lago Viedma**, Argentina
66 G 12 **Lagoa**, Portugal
58 H 12 **Lagoa dos Patos**, Brazil
55 I 23 **Lagoa Mangueira**, Brazil
59 G 14 **Lagoa Mirim**, Brazil/Uruguay
58 H 10 **Lagoa Vermelha**, Brazil
95 V 6 **Lagodekhi**, Georgia
120 J 12 **Lagonoy**, Philippines
120 K 13 **Lagonoy Gulf**, Philippines
66 G 12 **Lagos**, Portugal
129 O 13 **Lagos**, Nigeria
129 P 13 **Lagos**, Nigeria
45 P 10 **Lagos de Moreno**, Mexico
131 Q 11 **Lagosa**, Tanzania
134 H 4 **Lagrange**, WA, Australia
31 P 10 **Laguna**, NM, U.S.A.
58 J 11 **Laguna**, Brazil
47 R 6 **Laguna Bismuna**, Nicaragua
120 G 11 **Laguna de Bay**, Philippines
47 Q 5 **Laguna de Caratasca**, Honduras
45 O 11 **Laguna de Chapala**, Mexico
47 T 13 **Laguna de Chiriqui**, Panama
47 Q 7 **Laguna de Huaunta**, Nicaragua
47 R 9 **Laguna de Perlas**, Nicaragua
47 R 9 **Laguna de Perlas**, Nicaragua
53 K 17 **Laguna de San Luis**, Bolivia
45 X 12 **Laguna de Términos**, Mexico
81 J 19 **Laguna e Karavastasë**, Albania
47 P 4 **Laguna Ibans**, Honduras
47 R 7 **Laguna Karatá**, Nicaragua
27 Q 14 **Laguna Madre**, TX, U.S.A.
45 S 8 **Laguna Madre**, Mexico
53 J 17 **Laguna Rogaguado**, Bolivia
45 U 14 **Laguna Superior**, Mexico
47 R 6 **Laguna Taberis**, Nicaragua
76 G 7 **Laguna Veneta**, Italy
56 G 4 **Lagunas**, Chile
110 J 9 **Laha**, China
119 X 6 **Lahad Datu**, Malaysia
34 D 7 **Lahaina**, HI, U.S.A.
116 F 12 **Lahat**, Indonesia
114 D 7 **Lahe**, Myanmar
116 B 10 **Lahewa**, Indonesia
99 P 14 **Laḩij**, Yemen
73 E 18 **Lahn**, Germany
71 E 24 **Laholmsbukten**, Sweden
101 Y 9 **Lahore**, Pakistan
71 M 18 **Lahti**, Finland
129 W 11 **Laï**, Chad
114 J 11 **Lai Chau**, Vietnam
113 Q 7 **Laifeng**, China
65 O 4 **L'Aigle**, France
132 L 15 **Laingsburg**, Republic of South Africa
70 J 8 **Lainioälven**, Sweden
116 E 12 **Lais**, Indonesia
93 S 1 **Laishevo**, Russian Federation
113 W 2 **Laiwu**, China
111 G 20 **Laixi**, China
111 G 20 **Laiyang**, China
111 C 17 **Laiyuan**, China
111 G 19 **Laizhou**, China
111 G 19 **Laizhou Wan**, China
95 S 6 **Lajanurpekhi**, Georgia
58 H 12 **Lajeado**, Brazil
58 I 10 **Lajes**, Brazil
80 K 11 **Lajkovac**, Serbia and Montenegro
127 J 19 **Lake Abbe**, Ethiopia
32 I 13 **Lake Abert**, OR, U.S.A.
42 F 6 **Lake Abitibi**, ON, Canada
131 R 6 **Lake Albert**, Uganda/Democratic Republic of Congo
134 M 7 **Lake Amadeus**, NT, Australia
134 L 3 **Lake Argyle**, WA, Australia
18 I 8 **Lake Arthur**, LA, U.S.A.
36 M 9 **Lake Athabasca**, AB/SK, Canada
134 J 6 **Lake Auld**, WA, Australia
134 G 9 **Lake Austin**, WA, Australia
89 Q 13 **Lake Baikal**, Russian Federation
103 T 8 **Lake Balkhash**, Kazakhstan
134 I 9 **Lake Ballard**, WA, Australia
133 O 3 **Lake Bangweulu**, Zambia
134 H 9 **Lake Barlee**, WA, Australia
137 E 22 **Lake Benmore**, New Zealand
23 P 9 **Lake Benton**, MN, U.S.A.
19 T 5 **Lake Blackshear**, GA, U.S.A.
135 Q 9 **Lake Blanche**, SA, Australia
80 B 6 **Lake Bled**, Slovenia
121 L 23 **Lake Buluan**, Philippines
134 I 9 **Lake Carey**, WA, Australia
135 T 11 **Lake Cargelligo**, NSW, Australia
134 I 8 **Lake Carnegie**, WA, Australia
129 V 9 **Lake Chad**, Chad
14 L 5 **Lake Champlain**, VT, U.S.A.
18 H 7 **Lake Charles**, LA, U.S.A.
32 I 6 **Lake Chelan**, WA, U.S.A.
20 E 9 **Lake Chippewa**, WI, U.S.A.
16 J 8 **Lake City**, TN, U.S.A.
17 Q 12 **Lake City**, SC, U.S.A.
19 V 7 **Lake City**, FL, U.S.A.
20 K 12 **Lake City**, MI, U.S.A.
39 I 15 **Lake Claire**, AB, Canada
137 G 19 **Lake Coleridge**, New Zealand
27 S 9 **Lake Conroe**, TX, U.S.A.
74 H 5 **Lake Constance**, Switzerland
134 I 10 **Lake Cowan**, WA, Australia
16 I 7 **Lake Cumberland**, KY, U.S.A.
135 T 5 **Lake Dalrymple**, QLD, Australia
134 I 7 **Lake Disappointment**, WA, Australia
63 P 1 **Lake District**, U.K.
134 I 6 **Lake Dora**, WA, Australia
134 I 11 **Lake Dundas**, WA, Australia
131 Q 8 **Lake Edward**, Democratic Republic of Congo/Uganda
137 H 21 **Lake Ellesmere**, New Zealand
14 A 9 **Lake Erie**, PA, U.S.A.
21 M 16 **Lake Erie**, OH, U.S.A.
42 C 15 **Lake Erie**, ON, Canada
131 U 10 **Lake Eyasi**, Tanzania
135 O 8 **Lake Eyre North**, SA, Australia
135 O 9 **Lake Eyre South**, SA, Australia
27 S 5 **Lake Fork Reservoir**, TX, U.S.A.
135 Q 10 **Lake Frome**, SA, Australia
135 O 10 **Lake Gairdner**, SA, Australia
65 V 9 **Lake Geneva**, France/Switzerland
14 K 7 **Lake George**, NY, U.S.A.
19 W 9 **Lake George**, FL, U.S.A.
20 F 8 **Lake Gogebic**, MI, U.S.A.
135 S 15 **Lake Gordon**, TAS, Australia
134 H 11 **Lake Grace**, WA, Australia
134 K 5 **Lake Gregory**, WA, Australia
137 B 25 **Lake Hauroko**, New Zealand
30 H 11 **Lake Havasu City**, AZ, U.S.A.
137 D 22 **Lake Hawea**, New Zealand
134 I 11 **Lake Hope**, WA, Australia
134 L 7 **Lake Hopkins**, WA, Australia
20 L 10 **Lake Huron**, MI, U.S.A.
42 A 10 **Lake Huron**, ON, Canada
27 T 11 **Lake Jackson**, TX, U.S.A.
133 O 6 **Lake Kariba**, Zimbabwe
27 N 4 **Lake Kemp**, TX, U.S.A.
16 L 11 **Lake Keowee**, SC, U.S.A.
110 O 11 **Lake Khanka**, China
134 H 11 **Lake King**, WA, Australia
131 Q 9 **Lake Kivu**, Rwanda/Democratic Republic of Congo
28 L 2 **Lake Koocanusa**, MT, U.S.A.
131 S 7 **Lake Kyoga**, Uganda
90 F 9 **Lake Ladoga**, Russian Federation
121 K 21 **Lake Lanao**, Philippines
134 I 10 **Lake Lefroy**, WA, Australia
27 Q 5 **Lake Lewisville**, TX, U.S.A.
27 R 7 **Lake Limestone**, TX, U.S.A.
20 G 7 **Lake Linden**, MI, U.S.A.
27 S 9 **Lake Livingston**, TX, U.S.A.
39 I 20 **Lake Louise**, AB, Canada
134 L 6 **Lake MacDonald**, WA, Australia
134 L 6 **Lake Mackay**, WA, Australia
134 E 7 **Lake MacLeod**, WA, Australia
121 M 19 **Lake Mainit**, Philippines
133 R 4 **Lake Malawi**, Malawi
137 B 24 **Lake Manapouri**, New Zealand
40 I 10 **Lake Manitoba**, MB, Canada
131 U 10 **Lake Manyara**, Tanzania
50 K 3 **Lake Maracaibo**, Venezuela
17 P 13 **Lake Marion**, SC, U.S.A.
134 I 10 **Lake Marmion**, WA, Australia
19 Q 4 **Lake Martin**, AL, U.S.A.
17 W 9 **Lake Mattamuskeet**, NC, U.S.A.
134 M 9 **Lake Maurice**, SA, Australia
22 I 14 **Lake McConaughy**, NE, U.S.A.
30 G 9 **Lake Mead**, AZ/NV, U.S.A.
41 V 8 **Lake Melville**, NL, Canada
14 L 4 **Lake Memphremagog**, VT, U.S.A.
26 K 2 **Lake Meredith**, TX, U.S.A.

ountry ■ Internal administrative region: State/Province/Territory/Dependent territory · Capital city · Mountain range/ Undersea ridge · Mountain peak/ Volcano/Seamount · Geographic feature · Headland/Point/ Cape/Peninsula · Desert · Island/Island group · Antarctic base · Ocean · Sea · Bay/Gulf/Channel/Strait · Lake · Salt pan/Dry/ Intermittent lake · River

21 I 15 **Lake Michigan**, MI, U.S.A. ♒
134 J 9 **Lake Minigwal**, WA, Australia ♒
134 G 10 **Lake Moore**, WA, Australia ♒
17 P 13 **Lake Moultrie**, SC, U.S.A. ♒
17 N 12 **Lake Murray**, SC, U.S.A. ♒
138 A 5 **Lake Murray**, Papua New Guinea ♒
42 E 11 **Lake Muskoka**, ON, Canada ♒
131 P 13 **Lake Mweru**, Democratic Republic of Congo/Zambia ♒
126 F 12 **Lake Nasser**, Egypt ♒
131 U 9 **Lake Natron**, Tanzania ♒
120 G 13 **Lake Naujan**, Philippines ♒
134 L 7 **Lake Neale**, NT, Australia ♒
47 O 10 **Lake Nicaragua**, Nicaragua ♒
40 L 11 **Lake Nipigon**, ON, Canada ♒
42 E 9 **Lake Nipissing**, ON, Canada ♒
134 H 9 **Lake Noondie**, WA, Australia ♒
17 O 9 **Lake Norman**, NC, U.S.A. ♒
126 E 13 **Lake Nuba**, Sudan ♒
27 T 5 **Lake o' the Pines**, TX, U.S.A. ♒
22 J 9 **Lake Oahe**, SD, U.S.A. ♒
19 U 3 **Lake Oconee**, GA, U.S.A. ♒
25 U 5 **Lake of the Ozarks**, MO, U.S.A. ♒
40 J 11 **Lake of the Woods**, Canada/U.S.A. ♒
137 D 21 **Lake Ohau**, New Zealand ♒
82 B 13 **Lake Ohrid**, Macedonia (F.Y.R.O.M.) ♒
19 X 12 **Lake Okeechobee**, FL, U.S.A. ♒
90 H 9 **Lake Onega**, Russian Federation ♒
37 U 14 **Lake Ontario**, ON, Canada ♒
33 H 17 **Lake Oroville**, CA, U.S.A. ♒
25 T 11 **Lake Ouachita**, AR, U.S.A. ♒
32 K 12 **Lake Owyhee**, OR, U.S.A. ♒
27 S 6 **Lake Palestine**, TX, U.S.A. ♒
135 S 15 **Lake Pedder**, TAS, Australia ♒
84 I 7 **Lake Peipus**, Estonia ♒
14 K 6 **Lake Placid**, NY, U.S.A.
14 J 7 **Lake Pleasant**, NY, U.S.A.
18 L 8 **Lake Pontchartrain**, LA, U.S.A. ♒
137 B 25 **Lake Poteriteri**, New Zealand ♒
30 K 7 **Lake Powell**, UT, U.S.A. ♒
20 F 12 **Lake Poygan**, WI, U.S.A. ♒
82 C 13 **Lake Prespa**, Macedonia (F.Y.R.O.M.) ♒
90 D 12 **Lake Pskov**, Russian Federation ♒
137 E 21 **Lake Pukaki**, New Zealand ♒
134 I 10 **Lake Rebecca**, WA, Australia ♒
42 E 10 **Lake Rosseau**, ON, Canada ♒
136 M 10 **Lake Rotorua**, New Zealand ♒
131 S 12 **Lake Rukwa**, Tanzania ♒
22 I 3 **Lake Sakakawea**, ND, U.S.A. ♒
81 J 16 **Lake Scutari**, Serbia and Montenegro ♒
19 S 7 **Lake Seminole**, GA, U.S.A. ♒
21 F 19 **Lake Shelbyville**, IL, U.S.A. ♒
19 S 2 **Lake Sidney Lanier**, GA, U.S.A. ♒
42 F 12 **Lake Simcoe**, ON, Canada ♒
19 U 3 **Lake Sinclair**, GA, U.S.A. ♒
21 M 15 **Lake St Clair**, Canada/U.S.A. ♒
40 K 10 **Lake St Joseph**, ON, Canada ♒
133 Q 12 **Lake St Lucia**, Republic of South Africa ♒
31 S 11 **Lake Sumner**, NM, U.S.A. ♒
137 H 18 **Lake Sumner**, New Zealand ♒
13 S 5 **Lake Superior**, Canada/U.S.A. ♒
135 O 4 **Lake Sylvester**, NT, Australia ♒
120 G 12 **Lake Taal**, Philippines ♒
33 H 18 **Lake Tahoe**, CA, U.S.A. ♒
127 H 18 **Lake Tana**, Ethiopia ♒
131 Q 11 **Lake Tanganyika**, Africa ♒
136 M 11 **Lake Tarawera**, New Zealand ♒
136 L 12 **Lake Taupo**, New Zealand ♒
27 R 5 **Lake Tawakoni**, TX, U.S.A. ♒
137 B 23 **Lake Te Anau**, New Zealand ♒
137 E 21 **Lake Tekapo**, New Zealand
137 F 21 **Lake Tekapo**, New Zealand ♒
25 O 13 **Lake Texoma**, OK, U.S.A. ♒
96 G 8 **Lake Tiberias**, Israel ♒
53 H 19 **Lake Titicaca**, Peru ♒
135 P 10 **Lake Torrens**, SA, Australia ♒
131 U 5 **Lake Turkana**, Ethiopia/Kenya ♒
100 F 3 **Lake Urmia**, Iran ♒
131 S 8 **Lake Victoria**, Africa ♒
129 N 12 **Lake Volta**, Ghana ♒
137 K 16 **Lake Wairarapa**, New Zealand ♒
137 C 23 **Lake Wakatipu**, New Zealand ♒
19 W 10 **Lake Wales**, FL, U.S.A.
23 R 4 **Lake Walker**, MN, U.S.A. ♒
137 D 22 **Lake Wanaka**, New Zealand ♒
134 I 8 **Lake Wells**, WA, Australia ♒
134 L 5 **Lake White**, WA, Australia ♒
27 P 7 **Lake Whitney**, TX, U.S.A. ♒
20 G 12 **Lake Winnebago**, WI, U.S.A. ♒
23 R 4 **Lake Winnibigoshish**, MN, U.S.A. ♒
40 I 9 **Lake Winnipeg**, MB, Canada ♒
40 H 8 **Lake Winnipegosis**, MB, Canada ♒
15 O 7 **Lake Winnipesaukee**, NH, U.S.A. ♒
19 Y 12 **Lake Worth**, FL, U.S.A.
135 R 8 **Lake Yamma Yamma**, QLD, Australia ♒
139 Z 12 **Lakeba**, Fiji ✱
19 U 6 **Lakeland**, GA, U.S.A.
19 W 10 **Lakeland**, FL, U.S.A.
135 S 3 **Lakeland**, QLD, Australia
135 T 13 **Lakes Entrance**, VIC, Australia
32 E 12 **Lakeside**, OR, U.S.A.
33 I 14 **Lakeview**, OR, U.S.A.
14 C 10 **Lakewood**, NY, U.S.A.
14 J 14 **Lakewood**, NJ, U.S.A.
31 R 4 **Lakewood**, CO, U.S.A.
90 F 9 **Lakhdenpokh'ya**, Russian Federation
106 M 9 **Lakhimpur**, India
105 F 15 **Lakhnadon**, India
105 A 14 **Lakhpat**, India
101 V 8 **Lakki**, Pakistan
83 E 23 **Lakonikos Kolpos**, Greece ≈
117 S 15 **Lakor**, Indonesia ✱
22 M 3 **Lakota**, ND, U.S.A.
128 J 13 **Lakota**, Côte d'Ivoire
70 L 5 **Laksefjorden**, Norway ≈
70 K 6 **Lakselv**, Norway
105 A 22 **Lakshadweep**, India ▣
80 G 10 **Laktaši**, Bosnia and Herzegovina
120 H 6 **Lal-Lo**, Philippines
82 L 11 **Lalapaşa**, Turkey
94 B 6 **Lalapaşa**, Turkey
130 E 7 **Lalara**, Gabon
100 G 8 **Lālī**, Iran
127 I 19 **Lalībela**, Ethiopia
117 R 14 **Laliki**, Indonesia
66 I 2 **Lalín**, Spain
110 K 11 **Lalin**, China
117 O 13 **Laloa**, Indonesia
115 K 16 **Lam Pao Reservoir**, Thailand ♒
119 X 6 **Lamag**, Malaysia
25 S 6 **Lamar**, MO, U.S.A.
75 S 4 **Lambach**, Austria
64 J 5 **Lamballe**, France
130 E 8 **Lambaréné**, Gabon
52 A 13 **Lambayeque**, Peru
132 J 14 **Lambert's Bay**, Republic of South Africa
63 S 10 **Lambourn**, U.K.
29 W 7 **Lame Deer**, MT, U.S.A.
66 H 5 **Lamego**, Portugal
139 R 11 **Lamen**, Vanuatu
26 J 6 **Lamesa**, TX, U.S.A.
77 M 20 **Lamezia**, Italy
83 E 18 **Lamia**, Greece
121 N 23 **Lamigan Point**, Philippines ▶
121 H 23 **Lamitan**, Philippines
139 Y 11 **Lamiti**, Fiji
117 T 10 **Lamlam**, Indonesia
120 H 11 **Lamon Bay**, Philippines ≈
115 G 15 **Lampang**, Thailand
27 P 8 **Lampasas**, TX, U.S.A.
45 Q 6 **Lampazos**, Mexico
62 M 8 **Lampeter**, U.K.
115 G 14 **Lamphun**, Thailand
116 G 13 **Lampung**, Indonesia ▣
131 X 9 **Lamu**, Kenya
113 Z 12 **Lan Yü**, Taiwan ✱
34 C 7 **Lanai**, HI, U.S.A. ✱
34 D 8 **Lanai City**, HI, U.S.A.
119 V 6 **Lanas**, Malaysia
115 F 22 **Lanbi Kyun**, Myanmar ✱
121 I 20 **Lanboyan Point**, Philippines ▶
14 G 14 **Lancaster**, PA, U.S.A.
15 N 6 **Lancaster**, NH, U.S.A.
17 O 11 **Lancaster**, SC, U.S.A.
21 E 14 **Lancaster**, WI, U.S.A.
21 M 19 **Lancaster**, OH, U.S.A.
25 U 1 **Lancaster**, MO, U.S.A.
33 J 24 **Lancaster**, CA, U.S.A.
63 P 1 **Lancaster**, U.K.
37 P 4 **Lancaster Sound**, NU, Canada ≈
143 N 8 **Lancaster Sound**, Arctic Ocean ≈
134 F 11 **Lancelin**, WA, Australia
95 R 6 **Lanch'khut'i**, Georgia
76 J 13 **Lanciano**, Italy
57 F 16 **Lanco**, Chile
111 G 20 **Lancun**, China
73 L 23 **Landau an der Isar**, Germany
73 E 21 **Landau in der Pfalz**, Germany
74 K 7 **Landeck**, Austria
29 T 12 **Lander**, WY, U.S.A.
68 I 5 **Landerum**, Netherlands
105 N 20 **Landfall Island**, India ✱
74 I 8 **Landquart**, Switzerland
36 L 3 **Lands End**, NT, Canada ▶
62 I 15 **Land's End**, U.K. ▶
73 I 24 **Landsberg**, Germany
73 K 23 **Landshut**, Germany
109 Q 6 **Lang Shan**, China ▲▲
114 M 11 **Lang Son**, Vietnam
115 G 23 **Lang Suan**, Thailand
22 M 2 **Langdon**, ND, U.S.A.
74 L 7 **Längenfeld**, Austria
75 W 3 **Langenlois**, Austria
74 E 7 **Langenthal**, Switzerland
72 D 10 **Langeoog**, Germany ✱
88 L 10 **Langepas**, Russian Federation
111 E 17 **Langfang**, China
70 B 11 **Langjökull**, Iceland ◇
118 A 4 **Langkawi**, Malaysia ✱
119 V 4 **Langkon**, Malaysia
20 G 10 **Langlade**, WI, U.S.A.
32 E 12 **Langlois**, OR, U.S.A.
74 E 8 **Langnau**, Switzerland
65 R 12 **Langogne**, France
64 M 12 **Langon**, France
70 G 8 **Langøya**, Norway ✱
65 U 6 **Langres**, France
116 C 8 **Langsa**, Indonesia
69 M 25 **Langsur**, Luxembourg
129 S 12 **Langtang**, Nigeria
107 W 11 **Langting**, India
65 Q 14 **Languedoc-Roussillon**, France ▣
113 O 6 **Langzhong**, China
62 K 14 **Lanivet**, U.K.
95 Y 10 **Länkäran**, Azerbaijan
64 I 4 **Lannion**, France
14 I 13 **Lansdale**, PA, U.S.A.
21 K 14 **Lansing**, MI, U.S.A.
70 J 11 **Lansjärv**, Sweden
113 Q 4 **Lantian**, China
77 C 18 **Lanusei**, Italy
110 K 10 **Lanxi**, China
113 Y 7 **Lanxi**, China
113 N 2 **Lanzhou**, China
114 K 11 **Lao Cai**, Vietnam
120 F 6 **Laoag**, Philippines
121 L 14 **Laoang**, Philippines
110 N 12 **Laoheishan**, China
113 S 5 **Laohekou**, China
111 K 15 **Laoling**, China
65 R 3 **Laon**, France
115 K 14 **Laos**, Asia □
110 M 13 **Laotougou**, China
111 J 15 **Laotuding Shan**, China ▲
58 I 9 **Lapa**, Brazil
121 F 24 **Lapac**, Philippines ✱
58 C 10 **Lapachito**, Argentina
129 Q 12 **Lapai**, Nigeria
65 S 9 **Lapalisse**, France
121 E 24 **Laparan**, Philippines ✱
71 K 15 **Lappajärvi**, Finland ♒
71 N 18 **Lappeenranta**, Finland
70 I 11 **Lappland**, Sweden ◇
94 B 8 **Lâpseki**, Turkey
89 R 6 **Laptev Sea**, Russian Federation ∿
121 K 17 **Lapu-Lapu**, Philippines
71 K 16 **Lapua**, Finland
78 N 11 **Łapy**, Poland
76 I 13 **L'Aquila**, Italy
100 K 12 **Lār**, Iran
101 Q 9 **Lar Koh**, Afghanistan ▲
50 L 2 **Lara**, Venezuela ▣
124 H 6 **Larache**, Morocco
100 L 13 **Lārak**, Iran ✱
29 Y 14 **Laramie**, WY, U.S.A.
29 X 13 **Laramie**, WY, U.S.A. ʃ
29 W 12 **Laramie Mountains**, WY, U.S.A. ▲▲
58 G 8 **Laranjeiras do Sul**, Brazil
117 P 15 **Larantuka**, Indonesia
117 U 14 **Larat**, Indonesia ✱
27 N 13 **Laredo**, TX, U.S.A.
67 P 1 **Laredo**, Spain
68 I 11 **Laren**, Netherlands
19 V 11 **Largo**, FL, U.S.A.
60 G 13 **Largs**, U.K.
100 G 3 **Lārī**, Iran
23 N 3 **Larimore**, ND, U.S.A.
83 E 16 **Larisa**, Greece
101 U 12 **Larkana**, Pakistan
94 I 15 **Larnaka**, Cyprus
61 F 15 **Larne**, U.K.
24 K 5 **Larned**, KS, U.S.A.
135 N 3 **Larrimah**, NT, Australia
145 W 5 **Lars Christensen Coast**, Antarctica ◇
144 I 4 **Larsen Ice Shelf**, Antarctica ◇
38 J 6 **Larsen Sound**, NU, Canada ≈
71 C 21 **Larvik**, Norway
31 T 6 **Las Animas**, CO, U.S.A.
51 P 4 **Las Bonitas**, Venezuela
31 P 14 **Las Cruces**, NM, U.S.A.
59 D 17 **Las Flores**, Argentina
56 G 11 **Las Heras**, Argentina
44 M 7 **Las Herreras**, Mexico
57 G 21 **Las Horquetas**, Argentina
57 G 15 **Las Lajas**, Argentina
52 A 11 **Las Lomas**, Peru
56 L 6 **Las Lomitas**, Argentina
57 H 21 **Las Martinetas**, Argentina
47 U 15 **Las Palmas**, Panama
67 Q 8 **Las Pedroñeras**, Spain
59 E 16 **Las Piedras**, Uruguay
47 O 6 **Las Planchas**, Honduras
57 H 18 **Las Plumas**, Argentina
59 A 14 **Las Rosas**, Argentina
47 W 15 **Las Tablas**, Panama
56 I 8 **Las Termas**, Argentina
47 N 6 **Las Trojes**, Honduras
48 L 6 **Las Tunas**, Cuba
44 M 10 **Las Varas**, Mexico
59 A 14 **Las Varillas**, Argentina
31 R 9 **Las Vegas**, NM, U.S.A.
33 M 22 **Las Vegas**, NV, U.S.A.
59 F 15 **Lascano**, Uruguay
114 F 10 **Lashio**, Myanmar
101 R 9 **Lashkar Gāh**, Afghanistan
79 I 14 **Łask**, Poland
33 H 16 **Lassen Peak**, CA, U.S.A. ▲
144 K 5 **Lassiter Coast**, Antarctica ◇
31 T 4 **Last Chance**, CO, U.S.A.
130 F 8 **Lastoursville**, Gabon
81 F 15 **Lastovo**, Croatia ✱
81 E 15 **Lastovski Kanal**, Croatia ≈
139 P 7 **Lata**, Solomon Islands
52 B 9 **Latacunga**, Ecuador
144 I 6 **Lataday Island**, Antarctica ✱
42 E 8 **Latchford**, ON, Canada
140 I 10 **Late**, Tonga ✱
105 I 14 **Latehar**, India
77 N 16 **Laterza**, Italy
77 H 15 **Latina**, Italy
76 H 6 **Latisana**, Italy
105 E 17 **Latur**, India
84 F 10 **Latvia**, Europe □
70 B 10 **Laugarbakki**, Iceland
62 L 9 **Laugharne**, U.K.
84 C 13 **Laukuva**, Lithuania
62 L 14 **Launceston**, U.K.
135 T 15 **Launceston**, TAS, Australia
114 F 7 **Launggyaung**, Myanmar
115 F 19 **Launglon Bok Islands**, Myanmar ✱
120 G 10 **Laur**, Philippines
135 S 3 **Laura**, QLD, Australia
19 N 5 **Laurel**, MS, U.S.A.
23 O 12 **Laurel**, NE, U.S.A.
29 T 7 **Laurel**, MT, U.S.A.
16 M 11 **Laurens**, SC, U.S.A.
37 V 11 **Laurentian Mountains**, QC, Canada ▲▲
77 L 17 **Lauria**, Italy
144 I 1 **Laurie Island**, South Orkney Islands ✱
17 Q 11 **Laurinburg**, NC, U.S.A.
77 K 17 **Laurino**, Italy
137 G 21 **Lauriston**, New Zealand
74 B 9 **Lausanne**, Switzerland
116 H 8 **Laut**, Indonesia ✱
116 M 13 **Laut**, Indonesia ✱
139 W 11 **Lautoka**, Fiji
68 L 5 **Lauwersmeer**, Netherlands ♒
42 K 10 **Laval**, QC, Canada
64 M 6 **Laval**, France
59 F 15 **Lavalleja**, Uruguay ▣
75 U 8 **Lavamünd**, Austria
100 H 11 **Lāvar**, Iran
77 L 15 **Lavello**, Italy
63 Y 8 **Lavenham**, U.K.
24 J 8 **Laverne**, OK, U.S.A.
134 I 9 **Laverton**, WA, Australia
71 A 17 **Lavik**, Norway
29 T 6 **Lavina**, MT, U.S.A.
144 H 5 **Lavoisier Island**, Antarctica ✱
58 M 5 **Lavras**, Brazil
83 H 21 **Lavrio**, Greece
145 X 3 **Law Promontory**, Antarctica ▶
114 E 8 **Lawa**, Myanmar
119 T 6 **Lawas**, Malaysia
99 Q 14 **Lawdar**, Yemen
128 L 11 **Lawra**, Ghana
15 O 9 **Lawrence**, MA, U.S.A.
25 Q 4 **Lawrence**, KS, U.S.A.
137 E 24 **Lawrence**, New Zealand
16 E 10 **Lawrenceburg**, TN, U.S.A.
17 S 7 **Lawrenceville**, VA, U.S.A.
21 H 20 **Lawrenceville**, IL, U.S.A.
24 L 12 **Lawton**, OK, U.S.A.
99 R 7 **Laylá**, Saudi Arabia
33 F 17 **Laytonville**, CA, U.S.A.
45 O 13 **Lázaro Cárdenas**, Mexico
56 O 12 **Lazcano**, Uruguay
76 G 13 **Lazio**, Italy ▣
89 U 9 **Lazo**, Russian Federation
87 S 10 **Lazurne**, Ukraine
65 O 8 **Le Blanc**, France
65 Q 15 **Le Boulou**, France
74 B 9 **Le Brassus**, Switzerland
65 N 3 **Le Havre**, France
125 P 5 **Le Kef**, Tunisia
74 C 7 **Le Locle**, Switzerland
65 N 6 **Le Mans**, France
23 P 11 **Le Mars**, IA, U.S.A.
64 L 5 **Le Mont-St-Michel**, France
77 M 15 **Le Murge**, Italy ▲▲
64 J 7 **Le Palais**, France
65 S 11 **Le-Puy-en-Velay**, France
23 R 8 **Le Sueur**, MN, U.S.A.
65 P 1 **Le Touquet-Paris-Plage**, France
65 O 2 **Le Tréport**, France
65 R 13 **Le Vigan**, France
63 U 5 **Leadenham**, U.K.
39 L 19 **Leader**, SK, Canada
40 I 7 **Leaf Rapids**, MB, Canada
42 B 15 **Leamington**, ON, Canada
27 P 9 **Leander**, TX, U.S.A.
134 E 7 **Learmonth**, WA, Australia
69 F 22 **L'Eau d'Heure**, Belgium ♒
25 R 3 **Leavenworth**, KS, U.S.A.
32 I 7 **Leavenworth**, WA, U.S.A.
78 H 7 **Łeba**, Poland
121 K 23 **Lebak**, Philippines
81 N 14 **Lebane**, Serbia and Montenegro
14 G 13 **Lebanon**, PA, U.S.A.
14 M 7 **Lebanon**, NH, U.S.A.
16 G 8 **Lebanon**, TN, U.S.A.
16 M 7 **Lebanon**, VA, U.S.A.
21 I 18 **Lebanon**, IN, U.S.A.
25 U 6 **Lebanon**, MO, U.S.A.
32 G 11 **Lebanon**, OR, U.S.A.
96 H 6 **Lebanon**, Asia □
103 N 12 **Lebap**, Turkmenistan
103 O 14 **Lebapskiy Velayat**, Turkmenistan ▣
33 J 23 **Lebec**, CA, U.S.A.
92 L 4 **Lebedyan'**, Russian Federation
87 T 3 **Lebedyn**, Ukraine
130 M 5 **Lebo**, Democratic Republic of Congo
78 H 8 **Lębork**, Poland
133 O 10 **Lebowakgomo**, Republic of South Africa
66 K 13 **Lebrija**, Spain
57 E 14 **Lebu**, Chile
77 O 17 **Lecce**, Italy
76 D 6 **Lecco**, Italy
74 J 7 **Lech**, Austria
83 C 20 **Lechaina**, Greece
113 T 11 **Lechang**, China
63 S 10 **Lechlade**, U.K.
74 K 7 **Lechtaler Alpen**, Austria ▲▲
72 F 7 **Leck**, Germany
18 I 6 **Lecompte**, LA, U.S.A.
79 N 14 **Łęczna**, Poland
78 I 13 **Łęczyca**, Poland
63 Q 9 **Ledbury**, U.K.
66 K 5 **Ledesma**, Spain
61 B 21 **Lee**, Republic of Ireland ʃ
33 J 19 **Lee Vining**, CA, U.S.A.
19 Q 3 **Leeds**, AL, U.S.A.
63 S 2 **Leeds**, U.K.
63 R 5 **Leek**, U.K.
72 D 11 **Leer**, Germany
68 I 13 **Leerdam**, Netherlands
25 S 4 **Lees Summit**, MO, U.S.A.
17 T 3 **Leesburg**, VA, U.S.A.
19 W 9 **Leesburg**, FL, U.S.A.
84 G 5 **Leesi**, Estonia
18 H 6 **Leesville**, LA, U.S.A.
135 T 12 **Leeton**, NSW, Australia
132 L 14 **Leeu-Gamka**, Republic of South Africa
68 K 6 **Leeuwarden**, Netherlands
49 W 7 **Leeward Islands**, Caribbean Sea ✱
94 H 15 **Lefka**, Cyprus
83 G 26 **Lefka Ori**, Greece ▲▲
83 B 18 **Lefkada**, Greece
83 B 18 **Lefkada**, Greece ✱
83 A 16 **Lefkimmi**, Greece
120 K 13 **Legaspi**, Philippines
33 E 16 **Leggett**, CA, U.S.A.
69 J 24 **Léglise**, Belgium
76 F 7 **Legnago**, Italy
79 F 15 **Legnica**, Poland
131 N 6 **Leguga**, Democratic Republic of Congo
106 J 3 **Leh**, India
14 G 12 **Lehighton**, PA, U.S.A.
101 W 10 **Leiah**, Pakistan
75 W 8 **Leibnitz**, Austria
63 T 6 **Leicester**, U.K.
135 Q 4 **Leichhardt**, QLD, Australia ʃ
68 G 12 **Leiden**, Netherlands
136 K 7 **Leigh**, New Zealand
135 P 9 **Leigh Creek**, SA, Australia
63 U 9 **Leighton Buzzard**, U.K.
113 Q 9 **Leigong Shan**, China ▲
68 G 12 **Leimuiden**, Netherlands
73 G 14 **Leine**, Germany ʃ
73 H 16 **Leinefelde**, Germany
61 D 19 **Leinster**, Republic of Ireland ▣
134 H 9 **Leinster**, WA, Australia
83 L 21 **Leipsoi**, Greece ✱
73 K 16 **Leipzig**, Germany
71 C 18 **Leira**, Norway
66 G 7 **Leiria**, Portugal
71 A 19 **Leirvik**, Norway
84 D 7 **Leisi**, Estonia
16 G 6 **Leitchfield**, KY, U.S.A.
113 T 10 **Leiyang**, China
70 E 13 **Leka**, Norway ✱
130 M 8 **Lekatero**, Democratic Republic of Congo
70 F 9 **Leknes**, Norway
130 G 9 **Lékoni**, Gabon
130 G 9 **Lékoumou**, Congo ▣
71 G 19 **Leksand**, Sweden
18 K 3 **Leland**, MS, U.S.A.
68 J 10 **Lelystad**, Netherlands
138 I 4 **Lemankoa**, Papua New Guinea
94 H 15 **Lemesos**, Cyprus
73 F 14 **Lemgo**, Germany
41 T 3 **Lemieux Islands**, NU, Canada ✱
68 K 8 **Lemmer**, Netherlands
22 I 7 **Lemmon**, SD, U.S.A.
71 B 24 **Lemvig**, Denmark
115 C 15 **Lemyethna**, Myanmar
89 S 11 **Lena**, Russian Federation ʃ
55 M 15 **Lençóis**, Brazil
80 E 6 **Lendava**, Slovenia
90 G 7 **Lendery**, Russian Federation
108 M 7 **Lenghu**, China
113 S 9 **Lengshuijiang**, China
113 S 10 **Lengshuitan**, China
118 D 10 **Lenik**, Malaysia ʃ
103 T 12 **Lenin Peak**, Kyrgyzstan ▲
87 W 11 **Lenine**, Ukraine
145 S 15 **Leningradskaya**, Antarctica ⁙
90 F 10 **Leningradskaya Oblast'**, Russian Federation ▣
89 Y 5 **Leningradskiy**, Russian Federation
93 T 2 **Leninogorsk**, Russian Federation
103 Y 4 **Leninogorsk**, Kazakhstan
93 P 8 **Leninsk**, Russian Federation
103 U 3 **Lenīnskīy**, Kazakhstan
91 N 12 **Leninskoye**, Russian Federation
102 H 5 **Leninskoye**, Kazakhstan
103 P 2 **Leninskoye**, Kazakhstan
76 D 6 **Lenna**, Italy
73 E 16 **Lennestadt**, Germany
17 N 9 **Lenoir**, NC, U.S.A.
65 Q 1 **Lens**, France
69 E 20 **Lens**, Belgium
89 R 11 **Lensk**, Russian Federation
95 S 5 **Lentekhi**, Georgia
79 F 24 **Lenti**, Hungary
85 G 16 **Lentvaris**, Lithuania
88 G 7 **Lent'yevo**, Russian Federation
115 G 21 **Lenya**, Myanmar
128 L 10 **Léo**, Burkina Faso
75 V 6 **Leoben**, Austria
75 X 4 **Leobersdorf**, Austria
63 Q 8 **Leominster**, U.K.
45 P 10 **León**, Mexico
46 M 9 **León**, Nicaragua
64 L 13 **Léon**, France
66 L 2 **León**, Spain
27 R 5 **Leonard**, TX, U.S.A.
83 F 22 **Leonidi**, Greece
134 I 9 **Leonora**, WA, Australia
58 N 6 **Leopoldina**, Brazil
87 N 10 **Leova**, Moldova
133 N 9 **Lephepe**, Botswana
113 W 7 **Leping**, China
103 W 7 **Lepsy**, Kazakhstan
83 E 15 **Leptokarya**, Greece
77 I 22 **Lercara Friddi**, Italy
128 K 8 **Léré**, Mali
129 R 11 **Lere**, Nigeria
129 V 11 **Léré**, Chad
95 Y 10 **Lerik**, Azerbaijan
67 O 3 **Lerma**, Spain
74 L 6 **Lermoos**, Austria
83 M 22 **Leros**, Greece ✱
60 J 4 **Lerwick**, U.K.
49 N 8 **Les Cayes**, Haiti
20 K 9 **Les Cheneaux Islands**, MI, U.S.A. ✱
43 P 6 **Les Escoumins**, QC, Canada
64 L 8 **Les Herbiers**, France
43 R 5 **Les Méchins**, QC, Canada
65 V 13 **Les Mées**, France
64 K 8 **Les Sables-d'Olonne**, France
65 S 12 **Les Vans**, France
83 J 17 **Lesbos**, Greece ✱
112 M 7 **Leshan**, China
91 N 6 **Leshukonskoye**, Russian Federation
81 N 14 **Leskovac**, Serbia and Montenegro
81 L 21 **Leskovik**, Albania
21 K 15 **Leslie**, MI, U.S.A.
29 N 10 **Leslie**, ID, U.S.A.
79 E 15 **Leśna**, Poland
89 O 12 **Lesosibirsk**, Russian Federation
133 N 13 **Lesotho**, Africa □
89 V 15 **Lesozavodsk**, Russian Federation
64 L 11 **Lesparre-Médoc**, France
49 S 12 **Lesser Antilles**, Caribbean Sea ✱
95 R 7 **Lesser Caucasus**, Georgia ▲▲
39 I 17 **Lesser Slave Lake**, AB, Canada ♒
69 E 20 **Lessines**, Belgium
71 L 15 **Lestijärvi**, Finland ♒
71 K 14 **Lestijoki**, Finland ʃ
78 F 13 **Leszno**, Poland
39 K 21 **Lethbridge**, AB, Canada
51 T 7 **Lethem**, Guyana
117 R 15 **Leti**, Indonesia ✱
50 L 13 **Leticia**, Colombia
90 J 5 **Letniy Navolok**, Russian Federation
115 D 15 **Letpadan**, Myanmar
115 F 21 **Letsok-aw Kyun**, Myanmar ✱
132 J 4 **Léua**, Angola
73 H 25 **Leutkirch**, Germany
69 H 19 **Leuven**, Belgium
69 D 20 **Leuze-en-Hainaut**, Belgium
83 F 19 **Levadeia**, Greece
76 D 9 **Levanto**, Italy
93 R 15 **Levashi**, Russian Federation
26 I 5 **Levelland**, TX, U.S.A.
63 V 2 **Leven**, U.K.
73 C 17 **Leverkusen**, Germany
79 I 21 **Levice**, Slovakia
83 E 21 **Levidi**, Greece
83 L 22 **Levitha**, Greece ✱
14 I 13 **Levittown**, PA, U.S.A.
79 K 19 **Levoča**, Slovakia
82 J 7 **Levski**, Bulgaria
139 X 11 **Levuka**, Fiji
17 X 3 **Lewes**, DE, U.S.A.
63 W 13 **Lewes**, U.K.
23 N 11 **Lewis and Clark Lake**, SD, U.S.A. ♒
28 M 2 **Lewis Range**, MT, U.S.A. ▲▲
19 P 2 **Lewis Smith Lake**, AL, U.S.A. ♒
16 E 7 **Lewisburg**, KY, U.S.A.
16 F 10 **Lewisburg**, TN, U.S.A.
17 P 5 **Lewisburg**, WV, U.S.A.
15 P 6 **Lewiston**, ME, U.S.A.
28 J 6 **Lewiston**, ID, U.S.A.
14 E 13 **Lewistown**, PA, U.S.A.
29 S 5 **Lewistown**, MT, U.S.A.
16 I 5 **Lexington**, KY, U.S.A.
16 C 9 **Lexington**, TN, U.S.A.
17 P 9 **Lexington**, NC, U.S.A.
17 Q 5 **Lexington**, VA, U.S.A.
22 L 14 **Lexington**, NE, U.S.A.
32 I 10 **Lexington**, OR, U.S.A.
17 V 4 **Lexington Park**, MD, U.S.A.
63 P 3 **Leyland**, U.K.
121 L 16 **Leyte**, Philippines ✱
121 M 16 **Leyte Gulf**, Philippines ≈
79 N 17 **Leżajsk**, Poland
81 J 17 **Lezhë**, Albania
113 N 6 **Lezhi**, China
92 I 5 **L'gov**, Russian Federation
112 K 7 **Lhabo**, China
108 K 10 **Lhasa**, China
108 J 10 **Lhazê**, China
108 J 9 **Lhazhong**, China
116 C 8 **Lhokseumawe**, Indonesia
116 C 8 **Lhoksukon**, Indonesia
67 X 5 **L'Hospitalet de Llobregat**, Spain
113 W 10 **Liancheng**, China
121 N 20 **Lianga**, Philippines
111 B 16 **Liangcheng**, China
113 O 4 **Liangdang**, China
112 I 10 **Lianghe**, China
113 Q 7 **Lianghe**, China
113 N 4 **Lianghekou**, China
113 P 6 **Liangping**, China
113 U 9 **Lianhua**, China
113 Q 13 **Lianjiang**, China
113 X 9 **Lianjiang**, China
113 U 11 **Lianping**, China
111 G 16 **Lianshan**, China
113 S 11 **Lianshan**, China
113 X 4 **Lianshui**, China
113 X 3 **Lianyungang**, China
113 T 11 **Lianzhou**, China
113 U 2 **Liaocheng**, China
111 I 17 **Liaodong Bandao**, China ▶
111 H 16 **Liaodong Wan**, China ≈
112 M 10 **Liaohu**, China
111 I 15 **Liaoning**, China ▣
111 I 15 **Liaoyang**, China
111 J 14 **Liaoyuan**, China
39 C 14 **Liard**, YT, Canada ʃ
39 D 15 **Liard Plateau**, BC, Canada ◇
101 S 14 **Liāri**, Pakistan
50 I 6 **Libano**, Colombia
28 L 2 **Libby**, MT, U.S.A.
130 J 5 **Libenge**, Democratic Republic of Con
24 H 7 **Liberal**, KS, U.S.A.
79 D 16 **Liberec**, Czech Republic
47 O 11 **Liberia**, Costa Rica
128 H 13 **Liberia**, Africa □
50 M 4 **Libertad**, Venezuela
21 K 19 **Liberty**, IN, U.S.A.
69 I 24 **Libin**, Belgium
120 J 12 **Libmanan**, Philippines
113 P 10 **Libo**, China
64 M 11 **Libourne**, France
69 J 24 **Libramont**, Belgium
81 K 18 **Librazhd**, Albania
130 D 7 **Libreville**, Gabon ⌂
125 S 10 **Libya**, Africa □
125 X 10 **Libyan Desert**, Libya ◇
127 B 13 **Libyan Desert**, Sudan ◇
125 W 7 **Libyan Plateau**, Libya ◇
126 C 8 **Libyan Plateau**, Egypt ◇
56 F 13 **Licantén**, Chile
77 J 23 **Licata**, Italy
95 Q 11 **Lice**, Turkey
63 S 6 **Lichfield**, U.K.
133 R 4 **Lichinga**, Mozambique
133 N 11 **Lichtenburg**, Republic of South Africa
73 I 19 **Lichtenfels**, Germany
68 M 13 **Lichtenvoorde**, Netherlands
69 C 18 **Lichtervelde**, Belgium
113 Q 7 **Lichuan**, China
113 W 9 **Lichuan**, China
25 V 6 **Licking**, MO, U.S.A.
33 K 20 **Lida**, NV, U.S.A.
85 G 17 **Lida**, Belarus
71 E 21 **Lidköping**, Sweden
77 G 14 **Lido di Ostia**, Italy
78 J 10 **Lidzbark**, Poland
78 K 9 **Lidzbark Warmiński**, Poland
74 I 7 **Liechtenstein**, Europe □
69 K 21 **Liège**, Belgium ▣
69 J 20 **Liège**, Belgium
71 O 15 **Lieksa**, Finland
75 P 8 **Lienz**, Austria
84 B 11 **Liepāja**, Latvia
69 G 17 **Lier**, Belgium
74 E 6 **Liestal**, Switzerland
71 M 16 **Lievestuore**, Finland
75 T 6 **Liezen**, Austria
130 M 6 **Lifanga**, Democratic Republic of Cong
61 E 18 **Liffey**, Republic of Ireland ʃ
139 Q 13 **Lifou**, New Caledonia ✱
120 J 13 **Ligao**, Philippines
44 I 7 **Ligui**, Mexico
76 C 8 **Liguria**, Italy ▣
76 A 12 **Ligurian Sea**, Europe ∿
138 H 3 **Lihir Group**, Papua New Guinea ✱
138 H 3 **Lihir Island**, Papua New Guinea ✱
34 A 6 **Lihue**, HI, U.S.A.
84 F 7 **Lihula**, Estonia
112 J 9 **Lijiang**, China
131 O 14 **Likasi**, Democratic Republic of Congo
130 M 6 **Likati**, Democratic Republic of Congo
90 H 13 **Likhoslavl'**, Russian Federation
141 Y 2 **Likiep**, Marshall Islands ✱
130 K 8 **Likolia**, Democratic Republic of Cong
130 I 6 **Likouala**, Congo ▣
116 I 10 **Liku**, Indonesia
113 T 9 **Liling**, China
65 R 1 **Lille**, France
69 H 17 **Lille**, Belgium
71 D 18 **Lillehammer**, Norway
39 G 21 **Lillooet**, BC, Canada
133 R 5 **Lilongwe**, Malawi ⌂
121 I 21 **Liloy**, Philippines
21 L 17 **Lima**, OH, U.S.A.
29 O 9 **Lima**, MT, U.S.A.
53 C 16 **Lima**, Peru ⌂
53 C 16 **Lima**, Peru ▣
55 G 19 **Lima**, Paraguay
99 X 5 **Limah**, Oman
57 G 16 **Limay**, Argentina ʃ
57 I 14 **Limay Mahuida**, Argentina
119 T 6 **Limbang**, Malaysia
84 F 10 **Limbaži**, Latvia
69 K 16 **Limburg**, Netherlands ▣
69 I 18 **Limburg**, Belgium ▣
73 E 18 **Limburg**, Germany
71 F 18 **Limedsforsen**, Sweden
58 K 6 **Limeira**, Brazil
61 C 19 **Limerick**, Republic of Ireland
15 S 1 **Limestone**, ME, U.S.A.
71 B 23 **Limfjorden**, Denmark ≈
70 L 13 **Liminka**, Finland
71 F 23 **Limmared**, Sweden
135 O 2 **Limmen Bight**, NT, Australia ≈
83 G 18 **Limni**, Greece
83 D 14 **Limni Aliakmonas**, Greece ♒
82 F 12 **Limni Kerkinitis**, Greece ♒
83 D 18 **Limni Trichonida**, Greece ♒
82 D 13 **Limni Vegoritis**, Greece ♒
83 I 15 **Limnos**, Greece ✱
65 O 10 **Limoges**, France
31 T 4 **Limon**, CO, U.S.A.
47 S 12 **Limón**, Costa Rica
76 A 9 **Limone Piemonte**, Italy
65 O 10 **Limousin**, France ▣
65 Q 15 **Limoux**, France
133 P 9 **Limpopo**, Mozambique/Botswana ʃ
90 H 1 **Linakhamari**, Russian Federation
113 Y 6 **Lin'an**, China
121 K 23 **Linao Bay**, Philippines ≈
121 K 23 **Linao Point**, Philippines ▶
121 E 16 **Linapacan**, Philippines ✱
121 E 15 **Linapacan Strait**, Philippines ≈
45 Q 8 **Linares**, Mexico
56 F 13 **Linares**, Chile
67 O 11 **Linares**, Spain
83 I 18 **Linaria**, Greece
112 J 11 **Lincang**, China
113 V 8 **Linchuan**, China
15 R 4 **Lincoln**, ME, U.S.A.

□ Country ▣ Internal administrative region: State/Province/Territory/Dependent territory ⌂ Capital city ▲▲ Mountain range/Undersea ridge ▲ Mountain peak/Volcano/Seamount ◇ Geographic feature ▶ Headland/Point/Cape/Peninsula ◓ Desert ✱ Island/Island group ⁙ Antarctic base ◎ Ocean ∿ Sea ≈ Bay/Gulf/Channel/Strait ♒ Lake ⚑ Salt pan/Dry/Intermittent lake ʃ

M

Country | Internal administrative region: State/Province/Territory/Dependent territory | Capital city | Mountain range/Undersea ridge | Mountain peak/Volcano/Seamount | Geographic feature | Headland/Point/Cape/Peninsula | Desert | Island/Island group | Antarctic base | Ocean | Sea | Bay/Gulf/Channel/Strait | Lake | Salt pan/Dry/Intermittent lake | River

Country · Internal administrative region: State/Province/Territory/Dependent territory · Capital city · Mountain range/Undersea ridge · Mountain peak/Volcano/Seamount · Geographic feature · Headland/Point/Cape/Peninsula · Desert · Island/Island group · Antarctic base · Ocean · Sea · Bay/Gulf/Channel/Strait · Lake · Salt pan/Dry/Intermittent lake · R

Q 5 Marks, Russian Federation
J 6 Marksville, LA, U.S.A.
K 19 Marktredwitz, Germany
N 8 Marla, SA, Australia
S 11 Marlborough, U.K.
V 6 Marlborough, QLD, Australia
I 17 Marlborough, New Zealand ▣
S 10 Marlborough Downs, U.K. ◇
Q 8 Marlin, TX, U.S.A.
P 4 Marlinton, WV, U.S.A.
U 10 Marlow, U.K.
C 19 Marmagao, India
N 12 Marmande, France
C 8 Marmara, Turkey
C 8 Marmara, Turkey 🏝
N 13 Marmaraereğlisi, Turkey
C 13 Marmaris, Turkey
G 5 Marmolada, Italy ▲
F 9 Marne, Germany
U 7 Marneuli, Georgia
X 12 Maro, Chad
N 8 Maroa, Venezuela
Z 6 Maroantsetra, Madgascar
Z 5 Maromokotro, Madgascar ▲
P 7 Marondera, Zimbabwe
X 8 Maroni, French Guiana ᔕ
W 8 Maroochydore, QLD, Australia
O 5 Maroon Peak, CO, U.S.A. ▲
I 6 Maropiu, New Zealand
N 13 Maros, Indonesia
V 11 Maroua, Cameroon
X 6 Marovoay, Madgascar
W 15 Marquesas Keys, FL, U.S.A. 🏝
H 8 Marquette, MI, U.S.A.
R 8 Marquez, TX, U.S.A.
A 17 Marra Plateau, Sudan ◇
G 10 Marradi, Italy
G 8 Marrakech, Morocco
S 15 Marrawah, TAS, Australia
P 9 Marree, SA, Australia
S 7 Marromeu, Mozambique
S 4 Marrupa, Mozambique
W 8 Marsa al Burayqah, Libya
G 11 Marsa Alam, Egypt
C 7 Marsa Matrûh, Egypt
V 6 Marsabit, Kenya
G 22 Marsala, Italy
H 8 Marsdiep, Netherlands ≈
U 14 Marseille, France
L 1 Marsh Harbour, The Bahamas
J 8 Marsh Island, LA, U.S.A. 🏝
P 9 Marshall, MN, U.S.A.
T 3 Marshall, MO, U.S.A.
U 9 Marshall, AR, U.S.A.
T 6 Marshall, TX, U.S.A.
W 4 Marshall Islands, Oceania ▣
T 12 Marshalltown, IA, U.S.A.
E 11 Marshfield, WI, U.S.A.
V 4 Martanai Besar, Malaysia 🏝
L 12 Martapura, Indonesia
F 13 Martapura, Indonesia
K 24 Martelange, Belgium
F 8 Marten River, ON, Canada
O 11 Martha's Vineyard, MA, U.S.A. 🏝
C 10 Martigny, Switzerland
C 8 Martin, TN, U.S.A.
I 11 Martin, SD, U.S.A.
I 19 Martin, Slovakia
K 10 Martin Peninsula, Antarctica ▶
N 16 Martina Franca, Italy
L 16 Martinborough, New Zealand
S 11 Martínez, Mexico
Y 11 Martinique, France, France ▣
Y 10 Martinique Passage, Dominica ≈
F 19 Martino, Greece
O 18 Martins Ferry, OH, U.S.A.
S 2 Martinsburg, WV, U.S.A.
Q 7 Martinsville, VA, U.S.A.
I 20 Martinsville, IN, U.S.A.
L 14 Marton, New Zealand
K 4 Martuk, Kazakhstan
U 9 Martuni, Armenia
E 19 Marugame, Japan
O 14 Maruim, Brazil
N 14 Mary, Turkmenistan
W 8 Maryborough, QLD, Australia
T 3 Maryland, U.S.A. ▣
J 6 Marysvale, UT, U.S.A.
L 18 Marysville, OH, U.S.A.
O 2 Marysville, KS, U.S.A.
H 6 Marysville, WA, U.S.A.
G 18 Marysville, CA, U.S.A.
J 9 Maryville, TN, U.S.A.
R 1 Maryville, MO, U.S.A.
N 15 Maryyskiy Velayat, Turkmenistan ▣
G 6 Masagua, Guatemala
R 8 Masaka, Uganda
L 13 Masalembu Besar, Indonesia 🏝
L 13 Masalembu Kecil, Indonesia 🏝
Y 10 Masalli, Azerbaijan
O 12 Masamba, Indonesia
M 21 Masan, South Korea
W 14 Masasi, Tanzania
L 21 Masavi, Bolivia
N 9 Masaya, Nicaragua
J 14 Masbate, Philippines
J 15 Masbate, Philippines 🏝
N 12 Maseru, Lesotho ♜
S 1 Masham, U.K.
O 6 Mashhad, Iran
L 10 Mashīz, Iran
P 6 Mashonaland Central, Zimbabwe ▣
Q 6 Mashonaland East, Zimbabwe ▣
O 6 Mashonaland West, Zimbabwe ▣
K 7 Masi, Norway
J 10 Masi-Manimba, Democratic Republic of Congo
J 6 Masiáca, Mexico
R 7 Masindi, Uganda
T 9 Masis, Armenia
E 14 Masisea, Peru
G 8 Masjed Soleymān, Iran
D 11 Maslenica, Croatia
S 13 Masna'ah, Yemen
W 7 Masoarivo, Madgascar
M 3 Mason, WV, U.S.A.
N 9 Mason, TX, U.S.A.
B 26 Mason Bay, New Zealand ≈
F 18 Mason City, IL, U.S.A.
T 10 Mason City, IA, U.S.A.
E 10 Massa, Italy
F 12 Massa Marittimo, Italy
N 9 Massachusetts, U.S.A. ▣
15 O 9 Massachusetts Bay, MA, U.S.A. ≈
129 V 10 Massaguet, Chad
129 W 9 Massakory, Chad
133 Q 9 Massangena, Mozambique
133 R 4 Massangulo, Mozambique
127 I 16 Massawa, Eritrea
127 I 16 Massawa Channel, Eritrea ≈
14 I 5 Massena, NY, U.S.A.
129 W 10 Massenya, Chad
39 C 19 Masset, BC, Canada
42 C 9 Massey, ON, Canada
65 R 11 Massif Central, France ▲▲
49 N 8 Massif de la Hotte, Haiti ▲▲
129 S 6 Massif de L'aïr, Niger ▲▲
130 L 3 Massif des Bongo, Central African Republic ▲▲
129 Z 8 Massif du Kapka, Chad ▲▲
128 G 10 Massif du Tamgué, Guinea ▲
130 H 4 Massif du Yadé, Central African Republic ▲▲
129 Z 7 Massif Ennedi, Chad ▲▲
128 J 10 Massigui, Mali
133 R 9 Massinga, Mozambique
133 Q 10 Massingir, Mozambique
145 Y 9 Masson Island, Antarctica 🏝
98 L 8 Mastābah, Saudi Arabia
95 Z 8 Mastağa, Azerbaijan
137 L 15 Masterton, New Zealand
48 K 2 Mastic Point, The Bahamas
101 W 5 Mastuj, Pakistan
101 T 11 Mastung, Pakistan
98 L 7 Mastūrah, Saudi Arabia
123 C 19 Masuda, Japan
133 P 8 Masvingo, Zimbabwe
133 P 8 Masvingo, Zimbabwe ▣
96 H 4 Maşyāf, Syria
85 E 21 Masyevichy, Belarus
140 H 8 Matā 'Utu, Wallis and Futuna Islands ♜
133 N 7 Matabeleland North, Zimbabwe ▣
133 O 8 Matabeleland South, Zimbabwe ▣
42 E 7 Matachewan, ON, Canada
130 G 11 Matadi, Democratic Republic of Congo
26 L 4 Matador, TX, U.S.A.
47 N 8 Matagalpa, Nicaragua
41 P 11 Matagami, QC, Canada
27 R 12 Matagorda Bay, TX, U.S.A. ≈
27 R 12 Matagorda Island, TX, U.S.A. 🏝
27 R 12 Matagorda Peninsula, TX, U.S.A. ▶
103 U 5 Matak, Kazakhstan
116 G 9 Matak, Indonesia 🏝
136 M 9 Matakana Island, New Zealand 🏝
136 O 10 Matakaoa Point, New Zealand ▶
132 H 5 Matala, Angola
128 F 8 Matam, Senegal
136 L 10 Matamata, New Zealand
129 R 9 Matamey, Niger
45 S 7 Matamoros, Mexico
121 I 23 Matanal Point, Philippines ▶
43 Q 5 Matane, QC, Canada
48 H 4 Matanzas, Cuba
105 G 25 Matara, Sri Lanka
83 C 19 Mataragka, Greece
116 L 15 Mataram, Indonesia
135 N 2 Mataranka, NT, Australia
67 X 4 Mataró, Spain
136 M 10 Matata, New Zealand
137 D 25 Mataura, New Zealand
137 C 24 Mataura, New Zealand ᔕ
136 N 11 Matawai, New Zealand
103 W 8 Matay, Kazakhstan
53 L 17 Mategua, Bolivia
45 Q 9 Matehuala, Mexico
131 V 14 Matemanga, Tanzania
77 M 16 Matera, Italy
79 N 21 Mátészalka, Hungary
125 Q 5 Mateur, Tunisia
42 E 6 Matheson, ON, Canada
17 V 6 Mathews, VA, U.S.A.
27 P 13 Mathis, TX, U.S.A.
106 I 9 Mathura, India
121 N 22 Mati, Philippines
55 L 15 Matias Cardoso, Brazil
41 T 8 Matimekosh, QC, Canada
47 R 12 Matina, Costa Rica
84 G 9 Matīši, Latvia
101 U 14 Matli, Pakistan
63 S 5 Matlock, U.K.
121 K 14 Matnog, Philippines
55 H 14 Mato Grosso, Brazil ▣
58 F 6 Mato Grosso do Sul, Brazil ▣
66 H 5 Matosinhos, Portugal
75 P 8 Matrei in Osttirol, Austria
132 J 15 Matroosberg, Republic of South Africa ▲
113 Y 10 Matsu Tao, Taiwan 🏝
123 D 18 Matsue, Japan
122 I 8 Matsumae, Japan
123 I 16 Matsumoto, Japan
123 H 18 Matsusaka, Japan
123 D 20 Matsuyama, Japan
42 F 9 Mattawa, ON, Canada
15 R 4 Mattawamkeag, ME, U.S.A.
33 M 15 Matterhorn, NV, U.S.A. ▲
74 D 11 Matterhorn, Switzerland ▲
75 Y 5 Mattersburg, Austria
139 S 14 Matthew Island, Vanuatu 🏝
49 N 6 Matthew Town, The Bahamas
75 Q 4 Mattighofen, Austria
21 G 19 Mattoon, IL, U.S.A.
119 O 9 Matu, Malaysia
53 D 16 Matucana, Peru
139 Y 12 Matuku, Fiji 🏝
132 I 4 Matumbo, Angola
51 R 3 Maturín, Venezuela
117 Q 8 Matutuang, Indonesia 🏝
107 O 11 Mau, India
104 F 13 Mau Rampur, India
133 S 5 Maúa, Mozambique
65 S 2 Maubeuge, France
115 D 16 Maubin, Myanmar
106 L 11 Maudaha, India
54 G 11 Maués, Brazil
140 A 5 Maug Islands, Northern Mariana Islands 🏝
107 N 12 Mauganj, India
34 D 7 Maui, HI, U.S.A. 🏝
141 P 10 Mauke, Cook Islands 🏝
56 F 13 Maule, Chile ▣
57 F 17 Maullín, Chile
21 L 16 Maumee, OH, U.S.A.
132 L 8 Maun, Botswana
34 E 8 Mauna Kea, HI, U.S.A. ▲
34 E 9 Mauna Loa, HI, U.S.A. ▲
136 J 6 Maungatapere, New Zealand
115 F 19 Maungmagan Islands, Myanmar 🏝
32 H 10 Maupin, OR, U.S.A.
65 Q 11 Mauriac, France
128 F 6 Mauritania, Africa ▣
11 Q 11 Mauritius, Indian Ocean ▣
20 E 13 Mauston, WI, U.S.A.
75 R 7 Mauterndorf, Austria
131 O 6 Mava, Democratic Republic of Congo
133 S 4 Mavago, Mozambique
132 J 6 Mavengue, Angola
132 K 6 Mavinga, Angola
130 I 11 Mawanga, Democratic Republic of Congo
113 P 10 Mawei, China
145 X 4 Mawson, Antarctica ⁙
145 W 4 Mawson Coast, Antarctica ◇
145 T 15 Mawson Peninsula, Antarctica ▶
22 J 4 Max, ND, U.S.A.
56 I 8 Maxán, Argentina
45 Y 10 Maxcanú, Mexico
71 K 15 Maxmo, Finland
89 U 11 Maya, Russian Federation ᔕ
112 M 4 Maya, China
116 I 11 Maya, Indonesia 🏝
46 I 4 Maya Mountains, Guatemala ▲▲
49 O 4 Mayaguana Island, The Bahamas 🏝
49 T 8 Mayagüez, Puerto Rico
129 R 9 Mayahi, Niger
103 T 14 Mayakovskogo, Tajikistan ▲
130 H 10 Mayama, Congo
100 L 5 Mayamey, Iran
127 I 18 Maych'ew, Ethiopia
127 M 19 Maydh, Somalia
64 M 5 Mayenne, France
16 C 7 Mayfield, KY, U.S.A.
137 F 21 Mayfield, New Zealand
82 M 11 Mayha Dağl, Turkey ▲
31 R 13 Mayhill, NM, U.S.A.
103 U 4 Maykain, Kazakhstan
92 L 12 Maykop, Russian Federation
103 T 11 Mayluu-Suu, Kyrgyzstan
103 N 8 Maylybas, Kazakhstan
114 E 11 Maymyo, Myanmar
93 R 3 Mayna, Russian Federation
19 U 8 Mayo, FL, U.S.A.
38 B 12 Mayo, YT, Canada
129 T 12 Mayo-Belwa, Nigeria
129 V 11 Mayo-Kébbi, Chad ▣
130 F 9 Mayoko, Congo
59 B 19 Mayor Buratovich, Argentina
136 M 9 Mayor Island, New Zealand 🏝
55 F 17 Mayor Pablo Lagerenza, Paraguay
133 X 4 Mayotte, France 🏝
120 G 5 Mayraira Point, Philippines ▶
75 N 7 Mayrhofen, Austria
89 U 13 Mayskiy, Russian Federation
103 V 4 Mayskoye, Kazakhstan
16 J 4 Maysville, KY, U.S.A.
121 E 16 Maytiguid, Philippines 🏝
117 R 10 Mayu, Indonesia 🏝
130 E 10 Mayumba, Gabon
22 K 15 Maywood, NE, U.S.A.
59 A 18 Maza, Argentina
133 N 5 Mazabuka, Zambia
32 I 5 Mazama, WA, U.S.A.
65 Q 14 Mazamet, France
52 F 10 Mazán, Peru
100 J 5 Māzandarān, Iran ▣
108 G 7 Mazar, China
101 T 5 Mazār-e Sharīf, Afghanistan
77 G 22 Mazara del Vallo, Italy
67 R 12 Mazarrón, Spain
44 J 4 Mazatán, Mexico
46 F 6 Mazatenango, Guatemala
44 L 9 Mazatlán, Mexico
30 J 11 Mazatzal Peak, AZ, U.S.A. ▲
84 D 12 Mažeikiai, Lithuania
84 D 9 Mazirbe, Latvia
44 J 4 Mazocahui, Mexico
131 W 12 Mazomora, Tanzania
133 P 9 Mazunga, Zimbabwe
85 L 21 Mazyr, Belarus
133 P 11 Mbabane, Swaziland ♜
128 K 12 Mbahiakro, Côte d'Ivoire
130 J 5 Mbaïki, Central African Republic
129 V 15 Mbalam, Cameroon
131 T 7 Mbale, Uganda
129 T 15 Mbalmayo, Cameroon
138 M 7 Mbalo, Solomon Islands
131 T 14 Mbamba Bay, Tanzania
130 J 8 Mbandaka, Democratic Republic of Congo
129 S 14 Mbanga, Cameroon
132 G 1 M'banza Congo, Angola
130 H 11 Mbanza-Ngungu, Democratic Republic of Congo
131 R 8 Mbarara, Uganda
130 J 5 Mbata, Central African Republic
131 S 12 Mbeya, Tanzania ▣
131 T 13 Mbeya, Tanzania
130 F 9 Mbigou, Gabon
131 U 14 Mbinga, Tanzania
133 P 8 Mbizi, Zimbabwe
131 O 4 Mboki, Central African Republic
130 G 7 Mbomo, Congo
130 M 4 Mbomou, Central African Republic ▣
128 D 8 Mbour, Senegal
128 G 8 Mbout, Mauritania
131 S 13 Mbozi, Tanzania
130 M 11 Mbuji-Mayi, Democratic Republic of Congo
131 U 10 Mbulu, Tanzania
131 U 12 Mbuyuni, Tanzania
43 R 10 McAdam, NB, Canada
25 P 11 McAlester, OK, U.S.A.
27 P 15 McAllen, TX, U.S.A.
17 P 11 McBee, SC, U.S.A.
39 G 19 McBride, BC, Canada
28 K 8 McCall, ID, U.S.A.
26 J 8 McCamey, TX, U.S.A.
29 P 12 McCammon, ID, U.S.A.
38 I 5 McClintock Channel, NU, Canada ≈
14 F 12 McClure, PA, U.S.A.
36 L 4 McClure Strait, NT, Canada ≈
143 O 6 McClure Strait Gulf, Arctic Ocean ≈
22 K 4 McClusky, ND, U.S.A.
18 L 6 McComb, MS, U.S.A.
22 K 15 McCook, NE, U.S.A.
16 M 12 McCormick, SC, U.S.A.
33 K 14 McDermitt, NV, U.S.A.
25 X 13 McGehee, AR, U.S.A.
33 N 17 McGill, NV, U.S.A.
43 S 9 McGivney, NB, Canada
35 P 8 McGrath, AK, U.S.A.
131 X 13 Mchinga, Tanzania
133 Q 4 Mchinji, Malawi
22 J 7 McIntosh, SD, U.S.A.
140 I 4 McKean, Kiribati 🏝
16 C 8 McKenzie, TN, U.S.A.
35 R 7 McKinley Park, AK, U.S.A.
27 Q 5 McKinney, TX, U.S.A.
22 J 7 McLaughlin, SD, U.S.A.
21 G 21 McLeansboro, IL, U.S.A.
39 F 18 McLeod Lake, BC, Canada
115 F 21 McLeods Island, Myanmar 🏝
20 J 9 McMillan, MI, U.S.A.
16 H 9 McMinnville, TN, U.S.A.
32 F 10 McMinnville, OR, U.S.A.
145 R 12 McMurdo, Antarctica ⁙
25 N 5 Mcpherson, KS, U.S.A.
19 U 5 McRae, GA, U.S.A.
133 O 14 Mdantsane, Republic of South Africa
24 I 7 Meade, KS, U.S.A.
35 O 3 Meade, AK, U.S.A. ᔕ
39 L 17 Meadow Lake, SK, Canada
14 B 10 Meadville, PA, U.S.A.
66 H 6 Mealhada, Portugal
41 V 8 Mealy Mountains, NL, Canada ▲▲
65 Q 4 Meaux, France
33 L 25 Mecca, CA, U.S.A.
98 M 8 Mecca, Saudi Arabia
69 G 18 Mechelen, Belgium
124 L 7 Mecheria, Algeria
94 K 8 Mecitözü, Turkey
72 K 10 Mecklenburg-Vorpommern, Germany ▣
72 J 8 Mecklenburger Bucht, Germany ≈
133 T 4 Mecula, Mozambique
116 C 9 Medan, Indonesia
59 B 19 Médanos, Argentina
124 M 5 Médéa, Algeria
50 G 5 Medellín, Colombia
68 I 9 Medemblik, Netherlands
125 R 7 Medenine, Tunisia
128 E 7 Mederdra, Mauritania
20 E 11 Medford, WI, U.S.A.
32 F 13 Medford, OR, U.S.A.
56 I 12 Media Luna, Argentina
86 I 10 Mediaş, Romania
76 G 9 Medicina, Italy
29 X 13 Medicine Bow, WY, U.S.A.
39 K 20 Medicine Hat, AB, Canada
24 L 7 Medicine Lodge, KS, U.S.A.
14 D 8 Medina, NY, U.S.A.
22 L 5 Medina, ND, U.S.A.
98 M 6 Medina, Saudi Arabia
66 M 4 Medina de Rioseco, Spain
66 M 5 Medina del Campo, Spain
128 F 9 Medina Gounas, Senegal
67 Q 5 Medinaceli, Spain
107 R 14 Medinipur, India
85 G 16 Mednínkai, Lithuania
130 E 7 Médouneu, Gabon
81 M 15 Medveđa, Serbia and Montenegro
90 H 8 Medvezh'yegorsk, Russian Federation
92 J 2 Medyn', Russian Federation
134 G 8 Meekatharra, WA, Australia
31 N 4 Meeker, CO, U.S.A.
69 H 16 Meer, Belgium
68 I 13 Meerkerk, Netherlands
69 J 19 Meerssen, Belgium
106 J 8 Meerut, India
29 T 10 Meeteetse, WY, U.S.A.
127 I 23 Mēga, Ethiopia
127 H 23 Mega Escarpment, Ethiopia ▲▲
127 J 21 Megalo, Ethiopia
83 D 21 Megalopoli, Greece
83 B 18 Meganisi, Greece 🏝
83 G 20 Megara, Greece
107 V 11 Meghalaya, India ▣
107 U 13 Meghna Shahbazpur, Bangladesh ᔕ
95 V 10 Meghri, Azerbaijan
94 D 14 Megisti, Greece 🏝
86 G 12 Mehadica, Romania
70 L 5 Mehamn, Norway
101 U 13 Mehar, Pakistan
107 O 10 Mehndawal, India
100 L 8 Mehr Jān, Iran
100 F 7 Mehrān, Iran
113 Y 7 Meicheng, China
129 U 13 Meiganga, Cameroon
112 M 8 Meigu, China
111 K 14 Meihekou, China
114 D 12 Meiktila, Myanmar
73 H 18 Meiningen, Germany
112 M 7 Meishan, China
73 M 16 Meissen, Germany
110 M 9 Meixi, China
113 V 11 Meizhou, China
56 H 9 Mejicana, Argentina ▲
56 F 5 Mejillones, Chile
141 Z 2 Mejit Island, Marshall Islands 🏝
130 G 7 Mékambo, Gabon
127 I 18 Mek'elē, Ethiopia
128 D 8 Mékhé, Senegal
101 U 10 Mekhtar, Pakistan
124 I 7 Meknès, Morocco
115 L 20 Mekong, Asia ᔕ
118 C 10 Melaka, Malaysia
118 C 9 Melaka, Malaysia ▣
119 U 6 Melalap, Malaysia
138 H 2 Melanesia, Oceania ◇
19 X 10 Melbourne, FL, U.S.A.
25 W 9 Melbourne, AR, U.S.A.
135 S 13 Melbourne, VIC, Australia
46 J 2 Melchor de Mencos, Guatemala
42 B 9 Meldrum Bay, ON, Canada
93 W 3 Meleuz, Russian Federation
129 X 10 Mélfi, Chad
39 M 17 Melfort, SK, Canada
66 I 2 Melide, Spain
83 D 22 Meligalas, Greece
67 P 15 Melilla, Spain
56 F 12 Melipilla, Chile
40 H 10 Melita, MB, Canada
77 L 22 Melito di Porto Salvo, Italy
87 V 9 Melitopol', Ukraine
82 I 12 Melivoia, Greece
75 V 4 Melk, Austria
127 I 23 Melka Guba, Ethiopia
63 R 11 Melksham, U.K.
74 J 7 Mellau, Austria
69 E 18 Melle, Belgium
20 E 9 Mellen, WI, U.S.A.
71 E 21 Mellerud, Sweden
22 M 8 Mellette, SD, U.S.A.
72 E 10 Mellum, Germany 🏝
79 D 17 Mělník, Czech Republic
59 G 14 Melo, Uruguay
29 O 7 Melrose, MT, U.S.A.
29 U 5 Melstone, MT, U.S.A.
70 L 10 Meltaus, Finland
135 S 13 Melton, VIC, Australia
63 U 6 Melton Mowbray, U.K.
65 Q 5 Melun, France
127 E 19 Melut, Sudan
39 O 18 Melville, SK, Canada
37 N 4 Melville Island, NU, Canada 🏝
134 M 1 Melville Island, NT, Australia 🏝
41 O 1 Melville Peninsula, NU, Canada ▶
116 J 11 Memala, Indonesia
133 U 5 Memba, Mozambique
117 X 11 Memberamo, Indonesia ᔕ
73 H 25 Memmingen, Germany
116 I 10 Mempawah, Indonesia
16 A 10 Memphis, TN, U.S.A.
26 L 3 Memphis, TX, U.S.A.
25 S 12 Mena, AR, U.S.A.
87 R 2 Mena, Ukraine
62 M 4 Menai Bridge, U.K.
129 O 8 Ménaka, Mali
117 Q 11 Menanga, Indonesia
65 R 12 Mende, France
127 I 22 Mendebo Mountains, Ethiopia ▲▲
127 I 17 Mendefera, Eritrea
143 S 6 Mendeleyev Ridge, Arctic Ocean ▲▲
93 T 1 Mendeleyevsk, Russian Federation
18 M 5 Mendenhall, MS, U.S.A.
45 R 7 Méndez, Mexico
127 G 20 Mendī, Ethiopia
138 B 5 Mendi, Papua New Guinea
63 P 11 Mendip Hills, U.K. ▲▲
33 E 17 Mendocino, CA, U.S.A.
21 F 16 Mendota, IL, U.S.A.
56 H 11 Mendoza, Argentina
56 H 12 Mendoza, Argentina ▣
69 B 19 Menen, Belgium
141 U 1 Meneng Point, Nauru ▶
77 H 22 Menfi, Italy
119 U 5 Mengalum, Malaysia 🏝
113 V 4 Mengcheng, China
116 G 13 Menggala, Indonesia
112 J 13 Menghai, China
112 K 13 Mengla, China
113 R 11 Mengshan, China
113 W 2 Mengyin, China
112 J 13 Mengzhe, China
112 M 12 Mengzi, China
135 R 10 Menindee, NSW, Australia
135 R 10 Menindee Lake, NSW, Australia ◣
89 S 9 Menkere, Russian Federation
21 G 14 Menomonee Falls, WI, U.S.A.
132 I 5 Menongue, Angola
116 G 12 Mentok, Indonesia
109 P 7 Menyuan, China
93 U 1 Menzelinsk, Russian Federation
134 I 10 Menzies, WA, Australia
68 L 9 Meppel, Netherlands
72 D 12 Meppen, Germany
64 G 5 Mer d'Iroise, France 🌊
116 G 13 Merak, Indonesia
76 F 5 Merano, Italy
117 Y 15 Merauke, Indonesia
50 F 8 Mercaderes, Colombia
33 H 20 Merced, CA, U.S.A.
58 D 11 Mercedes, Argentina
59 D 15 Mercedes, Uruguay
14 A 11 Mercer, PA, U.S.A.
20 E 9 Mercer, WI, U.S.A.
136 L 8 Mercury Bay, New Zealand ≈
136 L 8 Mercury Islands, New Zealand 🏝
139 R 9 Mere Lava, Vanuatu 🏝
127 N 23 Mereeg, Somalia
136 K 9 Meremere, New Zealand
115 F 20 Mergui, Myanmar
115 E 21 Mergui Archipelago, Myanmar 🏝
82 L 12 Meriş, Turkey
45 Y 10 Mérida, Mexico
50 K 4 Mérida, Venezuela ▣
50 L 4 Mérida, Venezuela
66 K 9 Mérida, Spain
14 L 11 Meriden, CT, U.S.A.
19 N 5 Meridian, MS, U.S.A.
124 J 8 Meridja, Algeria
71 J 17 Merikarvia, Finland
73 I 24 Mering, Germany
140 I 15 Merir, Palau 🏝
119 R 9 Merit, Malaysia
103 T 10 Merke, Kazakhstan
85 F 17 Merkinė, Lithuania
127 E 15 Merowe, Sudan
134 H 11 Merredin, WA, Australia
20 F 10 Merrill, WI, U.S.A.
22 I 11 Merriman, NE, U.S.A.
39 G 21 Merritt, BC, Canada
19 X 10 Merritt Island, FL, U.S.A. 🏝
127 J 17 Mersa Fatma, Eritrea
127 I 16 Mersa Gulbub, Eritrea
69 L 25 Mersch, Luxembourg
63 Y 9 Mersea Island, U.K. 🏝
63 P 4 Mersey, U.K. ᔕ
94 J 13 Mersin, Turkey
118 E 9 Mersing, Malaysia
84 E 10 Mērsrags, Latvia
104 C 12 Merta, India
63 O 10 Merthyr Tydfil, U.K.
131 W 7 Merti, Kenya
66 I 11 Mértola, Portugal
131 V 9 Meru, Tanzania ▲
131 V 7 Meru, Kenya
119 W 7 Merutai, Malaysia
94 K 8 Merzifon, Turkey
73 B 21 Merzig, Germany
30 J 12 Mesa, AZ, U.S.A.
31 S 12 Mesa, NM, U.S.A.
45 P 9 Mesa Central, Mexico ▲▲
23 S 4 Mesabi Range, MN, U.S.A. ▲▲
77 O 16 Mesagne, Italy
73 E 16 Meschede, Germany
20 J 12 Mesick, MI, U.S.A.
83 F 14 Mesimeri, Greece
74 H 10 Mesocco, Switzerland
83 C 19 Mesolongi, Greece
58 D 13 Mesopotamia, Argentina ◇
27 Q 6 Mesquite, TX, U.S.A.
33 N 21 Mesquite, NV, U.S.A.
125 N 7 Messaad, Algeria
77 L 21 Messina, Italy
133 P 9 Messina, Republic of South Africa
83 D 22 Messiniakos Kolpos, Greece ≈
82 G 11 Mesta, Bulgaria ᔕ
76 G 7 Mestre, Italy
50 J 7 Meta, Colombia ▣
50 M 6 Meta, Colombia ᔕ
41 R 3 Meta Incognita Peninsula, NU, Canada ▶
42 M 6 Métabetchouan, QC, Canada
18 L 8 Metairie, LA, U.S.A.
56 I 6 Metán, Argentina
133 R 4 Metangula, Mozambique
46 I 6 Metapan, El Salvador
133 S 5 Metarica, Mozambique
43 S 12 Meteghan, NS, Canada
127 H 18 Metema, Ethiopia
138 G 3 Meteran, Papua New Guinea
137 G 20 Methven, New Zealand
81 G 14 Metković, Croatia
125 P 7 Metlaoui, Tunisia
133 U 4 Metoro, Mozambique
116 G 13 Metro, Indonesia
21 F 23 Metropolis, IL, U.S.A.
83 C 16 Metsovo, Greece
127 G 21 Metu, Ethiopia
65 V 4 Metz, France
69 H 21 Meuse, Belgium ᔕ
62 K 15 Mevagissey, U.K.
27 R 7 Mexia, TX, U.S.A.
44 F 2 Mexicali, Mexico
30 L 7 Mexican Hat, UT, U.S.A.
14 G 7 Mexico, NY, U.S.A.
25 V 3 Mexico, MO, U.S.A.
45 N 8 Mexico, North America ▣
45 Q 12 México, Mexico ▣
45 R 12 Mexico City, Mexico ♜
101 R 6 Meymaneh, Afghanistan
100 I 7 Meymeh, Iran
45 V 13 Mezcalapa, Mexico ᔕ
82 G 8 Mezdra, Bulgaria
90 M 5 Mezen', Russian Federation ᔕ
90 M 5 Mezen', Russian Federation
90 M 4 Mezenskaya Guba, Russian Federation ≈
45 S 7 Mezquital, Mexico
133 Q 4 Mfuwe, Zambia
77 K 25 Mgarr, Malta
133 Q 11 Mhlume, Swaziland
123 C 19 Mi-shima, Japan 🏝
121 H 17 Miagao, Philippines
45 T 14 Miahuatlán, Mexico
66 L 9 Miajadas, Spain
19 Y 13 Miami, FL, U.S.A.
25 R 7 Miami, OK, U.S.A.
19 Y 13 Miami Beach, FL, U.S.A.
101 X 10 Mian Chanmum, Pakistan
100 F 4 Miandowāb, Iran
133 X 8 Miandrivazo, Madgascar
110 H 8 Mianduhe, China
100 G 4 Miāneh, Iran
117 R 8 Miangas, Indonesia 🏝
121 O 24 Miangas, Philippines 🏝
112 L 8 Mianning, China
78 G 8 Mianowice, Poland
101 W 8 Mianwali, Pakistan
113 O 4 Mianxian, China
113 N 6 Mianyang, China
111 G 18 Miaodao Qundao, China 🏝
113 Z 11 Miaoli, Taiwan
133 Y 8 Miarinarivo, Madgascar
88 I 11 Miass, Russian Federation
78 G 9 Miastko, Poland
113 O 5 Micang Shan, China ▲▲
79 M 20 Michalovce, Slovakia
20 J 12 Michigan, U.S.A. ▣
21 I 16 Michigan City, IN, U.S.A.
42 A 7 Michipicoten Bay, ON, Canada ≈
40 M 12 Michipicoten Island, ON, Canada 🏝
42 A 6 Michipicoten River, ON, Canada
45 O 12 Michoacán, Mexico ▣
92 M 4 Michurinsk, Russian Federation
47 P 9 Mico, Nicaragua ᔕ
49 Z 11 Micoud, St Lucia
107 O 8 Mid Western, Nepal ▣
116 H 9 Midai, Indonesia 🏝
69 D 15 Middelburg, Netherlands
132 M 14 Middelburg, Republic of South Africa
68 H 8 Middenmeer, Netherlands
105 N 21 Middle Andaman, India 🏝
137 E 24 Middlemarch, New Zealand
135 U 6 Middlemount, QLD, Australia
16 K 7 Middlesboro, KY, U.S.A.
61 K 15 Middlesbrough, U.K.
46 K 2 Middlesex, Belize
16 B 10 Middleton, TN, U.S.A.
43 T 10 Middleton, NS, Canada
135 Q 6 Middleton, QLD, Australia
14 J 11 Middletown, NY, U.S.A.
14 J 13 Middletown, NJ, U.S.A.
14 L 11 Middletown, CT, U.S.A.
17 W 2 Middletown, DE, U.S.A.
63 Q 4 Middlewich, U.K.
124 I 7 Midelt, Morocco
63 U 12 Midhurst, U.K.
65 O 14 Midi-Pyrénées, France ▣
20 K 13 Midland, MI, U.S.A.
26 J 7 Midland, TX, U.S.A.
42 E 11 Midland, ON, Canada
133 O 7 Midlands, Zimbabwe ▣
27 Q 6 Midlothian, TX, U.S.A.
133 X 10 Midongy Atsimo, Madgascar
121 L 22 Midsayap, Philippines
29 X 11 Midwest, WY, U.S.A.
25 N 10 Midwest City, OK, U.S.A.
46 K 1 Midwinters Lagoon, Belize ◣
95 Q 12 Midyat, Turkey
82 F 7 Midzhur, Bulgaria ▲
123 D 21 Mie, Japan
78 F 12 Międzychód, Poland
78 N 13 Międzyrzec Podlaski, Poland
78 E 12 Międzyrzecz, Poland
79 L 17 Mielec, Poland
131 V 13 Miembwe, Tanzania
66 L 1 Mieres, Spain
69 J 16 Mierlo, Netherlands
78 I 7 Mierzeja Helska, Poland ▶
78 I 8 Mierzeja Wiślana, Poland ▶
113 O 3 Migang Shan, China ▲
107 Y 8 Miging, India
76 G 8 Migliarino, Italy
45 O 8 Miguel Auza, Mexico
47 V 13 Miguel de la Borda, Panama
114 C 13 Migyaunye, Myanmar
123 E 19 Mihara, Japan
68 H 12 Mijdrecht, Netherlands
85 I 21 Mikashevichy, Belarus

[…]ountry ▣ Internal administrative region: State/Province/Territory/Dependent territory ♜ Capital city ▲▲ Mountain range/ Undersea ridge ▲ Mountain peak/ Volcano/Seamount ◇ Geographic feature ▶ Headland/Point/ Cape/Peninsula ◖ Desert 🏝 Island/Island group ⁙ Antarctic base ◎ Ocean 🌊 Sea ≈ Bay/Gulf/Channel/Strait ◣ Lake ▚ Salt pan/Dry/ Intermittent lake ᔕ River

92 L 2 **Mikhaylov**, Russian Federation
93 O 7 **Mikhaylovka**, Russian Federation
103 U 2 **Mikhaylovka**, Kazakhstan
88 L 13 **Mikhaylovskiy**, Russian Federation
145 Y 7 **Mikhaytov Island**, Antarctica ✱
71 N 17 **Mikkeli**, Finland
131 V 12 **Mikumi**, Tanzania
91 P 8 **Mikun'**, Russian Federation
123 L 18 **Mikura-jima**, Japan ✱
23 S 6 **Milaca**, MN, U.S.A.
105 B 25 **Miladhunmadulu Atoll**, Maldives ✱
16 B 8 **Milan**, TN, U.S.A.
25 T 1 **Milan**, MO, U.S.A.
76 C 7 **Milan**, Italy
133 S 6 **Milange**, Mozambique
80 N 11 **Milanovac**, Serbia and Montenegro
94 B 12 **Milas**, Turkey
85 H 19 **Milavidy**, Belarus
23 O 8 **Milbank**, SD, U.S.A.
15 R 5 **Milbridge**, ME, U.S.A.
63 W 7 **Mildenhall**, U.K.
135 R 11 **Mildura**, VIC, Australia
112 M 11 **Mile**, China
127 J 19 **Mīlē**, Ethiopia
135 V 8 **Miles**, QLD, Australia
29 X 6 **Miles City**, MT, U.S.A.
14 I 11 **Milford**, PA, U.S.A.
14 L 12 **Milford**, CT, U.S.A.
15 N 10 **Milford**, MA, U.S.A.
15 N 8 **Milford**, NH, U.S.A.
17 W 3 **Milford**, DE, U.S.A.
30 I 6 **Milford**, UT, U.S.A.
62 K 9 **Milford Haven**, U.K.
25 N 3 **Milford Lake**, KS, U.S.A. ∽
137 A 22 **Milford Sound**, New Zealand ≈
137 B 22 **Milford Sound**, New Zealand
141 Z 4 **Mili**, Marshall Islands ✱
79 G 14 **Milicz**, Poland
134 M 1 **Milikapiti**, NT, Australia
89 Z 11 **Mil'kovo**, Russian Federation
41 P 3 **Mill Island**, NU, Canada ✱
145 Y 10 **Mill Island**, Antarctica ✱
65 R 13 **Millau**, France
23 R 6 **Mille Lacs**, MN, U.S.A. ∽
19 U 4 **Milledgeville**, GA, U.S.A.
141 S 6 **Millennium**, Kiribati ✱
92 M 8 **Millerovo**, Russian Federation
14 F 13 **Millersburg**, PA, U.S.A.
21 N 17 **Millersburg**, OH, U.S.A.
76 B 9 **Millesimo**, Italy
135 Q 13 **Millicent**, SA, Australia
15 R 3 **Millinocket**, ME, U.S.A.
19 O 3 **Millport**, AL, U.S.A.
38 G 13 **Mills Lake**, NT, Canada ∽
43 R 10 **Milltown**, NB, Canada
61 B 19 **Milltown Malbay**, Republic of Ireland
14 I 15 **Millville**, NJ, U.S.A.
21 M 18 **Millwood**, OH, U.S.A.
25 T 13 **Millwood Lake**, AR, U.S.A. ∽
138 G 7 **Milne Bay**, Papua New Guinea ≈
138 H 7 **Milne Bay**, Papua New Guinea ▣
63 P 1 **Milnthorpe**, U.K.
15 Q 4 **Milo**, ME, U.S.A.
83 H 23 **Milos**, Greece ✱
87 Z 4 **Milove**, Ukraine
14 F 12 **Milton**, PA, U.S.A.
19 P 7 **Milton**, FL, U.S.A.
137 E 25 **Milton**, New Zealand
32 K 9 **Milton-Freewater**, OR, U.S.A.
63 U 9 **Milton Keynes**, U.K.
25 N 3 **Miltonvale**, KS, U.S.A.
21 H 14 **Milwaukee**, WI, U.S.A.
64 L 13 **Mimizan**, France
130 F 8 **Mimongo**, Gabon
112 M 7 **Min**, China ʃ
33 K 19 **Mina**, NV, U.S.A.
99 W 5 **Mina Jebel Ali**, United Arab Emirates
99 S 3 **Minā' Sa'ūd**, Kuwait
100 M 13 **Mīnāb**, Iran
123 B 23 **Minamata**, Japan
48 K 5 **Minas**, Cuba
59 F 15 **Minas**, Uruguay
43 U 10 **Minas Basin**, NS, Canada ≈
43 T 10 **Minas Channel**, NS, Canada ≈
58 F 13 **Minas de Corrales**, Uruguay
48 F 4 **Minas de Matahambre**, Cuba
55 L 16 **Minas Gerais**, Brazil ▣
45 V 13 **Minatitlán**, Mexico
114 C 13 **Minbu**, Myanmar
57 F 18 **Minchinmávida**, Chile ▲
121 M 21 **Mindanao**, Philippines ✱
121 K 22 **Mindanao**, Philippines ʃ
73 H 24 **Mindelheim**, Germany
18 H 4 **Minden**, LA, U.S.A.
42 F 11 **Minden**, ON, Canada
72 F 13 **Minden**, Germany
120 G 13 **Mindoro**, Philippines ✱
121 F 14 **Mindoro Strait**, Philippines ≈
123 C 20 **Mine**, Japan
61 D 20 **Mine Head**, Republic of Ireland ▶
63 N 11 **Minehead**, U.K.
27 S 6 **Mineola**, TX, U.S.A.
27 O 6 **Mineral Wells**, TX, U.S.A.
93 O 13 **Mineral'nyye Vody**, Russian Federation
30 I 6 **Minersville**, UT, U.S.A.
77 M 15 **Minervino Murge**, Italy
131 P 14 **Minga**, Democratic Republic of Congo
95 W 8 **Mingäşşevir**, Azerbaijan
95 W 7 **Mingäçevir Su Anbari**, Azerbaijan ∽
130 L 4 **Mingala**, Central African Republic
134 G 10 **Mingenew**, WA, Australia
113 T 5 **Minggang**, China
114 D 9 **Mingin Range**, Myanmar ▲▲
110 K 10 **Mingshui**, China
60 D 11 **Mingulay**, U.K. ✱
113 W 9 **Mingxi**, China
115 D 15 **Minhla**, Myanmar
113 X 10 **Minhou**, China
105 B 24 **Minicoy Island**, India ✱
29 N 12 **Minidoka**, ID, U.S.A.
134 F 7 **Minilya Bridge Roadhouse**, WA, Australia
106 H 2 **Minimarg**, India
94 C 8 **Gönen**, Turkey
128 I 11 **Mininian**, Côte d'Ivoire
109 P 7 **Minle**, China
129 Q 11 **Minna**, Nigeria
23 R 8 **Minneapolis**, MN, U.S.A.
24 J 6 **Minneola**, KS, U.S.A.
23 O 6 **Minnesota**, U.S.A. ▣
23 R 8 **Minnesota**, MN, U.S.A. ʃ
67 Z 7 **Minorca**, Spain ✱
22 J 3 **Minot**, ND, U.S.A.
85 J 17 **Minsk**, Belarus ♜
78 L 13 **Mińsk Mazowiecki**, Poland
85 J 18 **Minskaya Voblasts'**, Belarus ▣
129 U 14 **Minta**, Cameroon
35 Q 7 **Minto**, AK, U.S.A.
43 S 9 **Minto**, NB, Canada
38 F 7 **Minto Inlet**, NT, Canada ≈
39 N 20 **Minton**, SK, Canada
77 J 15 **Minturno**, Italy
107 Z 8 **Minutang**, India
130 F 6 **Minvoul**, Gabon
109 Q 9 **Minxian**, China
93 X 1 **Minyar**, Russian Federation
107 Z 9 **Minzong**, India
20 L 11 **Mio**, MI, U.S.A.
85 H 18 **Mir**, Belarus
66 H 6 **Mira**, Portugal
54 J 13 **Miracema do Tocantins**, Brazil
101 V 8 **Miram Shah**, Pakistan
59 D 18 **Miramar**, Argentina
43 T 7 **Miramichi Bay**, NB, Canada ≈
65 N 12 **Miramont-de-Guyenne**, France
51 O 3 **Miranda**, Venezuela ▣
55 G 17 **Miranda**, Brazil
67 P 2 **Miranda de Ebro**, Spain
66 J 4 **Mirandela**, Portugal
58 H 5 **Mirandópolis**, Brazil
81 M 20 **Miras**, Albania
99 X 11 **Mirbāţ**, Oman
119 R 7 **Miri**, Malaysia
135 V 7 **Miriam Vale**, QLD, Australia
101 P 11 **Mīrjāveh**, Iran
145 Y 8 **Mirny**, Antarctica ⁘
89 R 11 **Mirnyy**, Russian Federation
78 F 10 **Mirosławiec**, Poland
101 U 14 **Mirpur Khas**, Pakistan
101 U 15 **Mirpur Sakro**, Pakistan
127 N 22 **Mirsale**, Somalia
83 F 22 **Mirtoö Pelagos**, Greece ◭
107 N 12 **Mirzapur**, India
123 D 21 **Misaki**, Japan
122 K 9 **Misawa**, Japan
43 U 6 **Miscou Island**, NB, Canada ✱
101 Y 5 **Misgar**, Pakistan
106 H 1 **Misgar**, India
105 O 24 **Misha**, India
110 N 11 **Mishan**, China
107 Z 8 **Mishmi Hills**, India ▲▲
138 C 5 **Misiki**, Papua New Guinea
58 F 10 **Misiones**, Argentina ▣
99 O 6 **Miskah**, Saudi Arabia
79 L 21 **Miskolc**, Hungary
117 T 11 **Misoöl**, Indonesia ✱
125 T 7 **Mişrātah**, Libya
22 J 11 **Mission**, SD, U.S.A.
41 N 9 **Missisa Lake**, ON, Canada ∽
42 E 13 **Mississauga**, ON, Canada
13 S 11 **Mississippi**, U.S.A., U.S.A. ʃ
18 K 3 **Mississippi**, U.S.A. ▣
18 M 9 **Mississippi Delta**, LA, U.S.A. ◇
18 M 7 **Mississippi Sound**, MS, U.S.A. ≈
29 N 5 **Missoula**, MT, U.S.A.
124 J 7 **Missour**, Morocco
12 M 5 **Missouri**, U.S.A., U.S.A. ʃ
25 S 5 **Missouri**, U.S.A. ▣
27 S 10 **Missouri City**, TX, U.S.A.
23 P 12 **Missouri Valley**, IA, U.S.A. ◇
41 R 11 **Mistassini**, QC, Canada
75 Y 2 **Mistelbach**, Austria
48 F 7 **Misteriosa Bank**, Cayman Islands ≈
87 Y 5 **Mistky**, Ukraine
54 H 8 **Mitaraka**, Brazil ▲
23 N 10 **Mitchell**, SD, U.S.A.
32 I 11 **Mitchell**, OR, U.S.A.
135 R 3 **Mitchell**, QLD, Australia ʃ
135 T 8 **Mitchell**, QLD, Australia
61 C 20 **Mitchelstown**, Republic of Ireland
101 V 15 **Mithi**, Pakistan
141 P 10 **Mitiaro**, Cook Islands ✱
123 L 15 **Mito**, Japan
131 W 13 **Mitole**, Tanzania
122 K 6 **Mitsuishi**, Japan
123 A 20 **Mitsushima**, Japan
74 J 7 **Mittelberg**, Austria
74 L 8 **Mittelberg**, Austria
75 P 7 **Mittersill**, Austria
73 M 26 **Mittlespitze**, Germany ▲
50 L 9 **Mitú**, Colombia
131 P 13 **Mitwaba**, Democratic Republic of Congo
130 E 7 **Mitzic**, Gabon
123 K 17 **Miura**, Japan
123 L 18 **Miyake-jima**, Japan ✱
122 L 10 **Miyako**, Japan
123 O 26 **Miyako-jima**, Japan ✱
123 N 26 **Miyako-rettō**, Japan ✱
123 C 23 **Miyakonojō**, Japan
102 J 5 **Miyaly**, Kazakhstan
123 D 23 **Miyazaki**, Japan
123 G 17 **Miyazu**, Japan
123 D 19 **Miyoshi**, Japan
111 E 16 **Miyun**, China
127 G 21 **Mīzan Teferī**, Ethiopia
125 S 8 **Mizdah**, Libya
61 A 21 **Mizen Head**, Republic of Ireland ▶
86 I 6 **Mizhhir''ya**, Ukraine
113 R 1 **Mizhi**, China
86 L 12 **Mizil**, Romania
82 G 7 **Miziya**, Bulgaria
107 W 13 **Mizoram**, India ▣
96 E 11 **Mizpe Ramon**, Israel
145 T 3 **Mizuho**, Antarctica ⁘
71 F 22 **Mjölby**, Sweden
131 W 11 **Mkata**, Tanzania
131 W 10 **Mkomazi**, Tanzania
133 O 4 **Mkushi**, Zambia
79 D 16 **Mladá Boleslav**, Czech Republic
80 L 11 **Mladenovac**, Serbia and Montenegro
78 K 11 **Mława**, Poland
81 G 15 **Mljet**, Croatia ✱
81 F 15 **Mljetski Kanal**, Croatia ≈
70 F 11 **Mo i Rana**, Norway
49 N 6 **Moa**, Cuba
117 S 14 **Moa**, Indonesia ✱
135 R 1 **Moa Island**, QLD, Australia ✱
30 M 5 **Moab**, UT, U.S.A.
139 Y 12 **Moala**, Fiji ✱
133 Q 10 **Moamba**, Mozambique
137 G 18 **Moana**, New Zealand
130 F 8 **Moanda**, Gabon
100 I 8 **Mobārakeh**, Iran
130 L 5 **Mobaye**, Central African Republic
130 L 5 **Mobayi-Mbongo**, Democratic Republic of Congo
25 U 3 **Moberly**, MO, U.S.A.
19 O 7 **Mobile**, AL, U.S.A.
19 O 7 **Mobile Bay**, AL, U.S.A. ≈
22 K 7 **Mobridge**, SD, U.S.A.
114 L 12 **Môc Châu**, Vietnam
49 Q 7 **Moca**, Dominican Republic
133 U 5 **Moçambique**, Mozambique
99 O 14 **Mocha**, Yemen
133 U 3 **Mocimboa da Praia**, Mozambique
132 H 4 **Môco**, Angola ▲
50 G 9 **Mocoa**, Colombia
58 K 5 **Mococa**, Brazil
44 M 4 **Moctezuma**, Mexico
133 S 6 **Mocuba**, Mozambique
65 W 11 **Modane**, France
30 H 6 **Modena**, UT, U.S.A.
76 F 8 **Modena**, Italy
33 H 20 **Modesto**, CA, U.S.A.
46 J 4 **Modesto Méndez**, Guatemala
77 K 24 **Modica**, Italy
75 X 4 **Mödling**, Austria
109 R 3 **Modot**, Mongolia
80 H 10 **Modriča**, Bosnia and Herzegovina
135 S 13 **Moe**, VIC, Australia
136 K 7 **Moehau**, New Zealand ▲
51 X 6 **Moengo**, Suriname
73 C 15 **Moers**, Germany
106 H 6 **Moga**, India
127 M 24 **Mogadishu**, Somalia ♜
130 J 6 **Mogalo**, Democratic Republic of Congo
122 J 12 **Mogami**, Japan ʃ
114 E 8 **Mogaung**, Myanmar
58 J 5 **Mogi-Guaçu**, Brazil ʃ
82 C 12 **Mogila**, Macedonia (F.Y.R.O.M.)
78 H 12 **Mogilno**, Poland
133 U 5 **Mogincual**, Mozambique
89 S 13 **Mogocha**, Russian Federation
127 E 20 **Mogogh**, Sudan
114 E 10 **Mogok**, Myanmar
47 N 7 **Mogotón**, Nicaragua ▲
110 H 9 **Moguqi**, China
79 I 26 **Mohács**, Hungary
124 H 7 **Mohammedia**, Morocco
14 J 8 **Mohawk**, NY, U.S.A. ʃ
110 H 4 **Mohe**, China
133 W 4 **Mohéli**, Comoros ✱
132 K 7 **Mohembo**, Botswana
143 R 13 **Mohns Ridge**, Arctic Ocean ▲▲
114 E 9 **Mohnyin**, Myanmar
53 H 18 **Moho**, Peru
131 W 13 **Mohoro**, Tanzania
86 M 6 **Mohyliv-Podil's'kyy**, Ukraine
107 X 12 **Moirang**, India
83 I 26 **Moires**, Greece
58 B 13 **Moisés Ville**, Argentina
43 S 3 **Moisie**, QC, Canada
129 X 12 **Moïssala**, Chad
33 J 23 **Mojave**, CA, U.S.A.
33 K 23 **Mojave Desert**, CA, U.S.A. ◇
112 K 12 **Mojiang**, China
123 C 20 **Mojikō**, Japan
81 J 14 **Mojkovac**, Serbia and Montenegro
107 X 10 **Mokokchung**, India
137 D 25 **Mokoreta**, New Zealand ▲
111 L 21 **Mokp'o**, South Korea
129 P 11 **Mokwa**, Nigeria
69 I 17 **Mol**, Belgium
77 N 15 **Mola di Bari**, Italy
45 R 11 **Molango**, Mexico
83 F 23 **Molaoi**, Greece
80 B 11 **Molat**, Croatia ✱
71 B 15 **Molde**, Norway
87 N 9 **Moldova**, Europe □
43 T 11 **Molega Lake**, NS, Canada ∽
130 K 5 **Molegbe**, Democratic Republic of Congo
132 M 10 **Molepolole**, Botswana
85 G 14 **Molètai**, Lithuania
77 M 15 **Molfetta**, Italy
67 R 6 **Molina de Aragón**, Spain
21 E 16 **Moline**, IL, U.S.A.
25 P 7 **Moline**, KS, U.S.A.
131 R 12 **Moliro**, Democratic Republic of Congo
77 K 14 **Molise**, Italy ▣
77 L 17 **Moliterno**, Italy
75 Q 8 **Möll**, Austria ʃ
53 F 20 **Mollendo**, Peru
67 V 4 **Mollerussa**, Spain
72 I 10 **Mölln**, Germany
87 V 8 **Molochans'k**, Ukraine
87 V 9 **Molochnyy Lyman**, Ukraine ∽
145 V 2 **Molodezhnaya**, Antarctica ⁘
103 T 4 **Molodezhnyy**, Kazakhstan
34 D 7 **Molokai**, HI, U.S.A. ✱
83 E 18 **Molos**, Greece
129 V 15 **Moloundou**, Cameroon
133 N 13 **Molteno**, Republic of South Africa
117 U 14 **Molu**, Indonesia ✱
117 Q 11 **Molucca Sea**, Indonesia ◭
117 T 10 **Moluccas**, Indonesia ✱
133 S 5 **Molumbo**, Mozambique
133 T 6 **Moma**, Mozambique
131 X 10 **Mombasa**, Kenya
107 X 12 **Mombi New**, India
82 J 12 **Momchilgrad**, Bulgaria
120 H 12 **Mompog Passage**, Philippines ≈
130 L 8 **Mompono**, Democratic Republic of Congo
50 I 3 **Mompós**, Colombia
89 U 8 **Momskiy Khrebet**, Russian Federation ▲▲
71 E 26 **Møn**, Denmark ✱
115 E 16 **Mon**, Myanmar ▣
65 X 13 **Monaco**, Monaco ♜
65 W 13 **Monaco**, Europe □
51 R 3 **Monagas**, Venezuela ▣
26 I 8 **Monahans**, TX, U.S.A.
133 U 5 **Monapo**, Mozambique
77 B 19 **Monastir**, Italy
125 R 6 **Monastir**, Tunisia
122 K 6 **Monbetsu**, Japan
129 U 11 **Monboré**, Cameroon
90 H 3 **Monchegorsk**, Russian Federation
73 B 16 **Mönchengladbach**, Germany
75 Y 4 **Mönchhof**, Austria
17 Q 14 **Moncks Corner**, SC, U.S.A.
45 P 6 **Monclova**, Mexico
43 U 9 **Moncton**, NB, Canada
77 I 21 **Mondello**, Italy
130 L 6 **Mondjamboli**, Democratic Republic of Congo
129 V 9 **Mondo**, Chad
66 J 1 **Mondoñedo**, Spain
76 A 9 **Mondovi**, Italy
77 I 15 **Mondragone**, Italy
75 R 5 **Mondsee**, Austria
83 F 23 **Monemvasia**, Greece
14 B 13 **Monessen**, PA, U.S.A.
66 J 2 **Monforte**, Spain
66 I 9 **Monforte**, Portugal
114 N 11 **Mong Cai**, Vietnam
114 F 13 **Mong Hang**, Myanmar
114 H 12 **Mong Hpayak**, Myanmar
114 F 11 **Mong Hsu**, Myanmar
114 F 11 **Mong Kung**, Myanmar
114 E 10 **Möng Mir**, Myanmar
114 F 13 **Mong Pan**, Myanmar
114 G 12 **Mong Ping**, Myanmar
114 G 12 **Mong Pu**, Myanmar
114 F 11 **Mong Yai**, Myanmar
130 M 5 **Monga**, Democratic Republic of Congo
127 E 22 **Mongalla**, Sudan
107 V 10 **Mongar**, Bhutan
131 Q 6 **Mongbwalu**, Democratic Republic of Congo
76 A 9 **Mongioie**, Italy ▲
129 X 10 **Mongo**, Chad
109 N 4 **Mongolia**, Asia □
129 T 15 **Mongomo**, Equatorial Guinea
129 U 10 **Mongonu**, Nigeria
101 W 7 **Mongora**, Pakistan
129 Z 10 **Mongororo**, Chad
132 L 5 **Mongu**, Zambia
20 F 10 **Monico**, WI, U.S.A.
46 I 6 **Monjas**, Guatemala
134 E 8 **Monkey Mia**, WA, Australia
121 N 21 **Monkeyo**, Philippines
78 N 10 **Mońki**, Poland
130 L 9 **Monkoto**, Democratic Republic of Congo
21 E 17 **Monmouth**, IL, U.S.A.
63 P 9 **Monmouth**, U.K.
33 J 19 **Mono Lake**, CA, U.S.A. ∽
15 Q 11 **Monomoy Island**, MA, U.S.A. ✱
77 N 15 **Monopoli**, Italy
79 J 23 **Monor**, Hungary
129 Z 7 **Monou**, Chad
65 O 12 **Monpazier**, France
67 S 6 **Monreal del Campo**, Spain
14 J 11 **Monroe**, NY, U.S.A.
17 P 10 **Monroe**, NC, U.S.A.
18 J 4 **Monroe**, LA, U.S.A.
21 L 15 **Monroe**, MI, U.S.A.
21 F 15 **Monroe**, WI, U.S.A.
25 V 2 **Monroe City**, MO, U.S.A.
21 I 20 **Monroe Lake**, IN, U.S.A. ∽
14 B 13 **Monroeville**, PA, U.S.A.
19 P 6 **Monroeville**, AL, U.S.A.
128 G 13 **Monrovia**, Liberia ♜
69 E 21 **Mons**, Belgium
73 B 18 **Monschau**, Germany
68 F 13 **Monster**, Netherlands
65 W 9 **Mont Blanc**, France/Switzerland ▲
129 S 14 **Mont Cameroun**, Cameroon ▲
41 S 10 **Mont de Babel**, QC, Canada ▲
64 M 13 **Mont-de-Marsan**, France
143 O 13 **Mont Forel**, Greenland ▲
130 E 8 **Mont Iboundji**, Gabon ▲
43 S 5 **Mont Jacques Cartier**, QC, Canada ▲
43 Q 6 **Mont-Joli**, QC, Canada
42 J 9 **Mont-Laurier**, QC, Canada
43 S 5 **Mont Louis**, QC, Canada
65 W 12 **Mont Pelat**, France ▲
51 Y 8 **Mont St-Marcel**, French Guiana ▲
125 O 13 **Mont Tahat**, Algeria ▲
65 W 11 **Mont Thabor**, France ▲
130 M 2 **Mont Toussoro**, Central African Republic ▲
65 U 13 **Mont Ventoux**, France ▲
41 T 9 **Mont Wright**, QC, Canada ▲
41 R 9 **Mont Yapeitso**, QC, Canada ▲
35 S 10 **Montague Island**, AK, U.S.A. ✱
64 L 8 **Montaigu**, France
67 S 6 **Montalbán**, Spain
76 F 13 **Montalto di Castro**, Italy
52 C 10 **Montalvo**, Ecuador
29 Q 5 **Montana**, U.S.A. ▣
82 G 7 **Montana**, Bulgaria ▣
82 F 7 **Montana**, Bulgaria
47 P 5 **Montañas de Colón**, Honduras ▲▲
65 Q 6 **Montargis**, France
65 O 13 **Montauban**, France
14 M 12 **Montauk**, NY, U.S.A.
15 N 12 **Montauk Point**, NY, U.S.A. ▶
65 S 6 **Montbard**, France
65 V 6 **Montbéliard**, France
67 V 5 **Montblanc**, Spain
65 S 8 **Montceau-les-Mines**, France
54 H 10 **Monte Alegre**, Brazil
76 J 13 **Monte Amaro**, Italy ▲
55 M 16 **Monte Azul**, Brazil
52 E 12 **Monte Bello**, Peru
57 F 24 **Monte Burney**, Chile ▲
65 X 13 **Monte Carlo**, Monaco
76 I 13 **Monte Carno**, Italy ▲
58 D 12 **Monte Caseros**, Argentina
65 Y 14 **Monte Cinto**, France ▲
49 P 6 **Monte Cristi**, Dominican Republic
57 H 25 **Monte Darwin**, Chile ▲
57 H 24 **Monte Dinero**, Argentina
65 Y 15 **Monte Incudine**, France ▲
57 F 19 **Monte Macá**, Chile ▲
57 F 18 **Monte Melimoyu**, Chile ▲
77 J 15 **Monte Miletto**, Italy ▲
55 N 16 **Monte Pascoal**, Brazil ▲
56 K 7 **Monte Quemado**, Argentina
65 Y 15 **Monte Rotondo**, France ▲
77 L 14 **Monte Sant'Angelo**, Italy
55 N 14 **Monte Santo**, Brazil
76 A 8 **Monte Viso**, Italy ▲
31 Q 7 **Monte Vista**, CO, U.S.A.
42 J 10 **Montebello**, QC, Canada
134 F 6 **Montebello Islands**, WA, Australia ✱
58 F 9 **Montecarlo**, Argentina
76 F 13 **Montefiascone**, Italy
48 K 8 **Montego Bay**, Jamaica
65 T 12 **Montélimar**, France
20 F 13 **Montello**, WI, U.S.A.
66 H 9 **Montemor-o-nova**, Portugal
45 Q 7 **Montemorelos**, Mexico
58 G 12 **Montenegro**, Brazil
81 I 15 **Montenegro**, Serbia and Montenegro ▣
133 T 4 **Montepuez**, Mozambique
17 Q 4 **Monterey**, VA, U.S.A.
33 G 21 **Monterey**, CA, U.S.A.
33 G 21 **Monterey Bay**, CA, U.S.A. ≈
50 H 4 **Montería**, Colombia
53 L 20 **Montero**, Bolivia
45 Q 7 **Monterrey**, Mexico
55 L 16 **Montes Claros**, Brazil
23 P 8 **Montevideo**, MN, U.S.A.
59 E 16 **Montevideo**, Uruguay ♜
24 I 6 **Montezuma**, KS, U.S.A.
19 R 5 **Montgomery**, AL, U.S.A.
63 O 7 **Montgomery**, U.K.
74 C 10 **Monthey**, Switzerland
14 I 11 **Monticello**, NY, U.S.A.
16 I 7 **Monticello**, KY, U.S.A.
18 L 6 **Monticello**, MS, U.S.A.
23 V 11 **Monticello**, IA, U.S.A.
25 V 2 **Monticello**, MO, U.S.A.
25 W 13 **Monticello**, AR, U.S.A.
30 M 6 **Monticello**, UT, U.S.A.
66 G 9 **Montijo**, Portugal
65 P 9 **Montluçon**, France
65 R 4 **Montmirail**, France
135 V 7 **Monto**, QLD, Australia
67 N 11 **Montoro**, Spain
14 L 6 **Montpelier**, VT, U.S.A.
29 Q 13 **Montpelier**, ID, U.S.A.
65 S 14 **Montpellier**, France
42 L 10 **Montréal**, QC, Canada
39 M 17 **Montreal Lake**, SK, Canada
39 M 17 **Montreal Lake**, SK, Canada ∽
42 A 8 **Montreal River**, ON, Canada
74 C 9 **Montreux**, Switzerland
14 H 10 **Montrose**, PA, U.S.A.
25 W 14 **Montrose**, AR, U.S.A.
31 O 6 **Montrose**, CO, U.S.A.
60 J 11 **Montrose**, U.K.
129 S 7 **Monts Bagzane**, Niger ▲
125 Q 7 **Monts des Ksour**, Tunisia ▲▲
125 N 12 **Monts du Mouydir**, Algeria ◇
131 Q 12 **Monts Mitumba**, Democratic Republic of Congo ▲▲
131 O 13 **Monts Mulumbe**, Democratic Republic of Congo ▲▲
43 P 8 **Monts Notre Dame**, QC, Canada ▲▲
49 X 9 **Montserrat**, U.K. ▣
67 N 5 **Montuenga**, Spain
30 M 7 **Monument Valley**, UT, U.S.A. ◇
130 L 6 **Monveda**, Democratic Republic of Congo
114 D 11 **Monywa**, Myanmar
76 C 6 **Monza**, Italy
53 D 14 **Monzón**, Peru
67 U 4 **Monzón**, Spain
133 N 10 **Mookane**, Botswana
135 Q 9 **Moolawatana**, SA, Australia
135 Q 9 **Moomba**, SA, Australia
135 U 9 **Moonie**, QLD, Australia
134 G 10 **Moora**, WA, Australia
27 N 11 **Moore**, TX, U.S.A.
29 N 10 **Moore**, ID, U.S.A.
29 S 5 **Moore**, MT, U.S.A.
17 R 3 **Moorefield**, WV, U.S.A.
23 O 5 **Moorhead**, MN, U.S.A.
29 R 11 **Moose**, WY, U.S.A.
41 O 10 **Moose**, ON, Canada ʃ
35 R 10 **Moose Pass**, AK, U.S.A.
15 Q 3 **Moosehead Lake**, ME, U.S.A. ∽
41 O 10 **Moosonee**, ON, Canada
133 S 7 **Mopeia**, Mozambique
128 K 9 **Mopti**, Mali
128 L 9 **Mopti**, Mali ▣
101 T 8 **Moqor**, Afghanistan
53 G 20 **Moquegua**, Peru
53 H 19 **Moquegua**, Peru ▣
79 H 23 **Mór**, Hungary
31 R 9 **Mora**, NM, U.S.A.
66 H 9 **Mora**, Portugal
67 O 8 **Mora**, Spain
71 F 18 **Mora**, Sweden
129 V 10 **Mora**, Cameroon
106 K 8 **Moradabad**, India
133 W 7 **Morafenobe**, Madgascar
78 J 9 **Morąg**, Poland
46 J 5 **Morales**, Guatemala
133 Y 8 **Moramanga**, Madgascar
29 R 10 **Moran**, WY, U.S.A.
135 U 6 **Moranbah**, QLD, Australia
105 F 25 **Moratuwa**, Sri Lanka
79 G 17 **Morava**, Czech Republic ʃ
79 E 19 **Moravia**, Czech Republic ◇
79 E 19 **Moravské Budějovice**, Czech Republic
134 F 10 **Morawa**, WA, Australia
60 H 9 **Moray Firth**, U.K. ≈
46 L 5 **Morazán**, Honduras
73 C 20 **Morbach**, Germany
105 B 14 **Morbi**, India
75 Y 5 **Mörbisch**, Austria
77 J 15 **Morcone**, Italy
92 M 5 **Mordovo**, Russian Federation
22 I 8 **Moreau**, SD, U.S.A. ʃ
63 P 1 **Morecambe**, U.K.
63 P 1 **Morecambe Bay**, U.K. ≈
135 U 9 **Moree**, NSW, Australia
16 K 5 **Morehead**, KY, U.S.A.
138 A 6 **Morehead**, Papua New Guinea
17 U 11 **Morehead City**, NC, U.S.A.
45 P 11 **Morelia**, Mexico
67 T 6 **Morella**, Spain
45 R 12 **Morelos**, Mexico ▣
106 J 10 **Morena**, India
39 C 20 **Moresby Island**, BC, Canada ✱
63 S 9 **Moreton- in-Marsh**, U.K.
135 W 8 **Moreton Island**, QLD, Australia ✱
65 V 8 **Morez**, France
94 H 15 **Morfou**, Cyprus
94 G 15 **Morfou Bay**, Cyprus ≈
135 Q 11 **Morgan**, SA, Australia
18 K 8 **Morgan City**, LA, U.S.A.
33 G 20 **Morgan Hill**, CA, U.S.A.
17 V 8 **Morgans Corner**, NC, U.S.A.
17 N 9 **Morganton**, NC, U.S.A.
17 P 2 **Morgantown**, WV, U.S.A.
74 B 9 **Morges**, Switzerland
122 J 7 **Mori**, Japan
31 Q 10 **Moriarty**, NM, U.S.A.
118 B 9 **Morib**, Malaysia
128 H 11 **Moribaya**, Guinea
50 L 8 **Morichal**, Colombia
122 K 10 **Morioka**, Japan
64 I 4 **Morlaix**, France
77 M 18 **Mormanno**, Italy
135 P 3 **Mornington Island**, QLD, Australia ✱
101 U 13 **Moro**, Pakistan
121 J 22 **Moro Gulf**, Philippines ≈
138 E 5 **Morobe**, Papua New Guinea
138 E 5 **Morobe**, Papua New Guinea ▣
21 H 17 **Morocco**, IN, U.S.A.
124 F 8 **Morocco**, Africa □
86 K 1 **Morochne**, Ukraine
131 V 12 **Morogoro**, Tanzania ▣
131 V 12 **Morogoro**, Tanzania
45 P 11 **Moroleón**, Mexico
117 Q 14 **Moromaho**, Indonesia ✱
133 V 9 **Morombe**, Madgascar
48 J 5 **Morón**, Cuba
109 P 2 **Mörön**, Mongolia
52 C 10 **Morona**, Ecuador
52 C 10 **Morona-Santiago**, Ecuador ▣
133 W 8 **Morondava**, Madgascar
128 J 11 **Morondo**, Côte d'Ivoire
133 W 4 **Moroni**, Comoros ♜
117 S 9 **Morotai**, Indonesia ✱
131 T 6 **Moroto**, Uganda ▲
131 T 6 **Moroto**, Uganda
93 N 9 **Morozovsk**, Russian Federation
55 L 14 **Morpara**, Brazil
136 L 10 **Morrinsville**, New Zealand
23 P 7 **Morris**, MN, U.S.A.
40 I 11 **Morris**, MB, Canada
14 J 12 **Morristown**, NJ, U.S.A.
16 K 8 **Morristown**, TN, U.S.A.
33 H 22 **Morro Bay**, CA, U.S.A.
55 M 14 **Morro do Chapéu**, Brazil
93 N 3 **Morshanka**, Russian Federation
70 G 10 **Mørsvikboth**, Norway
65 N 5 **Mortagne-au-Perche**, France
62 M 12 **Morte Bay**, U.K. ≈
58 B 13 **Morteros**, Argentina
49 N 4 **Mortimer's**, The Bahamas
141 P 15 **Mortlock Islands**, Federated States of Micronesia ✱
26 I 4 **Morton**, TX, U.S.A.
32 G 8 **Morton**, WA, U.S.A.
131 T 5 **Morungole**, Uganda ▲
135 T 8 **Morven**, QLD, Australia
92 J 2 **Mosal'sk**, Russian Federation
29 U 5 **Mosby**, MT, U.S.A.
16 B 10 **Moscow**, TN, U.S.A.
28 J 5 **Moscow**, ID, U.S.A.
92 K 1 **Moscow**, Russian Federation ♜
145 X 12 **Moscow University Ice Shelf**, Antarctica ◇
73 C 19 **Mosel**, Germany ʃ
32 J 8 **Moses Lake**, WA, U.S.A. ∽
131 V 10 **Moshi**, Tanzania
87 R 5 **Moshny**, Ukraine
78 G 13 **Mosina**, Poland
70 F 12 **Mosjøen**, Norway
70 F 9 **Moskenesøy**, Norway ✱
92 K 1 **Moskovskaya Oblast'**, Russian Federation ▣
79 G 22 **Moson-magyaróvár**, Hungary
41 P 5 **Mosquito Bay**, QC, Canada ≈
47 R 8 **Mosquito Coast**, Nicaragua ◇
19 X 9 **Mosquito Lagoon**, FL, U.S.A. ∽
71 D 20 **Moss**, Norway
137 C 24 **Mossburn**, New Zealand
132 L 15 **Mossel Bay**, Republic of South Africa
130 F 9 **Mossendjo**, Congo
54 O 12 **Mossoró**, Brazil
124 L 6 **Mostaganem**, Algeria
81 G 14 **Mostar**, Bosnia and Herzegovina
58 I 13 **Mostardas**, Brazil
87 Q 8 **Mostove**, Ukraine
92 M 13 **Mostovskoy**, Russian Federation
86 H 4 **Mostys'ka**, Ukraine
97 R 2 **Mosul**, Iraq
127 I 19 **Mot'a**, Ethiopia
67 P 8 **Mota del Cuervo**, Spain
139 Q 9 **Mota Lava**, Vanuatu ✱
46 I 5 **Motagua**, Guatemala ʃ
85 G 21 **Motal'**, Belarus
71 F 21 **Motala**, Sweden
106 K 11 **Moth**, India
107 P 10 **Motihari**, India
67 R 8 **Motilla del Palancar**, Spain
136 M 10 **Motiti Island**, New Zealand ✱
67 Q 1 **Motrico**, Spain
86 G 12 **Motru**, Romania
122 I 7 **Motsuta-misaki**, Japan ▶
22 H 6 **Mott**, ND, U.S.A.
136 N 11 **Motu**, New Zealand ʃ
137 H 16 **Motueka**, New Zealand
136 J 12 **Motunui**, New Zealand
138 I 5 **Motupena Point**, Papua New Guinea
130 I 6 **Mouali Gbangba**, Congo
128 G 7 **Moudjéria**, Mauritania
71 K 17 **Mouhijärvi**, Finland
130 E 9 **Mouila**, Gabon
127 K 18 **Moulhoulê**, Djibouti
65 R 8 **Moulins**, France
115 F 16 **Moulmein**, Myanmar
19 O 2 **Moulton**, AL, U.S.A.
19 T 6 **Moultrie**, GA, U.S.A.
21 F 23 **Mound City**, IL, U.S.A.
25 Q 1 **Mound City**, MO, U.S.A.
129 W 12 **Moundou**, Chad
17 O 2 **Moundsville**, WV, U.S.A.
56 G 11 **Mount Aconcagua**, Argentina ▲
57 K 23 **Mt Adam**, Falkland Islands ▲
32 H 8 **Mt Adams**, WA, U.S.A. ▲
17 O 8 **Mount Airy**, NC, U.S.A.
138 E 6 **Mt Albert Edward**, Papua New Guinea ▲
145 Y 10 **Mt Amundsen**, Antarctica ▲
137 C 26 **Mt Anglem**, New Zealand ▲
121 M 22 **Mount Apo**, Philippines ▲
95 T 9 **Mt Ararat**, Turkey ▲
137 F 20 **Mt Arrowsmith**, New Zealand ▲
20 G 8 **Mt Arvon**, MI, U.S.A. ▲
137 C 22 **Mt Aspiring**, New Zealand ▲
39 J 20 **Mt Assiniboine**, BC, Canada ▲
134 F 7 **Mt Augustus**, WA, Australia ▲
121 G 14 **Mount Baco**, Philippines ▲
32 H 5 **Mt Baker**, WA, U.S.A. ▲
138 I 4 **Mt Balbi**, Papua New Guinea ▲
120 H 12 **Mount Banahao**, Philippines ▲
138 E 5 **Mt Bangeta**, Papua New Guinea ▲
30 H 8 **Mt Bangs**, AZ, U.S.A. ▲
134 H 12 **Mount Barker**, WA, Australia
134 K 3 **Mount Barnett Roadhouse**, WA, Australia
135 V 10 **Mt Barrington**, NSW, Australia ▲
41 V 7 **Mt Benedict**, NL, Canada ▲
144 M 11 **Mt Berlin**, Antarctica ▲
130 F 9 **Mt Berongou**, Congo ▲
35 T 8 **Mt Blackburn**, AK, U.S.A. ▲
135 T 12 **Mt Bogong**, VIC, Australia ▲
35 T 9 **Mt Bona**, AK, U.S.A. ▲
138 B 5 **Mt Bosavi**, Papua New Guinea ▲
134 J 4 **Mt Broome**, WA, Australia ▲
121 I 17 **Mount Canlaon**, Philippines ▲
121 L 14 **Mount Capotoah**, Philippines ▲

□ Country ▣ Internal administrative region: State/Province/Territory/Dependent territory ♜ Capital city ▲▲ Mountain range/Undersea ridge ▲ Mountain peak/Volcano/Seamount ◇ Geographic feature ▶ Headland/Point/Cape/Peninsula ◗ Desert ✱ Island/Island group ⁘ Antarctic base ◎ Ocean ◭ Sea ≈ Bay/Gulf/Channel/Strait ∽ Lake ⚑ Salt pan/Dry/Intermittent lake ʃ

C 22 **Mt Cardrona**, New Zealand ▲
S 7 **Mount Carleton**, NB, Canada ▲
I 21 **Mount Carmel**, IN, U.S.A.
F 8 **Mt Carmel**, Israel ▲
U 5 **Mt Caubvick**, NL, Canada ▲
N 9 **Mt Chapman**, Antarctica ▲
N 2 **Mount Cleveland**, MT, U.S.A. ▲
W 3 **Mt Codrington**, Antarctica ▲
H 19 **Mt Columbia**, BC/AB, Canada ▲
K 5 **Mt Coman**, Antarctica ▲
E 20 **Mount Cook**, New Zealand
E 20 **Mt Cook**, New Zealand ▲
W 4 **Mt Cook**, Antarctica ▲
J 20 **Mount Dapiak**, Philippines ▲
P 6 **Mount Darwin**, Zimbabwe
C 14 **Mt Davis**, PA, U.S.A. ▲
R 6 **Mount Desert Island**, ME, U.S.A.
Q 5 **Mt Doonerak**, AK, U.S.A. ▲
P 11 **Mt Douglas**, AK, U.S.A. ▲
E 2 **Mt Dremsel**, Papua New Guinea ▲
C 22 **Mt Earnslaw**, New Zealand ▲
Q 4 **Mount Elbert**, CO, U.S.A. ▲
W 3 **Mt Elkins**, Antarctica ▲
L 6 **Mt Ellen**, UT, U.S.A. ▲
Q 12 **Mt Erebus**, Antarctica ▲
D 5 **Mt Eruki**, Papua New Guinea ▲
K 22 **Mount Etna**, Italy ▲
N 6 **Mount Evans**, MT, U.S.A. ▲
R 9 **Mt Everest**, China/Nepal ▲
H 8 **Mt Fairweather**, Canada/U.S.A. ▲
D 12 **Mount Forest**, ON, Canada
L 10 **Mt Frakes**, Antarctica ▲
J 16 **Mt Fuji**, Japan ▲
Q 13 **Mount Gambier**, SA, Australia
C 5 **Mt Giluwe**, Papua New Guinea ▲
M 14 **Mt Graham**, AZ, U.S.A. ▲
L 9 **Mount Greylock**, MA, U.S.A. ▲
I 14 **Mount Guitinguitin**, Philippines ▲
L 9 **Mt Guyot**, TN, U.S.A. ▲
C 4 **Mount Hagen**, Papua New Guinea
G 13 **Mount Halcon**, Philippines ▲
S 7 **Mt Harper**, AK, U.S.A. ▲
P 5 **Mt Harvard**, CO, U.S.A. ▲
A 15 **Mt Hay**, BC, Canada ▲
S 7 **Mt Hayes**, AK, U.S.A. ▲
K 15 **Mt Hector**, New Zealand ▲
Q 10 **Mt Hehaṇ**, Burundi ▲
H 20 **Mt Herbert**, New Zealand ▲
H 7 **Mt Hermon**, Syria ▲
M 19 **Mount Hilonghilong**, Philippines ▲
H 10 **Mt Hood**, OR, U.S.A. ▲
F 14 **Mount Horeb**, WI, U.S.A.
Q 14 **Mt Humboldt**, New Caledonia ▲
U 14 **Mt Hunt**, Antarctica ▲
G 20 **Mount Hutt**, New Zealand
F 20 **Mt Hutt**, New Zealand ▲
Q 5 **Mount Isa**, QLD, Australia
J 12 **Mount Isarog**, Philippines ▲
K 5 **Mt Jackson**, Antarctica ▲
H 10 **Mt Jefferson**, OR, U.S.A. ▲
L 18 **Mt Jefferson**, NV, U.S.A. ▲
Q 3 **Mt Katahdin**, ME, U.S.A. ▲
P 11 **Mt Katmai**, AK, U.S.A. ▲
V 8 **Mt Kenya**, Kenya ▲
V 5 **Mt Kinabalu**, Malaysia ▲
Q 10 **Mt Kirkpatrick**, Antarctica ▲
T 13 **Mt Kosciuszko**, NSW, Australia ▲
I 12 **Mount Labo**, Philippines ▲
Q 12 **Mt Lister**, Antarctica ▲
H 9 **Mt Livermore**, TX, U.S.A. ▲
A 14 **Mt Logan**, YT, Canada ▲
B 23 **Mt Lyall**, New Zealand ▲
R 13 **Mt Mackintosh**, Antarctica ▲
G 9 **Mount Magnet**, WA, Australia
J 20 **Mount Malindang**, Philippines ▲
L 5 **Mt Mansfield**, VT, U.S.A. ▲
B 19 **Mount Mantalingajan**, Philippines ▲
R 9 **Mt Marcus Baker**, AK, U.S.A. ▲
J 6 **Mt Marcy**, NY, U.S.A. ▲
K 5 **Mt Marvine**, UT, U.S.A. ▲
L 23 **Mount Matutum**, Philippines ▲
M 10 **Mount Maunganui**, New Zealand
K 13 **Mount Mayon**, Philippines ▲
R 11 **Mt McClintock**, Antarctica ▲
M 8 **Mount McGuire**, ID, U.S.A. ▲
Q 8 **Mt McKinley**, AK, U.S.A. ▲
G 7 **Mt Meharry**, WA, Australia ▲
U 5 **Mt Menzies**, Antarctica ▲
S 3 **Mt Michelson**, AK, U.S.A. ▲
Q 10 **Mt Miller**, Antarctica ▲
R 14 **Mt Minto**, Antarctica ▲
M 9 **Mt Mitchell**, NC, U.S.A. ▲
M 8 **Mt Moore**, Antarctica ▲
A 14 **Mount Morris**, PA, U.S.A.
E 9 **Mount Morris**, NY, U.S.A.
T 7 **Mt Mulu**, Malaysia ▲
U 14 **Mt Murchison**, Antarctica ▲
D 14 **Mt Murray**, YT, Canada ▲
L 12 **Mt Ngauruhoe**, New Zealand ▲
T 10 **Mount Olive**, NC, U.S.A.
F 6 **Mt Olympus**, WA, U.S.A. ▲
E 15 **Mt Olympus**, Greece ▲
F 22 **Mt Orr**, New Zealand ▲
S 15 **Mt Ossa**, TAS, Australia ▲
P 13 **Mt Panié**, New Caledonia ▲
F 10 **Mount Pinatubo**, Philippines ▲
I 23 **Mt Pinos**, CA, U.S.A. ▲
B 13 **Mount Pleasant**, PA, U.S.A.
Q 14 **Mount Pleasant**, SC, U.S.A.
K 13 **Mount Pleasant**, MI, U.S.A.
V 13 **Mount Pleasant**, IA, U.S.A.
S 5 **Mount Pleasant**, TX, U.S.A.
K 4 **Mount Pleasant**, UT, U.S.A.
M 7 **Mt Popomanaseu**, Solomon Islands ▲
G 8 **Mount Pulog**, Philippines ▲
F 20 **Mt Queen Bess**, BC, Canada ▲
L 21 **Mount Ragang**, Philippines ▲
J 11 **Mt Ragged**, WA, Australia ▲
H 7 **Mt Rainier**, WA, U.S.A. ▲
C 16 **Mt Ratz**, BC, Canada ▲
H 19 **Mt Robson**, BC, Canada ▲
N 7 **Mt Rogers**, VA, U.S.A. ▲
F 19 **Mt Rolleston**, New Zealand ▲
S 6 **Mt Roraima**, Brazil/Guyana ▲
L 16 **Mt Ross**, New Zealand ▲
K 12 **Mt Ruapehu**, New Zealand ▲
G 10 **Mt Rushmore**, SD, U.S.A. ▲
X 9 **Mt Sandow**, Antarctica ▲
E 20 **Mt Saugstad**, BC, Canada ▲
L 11 **Mt Scott**, OK, U.S.A. ▲
G 13 **Mt Scott**, OR, U.S.A. ▲
N 8 **Mt Seelig**, Antarctica ▲
G 15 **Mount Shasta**, CA, U.S.A.
33 G 15 **Mt Shasta**, CA, U.S.A. ▲
120 G 6 **Mount Sicapoo**, Philippines ▲
144 L 10 **Mt Sidley**, Antarctica ▲
138 G 7 **Mt Simpson**, Papua New Guinea ▲
138 H 4 **Mt Sinewit**, Papua New Guinea ▲
144 K 11 **Mt Siple**, Antarctica ▲
38 D 13 **Mt Sir James MacBrian**, NT, Canada ▲
138 B 5 **Mt Sisa**, Papua New Guinea ▲
137 B 24 **Mt Solitary**, New Zealand ▲
145 S 14 **Mt Southard**, Antarctica ▲
35 T 9 **Mt St Elias**, AK, U.S.A. ▲
32 G 8 **Mt St Helens**, WA, U.S.A. ▲
137 D 22 **Mt St Mary**, New Zealand ▲
16 K 5 **Mount Sterling**, KY, U.S.A.
137 J 16 **Mt Stokes**, New Zealand ▲
145 X 9 **Mt Strathcona**, Antarctica ▲
138 E 5 **Mt Strong**, Papua New Guinea ▲
127 H 16 **Mount Suara**, Eritrea ▲
24 G 3 **Mount Sunflower**, KS, U.S.A. ▲
39 E 16 **Mt Sylvia**, BC, Canada ▲
138 D 5 **Mt Tabletop**, Papua New Guinea ▲
139 P 10 **Mt Tabwemasana**, Vanuatu ▲
138 J 5 **Mt Takuan**, Papua New Guinea ▲
136 J 12 **Mt Taranaki (Mt Egmont)**, New Zealand ▲
31 O 10 **Mt Taylor**, NM, U.S.A. ▲
30 H 9 **Mt Tipton**, AZ, U.S.A. ▲
136 L 12 **Mt Tongariro**, New Zealand ▲
35 Q 9 **Mt Torbert**, AK, U.S.A. ▲
124 G 8 **Mt Toubkal**, Morocco ▲
94 G 15 **Mount Troödos**, Cyprus ▲
30 I 8 **Mt Trumbull**, AZ, U.S.A. ▲
144 L 7 **Mt Tyree**, Antarctica ▲
138 G 4 **Mt Ulawun**, Papua New Guinea ▲
137 H 18 **Mt Una**, New Zealand ▲
14 E 13 **Mt Union**, PA, U.S.A.
57 L 23 **Mt Usborne**, Falkland Islands ▲
35 N 12 **Mt Veniaminof**, AK, U.S.A. ▲
19 O 6 **Mount Vernon**, AL, U.S.A.
21 F 21 **Mount Vernon**, IL, U.S.A.
21 G 22 **Mount Vernon**, IN, U.S.A.
21 M 18 **Mt Vernon**, OH, U.S.A.
25 S 7 **Mount Vernon**, MO, U.S.A.
32 H 6 **Mount Vernon**, WA, U.S.A.
145 T 3 **Mt Victor**, Antarctica ▲
114 C 12 **Mt Victoria**, Myanmar ▲
138 E 6 **Mt Victoria**, Papua New Guinea ▲
139 X 11 **Mt Victoria**, Fiji ▲
138 F 6 **Mt Victory**, Papua New Guinea ▲
36 I 12 **Mt Waddington**, BC, Canada ▲
15 N 6 **Mt Washington**, NH, U.S.A. ▲
33 K 21 **Mt Whitney**, CA, U.S.A. ▲
20 E 9 **Mt Whittlesey**, WI, U.S.A. ▲
138 C 4 **Mt Wilhelm**, Papua New Guinea ▲
39 D 16 **Mt Will**, BC, Canada ▲
31 O 7 **Mt Wilson**, CO, U.S.A. ▲
134 M 8 **Mt Woodroffe**, SA, Australia ▲
144 M 8 **Mt Woollard**, Antarctica ▲
35 T 8 **Mt Wrangell**, AK, U.S.A. ▲
134 M 6 **Mt Zeil**, NT, Australia ▲
31 P 2 **Mt Zirkel**, CO, U.S.A. ▲
28 K 11 **Mountain Home**, ID, U.S.A.
25 V 9 **Mountain View**, AR, U.S.A.
125 T 13 **Mountains of Tummo**, Libya ▲
62 J 15 **Mount's Bay**, U.K.
54 E 10 **Moura**, Brazil
66 I 10 **Moura**, Portugal
135 V 7 **Moura**, QLD, Australia
129 Z 10 **Mouraya**, Chad
128 I 9 **Mourdiah**, Mali
136 M 10 **Mourea**, New Zealand
69 C 19 **Mouscron**, Belgium
129 W 10 **Mousgougou**, Chad
127 K 18 **Moussa Ali**, Djibouti ▲
129 W 9 **Moussoro**, Chad
67 V 6 **Mouth of the Ebro**, Spain ◇
61 A 19 **Mouth of the Shannon**, Republic of Ireland ◇
113 Z 5 **Mouth of the Yangtze**, China ◇
54 J 9 **Mouths of the Amazon**, Brazil ◇
107 U 15 **Mouths of the Ganges**, Bangladesh ◇
105 H 19 **Mouths of the Godavari**, India ◇
101 T 15 **Mouths of the Indus**, Pakistan ◇
115 B 17 **Mouths of the Irrawaddy**, Myanmar ◇
105 G 19 **Mouths of the Krishna**, India ◇
115 M 23 **Mouths of the Mekong**, Vietnam ◇
129 Q 14 **Mouths of the Niger**, Nigeria ◇
74 D 7 **Moutier**, Switzerland
65 V 10 **Moûtiers**, France
83 D 17 **Mouzaki**, Greece
132 J 5 **Moxico**, Angola ■
127 I 23 **Moyale**, Ethiopia
124 H 8 **Moyen Atlas**, Morocco
129 X 11 **Moyen-Chari**, Chad ■
130 D 8 **Moyen-Ogooué**, Gabon ■
133 N 13 **Moyeni**, Lesotho
128 F 10 **Moyenne-Guinée**, Guinea ■
116 M 15 **Moyo**, Indonesia
131 R 5 **Moyo**, Uganda
52 C 12 **Moyobamba**, Peru
70 G 9 **Møysalen**, Norway ▲
103 T 9 **Moyynkum**, Kazakhstan
103 T 7 **Moyynty**, Kazakhstan
133 Q 9 **Mozambique**, Africa ■
133 T 8 **Mozambique Channel**, Mozambique
93 P 13 **Mozdok**, Russian Federation
92 J 1 **Mozhaysk**, Russian Federation
91 R 14 **Mozhga**, Russian Federation
131 Q 12 **Mpala**, Democratic Republic of Congo
131 R 11 **Mpanda**, Tanzania
132 M 7 **Mpandamatenga**, Botswana
130 H 9 **Mpé**, Congo
107 Z 9 **Mpen**, India
131 S 7 **Mpigi**, Uganda
133 P 3 **Mpika**, Zambia
133 P 2 **Mporokoso**, Zambia
130 H 9 **Mpouya**, Congo
133 O 10 **Mpumalanga**, Republic of South Africa ■
131 U 11 **Mpwapwa**, Tanzania
78 L 9 **Mrągowo**, Poland
93 W 3 **Mrakovo**, Russian Federation
82 D 12 **Mrešičko**, Macedonia (F.Y.R.O.M.)
80 F 11 **Mrkonjić-Grad**, Bosnia and Herzegovina
87 Q 2 **Mryn**, Ukraine
125 N 6 **M'sila**, Algeria
85 N 17 **Mstsislaw**, Belarus
131 W 14 **Mtama**, Tanzania
92 J 3 **Mtsensk**, Russian Federation
95 T 6 **Mts'khet'a**, Georgia
131 W 14 **Mtwara**, Tanzania ■
131 X 14 **Mtwara**, Tanzania
130 F 11 **Muanda**, Democratic Republic of Congo
115 L 15 **Muang Khammouan**, Laos
115 M 18 **Muang Không**, Laos
115 L 17 **Muang Khôngxédôn**, Laos
114 J 12 **Muang Khoua**, Laos
114 J 12 **Muang Ngoy**, Laos
114 I 11 **Muang Ou Nua**, Laos
114 H 13 **Muang Pakbeng**, Laos
115 K 14 **Muang Pakxan**, Laos
115 L 16 **Muang Phalan**, Laos
115 M 16 **Muang Phin**, Laos
115 I 14 **Muang Phôn-Hông**, Laos
114 H 12 **Muang Sing**, Laos
114 J 13 **Muang Souy**, Laos
115 I 14 **Muang Xaignabouri**, Laos
114 I 12 **Muang Xay**, Laos
118 C 10 **Muar**, Malaysia
118 D 9 **Muar**, Malaysia
116 E 12 **Muaraaman**, Indonesia
116 F 12 **Muarabeliti**, Indonesia
116 E 11 **Muarabungo**, Indonesia
116 F 13 **Muaradua**, Indonesia
116 F 12 **Muaraenim**, Indonesia
116 C 11 **Muarasiberut**, Indonesia
103 P 13 **Mubarek**, Uzbekistan
129 U 11 **Mubi**, Nigeria
63 P 7 **Much Wenlock**, U.K.
134 G 11 **Muchea**, WA, Australia
112 M 8 **Muchuan**, China
60 F 11 **Muck**, U.K.
133 U 4 **Mucojo**, Mozambique
132 K 3 **Muconda**, Angola
132 H 6 **Mucope**, Angola
94 J 10 **Mucur**, Turkey
55 N 17 **Mucuri**, Brazil
22 H 8 **Mud Butte**, SD, U.S.A.
118 A 5 **Muda**, Malaysia
110 M 12 **Mudanjiang**, China
94 D 8 **Mudanya**, Turkey
29 V 13 **Muddy Gap**, WY, U.S.A.
105 D 19 **Mudhol**, India
115 F 17 **Mudon**, Myanmar
127 N 21 **Mudug**, Somalia ■
133 U 3 **Mueda**, Mozambique
113 U 7 **Mufu Shan**, China
133 O 4 **Mufulira**, Zambia
132 M 4 **Mufumbwe**, Zambia
95 Y 9 **Muğan Düzü**, Azerbaijan ◇
133 S 6 **Mugeba**, Mozambique
107 O 12 **Mughal Sarai**, India
100 J 7 **Mūghār**, Iran
94 C 12 **Muğla**, Turkey
127 B 18 **Muhagiriya**, Sudan
126 G 13 **Muhammad Qol**, Sudan
97 O 7 **Muḩaywīr**, Iraq
145 Q 2 **Mühlig-Hofmann Mountains**, Antarctica
75 S 3 **Mühlviertel**, Austria
96 H 4 **Muḩradah**, Syria
84 E 7 **Muhu**, Estonia
131 P 8 **Muhulu**, Democratic Republic of Congo
127 G 22 **Mui**, Ethiopia
115 L 24 **Mui Ca Mau**, Vietnam ▶
133 T 5 **Muite**, Mozambique
86 H 6 **Mukacheve**, Ukraine
119 P 9 **Mukah**, Malaysia
119 P 9 **Mukah**, Malaysia
115 L 16 **Mukdahan**, Thailand
134 G 10 **Mukinbudin**, WA, Australia
116 E 12 **Mukomuko**, Indonesia
106 G 6 **Muktsar**, India
112 K 7 **Mula**, China
47 Z 13 **Mula-tupo**, Panama
105 L 18 **Mulakatholhu Atoll**, Maldives
110 L 11 **Mulan**, China
120 I 13 **Mulanay**, Philippines
133 R 6 **Mulanje**, Malawi
133 S 5 **Mulanje**, Malawi ▲
97 W 8 **Mūlat al Mashkhūr**, Iraq
106 I 3 **Mulbekh**, India
35 O 10 **Mulchatna**, AK, U.S.A.
57 F 14 **Mulchén**, Chile
29 Z 10 **Mule Creek**, WY, U.S.A.
131 S 9 **Muleba**, Tanzania
44 I 6 **Mulegé**, Mexico
26 I 4 **Muleshoe**, TX, U.S.A.
67 P 12 **Mulhacén**, Spain ▲
65 W 6 **Mulhouse**, France
110 M 11 **Muling**, China
60 F 12 **Mull**, U.K.
61 G 15 **Mull of Galloway**, U.K. ▶
61 F 14 **Mull of Kintyre**, U.K. ▶
60 F 13 **Mull of Oa**, U.K. ▶
134 F 9 **Mullewa**, WA, Australia
73 D 25 **Müllheim**, Germany
61 D 17 **Mullingar**, Republic of Ireland
62 J 15 **Mullion**, U.K.
132 M 6 **Mulobezi**, Zambia
105 F 15 **Multai**, India
101 W 10 **Multan**, Pakistan
130 M 5 **Muma**, Democratic Republic of Congo
101 O 14 **Mūmān**, Iran
105 B 17 **Mumbai**, India
132 L 5 **Mumbeji**, Zambia
132 G 3 **Mumbondo**, Angola
133 N 5 **Mumbwa**, Zambia
138 E 5 **Mumeng**, Papua New Guinea
93 R 11 **Mumra**, Russian Federation
45 Y 11 **Muna**, Mexico
117 P 13 **Muna**, Indonesia
104 A 12 **Munabao**, India
112 J 12 **Munai**, China
123 B 21 **Munakata**, Japan
102 H 9 **Munayshy**, Kazakhstan
39 E 15 **Muncho Lake**, BC, Canada
111 L 17 **Munch'ŏn**, North Korea
21 J 18 **Muncie**, IN, U.S.A.
14 F 11 **Muncy**, PA, U.S.A.
101 W 10 **Munda**, Pakistan
26 M 5 **Munday**, TX, U.S.A.
63 X 7 **Mundford**, U.K.
58 F 7 **Mundo Novo**, Brazil
134 K 10 **Mundrabilla**, WA, Australia
135 V 8 **Mundubbera**, QLD, Australia
67 Q 9 **Munera**, Spain
16 G 6 **Munfordville**, KY, U.S.A.
133 Q 6 **Mungári**, Mozambique
131 P 6 **Mungbere**, Democratic Republic of Congo
107 R 11 **Munger**, India
135 P 8 **Mungerannie Hotel**, SA, Australia
135 U 9 **Mungindi**, NSW, Australia
73 J 24 **Munich**, Germany
20 I 9 **Munising**, MI, U.S.A.
71 D 21 **Munkedal**, Sweden
61 B 20 **Munster**, Republic of Ireland ■
72 H 12 **Münster**, Germany
73 D 14 **Münster**, Germany
74 F 9 **Münster**, Switzerland
120 F 11 **Muntinglupa**, Philippines
70 N 11 **Muojärvi**, Finland
114 K 12 **Muong Het**, Laos
70 K 9 **Muonio**, Finland
111 H 19 **Muping**, China
96 K 8 **Muqāţ**, Jordan
99 Q 14 **Muqaybirah**, Yemen
95 T 10 **Muradiye**, Turkey
106 J 8 **Muradnagar**, India
118 A 13 **Murai Reservoir**, Singapore
122 J 13 **Murakami**, Japan
131 Q 9 **Muramvya**, Burundi
91 P 11 **Murashi**, Russian Federation
65 Q 11 **Murat**, France
95 R 10 **Murat**, Turkey
82 M 12 **Muratli**, Turkey
75 T 7 **Murau**, Austria
77 C 18 **Muravera**, Italy
100 I 8 **Murchek-Khort**, Iran
134 F 9 **Murchison**, WA, Australia
137 H 17 **Murchison**, New Zealand
134 F 9 **Murchison Roadhouse**, WA, Australia
67 R 11 **Murcia**, Spain ■
67 S 11 **Murcia**, Spain
22 J 10 **Murdo**, SD, U.S.A.
43 S 5 **Murdochville**, QC, Canada
75 W 8 **Mureck**, Austria
86 J 9 **Mureș**, Romania
65 O 14 **Muret**, France
16 F 9 **Murfreesboro**, TN, U.S.A.
17 U 8 **Murfreesboro**, NC, U.S.A.
103 U 13 **Murghob**, Tajikistan
135 V 8 **Murgon**, QLD, Australia
74 F 7 **Muri**, Switzerland
58 N 5 **Muriaé**, Brazil
132 K 3 **Muriege**, Angola
141 O 14 **Murilo Atoll**, Federated States of Micronesia
95 P 10 **Mürit Dağlari**, Turkey ▲
72 L 10 **Müritz**, Germany
136 O 12 **Muriwai**, New Zealand
90 I 2 **Murmansk**, Russian Federation
143 U 12 **Murmansk Rise**, Arctic Ocean
90 H 2 **Murmanskaya Oblast'**, Russian Federation ■
90 I 2 **Murmanskiy Bereg**, Russian Federation ◇
90 H 2 **Murmashi**, Russian Federation
93 N 1 **Murom**, Russian Federation
131 R 8 **Murongo**, Tanzania
122 J 7 **Muroran**, Japan
123 F 20 **Muroto**, Japan
123 F 21 **Muroto-zaki**, Japan ▶
16 J 10 **Murphy**, NC, U.S.A.
28 J 11 **Murphy**, ID, U.S.A.
16 C 7 **Murray**, KY, U.S.A.
135 R 12 **Murray**, NSW, Australia
135 Q 12 **Murray Bridge**, SA, Australia
43 W 9 **Murray Harbour**, PE, Canada
21 E 19 **Murrayville**, IL, U.S.A.
101 X 7 **Murree**, Pakistan
133 T 5 **Murrupula**, Mozambique
80 E 6 **Murska Sobota**, Slovenia
39 G 19 **Murtle Lake**, BC, Canada
105 B 17 **Murud**, India
136 M 11 **Murupara**, New Zealand
105 G 14 **Murwara**, India
135 W 9 **Murwillumbah**, NSW, Australia
125 S 11 **Murzūq**, Libya
75 W 5 **Mürzzuschlag**, Austria
95 Q 11 **Muș**, Turkey
84 E 12 **Mūša**, Lithuania
101 R 9 **Musa Qala**, Afghanistan
130 M 9 **Musadi**, Democratic Republic of Congo
82 G 10 **Musala**, Bulgaria ▲
97 X 9 **Musallam**, Iraq
111 M 14 **Musan**, North Korea
99 X 4 **Musandam Peninsula**, Oman ▶
99 P 14 **Musaymir**, Yemen
99 Z 6 **Muscat**, Oman
23 V 13 **Muscatine**, IA, U.S.A.
41 Y 9 **Musgrave Harbour**, NL, Canada
134 L 8 **Musgrave Ranges**, SA, Australia
101 U 8 **Mūshakī**, Afghanistan
96 I 10 **Mushāsh Ḩadraj**, Jordan
130 I 9 **Mushie**, Democratic Republic of Congo
138 C 3 **Mushu**, Papua New Guinea
21 I 14 **Muskegon**, MI, U.S.A.
25 Q 10 **Muskogee**, OK, U.S.A.
39 F 15 **Muskwa**, BC, Canada
127 G 15 **Musmar**, Sudan
131 T 8 **Musoma**, Tanzania
131 T 12 **Musombe**, Tanzania
41 W 10 **Musquaro**, QC, Canada
138 F 2 **Mussau Island**, Papua New Guinea
29 U 4 **Musselshell**, MT, U.S.A.
132 H 3 **Mussende**, Angola
65 N 11 **Mussidan**, France
94 C 9 **Mustafakemalpaşa**, Turkey
127 L 22 **Mustahīl**, Ethiopia
74 K 9 **Müstair**, Switzerland
49 Z 12 **Mustique**, St Vincent and the Grenadines
84 D 7 **Mustjala**, Estonia
84 H 8 **Mustla**, Estonia
84 I 7 **Mustvee**, Estonia
135 V 11 **Muswellbrook**, NSW, Australia
94 I 13 **Mut**, Turkey
126 D 11 **Mut**, Egypt
133 Q 7 **Mutare**, Zimbabwe
50 G 5 **Mutis**, Colombia
133 W 4 **Mutsamudu**, Comoros
131 N 14 **Mutshatsha**, Democratic Republic of Congo
122 K 8 **Mutsu**, Japan
122 J 8 **Mutsu-wan**, Japan
135 S 6 **Muttaburra**, QLD, Australia
137 B 26 **Muttonbird Islands**, New Zealand
105 F 20 **Muttukuru**, India
133 S 5 **Mutuali**, Mozambique
129 T 12 **Mutum Biyu**, Nigeria
105 G 24 **Mutur**, Sri Lanka
108 K 8 **Mutztag Feng**, China ▲
132 H 2 **Muxaluando**, Angola
132 F 3 **Muxima**, Angola
129 S 10 **Muya**, Nigeria
131 R 9 **Muyinga**, Burundi
102 L 10 **Muynak**, Uzbekistan
131 O 12 **Muyumba**, Democratic Republic of Congo
101 X 7 **Muzaffarabad**, Pakistan
101 W 10 **Muzaffargarh**, Pakistan
106 K 8 **Muzaffarnagar**, India
107 P 11 **Muzaffarpur**, India
64 J 6 **Muzillac**, France
45 P 5 **Múzquiz**, Mexico
129 T 15 **Mvangan**, Cameroon
127 D 22 **Mvolo**, Sudan
131 V 11 **Mvomero**, Tanzania
133 P 7 **Mvuma**, Zimbabwe
131 S 9 **Mwanza**, Tanzania ■
131 S 9 **Mwanza**, Tanzania
130 L 10 **Mweka**, Democratic Republic of Congo
133 O 3 **Mwenda**, Zambia
130 M 12 **Mwene-Ditu**, Democratic Republic of Congo
133 P 8 **Mwenezi**, Zimbabwe
131 P 9 **Mwenga**, Democratic Republic of Congo
130 M 13 **Mwimba**, Democratic Republic of Congo
132 M 3 **Mwinilunga**, Zambia
141 Q 15 **Mwokil**, Federated States of Micronesia
115 M 22 **My Tho**, Vietnam
85 I 15 **Myadzyel**, Belarus
19 V 11 **Myakka City**, FL, U.S.A.
114 C 12 **Myanmar (Burma)**, Asia ■
115 C 16 **Myaungmya**, Myanmar
114 D 12 **Myingyan**, Myanmar
115 F 19 **Myinmoletkat**, Myanmar ▲
114 E 8 **Myitkyina**, Myanmar
115 F 19 **Myitta**, Myanmar
114 D 12 **Myittha**, Myanmar
87 V 8 **Mykhaylivka**, Ukraine
86 I 5 **Mykolayiv**, Ukraine
87 R 9 **Mykolayiv**, Ukraine
83 J 21 **Mykonos**, Greece
83 J 21 **Mykonos**, Greece
91 P 5 **Myla**, Russian Federation
107 U 12 **Mymensingh**, Bangladesh
103 T 8 **Mynaral**, Kazakhstan
114 B 12 **Myohaung**, Myanmar
111 M 15 **Myŏnggan**, North Korea
84 J 13 **Myory**, Belarus
70 B 12 **Myrdalsjökull**, Iceland ◇
87 T 4 **Myrhorod**, Ukraine
83 I 15 **Myrina**, Greece
87 Q 4 **Myrne**, Ukraine
87 X 8 **Myrne**, Ukraine
17 R 13 **Myrtle Beach**, SC, U.S.A.
32 F 12 **Myrtle Creek**, OR, U.S.A.
32 E 12 **Myrtle Point**, OR, U.S.A.
89 X 10 **Mys Alevina**, Russian Federation ▶
89 X 14 **Mys Aniva**, Russian Federation ▶
87 T 13 **Mys Ayya**, Ukraine ▶
89 Y 5 **Mys Blossom**, Russian Federation ▶
87 W 12 **Mys Chauda**, Ukraine ▶
89 R 5 **Mys Chelyuskin**, Russian Federation ▶
89 W 10 **Mys Duga-Zapadnaya**, Russian Federation ▶
89 W 12 **Mys Elizavety**, Russian Federation ▶
89 Z 9 **Mys Govena**, Russian Federation ▶
90 M 2 **Mys Kanin Nos**, Russian Federation ▶
87 W 11 **Mys Kazantip**, Ukraine ▶
87 S 13 **Mys Khersones**, Ukraine ▶
89 X 14 **Mys Kril'on**, Russian Federation ▶
89 Y 5 **Mys Litke**, Russian Federation ▶
89 V 7 **Mys Lopatka**, Russian Federation ▶
89 Z 12 **Mys Lopatka**, Russian Federation ▶
89 Z 7 **Mys Navarin**, Russian Federation ▶
90 L 4 **Mys Orlovskiy**, Russian Federation ▶
102 H 10 **Mys Peschanyy**, Kazakhstan ▶
102 H 10 **Mys Sengirli**, Kazakhstan ▶
89 X 6 **Mys Shelagskiy**, Russian Federation ▶
89 Y 5 **Mys Shmidta**, Russian Federation
102 H 11 **Mys Suz**, Kazakhstan ▶
90 K 3 **Mys Svyatoy Nos**, Russian Federation ▶
89 X 13 **Mys Terpeniya**, Russian Federation ▶
89 X 10 **Mys Tolstoy**, Russian Federation ▶
102 G 8 **Mys Tyub-Karagan**, Kazakhstan ▶
87 S 12 **Mys Yevpatoriys'kyy**, Ukraine ▶
89 Y 10 **Mys Yuzhnyy**, Russian Federation ▶
89 N 5 **Mys Zhelaniya**, Russian Federation ▶
79 K 18 **Myślenice**, Poland
78 D 11 **Myślibórz**, Poland
105 D 21 **Mysore**, India
83 L 17 **Mytilini**, Greece
92 L 1 **Mytishchi**, Russian Federation
30 M 3 **Myton**, UT, U.S.A.
133 Q 3 **Mzimba**, Malawi
133 Q 3 **Mzuzu**, Malawi

N

114 F 10 **Na-lang**, Myanmar
68 F 13 **Naaldwijk**, Netherlands
34 E 9 **Naalehu**, HI, U.S.A.
124 K 7 **Naama**, Algeria
71 K 19 **Naantali**, Finland
68 I 11 **Naarden**, Netherlands
121 H 15 **Nabas**, Philippines
131 V 10 **Naberera**, Tanzania
93 U 1 **Naberezhnyye Chelny**, Russian Federation
35 T 8 **Nabesna**, AK, U.S.A.
125 Q 5 **Nabeul**, Tunisia
106 I 7 **Nabha**, India
117 W 12 **Nabire**, Indonesia
96 G 9 **Nāblus**, Israel
128 M 11 **Nabolo**, Ghana
139 X 11 **Nabouwalu**, Fiji
133 U 5 **Nacala**, Mozambique
46 L 7 **Nacaome**, Honduras
133 U 5 **Nacaroa**, Mozambique
113 P 13 **Nachen**, China
131 W 14 **Nachingwea**, Tanzania
104 B 11 **Nachna**, India
79 F 16 **Náchod**, Czech Republic
105 N 22 **Nachuge**, India
27 T 7 **Nacogdoches**, TX, U.S.A.
44 J 3 **Nacozari de García**, Mexico
139 W 11 **Nadi**, Fiji
105 C 15 **Nadiad**, India
95 V 9 **Nadirchanly**, Azerbaijan
86 E 10 **Nădlac**, Romania
124 J 6 **Nador**, Morocco
86 J 6 **Nadvirna**, Ukraine
88 L 8 **Nadym**, Russian Federation
71 D 26 **Naestved**, Denmark
83 D 19 **Nafpaktos**, Greece
83 F 21 **Nafplio**, Greece
99 P 5 **Nafy**, Saudi Arabia
126 F 11 **Nag' Hammadi**, Egypt
120 J 12 **Naga**, Philippines
107 Y 10 **Naga Hills**, India
123 D 20 **Nagahama**, Japan
123 H 17 **Nagahama**, Japan
105 D 18 **Nagaj**, India
107 Y 10 **Nagaland**, India ■
123 I 15 **Nagano**, Japan
123 J 14 **Nagaoka**, Japan
107 W 10 **Nagaon**, India
105 F 22 **Nagappattinam**, India
105 F 19 **Nagarjuna Sagar**, India
123 B 22 **Nagasaki**, Japan
123 C 20 **Nagato**, Japan
104 C 12 **Nagaur**, India
105 E 24 **Nagercoil**, India
101 R 13 **Nagha Kalat**, Pakistan
106 K 8 **Nagina**, India
123 N 24 **Nago**, Japan
106 L 12 **Nagod**, India
73 F 23 **Nagold**, Germany
91 Q 11 **Nagorsk**, Russian Federation
123 H 17 **Nagoya**, Japan
105 F 16 **Nagpur**, India
108 L 10 **Nagqu**, China
88 M 3 **Nagurskoye**, Russian Federation
79 G 25 **Nagyatád**, Hungary
79 M 21 **Nagyhalász**, Hungary
79 G 25 **Nagykanizsa**, Hungary
79 J 23 **Nagykáta**, Hungary
123 N 25 **Naha**, Japan
96 F 7 **Nahariyya**, Israel
20 I 10 **Nahma Junction**, MI, U.S.A.
96 H 3 **Nahr al Āşī**, Syria
97 U 7 **Nahr Diyālá**, Iraq
113 S 13 **Nahuo**, China
44 M 5 **Naica**, Mexico
86 F 12 **Naidăș**, Romania
63 R 10 **Nailsworth**, U.K.
111 G 14 **Naiman Qi**, China
41 U 7 **Nain**, NL, Canada
100 J 8 **Nā'īn**, Iran
105 G 15 **Nainpur**, India
60 H 10 **Nairn**, U.K.
131 V 8 **Nairobi**, Kenya
84 F 5 **Naissaar**, Estonia
131 U 8 **Naivasha**, Kenya
100 I 8 **Najafābād**, Iran
110 I 9 **Naji**, China
106 K 7 **Najibabad**, India
111 N 14 **Najin**, North Korea
99 P 11 **Najrān**, Saudi Arabia
123 A 22 **Nakadōri-shima**, Japan
123 E 21 **Nakamura**, Japan
123 I 15 **Nakano**, Japan
123 B 26 **Nakano-shima**, Japan
123 D 17 **Nakano-shima**, Japan
122 M 4 **Nakashibetsu**, Japan
131 S 7 **Nakasongola**, Uganda
123 C 21 **Nakatsu**, Japan
123 I 17 **Nakatsugawa**, Japan
127 I 16 **Nakfa**, Eritrea
126 F 8 **Nakhl**, Egypt
100 I 12 **Nakhl-e Taqī**, Iran
89 V 15 **Nakhodka**, Russian Federation
107 W 10 **Nakhola**, India
115 I 19 **Nakhon Nayok**, Thailand
115 K 15 **Nakhon Phanom**, Thailand
115 I 18 **Nakhon Ratchasima**, Thailand
115 G 17 **Nakhon Sawan**, Thailand
115 H 24 **Nakhon Si Thammarat**, Thailand
105 A 14 **Nakhtarana**, India
78 G 11 **Nakło nad Notecią**, Poland
35 O 11 **Naknek**, AK, U.S.A.
35 O 11 **Naknek Lake**, AK, U.S.A.
106 H 6 **Nakodar**, India
133 Q 2 **Nakonde**, Zambia
71 D 26 **Nakskov**, Denmark
71 F 16 **Näkten**, Sweden
131 U 8 **Nakuru**, Kenya
39 I 21 **Nakusp**, BC, Canada
101 S 12 **Nal**, Pakistan
93 O 14 **Nal'chik**, Russian Federation
105 A 14 **Naliya**, India
94 G 9 **Nallihan**, Turkey
125 R 8 **Nālūt**, Libya
108 L 10 **Nam Co**, China
114 M 13 **Nam Đinh**, Vietnam
115 J 14 **Nam Ngum Reservoir**, Laos
115 J 16 **Nam Phong**, Thailand
132 H 7 **Namacunde**, Angola
133 S 6 **Namacurra**, Mozambique
107 N 9 **Namai**, Nepal
23 S 2 **Namakan Lake**, MN, U.S.A.
105 E 22 **Namakkal**, India
131 V 9 **Namanga**, Kenya
103 S 11 **Namangan**, Uzbekistan
103 S 11 **Namangan Wiloyati**, Uzbekistan ■
133 U 5 **Namapa**, Mozambique
132 J 11 **Namaqualand**, Namibia ◇
138 G 3 **Namatanai**, Papua New Guinea
135 W 10 **Nambucca Heads**, NSW, Australia
107 R 9 **Namche Bazar**, Nepal
111 K 18 **Namch'ŏn**, North Korea
132 G 8 **Namib Desert**, Namibia ◇
132 F 6 **Namibe**, Angola
132 F 6 **Namibe**, Angola ■
132 H 9 **Namibia**, Africa ■
133 S 7 **Namidobe**, Mozambique
108 M 10 **Namjagbarwa**, China ▲
114 E 11 **Namlan**, Myanmar
117 R 12 **Namlea**, Indonesia
135 T 10 **Namoi**, NSW, Australia
141 O 15 **Namoluk**, Federated States of Micronesia
141 N 14 **Namonuito**, Federated States of Micronesia
141 X 4 **Namorik**, Marshall Islands
28 J 10 **Nampa**, ID, U.S.A.
128 K 8 **Nampala**, Mali
111 J 18 **Namp'o**, North Korea
133 U 5 **Nampula**, Mozambique
133 T 5 **Nampula**, Mozambique ■
114 F 12 **Namsang**, Myanmar
71 E 14 **Namsos**, Norway
89 T 10 **Namtsy**, Russian Federation
114 E 10 **Namtu**, Myanmar
141 X 3 **Namu**, Marshall Islands
133 S 5 **Namuli**, Mozambique ▲
133 T 4 **Namuno**, Mozambique
69 H 22 **Namur**, Belgium ■
69 H 21 **Namur**, Belgium
132 I 7 **Namutoni**, Namibia
133 N 6 **Namwala**, Zambia
111 L 21 **Namwŏn**, South Korea
114 E 6 **Namya Ra**, Myanmar
79 H 15 **Namysłów**, Poland

...ountry ■ Internal administrative region: State/Province/Territory/Dependent territory · Capital city · Mountain range/Undersea ridge · ▲ Mountain peak/Volcano/Seamount · ◇ Geographic feature · ▶ Headland/Point/Cape/Peninsula · Desert · Island/Island group · Antarctic base · Ocean · Sea · Bay/Gulf/Channel/Strait · Lake · Salt pan/Dry/Intermittent lake · River

115	H 14	**Nan**, Thailand
130	J 3	**Nana-Grébizi**, Central African Republic ▣
130	H 4	**Nana-Mambéré**, Central African Republic ▣
39	F 22	**Nanaimo**, BC, Canada
111	N 15	**Nanam**, North Korea
113	X 11	**Nan'an**, China
123	H 15	**Nanao**, Japan
113	O 6	**Nanbu**, China
110	M 9	**Nancha**, China
113	V 8	**Nanchang**, China
113	W 9	**Nancheng**, China
113	O 6	**Nanchong**, China
113	P 7	**Nanchuan**, China
105	O 24	**Nancowry**, India 🏝
65	V 4	**Nancy**, France
106	L 7	**Nanda Devi**, India ▲
113	P 11	**Nandan**, China
105	E 17	**Nanded**, India
105	C 15	**Nandurbar**, India
105	F 19	**Nandyal**, India
111	I 16	**Nanfen**, China
113	V 9	**Nanfeng**, China
108	L 11	**Nang**, China
129	U 14	**Nanga Eboko**, Cameroon
101	Y 6	**Nanga Parbat**, Pakistan ▲
121	F 16	**Nangalao**, Philippines 🏝
101	V 7	**Nangarhār**, Afghanistan ▣
116	J 11	**Nangatayap**, Indonesia
111	K 17	**Nangnim-sanmaek**, North Korea ▲▲
113	U 1	**Nangong**, China
112	H 5	**Nangqên**, China
131	W 13	**Nangulangwa**, Tanzania
112	K 10	**Nanhua**, China
113	Z 6	**Nanhui**, China
105	E 21	**Nanjangud**, India
113	X 5	**Nanjing**, China
113	U 10	**Nankang**, China
123	F 20	**Nankoku**, Japan
132	J 6	**Nankova**, Angola
113	U 2	**Nanle**, China
113	X 6	**Nanling**, China
113	P 12	**Nanning**, China
142	M 14	**Nanortalik**, Greenland
113	N 11	**Nanpan**, China ∫
111	G 16	**Nanpiao**, China
113	N 4	**Nanping**, China
113	Y 10	**Nanri Dao**, China 🏝
143	T 9	**Nansen Basin**, Arctic Ocean ◇
143	S 10	**Nansen Cordillera**, Arctic Ocean ▲▲
37	O 1	**Nansen Sound**, NU, Canada ≈
131	S 9	**Nansio**, Tanzania
64	L 7	**Nantes**, France
42	E 14	**Nanticoke**, ON, Canada
39	J 20	**Nanton**, AB, Canada
113	Y 5	**Nantong**, China
15	P 11	**Nantucket**, MA, U.S.A.
15	P 11	**Nantucket Island**, MA, U.S.A. 🏝
15	P 11	**Nantucket Sound**, MA, U.S.A. ≈
63	Q 5	**Nantwich**, U.K.
140	E 5	**Nanumanga**, Tuvalu 🏝
140	E 5	**Nanumea**, Tuvalu 🏝
134	E 6	**Nanutarra Roadhouse**, WA, Australia
113	S 7	**Nanxian**, China
113	U 11	**Nanxiong**, China
113	T 5	**Nanyang**, China
122	K 13	**Nanyo**, Japan
131	V 7	**Nanyuki**, Kenya
113	S 5	**Nanzhang**, China
113	S 4	**Nanzhao**, China
110	J 5	**Naodahan**, China
107	T 12	**Naogaon**, Bangladesh
106	H 4	**Naoshera**, India
33	G 19	**Napa**, CA, U.S.A.
38	H 9	**Napaktulik Lake**, NU, Canada ◣
136	N 13	**Napier**, New Zealand
145	W 3	**Napier Mountains**, Antarctica ▲▲
19	W 13	**Naples**, FL, U.S.A.
28	K 2	**Naples**, ID, U.S.A.
77	J 16	**Naples**, Italy
52	B 8	**Napo**, Ecuador ▣
52	D 9	**Napo**, Ecuador/Peru ∫
113	O 12	**Napo**, China
21	L 16	**Napoleon**, OH, U.S.A.
22	K 6	**Napoleon**, ND, U.S.A.
99	Q 13	**Naqūb**, Yemen
123	H 18	**Nara**, Japan
128	J 8	**Nara**, Mali
31	U 9	**Nara Visa**, NM, U.S.A.
85	I 15	**Narach**, Belarus
135	Q 13	**Naracoorte**, SA, Australia
105	G 17	**Narainpur**, India
110	C 12	**Naran Bulag**, China
52	B 10	**Naranjal**, Ecuador
52	D 11	**Naranjal**, Peru
45	S 10	**Naranjos**, Mexico
123	A 22	**Narao**, Japan
105	I 18	**Narasannapeta**, India
115	I 26	**Narathiwat**, Thailand
107	U 13	**Narayanganj**, Bangladesh
65	R 15	**Narbonne**, France
105	O 20	**Narcondam Island**, India 🏝
58	C 13	**Naré**, Argentina
37	Q 1	**Nares Strait**, NU, Canada ≈
78	L 11	**Narew**, Poland ∫
105	D 19	**Nargund**, India
132	J 10	**Narib**, Namibia
101	U 6	**Narin**, Afghanistan
50	F 9	**Nariño**, Colombia ▣
123	L 16	**Narita**, Japan
106	J 6	**Narkanda**, India
105	D 15	**Narmada**, India ∫
139	Y 12	**Naro**, Fiji
92	K 1	**Naro-Fominsk**, Russian Federation
131	U 8	**Narok**, Kenya
135	U 13	**Narooma**, NSW, Australia
135	U 10	**Narrabri**, NSW, Australia
135	T 12	**Narrandera**, NSW, Australia
134	G 11	**Narrogin**, WA, Australia
135	T 11	**Narromine**, NSW, Australia
17	O 6	**Narrows**, VA, U.S.A.
142	M 13	**Narsarsuaq**, Greenland
107	U 13	**Narsingdi**, Bangladesh
111	D 14	**Nart**, China
123	F 19	**Naruto**, Japan
84	J 5	**Narva**, Estonia
84	J 5	**Narva Bay**, Estonia ≈
120	F 7	**Narvacan**, Philippines
70	H 9	**Narvik**, Norway
91	P 3	**Nar'yan-Mar**, Russian Federation
103	T 11	**Naryn**, Kyrgyzstan ∫
103	V 11	**Naryn**, Kyrgyzstan
103	V 11	**Narynskaya Oblast'**, Kyrgyzstan ▣
92	J 4	**Naryshkino**, Russian Federation
139	Y 11	**Nasau**, Fiji
32	G 8	**Naselle**, WA, U.S.A.
105	C 16	**Nashik**, India
15	N 9	**Nashua**, NH, U.S.A.
29	W 3	**Nashua**, MT, U.S.A.
16	F 8	**Nashville**, TN, U.S.A.
21	F 21	**Nashville**, IL, U.S.A.
25	T 13	**Nashville**, AR, U.S.A.
80	H 8	**Našice**, Croatia
127	F 20	**Nasir**, Sudan
41	U 8	**Naskaupi**, NL, Canada ∫
107	P 12	**Nasmganj**, India
77	K 21	**Naso**, Italy
131	N 14	**Nasondoye**, Democratic Republic of Congo
129	R 12	**Nassarawa**, Nigeria ▣
48	L 2	**Nassau**, The Bahamas ▙
140	M 7	**Nassau**, Cook Islands 🏝
71	F 23	**Nässjö**, Sweden
41	Q 7	**Nastapoca**, QC, Canada ∫
41	P 7	**Nastapoka Islands**, ON, Canada 🏝
123	K 14	**Nasu-dake**, Japan ▲
120	F 12	**Nasugbu**, Philippines
133	N 8	**Nata**, Botswana
50	H 7	**Natagaima**, Colombia
54	O 12	**Natal**, Brazil
116	C 10	**Natal**, Indonesia
100	I 7	**Naṭanz**, Iran
43	V 3	**Natashquan**, QC, Canada
18	K 6	**Natchez**, MS, U.S.A.
18	I 5	**Natchitoches**, LA, U.S.A.
138	D 7	**National Capital District**, Papua New Guinea ▣
129	N 11	**Natitingou**, Benin
122	K 12	**Natori**, Japan
14	B 12	**Natrona Heights**, PA, U.S.A.
105	E 23	**Nattam**, India
115	E 14	**Nattaung**, Myanmar ▲
116	H 9	**Natuna Besar**, Indonesia 🏝
132	I 10	**Nauchas**, Namibia
74	K 8	**Nauders**, Austria
72	L 13	**Nauen**, Germany
104	C 11	**Naukh**, India
141	U 1	**Nauru**, Oceania □
52	E 11	**Nauta**, Peru
45	T 11	**Nautla**, Mexico
101	R 9	**Nauzad**, Afghanistan
67	N 8	**Navahermosa**, Spain
85	H 18	**Navahrudak**, Belarus
31	O 8	**Navajo Lake**, NM, U.S.A. ◣
30	L 7	**Navajo Mount**, UT, U.S.A. ▲
121	K 16	**Naval**, Philippines
66	L 7	**Navalmoral de la Mata**, Spain
85	K 14	**Navapolatsk**, Belarus
67	R 2	**Navarra**, Spain ▣
49	N 7	**Navassa Island**, U.S.A., U.S.A. 🏝
85	G 18	**Navavel'nya**, Belarus
56	F 12	**Navidad**, Chile
105	A 14	**Navlakhi**, India
92	I 4	**Navlya**, Russian Federation
103	P 12	**Navoi**, Uzbekistan
44	J 6	**Navojoa**, Mexico
105	C 16	**Navsari**, India
139	W 12	**Navua**, Fiji
96	H 8	**Nawá**, Syria
107	S 12	**Nawabganj**, Bangladesh
107	U 12	**Nawabganj**, Bangladesh
101	U 13	**Nawabshah**, Pakistan
107	Q 12	**Nawada**, India
101	T 9	**Nāwah**, Afghanistan
106	H 9	**Nawalgarh**, India
105	H 16	**Nawapara**, India
114	F 10	**Nawngleng**, Myanmar
103	O 10	**Nawoiy Wiloyati**, Uzbekistan ▣
95	V 10	**Naxşşivan**, Azerbaijan
113	N 8	**Naxi**, China
83	J 22	**Naxos**, Greece
83	J 22	**Naxos**, Greece 🏝
50	G 7	**Naya**, Colombia
101	T 7	**Nayak**, Afghanistan
45	N 10	**Nayar**, Mexico
44	M 10	**Nayarit**, Mexico ▣
122	K 4	**Nayoro**, Japan
105	F 20	**Nayudupeta**, India
96	G 8	**Nazareth**, Israel
53	E 18	**Nazca**, Peru
123	O 22	**Naze**, Japan
94	C 11	**Nazilli**, Turkey
93	P 14	**Nazran'**, Russian Federation
127	I 20	**Nazrēt**, Ethiopia
99	Y 7	**Nazwá**, Oman
133	O 2	**Nchelenge**, Zambia
132	K 9	**Ncojane**, Botswana
129	T 15	**Ncue**, Equatorial Guinea
132	G 3	**N'dalatando**, Angola
129	O 11	**Ndali**, Benin
130	K 3	**Ndélé**, Central African Republic
129	V 14	**Ndélélé**, Cameroon
130	E 9	**Ndendé**, Gabon
139	P 7	**Ndeni**, Solomon Islands 🏝
129	V 10	**Ndjamena**, Chad ▙
130	E 8	**Ndjolé**, Gabon
130	G 8	**Ndjounou**, Gabon
133	O 4	**Ndola**, Zambia
131	Q 6	**Nduye**, Democratic Republic of Congo
83	F 17	**Nea Anchialos**, Greece
83	F 15	**Nea Moudania**, Greece
82	G 13	**Nea Zichni**, Greece
32	F 6	**Neah Bay**, WA, U.S.A.
83	F 23	**Neapoli**, Greece
83	K 26	**Neapoli**, Greece
34	B 11	**Near Islands**, AK, U.S.A. 🏝
63	N 10	**Neath**, U.K.
131	R 6	**Nebbi**, Uganda
128	M 10	**Nebbou**, Burkina Faso
102	I 12	**Nebitdag**, Turkmenistan
22	H 13	**Nebraska**, U.S.A. ▣
23	P 15	**Nebraska City**, NE, U.S.A.
20	E 12	**Necedah**, WI, U.S.A.
27	T 7	**Neches**, TX, U.S.A. ∫
73	F 21	**Neckar**, Germany ∫
59	D 19	**Necochea**, Argentina
129	X 8	**Nédéley**, Chad
69	K 17	**Nederweert**, Netherlands
87	T 3	**Nedryhayliv**, Ukraine
29	T 10	**Needle Mountain**, WY, U.S.A. ▲
33	N 24	**Needles**, CA, U.S.A.
40	H 10	**Neepawa**, MB, Canada
95	Z 9	**Neftşşala**, Azerbaijan
91	S 14	**Neftekamsk**, Russian Federation
93	P 12	**Neftekumsk**, Russian Federation
88	L 10	**Nefteyugansk**, Russian Federation
62	L 5	**Nefyn**, U.K.
132	G 2	**Negage**, Angola
116	L 15	**Negara**, Indonesia
127	I 21	**Negēlē**, Ethiopia
127	I 22	**Negēlē**, Ethiopia
118	C 9	**Negeri Sembilan**, Malaysia ▣
96	E 12	**Negev**, Israel ◇
131	W 15	**Negomane**, Tanzania
105	F 25	**Negombo**, Sri Lanka
80	O 11	**Negotin**, Serbia and Montenegro
86	I 12	**Negreni**, Romania
52	A 11	**Negritos**, Peru
57	H 15	**Negro**, South America ∫
121	I 18	**Negros**, Philippines 🏝
87	N 14	**Negru Vodă**, Romania
101	O 9	**Nehbandān**, Iran
110	J 8	**Nehe**, China
86	K 11	**Nehoiu**, Romania
132	H 6	**Nehone**, Angola
140	J 10	**Neiafu**, Tonga
49	P 8	**Neiba**, Dominican Republic
113	N 7	**Neijiang**, China
105	N 22	**Neill Island**, India 🏝
50	H 8	**Neiva**, Colombia
113	S 4	**Neixiang**, China
45	T 14	**Nejapa Tequisistlán**, Mexico
127	H 20	**Nek'emtē**, Ethiopia
90	F 14	**Nelidovo**, Russian Federation
23	N 12	**Neligh**, NE, U.S.A.
105	G 20	**Nellore**, India
39	I 21	**Nelson**, BC, Canada
137	I 16	**Nelson**, New Zealand
137	I 16	**Nelson**, New Zealand ▣
135	V 11	**Nelson Bay**, NSW, Australia
133	P 10	**Nelspruit**, Republic of South Africa
121	E 16	**Nelyan Point**, Philippines ▶
128	J 7	**Néma**, Mauritania
85	D 15	**Neman**, Lithuania ∫
85	C 15	**Neman**, Russian Federation
129	Q 14	**Nembe**, Nigeria
83	E 20	**Nemea**, Greece
85	G 15	**Nemenčinė**, Lithuania
122	N 4	**Nemuro**, Japan
122	N 4	**Nemuro-hantō**, Japan ▶
122	M 3	**Nemuro-kaikyō**, Japan ≈
122	N 4	**Nemuro-wan**, Japan ≈
87	N 6	**Nemyriv**, Ukraine
35	R 7	**Nenana**, AK, U.S.A.
118	E 8	**Nenasi**, Malaysia
91	R 2	**Nenetskiy Avtonomnyy Okrug**, Russian Federation ▣
110	J 8	**Nenjiang**, China
123	H 17	**Neo**, Japan
83	L 20	**Neo Karlovasi**, Greece
23	Q 13	**Neola**, IA, U.S.A.
107	O 8	**Nepal**, Asia □
106	M 9	**Nepalganj**, Nepal
42	I 11	**Nepean**, ON, Canada
79	B 18	**Nepomuk**, Czech Republic
89	S 14	**Nerchinsk**, Russian Federation
84	G 12	**Nereta**, Latvia
81	G 14	**Neretva**, Bosnia and Herzegovina ∫
132	K 6	**Neriquinha**, Angola
85	F 15	**Neris**, Lithuania ∫
67	N 13	**Nerja**, Spain
89	T 12	**Neryungri**, Russian Federation
68	K 5	**Nes**, Netherlands
82	N 9	**Nesebŭr**, Bulgaria
24	J 5	**Ness City**, KS, U.S.A.
85	D 15	**Nesterov**, Russian Federation
40	J 11	**Nestor Falls**, ON, Canada
82	H 12	**Nestos**, Greece ∫
96	F 8	**Netanya**, Israel
68	H 10	**Netherlands**, Europe □
49	S 12	**Netherlands Antilles**, The Netherlands, The Netherlands ▣
41	Q 2	**Nettilling Lake**, NU, Canada ◣
73	J 23	**Neuberg**, Germany
72	M 10	**Neubrandenburg**, Germany
72	J 9	**Neubukow**, Germany
74	C 7	**Neuchâtel**, Switzerland
72	M 13	**Neuenhagen**, Germany
65	U 5	**Neufchâteau**, France
69	J 24	**Neufchâteau**, Belgium
65	O 2	**Neufchâtel-en-Bray**, France
75	S 3	**Neufelden**, Austria
75	W 4	**Neulengbach**, Austria
73	J 21	**Neumarkt**, Germany
145	O 1	**Neumayer**, Antarctica ⠿
72	H 9	**Neumünster**, Germany
65	P 6	**Neung-sur-Beuvron**, France
73	C 21	**Neunkirchen**, Germany
75	W 5	**Neunkirchen**, Austria
57	H 15	**Neuquén**, Argentina
57	G 15	**Neuquén**, Argentina ▣
57	G 14	**Neuquén**, Argentina ∫
72	L 12	**Neuruppin**, Germany
75	Y 5	**Neusiedler See**, Austria ◣
73	C 16	**Neuss**, Germany
72	G 13	**Neustadt**, Germany
72	I 9	**Neustadt**, Germany
73	J 17	**Neustadt**, Germany
73	K 22	**Neustadt**, Germany
73	E 21	**Neustadt**, Germany
73	I 20	**Neustadt an der Aisch**, Germany
72	L 11	**Neustrelitz**, Germany
72	F 9	**Neuwerk**, Germany 🏝
73	D 18	**Neuwied**, Germany
25	S 6	**Nevada**, MO, U.S.A.
33	J 18	**Nevada**, U.S.A., U.S.A. ▣
33	H 17	**Nevada City**, CA, U.S.A.
45	N 12	**Nevada de Colima**, Mexico ▲
53	F 19	**Nevado Ampato**, Peru ▲
56	G 13	**Nevado Campanario**, Argentina ▲
53	F 18	**Nevado Coropuna**, Peru ▲
56	H 5	**Nevado de Chañi**, Argentina ▲
56	H 5	**Nevado de Poquis**, Chile ▲
45	Q 12	**Nevado de Tolúca**, Mexico ▲
50	H 8	**Nevado del Huila**, Colombia ▲
50	I 6	**Nevado del Ruiz**, Colombia ▲
53	C 14	**Nevado Huascarán**, Peru ▲
53	I 19	**Nevado Illampu**, Bolivia ▲
56	H 8	**Nevado Ojos del Salado**, Argentina ▲
53	I 20	**Nevado Sajama**, Bolivia ▲
56	H 6	**Nevados de Cachi**, Argentina ▲
90	E 14	**Nevel'**, Russian Federation
65	R 8	**Nevers**, France
93	N 12	**Nevinnomyssk**, Russian Federation
49	X 8	**Nevis**, St Kitts and Nevis 🏝
94	J 11	**Nevşehir**, Turkey
19	N 2	**New Albany**, MS, U.S.A.
21	J 21	**New Albany**, IN, U.S.A.
63	T 12	**New Alresford**, U.K.
51	V 5	**New Amsterdam**, Guyana
15	O 11	**New Bedford**, MA, U.S.A.
17	U 10	**New Bern**, NC, U.S.A.
27	T 4	**New Boston**, TX, U.S.A.
27	P 10	**New Braunfels**, TX, U.S.A.
138	F 4	**New Britain**, Papua New Guinea 🏝
43	S 8	**New Brunswick**, Canada ▣
139	N 14	**New Caledonia**, New Caledonia 🏝
139	O 15	**New Caledonia**, France ▣
43	T 6	**New Carlisle**, QC, Canada
14	A 11	**New Castle**, PA, U.S.A.
16	H 4	**New Castle**, KY, U.S.A.
14	J 12	**New City**, NY, U.S.A.
106	J 8	**New Delhi**, India ▙
17	N 13	**New Ellenton**, SC, U.S.A.
15	N 9	**New England**, NH, U.S.A. ◇
63	S 12	**New Forest**, U.K. ◇
138	K 6	**New Georgia**, Solomon Islands 🏝
138	J 6	**New Georgia Islands**, Solomon Islands 🏝
138	K 5	**New Georgia Sound**, Solomon Islands ≈
43	W 9	**New Glasgow**, NS, Canada
138	A 4	**New Guinea**, Indonesia/Papua New Guinea 🏝
15	N 7	**New Hampshire**, U.S.A. ▣
138	G 2	**New Hanover**, Papua New Guinea 🏝
14	L 11	**New Haven**, CT, U.S.A.
39	D 18	**New Hazelton**, BC, Canada
18	J 8	**New Iberia**, LA, U.S.A.
138	G 3	**New Ireland**, Papua New Guinea 🏝
138	H 2	**New Ireland**, Papua New Guinea ▣
14	I 14	**New Jersey**, U.S.A. ▣
21	N 19	**New Lexington**, OH, U.S.A.
42	F 7	**New Liskeard**, ON, Canada
14	M 11	**New London**, CT, U.S.A.
20	G 12	**New London**, WI, U.S.A.
17	R 4	**New Market**, VA, U.S.A.
28	J 8	**New Meadows**, ID, U.S.A.
31	O 11	**New Mexico**, U.S.A. ▣
135	S 15	**New Norfolk**, TAS, Australia
18	L 8	**New Orleans**, LA, U.S.A.
21	N 18	**New Philadelphia**, OH, U.S.A.
33	I 14	**New Pine Creek**, CA, U.S.A.
136	J 12	**New Plymouth**, New Zealand
48	K 2	**New Providence**, The Bahamas 🏝
62	L 8	**New Quay**, U.K.
43	S 6	**New Richmond**, QC, Canada
18	K 7	**New Roads**, LA, U.S.A.
14	K 12	**New Rochelle**, NY, U.S.A.
22	L 4	**New Rockford**, ND, U.S.A.
63	Y 12	**New Romney**, U.K.
43	U 11	**New Ross**, NS, Canada
61	E 20	**New Ross**, Republic of Ireland
89	T 6	**New Siberia Islands**, Russian Federation 🏝
19	X 9	**New Smyrna Beach**, FL, U.S.A.
135	T 10	**New South Wales**, Australia ▣
22	H 3	**New Town**, ND, U.S.A.
23	R 9	**New Ulm**, MN, U.S.A.
14	F 9	**New York**, U.S.A. ▣
14	K 12	**New York**, NY, U.S.A.
137	I 14	**New Zealand**, Oceania □
131	W 14	**Newala**, Tanzania
14	J 12	**Newark**, NJ, U.S.A.
14	F 8	**Newark**, NY, U.S.A.
17	W 2	**Newark**, DE, U.S.A.
21	N 18	**Newark**, OH, U.S.A.
33	M 17	**Newark Lake**, NV, U.S.A. ◣
63	U 5	**Newark-on-Trent**, U.K.
32	G 10	**Newberg**, OR, U.S.A.
17	N 12	**Newberry**, SC, U.S.A.
42	I 11	**Newboro**, ON, Canada
14	J 11	**Newburgh**, NY, U.S.A.
63	T 11	**Newbury**, U.K.
15	O 9	**Newburyport**, MA, U.S.A.
63	P 1	**Newby Bridge**, U.K.
29	Z 10	**Newcastle**, WY, U.S.A.
42	F 12	**Newcastle**, ON, Canada
43	S 8	**Newcastle**, NB, Canada
61	F 16	**Newcastle**, U.K.
135	V 11	**Newcastle**, NSW, Australia
62	L 9	**Newcastle Emlyn**, U.K.
63	Q 5	**Newcastle-under-Lyme**, U.K.
61	J 15	**Newcastle upon Tyne**, U.K.
14	D 8	**Newfane**, NY, U.S.A.
41	X 10	**Newfoundland**, NL, Canada 🏝
41	V 9	**Newfoundland and Labrador**, Canada ▣
63	W 13	**Newhaven**, U.K.
21	G 19	**Newman**, IL, U.S.A.
134	H 7	**Newman**, WA, Australia
15	O 8	**Newmarket**, NH, U.S.A.
42	E 12	**Newmarket**, ON, Canada
63	W 8	**Newmarket**, U.K.
19	S 3	**Newnan**, GA, U.S.A.
14	F 13	**Newport**, PA, U.S.A.
14	M 5	**Newport**, VT, U.S.A.
14	M 8	**Newport**, NH, U.S.A.
15	N 11	**Newport**, RI, U.S.A.
16	K 9	**Newport**, TN, U.S.A.
25	W 10	**Newport**, AR, U.S.A.
32	F 10	**Newport**, OR, U.S.A.
32	L 6	**Newport**, WA, U.S.A.
62	K 8	**Newport**, U.K.
63	T 13	**Newport**, U.K.
63	Q 6	**Newport**, U.K.
62	K 8	**Newport Bay**, U.K. ≈
17	V 7	**Newport News**, VA, U.S.A.
63	U 8	**Newport Pagnell**, U.K.
62	J 14	**Newquay**, U.K.
61	F 16	**Newry**, U.K.
15	O 10	**Newton**, MA, U.S.A.
23	T 13	**Newton**, IA, U.S.A.
25	N 5	**Newton**, KS, U.S.A.
63	Q 2	**Newton**, U.K.
63	N 14	**Newton Abbot**, U.K.
61	G 15	**Newton Stewart**, U.K.
63	O 7	**Newtown**, U.K.
90	M 13	**Neya**, Russian Federation
100	J 8	**Neyestānak**, Iran
101	N 6	**Neyshābūr**, Iran
105	E 24	**Neyyattinkara**, India
116	I 10	**Ngabang**, Indonesia
130	H 10	**Ngabé**, Congo
114	E 7	**Ngagahtawng**, Myanmar
140	J 14	**Ngajangel**, Palau 🏝
129	V 10	**Ngala**, Nigeria
129	W 11	**Ngam**, Chad
129	W 10	**Ngama**, Chad
132	L 8	**Ngamiland**, Botswana ▣
127	E 23	**Ngangala**, Sudan
108	I 8	**Nganglong Kangri**, China ▲
115	H 14	**Ngao**, Thailand
129	U 13	**Ngaoundal**, Cameroon
129	U 12	**Ngaoundéré**, Cameroon
131	R 9	**Ngara**, Tanzania
130	H 6	**Ngbala**, Congo
141	P 15	**Ngetik Atoll**, Federated States of Micronesia 🏝
138	L 6	**Nggatokae**, Solomon Islands 🏝
130	H 9	**Ngo**, Congo
115	O 18	**Ngoc Linh**, Vietnam ▲
129	U 12	**Ngong**, Cameroon
130	I 5	**Ngoto**, Central African Republic
130	E 9	**Ngounié**, Gabon ▣
129	W 9	**Ngoura**, Chad
129	U 8	**Ngourti**, Niger
131	N 4	**Ngouyo**, Central African Republic
130	H 5	**Nguia Bouar**, Central African Republic
129	U 9	**Nguigmi**, Niger
134	L 1	**Nguiu**, NT, Australia
135	O 2	**Ngukurr**, NT, Australia
140	J 14	**Ngulu**, Federated States of Micronesia 🏝
133	P 8	**Ngundu**, Zimbabwe
129	S 9	**Nguru**, Nigeria
114	M 11	**Nguyên**, Vietnam
115	O 20	**Nha Trang**, Vietnam
133	R 7	**Nhamatanda**, Mozambique
54	G 10	**Nhamundá**, Brazil
132	I 4	**N'harea**, Angola
135	R 12	**Nhill**, VIC, Australia
135	O 1	**Nhulunbuy**, NT, Australia
131	P 7	**Nia-Nia**, Democratic Republic of Congo
14	C 8	**Niagara Falls**, NY, U.S.A.
42	F 13	**Niagara Falls**, ON, Canada
119	R 7	**Niah**, Malaysia
107	P 9	**Niak**, Nepal
129	P 9	**Niamey**, Niger ▙
131	P 5	**Niangara**, Democratic Republic of Congo
113	O 3	**Niangniangba**, China
128	K 11	**Niangoloko**, Burkina Faso
110	I 9	**Nianzishan**, China
130	F 9	**Niari**, Congo ▣
116	B 10	**Nias**, Indonesia 🏝
133	S 4	**Niassa**, Mozambique ▣
141	U 1	**Nibok**, Nauru
47	P 8	**Nicaragua**, North America □
77	M 19	**Nicastro**, Italy
65	X 13	**Nice**, France
19	Q 7	**Niceville**, FL, U.S.A.
123	D 23	**Nichinan**, Japan
17	R 12	**Nichols**, SC, U.S.A.
105	N 24	**Nicobar Islands**, India 🏝
77	J 22	**Nicosia**, Italy
94	H 15	**Nicosia**, Cyprus ▙
47	O 12	**Nicoya**, Costa Rica
79	K 16	**Nida**, Poland ∫
85	B 14	**Nida**, Lithuania
82	D 13	**Nidže Kožuf**, Macedonia (F.Y.R.O.M.) ▲▲
78	K 10	**Nidzica**, Poland
72	F 7	**Niebüll**, Germany
69	M 25	**Niederanven**, Luxembourg
75	U 3	**Niederösterreich**, Austria ▣
72	F 12	**Niedersachsen**, Germany ▣
79	M 15	**Niedrzwica**, Poland
130	H 4	**Niem**, Central African Republic
72	G 13	**Nienburg**, Germany
73	O 16	**Niesky**, Germany
68	K 11	**Nieuw-Milligen**, Netherlands
51	V 6	**Nieuw Nickerie**, Suriname
68	I 13	**Nieuwegein**, Netherlands
69	E 15	**Nieuwerkerk**, Netherlands
68	G 13	**Nieuwerkerk aan den IJssel**, Netherlands
68	N 6	**Nieuwolda**, Netherlands
69	A 17	**Nieuwpoort**, Belgium
94	J 12	**Niğde**, Turkey
129	R 8	**Niger**, Africa □
129	Q 11	**Niger**, Nigeria ▣
129	Q 12	**Niger**, Africa ∫
129	R 11	**Nigeria**, Africa □
122	K 13	**Nihonmatsu**, Japan
123	K 18	**Nii-jima**, Japan 🏝
122	J 13	**Niigata**, Japan
123	I 15	**Niigata-yake-yama**, Japan ▲
123	E 20	**Niihama**, Japan
34	A 7	**Niihau**, HI, U.S.A. 🏝
123	E 18	**Niimi**, Japan
122	J 13	**Niitsu**, Japan
67	Q 13	**Níjar**, Spain
68	J 12	**Nijkerk**, Netherlands
69	K 14	**Nijmegen**, Netherlands
68	M 11	**Nijverdal**, Netherlands
83	E 16	**Nikaia**, Greece
90	H 1	**Nikel'**, Russian Federation
70	I 9	**Nikkaluokta**, Sweden
129	O 11	**Nikki**, Benin
123	K 14	**Nikkō**, Japan
89	W 12	**Nikolayevsk-na-Amure**, Russian Federation
93	Q 3	**Nikol'sk**, Russian Federation
82	I 7	**Nikopol**, Bulgaria
87	U 8	**Nikopol'**, Ukraine
94	M 8	**Niksar**, Turkey
101	O 13	**Nīkshahr**, Iran
81	I 15	**Nikšić**, Serbia and Montenegro
140	I 4	**Nikumaroro**, Kiribati 🏝
140	E 3	**Nikunau**, Kiribati 🏝
117	T 14	**Nila**, Indonesia 🏝
105	L 18	**Nilandhoo Atoll**, Maldives 🏝
126	E 10	**Nile**, Egypt/Sudan ∫
127	F 16	**Nile**, Sudan ▣
126	E 7	**Nile Delta**, Egypt ◇
21	I 16	**Niles**, MI, U.S.A.
45	U 14	**Niltepec**, Mexico
128	I 12	**Nimba Mountains**, Côte d'Ivoire/Guinea ▲
65	S 13	**Nîmes**, France
101	Q 10	**Nīmrūz**, Afghanistan ▣
127	E 23	**Nimule**, Sudan
132	K 5	**Ninda**, Angola
105	A 23	**Nine Degree Channel**, India ≈
110	M 12	**Ning'an**, China
113	Z 7	**Ningbo**, China
111	F 15	**Ningcheng**, China
113	Y 9	**Ningde**, China
113	V 9	**Ningdu**, China
113	X 6	**Ningguo**, China
113	Z 7	**Ninghai**, China
113	W 10	**Ninghua**, China
109	R 14	**Ningming**, China
112	L 9	**Ningnan**, China
113	O 5	**Ningqiang**, China
113	Q 4	**Ningshan**, China
113	O 2	**Ningxia**, China ▣
113	P 3	**Ningxian**, China
113	S 8	**Ningxiang**, China
113	S 10	**Ningyuan**, China
114	M 13	**Ninh Binh**, Vietnam
115	O 20	**Ninh Hoa**, Vietnam
138	C 2	**Ninigo Group**, Papua New Guinea 🏝
122	K 9	**Ninohe**, Japan
22	I 11	**Niobrara**, NE, U.S.A. ∫
23	N 12	**Niobrara**, NE, U.S.A.
107	X 9	**Nioko**, India
128	J 9	**Niono**, Mali
128	H 8	**Nioro**, Mali
64	M 9	**Niort**, France
39	M 17	**Nipawin**, SK, Canada
40	L 11	**Nipigon**, ON, Canada
33	M 23	**Nipton**, CA, U.S.A.
105	F 17	**Nirmal**, India
107	R 11	**Nirmali**, India
80	N 13	**Niš**, Serbia and Montenegro
97	U 14	**Nişāb**, Iraq
99	Q 13	**Nişab**, Yemen
123	C 25	**Nishino-omote**, Japan
123	F 18	**Nishiwaki**, Japan
123	C 22	**Nisi-mera**, Japan
79	M 16	**Nisko**, Poland
71	E 24	**Nissan**, Sweden ∫
138	I 4	**Nissan Island**, Papua New Guinea 🏝
71	B 20	**Nisser**, Norway ◣
83	M 23	**Nisyros**, Greece 🏝
123	E 18	**Nita**, Japan
58	N 7	**Niterói**, Brazil
79	H 21	**Nitra**, Slovakia
140	I 9	**Niua Group**, Tonga 🏝
140	I 9	**Niuafo'ou**, Tonga 🏝
140	I 9	**Niuatoputapu**, Tonga 🏝
140	K 10	**Niue**, Niue 🏝
140	K 10	**Niue**, New Zealand ▣
110	H 5	**Niu'erhe**, China
140	G 7	**Niulakita**, Tuvalu 🏝
140	F 5	**Niutao**, Tuvalu 🏝
69	F 20	**Nivelles**, Belgium
25	T 7	**Nixa**, MO, U.S.A.
27	P 11	**Nixon**, TX, U.S.A.
105	E 17	**Nizam Sagar**, India ◣
105	F 17	**Nizamabad**, India
90	M 13	**Nizhegorodskaya Oblast'**, Russian Federation ▣
93	S 1	**Nizhnekamsk**, Russian Federation
89	O 13	**Nizhneudinsk**, Russian Federation
88	L 10	**Nizhnevartovsk**, Russian Federation
89	T 7	**Nizhneyyansk**, Russian Federation
93	N 8	**Nizhniy Chir**, Russian Federation
93	O 3	**Nizhniy Lomov**, Russian Federation
93	P 1	**Nizhniy Novgorod**, Russian Federation
88	J 10	**Nizhniy Tagil**, Russian Federation
91	N 4	**Nizhnyaya Pesha**, Russian Federation
89	N 9	**Nizhnyaya Tunguska**, Russian Federation ∫
87	R 2	**Nizhyn**, Ukraine
94	M 13	**Nizip**, Turkey
81	I 14	**Njegoš**, Serbia and Montenegro ▲
133	P 12	**Njesuthi**, Lesotho ▲
131	W 13	**Njinjo**, Tanzania
131	T 13	**Njombe**, Tanzania
131	R 12	**Nkasi**, Tanzania
133	O 7	**Nkayi**, Zimbabwe
133	R 3	**Nkhata Bay**, Malawi
133	R 4	**Nkhotakota**, Malawi
131	R 11	**Nkondwe**, Tanzania
129	S 14	**Nkongsamba**, Cameroon
132	J 7	**Nkurenkuru**, Namibia
114	F 8	**Nmai Hka**, Myanmar ∫
105	J 15	**Noamundi**, India
123	D 22	**Nobeoka**, Japan
122	J 7	**Noboribetsu**, Japan
55	G 15	**Nobres**, Brazil
135	R 8	**Noccundra**, QLD, Australia
45	S 13	**Nochixtlán**, Mexico
77	N 16	**Noci**, Italy
123	K 15	**Noda**, Japan
42	E 9	**Noelville**, ON, Canada
30	K 15	**Nogales**, AZ, U.S.A.
44	I 3	**Nogales**, Mexico
65	O 5	**Nogent-le-Rotrou**, France
89	O 10	**Noginsk**, Russian Federation
92	L 1	**Noginsk**, Russian Federation
59	C 14	**Nogoyá**, Argentina
106	H 8	**Nohar**, India
73	C 20	**Nohfelden**, Germany
66	H 2	**Noia**, Spain
64	K 7	**Noirmoutier-en-l'Île**, France
123	L 17	**Nojima-zaki**, Japan ▶
101	Q 12	**Nok Kundi**, Pakistan
104	C 11	**Nokha**, India
71	L 18	**Nokia**, Finland
129	V 9	**Nokou**, Chad
107	U 11	**Nokrek Peak**, India ▲
77	J 16	**Nola**, Italy
130	H 5	**Nola**, Central African Republic
91	P 13	**Nolinsk**, Russian Federation
123	B 24	**Noma-misaki**, Japan ▶
34	M 7	**Nome**, AK, U.S.A.
123	B 22	**Nomo-zaki**, Japan ▶
140	I 10	**Nomuka Group**, Tonga 🏝
141	O 14	**Nomwin**, Federated States of Micronesia 🏝
115	I 16	**Nong Bua Lamphu**, Thailand
115	J 15	**Nong Khai**, Thailand
110	J 12	**Nong'an**, China
107	V 11	**Nongstoin**, India
140	E 3	**Nonouti**, Kiribati 🏝
115	H 19	**Nonthaburi**, Thailand
65	N 10	**Nontron**, France
68	G 8	**Nooderhaaks**, Netherlands 🏝
69	I 15	**Noord-Brabant**, Netherlands ▣
68	H 9	**Noord-Holland**, Netherlands ▣
35	N 5	**Noorvik**, AK, U.S.A.
135	W 8	**Noosa Heads**, QLD, Australia
103	R 13	**Norak**, Tajikistan
121	L 23	**Norala**, Philippines
42	F 6	**Noranda**, QC, Canada
129	U 12	**Nord**, Cameroon ▣
70	I 6	**Nord-Kvaløy**, Norway 🏝
129	T 13	**Nord-Ouest**, Cameroon ▣
65	Q 1	**Nord-pas-de-Calais**, France ▣
143	U 11	**Nordaustlandet**, Svalbard 🏝
72	D 10	**Norden**, Germany
72	C 10	**Norderney**, Germany 🏝
72	F 8	**Norderoogsand**, Germany 🏝
71	B 17	**Nordfjordeid**, Norway
70	G 10	**Nordfold**, Norway
72	E 8	**Nordfriesische Inseln**, Germany ◇
73	I 15	**Nordhausen**, Germany
72	C 13	**Nordhorn**, Germany
70	K 5	**Nordkapp**, Norway ▶

□ Country ▣ Internal administrative region: State/Province/Territory/Dependent territory ▙ Capital city ▲▲ Mountain range/Undersea ridge ▲ Mountain peak/Volcano/Seamount ◇ Geographic feature ▶ Headland/Point/Cape/Peninsula ◓ Desert 🏝 Island/Island group ⠿ Antarctic base 🌊 Ocean ◤ Sea ≈ Bay/Gulf/Channel/Strait ◣ Lake ▛ Salt pan/Dry/Intermittent lake ∫

Page	Grid	Name
	P 8	**Nordkivu**, Democratic Republic of Congo ◘
	F 14	**Nordli**, Norway
	I 22	**Nördlingen**, Germany
	I 15	**Nordmaling**, Sweden
	B 15	**Nordmøre**, Norway 🏝
	B 16	**Nordøyane**, Norway 🏝
	E 15	**Nordrhein-Westfalen**, Germany ◘
	F 8	**Nordstrand**, Germany 🏝
	R 7	**Nordvik**, Russian Federation
	C 19	**Noresund**, Norway
	V 7	**Norfolk**, VA, U.S.A.
	N 12	**Norfolk**, NE, U.S.A.
	V 8	**Norfork Lake**, AR, U.S.A. ◢
	P 14	**Norias**, TX, U.S.A.
	O 8	**Noril'sk**, Russian Federation
	F 11	**Norland**, ON, Canada
	P 8	**Norlina**, NC, U.S.A.
	G 18	**Normal**, IL, U.S.A.
	N 10	**Norman**, OK, U.S.A.
	R 4	**Norman**, QLD, Australia ⌇
	D 11	**Norman Wells**, NT, Canada
	G 7	**Normanby Island**, Papua New Guinea 🏝
	L 4	**Normandy**, France ◘
	R 4	**Normanton**, QLD, Australia
	G 17	**Ñorquinco**, Argentina
	F 19	**Norra Ny**, Sweden
	G 12	**Norra Storfjället**, Sweden ▲
	G 14	**Norråker**, Sweden
	C 23	**Nørresundby**, Denmark
	J 8	**Norris Lake**, TN, U.S.A. ◢
	G 21	**Norrköping**, Sweden
	I 20	**Norrtälje**, Sweden
	I 11	**Norseman**, WA, Australia
	C 20	**Norsjø**, Norway ◢
	Q 10	**Norsup**, Vanuatu
	J 4	**Norte de Santander**, Colombia ◘
	L 9	**North Adams**, MA, U.S.A.
	N 20	**North Andaman**, India 🏝
	M 13	**North Augusta**, SC, U.S.A.
	A 21	**North Balabac Strait**, Philippines ≈
	L 18	**North Battleford**, SK, Canada
	F 9	**North Bay**, ON, Canada
	S 10	**North Belcher Islands**, NU, Canada 🏝
	E 12	**North Bend**, OR, U.S.A.
	T 7	**North Branch**, MN, U.S.A.
	P 5	**North Caicos**, Turks and Caicos Islands 🏝
	I 4	**North Cape**, New Zealand ▶
	P 9	**North Carolina**, U.S.A. ◘
	G 24	**North Central**, Sri Lanka ◘
	B 9	**North Channel**, ON, Canada ≈
	E 14	**North Channel**, Republic of Ireland/United Kingdom ≈
	P 14	**North Charleston**, SC, U.S.A.
	I 4	**North Dakota**, U.S.A. ◘
	U 12	**North Downs**, U.K. ◇
	B 9	**North East**, PA, U.S.A.
	N 8	**North East**, Botswana ◘
	X 6	**North-Eastern**, Kenya ◘
	Z 11	**North Foreland**, U.K. ▶
	M 15	**North Fork**, NV, U.S.A.
	J 7	**North Head**, New Zealand ▶
	V 6	**North Horr**, Kenya
	L 20	**North Huvadhu Atoll**, Maldives 🏝
	B 23	**North Island**, India 🏝
	H 1	**North Island**, Philippines 🏝
	M 11	**North Island**, New Zealand 🏝
	E 20	**North Islet**, Philippines 🏝
	M 17	**North Korea**, Asia ■
	X 9	**North Lakhimpur**, India
	L 17	**North Maalhosmadulu Atoll**, Maldives 🏝
	N 2	**North Magnetic Pole**, NU, Canada ◇
	L 16	**North Miladunmadulu Atoll**, Maldives 🏝
	G 13	**North Platte**, NE, U.S.A. ⌇
	L 11	**North Point**, MI, U.S.A. ▶
	R 7	**North Pole**, AK, U.S.A.
	S 8	**North Pole**, Arctic Ocean ◇
	K 10	**North Powder**, OR, U.S.A.
	N 21	**North Reef Island**, India 🏝
	J 9	**North Rim**, AZ, U.S.A.
	I 6	**North Ronaldsay**, U.K. 🏝
	K 18	**North Saskatchewan**, SK, Canada ⌇
	N 22	**North Sentinel Island**, India 🏝
	J 4	**North Solomons**, Papua New Guinea ◘
	W 3	**North Somercotes**, U.K.
	W 9	**North Stradbroke Island**, QLD, Australia 🏝
	J 12	**North Taranaki Bight**, New Zealand ≈
	O 9	**North Twin Island**, QC, Canada 🏝
	F 23	**North Ubian**, Philippines 🏝
	E 10	**North Uist**, U.K. 🏝
	D 18	**North Verde**, Philippines 🏝
	J 20	**North Vernon**, IN, U.S.A.
	Z 5	**North Walsham**, U.K.
	L 11	**North West**, Republic of South Africa ◘
	E 6	**North West Cape**, WA, Australia ▶
	W 6	**North West Frontier**, Pakistan ◘
	G 11	**North West Highlands**, U.K. ⛰
	F 24	**North Western**, Sri Lanka ◘
	M 4	**North-Western**, Zambia ◘
	F 13	**North York**, ON, Canada
	S 1	**Northallerton**, U.K.
	G 11	**Northam**, WA, Australia
	L 9	**Northampton**, MA, U.S.A.
	U 8	**Northampton**, U.K.
	E 9	**Northampton**, WA, Australia
	K 7	**Northeast Cape**, AK, U.S.A. ▶
	H 15	**Northeim**, Germany
	G 23	**Northern**, Sri Lanka ◘
	D 14	**Northern**, Sudan ◘
	G 11	**Northern**, Sierra Leone ◘
	M 12	**Northern**, Ghana ◘
	O 10	**Northern**, Republic of South Africa ◘
	P 3	**Northern**, Zambia ◘
	Q 3	**Northern**, Malawi ◘
	F 6	**Northern**, Papua New Guinea ◘
	C 20	**Northern Bahr el Ghazal**, Sudan ◘
	K 13	**Northern Cape**, Republic of South Africa ◘
	L 2	**Northern Cay**, Belize 🏝
	L 7	**Northern Cook Islands**, Cook Islands 🏝
	B 15	**Northern Darfur**, Sudan ◘
	L 8	**Northern Dvina**, Russian Federation ⌇
	E 15	**Northern Ireland**, U.K. ◘
	D 16	**Northern Kordofan**, Sudan ◘
	K 2	**Northern Lagoon**, Belize ◢
	Y 11	**Northern Lau Group**, Fiji 🏝
	A 6	**Northern Mariana Islands**, U.S.A. ◘
	D 8	**Northern Plain**, Italy ◇
	N 4	**Northern Territory**, Australia ◘
	S 8	**Northfield**, MN, U.S.A.
	J 6	**Northland**, New Zealand ◘
43	U 8	**Northumberland Strait**, PE, Canada ≈
14	J 8	**Northville**, NY, U.S.A.
34	K 7	**Northwest Cape**, AK, U.S.A. ▶
38	H 11	**Northwest Territories**, Canada ◘
63	Q 4	**Northwich**, U.K.
143	R 4	**Northwind Plain**, Arctic Ocean ◇
24	J 2	**Norton**, KS, U.S.A.
34	M 7	**Norton Sound**, AK, U.S.A. ≈
16	E 6	**Nortonville**, KY, U.S.A.
14	K 12	**Norwalk**, CT, U.S.A.
21	M 17	**Norwalk**, OH, U.S.A.
71	B 19	**Norway**, Europe ■
40	J 8	**Norway House**, MB, Canada
143	S 15	**Norwegian Basin**, Arctic Ocean ◇
71	A 16	**Norwegian Sea**, Norway ◗
14	M 11	**Norwich**, CT, U.S.A.
63	Z 6	**Norwich**, U.K.
82	N 9	**Nos Emine**, Bulgaria ▶
82	O 7	**Nos Kaliakra**, Bulgaria ▶
82	O 7	**Nos Shabla**, Bulgaria ▶
122	N 4	**Nosapu-misaki**, Japan ▶
122	I 2	**Noshappu-misaki**, Japan ▶
122	J 10	**Noshiro**, Japan
91	Q 2	**Nosovaya**, Russian Federation
101	O 11	**Noṣratābād**, Iran
60	I 8	**Noss Head**, U.K. ▶
128	I 9	**Nossombougou**, Mali
133	Y 5	**Nosy Bé**, Madgascar 🏝
133	Z 7	**Nosy Boraha**, Madgascar 🏝
133	Y 8	**Nosy-Varika**, Madgascar
30	I 4	**Notch Peak**, UT, U.S.A. ▲
78	E 11	**Noteć**, Poland ⌇
83	J 23	**Notio Aigaio**, Greece ◘
83	A 16	**Notio Steno Kerkyras**, Greece ≈
83	G 19	**Notios Evvoïkos Kolpos**, Greece ≈
77	K 24	**Noto**, Italy
123	H 15	**Noto-hantō**, Japan ▶
122	M 3	**Notoro-ko**, Japan ◢
41	Y 9	**Notre Dame Bay**, NL, Canada ≈
42	E 11	**Nottawasaga Bay**, ON, Canada ≈
41	P 10	**Nottaway**, QC, Canada ⌇
63	T 5	**Nottingham**, U.K.
41	P 4	**Nottingham Island**, NU, Canada 🏝
124	A 14	**Nouâdhibou**, Western Sahara
128	D 5	**Nouâdhibou**, Mauritania
128	E 6	**Nouakchott**, Mauritania ⌂
128	E 6	**Nouâmghâr**, Mauritania
115	N 17	**Nouei**, Vietnam
139	Q 14	**Nouméa**, New Caledonia ⌂
103	R 12	**Nov**, Tajikistan
55	J 15	**Nova**, Brazil
58	G 5	**Nova Alvorada**, Brazil
132	F 2	**Nova Caipemba**, Angola
58	N 6	**Nova Friburgo**, Brazil
80	G 9	**Nova Gradiška**, Croatia
58	M 6	**Nova Iguaçu**, Brazil
133	R 8	**Nova Mambone**, Mozambique
133	T 6	**Nova Nabúri**, Mozambique
87	R 8	**Nova Odesa**, Ukraine
43	W 10	**Nova Scotia**, Canada ◘
80	K 13	**Nova Varoš**, Serbia and Montenegro
82	K 9	**Nova Zagora**, Bulgaria
76	B 7	**Novara**, Italy
33	F 19	**Novato**, CA, U.S.A.
88	L 6	**Novaya Zemlya**, Russian Federation 🏝
79	H 22	**Nové Zámky**, Slovakia
90	G 12	**Novgorodskaya Oblast'**, Russian Federation ◘
87	S 1	**Novhorod-Sivers'kyy**, Ukraine
87	S 7	**Novhorodka**, Ukraine
80	K 8	**Novi Bečej**, Serbia and Montenegro
82	G 9	**Novi-Iskŭr**, Bulgaria
76	C 8	**Novi Ligure**, Italy
81	L 14	**Novi Pazar**, Serbia and Montenegro
82	M 7	**Novi Pazar**, Bulgaria
80	K 9	**Novi Sad**, Serbia and Montenegro
54	E 10	**Novo Airão**, Brazil
54	F 11	**Novo Aripuanã**, Brazil
58	H 12	**Novo Hamburgo**, Brazil
80	C 8	**Novo Mesto**, Slovenia
82	F 12	**Novo Selo**, Macedonia (F.Y.R.O.M.)
93	N 6	**Novoanninskiy**, Russian Federation
87	Q 6	**Novoarkhanhel's'k**, Ukraine
87	Y 8	**Novoazovs'k**, Ukraine
103	S 13	**Novobod**, Tajikistan
102	H 6	**Novobogatinskoye**, Kazakhstan
87	V 8	**Novobohdanivka**, Ukraine
93	Q 1	**Novocheboksarsk**, Russian Federation
92	L 9	**Novocherkassk**, Russian Federation
90	K 6	**Novodvinsk**, Russian Federation
86	M 3	**Novohrad-Volyns'kyy**, Ukraine
92	M 6	**Novokhopersk**, Russian Federation
93	S 4	**Novokuybyshevsk**, Russian Federation
88	M 13	**Novokuznetsk**, Russian Federation
145	R 1	**Novolazarevskaya**, Antarctica ⁙
87	V 6	**Novomoskovs'k**, Ukraine
92	L 3	**Novomoskovsk**, Russian Federation
93	N 6	**Novonikolayevskiy**, Russian Federation
93	P 8	**Novonikol'skoye**, Russian Federation
87	U 10	**Novoolekisiyivka**, Ukraine
87	U 7	**Novopokrovka**, Ukraine
87	Z 4	**Novopskov**, Ukraine
92	K 12	**Novorossiysk**, Russian Federation
89	Q 7	**Novorybnaya**, Russian Federation
87	T 11	**Novoselivs'ke**, Ukraine
93	V 4	**Novosergiyevka**, Russian Federation
92	L 9	**Novoshakhtinsk**, Russian Federation
88	M 12	**Novosibirsk**, Russian Federation
93	R 4	**Novospasskoye**, Russian Federation
87	U 10	**Novotroyits'ke**, Ukraine
87	Q 7	**Novoukrayinka**, Ukraine
93	R 6	**Novouzensk**, Russian Federation
92	G 4	**Novozybkov**, Russian Federation
85	M 18	**Novy Bykhaw**, Belarus
79	H 18	**Nový Jičín**, Czech Republic
91	P 4	**Novyy Bor**, Russian Federation
87	S 8	**Novyy Buh**, Ukraine
87	R 3	**Novyy Bykiv**, Ukraine
92	K 6	**Novyy Oskol**, Russian Federation
88	M 8	**Novyy Port**, Russian Federation
88	M 9	**Novyy Urengoy**, Russian Federation
89	V 13	**Novyy Urgal**, Russian Federation
79	I 15	**Nowa**, Poland
79	M 16	**Nowa Dęba**, Poland
79	F 16	**Nowa Ruda**, Poland
78	E 10	**Nowogard**, Poland
135	U 12	**Nowra**, NSW, Australia
101	W 6	**Nowshak**, Pakistan ▲
101	W 7	**Nowshera**, Pakistan
78	K 12	**Nowy Dwór Mazowiecki**, Poland
79	L 18	**Nowy Sącz**, Poland
79	K 18	**Nowy Targ**, Poland
88	M 9	**Noyabr'sk**, Russian Federation
65	R 3	**Noyon**, France
64	K 6	**Nozay**, France
130	I 8	**Nsambi**, Democratic Republic of Congo
133	R 6	**Nsanje**, Malawi
129	T 15	**Nsoc**, Equatorial Guinea
133	P 3	**Nsombo**, Zambia
129	Q 13	**Nsukka**, Nigeria
130	I 9	**Ntandembele**, Democratic Republic of Congo
133	R 5	**Ntcheu**, Malawi
130	D 7	**Ntoum**, Gabon
131	R 8	**Ntungamo**, Uganda
132	M 8	**Ntwetwe Pan**, Botswana ◢
112	J 9	**Nu Shan**, China ⛰
127	E 18	**Nuba Mountains**, Sudan ⛰
127	G 14	**Nubian Desert**, Sudan ◇
139	Y 10	**Nubu**, Fiji
45	U 13	**Nudo de Zempoaltépetl**, Mexico ▲
40	J 4	**Nueltin Lake**, NU, Canada ◢
46	K 5	**Nueva Arcadia**, Honduras
50	L 3	**Nueva Bolivia**, Venezuela
45	X 12	**Nueva Coahuila**, Mexico
51	P 2	**Nueva Esparta**, Venezuela ◘
56	I 13	**Nueva Galia**, Argentina
48	G 5	**Nueva Gerona**, Cuba
47	Q 10	**Nueva Guinea**, Nicaragua
52	C 8	**Nueva Loja**, Ecuador
57	G 19	**Nueva Lubecka**, Argentina
46	J 6	**Nueva Ocotepeque**, Honduras
56	L 6	**Nueva Pompeya**, Argentina
45	P 5	**Nueva Rosita**, Mexico
46	I 7	**Nueva San Salvador**, El Salvador
45	R 8	**Nueva Villa de Padilla**, Mexico
59	C 16	**Nueve de Julio**, Argentina
48	L 5	**Nuevitas**, Cuba
45	Q 6	**Nuevo Laredo**, Mexico
45	R 7	**Nuevo León**, Mexico ◘
127	O 20	**Nugaal**, Somalia ◘
138	J 3	**Nuguria Islands**, Papua New Guinea 🏝
106	I 9	**Nuh**, India
136	O 12	**Nuhaka**, New Zealand
140	F 5	**Nui**, Tuvalu 🏝
35	Q 3	**Nuiqsut**, AK, U.S.A.
138	J 5	**Nukiki**, Solomon Islands
138	B 3	**Nuku**, Papua New Guinea
140	I 11	**Nuku'alofa**, Tonga ⌂
140	F 6	**Nukufetau**, Tuvalu 🏝
140	G 6	**Nukulaelae**, Tuvalu 🏝
138	L 4	**Nukumanu Islands**, Papua New Guinea 🏝
140	K 6	**Nukunonu**, Tokelau Islands 🏝
140	J 6	**Nukunonu**, Tokelau Islands
141	P 15	**Nukuoro**, Federated States of Micronesia 🏝
102	M 10	**Nukus**, Uzbekistan
134	H 6	**Nullagine**, WA, Australia
134	M 10	**Nullarbor**, SA, Australia
134	L 10	**Nullarbor Plain**, WA, Australia ◇
111	F 15	**Nulu'erhu Shan**, China ⛰
107	R 9	**Num**, Nepal
117	V 11	**Num**, Indonesia 🏝
129	U 11	**Numan**, Nigeria
69	G 14	**Numansdorp**, Netherlands
123	J 15	**Numata**, Japan
123	K 17	**Numazu**, Japan
135	O 2	**Numbulwar**, NT, Australia
40	J 2	**Nunavut**, Canada ◘
63	S 7	**Nuneaton**, U.K.
107	X 12	**Nungba**, India
110	F 11	**Nungnain Sum**, China
34	L 9	**Nunivak Island**, AK, U.S.A. 🏝
89	Z 6	**Nunligran**, Russian Federation
68	K 11	**Nunspeet**, Netherlands
77	C 17	**Nuoro**, Italy
139	P 7	**Nupani**, Solomon Islands 🏝
99	N 5	**Nuqrah**, Saudi Arabia
50	G 6	**Nuquí**, Colombia
103	N 6	**Nura**, Kazakhstan
100	I 10	**Nūrābād**, Iran
103	P 12	**Nurata**, Uzbekistan
73	I 21	**Nuremberg**, Germany
44	J 5	**Nuri**, Mexico
93	S 2	**Nurlat**, Russian Federation
71	N 14	**Nurmes**, Finland
101	W 9	**Nurpur**, Pakistan
106	I 5	**Nurpur**, India
116	M 14	**Nusa Tenggara Barat**, Indonesia ◘
117	O 15	**Nusa Tenggara Timur**, Indonesia ◘
95	Q 13	**Nusaybin**, Turkey
101	S 11	**Nushki**, Pakistan
143	O 11	**Nuugaatsiaq**, Greenland
142	M 12	**Nuuk**, Greenland ⌂
143	N 11	**Nuussuaq**, Greenland ▶
143	O 10	**Nuussuaq**, Greenland
88	K 9	**Nyagan'**, Russian Federation
131	U 7	**Nyahururu**, Kenya
108	K 10	**Nyainqêntanglha**, China ▲
108	L 10	**Nyainqêntanglha Shan**, China ⛰
131	S 9	**Nyakaliro**, Tanzania
127	A 18	**Nyala**, Sudan
133	O 8	**Nyamandhiovu**, Zimbabwe
127	C 20	**Nyamlell**, Sudan
90	K 9	**Nyandoma**, Russian Federation
130	E 10	**Nyanga**, Gabon ◘
130	F 9	**Nyanga**, Congo
131	T 8	**Nyanza**, Kenya ◘
85	I 19	**Nyasvizh**, Belarus
133	O 7	**Nyathi**, Zimbabwe
115	E 15	**Nyaunglebin**, Myanmar
71	E 18	**Nybergsund**, Norway
71	C 25	**Nyborg**, Denmark
71	G 24	**Nybro**, Sweden
131	V 8	**Nyeri**, Kenya
127	E 20	**Nyerol**, Sudan
108	M 11	**Nyingchi**, China
79	N 22	**Nyírbátor**, Hungary
79	M 22	**Nyíregyháza**, Hungary
71	D 26	**Nykøbing**, Denmark
71	H 21	**Nyköping**, Sweden
71	H 21	**Nynäshamn**, Sweden
135	T 10	**Nyngan**, NSW, Australia
85	G 18	**Nyoman**, Belarus ⌇
74	A 9	**Nyon**, Switzerland
65	U 12	**Nyons**, France
91	S 10	**Nyrob**, Russian Federation
79	G 16	**Nysa**, Poland
122	J 10	**Nyūdō-zaki**, Japan ▶
131	P 11	**Nyunzu**, Democratic Republic of Congo
116	M 9	**Nyurang**, Indonesia
89	S 10	**Nyurba**, Russian Federation
89	S 11	**Nyuya**, Russian Federation
87	U 9	**Nyzhni Sirohozy**, Ukraine
87	U 9	**Nyzhni Torhayi**, Ukraine
87	U 11	**Nyzhn'ohirs'kyy**, Ukraine
130	E 10	**Nzambi**, Congo
131	S 10	**Nzega**, Tanzania
128	H 12	**Nzérékoré**, Guinea
132	F 2	**N'zeto**, Angola
131	P 10	**Nzingu**, Democratic Republic of Congo

O

Page	Grid	Name
122	H 8	**Ō-shima**, Japan 🏝
123	K 17	**Ō-shima**, Japan 🏝
34	C 7	**Oahu**, HI, U.S.A. 🏝
15	O 11	**Oak Bluffs**, MA, U.S.A.
30	J 4	**Oak City**, UT, U.S.A.
21	H 14	**Oak Creek**, WI, U.S.A.
31	P 3	**Oak Creek**, CO, U.S.A.
32	G 6	**Oak Harbor**, WA, U.S.A.
21	H 16	**Oak Lawn**, IL, U.S.A.
16	J 8	**Oak Ridge**, TN, U.S.A.
18	I 7	**Oakdale**, LA, U.S.A.
63	U 6	**Oakham**, U.K.
33	I 20	**Oakhurst**, CA, U.S.A.
17	Q 2	**Oakland**, MD, U.S.A.
23	P 13	**Oakland**, NE, U.S.A.
32	F 12	**Oakland**, OR, U.S.A.
33	G 19	**Oakland**, CA, U.S.A.
24	I 3	**Oakley**, KS, U.S.A.
29	N 13	**Oakley**, ID, U.S.A.
134	H 5	**Oakover**, WA, Australia ⌇
32	G 12	**Oakridge**, OR, U.S.A.
136	J 12	**Oakura**, New Zealand
136	J 6	**Oakura**, New Zealand
137	F 23	**Oamaru**, New Zealand
123	D 19	**Ōasa**, Japan
33	N 15	**Oasis**, NV, U.S.A.
145	R 14	**Oates Land**, Antarctica ◇
45	T 14	**Oaxaca**, Mexico
45	S 14	**Oaxaca**, Mexico ◘
88	L 10	**Ob'**, Russian Federation ⌇
42	B 5	**Oba**, ON, Canada
129	T 14	**Obala**, Cameroon
60	F 12	**Oban**, U.K.
137	D 23	**Obelisk**, New Zealand ▲
58	F 10	**Oberá**, Argentina
75	Q 8	**Oberdrauburg**, Austria
24	I 2	**Oberlin**, KS, U.S.A.
75	Q 5	**Oberndorf**, Austria
75	Q 4	**Oberösterreich**, Austria ◘
73	K 20	**Oberpfälzer Wald**, Germany ◇
75	Y 6	**Oberpullendorf**, Austria
73	H 26	**Oberstdorf**, Germany
75	R 8	**Obervellach**, Austria
75	X 6	**Oberwart**, Austria
117	S 11	**Obi**, Indonesia 🏝
54	G 10	**Óbidos**, Brazil
122	L 5	**Obihiro**, Japan
21	G 20	**Oblong**, IL, U.S.A.
89	U 14	**Obluch'ye**, Russian Federation
92	K 1	**Obninsk**, Russian Federation
131	O 4	**Obo**, Central African Republic
131	O 8	**Obokote**, Democratic Republic of Congo
85	K 14	**Obol'**, Belarus
87	S 5	**Obolon'**, Ukraine
78	G 12	**Oborniki**, Poland
130	H 8	**Obouya**, Congo
92	J 5	**Oboyan'**, Russian Federation
90	K 7	**Obozerskiy**, Russian Federation
78	E 12	**Obra**, Poland ⌇
80	K 11	**Obrenovac**, Serbia and Montenegro
33	F 14	**O'Brien**, OR, U.S.A.
82	N 7	**Obrochishte**, Bulgaria
94	H 11	**Obruk**, Turkey
88	L 8	**Obskaya**, Russian Federation ≈
143	X 10	**Obskaya Guba**, Arctic Ocean ≈
128	L 13	**Obuasi**, Ghana
87	P 4	**Obukhiv**, Ukraine
91	P 10	**Ob''yachevo**, Russian Federation
87	W 9	**Obytichna Kosa**, Ukraine ▶
87	V 10	**Obytichna Zatoka**, Ukraine ≈
19	W 9	**Ocala**, FL, U.S.A.
31	R 9	**Ocate**, NM, U.S.A.
136	K 6	**Ocean Beach**, New Zealand
14	J 15	**Ocean City**, NJ, U.S.A.
17	X 4	**Ocean City**, MD, U.S.A.
32	F 8	**Ocean Park**, WA, U.S.A.
19	N 7	**Ocean Springs**, MS, U.S.A.
33	K 26	**Oceanside**, CA, U.S.A.
87	Q 9	**Ochakiv**, Ukraine
95	Q 6	**Och'amch'ire**, Georgia
91	S 13	**Ocher**, Russian Federation
122	N 4	**Ochiishi-misaki**, Japan ▶
48	L 8	**Ocho Rios**, Jamaica
19	X 13	**Ochopee**, FL, U.S.A.
73	H 20	**Ochsenfurt**, Germany
19	U 5	**Ocilla**, GA, U.S.A.
19	U 5	**Ocmulgeee**, GA, U.S.A. ⌇
46	F 6	**Ocos**, Guatemala
45	W 13	**Ocosingo**, Mexico
47	N 7	**Ocotal**, Nicaragua
17	W 10	**Ocracoke Island**, NC, U.S.A. 🏝
53	J 21	**Ocurí**, Bolivia
123	D 18	**Ōda**, Japan
128	M 13	**Oda**, Ghana
122	J 9	**Ōdate**, Japan
123	K 17	**Odawara**, Japan
27	Q 13	**Odem**, TX, U.S.A.
66	G 11	**Odemira**, Portugal
94	C 11	**Ödemiş**, Turkey
71	C 25	**Odense**, Denmark
72	N 12	**Oder**, Germany/Poland ⌇
72	M 9	**Oderhaff**, Germany ≈
76	H 6	**Oderzo**, Italy
87	Q 10	**Odesa**, Ukraine
26	J 7	**Odessa**, TX, U.S.A.
32	J 7	**Odessa**, WA, U.S.A.
128	I 11	**Odienné**, Côte d'Ivoire
115	L 21	**Ôdôngk**, Cambodia
68	N 8	**Odoorn**, Netherlands
86	K 10	**Odorheiu Secuiesc**, Romania
79	K 14	**Odrzywół**, Poland
80	J 9	**Odžaci**, Serbia and Montenegro
54	M 12	**Oeiras**, Brazil
22	G 11	**Oelrichs**, SD, U.S.A.
73	K 18	**Oelsnitz**, Germany
135	N 1	**Oenpelli**, NT, Australia
95	P 8	**Of**, Turkey
96	E 10	**Ofaqim**, Israel
129	P 12	**Offa**, Nigeria
73	F 19	**Offenbach**, Germany
73	D 23	**Offenburg**, Germany
83	K 23	**Ofidoussa**, Greece 🏝
122	L 11	**Ōfunato**, Japan
122	J 10	**Oga**, Japan
122	K 11	**Ogachi**, Japan
127	M 21	**Ogadēn**, Ethiopia ◇
123	H 17	**Ogaki**, Japan
22	I 14	**Ogallala**, NE, U.S.A.
122	K 9	**Ogawara-ko**, Japan ◢
129	P 12	**Ogbomoso**, Nigeria
30	J 2	**Ogden**, UT, U.S.A.
19	W 4	**Ogeechee**, GA, U.S.A. ⌇
122	I 13	**Ogi**, Japan
38	A 10	**Ogilvie Mountains**, YT, Canada ⛰
129	S 13	**Ogoja**, Nigeria
40	M 10	**Ogoki**, ON, Canada ⌇
130	G 7	**Ogooué-Ivindo**, Gabon ◘
130	F 8	**Ogooué-Lolo**, Gabon ◘
130	D 8	**Ogooué-Maritime**, Gabon ◘
82	F 11	**Ograzden**, Macedonia (F.Y.R.O.M.) ⛰
84	F 11	**Ogre**, Latvia
80	C 9	**Ogulin**, Croatia
129	O 13	**Ogun**, Nigeria ◘
95	W 7	**Oğuz**, Azerbaijan
136	L 13	**Ohakune**, New Zealand
125	Q 10	**Ohanet**, Algeria
132	I 7	**Ohangwena**, Namibia ◘
137	K 15	**Ohau**, New Zealand
136	K 10	**Ohaupo**, New Zealand
56	F 12	**O'Higgins**, Chile ◘
13	U 9	**Ohio**, U.S.A., U.S.A. ⌇
79	B 16	**Ohře**, Czech Republic ⌇
82	B 12	**Ohrid**, Macedonia (F.Y.R.O.M.)
136	K 12	**Ohura**, New Zealand
54	I 8	**Oiapoque**, Brazil
54	I 8	**Oiapoque**, Brazil ⌇
41	S 1	**Oikiqtarjuaq**, NU, Canada
69	I 15	**Oirschot**, Netherlands
123	C 21	**Ōita**, Japan
83	E 18	**Oiti**, Greece ▲
20	D 10	**Ojibwa**, WI, U.S.A.
123	A 22	**Ojika-jima**, Japan 🏝
45	N 4	**Ojinaga**, Mexico
123	J 14	**Ojiya**, Japan
44	M 4	**Ojo de Laguna**, Mexico
138	A 4	**Ok Tedi**, Papua New Guinea
92	K 2	**Oka**, Russian Federation ⌇
117	Y 14	**Okaba**, Indonesia
132	I 9	**Okahandja**, Namibia
136	I 5	**Okaihau**, New Zealand
41	U 6	**Okak Islands**, NL, Canada 🏝
132	I 8	**Okakarara**, Namibia
132	I 8	**Okaputa**, Namibia
101	X 10	**Okara**, Pakistan
102	I 13	**Okarem**, Turkmenistan
137	E 19	**Okarito Lagoon**, New Zealand ≈
132	H 8	**Okaukuejo**, Namibia
132	J 7	**Okavango**, Namibia ◘
132	K 7	**Okavango**, Botswana ⌇
132	L 7	**Okavango Delta**, Botswana ◇
123	I 16	**Okaya**, Japan
123	F 19	**Okayama**, Japan
123	I 17	**Okazaki**, Japan
19	Y 11	**Okeechobee**, FL, U.S.A.
62	M 13	**Okehampton**, U.K.
89	W 12	**Okha**, Russian Federation
107	Q 9	**Okhaldhunga**, Nepal
91	S 13	**Okhansk**, Russian Federation
89	W 11	**Okhotsk**, Russian Federation
87	V 9	**Okhrimivka**, Ukraine
87	U 4	**Okhtyrka**, Ukraine
123	D 17	**Oki-shotō**, Japan 🏝
123	O 24	**Okinawa**, Japan 🏝
123	O 25	**Okinawa-shotō**, Japan 🏝
123	E 22	**Okino-shima**, Japan 🏝
123	N 23	**Okinoerabu-jima**, Japan 🏝
24	L 10	**Oklahoma**, U.S.A. ◘
25	N 10	**Oklahoma City**, OK, U.S.A.
25	Q 10	**Okmulgee**, OK, U.S.A.
130	G 8	**Okondja**, Gabon
130	H 8	**Okoyo**, Congo
115	D 15	**Okpo**, Myanmar
70	J 6	**Øksfjord**, Norway
91	P 3	**Oksino**, Russian Federation
89	Z 11	**Oktyabr'skiy**, Russian Federation
90	L 10	**Oktyabr'skiy**, Russian Federation
93	U 2	**Oktyabr'skiy**, Russian Federation
93	O 9	**Oktyabr'skiy**, Russian Federation
93	W 4	**Oktyabr'skoye**, Russian Federation
123	N 24	**Oku**, Japan
90	G 12	**Okulovka**, Russian Federation
122	H 7	**Okushiri-tō**, Japan 🏝
129	O 12	**Okuta**, Nigeria
25	T 11	**Ola**, AR, U.S.A.
47	V 14	**Olá**, Panama
84	F 11	**Olaine**, Latvia
33	K 22	**Olancha**, CA, U.S.A.
71	H 24	**Öland**, Sweden 🏝
135	Q 10	**Olary**, SA, Australia
25	R 4	**Olathe**, KS, U.S.A.
59	C 17	**Olavarría**, Argentina
79	G 15	**Oława**, Poland
77	C 16	**Olbia**, Italy
38	A 9	**Old Crow**, YT, Canada
29	R 9	**Old Faithful**, WY, U.S.A.
14	I 7	**Old Forge**, NY, U.S.A.
35	P 12	**Old Harbor**, AK, U.S.A.
61	C 21	**Old Head of Kinsale**, Republic of Ireland ▶
15	R 4	**Old Town**, ME, U.S.A.
39	N 19	**Old Wives Lake**, SK, Canada ◢
68	K 10	**Oldebroek**, Netherlands
72	E 11	**Oldenburg**, Germany
72	I 8	**Oldenburg in Holstein**, Germany
68	N 11	**Oldenzaal**, Netherlands
70	K 6	**Olderfjord**, Norway
63	R 3	**Oldham**, U.K.
14	D 10	**Olean**, NY, U.S.A.
78	M 9	**Olecko**, Poland
89	S 11	**Olekminsk**, Russian Federation
87	R 6	**Oleksandrivka**, Ukraine
87	W 7	**Oleksandrivka**, Ukraine
87	S 6	**Oleksandriya**, Ukraine
90	I 2	**Olenegorsk**, Russian Federation
89	R 8	**Olenëk**, Russian Federation ⌇
89	S 7	**Olenekskiy Zaliv**, Russian Federation ≈
87	S 11	**Olenevka**, Ukraine
90	I 4	**Olenitsa**, Russian Federation
79	G 15	**Oleśnica**, Poland
79	I 16	**Olesno**, Poland
86	M 2	**Olevs'k**, Ukraine
70	G 11	**Ølfjellet**, Norway ▲
108	M 2	**Ölgiy**, Mongolia
66	I 12	**Olhão**, Portugal
80	C 11	**Olib**, Croatia 🏝
58	J 5	**Olímpia**, Brazil
16	K 5	**Olive Hill**, KY, U.S.A.
66	J 9	**Olivenza**, Spain
39	L 14	**Oliver Lake**, SK, Canada ◢
23	Q 8	**Olivia**, MN, U.S.A.
93	P 7	**Ol'khovka**, Russian Federation
79	J 17	**Olkusz**, Poland
56	H 4	**Ollagüe**, Chile
63	T 4	**Ollerton**, U.K.
130	H 8	**Ollombo**, Congo
67	N 5	**Olmedo**, Spain
52	B 12	**Olmos**, Peru
21	G 21	**Olney**, IL, U.S.A.
27	O 5	**Olney**, TX, U.S.A.
79	G 18	**Olomouc**, Czech Republic
90	G 9	**Olonets**, Russian Federation
120	F 11	**Olongapo**, Philippines
64	M 14	**Oloron-Ste-Marie**, France
67	X 3	**Olot**, Spain
89	R 14	**Olovyannaya**, Russian Federation
85	K 18	**Ol'sa**, Belarus ⌇
78	K 9	**Olsztyn**, Poland
78	K 10	**Olsztynek**, Poland
86	I 10	**Olt**, Romania ⌇
74	E 6	**Olten**, Switzerland
86	L 13	**Oltenița**, Romania
95	R 8	**Oltu**, Turkey
121	I 22	**Olutanga**, Philippines 🏝
32	G 7	**Olympia**, WA, U.S.A.
89	Z 8	**Olyutorskiy**, Russian Federation
89	Z 9	**Olyutorskiy Zaliv**, Russian Federation ≈
127	H 17	**Om Hajēr**, Eritrea
122	J 8	**Ōma**, Japan
122	J 8	**Ōma-zaki**, Japan ▶
123	J 18	**Omae-zaki**, Japan ▶
122	K 11	**Ōmagari**, Japan
61	E 15	**Omagh**, U.K.
52	F 11	**Omaguas**, Peru
23	P 14	**Omaha**, NE, U.S.A.
132	J 9	**Omaheke**, Namibia ◘
32	J 6	**Omak**, WA, U.S.A.
137	D 23	**Omakau**, New Zealand
137	M 14	**Omakere**, New Zealand
95	U 6	**Omalo**, Georgia
99	Y 8	**Oman**, Asia ■
137	E 22	**Omarama**, New Zealand
132	I 9	**Omaruru**, Namibia
130	I 4	**Ombella-Mpoko**, Central African Republic ◘
130	D 9	**Omboué**, Gabon
127	F 16	**Omdurman**, Sudan
87	T 5	**Omel'nyk**, Ukraine
20	L 12	**Omer**, MI, U.S.A.
45	R 14	**Ometepec**, Mexico
100	G 9	**Omīdīyeh**, Iran
80	F 13	**Omiš**, Croatia
68	M 10	**Ommen**, Netherlands
109	Q 5	**Ömnögövi**, Mongolia ◘
127	G 22	**Omo Wenz**, Ethiopia ⌇
89	X 8	**Omolon**, Russian Federation ⌇
89	X 8	**Omolon**, Russian Federation
88	K 11	**Omsk**, Russian Federation
89	X 9	**Omsukchan**, Russian Federation
122	K 3	**Ōmū**, Japan
123	B 22	**Ōmura**, Japan
82	L 8	**Omurtag**, Bulgaria
132	G 7	**Omusati**, Namibia ◘
123	B 22	**Ōmuta**, Japan
91	Q 12	**Omutninsk**, Russian Federation
20	D 12	**Onalaska**, WI, U.S.A.
23	R 6	**Onamia**, MN, U.S.A.
20	K 10	**Onaway**, MI, U.S.A.
122	M 5	**Onbetsu**, Japan
132	G 6	**Oncócua**, Angola
132	H 7	**Ondangwa**, Namibia
79	M 19	**Ondava**, Slovakia ⌇
105	F 14	**Onder**, India
132	H 6	**Ondjiva**, Angola
129	P 13	**Ondo**, Nigeria
129	Q 13	**Ondo**, Nigeria ◘
109	S 4	**Öndörhaan**, Mongolia
105	K 20	**One and a Half Degree Channel**, Maldives ≈
90	J 7	**Onega**, Russian Federation
14	H 8	**Oneida**, NY, U.S.A.
14	H 8	**Oneida Lake**, NY, U.S.A. ◢
22	M 12	**O'Neill**, NE, U.S.A.
14	I 9	**Oneonta**, NY, U.S.A.
19	Q 2	**Oneonta**, AL, U.S.A.
86	L 10	**Onești**, Romania
90	I 6	**Onezhskaya Guba**, Russian Federation ≈
130	G 8	**Onga**, Gabon
136	K 12	**Ongarue**, New Zealand
109	Q 4	**Ongi**, Mongolia
111	K 18	**Ongjin**, North Korea
105	G 19	**Ongole**, India
95	S 6	**Oni**, Georgia
129	Q 13	**Onitsha**, Nigeria
89	U 11	**Onnes**, Russian Federation
123	H 16	**Ono**, Japan
139	X 12	**Ono**, Fiji 🏝
139	Z 13	**Ono-i-lau**, Fiji 🏝
123	B 21	**Ōnojō**, Japan
123	E 19	**Onomichi**, Japan
110	H 8	**Onor**, China
140	E 3	**Onotoa**, Kiribati 🏝
132	J 12	**Onseepkans**, Republic of South Africa
134	E 6	**Onslow**, WA, Australia
17	T 12	**Onslow Bay**, NC, U.S.A. ≈
32	L 11	**Ontario**, OR, U.S.A.
42	C 7	**Ontario**, Canada ◘
67	T 9	**Ontinyent**, Spain
20	F 8	**Ontonagon**, MI, U.S.A.
138	L 4	**Ontong Java Atoll**, Solomon Islands 🏝
135	O 8	**Oodnadatta**, SA, Australia
127	L 20	**Oodweyne**, Somalia
134	M 10	**Ooldea**, SA, Australia
25	Q 8	**Oologah Lake**, OK, U.S.A. ◢
69	D 18	**Oost-Vlaanderen**, Belgium ◘
68	I 6	**Oost-Vlieland**, Netherlands
69	B 17	**Oostende**, Belgium
68	J 5	**Oosterend**, Netherlands
69	H 15	**Oosterhout**, Netherlands
69	E 15	**Oosterschelde**, Netherlands ≈
69	C 15	**Oostersscheldekering**, Netherlands ≈
68	L 7	**Oosterwolde**, Netherlands
69	C 17	**Oostkamp**, Belgium
69	A 18	**Oostvleteren**, Belgium
115	L 23	**Ôp Luc**, Vietnam
131	N 8	**Opala**, Democratic Republic of Congo
91	O 11	**Oparino**, Russian Federation
79	L 16	**Opatów**, Poland
79	H 17	**Opava**, Czech Republic
19	S 4	**Opelika**, AL, U.S.A.
18	I 7	**Opelousas**, LA, U.S.A.
138	G 4	**Open Bay**, Papua New Guinea ≈
29	W 2	**Opheim**, MT, U.S.A.

■ Country ◘ Internal administrative region: State/Province/Territory/Dependent territory ⌂ Capital city ⛰ Mountain range/ Undersea ridge ▲ Mountain peak/ Volcano/Seamount ◇ Geographic feature ▶ Headland/Point/ Cape/Peninsula ◠ Desert 🏝 Island/Island group ⁙ Antarctic base ⊕ Ocean ◗ Sea ≈ Bay/Gulf/Channel/Strait ◢ Lake ⚑ Salt pan/Dry/ Intermittent lake ⌇ River

68 J 13 **Opheusden**, Netherlands
131 P 7 **Opienge**, Democratic Republic of Congo
87 U 4 **Opishnya**, Ukraine
90 D 13 **Opochka**, Russian Federation
79 K 14 **Opoczno**, Poland
79 H 16 **Opole**, Poland
102 J 8 **Opornyy**, Kazakhstan
136 N 10 **Opotiki**, New Zealand
19 Q 6 **Opp**, AL, U.S.A.
71 D 16 **Oppdal**, Norway
77 M 21 **Oppido Mamertina**, Italy
136 J 13 **Opunake**, New Zealand
132 G 7 **Opuwo**, Namibia
30 L 14 **Oracle**, AZ, U.S.A.
86 G 8 **Oradea**, Romania
106 K 11 **Orai**, India
30 L 9 **Oraibi**, AZ, U.S.A.
56 J 5 **Orán**, Argentina
124 K 6 **Oran**, Algeria
87 P 2 **Orane**, Ukraine
27 V 9 **Orange**, TX, U.S.A.
65 T 13 **Orange**, France
132 M 13 **Orange**, Republic of South Africa ∿
135 U 11 **Orange**, NSW, Australia
46 K 1 **Orange Walk**, Belize
17 O 13 **Orangeburg**, SC, U.S.A.
138 F 7 **Orangerie Bay**, Papua New Guinea ≈
42 E 12 **Orangeville**, ON, Canada
120 F 11 **Orani**, Philippines
72 L 12 **Oranienburg**, Germany
132 I 12 **Oranjemund**, Namibia
49 R 13 **Oranjestad**, Aruba ♜
132 M 8 **Orapa**, Botswana
121 M 15 **Oras**, Philippines
86 H 10 **Orăştie**, Romania
79 J 19 **Orava**, Slovakia ∿
86 F 11 **Oravița**, Romania
137 B 25 **Orawia**, New Zealand
76 F 13 **Orbetello**, Italy
135 T 13 **Orbost**, VIC, Australia
144 I 1 **Orcadas**, Antarctica ⁘
67 Q 10 **Orcera**, Spain
134 L 4 **Ord**, WA, Australia ∿
66 H 1 **Ordes**, Spain
94 M 8 **Ordu**, Turkey
31 T 6 **Ordway**, CO, U.S.A.
103 N 3 **Ordzhonikidze**, Kazakhstan
95 X 9 **Ordzonikidze**, Azerbaijan
79 A 17 **Ore Mountains**, Czech Republic ⛰
71 G 20 **Örebro**, Sweden
21 F 14 **Oregon**, WI, U.S.A.
32 H 12 **Oregon**, U.S.A., U.S.A. ▣
32 G 10 **Oregon City**, OR, U.S.A.
87 T 6 **Orel**, Ukraine ∿
92 J 3 **Orel**, Russian Federation
52 D 13 **Orellana**, Peru
94 C 12 **Ören**, Turkey
93 W 5 **Orenburg**, Russian Federation
93 V 4 **Orenburgskaya Oblast'**, Russian Federation ▣
59 C 19 **Orense**, Argentina
82 L 12 **Orestiada**, Greece
137 C 25 **Oreti**, New Zealand ∿
136 K 8 **Orewa**, New Zealand
31 Q 14 **Organ Peak**, NM, U.S.A. ▲
51 Y 6 **Organabo**, French Guiana
101 U 8 **Orgūn**, Afghanistan
87 N 8 **Orhei**, Moldova
67 S 2 **Orhi**, Spain ▲
46 M 6 **Orica**, Honduras
33 E 15 **Orick**, CA, U.S.A.
131 O 6 **Orientale**, Democratic Republic of Congo ▣
59 C 19 **Oriente**, Argentina
67 S 11 **Orihuela**, Spain
87 V 8 **Orikhiv**, Ukraine
87 V 5 **Oril'**, Ukraine ∿
87 V 5 **Oril'ka**, Ukraine
42 F 12 **Orillia**, ON, Canada
29 Y 12 **Orin**, WY, U.S.A.
51 O 4 **Orinoco**, Venezuela ∿
138 B 6 **Oriomo**, Papua New Guinea
105 I 16 **Orissa**, India ▣
84 E 7 **Orissaare**, Estonia
77 B 18 **Oristano**, Italy
71 O 16 **Orivesi**, Finland ☵
54 G 10 **Oriximiná**, Brazil
45 S 12 **Orizaba**, Mexico
71 E 24 **Örkelljunga**, Sweden
60 H 7 **Orkney Islands**, U.K. ⊕
26 H 7 **Orla**, TX, U.S.A.
58 K 5 **Orlândia**, Brazil
19 W 10 **Orlando**, FL, U.S.A.
15 P 10 **Orleans**, MA, U.S.A.
33 F 15 **Orleans**, CA, U.S.A.
65 P 6 **Orléans**, France
92 K 4 **Orlovskaya Oblast'**, Russian Federation ▣
93 N 10 **Orlovskiy**, Russian Federation
65 Q 4 **Orly**, France
101 R 14 **Ormara**, Pakistan
121 L 16 **Ormoc**, Philippines
19 X 9 **Ormond Beach**, FL, U.S.A.
63 P 3 **Ormskirk**, U.K.
83 G 14 **Ormylia**, Greece
78 K 9 **Orneta**, Poland
71 I 21 **Ornö**, Sweden ⊕
31 P 3 **Orno Peak**, CO, U.S.A. ▲
71 I 15 **Örnsköldsvik**, Sweden
128 K 10 **Orodara**, Burkina Faso
28 K 5 **Orofino**, ID, U.S.A.
109 P 4 **Orog Nuur**, Mongolia ☵
31 Q 14 **Orogrande**, NM, U.S.A.
141 P 15 **Oroluk**, Federated States of Micronesia ⊕
127 H 20 **Oromia**, Ethiopia ▣
43 S 9 **Oromocto**, NB, Canada
96 F 11 **Oron**, Israel
129 S 14 **Oron**, Nigeria
140 J 4 **Orona**, Kiribati ⊕
121 K 20 **Oroquieta**, Philippines
83 J 26 **Oros Kofinas**, Greece ▲
77 D 17 **Orosei**, Italy
79 L 25 **Orosháza**, Hungary
33 K 15 **Orovada**, NV, U.S.A.
33 G 17 **Oroville**, CA, U.S.A.
110 H 7 **Orqohan**, China
85 M 16 **Orsha**, Belarus
74 D 11 **Orsières**, Switzerland
88 H 11 **Orsk**, Russian Federation
86 G 12 **Orşova**, Romania
94 H 13 **Orta Toroslar**, Turkey ⛰
94 I 12 **Ortaköy**, Turkey
75 Y 3 **Orth an der Donau**, Austria
64 L 14 **Orthez**, France
53 I 16 **Orthon**, Bolivia ∿
66 I 1 **Ortigueira**, Spain
44 J 5 **Ortiz**, Mexico
76 J 13 **Ortona**, Italy
23 O 7 **Ortonville**, MN, U.S.A.
100 F 3 **Orūmīyeh**, Iran
53 J 20 **Oruro**, Bolivia
53 I 21 **Oruro**, Bolivia ▣
71 D 22 **Orust**, Sweden ⊕
76 G 12 **Orvieto**, Italy
144 K 6 **Orville Coast**, Antarctica ◇
21 O 16 **Orwell**, OH, U.S.A.
82 H 6 **Oryakhovo**, Bulgaria
76 D 7 **Orzinuovi**, Italy
78 M 9 **Orzysz**, Poland
91 S 13 **Osa**, Russian Federation
23 T 10 **Osage**, IA, U.S.A.
123 G 18 **Ōsaka**, Japan
123 G 18 **Ōsaka-wan**, Japan ≈
103 S 4 **Osakarovka**, Kazakhstan
24 L 3 **Osborne**, KS, U.S.A.
77 C 16 **Oschiri**, Italy
20 L 12 **Oscoda**, MI, U.S.A.
80 J 11 **Osečina**, Serbia and Montenegro
42 I 11 **Osgoode**, ON, Canada
103 T 12 **Osh**, Kyrgyzstan
132 H 7 **Oshakati**, Namibia
122 I 7 **Oshamambe**, Japan
132 H 7 **Oshana**, Namibia ▣
42 F 12 **Oshawa**, ON, Canada
122 L 12 **Oshika-hantō**, Japan ▶
132 H 7 **Oshikango**, Namibia
132 I 7 **Oshikoto**, Namibia ▣
122 I 7 **Oshima-hantō**, Japan ▶
20 G 12 **Oshkosh**, WI, U.S.A.
22 H 14 **Oshkosh**, NE, U.S.A.
129 P 12 **Oshogbo**, Nigeria
103 T 12 **Oshskaya Oblast'**, Kyrgyzstan ▣
130 K 10 **Oshwe**, Democratic Republic of Congo
80 I 8 **Osijek**, Croatia
23 T 13 **Oskaloosa**, IA, U.S.A.
71 G 23 **Oskarshamn**, Sweden
87 X 4 **Oskol**, Ukraine ∿
71 D 20 **Oslo**, Norway ♜
71 C 21 **Oslofjorden**, Norway ≈
94 J 8 **Osmancik**, Turkey
94 E 8 **Osmaneli**, Turkey
94 L 13 **Osmaniye**, Turkey
84 E 6 **Osmussaar**, Estonia ⊕
72 E 13 **Osnabrück**, Germany
82 D 10 **Osogovske Planine**, Macedonia (F.Y.R.O.M.) ⛰
58 I 12 **Osório**, Brazil
57 E 16 **Osorno**, Chile
67 N 3 **Osorno**, Spain
39 H 22 **Osoyoos**, BC, Canada
71 A 19 **Osøyra**, Norway
69 J 14 **Oss**, Netherlands
20 D 11 **Osseo**, WI, U.S.A.
89 Y 9 **Ossora**, Russian Federation
90 F 13 **Ostashkov**, Russian Federation
87 P 3 **Oster**, Ukraine
72 J 12 **Osterburg**, Germany
71 F 16 **Östersund**, Sweden
72 C 10 **Ostfriesische Inseln**, Germany ⊕
71 I 19 **Östhammar**, Sweden
76 F 8 **Ostiglia**, Italy
79 H 18 **Ostrava**, Czech Republic
78 J 9 **Ostróda**, Poland
86 L 4 **Ostroh**, Ukraine
78 L 11 **Ostrołęka**, Poland
89 Q 5 **Ostrov**, Russian Federation ⊕
90 D 13 **Ostrov**, Russian Federation
89 N 6 **Ostrov Arkitcheskogo Instituta**, Russian Federation ⊕
89 X 6 **Ostrov Ayon**, Russian Federation ⊕
89 T 6 **Ostrov Bel'kovskiy**, Russian Federation ⊕
88 M 6 **Ostrov Belyy**, Russian Federation ⊕
89 U 5 **Ostrov Bennetta**, Russian Federation ⊕
89 Z 10 **Ostrov Beringa**, Russian Federation ⊕
89 U 6 **Ostrov Bol'shaya Lyakhovskiy**, Russian Federation ⊕
89 R 7 **Ostrov Bol'shoy Begichev**, Russian Federation ⊕
95 Z 8 **Ostrov Bulla**, Azerbaijan ⊕
91 R 1 **Ostrov Dolgiy**, Russian Federation ⊕
89 N 4 **Ostrov Dzheksona**, Russian Federation ⊕
90 D 10 **Ostrov Gogland**, Russian Federation ⊕
89 O 3 **Ostrov Greem-Bell**, Russian Federation ⊕
89 O 5 **Ostrov Isachenko**, Russian Federation ⊕
89 Y 14 **Ostrov Iturup**, Russian Federation ⊕
89 Z 9 **Ostrov Karaginskiy**, Russian Federation ⊕
90 I 1 **Ostrov Kil'din**, Russian Federation ⊕
91 O 2 **Ostrov Kolguyev**, Russian Federation ⊕
89 P 4 **Ostrov Komsomolets**, Russian Federation ⊕
89 T 6 **Ostrov Kotel'nyy**, Russian Federation ⊕
102 G 8 **Ostrov Kulaly**, Kazakhstan ⊕
89 Y 14 **Ostrov Kunashir**, Russian Federation ⊕
89 U 6 **Ostrov Malyy Lyakhovskiy**, Russian Federation ⊕
89 R 5 **Ostrov Malyy Taymyr**, Russian Federation ⊕
89 Z 10 **Ostrov Mednyy**, Russian Federation ⊕
88 K 6 **Ostrov Mezhdusharskiy**, Russian Federation ⊕
90 L 4 **Ostrov Morzhovets**, Russian Federation ⊕
89 U 6 **Ostrov Novaya Sibir'**, Russian Federation ⊕
102 H 12 **Ostrov Ogurchinskiy**, Turkmenistan ⊕
89 P 5 **Ostrov Oktyabr'skoy Revolyutsii**, Russian Federation ⊕
89 N 7 **Ostrov Oleniy**, Russian Federation ⊕
89 Z 12 **Ostrov Onekotan**, Russian Federation ⊕
89 Z 12 **Ostrov Paramushir**, Russian Federation ⊕
89 P 4 **Ostrov Pioner**, Russian Federation ⊕
89 N 3 **Ostrov Rudol'fa**, Russian Federation ⊕
89 Z 13 **Ostrov Shiashkotan**, Russian Federation ⊕
89 P 4 **Ostrov Shmidta**, Russian Federation ⊕
89 N 7 **Ostrov Sibiryakova**, Russian Federation ⊕
89 Z 13 **Ostrov Simushir**, Russian Federation ⊕
89 T 6 **Ostrov Stolbovoy**, Russian Federation ⊕
89 Y 14 **Ostrov Urup**, Russian Federation ⊕
89 O 4 **Ostrov Ushakova**, Russian Federation ⊕
89 O 5 **Ostrov Uyedineniya**, Russian Federation ⊕
91 R 1 **Ostrov Vaygach**, Russian Federation ⊕
89 N 6 **Ostrov Vil'kitskogo**, Russian Federation ⊕
89 O 4 **Ostrov Vise**, Russian Federation ⊕
102 L 9 **Ostrov Vozrozhdeniya**, Uzbekistan ⊕
89 V 5 **Ostrov Zhokhova**, Russian Federation ⊕
89 U 5 **Ostrova De-Longa**, Russian Federation ⊕
89 O 6 **Ostrova Izvestiy Ts. I. K.**, Russian Federation ⊕
89 W 6 **Ostrova Medvezh'i**, Russian Federation ⊕
102 H 8 **Ostrova Tyulen'i**, Kazakhstan ⊕
90 L 13 **Ostrovskoye**, Russian Federation
78 M 11 **Ostrów Mazowiecki**, Poland
79 H 14 **Ostrów Wielkopolski**, Poland
79 L 15 **Ostrowiec Świętokrzyski**, Poland
79 H 14 **Ostrzeszów**, Poland
72 M 8 **Ostseebad Göhren**, Germany
75 O 8 **Osttirol**, Austria ▣
77 O 16 **Ostuni**, Italy
82 I 8 **Osŭm**, Bulgaria ∿
123 C 24 **Ōsumi-hantō**, Japan ▶
123 C 24 **Ōsumi-kaikyō**, Japan ≈
123 B 25 **Ōsumi-shotō**, Japan ⊕
129 P 13 **Osun**, Nigeria ▣
66 M 12 **Osuna**, Spain
14 G 7 **Oswego**, NY, U.S.A.
63 P 6 **Oswestry**, U.K.
87 W 9 **Osypenko**, Ukraine
137 E 22 **Otago**, New Zealand ▣
137 F 24 **Otago Peninsula**, New Zealand ▶
136 J 6 **Otaika**, New Zealand
137 K 15 **Otaki**, New Zealand
103 U 9 **Otar**, Kazakhstan
122 J 5 **Otaru**, Japan
52 B 8 **Otavalo**, Ecuador
132 I 8 **Otavi**, Namibia
123 K 14 **Ōtawara**, Japan
137 E 22 **Otematata**, New Zealand
84 H 8 **Otepää**, Estonia
32 J 8 **Othello**, WA, U.S.A.
83 A 15 **Othonoi**, Greece ⊕
137 G 19 **Otira**, New Zealand
132 I 8 **Otjiwarongo**, Namibia
132 J 8 **Otjozondjupa**, Namibia ▣
63 S 2 **Otley**, U.K.
109 R 7 **Otog Qi**, China
122 J 3 **Otoineppu**, Japan
136 K 11 **Otorohanga**, New Zealand
137 E 20 **Otorokua Point**, New Zealand ▶
71 B 20 **Otra**, Norway ∿
77 O 17 **Otranto**, Italy
89 Y 7 **Otrozhnyy**, Russian Federation
21 J 15 **Otsego**, MI, U.S.A.
123 G 18 **Ōtsu**, Japan
71 D 17 **Otta**, Norway
21 F 17 **Ottawa**, IL, U.S.A.
25 Q 4 **Ottawa**, KS, U.S.A.
42 I 10 **Ottawa**, ON, Canada ♜
42 H 9 **Ottawa**, QC, Canada ∿
37 S 9 **Ottawa Islands**, NU, Canada ⊕
71 G 25 **Ottenby**, Sweden
75 V 3 **Ottenschlag**, Austria
72 F 10 **Otterndorf**, Germany
76 D 8 **Ottone**, Italy
23 U 14 **Ottumwa**, IA, U.S.A.
129 R 13 **Otukpa**, Nigeria
129 R 13 **Otukpo**, Nigeria
56 K 8 **Otumpa**, Argentina
78 L 13 **Otwock**, Poland
74 K 8 **Ötztaler Alpen**, Austria ⛰
122 K 10 **Ōu-sanmyaku**, Japan ⛰
25 U 13 **Ouachita**, AR, U.S.A. ∿
25 S 11 **Ouachita Mountains**, AR, U.S.A. ⛰
128 G 5 **Ouadâne**, Mauritania
130 L 3 **Ouadda**, Central African Republic
129 Y 9 **Ouaddaï**, Chad ▣
128 M 10 **Ouagadougou**, Burkina Faso ♜
128 L 9 **Ouahigouya**, Burkina Faso
130 K 4 **Ouaka**, Central African Republic ▣
128 J 7 **Oualâta**, Mauritania
129 O 9 **Ouallam**, Niger
51 Z 7 **Ouanary**, French Guiana
131 O 4 **Ouanda**, Central African Republic
130 J 3 **Ouandago**, Central African Republic
130 M 2 **Ouandja**, Central African Republic
130 L 5 **Ouango**, Central African Republic
128 K 11 **Ouangolodougou**, Côte d'Ivoire
129 N 10 **Ouargaye**, Burkina Faso
125 O 8 **Ouargla**, Algeria
69 F 14 **Oude-Tonge**, Netherlands
69 D 19 **Oudenaarde**, Belgium
132 L 15 **Oudtshoorn**, Republic of South Africa
124 H 7 **Oued Zem**, Morocco
128 I 10 **Ouélésébougou**, Mali
130 H 7 **Ouésso**, Congo
129 T 13 **Ouest**, Cameroon ▣
130 I 3 **Ouham**, Central African Republic ▣
130 H 3 **Ouham-Pendé**, Central African Republic ▣
124 K 6 **Oujda**, Morocco
128 G 5 **Oujeft**, Mauritania
124 G 9 **Oulad Teïma**, Morocco
128 G 8 **Ould Yenjé**, Mauritania
125 N 7 **Ouled Djellal**, Algeria
70 L 13 **Oulu**, Finland
71 M 14 **Oulujärvi**, Finland ☵
70 L 13 **Oulujoki**, Finland ∿
129 Y 8 **Oum-Chalouba**, Chad
125 O 6 **Oum el Bouaghi**, Algeria
129 Y 9 **Oum-Hadjer**, Chad
124 F 8 **Ounara**, Morocco
70 K 10 **Ounasjoki**, Finland ∿
63 U 7 **Oundle**, U.K.
129 X 6 **Ounianga Kébir**, Chad
129 Y 6 **Ounianga Sérir**, Chad
110 J 4 **Oupu**, China
71 C 18 **Øure Ardel**, Norway
66 I 3 **Ourense**, Spain
54 N 13 **Ouricurí**, Brazil
55 J 19 **Ourinhos**, Brazil
69 J 22 **Ourthe**, Belgium ∿
63 T 2 **Ouse**, U.K. ∿
61 D 10 **Outer Hebrides**, U.K. ⊕
20 E 8 **Outer Island**, WI, U.S.A. ⊕
20 I 10 **Outer Island**, MI, U.S.A. ⊕
132 I 8 **Outjo**, Namibia
137 E 24 **Outram**, New Zealand
139 Q 13 **Ouvéa**, New Caledonia ⊕
135 R 12 **Ouyen**, VIC, Australia
94 I 14 **Ovacik**, Turkey
139 X 11 **Ovalau**, Fiji ⊕
56 F 10 **Ovalle**, Chile
132 G 7 **Ovamboland**, Namibia ◇
130 F 7 **Ovan**, Gabon
66 H 5 **Ovar**, Portugal
129 U 15 **Oveng**, Cameroon
69 G 19 **Overijse**, Belgium
68 M 11 **Overijssel**, Netherlands ▣
70 K 11 **Överkalix**, Sweden
25 R 4 **Overland Park**, KS, U.S.A.
134 F 8 **Overlander Roadhouse**, WA, Australia
69 J 17 **Overpelt**, Belgium
33 N 21 **Overton**, NV, U.S.A.
87 N 13 **Ovidiu**, Romania
49 Q 8 **Oviedo**, Dominican Republic
66 L 1 **Oviedo**, Spain
84 C 9 **Ovišrags**, Latvia ▶
109 P 4 **Övörhangay**, Mongolia ▣
70 J 9 **Övre Soppero**, Sweden
87 O 2 **Ovruch**, Ukraine
137 E 25 **Owaka**, New Zealand
130 H 8 **Owando**, Congo
123 H 19 **Owase**, Japan
23 S 9 **Owatonna**, MN, U.S.A.
137 C 26 **Owen Head**, New Zealand ▶
115 F 21 **Owen Island**, Myanmar ⊕
137 H 17 **Owen River**, New Zealand
42 D 11 **Owen Sound**, ON, Canada
138 E 6 **Owen Stanley Range**, Papua New Guinea ⛰
33 K 21 **Owens Lake**, CA, U.S.A. ☵
16 E 5 **Owensboro**, KY, U.S.A.
129 R 14 **Owerri**, Nigeria
129 Q 13 **Owo**, Nigeria
21 L 14 **Owosso**, MI, U.S.A.
32 K 13 **Owyhee**, OR, U.S.A. ∿
33 M 14 **Owyhee**, NV, U.S.A.
39 O 19 **Oxbow**, SK, Canada
71 H 21 **Oxelösund**, Sweden
14 H 9 **Oxford**, NY, U.S.A.
17 S 8 **Oxford**, NC, U.S.A.
18 M 2 **Oxford**, MS, U.S.A.
21 L 14 **Oxford**, MI, U.S.A.
63 S 10 **Oxford**, U.K.
137 G 20 **Oxford**, New Zealand
33 I 24 **Oxnard**, CA, U.S.A.
63 W 11 **Oxted**, U.K.
103 U 12 **Oy Tal**, Kyrgyzstan
123 H 15 **Oyabe**, Japan
123 K 15 **Oyama**, Japan
130 E 7 **Oyem**, Gabon
39 K 19 **Oyen**, AB, Canada
71 D 20 **Øyeren**, Norway ☵
129 P 12 **Oyo**, Nigeria ▣
129 P 12 **Oyo**, Nigeria
130 H 8 **Oyo**, Congo
53 C 15 **Oyón**, Peru
114 A 13 **Oyster Island**, Myanmar ⊕
95 T 11 **Özalp**, Turkey
121 K 21 **Ozamiz**, Philippines
25 T 10 **Ozark**, AR, U.S.A.
25 T 7 **Ozark**, MO, U.S.A.
25 S 8 **Ozark Plateau**, MO, U.S.A. ◇
79 K 21 **Ózd**, Hungary
89 Z 12 **Ozernovskiy**, Russian Federation
92 H 1 **Ozernyy**, Russian Federation
103 Q 9 **Ozero Akzhaykyn**, Kazakhstan ☵
103 X 7 **Ozero Alakol'**, Kazakhstan ☵
102 G 5 **Ozero Aralsor**, Kazakhstan ☵
103 Q 12 **Ozero Aydarkul'**, Uzbekistan ☵
90 I 10 **Ozero Beloye**, Russian Federation ☵
90 F 12 **Ozero Il'men'**, Russian Federation ☵
90 H 3 **Ozero Imandra**, Russian Federation ☵
102 I 6 **Ozero Inder**, Kazakhstan ☵
102 I 5 **Ozero Itmurinkol'**, Kazakhstan ☵
103 R 8 **Ozero Karakoyyn**, Kazakhstan ☵
103 U 5 **Ozero Karasor**, Kazakhstan ☵
90 H 4 **Ozero Kovdozero**, Russian Federation ☵
90 J 8 **Ozero Kozhozero**, Russian Federation ☵
90 K 11 **Ozero Kubenskoye**, Russian Federation ☵
103 P 3 **Ozero Kusmurun**, Kazakhstan ☵
90 J 9 **Ozero Lacha**, Russian Federation ☵
90 G 7 **Ozero Leksozero**, Russian Federation ☵
90 I 3 **Ozero Lovozero**, Russian Federation ☵
93 O 10 **Ozero Manych-Gudilo**, Russian Federation ☵
103 Z 5 **Ozero Markakol'**, Kazakhstan ☵
90 G 4 **Ozero Pyaozero**, Russian Federation ☵
103 X 7 **Ozero Sasykkol**, Kazakhstan ☵
90 H 7 **Ozero Segozerskoye**, Russian Federation ☵
89 Y 14 **Ozero Shikotan**, Russian Federation ⊕
103 S 2 **Ozero Siletiteniz**, Kazakhstan ☵
103 P 8 **Ozero Solonchak**, Kazakhstan ☵
89 Q 6 **Ozero Taymyr**, Russian Federation ☵
103 S 2 **Ozero Teke**, Kazakhstan ☵
103 Q 5 **Ozero Tengiz**, Kazakhstan ☵
90 G 5 **Ozero Topozero**, Russian Federation ☵
103 S 2 **Ozero Ul'ken Karoy**, Kazakhstan ☵
90 I 3 **Ozero Umbozero**, Russian Federation ☵
90 J 8 **Ozero Vodlozero**, Russian Federation ☵
90 J 10 **Ozero Vozhe**, Russian Federation ☵
90 I 7 **Ozero Vygozero**, Russian Federation ☵
87 N 11 **Ozero Yalpuh**, Ukraine ☵
103 Y 6 **Ozero Zaysan**, Kazakhstan ☵
85 C 16 **Ozersk**, Russian Federation
92 L 2 **Ozery**, Russian Federation
103 T 12 **Özgön**, Kyrgyzstan
77 C 16 **Ozieri**, Italy
79 H 16 **Ozimek**, Poland
93 S 5 **Ozinki**, Russian Federation
26 K 9 **Ozona**, TX, U.S.A.
78 J 13 **Ozorków**, Poland
123 D 21 **Ōzu**, Japan
45 S 10 **Ozuluama**, Mexico
95 R 7 **Ozurget'i**, Georgia

P

115 F 16 **Pa-an**, Myanmar
139 R 11 **Paama**, Vanuatu ⊕
142 M 13 **Paamiut**, Greenland
132 J 15 **Paarl**, Republic of South Africa
79 J 14 **Pabianice**, Poland
107 T 13 **Pabna**, Bangladesh
85 G 15 **Pabradė**, Lithuania
52 B 13 **Pacasmayo**, Peru
83 K 24 **Pachia**, Greece ⊕
77 K 24 **Pachino**, Italy
53 E 14 **Pachitea**, Peru ∿
83 H 26 **Páchnes**, Greece ▲
45 R 11 **Pachuca**, Mexico
8 C 9 **Pacific Ocean**, 0 ◎
121 K 17 **Pacijan**, Philippines ⊕
135 R 10 **Packsaddle**, NSW, Australia
32 H 8 **Packwood**, WA, U.S.A.
47 X 13 **Pacora**, Panama
116 D 11 **Padang**, Indonesia
116 D 10 **Padangsidimpuan**, Indonesia
116 I 11 **Padangtikar**, Indonesia ⊕
90 H 7 **Padany**, Russian Federation
119 U 6 **Padas**, Malaysia ∿
53 K 23 **Padcaya**, Bolivia
73 F 15 **Paderborn**, Germany
53 K 21 **Padilla**, Bolivia
86 L 12 **Padina**, Romania
76 G 7 **Padova**, Italy
27 Q 14 **Padre Island**, TX, U.S.A. ⊕
77 D 16 **Padru**, Italy
62 K 14 **Padstow**, U.K.
16 C 6 **Paducah**, KY, U.S.A.
26 M 4 **Paducah**, TX, U.S.A.
106 J 4 **Padum**, India
111 L 14 **Paektu-san**, China/North Korea ▲
111 J 19 **Paengnyŏng-do**, South Korea ⊕
136 L 9 **Paeroa**, New Zealand
94 G 15 **Pafos**, Cyprus
133 P 9 **Pafuri**, Mozambique
80 C 11 **Pag**, Croatia
80 C 11 **Pag**, Croatia ⊕
54 H 11 **Paga-Conta**, Brazil
121 J 21 **Pagadian**, Philippines
116 D 12 **Pagai Selatan**, Indonesia ⊕
116 D 12 **Pagai Utara**, Indonesia ⊕
140 B 6 **Pagan**, Northern Mariana Islands ⊕
83 F 17 **Pagasitikos Kolpos**, Greece ≈
116 L 12 **Pagatan**, Indonesia
82 L 13 **Pağayiğit**, Turkey
30 K 8 **Page**, AZ, U.S.A.
85 C 14 **Pagėgiai**, Lithuania
17 P 11 **Pageland**, SC, U.S.A.
140 K 8 **Pago Pago**, American Samoa ♜
31 P 7 **Pagosa Springs**, CO, U.S.A.
108 K 11 **Pagri**, China
118 D 8 **Pahang**, Malaysia ▣
118 D 8 **Pahang**, Malaysia ∿
137 L 15 **Pahiatua**, New Zealand
105 N 21 **Pahlagaon**, India
115 F 14 **Pai**, Thailand
84 G 7 **Paide**, Estonia
63 N 14 **Paignton**, U.K.
136 J 5 **Paihia**, New Zealand
71 M 17 **Päijänne**, Finland ☵
115 J 20 **Pailin**, Cambodia
57 F 16 **Paillaco**, Chile
64 J 4 **Paimpol**, France
116 D 11 **Painan**, Indonesia
21 O 16 **Painesville**, OH, U.S.A.
30 K 9 **Painted Desert**, AZ, U.S.A. ◇
16 L 5 **Paintsville**, KY, U.S.A.
67 Q 2 **País Vasco**, Spain ▣
32 I 13 **Paisley**, OR, U.S.A.
52 A 12 **Paita**, Peru
70 K 10 **Pajala**, Sweden
115 I 18 **Pak Thong Chai**, Thailand
51 Q 7 **Pakaraima Mountains**, Brazil/Venezuela ⛰
42 E 10 **Pakesley**, ON, Canada
129 R 10 **Paki**, Nigeria
101 U 12 **Pakistan**, Asia □
114 C 12 **Pakokku**, Myanmar
79 I 25 **Paks**, Hungary
101 U 8 **Paktīā**, Afghanistan ▣
101 U 9 **Paktīkā**, Afghanistan ▣
115 L 18 **Pakxé**, Laos
129 V 11 **Pala**, Chad
27 S 12 **Palacios**, TX, U.S.A.
53 K 17 **Palacios**, Bolivia
67 Y 4 **Palafrugell**, Spain
94 H 15 **Palaichóri**, Cyprus
83 G 26 **Palaiochora**, Greece
83 B 18 **Palairos**, Greece
106 I 5 **Palam Pur**, India
83 D 16 **Palamas**, Greece
67 Y 4 **Palamós**, Spain
89 Y 9 **Palana**, Russian Federation
120 I 7 **Palanan**, Philippines
120 I 7 **Palanan Point**, Philippines ▶
84 B 13 **Palanga**, Lithuania
116 K 12 **Palangkaraya**, Indonesia
105 B 14 **Palanpur**, India
133 N 9 **Palapye**, Botswana
101 X 6 **Palas**, Pakistan
19 W 8 **Palatka**, FL, U.S.A.
89 X 10 **Palatka**, Russian Federation
77 C 15 **Palau**, Italy
140 I 15 **Palau**, Oceania □
140 I 15 **Palau Islands**, Palau ⊕
120 H 5 **Palaui**, Philippines ⊕
115 F 19 **Palauk**, Myanmar
115 F 20 **Palaw**, Myanmar
121 D 19 **Palawan**, Philippines ⊕
121 B 19 **Palawan Passage**, Philippines ≈
84 F 6 **Paldiski**, Estonia
117 O 10 **Paleleh**, Indonesia
116 G 12 **Palembang**, Indonesia
33 M 25 **Palen Dry Lake**, CA, U.S.A. ☵
57 F 18 **Palena**, Chile
67 N 3 **Palencia**, Spain
77 I 21 **Palermo**, Italy
27 S 7 **Palestine**, TX, U.S.A.
96 F 10 **Palestine**, Israel ◇
114 B 12 **Paletwa**, Myanmar
105 D 22 **Palghat**, India
132 G 8 **Palgrave Point**, Namibia ▶
104 C 13 **Pali**, India
141 P 15 **Palikir**, Federated States of Micronesia ♜
121 K 23 **Palimbang**, Philippines
69 I 24 **Paliseul**, Belgium
105 B 15 **Palitana**, India
105 F 23 **Palk Strait**, Sri Lanka ≈
105 I 17 **Palkonda**, India
93 Q 7 **Pallasovka**, Russian Federation
105 G 21 **Pallavaram**, India
131 T 7 **Pallisa**, Uganda
29 Q 11 **Pallisades Reservoir**, ID, U.S.A. ☵
137 K 16 **Palliser Bay**, New Zealand ≈
106 G 8 **Pallu**, India
33 L 25 **Palm Springs**, CA, U.S.A.
67 Y 8 **Palma**, Spain
66 M 11 **Palma del Río**, Spain
48 M 6 **Palma Soriano**, Cuba
47 R 13 **Palmar**, Costa Rica
58 I 12 **Palmares do Sul**, Brazil
54 K 13 **Palmas**, Brazil
58 H 9 **Palmas**, Brazil
33 J 24 **Palmdale**, CA, U.S.A.
58 G 10 **Palmeira das Missões**, Brazil
54 L 12 **Palmeiras**, Brazil
58 I 8 **Palmeiras**, Brazil
35 Q 9 **Palmer**, AK, U.S.A.
144 H 4 **Palmer**, Antarctica ⁘
144 I 5 **Palmer Land**, Antarctica ◇
134 L 1 **Palmerston**, NT, Australia
137 F 24 **Palmerston**, New Zealand
141 N 10 **Palmerston**, Cook Islands ⊕
137 L 15 **Palmerston North**, New Zealand
77 L 21 **Palmi**, Italy
50 H 7 **Palmira**, Colombia
96 K 5 **Palmyra**, Syria
33 F 20 **Palo Alto**, CA, U.S.A.
47 Z 15 **Palo de las Letras**, Panama
50 G 4 **Palo de las Letras**, Colombia
56 M 7 **Palo Santo**, Argentina
119 O 9 **Paloh**, Malaysia
127 F 19 **Paloich**, Sudan
70 K 9 **Palojoensuu**, Finland
53 H 18 **Palomani**, Peru ▲
45 U 13 **Palomares**, Mexico
117 O 12 **Palopo**, Indonesia
53 E 18 **Palpa**, Peru
95 P 11 **Palu**, Turkey
117 N 11 **Palu**, Indonesia
117 O 15 **Palu**, Indonesia ⊕
120 F 13 **Paluan**, Philippines
116 H 14 **Pamanukan**, Indonesia
117 X 12 **Pamdai**, Indonesia
105 H 15 **Pamgarh**, India
75 Z 5 **Pamhagen**, Austria
65 P 15 **Pamiers**, France
103 U 14 **Pamir**, Tajikistan ◇
17 V 10 **Pamlico Sound**, NC, U.S.A. ≈
26 L 2 **Pampa**, TX, U.S.A.
56 K 7 **Pampa de los Guanacos**, Argentina
53 K 20 **Pampa Grande**, Bolivia
56 I 13 **Pampas**, Argentina ◇
50 J 5 **Pamplona**, Colombia
67 R 2 **Pamplona**, Spain
106 I 3 **Pampur**, India
94 E 8 **Pamukova**, Turkey
21 F 20 **Pana**, IL, U.S.A.
130 F 9 **Pana**, Gabon
45 Z 10 **Panabá**, Mexico
121 H 21 **Panabutan Bay**, Philippines ≈
33 N 20 **Panaca**, NV, U.S.A.
121 D 18 **Panagtaran Point**, Philippines ▶
82 H 9 **Panagyurishte**, Bulgaria
116 G 14 **Panaitan**, Indonesia ⊕
105 C 19 **Panaji**, India
47 V 14 **Panama**, North America □
47 W 13 **Panama Canal**, Panama ∿
19 R 8 **Panama City**, FL, U.S.A.
47 X 14 **Panama City**, Panama ♜
121 L 18 **Panaon**, Philippines ⊕
121 I 16 **Panay**, Philippines ⊕
121 I 18 **Panay Gulf**, Philippines ≈
80 L 10 **Pančevo**, Serbia and Montenegro
86 F 9 **Pâncota**, Romania
133 R 10 **Panda**, Mozambique
120 K 12 **Pandan**, Philippines
121 I 15 **Pandan**, Philippines
121 B 20 **Pandanan**, Philippines ⊕
116 L 11 **Pandang**, Indonesia
116 G 14 **Pandeglang**, Indonesia
84 G 13 **Pandėlys**, Lithuania
105 D 18 **Pandharpur**, India
105 F 15 **Pandhurna**, India
53 I 16 **Pando**, Bolivia ▣
47 S 12 **Pandora**, Costa Rica
107 V 11 **Pandu**, India
130 J 5 **Pandu**, Democratic Republic of Congo
84 F 13 **Panevėžys**, Lithuania
115 G 15 **Pang**, Thailand
131 O 6 **Panga**, Democratic Republic of Congo
140 I 10 **Pangai**, Tonga
131 W 11 **Pangani**, Tanzania
121 I 21 **Panganuran**, Philippines
131 O 9 **Pangi**, Democratic Republic of Congo
116 C 9 **Pangkalanbrandan**, Indonesia
116 J 12 **Pangkalanbuun**, Indonesia
116 G 12 **Pangkalpinang**, Indonesia
118 A 7 **Pangkor**, Malaysia ⊕
121 K 19 **Panglao**, Philippines ⊕
41 S 2 **Pangnirtung**, NU, Canada
130 L 3 **Pangonda**, Central African Republic
110 I 4 **Pangu**, China
57 F 16 **Panguipulli**, Chile
30 J 6 **Panguitch**, UT, U.S.A.
138 J 5 **Panguna**, Papua New Guinea
121 F 23 **Pangutaran**, Philippines ⊕
121 F 23 **Pangutaran Group**, Philippines ⊕
26 K 2 **Panhandle**, TX, U.S.A.
131 P 12 **Pania-Mwanga**, Democratic Republic of Congo
106 I 7 **Panipat**, India
103 R 14 **Panj**, Tajikistan
101 T 7 **Panjāb**, Afghanistan
103 Q 13 **Panjakent**, Tajikistan
101 R 13 **Panjgur**, Pakistan
111 H 15 **Panjin**, China
129 S 11 **Pankshin**, Nigeria
106 L 12 **Panna**, India
107 X 10 **Golaghat**, India
134 F 6 **Pannawonica**, WA, Australia
58 H 5 **Panorama**, Brazil
111 K 14 **Panshi**, China
118 A 7 **Pantai Remis**, Malaysia
55 G 17 **Pantanal**, Brazil ◇
117 Q 15 **Pantar**, Indonesia ⊕
77 G 24 **Pantelleria**, Italy
117 Q 15 **Pantemakassar**, East Timor
114 C 9 **Pantha**, Myanmar
116 D 10 **Panti**, Indonesia
45 S 10 **Pánuco**, Mexico
45 R 10 **Pánuco**, Mexico ∿
113 N 10 **Panxian**, China
112 L 9 **Panzhihua**, China
130 J 12 **Panzi**, Democratic Republic of Congo
46 I 5 **Panzos**, Guatemala
77 M 19 **Paola**, Italy
21 I 21 **Paoli**, IN, U.S.A.
79 G 23 **Pápa**, Hungary
60 I 6 **Papa Westray**, U.K. ⊕
55 F 14 **Papagaio**, Brazil ∿
136 L 12 **Papakai**, New Zealand
136 J 7 **Paparoa**, New Zealand
72 D 11 **Papenburg**, Germany
23 P 14 **Papillion**, NE, U.S.A.
84 G 13 **Papilys**, Lithuania
56 F 6 **Paposo**, Chile
105 H 17 **Pappadahandi**, India

□ Country ▣ Internal administrative region: State/Province/Territory/Dependent territory ♜ Capital city ⛰ Mountain range/Undersea ridge ▲ Mountain peak/Volcano/Seamount ◇ Geographic feature ▶ Headland/Point/Cape/Peninsula ◗ Desert ⊕ Island/Island group ⁘ Antarctic base ◎ Ocean ◒ Sea ≈ Bay/Gulf/Channel/Strait ☵ Lake ⚑ Salt pan/Dry/Intermittent lake ∿

H 5 Papua New Guinea, Oceania □
E 15 Papun, Myanmar
P 12 Paquera, Costa Rica
I 11 Pará, Brazil ▣
G 7 Paraburdoo, WA, Australia
V 8 Parachinar, Pakistan
M 12 Paraćin, Serbia and Montenegro
N 11 Paracuru, Brazil
I 7 Paradis, QC, Canada
J 16 Paradwip, India
K 10 Paragominas, Brazil
Y 9 Paragould, AR, U.S.A.
M 18 Paragua, Bolivia ∫
F 19 Paraguay, South America □
G 19 Paraguay, Paraguay ∫
O 13 Paraíba, Brazil ▣
N 6 Paraíba do Sul, Brazil ∫
K 19 Parainen, Finland
V 12 Paraíso, Mexico
W 12 Paraíso, Mexico
O 11 Parakou, Benin
X 6 Paramaribo, Suriname ⌂
B 16 Paramythia, Greece
K 14 Paranã, Brazil
L 10 Paraná, Argentina/Brazil ∫
C 13 Paraná, Argentina
H 8 Paraná, Brazil ▣
J 9 Paranaguá, Brazil
H 4 Paranaíba, Brazil
I 4 Paranaíba, Brazil ∫
I 18 Paranapanema, Brazil ∫
G 7 Paranavaí, Brazil
K 22 Parang, Philippines
L 17 Paraopeba, Brazil
T 4 Pārapāra, Iraq
M 7 Parati, Brazil
I 12 Parauapebas, Brazil
E 17 Parbhani, India
J 10 Parchim, Germany
N 14 Parczew, Poland
G 5 Pardoo Roadhouse, WA, Australia
E 17 Pardubice, Czech Republic
F 2 Pareh, Iran
H 4 Parengarenga Harbour, New Zealand ≈
K 7 Parent, QC, Canada
F 22 Pareora, New Zealand
N 12 Parepare, Indonesia
B 17 Parga, Greece
O 11 Parigi, Indonesia
G 10 Parintins, Brazil
J 5 Paris, KY, U.S.A.
D 8 Paris, TN, U.S.A.
H 19 Paris, IL, U.S.A.
S 4 Paris, TX, U.S.A.
Q 13 Paris, ID, U.S.A.
Q 4 Paris, France ⌂
L 10 Pārīz, Iran
E 9 Park Falls, WI, U.S.A.
Q 5 Park Rapids, MN, U.S.A.
K 17 Parkano, Finland
G 11 Parker, AZ, U.S.A.
N 3 Parkersburg, WV, U.S.A.
T 11 Parkes, NSW, Australia
N 11 Parkston, SD, U.S.A.
I 17 Parlakimidi, India
D 17 Parli, India
N 16 Parma, OH, U.S.A.
D 8 Parma, Italy
M 11 Parnaíba, Brazil
K 13 Parnaíba, Brazil ∫
E 18 Parnassos, Greece ▲
Z 4 Parndorf, Austria
E 22 Parnon, Greece ▲▲
F 8 Pärnu, Estonia
F 7 Pärnu-Jaagupi, Estonia
F 8 Pärnu laht, Estonia ≈
T 9 Paro, Bhutan
J 22 Paros, Greece ⸙
J 22 Paros, Greece
I 6 Parowan, UT, U.S.A.
W 5 Parramore Island, VA, U.S.A. ⸙
P 7 Parras, Mexico
Q 13 Parrita, Costa Rica
U 10 Parrsboro, NS, Canada
O 1 Parry Bay, NU, Canada ≈
N 4 Parry Channel, NU, Canada ≈
M 3 Parry Islands, NU, Canada ⸙
E 10 Parry Sound, ON, Canada
F 9 Parsęta, Poland ∫
D 9 Parsons, TN, U.S.A.
Q 7 Parsons, KS, U.S.A.
J 8 Partenen, Austria
M 8 Parthenay, France
I 20 Partizánske, Slovakia
W 4 Partney, U.K.
H 9 Paru, Brazil ∫
G 10 Paru de Oeste, Brazil ∫
D 12 Parvatsar, India
U 7 Parwān, Afghanistan ▣
L 19 Parychy, Belarus
T 10 Pasadena, TX, U.S.A.
J 24 Pasadena, CA, U.S.A.
B 8 Paşalimani, Turkey ⸙
D 12 Pasapuat, Indonesia
K 7 Pasaquina, El Salvador
N 7 Pascagoula, MS, U.S.A.
L 8 Paşcani, Romania
J 9 Pasco, WA, U.S.A.
D 15 Pasco, Peru ▣
J 13 Pascual, Philippines
N 10 Pasewalk, Germany
L 14 Pasfield Lake, SK, Canada ◒
G 11 Pasig, Philippines
Y 8 Pasighat, India
Q 9 Pasinler, Turkey
I 3 Pasión, Guatemala ∫
C 5 Pasir Mas, Malaysia
D 5 Pasir Putih, Malaysia
P 12 Paskūh, Iran
J 9 Pasłęk, Poland
J 8 Pasłęka, Poland ∫
Q 14 Pasni, Pakistan
H 2 Paso Caballos, Guatemala
H 18 Paso de Indios, Argentina
E 12 Paso de los Libres, Argentina
E 14 Paso de los Toros, Uruguay
R 13 Paso Real, Costa Rica
H 19 Paso Río Mayo, Argentina
H 22 Paso Robles, CA, U.S.A.
F 5 Passage Point, NT, Canada ▶
W 6 Passail, Austria
M 23 Passau, Germany
R 3 Passau, Austria
121 I 16 Passi, Philippines
58 H 10 Passo Fundo, Brazil
58 K 5 Passos, Brazil
85 I 15 Pastavy, Belarus
52 C 9 Pastaza, Ecuador ▣
50 G 9 Pasto, Colombia
101 Y 5 Pasu, Pakistan
116 K 14 Pasuruan, Indonesia
84 F 13 Pasvalys, Lithuania
121 G 24 Pata, Philippines ⸙
130 L 3 Pata, Central African Republic
57 G 22 Patagonia, Argentina ◇
105 B 14 Patan, India
105 F 14 Patan, India
107 Q 9 Patan, Nepal
117 S 10 Patani, Indonesia
63 Q 10 Patchway, U.K.
136 J 13 Patea, New Zealand
129 Q 12 Pategi, Nigeria
63 S 1 Pateley Bridge, U.K.
75 R 8 Paternion, Austria
77 K 22 Paterno, Italy
14 J 12 Paterson, NJ, U.S.A.
106 I 5 Pathankot, India
29 W 12 Pathfinder Reservoir, WY, U.S.A. ◒
115 G 22 Pathiu, Thailand
106 I 7 Patiala, India
121 G 24 Patikul, Philippines
107 Y 9 Patkroo Range, India ▲▲
83 L 21 Patmos, Greece ⸙
107 P 11 Patna, India
120 I 11 Patnanongan, Philippines ⸙
95 S 10 Patnos, Turkey
21 I 21 Patoka Lake, IN, U.S.A. ◒
54 O 12 Patos, Brazil
55 K 17 Patos de Minas, Brazil
56 H 9 Patquía, Argentina
83 D 19 Patra, Greece
83 C 19 Patraïkos Kolpos, Greece ≈
70 A 10 Patreksfjörður, Iceland
63 W 3 Patrington, U.K.
115 I 26 Pattani, Thailand
115 H 20 Pattaya, Thailand
15 R 3 Patten, ME, U.S.A.
107 U 14 Patuakhali, Bangladesh
47 P 5 Patuca, Honduras ∫
45 P 12 Pátzcuaro, Mexico
64 M 14 Pau, France
54 C 13 Pauini, Brazil
114 C 12 Pauk, Myanmar
38 E 8 Paulatuk, NT, Canada
54 O 13 Paulista, Brazil
54 N 13 Paulo Afonso, Brazil
25 N 11 Pauls Valley, OK, U.S.A.
114 C 9 Paungbyin, Myanmar
115 D 14 Paungde, Myanmar
106 K 7 Pauri, India
105 E 20 Pavagada, India
92 L 3 Pavelets, Russian Federation
76 C 7 Pavia, Italy
84 C 11 Pāvilosta, Latvia
82 J 8 Pavlikeni, Bulgaria
86 J 3 Pavlivka, Ukraine
103 U 4 Pavlodar, Kazakhstan ▣
103 U 3 Pavlodar, Kazakhstan
87 V 6 Pavlohrad, Ukraine
80 F 8 Pavlovac, Croatia
93 O 1 Pavlovo, Russian Federation
92 M 6 Pavlovsk, Russian Federation
92 L 11 Pavlovskaya, Russian Federation
76 F 9 Pavullo nel Frignano, Italy
118 A 15 Pawai, Singapore ⸙
25 P 8 Pawhuska, OK, U.S.A.
25 O 8 Pawnee, OK, U.S.A.
83 H 26 Paximadia, Greece ⸙
83 A 17 Paxoi, Greece ⸙
35 S 8 Paxson, AK, U.S.A.
115 E 15 Payagyi, Myanmar
116 D 11 Payakumbuh, Indonesia
74 C 8 Payerne, Switzerland
28 J 10 Payette, ID, U.S.A.
134 G 10 Paynes Find, WA, Australia
23 Q 7 Paynesville, MN, U.S.A.
64 L 6 Pays de la Loire, France ▣
58 E 13 Paysandu, Uruguay ▣
59 D 14 Paysandú, Uruguay
30 K 11 Payson, AZ, U.S.A.
30 K 3 Payson, UT, U.S.A.
116 G 12 Payung, Indonesia
50 K 6 Paz de Ariporo, Colombia
95 Q 7 Pazar, Turkey
94 F 7 Pazarbaşi Burnu, Turkey ▶
94 M 12 Pazarcik, Turkey
82 H 10 Pazardzhik, Bulgaria ▣
82 H 10 Pazardzhik, Bulgaria
80 A 9 Pazin, Croatia
39 H 16 Peace, AB, Canada ∫
39 H 17 Peace River, AB, Canada
30 H 9 Peach Springs, AZ, U.S.A.
33 F 16 Peanut, CA, U.S.A.
30 M 14 Pearce, AZ, U.S.A.
18 L 5 Pearl, MS, U.S.A. ∫
113 R 12 Pearl, China ∫
34 B 7 Pearl City, HI, U.S.A.
34 B 7 Pearl Harbor, HI, U.S.A. ≈
19 U 6 Pearson, GA, U.S.A.
37 N 2 Peary Channel, NU, Canada ≈
143 R 10 Peary Land, Greenland ◇
41 N 8 Peawanuck, ON, Canada
133 T 6 Pebane, Mozambique
52 G 10 Pebas, Peru
57 L 23 Pebble Island, Falkland Islands ⸙
81 K 15 Peć, Serbia and Montenegro
18 I 8 Pecan Island, LA, U.S.A.
91 P 3 Pechora, Russian Federation ∫
91 S 5 Pechora, Russian Federation
91 Q 2 Pechorskaya Guba, Russian Federation ≈
88 K 6 Pechorskoye More, Russian Federation ≋
26 H 8 Pecos, TX, U.S.A.
31 S 12 Pecos, NM/TX, U.S.A. ∫
69 C 20 Pecq, Belgium
79 H 26 Pécs, Hungary
47 W 15 Pedasí, Panama
49 P 8 Pedernales, Dominican Republic
132 F 6 Pediva, Angola
55 M 16 Pedra Azul, Brazil
55 E 14 Pedras Negras, Brazil
47 S 14 Pedregal, Panama
58 K 4 Pedregulho, Brazil
45 N 7 Pedriceña, Mexico
54 K 13 Pedro Afonso, Brazil
48 K 9 Pedro Bank, Jamaica ≈
56 G 5 Pedro de Valdivia, Chile
55 G 18 Pedro Juan Caballero, Paraguay
58 G 13 Pedro Osório, Brazil
21 M 20 Peebles, OH, U.S.A.
14 K 11 Peekskill, NY, U.S.A.
38 B 10 Peel, YT/NT, Canada ∫
61 G 16 Peel, U.K.
72 M 9 Peene, Germany ∫
72 M 8 Peenemünde, Germany
137 I 20 Pegasus Bay, New Zealand ≈
73 J 20 Pegnitz, Germany
115 D 15 Pegu, Myanmar ▣
115 E 16 Pegu, Myanmar
115 D 14 Pegu Yoma, Myanmar ▲▲
116 B 8 Pegunungan Barisan, Indonesia ▲▲
119 P 10 Pegunungan Boven Kapuas, Malaysia ▲▲
119 R 8 Pegunungan Dulit, Malaysia ▲▲
119 R 9 Pegunungan Hose, Malaysia ▲▲
119 T 10 Pegunungan Iran, Indonesia/Malaysia ▲▲
117 X 12 Pegunungan Maoke, Indonesia ▲▲
116 K 11 Pegunungan Muller, Indonesia ▲▲
116 J 11 Pegunungan Schwaner, Indonesia ▲▲
63 Z 11 Pegwell Bay, U.K. ≈
59 B 17 Pehuajó, Argentina
83 G 20 Peiraias, Greece
118 B 14 Peirce Reservoir, Singapore ◒
55 J 14 Peixe, Brazil
116 H 10 Pejantan, Indonesia ⸙
118 E 8 Pekan, Malaysia
116 E 10 Pekanbaru, Indonesia
118 B 8 Pelabuhan Kelang, Malaysia
119 X 5 Pelabuhan Sandakan, Malaysia ≈
116 M 10 Pelawanbesar, Indonesia
42 B 15 Pelee Island, ON, Canada ⸙
42 B 15 Pelee Point, ON, Canada ▶
117 P 11 Peleng, Indonesia ⸙
79 D 18 Pelhřimov, Czech Republic
48 K 1 Pelican Point, The Bahamas
82 C 13 Pelister, Macedonia (F.Y.R.O.M.) ▲
19 Q 3 Pell City, AL, U.S.A.
70 K 11 Pello, Finland
72 F 8 Pellworm, Germany ⸙
38 B 13 Pelly, YT, Canada ∫
40 M 1 Pelly Bay, NU, Canada
38 B 12 Pelly Crossing, YT, Canada
31 O 12 Pelona Mountain, NM, U.S.A. ▲
83 D 21 Peloponnese, Greece ▲▲
83 E 22 Peloponnisos, Greece ▣
58 H 13 Pelotas, Brazil
58 H 10 Pelotas, Brazil ∫
118 F 9 Pemanggil, Malaysia ⸙
116 I 10 Pemangkat, Indonesia
116 C 9 Pematangsiantar, Indonesia
133 N 6 Pemba, Zambia
133 U 4 Pemba, Mozambique
131 W 11 Pemba Channel, Tanzania ≈
131 X 11 Pemba Island, Tanzania ⸙
39 G 21 Pemberton, BC, Canada
134 G 12 Pemberton, WA, Australia
23 N 2 Pembina, ND, U.S.A.
20 G 10 Pembine, WI, U.S.A.
117 X 14 Pembre, Indonesia
42 H 10 Pembroke, ON, Canada
62 K 10 Pembroke, U.K.
63 O 9 Pen y Fan, U.K. ▲
63 R 1 Pen-y-ghent, U.K. ▲
67 N 1 Pena Prieta, Spain ▲
66 I 5 Penafiel, Portugal
67 N 4 Peñafiel, Spain
67 O 5 Peñalara, Spain ▲
54 L 11 Penalva, Brazil
58 I 5 Penápolis, Brazil
66 M 6 Peñaranda de Bracamonte, Spain
66 L 10 Peñarroya-Pueblonuevo, Spain
63 O 11 Penarth, U.K.
28 K 3 Pend Oreille Lake, ID, U.S.A. ◒
32 J 9 Pendleton, OR, U.S.A.
131 N 11 Penge, Democratic Republic of Congo
113 Y 12 P'enghu Tao, Taiwan ⸙
111 G 19 Penglai, China
113 P 7 Pengshui, China
114 B 12 Pengwa, Myanmar
113 O 6 Pengxi, China
116 L 15 Penida, Indonesia ⸙
57 G 25 Península Brecknock, Chile ▶
47 V 15 Península de Azuero, Panama ▶
57 G 25 Península de Brunswick, Chile ▶
47 O 12 Península de Nicoya, Costa Rica ▶
47 R 14 Península de Osa, Costa Rica ▶
57 E 20 Península de Taitao, Chile ▶
57 H 26 Península Hardy, Chile ▶
57 I 25 Península Mitre, Argentina ▶
53 D 18 Peninsula Paracas, Peru ▶
50 L 1 Peninsula Paraguaná, Venezuela ▶
57 E 21 Península Tres Montes, Chile ▶
57 J 17 Peninsula Valdés, Argentina ▶
59 B 19 Península Verde, Argentina ▶
57 E 22 Península Wharton, Chile ▶
43 S 6 Péninsule de Gaspé, QC, Canada ▶
41 P 5 Pèninsule d'Ungava, QC, Canada ▶
67 U 7 Peñíscola, Spain
97 V 3 Penjwin, Iraq
63 R 6 Penkridge, U.K.
64 H 6 Penmarch, France
76 J 13 Penne, Italy
145 Q 14 Pennell Coast, Antarctica ◇
61 I 14 Pennines, U.K. ▲▲
63 R 1 Pennines Dales, U.K. ◇
16 L 7 Pennington Gap, VA, U.S.A.
14 H 14 Pennsville, NJ, U.S.A.
14 E 12 Pennsylvania, U.S.A. ▣
135 N 10 Penong, SA, Australia
47 V 14 Penonomé, Panama
61 I 15 Penrith, U.K.
62 J 15 Penryn, U.K.
19 P 7 Pensacola, FL, U.S.A.
145 N 6 Pensacola Mountains, Antarctica ▲▲
53 M 18 Pensamiento, Bolivia
119 U 7 Pensiangan, Malaysia
139 R 10 Pentecost, Vanuatu ⸙
39 H 21 Penticton, BC, Canada
62 K 14 Pentire Point, U.K. ▶
135 T 5 Pentland, QLD, Australia
60 H 7 Pentland Firth, U.K. ≈
105 E 20 Penukonda, India
63 O 8 Penybont, U.K.
63 N 10 Penywaun, U.K.
93 P 4 Penza, Russian Federation
62 I 15 Penzance, U.K.
73 J 25 Penzberg, Germany
93 P 4 Penzenskaya Oblast', Russian Federation ▣
89 Y 9 Penzhinskaya Guba, Russian Federation ≈
21 F 17 Peoria, IL, U.S.A.
136 K 9 Pepepe, New Zealand
118 B 7 Perak, Malaysia ▣
118 B 7 Perak, Malaysia ∫
67 S 6 Perales del Alfambra, Spain
83 I 26 Perama, Greece
105 F 22 Perambalur, India
70 N 12 Peranka, Finland
43 U 6 Percé, QC, Canada
75 X 4 Perchtoldsdorf, Austria
134 J 5 Percival Lakes, WA, Australia ◒
86 H 6 Perechyn, Ukraine
50 H 6 Pereira, Colombia
58 H 5 Pereira Barreto, Brazil
93 N 8 Perelazovskiy, Russian Federation
93 S 5 Perelyub, Russian Federation
86 J 4 Peremyshlyany, Ukraine
87 V 5 Pereshchepyne, Ukraine
90 J 14 Pereslavl'-Zalesskiy, Russian Federation
93 V 5 Perevolotskiy, Russian Federation
87 Q 4 Pereyaslav-Khmel'nyts'kyy, Ukraine
33 H 14 Perez, CA, U.S.A.
75 T 4 Perg, Austria
59 C 15 Pergamino, Argentina
118 D 5 Perhentian Besar, Malaysia ⸙
71 K 15 Perhonjoki, Finland ∫
41 S 10 Péribonca, QC, Canada ∫
56 I 6 Perico, Argentina
44 L 7 Pericos, Mexico
65 O 11 Périgueux, France
83 H 17 Peristera, Greece ⸙
57 G 20 Perito Moreno, Argentina
72 K 11 Perleberg, Germany
118 A 4 Perlis, Malaysia ▣
91 T 12 Perm', Russian Federation
81 L 21 Përmet, Albania
91 T 12 Permskaya Oblast', Russian Federation ▣
80 B 11 Permuda, Croatia ⸙
54 O 13 Pernambuco, Brazil ▣
82 F 9 Pernik, Bulgaria ▣
82 F 9 Pernik, Bulgaria
75 W 5 Pernitz, Austria
45 S 12 Perote, Mexico
65 R 15 Perpignan, France
62 J 14 Perranporth, U.K.
27 O 5 Perrin, TX, U.S.A.
19 T 4 Perry, GA, U.S.A.
19 T 8 Perry, FL, U.S.A.
25 N 9 Perry, OK, U.S.A.
25 Q 3 Perry Lake, KS, U.S.A. ◒
26 L 1 Perryton, TX, U.S.A.
53 L 18 Perseverancia, Bolivia
99 T 3 Persian Gulf, Asia ≈
42 I 11 Perth, ON, Canada
60 I 12 Perth, U.K.
134 G 11 Perth, WA, Australia
64 L 9 Pertuis Breton, France ≈
64 L 9 Pertuis d'Antioche, France ≈
21 J 18 Peru, IN, U.S.A.
53 E 15 Peru, South America □
53 J 16 Perú, Bolivia
76 G 11 Perugia, Italy
58 D 12 Perugorría, Argentina
58 K 8 Peruíbe, Brazil
69 D 21 Peruwelz, Belgium
87 Q 7 Pervomays'k, Ukraine
87 T 11 Pervomays'ke, Ukraine
92 M 3 Pervomayskiy, Russian Federation
93 W 5 Pervomayskiy, Russian Federation
87 V 5 Pervomays'kyy, Ukraine
89 Y 8 Pervorechenskiy, Russian Federation
88 I 10 Pervoural'sk, Russian Federation
76 H 10 Pesaro, Italy
76 J 13 Pescara, Italy
101 W 7 Peshawar, Pakistan
81 L 17 Peshkopi, Albania
82 H 10 Peshtera, Bulgaria
103 R 9 Peski Muyunkum, Kazakhstan ◇
103 V 8 Peski Saryyesik-Atyrau, Kazakhstan ◇
103 U 9 Peski Taukum, Kazakhstan ◇
46 L 7 Pespire, Honduras
90 H 12 Pestovo, Russian Federation
96 F 9 Petah Tiqwa, Israel
83 D 22 Petalidi, Greece
33 F 19 Petaluma, CA, U.S.A.
69 K 26 Pètange, Luxembourg
45 P 13 Petatlán, Mexico
133 P 5 Petauke, Zambia
20 E 12 Petenwell Lake, WI, U.S.A. ◒
144 H 8 Peter I Island, Norway ⸙
39 K 16 Peter Pond Lake, SK, Canada ◒
42 B 6 Peterbell, ON, Canada
42 F 12 Peterborough, ON, Canada
63 V 7 Peterborough, U.K.
135 P 11 Peterborough, SA, Australia
60 J 10 Peterhead, U.K.
143 P 12 Petermann Bjerg, Greenland ▲
17 T 6 Petersburg, VA, U.S.A.
35 X 11 Petersburg, AK, U.S.A.
63 T 12 Petersfield, U.K.
43 T 9 Petitodiac, NB, Canada
39 F 15 Petitot, BC, Canada ∫
45 Z 11 Peto, Mexico
20 K 10 Petoskey, MI, U.S.A.
96 G 12 Petra, Jordan
82 F 12 Petrich, Bulgaria
87 P 9 Petrivka, Ukraine
87 U 9 Petrivka, Ukraine
50 J 4 Petrólea, Colombia
54 N 13 Petrolina, Brazil
103 R 1 Petropavlovsk, Kazakhstan
89 Z 11 Petropavlovsk-Kamchatskiy, Russian Federation
58 N 6 Petrópolis, Brazil
86 H 11 Petroşani, Romania
93 P 4 Petrovsk, Russian Federation
89 Q 14 Petrovsk-Zabaykal'skiy, Russian Federation
90 G 9 Petrozavodsk, Russian Federation
86 M 7 Petruşeni, Moldova
87 U 6 Petrykivka, Ukraine
68 G 9 Petten, Netherlands
27 P 12 Pettus, TX, U.S.A.
88 J 11 Petukhovo, Russian Federation
92 L 1 Petushki, Russian Federation
63 U 12 Petworth, U.K.
75 S 3 Peuerbach, Austria
116 C 8 Peureula, Indonesia
89 X 6 Pevek, Russian Federation
79 G 21 Pezinok, Slovakia
101 V 9 Pezu, Pakistan
73 J 23 Pfaffenhofen an der Ilm, Germany
73 F 22 Pforzheim, Germany
73 G 25 Pfullendorf, Germany
74 K 8 Pfunds, Austria
133 P 10 Phalaborwa, Republic of South Africa
101 X 8 Phalia, Pakistan
104 C 12 Phalodi, India
115 O 21 Phan Rang, Vietnam
115 O 21 Phan Ri, Vietnam
115 O 22 Phan Thiêt, Vietnam
115 K 15 Phang Khon, Thailand
115 F 24 Phangnga, Thailand
107 R 9 Phaplu, Nepal
115 H 25 Phatthalung, Thailand
115 H 14 Phayao, Thailand
19 R 4 Phenix City, AL, U.S.A.
115 H 20 Phet Buri, Thailand
115 I 16 Phetchabun, Thailand
115 H 17 Phichit, Thailand
14 I 14 Philadelphia, PA, U.S.A.
35 R 4 Philip Smith Mountains, AK, U.S.A. ▲▲
69 G 22 Philippeville, Belgium
17 P 3 Philippi, WV, U.S.A.
120 L 11 Philippine Sea, 0 ≋
121 F 20 Philippines, Asia □
29 O 6 Philipsburg, MT, U.S.A.
24 L 2 Phillipsburg, KS, U.S.A.
115 J 18 Phimai, Thailand
115 H 16 Phitsanulok, Thailand
115 L 21 Phnom Penh, Cambodia ⌂
115 K 21 Phnum Aôral, Cambodia ▲
115 J 20 Phnum Tumpôr, Cambodia ▲
30 I 12 Phoenix, AZ, U.S.A.
140 K 4 Phoenix, Kiribati ⸙
140 H 4 Phoenix Islands, Kiribati ⸙
115 J 17 Phon, Thailand
114 K 11 Phong Thô, Vietnam
114 I 11 Phôngsali, Laos
115 J 14 Phou Bia, Laos ▲
115 L 15 Phou Cô Pi, Laos ▲
114 I 13 Phou Houie Moc, Laos ▲
114 J 13 Phou San, Laos ▲
115 M 17 Phou Set, Laos ▲
115 K 14 Phou Xai Lai Leng, Laos/Vietnam ▲
115 H 15 Phrae, Thailand
115 K 22 Phsar Ream, Cambodia
115 N 16 Phu Lôc, Vietnam
114 M 12 Phu Ly, Vietnam
115 O 18 Phu My, Vietnam
115 O 19 Phu Nhon, Vietnam
114 L 12 Phu Tho, Vietnam
115 F 25 Phuket, Thailand
115 L 21 Phumi Banam, Cambodia
115 J 21 Phumi Kaôh Kŏng, Cambodia
115 M 21 Phumi Krêk, Cambodia
115 L 19 Phumi Mlu Prey, Cambodia
115 K 19 Phumi Moŭng, Cambodia
115 K 20 Phumi Prâmaôy, Cambodia
115 K 19 Phumi Sâmraông, Cambodia
115 K 22 Phumi Veal Renh, Cambodia
115 L 23 Phuoc Long, Vietnam
76 D 8 Piacenza, Italy
76 E 8 Piadena, Italy
111 A 17 Pianguan, China
78 L 13 Piaseczno, Poland
79 N 15 Piaski, Poland
86 L 9 Piatra Neamţ, Romania
54 L 13 Piauí, Brazil ▣
54 L 13 Piauí, Brazil ∫
127 F 21 Pibor Post, Sudan
49 P 8 Pic de la Selle, Haiti ▲
128 H 12 Pic de Tibé, Guinea ▲
65 O 15 Pic d'Estats, France/Spain ▲
64 L 15 Pic d'Orhy, France ▲
56 G 3 Pica, Chile
45 O 4 Picacho del Centinela, Mexico ▲
65 Q 3 Picardie, France ▣
18 M 7 Picayune, MS, U.S.A.
56 J 5 Pichanal, Argentina
57 J 15 Pichi Mahuida, Argentina
56 F 12 Pichilemu, Chile
44 J 8 Pichilingue, Mexico
52 B 8 Pichincha, Ecuador ▣
63 U 1 Pickering, U.K.
40 L 10 Pickle Lake, ON, Canada
22 M 11 Pickstown, SD, U.S.A.
129 S 15 Pico Basile, Equatorial Guinea ▲
50 K 4 Pico Bolívar, Venezuela ▲
50 I 2 Pico Cristóbal Colón, Colombia ▲
54 D 9 Pico da Neblina, Brazil ▲
58 N 5 Pico das Bandeiras, Brazil ▲
55 L 17 Pico de Itambé, Brazil ▲
45 S 12 Pico de Orizaba, Mexico ▲
130 B 7 Pico de São Tomé, São Tomé and Príncipe ▲
49 Q 7 Pico Duarte, Dominican Republic ▲
48 I 4 Pico San Juan, Cuba ▲
54 D 9 Pico Tamacuari, Brazil ▲
57 H 20 Pico Truncado, Argentina
48 L 6 Pico Turquino, Cuba ▲
54 M 12 Picos, Brazil
52 D 13 Picota, Peru
42 H 12 Picton, ON, Canada
137 J 16 Picton, New Zealand
43 W 9 Pictou, NS, Canada
57 G 15 Picún Leufú, Argentina
101 Q 14 Pidarak, Pakistan
86 J 5 Pidhaytsi, Ukraine
105 G 25 Pidurutalagala, Sri Lanka ▲
17 O 10 Piedmont, NC, U.S.A. ▲▲
19 R 3 Piedmont, AL, U.S.A.
66 L 6 Piedrahita, Spain
45 Q 5 Piedras Negras, Mexico
46 G 2 Piedras Negras, Guatemala
71 N 16 Pieksämäki, Finland
71 O 15 Pielinen, Finland ◒
76 B 8 Piemonte, Italy ▣
78 J 8 Pieniężno, Poland
22 J 9 Pierre, SD, U.S.A.
79 H 20 Piešt'any, Slovakia
133 P 11 Piet Retief, Republic of South Africa
133 P 12 Pietermaritzburg, Republic of South Africa
133 O 10 Pietersburg, Republic of South Africa
76 H 5 Pieve di Cadóre, Italy
57 K 14 Pigüé, Argentina
59 B 18 Pigüe, Argentina
106 L 9 Pihani, India
71 L 15 Pihtipudas, Finland
45 V 14 Pijijiapan, Mexico
103 W 11 Pik Dankova, Kyrgyzstan ▲
103 Y 10 Pik Khan-Tengri, Kazakhstan/Kyrgyzstan ▲
132 J 15 Piketberg, Republic of South Africa
21 M 20 Piketon, OH, U.S.A.
16 L 6 Pikeville, KY, U.S.A.
16 I 9 Pikeville, TN, U.S.A.
121 L 22 Pikit, Philippines
111 I 17 Pikou, China
130 I 7 Pikounda, Congo
59 D 17 Pila, Argentina
78 G 11 Piła, Poland
55 G 20 Pilar, Paraguay
59 D 15 Pilar, Argentina
121 H 23 Pilas, Philippines ⸙
134 H 6 Pilbara, WA, Australia ◇
57 G 17 Pilcaniyeu, Argentina
56 K 5 Pilcomayo, Argentina ∫
105 F 21 Pileru, India
120 J 13 Pili, Philippines
106 L 8 Pilibhit, India
79 K 14 Pilica, Poland ∫
53 G 17 Pillcopata, Peru
48 K 6 Pilón, Cuba
32 J 10 Pilot Rock, OR, U.S.A.
79 L 17 Pilzno, Poland
55 E 14 Pimenta Bueno, Brazil
67 T 4 Pina, Spain
120 H 13 Pinamalayan, Philippines
118 A 5 Pinang, Malaysia ▣
118 A 6 Pinang, Malaysia ⸙
119 V 6 Pinangah, Malaysia
48 F 4 Pinar del Río, Cuba
94 L 11 Pinarbaşi, Turkey
94 C 6 Pinarhisar, Turkey
63 V 6 Pinchbeck, U.K.
39 J 21 Pincher Creek, AB, Canada
101 X 9 Pindi Bhattian, Pakistan
101 W 8 Pindi Gheb, Pakistan
83 B 15 Pindus Mountains, Greece ▲▲
104 B 13 Pindwara, India
25 W 12 Pine Bluff, AR, U.S.A.
134 M 2 Pine Creek, NT, Australia
40 I 9 Pine Dock, MB, Canada
40 I 10 Pine Falls, MB, Canada
19 W 10 Pine Hills, FL, U.S.A.
38 H 13 Pine Point, NT, Canada
22 H 11 Pine Ridge, SD, U.S.A.
23 Q 5 Pine River, MN, U.S.A.
29 S 12 Pinedale, WY, U.S.A.
90 L 6 Pinega, Russian Federation
39 L 16 Pinehouse Lake, SK, Canada
83 E 16 Pineios, Greece ∫
27 U 8 Pineland, TX, U.S.A.
76 A 8 Pinerolo, Italy
18 I 6 Pineville, LA, U.S.A.
109 P 8 Ping'an, China
113 P 6 Pingchang, China
113 T 4 Pingdingshan, China
111 G 20 Pingdu, China
141 R 15 Pingelap, Federated States of Micronesia ⸙
113 P 12 Pingguo, China
113 W 11 Pinghe, China
113 Z 6 Pinghu, China
113 T 8 Pingjiang, China
113 R 11 Pingle, China
113 Q 5 Pingli, China
113 O 2 Pingliang, China
111 F 16 Pingquan, China
22 L 5 Pingree, ND, U.S.A.
113 T 13 Pingsha, China
113 Y 10 Pingtan, China
113 Z 12 P'ingtung, Taiwan
113 N 5 Pingwu, China
113 T 9 Pingxiang, China
113 O 13 Pingxiang, China
113 Z 8 Pingyang, China
113 S 1 Pingyao, China
113 W 2 Pingyi, China
113 V 2 Pingyin, China
54 L 10 Pinheiro, Brazil
58 G 13 Pinheiro Machado, Brazil
66 J 6 Pinhel, Portugal
63 N 13 Pinhoe, U.K.
116 C 10 Pini, Indonesia ⸙
134 G 11 Pinjarra, WA, Australia
114 D 9 Pinlebu, Myanmar
135 Q 12 Pinnaroo, SA, Australia
67 S 10 Pinoso, Spain
45 S 14 Pinotepa Nacional, Mexico
85 H 21 Pinsk, Belarus
56 G 3 Pintados, Chile
58 A 12 Pinto, Argentina
121 M 18 Pintuyan, Philippines
131 N 12 Piodi, Democratic Republic of Congo
76 E 12 Piombino, Italy
136 K 11 Piopio, New Zealand
79 J 14 Piotrków Trybunalski, Poland
83 H 17 Piperi, Greece ⸙
23 P 9 Pipestone, MN, U.S.A.
136 K 13 Pipiriki, New Zealand
21 L 18 Piqua, OH, U.S.A.
106 G 3 Pir Panjal Range, India ▲▲
58 K 6 Piracicaba, Brazil
58 I 8 Piraí do Sul, Brazil
58 J 6 Pirajuí, Brazil
58 C 9 Pirané, Argentina
55 I 16 Piranhas, Brazil
55 L 16 Pirapora, Brazil
107 S 11 Pirganj, Bangladesh
54 M 11 Piripiri, Brazil
73 D 21 Pirmasens, Germany
81 O 14 Pirot, Serbia and Montenegro
117 S 12 Piru, Indonesia
101 R 9 Pirzada, Afghanistan
76 E 10 Pisa, Italy
56 F 3 Pisagua, Chile
77 K 17 Pisciotta, Italy
53 D 17 Pisco, Peru
79 C 19 Písek, Czech Republic
53 M 17 Piso Firme, Bolivia
45 Z 10 Pisté, Mexico
77 M 17 Pisticci, Italy
76 F 10 Pistoia, Italy
78 M 10 Pisz, Poland
128 G 10 Pita, Guinea
41 U 9 Pitaga, NL, Canada
58 H 8 Pitanga, Brazil
10 C 12 Pitcairn Island, U.K. ▣
70 J 13 Piteå, Sweden
70 I 12 Piteälven, Sweden ≈
86 I 12 Piteşti, Romania
65 Q 6 Pithiviers, France

ountry ▣ Internal administrative region: State/Province/Territory/Dependent territory ⌂ Capital city ▲▲ Mountain range/Undersea ridge ▲ Mountain peak/Volcano/Seamount ◇ Geographic feature ▶ Headland/Point/Cape/Peninsula ◭ Desert ⸙ Island/Island group ⁙ Antarctic base ◎ Ocean ≋ Sea ≈ Bay/Gulf/Channel/Strait ◒ Lake ◪ Salt pan/Dry/Intermittent lake ∫ River

106	L 7	**Pithoragarh**, India
90	G 9	**Pitkyaranta**, Russian Federation
60	H 11	**Pitlochry**, U.K.
80	F 7	**Pitomača**, Croatia
57	F 15	**Pitrufquén**, Chile
39	D 19	**Pitt Island**, BC, Canada 🏝
69	C 18	**Pittem**, Belgium
105	B 22	**Pitti**, India 🏝
25	R 6	**Pittsburg**, KS, U.S.A.
14	B 13	**Pittsburgh**, PA, U.S.A.
14	L 9	**Pittsfield**, MA, U.S.A.
15	Q 5	**Pittsfield**, ME, U.S.A.
21	D 19	**Pittsfield**, IL, U.S.A.
54	J 13	**Pium**, Brazil
52	A 12	**Piura**, Peru
52	A 12	**Piura**, Peru ▣
87	Q 8	**Pivdennyy Buh**, Ukraine 〰
80	B 8	**Pivka**, Slovenia
76	D 5	**Piz Bernina**, Italy/Switzerland ▲
53	H 20	**Pizacoma**, Peru
129	Q 11	**Pizhi**, Nigeria
41	Y 11	**Placentia Bay**, NL, Canada ≃
121	K 15	**Placer**, Philippines
121	M 18	**Placer**, Philippines
33	H 18	**Placerville**, CA, U.S.A.
124	L 11	**Plaine du Tidikelt**, Algeria ◇
24	I 7	**Plains**, KS, U.S.A.
26	I 5	**Plains**, TX, U.S.A.
28	M 4	**Plains**, MT, U.S.A.
26	K 4	**Plainview**, TX, U.S.A.
24	K 3	**Plainville**, KS, U.S.A.
116	M 15	**Plampang**, Indonesia
81	H 14	**Plana**, Bosnia and Herzegovina
54	H 9	**Planalto de Maracanaquara**, Brazil ◇
132	I 5	**Planalto do Bié**, Angola ◇
55	H 15	**Planalto do Mato Grosso**, Brazil ⛰
133	T 4	**Planalto Moçambicano**, Mozambique ◇
22	M 10	**Plankiton**, SD, U.S.A.
27	Q 5	**Plano**, TX, U.S.A.
18	J 7	**Plaquemine**, LA, U.S.A.
66	K 7	**Plasencia**, Spain
43	R 8	**Plaster Rock**, NB, Canada
83	D 20	**Platanos**, Greece
129	S 12	**Plateau**, Nigeria ▣
131	O 14	**Plateau de La Manika**, Democratic Republic of Congo ◇
115	M 18	**Plateau des Bolovens**, Laos ◇
129	U 5	**Plateau du Djado**, Niger ◇
125	P 11	**Plateau du Fadnoun**, Algeria ◇
130	M 12	**Plateau du Kasai**, Democratic Republic of Congo ◇
129	T 4	**Plateau du Manguéni**, Niger ◇
124	M 10	**Plateau du Tademaït**, Algeria ◇
125	O 11	**Plateau du Tinrhert**, Algeria ◇
130	G 9	**Plateaux**, Congo ▣
80	K 10	**Platičevo**, Serbia and Montenegro
34	M 10	**Platinum**, AK, U.S.A.
50	I 3	**Plato**, Colombia
22	M 14	**Platte**, NE, U.S.A. 〰
21	E 14	**Platteville**, WI, U.S.A.
31	R 3	**Platteville**, CO, U.S.A.
14	K 5	**Plattsburgh**, NY, U.S.A.
73	K 18	**Plauen**, Germany
72	K 10	**Plauer See**, Germany ⛆
81	K 15	**Plav**, Serbia and Montenegro
92	K 3	**Plavsk**, Russian Federation
115	O 19	**Plây Cu**, Vietnam
45	S 7	**Playa Lauro Villar**, Mexico
31	N 15	**Playas Lake**, NM, U.S.A. ⛆
25	R 5	**Pleasanton**, KS, U.S.A.
27	O 11	**Pleasanton**, TX, U.S.A.
79	C 20	**Plechý**, Czech Republic ▲
29	Y 1	**Plentywood**, MT, U.S.A.
90	K 8	**Plesetsk**, Russian Federation
78	H 13	**Pleszew**, Poland
82	I 7	**Pleven**, Bulgaria ▣
82	I 7	**Pleven**, Bulgaria
80	D 10	**Plitvica Selo**, Croatia
80	J 13	**Pljevlja**, Serbia and Montenegro
78	J 12	**Płock**, Poland
80	G 13	**Pločno**, Bosnia and Herzegovina ▲
64	K 6	**Ploërmel**, France
86	K 12	**Ploiești**, Romania
83	L 18	**Plomari**, Greece
72	H 9	**Plön**, Germany
78	K 12	**Płońsk**, Poland
85	H 21	**Plotnitsa**, Belarus
78	E 9	**Płoty**, Poland
64	H 4	**Ploudalmézeau**, France
82	I 10	**Plovdiv**, Bulgaria ▣
82	I 10	**Plovdiv**, Bulgaria
76	G 7	**Plove di Sacco**, Italy
28	J 4	**Plummer**, ID, U.S.A.
133	O 8	**Plumtree**, Zimbabwe
84	C 13	**Plungė**, Lithuania
81	I 14	**Plužine**, Serbia and Montenegro
85	J 16	**Plyeshchanitsy**, Belarus
15	O 10	**Plymouth**, MA, U.S.A.
20	G 13	**Plymouth**, WI, U.S.A.
21	I 16	**Plymouth**, IN, U.S.A.
49	X 9	**Plymouth**, Montserrat ♜
62	M 15	**Plymouth**, U.K.
62	M 14	**Plympton**, U.K.
90	E 12	**Plyussa**, Russian Federation
79	B 18	**Plzeň**, Czech Republic
78	F 12	**Pniewy**, Poland
76	E 8	**Po**, Italy 〰
128	M 10	**Pô**, Burkina Faso
76	H 8	**Po Delta**, Italy ◇
25	X 8	**Pocahontas**, AR, U.S.A.
29	O 12	**Pocatello**, ID, U.S.A.
92	H 3	**Pochep**, Russian Federation
92	H 2	**Pochinok**, Russian Federation
73	M 23	**Pocking**, Germany
63	U 2	**Pocklington**, U.K.
21	F 20	**Pocohontas**, IL, U.S.A.
17	V 5	**Pocomoke City**, MD, U.S.A.
55	G 16	**Poconé**, Brazil
58	L 5	**Poços de Caldas**, Brazil
80	N 12	**Podgorac**, Serbia and Montenegro
92	L 6	**Podgorenskiy**, Russian Federation
81	J 16	**Podgorica**, Serbia and Montenegro
89	N 11	**Podkamennaya Tunguska**, Russian Federation
93	Q 5	**Podlesnoye**, Russian Federation
92	K 1	**Podol'sk**, Russian Federation
128	E 7	**Podor**, Senegal
81	M 14	**Podujevo**, Serbia and Montenegro
79	G 22	**Podunajská nížina**, Slovakia ◇
132	K 13	**Pofadder**, Republic of South Africa
76	F 8	**Poggio Rusco**, Italy
81	L 19	**Pogradec**, Albania
111	N 20	**P'ohang**, South Korea
70	L 13	**Pohjois-Ii**, Finland
141	P 15	**Pohnpei**, Federated States of Micronesia 🏝
141	P 15	**Pohnpei**, Federated States of Micronesia ▣
93	N 4	**Poim**, Russian Federation
20	G 8	**Point Abbaye**, MI, U.S.A. ▶
33	E 18	**Point Arena**, CA, U.S.A.
33	E 18	**Point Arena**, CA, U.S.A. ▶
18	K 9	**Point au Fer Island**, LA, U.S.A. 🏝
35	P 2	**Point Barrow**, AK, U.S.A. ▶
33	H 24	**Point Conception**, CA, U.S.A. ▶
20	I 10	**Point Detour**, MI, U.S.A. ▶
35	O 2	**Point Franklin**, AK, U.S.A. ▶
34	M 4	**Point Hope**, AK, U.S.A.
35	N 3	**Point Lay**, AK, U.S.A.
62	M 3	**Point Lynas**, U.K. ▶
105	G 23	**Point Pedro**, Sri Lanka ▶
14	J 14	**Point Pleasant**, NJ, U.S.A.
16	M 4	**Point Pleasant**, WV, U.S.A.
33	F 19	**Point Reyes**, CA, U.S.A. ▶
32	G 5	**Point Roberts**, WA, U.S.A.
134	F 5	**Point Samson**, WA, Australia
33	E 14	**Point St George**, CA, U.S.A. ▶
20	I 10	**Point Sturgeon**, WI, U.S.A. ▶
33	G 21	**Point Sur**, CA, U.S.A. ▶
49	Y 9	**Pointe-à-Pitre**, Guadeloupe, France
20	M 12	**Pointe Aux Barques**, MI, U.S.A. ▶
51	Z 6	**Pointe Béhague**, French Guiana ▶
64	L 3	**Pointe de Barfleur**, France ▶
43	W 4	**Pointe de l'Est**, QC, Canada 🏝
43	T 4	**Pointe de l'Ouest**, QC, Canada 🏝
64	H 6	**Pointe de Penmarch**, France ▶
64	K 7	**Pointe de St-Gildas**, France ▶
64	G 5	**Pointe de St-Mathieu**, France ▶
64	G 5	**Pointe du Raz**, France ▶
130	E 10	**Pointe-Noire**, Congo
76	B 8	**Poirino**, Italy
65	N 8	**Poitiers**, France
64	M 9	**Poitou-Charentes**, France ▣
65	P 3	**Poix-de-Picardie**, France
78	K 10	**Pojezierze Mazurskie**, Poland ⛰
53	K 20	**Pojo**, Bolivia
104	B 12	**Pokaran**, India
136	K 9	**Pokeno**, New Zealand
107	O 9	**Pokhara**, Nepal
93	T 3	**Pokhvistnevo**, Russian Federation
70	L 9	**Pokka**, Finland
131	O 6	**Poko**, Democratic Republic of Congo
89	T 11	**Pokrovsk**, Russian Federation
92	K 9	**Pokrovskoye**, Russian Federation
100	J 10	**Pol-e Fāsā**, Iran
101	U 6	**Pol-e Khomrī**, Afghanistan
79	J 20	**Polana**, Slovakia ▲
78	F 11	**Poland**, Europe □
78	G 9	**Polanów**, Poland
94	G 9	**Polatli**, Turkey
85	K 14	**Polatsk**, Belarus
143	R 9	**Pole Plain**, Arctic Ocean ◇
117	N 12	**Polewali**, Indonesia
113	X 2	**Poli**, China
129	U 12	**Poli**, Cameroon
78	D 10	**Police**, Poland
83	K 17	**Polichnitos**, Greece
65	U 8	**Poligny**, France
120	H 11	**Polillo**, Philippines 🏝
120	H 10	**Polillo Islands**, Philippines 🏝
120	H 10	**Polillo Strait**, Philippines ≃
94	G 15	**Polis**, Cyprus
87	O 2	**Polis'ke**, Ukraine
105	E 22	**Pollachi**, India
67	Y 7	**Pollença**, Spain
136	J 9	**Pollok**, New Zealand
87	W 8	**Polohy**, Ukraine
121	L 23	**Polomoloc**, Philippines
105	G 24	**Polonnaruwa**, Sri Lanka
86	M 4	**Polonne**, Ukraine
86	H 12	**Polovragi**, Romania
62	L 15	**Polperro**, U.K.
82	J 7	**Polski Trŭmbesh**, Bulgaria
28	M 4	**Polson**, MT, U.S.A.
87	U 5	**Poltava**, Ukraine
84	H 7	**Põltsamaa**, Estonia
90	M 4	**Poluostrov Kanin**, Russian Federation ▶
90	I 1	**Poluostrov Rybachiy**, Russian Federation ▶
89	O 7	**Poluostrov Taymyr**, Russian Federation ▶
88	M 7	**Poluostrov Yamal**, Russian Federation ▶
84	I 8	**Põlva**, Estonia
83	I 23	**Polyaigos**, Greece 🏝
90	I 1	**Polyarnyy**, Russian Federation
91	T 5	**Polyarnyy Ural**, Russian Federation ⛰
83	G 14	**Polygyros**, Greece
82	E 13	**Polykastro**, Greece
140	F 3	**Polynesia**, Oceania ◇
66	H 7	**Pombal**, Portugal
133	R 9	**Pomene**, Mozambique
78	F 9	**Pomerania**, Poland ⛰
21	N 20	**Pomeroy**, OH, U.S.A.
138	G 4	**Pomio**, Papua New Guinea
72	N 9	**Pommersche Bucht**, Germany ≃
33	K 24	**Pomona**, CA, U.S.A.
46	K 3	**Pomona**, Belize
82	N 9	**Pomorie**, Bulgaria
90	I 6	**Pomorskiy Bereg**, Russian Federation ◇
91	O 3	**Pomorskiy Proliv**, Russian Federation ≃
19	Y 13	**Pompano Beach**, FL, U.S.A.
77	J 16	**Pompei**, Italy
25	N 8	**Ponca City**, OK, U.S.A.
49	U 8	**Ponce**, Puerto Rico
24	M 8	**Pond Creek**, OK, U.S.A.
105	H 19	**Pondicherry**, India ▣
46	M 9	**Poneloya**, Nicaragua
66	K 2	**Ponferrada**, Spain
79	M 15	**Poniatowa**, Poland
93	V 3	**Ponomarevka**, Russian Federation
90	L 4	**Ponoy**, Russian Federation
121	L 17	**Ponson**, Philippines 🏝
69	F 21	**Pont-à-Celles**, Belgium
65	U 4	**Pont-à-Mousson**, France
76	A 7	**Pont-Canavese**, Italy
55	N 17	**Ponta da Baleia**, Brazil ▶
133	R 10	**Ponta da Barra**, Mozambique ▶
133	R 9	**Ponta da Barra Falsa**, Mozambique ▶
132	F 2	**Ponta das Palmeirinhas**, Angola ▶
132	F 4	**Ponta das Salinas**, Angola ▶
132	F 6	**Ponta do Enfião**, Angola ▶
58	I 8	**Ponta Grossa**, Brazil
58	J 11	**Ponta Imbituba**, Brazil ▶
55	H 18	**Ponta Porã**, Brazil
133	S 7	**Ponta Timbué**, Mozambique ▶
65	V 8	**Pontarlier**, France
64	K 7	**Pontchâteau**, France
55	K 14	**Ponte Alta do Tocantins**, Brazil
66	H 4	**Ponte da Barca**, Portugal
66	H 4	**Ponte de Lima**, Portugal
66	H 8	**Ponte de Sor**, Portugal
66	H 3	**Ponteareas**, Spain
76	I 5	**Pontebba**, Italy
63	T 3	**Pontefract**, U.K.
55	F 15	**Pontes e Lacerda**, Brazil
66	H 2	**Pontevedra**, Spain
21	G 17	**Pontiac**, IL, U.S.A.
21	M 14	**Pontiac**, MI, U.S.A.
118	E 10	**Pontian Kechil**, Malaysia
116	I 11	**Pontianak**, Indonesia
64	J 5	**Pontivy**, France
65	P 4	**Pontoise**, France
40	I 8	**Ponton**, MB, Canada
19	N 2	**Pontotoc**, MS, U.S.A.
76	D 9	**Pontremoli**, Italy
67	V 4	**Ponts**, Spain
63	O 10	**Pontypool**, U.K.
63	O 10	**Pontypridd**, U.K.
47	V 15	**Ponuga**, Panama
85	J 15	**Ponya**, Belarus 〰
135	O 11	**Poochera**, SA, Australia
130	H 9	**Pool**, Congo ▣
63	R 13	**Poole**, U.K.
63	R 14	**Poole Bay**, U.K. ≃
135	R 11	**Pooncarie**, NSW, Australia
136	K 6	**Poor Knights Islands**, New Zealand 🏝
87	V 6	**Popasne**, Ukraine
50	G 8	**Popayán**, Colombia
84	C 10	**Pope**, Latvia
69	A 19	**Poperinge**, Belgium
29	X 3	**Poplar**, MT, U.S.A.
25	Y 7	**Poplar Bluff**, MO, U.S.A.
18	M 7	**Poplarville**, MS, U.S.A.
45	R 12	**Popocatépetl**, Mexico ▲
130	I 11	**Popokabaka**, Democratic Republic of Congo
76	I 13	**Popoli**, Italy
138	E 6	**Popondetta**, Papua New Guinea
82	L 7	**Popovo**, Bulgaria
79	K 19	**Poprad**, Slovakia
46	I 3	**Poptún**, Guatemala
137	M 14	**Porangahau**, New Zealand
55	J 15	**Porangatu**, Brazil
105	A 15	**Porbandar**, India
76	H 6	**Pordenone**, Italy
80	A 9	**Porec**, Croatia
93	Q 2	**Poretskoye**, Russian Federation
138	B 4	**Porgera**, Papua New Guinea
71	J 18	**Pori**, Finland
137	K 16	**Porirua**, New Zealand
70	I 11	**Porjus**, Sweden
90	E 12	**Porkhov**, Russian Federation
63	N 12	**Porlock**, U.K.
135	R 2	**Pormpuraaw**, QLD, Australia
64	K 7	**Pornic**, France
121	L 17	**Poro**, Philippines 🏝
89	X 13	**Poronaysk**, Russian Federation
83	G 21	**Poros**, Greece
85	F 19	**Porozava**, Belarus
145	W 13	**Porpoise Bay**, Antarctica ≃
74	C 6	**Porrentruy**, Switzerland
76	E 9	**Porreta Terme**, Italy
70	K 6	**Porsangen**, Norway ≃
71	C 20	**Porsgrunn**, Norway
49	N 8	**Port-à-Piment**, Haiti
39	F 22	**Port Alberni**, BC, Canada
133	N 15	**Port Alfred**, Republic of South Africa
32	G 6	**Port Angeles**, WA, U.S.A.
48	L 8	**Port Antonio**, Jamaica
27	U 10	**Port Arthur**, TX, U.S.A.
135	T 15	**Port Arthur**, TAS, Australia
49	O 7	**Port-au-Prince**, Haiti ♜
135	P 10	**Port Augusta**, SA, Australia
132	K 15	**Port Beaufort**, Republic of South Africa
131	S 7	**Port Bell**, Uganda
105	N 22	**Port Blair**, India
27	T 10	**Port Bolivar**, TX, U.S.A.
42	D 14	**Port Burwell**, ON, Canada
107	T 14	**Port Canning**, India
43	R 4	**Port-Cartier**, QC, Canada
137	F 24	**Port Chalmers**, New Zealand
19	W 12	**Port Charlotte**, FL, U.S.A.
21	M 16	**Port Clinton**, OH, U.S.A.
42	F 14	**Port Colborne**, ON, Canada
49	O 6	**Port-de-Paix**, Haiti
118	C 9	**Port Dickson**, Malaysia
135	T 3	**Port Douglas**, QLD, Australia
133	P 13	**Port Edward**, Republic of South Africa
42	C 11	**Port Elgin**, ON, Canada
43	U 9	**Port Elgin**, NB, Canada
133	N 15	**Port Elizabeth**, Republic of South Africa
62	M 10	**Port Eynon**, U.K.
136	L 7	**Port Fitzroy**, New Zealand
130	D 8	**Port-Gentil**, Gabon
18	L 5	**Port Gibson**, MS, U.S.A.
60	G 13	**Port Glasgow**, U.K.
35	P 10	**Port Graham**, AK, U.S.A.
129	R 14	**Port Harcourt**, Nigeria
39	E 21	**Port Hardy**, BC, Canada
43	X 9	**Port Hawkesbury**, NS, Canada
134	G 5	**Port Hedland**, WA, Australia
35	N 12	**Port Heiden**, AK, U.S.A.
46	K 4	**Port Honduras**, Belize ≃
20	M 12	**Port Hope**, MI, U.S.A.
41	X 8	**Port Hope Simpson**, NL, Canada
48	M 3	**Port Howe**, The Bahamas
21	M 14	**Port Huron**, MI, U.S.A.
62	K 14	**Port Isaac Bay**, U.K. ≃
27	Q 15	**Port Isabel**, TX, U.S.A.
92	K 10	**Port Katon**, Russian Federation
27	R 12	**Port Lavaca**, TX, U.S.A.
135	O 12	**Port Lincoln**, SA, Australia
128	F 11	**Port Loko**, Sierra Leone
11	Q 11	**Port Louis**, Mauritius ♜
135	V 10	**Port Macquarie**, NSW, Australia
43	T 4	**Port-Menier**, QC, Canada
138	E 6	**Port Moresby**, Papua New Guinea ♜
49	N 3	**Port Nelson**, The Bahamas
132	I 13	**Port Nolloth**, Republic of South Africa
60	F 8	**Port of Ness**, U.K.
49	Y 14	**Port of Spain**, Trinidad and Tobago ♜
32	E 13	**Port Orford**, OR, U.S.A.
137	B 26	**Port Pegasus**, New Zealand ≃
135	P 11	**Port Pirie**, SA, Australia
17	P 15	**Port Royal**, SC, U.S.A.
17	U 4	**Port Royal**, VA, U.S.A.
17	P 15	**Port Royal Sound**, SC, U.S.A. ≃
126	F 7	**Port Said**, Egypt
20	M 13	**Port Sanilac**, MI, U.S.A.
133	P 13	**Port Shepstone**, Republic of South Africa
19	R 8	**Port St Joe**, FL, U.S.A.
133	O 14	**Port St Johns**, Republic of South Africa
57	K 24	**Port Stephens**, Falkland Islands
127	H 14	**Port Sudan**, Sudan
18	M 9	**Port Sulphur**, LA, U.S.A.
63	N 10	**Port Talbot**, U.K.
65	R 15	**Port-Vendres**, France
139	Q 11	**Port Vila**, Vanuatu ♜
136	K 9	**Port Waikato**, New Zealand
135	P 11	**Port Wakefield**, SA, Australia
118	A 6	**Port Weld**, Malaysia
135	S 14	**Port Welshpool**, VIC, Australia
61	E 16	**Portadown**, U.K.
20	F 13	**Portage**, WI, U.S.A.
40	I 10	**Portage la Praire**, MB, Canada
66	I 9	**Portalegre**, Portugal ▣
66	I 8	**Portalegre**, Portugal
31	U 11	**Portales**, NM, U.S.A.
67	Y 3	**Portbou**, Spain
63	T 13	**Portchester**, U.K.
55	L 16	**Porteirinha**, Brazil
54	I 10	**Portel**, Brazil
66	I 10	**Portel**, Portugal
33	J 22	**Porterville**, CA, U.S.A.
63	O 10	**Porth**, U.K.
63	N 11	**Porthcawl**, U.K.
62	M 5	**Porthmadog**, U.K.
83	B 20	**Porthmos Zakynthou**, Greece ≃
67	W 9	**Portinatx**, Spain
63	P 10	**Portishead**, U.K.
15	P 7	**Portland**, ME, U.S.A.
21	K 18	**Portland**, IN, U.S.A.
27	Q 13	**Portland**, TX, U.S.A.
32	G 9	**Portland**, OR, U.S.A.
135	Q 13	**Portland**, VIC, Australia
136	O 13	**Portland Island**, New Zealand 🏝
61	D 18	**Portlaoise**, Republic of Ireland
66	H 5	**Porto**, Portugal ▣
66	H 5	**Porto**, Portugal
54	I 11	**Porto Alegre**, Brazil
58	H 12	**Porto Alegre**, Brazil
132	G 3	**Porto Amboim**, Angola
55	H 15	**Porto Artur**, Brazil
58	J 10	**Porto Belo**, Brazil
54	I 10	**Pôrto de Moz**, Brazil
55	G 14	**Porto dos Gaúchos**, Brazil
77	I 23	**Porto Empedocle**, Italy
55	F 16	**Porto Esperidião**, Brazil
54	K 12	**Porto Franco**, Brazil
54	I 9	**Porto Grande**, Brazil
55	G 16	**Porto Jofre**, Brazil
55	G 18	**Porto Murtinho**, Brazil
129	O 13	**Porto-Novo**, Benin ♜
76	I 11	**Porto Recanati**, Italy
76	I 11	**Porto San Giorgio**, Italy
58	G 6	**Porto São José**, Brazil
55	N 16	**Porto Seguro**, Brazil
77	B 16	**Porto Torres**, Italy
65	Y 15	**Porto-Vecchio**, France
54	D 13	**Porto Velho**, Brazil
47	W 13	**Portobelo**, Panama
76	E 12	**Portoferraio**, Italy
33	H 17	**Portola**, CA, U.S.A.
52	B 9	**Portoviejo**, Ecuador
60	F 10	**Portree**, U.K.
15	O 8	**Portsmouth**, NH, U.S.A.
17	V 7	**Portsmouth**, VA, U.S.A.
21	M 20	**Portsmouth**, OH, U.S.A.
49	Y 10	**Portsmouth**, Dominica
63	T 13	**Portsmouth**, U.K.
70	L 9	**Porttipahdan tekojärvi**, Finland ⛆
66	G 12	**Portugal**, Europe □
50	M 3	**Portuguesa**, Venezuela ▣
57	H 25	**Porvenir**, Chile
71	M 19	**Porvoo**, Finland
111	K 20	**Poryŏng**, South Korea
58	E 10	**Posadas**, Argentina
74	J 10	**Poschiavo**, Switzerland
90	J 12	**Poshekhon'ye**, Russian Federation
100	L 8	**Posht-e Badam**, Iran
70	M 11	**Posio**, Finland
117	O 11	**Poso**, Indonesia
95	R 7	**Posof**, Turkey
111	L 22	**Posŏng**, South Korea
52	A 10	**Posorja**, Ecuador
55	K 15	**Posse**, Brazil
27	O 5	**Possum Kingdom Lake**, TX, U.S.A. ⛆
26	K 5	**Post**, TX, U.S.A.
124	L 13	**Post Weygand**, Algeria
80	B 8	**Postojna**, Slovenia
23	U 10	**Postville**, IA, U.S.A.
80	G 13	**Posušje**, Bosnia and Herzegovina
121	I 17	**Potatan**, Philippines
25	R 11	**Poteau**, OK, U.S.A.
27	O 11	**Poteet**, TX, U.S.A.
77	L 16	**Potenza**, Italy
67	N 1	**Potes**, Spain
95	Q 6	**P'ot'i**, Georgia
129	T 10	**Potiskum**, Nigeria
28	J 5	**Potlatch**, ID, U.S.A.
17	U 4	**Potomac**, MD, U.S.A. 〰
25	X 5	**Potosi**, MO, U.S.A.
53	J 21	**Potosí**, Bolivia
53	J 23	**Potosí**, Bolivia ▣
14	I 5	**Potsdam**, NY, U.S.A.
72	M 13	**Potsdam**, Germany
14	H 13	**Pottstown**, PA, U.S.A.
14	G 12	**Pottsville**, PA, U.S.A.
105	H 25	**Pottuvil**, Sri Lanka
101	W 8	**Potwar Plateau**, Pakistan ◇
14	J 10	**Poughkeepsie**, NY, U.S.A.
136	M 13	**Poukawa**, New Zealand
63	P 2	**Poulton-le-Fylde**, U.K.
139	O 13	**Poum**, New Caledonia
20	G 11	**Pound**, WI, U.S.A.
58	L 6	**Pouso Alegre**, Brazil
115	K 20	**Poŭthisăt**, Cambodia
136	O 12	**Poverty Bay**, New Zealand ≃
66	H 4	**Póvoa de Varzim**, Portugal
93	N 6	**Povorino**, Russian Federation
29	Y 6	**Powder**, MT, U.S.A. 〰
29	W 11	**Powder River**, WY, U.S.A.
29	X 8	**Powder River Basin**, WY, U.S.A. ◇
29	T 9	**Powell**, WY, U.S.A.
39	F 21	**Powell River**, BC, Canada
20	H 10	**Powers**, MI, U.S.A.
17	S 6	**Powhatan**, VA, U.S.A.
21	O 18	**Powhatan Point**, OH, U.S.A.
112	K 4	**Powo**, China
118	A 14	**Poyan Reservoir**, Singapore ⛆
113	V 7	**Poyang Hu**, China ⛆
109	U 11	**PoyangHu**, China ⛆
75	Y 2	**Poysdorf**, Austria
45	S 11	**Poza Rica**, Mexico
94	J 12	**Pozanti**, Turkey
80	M 10	**Požarevac**, Serbia and Montenegro
80	K 12	**Požega**, Serbia and Montenegro
80	G 9	**Požega**, Croatia
78	G 12	**Poznań**, Poland
67	P 11	**Pozo Alcón**, Spain
55	G 19	**Pozo Colorado**, Paraguay
53	M 20	**Pozo del Tigre**, Bolivia
56	J 8	**Pozo Hondo**, Argentina
66	M 10	**Pozoblanco**, Spain
77	K 24	**Pozzallo**, Italy
116	F 12	**Prabumulih**, Indonesia
115	G 21	**Prachuap Khiri Khan**, Thailand
79	G 17	**Praděd**, Czech Republic ▲
65	Q 15	**Prades**, France
55	N 16	**Prado**, Brazil
75	O 7	**Prägraten**, Austria
79	C 17	**Prague**, Czech Republic ♜
10	K 8	**Praia**, Cape Verde ♜
54	H 10	**Prainha**, Brazil
32	J 11	**Prairie City**, OR, U.S.A.
115	J 18	**Prakhon Chai**, Thailand
84	G 5	**Prangli**, Estonia 🏝
116	D 9	**Prapat**, Indonesia
115	J 18	**Prasat**, Thailand
58	J 4	**Prata**, Brazil
76	F 10	**Prato**, Italy
24	L 6	**Pratt**, KS, U.S.A.
19	Q 4	**Prattville**, AL, U.S.A.
63	N 15	**Prawle Point**, U.K. ▶
116	L 15	**Praya**, Indonesia
85	J 14	**Prazaroki**, Belarus
75	S 7	**Predlitz**, Austria
75	T 3	**Pregarten**, Austria
84	I 12	**Preiļi**, Latvia
27	P 14	**Premont**, TX, U.S.A.
20	E 10	**Prentice**, WI, U.S.A.
72	M 11	**Prenzlau**, Germany
115	B 18	**Preparis Island**, Myanmar 🏝
115	B 17	**Preparis North Channel**, Myanmar ≃
115	B 18	**Preparis South Channel**, Myanmar ≃
79	G 18	**Přerov**, Czech Republic
45	W 14	**Presa de la Angostura**, Mexico ⛆
45	P 12	**Presa del Infiernillo**, Mexico ⛆
45	T 13	**Presa Miguel Alemán**, Mexico ⛆
45	V 13	**Presa Nezahualcóyotl**, Mexico ⛆
30	I 11	**Prescott**, AZ, U.S.A.
42	J 11	**Prescott**, ON, Canada
137	A 25	**Preservation Inlet**, New Zealand ≃
81	N 16	**Preševo**, Serbia and Montenegro
58	B 10	**Presidencia Roque Sáenz Peña**, Argentina
58	C 10	**Presidente de la Plaza**, Argentina
54	L 11	**Presidente Dutra**, Brazil
58	H 6	**Presidente Epitácio**, Brazil
58	I 6	**Presidente Prudente**, Brazil
58	H 6	**Presidente Venceslau**, Brazil
26	H 10	**Presidio**, TX, U.S.A.
103	Q 2	**Presnovka**, Kazakhstan
79	L 19	**Prešov**, Slovakia
15	R 1	**Presque Isle**, ME, U.S.A.
63	O 4	**Prestatyn**, U.K.
128	L 13	**Prestea**, Ghana
23	U 9	**Preston**, MN, U.S.A.
25	T 6	**Preston**, MO, U.S.A.
29	P 13	**Preston**, ID, U.S.A.
63	P 2	**Preston**, U.K.
16	K 6	**Prestonburg**, KY, U.S.A.
133	O 10	**Pretoria**, Republic of South Africa ♜
83	B 17	**Preveza**, Greece
34	J 11	**Pribilof Islands**, AK, U.S.A. 🏝
80	J 13	**Priboj**, Serbia and Montenegro
79	C 18	**Příbram**, Czech Republic
30	L 4	**Price**, UT, U.S.A.
85	E 16	**Prienai**, Lithuania
132	L 13	**Prieska**, Republic of South Africa
28	K 2	**Priest Lake**, ID, U.S.A. ⛆
28	J 3	**Priest River**, ID, U.S.A.
79	I 20	**Prievidza**, Slovakia
80	F 10	**Prijedor**, Bosnia and Herzegovina
80	J 13	**Prijepolje**, Serbia and Montenegro
82	D 12	**Prilep**, Macedonia (F.Y.R.O.M.)
85	A 15	**Primorsk**, Russian Federation
90	E 10	**Primorsk**, Russian Federation
82	N 10	**Primorsko**, Bulgaria
92	J 11	**Primorsko-Akhtarsk**, Russian Federation
39	K 17	**Primrose Lake**, SK, Canada ⛆
39	M 17	**Prince Albert**, SK, Canada
132	L 15	**Prince Albert**, Republic of South Africa
38	G 6	**Prince Albert Peninsula**, NT, Canada ▶
38	F 7	**Prince Albert Sound**, NT, Canada ≃
41	P 1	**Prince Charles Island**, NU, Canada 🏝
145	V 5	**Prince Charles Mountains**, Antarctica ⛰
43	V 8	**Prince Edward Island**, PE, Canada 🏝
43	V 8	**Prince Edward Island**, Canada, Canada ▣
17	V 4	**Prince Frederick**, MD, U.S.A.
17	U 6	**Prince George**, VA, U.S.A.
39	F 18	**Prince George**, BC, Canada
145	U 2	**Prince Harald Coast**, Antarctica ◇
35	X 12	**Prince of Wales Island**, AK, U.S.A. 🏝
38	J 5	**Prince of Wales Island**, NU, Canada 🏝
135	R 1	**Prince of Wales Island**, QLD, Australia 🏝
38	F 6	**Prince of Wales Strait**, NT, Canada ≃
36	M 3	**Prince Patrick Island**, NT, Canada 🏝
37	P 5	**Prince Regent Inlet**, NU, Canada ≃
39	C 18	**Prince Rupert**, BC, Canada
35	S 9	**Prince William Sound**, AK, U.S.A. ≃
17	W 4	**Princess Anne**, MD, U.S.A.
145	P 2	**Princess Astrid Coast**, Antarctica ◇
135	S 2	**Princess Charlotte Bay**, QLD, Australia ≃
145	V 7	**Princess Elizabeth Land**, Antarctica ◇
145	R 2	**Princess Ragnhild Coast**, Antarctica ◇
39	D 19	**Princess Royal Island**, BC, Canada 🏝
14	I 13	**Princeton**, NJ, U.S.A.
16	D 6	**Princeton**, KY, U.S.A.
17	O 6	**Princeton**, WV, U.S.A.
21	F 16	**Princeton**, IL, U.S.A.
21	H 21	**Princeton**, IN, U.S.A.
25	T 1	**Princeton**, MO, U.S.A.
32	J 12	**Princeton**, OR, U.S.A.
130	C 7	**Príncipe**, São Tomé and Príncipe 🏝
32	H 11	**Prineville**, OR, U.S.A.
69	G 15	**Prinsenbeek**, Netherlands
47	R 7	**Prinzapolca**, Nicaragua
47	P 7	**Prinzapolka**, Nicaragua 〰
90	F 9	**Priozersk**, Russian Federation
85	L 22	**Pripet**, Belarus 〰
85	H 21	**Pripet Marshes**, Belarus ◇
80	E 9	**Priseka**, Croatia ▲
81	M 15	**Priština**, Serbia and Montenegro
72	K 11	**Pritzwalk**, Germany
65	T 12	**Privas**, France
80	C 11	**Privlaka**, Croatia
93	P 7	**Privolzhskaya Vozvyshennost'**, Russian Federation ◇
93	R 4	**Privolzh'ye**, Russian Federation
93	O 11	**Priyutnoye**, Russian Federation
81	L 16	**Prizren**, Serbia and Montenegro
77	I 22	**Prizzi**, Italy
80	G 10	**Prnjavor**, Bosnia and Herzegovina
116	K 14	**Probolinggo**, Indonesia
27	O 7	**Proctor**, TX, U.S.A.
27	O 7	**Proctor Lake**, TX, U.S.A. ⛆
51	W 6	**Professor van Blommestein Meer**, Suriname ⛆
69	G 21	**Profondeville**, Belgium
45	Y 10	**Progreso**, Mexico
46	L 5	**Progreso**, Honduras
33	G 15	**Project City**, CA, U.S.A.
93	O 13	**Prokhladnyy**, Russian Federation
81	J 16	**Prokletije**, Albania ⛰
81	N 14	**Prokuplje**, Serbia and Montenegro
89	T 7	**Proliv Dmitriya Lapteva**, Russian Federation ≃
88	K 6	**Proliv Karskiye Vorota**, Russian Federation ≃
89	X 5	**Proliv Longa**, Russian Federation ≃
89	P 5	**Proliv Vil'kitskogo**, Russian Federation ≃
143	V 7	**Proliv Vil'kitskogo**, Arctic Ocean ≃
77	L 14	**Promontorio del Gargano**, Italy ▶
85	N 18	**Pronya**, Belarus 〰
135	T 5	**Proserpine**, QLD, Australia
78	H 13	**Prosna**, Poland 〰
32	G 13	**Prospect**, OR, U.S.A.
121	M 20	**Prosperidad**, Philippines
79	G 18	**Prostějov**, Czech Republic
82	M 8	**Provadiya**, Bulgaria
65	U 14	**Provence**, France ◇
65	V 13	**Provence-Alpes-Côte-d'Azur**, France
15	N 10	**Providence**, RI, U.S.A.
16	E 6	**Providence**, KY, U.S.A.
89	Z 6	**Provideniya**, Russian Federation
15	P 10	**Provincetown**, MA, U.S.A.
65	R 5	**Provins**, France
30	K 3	**Provo**, UT, U.S.A.
58	H 8	**Prudentópolis**, Brazil
35	R 3	**Prudhoe Bay**, AK, U.S.A.
79	H 17	**Prudnik**, Poland
73	B 19	**Prüm**, Germany
86	I 12	**Prundeni**, Romania
78	K 13	**Pruszków**, Poland
86	L 7	**Prut**, Moldova 〰
74	L 7	**Prutz**, Austria
85	F 20	**Pruzhany**, Belarus
87	V 9	**Pryazovs'ke**, Ukraine
145	X 6	**Prydz Bay**, Antarctica ≃
87	R 3	**Pryluky**, Ukraine
87	W 9	**Prymors'k**, Ukraine
87	O 11	**Prymors'ke**, Ukraine
87	V 11	**Prymors'kyy**, Ukraine
87	P 2	**Pryp"yat**, Ukraine 〰
78	L 11	**Przasnysz**, Poland
79	J 15	**Przedbórz**, Poland
79	N 17	**Przemyśl**, Poland
79	N 17	**Przeworsk**, Poland
83	G 19	**Psachna**, Greece
83	J 18	**Psara**, Greece 🏝
92	L 13	**Psebay**, Russian Federation
90	D 12	**Pskov**, Russian Federation
90	D 13	**Pskovskaya Oblast'**, Russian Federation ▣
103	N 4	**Pskovskiy**, Kazakhstan
87	T 3	**Ps'ol**, Ukraine 〰
83	D 14	**Ptolemaïda**, Greece
85	K 21	**Ptsich**, Belarus 〰
85	K 21	**Ptsich**, Belarus
80	D 6	**Ptuj**, Slovenia
115	H 14	**Pua**, Thailand
113	N 10	**Pu'an**, China
52	G 10	**Puca Urco**, Peru
53	E 14	**Pucallpa**, Peru
113	Q 3	**Pucheng**, China
113	X 8	**Pucheng**, China
90	L 14	**Puchezh**, Russian Federation
111	L 19	**Puch'ŏn**, South Korea
121	H 15	**Pucio Point**, Philippines ▶
86	J 12	**Pucioasa**, Romania
57	F 15	**Pucón**, Chile
70	M 12	**Pudasjärvi**, Finland
63	Q 13	**Puddletown**, U.K.
90	I 9	**Pudozh**, Russian Federation
45	R 12	**Puebla**, Mexico
45	S 13	**Puebla**, Mexico ▣
66	K 3	**Puebla de Sanabria**, Spain
31	S 6	**Pueblo**, CO, U.S.A.
67	Q 11	**Pueblo de Don Fadrique**, Spain
33	K 14	**Pueblo Mountain**, OR, U.S.A. ▲
47	N 7	**Pueblo Nuevo**, Nicaragua
47	N 5	**Pueblo Viejo**, Honduras
57	I 15	**Puelches**, Argentina
57	H 14	**Puelén**, Argentina
112	K 12	**Pu'er**, China
44	G 3	**Puertecitos**, Mexico
57	F 20	**Puerto Aisen**, Chile
50	L 11	**Puerto Alfonso**, Colombia
45	T 15	**Puerto Ángel**, Mexico
47	S 14	**Puerto Armuelles**, Panama
50	H 9	**Puerto Asís**, Colombia
51	N 6	**Puerto Ayacucho**, Venezuela
53	B 19	**Puerto Ayora**, Ecuador
53	C 19	**Puerto Baquerizo Moreno**, Ecuador
46	K 4	**Puerto Barrios**, Guatemala
58	C 10	**Puerto Bermejo**, Argentina
50	I 5	**Puerto Berrío**, Colombia
51	N 2	**Puerto Cabello**, Venezuela
47	R 7	**Puerto Cabezas**, Nicaragua
47	S 5	**Puerto Cabo Gracias á Dios**, Nicaragua
51	N 6	**Puerto Carreño**, Colombia
53	J 16	**Puerto Cavinas**, Bolivia
57	F 19	**Puerto Cisnes**, Chile
57	H 23	**Puerto Coig**, Argentina
46	K 4	**Puerto Cortés**, Honduras
47	R 13	**Puerto Cortés**, Costa Rica
44	H 3	**Puerto de Lobos**, Mexico
45	S 14	**Puerto Escondido**, Mexico
52	D 9	**Puerto Francisco de Orellana**, Ecuador
53	K 16	**Puerto Génova**, Bolivia
53	K 20	**Puerto Grether**, Bolivia
57	I 26	**Puerto Harberton**, Argentina
53	I 17	**Puerto Heath**, Bolivia
51	N 7	**Puerto Inírida**, Colombia
56	K 5	**Puerto Irigoyen**, Argentina
47	O 12	**Puerto Jesus**, Costa Rica
50	I 10	**Puerto Leguizamo**, Colombia

□ Country ▣ Internal administrative region: State/Province/Territory/Dependent territory ♜ Capital city ⛰ Mountain range/Undersea ridge ▲ Mountain peak/Volcano/Seamount ◇ Geographic feature ▶ Headland/Point/Cape/Peninsula ◓ Desert 🏝 Island/Island group ⁙ Antarctic base 🌊 Ocean ∿ Sea ≃ Bay/Gulf/Channel/Strait ⛆ Lake ◩ Salt pan/Dry/Intermittent lake 〰

Q 5 Puerto Lempira, Honduras
H 4 Puerto Libertad, Mexico
I 17 Puerto Lobos, Argentina
K 1 Puerto Lopez, Colombia
A 9 Puerto López, Ecuador
W 15 Puerto Madero, Mexico
I 18 Puerto Madryn, Argentina
H 16 Puerto Maldonado, Peru
A 11 Puerto Máncora, Peru
F 17 Puerto Montt, Chile
L 8 Puerto Morazáno, Nicaragua
B 14 Puerto Morin, Peru
F 24 Puerto Natáles, Chile
L 6 Puerto Nuevo, Colombia
Z 14 Puerto Obaldia, Panama
L 5 Puerto Padre, Cuba
N 5 Puerto Páez, Venezuela
D 11 Puerto Pardo, Peru
G 2 Puerto Peñasco, Mexico
J 10 Puerto Pizarro, Colombia
Q 6 Puerto Plata, Dominican Republic
F 15 Puerto Portillo, Peru
D 18 Puerto Princesa, Philippines
Q 13 Puerto Quepos, Costa Rica
T 8 Puerto Rico, U.S.A., U.S.A.
F 10 Puerto Rico, Argentina
H 22 Puerto San Julián, Argentina
M 9 Puerto Sandino, Nicaragua
H 22 Puerto Santa Cruz, Argentina
G 18 Puerto Sastre, Paraguay
K 17 Puerto Siles, Bolivia
H 10 Puerto Socorro, Peru
O 21 Puerto Suárez, Bolivia
M 11 Puerto Vallarta, Mexico
E 15 Puerto Victoria, Peru
S 12 Puerto Viejo, Costa Rica
A 19 Puerto Villamil, Ecuador
I 19 Puerto Visser, Argentina
H 25 Puerto Yartou, Chile
N 10 Puertollano, Spain
R 5 Pugachev, Russian Federation
L 9 Puge, China
G 6 Puget Sound, WA, U.S.A.
M 15 Puglia, Italy
V 9 Pugwash, NS, Canada
O 16 Puhos, Finland
W 3 Puigcerdà, Spain
P 15 Puigmal, France
X 3 Puigmal d'Err, Spain
G 12 Pujehun, Sierra Leone
M 7 Pukapuka, Cook Islands
H 7 Pukatawagan, MB, Canada
M 16 Pukch'ŏng, North Korea
K 16 Pukë, Albania
K 9 Pukekohe, New Zealand
E 19 Pukekura, New Zealand
L 16 Puksubaek-san, North Korea
C 19 Pula, Italy
A 10 Pula, Croatia
J 22 Pulacayo, Bolivia
N 10 Pulai, Indonesia
J 15 Pulanduta Point, Philippines
L 12 Pulangpisau, Indonesia
N 15 Pulap, Federated States of Micronesia
G 7 Pulaski, NY, U.S.A.
E 10 Pulaski, TN, U.S.A.
O 7 Pulaski, VA, U.S.A.
X 14 Pulau Dolak, Indonesia
Y 7 Pulau Gaya, Malaysia
N 9 Pulau Maratua, Indonesia
N 15 Pulawat, Federated States of Micronesia
M 16 Puławy, Poland
V 13 Pulborough, U.K.
M 14 Pulkkila, Finland
L 8 Pullman, WA, U.S.A.
I 15 Pulo Anna, Palau
L 12 Pułtusk, Poland
I 17 Pulu, China
P 10 Pülümür, Turkey
N 15 Pulusuk, Federated States of Micronesia
H 6 Puna de Atacama, Argentina
F 18 Punakaiki, New Zealand
U 9 Punakha, Bhutan
J 20 Punata, Bolivia
W 12 Puncak Jaya, Indonesia
Y 13 Puncak Mandala, Indonesia
X 13 Puncak Trikora, Indonesia
I 7 Pundri, India
C 17 Pune, India
B 13 Punggol, Singapore
M 15 P'ungsan, North Korea
O 8 Punia, Democratic Republic of Congo
X 10 Punjab, Pakistan
H 6 Punjab, India
H 19 Puno, Peru
G 18 Puno, Peru
G 6 Punta Abreojos, Mexico
N 19 Punta Alice, Italy
Z 11 Punta Allen, Mexico
L 15 Punta Almina, Spain
B 19 Punta Alta, Argentina
J 9 Punta Arena, Mexico
G 25 Punta Arenas, Chile
E 19 Punta Atico, Peru
F 3 Punta Baja, Mexico
B 21 Punta Bermeja, Argentina
S 15 Punta Burica, Costa Rica
S 12 Punta Cahuita, Costa Rica
H 2 Punta Canoas, Colombia
B 15 Punta Caprara, Italy
N 4 Punta Caxinas, Honduras
F 7 Punta Chirambirá, Colombia
L 8 Punta Cosigüina, Nicaragua
F 12 Punta Curaumilla, Chile
H 24 Punta de Arenas, Argentina
P 13 Punta de las Entinas, Spain
M 11 Punta de Mita, Mexico
R 9 Punta de Perlas, Nicaragua
N 6 Punta de Quemado, Cuba
R 10 Punta del Mono, Nicaragua
G 15 Punta del Palmar, Uruguay
J 18 Punta Delgada, Argentina
H 22 Punta Desengaño, Argentina
F 5 Punta Eugenia, Mexico
A 8 Punta Galera, Ecuador
E 16 Punta Galera, Chile
K 1 Punta Gallinas, Colombia
Y 15 Punta Garachiné, Panama
J 4 Punta Gorda, Belize
R 10 Punta Gorda, Nicaragua
R 6 Punta Gorda, Nicaragua
56 F 2 Punta Gorda, Chile
47 O 12 Punta Guiones, Costa Rica
45 Z 11 Punta Herrero, Mexico
56 F 5 Punta Jorjino, Chile
57 E 14 Punta Lavapié, Chile
56 F 10 Punta Lengua de Vaca, Chile
57 H 23 Punta León, Argentina
47 W 15 Punta Mala, Panama
50 E 9 Punta Manglares, Colombia
47 X 12 Punta Manzanillo, Panama
47 V 15 Punta Mariato, Panama
66 L 14 Punta Marroqui, Spain
57 I 21 Punta Medanosa, Argentina
52 A 12 Punta Negro, Peru
57 J 18 Punta Ninfas, Argentina
57 J 17 Punta Norte, Argentina
57 J 17 Punta Norte, Argentina
52 A 11 Punta Pariñas, Peru
47 Q 4 Punta Patuca, Honduras
44 G 4 Punta Prieta, Mexico
59 B 21 Punta Rasa, Argentina
50 F 8 Punta Reyes, Colombia
45 U 12 Punta Roca Partida, Mexico
44 J 6 Punta Rosa, Mexico
46 L 4 Punta Sal, Honduras
53 C 16 Punta Salinasó Lachay, Peru
44 G 6 Punta San Hipólito, Mexico
46 J 8 Punta San Juan, El Salvador
47 Q 14 Punta San Pedro, Costa Rica
52 A 10 Punta Santa Elena, Ecuador
53 D 18 Punta Santa Maria, Peru
59 E 17 Punta Sur, Argentina
45 N 13 Punta Tejupan, Mexico
56 F 12 Punta Topocalma, Chile
47 O 12 Puntarenas, Costa Rica
50 L 2 Punto Fijo, Venezuela
14 C 12 Punxsutawney, PA, U.S.A.
70 M 13 Puolanka, Finland
137 H 15 Puponga, New Zealand
109 T 11 Puqi, China
53 E 18 Puquio, Peru
56 G 8 Puquios, Chile
106 L 9 Puranpur, India
138 C 6 Puratu Island, Papua New Guinea
75 Y 4 Purbach, Austria
84 G 5 Purekkari neem, Estonia
57 F 15 Purén, Chile
105 J 17 Puri, India
75 X 3 Purkersdorf, Austria
68 H 10 Purmerend, Netherlands
107 R 11 Purnia, India
57 E 17 Purranque, Chile
45 P 12 Puruarán, Mexico
116 L 11 Purukcahu, Indonesia
107 Q 13 Puruliya, India
54 D 12 Purus, Brazil
71 O 16 Puruvesi, Finland
82 J 10 Pŭrvomay, Bulgaria
116 H 14 Purwakarta, Indonesia
119 O 10 Pusa, Malaysia
111 N 21 Pusan, South Korea
121 O 22 Pusan Point, Philippines
93 Q 6 Pushkino, Russian Federation
90 D 14 Pustoshka, Russian Federation
109 W 13 Putai, Taiwan
114 F 6 Putao, Myanmar
136 L 10 Putaruru, New Zealand
113 X 10 Putian, China
53 H 18 Putina, Peru
136 N 12 Putorino, New Zealand
56 G 2 Putre, Chile
105 F 24 Puttalam, Sri Lanka
68 J 11 Putten, Netherlands
72 I 8 Puttgarden, Germany
105 D 21 Puttur, India
50 H 9 Putumayo, Colombia
50 J 11 Putumayo, Colombia
116 K 10 Putusibau, Indonesia
87 T 2 Putyvl', Ukraine
71 M 17 Puula, Finland
71 N 17 Puumala, Finland
41 P 5 Puvurnituq, QC, Canada
113 R 2 Puxian, China
113 U 2 Puyang, China
57 F 16 Puyehue, Chile
52 C 9 Puyo, Ecuador
137 A 25 Puysegur Point, New Zealand
91 R 8 Puzla, Russian Federation
131 W 12 Pwani, Tanzania
131 Q 13 Pweto, Democratic Republic of Congo
62 M 5 Pwllheli, U.K.
90 K 5 Pyalitsa, Russian Federation
90 I 8 Pyal'ma, Russian Federation
115 D 17 Pyapon, Myanmar
89 O 6 Pyasinskiy Zaliv, Russian Federation
93 O 13 Pyatigorsk, Russian Federation
87 T 6 P"yatykhatky, Ukraine
114 D 12 Pyawbwe, Myanmar
115 C 14 Pyè, Myanmar
85 K 21 Pyetrykaw, Belarus
71 L 14 Pyhäjoki, Finland
71 M 15 Pyhäsalmi, Finland
71 O 16 Pyhäselkä, Finland
70 M 10 Pyhätunturin, Finland
114 D 13 Pyinmana, Myanmar
83 D 22 Pylos, Greece
111 J 18 P'yŏngang, North Korea
111 K 17 P'yŏngsong, North Korea
111 M 19 P'yŏngt'aek, South Korea
111 J 17 P'yŏngyang, North Korea
16 I 16 Pyramid Lake, NV, U.S.A.
64 K 15 Pyrenees, France/Spain
83 E 15 Pyrgetos, Greece
83 K 19 Pyrgi, Greece
83 C 21 Pyrgos, Greece
87 R 4 Pyryatyn, Ukraine
78 D 11 Pyrzyce, Poland
85 J 15 Pyshna, Belarus
87 V 7 Pys'menne, Ukraine
90 D 13 Pytalovo, Russian Federation
71 C 16 Pyttegga, Norway
115 D 14 Pyu, Myanmar

Q

98 L 7 Qaḍimah, Saudi Arabia
97 U 4 Qādir Karam, Iraq
110 F 8 Qagan, China
110 B 13 Qagan Nur, China
110 C 13 Qagan Nur, China
110 J 11 Qagan Nur, China
111 C 14 Qagan Nur, China
110 B 13 Qagan Teg, China
112 J 4 Qagca, China
101 R 6 Qaisar, Afghanistan
97 U 2 Qalā Diza, Iraq
103 S 13 Qal'aikhum, Tajikistan
99 W 14 Qalansiyah, Yemen
101 T 9 Qalāt, Afghanistan
97 W 12 Qal'at Abū Ghar, Iraq
98 J 4 Qal'at Aẓlam, Saudi Arabia
96 H 4 Qal'at al Ḥiṣn, Syria
99 O 9 Qal'at Bīshah, Saudi Arabia
97 Y 10 Qal'at Ṣāliḥ, Iraq
97 W 9 Qal'at Sukkār, Iraq
101 Q 7 Qal'eh-ye, Afghanistan
96 F 9 Qalqilya, Israel
38 M 9 Qamanittuaq, NU, Canada
112 I 6 Qamdo, China
125 W 8 Qaminis, Libya
127 O 18 Qandala, Somalia
95 V 10 Qapiciğ Dağl, Armenia
97 U 5 Qara Tepe, Iraq
98 M 3 Qārah, Saudi Arabia
97 Q 1 Qaratshuk, Syria
127 N 20 Qardho, Somalia
103 U 13 Qarokŭl, Tajikistan
110 H 10 Qarsan, China
103 P 13 Qashqadaryo Wiloyati, Uzbekistan
111 A 16 Qasq, China
96 I 9 Qaṣr al Azraq, Jordan
96 H 10 Qaṣr al Kharānah, Jordan
99 S 2 Qaṣr aṣ Ṣabiyah, Kuwait
126 D 10 Qaṣr Farafra, Egypt
99 Q 8 Qaṣr Ḥimām, Saudi Arabia
125 S 11 Qaṣr Larocu, Libya
96 H 7 Qaṭanā, Syria
99 U 5 Qatar, Asia
100 K 11 Qaṭrūyeh, Iran
126 C 9 Qattâra Depression, Egypt
95 W 7 Qax, Azerbaijan
101 N 8 Qāyen, Iran
97 S 3 Qayyārah, Iraq
95 U 7 Qazax, Azerbaijan
95 Y 8 Qazimämmäd, Azerbaijan
100 H 5 Qazvīn, Iran
100 H 5 Qazvīn, Iran
126 F 10 Qena, Egypt
143 N 12 Qeqertarsuaq, Greenland
100 L 13 Qeshm, Iran
100 L 13 Qeshm, Iran
112 K 6 Qêyi, China
100 J 13 Qeys, Iran
96 E 11 Qeẓi'ot, Israel
110 J 12 Qian'an, China
113 P 7 Qianjiang, China
113 T 6 Qianjiang, China
112 L 6 Qianning, China
112 K 10 Qiansuo, China
112 M 7 Qianwei, China
111 F 17 Qianxi, China
113 O 9 Qianxi, China
113 P 3 Qianxian, China
113 P 3 Qianyang, China
113 Q 2 Qiaozhen, China
113 V 7 Qichun, China
113 S 9 Qidong, China
113 Z 5 Qidong, China
109 N 9 Qidukou, China
108 J 7 Qiemo, China
113 O 7 Qijiang, China
108 M 5 Qijiaojing, China
101 Q 12 Qila Ladgasht, Pakistan
101 P 11 Qila Safed, Pakistan
101 U 10 Qila Saifullah, Pakistan
109 N 7 Qilian Shan, China
113 W 7 Qimen, China
113 P 4 Qin Ling, China
113 O 3 Qin'an, China
110 L 10 Qing'an, China
111 J 20 Qingdao, China
110 K 10 Qinggang, China
109 N 8 Qinghai, China
109 O 8 Qinghai Hu, China
111 I 20 Qingjian, China
111 F 16 Qinglong, China
111 N 16 Qingshuihe, China
113 Y 8 Qingtian, China
113 S 1 Qingxu, China
113 P 2 Qingyang, China
111 J 15 Qingyuan, China
113 J 12 Qingyuan, China
113 X 8 Qingyuan, China
112 J 10 Qingzhou, China
111 G 17 Qinhuangdao, China
113 S 1 Qinxian, China
113 T 3 Qinyang, China
113 S 2 Qinyuan, China
113 Q 13 Qinzhou, China
113 R 15 Qionghai, China
112 M 6 Qionglai, China
112 L 5 Qionglai Shan, China
110 G 5 Qiqian, China
110 I 10 Qiqihar, China
100 J 11 Qīr, Iran
96 F 10 Qiryat Gat, Israel
99 U 12 Qishn, Yemen
108 L 5 Qitai, China
110 N 10 Qitaihe, China
112 M 11 Qiubei, China
111 G 19 Qixia, China
113 S 1 Qixian, China
113 U 3 Qixian, China
110 G 4 Qiyahe, China
113 S 9 Qiyang, China
110 J 7 Qizhan, China
103 V 14 Qizilrabot, Tajikistan
100 J 5 Qolleh-ye Damāvand, Iran
100 I 6 Qom, Iran
100 I 6 Qom, Iran
127 O 21 Qooriga Neegro, Somalia
102 L 10 Qoraqalpoghiston Respublikasi, Uzbekistan
96 H 5 Qornet es Saouda, Lebanon
97 T 2 Qosh Tepe, Iraq
14 M 9 Quabbin Reservoir, MA, U.S.A.
72 E 12 Quakenbrück, Germany
115 K 23 Quân Đao Nam Du, Vietnam
113 S 4 Quanbao Shan, China
115 O 17 Quang Ngai, Vietnam
115 N 16 Quang Tri, Vietnam
113 X 11 Quanzhou, China
113 S 10 Quanzhou, China
41 R 5 Quaqtaq, QC, Canada
58 E 12 Quarai, Brazil
137 D 25 Quarry Hills, New Zealand
77 C 19 Quartu Sant'Elena, Italy
33 M 20 Quartzite Mountain, NV, U.S.A.
30 G 12 Quartzsite, AZ, U.S.A.
95 X 7 Quba, Azerbaijan
101 N 5 Quchan, Iran
96 K 4 Qudaym, Syria
135 U 12 Queanbeyan, NSW, Australia
42 K 7 Québec, Canada
43 N 8 Québec, QC, Canada
73 I 15 Quedlinburg, Germany
39 C 19 Queen Charlotte, BC, Canada
57 J 23 Queen Charlotte Bay, Falkland Islands
39 B 19 Queen Charlotte Islands, BC, Canada
39 D 20 Queen Charlotte Sound, BC, Canada
36 M 3 Queen Elizabeth Islands, NU, Canada
145 W 8 Queen Mary Land, Antarctica
40 J 1 Queen Maud Gulf, NU, Canada
145 O 3 Queen Maud Land, Antarctica
145 O 9 Queen Maud Mountains, Antarctica
135 R 6 Queensland, Australia
135 S 15 Queenstown, TAS, Australia
137 C 23 Queenstown, New Zealand
32 F 7 Queets, WA, U.S.A.
132 I 2 Quela, Angola
133 S 7 Quelimane, Mozambique
57 F 18 Quellón, Chile
31 N 11 Quemado, NM, U.S.A.
57 F 17 Quemchi, Chile
59 D 19 Quequén, Argentina
45 Q 11 Querétaro, Mexico
45 Q 11 Querétaro, Mexico
73 J 14 Querfurt, Germany
67 P 11 Quesada, Spain
39 G 19 Quesnel, BC, Canada
39 G 19 Quesnel Lake, BC, Canada
101 T 10 Quetta, Pakistan
57 F 16 Queule, Chile
52 A 9 Quevedo, Ecuador
46 F 5 Quezaltenango, Guatemala
46 J 6 Quezaltepeque, Guatemala
121 C 19 Quezon, Philippines
120 G 11 Quezon City, Philippines
124 I 6 Quezzane, Morocco
113 V 2 Qufu, China
114 L 13 Qui Châu, Vietnam
115 O 19 Qui Nhon, Vietnam
132 G 2 Quibaxe, Angola
50 G 6 Quibdó, Colombia
64 J 6 Quiberon, France
72 H 10 Quickborn, Germany
69 D 21 Quiévrechain, Belgium
55 G 20 Quiindy, Paraguay
132 G 5 Quilengues, Angola
39 N 18 Quill Lakes, SK, Canada
53 F 17 Quillabamba, Peru
56 G 4 Quillagua, Chile
65 Q 15 Quillan, France
59 D 16 Quilmes, Argentina
105 D 24 Quilon, India
135 S 8 Quilpie, QLD, Australia
56 F 11 Quilpue, Chile
132 H 1 Quimbele, Angola
56 K 8 Quimilí, Argentina
64 H 6 Quimper, France
64 I 6 Quimperlé, France
32 F 7 Quinault, WA, U.S.A.
53 G 17 Quince Mil, Peru
19 S 7 Quincy, FL, U.S.A.
21 D 19 Quincy, IL, U.S.A.
33 H 17 Quincy, CA, U.S.A.
56 I 11 Quines, Argentina
133 U 6 Quinga, Mozambique
34 M 10 Quinhagak, AK, U.S.A.
121 G 16 Quiniluban, Philippines
45 Z 11 Quintana Roo, Mexico
67 P 8 Quintanar, Spain
132 F 1 Quinzau, Angola
133 U 3 Quionga, Mozambique
132 G 5 Quipungo, Angola
57 F 14 Quirihue, Chile
53 K 21 Quiroga, Bolivia
59 B 16 Quiroga, Argentina
132 I 3 Quitapa, Angola
132 H 6 Quiteve, Angola
19 N 5 Quitman, MS, U.S.A.
19 T 7 Quitman, GA, U.S.A.
52 B 8 Quito, Ecuador
54 N 11 Quixadá, Brazil
112 M 10 Qujing, China
103 Q 13 Qullai Chimtarha, Tajikistan
103 S 13 Qullai Garmo, Tajikistan
103 T 14 Qullai Karl Marks, Tajikistan
112 I 5 Qu'nyido, China
135 P 10 Quorn, SA, Australia
99 Z 6 Qurayat, Oman
103 R 14 Qŭrghonteppa, Tajikistan
58 I 7 Qurinhos, Brazil
95 X 7 Qusar, Azerbaijan
99 T 13 Qusāy'ir, Yemen
126 G 10 Quseir, Egypt
113 P 6 Quxian, China
113 X 7 Quzhou, China
113 U 2 Quzhou, China
113 P 2 Quzi, China
95 V 6 Qvareli, Georgia

R

75 V 2 Raabs an der Thaya, Austria
70 L 13 Raahe, Finland
68 L 11 Raalte, Netherlands
116 L 14 Raas, Indonesia
80 C 10 Rab, Croatia
80 C 10 Rab, Croatia
79 K 18 Raba, Poland
79 G 23 Rába, Hungary
117 N 15 Raba, Indonesia
127 F 18 Rabak, Sudan
77 J 26 Rabat, Malta
124 H 7 Rabat, Morocco
138 H 3 Rabaul, Papua New Guinea
134 L 5 Rabbit Flat Roadhouse, NT, Australia
116 B 9 Rabi, Indonesia
139 Y 11 Rabi, Fiji
98 L 7 Rābigh, Saudi Arabia
46 H 5 Rabinal, Guatemala
79 K 16 Rabka, Poland
18 L 8 Raceland, LA, U.S.A.
115 L 23 Rach Gia, Vietnam
27 P 15 Rachal, TX, U.S.A.
79 H 17 Racibórz, Poland
21 H 14 Racine, WI, U.S.A.
99 P 13 Radā', Yemen
85 I 17 Radashkovichy, Belarus
16 G 5 Radcliff, KY, U.S.A.
86 J 4 Radekhiv, Ukraine
17 O 7 Radford, VA, U.S.A.
105 B 14 Radhanpur, India
93 R 4 Radishchevo, Russian Federation
41 P 9 Radisson, QC, Canada
50 E 8 Rado de Tumaco, Colombia
79 L 14 Radom, Poland
127 B 19 Radom, Sudan
82 F 9 Radomir, Bulgaria
79 J 15 Radomsko, Poland
82 L 11 Radovets, Bulgaria
82 E 11 Radoviš, Macedonia (F.Y.R.O.M.)
75 R 6 Radstadt, Austria
85 F 17 Radun', Belarus
84 E 13 Radviliškis, Lithuania
78 N 13 Radzyń Podlaski, Poland
106 M 11 Rae Bareli, India
38 H 12 Rae-Edzo, NT, Canada
38 G 11 Rae Lakes, NT, Canada
17 R 10 Raeford, NC, U.S.A.
137 D 24 Raes Junction, New Zealand
136 K 13 Raetihi, New Zealand
58 B 13 Rafaela, Argentina
99 O 2 Rafḥā', Saudi Arabia
83 H 20 Rafina, Greece
100 L 10 Rafsanjān, Iran
127 B 20 Raga, Sudan
120 I 12 Ragay Gulf, Philippines
63 P 10 Raglan, U.K.
136 K 10 Raglan, New Zealand
18 H 7 Ragley, LA, U.S.A.
77 K 23 Ragusa, Italy
117 P 13 Raha, Indonesia
85 M 19 Rahachow, Belarus
127 F 17 Rahad Canal, Sudan
129 S 11 Rahama, Nigeria
101 V 12 Rahimyar Khan, Pakistan
100 H 6 Rāhjerd, Iran
106 I 6 Rahon, India
105 E 19 Raichur, India
107 S 11 Raiganj, India
105 H 15 Raigarh, India
117 O 15 Raijua, Indonesia
39 G 15 Rainbow Lake, AB, Canada
23 R 2 Rainy Lake, MN, U.S.A.
71 J 15 Raippaluoto, Finland
105 G 16 Raipur, India
105 G 16 Raj-Nandgaon, India
105 I 15 Rajagangapur, India
105 H 18 Rajahmundry, India
119 P 10 Rajang, Malaysia
101 V 11 Rajanpur, Pakistan
105 E 23 Rajapalaiyam, India
105 C 18 Rajapur, India
106 G 8 Rajasthan, India
107 Q 12 Rajauli, India
107 R 10 Rajbiraj, Nepal
106 H 8 Rajgarh, India
105 B 15 Rajkot, India
105 D 15 Rajpur, India
107 T 12 Rajshahi, Bangladesh
107 T 12 Rajshahi, Bangladesh
141 O 6 Rakahanga, Cook Islands
131 R 8 Rakai, Uganda
137 G 21 Rakaia, New Zealand
137 F 20 Rakaia, New Zealand
86 I 7 Rakhiv, Ukraine
113 Q 6 Three Gorges Dam, China
103 P 6 Rakhmet, Kazakhstan
79 C 17 Rakovník, Czech Republic
84 H 6 Rakvere, Estonia
17 S 9 Raleigh, NC, U.S.A.
17 V 11 Raleigh Bay, NC, U.S.A.
141 W 2 Ralik Chain, Marshall Islands
26 K 4 Ralls, TX, U.S.A.
100 I 5 Rām-Sar, Iran
47 Q 9 Rama, Nicaragua
96 G 7 Rama, Israel
96 F 9 Ramallah, Israel
105 F 23 Ramanathapuram, India
105 H 14 Ramanuj Ganj, India
138 E 2 Rambutyo Island, Papua New Guinea
62 L 15 Rame Head, U.K.
107 Q 10 Ramechhap, Nepal
92 L 1 Ramenskoye, Russian Federation
90 H 13 Rameshki, Russian Federation
107 Q 13 Ramgarh, India
107 V 13 Ramgarh, Bangladesh
100 H 9 Rāmhormoz, Iran
135 O 1 Ramingining, NT, Australia
96 F 9 Ramla, Israel
99 Q 13 Ramlat as Sab'atayn, Yemen
99 P 11 Ramlat Dahm, Yemen
96 G 13 Ramm, Jordan
106 K 8 Ramnagar, India
86 L 11 Râmnicu Sărat, Romania
86 I 11 Râmnicu Vâlcea, Romania
47 P 12 Ramon, Costa Rica
33 L 26 Ramona, CA, U.S.A.
106 K 8 Rampur, India
106 K 6 Rampur, India
107 S 12 Rampur Hat, India
115 B 14 Ramree Island, Myanmar
42 C 7 Ramsey, ON, Canada
61 H 16 Ramsey, U.K.
62 J 9 Ramsey Island, U.K.
42 C 8 Ramsey Lake, ON, Canada
63 Z 12 Ramsgate, U.K.
100 G 9 Rāmshīr, Iran
71 G 17 Ramsjö, Sweden
107 W 15 Ramu, Bangladesh
138 C 4 Ramu, Papua New Guinea
104 D 13 Rana Pratap Sagar, India
56 G 12 Rancagua, Chile
69 F 23 Rance, Belgium
105 I 14 Ranchi, India
45 O 9 Rancho Grande, Mexico
77 K 22 Randazzo, Italy
71 C 24 Randers, Denmark
70 H 11 Randijaure, Sweden
128 F 8 Ranérou, Senegal
137 E 23 Ranfurly, New Zealand
115 I 26 Rangae, Thailand
107 V 14 Rangamati, Bangladesh
107 W 10 Rangapara North, India
136 I 5 Rangaunu Bay, New Zealand
15 O 5 Rangeley, ME, U.S.A.
31 N 3 Rangely, CO, U.S.A.
27 O 6 Ranger, TX, U.S.A.
42 B 8 Ranger, ON, Canada
107 V 10 Rangia, India
136 L 12 Rangipo, New Zealand
136 K 9 Rangiriri, New Zealand
136 M 12 Rangitaiki, New Zealand
137 F 21 Rangitata, New Zealand
136 L 13 Rangitikei, New Zealand
115 E 16 Rangoon, Myanmar
107 T 11 Rangpur, Bangladesh
46 K 3 Ranguana Cay, Belize
105 D 20 Ranibennur, India
107 R 13 Raniganj, India
26 K 8 Rankin, TX, U.S.A.
40 L 4 Rankin Inlet, NU, Canada
105 A 14 Rann of Kachchh, India
93 U 5 Ranneye, Russian Federation
133 W 9 Ranohira, Madgascar
115 F 23 Ranong, Thailand
138 J 6 Ranongga, Solomon Islands
115 H 25 Ranot, Thailand
117 V 11 Ransiki, Indonesia
116 L 12 Rantau, Indonesia
21 G 18 Rantoul, IL, U.S.A.
70 M 12 Ranua, Finland
97 U 12 Rānya, Iraq
110 O 9 Raohe, China
76 C 9 Rapallo, Italy
105 A 14 Rapar, India
22 G 9 Rapid City, SD, U.S.A.
20 H 9 Rapid River, MI, U.S.A.
84 I 8 Rāpina, Estonia
84 G 6 Rapla, Estonia
74 H 7 Rapperswil, Switzerland
120 K 13 Rapurapu, Philippines
14 I 7 Raquette Lake, NY, U.S.A.
141 O 11 Rarotonga, Cook Islands
126 F 9 Râs, Egypt
98 K 6 Rās Abū Madd, Saudi Arabia
126 H 13 Rās Abu Shagara, Sudan
99 Z 9 Rās ad Daqm, Oman
97 N 1 Ra's al 'Ayn, Syria
96 H 3 Rās al Basīṭ, Syria
99 Z 7 Rās al Ḥadd, Oman
99 Z 7 Rās al Ḥadd, Oman
99 S 13 Rās al Kalb, Yemen
99 X 5 Rās al Khaimah, United Arab Emirates
99 Z 10 Rās al Madrakah, Oman
99 S 3 Rās al Mish'āb, Saudi Arabia
125 Y 7 Rās al Muraysah, Libya
126 B 7 Rās al Muraysah, Egypt
96 G 12 Rās an Naqb, Jordan
98 I 3 Rās ash Shaykh Humayd, Saudi Arabia
125 X 7 Rās at Tin, Libya
99 S 4 Rās az Zawr, Saudi Arabia
99 O 15 Rās Bāb al Mandab, Yemen
126 G 12 Rās Banās, Egypt
98 K 6 Rās Baridī, Saudi Arabia
127 O 22 Rās Cabaad, Somalia
127 O 18 Rās Caluula, Somalia
127 O 18 Rās Caseyr, Somalia
127 I 18 Rās Dashen, Ethiopia
127 O 20 Rās Durdura, Somalia
100 G 10 Rās-e Barkan, Iran
100 H 11 Rās-e Halileh, Iran
101 N 14 Rās-e Meydani, Iran
126 D 7 Rās el Kanâyis, Egypt
128 K 7 Rās el Mâ, Mali
99 V 12 Rās Fartak, Yemen
127 O 20 Rās Gabbac, Somalia
126 H 13 Rās Hardârba, Sudan
98 L 8 Rās Ḥāṭibah, Saudi Arabia
127 O 21 Rās Illig, Somalia
99 O 13 Rās 'Īsá, Yemen
101 Q 14 Rās Jaddi, Pakistan
100 M 14 Rās Jagin, Iran
98 K 5 Rās Karkūmā, Saudi Arabia
127 I 15 Rās Kasar, Sudan/Eritrea
127 M 19 Rās Khansiir, Somalia
127 O 20 Rās Macbar, Somalia
99 X 11 Rās Mirbāṭ, Oman
99 X 14 Rās Momi, Yemen
101 T 15 Rās Muari, Pakistan
126 G 10 Rās Muhammad, Egypt
99 X 11 Rās Naws, Oman
124 A 14 Rās Nouâdhibou, Western Sahara
128 E 5 Rās Nouâdhibou, Mauritania
101 P 14 Ras Nuh, Pakistan
101 R 14 Ras Ormara, Pakistan
100 H 11 Ras osh Shaṭṭ, Iran
99 W 11 Rās Sājir, Oman
99 Y 10 Rās Ṣawqirah, Oman
131 X 9 Ras Shaka, Kenya
99 Y 10 Rās Sharbithāt, Oman
99 V 14 Rās Shu'ab, Yemen
99 Z 9 Rās Ṣirāb, Oman
127 N 19 Rās Surud, Somalia
99 S 3 Rās Tanāqib, Saudi Arabia
99 T 4 Rās Tannūrah, Saudi Arabia
128 E 6 Rās Timirist, Mauritania
127 O 19 Rās Xaafuun, Somalia
121 C 19 Rasa, Philippines
85 D 14 Raseiniai, Lithuania
127 E 19 Rashad, Sudan
87 T 4 Rashivka, Ukraine
100 K 6 Rashm, Iran
100 H 4 Rasht, Iran
115 K 17 Rasi Salai, Thailand
81 L 14 Raška, Serbia and Montenegro
101 Q 11 Raskoh, Pakistan
40 I 1 Rasmussen Basin, NU, Canada
38 L 7 Rasmussen Bay, NU, Canada
85 L 16 Rasna, Belarus
86 J 11 Râșnov, Romania
93 N 4 Rasskazovo, Russian Federation
73 E 22 Rastatt, Germany
70 L 6 Rásttigáisa, Norway
115 G 19 Rat Buri, Thailand
34 C 13 Rat Island, AK, U.S.A.
34 C 12 Rat Islands, AK, U.S.A.
137 L 14 Rata, New Zealand
141 X 2 Ratak Chain, Marshall Islands
106 H 9 Ratangarh, India
71 F 16 Rätansbyn, Sweden
106 L 11 Rath, India
114 A 12 Rathedaung, Myanmar
72 K 13 Rathenow, Germany
105 D 14 Ratlam, India
105 C 18 Ratnagiri, India
105 G 25 Ratnapura, Sri Lanka
86 J 1 Ratne, Ukraine
101 U 12 Rato Dero, Pakistan
31 S 8 Raton, NM, U.S.A.
75 N 6 Rattenberg, Austria
118 C 8 Raub, Malaysia
59 D 17 Rauch, Argentina
99 R 2 Raudhatain, Kuwait

Country ▪ Internal administrative region: State/Province/Territory/Dependent territory ▪ Capital city ▪ Mountain range/Undersea ridge ▪ Mountain peak/Volcano/Seamount ◆ Geographic feature ▶ Headland/Point/Cape/Peninsula ▪ Desert ▪ Island/Island group ▪ Antarctic base ▪ Ocean ▪ Sea ▪ Bay/Gulf/Channel/Strait ▪ Lake ▪ Salt pan/Dry/Intermittent lake ▪ River

136 O 11 **Raukumara Range**, New Zealand ▲▲
71 J 18 **Rauma**, Finland
105 I 15 **Raurkela**, India
122 M 3 **Rausu**, Japan
136 O 10 **Rautoria**, New Zealand
86 I 3 **Rava-Rus'ka**, Ukraine
28 M 4 **Ravalli**, MT, U.S.A.
100 M 9 **Rāvar**, Iran
69 H 16 **Ravels**, Belgium
33 I 16 **Ravendale**, CA, U.S.A.
76 G 9 **Ravenna**, Italy
73 G 25 **Ravensburg**, Germany
135 T 4 **Ravenshoe**, QLD, Australia
134 H 11 **Ravensthorpe**, WA, Australia
101 X 10 **Ravi**, Pakistan ∿
103 N 14 **Ravnina**, Turkmenistan
97 Q 5 **Rāwah**, Iraq
101 W 8 **Rawalpindi**, Pakistan
97 T 1 **Rawāndiz**, Iraq
117 U 11 **Rawas**, Indonesia
106 G 8 **Rawatsar**, India
79 G 14 **Rawicz**, Poland
134 K 10 **Rawlinna**, WA, Australia
29 V 13 **Rawlins**, WY, U.S.A.
57 I 18 **Rawson**, Argentina
109 N 11 **Rawu**, China
22 H 3 **Ray**, ND, U.S.A.
96 H 6 **Rayak**, Lebanon
89 U 14 **Raychikhinsk**, Russian Federation
99 P 12 **Raydah**, Yemen
93 V 2 **Rayevskiy**, Russian Federation
63 Y 10 **Rayleigh**, U.K.
32 F 8 **Raymond**, WA, U.S.A.
27 P 15 **Raymondville**, TX, U.S.A.
115 I 20 **Rayong**, Thailand
18 J 4 **Rayville**, LA, U.S.A.
101 V 8 **Razani**, Pakistan
82 L 7 **Razgrad**, Bulgaria ▣
82 L 7 **Razgrad**, Bulgaria
82 G 11 **Razlog**, Bulgaria
14 H 13 **Reading**, PA, U.S.A.
21 K 20 **Reading**, OH, U.S.A.
63 U 11 **Reading**, U.K.
20 E 13 **Readstown**, WI, U.S.A.
56 J 13 **Realicó**, Argentina
115 J 20 **Reăng Kesei**, Cambodia
125 Q 8 **Rebaa**, Algeria
70 I 7 **Rebbenesøy**, Norway ✱
125 W 12 **Rebiana Sand Sea**, Libya ◇
90 G 7 **Reboly**, Russian Federation
122 I 3 **Rebun-tō**, Japan ✱
85 M 20 **Rechytsa**, Belarus
54 O 13 **Recife**, Brazil
57 F 14 **Recinto**, Chile
58 C 12 **Reconquista**, Argentina
56 I 9 **Recreo**, Argentina
13 P 12 **Red**, TX, U.S.A. ∿
114 K 11 **Red**, Asia ∿
16 H 10 **Red Bank**, TN, U.S.A.
19 O 2 **Red Bay**, AL, U.S.A.
41 X 8 **Red Bay**, NL, Canada
33 G 16 **Red Bluff**, CA, U.S.A.
22 M 15 **Red Cloud**, NE, U.S.A.
39 J 19 **Red Deer**, AB, Canada
24 J 7 **Red Hills**, KS, U.S.A. ◇
30 H 9 **Red Lake**, AZ, U.S.A. ◣
40 J 10 **Red Lake**, ON, Canada
29 S 8 **Red Lodge**, MT, U.S.A.
126 H 11 **Red Sea**, Africa/Asia ◒
127 G 14 **Red Sea**, Sudan ▣
23 T 8 **Red Wing**, MN, U.S.A.
118 D 5 **Redang**, Malaysia ✱
61 K 15 **Redcar**, U.K.
33 G 16 **Redding**, CA, U.S.A.
63 R 8 **Redditch**, U.K.
54 J 12 **Redenção**, Brazil
54 L 13 **Redenção do Gurguéia**, Brazil
22 M 8 **Redfield**, SD, U.S.A.
90 H 14 **Redkino**, Russian Federation
33 K 24 **Redlands**, CA, U.S.A.
32 H 11 **Redmond**, OR, U.S.A.
21 L 20 **Redoak**, OH, U.S.A.
62 J 15 **Redruth**, U.K.
23 Q 8 **Redwood Falls**, MN, U.S.A.
33 F 17 **Redwood Valley**, CA, U.S.A.
20 J 13 **Reed City**, MI, U.S.A.
22 H 6 **Reeder**, ND, U.S.A.
32 E 11 **Reedsport**, OR, U.S.A.
17 V 5 **Reedville**, VA, U.S.A.
137 G 17 **Reefton**, New Zealand
73 B 15 **Rees**, Germany
95 N 9 **Refahiye**, Turkey
19 O 3 **Reform**, AL, U.S.A.
27 Q 12 **Refugio**, TX, U.S.A.
78 E 9 **Rega**, Poland ∿
73 M 22 **Regen**, Germany
73 K 22 **Regensburg**, Germany
124 L 11 **Reggane**, Algeria
76 E 8 **Reggio**, Italy
77 L 21 **Reggio di Calabria**, Italy
86 J 9 **Reghin**, Romania
39 N 19 **Regina**, SK, Canada
101 R 10 **Registan**, Afghanistan ◇
58 K 8 **Registro**, Brazil
107 X 8 **Regong**, India
66 I 10 **Reguengos de Monsaraz**, Portugal
132 I 10 **Rehoboth**, Namibia
17 X 3 **Rehoboth Beach**, DE, U.S.A.
17 Q 8 **Reidsville**, NC, U.S.A.
63 V 11 **Reigate**, U.K.
65 S 3 **Reims**, France
74 F 7 **Reinach**, Switzerland
39 M 16 **Reindeer**, SK, Canada ∿
39 M 14 **Reindeer Lake**, SK, Canada ◣
67 N 2 **Reinosa**, Spain
75 Y 2 **Reinthal**, Austria
38 J 12 **Reliance**, NT, Canada
124 L 6 **Relizane**, Algeria
125 Q 8 **Remada**, Tunisia
73 C 18 **Remagen**, Germany
116 J 14 **Rembang**, Indonesia
125 Q 8 **Remel el Abiod**, Tunisia ▲▲
69 M 26 **Remich**, Luxembourg
21 H 17 **Remington**, IN, U.S.A.
65 V 6 **Remiremont**, France
93 O 10 **Remontnoye**, Russian Federation
73 C 16 **Remscheid**, Germany
114 F 6 **Renam**, Myanmar
21 F 21 **Rend Lake**, IL, U.S.A. ◣
138 K 6 **Rendova**, Solomon Islands ✱
72 G 8 **Rendsburg**, Germany
42 H 10 **Renfrew**, ON, Canada
116 E 11 **Rengat**, Indonesia
56 G 12 **Rengo**, Chile
113 T 10 **Renhua**, China
87 N 11 **Reni**, Ukraine
135 Q 11 **Renmark**, SA, Australia
138 L 8 **Rennell**, Solomon Islands ✱
64 L 5 **Rennes**, France
40 J 10 **Rennie**, MB, Canada
33 I 17 **Reno**, NV, U.S.A.
14 E 11 **Renovo**, PA, U.S.A.
111 D 18 **Renqiu**, China
113 N 7 **Renshou**, China
117 O 15 **Reo**, Indonesia
103 N 13 **Repetek**, Turkmenistan
54 F 10 **Represa de Balbina**, Brazil ◣
58 H 9 **Represa de Foz de Areia**, Brazil ◣
58 L 5 **Represa de Furnas**, Brazil ◣
58 F 8 **Represa de Itaipu**, Brazil/Paraguay ◣
58 G 8 **Represa de Salto Santiago**, Brazil ◣
58 G 7 **Represa Ilha Grande**, Brazil ◣
58 H 4 **Represa Porto Primavera**, Brazil ◣
58 I 3 **Represa São Simão**, Brazil ◣
55 J 15 **Represa Serra da Mesa**, Brazil ◣
55 L 17 **Represa Três Marias**, Brazil ◣
54 J 11 **Represa Tucuruí**, Brazil ◣
46 L 5 **Repressa el Cajón**, Honduras ◣
20 G 9 **Republic**, MI, U.S.A.
32 J 6 **Republic**, WA, U.S.A.
132 M 12 **Republic of South Africa**, Africa □
80 F 10 **Republica Srpska**, Bosnia and Herzegovina ▣
41 N 2 **Repulse Bay**, NU, Canada
52 E 12 **Requena**, Peru
67 S 8 **Requena**, Spain
65 Q 13 **Réquista**, France
94 M 9 **Reşadiye**, Turkey
95 S 11 **Reşadiye**, Turkey
82 C 12 **Resen**, Macedonia (F.Y.R.O.M.)
58 H 8 **Reserva**, Brazil
31 N 12 **Reserve**, NM, U.S.A.
42 I 8 **Réservoir Baskatong**, QC, Canada ◣
42 I 8 **Réservoir Cabonga**, QC, Canada ◣
42 H 8 **Réservoir Dozois**, QC, Canada ◣
42 K 6 **Réservoir Gouin**, QC, Canada ◣
41 P 9 **Réservoir la Grande Deux**, QC, Canada ◣
41 Q 9 **Réservoir la Grande Trois**, QC, Canada ◣
43 P 4 **Réservoir Manic Trois**, QC, Canada ◣
43 P 2 **Réservoir Manicouagan**, QC, Canada ◣
41 Q 9 **Réservoir Opinaca**, QC, Canada ◣
43 O 4 **Réservoir Outardes Quatre**, QC, Canada ◣
43 N 4 **Réservoir Pipmuacan**, QC, Canada ◣
87 T 5 **Reshetylivka**, Ukraine
58 C 10 **Resistencia**, Argentina
86 F 11 **Reşiţa**, Romania
78 E 9 **Resko**, Poland
37 P 4 **Resolute Bay**, NU, Canada
41 T 4 **Resolution Island**, NU, Canada ✱
137 A 24 **Resolution Island**, New Zealand ✱
92 L 12 **Respublika Adygeya**, Russian Federation ▣
88 M 13 **Respublika Altay**, Russian Federation ▣
93 W 2 **Respublika Bashkortostan**, Russian Federation ▣
89 R 13 **Respublika Buryatiya**, Russian Federation ▣
93 R 15 **Respublika Dagestan**, Russian Federation ▣
93 Q 10 **Respublika Kalmykiya**, Russian Federation ▣
90 H 6 **Respublika Kareliya**, Russian Federation ▣
89 N 13 **Respublika Khakasiya**, Russian Federation ▣
91 R 7 **Respublika Komi**, Russian Federation ▣
91 O 14 **Respublika Mariy El**, Russian Federation ▣
93 O 3 **Respublika Mordoviya**, Russian Federation ▣
89 R 10 **Respublika Sakha**, Russian Federation ▣
93 O 14 **Respublika Severnaya Osetiya-Alaniya**, Russian Federation ▣
93 S 1 **Respublika Tatarstan**, Russian Federation ▣
89 O 13 **Respublika Tyva**, Russian Federation ▣
46 F 6 **Retalhuleu**, Guatemala
56 F 13 **Retén Llico**, Chile
63 T 4 **Retford**, U.K.
65 S 3 **Rethel**, France
83 H 26 **Rethymno**, Greece
75 W 2 **Retz**, Austria
11 Q 11 **Réunion**, France ▣
73 G 23 **Reutlingen**, Germany
74 L 6 **Reutte**, Austria
22 H 7 **Reva**, SD, U.S.A.
65 P 14 **Revel**, France
39 H 20 **Revelstoke**, BC, Canada
52 A 12 **Reventazón**, Peru
96 E 11 **Revivim**, Israel
106 M 12 **Rewa**, India
106 I 9 **Rewari**, India
29 P 10 **Rexburg**, ID, U.S.A.
53 I 18 **Reyes**, Bolivia
70 A 11 **Reykanestá**, Iceland ▶
143 N 14 **Reykjanes Basin**, Arctic Ocean ◇
143 N 15 **Reykjanes Ridge**, Arctic Ocean ▲▲
70 B 11 **Reykjavík**, Iceland ⌂
45 R 7 **Reynosa**, Mexico
84 I 12 **Rēzekne**, Latvia
87 N 8 **Rezina**, Moldova
80 N 12 **Rgotina**, Serbia and Montenegro
63 N 8 **Rhayader**, U.K.
72 D 13 **Rheine**, Germany
74 E 6 **Rheinfelden**, Switzerland
73 D 20 **Rheinland-Pfalz**, Germany ▣
74 H 9 **Rheinwaldhorn**, Switzerland ▲
65 W 5 **Rhine**, Europe ∿
20 F 10 **Rhinelander**, WI, U.S.A.
131 R 6 **Rhino Camp**, Uganda
72 K 12 **Rhinow**, Germany
69 H 21 **Rhisnes**, Belgium
15 N 11 **Rhode Island**, U.S.A. ▣
15 O 11 **Rhode Island Sound**, RI, U.S.A. ≈
83 O 24 **Rhodes**, Greece ✱
82 G 11 **Rhodope Mountains**, Bulgaria ▲▲
73 G 19 **Rhön**, Germany ▲▲
63 N 10 **Rhondda**, U.K. ◇
65 T 12 **Rhône**, France/Switzerland ∿
65 U 11 **Rhône-Alpes**, France ▣
63 O 5 **Rhosllanerchrugog**, U.K.
62 L 10 **Rhossili**, U.K.
61 I 18 **Rhyl**, U.K.
63 O 4 **Rhyl**, U.K.
129 S 15 **Riaba**, Equatorial Guinea
54 K 12 **Riachão**, Brazil
55 L 14 **Riachão das Neves**, Brazil
55 J 15 **Rialma**, Brazil
66 G 2 **Rías Bajas**, Spain ◇
116 E 10 **Riau**, Indonesia ▣
67 O 5 **Riaza**, Spain
55 H 18 **Ribas do Rio Pardo**, Brazil
133 T 5 **Ribáuè**, Mozambique
63 Q 2 **Ribble**, U.K. ∿
71 B 25 **Ribe**, Denmark
58 J 8 **Ribeira**, Brazil ∿
66 G 2 **Ribeira**, Spain
58 K 5 **Ribeirão Preto**, Brazil
53 J 16 **Riberalta**, Bolivia
67 X 3 **Ribes de Freser**, Spain
80 C 8 **Ribnica**, Slovenia
87 O 8 **Rîbniţa**, Moldova
72 K 8 **Ribnitz-Damgarten**, Germany
44 L 4 **Ricardo Flores Magón**, Mexico
76 H 10 **Riccione**, Italy
20 D 10 **Rice Lake**, WI, U.S.A.
25 S 11 **Rich Mountain**, AR, U.S.A. ▲
19 U 2 **Richard B. Russell Lake**, GA, U.S.A. ◣
128 E 7 **Richard Toll**, Senegal
133 Q 12 **Richards Bay**, Republic of South Africa
17 O 11 **Richburn**, SC, U.S.A.
28 M 11 **Richfield**, ID, U.S.A.
14 I 8 **Richfield Springs**, NY, U.S.A.
43 T 8 **Richibucto**, NB, Canada
27 R 7 **Richland**, TX, U.S.A.
20 E 13 **Richland Center**, WI, U.S.A.
16 M 7 **Richlands**, VA, U.S.A.
16 J 5 **Richmond**, KY, U.S.A.
17 T 6 **Richmond**, VA, U.S.A.
42 M 10 **Richmond**, QC, Canada
132 L 13 **Richmond**, Republic of South Africa
135 S 5 **Richmond**, QLD, Australia
137 I 16 **Richmond**, New Zealand
19 W 5 **Richmond Hill**, GA, U.S.A.
137 H 17 **Richmond Range**, New Zealand ▲▲
63 V 10 **Richmond upon Thames**, U.K.
28 K 13 **Riddle**, ID, U.S.A.
33 K 22 **Ridgecrest**, CA, U.S.A.
17 N 15 **Ridgeland**, SC, U.S.A.
14 D 11 **Ridgway**, PA, U.S.A.
75 R 4 **Ried im Innkreis**, Austria
73 G 24 **Riedlingen**, Germany
73 M 16 **Riesa**, Germany
84 C 13 **Rietavas**, Lithuania
76 H 13 **Rieti**, Italy
31 O 4 **Rifle**, CO, U.S.A.
70 C 9 **Rifstangi**, Iceland ▶
131 U 6 **Rift Valley**, Kenya ▣
129 V 9 **Rig-Rig**, Chad
84 F 11 **Rīga**, Latvia ⌂
28 K 7 **Riggins**, ID, U.S.A.
84 E 6 **Riguldi**, Estonia
145 N 3 **Riiser-Larsen Ice Shelf**, Antarctica ◇
145 U 2 **Riiser-Larsen Peninsula**, Antarctica ▶
84 F 6 **Riisipere**, Estonia
129 Q 10 **Rijau**, Nigeria
80 B 9 **Rijeka**, Croatia
68 M 11 **Rijssen**, Netherlands
122 L 4 **Rikubetsu**, Japan
82 G 10 **Rila**, Bulgaria ▲▲
25 O 3 **Riley**, KS, U.S.A.
32 J 12 **Riley**, OR, U.S.A.
69 F 16 **Rilland**, Netherlands
79 K 21 **Rimavská Sobota**, Slovakia
76 H 10 **Rimini**, Italy
43 Q 6 **Rimouski**, QC, Canada
117 N 15 **Rinca**, Indonesia ✱
112 K 6 **Rinda**, China
83 J 21 **Rineia**, Greece ✱
104 D 12 **Ringas**, India
18 H 4 **Ringgold**, LA, U.S.A.
27 P 4 **Ringgold**, TX, U.S.A.
129 S 10 **Ringim**, Nigeria
71 B 24 **Ringkøbing**, Denmark
24 M 12 **Ringling**, OK, U.S.A.
29 R 6 **Ringling**, MT, U.S.A.
71 D 25 **Ringsted**, Denmark
70 I 7 **Ringvassøy**, Norway ✱
63 S 13 **Ringwood**, U.K.
54 C 13 **Rio Branco**, Brazil
58 J 8 **Rio Branco do Sul**, Brazil
55 H 18 **Rio Brilhante**, Brazil
57 F 16 **Río Bueno**, Chile
49 Z 14 **Rio Claro**, Trinidad and Tobago
58 K 6 **Rio Claro**, Brazil
59 A 19 **Río Colorado**, Argentina
56 J 11 **Río Cuarto**, Argentina
58 N 7 **Rio de Janeiro**, Brazil
58 N 6 **Rio de Janeiro**, Brazil ▣
47 U 15 **Río de Jesús**, Panama
58 I 10 **Rio do Sul**, Brazil
57 H 23 **Río Gallegos**, Argentina
12 L 12 **Rio Grande**, U.S.A., U.S.A. ∿
45 O 8 **Río Grande**, Mexico
57 I 25 **Río Grande**, Argentina
59 H 14 **Rio Grande**, Brazil
27 O 15 **Rio Grande City**, TX, U.S.A.
45 N 10 **Río Grande de Santiago**, Mexico ∿
54 O 12 **Rio Grande do Norte**, Brazil ▣
58 F 11 **Rio Grande do Sul**, Brazil ▣
47 W 14 **Río Hato**, Panama
58 G 12 **Rio Jacuí**, Brazil ∿
45 Z 10 **Río Lagartos**, Mexico
66 G 8 **Rio Maior**, Portugal
53 J 21 **Río Mulatos**, Bolivia
57 I 16 **Río Negro**, Argentina ▣
58 I 9 **Rio Negro**, Brazil
59 D 14 **Río Negro**, Uruguay ▣
58 H 12 **Rio Pardo**, Brazil
31 P 10 **Rio Rancho**, NM, U.S.A.
52 D 10 **Río Tigre**, Peru
121 B 20 **Rio Tuba**, Philippines
45 Q 10 **Río Verde**, Mexico
55 I 17 **Rio Verde**, Brazil
57 G 24 **Rio Verde**, Chile
52 B 9 **Riobamba**, Ecuador
50 J 2 **Ríohacha**, Colombia
52 C 12 **Rioja**, Peru
65 R 10 **Riom**, France
67 Q 10 **Riópar**, Spain
87 Q 1 **Ripky**, Ukraine
16 A 9 **Ripley**, TN, U.S.A.
17 N 4 **Ripley**, WV, U.S.A.
21 L 20 **Ripley**, OH, U.S.A.
63 S 1 **Ripley**, U.K.
63 S 5 **Ripley**, U.K.
67 X 3 **Ripoll**, Spain
63 S 1 **Ripon**, U.K.
69 K 15 **Rips**, Netherlands
86 M 7 **Rîşcani**, Moldova
47 S 13 **Risco**, Panama ∿
122 I 3 **Rishiri-tō**, Japan ✱
122 I 3 **Rishiri-yama**, Japan ▲
96 F 9 **Rishon Le Ẕiyyon**, Israel
71 D 15 **Rissa**, Norway
71 N 17 **Ristiina**, Finland
70 N 13 **Ristijärvi**, Finland
84 C 6 **Ristna**, Estonia
105 N 21 **Ritchie's Archipelago**, India ✱
32 K 7 **Ritzville**, WA, U.S.A.
76 F 6 **Riva del Garda**, Italy
56 K 6 **Rivadavia**, Argentina
56 G 9 **Rivadavia**, Chile
59 A 16 **Rivadavia**, Argentina
47 N 10 **Rivas**, Nicaragua
128 H 13 **River Cess**, Liberia
20 C 11 **River Falls**, WI, U.S.A.
59 E 16 **River Plate**, Argentina/Uruguay ∿
58 F 13 **Rivera**, Brazil
58 F 13 **Rivera**, Uruguay
58 E 13 **Rivera**, Uruguay ▣
59 A 18 **Rivera**, Argentina
14 L 12 **Riverhead**, NY, U.S.A.
20 H 12 **Rivers**, WI, U.S.A.
129 Q 14 **Rivers**, Nigeria ▣
137 D 24 **Riversdale**, New Zealand
137 L 16 **Riversdale Beach**, New Zealand
27 S 8 **Riverside**, TX, U.S.A.
33 K 25 **Riverside**, CA, U.S.A.
29 U 11 **Riverton**, WY, U.S.A.
43 U 9 **Riverview**, NB, Canada
27 P 14 **Riviera**, TX, U.S.A.
43 T 5 **Rivière-au-Renard**, QC, Canada
41 Q 7 **Rivière aux Feuilles**, QC, Canada ∿
41 R 7 **Rivière aux Mélèzes**, QC, Canada ∿
43 V 4 **Rivière-aux-Saumons**, QC, Canada
43 P 7 **Rivière-du-Loup**, QC, Canada
43 R 4 **Rivière-Pentecôte**, QC, Canada
49 Z 11 **Rivière-Pilote**, Martinique
86 L 3 **Rivne**, Ukraine
76 A 7 **Rivoli**, Italy
132 K 6 **Rivungo**, Angola
99 R 6 **Riyadh**, Saudi Arabia ⌂
95 P 8 **Rize**, Turkey
113 X 2 **Rizhao**, China
94 J 15 **Rizokarpason**, Cyprus
49 V 7 **Road Town**, Virgin Islands, U.K. ⌂
30 M 5 **Roan Plateau**, UT, U.S.A. ◇
65 S 9 **Roanne**, France
13 W 9 **Roanoake**, VA, U.S.A.
17 Q 6 **Roanoke**, VA, U.S.A.
19 R 4 **Roanoke**, AL, U.S.A.
17 W 9 **Roanoke Island**, NC, U.S.A. ✱
17 T 8 **Roanoke Rapids**, NC, U.S.A.
47 N 3 **Roatán**, Honduras
63 O 10 **Roath**, U.K.
135 S 14 **Robbins Island**, TAS, Australia ✱
25 R 10 **Robert S. Kerr Reservoir**, OK, U.S.A. ◣
145 R 14 **Roberts Butte**, Antarctica ▲
107 O 12 **Robertsganj**, India
144 I 3 **Robertson Island**, Antarctica ✱
128 G 13 **Robertsport**, Liberia
42 M 6 **Roberval**, QC, Canada
135 R 12 **Robinvale**, VIC, Australia
67 Q 9 **Robledo**, Spain
40 H 9 **Roblin**, MB, Canada
53 N 21 **Robore**, Bolivia
27 P 13 **Robstown**, TX, U.S.A.
77 J 14 **Roccaraso**, Italy
59 F 15 **Rocha**, Uruguay
59 G 15 **Rocha**, Uruguay ▣
63 R 3 **Rochdale**, U.K.
65 O 10 **Rochechouart**, France
55 H 17 **Rochedo**, Brazil
64 L 9 **Rochefort**, France
69 I 23 **Rochefort**, Belgium
90 M 8 **Rochegda**, Russian Federation
14 E 8 **Rochester**, NY, U.S.A.
15 O 8 **Rochester**, NH, U.S.A.
21 I 17 **Rochester**, IN, U.S.A.
23 T 9 **Rochester**, MN, U.S.A.
63 X 11 **Rochester**, U.K.
137 D 24 **Rock and Pillar Range**, New Zealand ▲▲
21 E 16 **Rock Falls**, IL, U.S.A.
17 O 11 **Rock Hill**, SC, U.S.A.
29 T 14 **Rock Springs**, WY, U.S.A.
29 W 5 **Rock Springs**, MT, U.S.A.
27 Q 9 **Rockdale**, TX, U.S.A.
21 F 15 **Rockford**, IL, U.S.A.
135 V 7 **Rockhampton**, QLD, Australia
17 Q 11 **Rockingham**, NC, U.S.A.
22 L 2 **Rocklake**, ND, U.S.A.
15 Q 6 **Rockland**, ME, U.S.A.
21 H 22 **Rockport**, IN, U.S.A.
32 H 6 **Rockport**, WA, U.S.A.
26 M 10 **Rocksprings**, TX, U.S.A.
21 H 19 **Rockville**, IN, U.S.A.
23 R 12 **Rockwell City**, IA, U.S.A.
16 I 9 **Rockwood**, TN, U.S.A.
42 B 8 **Rocky Island Lake**, ON, Canada ◣
17 T 8 **Rocky Mount**, NC, U.S.A.
29 O 3 **Rocky Mountain**, MT, U.S.A. ▲
39 I 19 **Rocky Mountain House**, AB, Canada
12 J 4 **Rocky Mountains**, MT, U.S.A. ▲▲
132 G 8 **Rocky Point**, Namibia ▶
31 N 15 **Rodeo**, NM, U.S.A.
56 G 10 **Rodeo**, Argentina
65 Q 12 **Rodez**, France
73 L 21 **Roding**, Germany
86 J 8 **Rodna**, Romania
82 H 13 **Rodolivos**, Greece
83 O 23 **Rodos**, Greece
11 R 11 **Rodrigues Island**, Mauritius ▣
134 F 6 **Roebourne**, WA, Australia
134 I 4 **Roebuck Bay**, WA, Australia ≈
134 I 4 **Roebuck Plains Roadhouse**, WA, Australia
69 K 17 **Roermond**, Netherlands
41 N 3 **Roes Welcome Sound**, NU, Canada ≈
69 A 18 **Roesbrugge-Haringe**, Belgium
69 B 18 **Roeselare**, Belgium
77 L 17 **Rofrano**, Italy
80 I 13 **Rogatica**, Bosnia and Herzegovina
25 S 8 **Rogers**, AR, U.S.A.
20 L 10 **Rogers City**, MI, U.S.A.
33 K 23 **Rogers Lake**, CA, U.S.A. ◣
28 M 13 **Rogerson**, ID, U.S.A.
65 Y 14 **Rogliano**, France
77 M 19 **Rogliano**, Italy
86 J 5 **Rohatyn**, Ukraine
75 S 3 **Rohrbach**, Austria
101 U 12 **Rohri**, Pakistan
106 I 8 **Rohtak**, India
84 E 6 **Rohuküla**, Estonia
115 K 17 **Roi Et**, Thailand
107 Z 8 **Roing**, India
84 D 10 **Roja**, Latvia
59 B 15 **Rojas**, Argentina
84 G 13 **Rokiškis**, Lithuania
122 K 8 **Rokkasho**, Japan
123 H 14 **Rokkō-zaki**, Japan ▶
86 M 2 **Rokytne**, Ukraine
71 A 19 **Røldal**, Norway
25 W 5 **Rolla**, MO, U.S.A.
74 B 9 **Rolle**, Switzerland
135 U 7 **Rolleston**, QLD, Australia
42 F 7 **Rollet**, QC, Canada
70 K 5 **Rolvsøya**, Norway ✱
13 O 15 **Roma**, TX, U.S.A.
117 R 14 **Roma**, Indonesia ✱
135 U 8 **Roma**, QLD, Australia
86 G 10 **Romania**, Europe □
89 R 13 **Romanovka**, Russian Federation
121 I 14 **Romblon**, Philippines
121 I 14 **Romblon**, Philippines ✱
121 H 14 **Romblon Passage**, Philippines ≈
14 H 8 **Rome**, NY, U.S.A.
19 R 2 **Rome**, GA, U.S.A.
77 H 14 **Rome**, Italy ⌂
21 M 14 **Romeo**, MI, U.S.A.
63 W 10 **Romford**, U.K.
65 R 5 **Romilly-sur-Seine**, France
17 R 2 **Romney**, WV, U.S.A.
87 S 3 **Romny**, Ukraine
71 B 25 **Rømø**, Denmark ✱
93 P 2 **Romodanovo**, Russian Federation
65 P 7 **Romorantin-Lanthenay**, France
118 D 9 **Rompin**, Malaysia ∿
63 S 12 **Romsey**, U.K.
115 M 15 **Ron**, Vietnam
66 M 13 **Ronda**, Spain
50 K 5 **Rondón**, Colombia
55 E 14 **Rondônia**, Brazil ▣
55 H 16 **Rondonópolis**, Brazil
113 Q 11 **Rong'an**, China
112 J 5 **Rongbaca**, China
111 I 19 **Rongcheng**, China
141 W 1 **Rongelap Atoll**, Marshall Islands ✱
113 Q 10 **Rongjiang**, China
141 X 1 **Rongrik**, Marshall Islands ✱
113 R 12 **Rongxian**, China
71 F 26 **Rønne**, Denmark
144 I 7 **Ronne Entrance**, Antarctica ≈
144 L 7 **Ronne Ice Shelf**, Antarctica ◇
71 G 24 **Ronneby**, Sweden
71 F 15 **Rönnöfors**, Sweden
69 D 19 **Ronse**, Belgium
106 J 7 **Roorkee**, India
69 G 15 **Roosendaal**, Netherlands
30 K 12 **Roosevelt**, AZ, U.S.A.
145 O 11 **Roosevelt Island**, Antarctica ✱
79 M 17 **Ropczyce**, Poland
135 N 2 **Roper Bar**, NT, Australia
64 M 13 **Roquefort**, France
54 E 8 **Roraima**, Brazil ▣
71 E 16 **Røros**, Norway
87 Q 5 **Ros'**, Ukraine ∿
52 B 8 **Rosa Zárate**, Ecuador
48 I 9 **Rosalind Bank**, Jamaica ≈
58 G 6 **Rosana**, Brazil
44 M 9 **Rosario**, Mexico
50 K 3 **Rosario**, Venezuela
59 C 14 **Rosario**, Argentina
120 F 9 **Rosario**, Philippines
120 G 12 **Rosario**, Philippines
48 E 8 **Rosario Bank**, Cayman Islands ≈
56 J 7 **Rosario de la Frontera**, Argentina
58 F 12 **Rosário do Sul**, Brazil
44 E 2 **Rosarito**, Mexico
44 G 5 **Rosarito**, Mexico
44 I 6 **Rosarito**, Mexico
77 L 20 **Rosarno**, Italy
22 L 7 **Roscoe**, SD, U.S.A.
26 L 6 **Roscoe**, TX, U.S.A.
20 K 11 **Roscommon**, MI, U.S.A.
61 C 17 **Roscommon**, Republic of Ireland
61 D 19 **Roscrea**, Republic of Ireland
140 L 8 **Rose**, American Samoa ✱
30 M 12 **Rose Peak**, AZ, U.S.A. ▲
49 Y 10 **Roseau**, Dominica ⌂
32 F 12 **Roseburg**, OR, U.S.A.
69 H 22 **Rosée**, Belgium
127 G 19 **Roseires Reservoir**, Sudan ◣
27 S 10 **Rosenburg**, TX, U.S.A.
73 K 25 **Rosenheim**, Germany
67 Y 3 **Roses**, Spain
76 J 12 **Roseto degli Abruzzi**, Italy
39 L 19 **Rosetown**, SK, Canada
21 D 17 **Roseville**, IL, U.S.A.
132 I 12 **Rosh Pinah**, Namibia
76 E 11 **Rosignano Marittimo**, Italy
86 J 13 **Roşiori de Vede**, Romania
92 H 2 **Roslavl'**, Russian Federation
90 M 11 **Roslvatino**, Russian Federation
135 T 15 **Ross**, TAS, Australia
137 F 19 **Ross**, New Zealand
145 O 11 **Ross Ice Shelf**, Antarctica ◇
145 Q 12 **Ross Island**, Antarctica ✱
63 Q 9 **Ross-on-Wye**, U.K.
38 C 13 **Ross River**, YT, Canada
145 N 12 **Ross Sea**, Antarctica ◒
61 C 15 **Rossan Point**, Republic of Ireland ▶
138 I 7 **Rossel Island**, Papua New Guinea ✱
61 E 20 **Rosslare**, Republic of Ireland
128 E 7 **Rosso**, Mauritania
92 L 7 **Rossosh'**, Russian Federation
70 F 12 **Røssvatnet**, Norway ◣
100 J 13 **Rostāq**, Iran
72 J 9 **Rostock**, Germany
90 J 14 **Rostov**, Russian Federation
92 L 10 **Rostov-na-Donu**, Russian Federation
92 M 9 **Rostovskaya Oblast'**, Russian Federation ▣
19 S 2 **Roswell**, GA, U.S.A.
31 S 12 **Roswell**, NM, U.S.A.
140 A 9 **Rota**, Northern Mariana Islands ✱
117 P 15 **Rote**, Indonesia ✱
72 G 11 **Rotenburg**, Germany
73 E 17 **Rothaargebirge**, Germany ▲▲
73 H 21 **Rothenburg ob der Tauber**, Germany
144 H 5 **Rothera**, Antarctica ⁙
63 S 4 **Rotherham**, U.K.
144 I 6 **Rothschild Island**, Antarctica ✱
63 U 7 **Rothwell**, U.K.
117 P 15 **Roti**, Indonesia
137 G 19 **Rotomanu**, New Zealand
77 N 17 **Rotondella**, Italy
136 M 11 **Rotorua**, New Zealand
75 T 6 **Rottenmann**, Austria
68 G 13 **Rotterdam**, Netherlands
68 M 5 **Rottumeroog**, Netherlands ✱
68 L 4 **Rottumerplaat**, Netherlands ✱
73 F 24 **Rottweil**, Germany
139 W 8 **Rotuma**, Fiji ✱
65 Q 1 **Roubaix**, France
65 O 3 **Rouen**, France
16 F 6 **Rough River Lake**, KY, U.S.A. ◣
27 P 9 **Round Rock**, TX, U.S.A.
30 M 8 **Round Rock**, AZ, U.S.A.
29 T 6 **Roundup**, MT, U.S.A.
60 I 6 **Rousay**, U.K. ✱
42 F 7 **Rouyn**, QC, Canada
70 L 11 **Rovaniemi**, Finland
90 L 9 **Rovdino**, Russian Federation
87 Z 7 **Roven'ky**, Ukraine
74 H 10 **Roveredo**, Switzerland
76 F 6 **Rovereto**, Italy
115 L 19 **Rôvieng Tbong**, Cambodia
76 G 8 **Rovigo**, Italy
86 H 12 **Rovinari**, Romania
80 A 9 **Rovinj**, Croatia
93 Q 6 **Rovnoye**, Russian Federation
17 R 11 **Rowland**, NC, U.S.A.
41 O 1 **Rowley Island**, NU, Canada ✱
121 I 16 **Roxas**, Philippines
121 E 17 **Roxas**, Philippines
121 H 14 **Roxas**, Philippines
17 R 8 **Roxboro**, NC, U.S.A.
135 P 10 **Roxby Downs**, SA, Australia
29 T 4 **Roy**, MT, U.S.A.
31 S 9 **Roy**, NM, U.S.A.
63 S 8 **Royal Leamington Spa**, U.K.
63 X 12 **Royal Tunbridge Wells**, U.K.
14 M 7 **Royalton**, VT, U.S.A.
64 L 10 **Royan**, France
65 Q 3 **Roye**, France
19 U 2 **Royston**, GA, U.S.A.
63 W 9 **Royston**, U.K.
81 L 15 **Rožaje**, Serbia and Montenegro
78 L 11 **Różan**, Poland
87 T 11 **Rozdol'ne**, Ukraine
79 K 20 **Rožňava**, Slovakia
68 F 13 **Rozenburg**, Netherlands
68 K 13 **Rozendaal**, Netherlands
86 K 3 **Rozhyshche**, Ukraine
81 K 17 **Rrëshen**, Albania
93 O 5 **Rtishchevo**, Russian Federation
63 P 5 **Ruabon**, U.K.
132 G 7 **Ruacana**, Namibia
137 L 14 **Ruahine Range**, New Zealand ▲▲
136 J 6 **Ruakaka**, New Zealand
137 C 26 **Ruapuke Island**, New Zealand ✱
136 M 11 **Ruatahuna**, New Zealand
136 J 7 **Ruawai**, New Zealand
99 Q 10 **Rub' al Khālī**, Saudi Arabia ◇
87 Y 5 **Rubizhne**, Ukraine
88 L 13 **Rubtsovsk**, Russian Federation
35 P 7 **Ruby**, AK, U.S.A.
33 M 17 **Ruby Mountains**, NV, U.S.A. ▲▲
86 J 11 **Rucăr**, Romania
84 B 12 **Rucava**, Latvia
113 U 10 **Rucheng**, China
17 S 4 **Ruckersville**, VA, U.S.A.
101 Q 11 **Rudbar**, Afghanistan
92 G 1 **Rudnya**, Russian Federation
93 P 6 **Rudnya**, Russian Federation
103 O 3 **Rudnyy**, Kazakhstan
73 J 17 **Rudolstadt**, Germany
113 Z 5 **Rudong**, China
65 P 2 **Rue**, France
127 F 17 **Rufa'a**, Sudan
65 N 9 **Ruffec**, France
59 A 16 **Rufino**, Argentina
133 O 5 **Rufunsa**, Zambia
113 Y 5 **Rugao**, China
22 K 3 **Rugby**, ND, U.S.A.
61 K 20 **Rugby**, U.K.
63 T 7 **Rugby**, U.K.
63 R 6 **Rugeley**, U.K.
72 L 8 **Rügen**, Germany ✱
131 Q 8 **Ruhengeri**, Rwanda
84 E 9 **Ruhnu**, Estonia ✱
113 Z 8 **Rui'an**, China
113 V 7 **Ruichang**, China
31 R 13 **Ruidoso**, NM, U.S.A.
113 V 10 **Ruijin**, China
112 H 11 **Ruili**, China
131 U 12 **Ruipa**, Tanzania
44 M 10 **Ruiz**, Mexico
84 G 9 **Rūjiena**, Latvia
70 N 11 **Ruka**, Finland
131 R 12 **Rukwa**, Tanzania ▣
60 E 11 **Rum**, U.K. ✱
49 N 3 **Rum Cay**, The Bahamas ✱
80 K 10 **Ruma**, Serbia and Montenegro
99 R 5 **Rumāh**, Saudi Arabia
97 Y 12 **Rumaila**, Iraq
127 D 21 **Rumbek**, Sudan
138 A 4 **Rumginae**, Papua New Guinea
122 J 4 **Rumoi**, Japan
133 R 3 **Rumphi**, Malawi
113 U 4 **Runan**, China
63 P 4 **Runcorn**, U.K.
132 J 7 **Rundu**, Namibia
131 P 6 **Rungu**, Democratic Republic of Congo
131 T 12 **Rungwa**, Tanzania
112 L 4 **Ru'nying**, China
71 O 17 **Ruokolahti**, Finland
108 K 6 **Ruoqiang**, China
70 M 6 **Ruostefjelbma**, Norway
116 E 10 **Rupat**, Indonesia ✱
86 J 10 **Rupea**, Romania
17 O 5 **Rupert**, WV, U.S.A.
144 M 12 **Ruppert Coast**, Antarctica ◇
53 I 18 **Rurrenabaque**, Bolivia
133 Q 7 **Rusape**, Zimbabwe
86 I 7 **Ruscova**, Romania
82 K 6 **Ruse**, Bulgaria ▣
82 K 6 **Ruse**, Bulgaria
111 H 20 **Rushan**, China
63 U 8 **Rushden**, U.K.
21 D 18 **Rushville**, IL, U.S.A.
85 C 14 **Rusnė**, Lithuania
84 I 12 **Rušonu ezers**, Latvia ◣
16 L 4 **Russell**, KY, U.S.A.
24 L 4 **Russell**, KS, U.S.A.
138 L 6 **Russell Islands**, Solomon Islands ✱
16 H 7 **Russell Springs**, KY, U.S.A.

□ Country ▣ Internal administrative region: State/Province/Territory/Dependent territory ⌂ Capital city ▲▲ Mountain range/Undersea ridge ▲ Mountain peak/Volcano/Seamount ◇ Geographic feature ▶ Headland/Point/Cape/Peninsula ☗ Desert ✱ Island/Island group ⁙ Antarctic base ≋ Ocean ◒ Sea ≈ Bay/Gulf/Channel/Strait ◣ Lake ◤ Salt pan/Dry/Intermittent lake ∿ R

F 7 **Russellville**, KY, U.S.A.
O 2 **Russellville**, AL, U.S.A.
U 10 **Russellville**, AR, U.S.A.
J 9 **Russian Federation**, Europe □
M 12 **Russkaya**, Antarctica ⁙
V 7 **Russkoye Ust'ye**, Russian Federation
U 7 **Rust'avi**, Georgia
N 11 **Rustenburg**, Republic of South Africa
I 4 **Ruston**, LA, U.S.A.
C 17 **Ruten**, Norway ▲
O 15 **Ruteng**, Indonesia
M 18 **Ruth**, NV, U.S.A.
M 10 **Rutherfordton**, NC, U.S.A.
L 7 **Rutland**, VT, U.S.A.
N 22 **Rutland Island**, India 🏝
H 8 **Rutog**, China
D 9 **Rutter**, ON, Canada
R 15 **Rutul**, Russian Federation
M 12 **Ruurlo**, Netherlands
U 14 **Ruvuma**, Tanzania ▣
S 3 **Ruvuma**, Mozambique/Tanzania ∿
V 6 **Ruweis**, United Arab Emirates
P 3 **Ruzayevka**, Russian Federation
F 19 **Ruzhany**, Belarus
J 19 **Ružomberok**, Slovakia
Q 9 **Rwanda**, Africa □
M 2 **Ryazan'**, Russian Federation
M 2 **Ryazanskaya Oblast'**, Russian Federation ▣
M 3 **Ryazhsk**, Russian Federation
J 7 **Ryberg Peninsula**, Antarctica ▶
J 13 **Rybinsk**, Russian Federation
I 12 **Rybinsk Reservoir**, Russian Federation ◢
I 17 **Rybnik**, Poland
T 13 **Ryde**, U.K.
Y 12 **Rye**, U.K.
S 13 **Rye**, VIC, Australia
Y 13 **Rye Bay**, U.K. ≈
T 6 **Ryegate**, MT, U.S.A.
M 14 **Ryki**, Poland
I 5 **Ryl'sk**, Russian Federation
I 13 **Ryōtsu**, Japan
J 11 **Rypin**, Poland
N 24 **Ryukyu Islands**, Japan 🏝
D 12 **Rzepin**, Poland
M 17 **Rzeszów**, Poland
G 14 **Rzhev**, Russian Federation

L 13 **'s-Heerenberg**, Netherlands
I 14 **'s-Hertogenbosch**, Netherlands
I 5 **Sa de las Minas**, Guatemala ▲▲
M 22 **Sa Đec**, Vietnam
D 18 **Sa del Tandil**, Argentina ▲▲
I 19 **Sa Kaeo**, Thailand
K 24 **Saacow**, Somalia
J 15 **Saale**, Germany ∿
J 18 **Saalfeld**, Germany
Q 6 **Saalfelden**, Austria
C 21 **Saarbrücken**, Germany
B 20 **Saarburg**, Germany
D 9 **Sääre**, Estonia
D 8 **Saaremaa**, Estonia 🏝
L 16 **Saarijärvi**, Finland
C 21 **Saarland**, Germany ▣
E 10 **Saas Fee**, Switzerland
J 6 **Sab' Ābār**, Syria
W 8 **Saba**, Netherlands Antilles 🏝
J 10 **Šabac**, Serbia and Montenegro
W 4 **Sabadell**, Spain
G 16 **Sabae**, Japan
W 6 **Sabah**, Malaysia ▣
E 12 **Sabalgarh**, India
M 7 **Sabamagrande**, Honduras
L 3 **Sabana Grande**, Venezuela
I 2 **Sabanalarga**, Colombia
L 3 **Sabaneta**, Venezuela
B 8 **Sabang**, Indonesia
G 7 **Sabangan**, Philippines
L 9 **Săbăoani**, Romania
G 25 **Sabaragamuwa**, Sri Lanka ▣
H 15 **Sabaudia**, Italy
I 21 **Sabaya**, Bolivia
H 9 **Şabḩā**, Jordan
T 11 **Sabhā**, Libya
N 11 **Sabinal**, TX, U.S.A.
T 3 **Sabiñánigo**, Spain
Q 6 **Sabinas Hidalgo**, Mexico
H 6 **Sabine**, LA, U.S.A. ∿
H 8 **Sabine Lake**, LA, U.S.A. ◢
T 8 **Sabkhat al Hayshah**, Libya ◢
X 9 **Sabkhat al Qunayyin**, Libya ◢
W 9 **Sabkhat Ghuzayyil**, Libya ◢
F 14 **Sablayan**, Philippines
S 9 **Sabon Kafi**, Niger
M 13 **Sabres**, France
X 12 **Sabrina Coast**, Antarctica ◇
H 2 **Sabtang**, Philippines 🏝
J 6 **Sabugal**, Portugal
N 11 **Sabulu**, Indonesia
O 11 **Şabyā**, Saudi Arabia
M 6 **Sabzevār**, Iran
K 10 **Sacajawea Peak**, OR, U.S.A. ▲
Q 6 **Sacedón**, Spain
M 21 **Sach'ŏn**, South Korea
M 16 **Sachsen**, Germany ▣
J 12 **Sachsen-Anhalt**, Germany ▣
G 6 **Sackets Harbor**, NY, U.S.A.
V 2 **Saco**, MT, U.S.A.
I 22 **Sacol**, Philippines 🏝
G 19 **Sacramento**, CA, U.S.A.
G 17 **Sacramento**, CA, U.S.A. ∿
R 13 **Sacramento Mountains**, NM, U.S.A. ▲▲
G 16 **Sacramento Valley**, CA, U.S.A. ◇
I 5 **Şadad**, Syria
O 11 **Şa'dah**, Yemen
H 26 **Sadao**, Thailand
E 18 **Sadaseopet**, India
V 4 **Sadd Darband-i Khān**, Iraq ◢
T 8 **Saddat al Hindīyah**, Iraq
X 11 **Şadḩ**, Oman
G 20 **Sadi**, Ethiopia
V 12 **Sadiqabad**, Pakistan
Y 9 **Sadiya**, India
I 13 **Sadoga-shima**, Japan 🏝
U 11 **Sadove**, Ukraine
P 9 **Sadovoye**, Russian Federation
V 4 **Safed Khirs**, Afghanistan ▲▲
P 7 **Safed Koh**, Afghanistan ▲▲
E 21 **Säffle**, Sweden
L 13 **Safford**, AZ, U.S.A.
X 8 **Saffron Walden**, U.K.
124 G 8 **Safi**, Morocco
101 O 10 **Safidabeh**, Iran
96 H 4 **Şāfītā**, Syria
92 I 1 **Safonovo**, Russian Federation
97 Z 12 **Safwān**, Iraq
138 E 4 **Sag Sag**, Papua New Guinea
108 I 10 **Saga**, China
123 B 21 **Saga**, Japan
123 E 21 **Saga**, Japan
122 K 12 **Sagae**, Japan
114 C 10 **Sagaing**, Myanmar ▣
114 D 11 **Sagaing**, Myanmar
123 K 17 **Sagami-nada**, Japan ≈
123 K 16 **Sagami-wan**, Japan ≈
23 U 2 **Saganaga Lake**, MN, U.S.A. ◢
115 F 21 **Saganthif Kyun**, Myanmar 🏝
105 F 14 **Sagar**, India
89 S 7 **Sagastyr**, Russian Federation
107 P 10 **Sagauli**, India
100 L 8 **Saghand**, Iran
20 L 13 **Saginaw**, MI, U.S.A.
20 L 13 **Saginaw Bay**, MI, U.S.A. ≈
102 J 6 **Sagiz**, Kazakhstan
20 G 9 **Sagola**, MI, U.S.A.
67 P 11 **Sagra**, Spain ▲
66 G 12 **Sagres**, Portugal
114 C 13 **Sagu**, Myanmar
48 M 6 **Sagua de Tánamo**, Cuba
48 J 4 **Sagua la Grande**, Cuba
31 Q 6 **Saguache**, CO, U.S.A.
43 N 6 **Saguenay**, QC, Canada
43 N 6 **Saguenay**, QC, Canada ∿
67 T 8 **Sagunto**, Spain
35 R 3 **Sagwon**, AK, U.S.A.
96 H 9 **Saḩāb**, Jordan
124 I 13 **Sahara**, Algeria ◇
106 J 7 **Saharanpur**, India
107 R 11 **Saharsa**, India
95 V 10 **Şahbuz**, Azerbaijan
128 M 9 **Sahel**, Burkina Faso ◇
107 S 12 **Sahibganj**, India
101 X 10 **Sahiwal**, Pakistan
101 W 9 **Sahiwal**, Pakistan
101 O 9 **Sahlābād**, Iran
97 T 12 **Şaḩrā' al Ḩijāra**, Iraq ◇
44 J 4 **Sahuaripa**, Mexico
45 O 11 **Sahuayo**, Mexico
127 B 20 **Sa'id Bundas**, Sudan
96 G 6 **Saïda**, Lebanon
124 L 6 **Saïda**, Algeria
138 D 4 **Saidor**, Papua New Guinea
107 T 11 **Saidpur**, Bangladesh
123 E 17 **Saigō**, Japan
107 X 14 **Saiha**, India
111 B 14 **Saihan Tal**, China
123 E 20 **Saijō**, Japan
123 D 21 **Saiki**, Japan
71 N 17 **Saimaa**, Finland ◢
101 P 11 **Saindak**, Pakistan
60 J 13 **St Abb's Head**, U.K. ▶
75 W 5 **St Aegyd am Neuwalde**, Austria
62 J 15 **St Agnes**, U.K.
65 O 7 **St-Aignan**, France
16 M 4 **St Albans**, WV, U.S.A.
41 Y 10 **St Alban's**, NL, Canada
63 V 10 **St Albans**, U.K.
63 R 14 **St Alban's Head**, U.K. ▶
65 Q 8 **St-Amand-Montrond**, France
65 U 9 **St-Amour**, France
75 U 8 **St Andrä**, Austria
19 X 6 **St Andrew Sound**, GA, U.S.A. ≈
60 I 12 **St Andrews**, U.K.
43 R 5 **Ste-Anne-des-Monts**, QC, Canada
41 X 9 **St Anthony**, NL, Canada
74 K 7 **St Anton am Arlberg**, Austria
135 R 13 **St Arnaud**, VIC, Australia
137 H 17 **St Arnaud**, New Zealand
63 O 4 **St Asaph**, U.K.
41 W 9 **St-Augustin**, QC, Canada
19 W 8 **St Augustine**, FL, U.S.A.
62 K 15 **St Austell**, U.K.
62 K 15 **St Austell Bay**, U.K. ≈
49 X 8 **St Barthélémy**, France, France 🏝
65 N 15 **St-Béat**, France
62 J 9 **St Bride's Bay**, U.K. ≈
64 J 5 **St-Brieuc**, France
65 O 6 **St-Calais**, France
42 F 13 **St Catharines**, ON, Canada
63 T 14 **St Catherine's Point**, U.K. ▶
65 P 12 **St-Céré**, France
25 X 4 **St Charles**, MO, U.S.A.
29 Q 13 **Saint Charles**, ID, U.S.A.
62 L 9 **St Clears**, U.K.
23 R 7 **St Cloud**, MN, U.S.A.
49 V 8 **St Croix**, Virgin Islands, U.S.A. 🏝
20 C 10 **St Croix Falls**, WI, U.S.A.
43 O 9 **St-Damien-de-Buckland**, QC, Canada
62 J 9 **St David's**, U.K.
62 J 9 **St David's Head**, U.K. ▶
65 W 5 **St-Dié**, France
65 T 5 **St Dizier**, France
65 T 10 **St-Étienne**, France
49 X 8 **St Eusatius**, Netherlands Antilles 🏝
43 P 6 **St-Fabien**, QC, Canada
42 M 6 **St-Félicien**, QC, Canada
65 S 6 **St-Florentin**, France
65 R 11 **St-Flour**, France
24 G 2 **St Francis**, KS, U.S.A.
74 I 6 **St Gallen**, Switzerland
65 N 15 **St-Gaudens**, France
17 P 14 **St George**, SC, U.S.A.
30 H 7 **St George**, UT, U.S.A.
43 S 10 **St George**, NB, Canada
135 U 9 **St George**, QLD, Australia
19 S 8 **St George Island**, FL, U.S.A. 🏝
34 J 11 **St George Island**, AK, U.S.A. 🏝
75 U 3 **St Georgen**, Austria
43 O 9 **St-Georges**, QC, Canada
49 Y 13 **St George's**, Grenada ♜
51 Y 7 **St Georges**, French Guiana
41 W 11 **St Georges Bay**, NL, Canada ≈
43 X 9 **St George's Bay**, NS, Canada ≈
61 E 21 **St George's Channel**, Republic of Ireland/United Kingdom ≈
138 H 3 **St George's Channel**, Papua New Guinea ≈
75 R 5 **St Gilgen**, Austria
69 F 17 **St-Gillis-Waas**, Belgium
65 O 15 **St-Girons**, France
62 K 10 **St Govan's Head**, U.K. ▶
20 K 12 **Saint Helen**, MI, U.S.A.
10 L 11 **St Helena**, U.K. ▣
132 J 14 **Saint Helena Bay**, Republic of South Africa ≈
17 P 15 **St Helena Sound**, SC, U.S.A. ≈
32 F 9 **St Helens**, OR, U.S.A.
63 P 3 **St Helens**, U.K.
135 T 15 **St Helens**, TAS, Australia
61 J 26 **St Helier**, U.K.
69 J 23 **St-Hubert**, Belgium
42 L 10 **St-Hyacinthe**, QC, Canada
20 K 10 **St Ignace**, MI, U.S.A.
62 I 15 **St Ives**, U.K.
63 W 7 **St Ives**, U.K.
62 J 15 **St Ives Bay**, U.K. ≈
68 J 6 **St Jacobiparochie**, Netherlands
75 O 8 **St Jakob**, Austria
64 K 14 **St-Jean-de-Luz**, France
65 V 11 **St-Jean-de-Maurienne**, France
64 K 8 **St-Jean-de-Monts**, France
43 O 8 **St-Jean-de-Port-Joli**, QC, Canada
42 L 11 **St-Jean-sur-Richelieu**, QC, Canada
42 K 10 **St-Jérôme**, QC, Canada
75 P 6 **St Johann in Tirol**, Austria
24 L 5 **St John**, KS, U.S.A.
41 U 13 **St John**, NB, Canada
43 S 10 **Saint John**, NB, Canada
49 V 8 **St John**, Virgin Islands, U.S.A. 🏝
21 K 14 **Saint Johns**, MI, U.S.A.
30 M 11 **St Johns**, AZ, U.S.A.
41 Z 10 **St John's**, NL, Canada
49 Y 9 **St John's**, Antigua and Barbuda ♜
16 E 10 **St Joseph**, TN, U.S.A.
18 K 5 **St Joseph**, LA, U.S.A.
25 R 2 **St Joseph**, MO, U.S.A.
19 R 8 **St Joseph Bay**, FL, U.S.A. ≈
27 Q 13 **St Joseph Island**, TX, U.S.A. 🏝
42 A 9 **St Joseph Island**, ON, Canada 🏝
42 J 10 **St-Jovité**, QC, Canada
65 O 10 **St-Junien**, France
62 J 15 **St Keverne**, U.K.
49 X 8 **St Kitts**, St Kitts and Nevis 🏝
49 X 9 **St Kitts and Nevis**, North America □
51 X 6 **St-Laurent-du-Maroni**, French Guiana
37 W 11 **St Lawrence**, QC, Canada ∿
34 K 7 **St Lawrence Island**, AK, U.S.A. 🏝
69 K 25 **St-Léger**, Belgium
42 M 9 **St-Léonard**, QC, Canada
43 Q 8 **St-Léonard**, NB, Canada
64 L 4 **St-Lô**, France
25 X 4 **St Louis**, MO, U.S.A.
128 D 7 **St-Louis**, Senegal
49 Z 11 **St Lucia**, North America □
49 Y 11 **St Lucia Channel**, St Lucia ≈
49 W 8 **St Maarten**, Netherlands Antilles 🏝
64 K 4 **St-Malo**, France
49 O 7 **St Marc**, Haiti
65 P 8 **St-Marcel**, France
69 E 19 **St-Maria-Lierde**, Belgium
43 N 9 **Ste-Marie**, QC, Canada
19 T 7 **St Marks**, FL, U.S.A.
49 X 8 **St Martin**, France, France 🏝
135 P 10 **St Mary Peak**, SA, Australia ▲
25 P 3 **Saint Marys**, KS, U.S.A.
41 Z 11 **St Mary's Bay**, NL, Canada ≈
34 J 9 **St Matthew Island**, AK, U.S.A. 🏝
138 F 2 **St Matthias Group**, Papua New Guinea 🏝
62 K 15 **St Mawes**, U.K.
64 M 9 **St-Maxient-l'École**, France
65 W 14 **Ste-Maxime**, France
75 R 7 **St Michael**, Austria
75 U 6 **St Michael**, Austria
42 K 9 **St-Michel-des-Saints**, QC, Canada
74 J 9 **St Moritz**, Switzerland
64 K 7 **St-Nazaire**, France
63 V 8 **St Neots**, U.K.
69 F 17 **St-Niklaas**, Belgium
74 E 10 **St Niklaus**, Switzerland
75 S 6 **St Nikolai**, Austria
65 Q 1 **St-Omer**, France
43 O 8 **St-Pacôme**, QC, Canada
64 L 14 **St-Palais**, France
43 O 7 **St-Pascal**, QC, Canada
22 M 14 **St Paul**, NE, U.S.A.
23 S 8 **St Paul**, MN, U.S.A.
34 J 11 **St Paul Island**, AK, U.S.A. 🏝
43 Y 7 **St Paul Island**, NS, Canada 🏝
72 F 8 **St Peter-Ording**, Germany
61 J 25 **St Peter Port**, U.K.
43 Y 9 **St Peter's**, NS, Canada
43 W 8 **St Peters**, PE, Canada
19 V 11 **St Petersburg**, FL, U.S.A.
90 F 10 **St Petersburg**, Russian Federation
37 Z 10 **St-Pierre**, St Pierre and Miquelon ♜
41 Y 11 **St-Pierre**, France, Canada
41 X 11 **St Pierre and Miquelon**, France ▣
64 L 9 **St-Pierre-d'Oléron**, France
64 I 4 **St-Pol-de-Léon**, France
75 W 4 **St Pölten**, Austria
65 Q 14 **St-Pons-de-Thomiéres**, France
65 R 9 **St-Pourçain-sur-Sioule**, France
43 Q 7 **St Quentin**, NB, Canada
65 R 2 **St-Quentin**, France
65 W 14 **St-Raphaël**, France
28 L 4 **Saint Regis**, MT, U.S.A.
43 O 7 **St Siméon**, QC, Canada
17 Q 13 **St Stephen**, SC, U.S.A.
35 W 10 **St Terese**, AK, U.S.A.
42 L 10 **Ste-Thérese**, QC, Canada
42 C 14 **St Thomas**, ON, Canada
49 V 8 **St Thomas**, Virgin Islands, U.S.A. 🏝
43 N 8 **St-Tite-des-Caps**, QC, Canada
65 W 14 **St-Tropez**, France
69 I 19 **St-Truiden**, Belgium
65 O 2 **St-Valery-en-Caux**, France
75 T 8 **St Veit an der Glan**, Austria
49 Y 12 **St Vincent**, St Vincent and the Grenadines 🏝
49 X 12 **St Vincent and the Grenadines**, North America □
19 R 8 **St Vincent Island**, FL, U.S.A. 🏝
49 Y 11 **St Vincent Passage**, St Lucia ≈
39 L 17 **St Walburg**, SK, Canada
49 Z 10 **Sainte-Marie**, Martinique
49 Y 9 **Sainte-Rose**, Guadeloupe, France
64 M 10 **Saintes**, France
140 A 8 **Saipan**, Northern Mariana Islands ♜
140 A 8 **Saipan**, Northern Mariana Islands 🏝
114 B 11 **Saitlai**, Myanmar
123 C 23 **Saito**, Japan
53 H 20 **Sajama**, Bolivia
124 J 6 **Saka**, Morocco
123 G 18 **Sakai**, Japan
123 F 19 **Sakaide**, Japan
123 E 18 **Sakaiminato**, Japan
98 M 2 **Sakākah**, Saudi Arabia
133 W 9 **Sakaraha**, Madgascar
128 K 12 **Sakassou**, Côte d'Ivoire
122 J 12 **Sakata**, Japan
89 X 13 **Sakhalin**, Russian Federation 🏝
95 W 7 **Şäki**, Azerbaijan
129 O 12 **Saki**, Nigeria
85 D 15 **Šakiai**, Lithuania
123 M 26 **Sakishima-shotō**, Japan 🏝
115 K 16 **Sakon Nakhon**, Thailand
101 U 14 **Sakrand**, Pakistan
132 K 13 **Sakrivier**, Republic of South Africa
123 J 15 **Saku**, Japan
123 L 16 **Sakura**, Japan
87 T 12 **Saky**, Ukraine
71 H 20 **Sala**, Sweden
42 K 11 **Salaberry-de-Valleyfield**, QC, Canada
84 F 9 **Salacgrīva**, Latvia
58 D 11 **Saladas**, Argentina
59 C 16 **Saladillo**, Argentina
45 P 5 **Salado**, Mexico ∿
58 B 12 **Salado**, Argentina ∿
128 I 11 **Saladou**, Guinea
128 M 12 **Salaga**, Ghana
97 T 2 **Salahuddin**, Iraq
129 W 8 **Salal**, Chad
126 H 13 **Salâla**, Sudan
99 W 11 **Şalālah**, Oman
46 H 5 **Salamá**, Guatemala
14 D 10 **Salamanca**, NY, U.S.A.
56 F 11 **Salamanca**, Chile
66 L 5 **Salamanca**, Spain
129 Y 10 **Salamat**, Chad ▣
96 I 4 **Salamīyah**, Syria
84 C 12 **Salantai**, Lithuania
56 H 6 **Salar de Arizaro**, Argentina ◢
56 H 4 **Salar de Ascotán**, Chile ◢
56 G 5 **Salar de Atacama**, Chile ◢
53 I 21 **Salar de Coipasa**, Bolivia ◢
53 I 22 **Salar de Uyuni**, Bolivia ◢
67 O 3 **Salas de los Infantes**, Spain
116 J 14 **Salatiga**, Indonesia
93 W 3 **Salavat**, Russian Federation
117 T 11 **Salawati**, Indonesia 🏝
105 A 15 **Salaya**, India
117 O 13 **Salayar**, Indonesia 🏝
63 N 15 **Salcombe**, U.K.
132 J 15 **Saldanha**, Republic of South Africa
84 D 11 **Saldus**, Latvia
135 T 13 **Sale**, VIC, Australia
88 L 8 **Salekhard**, Russian Federation
15 O 9 **Salem**, MA, U.S.A.
21 F 21 **Salem**, IL, U.S.A.
25 W 6 **Salem**, MO, U.S.A.
30 K 3 **Salem**, UT, U.S.A.
32 G 10 **Salem**, OR, U.S.A.
105 E 22 **Salem**, India
77 H 22 **Salemi**, Italy
77 O 16 **Salentina Peninsula**, Italy ▶
77 K 16 **Salerno**, Italy
63 Q 3 **Salford**, U.K.
79 J 21 **Salgótarján**, Hungary
54 N 13 **Salgueiro**, Brazil
124 L 11 **Sali**, Algeria
117 R 9 **Salibabu**, Indonesia 🏝
31 Q 5 **Salida**, CO, U.S.A.
85 J 20 **Salihorsk**, Belarus
133 R 4 **Salima**, Malawi
25 N 4 **Salina**, KS, U.S.A.
30 J 5 **Salina**, UT, U.S.A.
45 U 14 **Salina Cruz**, Mexico
57 I 16 **Salina Gualicho**, Argentina ◢
33 G 21 **Salinas**, CA, U.S.A.
45 P 9 **Salinas**, Mexico
52 A 10 **Salinas**, Ecuador
56 I 5 **Salinas Grandes**, Argentina ◢
54 K 9 **Salinópolis**, Brazil
17 W 4 **Salisbury**, MD, U.S.A.
17 P 9 **Salisbury**, NC, U.S.A.
63 S 12 **Salisbury**, U.K.
41 P 3 **Salisbury Island**, NU, Canada 🏝
63 R 12 **Salisbury Plain**, U.K. ◇
86 I 11 **Săliște**, Romania
96 I 8 **Şalkhad**, Syria
67 W 4 **Sallent**, Spain
59 A 17 **Salliqueló**, Argentina
25 R 10 **Sallisaw**, OK, U.S.A.
41 Q 4 **Salluit**, QC, Canada
107 N 9 **Sallyana**, Nepal
97 U 7 **Salmān Pāk**, Iraq
100 E 3 **Salmās**, Iran
84 D 8 **Salme**, Estonia
28 L 7 **Salmon**, ID, U.S.A. ∿
29 N 8 **Salmon**, ID, U.S.A.
39 H 21 **Salmon Arm**, BC, Canada
28 M 8 **Salmon River Mountains**, ID, U.S.A. ▲▲
71 L 19 **Salo**, Finland
76 E 6 **Salò**, Italy
65 U 14 **Salon-de-Provence**, France
86 F 9 **Salonta**, Romania
56 I 10 **Salsacate**, Argentina
92 M 11 **Sal'sk**, Russian Federation
30 K 12 **Salt**, AZ, U.S.A. ∿
26 F 7 **Salt Basin**, TX, U.S.A. ◢
26 F 7 **Salt Flat**, TX, U.S.A.
30 J 2 **Salt Lake City**, UT, U.S.A.
101 W 8 **Salt Range**, Pakistan ◇
56 I 6 **Salta**, Argentina
56 I 6 **Salta**, Argentina ▣
62 M 14 **Saltash**, U.K.
45 P 7 **Saltillo**, Mexico
58 D 13 **Salto**, Uruguay
58 E 13 **Salto**, Uruguay ▣
59 C 15 **Salto**, Argentina
55 H 19 **Salto del Guairá**, Paraguay
33 M 25 **Salton Sea**, CA, U.S.A. ◢
71 J 19 **Saltvik**, Finland
17 N 12 **Saluda**, SC, U.S.A.
96 M 2 **Salūq**, Syria
121 N 20 **Salvacion**, Philippines
55 N 15 **Salvador**, Brazil
56 J 4 **Salvador Mazza**, Argentina
99 T 6 **Salwah**, Saudi Arabia
114 F 13 **Salween**, Myanmar ∿
16 L 5 **Salyersville**, KY, U.S.A.
75 Q 7 **Salzburg**, Austria ▣
75 Q 5 **Salzburg**, Austria
73 H 14 **Salzgitter**, Germany
75 Q 5 **Salzkammergut**, Austria ▲▲
72 I 12 **Salzwedel**, Germany
115 G 16 **Sam Ngao**, Thailand
27 U 7 **Sam Rayburn Reservoir**, TX, U.S.A. ◢
114 M 13 **Sâm Son**, Vietnam
53 K 21 **Samaipata**, Bolivia
121 M 22 **Samal**, Philippines 🏝
121 H 23 **Samales Group**, Philippines 🏝
126 E 9 **Samâlût**, Egypt
49 R 7 **Samaná**, Dominican Republic
101 T 6 **Samangān**, Afghanistan ▣
121 L 15 **Samar**, Philippines 🏝
93 T 3 **Samara**, Russian Federation ∿
93 S 3 **Samara**, Russian Federation
138 G 7 **Samarai**, Papua New Guinea
116 M 11 **Samarinda**, Indonesia
103 Q 13 **Samarkand**, Uzbekistan
103 P 12 **Samarqand Wiloyati**, Uzbekistan ▣
97 S 6 **Sāmarrā'**, Iraq
93 T 4 **Samarskaya Oblast'**, Russian Federation ▣
103 Y 5 **Samarskoye**, Kazakhstan
107 Q 11 **Samastipur**, India
95 Y 8 **Şamaxi**, Azerbaijan
131 O 10 **Samba**, Democratic Republic of Congo
132 H 2 **Samba Cajú**, Angola
105 I 16 **Sambalpur**, India
116 I 10 **Sambas**, Indonesia
133 Z 5 **Sambava**, Madgascar
86 H 5 **Sambir**, Ukraine
69 E 22 **Sambre**, Belgium ∿
111 N 19 **Samch'ŏk**, South Korea
133 O 3 **Samfya**, Zambia
111 M 15 **Samjiyŏn**, North Korea
95 V 8 **Şämkir**, Azerbaijan
125 T 11 **Samnū**, Libya
140 J 7 **Samoa**, Oceania □
140 J 8 **Samoan Islands**, Samoa/American Samoa 🏝
80 D 8 **Samobor**, Croatia
82 G 10 **Samokov**, Bulgaria
79 G 21 **Šamorín**, Slovakia
83 M 20 **Samos**, Greece
83 L 20 **Samos**, Greece 🏝
83 I 14 **Samotharaki**, Greece 🏝
116 K 12 **Sampit**, Indonesia
138 H 4 **Sampun**, Papua New Guinea
131 P 13 **Sampwe**, Democratic Republic of Congo
71 D 25 **Samsø**, Denmark 🏝
115 H 19 **Samut Prakan**, Thailand
115 H 19 **Samut Sakhon**, Thailand
115 H 19 **Samut Songkhram**, Thailand
79 N 19 **San**, Poland ∿
128 K 9 **San**, Mali
59 D 18 **San Agustín**, Argentina
56 H 10 **San Agustín de Valle Fértil**, Argentina
33 H 19 **San Andreas**, CA, U.S.A.
46 I 2 **San Andrēs**, Guatemala
53 K 18 **San Andrés**, Bolivia
120 I 13 **San Andres**, Philippines
120 K 13 **San Andres**, Philippines
31 Q 12 **San Andres Mountains**, NM, U.S.A. ▲▲
45 U 12 **San Andrés Tuxtla**, Mexico
26 M 8 **San Angelo**, TX, U.S.A.
27 O 11 **San Antonio**, TX, U.S.A.
27 P 11 **San Antonio**, TX, U.S.A. ∿
31 P 12 **San Antonio**, NM, U.S.A.
46 J 3 **San Antonio**, Belize
46 J 5 **San Antonio**, Honduras
46 L 6 **San Antonio**, Honduras
51 N 8 **San Antonio**, Venezuela
51 Q 3 **San Antonio**, Venezuela
56 H 11 **San Antonio**, Argentina
56 I 9 **San Antonio**, Argentina
56 F 12 **San Antonio**, Chile
120 F 11 **San Antonio**, Philippines
67 W 9 **San Antonio Abad**, Spain
121 B 20 **San Antonio Bay**, Philippines ≈
56 I 6 **San Antonio de los Cobres**, Argentina
46 M 6 **San Antonio de Oriente**, Honduras
57 J 16 **San Antonio Oeste**, Argentina
76 J 12 **San Benedetto del Tronto**, Italy
74 H 9 **San Bernadino**, Switzerland
33 K 24 **San Bernardino**, CA, U.S.A.
33 K 24 **San Bernardino Mountains**, CA, U.S.A. ▲▲
121 K 14 **San Bernardino Strait**, Philippines ≈
56 G 12 **San Bernardo**, Chile
44 K 7 **San Blas**, Mexico
53 J 18 **San Borja**, Bolivia
56 K 6 **San Camilo**, Argentina
44 H 7 **San Carlos**, Mexico
47 Q 12 **San Carlos**, Costa Rica
47 P 10 **San Carlos**, Nicaragua
47 W 14 **San Carlos**, Panama
51 O 9 **San Carlos**, Venezuela
53 L 20 **San Carlos**, Bolivia
57 F 14 **San Carlos**, Chile
59 F 16 **San Carlos**, Uruguay
120 G 9 **San Carlos**, Philippines
121 J 17 **San Carlos**, Philippines
57 G 17 **San Carlos de Bariloche**, Argentina
59 B 17 **San Carlos de Bolívar**, Argentina
77 O 16 **San Cataldo**, Italy
33 K 25 **San Clemente**, CA, U.S.A.
56 F 13 **San Clemente**, Chile
33 J 26 **San Clemente Island**, CA, U.S.A. 🏝
46 H 5 **San Crisóbal Verapez**, Guatemala
50 J 11 **San Cristóbal**, Colombia
50 K 4 **San Cristóbal**, Venezuela
56 K 9 **San Cristóbal**, Argentina
58 B 12 **San Cristobal**, Argentina
139 N 7 **San Cristobal**, Solomon Islands 🏝
45 W 13 **San Cristóbal de las Casas**, Mexico
46 I 6 **San Cristobal Frontera**, Guatemala
27 P 13 **San Diego**, TX, U.S.A.
33 K 26 **San Diego**, CA, U.S.A.
76 H 7 **San Donà di Piave**, Italy
44 G 3 **San Felipe**, Mexico
45 P 10 **San Felipe**, Mexico
50 M 2 **San Felipe**, Venezuela
56 G 11 **San Felipe**, Chile
33 J 24 **San Fernando**, CA, U.S.A.
44 G 4 **San Fernando**, Mexico
45 S 8 **San Fernando**, Mexico
49 Y 14 **San Fernando**, Trinidad and Tobago
56 G 12 **San Fernando**, Chile
59 D 15 **San Fernando**, Argentina
66 K 13 **San Fernando**, Spain
120 F 10 **San Fernando**, Philippines
120 F 8 **San Fernando**, Philippines
51 N 4 **San Fernando de Apure**, Venezuela
51 N 7 **San Fernando de Atabapo**, Venezuela
33 F 19 **San Francisco**, CA, U.S.A.
58 B 13 **San Francisco**, Argentina
33 G 19 **San Francisco Bay**, CA, U.S.A. ≈
56 J 9 **San Francisco del Chañar**, Argentina
46 L 7 **San Francisco Gotera**, El Salvador
67 W 10 **San Francisco Javier**, Spain
52 C 8 **San Gabriel**, Ecuador
49 T 8 **San Germán**, Puerto Rico
76 E 11 **San Gimignano**, Italy
77 N 19 **San Giovanni in Fiore**, Italy
44 H 6 **San Ignacio**, Mexico
46 J 2 **San Ignacio**, Belize
52 B 12 **San Ignacio**, Peru
53 J 18 **San Ignacio**, Bolivia
53 M 19 **San Ignacio**, Bolivia
120 H 9 **San Ildefonso Peninsula**, Philippines ▶
47 Q 13 **San Isidro**, Costa Rica
121 K 14 **San Jacinto**, Philippines
53 K 18 **San Javier**, Bolivia
58 B 13 **San Javier**, Argentina
33 G 19 **San Joaquin**, CA, U.S.A. ∿
33 H 20 **San Joaquin Valley**, CA, U.S.A. ◇
59 B 14 **San Jorge**, Argentina
21 F 18 **San Jose**, IL, U.S.A.
31 R 10 **San Jose**, NM, U.S.A.
33 G 20 **San Jose**, CA, U.S.A.
46 H 7 **San José**, Guatemala
46 M 5 **San José**, Honduras
47 Q 12 **San José**, Costa Rica ♜
59 E 15 **San José**, Uruguay ▣
120 G 9 **San Jose**, Philippines
121 G 14 **San Jose**, Philippines
140 A 8 **San Jose**, Northern Mariana Islands
121 H 17 **San Jose de Buenavista**, Philippines
53 N 20 **San José de Chiquitos**, Bolivia
58 D 12 **San José de Feliciano**, Argentina
44 J 4 **San José de Gracia**, Mexico
56 H 10 **San José de Jáchal**, Argentina
56 J 10 **San José de la Dormida**, Argentina
59 E 15 **San José de Mayo**, Uruguay
53 D 16 **San José de Quero**, Peru
45 Q 8 **San José de Raíces**, Mexico
44 J 9 **San José del Cabo**, Mexico
50 J 8 **San José del Guaviare**, Colombia
45 T 13 **San Juan**, Mexico
47 Q 11 **San Juan**, Nicaragua ∿
49 U 7 **San Juan**, Puerto Rico ♜
49 Q 7 **San Juan**, Dominican Republic
56 H 10 **San Juan**, Argentina
56 G 10 **San Juan**, Argentina ▣
55 G 20 **San Juan Bautista**, Paraguay
51 N 3 **San Juan de los Morros**, Venezuela
57 J 25 **San Juan de Salvamento**, Argentina
47 Q 11 **San Juan del Norte**, Nicaragua
45 Q 11 **San Juan del Río**, Mexico
47 N 10 **San Juan del Sur**, Nicaragua
46 G 4 **San Juan Ixcoy**, Guatemala
31 P 7 **San Juan Mountains**, CO, U.S.A. ▲▲
44 H 6 **San Juanico**, Mexico
56 L 10 **San Justo**, Argentina
46 L 7 **San Lorenzo**, Honduras
52 B 7 **San Lorenzo**, Ecuador
53 J 18 **San Lorenzo**, Bolivia
53 H 16 **San Lorenzo**, Peru
59 B 14 **San Lorenzo**, Argentina
44 H 6 **San Lucas**, Mexico
44 J 9 **San Lucas**, Mexico
53 K 22 **San Lucas**, Bolivia
56 I 11 **San Luis**, Argentina
56 I 12 **San Luis**, Argentina ▣
45 Q 10 **San Luis de la Paz**, Mexico
58 D 10 **San Luis del Palmar**, Argentina
33 H 23 **San Luis Obispo**, CA, U.S.A.
31 P 6 **San Luis Peak**, CO, U.S.A. ▲
45 P 10 **San Luis Potosí**, Mexico
45 P 9 **San Luis Potosí**, Mexico ▣
44 G 1 **San Luis Río Colorado**, Mexico
44 H 3 **San Luisito**, Mexico
27 P 10 **San Marcos**, TX, U.S.A.
45 R 14 **San Marcos**, Mexico
46 F 5 **San Marcos**, Guatemala
46 M 7 **San Marcos de Colón**, Honduras
76 H 10 **San Marino**, Europe □
52 C 13 **San Martín**, Peru ▣
53 L 18 **San Martín**, Bolivia ∿
56 H 11 **San Martín**, Argentina
56 I 9 **San Martín**, Argentina
144 I 5 **San Martin**, Antarctica ⁙
57 G 16 **San Martín de Los Andes**, Argentina
67 N 6 **San Martín de Valdeiglesias**, Spain
33 F 20 **San Mateo**, CA, U.S.A.
46 F 4 **San Mateo Ixtatán**, Guatemala
53 O 19 **San Matías**, Bolivia
46 K 7 **San Miguel**, El Salvador
47 X 14 **San Miguel**, Panama
53 M 20 **San Miguel**, Bolivia
53 L 18 **San Miguel**, Bolivia ∿
120 J 12 **San Miguel Bay**, Philippines ≈
53 J 19 **San Miguel de Huachi**, Bolivia
56 J 7 **San Miguel de Tucumán**, Argentina
59 C 16 **San Miguel del Monte**, Argentina
33 H 24 **San Miguel Island**, CA, U.S.A. 🏝
121 C 21 **San Miguel Islands**, Philippines 🏝
47 P 10 **San Miguelito**, Nicaragua
47 X 13 **San Miguelito**, Panama
59 B 15 **San Nicolás de los Arroyos**, Argentina
33 I 25 **San Nicolas Island**, CA, U.S.A. 🏝
77 C 18 **San Nicoló Gerrei**, Italy
53 L 19 **San Pablo**, Bolivia
120 G 12 **San Pablo**, Philippines
44 J 8 **San Pedro**, Mexico
46 L 1 **San Pedro**, Belize
56 I 6 **San Pedro**, Argentina
58 F 9 **San Pedro**, Argentina
59 C 15 **San Pedro**, Argentina
121 G 14 **San Pedro**, Philippines
128 J 14 **San-Pédro**, Côte d'Ivoire
46 H 4 **San Pedro Carchá**, Guatemala
45 O 7 **San Pedro de las Colonias**, Mexico
49 R 7 **San Pedro de Macoris**, Dominican Republic
67 S 11 **San Pedro del Pinatar**, Spain
46 K 4 **San Pedro Sula**, Honduras
44 F 3 **San Quintín**, Mexico
47 P 11 **San Rafael**, Costa Rica
56 H 12 **San Rafael**, Argentina
47 N 7 **San Rafael del Norte**, Nicaragua
53 K 17 **San Ramón**, Bolivia
53 M 20 **San Ramón**, Bolivia
76 A 10 **San Remo**, Italy
27 O 8 **San Saba**, TX, U.S.A.
46 J 7 **San Salvador**, El Salvador ♜
49 N 3 **San Salvador**, The Bahamas 🏝
58 D 13 **San Salvador**, Argentina
56 I 5 **San Salvador de Jujuy**, Argentina
57 H 25 **San Sebastián**, Argentina
77 L 14 **San Severo**, Italy
33 G 22 **San Simeon**, CA, U.S.A.
44 F 2 **San Vicente**, Mexico
46 J 7 **San Vicente**, El Salvador
120 H 5 **San Vicente**, Philippines

[...]ountry □ Internal administrative region: State/Province/Territory/Dependent territory ▣ ♜ Capital city ▲▲ Mountain range/Undersea ridge ▲ Mountain peak/Volcano/Seamount ◇ Geographic feature ▶ Headland/Point/Cape/Peninsula ◓ Desert 🏝 Island/Island group ⁙ Antarctic base ◎ Ocean ◑ Sea ≈ Bay/Gulf/Channel/Strait ◢ Lake ⚑ Salt pan/Dry/Intermittent lake ∿ River

Country · Internal administrative region: State/Province/Territory/Dependent territory · Capital city · Mountain range/Undersea ridge · Mountain peak/Volcano/Seamount · Geographic feature · Headland/Point/Cape/Peninsula · Desert · Island/Island group · Antarctic base · Ocean · Sea · Bay/Gulf/Channel/Strait · Lake · Salt pan/Dry/Intermittent lake

G 19 **Sennan**, Japan
F 18 **Sennar**, Sudan
G 18 **Sennar**, Sudan ■
I 15 **Sennen**, U.K.
H 6 **Senneterre**, QC, Canada
G 25 **Seno Otway**, Chile ↘
F 24 **Seno Skyring**, Chile ↘
R 5 **Sens**, France
K 7 **Sensuntepeque**, El Salvador
K 7 **Senta**, Serbia and Montenegro
G 5 **Sentinel Butte**, ND, U.S.A. ▲
A 15 **Sentosa**, Singapore ⁂
F 15 **Seoni**, India
L 19 **Seoul**, South Korea ⌂
C 9 **Sepang**, Malaysia
L 14 **Sepanjang**, Indonesia ⁂
H 15 **Separation Point**, New Zealand ▶
M 10 **Sepasu**, Indonesia
B 3 **Sepik**, Papua New Guinea ∽
R 9 **Seping**, Malaysia ∽
W 9 **Seppa**, India
S 4 **Sept-Îles**, QC, Canada
H 10 **Septemvri**, Bulgaria
N 7 **Serafimovich**, Russian Federation
J 20 **Seraing**, Belgium
S 12 **Seram**, Indonesia ⁂
S 12 **Seram Sea**, Indonesia ◗
G 13 **Serang**, Indonesia
I 9 **Serasan**, Indonesia ⁂
L 12 **Serbia**, Serbia and Montenegro ■
L 13 **Serbia and Montenegro**, Europe ■
J 18 **Serdo**, Ethiopia
O 4 **Serdobsk**, Russian Federation
Y 4 **Serebryansk**, Kazakhstan
H 21 **Sereď**, Slovakia
I 4 **Seredyna-Buda**, Russian Federation
I 10 **Şereflikoçhisar**, Turkey
C 9 **Seremban**, Malaysia
T 9 **Serengeti Plain**, Tanzania ◇
P 4 **Serenje**, Zambia
K 5 **Seret**, Ukraine ∽
P 1 **Sergach**, Russian Federation
S 4 **Sergelen**, Mongolia
Q 2 **Sergeyevka**, Kazakhstan
N 14 **Sergipe**, Brazil ■
L 1 **Sergiyev Posad**, Russian Federation
F 9 **Seri Buat**, Malaysia ⁂
S 6 **Seria**, Brunei
I 22 **Serifos**, Greece ⁂
F 13 **Serik**, Turkey
A 6 **Serki**, Papua New Guinea
S 14 **Sermata**, Indonesia ⁂
P 14 **Sernur**, Russian Federation
Q 12 **Serón**, Spain
K 7 **Seronga**, Botswana
J 9 **Serov**, Russian Federation
N 9 **Serowe**, Botswana
I 11 **Serpa**, Portugal
Y 14 **Serpent's Mouth**, Trinidad and Tobago ≈
K 2 **Serpukhov**, Russian Federation
O 5 **Serra**, Brazil
G 6 **Serra da Chela**, Angola ⛰
G 9 **Serra da Fartura**, Brazil ⛰
M 11 **Serra da Ibiapaba**, Brazil ⛰
L 6 **Serra da Mantiqueira**, Brazil ⛰
F 8 **Serra das Araras**, Brazil ⛰
F 12 **Serra das Encantadas**, Brazil ⛰
F 10 **Serra de Misiones**, Argentina ⛰
I 8 **Serra de Paranapiacaba**, Brazil ⛰
F 6 **Serra de Santa Bárbara**, Brazil ⛰
G 12 **Serra do Cachimbo**, Brazil ⛰
F 12 **Serra do Canguçu**, Brazil ⛰
H 8 **Serra do Cavernoso**, Brazil ⛰
H 9 **Serra do Espigão**, Brazil ⛰
L 17 **Serra do Espinhaço**, Brazil ⛰
F 11 **Serra do Espinilho**, Brazil ⛰
I 11 **Serra do Mar**, Brazil ⛰
H 6 **Serra do Mirante**, Brazil ⛰
H 15 **Serra do Roncador**, Brazil ⛰
D 14 **Serra dos Parecis**, Brazil ⛰
H 8 **Serra Geral**, Brazil ⛰
M 20 **Serra San Bruno**, Italy
X 13 **Serranía de Majé**, Panama ⛰
Z 13 **Serranía del Darién**, Panama ⛰
Y 15 **Serranía del Sapo**, Panama ⛰
Q 5 **Serranía Turagua**, Venezuela ▲
I 10 **Serranilla Bank**, Jamaica ≈
I 17 **Serranópolis**, Brazil
G 13 **Serres**, Greece
I 10 **Serrezuela**, Argentina
N 14 **Serrinha**, Brazil
J 5 **Sertãozinho**, Brazil
K 5 **Sêrtar**, China
T 14 **Serua**, Indonesia ⁂
W 11 **Serui**, Indonesia
D 15 **Servia**, Greece
S 11 **Sesepe**, Indonesia
H 8 **Sesfontein**, Namibia
M 6 **Sesheke**, Zambia
F 10 **Sesimbra**, Portugal
K 12 **Seskar Furö**, Sweden ⁂
K 5 **Sessa**, Angola
D 9 **Sestri Levante**, Italy
A 8 **Sestriere**, Italy
E 8 **Sesvete**, Croatia
I 7 **Setana**, Japan
S 14 **Sète**, France
L 17 **Sete Lagoas**, Brazil
O 22 **Seteuchi**, Japan
O 5 **Sétif**, Algeria
I 17 **Seto**, Japan
E 20 **Seto naikai**, Japan ◗
H 7 **Settat**, Morocco
D 9 **Setté Cama**, Gabon
Q 1 **Settle**, U.K.
G 10 **Setubal**, Portugal ■
G 9 **Setúbal**, Portugal
U 8 **Sevana Lich**, Armenia ↘
T 12 **Sevastopol'**, Ukraine
E 18 **Seven Sisters**, BC, Canada ▲
J 10 **Seven Sisters Peaks**, BC, Canada ▲
W 11 **Sevenoaks**, U.K.
M 8 **Severn**, ON, Canada ∽
Q 10 **Severn**, U.K. ∽
K 8 **Severn Lake**, ON, Canada ↘
Q 4 **Severnaya Zemlya**, Russian Federation ⁂
T 2 **Severnoye**, Russian Federation
U 2 **Severnyy**, Russian Federation
X 6 **Severnyy Anyuyskiy Khrebet**, Russian Federation ⛰
Q 2 **Severnyy Kazakhstan**, Kazakhstan ■
T 7 **Severnyy Ural**, Russian Federation ⛰
89 Z 12 **Severo-Kuril'sk**, Russian Federation
89 P 7 **Severo-Sibirskaya Nizmennost'**, Russian Federation ◇
89 O 11 **Severo-Yeniseyskiy**, Russian Federation
89 R 12 **Severobaykal'sk**, Russian Federation
90 K 6 **Severodvinsk**, Russian Federation
90 I 2 **Severomorsk**, Russian Federation
30 I 4 **Sevier**, UT, U.S.A. ∽
30 I 5 **Sevier Lake**, UT, U.S.A. ↘
16 K 9 **Sevierville**, TN, U.S.A.
50 H 7 **Sevilla**, Colombia
66 K 12 **Seville**, Spain
82 I 8 **Sevlievo**, Bulgaria
80 D 7 **Sevnica**, Slovenia
35 R 10 **Seward**, AK, U.S.A.
34 M 5 **Seward Peninsula**, AK, U.S.A. ▶
88 M 7 **Seyakha**, Russian Federation
45 X 11 **Seybaplaya**, Mexico
11 Q 10 **Seychelles**, Indian Ocean ■
103 N 13 **Seydi**, Turkmenistan
94 G 12 **Seydisehir**, Turkey
70 D 10 **Seyðisfjörður**, Iceland
94 K 12 **Seyhan**, Turkey ∽
87 S 2 **Seym**, Ukraine ∽
27 N 5 **Seymour**, TX, U.S.A.
135 S 13 **Seymour**, VIC, Australia
101 U 7 **Seyyedābād**, Afghanistan
65 R 5 **Sézanne**, France
77 H 15 **Sezze**, Italy
83 H 26 **Sfakia**, Greece
125 R 6 **Sfax**, Tunisia
113 Q 4 **Shaanxi**, China ■
127 M 23 **Shabeellaha Dhexe**, Somalia ■
127 L 24 **Shabeellaha Hoose**, Somalia ■
82 O 7 **Shabla**, Bulgaria
131 P 9 **Shabunda**, Democratic Republic of Congo
99 R 13 **Shabwah**, Yemen
108 H 6 **Shache**, China
145 Q 11 **Shackleton Coast**, Antarctica ◇
145 Y 9 **Shackleton Ice Shelf**, Antarctica ◇
145 N 6 **Shackleton Range**, Antarctica ⛰
26 G 10 **Shafter**, TX, U.S.A.
63 R 12 **Shaftesbury**, U.K.
137 F 24 **Shag Point**, New Zealand ▶
118 B 8 **Shah Alam**, Malaysia
101 T 9 **Shāh Jūy**, Afghanistan
96 I 8 **Shahbā'**, Syria
101 U 14 **Shahdapur**, Pakistan
105 G 14 **Shahdol**, India
113 U 1 **Shahe**, China
107 N 11 **Shahganj**, India
106 L 9 **Shahjahanpur**, India
105 E 19 **Shahpur**, India
100 H 8 **Shahr-e Kord**, Iran
101 S 9 **Shahr-i-Safa**, Afghanistan
101 R 7 **Shahrak**, Afghanistan
101 O 8 **Shāhrakht**, Iran
100 I 8 **Shahrezā**, Iran
103 R 14 **Shahrtuz**, Tajikistan
100 L 5 **Shāhrūd**, Iran
103 R 14 **Shakh**, Tajikistan
92 J 1 **Shakhovskaya**, Russian Federation
103 Q 13 **Shakhrisabz**, Uzbekistan
103 S 5 **Shakhtinsk**, Kazakhstan
92 L 9 **Shakhty**, Russian Federation
102 L 6 **Shakhty**, Kazakhstan
91 N 13 **Shakhun'ya**, Russian Federation
122 I 6 **Shakotan-hantō**, Japan ▶
122 I 5 **Shakotan-misaki**, Japan ▶
103 V 3 **Shalday**, Kazakhstan
93 Q 14 **Shali**, Russian Federation
17 S 12 **Shallotte**, NC, U.S.A.
112 J 5 **Shaluli Shan**, China ⛰
40 L 7 **Shamattawa**, MB, Canada
99 W 6 **Shamis**, United Arab Emirates
106 J 8 **Shamli**, India
14 G 12 **Shamokin**, PA, U.S.A.
26 M 2 **Shamrock**, TX, U.S.A.
114 F 12 **Shan**, Myanmar ■
114 E 12 **Shan Plateau**, Myanmar ◇
113 W 2 **Shandong**, China ■
111 H 19 **Shandong Bandao**, China ▶
97 V 7 **Shandrūkh**, Iraq
113 U 4 **Shangcai**, China
113 U 5 **Shangcheng**, China
113 T 13 **Shangchuan Dao**, China ⁂
111 C 15 **Shangdu**, China
110 L 9 **Shangganling**, China
113 U 8 **Shanggao**, China
109 X 10 **Shanghai**, China ■
113 Z 5 **Shanghai**, China
113 W 11 **Shanghang**, China
111 E 19 **Shanghe**, China
110 G 7 **Shangkuli**, China
113 R 4 **Shangnan**, China
132 L 6 **Shangombo**, Zambia
113 U 3 **Shangqiu**, China
113 W 8 **Shangrao**, China
113 Y 7 **Shangyu**, China
112 J 12 **Shangyun**, China
110 L 11 **Shangzhi**, China
113 R 4 **Shangzhou**, China
111 G 17 **Shanhaiguan**, China
110 L 12 **Shanhetun**, China
129 T 11 **Shani**, Nigeria
32 I 10 **Shaniko**, OR, U.S.A.
63 T 14 **Shanklin**, U.K.
61 D 17 **Shannon**, Republic of Ireland ∽
137 L 15 **Shannon**, New Zealand
89 V 12 **Shantarskiye Ostrova**, Russian Federation ⁂
113 W 12 **Shantou**, China
113 V 12 **Shanwei**, China
113 S 2 **Shanxi**, China ■
113 V 3 **Shanxian**, China
113 R 4 **Shanyang**, China
111 B 17 **Shanyin**, China
113 S 9 **Shaodong**, China
113 T 11 **Shaoguan**, China
113 W 9 **Shaowu**, China
113 Y 6 **Shaoxing**, China
113 S 9 **Shaoyang**, China
113 S 13 **Shapa**, China
60 I 7 **Shapinsay**, U.K. ⁂
99 Q 5 **Shaqrā'**, Saudi Arabia
103 X 5 **Shar**, Kazakhstan
127 C 18 **Sharafa**, Sudan
103 Q 11 **Shardara**, Kazakhstan
109 N 4 **Sharga**, Mongolia
122 M 4 **Shari**, Japan
99 X 5 **Sharjah**, United Arab Emirates
134 E 8 **Shark Bay**, WA, Australia ≈
85 I 14 **Sharkawshchyna**, Belarus
99 U 13 **Sharkhāt**, Yemen
93 V 3 **Sharlyk**, Russian Federation
126 G 9 **Sharm el Sheikh**, Egypt
24 H 4 **Sharon Springs**, KS, U.S.A.
91 N 13 **Shar'ya**, Russian Federation
127 I 21 **Shashemenē**, Ethiopia
33 G 15 **Shasta Lake**, CA, U.S.A. ↘
93 O 2 **Shatki**, Russian Federation
93 N 3 **Shatsk**, Russian Federation
97 Z 12 **Shaṭṭ al 'Arab**, Iraq ∽
24 J 8 **Shattuck**, OK, U.S.A.
20 G 11 **Shawano**, WI, U.S.A.
25 N 10 **Shawnee**, OK, U.S.A.
113 X 9 **Shaxian**, China
103 R 10 **Shayan**, Kazakhstan
113 S 6 **Shayang**, China
98 K 5 **Shaybārā**, Saudi Arabia ⁂
97 X 8 **Shaykh Jūwī**, Iraq
97 W 8 **Shaykh Sa'd**, Iraq
103 T 14 **Shazud**, Tajikistan
87 Z 5 **Shchastya**, Ukraine
92 K 3 **Shchekino**, Russian Federation
103 V 3 **Shcherbakty**, Kazakhstan
92 J 5 **Shchigry**, Russian Federation
87 R 1 **Shchors**, Ukraine
103 R 3 **Shchuchinsk**, Kazakhstan
85 F 18 **Shchuchyn**, Belarus
92 J 6 **Shebekino**, Russian Federation
127 L 25 **Shebeli**, Somalia/Ethiopia ∽
20 H 13 **Sheboygan**, WI, U.S.A.
43 U 9 **Shediac**, NB, Canada
63 Y 11 **Sheerness**, U.K.
43 W 10 **Sheet Harbour**, NS, Canada
96 F 8 **Shefar'am**, Israel
19 O 1 **Sheffield**, AL, U.S.A.
63 S 4 **Sheffield**, U.K.
113 N 6 **Shehong**, China
101 Y 9 **Shekhupura**, Pakistan
43 T 12 **Shelburne**, NS, Canada
29 P 2 **Shelby**, MT, U.S.A.
16 F 9 **Shelbyville**, TN, U.S.A.
21 F 20 **Shelbyville**, IL, U.S.A.
21 J 19 **Shelbyville**, IN, U.S.A.
23 Q 11 **Sheldon**, IA, U.S.A.
43 S 3 **Sheldrake**, QC, Canada
35 O 12 **Shelikof Strait**, AK, U.S.A. ≈
32 G 7 **Shelton**, WA, U.S.A.
103 X 4 **Shemonaikha**, Kazakhstan
34 C 11 **Shemya Island**, AK, U.S.A. ⁂
23 Q 14 **Shenandoah**, IA, U.S.A.
17 R 4 **Shenandoah Mountains**, VA, U.S.A. ⛰
129 S 12 **Shendam**, Nigeria
127 F 16 **Shendi**, Sudan
113 Z 7 **Shengzhou**, China
110 J 12 **Shenjingzi**, China
90 L 9 **Shenkursk**, Russian Federation
113 U 4 **Shenqiu**, China
111 H 15 **Shenyang**, China
113 U 13 **Shenzhen**, China
16 H 5 **Sheperdsville**, KY, U.S.A.
86 M 4 **Shepetivka**, Ukraine
139 R 11 **Shepherd Islands**, Vanuatu ⁂
135 S 12 **Shepparton**, VIC, Australia
63 Q 12 **Shepton Mallet**, U.K.
63 Q 12 **Sherborne**, U.K.
128 F 12 **Sherbro Island**, Sierra Leone ⁂
42 M 10 **Sherbrooke**, QC, Canada
43 X 10 **Sherbrooke**, NS, Canada
127 F 15 **Shereiq**, Sudan
104 B 12 **Shergarh**, India
107 P 12 **Sherghati**, India
25 V 12 **Sheridan**, AR, U.S.A.
29 V 9 **Sheridan**, WY, U.S.A.
27 R 4 **Sherman**, TX, U.S.A.
15 R 3 **Sherman Mills**, ME, U.S.A.
107 U 11 **Sherpur**, Bangladesh
63 T 5 **Sherwood Forest**, U.K. ◇
60 J 4 **Shetland Islands**, U.K. ⁂
102 H 9 **Shetpe**, Kazakhstan
127 G 21 **Shewa Gīmīra**, Ethiopia
113 X 7 **Shexian**, China
113 Y 4 **Sheyang**, China
22 M 4 **Sheyenne**, ND, U.S.A. ∽
100 J 13 **Sheykh Sho'eyb**, Iran ⁂
60 F 9 **Shiant Islands**, U.K. ⁂
99 S 12 **Shibām**, Yemen
122 J 13 **Shibata**, Japan
110 J 4 **Shibazhan**, China
122 M 4 **Shibecha**, Japan
122 K 4 **Shibetsu**, Japan
122 M 4 **Shibetsu**, Japan
126 E 8 **Shibîn el Kôm**, Egypt
111 I 17 **Shicheng Dao**, China ⁂
111 I 20 **Shidao**, China
112 J 9 **Shigu**, China
108 K 4 **Shihezi**, China
122 L 5 **Shihoro**, Japan
123 C 22 **Shiiba**, Japan
111 C 18 **Shijiazhuang**, China
122 J 7 **Shikabe**, Japan
101 U 12 **Shikarpur**, Pakistan
123 K 18 **Shikine-shima**, Japan ⁂
106 J 10 **Shikohabad**, India
123 E 20 **Shikoku**, Japan ⁂
123 E 21 **Shikoku-sanchi**, Japan ⛰
122 J 6 **Shikotsu-ko**, Japan ↘
107 S 10 **Shiliguri**, India
107 V 11 **Shillong**, India
113 Q 12 **Shilong**, China
92 M 2 **Shilovo**, Russian Federation
123 B 22 **Shimabara**, Japan
89 U 13 **Shimanovsk**, Russian Federation
127 M 19 **Shimbiris**, Somalia ▲
123 J 17 **Shimizu**, Japan
106 J 6 **Shimla**, India
123 B 24 **Shimo-Koshiki-jima**, Japan ⁂
123 K 17 **Shimoda**, Japan
105 C 20 **Shimoga**, India
122 J 8 **Shimokita-hantō**, Japan ▶
123 B 20 **Shimonoseki**, Japan
101 Y 5 **Shimshal**, Pakistan
106 I 1 **Shimshal**, India
90 E 12 **Shimsk**, Russian Federation
101 Q 8 **Shīndand**, Afghanistan
114 E 7 **Shingbwiyang**, Myanmar
20 I 9 **Shingleton**, MI, U.S.A.
123 H 19 **Shingū**, Japan
122 K 12 **Shinjō**, Japan
122 K 5 **Shintoku**, Japan
131 T 10 **Shinyanga**, Tanzania ■
131 T 10 **Shinyanga**, Tanzania
122 K 12 **Shiogama**, Japan
123 I 16 **Shiojiri**, Japan
123 N 26 **Shiokawa**, Japan
123 H 20 **Shiono-misaki**, Japan ▶
123 L 14 **Shioya-zaki**, Japan ▶
112 L 11 **Shiping**, China
63 S 2 **Shipley**, U.K.
31 N 8 **Shiprock**, NM, U.S.A.
31 N 8 **Shiprock Peak**, NM, U.S.A. ▲
113 Z 7 **Shipu**, China
113 Q 4 **Shiquan**, China
100 J 9 **Shīr Kūh**, Iran ▲
122 J 8 **Shirakami-misaki**, Japan ▶
123 K 14 **Shirakawa**, Japan
122 M 5 **Shiranuka**, Japan
145 N 11 **Shirase Coast**, Antarctica ◇
100 I 10 **Shīrāz**, Iran
122 M 3 **Shiretoko-hantō**, Japan ▶
122 M 3 **Shiretoko-misaki**, Japan ▶
122 K 8 **Shiriya-zaki**, Japan ▶
14 L 12 **Shirley**, NY, U.S.A.
122 K 12 **Shiroishi**, Japan
129 R 11 **Shiroro Reservoir**, Nigeria ↘
101 N 5 **Shīrvān**, Iran
110 J 5 **Shisanzhan**, China
34 L 13 **Shishaldin Volcano**, AK, U.S.A. ▲
34 M 5 **Shishmaref**, AK, U.S.A.
113 S 7 **Shishou**, China
110 J 5 **Shisizhan**, China
113 T 11 **Shitan**, China
104 B 12 **Shiv**, India
104 E 13 **Shivpuri**, India
110 G 6 **Shiwei**, China
113 R 5 **Shiyan**, China
110 J 6 **Shiyizhan**, China
112 M 11 **Shizong**, China
122 L 11 **Shizugawa**, Japan
109 R 7 **Shizuishan**, China
123 J 17 **Shizuoka**, Japan
85 M 16 **Shklow**, Belarus
81 J 16 **Shkodër**, Albania
81 J 19 **Shkumbin**, Albania ∽
123 D 19 **Shōbara**, Japan
123 F 19 **Shodo-shima**, Japan ⁂
122 J 5 **Shokanbetsu-dake**, Japan ▲
103 O 4 **Sholaksay**, Kazakhstan
103 R 9 **Shollakorgan**, Kazakhstan
101 S 14 **Shorap**, Pakistan
138 J 5 **Shortland Island**, Solomon Islands ⁂
122 J 4 **Shosanbetsu**, Japan
28 M 12 **Shoshone**, ID, U.S.A.
33 L 22 **Shoshone**, CA, U.S.A.
33 K 18 **Shoshone Mountains**, NV, U.S.A. ⛰
29 U 11 **Shoshoni**, WY, U.S.A.
87 S 1 **Shostka**, Ukraine
113 X 7 **Shouchang**, China
113 V 5 **Shouxian**, China
113 T 1 **Shouyang**, China
30 L 11 **Show Low**, AZ, U.S.A.
127 G 17 **Showak**, Sudan
90 M 3 **Shoyna**, Russian Federation
90 K 9 **Shozhma**, Russian Federation
18 H 4 **Shreveport**, LA, U.S.A.
63 P 6 **Shrewsbury**, U.K.
103 T 10 **Shu**, Kazakhstan
97 Y 11 **Shu'aiba**, Iraq
112 M 5 **Shuajingsi**, China
110 J 11 **Shuangcheng**, China
113 S 9 **Shuangfeng**, China
112 J 11 **Shuangjiang**, China
110 I 13 **Shuangliao**, China
110 N 10 **Shuangyashan**, China
102 L 6 **Shubarkuduk**, Kazakhstan
113 V 6 **Shucheng**, China
110 L 12 **Shulan**, China
87 Y 5 **Shul'hynka**, Ukraine
35 N 13 **Shumagin Islands**, AK, U.S.A. ⁂
102 L 10 **Shumanay**, Uzbekistan
82 M 7 **Shumen**, Bulgaria ■
82 L 8 **Shumen**, Bulgaria
93 Q 1 **Shumerlya**, Russian Federation
88 I 11 **Shumikha**, Russian Federation
85 L 14 **Shumilina**, Belarus
113 X 9 **Shunchang**, China
113 T 12 **Shunde**, China
35 O 5 **Shungnak**, AK, U.S.A.
111 B 17 **Shuozhou**, China
99 Q 14 **Shuqrah**, Yemen
100 I 7 **Shūr Āb**, Iran
101 N 11 **Shūr Gaz**, Iran
100 M 7 **Shūrāb**, Iran
133 P 7 **Shurugwi**, Zimbabwe
101 O 9 **Shusf**, Iran
100 G 8 **Shūsh**, Iran
100 G 8 **Shushtar**, Iran
46 I 5 **Shutaque**, Guatemala ∽
90 K 14 **Shuya**, Russian Federation
113 X 3 **Shuyang**, China
114 D 11 **Shwebo**, Myanmar
103 R 11 **Shymkent**, Kazakhstan
106 K 3 **Shyok**, India
87 S 8 **Shyroke**, Ukraine
87 T 4 **Shyshaky**, Ukraine
85 J 19 **Shyshchytsy**, Belarus
115 G 18 **Si Nakarin Reservoir**, Thailand ↘
115 H 20 **Si Racha**, Thailand
117 V 14 **Sia**, Indonesia
101 Q 13 **Siahan Range**, Pakistan ⛰
101 Y 8 **Sialkot**, Pakistan
138 E 5 **Sialum**, Papua New Guinea
116 G 9 **Siantan**, Indonesia ⁂
121 N 18 **Siargao**, Philippines ⁂
121 G 24 **Siasi**, Philippines
121 G 25 **Siasi**, Philippines ⁂
138 E 4 **Siassi**, Papua New Guinea
83 D 15 **Siatista**, Greece
121 J 19 **Siaton**, Philippines
117 Q 9 **Siau**, Indonesia ⁂
84 E 13 **Šiaulėnai**, Lithuania
84 E 13 **Šiauliai**, Lithuania
120 H 1 **Siayan**, Philippines ⁂
77 M 18 **Sibari**, Italy
121 G 15 **Sibay**, Philippines ⁂
80 D 13 **Šibenik**, Croatia
89 N 9 **Siberia**, Russian Federation ◇
116 C 11 **Siberut**, Indonesia ⁂
101 T 11 **Sibi**, Pakistan
138 B 6 **Sibidiri**, Papua New Guinea
130 G 10 **Sibiti**, Congo
86 I 10 **Sibiu**, Romania
23 P 10 **Sibley**, IA, U.S.A.
117 N 10 **Siboa**, Indonesia
116 C 10 **Sibolga**, Indonesia
107 Y 10 **Sibsagar**, India
63 W 5 **Sibsey**, U.K.
118 F 9 **Sibu**, Malaysia ⁂
119 P 9 **Sibu**, Malaysia
121 H 22 **Sibuco**, Philippines
121 H 22 **Sibuco Bay**, Philippines ≈
121 J 21 **Sibuguey**, Philippines ∽
121 I 22 **Sibuguey Bay**, Philippines ≈
130 J 4 **Sibut**, Central African Republic
121 D 25 **Sibutu**, Philippines ⁂
121 D 26 **Sibutu Group**, Philippines ⁂
121 E 25 **Sibutu Passage**, Philippines ≈
121 I 14 **Sibuyan**, Philippines ⁂
121 I 14 **Sibuyan Sea**, Philippines ◗
53 I 20 **Sicasica**, Bolivia
115 G 24 **Sichon**, Thailand
112 M 6 **Sichuan**, China ■
113 O 7 **Sichuan Basin**, China ◇
77 J 23 **Sicilia**, Italy ■
77 F 21 **Sicilian Channel**, Italy/Tunisia ≈
77 I 22 **Sicily**, Italy ⁂
47 P 4 **Sico**, Honduras
47 O 5 **Sico**, Honduras ∽
80 J 9 **Šid**, Serbia and Montenegro
124 L 6 **Sid**, Algeria
77 M 21 **Siderno**, Italy
107 N 12 **Sidhi**, India
124 L 6 **Sidi Ali**, Algeria
126 C 7 **Sidi Barrani**, Egypt
124 K 6 **Sidi Bel Abbès**, Algeria
124 G 7 **Sidi-Bennour**, Morocco
125 Q 6 **Sidi Bouzid**, Tunisia
124 F 9 **Sidi Ifni**, Morocco
124 I 6 **Sidi Kacem**, Morocco
124 G 7 **Sidi-Smaïl**, Morocco
116 C 9 **Sidikalang**, Indonesia
82 G 12 **Sidirokastro**, Greece
63 O 13 **Sidmouth**, U.K.
22 H 14 **Sidney**, NE, U.S.A.
29 Z 3 **Sidney**, MT, U.S.A.
128 I 10 **Sido**, Mali
55 H 18 **Sidrolândia**, Brazil
78 M 13 **Siedlce**, Poland
73 E 17 **Siegen**, Germany
115 K 19 **Siem Reap**, Cambodia
78 N 12 **Siemiatycze**, Poland
115 M 19 **Siempang**, Cambodia
76 F 11 **Siena**, Italy
79 I 14 **Sieradz**, Poland
78 J 11 **Sierpc**, Poland
26 F 8 **Sierra Blanca**, TX, U.S.A.
26 F 8 **Sierra Blanca**, TX, U.S.A. ▲
57 H 16 **Sierra Colorada**, Argentina
46 M 6 **Sierra de Agalta**, Honduras ⛰
57 H 14 **Sierra de Auca Mahuida**, Argentina ▲
44 G 5 **Sierra de Camalli**, Mexico ▲
44 F 2 **Sierra de Juárez**, Mexico ⛰
46 M 6 **Sierra de la Esperanza**, Honduras ⛰
59 A 18 **Sierra de la Ventana**, Argentina ⛰
45 S 14 **Sierra de Miahuatlán**, Mexico ⛰
26 F 7 **Sierra Diablo**, TX, U.S.A. ⛰
57 I 17 **Sierra Grande**, Argentina
128 G 11 **Sierra Leone**, Africa ■
45 V 14 **Sierra Madre**, Mexico ⛰
120 G 9 **Sierra Madre**, Philippines ⛰
45 P 13 **Sierra Madre del Sur**, Mexico ⛰
44 K 4 **Sierra Madre Occidental**, Mexico ⛰
45 P 5 **Sierra Madre Oriental**, Mexico ⛰
48 L 6 **Sierra Maestra**, Cuba ⛰
51 N 6 **Sierra Maigualida**, Venezuela ⛰
66 K 11 **Sierra Morena**, Spain ⛰
33 G 17 **Sierra Nevada**, CA, U.S.A. ⛰
56 H 7 **Sierra Nevada**, Argentina ▲
51 P 6 **Sierra Parima**, Venezuela ⛰
44 F 2 **Sierra San Pedro Martir**, Mexico ⛰
51 O 10 **Sierra Tapirapecó**, Venezuela ⛰
26 F 8 **Sierra Vieja**, TX, U.S.A. ⛰
30 L 15 **Sierra Vista**, AZ, U.S.A.
56 I 11 **Sierras de Córdoba**, Argentina ⛰
74 D 10 **Sierre**, Switzerland
71 L 14 **Sievi**, Finland
83 I 22 **Sifnos**, Greece ⁂
139 W 12 **Sigatoka**, Fiji
143 N 11 **Sigguup Nunaa**, Greenland ▶
86 I 7 **Sighetu Marmației**, Romania
86 J 10 **Sighișoara**, Romania
116 B 8 **Sigli**, Indonesia
70 C 9 **Siglufjörður**, Iceland
121 I 16 **Sigma**, Philippines
73 F 24 **Sigmaringen**, Germany
69 L 20 **Signal de Botrange**, Belgium ▲
30 H 7 **Signal Peak**, UT, U.S.A. ▲
144 H 1 **Signy**, Antarctica ⁙
46 L 6 **Siguatepeque**, Honduras
67 S 2 **Sigüés**, Spain
128 H 10 **Siguiri**, Guinea
84 G 10 **Sigulda**, Latvia
113 W 4 **Sihong**, China
105 G 14 **Sihora**, India
53 C 14 **Sihuas**, Peru
113 T 12 **Sihui**, China
71 N 15 **Siilinjärvi**, Finland
95 R 12 **Siirt**, Turkey
139 N 6 **Sikaiana**, Solomon Islands ⁂
106 G 9 **Sikar**, India
128 J 10 **Sikasso**, Mali
128 J 10 **Sikasso**, Mali ■
114 E 9 **Sikaw**, Myanmar
25 Z 7 **Sikeston**, MO, U.S.A.
89 W 15 **Sikhote-Alin'**, Russian Federation ⛰
83 J 23 **Sikinos**, Greece ⁂
107 S 9 **Sikkim**, India ■
79 H 26 **Siklós**, Hungary
89 S 8 **Siktyakh**, Russian Federation
121 M 14 **Sila Point**, Philippines ▶
76 E 5 **Silandro**, Italy
121 J 17 **Silay**, Philippines
80 B 11 **Silba**, Croatia ⁂
107 W 12 **Silchar**, India
17 Q 9 **Siler City**, NC, U.S.A.
79 D 14 **Silesia**, Poland ◇
125 N 14 **Silet**, Algeria
106 M 8 **Silgarhi**, Nepal
94 I 14 **Silifke**, Turkey
104 K 12 **Siliguri**, India
113 P 12 **Silin**, China
108 K 9 **Siling Co**, China ↘
82 M 6 **Silistra**, Bulgaria ■
82 M 6 **Silistra**, Bulgaria
94 D 7 **Silivri**, Turkey
71 F 18 **Siljan**, Sweden ↘
67 T 8 **Silla**, Spain
84 J 6 **Sillamäe**, Estonia
75 P 9 **Sillian**, Austria
25 S 9 **Siloam Springs**, AR, U.S.A.
27 U 9 **Silsbee**, TX, U.S.A.
85 C 14 **Šilutė**, Lithuania
95 Q 11 **Silvan**, Turkey
95 Q 11 **Silvan Baraji**, Turkey ↘
105 C 16 **Silvassa**, India
23 U 4 **Silver Bay**, MN, U.S.A.
31 N 13 **Silver City**, NM, U.S.A.
32 H 12 **Silver Lake**, OR, U.S.A.
136 K 8 **Silverdale**, New Zealand
63 T 8 **Silverstone**, U.K.
66 H 12 **Silves**, Portugal
45 Y 12 **Silvituc**, Mexico
74 J 8 **Silvretta Gruppe**, Switzerland ⛰
93 X 1 **Sim**, Russian Federation
112 J 12 **Simao**, China
121 H 14 **Simara**, Philippines ⁂
94 D 10 **Simav**, Turkey
130 M 7 **Simba**, Democratic Republic of Congo
138 C 4 **Simbai**, Papua New Guinea
42 D 14 **Simcoe**, ON, Canada
127 I 18 **Simēn Mountains**, Ethiopia ⛰
116 A 9 **Simeuluë**, Indonesia ⁂
87 U 12 **Simferopol'**, Ukraine
105 H 15 **Simga**, India
33 J 24 **Simi Valley**, CA, U.S.A.
107 N 7 **Simikot**, Nepal
18 J 6 **Simmesport**, LA, U.S.A.
29 P 4 **Simms**, MT, U.S.A.
85 E 16 **Simnas**, Lithuania
70 M 11 **Simojärvi**, Finland ↘
54 M 13 **Simplício Mendes**, Brazil
74 F 10 **Simplon**, Switzerland
29 R 2 **Simpson**, MT, U.S.A.
135 P 7 **Simpson Desert**, NT, Australia ◇
38 M 5 **Simpson Peninsula**, NU, Canada ▶
107 P 10 **Simra**, Nepal
71 F 25 **Simrishamn**, Sweden
119 N 10 **Simunjan**, Malaysia
121 E 25 **Simunul**, Philippines ⁂
127 M 22 **Sina Dhaqa**, Somalia
116 B 9 **Sinabang**, Indonesia
120 H 9 **Sinadipan**, Philippines
126 F 9 **Sinai**, Egypt ◇
44 K 7 **Sinaloa**, Mexico ■
125 R 8 **Sīnāwin**, Libya
114 E 8 **Sinbo**, Myanmar
114 C 12 **Sinbyugyun**, Myanmar
94 M 10 **Sincan**, Turkey
50 H 3 **Sincelejo**, Colombia
101 U 13 **Sind**, Pakistan ■
104 E 13 **Sind**, India ∽
101 W 10 **Sind Sāgar Doāb**, Pakistan ◇
121 J 20 **Sindañgan**, Philippines
121 I 20 **Sindangan Bay**, Philippines ≈
116 H 14 **Sindangbarang**, Indonesia
84 F 8 **Sindi**, Estonia
91 Q 8 **Sindor**, Russian Federation
66 G 10 **Sines**, Portugal
128 J 13 **Sinfra**, Côte d'Ivoire
115 H 18 **Sing Buri**, Thailand
127 F 18 **Singa**, Sudan
106 M 9 **Singahi**, India
118 B 14 **Singapore**, Singapore ⌂
118 B 15 **Singapore**, Asia ■
116 L 15 **Singaraja**, Indonesia
105 G 20 **Singaray-akonda**, India
73 F 25 **Singen**, Germany
87 N 8 **Sîngerei**, Moldova
131 T 12 **Singida**, Tanzania ■
131 T 10 **Singida**, Tanzania
114 D 7 **Singkaling Hkamti**, Myanmar
117 O 13 **Singkang**, Indonesia
116 I 10 **Singkawang**, Indonesia
116 F 11 **Singkep**, Indonesia ⁂
135 V 11 **Singleton**, NSW, Australia
107 V 11 **Singra**, India
77 D 16 **Siniscola**, Italy
80 E 13 **Sinj**, Croatia
117 O 13 **Sinjai**, Indonesia
97 P 2 **Sinjār**, Iraq
114 E 9 **Sinkan**, Myanmar
127 H 15 **Sinkat**, Sudan
111 J 17 **Sinmi-do**, North Korea ⁂
55 H 14 **Sinop**, Brazil
94 K 6 **Sinop**, Turkey
94 K 6 **Sinop Burnu**, Turkey ▶
111 M 16 **Sinp'o**, North Korea
111 L 18 **Sinp'yŏng**, North Korea
116 J 10 **Sintang**, Indonesia
27 Q 13 **Sinton**, TX, U.S.A.
66 F 9 **Sintra**, Portugal
111 J 16 **Sinŭiju**, North Korea
127 O 20 **Sinujiif**, Somalia
34 L 6 **Sinuk**, AK, U.S.A.
121 H 21 **Siocon**, Philippines
79 H 24 **Siófok**, Hungary
74 D 10 **Sion**, Switzerland
23 P 12 **Sioux City**, IA, U.S.A.
23 O 10 **Sioux Falls**, SD, U.S.A.
40 K 10 **Sioux Lookout**, ON, Canada
46 G 7 **Sipacate**, Guatemala
119 Y 7 **Sipadan**, Malaysia ⁂
121 I 18 **Sipalay**, Philippines
110 J 13 **Siping**, China
119 U 6 **Sipitang**, Malaysia
40 J 7 **Sipiwesk**, MB, Canada
145 O 11 **Siple Coast**, Antarctica ◇
144 K 11 **Siple Island**, Antarctica ⁂
116 D 12 **Sipura**, Indonesia ⁂
47 P 8 **Siquia**, Nicaragua
47 P 9 **Siquia**, Nicaragua ∽
121 K 19 **Siquijor**, Philippines ⁂
47 R 12 **Siquirres**, Costa Rica
135 P 2 **Sir Edward Pellew Group**, NT, Australia ⁂
71 A 21 **Sira**, Norway
105 E 20 **Sira**, India
107 T 12 **Sirajganj**, Bangladesh
103 R 12 **Sirdaryo Wiloyati**, Uzbekistan ■
86 L 7 **Siret**, Romania
107 Q 10 **Sirha**, Nepal
100 L 13 **Sīrīk**, Iran
115 H 15 **Sirikit Reservoir**, Thailand ↘
100 L 11 **Sīrjān**, Iran
95 R 12 **Şirnak**, Turkey
100 J 13 **Sirri**, Iran ⁂
106 H 7 **Sirsa**, India
105 D 20 **Sirsi**, India
105 F 17 **Sirsilla**, India
125 U 8 **Sirte**, Libya
85 G 15 **Širvintos**, Lithuania
97 V 4 **Sirwan**, Iraq ∽
80 E 8 **Sisak**, Croatia

Country ■ Internal administrative region: State/Province/Territory/Dependent territory ⌂ Capital city ⛰ Mountain range/Undersea ridge ▲ Mountain peak/Volcano/Seamount ◇ Geographic feature ▶ Headland/Point/Cape/Peninsula ◒ Desert ⁂ Island/Island group ⁙ Antarctic base ◎ Ocean ◗ Sea ≈ Bay/Gulf/Channel/Strait ↘ Lake ▞ Salt pan/Dry/Intermittent lake ∽ River

115 K 18 Sisaket, Thailand
113 P 3 Sishilipu, China
95 V 9 Sisian, Armenia
115 J 19 Sisŏphŏn, Cambodia
138 B 3 Sissano, Papua New Guinea
23 O 7 Sisseton, SD, U.S.A.
101 P 13 Sīstān Va Balūchestān, Iran ▣
66 L 7 Sistema Central, Spain ⛰
67 O 4 Sistema Ibérico, Spain ⛰
67 N 12 Sistemas Béticos, Spain ⛰
65 V 13 Sisteron, France
32 H 11 Sisters, OR, U.S.A.
105 N 22 Sisters, India ✽
107 V 14 Sitakunda, Bangladesh
106 L 9 Sitapur, India
83 K 26 Siteia, Greece
67 W 5 Sitges, Spain
35 W 11 Sitka, AK, U.S.A.
115 D 14 Sittang, Myanmar ∿
69 K 18 Sittard, Netherlands
63 Y 11 Sittingbourne, U.K.
114 B 13 Sittwe, Myanmar
47 P 7 Siuna, Nicaragua
107 R 13 Siuri, India
105 F 23 Sivaganga, India
100 J 10 Sivand, Iran
94 M 9 Sivas, Turkey
95 O 12 Siverek, Turkey
87 Y 5 Sivers'k, Ukraine
90 E 11 Siverskiy, Russian Federation
94 G 10 Sivrihisar, Turkey
117 O 12 Siwa, Indonesia
126 B 9 Siwa, Egypt
126 B 8 Siwa Oasis, Egypt ◇
106 J 6 Siwalik Range, India ⛰
107 P 11 Siwan, India
20 J 13 Six Lakes, MI, U.S.A.
47 S 13 Sixaola, Costa Rica
113 W 4 Sixian, China
113 W 4 Siyang, China
95 Y 7 Siyäzän, Azerbaijan
71 D 25 Sjaelland, Denmark ✽
81 K 14 Sjenica, Serbia and Montenegro
87 S 10 Skadovs'k, Ukraine
71 C 22 Skagen, Denmark
71 B 23 Skagerrak, Denmark ≈
35 W 9 Skagway, AK, U.S.A.
83 E 22 Skala, Greece
86 L 6 Skala-Podil's'ka, Ukraine
71 E 24 Skälderviken, Sweden ≈
83 H 17 Skantzoura, Greece ✽
101 Y 6 Skardu, Pakistan
106 I 2 Skardu, India
71 A 19 Skare, Norway
79 L 15 Skarżysko-Kamienna, Poland
124 C 12 Skaymat, Western Sahara
63 X 4 Skegness, U.K.
70 J 13 Skellefteå, Sweden
71 D 20 Ski, Norway
83 F 17 Skiathos, Greece ✽
83 G 17 Skiathos, Greece
70 I 7 Skibotn, Norway
85 F 18 Skidal', Belarus
71 C 20 Skien, Norway
78 K 13 Skierniewice, Poland
125 O 5 Skikda, Algeria
63 V 2 Skipsea, U.K.
63 R 2 Skipton, U.K.
71 B 24 Skive, Denmark
83 F 16 Sklithro, Greece
62 J 10 Skokholm Island, U.K. ✽
86 I 5 Skole, Ukraine
62 J 9 Skomer Island, U.K. ✽
83 G 17 Skopelos, Greece ✽
83 G 17 Skopelos, Greece
82 D 10 Skopje, Macedonia (F.Y.R.O.M.) ♜
71 F 22 Skövde, Sweden
89 T 13 Skovorodino, Russian Federation
15 P 5 Skowhegan, ME, U.S.A.
71 D 20 Skrimfjell, Norway ▲
84 C 11 Skrunda, Latvia
71 A 20 Skudeneshavn, Norway
133 P 10 Skukuza, Republic of South Africa
84 C 12 Skuodas, Lithuania
87 O 5 Skvyra, Ukraine
78 E 12 Skwierzyna, Poland
60 F 10 Skye, U.K. ✽
83 H 18 Skyropoula, Greece ✽
83 I 18 Skyros, Greece
83 H 18 Skyros, Greece ✽
71 D 25 Slagelse, Denmark
35 S 8 Slana, AK, U.S.A.
61 E 19 Slaney, Republic of Ireland ∿
90 D 11 Slantsy, Russian Federation
80 G 8 Slatina, Croatia
86 I 13 Slatina, Romania
25 K 5 Slaton, TX, U.S.A.
89 Y 8 Slautnoye, Russian Federation
36 M 9 Slave, NT, Canada ∿
129 O 13 Slave Coast, Nigeria ◇
39 I 17 Slave Lake, AB, Canada
80 G 8 Slavonija, Croatia ⛰
80 H 9 Slavonski Brod, Croatia
92 K 12 Slavyansk-na-Kubani, Russian Federation
85 N 18 Slawharad, Belarus
78 G 8 Sławno, Poland
63 V 5 Sleaford, U.K.
41 O 7 Sleeper Island, ON, Canada ✽
37 S 9 Sleeper Islands, NU, Canada ✽
78 H 12 Ślesin, Poland
14 J 10 Slide Mountain, NY, U.S.A. ▲
18 M 8 Slidell, LA, U.S.A.
61 C 16 Sligo, Republic of Ireland
61 C 16 Sligo Bay, Republic of Ireland ≈
82 L 9 Sliven, Bulgaria ▣
82 K 9 Sliven, Bulgaria
82 K 6 Slivo Pole, Bulgaria
80 E 7 Sljeme, Croatia ▲
87 O 7 Slobidka, Ukraine
91 P 12 Slobodskoy, Russian Federation
86 M 13 Slobozia, Romania
68 N 6 Slochteren, Netherlands
78 B 16 Slogen, Norway ▲
79 K 17 Słomniki, Poland
85 G 19 Slonim, Belarus
68 J 8 Slotermeer, Netherlands ◡
63 U 10 Slough, U.K.
79 I 21 Slovak Ore Mountains, Slovakia ⛰
79 I 20 Slovakia, Europe □
81 N 2 Slovechne, Ukraine
80 C 7 Slovenia, Europe □
80 D 6 Slovenska Bistrica, Slovenia
87 X 5 Slov"yans'k, Ukraine
85 L 22 Slovyechna, Belarus ∿
78 D 12 Słubice, Poland
86 L 2 Sluch, Ukraine ∿
69 C 16 Sluis, Netherlands
78 H 13 Słupca, Poland
78 G 8 Słupsk, Poland
70 H 13 Slussfors, Sweden
85 J 19 Slutsk, Belarus
61 A 17 Slyne Head, Republic of Ireland ▶
89 P 14 Slyudyanka, Russian Federation
15 P 7 Small Point, ME, U.S.A. ▶
41 U 8 Smallwood Reservoir, NL, Canada ◡
85 J 17 Smalyavichy, Belarus
85 H 16 Smarhon', Belarus
80 L 10 Smederevo, Serbia and Montenegro
80 M 11 Smederevska Palanka, Serbia and Montenegro
87 R 5 Smila, Ukraine
85 J 17 Smilavichy, Belarus
84 H 10 Smiltene, Latvia
24 L 2 Smith Center, KS, U.S.A.
41 P 5 Smith Island, NU, Canada ✽
33 E 14 Smith River, CA, U.S.A.
37 Q 2 Smith Sound, NU, Canada ≈
42 I 11 Smiths Falls, ON, Canada
25 R 12 Smithville, OK, U.S.A.
24 L 4 Smoky Hill, KS, U.S.A. ∿
24 K 3 Smoky Hills, KS, U.S.A. ◇
71 C 15 Smøla, Norway ✽
92 H 1 Smolensk, Russian Federation
92 I 1 Smolenskaya Oblast', Russian Federation ▣
92 H 1 Smolensko-Moskovskaya Vozvyshennost', Russian Federation ◇
83 C 15 Smolikas, Greece ▲
82 I 11 Smolyan, Bulgaria ▣
82 I 12 Smolyan, Bulgaria
29 Q 12 Smoot, WY, U.S.A.
42 D 5 Smooth Rock Falls, ON, Canada
82 L 8 Smyadovo, Bulgaria
144 J 7 Smyley Island, Antarctica ✽
17 W 2 Smyrna, DE, U.S.A.
70 D 10 Snaefell, Iceland ▲
70 C 11 Snaekollur, Iceland ▲
63 T 3 Snaith, U.K.
29 P 10 Snake, ID/WA, U.S.A. ∿
31 M 12 Snake River Plain, ID, U.S.A. ◇
71 E 14 Snåsvatn, Norway ◡
68 J 7 Sneek, Netherlands
68 K 7 Sneekermeer, Netherlands ◡
70 A 11 Snæfellsjökull, Iceland ▲
63 X 5 Snettisham, U.K.
89 O 8 Snezhnogorsk, Russian Federation
79 E 16 Sněžka, Czech Republic ▲
87 S 9 Snihurivka, Ukraine
79 M 19 Snina, Slovakia
71 C 16 Snöhetta, Norway ▲
71 B 20 Snønuten, Norway ▲
71 C 16 Snota, Norway ▲
17 W 4 Snow Hill, MD, U.S.A.
38 L 12 Snowbird Lake, NT, Canada ◡
62 M 5 Snowdon, U.K. ▲
30 L 11 Snowflake, AZ, U.S.A.
144 I 3 Snowhill Island, Antarctica ✽
28 L 3 Snowshoe Peak, MT, U.S.A. ▲
30 J 1 Snowville, UT, U.S.A.
49 O 4 Snug Corner, The Bahamas
41 X 8 Snug Harbour, NL, Canada
115 M 20 Snuŏl, Cambodia
86 K 6 Snyatyn, Ukraine
24 K 12 Snyder, OK, U.S.A.
26 L 6 Snyder, TX, U.S.A.
133 X 6 Soalala, Madgascar
111 L 22 Soan-kundo, South Korea ✽
133 Z 6 Soanierana-Ivongo, Madgascar
111 M 21 Sobaek-sanmaek, South Korea ⛰
127 E 20 Sobat, Sudan ∿
79 C 19 Soběslav, Czech Republic
54 M 11 Sobral, Brazil
115 M 23 Soc Trăng, Vietnam
78 K 13 Sochaczew, Poland
92 L 13 Sochi, Russian Federation
82 G 13 Sochos, Greece
56 H 6 Socompa, Argentina
31 P 12 Socorro, NM, U.S.A.
50 I 5 Socorro, Colombia
99 W 14 Socotra, Yemen ✽
33 M 23 Soda Lake, CA, U.S.A. ◡
29 Q 12 Soda Springs, ID, U.S.A.
70 L 10 Sodankylä, Finland
71 H 18 Söderhamn, Sweden
127 D 17 Sodiri, Sudan
127 H 21 Sodo, Ethiopia
117 Q 15 Soë, Indonesia
133 P 9 Soekmekaar, Republic of South Africa
84 D 7 Soela Väin, Estonia ≈
68 I 12 Soest, Netherlands
83 D 17 Sofades, Greece
133 R 7 Sofala, Mozambique ▣
82 G 9 Sofia, Bulgaria ♜
83 F 20 Sofiko, Greece
82 H 9 Sofiya, Bulgaria ▣
87 T 7 Sofiyivka, Ukraine
108 M 10 Sog, China
50 J 6 Sogamoso, Colombia
71 A 17 Sognefjorden, Norway ∿
121 L 17 Sogod, Philippines
111 L 23 Sŏgwip'o, South Korea
126 E 10 Sohâg, Egypt
63 W 7 Soham, U.K.
105 I 16 Sohapur, India
101 X 8 Sohawa, Pakistan
69 J 21 Soheit-Tinlot, Belgium
69 F 20 Soignies, Belgium
65 R 3 Soissons, France
123 E 19 Sōja, Japan
121 I 18 Sojoton Point, Philippines ▶
111 M 18 Sokch'o, South Korea
94 B 11 Söke, Turkey
103 S 12 Sokh, Uzbekistan
95 O 5 Sokhumi, Georgia
80 N 13 Sokobanja, Serbia and Montenegro
129 N 12 Sokodé, Togo
90 K 11 Sokol, Russian Federation
80 I 12 Sokolac, Bosnia and Herzegovina
87 P 6 Sokolivka, Ukraine
78 O 10 Sokółka, Poland
128 J 8 Sokolo, Mali
87 U 9 Sokolohirne, Ukraine
78 M 12 Sokołów Podlaski, Poland
129 P 9 Sokoto, Nigeria
129 P 9 Sokoto, Nigeria ▣
93 V 5 Sol'-Iletsk, Russian Federation
106 J 6 Solan, India
137 A 26 Solander Island, New Zealand ✽
105 D 18 Solapur, India
87 N 7 Soldăneşti, Moldova
74 L 8 Sölden, Austria
33 G 21 Soledad, CA, U.S.A.
50 I 2 Soledad, Colombia
58 H 11 Soledade, Brazil
65 Y 15 Solenzara, France
95 Q 10 Solhan, Turkey
90 L 12 Soligalich, Russian Federation
63 S 7 Solihull, U.K.
91 T 10 Solikamsk, Russian Federation
54 D 11 Solimões, Brazil ∿
73 C 16 Solingen, Germany
95 Y 6 Şollar, Azerbaijan
71 H 15 Sollefteå, Sweden
67 Y 7 Soller, Spain
86 L 5 Soloblovtsi, Ukraine
116 D 11 Solok, Indonesia
46 G 5 Sololá, Guatemala
139 O 6 Solomon Islands, Oceania □
138 G 6 Solomon Sea, Solomon Islands/Papua New Guinea ≋
15 P 5 Solon, ME, U.S.A.
110 H 10 Solon, China
20 D 9 Solon Springs, WI, U.S.A.
117 P 15 Solor, Indonesia ✽
92 M 2 Solotcha, Russian Federation
74 E 7 Solothurn, Switzerland
90 I 6 Solovetskiy, Russian Federation ✽
90 I 5 Solovetskiye Ostrova, Russian Federation ✽
79 I 24 Solt, Hungary
80 E 13 Šolta, Croatia ✽
100 I 6 Soltānābād, Iran
101 N 5 Soltānābād, Iran
72 G 12 Soltau, Germany
90 E 12 Sol'tsy, Russian Federation
61 H 15 Solway Firth, U.K. ≈
133 N 4 Solwezi, Zambia
94 C 9 Soma, Turkey
122 L 13 Sōma, Japan
127 M 22 Somali, Ethiopia ▣
127 K 24 Somalia, Africa □
82 K 2 Sombo, Angola
80 I 8 Sombor, Serbia and Montenegro
69 G 21 Sombreffe, Belgium
45 N 9 Sombrerete, Mexico
57 H 24 Sombrero, Chile
86 H 8 Şomcuta Mare, Romania
104 C 12 Somdari, India
69 K 16 Someren, Netherlands
83 M 3 Somers, MT, U.S.A.
16 I 7 Somerset, KY, U.S.A.
21 N 19 Somerset, OH, U.S.A.
31 O 5 Somerset, CO, U.S.A.
37 P 4 Somerset Island, NU, Canada ✽
14 H 11 Somersville, PA, U.S.A.
14 J 13 Somerville, NJ, U.S.A.
27 R 9 Somerville, TX, U.S.A.
27 Q 9 Somerville Lake, TX, U.S.A. ◡
97 Y 9 Somesh, Iraq
73 I 16 Sömmerda, Germany
70 E 12 Sømna, Norway ✽
139 Y 11 Somosomo, Fiji
46 M 8 Somotillo, Nicaragua
105 I 17 Sompeta, India
69 J 15 Son, Netherlands
107 N 12 Son, India ∿
114 K 12 Son La, Vietnam
47 U 15 Soná, Panama
111 J 17 Sŏnch'ŏn, North Korea
71 C 26 Sønderborg, Denmark
73 I 16 Sonderhausen, Germany
76 D 5 Sondrio, Italy
119 Q 10 Song, Malaysia
115 O 19 Sông Cau, Vietnam
115 L 24 Sông Đốc, Vietnam
111 G 16 Song Range, China ⛰
113 T 9 Songbai, China
131 U 14 Songea, Tanzania
110 K 13 Songhua Hu, China ◡
115 H 25 Songkhla, Thailand
110 G 9 Songling, China
112 L 10 Songming, China
111 K 18 Songnim, North Korea
132 G 1 Songo, Angola
133 Q 5 Songo, Mozambique
112 M 5 Songpan, China
107 U 11 Songsak, India
113 Y 9 Songxi, China
113 S 4 Songxian, China
110 J 11 Songyuan, China
113 S 7 Songzi, China
110 C 13 Sonid Zuoqi, China
106 J 8 Sonipat, India
101 T 14 Sonmiani, Pakistan
101 S 14 Sonmiani Bay, Pakistan ≈
44 H 2 Sonoita, Mexico
26 L 9 Sonora, TX, U.S.A.
33 H 19 Sonora, CA, U.S.A.
44 I 4 Sonora, Mexico ▣
44 I 4 Sonora, Mexico ∿
30 G 13 Sonoran Desert, AZ, U.S.A. ◇
46 I 7 Sonsonate, El Salvador
140 I 15 Sonsorol Islands, Palau ✽
89 Z 10 Sopka Klyuchevskaya, Russian Federation ▲
89 Z 11 Sopka Koryakskaya, Russian Federation ▲
89 Z 10 Sopka Shiveluch, Russian Federation ▲
78 I 8 Sopot, Poland
79 F 22 Sopron, Hungary
87 T 1 Sopych, Ukraine
145 S 2 Sor Rondane Mountains, Antarctica ⛰
77 I 14 Sora, Italy
111 M 18 Sŏrak-san, South Korea ▲
67 Q 13 Sorbas, Spain
42 L 10 Sorel, QC, Canada
94 K 9 Sorgun, Turkey
67 Q 4 Soria, Spain
59 D 15 Soriano, Uruguay ▣
105 J 16 Soro, India
58 K 7 Sorocaba, Brazil
93 U 4 Sorochinsk, Russian Federation
140 K 15 Sorol, Federated States of Micronesia ✽
117 T 11 Sorong, Indonesia
131 T 7 Soroti, Uganda
70 J 6 Sørøya, Norway ✽
70 J 6 Sørøysundet, Norway ≈
77 J 16 Sorrento, Italy
70 N 9 Sorsatunturi, Finland ▲
70 H 12 Sorsele, Sweden
120 K 13 Sorsogon, Philippines
90 F 8 Sortavala, Russian Federation
70 G 8 Sortland, Norway
70 F 9 Sørvågen, Norway
133 O 10 Soshanguve, Republic of South Africa
91 Q 7 Sosnogorsk, Russian Federation
90 H 6 Sosnovets, Russian Federation
90 K 4 Sosnovka, Russian Federation
90 F 10 Sosnovo, Russian Federation
90 E 10 Sosnovyy Bor, Russian Federation
79 J 17 Sosnowiec, Poland
87 R 2 Sosnytsya, Ukraine
88 J 10 Sos'va, Russian Federation
71 N 14 Sotkamo, Finland
56 I 10 Soto, Argentina
45 R 9 Soto la Marina, Mexico
71 A 18 Sotra, Norway ✽
45 Y 10 Sotuta, Mexico
130 G 6 Souanké, Congo
128 J 13 Soubré, Côte d'Ivoire
83 H 26 Souda, Greece
82 K 12 Soufli, Greece
128 G 11 Souguéta, Guinea
65 P 11 Souillac, France
125 P 5 Souk Ahras, Algeria
124 I 6 Souk el Arbaâ du Rharb, Morocco
64 L 10 Soulac-sur-Mer, France
96 F 7 Soûr, Lebanon
53 G 18 Source of the Amazon, Peru ◇
54 J 10 Soure, Brazil
43 W 8 Souris, PE, Canada
54 N 12 Sousa, Brazil
125 Q 6 Sousse, Tunisia
105 N 22 South Andaman, India ✽
135 O 9 South Australia, Australia ▣
31 P 12 South Baldy, NM, U.S.A. ▲
21 M 16 South Bass Island, OH, U.S.A. ✽
42 C 10 South Baymouth, ON, Canada
21 J 16 South Bend, IN, U.S.A.
17 R 7 South Boston, VA, U.S.A.
17 O 12 South Carolina, U.S.A. ▣
109 T 15 South China Sea, Asia ≋
22 H 8 South Dakota, U.S.A. ▣
63 U 12 South Downs, U.K. ◇
132 M 10 South East, Botswana ▣
135 S 15 South East Cape, TAS, Australia ▶
31 P 6 South Fork, CO, U.S.A.
33 E 16 South Fork, CA, U.S.A.
145 T 9 South Geomagnetic Pole, Antarctica ◇
107 V 14 South Hatia Island, Bangladesh ✽
21 I 15 South Haven, MI, U.S.A.
40 K 4 South Henik Lake, NU, Canada ◡
17 S 7 South Hill, VA, U.S.A.
131 V 6 South Horr, Kenya
105 L 20 South Huvadhu Atoll, Maldives ✽
37 P 10 South Indian Lake, MB, Canada
105 B 23 South Island, India ✽
137 G 19 South Island, New Zealand ✽
121 E 20 South Islet, Philippines ✽
40 I 11 South Junction, MB, Canada
111 K 20 South Korea, Asia □
33 I 18 South Lake Tahoe, CA, U.S.A.
105 M 17 South Maalhosmadulu Atoll, Maldives ✽
145 V 14 South Magnetic Pole, Antarctica ◇
105 L 18 South Male Atoll, Maldives ✽
105 L 17 South Miladunmadulu Atoll, Maldives ✽
63 N 12 South Molton, U.K.
48 K 8 South Negril Point, Jamaica ▶
144 H 1 South Orkney Islands, U.K. ✽
15 O 6 South Paris, ME, U.S.A.
31 T 3 South Platte, CO, U.S.A. ∿
20 L 11 South Point, MI, U.S.A. ▶
145 P 8 South Pole, Antarctica ◇
42 F 10 South River, ON, Canada
60 I 7 South Ronaldsay, U.K. ✽
39 L 19 South Saskatchewan, SK, Canada ∿
144 G 3 South Shetland Islands, U.K. ✽
61 K 15 South Shields, U.K.
16 L 4 South Shore, KY, U.S.A.
41 P 1 South Spicer Island, NU, Canada ✽
136 J 13 South Taranaki Bight, New Zealand ≈
41 P 9 South Twin Island, QC, Canada ✽
60 D 10 South Uist, U.K. ✽
137 B 26 South West Cape, New Zealand ▶
14 M 12 Southampton, NY, U.S.A.
63 T 13 Southampton, U.K.
41 N 3 Southampton Island, NU, Canada ✽
14 M 10 Southbridge, MA, U.S.A.
39 M 15 Southend, SK, Canada
63 Y 10 Southend-on-Sea, U.K.
105 G 26 Southern, Sri Lanka ▣
127 G 22 Southern, Ethiopia ▣
128 G 13 Southern, Sierra Leone ▣
132 L 10 Southern, Botswana ▣
133 N 6 Southern, Zambia ▣
133 R 5 Southern, Malawi ▣
137 C 22 Southern Alps, New Zealand ⛰
141 O 10 Southern Cook Islands, Cook Islands ✽
134 H 10 Southern Cross, WA, Australia
127 A 19 Southern Darfur, Sudan ▣
138 B 5 Southern Highlands, Papua New Guinea ▣
40 J 6 Southern Indian Lake, MB, Canada ◡
40 J 6 Southern Indian Lake, MB, Canada
127 E 19 Southern Kordofan, Sudan ▣
46 K 2 Southern Lagoon, Belize ≈
139 Y 12 Southern Lau Group, Fiji ✽
141 R 6 Southern Line Islands, Kiribati ✽
46 L 2 Southern Long Cays, Belize ✽
61 H 14 Southern Uplands, U.K. ⛰
39 N 19 Southey, SK, Canada
38 O 7 Southampton Island, NU, Canada ✽
137 C 24 Southland, New Zealand ▣
17 T 12 Southport, NC, U.S.A.
63 O 3 Southport, U.K.
135 S 15 Southport, TAS, Australia
138 D 2 Southwest Point, Papua New Guinea ▶
63 Z 7 Southwold, U.K.
77 M 20 Soverato, Italy
77 M 19 Soveria Mannelli, Italy
85 C 15 Sovetsk, Russian Federation
91 P 13 Sovetsk, Russian Federation
88 J 9 Sovetskiy, Russian Federation
133 N 8 Sowa Pan, Botswana ▱
133 N 11 Soweto, Republic of South Africa
122 J 2 Sōya-misaki, Japan ▶
122 J 2 Sōya-wan, Japan ≈
45 W 13 Soyaló, Mexico
132 F 1 Soyo, Angola
85 N 18 Sozh, Belarus ∿
82 N 9 Sozopol, Bulgaria
69 K 21 Spa, Belgium
144 J 6 Spaatz Island, Antarctica ✽
103 O 8 Space Launching Center, Kazakhstan
67 Q 8 Spain, Europe □
63 W 6 Spalding, U.K.
42 C 9 Spanish, ON, Canada
33 I 17 Sparks, NV, U.S.A.
16 H 9 Sparta, TN, U.S.A.
17 O 8 Sparta, NC, U.S.A.
16 M 11 Spartanburg, SC, U.S.A.
83 E 22 Sparti, Greece
39 J 21 Sparwood, BC, Canada
92 I 2 Spas-Demensk, Russian Federation
92 M 2 Spas-Klepiki, Russian Federation
89 V 15 Spassk-Dal'niy, Russian Federation
22 G 9 Spearfish, SD, U.S.A.
26 K 1 Spearman, TX, U.S.A.
49 Z 12 Speightstown, Barbados
23 Q 11 Spencer, IA, U.S.A.
135 O 11 Spencer Gulf, SA, Australia ≈
137 C 24 Spencer Peak, New Zealand ▲
83 F 22 Spetses, Greece ✽
83 F 22 Spetses, Greece
60 H 10 Spey, U.K. ∿
73 E 21 Speyer, Germany
72 D 9 Spiekeroog, Germany ✽
75 W 8 Spielfeld, Austria
74 E 9 Spiez, Switzerland
83 I 26 Spili, Greece
101 S 10 Spin, Afghanistan
77 M 16 Spinazzola, Italy
136 J 14 Spirits Bay, New Zealand ≈
39 L 18 Spiritwood, SK, Canada
25 R 11 Spiro, OK, U.S.A.
95 T 8 Spitak, Armenia
143 U 11 Spitsbergen, Svalbard ✽
75 R 8 Spittal, Austria
75 V 3 Spitz, Austria
27 T 9 Splendora, TX, U.S.A.
80 E 13 Split, Croatia
74 I 9 Splügen, Switzerland
63 S 2 Spofforth, U.K.
84 I 13 Špoģi, Latvia
32 K 7 Spokane, WA, U.S.A.
76 H 12 Spoleto, Italy
20 C 9 Spooner, WI, U.S.A.
29 X 8 Spotted Horse, WY, U.S.A.
32 K 7 Sprague, WA, U.S.A.
32 J 10 Spray, OR, U.S.A.
80 H 10 Spreča, Bosnia and Herzegovina ∿
69 J 21 Sprimont, Belgium
19 V 10 Spring Hill, FL, U.S.A.
21 I 14 Spring Lake, MI, U.S.A.
132 J 13 Springbok, Republic of South Africa
25 S 9 Springdale, AR, U.S.A.
41 X 10 Springdale, NL, Canada
31 S 8 Springer, NM, U.S.A.
14 L 10 Springfield, MA, U.S.A.
14 M 8 Springfield, VT, U.S.A.
16 F 8 Springfield, TN, U.S.A.
21 F 19 Springfield, IL, U.S.A.
21 L 19 Springfield, OH, U.S.A.
23 Q 9 Springfield, MN, U.S.A.
25 T 7 Springfield, MO, U.S.A.
31 U 7 Springfield, CO, U.S.A.
32 G 11 Springfield, OR, U.S.A.
43 V 9 Springhill, NS, Canada
137 G 18 Springs Junction, New Zealand
135 U 7 Springsure, QLD, Australia
14 D 9 Springville, NY, U.S.A.
17 Q 3 Spruce Knob, WV, U.S.A. ▲
33 N 16 Spruce Mountain, NV, U.S.A. ▲
69 G 15 Sprundel, Netherlands
63 W 3 Spurn Head, U.K. ▶
137 I 18 Spy Glass Point, New Zealand ▶
39 G 21 Squamish, BC, Canada
80 J 8 Srbobran, Serbia and Montenegro
115 K 22 Srê Âmbel, Cambodia
89 Y 9 Sredinnyy Khrebet, Russian Federation ⛰
82 M 6 Sredishte, Bulgaria
89 W 8 Srednekolymsk, Russian Federation
92 J 3 SredneŠRusskaya Vozvyshennost', Russian Federation ◇
91 T 10 Sredniy Ural, Russian Federation ⛰
82 H 9 Srednogorie, Bulgaria
78 G 13 Śrem, Poland
89 S 13 Sretensk, Russian Federation
119 O 11 Sri Aman, Malaysia
105 F 25 Sri Jayewardenepura Kotte, Sri Lanka ♜
105 H 23 Sri Lanka, Asia □
105 I 18 Srikakulam, India
107 V 12 Srimangal, Bangladesh
106 H 3 Srinagar, India
106 K 7 Srinagar, India
78 G 13 Środa Wielkopolska, Poland
72 G 10 Stade, Germany
71 A 16 Stadlandet, Norway ▶
68 N 7 Stadskanaal, Netherlands
63 R 6 Stafford, U.K.
14 M 10 Stafford Springs, CT, U.S.A.
75 S 6 Stainach, Austria
63 V 11 Staines, U.K.
75 V 8 Stainz, Austria
87 Y 6 Stakhanov, Ukraine
75 Q 8 Stall, Austria
79 M 16 Stalowa Wola, Poland
14 K 12 Stamford, CT, U.S.A.
14 J 9 Stamford, NY, U.S.A.
26 M 5 Stamford, TX, U.S.A.
63 V 6 Stamford, U.K.
63 U 1 Stamford Bridge, U.K.
132 J 10 Stampriet, Namibia
74 L 7 Stams, Austria
25 R 1 Stanberry, MO, U.S.A.
133 O 11 Standerton, Republic of South Africa
20 L 13 Standish, MI, U.S.A.
29 R 5 Stanford, MT, U.S.A.
133 P 12 Stanger, Republic of South Africa
87 R 9 Stanislav, Ukraine
22 H 3 Stanley, ND, U.S.A.
28 L 9 Stanley, ID, U.S.A.
57 L 24 Stanley, Falkland Islands ♜
89 S 12 Stanovoy Khrebet, Russian Federation ⛰
89 R 12 Stanovoye Nagor'ye, Russian Federation ◇
135 V 9 Stanthorpe, QLD, Australia
16 J 5 Stanton, KY, U.S.A.
63 Y 7 Stanton, U.K.
68 L 9 Staphorst, Netherlands
63 T 5 Stapleford, U.K.
22 K 13 Stapleton, NE, U.S.A.
75 L 19 Stará-Lubovna, Slovakia
82 J 9 Stara Zagora, Bulgaria ▣
82 J 9 Stara-Zagora, Bulgaria
79 L 15 Starachowice, Poland
90 F 12 Staraya Russa, Russian Federation
141 Q 5 Starbuck Island, Kiribati ✽
78 E 10 Stargard-Szczeciński, Poland
90 G 14 Staritsa, Russian Federation
19 V 8 Starke, FL, U.S.A.
19 N 3 Starkville, MS, U.S.A.
73 I 25 Starnberger See, Germany ◡
82 N 8 Staro Oryakhovo, Bulgaria
87 Y 5 Starobil's'k, Ukraine
78 I 9 Starogard Gdański, Poland
86 M 4 Starokostyantyniv, Ukraine
92 K 10 Starominskaya, Russian Federation
92 J 12 Starotitarovskaya, Russian Federation
87 V 5 Starovirivka, Ukraine
63 N 15 Start Bay, U.K. ≈
63 N 15 Start Point, U.K. ▶
87 V 12 Staryy Krym, Ukraine
88 L 9 Staryy Nadym, Russian Federation
92 K 5 Staryy Oskol, Russian Federation
87 W 4 Staryy Saltiv, Ukraine
85 K 19 Staryya Darohi, Belarus
79 L 16 Staszów, Poland
14 E 12 State College, PA, U.S.A.
14 J 13 Staten Island, NY, U.S.A. ✽
17 O 9 Statesville, NC, U.S.A.
143 R 10 Station Nord, Greenland
71 A 20 Stavanger, Norway
63 S 4 Staveley, U.K.
137 F 20 Staveley, New Zealand
69 E 15 Stavenisse, Netherlands
93 N 12 Stavropol', Russian Federation
93 N 11 Stavropol'skiy Kray, Russian Federation ▣
83 G 14 Stavros, Greece
78 M 10 Stawiski, Poland
78 H 13 Stawiszyn, Poland
31 P 3 Steamboat Springs, CO, U.S.A.
16 I 7 Stearns, KY, U.S.A.
34 M 7 Stebbins, AK, U.S.A.
144 J 5 Steele Island, Antarctica ✽
39 H 14 Steen River, AB, Canada
69 F 15 Steenbergen, Netherlands
33 J 14 Steens Mountain, OR, U.S.A. ▲
68 K 9 Steenwijk, Netherlands
134 E 8 Steep Point, WA, Australia ▶
38 H 4 Stefansson Island, NU, Canada ✽
75 X 7 Stegersbach, Austria
86 G 9 Ştei, Romania
75 V 7 Steiermark, Austria ▣
40 I 10 Steinbach, MB, Canada
69 K 25 Steinfort, Luxembourg
73 D 14 Steinfurt, Germany
132 J 13 Steinkopf, Republic of South Africa
69 E 14 Stellendam, Netherlands
65 T 3 Stenay, France
72 K 13 Stendal, Germany
84 D 10 Stende, Latvia
83 F 25 Steno Antikythiro, Greece ≈
83 F 23 Steno Elafonisou, Greece ≈
83 M 24 Steno Karpathou, Greece ≈
86 L 2 Stepan', Ukraine
27 O 7 Stephenville, TX, U.S.A.
41 X 10 Stephenville, NL, Canada
103 S 3 Stepnogorsk, Kazakhstan
93 P 13 Stepnoye, Russian Federation
80 K 11 Stepojevac, Serbia and Montenegro
83 F 19 Sterea Ellas, Greece ▣
22 K 5 Sterling, ND, U.S.A.
31 T 2 Sterling, CO, U.S.A.
26 L 7 Sterling City, TX, U.S.A.
21 M 14 Sterling Heights, MI, U.S.A.
17 T 3 Sterling Park, VA, U.S.A.
93 W 2 Sterlitamak, Russian Federation
39 J 19 Stettler, AB, Canada
21 O 18 Steubenville, OH, U.S.A.
63 V 9 Stevenage, U.K.
20 F 11 Stevens Point, WI, U.S.A.
35 R 6 Stevens Village, AK, U.S.A.
19 Q 1 Stevenson, AL, U.S.A.
35 Q 11 Stevenson Entrance, AK, U.S.A. ≈
39 D 17 Stewart, BC, Canada
137 C 26 Stewart Island, New Zealand ✽
23 T 9 Stewartville, MN, U.S.A.
43 V 10 Stewiacke, NS, Canada
75 T 4 Steyr, Austria
68 K 6 Stiens, Netherlands
20 H 11 Stiles Junction, WI, U.S.A.
63 T 1 Stillington, U.K.
25 N 9 Stillwater, OK, U.S.A.
33 J 18 Stillwater Range, NV, U.S.A. ⛰
80 G 12 Štilt, Bosnia and Herzegovina ▲
63 V 7 Stilton, U.K.
26 K 1 Stinnett, TX, U.S.A.
82 E 11 Štip, Macedonia (F.Y.R.O.M.)
60 H 12 Stirling, U.K.
70 J 6 Stjernøya, Norway ✽
73 F 25 Stockach, Germany
75 X 3 Stockerau, Austria
71 H 21 Stockholm, Sweden ♜
63 R 4 Stockport, U.K.
63 S 3 Stocksbridge, U.K.
24 K 3 Stockton, KS, U.S.A.
25 T 6 Stockton, MO, U.S.A.
33 H 19 Stockton, CA, U.S.A.
20 E 8 Stockton Island, WI, U.S.A. ✽
25 S 6 Stockton Lake, MO, U.S.A. ◡
26 J 9 Stockton Plateau, TX, U.S.A. ◇
78 M 13 Stoczek, Poland
79 B 18 Stod, Czech Republic
115 M 19 Stœng Trêng, Cambodia
63 R 5 Stoke-on-Trent, U.K.
80 N 11 Stol, Serbia and Montenegro ▲
88 L 5 Stolbovoy, Russian Federation
85 I 21 Stolin, Belarus
63 R 5 Stone, U.K.
42 G 9 Stonecliffe, ON, Canada
60 J 11 Stonehaven, U.K.
17 T 7 Stony Creek, VA, U.S.A.
37 N 10 Stony Rapids, SK, Canada
35 O 9 Stony River, AK, U.S.A.
70 I 12 Storavan, Sweden ◡
71 A 19 Stord, Norway ✽
71 C 25 Store Baelt, Denmark ≈
71 D 15 Støren, Norway
70 G 11 Storjord, Norway
38 H 5 Storkerson Peninsula, NU, Canada ▶
71 E 15 Storlien, Sweden
23 Q 11 Storm Lake, IA, U.S.A.
60 F 8 Stornoway, U.K.
91 P 9 Storozhevsk, Russian Federation
86 K 7 Storozhynets', Ukraine

□ Country ▣ Internal administrative region: State/Province/Territory/Dependent territory ♜ Capital city ⛰ Mountain range/Undersea ridge ▲ Mountain peak/Volcano/Seamount ◇ Geographic feature ▶ Headland/Point/Cape/Peninsula ◠ Desert ✽ Island/Island group ⁙ Antarctic base Ⓞ Ocean ≋ Sea ≈ Bay/Gulf/Channel/Strait ◡ Lake ▱ Salt pan/Dry/Intermittent lake ∿ R…

	F 15	**Storsjön**, Sweden ⛆
	H 6	**Stortemelk**, Netherlands ≈
	H 13	**Storuman**, Sweden
	H 13	**Storuman**, Sweden ⛆
	X 9	**Stour**, U.K. ∫
	R 7	**Stourbridge**, U.K.
	Q 7	**Stourport-on-Severn**, U.K.
	J 9	**Stout Lake**, ON, Canada ⛆
	S 9	**Stow-on-the-Wold**, U.K.
	I 18	**Stowbtsy**, Belarus
	Y 8	**Stowmarket**, U.K.
	D 15	**Strabane**, U.K.
	S 15	**Strahan**, TAS, Australia
	J 25	**Straimont**, Belgium
	X 9	**Strait of Belle Isle**, NL, Canada ≈
	C 15	**Strait of Bonifacio**, Italy ≈
	X 9	**Strait of Canso**, NS, Canada ≈
	Z 13	**Strait of Dover**, France/United Kingdom ≈
	F 21	**Strait of Georgia**, BC, Canada ≈
	K 15	**Strait of Gibraltar**, Africa/Spain ≈
	K 14	**Strait of Hormuz**, Iran ≈
	F 3	**Strait of Juan de Fuco**, OR, U.S.A. ≈
	G 25	**Strait of Magellan**, Chile ≈
	B 9	**Strait of Malacca**, Indonesia/Malaysia ≈
	Y 15	**Straits of Florida**, Cuba/U.S.A ≈
	C 19	**Strakonice**, Czech Republic
	L 8	**Stralsund**, Germany
	F 16	**Strangford Lough**, U.K. ⛆
	H 20	**Strängnäs**, Sweden
	G 15	**Stranraer**, U.K.
	X 4	**Strasbourg**, France
	R 3	**Strasburg**, VA, U.S.A.
	R 5	**Strasswalchen**, Austria
	N 11	**Stratford**, OK, U.S.A.
	J 1	**Stratford**, TX, U.S.A.
	D 13	**Stratford**, ON, Canada
	J 13	**Stratford**, New Zealand
	S 8	**Stratford-upon-Avon**, U.K.
	S 15	**Strathgordon**, TAS, Australia
	C 14	**Strathroy**, ON, Canada
	O 4	**Stratton**, ME, U.S.A.
	L 8	**Stratton Mountain**, VT, U.S.A. ▲
	L 22	**Straubing**, Germany
	A 9	**Straumnes**, Iceland ▶
	K 11	**Strawberry Mountain**, OR, U.S.A. ▲
	L 3	**Strawberry Reservoir**, UT, U.S.A. ⛆
	N 11	**Streaky Bay**, SA, Australia
	G 12	**Strehaia**, Romania
	G 9	**Strenči**, Latvia
	C 6	**Stresa**, Italy
	L 22	**Stretta di Messina**, Italy ≈
	N 13	**Strevell**, ID, U.S.A.
	B 18	**Stříbro**, Czech Republic
	A 5	**Strickland**, Papua New Guinea ∫
	B 20	**Stroeder**, Argentina
	L 20	**Stromboli**, Italy ▲
	I 7	**Stromness**, U.K.
	N 14	**Stromsburg**, NE, U.S.A.
	D 21	**Strömstad**, Sweden
	G 15	**Strömsund**, Sweden
	I 7	**Stronsay**, U.K. 🏝
	O 9	**Stroud**, OK, U.S.A.
	R 10	**Stroud**, U.K.
	I 12	**Stroudsburg**, NJ, U.S.A.
	B 24	**Struer**, Denmark
	B 12	**Struga**, Macedonia (F.Y.R.O.M.)
	F 11	**Struma**, Bulgaria ∫
	K 8	**Strumble Head**, U.K. ▶
	E 12	**Strumica**, Macedonia (F.Y.R.O.M.)
	I 5	**Stryy**, Ukraine
	H 16	**Strzelce Opolskie**, Poland
	G 16	**Strzelin**, Poland
	H 12	**Strzelno**, Poland
	Y 11	**Stuart**, FL, U.S.A.
	L 7	**Stubaier Alpen**, Austria ⛰
	R 8	**Studley**, U.K.
	L 2	**Stupino**, Russian Federation
	S 15	**Sturge Island**, Antarctica 🏝
	H 11	**Sturgeon Bay**, WI, U.S.A.
	E 9	**Sturgeon Falls**, ON, Canada
	G 9	**Sturgis**, SD, U.S.A.
	Q 12	**Sturminster Newton**, U.K.
	I 22	**Štúrovo**, Slovakia
	Q 8	**Sturt Stony Desert**, SA, Australia ◇
	N 14	**Stutterheim**, Republic of South Africa
	W 12	**Stuttgart**, AR, U.S.A.
	F 23	**Stuttgart**, Germany
	A 10	**Stykkishólmur**, Iceland
	E 18	**Stylida**, Greece
	H 21	**Styr**, Belarus/Ukraine ∫
	R 8	**Suai**, Malaysia
	H 14	**Suakin**, Sudan
	K 12	**Suana**, Democratic Republic of Congo
	Z 11	**Suao**, Taiwan
	H 9	**Subi Besar**, Indonesia 🏝
	H 14	**Subiaco**, Italy
	I 6	**Sublette**, KS, U.S.A.
	J 7	**Subotica**, Serbia and Montenegro
	F 13	**Subrag**, China
	L 8	**Suceava**, Romania
	K 7	**Sucevița**, Romania
	N 10	**Suchowola**, Poland
	I 4	**Sucre**, Colombia ▣
	Q 3	**Sucre**, Venezuela ▣
	K 21	**Sucre**, Bolivia ▟
	C 8	**Sucumbíos**, Ecuador ▣
	F 11	**Sucunduri**, Brazil ∫
	H 4	**Sucuriú**, Brazil ∫
	T 15	**Sud**, Cameroon ▣
	P 9	**Sud-Kivu**, Democratic Republic of Congo ▣
	S 14	**Sud-Ouest**, Cameroon ▣
	V 12	**Sudak**, Ukraine
	B 19	**Sudan**, Africa □
	D 9	**Sudbury**, ON, Canada
	X 8	**Sudbury**, U.K.
	D 21	**Sudd**, Sudan ◇
	E 8	**Süderoogsand**, Germany 🏝
	E 16	**Sudeten**, Czech Republic ⛰
	M 1	**Sudogda**, Russian Federation
	I 5	**Sudzha**, Russian Federation
	T 8	**Sueca**, Spain
	F 8	**Suez**, Egypt
	F 8	**Suez Canal**, Egypt ◇
	V 7	**Suffolk**, VA, U.S.A.
	S 10	**Sugar Land**, TX, U.S.A.
	N 18	**Sugbuhan Point**, Philippines ▶
	H 9	**Sugehe**, China
	H 5	**Sugun**, China
	Q 7	**Suhait**, China
	Y 6	**Şuḩār**, Oman
	S 4	**Sühbaatar**, Mongolia ▣
109	Q 2	**Sühbaatar**, Mongolia
73	I 18	**Suhl**, Germany
80	F 12	**Šuica**, Bosnia and Herzegovina
113	X 8	**Suichang**, China
113	U 10	**Suichuan**, China
113	R 1	**Suide**, China
105	B 14	**Suigam**, India
110	K 10	**Suihua**, China
112	M 8	**Suijiang**, China
110	K 9	**Suileng**, China
113	O 6	**Suining**, China
113	R 10	**Suining**, China
65	T 4	**Suippes**, France
61	D 20	**Suir**, Republic of Ireland ∫
113	R 14	**Suixi**, China
113	V 4	**Suixi**, China
113	U 3	**Suixian**, China
113	P 8	**Suiyang**, China
111	G 16	**Suizhong**, China
113	T 5	**Suizhou**, China
101	U 15	**Sujawal**, Pakistan
116	H 14	**Sukabumi**, Indonesia
116	I 11	**Sukadana**, Indonesia
123	K 14	**Sukagawa**, Japan
116	J 12	**Sukaramai**, Indonesia
119	X 5	**Sukau**, Malaysia
71	M 14	**Sukeva**, Finland
92	J 2	**Sukhinichi**, Russian Federation
90	M 10	**Sukhona**, Russian Federation ∫
115	G 16	**Sukhothai**, Thailand
101	U 12	**Sukkur**, Pakistan
125	U 10	**Sūknah**, Libya
132	I 8	**Sukses**, Namibia
91	T 13	**Suksun**, Russian Federation
123	E 21	**Sukumo**, Japan
71	A 17	**Sula**, Norway 🏝
87	S 4	**Sula**, Ukraine ∫
117	R 12	**Sulabesi**, Indonesia 🏝
101	U 12	**Sulaiman Ranges**, Pakistan ⛰
93	R 14	**Sulak**, Russian Federation
121	M 15	**Sulat**, Philippines
117	O 12	**Sulawesi**, Indonesia 🏝
117	N 13	**Sulawesi Selatan**, Indonesia ▣
117	P 12	**Sulawesi Tengah**, Indonesia ▣
117	P 14	**Sulawesi Tenggara**, Indonesia ▣
117	P 10	**Sulawesi Utara**, Indonesia ▣
97	U 4	**Sulaymān Beg**, Iraq
78	E 13	**Sulechów**, Poland
129	R 12	**Suleja**, Nigeria
79	J 15	**Sulejów**, Poland
72	F 12	**Sulingen**, Germany
52	A 12	**Sullana**, Peru
19	O 3	**Sulligent**, AL, U.S.A.
21	H 20	**Sullivan**, IN, U.S.A.
25	W 5	**Sullivan**, MO, U.S.A.
82	L 11	**Süloğlu**, Turkey
18	H 7	**Sulphur**, LA, U.S.A.
25	O 12	**Sulphur**, OK, U.S.A.
42	B 7	**Sultan**, ON, Canada
125	W 8	**Sultan**, Libya
94	I 11	**Sultanhani**, Turkey
107	N 10	**Sultanpur**, India
121	E 26	**Sulu Archipelago**, Philippines 🏝
117	O 7	**Sulu Sea**, Malaysia/Philippines ◗
121	N 17	**Suluan**, Philippines 🏝
94	G 10	**Sülüklü**, Turkey
103	R 12	**Sülüktü**, Kyrgyzstan
125	W 7	**Sulunḩah**, Libya
125	W 7	**Sulūq**, Libya
73	K 20	**Sulzbach-Rosenberg**, Germany
145	N 12	**Sulzberger Bay**, Antarctica ≈
116	D 11	**Sumatera Barat**, Indonesia ▣
116	F 12	**Sumatera Selatan**, Indonesia ▣
116	D 9	**Sumatera Utara**, Indonesia ▣
116	F 10	**Sumatra**, Indonesia 🏝
117	N 15	**Sumba**, Indonesia 🏝
117	N 14	**Sumbawa**, Indonesia 🏝
116	M 15	**Sumbawabesar**, Indonesia
131	R 12	**Sumbawanga**, Tanzania
132	G 4	**Sumbe**, Angola
133	O 2	**Sumbu**, Zambia
60	J 5	**Sumburgh Head**, U.K. ▶
112	K 7	**Sumdo**, China
100	H 4	**Sume'eh Sarā**, Iran
127	C 20	**Sumeih**, Sudan
116	K 14	**Sumenep**, Indonesia
123	O 22	**Sumiyō**, Japan
97	R 1	**Summēl**, Iraq
32	I 13	**Summer Lake**, OR, U.S.A. ⛆
17	P 14	**Summerville**, SC, U.S.A.
19	R 2	**Summerville**, GA, U.S.A.
39	E 15	**Summit Lake**, BC, Canada
123	G 19	**Sumoto**, Japan
79	G 17	**Šumperk**, Czech Republic
114	F 7	**Sumprabum**, Myanmar
95	Z 8	**Sumqayit**, Azerbaijan
17	P 12	**Sumter**, SC, U.S.A.
87	U 3	**Sumy**, Ukraine
33	K 25	**Sun City**, CA, U.S.A.
107	Q 9	**Sun Kosi**, Nepal ∫
91	P 13	**Suna**, Russian Federation
122	J 5	**Sunagawa**, Japan
111	K 17	**Sunan**, North Korea
99	X 6	**Şunaynah**, Oman
29	P 2	**Sunburst**, MT, U.S.A.
21	M 18	**Sunbury**, OH, U.S.A.
58	B 13	**Sunchales**, Argentina
111	L 21	**Sunch'ŏn**, South Korea
116	G 13	**Sunda Strait**, Indonesia ≈
29	Z 9	**Sundance**, WY, U.S.A.
107	S 14	**Sundarbans**, India ◇
61	K 15	**Sunderland**, U.K.
94	F 9	**Sündiken Dağlari**, Turkey
71	H 17	**Sundsvall**, Sweden
131	W 10	**Sunga**, Tanzania
118	B 8	**Sungai Besar**, Malaysia
116	D 8	**Sungai Petani**, Malaysia
116	E 11	**Sungaidareh**, Indonesia
116	E 11	**Sungaipenuh**, Indonesia
118	A 5	**Sungei Petani**, Malaysia
118	B 13	**Sungei Seletar Reservoir**, Singapore ⛆
130	I 8	**Sungu**, Democratic Republic of Congo
94	J 9	**Sungurlu**, Turkey
50	H 6	**Sunia**, Colombia
71	E 20	**Sunne**, Sweden
32	I 8	**Sunnyside**, WA, U.S.A.
33	G 20	**Sunnyvale**, CA, U.S.A.
135	W 8	**Sunshine Coast**, QLD, Australia ◇
89	S 11	**Suntar**, Russian Federation
101	P 14	**Suntsar**, Pakistan
110	K 7	**Sunwu**, China
128	L 12	**Sunyani**, Ghana
123	C 20	**Suō-nada**, Japan ≈
70	N 13	**Suomussalmi**, Finland
115	L 21	**Suŏng**, Cambodia
90	G 8	**Suoyarvi**, Russian Federation
20	C 8	**Superior**, WI, U.S.A.
30	K 13	**Superior**, AZ, U.S.A.
95	R 10	**Süphan Dağt**, Turkey ▲
117	W 11	**Supiori**, Indonesia 🏝
17	S 12	**Suppli**, NC, U.S.A.
97	X 11	**Sūq ash Shuyūkh**, Iraq
113	W 4	**Suqian**, China
47	R 14	**Sur**, Costa Rica
99	Z 7	**Şūr**, Oman
93	Q 2	**Sura**, Russian Federation ∫
95	Z 7	**Şuraabad**, Azerbaijan
101	S 12	**Surab**, Pakistan
116	K 14	**Surabaya**, Indonesia
116	J 14	**Surakarta**, Indonesia
121	L 23	**Surallah**, Philippines
105	C 15	**Surat**, India
135	U 8	**Surat**, QLD, Australia
115	G 23	**Surat Thani**, Thailand
106	G 7	**Suratgarh**, India
85	M 14	**Surazh**, Belarus
92	H 3	**Surazh**, Russian Federation
97	U 3	**Sūrdāsh**, Iraq
86	M 12	**Surdila-Greci**, Romania
81	N 15	**Surdulica**, Serbia and Montenegro
105	B 15	**Surendranagar**, India
14	J 14	**Surf City**, NJ, U.S.A.
135	W 9	**Surfers Paradise**, QLD, Australia
48	H 4	**Surgidero de Batabanó**, Cuba
88	L 10	**Surgut**, Russian Federation
105	F 18	**Suriapet**, India
121	M 18	**Surigao**, Philippines
121	M 18	**Surigao Strait**, Philippines ≈
115	K 18	**Surin**, Thailand
51	V 7	**Suriname**, Suriname □
106	M 8	**Surkhet**, Nepal
103	Q 14	**Surkhondaryo Wiloyati**, Uzbekistan ▣
95	O 8	**Sürmene**, Turkey
93	N 8	**Surovikino**, Russian Federation
74	F 7	**Sursee**, Switzerland
93	Q 2	**Surskoye**, Russian Federation
70	B 12	**Surtsey**, Iceland 🏝
95	N 13	**Sürüş**, Turkey
123	J 17	**Suruga-wan**, Japan ≈
116	E 12	**Surulangun**, Indonesia
76	A 7	**Susa**, Italy
95	W 9	**Şuşa**, Azerbaijan
123	C 19	**Susa**, Japan
81	E 15	**Sušac**, Croatia 🏝
80	B 11	**Susak**, Croatia 🏝
123	E 21	**Susaki**, Japan
123	G 20	**Susami**, Japan
100	G 8	**Sūsangerd**, Iran
33	H 16	**Susanville**, CA, U.S.A.
74	J 8	**Susch**, Switzerland
95	N 9	**Suşehri**, Turkey
115	G 25	**Suso**, Thailand
14	F 13	**Susquehanna**, PA, U.S.A. ∫
56	I 5	**Susques**, Argentina
43	T 10	**Sussex**, NB, Canada
39	E 17	**Sustut Peak**, BC, Canada ▲
89	W 9	**Susuman**, Russian Federation
108	M 3	**Sutay Uul**, Mongolia ▲
132	K 14	**Sutherland**, Republic of South Africa
32	F 12	**Sutherlin**, OR, U.S.A.
101	W 11	**Sutlej**, Pakistan ∫
17	O 4	**Sutton**, WV, U.S.A.
63	S 7	**Sutton Coldfield**, U.K.
63	T 5	**Sutton in Ashfield**, U.K.
41	N 8	**Sutton Ridges**, ON, Canada ⛰
122	I 6	**Suttsu**, Japan
109	Q 3	**Süüj**, Mongolia
84	H 9	**Suur Munamägi**, Estonia ▲
103	U 11	**Suusamyr**, Kyrgyzstan
139	X 12	**Suva**, Fiji ▟
87	O 11	**Suvorove**, Ukraine
78	N 8	**Suwałki**, Poland
115	K 17	**Suwannaphum**, Thailand
123	B 26	**Suwanose-jima**, Japan 🏝
141	N 8	**Suwarrow**, Cook Islands 🏝
96	G 9	**Suwayliḩ**, Jordan
111	L 19	**Suwon**, South Korea
103	R 9	**Suzak**, Kazakhstan
123	I 15	**Suzaka**, Japan
90	K 14	**Suzdal'**, Russian Federation
113	Y 6	**Suzhou**, China
113	V 4	**Suzhou**, China
123	H 14	**Suzu**, Japan
123	H 14	**Suzu-misaki**, Japan ▶
123	H 18	**Suzuka**, Japan
143	S 10	**Svalbard**, Norway ▣
71	F 26	**Svaneke**, Denmark
70	J 10	**Svappavaara**, Sweden
70	J 12	**Svartlå**, Sweden
87	Y 5	**Svatove**, Ukraine
115	M 21	**Svay Rieng**, Cambodia
84	G 13	**Svėdasai**, Lithuania
71	F 17	**Sveg**, Sweden
85	C 14	**Švėkšna**, Lithuania
71	C 26	**Svendborg**, Denmark
71	F 16	**Svenstavik**, Sweden
87	Z 6	**Sverdlovs'k**, Ukraine
37	N 2	**Sverdrup Channel**, NU, Canada ≈
82	E 11	**Sveti Nikole**, Macedonia (F.Y.R.O.M.)
89	W 14	**Svetlaya**, Russian Federation
93	N 12	**Svetlograd**, Russian Federation
85	A 15	**Svetlyy**, Russian Federation
90	E 9	**Svetogorsk**, Russian Federation
70	C 11	**Svíahnúkar**, Iceland ▲
79	M 19	**Svidnik**, Slovakia
82	K 11	**Svilengrad**, Bulgaria
85	H 15	**Svir**, Belarus
82	J 7	**Svishtov**, Bulgaria
85	F 19	**Svislach**, Belarus
79	F 18	**Svitavy**, Czech Republic
89	U 13	**Svobodnyy**, Russian Federation
82	G 8	**Svoge**, Bulgaria
80	N 13	**Svrljig**, Serbia and Montenegro
85	L 20	**Svyetlahorsk**, Belarus
73	F 24	**Swabian Alp**, Germany ⛰
63	X 6	**Swaffham**, U.K.
140	K 7	**Swains**, American Samoa 🏝
19	V 4	**Swainsboro**, GA, U.S.A.
132	H 9	**Swakopmund**, Namibia
63	S 1	**Swale**, U.K. ∫
139	Q 7	**Swallow Islands**, Solomon Islands 🏝
135	R 12	**Swan Hill**, VIC, Australia
40	H 9	**Swan River**, MB, Canada
63	R 14	**Swanage**, U.K.
17	V 9	**Swanquarter**, NC, U.S.A.
15	R 6	**Swans Island**, ME, U.S.A. 🏝
62	M 10	**Swansea**, U.K.
135	T 15	**Swansea**, TAS, Australia
135	V 11	**Swansea**, NSW, Australia
78	G 12	**Swarzędz**, Poland
133	P 11	**Swaziland**, Africa □
71	F 22	**Sweden**, Europe □
32	G 11	**Sweet Home**, OR, U.S.A.
16	J 9	**Sweetwater**, TN, U.S.A.
26	L 6	**Sweetwater**, TX, U.S.A.
132	K 15	**Swellendam**, Republic of South Africa
79	N 15	**Świdnik**, Poland
78	E 9	**Świdwin**, Poland
78	E 13	**Świebodzin**, Poland
78	I 10	**Świecie**, Poland
39	M 20	**Swift Current**, SK, Canada
63	S 10	**Swindon**, U.K.
63	V 5	**Swineshead**, U.K.
78	D 9	**Świnoujście**, Poland
74	B 8	**Switzerland**, Europe □
90	K 11	**Syamzha**, Russian Federation
85	L 15	**Syanno**, Belarus
90	G 10	**Syas'troy**, Russian Federation
92	I 1	**Sychevka**, Russian Federation
79	H 15	**Syców**, Poland
43	Y 8	**Sydney**, NS, Canada
135	V 11	**Sydney**, NSW, Australia
87	Y 5	**Syeverodonets'k**, Ukraine
72	F 12	**Syke**, Germany
91	P 9	**Syktyvkar**, Russian Federation
19	R 3	**Sylacauga**, AL, U.S.A.
107	W 12	**Sylhet**, Bangladesh
107	V 12	**Sylhet**, Bangladesh ▣
72	E 7	**Sylt**, Germany 🏝
16	K 10	**Sylva**, NC, U.S.A.
19	W 4	**Sylvania**, GA, U.S.A.
19	T 6	**Sylvester**, GA, U.S.A.
83	N 23	**Symi**, Greece 🏝
87	V 6	**Synel'nykove**, Ukraine
71	C 18	**Synnfjell**, Norway ▲
91	S 5	**Synya**, Russian Federation
145	U 2	**Syowa**, Antarctica ⁙
14	G 8	**Syracuse**, NY, U.S.A.
24	G 5	**Syracuse**, KS, U.S.A.
77	L 23	**Syracuse**, Italy
103	Q 10	**Syrdar'ya**, Kazakhstan ∫
96	K 4	**Syria**, Asia □
115	D 16	**Syriam**, Myanmar
96	K 8	**Syrian Desert**, Jordan ◇
83	L 24	**Syrna**, Greece 🏝
83	I 21	**Syros**, Greece 🏝
71	N 15	**Syväri**, Finland ⛆
93	R 3	**Syzran'**, Russian Federation
78	F 12	**Szamotuły**, Poland
78	D 10	**Szczecin**, Poland
78	F 9	**Szczecinek**, Poland
79	J 16	**Szczekociny**, Poland
78	M 10	**Szczuczyn**, Poland
78	L 10	**Szczytno**, Poland
79	K 25	**Szeged**, Hungary
79	L 24	**Szeghalom**, Hungary
79	I 23	**Székesfehervár**, Hungary
79	I 25	**Szekszárd**, Hungary
79	K 24	**Szentes**, Hungary
79	H 26	**Szentőrinc**, Hungary
79	L 21	**Szerencs**, Hungary
79	K 23	**Szolnok**, Hungary
79	F 23	**Szombathely**, Hungary
79	E 14	**Szprotawa**, Poland
78	H 11	**Szubin**, Poland

T

114	F 12	**Ta-Kaw**, Myanmar
114	I 11	**Ta Loung San**, Laos ▲
120	K 13	**Tabaco**, Philippines
138	H 3	**Tabar Islands**, Papua New Guinea 🏝
100	M 8	**Ţabas**, Iran
45	V 12	**Tabasco**, Mexico ▣
100	M 10	**Tabāsīn**, Iran
54	B 11	**Tabatinga**, Brazil
124	J 10	**Tabelbala**, Algeria
39	K 20	**Taber**, AB, Canada
131	P 7	**Tabili**, Democratic Republic of Congo
140	E 3	**Tabiteuea**, Kiribati 🏝
121	H 14	**Tablas**, Philippines 🏝
121	H 15	**Tablas Strait**, Philippines ≈
121	D 18	**Table Point**, Philippines ▶
25	S 8	**Table Rock Reservoir**, MO, U.S.A. ⛆
79	D 19	**Tábor**, Czech Republic
131	S 11	**Tabora**, Tanzania ▣
131	S 11	**Tabora**, Tanzania
103	R 12	**Taboshar**, Tajikistan
128	I 14	**Tabou**, Côte d'Ivoire
100	F 3	**Tabrīz**, Iran
141	P 1	**Tabuaeran**, Kiribati 🏝
138	A 4	**Tabubil**, Papua New Guinea
98	K 3	**Tabūk**, Saudi Arabia
120	G 7	**Tabuk**, Philippines
108	J 3	**Tacheng**, China
50	K 5	**Tachira**, Venezuela ▣
121	L 16	**Tacloban**, Philippines
50	L 11	**Tacna**, Colombia
53	H 20	**Tacna**, Peru
53	H 20	**Tacna**, Peru ▣
56	J 6	**Taco Pozo**, Argentina
32	G 7	**Tacoma**, WA, U.S.A.
14	K 10	**Taconic Range**, NY, U.S.A. ⛰
46	H 5	**Tactic**, Guatemala
58	E 13	**Tacuarembó**, Uruguay
59	E 14	**Tacuarembo**, Uruguay ▣
121	L 23	**Tacurong**, Philippines
63	T 2	**Tadcaster**, U.K.
139	Q 14	**Tadine**, New Caledonia
125	N 12	**Tadjmout**, Algeria
127	K 19	**Tadjoura**, Djibouti
124	M 7	**Tadjrouna**, Algeria
43	O 7	**Tadoussac**, QC, Canada
105	E 20	**Tadpatri**, India
111	M 18	**T'aebaek-sanmaek**, North Korea/South Korea ⛰
111	J 19	**Taech'ŏng-do**, South Korea 🏝
111	M 20	**Taegu**, South Korea
111	K 22	**Taehŭksan-kundo**, South Korea 🏝
111	L 20	**Taejŏn**, South Korea
111	L 23	**Taejŏng**, South Korea
67	R 3	**Tafalla**, Spain
56	I 7	**Tafi Viejo**, Argentina
124	F 9	**Tafraoute**, Morocco
100	K 9	**Taft**, Iran
105	O 24	**Tafwap**, India
127	E 14	**Tagab**, Sudan
92	L 10	**Taganrog**, Russian Federation
128	H 6	**Tagant**, Mauritania ▣
123	C 21	**Tagawa**, Japan
121	K 18	**Tagbilaran**, Philippines
124	K 9	**Taghit**, Algeria
39	B 15	**Tagish Lake**, BC, Canada ⛆
103	O 15	**Tagtabazar**, Turkmenistan
55	K 14	**Taguatinga**, Brazil
138	H 8	**Tagula**, Papua New Guinea
138	H 8	**Tagula Island**, Papua New Guinea 🏝
121	M 22	**Tagum**, Philippines
110	J 5	**Tahe**, China
33	I 18	**Tahoe City**, CA, U.S.A.
26	K 5	**Tahoka**, TX, U.S.A.
32	F 7	**Taholah**, WA, U.S.A.
136	K 12	**Tahora**, New Zealand
129	Q 8	**Tahoua**, Niger
129	Q 8	**Tahoua**, Niger ▣
97	V 9	**Taḩrīr**, Iraq
100	M 11	**Tahrūd**, Iran
126	E 10	**Tahta**, Egypt
94	K 13	**Tahtali Dağlari**, Turkey ⛰
53	I 16	**Tahuamanu**, Bolivia ∫
117	Q 9	**Tahulandang**, Indonesia 🏝
117	Q 9	**Tahuna**, Indonesia
136	L 9	**Tahuna**, New Zealand
128	I 13	**Taï**, Côte d'Ivoire
113	Y 6	**Tai Hu**, China ⛆
113	V 2	**Tai'an**, China
113	P 4	**Taibai**, China
113	Q 2	**Taibai**, China
113	P 4	**Taibai Shan**, China ▲
113	Y 11	**T'aichung**, Taiwan
137	E 24	**Taieri**, New Zealand ∫
83	E 22	**Taigetos**, Greece ⛰
113	S 1	**Taigu**, China
113	T 2	**Taihang Shan**, China ⛰
136	L 13	**Taihape**, New Zealand
113	U 9	**Taihe**, China
113	V 4	**Taihe**, China
113	V 6	**Taihu**, China
113	U 4	**Taikang**, China
115	D 16	**Taikkyi**, Myanmar
110	I 10	**Tailai**, China
135	Q 12	**Tailem Bend**, SA, Australia
60	H 9	**Tain**, U.K.
113	Z 12	**T'ainan**, Taiwan
113	Z 10	**Taipei**, Taiwan ▟
113	O 13	**Taiping**, China
113	U 12	**Taiping**, China
118	B 6	**Taiping**, Malaysia
110	G 9	**Taiping Ling**, China ▲
123	B 26	**Taira-jima**, Japan 🏝
136	L 9	**Tairua**, New Zealand
100	E 6	**Tairuq**, Iran
116	E 13	**Tais**, Indonesia
113	T 13	**Taishan**, China
113	Z 12	**T'aitung**, Taiwan
70	M 12	**Taivalkoski**, Finland
113	Y 11	**Taiwan**, Asia □
113	Y 12	**Taiwan Strait**, Taiwan/China ≈
110	I 6	**Taiyanggou**, China
113	S 1	**Taiyuan**, China
113	Y 5	**Taizhou**, China
113	Z 7	**Taizhou**, China
99	P 14	**Ta'izz**, Yemen
125	T 12	**Tajarḩī**, Libya
103	S 13	**Tajikistan**, Asia □
123	K 14	**Tajima**, Japan
44	I 3	**Tajitos**, Mexico
66	L 7	**Tajo**, Spain ∫
115	G 16	**Tak**, Thailand
100	G 5	**Takāb**, Iran
131	X 6	**Takabba**, Kenya
137	I 15	**Takaka**, New Zealand
123	F 19	**Takamatsu**, Japan
123	D 23	**Takanabe**, Japan
123	H 15	**Takaoka**, Japan
136	J 8	**Takapuna**, New Zealand
123	B 26	**Takara-jima**, Japan 🏝
123	J 15	**Takasaki**, Japan
132	M 10	**Takatokwane**, Botswana
123	G 18	**Takatsuki**, Japan
123	E 21	**Takatsuki-yama**, Japan ▲
123	H 16	**Takayama**, Japan
123	C 25	**Take-shima**, Japan 🏝
123	G 17	**Takefu**, Japan
116	B 8	**Takengon**, Indonesia
123	B 21	**Takeo**, Japan
100	H 5	**Tākestān**, Iran
123	C 22	**Taketa**, Japan
115	L 22	**Takêv**, Cambodia
101	V 6	**Takhār**, Afghanistan ▣
101	S 10	**Takhta Pul Post**, Afghanistan
122	J 5	**Takikawa**, Japan
122	K 4	**Takinoue**, Japan
138	G 3	**Takis**, Papua New Guinea
39	E 18	**Takla Lake**, BC, Canada ⛆
108	H 6	**Taklimakan Desert**, China ◇
128	M 14	**Takoradi**, Ghana
89	R 12	**Taksimo**, Russian Federation
115	F 24	**Takua Pa**, Thailand
129	S 12	**Takum**, Nigeria
141	P 10	**Takutea**, Cook Islands 🏝
138	K 4	**Takuu Islands**, Papua New Guinea 🏝
59	F 15	**Tala**, Uruguay
56	H 10	**Talacasto**, Argentina
85	L 16	**Talachyn**, Belarus
101	W 8	**Talagang**, Pakistan
105	F 23	**Talaimannar**, Sri Lanka
116	G 12	**Talangbatu**, Indonesia
52	A 11	**Talara**, Peru
103	T 10	**Talas**, Kyrgyzstan
138	F 4	**Talasea**, Papua New Guinea
103	T 11	**Talasskaya Oblast'**, Kyrgyzstan ▣
66	M 7	**Talavera de la Reina**, Spain
56	F 13	**Talca**, Chile
57	E 14	**Talcahuano**, Chile
105	J 16	**Talcher**, India
103	W 8	**Taldykorgan**, Kazakhstan
103	V 10	**Talgar**, Kazakhstan
63	O 9	**Talgarth**, U.K.
127	E 22	**Tali Post**, Sudan
117	Q 11	**Taliabu**, Indonesia 🏝
121	K 18	**Talibon**, Philippines
105	D 19	**Talikota**, India
103	P 13	**Talimardzhan**, Uzbekistan
95	W 10	**Talish Mountains**, Azerbaijan ⛰
116	L 15	**Taliwang**, Indonesia
97	Q 2	**Tall 'Afar**, Iraq
96	K 1	**Tall al Aḩmar**, Syria
97	W 11	**Tall al Laḩm**, Iraq
97	O 1	**Tall Baydar**, Syria
96	J 7	**Tall Ghāb**, Syria ▲
97	Q 2	**Tall Ḩuqnah**, Iraq
97	R 2	**Tall Kayf**, Iraq
97	Q 1	**Tall Kūjik**, Syria
96	L 7	**Tall Salāh**, Jordan ▲
97	N 1	**Tall Tamir**, Syria
97	Q 1	**Tall 'Uwaynāt**, Iraq
19	S 7	**Tallahassee**, FL, U.S.A.
84	F 5	**Tallinn**, Estonia ▟
18	K 5	**Tallulah**, LA, U.S.A.
86	I 11	**Tălmaciu**, Romania
124	G 8	**Talmest**, Morocco
87	P 6	**Tal'ne**, Ukraine
127	E 19	**Talodi**, Sudan
101	V 5	**Tāloqān**, Afghanistan
109	O 4	**Talshand**, Mongolia
84	D 10	**Talsi**, Latvia
56	F 7	**Taltal**, Chile
117	P 10	**Taludaa**, Indonesia
116	E 11	**Taluk**, Indonesia
115	O 17	**Tam Ky**, Vietnam
128	M 11	**Tamale**, Ghana
140	E 3	**Tamana**, Kiribati 🏝
124	F 8	**Tamanar**, Morocco
125	T 11	**Tamanhint**, Libya
125	O 14	**Tamanrasset**, Algeria
114	D 8	**Tamanthi**, Myanmar
62	L 14	**Tamar**, U.K. ∫
79	H 25	**Tamási**, Hungary
45	R 9	**Tamaulipas**, Mexico ▣
45	R 10	**Tamazunchale**, Mexico
128	F 9	**Tambacounda**, Senegal
116	H 10	**Tambelan Besar**, Indonesia 🏝
88	M 7	**Tambey**, Russian Federation
119	Z 6	**Tambisan**, Malaysia
53	G 20	**Tambo**, Peru ∫
135	T 7	**Tambo**, QLD, Australia
52	A 12	**Tambo Grande**, Peru
133	W 7	**Tambohorano**, Madgascar
131	N 4	**Tamboura**, Central African Republic
93	N 4	**Tambov**, Russian Federation
93	N 4	**Tambovskaya Oblast'**, Russian Federation ▣
119	V 5	**Tambunan**, Malaysia
127	C 22	**Tambura**, Sudan
128	H 7	**Tâmchekket**, Mauritania
105	F 22	**Tamil Nadu**, India ▣
74	I 8	**Tamins**, Switzerland
80	L 10	**Tamiš**, Serbia and Montenegro ∫
71	L 20	**Tammisaari**, Finland
19	V 10	**Tampa**, FL, U.S.A.
19	U 11	**Tampa Bay**, FL, U.S.A. ≈
71	L 17	**Tampere**, Finland
45	S 10	**Tampico**, Mexico
118	C 9	**Tampin**, Malaysia
118	B 14	**Tampines**, Singapore
99	Q 9	**Tamrah**, Saudi Arabia
52	F 11	**Tamshiyacu**, Peru
75	S 7	**Tamsweg**, Austria
63	S 6	**Tamworth**, U.K.
135	U 10	**Tamworth**, NSW, Australia
115	M 22	**Tân An**, Vietnam
124	E 10	**Tan-Tan**, Morocco
70	M 6	**Tana Bru**, Norway
123	G 20	**Tanabe**, Japan
34	E 13	**Tanaga Island**, AK, U.S.A. 🏝
118	C 5	**Tanah Merah**, Malaysia
116	C 11	**Tanahbala**, Indonesia 🏝
116	M 11	**Tanahgrogot**, Indonesia
117	O 14	**Tanahjampea**, Indonesia 🏝
116	C 11	**Tanahmasa**, Indonesia 🏝
106	L 8	**Tanakpur**, India
134	M 5	**Tanami Desert**, NT, Australia ◇
35	Q 6	**Tanana**, AK, U.S.A.
111	M 16	**Tanch'ŏn**, North Korea
107	N 10	**Tanda**, India
128	L 12	**Tanda**, Côte d'Ivoire
121	N 19	**Tandag**, Philippines
86	M 12	**Tăndărei**, Romania
119	V 4	**Tandek**, Malaysia
59	D 18	**Tandil**, Argentina
129	W 11	**Tandjilé**, Chad ▣
101	U 14	**Tando Adam**, Pakistan
123	C 25	**Tanega-shima**, Japan 🏝
79	N 16	**Tanew**, Poland ∫
124	K 15	**Tanezrouft**, Algeria ⛰
131	W 11	**Tanga**, Tanzania ▣
131	W 11	**Tanga**, Tanzania
138	H 3	**Tanga Islands**, Papua New Guinea 🏝
112	L 9	**Tangdan**, China
112	L 4	**Tanggor**, China
108	K 9	**Tanggula Shan**, China ⛰
113	S 5	**Tanghe**, China
124	I 6	**Tangier**, Morocco
17	W 5	**Tangier Island**, VA, U.S.A. 🏝
113	U 10	**Tangjiang**, China
118	B 14	**Tanglin**, Singapore
123	F 17	**Tango**, Japan
136	N 13	**Tangoio**, New Zealand
108	J 9	**Tangra Yumco**, China ⛆
116	B 8	**Tangse**, Indonesia
111	F 17	**Tangshan**, China
113	U 2	**Tangyin**, China
110	M 10	**Tangyuan**, China
133	V 9	**Tanjona Ankaboa**, Madgascar ▶
133	Z 4	**Tanjona Bobaomby**, Madgascar ▶
133	Z 6	**Tanjona Masoala**, Madgascar ▶
133	W 6	**Tanjona Vilanandro**, Madgascar ▶
133	W 11	**Tanjona Vohimena**, Madgascar ▶
116	L 11	**Tanjung**, Indonesia
117	O 10	**Tanjung Arus**, Indonesia ▶
118	A 7	**Tanjung Beras Basah**, Malaysia ▶
119	X 5	**Tanjung Bidadari**, Malaysia ▶
116	J 14	**Tanjung Bugel**, Indonesia ▶
116	F 13	**Tanjung Cina**, Indonesia ▶
118	M 10	**Tanjung Datu**, Malaysia ▶
117	X 11	**Tanjung d'Urville**, Indonesia ▶
118	E 7	**Tanjung Gelang**, Malaysia ▶
116	G 14	**Tanjung Guhakolak**, Indonesia ▶
119	O 9	**Tanjung Jerijih**, Malaysia ▶
117	O 10	**Tanjung Kandi**, Indonesia ▶
119	Q 8	**Tanjung Kidurong**, Malaysia ▶
117	O 13	**Tanjung Koku**, Indonesia ▶
116	L 13	**Tanjung Layar**, Indonesia ▶
117	S 11	**Tanjung Libobo**, Indonesia ▶
116	G 12	**Tanjung Lumut**, Indonesia ▶
117	N 10	**Tanjung Mangkalihat**, Indonesia ▶
116	L 15	**Tanjung Mebulu**, Indonesia ▶
116	I 10	**Tanjung Mungguresak**, Indonesia ▶
117	R 12	**Tanjung Palpetu**, Indonesia ▶
119	R 8	**Tanjung Payung**, Malaysia ▶
119	N 10	**Tanjung Po**, Malaysia ▶
116	J 12	**Tanjung Puting**, Indonesia ▶
118	E 9	**Tanjung Resang**, Malaysia ▶
116	I 12	**Tanjung Sambar**, Indonesia ▶
116	L 13	**Tanjung Selatan**, Indonesia ▶

□ Country ▣ Internal administrative region: State/Province/Territory/Dependent territory ▟ Capital city ⛰ Mountain range/Undersea ridge ▲ Mountain peak/Volcano/Seamount ◇ Geographic feature ▶ Headland/Point/Cape/Peninsula ⌓ Desert 🏝 Island/Island group ⁙ Antarctic base 🌊 Ocean ◗ Sea ≈ Bay/Gulf/Channel/Strait ⛆ Lake ▚ Salt pan/Dry/Intermittent lake ∫ River

119	V 4	**Tanjung Simpang Mangayau**, Malaysia ▶
119	N 10	**Tanjung Sipang**, Malaysia ▶
119	O 9	**Tanjung Sirik**, Malaysia ▶
117	S 9	**Tanjung Sopi**, Indonesia ▶
119	W 4	**Tanjung Sugut**, Malaysia ▶
119	W 4	**Tanjung Sumangat**, Malaysia ▶
118	C 9	**Tanjung Tuan**, Malaysia ▶
117	X 15	**Tanjung Vals**, Indonesia ▶
117	R 12	**Tanjung Waka**, Indonesia ▶
116	H 12	**Tanjungpandan**, Indonesia
116	F 10	**Tanjungpinang**, Indonesia
116	L 9	**Tanjungredeb**, Indonesia
116	M 9	**Tanjungselor**, Indonesia
101	V 9	**Tank**, Pakistan
106	K 3	**Tankse**, India
139	R 12	**Tanna**, Vanuatu ✱
121	J 18	**Tañon Strait**, Philippines ≈
129	S 8	**Tanout**, Niger
107	O 9	**Tansen**, Nepal
126	E 8	**Tanta**, Egypt
96	F 8	**Tantura**, Israel
34	L 9	**Tanunak**, AK, U.S.A.
131	S 11	**Tanzania**, Africa □
113	S 8	**Taojiang**, China
110	I 11	**Taonan**, China
77	L 21	**Taormina**, Italy
31	R 8	**Taos**, NM, U.S.A.
128	L 4	**Taoudenni**, Mali
124	I 6	**Taounate**, Morocco
124	J 6	**Taourirt**, Morocco
124	J 9	**Taouz**, Morocco
113	Z 10	**T'aoyüan**, Taiwan
113	S 8	**Taoyuan**, China
84	H 6	**Tapa**, Estonia
45	W 15	**Tapachula**, Mexico
54	G 11	**Tapajós**, Brazil ∫
116	C 9	**Tapaktuan**, Indonesia
59	C 17	**Tapalqué**, Argentina
116	D 12	**Tapan**, Indonesia
137	D 24	**Tapanui**, New Zealand
54	E 12	**Tapauá**, Brazil
54	C 12	**Tapauá**, Brazil ∫
58	G 11	**Tapera**, Brazil
58	H 12	**Tapes**, Brazil
128	H 13	**Tapeta**, Liberia
57	G 23	**Tapi Aike**, Argentina
66	K 1	**Tapia de Casariego**, Spain
107	R 9	**Taplejung**, Nepal
79	G 24	**Tapolca**, Hungary
17	U 5	**Tappahannock**, VA, U.S.A.
122	J 8	**Tappi-zaki**, Japan ▶
121	G 24	**Tapul**, Philippines
121	G 24	**Tapul Group**, Philippines ✱
97	T 3	**Ţaqţaq**, Iraq
58	H 11	**Taquari**, Brazil ∫
58	J 5	**Taquaritinga**, Brazil
129	T 12	**Taraba**, Nigeria ▣
97	W 9	**Tarād al Kahf**, Iraq
136	M 13	**Taradale**, New Zealand
125	T 11	**Tarāghin**, Libya
116	M 9	**Tarakan**, Indonesia
123	N 26	**Tarana-jima**, Japan ✱
136	J 12	**Taranaki**, New Zealand ▣
67	P 7	**Tarancón**, Spain
60	E 9	**Taransay**, U.K. ✱
77	N 17	**Taranto**, Italy
50	M 12	**Tarapacá**, Colombia
56	G 3	**Tarapacá**, Chile ▣
52	D 13	**Tarapoto**, Peru
54	B 9	**Taraquá**, Brazil
65	T 9	**Tarare**, France
87	P 5	**Tarashcha**, Ukraine
125	Q 12	**Tarat**, Algeria
53	H 20	**Tarata**, Peru
54	B 13	**Tarauacá**, Brazil
54	B 13	**Tarauacá**, Brazil ∫
140	D 2	**Tarawa**, Kiribati ✱
136	M 12	**Tarawera**, New Zealand
103	S 10	**Taraz**, Kazakhstan
67	R 4	**Tarazona**, Spain
103	X 6	**Tarbagatay**, Kazakhstan
60	H 9	**Tarbat Ness**, U.K. ▶
101	X 7	**Tarbela Reservoir**, Pakistan ◣
60	E 9	**Tarbert**, U.K.
60	F 13	**Tarbert**, U.K.
61	B 19	**Tarbert**, Republic of Ireland
65	N 14	**Tarbes**, France
80	H 12	**Tarčin**, Bosnia and Herzegovina
135	O 10	**Tarcoola**, SA, Australia
135	V 11	**Taree**, NSW, Australia
89	O 7	**Tareya**, Russian Federation
124	D 10	**Tarfaya**, Morocco
86	J 12	**Târgovişte**, Romania
86	H 11	**Târgu Jiu**, Romania
86	J 9	**Târgu Mureş**, Romania
86	K 10	**Târgu Secuiesc**, Romania
125	S 8	**Tarhūnah**, Libya
99	W 6	**Tarif**, United Arab Emirates
66	L 14	**Tarifa**, Spain
120	I 8	**Tarigtig Point**, Philippines ▶
53	K 23	**Tarija**, Bolivia
53	K 23	**Tarija**, Bolivia ▣
53	K 23	**Tarija**, Bolivia ∫
108	I 6	**Tarim Basin**, China ◇
108	I 5	**Tarim He**, China ∫
131	T 8	**Tarime**, Tanzania
101	S 8	**Tarin Kowt**, Afghanistan
117	X 12	**Taritatu**, Indonesia ∫
88	M 9	**Tarko-Sale**, Russian Federation
128	L 14	**Tarkwa**, Ghana
120	F 10	**Tarlac**, Philippines
120	F 9	**Tarlac**, Philippines ∫
79	M 16	**Tarnobrzeg**, Poland
79	N 16	**Tarnogród**, Poland
90	L 10	**Tarnogskiy Gorodok**, Russian Federation
79	L 17	**Tarnów**, Poland
71	H 19	**Tärnsjö**, Sweden
100	L 12	**Ţārom**, Iran
135	U 8	**Taroom**, QLD, Australia
124	G 9	**Taroudannt**, Morocco
19	V 10	**Tarpon Springs**, FL, U.S.A.
48	M 2	**Tarpum Bay**, The Bahamas
76	G 13	**Tarquinia**, Italy
135	N 4	**Tarrabool Lake**, NT, Australia ◣
67	V 5	**Tarragona**, Spain
129	X 5	**Tarso Emissi**, Chad ▲
94	J 13	**Tarsus**, Turkey
56	J 5	**Tartagal**, Argentina
58	C 11	**Tartagal**, Argentina
84	I 8	**Tartu**, Estonia
96	H 4	**Ţarţūs**, Syria
122	J 6	**Tarumae-san**, Japan ▲
123	C 24	**Tarumizu**, Japan
116	C 9	**Tarutung**, Indonesia
87	O 10	**Tarutyne**, Ukraine
76	I 5	**Tarvisio**, Italy
89	T 10	**Tas-Tumas**, Russian Federation
103	P 9	**Tasbuget**, Kazakhstan
103	T 11	**Tash-Kömür**, Kyrgyzstan
95	T 7	**Tashir**, Armenia
103	R 11	**Tashkent**, Uzbekistan ⌂
103	N 15	**Tashkepri**, Turkmenistan
118	D 6	**Tasik Kenyir**, Malaysia ◣
118	B 5	**Tasik Temengor**, Malaysia ◣
41	R 6	**Tasiujaq**, QC, Canada
143	O 11	**Tasiusaq**, Greenland
129	T 8	**Tasker**, Niger
103	X 6	**Taskesken**, Kazakhstan
94	J 7	**Taşköprü**, Turkey
138	G 2	**Taskul**, Papua New Guinea
95	S 10	**Taşlişşay**, Turkey
137	H 16	**Tasman**, New Zealand ▣
137	I 15	**Tasman Bay**, New Zealand ≈
135	T 15	**Tasman Peninsula**, TAS, Australia ▶
135	U 15	**Tasman Sea**, Australia/New Zealand ∽
135	R 15	**Tasmania**, Australia ▣
94	L 8	**Taşova**, Turkey
129	Q 7	**Tassara**, Niger
125	N 15	**Tassili du Hoggar**, Algeria ◇
125	O 11	**Tassili n'Ajjer**, Algeria ◇
54	L 13	**Tasso Fragoso**, Brazil
79	I 22	**Tata**, Hungary
124	G 9	**Tata**, Morocco
79	I 22	**Tatabánya**, Hungary
125	Q 7	**Tataouine**, Tunisia
87	O 11	**Tatarbunary**, Ukraine
88	L 12	**Tatarsk**, Russian Federation
89	W 13	**Tatarskiy Proliv**, Russian Federation ≈
119	Q 9	**Tatau**, Malaysia
123	L 17	**Tateyama**, Japan
39	H 14	**Tathlina Lake**, NT, Canada ◣
99	O 9	**Tathlīth**, Saudi Arabia
114	D 13	**Tatkon**, Myanmar
39	F 20	**Tatla Lake**, BC, Canada
94	I 15	**Tatlisu**, Cyprus
79	J 19	**Tatra Mountains**, Slovakia ▲▲
101	U 15	**Tatta**, Pakistan
103	T 10	**Tatti**, Kazakhstan
31	U 12	**Tatum**, NM, U.S.A.
95	R 11	**Tatvan**, Turkey
54	N 12	**Taua**, Brazil
58	L 7	**Taubaté**, Brazil
102	H 9	**Tauchik**, Kazakhstan
73	F 18	**Taufstein**, Germany ▲
25	X 6	**Taum Sauk Mountain**, MO, U.S.A. ▲
136	K 12	**Taumarunui**, New Zealand
114	E 12	**Taunggyi**, Myanmar
114	F 11	**Taunglau**, Myanmar
114	D 12	**Taungtha**, Myanmar
115	C 14	**Taunqup**, Myanmar
101	V 10	**Taunsa**, Pakistan
15	N 10	**Taunton**, MA, U.S.A.
63	O 12	**Taunton**, U.K.
73	D 19	**Taunus**, Germany ◇
136	K 10	**Taupiri**, New Zealand
136	M 11	**Taupo**, New Zealand
85	C 14	**Tauragė**, Lithuania
136	M 10	**Tauranga**, New Zealand
77	M 21	**Taurianova**, Italy
136	H 5	**Tauroa Point**, New Zealand ▶
94	F 13	**Taurus Mountains**, Turkey ▲▲
67	S 4	**Tauste**, Spain
141	Z 8	**Tautira**, French Polynesia
89	X 10	**Tauyskaya Guba**, Russian Federation ≈
94	D 12	**Tavas**, Turkey
88	J 10	**Tavda**, Russian Federation
63	Z 6	**Taverham**, U.K.
67	T 9	**Tavernes de la Valldigna**, Spain
139	Y 11	**Taveuni**, Fiji ✱
66	I 12	**Tavira**, Portugal
62	M 14	**Tavistock**, U.K.
115	F 19	**Tavoy**, Myanmar
115	F 19	**Tavoy Point**, Myanmar ▶
94	E 9	**Tavşanli**, Turkey
62	M 12	**Taw**, U.K. ∫
105	E 15	**Tawa Reservoir**, India ◣
107	V 9	**Tawang**, India
20	L 12	**Tawas City**, MI, U.S.A.
119	X 7	**Tawau**, Malaysia
63	N 10	**Tawe**, U.K. ∫
121	E 25	**Tawitawi**, Philippines ✱
113	Z 12	**Tawu**, Taiwan
45	Q 12	**Taxco**, Mexico
108	G 6	**Taxkorgan**, China
60	H 12	**Tay**, U.K. ∫
115	M 21	**Tây Ninh**, Vietnam
120	H 12	**Tayabas Bay**, Philippines ≈
127	L 23	**Tayeeglow**, Somalia
109	O 4	**Taygan**, Mongolia
22	L 13	**Taylor**, NE, U.S.A.
27	Q 9	**Taylor**, TX, U.S.A.
17	O 9	**Taylorsville**, NC, U.S.A.
21	F 19	**Taylorville**, IL, U.S.A.
98	L 4	**Taymā'**, Saudi Arabia
102	I 5	**Taypak**, Kazakhstan
89	O 12	**Tayshet**, Russian Federation
121	E 17	**Taytay**, Philippines
121	E 17	**Taytay Bay**, Philippines ≈
121	M 17	**Taytay Point**, Philippines ▶
110	I 5	**Tayuan**, China
101	O 7	**Tayyebād**, Iran
103	R 2	**Tayynsha**, Kazakhstan
89	N 8	**Taz**, Russian Federation ∫
124	J 7	**Taza**, Morocco
97	T 4	**Tāza Khurmātū**, Iraq
124	H 9	**Tazenakht**, Morocco
16	K 8	**Tazewell**, TN, U.S.A.
125	X 11	**Tāzirbū**, Libya
88	M 8	**Tazovskiy**, Russian Federation
124	H 9	**Tazzarine**, Morocco
124	J 8	**Tazzouguert**, Morocco
95	U 7	**T'Bilisi**, Georgia ⌂
129	T 12	**Tchabal Mbabo**, Cameroon ▲
130	E 9	**Tchibanga**, Gabon
129	Q 8	**Tchin-Tabaradene**, Niger
129	V 12	**Tcholliré**, Cameroon
78	I 9	**Tczew**, Poland
137	B 24	**Te Anau**, New Zealand
136	O 10	**Te Araroa**, New Zealand
136	N 10	**Te Kaha**, New Zealand
136	H 4	**Te Kao**, New Zealand
136	O 12	**Te Kapu**, New Zealand ▲
136	O 11	**Te Karaka**, New Zealand
137	L 17	**Te Kaukau Point**, New Zealand ▶
136	K 11	**Te Kuiti**, New Zealand
136	M 12	**Te Pohue**, New Zealand
136	M 10	**Te Puke**, New Zealand
136	I 6	**Te Raupa**, New Zealand ▲
136	N 10	**Te Teko**, New Zealand
137	B 25	**Te Waewae**, New Zealand
137	A 25	**Te Waewae Bay**, New Zealand ≈
44	M 9	**Teacapán**, Mexico
141	Z 8	**Teahupoo**, French Polynesia
45	W 13	**Teapa**, Mexico
117	X 11	**Teba**, Indonesia
119	N 11	**Tebedu**, Malaysia
92	M 14	**Teberda**, Russian Federation
125	P 6	**Tébessa**, Algeria
95	U 6	**Tebulos Mt'a**, Georgia/Russian Federation ▲
44	F 2	**Tecate**, Mexico
128	L 12	**Techiman**, Ghana
87	N 13	**Techirghiol**, Romania
83	C 17	**Techniti Limni Kremaston**, Greece ◣
57	G 18	**Tecka**, Argentina
45	N 12	**Tecomán**, Mexico
44	J 5	**Tecoripa**, Mexico
45	Q 13	**Técpan**, Mexico
86	M 11	**Tecuci**, Romania
127	L 23	**Ted**, Somalia
102	M 14	**Tedzhen**, Turkmenistan
89	N 14	**Teeli**, Russian Federation
61	J 16	**Tees**, U.K. ∫
54	D 11	**Tefé**, Brazil
116	I 14	**Tegal**, Indonesia
69	L 16	**Tegelen**, Netherlands
129	Q 11	**Tegina**, Nigeria
139	Q 9	**Tégua**, Vanuatu ✱
46	L 6	**Tegucigalpa**, Honduras ⌂
33	J 23	**Tehachapi**, CA, U.S.A.
100	I 5	**Tehrān**, Iran ▣
100	I 6	**Tehran**, Iran ⌂
106	K 7	**Tehri**, India
45	S 12	**Tehuacán**, Mexico
141	W 9	**Tehuata**, French Polynesia ✱
127	B 16	**Teiga Plateau**, Sudan ◇
63	N 14	**Teignmouth**, U.K.
86	H 10	**Teiuş**, Romania
46	F 5	**Tejutla**, Guatemala
103	W 8	**Tekeli**, Kazakhstan
103	X 10	**Tekes**, Kazakhstan
108	H 7	**Tekilitag**, China ▲
82	N 13	**Tekirdağ**, Turkey ▣
94	C 7	**Tekirdağ**, Turkey
117	P 11	**Teku**, Indonesia
96	E 9	**Tel Aviv-Jaffa**, Israel
46	L 4	**Tela**, Honduras
124	K 6	**Télagh**, Algeria
129	O 8	**Télataï**, Mali
95	U 6	**T'elavi**, Georgia
45	Y 10	**Telchac Puerto**, Mexico
86	I 8	**Telciu**, Romania
138	A 4	**Telefomin**, Papua New Guinea
58	I 8	**Telêmaco Borba**, Brazil
87	N 8	**Teleneşti**, Moldova
54	G 13	**Teles Pires**, Brazil ∫
33	K 22	**Telescope Peak**, CA, U.S.A. ▲
134	I 6	**Telfer**, WA, Australia
63	Q 6	**Telford**, U.K.
74	L 7	**Telfs**, Austria
34	L 6	**Teller**, AK, U.S.A.
97	W 10	**Telloh**, Iraq
31	O 6	**Telluride**, CO, U.S.A.
87	Y 8	**Tel'manove**, Ukraine
118	A 14	**Telok Blangah**, Singapore
57	I 17	**Telsen**, Argentina
84	C 13	**Telšiai**, Lithuania
118	B 7	**Teluk Anson**, Malaysia
117	U 12	**Teluk Beru**, Indonesia ≈
117	O 12	**Teluk Bone**, Indonesia ≈
117	W 12	**Teluk Cenderawasih**, Indonesia ≈
119	N 10	**Teluk Datu**, Malaysia ≈
117	V 12	**Teluk Kamrau**, Indonesia ≈
119	U 5	**Teluk Kimanis**, Malaysia ≈
116	J 12	**Teluk Kumai**, Indonesia ≈
119	X 5	**Teluk Labuk**, Malaysia ≈
119	X 6	**Teluk Lahad Datu**, Malaysia ≈
119	V 4	**Teluk Marudu**, Malaysia ≈
119	W 4	**Teluk Paitan**, Malaysia ≈
116	G 14	**Teluk Palabuhanratu**, Indonesia ≈
117	O 11	**Teluk Poso**, Indonesia ≈
116	K 12	**Teluk Sampit**, Indonesia ≈
116	I 11	**Teluk Sukadana**, Indonesia ≈
117	O 11	**Teluk Tomini**, Indonesia ≈
116	I 11	**Telukbatang**, Indonesia
116	C 10	**Telukdalam**, Indonesia
119	W 5	**Telupid**, Malaysia
129	N 13	**Tema**, Ghana
42	E 8	**Temagami Lake**, ON, Canada ◣
141	W 11	**Tematangi**, French Polynesia ✱
117	W 13	**Tembagapura**, Indonesia
116	F 11	**Tembilahan**, Indonesia
133	O 11	**Tembisa**, Republic of South Africa
67	O 8	**Tembleque**, Spain
132	H 2	**Tembo Aluma**, Angola
33	K 25	**Temecula**, CA, U.S.A.
128	M 7	**Téméra**, Mali
80	K 9	**Temerin**, Serbia and Montenegro
118	D 8	**Temerloh**, Malaysia
103	T 5	**Temirtau**, Kazakhstan
42	F 9	**Temiscaming**, QC, Canada
93	O 2	**Temnikov**, Russian Federation
135	T 12	**Temora**, NSW, Australia
44	L 4	**Temósachic**, Mexico
139	Q 7	**Temotu**, Solomon Islands ▣
30	J 13	**Tempe**, AZ, U.S.A.
27	Q 8	**Temple**, TX, U.S.A.
62	M 8	**Temple Bar**, U.K.
62	K 9	**Templeton**, U.K.
132	I 5	**Tempué**, Angola
92	J 12	**Temryuk**, Russian Federation
87	X11	**Temryukskiy Zaliv**, Ukraine ≈
57	F 15	**Temuco**, Chile
137	F 21	**Temuka**, New Zealand
105	M 23	**Ten Degree Channel**, India ≈
19	W 13	**Ten Thousand Islands**, FL, U.S.A. ✱
52	C 9	**Tena**, Ecuador
128	K 11	**Téna Kourou**, Burkina Faso ▲
27	U 7	**Tenaha**, TX, U.S.A.
105	G 19	**Tenali**, India
141	Y 11	**Tenararo**, French Polynesia ✱
115	F 20	**Tenasserim**, Myanmar ▣
63	Q 8	**Tenbury Wells**, U.K.
62	L 10	**Tenby**, U.K.
127	J 19	**Tendaho**, Ethiopia
127	E 18	**Tendelti**, Sudan
122	K 12	**Tendō**, Japan
29	N 8	**Tendoy**, ID, U.S.A.
124	K 7	**Tendrara**, Morocco
128	K 9	**Ténenkou**, Mali
129	T 5	**Ténéré du Tafassâsset**, Niger ◇
124	L 5	**Ténès**, Algeria
112	I 10	**Tengchong**, China
118	E 6	**Tenggul**, Malaysia ✱
128	J 11	**Tengréla**, Côte d'Ivoire
113	R 12	**Tengxian**, China
113	W 3	**Tengzhou**, China
19	U 8	**Tenille**, FL, U.S.A.
131	O 14	**Tenke**, Democratic Republic of Congo
135	O 5	**Tennant Creek**, NT, Australia
16	C 9	**Tennessee**, U.S.A. ▣
16	C 10	**Tennessee**, TN, U.S.A. ∫
69	J 23	**Tenneville**, Belgium
70	M 10	**Tenniöjoki**, Finland ∫
70	L 7	**Tenojoki**, Finland ∫
119	U 6	**Tenom**, Malaysia
45	X 13	**Tenosique**, Mexico
123	I 17	**Tenryū**, Japan
123	I 17	**Tenryū**, Japan ∫
63	Y 12	**Tenterden**, U.K.
135	V 9	**Tenterfield**, NSW, Australia
58	H 6	**Teodoro Sampaio**, Brazil
55	M 17	**Teófilo Otôni**, Brazil
121	G 23	**Teomabal**, Philippines ✱
117	T 14	**Tepa**, Indonesia
45	O 11	**Tepatitlán**, Mexico
81	K 21	**Tepelenë**, Albania
44	M 10	**Tepic**, Mexico
79	C 16	**Teplice**, Czech Republic
141	W 8	**Tepoto**, French Polynesia ✱
45	N 11	**Tequila**, Mexico
68	O 8	**Ter Apel**, Netherlands
129	N 9	**Téra**, Niger
141	O 1	**Teraina**, Kiribati ✱
76	I 12	**Teramo**, Italy
68	M 13	**Terborg-Silvolde**, Netherlands
95	P 9	**Tercan**, Turkey
86	G 11	**Teregova**, Romania
93	Q 14	**Terek**, Russian Federation ∫
103	Z 5	**Terekty**, Kazakhstan
118	E 6	**Terengganu**, Malaysia ▣
103	P 9	**Terenozek**, Kazakhstan
54	M 11	**Teresina**, Brazil
58	N 6	**Teresópolis**, Brazil
78	O 13	**Terespol**, Poland
105	N 24	**Teressa Island**, India ✱
65	R 3	**Tergnier**, France
26	H 11	**Terlingua**, TX, U.S.A.
94	M 8	**Terme**, Turkey
103	Q 14	**Termez**, Uzbekistan
77	I 21	**Termini Imerese**, Italy
129	T 8	**Termit-Kaoboul**, Niger
117	R 10	**Ternate**, Indonesia
69	E 16	**Terneuzen**, Netherlands
76	H 13	**Terni**, Italy
87	P 6	**Ternivka**, Ukraine
86	K 5	**Ternopil'**, Ukraine
87	T 2	**Terny**, Ukraine
132	L 11	**Terra Firma**, Republic of South Africa
145	R 13	**Terra Nova Bay**, Antarctica ⁙
39	E 18	**Terrace**, BC, Canada
40	M 12	**Terrace Bay**, ON, Canada
77	H 15	**Terracina**, Italy
70	E 13	**Terråk**, Norway
77	B 18	**Terralba**, Italy
21	H 20	**Terre Haute**, IN, U.S.A.
27	R 6	**Terrell**, TX, U.S.A.
29	P 10	**Terreton**, ID, U.S.A.
63	W 6	**Terrington St Clement**, U.K.
18	L 5	**Terry**, MS, U.S.A.
29	X 5	**Terry**, MT, U.S.A.
68	I 5	**Terschelling**, Netherlands ✱
103	V 11	**Terskey Ala-Too**, Kyrgyzstan ▲▲
90	J 5	**Terskiy Bereg**, Russian Federation ◇
77	D 18	**Tertenia**, Italy
67	S 7	**Teruel**, Spain
115	G 26	**Terutao**, Thailand ✱
82	M 6	**Tervel**, Bulgaria
127	H 17	**Teseney**, Eritrea
122	M 4	**Teshikaga**, Japan
122	J 3	**Teshio**, Japan
122	J 3	**Teshio**, Japan ∫
122	J 3	**Teshio-sanchi**, Japan ▲▲
39	C 15	**Teslin Lake**, BC, Canada ◣
124	L 15	**Tessalit**, Algeria
129	N 6	**Tessalit**, Mali
129	R 9	**Tessaoua**, Niger
72	K 9	**Tessin**, Germany
63	S 12	**Test**, U.K. ∫
63	R 10	**Tetbury**, U.K.
133	R 6	**Tete**, Mozambique
133	Q 5	**Tete**, Mozambique ▣
39	G 19	**Tête Jaune Cache**, BC, Canada
138	K 6	**Tetepare**, Solomon Islands ✱
87	P 3	**Teteriv**, Ukraine ∫
72	K 9	**Teterow**, Germany
141	T 9	**Tetiaroa**, French Polynesia ✱
67	Q 12	**Tetica de Becares**, Spain ▲
87	O 5	**Tetiyiv**, Ukraine
63	W 3	**Tetney**, U.K.
29	R 11	**Teton Range**, WY, U.S.A. ▲▲
124	I 6	**Tétouan**, Morocco
82	C 10	**Tetovo**, Macedonia (F.Y.R.O.M.)
141	Z 8	**Tetufera**, French Polynesia ▲
93	R 2	**Tetyushi**, Russian Federation
123	B 24	**Teuchi**, Japan
117	S 14	**Teun**, Indonesia ✱
122	J 4	**Teuri-tō**, Japan ✱
47	O 9	**Teustepe**, Nicaragua
112	M 3	**Têwo**, China
25	S 14	**Texarkana**, AR, U.S.A.
27	U 4	**Texarkana**, TX, U.S.A.
26	L 8	**Texas**, U.S.A. ▣
135	V 9	**Texas**, QLD, Australia
27	T 10	**Texas City**, TX, U.S.A.
68	H 7	**Texel**, Netherlands ✱
24	G 8	**Texhoma**, OK, U.S.A.
46	I 6	**Texistepeque**, El Salvador
26	I 1	**Texline**, TX, U.S.A.
90	K 14	**Teykovo**, Russian Federation
107	W 10	**Tezpur**, India
107	Z 9	**Tezu**, India
124	F 11	**Tfaritiy**, Western Sahara
115	K 18	**Tha Tum**, Thailand
133	O 12	**Thabana-Ntlenyana**, Lesotho ▲
133	N 10	**Thabazimbi**, Republic of South Africa
114	M 12	**Thai Binh**, Vietnam
114	L 11	**Thai Nguyên**, Vietnam
115	G 17	**Thailand**, Asia □
107	S 11	**Thakurgaon**, Bangladesh
101	V 8	**Thal**, Pakistan
115	H 25	**Thale Luang**, Thailand ◣
135	U 9	**Thallon**, QLD, Australia
99	W 11	**Thamarīt**, Oman
63	T 10	**Thame**, U.K.
63	X 10	**Thames**, U.K. ∫
136	L 9	**Thames**, New Zealand
115	F 23	**Than Kyun**, Myanmar ✱
115	F 17	**Thanbyuzayat**, Myanmar
105	B 17	**Thane**, India
106	I 7	**Thanesar**, India
114	M 13	**Thanh Hoa**, Vietnam
105	F 22	**Thanjavur**, India
115	G 21	**Thap Sakae**, Thailand
104	B 12	**Thar Desert**, India/Pakistan ◇
135	S 9	**Thargomindah**, QLD, Australia
97	R 6	**Tharthar**, Iraq
99	W 7	**Tharwānīyyah**, United Arab Emirates
82	I 13	**Thasos**, Greece
83	I 14	**Thasos**, Greece ✱
115	E 16	**Thaton**, Myanmar
115	F 20	**Thayawthadangyi Kyun**, Myanmar ✱
115	C 14	**Thayetmyo**, Myanmar
29	Q 12	**Thayne**, WY, U.S.A.
63	Z 6	**The Broads**, U.K. ◇
32	H 9	**The Dalles**, OR, U.S.A.
63	V 6	**The Fens**, U.K. ◇
126	E 11	**The Great Oasis**, Egypt ◇
49	Z 12	**The Grenadines**, St Vincent and the Grenadines ✱
68	F 12	**The Hague**, Netherlands ⌂
137	E 21	**The Hunters Hills**, New Zealand ▲▲
60	F 9	**The Minch**, U.K. ≈
62	M 10	**The Mumbles**, U.K.
63	Z 9	**The Naze**, U.K. ▶
63	S 14	**The Needles**, U.K. ▶
40	H 8	**The Pas**, MB, Canada
49	Y 11	**The Pitons**, St Lucia ▲
63	S 13	**The Solent**, U.K. ≈
114	F 7	**The Triangle**, Myanmar ◇
49	X 8	**The Valley**, Anguilla ⌂
63	W 5	**The Wash**, U.K. ≈
63	X 12	**The Weald**, U.K. ◇
27	S 9	**The Woodlands**, TX, U.S.A.
22	K 13	**Thedford**, NE, U.S.A.
115	F 21	**Theinkun**, Myanmar
30	K 12	**Theodore Roosevelt Lake**, AZ, U.S.A. ◣
83	F 15	**Thermaïkos Kolpos**, Greece ≈
29	U 10	**Thermopolis**, WY, U.S.A.
83	E 18	**Thermopyles**, Greece
38	E 6	**Thesiger Bay**, NT, Canada ≈
83	E 17	**Thessalia**, Greece ▣
42	A 9	**Thessalon**, ON, Canada
83	F 14	**Thessaloniki**, Greece
63	Y 7	**Thetford**, U.K.
43	N 9	**Thetford Mines**, QC, Canada
18	L 8	**Thibodaux**, LA, U.S.A.
23	P 3	**Thief River Falls**, MN, U.S.A.
65	R 10	**Thiers**, France
128	D 8	**Thiès**, Senegal
131	V 8	**Thika**, Kenya
105	L 16	**Thiladhunmathee Atoll**, Maldives ✱
107	T 9	**Thimphu**, Bhutan ⌂
139	P 14	**Thio**, New Caledonia
65	V 3	**Thionville**, France
83	J 24	**Thira**, Greece ✱
83	J 23	**Thira**, Greece
83	J 23	**Thirasia**, Greece ✱
63	T 1	**Thirsk**, U.K.
71	B 23	**Thisted**, Denmark
83	G 19	**Thiva**, Greece
65	O 10	**Thiviers**, France
115	G 15	**Thoen**, Thailand
114	H 13	**Thoeng**, Thailand
133	P 9	**Thohoyandou**, Republic of South Africa
17	Q 3	**Thomas**, WV, U.S.A.
19	S 4	**Thomaston**, GA, U.S.A.
19	P 5	**Thomasville**, AL, U.S.A.
19	T 7	**Thomasville**, GA, U.S.A.
69	L 22	**Thommen**, Belgium
30	M 5	**Thompson**, UT, U.S.A.
40	J 7	**Thompson**, MB, Canada
28	L 4	**Thompson Falls**, MT, U.S.A.
19	V 3	**Thomson**, GA, U.S.A.
135	R 7	**Thomson**, QLD, Australia ∫
65	V 9	**Thonon-les-Bains**, France
63	Q 10	**Thornbury**, U.K.
61	H 14	**Thornhill**, U.K.
145	R 2	**Thorshavnheiane**, Antarctica ▲▲
64	M 8	**Thouars**, France
33	N 15	**Thousand Springs**, NV, U.S.A.
83	I 14	**Thrakiko Pelagos**, Greece ∽
29	Q 7	**Three Forks**, MT, U.S.A.
135	S 14	**Three Hummock Island**, TAS, Australia ✱
136	G 3	**Three Kings Islands**, New Zealand ✱
115	F 18	**Three Pagodas Pass**, Thailand ◇
21	J 16	**Three Rivers**, MI, U.S.A.
27	P 12	**Three Rivers**, TX, U.S.A.
27	N 5	**Throckmorton**, TX, U.S.A.
115	M 21	**Thu Dâu Môt**, Vietnam
69	F 21	**Thuin**, Belgium
143	P 9	**Thule**, Greenland
133	O 9	**Thuli**, Zimbabwe
74	E 8	**Thun**, Switzerland
20	M 11	**Thunder Bay**, MI, U.S.A. ≈
40	L 12	**Thunder Bay**, ON, Canada
74	E 8	**Thuner See**, Switzerland ◣
115	G 24	**Thung Song**, Thailand
73	J 17	**Thüringen**, Germany ▣
73	H 17	**Thüringer Wald**, Germany ◇
61	D 19	**Thurles**, Republic of Ireland
135	R 1	**Thursday Island**, QLD, Australia
60	H 8	**Thurso**, U.K.
144	J 9	**Thurston Island**, Antarctica ✱
74	I 9	**Thusis**, Switzerland
135	N 6	**Ti Tree**, NT, Australia
108	H 5	**Tian Shan**, China ▲▲
113	X 5	**Tianchang**, China
113	P 12	**Tiandeng**, China
113	P 11	**Tian'e**, China
111	E 17	**Tianjin**, China
111	E 17	**Tianjin Shi**, China ▣
109	O 8	**Tianjun**, China
113	O 11	**Tianlin**, China
113	T 6	**Tianmen**, China
110	M 13	**Tianqiaoling**, China
112	L 7	**Tianquan**, China
110	G 13	**Tianshan**, China
113	O 3	**Tianshui**, China
113	Z 7	**Tiantai**, China
113	O 12	**Tianyang**, China
113	Q 9	**Tianzhu**, China
124	L 6	**Tiaret**, Algeria
139	O 13	**Tiari**, New Caledonia
128	K 13	**Tiassalé**, Côte d'Ivoire
58	I 7	**Tibagi**, Brazil ∫
129	U 13	**Tibati**, Cameroon
29	Q 3	**Tiber Reservoir**, MT, U.S.A. ◣
96	G 8	**Tiberias**, Israel
129	W 5	**Tibesti**, Chad ▲▲
108	J 8	**Tibet**, China ▣
121	H 16	**Tibiao**, Philippines
135	R 9	**Tibooburra**, NSW, Australia
107	O 8	**Tibrikot**, Nepal
121	K 14	**Ticao**, Philippines ✱
128	I 6	**Tichît**, Mauritania
124	C 14	**Tichla**, Western Sahara
74	G 10	**Ticino**, Switzerland ▣
14	K 7	**Ticonderoga**, NY, U.S.A.
45	Y 11	**Ticul**, Mexico
135	S 14	**Tidal River**, VIC, Australia
114	B 10	**Tiddim**, Myanmar
105	O 24	**Tiden**, India
128	G 6	**Tidjikja**, Mauritania
111	I 14	**Tiefa**, China
74	I 9	**Tiefencastel**, Switzerland
68	J 13	**Tiel**, Netherlands
110	L 10	**Tieli**, China
111	J 14	**Tieling**, China
108	I 7	**Tielongtan**, China
114	N 11	**Tiên Yên**, Vietnam
69	H 19	**Tienen**, Belgium
73	E 25	**Tiengen**, Germany
71	H 19	**Tierp**, Sweden
31	P 8	**Tierra Amarilla**, NM, U.S.A.
45	R 13	**Tierra Colorada**, Mexico
57	I 25	**Tierra del Fuego**, Argentina ▣
58	K 7	**Tietê**, Brazil
58	I 5	**Tietê**, Brazil ∫
21	M 17	**Tiffin**, OH, U.S.A.
117	R 10	**Tifore**, Indonesia ✱
19	U 6	**Tifton**, GA, U.S.A.
117	R 12	**Tifu**, Indonesia
119	U 5	**Tiga**, Malaysia ✱
139	Q 13	**Tiga**, New Caledonia ✱
32	L 6	**Tiger**, WA, U.S.A.
87	O 9	**Tighina**, Moldova
129	U 12	**Tignère**, Cameroon
43	U 7	**Tignish**, PE, Canada
127	H 17	**Tigray**, Ethiopia ▣
52	D 10	**Tigre**, Peru ∫
95	P 12	**Tigris**, Iraq/Turkey ∫
128	E 7	**Tiguent**, Mauritania
136	L 11	**Tihoi**, New Zealand
106	J 9	**Tijara**, India
125	R 8	**Tījī**, Libya
44	E 1	**Tijuana**, Mexico
46	I 2	**Tikal**, Guatemala
141	T 8	**Tikehau**, French Polynesia ✱
141	V 8	**Tikei**, French Polynesia ✱
92	L 11	**Tikhoretsk**, Russian Federation
90	G 11	**Tikhvin**, Russian Federation
136	O 10	**Tikitiki**, New Zealand
139	R 8	**Tikopia**, Solomon Islands ✱
97	S 5	**Tikrīt**, Iraq
90	G 6	**Tiksha**, Russian Federation
89	S 7	**Tiksi**, Russian Federation
69	I 15	**Tilburg**, Netherlands
63	X 11	**Tilbury**, U.K.
56	I 5	**Tilcara**, Argentina
27	O 12	**Tilden**, TX, U.S.A.
129	P 8	**Tilemsès**, Niger
129	O 9	**Tillabéri**, Niger
129	O 9	**Tillabéri**, Niger ▣
32	F 9	**Tillamook**, OR, U.S.A.
105	O 24	**Tillanchong Island**, India ✱
39	K 20	**Tilley**, AB, Canada
129	P 8	**Tillia**, Niger
19	O 7	**Tillmans Corner**, AL, U.S.A.
42	D 14	**Tillsonburg**, ON, Canada
129	O 8	**Tiloa**, Niger
56	H 5	**Tilomonte**, Chile
83	N 23	**Tilos**, Greece ✱
125	N 7	**Tilrhemt**, Algeria
92	K 5	**Tim**, Russian Federation
126	E 10	**Tima**, Egypt
91	O 3	**Timanskiy Kryazh**, Russian Federation ◇
95	S 10	**Timar**, Turkey
137	F 22	**Timaru**, New Zealand
93	T 3	**Timashevo**, Russian Federation
92	K 11	**Timashevsk**, Russian Federation
18	L 9	**Timbalier Bay**, LA, U.S.A.
128	I 8	**Timbedgha**, Mauritania
134	M 3	**Timber Creek**, NT, Australia
128	L 7	**Timbuktu**, Mali
119	X 6	**Timbun Mata**, Malaysia ✱
128	M 6	**Timétrine**, Mali
129	R 7	**Timia**, Niger
124	L 10	**Timimoun**, Algeria
103	P 2	**Timiryazevo**, Kazakhstan
86	G 11	**Timiş**, Romania ∫
86	F 10	**Timişoara**, Romania
42	D 6	**Timmins**, ON, Canada
20	E 10	**Timms Hill**, WI, U.S.A. ▲
141	Z 12	**Timoé**, French Polynesia ✱
17	U 2	**Timonium**, MD, U.S.A.
117	Q 15	**Timor**, Indonesia ✱
134	K 1	**Timor Sea**, Australia/Indonesia ∽
59	A 16	**Timote**, Argentina
124	K 10	**Timoudi**, Algeria
71	H 16	**Timrå**, Sweden
51	N 3	**Tinaco**, Venezuela
96	L 2	**Tinah**, Syria
120	J 12	**Tinambac**, Philippines
105	F 21	**Tindivanam**, India
124	G 10	**Tindouf**, Algeria
66	K 1	**Tineo**, Spain
124	I 8	**Tinerhir**, Morocco
124	H 10	**Tinfouchy**, Algeria
118	F 9	**Tinggi**, Malaysia ✱
53	D 14	**Tingo Maria**, Peru
140	A 8	**Tinian**, Northern Mariana Islands ✱
119	S 8	**Tinjar**, Malaysia ∫
56	H 8	**Tinogasta**, Argentina
83	J 21	**Tinos**, Greece ✱
83	J 21	**Tinos**, Greece
107	Y 9	**Tinsukia**, India
39	E 18	**Tintagel**, BC, Canada
62	K 13	**Tintagel**, U.K.
128	H 7	**Tîntâne**, Mauritania
56	K 7	**Tintina**, Argentina
22	H 3	**Tioga**, ND, U.S.A.
118	F 9	**Tioman**, Malaysia ✱
76	E 6	**Tione di Trento**, Italy
14	C 11	**Tionesta**, PA, U.S.A.

□ Country ▣ Internal administrative region: State/Province/Territory/Dependent territory ⌂ Capital city ▲▲ Mountain range/Undersea ridge ▲ Mountain peak/Volcano/Seamount ◇ Geographic feature ▶ Headland/Point/Cape/Peninsula ● Desert ✱ Island/Island group ⁙ Antarctic base 〰 Ocean ∽ Sea ≈ Bay/Gulf/Channel/Strait ◣ Lake ⚑ Salt pan/Dry/Intermittent lake ∫

M 12 **Tip Top Hill**, ON, Canada ▲
N 9 **Tipitapa**, Nicaragua
C 19 **Tipperary**, Republic of Ireland
U 4 **Tipton**, MO, U.S.A.
A 8 **Tiptonville**, TN, U.S.A.
D 21 **Tiptur**, India
Q 12 **Tiquicheo**, Mexico
G 6 **Tiquisate**, Guatemala
K 18 **Tirana**, Albania ■
E 5 **Tirano**, Italy
O 9 **Tiraspol**, Moldova
L 10 **Tirau**, New Zealand
L 15 **Tiraumea**, New Zealand
N 8 **Tirebolu**, Turkey
E 12 **Tiree**, U.K. ✱
I 3 **Tiris Zemmour**, Mauritania ▣
K 7 **Tirol**, Austria ▣
L 2 **Tiroungoulou**, Central African Republic
K 11 **Tirua Point**, New Zealand ▶
E 24 **Tiruchchendur**, India
F 22 **Tiruchchirappalli**, India
E 24 **Tirunelveli**, India
F 21 **Tirupati**, India
E 22 **Tiruppur**, India
E 22 **Tiruvannamalai**, India
G 21 **Tiruvottiyur**, India
K 8 **Tisa**, Serbia and Montenegro ∿
E 24 **Tisaiyanvilai**, India
M 6 **Tissemsilt**, Algeria
L 22 **Tiszafüred**, Hungary
L 22 **Tiszaújváros**, Hungary
M 21 **Tiszavasvári**, Hungary
O 13 **Tit**, Algeria
S 7 **Tit-Ary**, Russian Federation
H 16 **Titlagarh**, India
E 11 **Titov Drvar**, Bosnia and Herzegovina
D 10 **Titova Korenica**, Croatia
L 24 **Tittmoning**, Germany
J 12 **Titu**, Romania
B 10 **Titusville**, PA, U.S.A.
X 9 **Titusville**, FL, U.S.A.
C 12 **Tivari**, India
N 13 **Tiverton**, U.K.
K 5 **Tiyās**, Syria
N 5 **Tizi Ouzou**, Algeria
Z 10 **Tizimín**, Mexico
F 9 **Tiznit**, Morocco
K 8 **Tjeukemeer**, Netherlands ◣
D 22 **Tjörn**, Sweden ✱
E 12 **Tjøtta**, Norway
J 8 **Tjukayirla Roadhouse**, WA, Australia
T 13 **Tlacolula**, Mexico
R 12 **Tlalnepantla**, Mexico
R 12 **Tlaxcala**, Mexico ▣
S 13 **Tlaxiaco**, Mexico
K 6 **Tlemcen**, Algeria
N 10 **Tlokweng**, Botswana
Q 15 **Tlyarata**, Russian Federation
U 11 **Tmassah**, Libya
F 5 **Tmeïmîchât**, Mauritania
K 17 **To-shima**, Japan ✱
B 14 **Toa Payoh**, Singapore
Z 7 **Toamasina**, Madgascar
Y 7 **Toamasina**, Madgascar ▣
U 9 **Toau**, French Polynesia ✱
I 5 **Toba**, China
T 10 **Toba and Kakar Ranges**, Pakistan ▲▲
Z 13 **Tobago**, Trinidad and Tobago ✱
R 10 **Tobarra**, Spain
P 6 **Tobermorey**, NT, Australia
C 10 **Tobermory**, ON, Canada
E 11 **Tobermory**, U.K.
M 17 **Tobin Lake**, SK, Canada ◣
G 12 **Toboali**, Indonesia
N 3 **Tobol**, Kazakhstan
K 10 **Tobol'sk**, Russian Federation
Y 7 **Tobruk**, Libya
P 2 **Tobseda**, Russian Federation
J 11 **Tocantins**, Brazil ∿
J 14 **Tocantins**, Brazil ▣
L 11 **Toccoa**, SC, U.S.A.
U 2 **Toccoa**, GA, U.S.A.
K 6 **Toco**, Honduras ∿
G 4 **Toco**, Chile
H 5 **Toconao**, Chile
F 4 **Tocopilla**, Chile
H 12 **Todi**, Italy
R 3 **Todmorden**, U.K.
J 7 **Todohokke**, Japan
J 9 **Todos Santos**, Mexico
K 19 **Todos Santos**, Bolivia
C 26 **Toetoes Bay**, New Zealand ≈
R 15 **Tofol**, Federated States of Micronesia
I 10 **Tofua**, Tonga ✱
Q 9 **Toga**, Vanuatu ✱
L 16 **Tōgane**, Japan
M 20 **Togdheer**, Somalia ▣
H 15 **Togi**, Japan
N 10 **Togiak**, AK, U.S.A.
P 11 **Togian**, Indonesia ✱
N 12 **Togo**, Africa □
M 3 **Tögrög**, Mongolia
M 7 **Toguz**, Kazakhstan
N 9 **Tohatchi**, NM, U.S.A.
Y 8 **Tohiea**, French Polynesia ▲
J 17 **Toi**, Japan
D 24 **Toi-misaki**, Japan ▶
E 18 **Tōjō**, Japan
T 7 **Tok**, AK, U.S.A.
I 18 **Tōkai**, Japan
J 14 **Tōkamachi**, Japan
H 15 **Tokar**, Sudan
B 26 **Tokara-rettō**, Japan ✱
F 23 **Tokarahi**, New Zealand
N 25 **Tokasiki-jima**, Japan ✱
L 9 **Tokat**, Turkey
K 19 **Tŏkchŏk-to**, South Korea ✱
J 5 **Tokelau Islands**, New Zealand ▣
K 12 **Tokirima**, New Zealand
L 5 **Tokkachi**, Japan ∿
V 8 **Tokmak**, Ukraine
O 11 **Tokomaru Bay**, New Zealand
L 4 **Tokoro**, Japan ∿
L 11 **Tokoroa**, New Zealand
H 11 **Tokounuo**, Guinea
T 11 **Toktogul**, Kyrgyzstan
I 10 **Toku**, Tonga ✱
N 22 **Toku-no-shima**, Japan ✱
N 22 **Tokunoshima**, Japan
F 19 **Tokushima**, Japan
D 20 **Tokuyama**, Japan
K 16 **Tokyo**, Japan ■
K 16 **Tōkyō-wan**, Japan ≈

101 S 6 **Tokzār**, Afghanistan
136 O 11 **Tolaga Bay**, New Zealand
133 X 11 **Tôlanaro**, Madgascar
93 W 2 **Tolbazy**, Russian Federation
108 M 3 **Tolbo**, Mongolia
47 U 14 **Tolé**, Panama
103 T 9 **Tole Bi**, Kazakhstan
21 L 16 **Toledo**, OH, U.S.A.
32 F 10 **Toledo**, OR, U.S.A.
58 G 8 **Toledo**, Brazil
67 O 7 **Toledo**, Spain
121 J 17 **Toledo**, Philippines
18 H 6 **Toledo Bend Reservoir**, LA, U.S.A. ◣
108 J 3 **Toli**, China
133 V 10 **Toliara**, Madgascar
133 W 9 **Toliara**, Madgascar ▣
50 H 7 **Tolima**, Colombia ▣
117 O 10 **Tolitoli**, Indonesia
103 U 10 **Tolmak**, Kyrgyzstan
76 H 5 **Tolmezzo**, Italy
80 A 7 **Tolmin**, Slovenia
79 I 25 **Tolna**, Hungary
130 J 9 **Tolo**, Democratic Republic of Congo
121 I 19 **Tolong Bay**, Philippines ≈
67 R 1 **Tolosa**, Spain
45 Q 12 **Toluca**, Mexico
77 M 16 **Tolve**, Italy
93 R 3 **Tol'yatti**, Russian Federation
133 O 9 **Tom Burke**, Republic of South Africa
134 G 6 **Tom Price**, WA, Australia
20 E 12 **Tomah**, WI, U.S.A.
122 K 6 **Tomakomai**, Japan
122 J 4 **Tomamae**, Japan
119 Y 6 **Tomanggong**, Malaysia
119 U 6 **Tomani**, Malaysia
103 U 7 **Tomar**, Kazakhstan
92 J 6 **Tomarovka**, Russian Federation
94 K 11 **Tomarza**, Turkey
79 O 16 **Tomaszów Lubelski**, Poland
79 K 14 **Tomaszów Mazowiecki**, Poland
44 M 11 **Tomatlán**, Mexico
19 O 5 **Tombigbee**, AL, U.S.A. ∿
132 F 1 **Tomboco**, Angola
128 L 7 **Tombouctou**, Mali ▣
30 L 15 **Tombstone**, AZ, U.S.A.
132 F 6 **Tombua**, Angola
57 F 14 **Tomé**, Chile
117 Q 13 **Tomea**, Indonesia ✱
67 P 9 **Tomelloso**, Spain
103 Q 9 **Tomenaryk**, Kazakhstan
122 L 13 **Tomioka**, Japan
50 M 6 **Tomo**, Colombia ∿
130 H 6 **Tomori**, Central African Republic
14 J 14 **Toms River**, NJ, U.S.A.
88 M 12 **Tomsk**, Russian Federation
89 V 9 **Tomtor**, Russian Federation
117 U 12 **Tomu**, Indonesia
123 N 25 **Tonaki-jima**, Japan ✱
45 V 14 **Tonalá**, Mexico
54 C 11 **Tonantins**, Brazil
32 J 5 **Tonasket**, WA, U.S.A.
14 D 8 **Tonawanda**, NY, U.S.A.
63 W 11 **Tonbridge**, U.K.
117 Q 10 **Tondano**, Indonesia
71 B 26 **Tønder**, Denmark
144 K 10 **Toney Mountain**, Antarctica ▲
140 I 9 **Tonga**, Oceania □
113 X 11 **Tong'an**, China
141 P 6 **Tongareva**, Cook Islands ✱
140 I 11 **Tongatapu**, Tonga ✱
140 H 12 **Tongatapu Group**, Tonga ✱
113 T 5 **Tongbai**, China
110 K 9 **Tongbei**, China
113 W 6 **Tongcheng**, China
111 M 17 **T'ongch'ŏn**, North Korea
113 Q 3 **Tongchuan**, China
113 R 10 **Tongdao**, China
69 J 19 **Tongeren**, Belgium
113 U 8 **Tonggu**, China
113 R 3 **Tongguan**, China
113 T 8 **Tongguan**, China
111 N 19 **Tonghae**, South Korea
112 L 11 **Tonghai**, China
110 L 10 **Tonghe**, China
111 K 15 **Tonghua**, China
110 O 9 **Tongjiang**, China
110 H 13 **Tongliao**, China
113 W 6 **Tongling**, China
139 R 11 **Tongoa**, Vanuatu ✱
121 H 24 **Tongquil**, Philippines ✱
113 Q 9 **Tongren**, China
113 Q 15 **Tongshi**, China
60 H 8 **Tongue**, U.K.
113 N 3 **Tongwei**, China
111 E 17 **Tongxian**, China
109 Q 8 **Tongxin**, China
110 E 13 **Tongxing**, China
110 I 12 **Tongyu**, China
113 O 8 **Tongzi**, China
44 J 5 **Tónichi**, Mexico
127 D 21 **Tonj**, Sudan
104 D 12 **Tonk**, India
100 I 5 **Tonkābon**, Iran
114 L 11 **Tonkin**, Vietnam ◇
115 K 20 **Tônlé Sab**, Cambodia ◣
65 S 6 **Tonnerre**, France
72 F 8 **Tönning**, Germany
33 K 19 **Tonopah**, NV, U.S.A.
47 V 15 **Tonosí**, Panama
71 D 20 **Tønsberg**, Norway
30 J 3 **Tooele**, UT, U.S.A.
135 V 9 **Toowoomba**, QLD, Australia
127 O 18 **Tooxin**, Somalia
134 M 3 **Top Springs**, NT, Australia
25 Q 4 **Topeka**, KS, U.S.A.
86 J 9 **Toplița**, Romania
33 N 24 **Topock**, CA, U.S.A.
82 C 12 **Topolčani**, Macedonia (F.Y.R.O.M.)
44 K 7 **Topolobampo**, Mexico
82 K 10 **Topolovgrad**, Bulgaria
87 N 3 **Toporyshche**, Ukraine
63 N 13 **Topsham**, U.K.
136 J 7 **Topuni**, New Zealand
63 N 14 **Tor Bay**, U.K. ≈
94 B 11 **Torbali**, Turkey
101 O 7 **Torbat-e Heydarīyeh**, Iran
101 O 6 **Torbat-e Jām**, Iran
66 M 4 **Tordesillas**, Spain
70 K 12 **Töre**, Sweden
87 Y 7 **Torez**, Ukraine
73 L 15 **Torgau**, Germany
72 N 10 **Torgelow**, Germany
103 O 5 **Torghay**, Kazakhstan

69 B 18 **Torhout**, Belgium
127 E 23 **Torit**, Sudan
90 E 11 **Torkovichi**, Russian Federation
70 I 9 **Torneälven**, Sweden ∿
70 I 9 **Torneträsk**, Sweden ◣
70 I 9 **Torneträsk**, Sweden
41 T 5 **Torngat Mountains**, QC, Canada ▲▲
26 E 8 **Tornillo**, TX, U.S.A.
70 K 12 **Tornio**, Finland
59 B 18 **Tornquist**, Argentina
66 M 4 **Toro**, Spain
129 S 11 **Toro**, Nigeria
33 L 25 **Toro Peak**, CA, U.S.A. ▲
129 O 9 **Torodi**, Niger
138 J 5 **Torokina**, Papua New Guinea
79 K 23 **Törökszentmiklós**, Hungary
42 F 13 **Toronto**, ON, Canada
90 F 14 **Toropets**, Russian Federation
131 T 7 **Tororo**, Uganda
62 L 15 **Torpoint**, U.K.
63 N 14 **Torquay**, U.K.
67 N 3 **Torquemada**, Spain
33 J 25 **Torrance**, CA, U.S.A.
66 H 10 **Torrão**, Portugal
67 V 3 **Torre de Cadí**, Spain
66 J 5 **Torre de Moncorvo**, Portugal
66 M 13 **Torrecilla**, Spain ▲
67 O 1 **Torrelavega**, Spain
45 O 7 **Torreón**, Mexico
58 I 11 **Torres**, Brazil
139 P 9 **Torres Islands**, Vanuatu ✱
66 H 8 **Torres Novas**, Portugal
117 Y 15 **Torres Strait**, Asia/Oceania ≈
66 G 8 **Torres Vedras**, Portugal
67 T 11 **Torrevieja**, Spain
138 A 3 **Torricelli Mountains**, Papua New Guinea ▲▲
76 C 9 **Torriglia**, Italy
14 L 10 **Torrington**, CT, U.S.A.
29 Z 13 **Torrington**, WY, U.S.A.
71 F 14 **Torrön**, Sweden ◣
71 E 19 **Torsby**, Sweden
57 F 21 **Tortel**, Chile
103 T 4 **Tortkuduk**, Kazakhstan
49 V 8 **Tortola**, Virgin Islands, U.K. ✱
95 Q 9 **Tortum**, Turkey
100 L 6 **Ţorūd**, Iran
95 O 8 **Torul**, Turkey
78 H 11 **Toruń**, Poland
84 H 9 **Tõrva**, Estonia
90 H 14 **Torzhok**, Russian Federation
123 E 20 **Tosa**, Japan
123 F 21 **Tosa-wan**, Japan ≈
123 E 21 **Tosashimizu**, Japan
70 F 13 **Tosbotn**, Norway
132 M 11 **Tosca**, Republic of South Africa
76 F 11 **Toscana**, Italy ▣
103 R 11 **Toshkent Wiloyati**, Uzbekistan ▣
58 B 12 **Tostado**, Argentina
84 F 8 **Tõstamaa**, Estonia
72 G 11 **Tostedt**, Germany
94 J 8 **Tosya**, Turkey
67 R 11 **Totana**, Spain
90 L 11 **Tot'ma**, Russian Federation
63 N 14 **Totnes**, U.K.
51 V 6 **Totness**, Suriname
56 F 8 **Totoral**, Chile
139 Y 12 **Totoya**, Fiji ✱
93 U 4 **Totskoye**, Russian Federation
123 F 17 **Tottori**, Japan
128 I 12 **Touba**, Côte d'Ivoire
128 E 8 **Touba**, Senegal
129 V 12 **Touboro**, Cameroon
128 L 9 **Tougan**, Burkina Faso
125 O 7 **Touggourt**, Algeria
128 G 10 **Tougué**, Guinea
139 P 13 **Touho**, New Caledonia
128 H 8 **Touil**, Mauritania
128 H 9 **Toukoto**, Mali
65 U 4 **Toul**, France
65 V 15 **Toulon**, France
65 P 14 **Toulouse**, France
128 J 13 **Toumodi**, Côte d'Ivoire
129 U 12 **Toungo**, Nigeria
115 E 14 **Toungoo**, Myanmar
129 V 9 **Tourba**, Chad
69 C 20 **Tournai**, Belgium
53 E 14 **Tournavista**, Peru
65 T 11 **Tournon-sur-Rhône**, France
65 T 8 **Tournus**, France
54 O 12 **Touros**, Brazil
65 N 7 **Tours**, France
109 Q 3 **Töv**, Mongolia ▣
92 J 2 **Tovarkovo**, Russian Federation
95 U 7 **Tovuz**, Azerbaijan
122 K 9 **Towada**, Japan
122 K 9 **Towada-ko**, Japan ◣
14 G 10 **Towanda**, PA, U.S.A.
63 T 8 **Towcester**, U.K.
22 J 3 **Towner**, ND, U.S.A.
29 Q 6 **Townsend**, MT, U.S.A.
135 T 4 **Townsville**, QLD, Australia
127 G 22 **Towot**, Sudan
17 U 2 **Towson**, MD, U.S.A.
122 J 6 **Tōya-ko**, Japan ◣
26 H 8 **Toyah**, TX, U.S.A.
123 H 15 **Toyama**, Japan
123 H 14 **Toyama-wan**, Japan ≈
91 N 9 **Toyma**, Russian Federation
123 I 18 **Toyohashi**, Japan
123 F 17 **Toyooka**, Japan
46 L 4 **Toyós**, Honduras
123 I 17 **Toyota**, Japan
125 P 7 **Tozeur**, Tunisia
95 S 6 **Tqibuli**, Georgia
95 Q 5 **Tqvarch'eli**, Georgia
115 M 23 **Tra Vinh**, Vietnam
66 K 4 **Trabazos**, Spain
95 O 8 **Trabzon**, Turkey
75 W 4 **Traisen**, Austria
61 B 20 **Tralee**, Republic of Ireland
71 F 22 **Tranås**, Sweden
56 I 7 **Trancas**, Argentina
115 G 25 **Trang**, Thailand
117 V 14 **Trangan**, Indonesia ✱
58 E 13 **Tranqueras**, Uruguay
145 N 7 **Transantarctic Mountains**, Antarctica ▲▲
86 G 10 **Transylvania**, Romania ◇
86 G 11 **Transylvanian Alps**, Romania ▲▲
86 H 8 **Transylvanian Basin**, Romania ◇
77 H 21 **Trapani**, Italy
128 F 6 **Trarza**, Mauritania ▣
107 V 9 **Trashigang**, Bhutan

115 J 20 **Trat**, Thailand
75 T 4 **Traun**, Austria
75 S 5 **Traunsee**, Austria ◣
72 I 9 **Travemünde**, Germany
20 J 11 **Traverse City**, MI, U.S.A.
76 D 8 **Travo**, Italy
63 N 5 **Trawsfynydd**, U.K.
138 J 5 **Treasury Islands**, Solomon Islands ✱
79 E 19 **Třebíč**, Czech Republic
81 H 15 **Trebinje**, Bosnia and Herzegovina
79 M 20 **Trebišov**, Slovakia
137 C 22 **Treble Cone**, New Zealand ▲
80 C 8 **Trebnje**, Slovenia
105 B 22 **Tree Island**, India ✱
62 K 15 **Tregony**, U.K.
59 G 14 **Treinta y Tres**, Uruguay
59 F 14 **Treinta y Tres**, Uruguay ▣
57 I 18 **Trelew**, Argentina
71 E 26 **Trelleborg**, Sweden
62 M 6 **Tremadog Bay**, U.K. ≈
30 J 1 **Tremonton**, UT, U.S.A.
20 I 9 **Trenary**, MI, U.S.A.
79 H 20 **Trenčín**, Slovakia
59 A 17 **Trenque Lauquen**, Argentina
63 U 5 **Trent**, U.K. ∿
76 F 5 **Trentino-Alto Adige**, Italy ▣
76 F 6 **Trento**, Italy
14 I 13 **Trenton**, NJ, U.S.A.
25 T 2 **Trenton**, MO, U.S.A.
42 H 12 **Trenton**, ON, Canada
41 Z 11 **Trepassey**, NL, Canada
59 C 18 **Tres Arroyos**, Argentina
54 E 12 **Três Casas**, Brazil
57 H 21 **Tres Cerros**, Argentina
58 L 6 **Três Corações**, Brazil
50 H 9 **Tres Esquinas**, Colombia
58 B 9 **Tres Isletas**, Argentina
58 H 5 **Três Lagoas**, Brazil
57 G 22 **Tres Lagos**, Argentina
45 V 14 **Tres Picos**, Mexico
31 Q 8 **Tres Piedras**, NM, U.S.A.
46 K 4 **Tres Puntas**, Guatemala ▶
58 N 6 **Três Rios**, Brazil
71 D 18 **Tretten**, Norway
76 D 7 **Treviglio**, Italy
76 G 6 **Treviso**, Italy
62 K 14 **Trevose Head**, U.K. ▶
81 N 16 **Trgovište**, Serbia and Montenegro
83 M 24 **Tria Nisia**, Greece ✱
24 G 4 **Tribune**, KS, U.S.A.
105 D 22 **Trichur**, India
75 T 6 **Trieben**, Austria
73 B 20 **Trier**, Germany
76 I 7 **Trieste**, Italy
80 A 6 **Triglav**, Slovenia ▲
83 D 16 **Trikala**, Greece
105 G 24 **Trincomalee**, Sri Lanka
31 S 7 **Trinidad**, CO, U.S.A.
48 I 5 **Trinidad**, Cuba
49 Z 14 **Trinidad**, Trinidad and Tobago ✱
53 K 18 **Trinidad**, Bolivia
59 E 15 **Trinidad**, Uruguay
49 Y 13 **Trinidad and Tobago**, North America □
27 T 9 **Trinity**, TX, U.S.A. ∿
41 Z 10 **Trinity Bay**, NL, Canada ≈
35 P 12 **Trinity Islands**, AK, U.S.A. ✱
83 E 21 **Tripoli**, Greece
96 G 5 **Tripoli**, Lebanon
125 S 7 **Tripoli**, Libya ■
107 V 13 **Tripura**, India ▣
72 F 9 **Trischen**, Germany ✱
10 L 12 **Tristan da Cunha**, U.K. ▣
46 M 8 **Triunfo**, Honduras
105 D 24 **Trivandrum**, India
77 K 14 **Trivento**, Italy
79 G 21 **Trnava**, Slovakia
138 G 6 **Trobriand Islands**, Papua New Guinea ✱
103 P 2 **Troebratskåy**, Kazakhstan
70 F 12 **Trofors**, Norway
80 E 13 **Trogir**, Croatia
80 E 12 **Troglav**, Bosnia and Herzegovina ▲
80 F 12 **Troglav**, Croatia ▲
77 L 15 **Troia**, Italy
43 P 7 **Trois-Pistoles**, QC, Canada
69 K 21 **Trois-Ponts**, Belgium
42 L 9 **Trois-Rivières**, QC, Canada
88 I 11 **Troitsk**, Russian Federation
91 S 8 **Troitsko-Pechorsk**, Russian Federation
71 E 22 **Trollhättan**, Sweden
54 G 9 **Trombetas**, Brazil ∿
133 N 13 **Trompsburg**, Republic of South Africa
70 I 7 **Tromsø**, Norway
71 D 15 **Trondheim**, Norway
71 D 15 **Trondheimsfjorden**, Norway ≈
107 U 9 **Trongsa**, Bhutan
61 G 14 **Troon**, U.K.
83 D 20 **Tropaia**, Greece
77 L 20 **Tropea**, Italy
87 U 3 **Trostyanets'**, Ukraine
20 K 9 **Trout Lake**, MI, U.S.A.
39 F 14 **Trout Lake**, NT, Canada ◣
40 K 10 **Trout Lake**, ON, Canada ◣
29 S 9 **Trout Peak**, WY, U.S.A. ▲
63 R 11 **Trowbridge**, U.K.
14 K 9 **Troy**, NY, U.S.A.
19 Q 5 **Troy**, AL, U.S.A.
25 X 3 **Troy**, MO, U.S.A.
28 K 2 **Troy**, MT, U.S.A.
33 M 19 **Troy Peak**, NV, U.S.A. ▲
82 I 8 **Troyan**, Bulgaria
65 S 5 **Troyes**, France
87 Y 4 **Troyits'ke**, Ukraine
31 R 9 **Truchas Peak**, NM, U.S.A. ▲
33 I 17 **Truckee**, CA, U.S.A.
47 N 4 **Trujillo**, Honduras
50 L 3 **Trujillo**, Venezuela ▣
53 B 14 **Trujillo**, Peru
66 L 8 **Trujillo**, Spain
82 E 9 **Trŭn**, Bulgaria
43 V 10 **Truro**, NS, Canada
62 J 15 **Truro**, U.K.
39 F 16 **Trutch**, BC, Canada
31 P 13 **Truth Or Consequences**, NM, U.S.A.
82 J 9 **Tryavna**, Bulgaria
22 J 13 **Tryon**, NE, U.S.A.
80 D 10 **Tržac**, Bosnia and Herzegovina
78 F 11 **Trzcianka**, Poland
78 E 12 **Trzciel**, Poland
79 G 15 **Trzebnica**, Poland
80 B 6 **Tržič**, Slovenia
109 U 3 **Tsagaannuur**, Mongolia
93 Q 9 **Tsagan Aman**, Russian Federation
70 I 9 **Tsåktso**, Sweden ▲

95 T 7 **Ts'alka**, Georgia
82 N 10 **Tsarevo**, Bulgaria
87 U 6 **Tsarychanka**, Ukraine
109 N 4 **Tseel**, Mongolia
92 M 10 **Tselina**, Russian Federation
132 J 11 **Tses**, Namibia
132 L 9 **Tsetseng**, Botswana
129 N 13 **Tsévié**, Togo
132 L 11 **Tshabong**, Botswana
132 L 10 **Tshane**, Botswana
130 F 11 **Tshela**, Democratic Republic of Congo
130 L 12 **Tshibala**, Democratic Republic of Congo
130 L 13 **Tshibwika**, Democratic Republic of Congo
130 K 11 **Tshikapa**, Democratic Republic of Congo
131 P 12 **Tshimbo**, Democratic Republic of Congo
133 Q 10 **Tshokwane**, Republic of South Africa
132 K 9 **Tshootsha**, Botswana
38 C 9 **Tsiigehtchic**, NT, Canada
93 N 9 **Tsimlyanskoye Reservoir**, Russian Federation ◣
132 L 11 **Tsineng**, Republic of South Africa
133 W 11 **Tsiombe**, Madgascar
133 W 7 **Tsiroanomandidy**, Madgascar
93 Q 1 **Tsivil'sk**, Russian Federation
95 T 6 **Ts'khinvali**, Georgia
95 V 7 **Tsnori**, Georgia
106 K 4 **Tso Morari Lake**, India ◣
133 O 13 **Tsolo**, Republic of South Africa
95 R 6 **Tsqaltubo**, Georgia
123 H 18 **Tsu**, Japan
123 L 15 **Tsuchiura**, Japan
122 J 8 **Tsugarū-kaikyō**, Japan ≈
123 D 21 **Tsukumi**, Japan
132 I 7 **Tsumeb**, Namibia
132 I 10 **Tsumis Park**, Namibia
132 J 8 **Tsumkwe**, Namibia
123 G 17 **Tsuruga**, Japan
123 F 20 **Tsurugi-san**, Japan ▲
122 J 12 **Tsuruoka**, Japan
123 A 20 **Tsushima**, Japan ✱
123 F 18 **Tsuyama**, Japan
133 N 11 **Tswelelang**, Republic of South Africa
85 N 20 **Tsyerakhowka**, Belarus
87 S 9 **Tsyurupyns'k**, Ukraine
39 F 14 **Tthenaagoo**, NT, Canada
136 N 12 **Tuai**, New Zealand
136 K 9 **Tuakau**, New Zealand
61 C 17 **Tuam**, Republic of Ireland
141 T 8 **Tuamotu Archipelago**, French Polynesia ✱
114 J 11 **Tuân Giao**, Vietnam
120 G 6 **Tuao**, Philippines
92 L 13 **Tuapse**, Russian Federation
119 U 5 **Tuaran**, Malaysia
118 A 14 **Tuas**, Singapore
140 J 8 **Tuasivi**, Samoa
30 K 9 **Tuba City**, AZ, U.S.A.
117 S 11 **Tubalai**, Indonesia ✱
116 J 14 **Tuban**, Indonesia
58 J 11 **Tubarão**, Brazil
96 G 8 **Tūbās**, Israel
121 E 20 **Tubbataha Reefs**, Philippines ✱
73 F 23 **Tübingen**, Germany
69 F 20 **Tubize**, Belgium
128 G 13 **Tubmanburg**, Liberia
141 T 12 **Tubuai**, French Polynesia ✱
53 O 21 **Tucavaca**, Bolivia
78 H 10 **Tuchola**, Poland
19 T 2 **Tucker**, GA, U.S.A.
30 K 14 **Tucson**, AZ, U.S.A.
56 I 8 **Tucumán**, Argentina ▣
31 T 10 **Tucumcari**, NM, U.S.A.
56 H 10 **Tucunuco**, Argentina
54 J 11 **Tucuruí**, Brazil
67 R 3 **Tudela**, Spain
84 I 6 **Tudu**, Estonia
107 Y 10 **Tuensang**, India
99 S 4 **Ţufayḩ**, Saudi Arabia
138 F 6 **Tufi**, Papua New Guinea
121 M 16 **Tugnug Point**, Philippines ▶
120 G 7 **Tuguegarao**, Philippines
89 V 13 **Tugur**, Russian Federation
136 K 12 **Tuhua**, New Zealand
66 H 3 **Tui**, Spain
127 M 21 **Tukayel**, Ethiopia
86 H 6 **Tukhol'ka**, Ukraine
103 U 14 **Tŭkhtamish**, Tajikistan
125 W 7 **Tūkrah**, Libya
38 C 8 **Tuktoyaktuk**, NT, Canada
84 E 11 **Tukums**, Latvia
131 T 13 **Tukuyu**, Tanzania
45 Q 9 **Tula**, Mexico
92 K 2 **Tula**, Russian Federation
138 M 6 **Tulaghi**, Solomon Islands
101 Q 8 **Tulak**, Afghanistan
45 R 11 **Tulancingo**, Mexico
33 I 22 **Tulare**, CA, U.S.A.
33 H 22 **Tulare Lake Bed**, CA, U.S.A. ◣
52 B 8 **Tulcán**, Ecuador
87 N 12 **Tulcea**, Romania
26 K 3 **Tulia**, TX, U.S.A.
110 H 6 **Tulihe**, China
38 E 11 **Tulit'a**, NT, Canada
16 G 10 **Tullahoma**, TN, U.S.A.
61 D 18 **Tullamore**, Republic of Ireland
65 P 11 **Tulle**, France
75 X 3 **Tulln**, Austria
18 J 5 **Tullos**, LA, U.S.A.
135 T 4 **Tully**, QLD, Australia
86 L 10 **Tulnici**, Romania
70 M 9 **Tulppio**, Finland
25 P 9 **Tulsa**, OK, U.S.A.
92 K 3 **Tul'skaya Oblast'**, Russian Federation ▣
89 P 13 **Tulun**, Russian Federation
138 J 4 **Tulun Islands**, Papua New Guinea ✱
47 O 8 **Tuma**, Nicaragua ∿
92 M 2 **Tuma**, Russian Federation
50 F 8 **Tumaco**, Colombia
130 M 9 **Tumba**, Democratic Republic of Congo
116 K 11 **Tumbangsamba**, Indonesia
52 A 11 **Tumbes**, Peru
39 G 18 **Tumbler Ridge**, BC, Canada
135 O 11 **Tumby Bay**, SA, Australia
111 M 14 **Tumen**, China ∿
51 S 5 **Tumeremo**, Venezuela
121 E 26 **Tumindao**, Philippines ✱
105 E 21 **Tumkur**, India
118 C 5 **Tumpat**, Malaysia
128 L 11 **Tumu**, Ghana
51 V 8 **Tumuc-Humac Mountains**, Brazil/Suriname ▲▲
95 O 10 **Tunceli**, Turkey
113 R 15 **Tunchang**, China

129 R 10 **Tundun-Wada**, Nigeria
131 V 14 **Tunduru**, Tanzania
82 J 9 **Tundzha**, Bulgaria ∿
129 S 12 **Tunga**, Nigeria
105 D 20 **Tungabhadra Reservoir**, India ◣
127 E 19 **Tungaru**, Sudan
121 I 22 **Tungawan**, Philippines
119 Z 6 **Tungku**, Malaysia
47 P 7 **Tungla**, Nicaragua
52 C 9 **Tungurahua**, Ecuador ▣
105 H 18 **Tuni**, India
18 L 1 **Tunica**, MS, U.S.A.
125 Q 5 **Tunis**, Tunisia ■
125 P 6 **Tunisia**, Africa □
50 J 6 **Tunja**, Colombia
47 P 7 **Tunki**, Nicaragua
70 F 13 **Tunnsjøen**, Norway ◣
63 W 2 **Tunstall**, U.K.
56 G 12 **Tunuyán**, Argentina
103 W 10 **Tüp**, Kyrgyzstan
58 I 6 **Tupã**, Brazil
141 R 9 **Tupai**, French Polynesia ✱
58 G 11 **Tupanciretã**, Brazil
19 N 2 **Tupelo**, MS, U.S.A.
54 J 13 **Tupiratins**, Brazil
53 J 23 **Tupiza**, Bolivia
14 I 6 **Tupper Lake**, NY, U.S.A. ◣
110 H 11 **Tuquan**, China
89 P 10 **Tura**, Russian Federation
107 U 11 **Tura**, India
103 S 10 **Tura-Ryskulova**, Kazakhstan
99 N 8 **Turabah**, Saudi Arabia
137 K 14 **Turakina**, New Zealand
137 K 16 **Turakirae Head**, New Zealand ▶
138 B 5 **Turama**, Papua New Guinea ∿
102 K 13 **Turan Lowland**, Turkmenistan ◇
136 L 12 **Turangi**, New Zealand
85 J 21 **Turaw**, Belarus
98 L 1 **Turayf**, Saudi Arabia
101 Q 14 **Turbat**, Pakistan
17 P 13 **Turbeville**, SC, U.S.A.
50 G 4 **Turbo**, Colombia
86 I 9 **Turda**, Romania
141 X 11 **Tureia**, French Polynesia ✱
78 I 13 **Turek**, Poland
103 T 4 **Turgay**, Kazakhstan
82 L 8 **Tŭrgovishte**, Bulgaria
82 L 8 **Turgovishte**, Bulgaria ▣
94 B 11 **Turgutlu**, Turkey
94 L 9 **Turhal**, Turkey
56 G 4 **Turi**, Chile
84 G 7 **Türi**, Estonia
67 S 8 **Turia**, Spain ∿
54 L 10 **Turiaçu**, Brazil
76 A 7 **Turin**, Italy
86 J 2 **Turiys'k**, Ukraine
86 H 5 **Turka**, Ukraine
94 B 8 **Türkeli**, Turkey ✱
103 Q 10 **Turkestan**, Kazakhstan
103 Q 12 **Turkestan Range**, Uzbekistan ▲▲
26 L 3 **Turkey**, TX, U.S.A.
94 M 10 **Turkey**, Asia/Europe □
93 O 5 **Turki**, Russian Federation
102 H 12 **Turkmenbashi**, Turkmenistan
102 M 12 **Turkmenistan**, Asia □
102 I 13 **Turkmenskiy Zaliv**, Turkmenistan ≈
94 L 12 **Türkoğlu**, Turkey
49 Q 4 **Turks and Caicos Islands**, U.K. ▣
49 Q 5 **Turks Islands**, Turks and Caicos Islands ✱
71 K 19 **Turku**, Finland
33 H 20 **Turlock**, CA, U.S.A.
46 L 2 **Turneffe Islands**, Belize ✱
69 H 16 **Turnhout**, Belgium
75 W 4 **Türnitz**, Austria
39 K 15 **Turnor Lake**, SK, Canada ◣
86 J 14 **Turnu Măgurele**, Romania
108 L 5 **Turpan**, China
108 L 5 **Turpan Depression**, China ◇
75 S 8 **Turrach**, Austria
25 Y 10 **Turrell**, AR, U.S.A.
47 R 12 **Turrialba**, Costa Rica
97 V 7 **Tursāq**, Iraq
102 M 11 **Turtkul'**, Uzbekistan
121 C 23 **Turtle Islands**, Philippines ✱
20 C 10 **Turtle Lake**, WI, U.S.A.
89 N 9 **Turukhansk**, Russian Federation
30 J 9 **Tusayan**, AZ, U.S.A.
19 O 3 **Tuscaloosa**, AL, U.S.A.
76 D 9 **Tuscan Archipelago**, Italy ✱
14 E 14 **Tuscarora Mountains**, PA, U.S.A. ▲▲
21 G 19 **Tuscola**, IL, U.S.A.
26 M 7 **Tuscola**, TX, U.S.A.
95 S 10 **Tutak**, Turkey
105 E 24 **Tuticorin**, India
119 S 6 **Tutong**, Brunei
82 L 6 **Tutrakan**, Bulgaria
22 K 5 **Tuttle**, ND, U.S.A.
25 O 3 **Tuttle Creek Reservoir**, KS, U.S.A. ◣
73 F 24 **Tuttlingen**, Germany
117 R 15 **Tutuala**, East Timor
140 K 8 **Tutuila**, American Samoa ✱
133 N 8 **Tutume**, Botswana
137 L 16 **Tuturumuri**, New Zealand
71 N 15 **Tuusniemi**, Finland
140 G 5 **Tuvalu**, Oceania □
98 L 7 **Tuwwal**, Saudi Arabia
45 O 12 **Tuxpan**, Mexico
45 S 11 **Tuxpan**, Mexico
45 V 14 **Tuxtla Gutiérrez**, Mexico
115 N 20 **Tuy Duc**, Vietnam
115 O 19 **Tuy Hoa**, Vietnam
114 L 11 **Tuyên Quang**, Vietnam
94 I 11 **Tuz Gölü**, Turkey ◣
97 U 4 **Tūz Khurmātū**, Iraq
80 I 11 **Tuzla**, Bosnia and Herzegovina
87 N 13 **Tuzla**, Romania
94 J 13 **Tuzla**, Turkey
90 H 14 **Tver'**, Russian Federation
90 H 13 **Tverskaya Oblast'**, Russian Federation ▣
79 J 19 **Tvrdošín**, Slovakia
82 K 9 **Tvŭrdista**, Bulgaria
60 J 13 **Tweed**, U.K. ∿
33 M 24 **Twentynine Palms**, CA, U.S.A.
29 P 7 **Twin Bridges**, MT, U.S.A.
19 V 4 **Twin City**, GA, U.S.A.
28 M 12 **Twin Falls**, ID, U.S.A.
28 M 9 **Twin Peaks**, ID, U.S.A. ▲
32 I 6 **Twisp**, WA, U.S.A.
137 E 21 **Twizel**, New Zealand
20 H 12 **Two**, WI, U.S.A.
79 I 17 **Tychy**, Poland

□ Country ▣ Internal administrative region: State/Province/Territory/Dependent territory ■ Capital city ▲▲ Mountain range/Undersea ridge ▲ Mountain peak/Volcano/Seamount ◇ Geographic feature ▶ Headland/Point/Cape/Peninsula ◭ Desert ✱ Island/Island group ⁙ Antarctic base ◎ Ocean ◒ Sea ≈ Bay/Gulf/Channel/Strait ◣ Lake ⊞ Salt pan/Dry/Intermittent lake ∿ River

27 S 6 **Tyler**, TX, U.S.A.
18 L 6 **Tylertown**, MS, U.S.A.
83 I 26 **Tympaki**, Greece
89 T 13 **Tynda**, Russian Federation
61 I 15 **Tyne**, U.K. ∫
16 J 6 **Tyner**, KY, U.S.A.
71 D 16 **Tynset**, Norway
71 D 19 **Tyrifjorden**, Norway ◣
83 E 16 **Tyrnavos**, Greece
14 D 12 **Tyrone**, PA, U.S.A.
77 E 15 **Tyrrhenian Sea**, Europe ◗
88 K 11 **Tyukalinsk**, Russian Federation
93 W 4 **Tyul'gan**, Russian Federation
88 J 10 **Tyumen'**, Russian Federation
62 M 9 **Tywi**, U.K. ∫

U

141 X 6 **Ua Huka**, French Polynesia 🏝
141 W 6 **Ua Pou**, French Polynesia 🏝
54 D 11 **Uarini**, Brazil
54 F 10 **Uatumã**, Brazil ∫
54 N 13 **Uauá**, Brazil
46 I 2 **Uaxactún**, Guatemala
55 L 18 **Ubá**, Brazil
58 N 5 **Ubá**, Brazil
55 N 15 **Ubaitaba**, Brazil
130 J 5 **Ubangi**, Central African Republic ∫
97 N 7 **Ubaylah**, Iraq
123 C 20 **Ube**, Japan
67 O 11 **Úbeda**, Spain
58 K 4 **Uberaba**, Brazil
58 J 3 **Uberlândia**, Brazil
73 F 25 **Überlingen**, Germany
118 B 13 **Ubin**, Singapore 🏝
115 I 16 **Ubolratna Reservoir**, Thailand ◣
133 Q 12 **Ubombo**, Republic of South Africa
115 L 17 **Ubon Ratchathani**, Thailand
131 N 8 **Ubundu**, Democratic Republic of Congo
53 E 14 **Ucayali**, Peru ▣
53 E 14 **Ucayali**, Peru ∫
69 F 19 **Uccle**, Belgium
89 P 10 **Uchami**, Russian Federation
103 X 7 **Ucharal**, Kazakhstan
123 C 24 **Uchinoura**, Japan
122 I 7 **Uchiura-wan**, Japan ≈
103 O 11 **Uchkuduk**, Uzbekistan
63 W 12 **Uckfield**, U.K.
29 W 9 **Ucross**, WY, U.S.A.
89 U 13 **Uda**, Russian Federation ∫
89 R 9 **Udachnyy**, Russian Federation
106 H 9 **Udaipur**, India
87 S 3 **Uday**, Ukraine ∫
80 D 11 **Udbina**, Croatia
71 D 22 **Uddevalla**, Sweden
70 H 12 **Uddjaure**, Sweden ◣
69 J 15 **Uden**, Netherlands
76 I 6 **Udine**, Italy
105 C 21 **Udipi**, India
91 R 13 **Udmurtskaya Respublika**, Russian Federation ▣
115 J 15 **Udon Thani**, Thailand
72 M 10 **Uecker**, Germany ∫
123 I 15 **Ueda**, Japan
130 L 5 **Uele**, Democratic Republic of Congo ∫
89 Z 5 **Uelen**, Russian Federation
89 Z 6 **Uel'kal'**, Russian Federation
72 I 12 **Uelzen**, Germany
123 H 18 **Ueno**, Japan
93 W 1 **Ufa**, Russian Federation ∫
93 W 1 **Ufa**, Russian Federation
84 D 10 **Ugāle**, Latvia
131 R 6 **Uganda**, Africa □
77 O 18 **Ugento**, Italy
89 W 13 **Uglegorsk**, Russian Federation
90 J 13 **Uglich**, Russian Federation
80 C 12 **Ugljan**, Croatia 🏝
89 Z 6 **Ugol'nyye**, Russian Federation
92 I 2 **Ugra**, Russian Federation
79 G 19 **Uherské Hradiště**, Czech Republic
21 O 18 **Uhrichsville**, OH, U.S.A.
60 F 10 **Uig**, U.K.
132 G 2 **Uíge**, Angola
132 G 1 **Uíge**, Angola ▣
111 L 18 **Uijongbu**, South Korea
102 J 5 **Uil**, Kazakhstan
91 T 13 **Uinskoye**, Russian Federation
30 L 3 **Uinta Mountains**, UT, U.S.A. ⛰
132 H 9 **Uis**, Namibia
68 H 11 **Uithoorn**, Netherlands
141 W 2 **Ujae**, Marshall Islands 🏝
79 M 22 **Újfehértó**, Hungary
123 G 18 **Uji**, Japan
123 B 24 **Uji-guntō**, Japan 🏝
123 K 14 **Ujiie**, Japan
105 D 14 **Ujjain**, India
117 N 13 **Ujung Pandang**, Indonesia
116 C 8 **Ujung Tamiang**, Indonesia ▶
129 Q 11 **Ukata**, Nigeria
123 O 22 **Uke-jima**, Japan 🏝
131 S 9 **Ukerewe Island**, Tanzania 🏝
91 Q 7 **Ukhta**, Russian Federation
139 N 7 **Uki**, Solomon Islands 🏝
32 J 10 **Ukiah**, OR, U.S.A.
33 F 17 **Ukiah**, CA, U.S.A.
85 F 14 **Ukmergė**, Lithuania
87 O 6 **Ukraine**, Europe □
132 G 4 **Uku**, Angola
123 A 21 **Uku-jima**, Japan 🏝
109 R 3 **Ulaanbaatar**, Mongolia ♜
108 M 2 **Ulaangom**, Mongolia
111 A 15 **Ulan Hua**, China
93 R 11 **Ulan Khol**, Russian Federation
89 Q 14 **Ulan-Ude**, Russian Federation
108 L 8 **Ulan Ul Hu**, China ◣
103 S 9 **Ulanbel'**, Kazakhstan
110 H 11 **Ulanhot**, China
82 N 12 **Ulaş**, Turkey
94 C 7 **Ulaş**, Turkey
94 M 10 **Ulaş**, Turkey
139 N 7 **Ulawa**, Solomon Islands 🏝
111 N 19 **Ulchin**, South Korea
81 J 17 **Ulcinj**, Serbia and Montenegro
109 T 2 **Uldz**, Mongolia ∫
109 S 3 **Uldz**, Mongolia
105 C 17 **Ulhasnagar**, India
110 E 11 **Uliastai**, China
109 O 3 **Uliastay**, Mongolia
140 K 14 **Ulithi**, Federated States of Micronesia 🏝
103 N 5 **Ul'kayak**, Kazakhstan ∫
135 U 12 **Ulladulla**, NSW, Australia
60 G 9 **Ullapool**, U.K.
111 O 19 **Ullŭng-do**, South Korea 🏝
73 H 24 **Ulm**, Germany
86 H 8 **Ulmeni**, Romania
80 H 13 **Ulog**, Bosnia and Herzegovina
133 R 5 **Ulongue**, Mozambique
111 N 20 **Ulsan**, South Korea
71 D 16 **Ulsberg**, Norway
61 D 15 **Ulster**, U.K. ▣
46 K 5 **Ulúa**, Honduras ∫
94 D 8 **Ulubat Gölü**, Turkey ◣
94 D 9 **Uludağ**, Turkey ▲
108 G 5 **Ulugqat**, China
94 J 12 **Ulukişla**, Turkey
141 N 14 **Ulul**, Federated States of Micronesia 🏝
133 P 12 **Ulundi**, Republic of South Africa
108 L 3 **Ulungur Hu**, China ◣
38 G 7 **Uluqsaqtuuq**, NT, Canada
134 M 7 **Uluru**, NT, Australia ▲
63 P 1 **Ulverston**, U.K.
87 P 7 **Ul'yanovka**, Ukraine
93 S 2 **Ul'yanovsk**, Russian Federation
93 S 3 **Ul'yanovskaya Oblast'**, Russian Federation ▣
103 T 5 **Ul'yanovskiy**, Kazakhstan
24 H 6 **Ulysses**, KS, U.S.A.
103 Q 6 **Ulytau**, Kazakhstan
80 A 8 **Umag**, Croatia
87 P 6 **Uman'**, Ukraine
101 V 14 **Umarkot**, Pakistan
32 J 9 **Umatilla**, WA, U.S.A.
90 I 4 **Umba**, Russian Federation
76 G 11 **Umbertide**, Italy
138 E 4 **Umboi Island**, Papua New Guinea 🏝
76 H 12 **Umbria**, Italy ▣
138 F 2 **Umbukul**, Papua New Guinea
71 J 15 **Umeå**, Sweden
71 I 14 **Umeälven**, Sweden ∫
93 N 4 **Umet**, Russian Federation
99 R 3 **Umgharah**, Kuwait
35 Q 4 **Umiat**, AK, U.S.A.
38 I 8 **Umingmaktok**, NU, Canada
133 P 13 **Umlazi**, Republic of South Africa
99 X 5 **Umm al Qaiwain**, United Arab Emirates
97 R 5 **Umm al Tūz**, Iraq
127 C 17 **Umm Bel**, Sudan
98 K 5 **Umm Lajj**, Saudi Arabia
97 Z 12 **Umm Qaşr**, Iraq
127 E 18 **Umm Ruwaba**, Sudan
125 Y 7 **Umm Sa'ad**, Libya
99 U 6 **Umm Sa'id**, Qatar
127 E 17 **Umm Saiyala**, Sudan
98 J 5 **Umm Urūmah**, Saudi Arabia 🏝
143 O 9 **Ummannaq**, Greenland
34 J 14 **Umnak Island**, AK, U.S.A. 🏝
132 I 4 **Umpulo**, Angola
133 O 14 **Umtata**, Republic of South Africa
129 R 13 **Umuahia**, Nigeria
58 F 7 **Umuarama**, Brazil
55 N 16 **Una**, Brazil
80 E 10 **Una**, Croatia/Bosnia and Herzegovina ∫
34 K 14 **Unalaska Island**, AK, U.S.A. 🏝
70 L 10 **Unari**, Finland ◣
70 L 10 **Unari**, Finland
117 O 11 **Unauna**, Indonesia 🏝
96 G 12 **'Unayzah**, Jordan
99 P 5 **'Unayzah**, Saudi Arabia
22 J 4 **Underwood**, ND, U.S.A.
138 F 4 **Unea Island**, Papua New Guinea 🏝
92 H 3 **Unecha**, Russian Federation
41 S 5 **Ungava Bay**, QC, Canada ≈
131 X 9 **Ungwana Bay**, Kenya ≈
58 H 9 **União da Vitória**, Brazil
80 B 10 **Unije**, Croatia 🏝
34 L 13 **Unimak Island**, AK, U.S.A. 🏝
34 J 13 **Unimak Pass**, AK, U.S.A. ≈
54 D 10 **Unini**, Brazil ∫
25 X 4 **Union**, MO, U.S.A.
14 B 10 **Union City**, PA, U.S.A.
16 B 8 **Union City**, TN, U.S.A.
19 R 5 **Union Springs**, AL, U.S.A.
14 B 14 **Uniontown**, PA, U.S.A.
25 T 1 **Unionville**, MO, U.S.A.
99 W 6 **United Arab Emirates**, Asia □
61 J 16 **United Kingdom**, Europe □
12 H 8 **United States of America**, North America □
32 K 11 **Unity**, OR, U.S.A.
75 P 6 **Unken**, Austria
106 L 10 **Unnao**, India
60 K 3 **Unst**, U.K. 🏝
47 O 11 **Upala**, Costa Rica
51 R 4 **Upata**, Venezuela
63 S 11 **Upavon**, U.K.
132 K 12 **Upington**, Republic of South Africa
105 A 15 **Upleta**, India
140 J 8 **Upolu**, Samoa 🏝
34 E 8 **Upolu Point**, HI, U.S.A. ▶
14 H 14 **Upper Darby**, PA, U.S.A.
128 M 11 **Upper East**, Ghana ▣
137 K 16 **Upper Hutt**, New Zealand
32 G 13 **Upper Klamath Lake**, OR, U.S.A. ◣
33 I 14 **Upper Lake**, CA, U.S.A. ◣
127 F 20 **Upper Nile**, Sudan ▣
23 Q 3 **Upper Red Lake**, MN, U.S.A. ◣
21 L 17 **Upper Sandusky**, OH, U.S.A.
128 L 11 **Upper West**, Ghana ▣
71 H 20 **Uppsala**, Sweden
40 K 11 **Upsala**, ON, Canada
106 J 4 **Upshi**, India
29 Z 9 **Upton**, WY, U.S.A.
99 N 5 **'Uqlat aş Şuqūr**, Saudi Arabia
97 N 6 **Uqlat Şawāb**, Iraq
109 R 6 **Urad Houqi**, China
122 L 5 **Urahoro**, Japan
122 L 6 **Urakawa**, Japan
93 V 5 **Ural**, Kazakhstan/Russian Federation ∫
88 I 11 **Ural Mountains**, Russian Federation ⛰
88 G 10 **Ural'sk**, Russian Federation
102 I 4 **Ural'sk**, Kazakhstan
96 I 2 **Urām aş Şughrá**, Syria
131 S 11 **Urambo**, Tanzania
135 P 5 **Urandangi**, QLD, Australia
55 L 15 **Urandi**, Brazil
31 N 6 **Uravan**, CO, U.S.A.
123 K 16 **Urawa**, Japan
88 J 9 **Uray**, Russian Federation
99 S 5 **Uray'irah**, Saudi Arabia
21 G 19 **Urbana**, IL, U.S.A.
76 G 10 **Urbania**, Italy
76 G 10 **Urbino**, Italy
53 G 17 **Urcos**, Peru
108 M 3 **Urdgol**, Mongolia
103 X 7 **Urdzhar**, Kazakhstan
63 S 1 **Ure**, U.K. ∫
91 N 13 **Uren'**, Russian Federation
88 M 9 **Urengoy**, Russian Federation
139 Q 9 **Uréparapara**, Vanuatu 🏝
102 M 11 **Urgench**, Uzbekistan
108 K 3 **Urho**, China
106 G 3 **Uri**, India
103 P 3 **Uritskiy**, Kazakhstan
68 J 9 **Urk**, Netherlands
94 A 10 **Urla**, Turkey
129 Q 13 **Uromi**, Nigeria
81 M 16 **Uroševac**, Serbia and Montenegro
103 R 12 **Üroteppa**, Tajikistan
109 P 5 **Urt**, Mongolia
44 K 5 **Uruáchic**, Mexico
55 J 15 **Uruaçu**, Brazil
45 P 12 **Uruapan**, Mexico
54 G 10 **Urucará**, Brazil
54 L 12 **Uruçuí**, Brazil
58 E 12 **Uruguaiana**, Brazil
56 O 8 **Uruguay**, South America ∫
59 F 14 **Uruguay**, South America □
108 K 5 **Ürümqi**, China
101 T 8 **Urūzgān**, Afghanistan ▣
93 N 6 **Uryupinsk**, Russian Federation
91 P 14 **Urzhum**, Russian Federation
86 L 12 **Urziceni**, Romania
87 X 9 **Urzuf**, Ukraine
91 S 4 **Usa**, Russian Federation ∫
123 C 21 **Usa**, Japan
121 F 24 **Usada**, Philippines 🏝
94 D 10 **Uşak**, Turkey
80 L 13 **Ušće**, Serbia and Montenegro
98 L 8 **'Usfān**, Saudi Arabia
98 M 8 **'Ushayrah**, Saudi Arabia
123 B 23 **Ushibuka**, Japan
103 W 8 **Ushtobe**, Kazakhstan
57 H 25 **Ushuaia**, Argentina
138 D 4 **Usino**, Papua New Guinea
91 S 4 **Usinsk**, Russian Federation
63 O 10 **Usk**, U.K. ∫
94 D 7 **Üsküdar**, Turkey
73 G 15 **Uslar**, Germany
92 M 5 **Usman'**, Russian Federation
84 C 10 **Usmas ezers**, Latvia ◣
91 O 7 **Usogorsk**, Russian Federation
89 Q 13 **Usol'ye-Sibirskoye**, Russian Federation
121 K 15 **Uson**, Philippines
87 W 7 **Uspenivka**, Ukraine
103 V 3 **Uspenka**, Kazakhstan
65 Q 10 **Ussel**, France
89 V 15 **Ussuriysk**, Russian Federation
89 Q 13 **Ust'-Barguzin**, Russian Federation
89 P 12 **Ust'-Ilimsk**, Russian Federation
89 Z 10 **Ust'-Kamchatsk**, Russian Federation
103 X 4 **Ust'-Kamenogorsk**, Kazakhstan
91 R 9 **Ust'-Kulom**, Russian Federation
89 P 12 **Ust'-Kut**, Russian Federation
89 T 8 **Ust'-Kuyga**, Russian Federation
89 U 11 **Ust'-Maya**, Russian Federation
91 R 9 **Ust'-Nem**, Russian Federation
89 V 9 **Ust'-Nera**, Russian Federation
89 R 7 **Ust'-Olenek**, Russian Federation
89 W 10 **Ust'-Omchug**, Russian Federation
90 L 7 **Ust'-Pinega**, Russian Federation
89 O 8 **Ust'-Port**, Russian Federation
91 P 5 **Ust'-Tsil'ma**, Russian Federation
103 O 2 **Ust'-Uyskoye**, Kazakhstan
90 L 8 **Ust'-Vayen'ga**, Russian Federation
79 C 16 **Ústí nad Labem**, Czech Republic
78 G 8 **Ustka**, Poland
92 L 12 **Ust'Labinsk**, Russian Federation
82 L 10 **Ustrem**, Bulgaria
78 F 8 **Ustronie Morskie**, Poland
79 N 18 **Ustrzyki Dolne**, Poland
102 J 9 **Ustyurt Plateau**, Kazakhstan ◇
90 I 12 **Ustyuzhna**, Russian Federation
46 K 8 **Usulután**, El Salvador
45 X 13 **Usumacinta**, Mexico ∫
117 W 13 **Uta**, Indonesia
30 J 4 **Utah**, U.S.A. ▣
30 J 3 **Utah Lake**, UT, U.S.A. ◣
31 T 9 **Ute Reservoir**, NM, U.S.A. ◣
85 G 14 **Utena**, Lithuania
131 W 12 **Utete**, Tanzania
115 H 17 **Uthai Thani**, Thailand
101 T 14 **Uthal**, Pakistan
14 I 8 **Utica**, NY, U.S.A.
46 M 4 **Utila**, Honduras
123 B 22 **Uto**, Japan
107 N 10 **Utraula**, India
68 H 12 **Utrecht**, Netherlands ▣
68 I 12 **Utrecht**, Netherlands
141 Y 1 **Utrik**, Marshall Islands 🏝
70 L 7 **Utsjoki**, Finland
123 K 15 **Utsunomiya**, Japan
93 Q 11 **Utta**, Russian Federation
106 L 10 **Uttar Pradesh**, India ▣
115 H 15 **Uttaradit**, Thailand
106 K 6 **Uttaranchal**, India ▣
106 K 6 **Uttarkashi**, India
108 K 3 **Utubulak**, China
139 Q 8 **Utupua**, Solomon Islands 🏝
141 S 9 **Uturoa**, French Polynesia
71 L 16 **Uurainen**, Finland
71 J 19 **Uusikaupunki**, Finland
105 G 25 **Uva**, Sri Lanka ▣
80 J 13 **Uvac**, Serbia and Montenegro ∫
26 M 11 **Uvalde**, TX, U.S.A.
85 M 20 **Uvaravichy**, Belarus
93 N 5 **Uvarovo**, Russian Federation
131 R 11 **Uvinza**, Tanzania
138 G 5 **Uvol**, Papua New Guinea
109 N 2 **Uvs**, Mongolia ▣
109 N 2 **Uvs Nuur**, Mongolia ◣
123 D 21 **Uwajima**, Japan
99 Y 7 **'Uwayfī**, Oman
125 S 10 **'Uwaynāt Wannīn**, Libya
89 O 12 **Uyar**, Russian Federation
109 R 5 **Üydzin**, Mongolia
129 R 14 **Uyo**, Nigeria
103 S 10 **Uyuk**, Kazakhstan
103 O 11 **Uzbekistan**, Asia □
85 I 18 **Uzda**, Belarus
65 P 10 **Uzerche**, France
65 T 13 **Uzès**, France
87 N 3 **Uzh**, Ukraine ∫
86 G 6 **Uzhhorod**, Ukraine
80 K 12 **Užice**, Serbia and Montenegro
103 V 10 **Uzunaghach**, Kazakhstan
94 B 7 **Uzunköprü**, Turkey
84 D 13 **Užventis**, Lithuania

V

132 M 12 **Vaal**, Republic of South Africa ∫
70 M 13 **Vaala**, Finland
69 L 19 **Vaals**, Netherlands
71 J 16 **Vaasa**, Finland
68 K 11 **Vaassen**, Netherlands
84 F 13 **Vabalninkas**, Lithuania
79 J 22 **Vác**, Hungary
58 I 11 **Vacaria**, Brazil
33 G 19 **Vacaville**, CA, U.S.A.
105 C 15 **Vadodara**, India
70 M 6 **Vadsø**, Norway
74 I 7 **Vaduz**, Liechtenstein ♜
138 K 5 **Vaghena**, Solomon Islands 🏝
70 H 8 **Vågsfjorden**, Norway ≈
79 H 19 **Váh**, Slovakia ∫
141 X 10 **Vahitahi**, French Polynesia 🏝
140 G 6 **Vaiaku**, Tuvalu ♜
31 Q 4 **Vail**, CO, U.S.A.
141 X 10 **Vairaatea**, French Polynesia 🏝
84 E 6 **Väiri**, Estonia ≈
140 F 5 **Vaitupu**, Tuvalu 🏝
130 M 2 **Vakaga**, Central African Republic ▣
65 W 10 **Val d'Isere**, France
42 G 7 **Val-d'Or**, QC, Canada
39 M 20 **Val Marie**, SK, Canada
74 D 10 **Valais**, Switzerland ▣
82 E 12 **Valandovo**, Macedonia (F.Y.R.O.M.)
83 H 18 **Valaxa**, Greece 🏝
57 I 16 **Valcheta**, Argentina
90 G 12 **Valday**, Russian Federation
67 P 9 **Valdepeñas**, Spain
66 M 3 **Valderas**, Spain
35 S 9 **Valdez**, AK, U.S.A.
57 F 16 **Valdivia**, Chile
19 U 7 **Valdosta**, GA, U.S.A.
71 C 18 **Valdres**, Norway ⛰
32 L 12 **Vale**, OR, U.S.A.
95 S 7 **Vale**, Georgia
86 G 8 **Valea lui Mihai**, Romania
55 N 15 **Valença**, Brazil
54 M 12 **Valença do Piauí**, Brazil
65 T 11 **Valence**, France
51 N 3 **Valencia**, Venezuela
67 S 8 **Valencia**, Spain ▣
67 T 8 **Valencia**, Spain
121 L 21 **Valencia**, Philippines
66 J 8 **Valencia de Alcántara**, Spain
66 L 3 **Valencia de Don Juan**, Spain
65 R 1 **Valenciennes**, France
22 K 11 **Valentine**, NE, U.S.A.
26 G 9 **Valentine**, TX, U.S.A.
76 C 8 **Valenza**, Italy
120 G 11 **Valenzuela**, Philippines
84 H 9 **Valga**, Estonia
80 K 11 **Valjevo**, Serbia and Montenegro
84 H 9 **Valka**, Latvia
69 J 16 **Valkenswaard**, Netherlands
87 V 4 **Valky**, Ukraine
45 Z 10 **Valladolid**, Mexico
67 N 4 **Valladolid**, Spain
77 L 15 **Vallata**, Italy
76 A 6 **Valle D'Aosta**, Italy ▣
51 N 3 **Valle de La Pascua**, Venezuela
50 G 7 **Valle Del Cauca**, Colombia ▣
45 T 13 **Valle Nacional**, Mexico
50 J 2 **Valledupar**, Colombia
43 O 9 **Vallée-Jonction**, QC, Canada
33 G 19 **Vallejo**, CA, U.S.A.
56 F 9 **Vallenar**, Chile
77 K 26 **Valletta**, Malta ♜
22 M 5 **Valley City**, ND, U.S.A.
32 I 13 **Valley Falls**, OR, U.S.A.
17 P 4 **Valley Head**, WV, U.S.A.
120 H 6 **Valley Head**, Philippines ▶
16 G 5 **Valley Station**, KY, U.S.A.
39 H 17 **Valleyview**, AB, Canada
76 G 9 **Valli di Comacchio**, Italy ◣
77 K 17 **Vallo della Lucania**, Italy
74 B 8 **Vallorbe**, Switzerland
67 V 5 **Valls**, Spain
84 G 9 **Valmiera**, Latvia
64 L 3 **Valognes**, France
85 H 17 **Valozhyn**, Belarus
105 E 23 **Valparai**, India
21 H 16 **Valparaiso**, IN, U.S.A.
56 F 11 **Valparaíso**, Chile
56 F 11 **Valparaíso**, Chile ▣
58 I 5 **Valparáiso**, Brazil
80 H 8 **Valpovo**, Croatia
74 H 9 **Vals**, Switzerland
105 C 16 **Valsad**, India
71 F 14 **Valsjöbyn**, Sweden
92 K 7 **Valuyki**, Russian Federation
66 J 11 **Valverde del Camino**, Spain
71 K 18 **Vammala**, Finland
95 S 11 **Van**, Turkey
15 R 1 **Van Buren**, ME, U.S.A.
25 X 7 **Van Buren**, MO, U.S.A.
115 O 19 **Vân Canh**, Vietnam
134 M 1 **Van Diemen Gulf**, NT, Australia ≈
95 S 11 **Van Gölü**, Turkey ◣
26 F 8 **Van Horn**, TX, U.S.A.
21 K 17 **Van Wert**, OH, U.S.A.
95 T 8 **Vanadzor**, Armenia
141 X 11 **Vanavana**, French Polynesia 🏝
89 P 11 **Vanavara**, Russian Federation
15 S 3 **Vanceboro**, ME, U.S.A.
32 G 9 **Vancouver**, WA, U.S.A.
39 G 22 **Vancouver**, BC, Canada
39 E 22 **Vancouver Island**, BC, Canada 🏝
21 F 20 **Vandalia**, IL, U.S.A.
135 P 3 **Vanderlin Island**, NT, Australia 🏝
105 F 21 **Vandivasi**, India
84 G 7 **Vändra**, Estonia
71 E 21 **Vänern**, Sweden ◣
71 E 22 **Vänersborg**, Sweden
133 Y 10 **Vangaindrano**, Madgascar
138 K 6 **Vangunu**, Solomon Islands 🏝
139 Q 8 **Vanikoro Islands**, Solomon Islands 🏝
138 A 3 **Vanimo**, Papua New Guinea
89 W 14 **Vanino**, Russian Federation
86 G 12 **Vânju Mare**, Romania
89 Z 5 **Vankarem**, Russian Federation
70 I 6 **Vanna**, Norway 🏝
64 J 6 **Vannes**, France
132 J 14 **Vanrhynsdorp**, Republic of South Africa
41 O 2 **Vansittart Island**, NU, Canada 🏝
71 L 19 **Vantaa**, Finland
139 Z 11 **Vanua Balavu**, Fiji 🏝
139 Q 9 **Vanua Lava**, Vanuatu 🏝
139 X 10 **Vanua Levu**, Fiji 🏝
139 S 11 **Vanuatu**, Oceania □
128 L 11 **Varalé**, Côte d'Ivoire
76 B 6 **Varallo**, Italy
100 I 6 **Varāmīn**, Iran
107 O 11 **Varanasi**, India
91 R 2 **Varandey**, Russian Federation
70 M 6 **Varangerfjorden**, Norway ≈
70 M 6 **Varangerhalvøya**, Norway ▶
85 I 14 **Varapayeva**, Belarus
80 E 7 **Varaždin**, Croatia
71 D 23 **Varberg**, Sweden
83 C 20 **Varda**, Greece
82 D 11 **Vardar**, Macedonia (F.Y.R.O.M.) ∫
71 B 25 **Varde**, Denmark
95 V 9 **Vardenis**, Armenia
70 N 6 **Vardø**, Norway
72 E 10 **Varel**, Germany
85 F 16 **Varėna**, Lithuania
76 C 6 **Varese**, Italy
86 J 8 **Vârful Ineu**, Romania ▲
86 J 11 **Vârful Moldoveanu**, Romania ▲
86 J 11 **Vârful Omu**, Romania ▲
86 G 11 **Vârful Peleaga**, Romania ▲
86 I 8 **Vârful Pietrosu**, Romania ▲
86 G 12 **Vârful Svinecea Mare**, Romania ▲
86 K 9 **Vârful Toaca**, Romania ▲
58 L 6 **Varginha**, Brazil
56 F 6 **Varillas**, Chile
71 N 16 **Varkaus**, Finland
83 G 20 **Varkiza**, Greece
71 E 20 **Värmeln**, Sweden ◣
82 N 8 **Varna**, Bulgaria ▣
82 N 8 **Varna**, Bulgaria
71 F 23 **Värnamo**, Sweden
84 D 13 **Varniai**, Lithuania
85 H 15 **Varnyany**, Belarus
95 Q 10 **Varto**, Turkey
76 C 8 **Varzi**, Italy
79 N 21 **Vásárosnamény**, Hungary
91 N 7 **Vashka**, Russian Federation ∫
85 L 21 **Vasilyevichy**, Belarus
86 M 9 **Vaslui**, Romania
20 L 13 **Vassar**, MI, U.S.A.
70 G 12 **Västansjö**, Sweden
71 G 17 **Västbäcka**, Sweden
71 G 20 **Västerås**, Sweden
71 E 18 **Västerdalälven**, Sweden ∫
71 G 23 **Västervik**, Sweden
76 K 13 **Vasto**, Italy
71 E 20 **Västra Silen**, Sweden ◣
79 F 24 **Vasvár**, Hungary
87 V 8 **Vasylivka**, Ukraine
87 P 4 **Vasyl'kiv**, Ukraine
87 V 7 **Vasyl'kivka**, Ukraine
65 P 7 **Vatan**, France
60 D 11 **Vatersay**, U.K. 🏝
77 H 14 **Vatican City**, Europe □
70 C 11 **Vatnajökull**, Iceland ◇
133 Y 8 **Vatomandry**, Madgascar
86 J 8 **Vatra Dornei**, Romania
71 F 22 **Vättern**, Sweden ◣
139 W 12 **Vatulele**, Fiji 🏝
74 B 9 **Vaud**, Switzerland ▣
31 R 11 **Vaughn**, NM, U.S.A.
50 L 9 **Vaupés**, Colombia ▣
65 S 14 **Vauvert**, France
140 J 10 **Vava'u Group**, Tonga 🏝
105 G 24 **Vavuniya**, Sri Lanka
85 M 17 **Vawkavichy**, Belarus
85 F 19 **Vawkavysk**, Belarus
71 F 24 **Växjö**, Sweden
95 U 9 **Vayk**, Armenia
72 E 12 **Vechta**, Germany
105 F 23 **Vedaranniyam**, India
86 K 14 **Vedea**, Romania
59 B 16 **Vedia**, Argentina
85 M 21 **Vedrych**, Belarus ∫
68 N 7 **Veendam**, Netherlands
68 J 13 **Veenendaal**, Netherlands
26 J 2 **Vega**, TX, U.S.A.
70 E 12 **Vega**, Norway 🏝
69 J 15 **Veghel**, Netherlands
105 L 19 **Veimandu Channel**, Maldives ≈
71 B 25 **Vejle**, Denmark
81 F 14 **Vela Luka**, Croatia
73 C 16 **Velbert**, Germany
75 S 9 **Velden**, Austria
80 C 10 **Velebit**, Croatia ⛰
80 C 6 **Velenje**, Slovenia
82 D 11 **Veles**, Macedonia (F.Y.R.O.M.)
67 Q 11 **Vélez Rubio**, Spain
80 M 10 **Velika**, Serbia and Montenegro ∫
80 D 8 **Velika Gorica**, Croatia
80 C 9 **Velika Kapela**, Croatia ⛰
80 D 9 **Velika Kladuša**, Bosnia and Herzegovina
90 E 12 **Velikiy Novgorod**, Russian Federation
91 N 10 **Velikiy Ustyug**, Russian Federation
90 E 14 **Velikiye Luki**, Russian Federation
82 J 8 **Veliko Tŭrnovo**, Bulgaria ▣
82 J 8 **Veliko Tŭrnovo**, Bulgaria
128 F 9 **Vélingara**, Senegal
82 H 10 **Velingrad**, Bulgaria
92 G 1 **Velizh**, Russian Federation
79 F 19 **Velká Bíteš**, Czech Republic
138 J 5 **Vella Lavella**, Solomon Islands 🏝
105 F 21 **Vellore**, India
83 G 22 **Velopoula**, Greece 🏝
90 L 10 **Vel'sk**, Russian Federation
22 J 3 **Velva**, ND, U.S.A.
87 R 9 **Velyka Korenykha**, Ukraine
87 T 8 **Velyka Lepetykha**, Ukraine
87 X 4 **Velykyy Burluk**, Ukraine
59 B 15 **Venado Tuerto**, Argentina
66 H 9 **Vendas Novas**, Portugal
91 O 7 **Vendinga**, Russian Federation
65 O 6 **Vendôme**, France
76 G 7 **Veneto**, Italy ▣
92 L 2 **Venev**, Russian Federation
51 N 5 **Venezuela**, Venezuela □
18 M 9 **Venice**, LA, U.S.A.
19 V 12 **Venice**, FL, U.S.A.
76 G 7 **Venice**, Italy
69 L 16 **Venlo**, Netherlands
69 K 15 **Venray**, Netherlands
84 C 11 **Venta**, Latvia/Lithuania ∫
133 N 13 **Venterstad**, Republic of South Africa
76 A 10 **Ventimiglia**, Italy
57 F 17 **Ventisquero**, Argentina ▲
63 T 14 **Ventnor**, U.K.
84 C 10 **Ventspils**, Latvia
33 I 24 **Ventura**, CA, U.S.A.
58 B 12 **Vera**, Argentina
67 R 12 **Vera**, Spain
45 T 12 **Veracruz**, Mexico
45 R 10 **Veracruz**, Mexico ▣
105 A 16 **Veraval**, India
76 C 6 **Verbania**, Italy
76 B 7 **Vercelli**, Italy
71 E 14 **Verdalsøra**, Norway
30 J 11 **Verde**, AZ, U.S.A. ∫
120 F 12 **Verde Island Passage**, Philippines ≈
65 T 4 **Verdun**, France
59 G 14 **Vergara**, Uruguay
14 L 6 **Vergennes**, VT, U.S.A.
87 U 8 **Verkhiniy Rohachyk**, Ukraine
91 N 12 **Verkhnespasskoye**, Russian Federatio
90 G 2 **Verkhnetulomskoye Vodokhranilishc** Russian Federation ◣
92 K 4 **Verkhov'ye**, Russian Federation
89 T 7 **Verkhoyanskiy Khrebet**, Russian Federation ⛰
39 K 18 **Vermilion**, AB, Canada
18 J 8 **Vermilion Bay**, LA, U.S.A. ≈
23 T 3 **Vermilion Lake**, MN, U.S.A. ◣
23 O 11 **Vermillion**, SD, U.S.A.
14 K 7 **Vermont**, U.S.A. ▣
144 H 4 **Vernadsky**, Antarctica ⁙
30 M 3 **Vernal**, UT, U.S.A.
42 E 9 **Verner**, ON, Canada
65 O 4 **Verneuil-sur-Avre**, France
19 O 3 **Vernon**, AL, U.S.A.
27 N 4 **Vernon**, TX, U.S.A.
30 J 3 **Vernon**, UT, U.S.A.
39 H 21 **Vernon**, BC, Canada
19 Y 11 **Vero Beach**, FL, U.S.A.
83 E 14 **Veroia**, Greece
76 F 7 **Verona**, Italy
59 E 16 **Verónica**, Argentina
21 J 20 **Versailles**, IN, U.S.A.
25 U 5 **Versailles**, MO, U.S.A.
65 P 4 **Versailles**, France
74 A 10 **Versoix**, Switzerland
48 K 5 **Vertientes**, Cuba
87 R 2 **Vertiyivka**, Ukraine
69 K 20 **Verviers**, Belgium
65 S 2 **Vervins**, France
39 M 20 **Verwood**, SK, Canada
65 Z 14 **Vescovato**, France
87 U 9 **Vesele**, Ukraine
92 M 10 **Veselovskoye Vodokhranilishche**, Rus Federation ◣
93 N 7 **Veshenskaya**, Russian Federation
65 V 6 **Vesoul**, France
19 Q 3 **Vestavia Hills**, AL, U.S.A.
71 A 21 **Vestbygd**, Norway
70 G 8 **Vesterålen**, Norway 🏝
70 G 9 **Vestfjorden**, Norway ≈
70 G 9 **Vestvågøy**, Norway 🏝
77 J 16 **Vesuvius**, Italy ▲
90 J 12 **Ves'yegonsk**, Russian Federation
79 H 24 **Veszprém**, Hungary
71 G 23 **Vetlanda**, Sweden
91 N 13 **Vetluga**, Russian Federation
90 M 14 **Vetluzhskiy**, Russian Federation
82 K 6 **Vetovo**, Bulgaria
76 G 13 **Vetralla**, Italy
82 M 9 **Vetren**, Bulgaria
69 A 17 **Veurne**, Belgium
74 C 9 **Vevey**, Switzerland
65 U 12 **Veynes**, France
94 K 8 **Vezirköprü**, Turkey
58 H 12 **Viamão**, Brazil
66 H 3 **Viana do Castelo**, Portugal ▣
66 H 4 **Viana do Castelo**, Portugal
69 L 24 **Vianden**, Luxembourg
68 I 13 **Vianen**, Netherlands
114 H 12 **Viangphoukha**, Laos
76 E 10 **Viareggio**, Italy
77 M 20 **Vibo Valentia**, Italy
71 C 24 **Viborg**, Denmark
67 X 4 **Vic**, Spain
64 M 14 **Vic-en-Bigorre**, France
76 F 7 **Vicenza**, Italy
50 M 6 **Vichada**, Colombia ▣
50 L 7 **Vichada**, Colombia ∫
65 R 9 **Vichy**, France
24 K 9 **Vici**, OK, U.S.A.
18 K 5 **Vicksburg**, MS, U.S.A.
58 N 5 **Viçosa**, Brazil
23 U 12 **Victor**, IA, U.S.A.
29 Q 11 **Victor**, ID, U.S.A.
135 P 12 **Victor Harbor**, SA, Australia
11 Q 10 **Victoria**, Seychelles ♜
27 Q 11 **Victoria**, TX, U.S.A.
39 F 22 **Victoria**, BC, Canada
46 L 5 **Victoria**, Honduras
59 B 14 **Victoria**, Argentina
120 F 10 **Victoria**, Philippines
134 M 3 **Victoria**, NT, Australia ∫
135 T 13 **Victoria**, Australia ▣
132 M 7 **Victoria Falls**, Zimbabwe
38 H 6 **Victoria Island**, NU, Canada 🏝
145 R 12 **Victoria Land**, Antarctica ◇
46 J 3 **Victoria Peak**, Belize ▲
121 C 19 **Victoria Peak**, Philippines ▲
134 M 3 **Victoria River**, NT, Australia
132 L 14 **Victoria West**, Republic of South Afric
42 M 10 **Victoriaville**, QC, Canada
56 I 13 **Victorica**, Argentina
33 K 24 **Victorville**, CA, U.S.A.
56 J 12 **Vicuña Mackenna**, Argentina
29 X 3 **Vida**, MT, U.S.A.
33 N 24 **Vidal**, CA, U.S.A.
86 J 13 **Videle**, Romania
66 I 10 **Vidigueira**, Portugal
82 E 6 **Vidin**, Bulgaria ▣
82 F 6 **Vidin**, Bulgaria
81 H 14 **Viduša**, Bosnia and Herzegovina ⛰
85 H 14 **Vidzy**, Belarus
59 B 21 **Viedma**, Argentina
84 D 12 **Viekšniai**, Lithuania
67 V 2 **Vielha**, Spain
69 K 22 **Vielsalm**, Belgium
17 N 3 **Vienna**, WV, U.S.A.
21 F 23 **Vienna**, IL, U.S.A.
25 V 5 **Vienna**, MO, U.S.A.
75 X 3 **Vienna**, Austria ♜
65 T 10 **Vienne**, France
115 J 15 **Vientiane**, Laos ♜
73 B 16 **Viersen**, Germany
74 F 8 **Vierwaldstätter See**, Switzerland ◣
65 P 7 **Vierzon**, France
84 G 12 **Viesīte**, Latvia
77 M 14 **Vieste**, Italy
114 L 12 **Viêt Tri**, Vietnam
70 I 10 **Vietas**, Sweden
114 L 13 **Vietnam**, Asia □
49 Z 11 **Vieux Fort**, St Lucia
120 K 12 **Viga**, Philippines
120 F 7 **Vigan**, Philippines

□ Country ▣ Internal administrative region: State/Province/Territory/Dependent territory ♜ Capital city ⛰ Mountain range/Undersea ridge ▲ Mountain peak/Volcano/Seamount ◇ Geographic feature ▶ Headland/Point/Cape/Peninsula ◠ Desert 🏝 Island/Island group ⁙ Antarctic base ◎ Ocean ◗ Sea ≈ Bay/Gulf/Channel/Strait ◣ Lake ⚑ Salt pan/Dry/Intermittent lake ∫ R

C 7 Vigevano, Italy
Z 11 Vigia Chico, Mexico
M 15 Vignemale, France/Spain ▲
H 3 Vigo, Spain
X 10 Vihari, Pakistan
L 19 Vihti, Finland
I 10 Viļaka, Latvia
I 11 Viļāni, Latvia
M 15 Viitasaari, Finland
H 5 Viitna, Estonia
G 19 Vijayawada, India
E 13 Vik, Norway
C 12 Vík, Iceland
G 11 Vikhren, Bulgaria ▲
K 18 Viking, AB, Canada
E 13 Vikna, Norway ✲
F 15 Vila Bela da Santíssima Trindade, Brazil
B 10 Vila Bittencourt, Brazil
R 6 Vila de Sena, Mozambique
G 12 Vila do Bispo, Portugal
G 9 Vila Franca de Xira, Portugal
J 5 Vila Nova de Foz Coa, Portugal
H 5 Vila Nova de Gaia, Portugal
F 9 Vila Novo Paraíso, Brazil
I 5 Vila Real, Portugal ◘
I 5 Vila Real, Portugal
O 5 Vila Velha, Brazil
K 22 Vilacaya, Bolivia
J 1 Vilalba, Spain
R 9 Vilanculos, Mozambique
E 23 Vilatikkulam, India
H 14 Vilhelmina, Sweden
F 14 Vilhena, Brazil
T 12 Viline, Ukraine
G 8 Viljandi, Estonia
D 15 Vilkaviškis, Lithuania
E 15 Vilkija, Lithuania
L 8 Villa, Argentina
K 22 Villa Abecia, Bolivia
M 3 Villa Ahumada, Mexico
B 10 Villa Angela, Argentina
B 10 Villa Berthet, Argentina
C 15 Villa Constitución, Argentina
J 10 Villa del Rosario, Argentina
I 11 Villa Dolores, Argentina
W 14 Villa Flores, Mexico
E 17 Villa Gesell, Argentina
I 7 Villa Insurgentes, Mexico
A 19 Villa Iris, Argentina
J 16 Villa Literno, Italy
A 14 Villa María, Argentina
I 22 Villa Martin, Bolivia
J 16 Villa Montes, Bolivia
M 6 Villa Ocampo, Mexico
C 11 Villa Ocampo, Argentina
J 9 Villa Ojo de Agua, Argentina
M 9 Villa Unión, Mexico
N 8 Villa Unión, Mexico
H 9 Villa Unión, Argentina
I 12 Villa Valeria, Argentina
K 2 Villablino, Spain
P 11 Villacarrillo, Spain
N 6 Villacastín, Spain
S 9 Villach, Austria
M 3 Villada, Spain
J 2 Villafranca del Bierzo, Spain
I 22 Villafrati, Italy
Q 8 Villagrán, Mexico
C 13 Villaguay, Argentina
W 13 Villahermosa, Mexico
T 10 Villajoyosa, Spain
J 16 Villálonga, Argentina
B 20 Villalonga, Argentina
M 4 Villalpando, Spain
B 16 Villanova Monteleone, Italy
P 10 Villanueva de los Infantes, Spain
J 16 Villány, Hungary
M 4 Villardefrades, Spain
F 15 Villarrica, Chile
Q 8 Villarrobledo, Spain
C 19 Villasimius, Italy
J 7 Villavicencio, Colombia
M 1 Villaviciosa de Asturias, Spain
K 23 Villazon, Bolivia
F 8 Ville-Marie, QC, Canada
P 12 Villefranche-de-Rouergue, France
T 9 Villefranche-sur-Saône, France
S 10 Villena, Spain
R 14 Villisca, IA, U.S.A.
G 16 Vilnius, Lithuania ♜
L 23 Vilsbiburg, Germany
M 23 Vilshofen, Germany
G 18 Vilvoorde, Belgium
I 15 Vilyeyka, Belarus
S 10 Vilyuy, Russian Federation ʃ
Q 10 Vilyuyskoye Vodokhranilishche, Russian Federation ∽
G 1 Vimianzo, Spain
N 4 Vimoutiers, France
E 11 Viña del Mar, Chile
R 6 Vinalhaven Island, ME, U.S.A. ✲
Z 6 Vinanivao, Madgascar
U 6 Vinarós, Spain
H 21 Vincennes, IN, U.S.A.
Y 11 Vincennes Bay, Antarctica ≈
C 15 Vindhya Ranges, India ▲▲
F 10 Vinga, Romania
L 14 Vinh, Vietnam
N 16 Vinh Linh, Vietnam
M 22 Vinh Long, Vietnam
L 23 Vinh Rach Gia, Vietnam ≈
J 4 Vinhais, Portugal
E 11 Vinica, Macedonia (F.Y.R.O.M.)
Q 8 Vinita, OK, U.S.A.
I 9 Vinkovci, Croatia
N 5 Vinnytsya, Ukraine
L 7 Vinson Massif, Antarctica ▲
G 10 Vinza, Congo
F 4 Vipiteno, Italy
K 13 Virac, Philippines
B 14 Viramgam, India
P 13 Viranşehir, Turkey
W 15 Virawah, Pakistan
H 10 Virden, MB, Canada
M 4 Vire, France
G 6 Virei, Angola
V 7 Virgin Corda, Virgin Islands, U.K. ✲
V 7 Virgin Islands, U.K. ◘
V 8 Virgin Islands, U.S.A. ◘
R 5 Virginia, MN, U.S.A.
Q 5 Virginia, U.S.A. ◘
E 19 Virginia, IL, U.S.A.
T 4 Virginia, MN, U.S.A.
133 N 12 Virginia, Republic of South Africa
135 N 1 Arnhem Land, NT, Australia ◇
17 W 7 Virginia Beach, VA, U.S.A.
29 P 8 Virginia City, MT, U.S.A.
33 I 18 Virginia City, NV, U.S.A.
42 F 7 Virginiatown, ON, Canada
71 N 18 Virojoki, Finland
80 G 8 Virovitica, Croatia
69 J 6 Virton, Belgium
84 E 7 Virtsu, Estonia
53 B 14 Virú, Peru
81 E 14 Vis, Croatia ✲
33 I 21 Visalia, CA, U.S.A.
121 J 15 Visayan Sea, Philippines ◒
71 H 23 Visby, Sweden
54 B 11 Visconde do Rio Branco, Brazil
37 N 4 Viscount Melville Sound, NU, Canada ≈
143 O 7 Viscount Melville Sound, Arctic Ocean ≈
69 K 19 Visé, Belgium
80 J 12 Višegrad, Bosnia and Herzegovina
66 I 6 Viseu, Portugal ◘
66 I 6 Viseu, Portugal
105 H 18 Vishakhapatnam, India
82 L 11 Vishegrad, Bulgaria ▲
103 S 4 Vishnevka, Kazakhstan
74 E 10 Visp, Switzerland
78 J 12 Vistula, Poland ʃ
85 A 16 Vistula Lagoon, Russian Federation ≈
87 S 8 Visun', Ukraine ʃ
82 I 7 Vit, Bulgaria ʃ
76 G 13 Viterbo, Italy
139 W 11 Viti Levu, Fiji ✲
66 K 5 Vitigudino, Spain
58 O 5 Vitória, Brazil
55 M 16 Vitória da Conquista, Brazil
54 I 10 Vitória do Xingu, Brazil
67 Q 2 Vitoria-Gasteiz, Spain
82 F 9 Vitosha, Bulgaria ▲▲
64 L 5 Vitré, France
65 T 4 Vitry-le-François, France
85 M 14 Vitsyebsk, Belarus
85 L 15 Vitsyebskaya Voblasts', Belarus ◘
70 J 10 Vittangi, Sweden
65 U 5 Vittel, France
77 J 23 Vittoria, Italy
66 J 1 Viveiro, Spain
67 T 7 Viver, Spain
133 O 9 Vivo, Republic of South Africa
65 N 9 Vivonne, France
82 N 11 Vize, Turkey
105 H 18 Vizianagaram, India
91 P 10 Vizinga, Russian Federation
86 M 12 Viziru, Romania
81 K 20 Vjosë, Albania ʃ
69 I 19 Vlaams Brabant, Belgium ◘
68 F 13 Vlaardingen, Netherlands
81 N 15 Vladičin Han, Serbia and Montenegro
93 P 14 Vladikavkaz, Russian Federation
92 M 1 Vladimir, Russian Federation
82 G 7 Vladimirovo, Bulgaria
89 V 15 Vladivostok, Russian Federation
68 O 7 Vlagtwedde, Netherlands
80 I 12 Vlasenica, Bosnia and Herzegovina
80 G 11 Vlašić, Bosnia and Herzegovina ▲
79 D 18 Vlašim, Czech Republic
81 N 14 Vlasotince, Serbia and Montenegro
68 H 6 Vlieland, Netherlands ✲
69 D 16 Vlissingen, Netherlands
81 J 20 Vlorë, Albania
79 C 18 Vltava, Czech Republic ʃ
75 R 4 Vöcklabruck, Austria
91 Q 7 Vodnyy, Russian Federation
129 T 12 Vogel Peak, Nigeria ▲
73 F 18 Vogelsberg, Germany ▲▲
133 Y 9 Vohilava, Madgascar
84 D 7 Võhma, Estonia
84 G 7 Võhma, Estonia
131 W 10 Voi, Kenya
86 I 11 Voineasa, Romania
128 H 12 Voinjama, Liberia
65 U 10 Voiron, France
75 V 7 Voitsberg, Austria
80 D 9 Vojnić, Croatia
80 J 9 Vojvodina, Serbia and Montenegro ◘
129 U 12 Voko, Cameroon
29 X 7 Volborg, MT, U.S.A.
46 H 6 Volcán Agua, Guatemala ▲
46 G 6 Volcán Antofalla, Argentina ▲
56 H 4 Volcán Apagado, Chile ▲
47 S 14 Volcán Barú, Panama ▲
56 G 8 Volcán Copiapó, Chile ▲
57 F 18 Volcán Corcovado, Chile ▲
52 B 9 Volcán Cotopaxi, Ecuador ▲
53 A 18 Volcán Darwin, Ecuador ▲
46 I 7 Volcán de Santa Ana, El Salvador ▲
45 W 15 Volcán de Tacaná, Mexico ▲
56 G 14 Volcán Domuyo, Argentina ▲
56 G 2 Volcán Guallatiri, Chile ▲
47 R 12 Volcán Irazu, Costa Rica ▲
53 A 18 Volcán La Cumbre, Ecuador ▲
57 F 16 Volcán Lanín, Argentina ▲
44 H 5 Volcán Las Tres Virgenes, Mexico ▲
56 H 5 Volcán Licancábur, Chile ▲
56 G 6 Volcán Llullaillaco, Chile ▲
47 P 11 Volcán Miravalles, Costa Rica ▲
53 G 19 Volcán Misti, Peru ▲
53 I 23 Volcán Ollagüe, Bolivia ▲
47 Q 12 Volcán Poás, Costa Rica ▲
56 G 12 Volcán San José, Chile ▲
52 B 10 Volcán Sangay, Ecuador ▲
50 G 8 Volcán Sotará, Colombia ▲
53 H 20 Volcán Tacora, Chile/Peru ▲
46 F 5 Volcán Tajumulco, Guatemala ▲
57 G 14 Volcán Tromen, Argentina ▲
57 F 16 Volcán Villarrica, Chile ▲
53 A 18 Volcán Wolf, Ecuador ▲
34 E 9 Volcano, HI, U.S.A.
91 R 8 Vol'dino, Russian Federation
68 I 10 Volendam, Netherlands
88 F 10 Volga, Russian Federation ʃ
93 O 8 VolgaŠDon Canal, Russian Federation ʃ
93 N 9 Volgodonsk, Russian Federation
93 P 8 Volgograd, Russian Federation
93 O 7 Volgogradskaya Oblast', Russian Federation ◘
93 Q 7 Volgogradskoye Vodokhranilishche, Russian Federation ∽
75 T 9 Völkermarkt, Austria
90 G 11 Volkhov, Russian Federation
87 X 7 Volnovakha, Ukraine
89 P 8 Volochanka, Russian Federation
86 L 5 Volochys'k, Ukraine
87 P 5 Volodarka, Ukraine
87 X 8 Volodars'ke, Ukraine
86 J 3 Volodymyr-Volyns'kyy, Ukraine
86 L 2 Volodymyrets', Ukraine
90 K 12 Vologda, Russian Federation
90 K 10 Vologodskaya Oblast', Russian Federation ◘
87 W 5 Volokhiv Yar, Ukraine
92 J 1 Volokolamsk, Russian Federation
92 K 6 Volokonovka, Russian Federation
83 F 17 Volos, Greece
87 Z 5 Voloshino, Ukraine
92 L 8 Voloshino, Russian Federation
92 K 3 Volovo, Russian Federation
93 Q 5 Vol'sk, Russian Federation
129 N 12 Volta, Ghana ◘
129 N 13 Volta, Ghana ʃ
58 M 6 Volta Redonda, Brazil
76 E 11 Volterra, Italy
91 L 7 Volzhsk, Russian Federation
93 P 8 Volzhskiy, Russian Federation
133 X 10 Vondrozo, Madgascar
83 B 18 Vonitsa, Greece
84 I 8 Võnnu, Estonia
68 J 12 Voorhuizen, Netherlands
68 G 12 Voorschoten, Netherlands
70 D 10 Vopnafjörður, Iceland
85 G 17 Voranava, Belarus
75 S 5 Vorchdorf, Austria
68 L 12 Vorden, Netherlands
71 D 26 Vordingborg, Denmark
83 K 18 Voreio Aigaio, Greece ◘
83 G 18 Voreioi Sporades, Greece ✲
83 F 18 Voreios Evvoïkos Kolpos, Greece ≈
143 T 15 Voring Plateau, Arctic Ocean ◇
91 U 2 Vorkuta, Russian Federation
84 E 6 Vormsi, Estonia ✲
92 L 5 Voronezh, Russian Federation
92 L 5 Voronezhskaya Oblast', Russian Federation ◘
87 U 4 Vorskla, Ukraine ʃ
84 G 8 Võrtsjärv, Estonia ∽
84 I 9 Võru, Estonia
103 S 12 Vorukh, Tajikistan
132 L 13 Vosburg, Republic of South Africa
103 R 14 Vose, Tajikistan
65 W 6 Vosges, France ▲▲
92 L 1 Voskresensk, Russian Federation
91 N 14 Voskresenskoye, Russian Federation
71 A 18 Voss, Norway
103 X 5 Vostochnyy Kazakhstan, Kazakhstan ◘
89 N 13 Vostochnyy Sayan, Russian Federation ▲▲
141 R 6 Vostok, Kiribati ✲
145 T 9 Vostok, Antarctica ⁙
91 R 13 Votkinsk, Russian Federation
91 S 13 Votkinskoye Vodokhranilishche, Russian Federation ∽
58 I 5 Votuporanga, Brazil
65 T 3 Vouziers, France
87 W 7 Vovcha, Ukraine ʃ
87 W 3 Vovchans'k, Ukraine
90 G 5 Voynitsa, Russian Federation
91 R 8 Voyvozh, Russian Federation
91 O 6 Vozhgora, Russian Federation
92 O 12 Voznesens'k, Ukraine
87 R 8 Vozsiyats'ke, Ukraine
85 J 20 Vozyera Chyrvonaye, Belarus ∽
87 P 8 Vradiyivka, Ukraine
81 N 15 Vranjska Banja, Serbia and Montenegro
79 M 20 Vranov nad Toplou, Slovakia
82 G 8 Vratsa, Bulgaria ◘
82 G 8 Vratsa, Bulgaria
80 B 7 Vrhnika, Slovenia
69 D 15 Vrouwenpolder, Netherlands
80 M 9 Vršac, Serbia and Montenegro
80 E 10 Vrtoče, Bosnia and Herzegovina
132 M 11 Vryburg, Republic of South Africa
133 P 12 Vryheid, Republic of South Africa
79 H 19 Vsetin, Czech Republic
81 M 15 Vučitrn, Serbia and Montenegro
69 I 15 Vught, Netherlands
87 X 7 Vuhledar, Ukraine
80 I 9 Vukovar, Croatia
91 S 6 Vuktyl', Russian Federation
133 P 11 Vukuzakhe, Republic of South Africa
89 Y 10 Vulkan Ichinskiy, Russian Federation ▲
115 N 22 Vung Tau, Vietnam
139 X 12 Vunisea, Fiji
71 M 18 Vuohijarvi, Finland ∽
70 J 11 Vuollerim, Sweden
70 H 11 Vuolvojaure, Sweden ∽
70 L 9 Vuotso, Finland
93 T 1 Vyatka, Russian Federation ʃ
93 S 1 Vyatskiye Polyany, Russian Federation
92 I 1 Vyaz'ma, Russian Federation
93 N 1 Vyazniki, Russian Federation
90 E 9 Vyborg, Russian Federation
91 N 9 Vychegda, Russian Federation ʃ
84 J 13 Vyerkhnyadzvinsk, Belarus
85 N 20 Vyetka, Belarus
85 K 14 Vyetryna, Belarus
85 H 20 Vyhanashchy, Belarus
93 N 2 Vyksa, Russian Federation
87 O 11 Vylkove, Ukraine
86 H 7 Vylok, Ukraine
90 E 11 Vyritsa, Russian Federation
86 K 4 Vyshnivets', Ukraine
90 I 12 Vyshniy-Volochek, Russian Federation
79 G 19 Vyškov, Czech Republic
85 E 12 Vysokaye, Belarus
87 O 2 Vystupovychi, Ukraine
90 I 10 Vytegra, Russian Federation

W

128 L 11 Wa, Ghana
69 I 14 Waal, Netherlands ʃ
69 I 14 Waalwijk, Netherlands
127 E 21 Waat, Sudan
138 C 4 Wabag, Papua New Guinea
39 I 16 Wabasca, AB, Canada ʃ
39 I 16 Wabasca-Desmarais, AB, Canada
21 J 17 Wabash, IN, U.S.A.
21 H 18 Wabash, IN/IL, U.S.A. ʃ
23 U 8 Wabasha, MN, U.S.A.
19 U 9 Waccasassa Bay, FL, U.S.A. ≈
27 Q 7 Waco, TX, U.S.A.
24 L 2 Waconda Lake, KS, U.S.A. ∽
101 S 13 Wad, Pakistan
127 C 18 Wad Banda, Sudan
127 F 16 Wad Hamid, Sudan
127 F 17 Wad Medani, Sudan
125 U 9 Waddān, Libya
68 H 6 Waddeneilanden, Netherlands ◇
68 H 8 Waddenzee, Netherlands ≈
62 K 14 Wadebridge, U.K.
23 Q 6 Wadena, MN, U.S.A.
74 G 7 Wädenswil, Switzerland
17 Q 10 Wadesboro, NC, U.S.A.
97 X 14 Wādī al Bāṭin, Iraq ʃ
99 T 12 Wādī al Masīlah, Yemen ʃ
96 G 9 Wādī as Sīr, Jordan
97 R 3 Wādī ath Tharthār, Iraq ʃ
126 E 13 Wadi Halfa, Sudan
97 O 7 Wādī Ḩawrān, Iraq ʃ
96 G 12 Wādī Mūsá, Jordan
19 V 4 Wadley, GA, U.S.A.
123 N 23 Wadomari, Japan
111 H 17 Wafangdian, China
68 K 13 Wageningen, Netherlands
40 M 2 Wager Bay, NU, Canada ≈
135 T 12 Wagga Wagga, NSW, Australia
134 G 11 Wagin, WA, Australia
74 G 7 Wägiteler See, Switzerland ∽
31 S 9 Wagon Mound, NM, U.S.A.
78 G 11 Wągrowiec, Poland
101 X 8 Wah, Pakistan
30 H 5 Wah Wah Mountains, UT, U.S.A. ▲▲
117 S 12 Wahai, Indonesia
136 L 10 Waharoa, New Zealand
127 D 20 Wahda, Sudan ◘
34 C 7 Wahiawa, HI, U.S.A.
23 O 6 Wahpeton, ND, U.S.A.
137 H 19 Waiau, New Zealand
137 H 18 Waiau, New Zealand ʃ
75 U 4 Waidhofen an der Ybbs, Austria
117 T 11 Waigeo, Indonesia ✲
136 I 5 Waiharara, New Zealand
136 O 11 Waihau Bay, New Zealand ≈
136 K 8 Waiheke Island, New Zealand ✲
136 L 9 Waihi, New Zealand
136 M 10 Waihirere, New Zealand
137 E 25 Waihola, New Zealand
117 N 15 Waikabubak, Indonesia
137 K 15 Waikanae, New Zealand
137 H 19 Waikari, New Zealand
136 K 11 Waikato, New Zealand ◘
137 F 24 Waikouaiti, New Zealand
34 D 7 Wailuku, HI, U.S.A.
137 G 16 Waimarie, New Zealand
137 G 22 Waimate, New Zealand
34 A 6 Waimea, HI, U.S.A.
34 B 7 Waimea, HI, U.S.A.
34 E 8 Waimea, HI, U.S.A.
63 X 5 Wainfleet All Saints, U.K.
117 O 15 Waingapu, Indonesia
136 L 16 Wainuioru, New Zealand
35 O 3 Wainwright, AK, U.S.A.
39 K 18 Wainwright, AB, Canada
136 M 11 Waiotapu, New Zealand
136 L 13 Waiouru, New Zealand
137 D 25 Waipahi, New Zealand
137 H 19 Waipara, New Zealand
137 M 14 Waipawa, New Zealand
136 J 7 Waipu, New Zealand
137 M 14 Waipukurau, New Zealand
137 I 17 Wairau, New Zealand ʃ
137 I 17 Wairau Valley, New Zealand
136 N 12 Wairoa, New Zealand
136 M 12 Waitahanui, New Zealand
136 L 9 Waitakaruru, New Zealand
136 J 8 Waitakere, New Zealand
137 E 22 Waitaki, New Zealand ʃ
137 F 24 Waitati, New Zealand
136 K 13 Waitotara, New Zealand
136 J 9 Waiuku, New Zealand
123 H 14 Wajima, Japan
130 K 7 Waka, Democratic Republic of Congo
123 G 17 Wakasa-wan, Japan ≈
123 G 19 Wakayama, Japan
24 J 3 WaKeeney, KS, U.S.A.
63 S 3 Wakefield, U.K.
123 F 19 Waki, Japan
122 J 8 Wakinosawa, Japan
122 J 3 Wakkanai, Japan
132 H 4 Waku-Kungo, Angola
138 J 4 Wakunai, Papua New Guinea
110 J 4 Walagan, China
79 F 16 Wałbrzych, Poland
135 V 10 Walcha, NSW, Australia
29 W 13 Walcott, WY, U.S.A.
78 F 10 Wałcz, Poland
31 Q 2 Walden, CO, U.S.A.
73 D 24 Waldkirch, Germany
17 U 4 Waldorf, MD, U.S.A.
32 F 11 Waldport, OR, U.S.A.
25 S 11 Waldron, AR, U.S.A.
73 E 25 Waldshut, Germany
117 P 11 Waleabahi, Indonesia ✲
63 N 8 Wales, U.K. ◘
69 L 25 Walferdange, Luxembourg
135 T 9 Walgett, NSW, Australia
144 K 9 Walgreen Coast, Antarctica ◇
131 P 8 Walikale, Democratic Republic of Congo
23 Q 4 Walker, MN, U.S.A.
33 J 18 Walker Lake, NV, U.S.A. ∽
22 H 9 Wall, SD, U.S.A.
32 K 9 Walla Walla, WA, U.S.A.
17 T 11 Wallace, NC, U.S.A.
28 K 4 Wallace, ID, U.S.A.
39 H 18 Wallace Mountain, AB, Canada ▲
41 B 14 Wallaceburg, ON, Canada
135 P 11 Wallaroo, SA, Australia
73 G 20 Walldürn, Germany
74 H 7 Wallensee, Switzerland ∽
140 I 8 Wallis, Wallis and Futuna Islands ✲
140 H 7 Wallis and Futuna Islands, France ◘
74 D 10 Walliser Alpen, Switzerland ▲▲
20 K 10 Walloon Lake, MI, U.S.A. ∽
25 X 9 Walnut Ridge, AR, U.S.A.
134 G 12 Walpole, WA, Australia
63 R 6 Walsall, U.K.
31 S 7 Walsenburg, CO, U.S.A.
105 H 18 Waltair, India
19 S 5 Walter F. George Reservoir, GA, U.S.A. ∽
17 O 14 Walterboro, SC, U.S.A.
63 W 10 Waltham Abbey, U.K.
63 U 6 Waltham on the Wolds, U.K.
43 U 10 Walton, NS, Canada
63 Z 9 Walton-on-the-Naze, U.K.
132 H 9 Walvis Bay, Namibia ≈
132 H 10 Walvis Bay, Namibia
117 Y 14 Wamal, Indonesia
130 L 8 Wamba, Democratic Republic of Congo
131 P 6 Wamba, Democratic Republic of Congo
47 P 5 Wampusirpi, Honduras
101 V 9 Wana, Pakistan
135 R 9 Wanaaring, NSW, Australia
137 D 22 Wanaka, New Zealand
113 U 9 Wan'an, China
117 W 13 Wanapiri, Indonesia
42 E 8 Wanapitei Lake, ON, Canada ∽
117 W 12 Wandai, Indonesia
143 S 10 Wandel Sea, Arctic Ocean ◒
112 I 11 Wanding, China
115 G 14 Wang Nua, Thailand
115 I 16 Wang Saphung, Thailand
136 K 13 Wanganui, New Zealand ʃ
137 K 14 Wanganui, New Zealand
135 S 12 Wangaratta, VIC, Australia
107 T 9 Wangdue-Phodrang, Bhutan
73 G 25 Wangen, Germany
72 E 9 Wangerooge, Germany ✲
113 S 11 Wanggao, China
117 P 13 Wangiwangi, Indonesia ✲
113 O 11 Wangmo, China
110 M 13 Wangqing, China
39 H 17 Wanham, AB, Canada
131 N 7 Wanie-Rukula, Democratic Republic of Congo
127 L 24 Wanlaweyn, Somalia
113 R 15 Wanning, China
47 P 5 Wanquibila, Honduras
63 S 10 Wantage, U.K.
113 Q 6 Wanxian, China
113 P 5 Wanyuan, China
113 U 8 Wanzai, China
21 L 18 Wapakoneta, OH, U.S.A.
32 I 8 Wapato, WA, U.S.A.
68 L 11 Wapenveld, Netherlands
25 Y 7 Wappapello Lake, MO, U.S.A. ∽
127 D 21 Warab, Sudan
127 D 21 Warab, Sudan ◘
134 K 7 Warakurna Roadhouse, WA, Australia
127 L 21 Warandab, Ethiopia
105 F 18 Warangal, India
63 W 7 Warboys, U.K.
73 F 15 Warburg, Germany
134 K 8 Warburton, WA, Australia
135 P 8 Warburton, SA, Australia ʃ
101 U 7 Wardag, Afghanistan ◘
105 F 16 Wardha, India
97 P 2 Wardīyah, Iraq
69 C 19 Waregem, Belgium
63 Q 13 Wareham, U.K.
69 I 20 Waremme, Belgium
72 L 10 Waren, Germany
73 E 14 Warendorf, Germany
135 V 6 Warginburra Peninsula, QLD, Australia ▶
135 V 9 Warialda, NSW, Australia
78 L 13 Warka, Poland
136 K 7 Warkworth, New Zealand
32 H 10 Warm Springs, OR, U.S.A.
33 L 19 Warm Springs, NV, U.S.A.
117 U 11 Warmandi, Indonesia
132 J 12 Warmbad, Namibia
63 R 11 Warminster, U.K.
134 K 3 Warmun, WA, Australia
72 K 8 Warnemünde, Germany
19 U 4 Warner Robins, GA, U.S.A.
69 B 19 Warneton, Belgium
105 F 16 Warora, India
135 Q 12 Warracknabeal, VIC, Australia
135 S 9 Warrego, QLD, Australia ʃ
14 C 10 Warren, PA, U.S.A.
21 M 15 Warren, MI, U.S.A.
21 O 17 Warren, OH, U.S.A.
23 O 3 Warren, MN, U.S.A.
27 T 9 Warren, TX, U.S.A.
25 T 4 Warrensburg, MO, U.S.A.
17 T 4 Warrenton, VA, U.S.A.
132 M 12 Warrenton, Republic of South Africa
129 Q 14 Warri, Nigeria
19 P 7 Warrington, FL, U.S.A.
63 Q 4 Warrington, U.K.
19 P 2 Warrior, AL, U.S.A.
135 R 13 Warrnambool, VIC, Australia
23 P 2 Warroad, MN, U.S.A.
14 E 9 Warsaw, NY, U.S.A.
17 T 10 Warsaw, NC, U.S.A.
21 J 17 Warsaw, IN, U.S.A.
25 T 5 Warsaw, MO, U.S.A.
78 L 13 Warsaw, Poland ♜
127 M 24 Warshiikh, Somalia
79 I 14 Warta, Poland ʃ
105 F 16 Warud, India
15 N 11 Warwick, RI, U.S.A.
63 S 8 Warwick, U.K.
135 V 9 Warwick, QLD, Australia
112 K 8 Warzhong, China
30 J 5 Wasatch Range, UT, U.S.A. ▲▲
32 I 9 Wasco, OR, U.S.A.
101 Q 13 Washap, Pakistan
20 E 8 Washburn, WI, U.S.A.
105 E 16 Washim, India
14 A 13 Washington, PA, U.S.A.
17 U 9 Washington, NC, U.S.A.
17 S 4 Washington, VA, U.S.A.
21 F 18 Washington, IL, U.S.A.
21 M 19 Washington, OH, U.S.A.
23 V 13 Washington, IA, U.S.A.
32 H 7 Washington, U.S.A., U.S.A. ◘
17 U 3 Washington, D.C., DC, U.S.A. ♜
20 I 10 Washington Island, WI, U.S.A. ✲
41 P 10 Waskaganish, QC, Canada
39 L 17 Waskesiu Lake, SK, Canada
47 Q 6 Waspán, Nicaragua
69 H 14 Waspik, Netherlands
128 F 9 Wassadou, Senegal
73 K 24 Wasserburg, Germany
73 G 18 Wasserkuppe, Germany ▲
138 E 4 Wasu, Papua New Guinea
138 B 6 Wasua, Papua New Guinea
117 O 13 Watampone, Indonesia
105 L 18 Wataru Channel, Maldives ≈
18 M 2 Water Valley, MS, U.S.A.
14 L 11 Waterbury, CT, U.S.A.
17 O 11 Wateree Lake, SC, U.S.A. ∽
61 D 20 Waterford, Republic of Ireland
62 J 14 Watergate Bay, U.K. ≈
23 U 11 Waterloo, IA, U.S.A.
42 D 13 Waterloo, ON, Canada
69 G 20 Waterloo, Belgium
63 U 13 Waterlooville, U.K.
20 F 9 Watersmeet, MI, U.S.A.
14 H 6 Watertown, NY, U.S.A.
23 N 8 Watertown, SD, U.S.A.
13 Z 5 Waterville, ME, U.S.A.
25 N 2 Waterville, KS, U.S.A.
32 I 7 Waterville, WA, U.S.A.
61 A 21 Waterville, Republic of Ireland
63 V 10 Watford, U.K.
22 G 3 Watford City, ND, U.S.A.
14 G 9 Watkins Glen, NY, U.S.A.
24 L 9 Watonga, OK, U.S.A.
131 O 8 Watsa, Democratic Republic of Congo
130 K 8 Watsi Kengo, Democratic Republic of Congo
39 M 18 Watson, SK, Canada
38 D 14 Watson Lake, YT, Canada
33 G 20 Watsonville, CA, U.S.A.
16 I 9 Watts Bar Lake, TN, U.S.A. ∽
74 H 7 Wattwil, Switzerland
127 C 21 Wau, Sudan
138 E 5 Wau, Papua New Guinea
135 N 5 Wauchope, NT, Australia
19 W 11 Wauchula, FL, U.S.A.
21 H 15 Waukegan, IL, U.S.A.
21 G 14 Waukesha, WI, U.S.A.
20 F 12 Waupaca, WI, U.S.A.
24 M 12 Waurika, OK, U.S.A.
20 F 11 Wausau, WI, U.S.A.
20 F 12 Wautoma, WI, U.S.A.
134 M 3 Wave Hill, NT, Australia
63 Z 7 Waveney, U.K. ʃ
14 G 10 Waverly, PA, U.S.A.
16 D 8 Waverly, TN, U.S.A.
23 P 14 Waverly, NE, U.S.A.
69 G 20 Wavre, Belgium
125 U 11 Wāw al Kabīr, Libya
42 A 6 Wawa, ON, Canada
47 Q 6 Wawa, Nicaragua ʃ
129 P 11 Wawa, Nigeria
138 B 5 Wawoi, Papua New Guinea ʃ
27 Q 6 Waxahachie, TX, U.S.A.
117 S 9 Wayabula, Indonesia
117 T 10 Wayag, Indonesia ✲
19 V 6 Waycross, GA, U.S.A.
16 D 10 Waynesboro, TN, U.S.A.
17 R 5 Waynesboro, VA, U.S.A.
19 N 6 Waynesboro, MS, U.S.A.
19 V 3 Waynesboro, GA, U.S.A.
16 L 10 Waynesville, NC, U.S.A.
24 L 8 Waynoka, OK, U.S.A.
129 V 10 Waza, Cameroon
101 T 8 Wazi Khwa, Afghanistan
101 Y 8 Wazirabad, Pakistan
78 H 10 Wda, Poland ʃ
139 Q 13 Wé, New Caledonia
24 K 10 Weatherford, OK, U.S.A.
33 F 15 Weaverville, CA, U.S.A.
40 M 9 Webequie, ON, Canada
14 F 8 Webster, NY, U.S.A.
138 G 7 Wedau, Papua New Guinea
57 K 24 Weddell Island, Falkland Islands ✲
144 K 5 Weddell Sea, Antarctica ◒
135 U 10 Wee Waa, NSW, Australia
33 G 15 Weed, CA, U.S.A.
14 D 11 Weedville, PA, U.S.A.
69 I 16 Weelde, Belgium
69 K 17 Weert, Netherlands
68 H 11 Weesp, Netherlands
78 L 8 Węgorzewo, Poland
78 M 12 Węgrów, Poland
116 B 8 Weh, Indonesia ✲
113 N 3 Wei, China ʃ
111 E 15 Weichang, China
73 K 20 Weiden, Germany
111 G 20 Weifang, China
111 I 19 Weihai, China
73 J 17 Weimar, Germany
113 Q 3 Weinan, China
113 N 9 Weining, China
135 R 1 Weipa, QLD, Australia
17 O 1 Weirton, WV, U.S.A.
28 J 9 Weiser, ID, U.S.A.
112 K 10 Weishan, China
113 V 3 Weishan Hu, China ∽
113 U 3 Weishi, China
19 R 2 Weiss Lake, AL, U.S.A. ∽
73 I 22 Weissenburg in Bayern, Germany
73 N 15 Weisswasser, Germany
69 L 23 Weiswampach, Luxembourg
75 U 2 Weitra, Austria
112 J 9 Weixi, China
113 N 8 Weixin, China
75 W 7 Weiz, Austria
78 H 8 Wejherowo, Poland
137 G 15 Wekakura Point, New Zealand ▶
17 N 6 Welch, WV, U.S.A.
127 I 19 Weldiya, Ethiopia
33 J 22 Weldon, CA, U.S.A.
127 H 21 Welk'īt'ē, Ethiopia
133 N 12 Welkom, Republic of South Africa
42 F 14 Welland Canal, ON, Canada ≈
105 G 25 Wellawaya, Sri Lanka
135 Q 3 Wellesley Islands, QLD, Australia ✲
69 I 23 Wellin, Belgium
63 V 8 Wellingborough, U.K.
63 Q 6 Wellington, U.K.
135 U 11 Wellington, NSW, Australia
137 L 16 Wellington, New Zealand ♜
137 L 16 Wellington, New Zealand ◘
33 M 15 Wells, NV, U.S.A.
63 P 12 Wells, U.K.
63 Y 5 Wells-next-the-Sea, U.K.
136 K 7 Wellsford, New Zealand
20 J 12 Wellston, MI, U.S.A.
75 S 4 Wels, Austria
63 O 6 Welshpool, U.K.
41 P 9 Wemindji, QC, Canada
32 J 7 Wenatchee, WA, U.S.A.
113 R 15 Wenchang, China
113 Y 8 Wencheng, China
128 L 12 Wenchi, Ghana
112 M 6 Wenchuan, China
30 H 12 Wenden, AZ, U.S.A.
73 E 17 Wenden, Germany
111 H 19 Wendeng, China
33 N 16 Wendover, NV, U.S.A.
63 U 10 Wendover, U.K.
74 E 9 Wengen, Switzerland
113 Z 8 Wenling, China
141 O 15 Weno, Federated States of Micronesia
21 F 17 Wenona, IL, U.S.A.
108 J 4 Wenquan, China
108 L 9 Wenquan, China
112 M 12 Wenshan, China
135 R 11 Wentworth, NSW, Australia
25 X 4 Wentzville, MO, U.S.A.
113 S 3 Wenxi, China
113 N 4 Wenxian, China

ountry ◘ Internal administrative region: State/Province/Territory/Dependent territory ♜ Capital city ▲▲ Mountain range/Undersea ridge ▲ Mountain peak/Volcano/Seamount ◇ Geographic feature ▶ Headland/Point/Cape/Peninsula ☗ Desert ✲ Island/Island group ⁙ Antarctic base ◎ Ocean ◒ Sea ≈ Bay/Gulf/Channel/Strait ∽ Lake ▚ Salt pan/Dry/Intermittent lake ʃ River

113 Y 8 **Wenzhou**, China
69 K 21 **Werbomont**, Belgium
132 L 10 **Werda**, Botswana
127 L 21 **Werdër**, Ethiopia
75 R 6 **Werfen**, Austria
73 E 15 **Werl**, Germany
73 K 21 **Wernberg-Köblitz**, Germany
73 I 15 **Wernigerode**, Germany
127 H 19 **Werota**, Ethiopia
73 H 16 **Werra**, Germany ∽
73 G 20 **Wertheim**, Germany
68 I 9 **Wervershoof**, Netherlands
73 B 15 **Wesel**, Germany
73 G 15 **Weser**, Germany ∽
15 S 4 **Wesley**, ME, U.S.A.
135 O 1 **Wessel Islands**, NT, Australia ♣
27 Q 7 **West**, TX, U.S.A.
144 L 7 **West Antarctica**, Antarctica ◇
96 G 9 **West Bank**, Israel ◇
18 M 9 **West Bay**, LA, U.S.A. ≈
19 Q 7 **West Bay**, FL, U.S.A.
20 G 13 **West Bend**, WI, U.S.A.
107 R 14 **West Bengal**, India ◘
63 T 5 **West Bridgford**, U.K.
63 R 7 **West Bromwich**, U.K.
29 Q 2 **West Butte**, MT, U.S.A. ▲
137 A 25 **West Cape**, New Zealand ▶
137 E 19 **West Coast**, New Zealand ◘
27 S 11 **West Columbia**, TX, U.S.A.
57 J 23 **West Falkland**, Falkland Islands ♣
140 M 15 **West Fayu**, Federated States of Micronesia ♣
29 N 2 **West Glacier**, MT, U.S.A.
15 S 4 **West Grand Lake**, ME, U.S.A. ◣
145 X 6 **West Ice Shelf**, Antarctica ◇
21 I 18 **West Lafayette**, IN, U.S.A.
62 L 14 **West Looe**, U.K.
42 C 14 **West Lorne**, ON, Canada
25 Y 10 **West Memphis**, AR, U.S.A.
138 F 5 **West New Britain**, Papua New Guinea ◘
133 P 8 **West Nicholson**, Zimbabwe
19 Z 12 **West Palm Beach**, FL, U.S.A.
25 V 8 **West Plains**, MO, U.S.A.
17 U 6 **West Point**, VA, U.S.A.
19 R 3 **West Point Lake**, AL, U.S.A. ◣
88 L 9 **West Siberian Plain**, Russian Federation ◇
68 I 6 **West-Terschelling**, Netherlands
23 U 10 **West Union**, IA, U.S.A.
17 O 3 **West Virginia**, U.S.A. ◘
69 A 18 **West-Vlaanderen**, Belgium ◘
135 T 11 **West Wyalong**, NSW, Australia
29 Q 9 **West Yellowstone**, MT, U.S.A.
20 D 13 **Westby**, WI, U.S.A.
31 R 6 **Westcliffe**, CO, U.S.A.
68 M 8 **Westerbork**, Netherlands
105 F 25 **Western**, Sri Lanka ◘
107 O 9 **Western**, Nepal ◘
128 L 13 **Western**, Ghana ◘
131 T 7 **Western**, Kenya ◘
132 L 6 **Western**, Zambia ◘
138 B 5 **Western**, Papua New Guinea ◘
138 J 6 **Western**, Solomon Islands ◘
128 F 12 **Western Area**, Sierra Leone ◘
134 J 7 **Western Australia**, Australia ◘
127 C 21 **Western Bahr el Ghazal**, Sudan ◘
132 L 14 **Western Cape**, Republic of South Africa ◘
127 A 17 **Western Darfur**, Sudan ◘
126 C 9 **Western Desert**, Egypt ◇
84 F 11 **Western Dvina**, Belarus/Latvia ∽
127 D 22 **Western Equatoria**, Sudan ◘
105 C 17 **Western Ghats**, India ▲▲
138 C 4 **Western Highlands**, Papua New Guinea ◘
127 D 19 **Western Kordofan**, Sudan ◘
124 C 12 **Western Sahara**, Africa □
69 D 16 **Westerschelde**, Netherlands ≈
14 B 9 **Westfield**, NY, U.S.A.
68 K 5 **Westgat**, Netherlands ≈
22 J 2 **Westhope**, ND, U.S.A.
69 G 16 **Westmalle**, Belgium
17 T 2 **Westminster**, MD, U.S.A.
17 O 3 **Weston**, WV, U.S.A.
63 O 11 **Weston-super-Mare**, U.K.
32 E 7 **Westport**, WA, U.S.A.
61 B 17 **Westport**, Republic of Ireland
137 G 17 **Westport**, New Zealand
40 H 8 **Westray**, MB, Canada
60 I 6 **Westray**, U.K. ♣
42 D 7 **Westree**, ON, Canada
21 I 16 **Westville**, IN, U.S.A.
62 L 12 **Westward Ho!**, U.K.
117 R 14 **Wetar**, Indonesia ♣
39 J 19 **Wetaskiwin**, AB, Canada
131 X 11 **Wete**, Tanzania
63 S 2 **Wetherby**, U.K.
73 E 18 **Wetzlar**, Germany
69 C 19 **Wevelgem**, Belgium
34 M 3 **Wevok**, AK, U.S.A.
19 S 8 **Wewahitchka**, FL, U.S.A.
138 C 3 **Wewak**, Papua New Guinea
25 O 11 **Wewoka**, OK, U.S.A.
61 E 20 **Wexford**, Republic of Ireland
39 N 19 **Weyburn**, SK, Canada
75 U 5 **Weyer Markt**, Austria
73 D 17 **Weyerbusch**, Germany
15 O 10 **Weymouth**, MA, U.S.A.
43 T 11 **Weymouth**, NS, Canada
63 Q 14 **Weymouth**, U.K.
63 Q 14 **Weymouth Bay**, U.K. ≈
38 G 12 **Wha Ti**, NT, Canada
136 M 11 **Whakamaru**, New Zealand
136 J 6 **Whakapara**, New Zealand
137 M 15 **Whakataki**, New Zealand
136 N 10 **Whakatane**, New Zealand
136 N 13 **Whakatu**, New Zealand
40 L 4 **Whale Cove**, NU, Canada
60 K 4 **Whalsay**, U.K. ♣
136 M 9 **Whangamata**, New Zealand
136 K 12 **Whangamomona**, New Zealand
137 H 15 **Whanganui Inlet**, New Zealand ≈
136 O 10 **Whangaparaoa**, New Zealand
136 O 11 **Whangara**, New Zealand
136 J 6 **Whangarei**, New Zealand
63 U 1 **Wharram le Street**, U.K.
26 M 2 **Wheeler**, TX, U.S.A.
19 P 1 **Wheeler Lake**, AL, U.S.A. ◣
31 R 8 **Wheeler Peak**, NM, U.S.A. ▲
33 N 18 **Wheeler Peak**, NV, U.S.A. ▲
17 O 1 **Wheeling**, WV, U.S.A.
21 G 15 **Wheeling**, IL, U.S.A.
136 L 8 **Whenuakite**, New Zealand
63 Q 1 **Whernside**, U.K. ▲
63 N 13 **Whiddon Down**, U.K.
136 I 6 **Whirinaki**, New Zealand
39 G 21 **Whistler**, BC, Canada
61 L 16 **Whitby**, U.K.
63 P 5 **Whitchurch**, U.K.
63 T 12 **Whitchurch**, U.K.
22 H 10 **White**, SD, U.S.A. ∽
41 X 10 **White Bay**, NL, Canada ≈
22 H 6 **White Butte**, ND, U.S.A. ▲
15 Q 3 **White Cap Mountain**, ME, U.S.A. ▲
32 G 13 **White City**, OR, U.S.A.
135 R 10 **White Cliffs**, NSW, Australia
43 X 8 **White Hill**, NS, Canada ▲
136 N 9 **White Island**, New Zealand ♣
18 I 8 **White Lake**, LA, U.S.A. ◣
33 K 20 **White Mountain**, CA, U.S.A. ▲
15 N 6 **White Mountains**, NH, U.S.A. ▲▲
127 F 18 **White Nile**, Sudan ◘
127 D 21 **White Nile**, Sudan ∽
32 I 9 **White Salmon**, OR, U.S.A.
90 I 5 **White Sea**, Russian Federation ◒
143 W 13 **White Sea**, Arctic Ocean ◒
17 P 5 **White Sulphur Springs**, WV, U.S.A.
29 R 6 **White Sulphur Springs**, MT, U.S.A.
128 M 10 **White Volta**, Ghana ∽
39 J 18 **Whitecourt**, AB, Canada
14 K 6 **Whiteface Mountain**, NY, U.S.A. ▲
28 M 2 **Whitefish**, MT, U.S.A.
20 K 8 **Whitefish Bay**, MI, U.S.A. ≈
20 J 8 **Whitefish Point**, MI, U.S.A.
14 K 7 **Whitehall**, NY, U.S.A.
20 D 12 **Whitehall**, WI, U.S.A.
61 H 15 **Whitehaven**, U.K.
39 B 14 **Whitehorse**, YT, Canada
30 L 12 **Whiteriver**, AZ, U.S.A.
16 A 10 **Whiteville**, TN, U.S.A.
17 S 11 **Whiteville**, NC, U.S.A.
31 N 13 **Whitewater Baldy**, NM, U.S.A. ▲
61 H 15 **Whithorn**, U.K.
17 N 11 **Whitmire**, SC, U.S.A.
42 G 10 **Whitney**, ON, Canada
62 L 15 **Whitsand Bay**, U.K. ≈
135 U 5 **Whitsunday Group**, QLD, Australia ♣
20 L 12 **Whittemore**, MI, U.S.A.
35 R 9 **Whittier**, AK, U.S.A.
63 V 7 **Whittlesey**, U.K.
38 K 12 **Wholdaia Lake**, NT, Canada ◣
135 P 11 **Whyalla**, SA, Australia
115 G 14 **Wiang Pa Pao**, Thailand
114 G 13 **Wiang Phran**, Thailand
42 D 11 **Wiarton**, ON, Canada
29 Z 5 **Wibaux**, MT, U.S.A.
25 N 6 **Wichita**, KS, U.S.A.
27 N 4 **Wichita**, TX, U.S.A. ∽
27 O 4 **Wichita Falls**, TX, U.S.A.
24 L 11 **Wichita Mountains**, OK, U.S.A. ▲▲
60 I 8 **Wick**, U.K.
30 I 12 **Wickenburg**, AZ, U.S.A.
63 Z 8 **Wickham Market**, U.K.
16 B 7 **Wickliffe**, KY, U.S.A.
61 F 19 **Wicklow Head**, Republic of Ireland ▶
63 P 4 **Widnes**, U.K.
73 E 15 **Wiedenbrück**, Germany
73 D 17 **Wiehl**, Germany
72 L 7 **Wiek**, Germany
78 L 10 **Wielbark**, Poland
79 I 15 **Wieluń**, Poland
75 X 5 **Wiener Neustadt**, Austria
79 M 14 **Wieprz**, Poland ∽
73 E 19 **Wiesbaden**, Germany
73 C 18 **Wiesemscheid**, Germany
73 F 21 **Wiesloch**, Germany
63 P 3 **Wigan**, U.K.
31 S 3 **Wiggins**, CO, U.S.A.
63 T 7 **Wigston**, U.K.
69 K 14 **Wijchen**, Netherlands
68 J 13 **Wijk bij Duurstede**, Netherlands
127 I 17 **Wik'ro**, Ethiopia
74 H 6 **Wil**, Switzerland
32 J 7 **Wilbur**, WA, U.S.A.
135 R 10 **Wilcannia**, NSW, Australia
72 E 12 **Wildeshausen**, Germany
74 D 9 **Wildhorn**, Switzerland ▲
75 W 8 **Wildon**, Austria
74 L 8 **Wildspitze**, Austria ▲
39 I 18 **Wildwood**, AB, Canada
51 V 7 **Wilhelmina Gebergte**, Suriname ▲▲
72 E 10 **Wilhelmshaven**, Germany
14 H 11 **Wilkes Barre**, PA, U.S.A.
145 W 13 **Wilkes Coast**, Antarctica ◇
145 V 12 **Wilkes Land**, Antarctica ◇
17 O 8 **Wilkesboro**, NC, U.S.A.
32 F 11 **Willamette**, OR, U.S.A. ∽
32 E 8 **Willapa Bay**, WA, U.S.A. ≈
21 M 17 **Willard**, OH, U.S.A.
31 Q 11 **Willard**, NM, U.S.A.
30 M 14 **Willcox**, AZ, U.S.A.
69 F 18 **Willebroek**, Belgium
49 S 13 **Willemstad**, Netherlands Antilles ♜
63 P 8 **Willersley**, U.K.
135 O 9 **William Creek**, SA, Australia
30 J 10 **Williams**, AZ, U.S.A.
33 G 18 **Williams**, CA, U.S.A.
134 G 11 **Williams**, WA, Australia
39 F 20 **Williams Lake**, BC, Canada
16 K 7 **Williamsburg**, KY, U.S.A.
17 U 6 **Williamsburg**, VA, U.S.A.
16 L 6 **Williamson**, KY, U.S.A.
14 F 11 **Williamsport**, PA, U.S.A.
17 U 9 **Williamston**, NC, U.S.A.
19 V 8 **Williston**, FL, U.S.A.
22 G 3 **Williston**, ND, U.S.A.
132 K 14 **Williston**, Republic of South Africa
39 F 17 **Williston Lake**, BC, Canada ◣
63 O 12 **Williton**, U.K.
33 F 17 **Willits**, CA, U.S.A.
23 Q 8 **Willmar**, MN, U.S.A.
33 F 15 **Willow Creek**, CA, U.S.A.
14 E 13 **Willow Hill**, PA, U.S.A.
25 V 7 **Willow Springs**, MO, U.S.A.
132 M 15 **Willowmore**, Republic of South Africa
33 G 17 **Willows**, CA, U.S.A.
17 W 1 **Wilmington**, DE, U.S.A.
17 T 12 **Wilmington**, NC, U.S.A.
21 G 17 **Wilmington**, IL, U.S.A.
21 L 19 **Wilmington**, OH, U.S.A.
21 O 17 **Wilmott**, OH, U.S.A.
63 R 4 **Wilmslow**, U.K.
17 T 9 **Wilson**, NC, U.S.A.
135 S 14 **Wilsons Promontory**, VIC, Australia ▶
15 P 5 **Wilton**, ME, U.S.A.
22 J 5 **Wilton**, ND, U.S.A.
63 R 12 **Wilton**, U.K.
69 K 24 **Wiltz**, Luxembourg
134 H 8 **Wiluna**, WA, Australia
137 M 15 **Wimbledon**, New Zealand
63 R 13 **Wimborne Minster**, U.K.
21 I 17 **Winamac**, IN, U.S.A.
133 N 12 **Winburg**, Republic of South Africa
63 Q 12 **Wincanton**, U.K.
63 Y 12 **Winchelsea**, U.K.
16 J 5 **Winchester**, KY, U.S.A.
16 G 10 **Winchester**, TN, U.S.A.
17 S 3 **Winchester**, VA, U.S.A.
28 K 6 **Winchester**, ID, U.S.A.
63 S 12 **Winchester**, U.K.
29 R 11 **Wind River Range**, WY, U.S.A. ▲▲
19 T 2 **Winder**, GA, U.S.A.
63 P 1 **Windermere**, U.K.
132 I 9 **Windhoek**, Namibia ♜
40 K 9 **Windigo Lake**, ON, Canada ◣
75 T 5 **Windischgarsten**, Austria
23 Q 10 **Windom**, MN, U.S.A.
135 R 7 **Windorah**, QLD, Australia
14 L 10 **Windsor**, CT, U.S.A.
17 U 8 **Windsor**, NC, U.S.A.
42 B 14 **Windsor**, ON, Canada
43 U 10 **Windsor**, NS, Canada
63 U 11 **Windsor**, U.K.
49 Z 9 **Windward Islands**, Caribbean ♣
49 N 7 **Windward Passage**, Cuba ≈
25 O 7 **Winfield**, KS, U.S.A.
42 C 12 **Wingham**, ON, Canada
29 S 4 **Winifred**, MT, U.S.A.
40 M 9 **Winisk**, ON, Canada ∽
41 N 8 **Winisk**, ON, Canada
115 F 17 **Winkana**, Myanmar
75 Q 8 **Winklern**, Austria
128 M 14 **Winneba**, Ghana
33 K 15 **Winnemucca**, NV, U.S.A.
33 J 16 **Winnemucca Lake**, NV, U.S.A. ◣
22 K 10 **Winner**, SD, U.S.A.
29 T 5 **Winnett**, MT, U.S.A.
42 G 8 **Winneway**, QC, Canada
18 I 5 **Winnfield**, LA, U.S.A.
27 U 10 **Winnie**, TX, U.S.A.
40 J 10 **Winnipeg**, MB, Canada
18 J 5 **Winnsboro**, LA, U.S.A.
13 S 12 **Winona**, MS, U.S.A.
23 U 9 **Winona**, MN, U.S.A.
68 O 7 **Winschoten**, Netherlands
72 H 11 **Winsen**, Germany
15 Q 5 **Winslow**, ME, U.S.A.
30 K 10 **Winslow**, AZ, U.S.A.
14 K 10 **Winsted**, CT, U.S.A.
17 P 8 **Winston-Salem**, NC, U.S.A.
19 W 9 **Winter Park**, FL, U.S.A.
23 S 13 **Winterset**, IA, U.S.A.
68 N 13 **Winterswijk**, Netherlands
74 G 6 **Winterthur**, Switzerland
17 U 8 **Winton**, NC, U.S.A.
135 R 6 **Winton**, QLD, Australia
137 C 25 **Winton**, New Zealand
63 W 6 **Wisbech**, U.K.
15 Q 6 **Wiscasset**, ME, U.S.A.
20 D 12 **Wisconsin**, U.S.A. ◘
20 E 12 **Wisconsin Rapids**, WI, U.S.A.
29 N 7 **Wisdom**, MT, U.S.A.
16 L 7 **Wise**, VA, U.S.A.
35 Q 5 **Wiseman**, AK, U.S.A.
22 L 6 **Wishek**, ND, U.S.A.
79 I 18 **Wisła**, Poland
72 J 9 **Wismar**, Germany
18 K 5 **Wisner**, LA, U.S.A.
65 X 4 **Wissembourg**, France
78 O 13 **Wisznice**, Poland
63 V 5 **Witham**, U.K. ∽
63 N 13 **Witheridge**, U.K.
63 W 2 **Withernsea**, U.K.
63 S 9 **Witney**, U.K.
20 F 11 **Wittenberg**, WI, U.S.A.
72 J 12 **Wittenberge**, Germany
72 I 10 **Wittenburg**, Germany
134 G 6 **Wittenoom**, WA, Australia
73 C 19 **Wittlich**, Germany
72 K 11 **Wittstock**, Germany
138 F 4 **Witu Islands**, Papua New Guinea ♣
132 J 9 **Witvlei**, Namibia
73 G 16 **Witzenhausen**, Germany
78 J 11 **Wkra**, Poland ∽
78 H 7 **Władysławowo**, Poland
78 I 12 **Włocławek**, Poland
79 O 14 **Włodawa**, Poland
79 J 15 **Włoszczowa**, Poland
135 T 12 **Wodonga**, VIC, Australia
79 K 16 **Wodzisław**, Poland
79 I 17 **Wodzisław Śląski**, Poland
68 H 12 **Woerden**, Netherlands
74 F 6 **Wohlen**, Switzerland
145 R 2 **Wohlthat Mountains**, Antarctica ▲▲
117 V 13 **Wokam**, Indonesia ♣
110 N 10 **Woken**, China
63 V 11 **Woking**, U.K.
63 U 11 **Wokingham**, U.K.
72 M 10 **Woldegk**, Germany
140 L 15 **Woleai**, Federated States of Micronesia ♣
130 F 6 **Woleu-Ntem**, Gabon ◘
29 P 5 **Wolf Creek**, MT, U.S.A.
35 P 6 **Wolf Mountain**, AK, U.S.A. ▲
29 X 3 **Wolf Point**, MT, U.S.A.
75 U 8 **Wolfsberg**, Austria
72 I 13 **Wolfsburg**, Germany
43 U 10 **Wolfville**, NS, Canada
72 M 9 **Wolgast**, Germany
74 F 7 **Wolhusen**, Switzerland
78 D 9 **Wolin**, Poland
39 L 14 **Wollaston Lake**, SK, Canada ◣
38 H 7 **Wollaston Peninsula**, NU, Canada ▶
135 P 3 **Wollogorang Roadhouse**, NT, Australia
135 U 12 **Wollongong**, NSW, Australia
79 F 14 **Wołów**, Poland
22 M 9 **Wolsey**, SD, U.S.A.
78 F 13 **Wolsztyn**, Poland
68 K 8 **Wolvega**, Netherlands
63 R 7 **Wolverhampton**, U.K.
134 G 10 **Wongan Hills**, WA, Australia
111 M 19 **Wonju**, South Korea
39 G 16 **Wonowon**, BC, Canada
111 L 17 **Wŏnsan**, North Korea
135 S 14 **Wonthaggi**, VIC, Australia
19 N 1 **Woodall Mountain**, MS, U.S.A. ▲
14 I 15 **Woodbine**, NJ, U.S.A.
19 V 6 **Woodbine**, GA, U.S.A.
17 T 4 **Woodbridge**, VA, U.S.A.
63 Z 8 **Woodbridge**, U.K.
32 G 10 **Woodburn**, OR, U.S.A.
137 H 20 **Woodend**, New Zealand
15 S 4 **Woodland**, ME, U.S.A.
32 G 9 **Woodland**, WA, U.S.A.
33 G 18 **Woodland**, CA, U.S.A.
138 H 6 **Woodlark Island**, Papua New Guinea ♣
20 E 9 **Woodruff**, WI, U.S.A.
21 O 19 **Woodsfield**, OH, U.S.A.
17 S 3 **Woodstock**, VA, U.S.A.
21 F 15 **Woodstock**, IL, U.S.A.
42 D 13 **Woodstock**, ON, Canada
43 R 9 **Woodstock**, NB, Canada
63 S 9 **Woodstock**, U.K.
137 H 16 **Woodstock**, New Zealand
18 K 6 **Woodville**, MS, U.S.A.
27 U 8 **Woodville**, TX, U.S.A.
137 L 14 **Woodville**, New Zealand
24 K 8 **Woodward**, OK, U.S.A.
117 W 11 **Woöi**, Indonesia
135 P 10 **Woomera**, SA, Australia
15 N 10 **Woonsocket**, RI, U.S.A.
134 F 8 **Wooramel Roadhouse**, WA, Australia
21 N 17 **Wooster**, OH, U.S.A.
127 L 19 **Woqooyi Galbeed**, Somalia ◘
15 N 10 **Worcester**, MA, U.S.A.
63 R 8 **Worcester**, U.K.
132 K 15 **Worcester**, Republic of South Africa
75 O 6 **Wörgl**, Austria
117 V 14 **Workai**, Indonesia ♣
61 H 15 **Workington**, U.K.
63 T 4 **Worksop**, U.K.
68 J 8 **Workum**, Netherlands
29 U 10 **Worland**, WY, U.S.A.
73 E 20 **Worms**, Germany
62 L 10 **Worms Head**, U.K. ▶
63 V 13 **Worthing**, U.K.
23 Q 10 **Worthington**, MN, U.S.A.
141 W 2 **Wotho**, Marshall Islands ♣
141 Y 2 **Wotje**, Marshall Islands ♣
117 O 12 **Wotu**, Indonesia
117 P 13 **Wowoni**, Indonesia ♣
63 V 4 **Wragby**, U.K.
89 Y 5 **Wrangel Island**, Russian Federation ♣
143 T 5 **Wrangel Sea**, Arctic Ocean ◒
35 Y 11 **Wrangell**, AK, U.S.A.
35 S 8 **Wrangell Mountains**, AK, U.S.A. ▲▲
63 W 5 **Wrangle**, U.K.
31 U 3 **Wray**, CO, U.S.A.
132 I 13 **Wreck Point**, Republic of South Africa ▶
19 V 3 **Wrens**, GA, U.S.A.
63 P 5 **Wrexham**, U.K.
29 X 10 **Wright**, WY, U.S.A.
121 L 15 **Wright**, Philippines
144 K 10 **Wright Island**, Antarctica ♣
27 T 5 **Wright Patman Lake**, TX, U.S.A. ◣
105 N 21 **Wrightmyo**, India
38 E 12 **Wrigley**, NT, Canada
79 G 15 **Wrocław**, Poland
78 F 12 **Wronki**, Poland
78 H 12 **Września**, Poland
78 F 13 **Wschowa**, Poland
113 P 7 **Wu**, China ∽
113 T 2 **Wu'an**, China
134 G 10 **Wubin**, WA, Australia
110 G 10 **Wuchagou**, China
110 L 12 **Wuchang**, China
111 A 15 **Wuchuan**, China
113 R 14 **Wuchuan**, China
111 F 14 **Wudan**, China
99 R 11 **Wuday'ah**, Saudi Arabia
111 E 19 **Wudi**, China
129 S 10 **Wudil**, Nigeria
112 L 10 **Wuding**, China
113 N 4 **Wudu**, China
113 R 7 **Wufeng**, China
113 R 9 **Wugang**, China
109 R 7 **Wuhai**, China
113 U 6 **Wuhan**, China
113 W 4 **Wuhe**, China
113 X 6 **Wuhu**, China
113 V 11 **Wuhua**, China
129 S 12 **Wukari**, Nigeria
111 H 20 **Wuleidao Wan**, China ≈
112 K 11 **Wuliang Shan**, China ▲▲
117 T 14 **Wuliaru**, Indonesia ♣
75 T 2 **Wullowitz**, Austria
129 S 13 **Wum**, Cameroon
112 M 10 **Wumeng Shan**, China ▲▲
113 P 12 **Wuming**, China
127 C 20 **Wun Rog**, Sudan
113 V 10 **Wuping**, China
73 C 16 **Wuppertal**, Germany
73 H 20 **Würzburg**, Germany
73 L 16 **Wurzen**, Germany
113 R 6 **Wushan**, China
113 T 11 **Wushi**, China
111 B 17 **Wutai Shan**, China ▲
69 G 16 **Wuustwezel**, Belgium
138 B 2 **Wuvulu Island**, Papua New Guinea ♣
113 W 6 **Wuwei**, China
113 Y 5 **Wuxi**, China
113 Q 6 **Wuxi**, China
113 P 13 **Wuxu**, China
113 R 12 **Wuxuan**, China
113 V 10 **Wuyi Shan**, China ▲▲
110 M 8 **Wuyiling**, China
113 X 8 **Wuyishan**, China
113 W 7 **Wuyuan**, China
111 A 17 **Wuzhai**, China
109 Q 7 **Wuzhong**, China
113 S 12 **Wuzhou**, China
135 T 8 **Wyandra**, QLD, Australia
63 P 8 **Wye**, U.K. ∽
63 Y 12 **Wye**, U.K.
134 K 3 **Wyndham**, WA, Australia
25 X 10 **Wynne**, AR, U.S.A.
29 V 8 **Wyola**, MT, U.S.A.
21 J 14 **Wyoming**, MI, U.S.A.
29 U 11 **Wyoming**, U.S.A. ◘
29 Q 11 **Wyoming Range**, WY, U.S.A. ▲▲
78 L 12 **Wyszków**, Poland
78 K 12 **Wyszogród**, Poland
17 O 7 **Wytheville**, VA, U.S.A.
79 M 15 **Wyżyna Lubelska**, Poland ▲▲
79 J 17 **Wyżyna Małopolska**, Poland ▲▲

X

45 Z 10 **X-Can**, Mexico
132 I 3 **Xá-Muteba**, Angola
127 O 19 **Xaafuun**, Somalia
46 G 4 **Xaclbal**, Guatemala ∽
95 Y 7 **Xaşşmaz**, Azerbaijan
133 Q 10 **Xai-Xai**, Mozambique
108 K 10 **Xainza**, China
114 K 13 **Xam Hua**, Laos
54 K 12 **Xambioá**, Brazil
132 G 6 **Xangongo**, Angola
95 W 9 **Xankändi**, Azerbaijan
73 B 15 **Xanten**, Germany
82 I 13 **Xanthi**, Greece
58 H 9 **Xanxeré**, Brazil
127 N 23 **Xarardheere**, Somalia
112 K 4 **Xar'oi**, China
67 T 9 **Xátiva**, Spain
108 J 11 **Xêgar**, China
21 L 19 **Xenia**, OH, U.S.A.
132 M 8 **Xhumo**, Botswana
110 E 12 **Xi Ujimqin Qi**, China
113 X 11 **Xiamen**, China
113 Q 4 **Xi'an**, China
113 Q 7 **Xianfeng**, China
113 T 10 **Xiang**, China ∽
112 J 7 **Xiangcheng**, China
113 S 5 **Xiangfan**, China
115 J 14 **Xiangkhoang**, Laos
115 J 14 **Xiangkhoang Plateau**, Laos ◇
113 Z 7 **Xiangshan**, China
113 X 3 **Xiangshui**, China
113 T 8 **Xiangtan**, China
113 V 8 **Xiangtang**, China
113 Y 7 **Xianju**, China
113 T 7 **Xianning**, China
113 T 7 **Xiantao**, China
113 W 8 **Xianxia Ling**, China ▲▲
113 Q 3 **Xianyang**, China
113 X 10 **Xianyou**, China
109 W 1 **Xiao Higgan Ling**, China ▲▲
110 K 6 **Xiao Hinggan Range**, China ▲▲
110 I 8 **Xiao'ergou**, China
113 U 6 **Xiaogan**, China
112 L 6 **Xiaojin**, China
113 V 3 **Xiaoxian**, China
113 S 1 **Xiaoyi**, China
113 Y 9 **Xiapu**, China
112 L 8 **Xichang**, China
113 N 12 **Xichou**, China
111 J 14 **Xifeng**, China
113 O 9 **Xifeng**, China
113 P 2 **Xifeng**, China
108 K 10 **Xigazê**, China
110 K 10 **Xiji**, China
110 B 13 **Xil**, China
113 N 11 **Xilin**, China
110 D 13 **Xilinhot**, China
109 O 6 **Ximiao**, China
110 F 9 **Xin Barag Zuoqi**, China
110 C 13 **Xin Hot**, China
111 J 15 **Xinbin**, China
111 E 14 **Xinbo**, China
113 S 11 **Xindu**, China
113 R 10 **Xing'an**, China
113 V 8 **Xingan**, China
111 G 16 **Xingcheng**, China
113 V 10 **Xingguo**, China
111 C 16 **Xinghe**, China
113 X 4 **Xinghua**, China
111 E 16 **Xinglong**, China
110 K 10 **Xinglongzhen**, China
113 V 11 **Xingning**, China
113 R 6 **Xingshan**, China
113 U 1 **Xingtai**, China
111 C 18 **Xingtang**, China
54 I 13 **Xingu**, Brazil ∽
54 J 12 **Xinguara**, Brazil
113 N 10 **Xingyi**, China
113 Q 9 **Xinhuang**, China
109 P 8 **Xining**, China
113 S 2 **Xinjiang**, China
108 I 6 **Xinjiang Uygur**, China ◘
112 M 6 **Xinjin**, China
110 O 8 **Xinlincun**, China
111 H 15 **Xinlitun**, China
112 K 6 **Xinlong**, China
111 I 15 **Xinmin**, China
110 M 8 **Xinqing**, China
113 S 9 **Xinshao**, China
113 W 2 **Xintai**, China
113 T 3 **Xinxiang**, China
113 S 12 **Xinxing**, China
113 U 5 **Xinyang**, China
113 W 3 **Xinyi**, China
113 Q 15 **Xinying**, China
113 U 9 **Xinyu**, China
108 J 4 **Xinyuan**, China
110 L 13 **Xinzhan**, China
110 H 7 **Xinzhangfang**, China
113 T 3 **Xinzheng**, China
109 R 6 **Xinzhoa**, China ▲
111 A 18 **Xinzhou**, China
113 T 4 **Xiping**, China
112 K 2 **Xiqing Shan**, China ▲▲
55 M 14 **Xique-Xique**, Brazil
113 O 8 **Xishui**, China
113 V 6 **Xishui**, China
128 E 10 **Xitole**, Guinea-Bissau
113 X 7 **Xiuning**, China
113 Q 8 **Xiushan**, China
113 U 7 **Xiushui**, China
113 T 3 **Xiuwu**, China
111 I 16 **Xiuyan**, China
113 S 4 **Xixia**, China
113 U 5 **Xixian**, China
113 P 5 **Xixiang**, China
111 H 17 **Xizhong Dao**, China ♣
127 M 19 **Xjis**, Somalia
95 U 10 **Xok**, Azerbaijan
115 N 21 **Xom Duc Hanh**, Vietnam
108 L 7 **Xorkol**, China
113 Q 7 **Xuan'en**, China
111 C 16 **Xuanhua**, China
112 M 10 **Xuanwei**, China
113 X 6 **Xuanzhou**, China
113 T 4 **Xuchang**, China
127 L 23 **Xuddur**, Somalia
127 N 20 **Xudun**, Somalia
113 W 3 **Xuecheng**, China
113 X 3 **Xugou**, China
110 L 7 **Xunhe**, China
110 L 7 **Xunke**, China
113 V 11 **Xunwu**, China
113 Q 5 **Xunyang**, China
113 Q 3 **Xunyi**, China
113 R 8 **Xupu**, China
113 R 14 **Xuwen**, China
113 N 8 **Xuyong**, China
113 W 3 **Xuzhou**, China
83 F 20 **Xylokastro**, Greece

Y

112 L 7 **Ya'an**, China
127 I 23 **Yabēlo**, Ethiopia
82 H 8 **Yablanitsa**, Bulgaria
129 P 10 **Yabo**, Nigeria
96 I 6 **Yabrūd**, Syria
110 L 12 **Yabuli**, China
32 F 11 **Yachats**, OR, U.S.A.
113 Q 15 **Yacheng**, China
53 L 23 **Yacuiba**, Bolivia
53 J 18 **Yacuma**, Bolivia ∽
110 I 8 **Yadong**, China
93 P 1 **Yadrin**, Russian Federation
123 M 26 **Yaeyama-rettō**, Japan ♣
125 S 8 **Yafran**, Libya
122 J 4 **Yagishiri-tō**, Japan ♣
89 W 9 **Yagodnoye**, Russian Federation
39 I 21 **Yahk**, BC, Canada
87 R 4 **Yahotyn**, Ukraine
130 M 7 **Yahuma**, Democratic Republic of Cong
123 J 17 **Yaizu**, Japan
112 K 6 **Yajiang**, China
130 J 5 **Yaka**, Central African Republic
110 G 8 **Yakeshi**, China
32 I 8 **Yakima**, WA, U.S.A.
101 Q 12 **Yakmach**, Pakistan
128 L 9 **Yako**, Burkina Faso
82 G 11 **Yakoruda**, Bulgaria
123 D 25 **Yaku-shima**, Japan ♣
122 I 7 **Yakumo**, Japan
35 U 10 **Yakutat**, AK, U.S.A.
89 T 10 **Yakutsk**, Russian Federation
87 V 9 **Yakymivka**, Ukraine
115 I 26 **Yala**, Thailand
131 N 8 **Yaleko**, Democratic Republic of Congo
130 M 4 **Yalinga**, Central African Republic
130 I 4 **Yaloké**, Central African Republic
94 E 8 **Yalova**, Turkey
87 U 13 **Yalta**, Ukraine
111 J 16 **Yalu**, China ∽
88 J 11 **Yalutorovsk**, Russian Federation
94 F 11 **Yalvaş**, Turkey
122 L 10 **Yamada**, Japan
123 C 22 **Yamaga**, Japan
122 K 12 **Yamagata**, Japan
123 C 20 **Yamaguchi**, Japan
93 X 2 **Yamantau**, Russian Federation ▲
123 N 22 **Yamato**, Japan
127 C 23 **Yambio**, Sudan
82 L 10 **Yambol**, Bulgaria ◘
82 L 9 **Yambol**, Bulgaria
88 M 8 **Yamburg**, Russian Federation
117 T 14 **Yamdena**, Indonesia ♣
120 H 1 **Y'ami**, Philippines ♣
128 K 13 **Yamoussoukro**, Côte d'Ivoire ♜
31 N 3 **Yampa**, CO, U.S.A. ∽
87 N 7 **Yampil'**, Ukraine
87 T 1 **Yampil'**, Ukraine
106 L 11 **Yamuna**, India ∽
108 L 11 **Yamzho Yumco**, China ◣
111 E 16 **Yan Shan**, China ▲▲
89 T 8 **Yana**, Russian Federation ∽
138 H 7 **Yanaba Island**, Papua New Guinea ♣
123 E 20 **Yanadani**, Japan
123 D 20 **Yanai**, Japan
105 H 19 **Yanam**, India
113 Q 2 **Yan'an**, China
91 S 14 **Yanaul**, Russian Federation
98 K 6 **Yanbu' al Baḩr**, Saudi Arabia
113 Y 4 **Yancheng**, China
109 N 7 **Yanchiwan**, China
113 R 1 **Yanchuan**, China
130 I 9 **Yandja**, Democratic Republic of Congo
130 K 3 **Yangalia**, Central African Republic
131 N 7 **Yangambi**, Democratic Republic of Congo
128 J 9 **Yangasso**, Mali
108 L 10 **Yangbajain**, China
112 J 10 **Yangbi**, China
113 S 3 **Yangcheng**, China
113 S 13 **Yangchun**, China
110 O 11 **Yanggang**, China
111 C 16 **Yanggao**, China
113 V 2 **Yanggu**, China
113 S 13 **Yangjiang**, China
113 T 1 **Yangquan**, China
113 T 11 **Yangshan**, China
113 R 11 **Yangshuo**, China
113 V 7 **Yangtze**, China ∽
112 L 11 **Yangwu**, China
113 P 4 **Yangxian**, China
113 U 7 **Yangxin**, China
111 M 18 **Yangyang**, South Korea
111 C 16 **Yangyuan**, China
113 X 5 **Yangzhou**, China
113 Q 8 **Yanhe**, China
110 M 13 **Yanji**, China
112 M 8 **Yanjin**, China
112 J 7 **Yanjing**, China
23 N 11 **Yankton**, SD, U.S.A.
112 J 8 **Yanmen**, China
111 D 16 **Yanqing**, China
111 E 19 **Yanshan**, China
112 M 12 **Yanshan**, China
113 R 11 **Yanshan**, China
113 W 8 **Yanshan**, China
89 T 7 **Yanskiy Zaliv**, Russian Federation ≈
111 H 19 **Yantai**, China
85 A 15 **Yantarnyy**, Russian Federation
110 K 13 **Yantongshan**, China
113 Y 8 **Yantou**, China
82 J 6 **Yantra**, Bulgaria ∽
113 X 3 **Yanweigang**, China
112 K 8 **Yanyuan**, China
113 V 2 **Yanzhou**, China
112 K 10 **Yao'an**, China
129 T 14 **Yaoundé**, Cameroon ♜
113 Q 3 **Yaoxian**, China
140 K 14 **Yap**, Federated States of Micronesia ♣
140 L 15 **Yap**, Federated States of Micronesia ◘
117 W 11 **Yapen**, Indonesia ♣
44 J 5 **Yaqui**, Mexico ∽
50 M 3 **Yaracuy**, Venezuela ◘
91 O 13 **Yaransk**, Russian Federation
94 E 14 **Yardimci Burnu**, Turkey ▶
95 Y 10 **Yardimli**, Azerbaijan
63 Z 6 **Yare**, U.K. ∽
141 U 1 **Yaren**, Nauru ♜
91 P 9 **Yarensk**, Russian Federation

□ Country ◘ Internal administrative region: State/Province/Territory/Dependent territory ♜ Capital city ▲▲ Mountain range/Undersea ridge ▲ Mountain peak/Volcano/Seamount ◇ Geographic feature ▶ Headland/Point/Cape/Peninsula ◢ Desert ♣ Island/Island group ⁙ Antarctic base ◎ Ocean ◒ Sea ≈ Bay/Gulf/Channel/Strait ◣ Lake ▛ Salt pan/Dry/Intermittent lake ∽ R

J 10 **Yari**, Colombia
P 13 **Yarīm**, Yemen
H 9 **Yaripo**, Brazil
H 6 **Yarkant He**, China
H 12 **Yarma**, Turkey
S 12 **Yarmouth**, NS, Canada
J 13 **Yaroslavl'**, Russian Federation
J 12 **Yaroslavskaya Oblast'**, Russian Federation
H 1 **Yartsevo**, Russian Federation
H 5 **Yarumal**, Colombia
W 11 **Yasawa Group**, Fiji
N 11 **Yashalta**, Russian Federation
R 10 **Yashi**, Nigeria
P 11 **Yashikera**, Nigeria
P 11 **Yashkul'**, Russian Federation
I 7 **Yasinya**, Ukraine
C 14 **Yasnoye**, Russian Federation
K 17 **Yasothon**, Thailand
U 12 **Yass**, NSW, Australia
I 9 **Yāsūj**, Iran
M 7 **Yasun Burnu**, Turkey
C 12 **Yatağan**, Turkey
Q 14 **Yaté**, New Caledonia
P 6 **Yates Center**, KS, U.S.A.
K 3 **Yathkyed Lake**, NU, Canada
N 7 **Yatolema**, Democratic Republic of Congo
C 22 **Yatsushiro**, Japan
F 10 **Yatta**, Israel
E 19 **Yauca**, Peru
G 18 **Yauri**, Peru
F 11 **Yavari**, Brazil/Peru
J 6 **Yávaros**, Mexico
F 16 **Yavatmal**, India
Z 14 **Yaviza**, Panama
Q 2 **Yavlenka**, Kazakhstan
I 4 **Yavoriv**, Ukraine
D 21 **Yawatahama**, Japan
K 9 **Yazd**, Iran
L 9 **Yazd**, Iran
I 9 **Yazd-e Khast**, Iran
O 8 **Yazdan**, Iran
N 11 **Yazihan**, Turkey
L 4 **Yazoo City**, MS, U.S.A.
U 4 **Ybbs an der Donau**, Austria
G 22 **Ydra**, Greece
G 21 **Ydra**, Greece
F 18 **Ye**, Myanmar
X 5 **Yebbi-Bou**, Chad
H 6 **Yecheng**, China
S 10 **Yecla**, Spain
K 5 **Yécora**, Mexico
D 14 **Yedashe**, Myanmar
I 14 **Yedy**, Belarus
K 23 **Yeed**, Somalia
X 11 **Yeehaw Junction**, FL, U.S.A.
H 11 **Yefimovskiy**, Russian Federation
K 4 **Yefremo**, Russian Federation
U 9 **Yeghegnadzor**, Armenia
V 5 **Yegindybulak**, Kazakhstan
N 12 **Yégué**, Togo
C 15 **Yegyi**, Myanmar
E 23 **Yei**, Sudan
D 22 **Yei**, Sudan
M 12 **Yeji**, Ghana
J 10 **Yekaterinburg**, Russian Federation
T 1 **Yelabuga**, Russian Federation
O 6 **Yelan'**, Russian Federation
R 8 **Yelanets'**, Ukraine
L 4 **Yelets**, Russian Federation
U 3 **Yeletskiy**, Russian Federation
H 8 **Yélimané**, Mali
T 3 **Yelkhovka**, Russian Federation
J 4 **Yell**, U.K.
R 2 **Yellow**, China
L 8 **Yellow Pine**, ID, U.S.A.
X 8 **Yellow Sea**, China
H 12 **Yellowknife**, NT, Canada
U 7 **Yellowstone**, MT, U.S.A.
S 9 **Yellowstone Lake**, WY, U.S.A.
O 2 **Yel'niki**, Russian Federation
N 14 **Yeloten**, Turkmenistan
L 21 **Yel'sk**, Belarus
P 11 **Yelwa**, Nigeria
O 15 **Yemassee**, SC, U.S.A.
T 12 **Yemen**, Asia
M 3 **Yemil'chyne**, Ukraine
K 8 **Yemtsa**, Russian Federation
P 8 **Yemva**, Russian Federation
L 11 **Yên Bai**, Vietnam
C 13 **Yenangyaung**, Myanmar
N 11 **Yendi**, Ghana
F 10 **Yénéganou**, Congo
G 6 **Yengisar**, China
H 7 **Yengo**, Congo
E 8 **Yenişehir**, Turkey
N 10 **Yenisey**, Russian Federation
X 9 **Yeniseykiy Zaliv**, Arctic Ocean
N 11 **Yeniseyskiy Kryazh**, Russian Federation
P 13 **Yeovil**, U.K.
K 5 **Yepachi**, Mexico
V 6 **Yeppoon**, QLD, Australia
L 13 **Yerbent**, Turkmenistan
Q 11 **Yerbogachen**, Russian Federation
T 9 **Yerevan**, Armenia
T 4 **Yereymentau**, Kazakhstan
J 18 **Yerington**, NV, U.S.A.
J 9 **Yerköy**, Turkey
D 17 **Yermala**, India
T 13 **Yerofey**, Russian Federation
F 11 **Yeroham**, Israel
R 5 **Yershov**, Russian Federation
C 11 **Yesagyo**, Myanmar
P 4 **Yesil'**, Kazakhstan
J 11 **Yeşilhisar**, Turkey
E 12 **Yeşilova**, Turkey
N 13 **Yessentuki**, Russian Federation
W 8 **Yevlax**, Azerbaijan
T 12 **Yevpatoriya**, Ukraine
T 4 **Yexian**, China
K 10 **Yeysk**, Russian Federation
L 13 **Yezyaryshcha**, Belarus
J 9 **Yi'an**, China
N 8 **Yibin**, China
R 6 **Yichang**, China
S 6 **Yicheng**, China
R 2 **Yichuan**, China
L 9 **Yichun**, China
U 8 **Yichun**, China
J 6 **Yidun**, China
U 8 **Yifeng**, China
Q 3 **Yijun**, China

110 J 8 **Yilaha**, China
110 M 10 **Yilan**, China
94 L 9 **Yildizeli**, Turkey
110 I 6 **Yilehuli Shan**, China
112 M 11 **Yiliang**, China
112 M 9 **Yiliang**, China
112 L 9 **Yimen**, China
110 L 11 **Yimianpo**, China
110 G 4 **Yimuhe**, China
113 W 2 **Yinan**, China
109 Q 7 **Yinchuan**, China
113 T 6 **Yingcheng**, China
113 T 11 **Yingde**, China
112 I 11 **Yingjiang**, China
112 M 7 **Yingjing**, China
111 H 16 **Yingkou**, China
113 O 6 **Yingshan**, China
113 T 6 **Yingshan**, China
113 V 5 **Yingshang**, China
113 W 8 **Yingtan**, China
111 B 17 **Yingxian**, China
108 J 4 **Yining**, China
113 P 8 **Yinjiang**, China
112 L 10 **Yipinglang**, China
113 P 9 **Yiquan**, China
127 E 22 **Yirol**, Sudan
110 G 10 **Yirxie**, China
113 Q 11 **Yishan**, China
113 X 2 **Yishui**, China
118 B 13 **Yishun**, Singapore
110 H 6 **Yitulihe**, China
113 Y 7 **Yiwu**, China
111 H 15 **Yixian**, China
110 J 4 **Yixiken**, China
113 Y 6 **Yixing**, China
113 S 8 **Yiyang**, China
113 W 8 **Yiyang**, China
113 W 2 **Yiyuan**, China
113 T 10 **Yizhang**, China
84 C 12 **Ylakiai**, Lithuania
70 L 12 **Yli-Kärppä**, Finland
70 K 11 **Ylitornio**, Finland
143 Q 11 **Ymer Nunatak**, Greenland
89 V 11 **Ynykchanskiy**, Russian Federation
129 T 10 **Yobe**, Nigeria
122 I 6 **Yobetsu-dake**, Japan
127 K 19 **Yoboki**, Djibouti
120 K 12 **Yog Point**, Philippines
116 I 14 **Yogyakarta**, Indonesia
116 I 15 **Yogyakarta**, Indonesia
123 F 17 **Yōka**, Japan
129 V 14 **Yokadouma**, Cameroon
123 N 21 **Yokate-jima**, Japan
123 H 18 **Yokkaichi**, Japan
129 U 13 **Yoko**, Cameroon
123 K 16 **Yokohama**, Japan
123 K 16 **Yokosuka**, Japan
122 K 11 **Yokote**, Japan
129 U 12 **Yola**, Nigeria
130 M 9 **Yolombo**, Democratic Republic of Congo
123 E 18 **Yonago**, Japan
123 L 26 **Yonaguni-jima**, Japan
122 K 13 **Yonezawa**, Japan
118 E 10 **Yong Peng**, Malaysia
113 W 10 **Yong'an**, China
113 V 4 **Yongcheng**, China
111 N 20 **Yŏngch'ŏn**, South Korea
113 O 7 **Yongchuan**, China
113 V 9 **Yongfeng**, China
113 R 11 **Yongfu**, China
111 M 19 **Yŏngju**, South Korea
113 Y 7 **Yongkang**, China
112 J 10 **Yongping**, China
112 L 10 **Yongren**, China
112 M 8 **Yongshan**, China
112 K 9 **Yongsheng**, China
113 R 8 **Yongshun**, China
113 T 10 **Yongxing**, China
113 U 9 **Yongxing**, China
113 V 7 **Yongxiu**, China
113 S 10 **Yongzhou**, China
14 K 12 **Yonkers**, NY, U.S.A.
14 F 14 **York**, PA, U.S.A.
19 O 4 **York**, AL, U.S.A.
23 N 14 **York**, NE, U.S.A.
42 E 13 **York**, ON, Canada
63 T 2 **York**, U.K.
134 G 11 **York**, WA, Australia
15 O 8 **York Harbor**, ME, U.S.A.
135 P 11 **Yorke Peninsula**, SA, Australia
135 O 12 **Yorketown**, SA, Australia
63 R 1 **Yorkshire Dales**, U.K.
63 U 1 **Yorkshire Wolds**, U.K.
39 N 18 **Yorkton**, SK, Canada
17 V 6 **Yorktown**, VA, U.S.A.
21 G 16 **Yorkville**, IL, U.S.A.
46 M 5 **Yoro**, Honduras
123 N 22 **Yoro-jima**, Japan
123 O 23 **Yoron-tō**, Japan
33 I 20 **Yosemite Village**, CA, U.S.A.
91 O 14 **Yoshkar-Ola**, Russian Federation
111 M 21 **Yŏsu**, South Korea
96 F 12 **Yotvata**, Israel
61 C 20 **Youghal**, Republic of Ireland
61 D 21 **Youghal Bay**, Republic of Ireland
56 M 11 **Young**, Uruguay
135 T 12 **Young**, NSW, Australia
145 S 15 **Young Island**, Antarctica
21 O 17 **Youngstown**, OH, U.S.A.
124 G 7 **Youssoufia**, Morocco
113 Q 8 **Youyang**, China
88 M 14 **Youyi Feng**, Russian Federation
63 Z 8 **Yoxford**, U.K.
94 J 9 **Yozgat**, Turkey
33 G 14 **Yreka**, CA, U.S.A.
138 F 2 **Ysabel Channel**, Papua New Guinea
71 E 26 **Ystad**, Sweden
63 N 9 **Ystalyfera**, U.K.
103 V 10 **Ysyk-Köl**, Kyrgyzstan
117 T 11 **Yu**, Indonesia
109 X 13 **Yü-Shan**, Taiwan
113 Z 11 **Yü Shan**, Taiwan
113 R 8 **Yuan**, China
113 Q 10 **Yuanbao Shan**, China
112 L 12 **Yuanjiang**, China
113 R 8 **Yuanling**, China
112 L 10 **Yuanmou**, China
111 B 18 **Yuanping**, China
113 S 3 **Yuanqu**, China
33 G 17 **Yuba City**, CA, U.S.A.
122 K 5 **Yūbari-sanchi**, Japan
45 Y 10 **Yucatán**, Mexico
45 Y 9 **Yucatan Channel**, Mexico

45 Y 11 **Yucatan Peninsula**, Mexico
113 T 1 **Yuci**, China
111 E 14 **Yudaokou**, China
110 H 4 **Yudi Shan**, China
134 M 6 **Yuendumu**, NT, Australia
113 Z 8 **Yueqing**, China
112 L 8 **Yuexi**, China
113 V 6 **Yuexi**, China
113 T 7 **Yueyang**, China
113 W 8 **Yugan**, China
91 S 1 **Yugorskiy Poluostrov**, Russian Federation
113 R 1 **Yuhebu**, China
113 V 8 **Yujiang**, China
89 X 7 **Yukagirskoye Ploskogor'ye**, Russian Federation
84 K 13 **Yukhavichy**, Belarus
92 J 2 **Yukhnov**, Russian Federation
130 K 10 **Yuki**, Democratic Republic of Congo
36 I 6 **Yukon**, YT, Canada
35 R 5 **Yukon Flats**, AK, U.S.A.
38 B 13 **Yukon Territory**, Canada
95 T 12 **Yüksekova**, Turkey
123 C 20 **Yukuhashi**, Japan
134 M 7 **Yulara**, NT, Australia
93 X 4 **Yuldybayevo**, Russian Federation
19 W 7 **Yulee**, FL, U.S.A.
113 Z 12 **Yüli**, Taiwan
109 S 7 **Yulin**, China
113 R 13 **Yulin**, China
112 K 9 **Yulongxue Shan**, China
30 G 13 **Yuma**, AZ, U.S.A.
130 I 9 **Yumbi**, Democratic Republic of Congo
131 O 8 **Yumbi**, Democratic Republic of Congo
109 O 7 **Yumen**, China
112 L 10 **Yun Gui Gaoyuan**, China
94 G 10 **Yunak**, Turkey
113 S 12 **Yunan**, China
34 I 14 **Yunaska Island**, AK, U.S.A.
113 R 3 **Yuncheng**, China
113 V 2 **Yuncheng**, China
113 S 12 **Yunfu**, China
53 J 20 **Yungas**, Bolivia
113 T 6 **Yunmeng**, China
112 K 11 **Yunnan**, China
135 Q 11 **Yunta**, SA, Australia
111 E 16 **Yunwu Shan**, China
113 R 5 **Yunxi**, China
112 J 11 **Yunxian**, China
113 R 5 **Yunxian**, China
113 W 11 **Yunxiao**, China
113 Q 6 **Yunyang**, China
113 P 9 **Yuping**, China
113 P 9 **Yuqing**, China
53 J 22 **Yura**, Bolivia
85 H 17 **Yuratsishki**, Belarus
88 M 12 **Yurga**, Russian Federation
52 D 12 **Yurimaguas**, Peru
91 R 11 **Yurla**, Russian Federation
91 O 12 **Yur'ya**, Russian Federation
90 J 14 **Yur'yev-Pol'skiy**, Russian Federation
90 L 14 **Yur'yevets**, Russian Federation
87 V 6 **Yur"yivka**, Ukraine
113 X 8 **Yushan**, China
90 H 6 **Yushkozero**, Russian Federation
110 K 12 **Yushu**, China
112 I 4 **Yushu**, China
93 Q 10 **Yusta**, Russian Federation
90 H 8 **Yustozero**, Russian Federation
95 Q 8 **Yusufeli**, Turkey
123 E 21 **Yusuhara**, Japan
108 I 7 **Yutian**, China
123 N 22 **Yuwan-dake**, Japan
113 O 1 **Yuwang**, China
112 L 11 **Yuxi**, China
112 M 11 **Yuxia**, China
111 B 18 **Yuxian**, China
111 C 17 **Yuxian**, China
113 Z 6 **Yuyao**, China
89 Y 14 **Yuzhno-Kuril'sk**, Russian Federation
89 X 14 **Yuzhno-Sakhalinsk**, Russian Federation
87 Q 7 **Yuzhnoukrayinsk**, Ukraine
103 R 9 **Yuzhnyy Kazakhstan**, Kazakhstan
113 T 4 **Yuzhou**, China
74 B 8 **Yverdon**, Switzerland
65 O 3 **Yvetot**, France
114 D 13 **Ywamun**, Myanmar
114 D 10 **Ywathit**, Myanmar

Z

68 H 10 **Zaandam**, Netherlands
89 S 14 **Zabaykal'sk**, Russian Federation
131 O 6 **Zabia**, Democratic Republic of Congo
99 O 13 **Zabīd**, Yemen
101 P 10 **Zābol**, Iran
79 I 17 **Zabrze**, Poland
101 T 8 **Zābul**, Afghanistan
46 J 5 **Zacapa**, Guatemala
46 K 6 **Zacapa**, Honduras
45 P 12 **Zacapu**, Mexico
45 O 9 **Zacatecas**, Mexico
45 O 8 **Zacatecas**, Mexico
46 J 7 **Zacatecoluca**, El Salvador
45 S 11 **Zacatlán**, Mexico
83 D 21 **Zacharo**, Greece
87 U 5 **Zachepylivka**, Ukraine
80 C 12 **Zadar**, Croatia
115 F 22 **Zadetkale Kyun**, Myanmar
115 F 23 **Zadetkyi Kyun**, Myanmar
108 M 9 **Zadoi**, China
83 L 24 **Zafora**, Greece
66 K 10 **Zafra**, Spain
124 F 10 **Zag**, Morocco
79 E 14 **Żagań**, Poland
126 E 8 **Zagazig**, Egypt
125 Q 5 **Zaghouan**, Tunisia
80 D 8 **Zagreb**, Croatia
100 G 6 **Zagros Mountains**, Iran
80 M 11 **Źagubica**, Serbia and Montenegro
108 K 9 **Za'gya**, China
101 O 11 **Zāhedān**, Iran
96 H 6 **Zahlé**, Lebanon
99 O 11 **Ẓahrān**, Saudi Arabia
97 T 13 **Ẓahrat al Baṭn**, Iraq
93 T 1 **Zainsk**, Russian Federation
132 F 1 **Zaire**, Angola
80 N 12 **Zaječar**, Serbia and Montenegro
97 R 1 **Zākhō**, Iraq
90 J 2 **Zakhrebetnoye**, Russian Federation
79 J 19 **Zakopane**, Poland
129 Y 10 **Zakouma**, Chad
83 B 20 **Zakynthos**, Greece
83 B 20 **Zakynthos**, Greece

97 N 3 **Zalābiyah**, Syria
79 F 24 **Zalaegerszeg**, Hungary
129 S 11 **Zalanga**, Nigeria
110 H 9 **Zalantun**, China
86 H 8 **Zalău**, Romania
78 D 9 **Zalew Szczeciński**, Poland
78 J 8 **Zalew Wiślany**, Poland
99 N 7 **Ẓalim**, Saudi Arabia
127 A 18 **Zalingei**, Sudan
86 K 6 **Zalischyky**, Ukraine
89 X 14 **Zaliv Aniva**, Russian Federation
102 I 11 **Zaliv Kara-Bogaz-Gol**, Turkmenistan
102 I 8 **Zaliv Komsomolets**, Kazakhstan
89 Z 6 **Zaliv Kresta**, Russian Federation
89 Y 9 **Zaliv Shelikhova**, Russian Federation
89 X 13 **Zaliv Terpeniya**, Russian Federation
87 R 10 **Zaliznyy Port**, Ukraine
69 I 14 **Zaltbommel**, Netherlands
90 E 13 **Zaluch'ye**, Russian Federation
39 G 15 **Zama Lake**, AB, Canada
99 R 12 **Zamakh**, Yemen
120 F 9 **Zambales Mountains**, Philippines
132 L 4 **Zambezi**, Zambia
133 R 6 **Zambezi**, Africa
133 S 6 **Zambézia**, Mozambique
132 M 5 **Zambia**, Africa
121 H 22 **Zamboanga**, Philippines
121 H 22 **Zamboanga Peninsula**, Philippines
46 L 6 **Zambrano**, Honduras
78 M 11 **Zambrów**, Poland
133 P 5 **Zambue**, Mozambique
129 Q 10 **Zamfara**, Nigeria
52 B 11 **Zamora**, Ecuador
52 B 11 **Zamora**, Ecuador
66 L 4 **Zamora**, Spain
52 B 11 **Zamora-Chinchipe**, Ecuador
45 O 11 **Zamora de Hidalgo**, Mexico
79 O 15 **Zamość**, Poland
130 G 9 **Zanaga**, Congo
21 N 19 **Zanesville**, OH, U.S.A.
128 J 10 **Zangasso**, Mali
106 J 4 **Zangla**, India
100 G 5 **Zanjān**, Iran
100 G 5 **Zanjān**, Iran
131 W 11 **Zanzibar**, Tanzania
131 W 11 **Zanzibar Channel**, Tanzania
131 X 11 **Zanzibar Island**, Tanzania
125 Q 12 **Zaouatallaz**, Algeria
113 T 5 **Zaoyang**, China
103 S 3 **Zaozernyy**, Kazakhstan
113 W 3 **Zaozhuang**, China
80 L 13 **Zapadna Morava**, Serbia and Montenegro
90 E 14 **Zapadnaya Dvina**, Russian Federation
102 I 4 **Zapadnyy Kazakhstan**, Kazakhstan
88 M 13 **Zapadnyy Sayan**, Russian Federation
57 G 15 **Zapala**, Argentina
27 N 14 **Zapata**, TX, U.S.A.
90 H 1 **Zapolyarnyy**, Russian Federation
87 V 7 **Zaporizhzhya**, Ukraine
95 V 7 **Zaqatala**, Azerbaijan
94 M 9 **Zara**, Turkey
103 O 11 **Zarafshan**, Uzbekistan
67 S 4 **Zaragoza**, Spain
100 L 10 **Zarand**, Iran
101 P 10 **Zaranj**, Afghanistan
84 H 13 **Zarasai**, Lithuania
95 Y 7 **Zarat**, Azerbaijan
59 D 15 **Zárate**, Argentina
51 P 3 **Zaraza**, Venezuela
101 U 8 **Zarghūn Shahr**, Afghanistan
129 R 10 **Zaria**, Nigeria
79 I 21 **Žarnovica**, Slovakia
79 D 14 **Żary**, Poland
125 Q 10 **Zarzaïtine**, Algeria
125 R 7 **Zarzis**, Tunisia
106 I 3 **Zaskar Mountains**, India
85 I 17 **Zaslawye**, Belarus
79 B 16 **Žatec**, Czech Republic
87 P 10 **Zatoka**, Ukraine
78 D 9 **Zatoka Pomorska**, Poland
27 T 8 **Zavalla**, TX, U.S.A.
69 G 19 **Zaventem**, Belgium
93 P 10 **Zavetnoye**, Russian Federation
79 J 16 **Zawiercie**, Poland
125 T 11 **Zawīlah**, Libya
125 W 8 **Zāwiyat Masūs**, Libya
103 Z 6 **Zaysan**, Kazakhstan
109 N 11 **Zayü**, China
103 O 6 **Zban**, Kazakhstan
86 K 4 **Zbarazh**, Ukraine
78 H 9 **Zblewo**, Poland
86 K 4 **Zboriv**, Ukraine
79 I 14 **Zduńska Wola**, Poland
140 B 7 **Zealandia Bank**, Northern Mariana Islands
101 V 5 **Zēbāk**, Afghanistan
97 T 1 **Zēbār**, Iraq
17 S 9 **Zebulon**, NC, U.S.A.
69 D 15 **Zeeland**, Netherlands
96 F 10 **Ze'elim**, Israel
72 M 11 **Zehdenick**, Germany
68 I 12 **Zeist**, Netherlands
73 K 17 **Zeitz**, Germany
80 H 13 **Zelena Gora**, Bosnia and Herzegovina
90 H 4 **Zelenoborskiy**, Russian Federation
90 E 10 **Zelenogorsk**, Russian Federation
92 K 1 **Zelenograd**, Russian Federation
85 A 14 **Zelenogradsk**, Russian Federation
93 O 13 **Zelenokumsk**, Russian Federation
80 E 7 **Zelina**, Croatia
75 Q 7 **Zell am See**, Austria
75 N 7 **Zell am Ziller**, Austria
84 I 10 **Zeltiņi**, Latvia
85 F 19 **Zel'va**, Belarus
69 E 17 **Zelzate**, Belgium
93 N 3 **Zemetchino**, Russian Federation
131 N 5 **Zémio**, Central African Republic
88 M 3 **Zemlya Aleksandry**, Russian Federation
88 M 3 **Zemlya Georga**, Russian Federation
112 I 4 **Zênda**, China
80 H 12 **Zenica**, Bosnia and Herzegovina
62 I 15 **Zennor**, U.K.
80 H 11 **Žepče**, Bosnia and Herzegovina
103 R 13 **Zerafshon**, Tajikistan
73 K 14 **Zerbst**, Germany
103 R 3 **Zerenda**, Kazakhstan
125 O 6 **Zeribet el Oued**, Algeria
74 E 11 **Zermatt**, Switzerland
74 J 9 **Zernez**, Switzerland
72 G 11 **Zeven**, Germany
68 L 13 **Zevenaar**, Netherlands

69 G 15 **Zevenbergen**, Netherlands
89 T 13 **Zeya**, Russian Federation
89 U 13 **Zeya**, Russian Federation
89 U 13 **Zeyskoye Vodokhranilishche**, Russian Federation
96 H 5 **Zgharta**, Lebanon
78 J 13 **Zgierz**, Poland
79 D 15 **Zgorzelec**, Poland
87 R 1 **Zhadove**, Ukraine
103 Q 4 **Zhaksy**, Kazakhstan
102 H 5 **Zhalpaktal**, Kazakhstan
103 T 9 **Zhambyl**, Kazakhstan
103 S 7 **Zhambyl**, Kazakhstan
103 Q 10 **Zhanakorgan**, Kazakhstan
103 U 6 **Zhanaortalyk**, Kazakhstan
102 I 10 **Zhanaozen**, Kazakhstan
103 R 10 **Zhanatas**, Kazakhstan
102 H 7 **Zhanbay**, Kazakhstan
110 L 8 **Zhanbei**, China
111 C 15 **Zhangbei**, China
110 K 6 **Zhangdiyingzi**, China
109 X 4 **Zhangguangcai Ling**, China
110 L 12 **Zhangguangcai Range**, China
103 X 5 **Zhangiztobe**, Kazakhstan
113 R 7 **Zhangjiajie**, China
111 C 16 **Zhangjiakou**, China
113 W 10 **Zhangping**, China
113 X 11 **Zhangpu**, China
113 V 8 **Zhangshu**, China
111 H 14 **Zhangwu**, China
109 P 7 **Zhangye**, China
113 X 11 **Zhangzhou**, China
113 S 2 **Zhangzi**, China
113 S 14 **Zhanjiang**, China
102 J 6 **Zhanterek**, Kazakhstan
112 M 10 **Zhanyi**, China
110 I 12 **Zhanyu**, China
113 W 11 **Zhao'an**, China
110 K 11 **Zhaodong**, China
112 L 8 **Zhaojue**, China
113 R 11 **Zhaoping**, China
113 T 12 **Zhaoqing**, China
112 M 9 **Zhaotong**, China
113 U 1 **Zhaoxian**, China
110 J 11 **Zhaoyuan**, China
110 J 11 **Zhaozhou**, China
108 J 10 **Zhari Namco**, China
102 K 6 **Zharkamys**, Kazakhstan
103 X 9 **Zharkent**, Kazakhstan
90 F 14 **Zharkovskiy**, Russian Federation
103 X 5 **Zharma**, Kazakhstan
87 P 5 **Zhashkiv**, Ukraine
113 Q 4 **Zhashui**, China
108 H 8 **Zhaxigang**, China
113 Y 7 **Zhejiang**, China
103 U 2 **Zhelezinka**, Kazakhstan
85 B 16 **Zheleznodorozhnyy**, Russian Federation
92 J 4 **Zheleznogorsk**, Russian Federation
107 U 10 **Zhemgang**, Bhutan
113 Q 4 **Zhen'an**, China
113 P 5 **Zhenba**, China
113 P 8 **Zheng'an**, China
113 X 9 **Zhenghe**, China
113 T 3 **Zhengzhou**, China
113 Z 6 **Zhenhai**, China
113 X 5 **Zhenjiang**, China
110 I 11 **Zhenlai**, China
113 O 10 **Zhenning**, China
113 Q 5 **Zhenping**, China
113 P 9 **Zhenyuan**, China
103 Q 7 **Zhezkazgan**, Kazakhstan
89 S 9 **Zhigansk**, Russian Federation
113 Q 9 **Zhijiang**, China
89 R 8 **Zhilinda**, Russian Federation
103 N 3 **Zhitikara**, Kazakhstan
92 I 3 **Zhizdra**, Russian Federation
85 M 19 **Zhlobin**, Belarus
87 N 6 **Zhmerynka**, Ukraine
101 U 10 **Zhob**, Pakistan
101 U 10 **Zhob**, Pakistan
85 K 17 **Zhodzina**, Belarus
112 J 8 **Zhongdian**, China
113 N 1 **Zhongning**, China
113 T 13 **Zhongshan**, China
145 X 6 **Zhongshan**, Antarctica
113 P 7 **Zhongxian**, China
113 S 6 **Zhongxiang**, China
110 J 6 **Zhongyaozhan**, China
113 V 1 **Zhoucun**, China
113 U 4 **Zhoukou**, China
113 Z 6 **Zhoushan**, China
113 Z 6 **Zhoushan Dao**, China
86 I 4 **Zhovkva**, Ukraine
87 P 8 **Zhovten'**, Ukraine
87 T 7 **Zhovti Vody**, Ukraine
111 I 17 **Zhuanghe**, China
112 I 4 **Zhubgyügoin**, China
113 X 2 **Zhucheng**, China
113 N 4 **Zhugqu**, China
113 T 13 **Zhuhai**, China
113 Y 7 **Zhuji**, China
92 I 3 **Zhukovka**, Russian Federation
113 U 5 **Zhumadian**, China
111 D 16 **Zhuolu**, China
111 B 16 **Zhuozi**, China
102 L 5 **Zhuryn**, Kazakhstan
113 R 5 **Zhushan**, China
113 R 5 **Zhuxi**, China
113 T 8 **Zhuzhou**, China
102 I 4 **Zhympity**, Kazakhstan
85 J 21 **Zhytkavichy**, Belarus
87 N 4 **Zhytomyr**, Ukraine
79 I 20 **Žiar nad Hronom**, Slovakia
97 S 1 **Zībār**, Iraq
111 E 20 **Zibo**, China
113 Q 1 **Zichang**, China
103 R 13 **Ziddí**, Tajikistan
79 G 16 **Ziębice**, Poland
78 E 13 **Zielona Góra**, Poland
69 E 15 **Zierikzee**, Netherlands
114 B 13 **Zigaing**, Myanmar
125 X 11 **Zighan**, Libya
115 D 14 **Zigon**, Myanmar
113 N 7 **Zigong**, China
129 V 8 **Ziguey**, Chad
113 R 6 **Zigui**, China
128 D 9 **Ziguinchor**, Senegal
112 K 7 **Zihag**, China
45 P 13 **Zihuatanejo**, Mexico
113 V 12 **Zijin**, China
94 K 9 **Zile**, Turkey
79 I 19 **Žilina**, Slovakia
125 V 10 **Zillah**, Libya

75 N 7 **Zillertaler Alpen**, Austria
84 J 12 **Zilupe**, Latvia
89 P 13 **Zima**, Russian Federation
133 N 6 **Zimba**, Zambia
133 O 7 **Zimbabwe**, Africa
128 G 12 **Zimmi**, Sierra Leone
86 J 14 **Zimnicea**, Romania
90 K 5 **Zimniy Bereg**, Russian Federation
93 N 10 **Zimovniki**, Russian Federation
129 S 9 **Zinder**, Niger
129 T 9 **Zinder**, Niger
99 Q 14 **Zinjibār**, Yemen
79 H 23 **Zirc**, Hungary
72 N 9 **Zirchow**, Germany
80 D 13 **Žirje**, Croatia
107 X 9 **Ziro**, India
45 Q 12 **Zitácuaro**, Mexico
113 N 6 **Zitong**, China
73 O 17 **Zittau**, Germany
80 I 11 **Živinice**, Bosnia and Herzegovina
127 I 21 **Ziway Hāyk'**, Ethiopia
113 T 10 **Zixing**, China
113 N 7 **Ziyang**, China
113 Q 5 **Ziyang**, China
113 R 10 **Ziyuan**, China
113 N 7 **Zizhong**, China
113 R 1 **Zizhou**, China
82 I 12 **Zlatograd**, Bulgaria
93 Y 1 **Zlatoust**, Russian Federation
79 H 19 **Zlín**, Czech Republic
125 S 7 **Zlīṭan**, Libya
79 I 14 **Złoczew**, Poland
78 G 10 **Złotów**, Poland
92 G 4 **Zlynka**, Russian Federation
79 G 14 **Żmigród**, Poland
87 W 4 **Zmiyiv**, Ukraine
103 W 4 **Znamenka**, Kazakhstan
78 H 11 **Żnin**, Poland
79 F 20 **Znojmo**, Czech Republic
68 G 12 **Zoetermeer**, Netherlands
112 J 5 **Zogqên**, China
112 M 4 **Zoigê**, China
69 I 18 **Zolder**, Belgium
87 V 3 **Zolochiv**, Ukraine
87 Y 6 **Zolote**, Ukraine
87 R 5 **Zolotonosha**, Ukraine
92 J 4 **Zolotukhino**, Russian Federation
130 J 5 **Zongo**, Democratic Republic of Congo
94 G 7 **Zonguldak**, Turkey
69 B 19 **Zonnebeke**, Belgium
66 L 8 **Zorita**, Spain
82 L 10 **Zornitsa**, Bulgaria
52 A 11 **Zorritos**, Peru
128 H 12 **Zorzor**, Liberia
69 E 19 **Zottegem**, Belgium
129 W 5 **Zouar**, Chad
128 G 4 **Zouérat**, Mauritania
113 S 8 **Zoushi**, China
80 K 9 **Zrenjanin**, Serbia and Montenegro
73 L 17 **Zschopau**, Germany
128 J 12 **Zuénoula**, Côte d'Ivoire
67 S 4 **Zuera**, Spain
99 V 10 **Ẓufār**, Oman
74 G 7 **Zug**, Switzerland
95 R 6 **Zugdidi**, Georgia
74 G 7 **Zuger See**, Switzerland
74 L 6 **Zugspitze**, Austria/Germany
129 Q 10 **Zugu**, Nigeria
69 F 14 **Zuid-Holland**, Netherlands
68 M 6 **Zuidhorn**, Netherlands
68 M 7 **Zuidlaardermeer**, Netherlands
50 K 3 **Zulia**, Venezuela
73 B 17 **Zülpich**, Germany
52 B 11 **Zumba**, Ecuador
133 P 5 **Zumbo**, Mozambique
111 F 16 **Zunhua**, China
31 N 10 **Zuni**, NM, U.S.A.
31 N 10 **Zuni Mountains**, NM, U.S.A.
113 O 9 **Zunyi**, China
113 T 1 **Zuoquan**, China
111 B 16 **Zuoyun**, China
74 J 9 **Zuoz**, Switzerland
80 I 9 **Županja**, Croatia
81 L 16 **Žur**, Serbia and Montenegro
101 P 6 **Zūrābād**, Iran
68 J 7 **Zurich**, Netherlands
74 G 6 **Zürich**, Switzerland
74 G 7 **Zürich See**, Switzerland
129 Q 10 **Zuru**, Nigeria
68 L 12 **Zutphen**, Netherlands
125 R 7 **Zuwārah**, Libya
87 Q 6 **Zvenyhorodka**, Ukraine
82 M 10 **Zvezdets**, Bulgaria
133 P 8 **Zvishavane**, Zimbabwe
79 J 20 **Zvolen**, Slovakia
80 I 11 **Zvornik**, Serbia and Montenegro
128 I 13 **Zwedru**, Liberia
74 D 9 **Zweisimmen**, Switzerland
75 V 3 **Zwettl**, Austria
73 L 17 **Zwickau**, Germany
79 N 16 **Zwierzyniec**, Poland
69 F 17 **Zwijndrecht**, Belgium
79 M 14 **Zwoleń**, Poland
18 H 5 **Zwolle**, LA, U.S.A.
68 L 10 **Zwolle**, Netherlands
85 J 16 **Zyembin**, Belarus
78 K 13 **Żyrardów**, Poland
89 W 8 **Zyryanka**, Russian Federation
89 N 10 **Zyryanovo**, Russian Federation
103 Y 4 **Zyryanovsk**, Kazakhstan
79 J 18 **Żywiec**, Poland

ountry · Internal administrative region: State/Province/Territory/Dependent territory · Capital city · Mountain range/Undersea ridge · Mountain peak/Volcano/Seamount · Geographic feature · Headland/Point/Cape/Peninsula · Desert · Island/Island group · Antarctic base · Ocean · Sea · Bay/Gulf/Channel/Strait · Lake · Salt pan/Dry/Intermittent lake · River

Acknowledgments

BONNIER PUBLISHING
Group Publisher John Owen

WELDON OWEN PTY LTD
Chief Executive Officer Sheena Coupe
Creative Director Sue Burk
Senior Vice President, International Sales Stuart Laurence
Vice President, Sales: North America Amy Kaneko
Administrator International Sales Kristine Ravn

Project Manager Sarah Anderson
Art Director Suzanne Keating

Project Editor/Text Scott Forbes
Editorial Assistant Karen Penzes

Designer Liz Murphy
Design Assistant Domenika Markovtzev
Initial Design Concept John Bull

Production Manager Todd Rechner
Production Coordinators Lisa Conway, Mike Crowton

Systems Administrator Margaret Hilliard
Editorial Coordinator Jennifer Losco

Picture Researcher Jo Collard

Maps Map Illustrations
Chief Cartographer Laurie Whiddon
Cartographic Team Bil Andersen, Andrew Davies, Kerrie deGruchy, Sydney Gubbay, Ian Faulkner, Brian Johnston, Brad McLean, Karen Reithmuller

Cityscape Illustrations Murray Zanoni
Information Graphics Andrew Davies, Suzanne Keating
Flags Flag Society of Australia

Weldon Owen would like to thank the following people for their assistance in the production of this book: Tony Burton (Flag Society of Australia), Jenni Bruce, Melanie Calabretta, Brendan Cotter, Janine Flew, Helen Flint, Angela Handley, Emma Hutchinson, Tessy Grabo, Global Forest Watch, Matthew Hall, Ralph Kelly (Flag Society of Australia), Professor Kim Lowell (Département des sciences du bois et de la forêt, Université Laval, Canada), Margaret McPhee, Rory Moore, Michael Nahas, Grace Newell, Sarah Plant (Puddingburn Publishing Services), Deborah Smith, Kiren Thandi, Shannon Tufui.

Notes

1. All population statistics quoted in this atlas are projected 2005 figures. National population statistics have been sourced from the U.S. Census Bureau. City population statistics have been sourced from the United Nations Population Division, World Urbanization Prospects: The 2001 Revision.
2. All city population statistics quoted in this atlas are of urban agglomerations. The combined population of a city and its suburbs is known as an urban agglomeration.
3. Billion is defined as 1,000 million (1,000,000,000) in this atlas.

Credits

Photo Credits

Key t=top; l=left; r=right; tl=top left; tc=top center; tr=top right; cl=center left; c=center; cr=center right; b=bottom; bl=bottom left; bc=bottom center; br=bottom right
AAP = Australian Associated Press; APL/Corbis = Australian Picture Library/Corbis; COR = Corel Corp.; DS = Digital Stock; GI = Getty Images; IOT = Images on Tap; N_L= NASA/Landsat; N_V = NASA/Visible Earth; NASA = National Aeronautics and Space Administration; PD = Photodisc; PE = PhotoEssentials; PL = photolibrary.com

2t Craig Mahew & Robert Simmon/NASA/GSFC **4**b DS; cl N_L; cr NASA/GSFC/MITI/ERSDAC/JAROS/US/Japan ASTER Science Team; tUSGS/EROS Data Center Satellite Systems Branch **6**tc, tc AV HRR/NDVI/Seawifs/MODIS/NCEP/DMSP/Sky2000 star catalog/AVHRR & Seawifs/Reto Stockli/Marit Jentoft-Nilsen; tl PL; tr GI; Globes N_V **7**tc, tc, tl AVHRR/NDVI/Seawifs/ ODIS/NCEP/DMSP/Sky2000 star catalog/AVHRR & Seawifs/Reto Stockli/Marit Jentoft-Nilsen; tr Jerry Stebbins; Globes N_V **10**bl APL/Corbis **11**br, tc, tl APL/Corbis **12**tc, tr APL/ Corbis **13**br GI; tl APL/Corbis **14**tc PD; tr APL/Corbis **15**c, cl GI; cl APL/Corbis **17**bc, cr APL/Corbis **18**c GI; cl DS **19**cr GI; tr DS **20**cl APL/Corbis **21**br, cr, tr APL/Corbis **23**br, tr APL/Corbis; cr PD **24**cl APL/Corbis **25**bl, tr APL/Corbis **26**br APL/Corbis **27**bc, tc, tc, tr APL/Corbis; tl PD **28**bc, br APL/Corbis; tc GI **31**tc, tr APL/Corbis **32**bc GI; br COR **33**bc, bl PD; cr APL/Corbis **34**bl, c, tc, tr GI; c PD **36**tc, tr APL/Corbis **37**br, cr APL/Corbis **38**cl GI; tl PD **39**bc, tc APL/Corbis **40**c GI; cl COR **41**br APL/Corbis; cr COR **42**br GI; tr APL/Corbis **43**tr GI **44**bc, br, cr APL/Corbis **45**tc, tl GI **46**br, cr APL/Corbis **47**c, tc, tl APL/Corbis **48**bl GI; cl APL/Corbis **50**bc APL/Corbis; br PD **51**bc, bl APL/Corbis; c GI **52**c GI; cl APL/Corbis **53**tl, cr PD; tr PE **55**bc, cr, tc APL/Corbis; bc, bl PD **56**cr APL/Corbis; br GI **57**tl, tr GI **58**cl, cr, tl, tr APL/Corbis **59**c APL/Corbis **60**bc APL/Corbis; br GI **61**tl GI **62**c, tc, tr APL/Corbis **63**br, tr APL/Corbis **65**br, cr GI; tr APL/Corbis; tr PD **66**c COR; cl IOT **68**bl APL/Corbis; cl COR; tl GI **69**tc APL/Corbis; tl IOT **71**c PE; cr GI **72**br GI **73**br APL/Corbis; tr GI **74**tc, tr GI **75**tl GI **77**tc, tr APL/Corbis **78**bc Georg Gerster; br GI **79**tr PE **81**c, cl, tc, tr APL/Corbis; tl GI **83**tc APL/Corbis; tl Guido Alberto Rossi **85**bc, cr, APL/Corbis; tr GI **86**br APL/Corbis **87**tc, tr APL/Corbis **88**tc GI; cl, tr APL/Corbis **90**bl, cl APL/Corbis **91**br, tc, tr APL/Corbis **92**c APL/Corbis **93**bc APL/Corbis; c GI **94**bl APL/Corbis **95**bc, bl APL/Corbis **96**br, cr GI **97**br, tr APL/Corbis; cr GI **98**br APL/Corbis **99**br, tr APL/Corbis; tc GI **100**cl, c, tc, tr APL/Corbis **101**br APL/Corbis **102**tc, tr APL/ Corbis **103**tr APL/Corbis **104**bc AAP/EPA AFPI; c APL/Corbis **105**c APL/Corbis **106**c, cl, cr APL/Corbis **107**bl APL/Corbis **108**bc AAP/Associated Press/XINHUA NEWS AGENCY; br, cl APL/Corbis; c PD **109**br PD **110**br, tl PD; cl, tc APL/Corbis **112**br AAP Image/EPA/Michael Reynolds; c, cl APL/Corbis **113**br GI **114**c, cl, cr APL/Corbis **115**tr APL/Corbis; cr PD **116**bc GI bl AAP/Associated Press AP cr APL/Corbis **118**cr, tr APL/Corbis **119**bl, tr APL/Corbis **120**br, cr APL/Corbis **121**bl, cr APL/Corbis **122**tc GI; tr APL/Corbis **123**bl, tl GI; cr, tc APL/Corbis **124**c, cl APL/Corbis **125**bc AAP/Associated Press; c APL/Corbis **126**cr APL/Corbis **127**cl, tl, tr APL/Corbis **128**cl APL/Corbis **129**br APL/Corbis **130**cl PL **131**br, cr APL/Corbis **133**bc, bl, c, tr APL/Corbis **134**br APL/Corbis **135**bl, cr, tr APL/Corbis **136**c, cr APL/Corbis **137**bl, bc, c, cl APL/Corbis **138**bc, br, cr, tr APL/Corbis **140**br, cl, tr APL/Corbis **141**bl, tc APL/Corbis **142**bc, br, c, cr, tr APL/Corbis **145**br, cr, tr APL/Corbis

Illustration Credits

Andrew Davies/Creative Communication: 12, 15, 16, 18, 21, 22, 24, 27, 28, 31, 32, 35, 36, 39, 40, 43, 44, 46, 49, 50, 52, 54, 57, 59, 60, 62, 64, 66, 68, 70, 72, 74, 76, 78, 81, 82, 84, 86, 91, 93, 95, 96, 98, 101, 102, 104, 106, 108, 111, 112, 114, 117, 119, 120, 122, 124, 126, 129, 131, 132, 134, 137, 139, 142, 144; **Map Illustrations:** 8, 10, 11, 15, 30, 33, 35, 36, 37, 38, 40, 42, 44, 46, 48, 50, 52, 54, 56, 58, 60, 62, 64, 66, 67, 68, 70, 71, 72, 74, 76, 78, 80, 82, 84, 86, 90, 92, 94, 96, 98, 100, 102, 104, 105, 106, 107, 108, 110, 112, 114, 116, 118, 120, 122, 124, 125, 126, 128, 130, 132, 134, 136, 138, 140, 141, 142, 144; **Suzanne Keating:** 1, 9; **Murray Zanoni:** 13, 19, 23, 24, 26, 30, 36, 40, 45, 47, 51, 55, 56, 59, 62, 63, 64, 68, 73, 74, 76, 78, 80, 82, 84, 87, 92, 94, 96, 98, 103, 107, 115, 117, 119, 120, 124, 127, 128, 130, 133, 135, 136, 142.